150 GREAT TECH PREP CAREERS

Second Edition

150 GREAT TECH PREP CAREERS

Second Edition

Checkmark Books®
An imprint of Infobase Publishing

150 Great Tech Prep Careers, Second Edition

Copyright © 2009 by Infobase Publishing

Checkmark Books
An imprint of Infobase Publishing, Inc.
132 West 31st Street
New York NY 10001

Library of Congress Cataloging-in-Publication Data

150 great tech prep careers. — 2nd ed.
    p. cm.
  Includes bibliographical references and index.
  ISBN-13: 978-0-8160-7733-5 (hc: alk. paper)
  ISBN-10: 0-8160-7733-9 (hc: alk. paper)
  ISBN-13: 978-0-8160-7734-2 (pbk.: alk. paper)
  ISBN-10: 8160-7734-7 (pbk.: alk. paper) 1. Vocational guidance—United States—Handbooks, manuals, etc. 2. Vocational school graduates—Employment—United States—Handbooks, manuals, etc. 3. High school graduates—Employment—United States—Handbooks, manuals, etc. I. Title: One hundred fifty great tech prep careers.
  HF5382.5.U5F76 2009
  331.702'33—dc22

                          2008034824

Text design by Mary Susan Ryan-Flynn
Cover design by Takeshi Takahashi

Printed in the United States of America

VB MSRF 10 9 8 7 6 5 4 3 2 1

TABLE OF CONTENTS

INTRODUCTION

Tech Prep, short for *technical preparation*, began with a federal education initiative to support career and technical education nationwide. In the Tech Prep model, vocational education is delivered via high school and postsecondary courses, and supplemented with workplace experience (training, mentoring, internships, or apprenticeships). Community businesses partner with area high schools and postsecondary institutions to provide field-training opportunities to students and to fill their own hiring needs. This school-to-work transition afforded by Tech Prep education is important in assuring the employment of future generations, as well as the health of the economy: nearly a third of the fastest growing careers require an associate's degree or a postsecondary vocational certificate, according to a 2006 Bureau of Labor Statistics report.

Career and technical education have been proven to increase the academic achievement and earnings of students: Career and technical education students take more and higher level math and science courses than general students, according to the National Research Center for Career and Technical Education. Just one year of postsecondary vocational education brought 5 to 8 percent higher earnings than the average high school graduate receives, according to the 2004 National Assessment of Vocational Education, from the U.S. Department of Education. Considering these facts, it should be no surprise that a third of U.S. college students are involved in career and technical education programs, according to the U.S. Department of Education. **150 Great Tech Prep Careers** presents comprehensive information on the broad range of high-growth, exciting careers open to Tech Prep graduates.

TECHNICAL EDUCATION: DEVELOPING A SKILLED WORKFORCE

Technical education has its roots in the very first type of vocational education: the apprenticeship. Dating back to ancient Greece, apprenticeships once taught reading and writing as well as the secrets of the trade. Today, apprenticeships are still fundamental in the many trades where training best involves an experienced "master" teaching his or her skills to an apprentice.

Technical education generally prepares students for a variety of areas, including agriculture, business and marketing, family and consumer sciences, health occupations, trade and industrial, public safety and security, and technology. Beginning in middle school, students take courses in areas such as family and consumer sciences and technology education. Students then progress to a more specialized technical program offered at a career and technical high school or general high schools. These courses are often supplemented by internships or apprenticeships. Some students may graduate high school and begin an apprenticeship or go into the workforce, where they will learn on the job. Other students choose to attend a postsecondary school, to obtain a diploma, certificate, or associate's degree in the specialty of their choosing.

Middle and High School

Students may take part in career learning as early as the sixth grade, with career awareness education, career days, trips to local employers, or job shadowing opportunities. Middle schools also frequently offer courses in work-related skills such as typing and computers.

After middle school, students may have the option to attend a vocational and technical high school if one is available locally. Vocational and technical high schools provide both academic and vocational education. Based on their interests, students choose a technical program to pursue. These programs often prepare students to take certification exams or enter apprenticeships upon graduation, going directly into the workforce. Some examples include automotive technology, commercial art and design, computer technology, construction technology, cosmetology, culinary arts, drafting/CAD, early childhood education, electrical, health occupations, and heating, ventilation, air conditioning, and refrigeration (HVAC/R).

Apprenticeships

Apprenticeships involve on-the-job learning under a skilled worker and offer the benefits technical instruction and mentorship while earning a living. Students may begin apprenticeships as early as 16, although 18 is the most common age for safety reasons. Apprenticeships may last from one to four years, and upon completion individuals receive a certificate and recognition as a qualified journeyworker in their field. Some postsecondary schools may apply credit for apprenticeship completion toward an associate's degree. Apprenticeships exist in health care, information technology, energy, aerospace, social services, transportation, and security.

Postsecondary Technical Institutes and Community Colleges

Technical education at the postsecondary level takes place at community colleges and postsecondary

TECH PREP: DID YOU KNOW?

- The number of students enrolled in career and technical education programs has grown 157% from 1999 to 2004, according to the U.S. Office of Vocational and Adult Education.

- There are more than 15 million career and technical education students in the United States, according to the U.S. Department of Education.

- Approximately 11,000 high schools, 1,400 career tech centers, and 9,400 postsecondary institutions offer career and technical education, according to the Association for Career and Technical Education.

technical institutes. Technical institutes typically offer diploma, certification, and/or associate's degree programs, ranging in length from under a year to two years. Individuals may choose a technical institute to gain the specialized training necessary for a specific career, from dental assisting to IT support. Community colleges generally offer certification and associate's degrees in a variety of areas. Students pursuing an occupational associate's degree may earn an Associate of Applied Science, Associate of Occupational Studies, Associate of Applied Arts, or an Associate of Applied Technology.

Acquiring postsecondary education pays: Individuals with an associate's degree had median weekly earnings of $740 in 2007; individuals with some postsecondary education earned $683 weekly; and those with a high school diploma earned $604 per week, according to the U.S. Bureau of Labor Statistics.

CAREERS FOR THE 21ST CENTURY

Technology and the global marketplace are constantly evolving, and employers require employees the latest skills and the most current training. Many of the hottest careers at the moment required specialized technological training and continuing education. Technical education meets these needs by preparing employees trained to fit these needs. The career fields below are expected to show strong growth through 2016, according to the U.S. Department of Labor, and should provide significant opportunities to the technically trained segment of the workforce.

Health Care

Health care was the largest industry in the United States in 2006, employing more than 14 million. Professional (such as doctors and nurses) and service (such as home health aides and dental hygienists) occupations make up the majority in this field. Most jobs in the field require less than four years of college education. Health care is expected to generate more employment than any other industry through 2016, adding 3 million jobs. This is due largely to the growing and aging population, the baby boomer generation in particular. Among the many health-related careers profiled in this book are Aerobics Instructors and Fitness Trainers, Cardiovascular Technologists, Dental Hygienists, Diagnostic Medical Sonographers, Dialysis Technicians, Electroneurodiagnostic Technologists, Histologic Technicians, Licensed Practical Nurses, Massage Therapists, Medical Transcriptionists, Occupational Therapy Assistants and Aides, and Yoga and Pilates Instructors.

Professional and Business Services

Professional and business services will add 4 million new jobs by 2016, according to the U.S. Department of Labor. Administrative and support services and waste management and remediation will add 2.1 million new jobs, while professional, scientific, and technical services will add 2.1 million new jobs. Some of the fastest growing careers are in this area: 360,000 new openings for administrative assistants and secretaries are expected by 2016, while employment of environmental technicians is expected to grow much faster than the average. Related careers profiled in this book include Bookkeeping and Accounting Clerks, Chemical Technicians, Customer Service Representatives, Energy Conservation Technicians, Environmental Technicians, Instrumentation Technicians, Laboratory Testing Technicians, Legal Secretaries, Office Administrators, Office Clerks, Paralegals, and Secretaries.

Leisure and Hospitality

Arts, entertainment, and recreation will add nearly 600,000 new jobs by 2016, a large portion of which will be in the amusement and gaming sector. Accommodation and food services will add 1.3 million new jobs by 2016, with major growth in food services and drinking places. Much of this growth will arise due to increasing incomes, growing awareness of the benefits of fitness, and public participation in the arts. Leisure and hospitality career opportunities profiled in this book include Audio Recording Engineers, Brewers, Broadcast

Engineers, Camera Operators, Cartoonists and Animators, Cooks and Chefs, Cruise Ship Workers, Desktop Publishing Specialists, Gaming Occupations, Graphic Designers, Photographers, Restaurant and Food Service Managers, and Travel Agents.

Trade and Transportation

Retail trade is expected to add 700,000 new jobs by 2016, and wholesale trade, 400,000. Retail sales representatives make up an estimated 40 percent of employment in the field. Transportation and warehousing are expected to add nearly 500,000 jobs by 2016. Truck transportation in particular will experience growth, while rail transportation will be on the decline. Some trade and transportation careers profiled in this book include Diesel Mechanics, Merchandise Displayers, Public Transportation Operators, Retail Managers, Retail Sales Workers, Sales Representatives, and Truck Drivers.

Financial Activities

Finance and insurance are expected to add 800,000 jobs by 2016, while real estate, rental, and leasing will add nearly 400,000. Real estate growth will reflect increased demand as the U.S. population grows. Careers profiled in this book include Assessors and Appraisers, Financial Institution Tellers, Clerks, and Related Workers, Insurance Policy Processing Workers, Real Estate Agents and Brokers, and Tax Preparers.

Information

The information sector, with some of highest-growth computer industries, will add 200,000 jobs by 2016. Internet publishing and broadcasting, software publishing, and wireless telecommunications in particular are expected to see growth. Related careers profiled in this book include Computer Support Specialists, Computer and Office Machine Service Technicians, Line Installers and Cable Splicers, Webmasters, and Wireless Service Technicians.

Construction

Construction is expected add more than 620,000 jobs by 2016. Nonresidential and road, bridge, and tunnel construction are projected to see the most growth during this period. Related careers in this book include Bricklayers and Stonemasons, Carpenters, Cement Masons, Construction Inspectors, Cost Estimators, Marble Setters, Tile Setters, and Terazzo Workers, Plasterers, Plumb-

CHANGE IN TOTAL EMPLOYMENT BY OCCUPATIONAL GROUP, 2006-2016	
Professional and Related	+16.7 percent
Service	+16.7 percent
Management, Business, and Financial	+10.4 percent
Construction and Extraction	+9.5 percent
Installation, Maintenance, and Repair	+9.3 percent
Sales and Related	+7.6 percent
Office and Administrative Support	+7.2 percent
Transportation and Material Moving	+4.5 percent
Farming, Fishing, and Forestry	-2.8 percent
Production	-4.9 percent

Source: U.S. Bureau of Labor Statistics

ers and Pipefitters, Roofers, Sheet Metal Workers, and Surveyors.

Installation, Maintenance, and Repair

Installation, maintenance, and repair occupations are projected to yield 550,000 new jobs by 2016. Related careers profiled in this book include Aircraft Mechanics, Automobile Collision Repairers, Automobile Service Technicians, Boilermakers and Boilermaker Mechanics, General Maintenance Mechanics, Locksmiths, Marine Services Technicians, Millwrights, and Musical Instrument Repairers and Tuners.

HOW TO USE THIS BOOK

Similar in form and content to the well-respected *Encyclopedia of Careers and Vocational Guidance*, **150 Great Tech Prep Careers** includes information on The Job, Requirements, Starting Out, Advancement, Work Environment, Earnings, Outlook, and sources of additional information for 150 careers.

With each article is a sidebar featuring information on recommended School Subjects, Personal Skills, Work Environment, the Minimum Education necessary to work in the field, Median Earnings, Certification or Licensing requirements, and the Outlook for the career field.

The *Overview* section is a brief introductory description of the duties and responsibilities involved in this career. Oftentimes, a career may have a variety of job titles. When this is the case, alternative career titles are presented.

The Job section describes an average day for a worker in this field, including primary and secondary duties; the types of tools, machinery, or equipment used to perform this job; and other types of workers interacted with on a daily basis. Growing subfields or subspecialties of this career are also discussed in detail.

The *Requirements* section describes the formal educational requirements—from high school diploma to advanced college degree—that are necessary to become employed in the field. This section provides information on how students can receive training if a college degree is not required, via on-the-job training, apprenticeships, the armed forces, or other activities. Explained here are certification, licensing, and continuing education requirements. Finally, the Requirements section recommends personal qualities that will be helpful to someone working in this field.

In the *Exploring* section, you will find a variety of suggestions for exploring the field—such as periodicals to read, Web sites to visit, summer jobs and programs to check out, volunteer opportunities, associations and clubs to join, and hobbies to explore—before you invest time and money in education and training.

The *Employers* section lists major employers of workers in the field.

The *Starting Out* section offers tips on how to land your first job, be it through newspaper ads, the Internet, college career services offices, or personal contacts, This section explains how the average person finds employment in this field.

The *Advancement* section describes the possible career path and the tools or experience you might need—advanced training or outside education—to move up in the career.

The *Earnings* section lists salary ranges for beginning, mid-range, and experienced workers in this field. Average starting salaries by educational achievement are also listed, when available. Fringe benefits, such as paid vacation and sick days, health insurance, pensions, and profit sharing plans, are covered.

In the *Work Environment* section, you will see what a typical day on the job is like. Is indoor or outdoor work required? Are safety measures and equipment such as protective clothing necessary? Is the job in a quiet office or on a noisy assembly line? What are the standard hours of work? Are overtime and weekend work often required? Is travel frequent? If so, to where, and for how long? This is a good place to gauge your true interest in the field.

The *Outlook* section predicts the potential long-term employment outlook for the field: which areas are growing because of technology and which are in decline. Most of this information is obtained from the Bureau of Labor Statistics. Job growth terms follow those used in the *Occupational Outlook Handbook*: growth much faster than the average means an increase of 21 percent or more; growth faster than the average means an increase of 14 to 20 percent; growth about as fast as the average means an increase of 7 to 13 percent.

In the last section, *For More Information*, you'll find the names, street addresses, phone numbers, email, and Web addresses of a variety of associations, government agencies, or unions that can provide further information regarding educational requirements, accreditation and certification, and other general career information.

Whether you are interested in education, business, health care, computers, or any other field, there is a chance for you to have a rewarding career in any number of related tech-prep careers. Read about the different opportunities available, and be sure to contact the organizations listed for more information.

IN CONCLUSION

Choosing a career involves research, preparation, and the proper education and training. Tech Prep confers practical skills and training while giving you an inside scoop on the real-world career of your choice. Do you want to be a nurse? An associate's degree in nursing will give you the training to become a Licensed Practical Nurse. Are you interested in auto repair? An apprenticeship will prepare you for a career as an Automobile Service Technician. Do you want to work in health care and learn on the job? Opt for a career as a dental assistant. Whatever your decision, the more education you receive, the closer you are to a rewarding and satisfying career.

ADULT DAY CARE COORDINATORS

OVERVIEW

Adult day care coordinators, also called *adult day services coordinators,* direct day service programs for adults who have physical or mental impairments or both. Clients of these programs are usually the elderly, although younger people with impairments, such as those recovering from strokes, may also participate in these programs. Coordinators oversee staff members who provide care, meals, and social activities to day care clients, and they serve as liaisons between their centers and their clients' families.

THE JOB

Adult day care coordinators direct adult day care centers. Although specific duties vary depending on the size of the center and the services it offers, the general responsibility of coordinators is to ensure that their centers provide the necessary care for clients. Such care may include attention to personal hygiene and providing meals, medications, therapies, and social activities. Adult day care centers differ from nursing homes in that clients receive care only during the day or early evening hours. Clients do not reside in such centers, as service is always designated as less than 24 hours a day.

Although coordinators working in small day care centers may actually perform some services for clients, this is not the norm. Instead, coordinators usually oversee various staff members who provide the care. A large center, for example, might have a nurse, physical therapist, social worker, cook, and several aides. Coordinators are responsible for staff hiring, training, and scheduling. They may meet with staff members either one-on-one or in group sessions to review and discuss plans for the clients.

Overseeing meal planning and preparation is also the responsibility of the adult day services coordinator. In most centers, clients are given a midday meal and usually juices and snacks in the morning and afternoon. Coordinators work with a cook or dietitian to develop well-rounded menus that take into account the nutritional needs of the clients, including any particular restrictions such as diabetic or low-sodium diets. The coordinator may also oversee purchasing and taking inventory of the center's food supply.

The coordinator schedules daily and weekly activities for the day care clients. Depending on the particular needs and abilities of the clients, a recreational schedule might include crafts, games, exercises, reading time, or movies. In some centers, clients are taken on outings to shopping centers, parks, or restaurants. The coordinator plans such outings, arranging for transportation and any reservations or special accommodations that may be necessary. Finally, the coordinator also organizes parties for special events, such as holidays and birthdays.

Finding new activities and visitors for the center is also part of the job. Coordinators might recruit volunteers to teach crafts or music to the clients. Often, church or civic groups come to such facilities to visit with clients. Some groups institute buddy programs, in which each group member pairs with a day care client to develop an ongoing relationship. The day care coordinator must authorize and monitor any group visits, activities, or programs.

In addition to planning and overseeing the activities of the center and its clients, the adult day care coordinator

QUICK FACTS

SCHOOL SUBJECTS
Family and consumer science
Psychology
Sociology

PERSONAL SKILLS
Helping/teaching
Leadership/management

WORK ENVIRONMENT
Primarily indoors
Primarily one location

MINIMUM EDUCATION LEVEL
Associate's degree

MEDIAN SALARY
$31,000

CERTIFICATION OR LICENSING
Required for certain positions

OUTLOOK
Much faster than the average

also works closely with client family members to make sure that each individual is receiving care that best fits his or her needs. This relationship with the client's family usually begins before the client is placed in the day care center.

When a family is considering placing an elderly relative in day care, they often have many questions about the center and its activities. The coordinator meets with family members to show them the center and explain how it is run. The coordinator also gathers information about the potential client, including names and phone numbers of doctors and people to contact in case of emergency; lists of medications taken and instructions on when and how they should be administered; and information on allergies, food choices, and daily habits and routines.

After the client is placed in the center, the coordinator may meet periodically with the client's family to update them on how the client is responding to the day care setting. If necessary, the coordinator may advise the family about social services, such as home health care, and refer them to other providers.

Adult day care coordinators may have other duties, depending on the center and how it is owned and operated. For example, they may be responsible for developing and adhering to a budget for the center. In centers licensed or certified by the state, coordinators may ensure that their centers remain in compliance with the regulations and have necessary documentation. They may also be responsible for general bookkeeping, bill payment, and office management.

In addition to supervising centers, coordinators may also promote and advertise the center to the community. This can involve fund-raising, preparing press releases, and speaking to various service clubs and other civic groups.

REQUIREMENTS
High School

Because this is a relatively new and growing field, there are no official requirements for becoming an adult day care coordinator. Some people have learned their skills on the job; others have taken courses in home nursing or health care; still others have completed bachelor's degrees in areas such as health and human services. As the need for and popularity of adult day care services continue to grow, more employers will begin to expect coordinators to have at least some formal education. While you are in high school, you should take classes that prepare you for postsecondary training. These include mathemat-

ics, business, and family and consumer science classes, as well as science classes, such as biology. To improve your understanding of people, take history, psychology, and sociology classes. Because communication is an important skill, English and speech classes are also good choices.

Postsecondary Training

Many employers prefer to hire candidates who meet the standards set by the National Adult Day Services Association (NADSA). In order to meet these standards, a coordinator must have a bachelor's degree in health or social services or a related field, with one year's supervisory experience in a social or health services setting. In preparation for such a career, a college student might choose occupational, recreational, or rehabilitation therapy, or social work or human development. An increasingly popular major for potential adult day care coordinators is gerontology, or geriatrics.

The Association for Gerontology in Higher Education publishes the *Directory of Educational Programs in Gerontology and Geriatrics*, which contains information on more than 750 programs available from the associate's to the post-doctorate level. Although specific courses vary from school to school, most programs consist of classes in social gerontology, biology and physiology of aging, psychology of aging, and sociology of aging. In addition to these four core classes, most programs offer elective courses in such areas as social policy, community services, nutrition and exercise, diversity in aging, health issues, death and dying, and ethics and life extension.

A practicum or field placement is also a part of most gerontology programs. This allows students to obtain experience working with both well-functioning elderly people and those with age-related disabilities.

Certification or Licensing

According to NADSA, there are currently no national standards regarding the qualifications for adult day services workers. NADSA does offer voluntary certification to program assistants. The National Certification Council for Activity Professionals also offers certification to qualified adult day care coordinators. Those who meet the professional standards earn the designation certified activity professional (CAP).

Regulations can vary by state. In some states, for example, the agency that a coordinator works for must be licensed or certified by the state department of health. Any adult day care center that receives payment from

Medicare or from other government agencies must be certified by the state department of health. In these cases, licensing requirements may include requirements for coordinators and other staff members. The trend is toward stricter standards.

Other Requirements

Regardless of what level of education a prospective coordinator has, there are certain personal characteristics that are necessary for success in this field. Compassion and an affinity for the elderly and people with disabilities are vital, as are patience and the desire to help others. You should also be organized and able to manage other workers effectively. Communication skills are very important since you will be working with staff, clients, regulatory agencies, and clients' families.

EXPLORING

There are several ways you can learn more about the career of adult day care coordinator. The first and easiest way is to check your local library for books or articles on aging in order to learn more about the elderly, their issues, and the services available to them. Next, visit a nursing home or adult day care center to experience firsthand what it is like to spend time with and interact with elderly people. Arrange a meeting with staff members and the center's coordinator to find out what their day-to-day jobs are like. Your high school guidance counselor may also be able to arrange for a coordinator to give a career talk at your school. Finally, get a volunteer position or part-time job in such a facility. This would allow you to gauge your aptitude for a career in adult day care work.

EMPLOYERS

Adult day care coordinators work at adult day care centers. These may be small or large. According to NASDA, there are more than 3,500 adult day care centers currently operating in the United States, providing care for 150,000 older Americans each day. Most of them are operated on a nonprofit or public basis, and many are affiliated with large organizations such as nursing homes, hospitals, or multipurpose senior organizations. Standards and work environments vary.

STARTING OUT

In looking for a position as an adult day care coordinator, candidates should first locate and contact all such programs in the area. Checking the local Yellow Pages under Nursing Homes, Residential Care Facilities, Aging Services, or Senior Citizens Services should provide a list of leads. The job seeker might either send a resume and cover letter or call these potential employers directly. Prospective coordinators should also watch for job openings listed in area newspapers and on organizations' Web sites.

Another means of finding job leads is to become affiliated with a professional association, such as the American Geriatrics Society, the American Association of Homes and Services for the Aging, the Gerontological Society of America, or the National Council on the Aging. Many of these organizations have monthly or quarterly newsletters that list job opportunities. Some may even have job banks or referral services.

Job seekers who have received associate's or bachelor's degrees should also check with the career placement offices at their colleges or universities.

ADVANCEMENT

Because the field of aging-related services continues to grow, the potential for advancement for adult day care coordinators is good. Some coordinators advance by transferring to a larger center that pays better wages. Others eventually start their own centers. Still others advance by moving into management positions in other, similar social service organizations, such as nursing homes, hospices, or government agencies on aging.

An adult day care coordinator might choose to return to school and complete a higher degree, often a master's degree in social work. For those who choose this option, there are many career opportunities in the field of social services. Social workers, for example, work with individuals and families dealing with AIDS, cancer, or other debilitating illnesses. They also work for agencies offering various types of counseling, rehabilitation, or crisis intervention.

EARNINGS

Starting salaries for this position depend partly on the experience and education of the coordinator and partly upon the size and location of the day care center. Larger centers located in metropolitan areas tend to offer the highest wages.

According to the Association for Gerontology in Higher Education, beginning annual salaries range from $18,000 to $31,000 for persons with a bachelor's degree and little experience. Generally, coordinators who do not have a bachelor's degree can expect to earn somewhat less. According to the Web site Salary.com, national averages for experienced adult day care directors are between $62,000 and $84,000 a year. These higher salaries reflect ample experience and continued education and training in this field.

In addition to salary, some coordinators are also offered a benefits package, which typically includes health insurance, paid vacation and sick days, and a retirement plan.

WORK ENVIRONMENT

Most adult day care centers have a schedule that corresponds to standard business hours. Most coordinators work a 40-hour week, Monday through Friday, with weekends off.

The coordinator's work environment will vary depending on the size and type of center he or she supervises. Some centers are fairly institutional, resembling children's day care centers or nursing homes. Others have a more residential feel, being carpeted and furnished like a private home. Regardless of the furnishings, the center is typically clean, well lit, and equipped with ramps, rails, and other devices that ensure the safety of clients.

Part of the coordinator's day may be spent in the center's common areas with clients and staff. He or she may also spend time working in an on-site office. If the staff members take clients on outings, the coordinator may accompany them.

Coordinators are on their feet much of the time, ensuring that meals and activities run smoothly and helping staff members when necessary. Attire for the job varies from center to center, ranging from very casual to standard office wear. Most coordinators, however, wear clothing that is comfortable and allows them freedom of movement.

Regardless of the size of the center, coordinators spend the majority of their time working with people, both staff members and day care clients. Working with clients is often very trying. Many of them may have had a stroke or have Alzheimer's disease, and they may be confused, uncooperative, or even hostile. The job may also be emotionally taxing for the coordinator who becomes attached to his or her clients. Most adults who use a day care center are elderly or permanently disabled; for this reason, day care staff must frequently deal with the decline and eventual death of their clients.

OUTLOOK

The career outlook for adult day care coordinators, as for all social assistance workers, is expected to be excellent through 2016. According to the U.S. Department of Labor, the number of human services and social assistance workers is projected to grow tremendously, with elder care being one of the fastest growing human services areas.

The main reason for this is that the senior citizen population is growing rapidly. According to the U.S. Census Bureau, approximately 35 million Americans were age 65 or older in 2001; the bureau projects this number to increase steadily, reaching approximately 82 million by 2050 as the baby boomer generation ages. This rapid growth has led to the development and increased popularity of aging-related services during the last several years. The increase in adult day care centers is one example of this trend. According to NADSA, there were only approximately 300 adult day care centers in existence by the late 1970s; today, there are more than 3,500. This growth should continue as Americans become increasingly aware of the diverse needs of the elderly and the various service options available to them. Adult day care is expected to be used more frequently as a cost-efficient and preferable alternative to nursing homes.

FOR MORE INFORMATION

For information on aging and services for the elderly, contact

American Association of Homes and Services for the Aging
2519 Connecticut Avenue, NW
Washington, DC 20008-1520
Tel: 202-783-2242
http://www.aahsa.org

AGHE, a section of the Gerontological Society of America, promotes education in the field of aging and offers a directory of gerontology and geriatrics programs. Visit the Web site http://www.careersinaging.com to read AGHE's Careers in Aging: Consider the Opportunities.

Association for Gerontology in Higher Education (AGHE)
1120 L Street, NW, Suite 901
Washington, DC 20005-1503
Tel: 202-289-9806
Email: aghetemp@aghe.org
http://www.aghe.org

For career information and student resources, contact
Gerontological Society of America
1120 L Street, NW, Suite 901
Washington, DC 20005-4018
Tel: 202-842-1275
Email: geron@geron.org
http://www.geron.org

For information on the history of adult day service and day service facts, contact

National Adult Day Services Association
85 South Washington Street
Seattle, WA 98104
Tel: 877-745-1440
Email: info@nadsa.org
http://www.nadsa.org

❏ AEROBICS INSTRUCTORS AND FITNESS TRAINERS

OVERVIEW

Aerobics instructors choreograph and teach aerobics classes of varying types. Classes are geared toward people with general good health as well as to specialized populations, including the elderly and those with specific health problems that affect their ability to exercise. Many people enjoy participating in the lively exercise routines set to music.

Depending on where they are employed, *fitness trainers* help devise health conditioning programs for clients, from professional athletes to average individuals looking for guidance. Fitness trainers motivate clients to follow prescribed exercise programs and monitor their progress. When injuries occur, either during training or sporting events, fitness trainers determine the extent of the injury and administer first aid for minor problems such as blisters, bruises, and scrapes. Following more serious injury, trainers may work with a physical therapist to help the athlete perform rehabilitative exercises.

There are approximately 235,000 aerobics instructors and fitness trainers employed in the United States.

THE JOB

There are three general levels of aerobics classes: low impact, moderate, and high intensity. A typical class starts with warm-up exercises (slow stretching movements to loosen up muscles), followed by 35 to 40 minutes of nonstop activity to raise the heart rate, and ending with a cool-down period of stretching and slower movements. Instructors teach class members to

QUICK FACTS

SCHOOL SUBJECTS
Health
Physical education
Theater/dance

PERSONAL SKILLS
Helping/teaching
Leadership/management

WORK ENVIRONMENT
Primarily indoors
Primarily one location

MINIMUM EDUCATION LEVEL
High school diploma

MEDIAN SALARY
$25,910

CERTIFICATION OR LICENSING
Required for certain positions

OUTLOOK
Much faster than the average

monitor their heart rates and listen to their bodies for signs of progress.

Aerobics instructors prepare activities prior to their classes. They choose exercises to work different muscles and accompany these movements to music during each phase of the program. Generally, instructors use upbeat music for the more intense exercise portion and more soothing music for the cool-down period. Instructors demonstrate each step of a sequence until the class can follow along. Additional sequences are added continuously as the class progresses, making up a longer routine that is set to music. Most classes are structured so that new participants can start in any given class. The instructor either faces the rest of the room or faces a mirror in order to observe class progress and ensure that participants do exercises correctly. Many aerobics instructors also lead toning and shaping classes. In these classes, the emphasis is not on aerobic activity but on working particular areas of the body. An instructor begins the class with a brief aerobic period followed by stretching and weight-bearing exercises that loosen and work major muscle groups.

In a health club, fitness trainers evaluate their clients' fitness level with physical examinations and fitness tests. Using various pieces of testing equipment, they determine such things as percentage of body fat and optimal heart and pulse rates. Clients fill out questionnaires about their medical background, general fitness level, and fitness goals. Fitness trainers use this information to design a customized workout plan using weights and other exercise options such as swimming and running to help clients meet these goals. Trainers also advise clients on weight control, diet, and general health. Some fitness trainers also work at the client's home or office. This convenient way of staying physically fit meets the needs of many busy, active adults today.

To start a client's exercise program, the trainer often demonstrates the proper use of weight-lifting equipment to reduce the chance of injury, especially if the client is a beginner. As the client uses the equipment, the trainer observes and corrects any problems before injury occurs. Preventing injury is extremely important, according to American Council on Exercise Certified Personal Trainer (CPT) Nicole Gutter. "It is a good idea to carry your own liability insurance. The bottom line is, know what you're doing because there is a huge risk of injury or even death for high-risk people," she says. "You should be insured in case anything beyond your control does happen."

Fitness trainers also use exercise tape to wrap weak or injured hands, feet, or other parts of the body. The heavy-duty tape helps strengthen and position the joint to prevent further injury or strain. Fitness trainers also help athletes with therapy or rehabilitation, using special braces or other equipment to support or protect the injured part until it heals. Trainers ensure that the athlete does not overuse a weak joint or muscle, risking further damage.

REQUIREMENTS
High School

Aerobics instructors and fitness trainers should hold a high school diploma. If you are interested in a fitness career, take courses in physical education, biology, and anatomy. In addition, be involved in sports, weight lifting, or dance activities to stay fit and learn to appreciate the value of exercise.

Postsecondary Training

Although it isn't always necessary, a college degree will make you more marketable in the fitness field. Typically, aerobics instructors do not need a college education to qualify for jobs; however, some employers may be more interested in candidates with a balance of ability and education.

Fitness trainers are usually required to have a bachelor's degree from an accredited athletic training program or a related program in physical education or health. These programs often require extensive internships that can range from 500 to 1,800 hours of hands-on experience. Essential college-level courses include anatomy, biomechanics, chemistry, first aid, health, kinesiology, nutrition, physics, physiology, psychology, and safety.

Tony Hinsberger, owner of Summit Fitness Personal Training, highly recommends getting a college degree in physiology, kinesiology, exercise science, or athletic training. "As an owner of a small personal training firm, I hire trainers," he says. "If I had to make a choice between equally experienced and qualified candidates, I would pick the one with a degree."

Certification or Licensing

Most serious fitness trainers and aerobics instructors become certified. Certification is not required in most states, but most clients and fitness companies expect these professionals to have credentials to prove their worth.

As a current employer of fitness professionals, Hinsberger recommends certification. "I only hire certified trainers," he says. "Most facilities require certification and there are many, many certifying agencies. Certification is also required by most liability insurance plans."

Certifying agencies include the following: Aerobics and Fitness Association of America, American College of Sports Medicine, American Council on Exercise, and National Academy of Sports Medicine. Since the risk of client injuries on the job is very real, aerobics instructors and fitness trainers should also be certified in cardiopulmonary resuscitation (CPR) before finding a job, or train as an emergency medical technician (EMT). These may also be requirements of certification.

The National Athletic Trainers' Association and the American Athletic Trainers Association certify fitness trainers who have graduated from accredited college programs or have completed the necessary internship following a degree in a related field.

Whichever career path they follow, aerobics instructors and fitness trainers are expected to keep up-to-date with their fields, becoming thoroughly familiar with the latest knowledge and safety practices. They must take continuing education courses and participate in seminars to keep their certification current.

Other Requirements

Aerobics instructors and fitness trainers are expected to be physically fit, but are not expected to be specimens of human perfection. For example, members of an aerobics class geared toward senior citizens may benefit from an older instructor.

EXPLORING

A visit to a health club, park district, or YMCA aerobics class is a good way to observe the work of fitness trainers and aerobics instructors. Part-time or summer jobs are sometimes available for high school students in these facilities. It may also be possible to volunteer in a senior citizen center where aerobics classes are offered.

"To explore this [career] path, I recommend working part time in a gym or fitness facility," Tony Hinsberger suggests. "Some clubs have an orientation position. People in this job take new members on a tour of the facility and show new members how to use the equipment safely. It typically doesn't require a degree, only on-site training."

If possible, enroll in an aerobics class or train with a fitness trainer to experience firsthand what their jobs entail and to see what makes a good instructor. Fitness trainer Brett Vicknair agrees: "I would encourage someone wanting to pursue a career as a personal trainer to get involved with working out first, maybe at a local fitness center, and take advantage of any help that is usually offered when someone first becomes a member."

Aerobics instructor workshops are taught to help prospective instructors gain experience. These are usually offered in adult education courses at such places as the YMCA. Unpaid apprenticeships are also a good way for future instructors to obtain supervised experience before teaching classes on their own. The facility may allow prospective aerobics instructors to take their training class for free if there is a possibility that they will work there in the future.

Opportunities for student fitness trainers are available in schools with fitness trainers on staff. This is an excellent way for students to observe and assist a professional fitness trainer on an ongoing basis.

EMPLOYERS

Most aerobics instructors work for fitness centers and gymnasiums. Most employers are for-profit businesses, but some are community-based, such as the YMCA or a family center. Other job possibilities can be found in corporate fitness centers, colleges, retirement centers, and resorts.

Some fitness trainers work in more than one facility. Others are self-employed and take clients on an appointment basis, working either in personal homes or in a public gym. Some fitness trainers will work with high-profile athletes on a one-on-one basis to meet specific fitness requirements.

"Trainers work in gyms or fitness centers, in private personal fitness centers where members are seen on an appointment basis only, and in country clubs, just to name some of the opportunities," Brett Vicknair says.

Most medium-to-large cities have one or more gyms or fitness centers; smaller towns may not have any such facilities. However, there may be limited openings at retirement homes, schools, and community centers in these small towns.

STARTING OUT

Students should use their schools' placement offices for information on available jobs. Often, facilities that provide training or internships will hire or provide job leads to individuals who have completed programs. Students can also find jobs through classified ads and by applying to health and fitness clubs, YMCAs, YWCAs, Jewish community centers, local schools, park districts, church groups, and other fitness organizations. Because exercise is understood to be a preventive measure for many health and medical problems, insurance companies often reward businesses that offer fitness facilities to their employees with lower insurance rates. As a result, students should consider nearby companies for prospective fitness instructor and trainer positions.

ADVANCEMENT

Experienced aerobics instructors can become instructor trainers, providing tips and insight on how to lead a class and what routines work well.

A bachelor's degree in sports physiology, exercise physiology, or business management is especially beneficial for those who want to advance to the position of health club director or to teach corporate wellness programs.

Fitness trainers working at schools can advance from assistant positions to head athletic director, which may involve relocating to another school. Fitness trainers can advance to instruct new fitness trainers in college. They also can work in sports medicine facilities, usually in rehabilitation work. In health clubs, fitness trainers can advance to become health club directors or work in administration. Often, fitness trainers who build up a reputation and a clientele go into business for themselves as personal trainers.

EARNINGS

Aerobics instructors are usually paid by the class and generally start out at about $10 per class. Experienced aerobics instructors can earn up to $50 or $60 per class. The U.S. Department of Labor reports that fitness workers such as aerobics instructors had median annual earnings of $25,910 in 2006. The lowest paid 10 percent earned less than $14,880, and the highest paid 10 percent earned more than $56,750 per year.

Although a sports season lasts only about six months, athletes train year-round to remain in shape and require trainers to guide them. Many personal trainers are paid on a client-by-client basis. Contracts are drawn up and the payment is agreed upon before the training starts. Some trainers get paid more or less depending on the results.

A compensation survey by health and fitness organization IDEA reports that many employers offer health insurance and paid sick and vacation time to full-time employees. They also may provide discounts on products sold in the club (such as shoes, clothes, and equipment) and free memberships to use the facility.

WORK ENVIRONMENT

Most weight training and aerobics classes are held indoors. Depending on the popularity of the class and/ or instructor, aerobics classes can get crowded and hectic at times. Instructors need to keep a level head and maintain a positive, outgoing personality in order to motivate people and keep them together. It is important that aerobics instructors make the class enjoyable yet challenging so that members will return class after class. They also need to be unaffected by complaints of class members, some of whom may find the routines too hard, too easy, or who may not like the music selections. Instructors need to realize that these complaints are not personal attacks.

Fitness trainers need to be able to work on a one-on-one basis with amateur and professional athletes and nonathletes. They may work with individuals who are in pain after an injury and must be able to coax them to use muscles they would probably rather not. Trainers must possess patience, especially for beginners or those who are not athletically inclined, and offer encouragement to help them along.

Most trainers find it rewarding to help others achieve fitness goals. "To truly be a great personal fitness trainer, first you must enjoy helping and being around people. I love being able to motivate and give my clients the knowledge to help them meet their fitness goals," Brett Vicknair says.

OUTLOOK

Because of the country's ever-expanding interest in health and fitness, the U.S. Department of Labor predicts that the job outlook for aerobics instructors should remain strong through 2016, with much faster than average growth. As the population ages, more opportunities will arise to work with the elderly in retirement homes. Large companies and corporations are also interested in keeping insurance costs down by hiring aerobics instructors to hold classes for their employees. The struggle with obesity in the United States will also have an effect on the popularity and demand for aerobics instructors. As communities, schools, and individuals attempt to shed the pounds, the need for fitness instructors and motivators will continue.

Fitness trainers are also in strong demand, especially at the high school level. Currently, some states require high schools to have a fitness trainer on staff. According to Brett Vicknair, home fitness trainers will remain in high demand. The convenience of being able to work out with a personal trainer before work, at lunch, early Saturday morning, or late Friday night make the use of a personal trainer a flexible option. With the hectic lifestyle of most people today, that aspect alone should keep personal training positions on the rise.

FOR MORE INFORMATION

For information on various certifications, contact the following organizations:

Aerobics and Fitness Association of America
15250 Ventura Boulevard, Suite 200
Sherman Oaks, CA 91403
Tel: 877-968-7263
Email: contactAFAA@afaa.com
http://www.afaa.com

National Athletic Trainers' Association
2952 Stemmons Freeway, Suite 200
Dallas, TX 75247-6916
Tel: 800-879-6282
http://www.nata.org

For free information and materials about sports medicine topics, contact
American College of Sports Medicine
PO Box 1440
Indianapolis, IN 46206-1440
Tel: 317-637-9200
http://www.acsm.org

For more information about certification and careers in fitness, contact ACE.
American Council on Exercise (ACE)
4851 Paramount Drive
San Diego, CA 92123
Tel: 888-825-3636
http://www.acefitness.org

For fitness facts and articles, visit IDEA's Web site.
IDEA: The Health and Fitness Association
10455 Pacific Center Court
San Diego, CA 92121
Tel: 800-999-4332
http://www.ideafit.com

AIRCRAFT MECHANICS

QUICK FACTS

SCHOOL SUBJECTS
Computer science
Technical/shop

PERSONAL SKILLS
Mechanical/manipulative
Technical/scientific

WORK ENVIRONMENT
Indoors and outdoors
One location with some travel

MINIMUM EDUCATION LEVEL
Some postsecondary training

MEDIAN SALARY
$47,736

CERTIFICATION OR LICENSING
Recommended

OUTLOOK
About as fast as the average

OVERVIEW

Aircraft mechanics examine, service, repair, and overhaul aircraft and aircraft engines. They also repair, replace, and assemble parts of the airframe (the structural parts of the plane other than the power plant or engine). There are about 138,000 aircraft mechanics working in the United States.

THE JOB

The work of aircraft mechanics employed by the commercial airlines may be classified into two categories: line maintenance mechanics and overhaul mechanics.

Line maintenance mechanics are all-around craft workers who make repairs on all parts of the plane. Working at the airport, they make emergency and other necessary repairs in the time between an aircraft's landing and when it takes off again. They may be told by the pilot, flight engineer, or head mechanic what repairs need to be made, or they may thoroughly inspect the plane themselves for oil leaks, cuts or dents in the surface and

tires, or any malfunction in the radio, radar, and light equipment. In addition, their duties include changing oil, cleaning spark plugs, and replenishing the hydraulic and oxygen systems. They work as fast as safety permits so the aircraft can be put back into service quickly.

Overhaul mechanics keep the aircraft in top operating condition by performing scheduled maintenance, making repairs, and conducting inspections required by the Federal Aviation Administration (FAA). Scheduled maintenance programs are based on the number of hours flown, calendar days, or a combination of these factors. Overhaul mechanics work at the airline's main overhaul base on either or both of the two major parts of the aircraft: the airframe, which includes wings, fuselage, tail assembly, landing gear, control cables, propeller assembly, and fuel and oil tanks; or the power plant, which may be a radial (internal combustion), turbojet, turboprop, or rocket engine.

Other specialties in this field are as follows.

Airframe mechanics work on parts of the aircraft other than the engine, inspecting the various components of the airframe for worn or defective parts. They check the sheet-metal surfaces, measure the tension of control cables, and check for rust, distortion, and cracks in the fuselage and wings. They consult manufacturers' manuals and the airline's maintenance manual for specifications and to determine whether repair or replacement is needed to correct defects or malfunctions. They also use specialized computer software to assist in determining the need, extent, and nature of repairs. Airframe mechanics repair, replace, and assemble parts using a variety of tools, including power shears, sheet-metal breakers, arc and acetylene welding equipment, rivet guns, and air or electric drills.

Aircraft powerplant mechanics inspect, service, repair, and overhaul the engine of the aircraft. Looking through specially designed openings while working from ladders or scaffolds, they examine an engine's external appearance for such problems as cracked cylinders, oil leaks, or cracks or breaks in the turbine blades. They also listen to the engine in operation to detect sounds indicating malfunctioning components, such as sticking or burned valves. The test equipment used to check the engine's operation includes ignition analyzers, compression checkers, distributor timers, and ammeters. If necessary, the mechanics remove the engine from the aircraft, using a hoist or a forklift truck, and take the engine apart. They use sensitive instruments to measure parts for wear and use X-ray and magnetic inspection equipment to check for invisible cracks. Worn or damaged parts are replaced or repaired, and the mechanics then reassemble and reinstall the engine.

Aircraft mechanics adjust and repair electrical wiring systems and aircraft accessories and instruments; inspect, service, and repair pneumatic and hydraulic systems; and handle various servicing tasks, such as flushing crankcases, cleaning screens, greasing moving parts, and checking brakes.

Mechanics may work on only one type of aircraft or on many different types, such as jets, propeller-driven planes, and helicopters. For greater efficiency, some specialize in one section, such as the electrical system, of a particular type of aircraft. Among other specialists, there are *airplane electricians; pneumatic testers and pressure sealer-and-testers; aircraft body repairers* and *bonded structures repairers,* such as *burnishers* and *bumpers;* and *air conditioning mechanics, aircraft rigging and controls mechanics, plumbing and hydraulics mechanics,* and *experimental-aircraft testing mechanics. Avionics technicians* are mechanics who specialize in the aircraft's electronic systems.

Mechanics who work for businesses that own their own aircraft usually handle all necessary repair and maintenance work. The planes, however, generally are small and the work is less complex than in repair shops.

In small, independent repair shops, mechanics must inspect and repair many different types of aircraft. The airplanes may include small commuter planes run by an aviation company, private company planes and jets, private individually owned aircraft, and planes used for flying instruction.

REQUIREMENTS
High School

The first requirement for prospective aircraft mechanics is a high school diploma. Courses in mathematics, physics, chemistry, and mechanical drawing are particularly helpful because they teach the principles involved in the operation of an aircraft, and this knowledge is often necessary to making the repairs. Machine shop, auto mechanics, or electrical shop are important courses for gaining many skills needed by aircraft mechanics.

Postsecondary Training

At one time, mechanics were able to acquire their skills through on-the-job training. This is rare today. Now most mechanics learn the job either in the armed forces or in trade schools approved by the FAA. The trade schools provide training with the necessary tools and equipment in programs that range in length from 18 to 24 months. In considering applicants for certification, the FAA sometimes accepts successful completion of such schooling in place of work experience, but the schools do not guarantee an FAA certificate. There are about 170 such schools in the United States.

The experience acquired by aircraft mechanics in the armed forces sometimes satisfies the work requirements for FAA certification, and veterans may be able to pass the exam with a limited amount of additional study. But jobs in the military service are usually too specialized to satisfy the FAA requirement for broad work experience. In that case, veterans applying for FAA approval will have to complete a training program at a trade school. Schools occasionally give some credit for material learned in the armed services. However, airlines are especially eager to hire aircraft mechanics with both military experience and a trade school education.

Certification or Licensing

FAA certification is necessary for certain types of aircraft mechanics and is usually required to advance beyond entry-level positions. Most mechanics who work on civilian aircraft have FAA authorization as airframe mechanics, power plant mechanics, or avionics repair specialists. Airframe mechanics are qualified to work on the fuselage, wings, landing gear, and other structural parts of the aircraft; power plant mechanics are qualified for work on the engine. Mechanics may qualify for both airframe and power plant licensing, allowing them to work on any part of the plane. Combination airframe and power plant mechanics with an inspector's certificate are permitted to certify inspection work done by other mechanics. Mechanics without certification must be supervised by certified mechanics.

FAA certification is granted only to aircraft mechanics with previous work experience: a minimum of 18 months for an airframe or power plant certificate and at least 30 months working with both engines and airframes for a combination certificate. To qualify for an inspector's certificate, mechanics must have held a combined airframe and power plant certificate for at least three years. In addition, all applicants for certification must pass written and oral tests and demonstrate their ability to do the work authorized by the certificate.

Other Requirements

Aircraft mechanics must be able to work with precision and meet rigid standards. Their physical condition is also important. They need more than average strength for lifting heavy parts and tools, as well as agility for reaching and climbing. And they should not be afraid of heights, since they may work on top of the wings and fuselages of large jet planes.

In addition to education and certification, union membership may be a requirement for some jobs, particularly for mechanics employed by major airlines. The principal unions organizing aircraft mechanics are the International Association of Machinists and Aerospace Workers and the Transport Workers Union of America. In addition, some mechanics are represented by the International Brotherhood of Teamsters, Chauffeurs, Warehousemen and Helpers of America.

EXPLORING

Working with electronic kits, tinkering with automobile engines, and assembling model airplanes are good ways of gauging your ability to do the kinds of work performed by aircraft mechanics. A guided tour of an airfield can give you a brief overall view of this industry. Even better would be a part-time or summer job with an airline in an area such as the baggage department. Small airports may also offer job opportunities for part-time, summer, or replacement workers. You may also earn a Student Pilot (SP) license at the age of 16 and may gain more insight into the basic workings of an airplane that way. Kits for building ultralight craft are also available and may provide even more insight into the importance of proper maintenance and repair.

EMPLOYERS

Of the roughly 138,000 aircraft mechanics currently employed in the United States, more than half work for air transportation companies, according to the U.S. Department of Labor. Each airline usually has one main overhaul base, where most of its mechanics are employed. These bases are found along the main airline routes or near large cities, including New York, Chicago, Los Angeles, Atlanta, San Francisco, and Miami.

About 16 percent of aircraft mechanics works for the federal government. Many of these mechanics are civilians employed at military aviation installations, while others work for the FAA, mainly in its headquarters in Oklahoma City. Other mechanics work for aircraft assembly firms. Most of the rest are general aviation mechanics employed by independent repair shops at airports around the country, by businesses that use their own planes for transporting employees or cargo, by certified supplemental airlines, or by crop-dusting and air-taxi firms.

STARTING OUT

High school graduates who wish to become aircraft mechanics may enter this field by enrolling in an FAA-approved trade school. (Note that there are schools offering this training that do not have FAA approval.) These schools generally have placement services available for their graduates.

Another method is to make direct application to the employment offices of companies providing air transportation and services or the local offices of the state employment service, although airlines prefer to employ people who have already completed training. Many airports are managed by private fixed-base operators, which also operate the airport's repair and maintenance facilities. The field may also be entered through enlistment in the armed forces.

ADVANCEMENT

Promotions depend in part on the size of the organization for which an aircraft mechanic works. The first promotion after beginning employment is usually based on merit and comes in the form of a salary increase. To advance further, many companies require the mechanic to have a combined airframe and power plant certificate, or perhaps an aircraft inspector's certificate.

Advancement could take the following route: journeyworker mechanic, head mechanic or crew chief, inspector, head inspector, and shop supervisor. With additional training, a mechanic may advance to engineering, administrative, or executive positions. In larger airlines, mechanics may advance to become flight engineers, then copilots and pilots. With business training, some mechanics open their own repair shops.

EARNINGS

Although some aircraft mechanics, especially at the entry level and at small businesses, earn little more than the minimum wage, the median annual income for aircraft mechanics was about $47,736 in 2006, according to the U.S. Department of Labor. The top 10 percent earned more than $71,780, while the bottom 10 percent earned $31,075 or less. Mechanics with airframe and power-plant certification earn more than those without it. Overtime, night shift, and holiday pay differentials are usually available and can greatly increase a mechanic's annual earnings.

Most major airlines are covered by union agreements. Their mechanics generally earn more than those working for other employers. Contracts usually include health insurance and often life insurance and retirement plans as well. An attractive fringe benefit for airline mechanics and their immediate families is free or reduced fares on their own and many other airlines. Mechanics working for the federal government also benefit from the greater job security of civil service and government jobs.

WORK ENVIRONMENT

Most aircraft mechanics work a five-day, 40-hour week. Their working hours, however, may be irregular and often include nights, weekends, and holidays, as airlines operate 24 hours a day. Extra work is required during holiday seasons.

When doing overhauling and major inspection work, aircraft mechanics generally work in hangars with adequate heat, ventilation, and lights. If the hangars are full, however, or if repairs must be made quickly, they may work outdoors, sometimes in unpleasant weather. Outdoor work is frequent for line maintenance mechanics, who work at airports, because they must make minor repairs and preflight checks at the terminal to save time. To maintain flight schedules, or to keep from inconveniencing customers in general aviation, the mechanics often have to work under time pressure.

The work is physically strenuous and demanding. Mechanics often have to lift or pull as much as 70 pounds of weight. They may stand, lie, or kneel in awkward positions, sometimes in precarious places such as on a scaffold or ladder.

Noise and vibration are common when testing engines. Regardless of the stresses and strains, aircraft mechanics are expected to work quickly and with great precision.

Although the power tools and test equipment are provided by the employer, mechanics may be expected to furnish their own hand tools.

OUTLOOK

Despite recent fluctuations in air travel, the outlook for aircraft mechanics should remain steady over the course of the next decade. Employment opportunities will open up due to fewer young workers entering the labor force, fewer entrants from the military, and more retirees leaving positions. But the job prospects will vary according to the type of employer. Less competition for jobs is likely to be found at smaller commuter and regional airlines, FAA repair stations, and in general aviation. These employers pay lower wages and fewer applicants compete for their positions, while higher paying airline positions, which also include travel benefits, are more in demand among qualified applicants. Mechanics who keep up with technological advancements in electronics, composite materials, and other areas will be in greatest demand.

Employment of aircraft mechanics is likely to increase about as fast as the average through 2016, according to the U.S. Department of Labor. The demand for air travel and the numbers of aircraft created are expected to increase due to population growth and rising incomes. However, employment growth will be affected by the use of automated systems that make the aircraft mechanic's job more efficient.

FOR MORE INFORMATION

For career books and information about high school student membership, national forums, and job fairs, contact

Aviation Information Resources Inc.
3800 Camp Creek Parkway, Suite 18-100
Atlanta, GA 30331
Tel: 800-JET-JOBS
http://www.jet-jobs.com

Professional Aviation Maintenance Association
400 Commonwealth Drive
Warrendale, PA 15096
Tel: 866-865-7262
Email: hq@pama.org
http://www.pama.org

AIRPORT SECURITY PERSONNEL

OVERVIEW

Airport security personnel is a blanket term describing all workers who protect the safety of passengers and staff in the nation's airports and aircraft. One of the largest group of personnel in this line of work is *security screeners,* who are responsible for identifying dangerous objects or hazardous materials in baggage, cargo, or on traveling passengers and preventing these objects and their carriers from boarding planes. Also included in this group of workers are *air marshals,* who act as on-board security agents, protecting passengers, pilots, and other airline staff in the case of any emergencies while in the air. More than 40,000 people are employed in airport security.

THE JOB

Protecting U.S. skies, airports, and passengers is a huge undertaking that requires many qualified, well-trained individuals in different security roles. The most visible airport security worker is the security screener, also called the *baggage and passenger screener.* These workers use computers, X-ray machines, and handheld scanners to screen bags and their owners passing through airport terminals. In addition to using technology to help them identify dangerous items, they also have to depend on their own eyesight to catch suspicious behavior and read the X-ray screens for signs of danger. These workers must be focused and alert, while also remaining personable and courteous to people being screened. The screening process can take a lot of time during high-volume travel days, and passengers waiting in line may be late for a flight, impatient, or simply rude. For this reason, security screeners must be people-oriented, able to manage crowds, and maintain composure in what can be stressful conditions.

The need for security is not limited to the ground. Air marshals, also called *security agents,* have the demanding

QUICK FACTS

SCHOOL SUBJECTS
Computer science
Government
Mathematics

PERSONAL SKILLS
Following instructions
Leadership/management

WORK ENVIRONMENT
Indoors and outdoors
Primarily multiple locations

MINIMUM EDUCATION LEVEL
Some postsecondary training

MEDIAN SALARY
$31,665

CERTIFICATION OR LICENSING
None

OUTLOOK
Faster than the average

job of protecting all airline passengers and staff from on-board threats, such as terrorists, bombs, or other weapons. These workers are often covert in their operations, meaning they may be dressed and seated like an average passenger and thereby surprise a potential attacker if the need arises. Much of the details of air marshal jobs are classified to protect national security, such as their exact number and identities, routes, and training procedures. However the basics of their job is much like that of a Secret Service agent. They must be attentive to all activity that goes on around them, identify potential threats to security, and deal with dangerous individuals or objects once exposed on board. The main difference between air marshals and other security agents is they must be trained and able to handle possible warfare in a confined space at 30,000 feet in the air.

Another airport security job of high importance is that of *security director.* These workers, employed by the federal government, are responsible for all security personnel within an airport. They oversee the hiring, training, and work of baggage and passenger screeners, air marshals, and other security guards. In the nation's largest airports, such as JFK in New York City or O'Hare in Chicago, directors are in charge of hundreds of workers. Because of their high level of responsibility, security directors often have previous experience in crisis management or law enforcement.

REQUIREMENTS
High School

To work in most airport security jobs, you should have at least a high school diploma. However, security screeners can sidestep this educational requirement with previous job experience in security. While in high school, take classes in history and government to familiarize yourself with previous events and political threats that have threatened our national security, such as foreign hijackers and terrorist operations. You should also be comfortable working with computers since most jobs in security involve a great deal of technology. Math classes can be beneficial because as a security worker, you must be analytical and observant to identify and catch dangers before they happen.

Postsecondary Training

All security workers, from screeners to directors, are highly trained before starting their jobs. Screeners are trained on how to operate and identify dangerous objects by using equipment such as X-ray machines and handheld wands. They also must be prepared to manage potentially dangerous individuals. Screeners currently receive 40 hours of training before their first day at work, and receive an additional 60 hours of training while on the job. This training period may be extended due to increased scrutiny on screeners' performance and heightened national security risks.

Air marshals are rigorously trained in classified training centers across the country; they usually come to the job with previous military or civilian police force experience. Similarly, security directors must have previous federal security experience and are trained for up to 400 hours before taking on the responsibility of directing an entire airport security staff.

Other Requirements

All airport security personnel have demanding jobs that require a calm demeanor under pressure. Screeners often have to stand for hours at a time and assist in lifting passengers' luggage onto the screening belt.

Their eyesight must be strong enough to detect even the smallest of possible threats displayed on a computer screen. To ensure that individuals can handle these demands, potential screeners face many physical and vision tests to ensure they are up to the job. All screeners must be U.S. citizens or nationals and pass tests evaluating mental abilities (English reading, writing, and speaking), visual observation (including color perception), hearing, and manual dexterity. Similarly, air marshals and directors of security must pass vision and hearing tests and be in good physical shape to face and dominate potential attackers.

EXPLORING

To explore this job, watch people at work the next time you are at the airport. Notice how many people are involved in screening luggage and passengers. While you should not talk to these screeners and other security staff while they are at work, you may be able to schedule an interview with security personnel while they are on break or perhaps over the phone. Talk to a teacher or your school's guidance counselor for help in arranging this.

You can also learn about security jobs at your local library or online. Explore the Web sites of the Federal Aviation Administration (FAA) for facts and job descriptions, changes in policy, and even summer camp opportunities. The link at the end of this article is a good place to start your research.

EMPLOYERS

In late 2001, airport and airline security was placed under the oversight of the federal government. While some screening jobs may still be handled by private companies, all security personnel are screened and trained under federal rules and regulations. This shift in responsibility was done to improve standards in security and ensure the safety of U.S. passengers and airline staff. The Transportation Security Administration (TSA) and the FAA are the employers of all airport security staff. According to the TSA, there are more than 43,000 people employed in airport security, approximately 28,000 of whom are security screeners working in the nation's airports.

STARTING OUT

Depending on the security level you want to be employed in, you can start out working with no more than a high school diploma and on-the-job training. Security screening jobs are a great way to start out in this line of work. These jobs provide front-line experience in airport security and can offer flexible part-time schedules.

Positions as air marshals or directors or security are not entry-level positions. If you are interested in one of these jobs, you will need previous experience with the police, U.S. military, or other position in which you have gained skills in protecting the lives of others.

ADVANCEMENT

Screening jobs have high turnover rates, and as a result, offer many chances for advancement. After a couple of years of experience in baggage and passenger screening, you can work into higher positions in management or busier traffic responsibility. Security managers may be responsible for hundreds of workers and oversee the hiring and training of new workers.

Positions as air marshals already offer a high level of responsibility, but qualified and talented individuals can advance into manager and director roles, responsible for hundreds and even thousands of workers.

The TSA Web site offers the Career Toolbox, an instrument that can help you plan your progress through various airport security careers in the TSA. See http://www.tsa.gov/join/benefits/benefits_career_toolbox.shtm for more details.

EARNINGS

Before airline security was adopted by the TSA, screeners were paid minimum wage. But to attract and retain qualified and dedicated workers, earnings have been raised considerably, with most full-time screeners earning salaries of $24,000 to $41,000 a year. Their pay increases as their level of experience and responsibility increases. According to Payscale.com, airline security screeners with between one and four years of experience earned a median annual salary of $31,665 in 2008. Air marshals and directors earn much more, with directors topping out at a salary of $150,000 or more—one of the highest salaries in government service.

WORK ENVIRONMENT

As previously stated, any job in airport security is demanding and stressful, especially during high periods of travel, such as the holidays. Screeners face physical challenges of standing, bending, and lifting during their shifts, while having to maintain total visual focus on their X-ray machines or while searching individual passengers by hand.

The job of air marshals can be extremely stressful. These workers must be prepared to overcome an attacker in a confined space without risking harm to any of the plane's passengers. In addition, air marshals must spend considerable time away from home.

OUTLOOK

With the new awareness of airline dangers following recent terrorist attacks, the employment of airport security personnel will grow at a faster-than-average rate. Despite better pay, security screeners still have high turnover rates due to the high demands involved with the job. This turnover will continue to create many new jobs in the future. While jobs as air marshals and security directors will not be as plentiful, there will always be a critical need for qualified and skilled individuals to protect airplanes and passengers from security threats.

FOR MORE INFORMATION

The FAA offers a wealth of information on its Web site, from airline accident statistics to career guidance. Visit the Education pages for information on summer camps for middle and high school students interested in aviation careers.

Federal Aviation Administration
800 Independence Avenue, SW
Washington, DC 20591
Tel: 866-835-5322
http://www.faa.gov

According to its Web site, the TSA "sets the standard for excellence in transportation security through its people, processes, and technologies." Explore the site for details on the nation's threat advisory level and tips on flying and packing safely.

Transportation Security Administration
TSA-21 Human Resources
601 South 12th Street
Arlington, VA 22202-4220
http://www.tsa.gov

ANIMAL CARETAKERS

OVERVIEW

Animal caretakers, as the name implies, take care of animals. The job responsibilities range from the day-to-day normal activities of caring for a healthy animal to caring for sick, injured, or aging animals. Daily animal care routines usually involve feeding and providing drinking water for each animal, making sure that their enclosure is clean, safe, appropriately warm, and, if needed, stocked

QUICK FACTS

SCHOOL SUBJECTS
Biology
Health

PERSONAL SKILLS
Following instructions
Helping/teaching

WORK ENVIRONMENT
Indoors and outdoors
One location with some travel

MINIMUM EDUCATION LEVEL
High school diploma

MEDIAN SALARY
$18,137

CERTIFICATION OR LICENSING
None available

OUTLOOK
Faster than the average

laboratory animal technicians, laboratory animal technologists, and *kennel technicians.*

Animal caretakers are employed in kennels, stables, pet stores, boarding facilities, walking services, shelters, sanctuaries, rescue centers, zoos, aquariums, veterinary facilities, and animal experimentation labs. They may also be employed by the federal government, state or local parks that have educational centers with live animals, the U.S. Department of Agriculture in programs such as quarantine centers for animals coming into the United States, and the Centers for Disease Control laboratories.

Almost every one of these employers expects the animal caretaker to provide the daily maintenance routine for animals. The caretaker may be responsible for one animal or one species, or may be required to handle many animals and many species. A veterinary assistant is likely to encounter dogs and cats, with the occasional bird or reptile. A *wildlife shelter worker* works with the local wild population. In most parts of the United States that means working with raccoons, skunks, porcupines, hunting birds, song birds, the occasional predator such as coyote or fox, and perhaps large animals such as bear, elk, moose, or deer.

Caretakers are responsible for some or all of the following tasks: selecting, mixing, and measuring out the appropriate food; providing water; cleaning the animal and the enclosure; changing bedding and groundcover if used; moving the animals from night facilities to day facilities or exercise spaces or different quarters; sterilizing facilities and equipment not in use; recording and filing statistics, medical reports, or lab reports on each animal; and providing general attention and affection to animals that need human contact.

The animal caretaker learns to recognize signs of illness such as lack of appetite, fatigue, skin sores, and changed behavior. They check the animals they can physically approach or handle for lumps, sores, fat, texture of the skin, fur, or feathers, and condition of the mouth. Since most animals do not exhibit signs of illness until they are very sick, it is important that the caretaker who sees the animal most regularly note any small change in the animal's physical or mental state.

The caretaker also maintains the animal's living quarters. For most animals in their care, this will be an enclosure of some type. The enclosure has to be safe and secure. The animal should not be able to injure itself within the enclosure, be able to escape, or have outside animals able to get into the enclosure. Small holes in an enclosure wall would not threaten a coyote, but small holes that a snake can pass through could

with materials to keep the animal active and engaged. Caretakers may be responsible for creating different enrichment materials so that the animal is challenged by new objects and activities. They may exercise or train the animals. They may assist veterinarians or other trained medical staff in working with animals that require treatment. Animal caretakers may also maintain the written records for each animal. These records can include weight, eating habits, behavior, medicines given, or treatment given. Animal caretakers hold about 157,000 jobs in the United States.

THE JOB

Animal caretakers perform the daily duties of animal care, which include feeding, grooming, cleaning, exercising, examining, and nurturing the individuals in their care. Depending on their specialty, these caretakers have titles such as *animal shelter workers, grooms, veterinary assistants, wildlife assistants, animal shelter attendants,*

threaten a rabbit. Horses can injure themselves in their stables and are vulnerable to a multitude of pasture injuries.

The quarters need to be the right size for the animal. If they are too large, the animal will feel threatened by the amount of open space, feeling it cannot protect the area adequately. Inappropriately small enclosures can be just as damaging. If the animal cannot get sufficient exercise within the enclosure, it will also suffer both psychologically and physically.

Caretakers set up and oversee enrichment activities that provide an animal with something to keep it engaged and occupied while in its home. For even the smallest rodent, enrichment activities are required. Most of us are familiar with enrichment toys for our pets. These are balls and squeaky toys for dogs and cats, bells and different foot surfaces for birds, and tunnels and rolling wheels for hamsters and gerbils. Wild animals require the same stimulation. Animal caretakers hide food in containers that require ingenuity and tools to open (ideal for a raccoon), or ropes and inner tubes for animals such as primates to swing on and play with.

Animals that can exercise are taken to specially designed areas for this purpose. For hunting birds this may mean flying on a creance (tether); for dogs it may mean a game of fetch in the yard. Horses may be lunged (run around), or hacked (ridden); they may also simply be turned out in a field to exercise themselves, but some form of training is useful to keep them in optimal riding condition. Domestic animal shelters, veterinarian offices, kennels, boarding facilities, and dog-walking services work predominantly with domesticated dogs and cats, and perhaps horses at boarding centers. Exercise often consists of walks or free runs within an enclosed space. The animal caretaker for these employers often works with a rotating population of animals, some of whom may be in their care only for a few hours or days, although some animals may be cared for over longer periods. Caretakers at sanctuaries, quarantines, laboratories, and such may care for the same animals for months or years.

It is also an unpleasant side of the job that in almost every facility, the caretaker will have to deal with the death of an animal in his or her care. For veterinary offices, shelters, and wildlife facilities of any type, animal deaths are a part of everyone's experience. Shelters may choose to euthanize (kill) animals that are beyond medical treatment, deemed unadoptable, or unmaintainable because of their condition or the facilities' inability to house them. But even for places without a euthanasia policy, any center working with older, injured, sick, or rescued animals is going to lose the battle to save some of them. For the animal caretaker, this may mean losing an animal that just came in that morning, or losing an animal that he or she fed every day for years. It can be as painful as losing one's own pet.

As an animal caretaker gains experience working with the animals, the responsibilities may increase. Caretakers may begin to perform tasks that either senior caretakers were performing or medical specialists were doing. This can include administering drugs; clipping nails, beaks, and wing feathers; banding wild animals with identification tags; and training the animal.

There are numerous clerical tasks that may also be part of the animal caretakers' routine. Beyond the medical reports made on the animals, animal caretakers may be required to screen people looking to take an animal home and write status reports or care plans. The animal caretaker may be responsible for communicating to an animal's owner the status of the animal in his or her care. Other clerical and administrative tasks may be required, depending on the facilities, the specific job, and the employer. But for most animal caretakers, the day is usually spent looking after the well-being of the animals.

REQUIREMENTS
High School

Students preparing for animal caretaker careers need a high school diploma. While in high school, classes in anatomy and physiology, science, and health are recommended. Students can obtain valuable information by taking animal science classes, if available. Any knowledge about animal breeds, behavior, and health is helpful. The basics of human nutrition, disease, reproduction, and aging help to give a background for learning about these topics for different species. A basic grasp of business and computer skills will help with the clerical tasks.

Postsecondary Training

There are two-year college programs in animal health that lead to an associate's degree. This type of program offers courses in anatomy and physiology, chemistry, mathematics, clinical pharmacology, pathology, radiology, animal care and handling, infectious diseases, biology, and current veterinary treatment. Students graduating from these programs go on to work in veterinary practices, shelters, zoos and aquariums, pharmaceutical companies, and laboratory research facilities. Students should look for programs accredited by the American Veterinary Medical Association.

Training programs and workshops are available through the Humane Society of the United States, the American Humane Association, and the National Animal Control Association. Although not required to become an animal caretaker, these workshops can provide valuable information about topics such as cruelty investigations, appropriate methods of euthanasia for shelter animals, proper guidelines for capturing animals, techniques for preventing problems with wildlife, and dealing with the public.

Apprenticing for the handling of wild hunting birds is required by most facilities. This can include having apprentices pursue a falconry license, which means apprenticing to a licensed falconer. Licenses for assistant laboratory animal technician, laboratory animal technician, and laboratory animal technologist are available through the American Association for Laboratory Animal Science and may be required by some employers.

A bachelor's degree is required for many jobs, particularly in zoos and aquariums. Degrees in wildlife management, biology, zoology, animal physiology, or other related fields are most useful.

Other Requirements

Animal caretakers should have great love, empathy, and respect for animals. They should have a strong interest in the environment. Patience, compassion, dependability, and the ability to work on repetitive, physically challenging, or unstimulating tasks without annoyance are essential characteristics for job satisfaction as an animal caretaker.

EXPLORING

Volunteering is the most effective method of experiencing the tasks of an animal caretaker. Most shelters, rescue centers, and sanctuaries, and some zoos, aquariums, and labs rely on volunteers to fill their staff. Opportunities as a volunteer may include the ability to work directly with animals in some or all of the capacities of a paid animal caretaker.

There is always a concern, sometimes justified, that an organization will never pay someone whose services they have gotten for free. You may not be able to get paid employment from the same organization for which you volunteered. But many organizations recognize the benefit of hiring prior volunteers: They get someone who already knows the institution, the system, and the preferred caretaking methods.

Volunteering also provides a line on your resume that demonstrates that you bring experience to your first paying job. It provides valuable references who can vouch for your skills with animals, your reliability, and your dedication to the field. Thus, you should treat any volunteer position with the same professionalism that you would a paid job.

Other avenues for exploration are interviewing people already in the position, or finding a paid position in a facility where animal caretakers work so you can see them in action. You may also begin by providing a pet walking or sitting service in your neighborhood, but be sure to only take on the number and kinds of animals you know you can handle successfully.

EMPLOYERS

There are many different types of facilities and businesses that employ animal caretakers, including veterinary offices, kennels, stables, breeding farms, boarding facilities, rescue centers, shelters, sanctuaries, zoos, aquariums, and pet stores. Other job opportunities for animal caretakers exist in government agencies and with state and local parks. This field is growing, and increasing job opportunities will be available all over the country for animal caretakers. Since pet ownership and interest in animals continues to increase, more and more jobs will become available with all kinds of employers, resulting in work in environments ranging from nonprofit organizations to retail stores to laboratories.

STARTING OUT

High school students who volunteer will be able to test the job before committing to it. They will also, as explained earlier, be able to get a job on their resume that demonstrates their experience in the field.

Two- and four-year college programs offer some placement assistance, but familiarity with the regional market for organizations that use animal caretakers will assist you in selecting places to target with your resume. Many animal caretakers work in veterinary offices and boarding facilities or kennels, but animal research laboratories also hire many caretakers. Other employers include the federal government, state governments, pharmaceutical companies, teaching hospitals, and food production companies.

ADVANCEMENT

Advancement depends on the job setting. There may be promotion opportunities to senior technician, supervisor, assistant facilities manager, or facilities manager. Some animal caretakers may open their own facilities or services. Services such as dog walking require little in the way of offices or equipment, so these are easy ways for animal caretakers to start on their own, with an established clientele that they bring from a previous position.

Laboratory workers can move from assistant technician to technician to technologist with increased education and experience. But for most promotions, more education is usually required.

EARNINGS

Animal caretakers earned a median salary of $18,137 in 2006, according to the *Occupational Outlook Handbook*. The top 10 percent earned more than $30,451, and the bottom 10 percent earned less than $13,644 a year.

Self-employed animal caretakers who provide dog walking, kennel, sitting, or other cottage industry services do not have salaries that are readily available for review, but in large cities, boarding a dog overnight can cost $25 to $40, with a minimum of three dogs usually at one facility. Dog walkers charge between $5 and $12 a dog. There is little overhead for either service, beyond perhaps providing food.

WORK ENVIRONMENT

Animals may either be kept indoors or outdoors, in any type of weather. Eagles don't come in from the rain, so animal caretakers caring for eagles still have to traipse outside to feed them when it's raining. Horses are turned out in the middle of the winter, so horse grooms still have to carry bales of hay to the pasture in the middle of January snowdrifts. Though currying, saddling, exercising, medicating, and cleaning up after a horse—or horses—may seem like a dream job to some, it is considerably less romantic to clean a stable day in and day out, regardless of weather.

Depending on the facilities, heavy lifting may be part of the job. You may have to lift crates, animals, food, equipment, or other items big enough to accommodate a large animal. The work can sometimes be hard, repetitive, and dirty. Cleaning enclosures and disinfecting spaces can involve hot or cold water and chemicals.

The work can also be dangerous, depending on the animals you work with. Although animals that are handled correctly and are treated with the proper respect and distance can be quite safe, situations can arise where the animal is unpredictable, or is frightened or cornered. Although this is more likely with animal caretakers working with wildlife populations, large dogs, horses, and cattle are quite capable of injuring and killing people. There is a certain physical risk involved in working with animals, which may be as minor as scratches from nails or bites, but can be as great as broken or crushed bones, or accidental death.

Many facilities require long workdays and workweeks, odd hours, weekend work, holiday work, and intermittent schedules. Depending on the hours of the facility, the services provided, and the staffing, there may be several shifts, including a graveyard shift. Animal caretakers should be prepared to work a changing schedule. The needs of animals don't cease for weekends and holidays.

Also, for many facilities, animals that require round-the-clock care have to be taken home with an animal caretaker who is willing to provide whatever service the animal needs, including waking every two hours to bottlefeed a newborn chimp.

OUTLOOK

The animal care field is expected to grow faster than the average through 2016, according to the U.S. Department of Labor. More people have pets and are more concerned with their pets' care. Since most households have all the adults in full-time employment, animals are left home alone longer than in earlier times. Dog-walking services, pet sitting and in-house care, boarding facilities, and kennels that provide assistance with the daily care of an animal for the working or traveling owner are far more prevalent and successful than before.

Veterinary services are also on the rise, with the increased number of pets and the increased awareness on the part of owners that vet services are essential to an animal's well-being.

There is a high turnover in the profession. This is due in part to the seasonal nature of some of the jobs, the low pay, and the lack of advancement opportunities in the field. Wildlife sanctuaries, release-and-rescue programs, shelters, and zoos and aquariums are heavily dependent on charitable contributions and fund-raising efforts. Staff employment can be tied to the rise and fall of donations. Many of these institutions rely heavily on volunteer labor. As such, the competitiveness for the paid jobs is quite high.

Positions as animal caretakers in zoos, aquariums, and rehabilitation and rescue centers are the most sought after, partly because of the ability to work with exotic and wild species. Aspiring animal caretakers will find few openings in these facilities.

Graduates of veterinary technician programs have the best employment prospects. Laboratory animal technicians and technologists also have good opportunities. Increasing concern for animal rights and welfare means that these facilities are staffing more professionals to operate their labs.

FOR MORE INFORMATION

For information about animal laboratory work and certification programs, contact

American Association for Laboratory Animal Science
9190 Crestwyn Hills Drive
Memphis, TN 38125
Tel: 901-754-8620
Email: info@aalas.org
http://www.aalas.org

For information on available training programs, such as the facility accreditation program, certification program for kennel operators, complete staff training program, and ethics program, contact

American Boarding Kennels Association
1702 East Pikes Peak Avenue
Colorado Springs, CO 80909
Tel: 719-667-1600
Email: info@abka.com
http://www.abka.com

For more information on careers, schools, and resources, contact AVMA.

American Veterinary Medical Association (AVMA)
1931 North Meacham Road, Suite 100
Schaumburg, IL 60173
Tel: 847-925-8070
Email: avmainfo@avma.org
http://www.avma.org

For information on working in animal control and for additional career and salary information on animal care jobs, contact

National Animal Control Association
P.O. Box 480851
Kansas City, MO 64148
Tel: 913-768-1319
http://www.nacanet.org

For information on the Student Career Experience Program, contact the U.S. Fish and Wildlife Service in your state or visit the following Web site:

U.S. Fish and Wildlife Service
http://www.fws.gov

ANIMAL HANDLERS

OVERVIEW

Anybody who works directly with animals, from the caretaker of your local park's petting zoo, to the activist who reintroduces wild animals to national parks, is an *animal handler*. Animal handlers care for, train, and study animals in such places as zoos, parks, research laboratories, animal breeding facilities, rodeos, and museums. An animal handler's job involves feeding the animals, cleaning their living and sleeping areas, preparing medications, and other aspects of basic care. A handler may also be actively involved in an animal's training, and in presenting animals to the public in shows and parks.

THE JOB

Wrangling an iguana for a movie production; preparing the diet for a zoo's new albino alligator; comforting bison to keep them from committing "suicide"; training cats for an animal-assisted therapy program at a nursing home—all these responsibilities, strange as they may seem, actually exist for some animal handlers. Many western states have long telephone book listings of animal handlers who rent out trained iguanas, horses, cougars, cattle, and other animals for movie productions. Zoos and marine animal parks hire highly trained keepers to feed, shelter, and protect some of the most exotic animals in the world. Bison, if not properly prepared for transport, can easily be provoked to stampede, sometimes killing themselves. And even cats can be a form of therapy, as people introduce their pets to elderly and ill patients who respond well to interaction with animals.

Whether taking on jobs like those listed above or working for a small park or large zoo, all animal handlers are called upon for the daily care and safety of animals. They may have special training in a particular animal or breed or work with a variety of animals. Jennifer Gales works in the petting zoo of Knotts Berry Farm in California, caring for the goats, ponies, rabbits, tortoises, and other animals visited every day. It is her responsibility to check the health of the animals, and to feed and water them. "You have to learn as much as you can about the animal's habits and personality," she says. "Every animal is different." With a wide knowledge of an animal's nutritional and exercise requirements, animal handlers make sure the animals in their care are well-fed, well-groomed, and healthy. They prepare food and formulas, which may include administering medications. Maintaining proper shelters for animals requires cleaning the area, ensuring good ventilation, and providing proper bedding. Animal handlers arrange for vaccinations, as well as look for diseases in their animals. They also prepare animals for transport, knowing how to use muzzles and kennels, and how to calm an animal. But an animal handler needs a rapport with the two-legged creatures as well; working with people is an important aspect of most animal care jobs, as many of these animals are kept for presentation and performance.

"Every day is different," Gales says, "because animals have good and bad days, just like people. There are days they just don't want to be touched at all, and they let you know it by their actions." The relationship between an animal and its handler can be very strong, particularly in training situations. Dogs trained for a police unit require specially certified trainers, and the dogs often both live and work alongside the officers to whom they are assigned. The same is true of handlers who train seeing-eye dogs or hearing-ear dogs: it is the handler's responsibility to train the animal to think of itself and its owner as one unit, thereby assuring it will watch out for both its own safety and that of its owner. Handlers who breed animals are often very devoted to the animals they place in other homes. They often interview prospective buyers, making sure the animal will have proper shelter, exercise, and feeding. Handlers who prepare animals for research in a lab must pay close attention to animal health, as well as their own; many states require health tests and immunizations of people who run the risk of catching diseases or illnesses from the animals they study.

REQUIREMENTS

High School

To prepare for a career as an animal handler, take biology, chemistry, and other science courses offered by your high school. The study of science will be important to any student of animals, as will the study of psychology and sociology. Knowing about animal nutrition, health, behavior, and biology will help you to understand the animals you care for, and how to best provide for them. And if you do choose to go on to college, most animal-related courses of study are science based.

Some may think of animal handlers as people who spend all their time separate from the rest of the community, communicating only with animals and limiting interaction with humans. However, nothing could be further from the truth—most animal handlers work actively with the public; they present the animals in

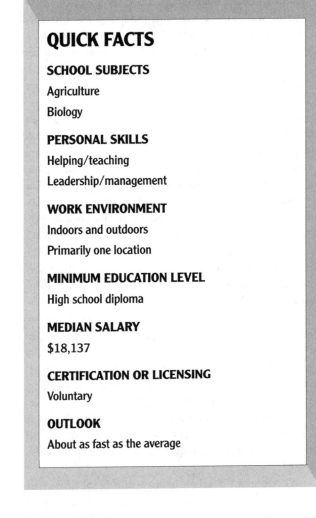

QUICK FACTS

SCHOOL SUBJECTS
Agriculture
Biology

PERSONAL SKILLS
Helping/teaching
Leadership/management

WORK ENVIRONMENT
Indoors and outdoors
Primarily one location

MINIMUM EDUCATION LEVEL
High school diploma

MEDIAN SALARY
$18,137

CERTIFICATION OR LICENSING
Voluntary

OUTLOOK
About as fast as the average

zoos and public programs, and may even perform with the animals. Join your speech and debate team, or your drama club, to prepare for speaking in front of groups of people.

Because so many animal programs, from petting zoos to animal therapy programs, rely on community support, there are many volunteer opportunities for high school students looking to work with animals. Zoos, parks, and museums need volunteers, as do kennels, shelters, and local chapters of the Humane Society. These organizations may even offer students paid part-time positions. If few opportunities exist in your area, check with the nearest zoo about summer internship programs for high school students.

Postsecondary Training

Though Jennifer Gales doesn't have a college degree, some of her coworkers at the Knotts Berry Farm petting zoo are pursuing degrees in the veterinary sciences. The value of a college degree depends on the work you do. Many animal handlers do not have degrees, but zoos often prefer to hire people with a postsecondary education. A degree can often determine promotions and pay raises among the workers of a zoo. Many universities offer degrees in animal sciences, zoology, and zoological sciences. There are also graduate degrees in zoology, which may require courses in physiology, animal behavior, and oceanography. Courses for animal science programs generally focus on animal research, but some programs allow students to create their own course plans to involve hands-on experience as an animal handler. The Santa Fe Community College in Gainesville, Florida, offers a unique and popular zoo animal technology program; students work toward an associate's degree while gaining a great deal of first-hand zoo experience. The students run an 80-species zoo entirely on their own and, upon graduation, enter bachelor's programs or other animal care jobs.

Some consider a job as an animal handler an internship in and of itself; after gaining experience in a petting zoo or teaching zoo, or working with a breeder or stable hand, some animal handlers pursue careers as zookeepers, veterinarians, and animal researchers. Most college animal science and zoology programs offer some hands-on experience with animals; in the case of the Santa Fe Community College mentioned above, an internship with the school's zoo is required along with the academic classes.

Many unpaid internships are available for those willing to volunteer their time to researchers and other animal professionals. Check with your local university and zoo to find out about opportunities to study animals in the wild, or to reintroduce animals to their native habitats.

Certification or Licensing

Some animal handlers in very specialized situations, such as patrol dog trainers and lab animal technicians, are required to pursue certification. The American Association for Laboratory Animal Sciences offers certification for those working with lab animals. But for the majority of animal handlers, no certification program exists. Accreditation is generally only required of the institutions and programs that hire animal handlers. The American Zoo and Aquarium Association offers accreditation, as well as memberships to individuals. Though members are required to have a certain amount of experience, membership is not mandatory for those working with animals.

Other Requirements

"I have always had a love for animals," Gales says. "The only ones I don't like are snakes—I need legs on animals." It is important for animal handlers to love the animals they care for. What might not be as apparent, however, is the need for animal handlers to enjoy working with people as well. Animal handlers are often required to present the animals to park and zoo visitors, and to serve as tour guides; they also work as instructors in zoo and museum education programs. Some animal handlers even perform alongside their trained animals in theme parks and shows. Some shows, such as marine animal shows, can be particularly strenuous, calling for very athletic trainers.

Working with animals on a daily basis requires patience and calmness since animals faced with unfamiliar situations are easily frightened. Animal handlers must be very knowledgeable about the needs and habits of all the animals in their care. Handlers are often called upon to transport animals, and they must know ways to best comfort them. Impatience may result in serious injury to both the animal and the handler.

EXPLORING

If you grew up with a family pet or have spent time on a farm, you're probably already very familiar with how to care for animals. But if you want to gain experience handling a large group of animals, contact your local zoo about volunteer or part-time positions. Many zoos have programs in place to introduce young people to the duties and responsibilities of an animal handler. If your local zoo doesn't have such a program, try to create your own: Contact zookeepers, express your interest in their work, and ask to "shadow" them for a few days.

Many part-time jobs are available to high school students interested in working with animals. Pet shops, petting zoos, stables, and kennels are likely to have a few after-school positions. In larger cities, you may be able to start your own animal care business as a dog walker or pet sitter. Some animal handlers work exclusively with movie production crews and other entertainment venues; you may be able to work as a temporary assistant on a production.

EMPLOYERS

Animal handlers are employed by zoos, aquariums, parks, animal shelters, movie studios, research laboratories, animal breeding facilities, rodeos, and museums. There are about 157,000 nonfarm animal care and service workers in the United States.

STARTING OUT

Jennifer Gales found it very easy to get her job with Knotts Berry Farm. "If you love animals," she said, "it just shows in what you say, and the way you talk about them. My interview was about an hour of me sitting there talking about animals." Depending on the area of animal care in which you want to work, you may be able to find many great opportunities. A high school job or internship is a good start; experience with animals is what is most important to employers hiring handlers. Any volunteering you've done will also look good to an employer because it shows that you have a personal dedication to the care of animals. Kennels, petting zoos, museums, and animal shelters often run classified ads in the newspaper; due to the lower pay and some of the hazards involved in handling animals, those positions are frequently available.

Jobs with zoos in major cities, or with animal shows, can be highly competitive. If you're hoping to work in a larger, more famous zoo, you should first pursue experience with a smaller zoo. Jobs working with marine mammals are also difficult to get; because there are few marine animal shows in the country (such as those performed at Sea World parks), you may first have to pursue experience with internships and college programs.

ADVANCEMENT

Most people who work with animals are not looking to climb any ladder of advancement. As a matter of fact, many people change from high-paying careers to lower paying animal care jobs just to do something they love. Much of the student body of the animal tech program at Santa Fe Community College is composed of people over thirty years old who have tried other careers. Some who have gained experience handling and training animals may start their own businesses, perhaps building their own stables of trained "actors" to hire out for area movie shoots, stage shows, parades, and other performances. Some animal handlers may pursue higher education while working full or part time, taking courses toward veterinary sciences degrees, or degrees in biology. With a degree, an animal handler may have a better chance at the higher paying, supervisory zookeeper positions. After years with a particular zoo, an animal handler can take on more responsibility and make decisions that influence the direction of the zoo.

EARNINGS

The opportunity to work directly with a variety of different animals is often reward enough for animal handlers. Someone who owns a stable of well-trained animals used in performances may be able to negotiate for large contracts, or a successful dog breeder may make a comfortable living with an established business, but most animal handlers make do with small salaries and hourly wages. The Santa Fe Community College advises the graduates of their animal technology program to expect between $15,000 and $18,500 annually. This wage varies according to region—in the colder Midwestern and Northern states, and in California, animal handlers can make more than those living in the Southeast. An experienced animal handler may draw an hourly wage of $16 to $20. Many full-time, salaried zoo positions include health benefits. The U.S. Department of Labor estimates that nonfarm animal handlers earned a median salary of $18,137 in 2006, with 10 percent earning less than $13,644 and 10 percent more than $30,451.

WORK ENVIRONMENT

Depending on the lives of the animals for which they care, handlers usually work both indoors and outdoors. But the indoors is often nothing more than an animal shelter, and not much different from the pens outdoors. Be prepared for smelly, messy, and dusty environments; if you have allergies, they'll be under constant assault. It will be both to your benefit, and the animal's, to make sure you work in well-ventilated areas. Some institutions, particularly animal research labs, require handlers to have immunizations and physicals before working with the animals. In addition to allergies, there is some danger of diseases transferred from animals to humans. These risks can be lessened with protective clothing like lab coats, gloves, and ventilated hoods.

The temperament of your animals will also affect your work environment. Handlers must be prepared for occasional scratches, bites, and kicks from animals with even the best dispositions. Though some animals can be very noisy when disturbed, handlers attempt to keep their animals' surroundings quiet and calm.

OUTLOOK

With the popularity of cable channels such as the Discovery Channel and Animal Planet, as well as feature films focusing on animals, the public's interest in animals is only likely to increase. Zoos, parks, and museums will benefit a great deal from any increased exposure the public has to the animal kingdom. Zoos must also compete with television as family entertainment, and therefore are constantly striving to improve their facilities with more exotic animals, better shelters, and more programs to involve the public directly with animals.

Concerns about the treatment of animals will perhaps lead to more stringent laws and certification requirements. Some activists hope to end the capture of animals for display in zoos; some even object to filming animals in the wild. But zoos are likely to continue to operate and expand, with zoo professionals arguing that zoo animals are often safer and receive better care than they would in their natural habitats. Individuals looking for work as animal handlers should have good prospects through 2016, according to the U.S. Department of Labor.

FOR MORE INFORMATION

For general information about zoos, aquariums, oceanariums, and wildlife parks, contact

American Zoo and Aquarium Association
8403 Colesville Road, Suite 710
Silver Spring, MD 20910-3314
Tel: 301-562-0777
http://www.aza.org

For information on their zoo animal technology program, and other career information, contact

Santa Fe Community College
3000 83rd Street NW
Gainesville, FL 32606
Tel: 352-395-5604
http://inst.sfcc.edu/~zoo

ANIMAL TRAINERS

OVERVIEW

Animal trainers teach animals to obey commands so the animals can be counted on to perform these tasks in given situations. The animals can be trained for up to several hundred commands, to compete in shows or races, to perform tricks that entertain audiences, to protect property, or to act as guides for the disabled. Animal trainers may work with several types of animals or specialize with one type. Approximately 43,000 animal trainers are employed in the United States.

THE JOB

Many animals are capable of being trained. The techniques used to train them are basically the same, regardless of the type of animal. Animal trainers conduct programs consisting primarily of repetition and reward to teach animals to behave in a particular manner and to do it consistently.

First, trainers evaluate an animal's temperament, ability, and aptitude to determine its trainability. Animals vary in personality, just as people do. Some animals are more stubborn, willful, or easily distracted and would not do well with rigid training programs. All animals can be trained at some level, but certain animals are more receptive to training; these animals are chosen for programs that demand great skill.

One of the most familiar examples is the seeing-eye dog, now usually called a companion animal for the blind. These dogs are trained with several hundred verbal commands to assist their human and to recognize potentially dangerous situations. The dog must be able to, without any command, walk his companion around obstacles on the sidewalk. The companion dog must be able to read street lights and know to cross at the green, and only after traffic has cleared. The dog must also not be tempted to run to greet other dogs, grab food, or behave as most pet dogs do. Very few dogs make it through the rigorous training program. The successful dogs have proved to be such aids to the visually impaired that similar programs have been developed to train dogs for people who are confined to a wheelchair, or are hearing impaired, or incapable of executing some aspect of a day-to-day routine where a dog can assist.

By painstakingly repeating routines many times and rewarding the animal when it does what is expected, animal trainers train an animal to obey or perform on command or, in certain situations, without command. In addition, animal trainers are responsible for the feeding, exercising, grooming, and general care of the animals, either handling the duties themselves or supervising other workers. In some training programs, trainers go to a job site and work with the animals; in other programs, such as the companion animal program, the animal lives with the trainer for the duration of the program.

Trainers usually specialize in one type of animal and are identified by this type of animal. *Dog trainers*, for example, may work with police dogs, training them to search for drugs or missing people. The programs to train drug-detecting dogs use different detection responses, but each dog is trained in only one response system. Some dogs are trained to behave passively when the scent is detected, with a quiet signal given to the accompanying police officer that drugs have been detected. The signal can be sitting next to the scent, pointing, or following. Other dogs are trained to dig, tear, and destroy containers that have the drug in them. As one animal trainer from the U.S. Customs office pointed out, these dogs may be nightmare pets because they can destroy a couch in seconds, but they make great drug-detecting dogs. The common breeds for companion dogs and police dogs are German shepherds, rottweilers, and Labrador retrievers.

Some dog trainers train guard dogs to protect private property; others train dogs for performance, where the dog may learn numerous stunts or movements with hand commands so that the dog can perform on a stage or in film without the audience hearing the commands spoken from offstage. Shepherding dogs are also trained with whistle or hand commands because commands may have to be given from some distance away from where the dog is working.

Dogs, partly because of the variety of breeds available and partly because of their nature to work for approval, have countless roles for which they are trained. Even pet dogs may be trained by animal trainers who work with owners to teach the dog routine commands that make walking the dog safer and easier, or break the dog of destructive or dangerous habits.

Horse trainers specialize in training horses for riding or for harness. They talk to and handle a horse gently to accustom it to human contact, gradually getting it to accept a harness, bridle, saddle, and other riding gear. Trainers teach horses to respond to commands that are either spoken or given by use of the reins and legs. Draft horses are conditioned to draw equipment either alone or as part of a team. Show horses are given special training to qualify them to perform in competitions. Horse trainers sometimes have to retrain animals that have developed bad habits, such as bucking or biting. Besides feeding, exercising, and grooming, these trainers may make arrangements for breeding the horses and help mares deliver their foals.

A highly specialized occupation in the horse-training field is that of *racehorse trainers*, who must create individualized training plans for every horse in their care. By studying the animal's performance record and becoming familiar with its behavior during workouts, trainers can adapt their training methods to take advantage of each animal's peculiarities. Like other animal trainers, racehorse trainers oversee the exercising, grooming, and feeding of their charges. They also clock the running time during workouts to determine when a

QUICK FACTS

SCHOOL SUBJECTS
Biology
Psychology

PERSONAL SKILLS
Following instructions
Helping/teaching

WORK ENVIRONMENT
Indoors and outdoors
One location with some travel

MINIMUM EDUCATION LEVEL
Some postsecondary training

MEDIAN SALARY
$26,312

CERTIFICATION OR LICENSING
Required by certain states

OUTLOOK
Faster than the average

horse is ready for competitive racing. Racehorse trainers coach jockeys on how best to handle a particular horse during a race and may give owners advice on purchasing horses.

Police horse trainers work with police horses to keep them from startling in crowds or responding to other animals in their presence. As with the police dogs, these animals require a very stable, calm personality that remains so no matter what the situation the animal works in.

Other animal trainers work with more exotic animals for performance or for health reasons. The dolphins and whales at the Shedd Aquarium in Chicago are trained to roll over, lift fins and tails, and open their mouths on command, so that much veterinary work can be done without anesthesia, which is always dangerous for animals. These skills are demonstrated for the public every day, so they function as a show for people, but the overriding reason for training the dolphins is to keep them healthy. Other training elements include teaching dolphins to retrieve items from the bottom of their pool, so that if any visitor throws or loses something in the pool, divers are not required to invade the dolphins' space.

Animal trainers work with hunting birds, training them to fly after an injury, or to hunt if the bird was found as a hatchling before a parent had trained it. Birds that are successfully trained to fly and hunt can be released into the wild; the others may remain in educational programs where they will perform for audiences. It is, however, illegal to keep any releasable hunting bird for more than one year in the United States.

Each species of animal is trained by using the instincts and reward systems that are appropriate to that species. Hunting birds are rewarded with food; they don't enjoy petting and do not respond warmly to human touch, unless they were hand-raised from hatching by humans. Dogs, on the other hand, respond immediately to petting and gentle handling, unless they were handled inappropriately or viciously by someone. Sea mammals respond to both food and physical contact.

Some animal species are generally difficult to train. Sea otters are extremely destructive naturally and do not train easily. African elephants are much more difficult to train than Asian elephants, and females are much more predictable and trainable than the larger males. Most circus elephants are Asian because elephants from this area are much easier to handle. Captive elephants, though, kill more handlers and keepers than every other species combined.

REQUIREMENTS
High School

For high school students interested in becoming an animal trainer, courses in anatomy, physiology, biology, and psychology will be helpful. Understanding how the body and mind work helps a trainer understand the best methods for training. Knowledge of psychology will help the trainer recognize behaviors in the animals they train as well as in the people whom the animals are helping.

Postsecondary Training

Although there are no formal education requirements to enter this field, some positions do have educational requirements that include a college degree. Animal trainers in circuses and the entertainment field may be required to have some education in animal psychology in addition to their caretaking experience. Zoo and aquarium animal trainers usually must have a bachelor's degree in a field related to animal management or animal physiology. Trainers of companion dogs prepare for their work in a three-year course of study at schools that train dogs and instruct the disabled owner-companion.

Most trainers begin their careers as keepers and gain on-the-job experience in evaluating the disposition, intelligence, and "trainability" of the animals they look after. At the same time, they learn to make friends with their charges, develop a rapport with them, and gain their confidence. The caretaking experience is an important building block in the education and success of an animal trainer. Although previous training experience may give job applicants an advantage in being hired, they still will be expected to spend time caring for the animals before advancing to a trainer position.

Establishments that hire trainers often require previous animal-keeping or equestrian experience, as proper care and feeding of animals is an essential part of a trainer's responsibilities. These positions serve as informal apprenticeships. The assistant may get to help an animal trainer on certain tasks but will be able to watch and learn from other tasks being performed around him or her. For example, racehorse trainers often begin as jockeys or grooms in training stables.

Certification or Licensing

Racehorse trainers must be licensed by the state in which they work. Otherwise, there are no special requirements for this occupation. However, certification by a professional association may lend credibility when you are under review by potential clients. While not mandatory for employment, certification in dog training by an agency such as the Certification Council for Professional Dog Trainers (CCPDT) may distinguish you from other trainers and lead to better business opportunities. Certification from CCPDT requires 300 hours of professional dog training experience; a high school diploma or its equivalent; references from a veterinarian, client, and professional colleague; and passing an exam covering the following five areas of knowledge: learning theory, instruction skills, husbandry, ethology, and equipment. For more information, visit http://www.ccpdt.org.

Other Requirements

Prospective animal trainers should like and respect animals and have a genuine interest in working with them. With most of the career options for an animal trainer, there is an underlying desire to help people as well. Most trained animals work with people to accomplish a goal, so the relationship between the animal, the trainer, and the owner or companion is an important one. It requires the trainer to be thoughtful, sensitive, and well-spoken. Also, the trainer should be prepared to work intensely with an animal and then have that animal go on to work somewhere else. The relationship with the trained animal may not be permanent, so separation is part of the trainer's job.

EXPLORING

Students wishing to enter this field would do well to learn as much as they can about animals, especially animal psychology, either through coursework or independent study. Interviews with animal trainers and tours of their workplaces might be arranged to provide firsthand information about the practical aspects of this occupation.

Volunteering offers an opportunity to begin training with animals and learning firsthand about the tasks and routines involved in managing animals, as well as training them. Part-time or volunteer work in animal shelters, pet-training programs, rescue centers, pet shops, or veterinary offices gives potential trainers a chance to discover whether they have the aptitude for working with animals. You can also gain experience in summer jobs as animal caretakers at zoos, aquariums, museums that feature live animal shows, amusement parks, and, for those with a special interest in horse racing, at stables.

EMPLOYERS

Animal trainers work for a wide variety of employers, including stables, dog-training and companion pet programs, zoos, aquariums and oceanariums, amusement parks, rescue centers, pet shops, and circuses. Many are self-employed, and a few very successful animal trainers work in the entertainment field, training animal "actors" or working with wild and/or dangerous animals. A number of these positions require a great deal of traveling and even relocating. Although some new zoos and aquariums may open and others may expand their facilities, the number of job opportunities for animal trainers at these facilities will remain relatively small. Companion programs that train animals to assist people who need help in daily living activities will employ an increasing number of trainers.

Tightened security measures around the globe have created demand for bomb-sniffing dogs and their trainers. An increasing number of animal trainers and handlers will be employed by government agencies such as the Federal Aviation Administration and U.S. Customs Service, Fortune 500 companies, amusement parks, and sports arenas.

STARTING OUT

People who wish to become animal trainers generally start out as animal keepers, stable workers, or caretakers and rise to the position of trainer only after acquiring experience within the ranks of an organization. You can enter the field by applying directly for a job as animal keeper, letting your employer or supervisor know of your ambition so you will eventually be considered for promotion. The same applies for volunteer positions. Learning as a volunteer is an excellent way to get hands-on experience, but you should be vocal in your interest in a paid position once you have gotten to know the staff and they have gotten to know you.

You should pay close attention to the training methods of any place at which you are considering working. No reputable organization, regardless of what it trains animals for, should use physical injury to train or discipline an animal. The techniques you learn at your first job determine the position you will qualify for after that. You want to be sure that you are witnessing and learning from an organization that has a sound philosophy and training method for working with animals.

The most coveted positions depend on the animals you want to work with. Sea mammals are a specialty of oceanariums and aquariums, and these positions are fiercely competitive. Dog training programs are probably the most plentiful and offer the widest range of training philosophies and techniques. There are numerous books on dog training methods that you should consult to know what the differences are.

FEMA works only with established dog and handler teams, who usually work within the emergency systems for the regional or local authorities in some capacity. These teams choose to also be trained within the FEMA guidelines.

ADVANCEMENT

Most establishments have very small staffs of animal trainers, which means that the opportunities for advancement are limited. The progression is from animal keeper to animal trainer. A trainer who directs or supervises others may be designated *head animal trainer* or *senior animal trainer*.

Some animal trainers go into business for themselves and, if successful, hire other trainers to work for them. Others become agents for animal acts. But promotion may mean moving from one organization to another and may require relocating to another city, depending on what animal you specialize in.

EARNINGS

Salaries of animal trainers can vary widely according to specialty and place of employment. Salaries ranged from $15,933 to $46,634 a year or more in 2006, according to the U.S. Department of Labor. The median salary for animal trainers was $26,312. Those who earn higher salaries are in upper management and spend more time running the business than working with animals.

In the field of racehorse training, however, trainers are paid an average fee of $35 to $50 a day for each horse, plus 10 percent of any money their horses win in races. Depending on the horse and the races it runs, this can exceed the average high-end earnings for a trainer. Show horse trainers may earn as much as $30,000 to $35,000 a year. Trainers in business for themselves set their own fees for teaching both horses and owners.

WORK ENVIRONMENT

The working hours for animal trainers vary considerably, depending on the type of animal, performance schedule, and whether travel is involved. For some trainers, such as those who work with show horses, give educational programs with hunting birds, or work with new animals being brought into zoos and aquariums, the hours can be long and quite irregular. Travel is common and will probably include responsibility for seeing to the animals' needs while on the road. This can include feeding, creative housing, and driving with the animal. For one program director of a rescue center that works with injured hawks, it means traveling frequently for educational shows with a suitcase full of frozen rats and chicks for food.

Much of the work is conducted outdoors. In winter, trainers may work indoors, but depending on the animal, they may continue outdoor training year-round. If the animal is expected to work or perform outdoors in winter, it has to be trained in winter as well. Companion animals have to cope with every type of weather, so the trainer is responsible for training and testing the animal accordingly.

Working with certain animals requires physical strength; for example, it takes arm strength to hold a falcon on your wrist for an hour, or to control an 80-pound dog who doesn't want to heel. Other aspects of the work may require lifting, bending, or extended periods of standing or swimming. Trainers of aquatic mammals, such as dolphins and seals, work in water and must feel comfortable in aquatic environments.

Patience is essential to the job as well. Just as people do, animals have bad days where they won't work well and respond to commands. So even the best trainer encounters days of frustration where nothing seems to go well. Trainers must spend long hours repeating routines and rewarding their pupils for performing well, while never getting angry with them or punishing them when they fail to do what is expected. Trainers must be able to exhibit the authority to keep animals under control without raising their voices or using physical force. Calmness under stress is particularly important when dealing with wild animals.

OUTLOOK

This field is expected to grow faster than the average through 2016, according to the U.S. Department of Labor. Although criticism of animals used for purely entertainment purposes has reduced the number used for shows and performances, programs have expanded for companion animals and animals used in work settings. Also, a growing number of animal owners are seeking training services for their pets.

An increased number of trainers will be needed to train the growing number of search-and-rescue and bomb-sniffing dog teams. The latter will be in demand to ensure the safety of airports, government buildings, corporations, amusement parks, sports facilities, and public utilities.

In all fields, applicants must be well qualified to overcome the heavy competition for available jobs. Some openings may be created as zoos and aquariums expand or provide more animal shows in an effort to increase revenue.

FOR MORE INFORMATION

For information on careers, contact
American Zoo and Aquarium Association
8403 Colesville Road, Suite 710
Silver Spring, MD 20910-3314
Tel: 301-562-0777
http://www.aza.org

Canine Companions for Independence is a non-profit organization that assists people with disabilities by providing trained assistance dogs and ongoing support.
Canine Companions for Independence
PO Box 446
Santa Rosa, CA 95402-0446
Tel: 800-572-2275
http://www.caninecompanions.org

The Delta Society currently provides certification programs in animal evaluation and in training animal handlers for animal-assisted therapy and companion animal training.

Delta Society
845 124th Avenue NE, Suite 101
Bellevue, WA 98055-2297
Tel: 425-679-5500
Email: info@deltasociety.org
http://www.deltasociety.org

ASSESSORS AND APPRAISERS

OVERVIEW

Assessors and appraisers collect and interpret data to make judgments about the value, quality, and use of property. Assessors are government officials who evaluate property for the express purpose of determining how much the real estate owner should pay the city or county government in property taxes. Appraisers evaluate the market value of property to help people make decisions about purchases, sales, investments, mortgages, or loans. Rural districts or small towns may have only a few assessors, while large cities or urban counties may have several hundred. Appraisers are especially in demand in large cities but also work in smaller communities. There are approximately 101,000 real estate assessors and appraisers employed in the United States.

THE JOB

Property is divided into two distinct types: real property and personal property. Real property is land and the structures built upon the land, while personal property includes all other types of possessions. Appraisers determine the value, quality, and use of real property and personal property based on selective research into market areas, the application of analytical techniques, and professional judgment derived from experience. In evaluating real property, they analyze the supply and demand for different types of property, such as residential dwellings, office buildings, shopping centers, industrial sites, and farms, to estimate their values. Appraisers analyze construction, condition, and functional design. They review public records of sales, leases, previous assessments, and other transactions pertaining to land and buildings to determine the market values, rents, and construction costs of similar properties. Appraisers collect information about neighborhoods, such as availability of gas, electricity, power lines, and transportation. They also may interview people familiar with the property and consider the cost of making improvements on the property.

Appraisers also must consider such factors as location and changes that might influence the future value of the property. A residence worth $300,000 in the suburbs may be worth only a fraction of that in the inner city or in a remote rural area. But that same suburban residence may depreciate in value if an airport will be built nearby. After conducting a thorough investigation, appraisers usually prepare a written report that documents their findings and conclusions.

Assessors perform the same duties as appraisers and then compute the amount of tax to be levied on property, using applicable tax tables. The primary responsibility of the assessor is to prepare an annual assessment roll, which lists all properties in a district and their assessed values.

QUICK FACTS

SCHOOL SUBJECTS
Computer science
English
Mathematics

PERSONAL SKILLS
Communication/ideas
Mechanical/manipulative

WORK ENVIRONMENT
Indoors and outdoors
Primarily multiple locations

MINIMUM EDUCATION LEVEL
Some postsecondary training

MEDIAN SALARY
$44,460

CERTIFICATION OR LICENSING
Recommended (certification)
Required for certain positions (licensing)

OUTLOOK
Faster than the average

To prepare the assessment roll, assessors and their staffs first must locate and identify all taxable property in the district. To do so, they prepare and maintain complete and accurate maps that show the size, shape, location, and legal description of each parcel of land. Next, they collect information about other features, such as zoning, soil characteristics, and availability of water, electricity, sewers, gas, and telephones. They describe each building and how land and buildings are used. This information is put in a parcel record.

Assessors also analyze relationships between property characteristics and sales prices, rents, and construction costs to produce valuation models or formulas. They use these formulas to estimate the value of every property as of the legally required assessment date. For example, assessors try to estimate the value of adding a bedroom to a residence or adding an acre to a farm, or how much competition from a new shopping center detracts from the value of a downtown department store. Finally, assessors prepare and certify an assessment roll listing all properties, owners, and assessed values and notify owners of the assessed value of their properties. Because taxpayers have the right to contest their assessments, assessors must be prepared to defend their estimates and methods.

Most appraisers deal with land and buildings, but some evaluate other items of value. Specialized appraisers evaluate antiques, gems and jewelry, machinery, equipment, aircraft, boats, oil and gas reserves, and businesses. These appraisers obtain special training in their areas of expertise but generally perform the same functions as real property appraisers.

Personal property assessors help the government levy taxes by preparing lists of personal property owned by businesses and, in a few areas, householders. In addition to listing the number of items, these assessors also estimate the value of taxable items.

REQUIREMENTS
High School

If you are interested in the fields of assessing or appraising, there are a number of courses you can take in high school to help prepare you for this work. Take plenty of math classes, since you will need to be comfortable working with numbers and making calculations. Accounting classes will also be helpful for the same reasons. English courses will help you develop your researching and writing skills as well as verbal skills. Take computer classes in order to become accustomed with a variety of software applications. Courses in civics or government may also be beneficial.

Postsecondary Training

Appraisers and assessors need a broad range of knowledge in such areas as equity and mortgage finance, architectural function, demographic statistics, and business trends. In addition, they must be competent writers and able to communicate effectively with people. In the past, some people have been able to enter these fields with only a high school education and learn specialized skills on the job. Today, however, most appraisers and assessors have at least some college education. As of 2008, assessors and appraisers working in states that require licensure must have at least a bachelor's degree or a substantial number of college-level courses, usually in a field such as economics, finance, or real estate. Training courses specific to the field are usually offered at community colleges or professional organizations such as the American Society of Appraisers, the Appraisal Institute, and the International Association of Assessing Officers.

A few colleges and universities, such as Lindenwood University (http://www.lindenwood.edu) in St. Charles, Missouri, now offer degrees in valuation sciences that will prepare you for this career. Other areas of undergraduate study to consider as preparation for this field include public administration and business administration, real estate and urban land economics, engineering, architecture, and computer science. Appraisers choosing to specialize in a particular area should have a solid background in that field.

Certification or Licensing

A number of professional organizations, such as the ASA and the AI, offer certification or designations in the field. It is highly recommended that you attain professional designation in order to enhance your standing in the field and demonstrate to consumers your level of expertise. To receive a designation, you will typically need to pass a written exam, demonstrate ethical behavior, and have completed a certain amount of education. To maintain your designation, you will also need to fulfill continuing education requirements.

Because appraisals used for federally regulated real estate transactions with a loan amount of $250,000 or more must be conducted by licensed appraisers, most appraisers now obtain a state license. As of 2008, the educational requirements for state licensure have been changed to 150 education hours and 2,000 hours of on-the-job training. In addition, some states—known as "mandatory states"—require real estate appraisers to be licensed even if the appraisers do not deal with federally regulated transactions. You will need to check with your state's regulatory agency to learn more about the exact requirements for your state. In addition to a license, some states may require assessors who are government employees to pass civil service tests or other examinations before they can start work. Continuing education is also a requirement for licensure.

Other Requirements

Good appraisers are skilled investigators and must be proficient at gathering data. They must be familiar with sources of information on such diverse topics as public records, construction materials, building trends, economic trends, and governmental regulations affecting use of property. They should know how to read survey drawings and blueprints and be able to identify features of building construction.

EXPLORING

One simple way you can practice the methods used by appraisers is to write a detailed analysis of something you are considering investing in, such as a car, a computer, or even which college to attend. Your analysis should include both the benefits and the shortcomings of the investment as well as your final recommendation. Is the car overpriced? Does one particular school offer a better value for you? By doing this, you will begin to get a feel for the researching and writing done by an appraiser. Another way to explore this career is to look for part-time or summer work with an appraisal firm. Some firms also have jobs as appraiser assistants or trainees. Working at county assessors' or treasurers' offices, financial institutions, or real estate companies also might provide experience. If you are interested in working with real estate, you may want to learn the particulars of building construction by finding summer work with a construction company.

EMPLOYERS

Assessors are public servants who are either elected or appointed to office. The United States is divided into assessment districts, with population size affecting the number of assessors in a given area. Appraisers are employed by private businesses, such as accounting firms, real estate companies, and financial institutions, and by larger assessors' offices. Appraisers also work at auction houses, art galleries, and antique shops; some also work in government offices or for U.S. Customs and Border Protection. Assessors' offices might employ administrators, property appraisers, mappers, systems analysts,

computer technicians, public relations specialists, word processors, and clerical workers. In small offices, one or two people might handle most tasks; in large offices, some with hundreds of employees, specialists are more common.

STARTING OUT

After you have acquired the necessary technical and mathematical knowledge in the classroom, you should apply to area appraisal firms, local county assessors, real estate brokers, or large accounting firms. Because assessing jobs are often civil service positions, they may be listed with government employment agencies. If you have graduated from a degree program in valuation sciences, your school's career services office should also be able to provide you with assistance in finding that first job.

ADVANCEMENT

Appraising is a dynamic field, affected yearly by new legislation and technology. To distinguish themselves in the business, top appraisers continue their education and pursue certification through the various national appraising organizations, such as the Appraisal Institute, the American Society of Appraisers, and the International Association of Assessing Officers. Certified appraisers are entrusted with the most prestigious projects and can command the highest fees. In addition to working on more and more prestigious projects, some appraisers advance by opening their own appraisal firms. Others may advance by moving to larger firms or agency offices, where they are more able to specialize.

EARNINGS

Income for assessors is influenced by their location and employer; their salaries generally increase as the population of their jurisdiction increases. For example, those working in large counties, such as Los Angeles County, may make up to $100,000 annually. Appraisers employed in the private sector tend to earn higher incomes than those in the public sector.

The average fee for appraisal of a standard residential property is about $300, but fees can range from $75 for a re-inspection of new construction or repairs to $600 for inspection of a small residential income property.

According to the U.S. Department of Labor, real estate appraisers and assessors earned a median salary of $44,460 in 2006. The lowest paid 10 percent earned $24,000 or less per year on average, while the highest paid earned $86,140 or more. Assessors and appraiser working in urban and coastal regions usually earn more than those working in rural locations.

Earnings at any level are enhanced by higher education and professional designations. Fringe benefits for both public and private employees usually include paid vacations and health insurance.

WORK ENVIRONMENT

Appraisers and assessors have a variety of working conditions, from the comfortable offices where they write and edit appraisal reports to outdoor construction sites, which they visit in both the heat of summer and the bitter cold of winter. Many appraisers spend mornings at their desks and afternoons in the field. Experienced appraisers may need to travel out of state.

Appraisers and assessors who work for a government agency or financial institution usually work 40-hour weeks, with overtime when necessary. Independent appraisers often can set their own schedules.

Appraisal is a very people-oriented occupation. Appraisers must be unfailingly cordial, and they have to deal calmly and tactfully with people who challenge their decisions (and are usually angry). Appraising can be a high-stress occupation because a considerable amount of money and important personal decisions ride on appraisers' calculations.

OUTLOOK

The U.S. Department of Labor estimates that employment of assessors and appraisers will grow faster than the average for all occupations through 2016. Due to recent events in the real estate industry, there is a large number of properties on the market to be assessed and appraised. This means a steady flow of work for these occupations. In general, assessors work in a fairly secure field. As long as governments levy property taxes, assessors will be needed to provide them with information. The real estate industry, however, is influenced dramatically by the overall health of the economy, so appraisers in real estate can expect to benefit during periods of growth and experience slowdowns during recessions and depressions.

FOR MORE INFORMATION

For information on education and professional designations, contact

American Society of Appraisers
555 Herndon Parkway, Suite 125
Herndon, VA 20170

Tel: 703-478-2228
Email: asainfo@appraisers.org
http://www.appraisers.org

Visit this organization's Web site for a listing of state real estate appraiser regulatory boards.

Appraisal Foundation
1155 15th Street, NW, Suite 1111
Washington, DC 20005-3517
Tel: 202-347-7722
Email: info@appraisalfoundation.org
http://www.appraisalfoundation.org

For information on professional designations, education, careers, and scholarships, contact

Appraisal Institute
550 West Van Buren Street, Suite 1000
Chicago, IL 60607
Tel: 312-335-4100
http://www.appraisalinstitute.org

For information on professional designations, education, and publications, contact

International Association of Assessing Officers
314 West 10th Street
Kansas City, MO 64105-1616
Tel: 816-701-8100
http://www.iaao.org

For information on education and appraisal careers, contact

National Association of Independent Fee Appraisers
401 North Michigan Avenue, Suite 2200
Chicago, IL 60611
Tel: 312-321-6830
Email: info@naifa.com
http://www.naifa.com

AUDIO RECORDING ENGINEERS

OVERVIEW

Audio recording engineers oversee the technical end of recording. They operate the controls of the recording equipment—often under the direction of a music producer—during the production of music recordings; film, television, and radio productions; and other mediums that require sound recording. Recording engineers monitor and operate electronic and computer consoles to make necessary adjustments, and solve technical problems as they occur during a recording session. They assure that the equipment is in optimal working order and obtain any additional equipment necessary for the recording. There are approximately 16,000 audio recording engineers working in the United States.

THE JOB

Audio recording engineers operate and maintain the equipment used in a sound recording studio. They record the following: music, live and in studios; speech, such as dramatic readings of novels or radio advertisements; and sound effects and dialogue used in television and film. They work in control rooms at master console boards often containing hundreds of dials, switches, meters, and lights, which the engineer reads and adjusts to achieve desired results during a recording. Today, the recording studio is often considered an extra instrument, and thus, the audio recording engineer becomes an extra musician in his or her ability to dramatically alter the final sound of the recording.

As the owner of Watchmen Studios in Lockport, New York, Doug White offers audio recording services, digital audio mastering, audio duplication, and Web site construction. "I record a lot of hardcore and metal," he says. "It makes up about 60 percent of what we do here." His clients include Bughouse, Big Hair, Tugboat Annie, and Slugfest. Watchmen Studios features separate drum, vocal, and guitar booths, and offers 24-, 16-, and 8-track recording. The studio even offers spare guitars. "I try to keep it to a nine-hour day," White says. "Some studio engineers work up to 12 hours a day, but I feel my work suffers after too long."

As recording engineers prepare to record a session, they ask the musicians and producer what style of music they will be playing and what type of sound and emotion they want reflected in the final recording. Audio recording engineers must find out what types of instruments and orchestration will be recorded to determine how to manage the recording session and what additional equipment will be needed. For example, each instrument or vocalist may require a special microphone. The recording of dialogue will take considerably less preparation.

Before the recording session, audio recording engineers test all microphones, chords, recording equipment, and amplifiers to ensure everything is operating correctly.

QUICK FACTS

SCHOOL SUBJECTS
Computer science
Music

PERSONAL SKILLS
Mechanical/manipulative
Technical/scientific

WORK ENVIRONMENT
Primarily indoors
Primarily one location

MINIMUM EDUCATION LEVEL
Some postsecondary training

MEDIAN SALARY
$43,010

CERTIFICATION OR LICENSING
Recommended

OUTLOOK
About as fast as the average

They load tape players and set recording levels. Microphones must be positioned in precise locations near the instrument or amplifier. They experiment with several different positions of the microphone and listen in the control room for the best sound. Depending on the size of the studio and the number of musicians or vocalists, audio recording engineers position musicians in various arrangements to obtain the best sound for the production. For smaller projects, such as three- to eight-piece bands, each instrument may be sectioned off in sound-proof rooms to ensure the sounds of one instrument do not "bleed" into the recording of another instrument. For more complex recording of larger orchestration, specialized microphones must be placed in exact locations to record one or several instruments.

Once audio recording engineers have the musicians in place and the microphones set, they instruct musicians to play a sample of their music. At the main console, they read the gauges and set recording levels for each instrument. Recording engineers must listen for sound imperfections, such as hissing, popping, "mike bleeding," and any other extraneous noises, and pinpoint their source. They turn console dials to adjust recording level, volume, tone, and effects. Depending on the problem, they may have to reposition either the microphone or the musician.

With the right sound and recording level of each microphone set, audio recording engineers prepare the recording equipment (either tape or digital). During the recording of a song or voice-over, they monitor the recording level of each microphone to ensure none of the tracks are too high, which results in distortion, or too low, which results in weak sound quality. Recording engineers usually record more than one "take" of a song. Before the mixing process, they listen to each take carefully and determine which one has the best sound. They often splice the best part of one take with the best part of another take.

In some recording sessions, two engineers work in the control room. One usually works with the recording equipment, and the other takes instruction from the producer. The engineers coordinate the ideas of the producer to create the desired sound. During each session, the volume, speed, intensity, and tone quality must be carefully monitored. Producers may delegate more responsibility to the recording engineer. Engineers often tell the musicians when to start and stop playing or when to redo a certain section. They may ask musicians or other studio technicians to move microphones or other equipment in the studio to improve sound quality.

After the recording is made, the individual tracks must be "mixed" to a master tape. When mixing, they balance each instrument in relation to the others. Together with the producer and the musicians, recording engineers listen to the song or piece several times with the instruments at different levels and decide on the best sound and consistency. At this stage, they also set equalization and manipulate sound, tone, intensity, effects, and speed of the recording. Mixing a record is often a tedious, time-consuming task that can take several weeks to complete, especially with some recordings that are 24 or more tracks. At a larger studio, this may be done exclusively by a *sound mixer*. Sound mixers exclusively study various mixing methodologies.

Audio recording engineers frequently perform maintenance and repair on their equipment. They must identify and solve common technical problems in the studio. They may have to rewire or move equipment when updating the studio with new equipment. They may write proposals for equipment purchases and studio design changes. Engineers are often assisted in many of the basic sound recording tasks by apprentices, also known as *studio technicians*.

Recording engineers at smaller studios may set studio times for musicians. They must keep a thorough account of the band or performer scheduled to play, the musical style of the band or performer, the specific equipment that will be needed, and any other special arrangements needed to make the session run smoothly. They make sure the studio is stocked with the right working accessory equipment, including cords, cables, microphones, amplifiers, tapes, tuners, and effect pedals.

REQUIREMENTS
High School

You should take music courses to learn an instrument, study voice, or learn composition. High school orchestras and bands are an excellent source for both practicing and studying music performance. You should also take classes in computer science, mathematics, business, and, if offered, electronics. A drama or broadcast journalism class may allow you access to a sound booth, and the opportunity to assist with audio engineering for live theatrical productions and radio programs.

Postsecondary Training

More than ever before, postsecondary training is an essential step for becoming a successful recording engineer. This is when you will make your first contacts and be introduced to many of the highly technical (and continually changing) aspects of the field. To learn about educational opportunities in the United States and abroad, visit the Web sites of the Audio Engineering Society (http://www.aes.org) or *Mix* magazine (http://mixonline.com).

Seminars and workshops offer the most basic level of education. This may be the best way to obtain an early, hands-on understanding of audio recording and prepare for entry-level apprentice positions. These programs are intended to introduce students to the equipment and technical aspects of the field, such as microphones, sound reinforcement, audio processing devices, tape and digital audiotape (DAT) machines, digital processing, and sound editing. Students will also become familiar with the newest technologies in the audio field, such as MIDI (musical instrument digital interface), synthesis, sampling, and current music software. A seminar can last from a couple of hours to several weeks. Many workshops are geared toward in-depth study of a certain aspect of recording such as mixing, editing, or music production.

Students looking for a more comprehensive course of study in specific areas of the recording industry can enroll in technical school or community college programs. Depending on the curriculum, these programs can take from several weeks to up to a year to complete. The most complete level of postsecondary education is a two- or four-year degree from a university. At many universities, students have access to state-of-the-art equipment and a teaching staff of knowledgeable professionals in the industry. Universities incorporate music, music technology, and music business in a comprehensive curriculum that prepare graduates to be highly competitive in the industry. Students can enroll in other non-audio courses, such as business, communications, marketing, and computers.

Certification or Licensing

In the broadcast industry, engineers can be certified by the Society of Broadcast Engineers (http://www.sbe. org). Certification is recommended because this step shows your dedication to the field and your level of competence. After completing technical training and meeting strict qualifications, you can also join this society as a member or associate member. Membership gives you access to educational seminars, conferences, and a weekly job line.

Other Requirements

Being a recording engineer requires both technical skills and communication skills. You must be patient, capable of working well with a variety of people, and possess the confidence to function in a leadership position. Excellent troubleshooting skills are essential for an audio recording engineer.

"A very powerful, outgoing personality is the number one qualification," Doug White says. "You're dealing every day with picky musicians who never will be happy with their work, so they look to you for verification." White emphasizes that engineers need an even temperament and endless patience. "You have to be able to handle all types of personalities with kid gloves," he says.

EXPLORING

One way to learn more about this field is to read publications that focus on audio recording. *Mix* magazine (http://mixonline.com) offers articles about education, technology, and production. Other publications that

provide useful information on the industry and audio recording techniques include *Remix* (http:// www.remix-mag.com), *Pro Sound News* (http://www.prosoundnews. com), and *Broadcast Engineering* (http:// www.broadcastengineering.com).

Any experience you can get working in or around music will provide excellent background for this field. You could take up an instrument in the school band or orchestra, or perform with your own band. You might also have the opportunity to work behind the scenes with a music group, serving as a business manager, helping set up sound systems, or working as a technician in a school sound recording studio or radio station.

Write or call record companies or recording studios to get more information; local studios can usually be found in the classified telephone directory, and others can be located in the music trade magazines. The National Academy of Recording Arts and Sciences (the organization responsible for the Grammy Awards) is one source for information on the industry. Numerous books and music trade magazines that cover music production are available at bookstores or libraries.

Doug White recommends that prospective recording engineers make appointments to interview working sound professionals. "Even if you have to buy an hour of studio time to sit with them and talk," he says, "it's worth the cost. Ask as much about the personal/social side of working with artists. Don't be dazzled by the equipment. Believe me, it's a very small part of the job."

EMPLOYERS

Though most major recording studios are located in metropolitan areas such as New York and Los Angeles, many cities across the country have vibrant music scenes. Talented, skilled engineers will always be in demand, no matter the size of the recording studio. They may be employed by a studio, or they may be self-employed, either contracting with studios or operating their own recording business. Engineers also work for broadcast companies, engineering sound for radio and TV programs. Some recording engineers work for video production companies and corporate media libraries, helping to create in-house company presentations and films.

STARTING OUT

After high school, seek experience as an intern or apprentice or begin postsecondary training in audio at a university or college or trade school. Because most professional recording studios and broadcasters prefer to offer apprenticeship positions to students who have some previous experience in audio, those who have completed some trade school courses may have better chances at landing jobs. Most university and college programs offer semester internship programs at professional recording studios as a way of earning credit. Professional trade associations also support internships for their members by either matching students with employers or funding internship expenses. Universities and trade schools also have job placement services for their graduates.

Before going into the business, Doug White got an associate's degree from the Art Institute of Atlanta. "But in this business," he says, "your education doesn't get you very far. Reputation and experience are usually what open doors."

Internships and apprenticeships play an important role in helping students establish personal connections. Students are often hired by the studios or stations with which they've interned, or their employer can make recommendations for other job openings at a different studio. Employers will often post entry-level openings at universities or trade schools, but very seldom will they advertise in a newspaper.

Most audio engineers begin their career in small studios as assistants, called *studio technicians,* and have varied responsibilities, which may entail anything from running out to pick up dinner for the musicians during a recording session, to helping the recording engineer in the mixing process. Positions in radio will also provide a good stepping-stone to a career in audio recording. Entry-level positions may be easier to come by at studios that specialize in educational recording and radio advertisements than at music recording studios.

ADVANCEMENT

Career advancement will depend upon an engineer's interests as well as on hard work and perseverance. They may advance to the higher paying, glamorous (yet high-pressure) position of *music producer,* either as an independent producer or working for a record label. Recording engineers may also advance to positions in the radio or television industries, which usually offer better pay than studio work. If engineers wish to stay in the field of audio recording, they can advance to managerial positions or choose to open their own recording studio.

The recording industry is continually changing in response to frequent technological breakthroughs. Recording engineers who adapt easily to such advances as digital recording and new computer software will have a better chance for success. Some recording engineers

may team up with producers who work independently of the studio. They may form their own company, allowing for greater flexibility and higher salaries.

EARNINGS

According to the U.S. Department of Labor, the median income for sound engineering technicians was approximately $43,010 in 2006. At the low end of the scale, about 10 percent of these workers made less than $21,050. The highest paid 10 percent made $90,770 or more. Audio engineers in the broadcast industry often earn higher salaries than those in the music industry. Generally, those working at television stations earned more than those working at radio stations.

Benefits packages will vary from business to business. Audio recording engineers employed by a recording company or by a broadcast station receive health insurance and paid vacation. Other benefits may include dental and eye care, life and disability insurance, and a pension plan.

WORK ENVIRONMENT

Recording studios can be comfortable places to work. They are usually air conditioned because of the sensitivity of the equipment. They may be loud or cramped, however, especially during recording sessions where many people are working in a small space. The work is not particularly demanding physically (except when recording engineers must move equipment), but there may be related stress depending on the personalities of the producer and the performers. Audio recording engineers must be able to follow directions from producers and must often give directions. Their work must be quick and precise, and the engineer must be able to work as part of a team. Depending on the type of recording business, some engineers may be required to record off-site, at live concerts, for example, or other places where the recording is to take place. Engineers can usually come to work dressed however they wish.

Engineers must have patience when working with performers. For the engineer, there are often long periods of waiting while the musicians or performers work out problems and try to perfect parts of their songs. Engineers will frequently have to record the same song or spoken-word piece several times after mistakes have been made in the presentation. In addition, the mixing process itself can become tedious for many engineers—especially if they are not fond of the music. During the mix, engineers must listen to the same song over and over again to assure a proper balance of the musical tracks, and they often try various mixes.

Working hours depend on the job. Some studios are open at night or on the weekends to accommodate the schedules of musicians and performers. Other studios and recording companies only operate during normal business hours. Engineers work between 40 and 60 hours a week and may frequently put in 12-hour workdays. Album or compact disc recordings typically take 300 to 500 hours each to record. In contrast, educational or language cassette recordings take only about 100 hours.

OUTLOOK

Employment in this field is expected to grow about as fast as the average through 2016, according to the U.S. Department of Labor. New computer technology (hardware and software) is rapidly changing the way many recording engineers perform their jobs, making the entire audio recording process easier. These technological advancements will negatively affect job prospects for entry-level studio technicians whose more mundane recording tasks will increasingly be performed by computers. However, technology will also have some beneficial impact. As American media expands through technology and markets such as digital cable and satellite radio continue to expand, opportunities for audio recording engineers will likewise increase.

With computer technology making the recording process faster, easier, and ideally better, this will free up time in the studio—time that the studio managers can book with more recording sessions, which in turn may require a larger staff. As this technology becomes affordable, though, some performers, particularly rock or jazz groups, may choose to record themselves. With computers doing most of the grunt work and allowing complete control and manipulation of sound, some of these "home" recordings (also called "low-fi" recordings) can sound just as good as a studio recording for certain music genres. However, to take full advantage of digital and multimedia technology, musicians will continue to seek out the expertise of studio professionals.

Competition for jobs will be steepest in high-paying urban areas. Audio recording engineers will find jobs more easily in small cities and towns.

FOR MORE INFORMATION

For information on graduate-level scholarships and audio recording schools and courses in the United States and abroad, contact
Audio Engineering Society
60 East 42nd Street, Room 2520
New York, NY 10165-2520

Tel: 212-661-8528
Email: HQ@aes.org
http://www.aes.org

For facts and statistics about the recording industry, contact
Recording Industry Association of America
1025 F Street, NW, 10th Floor
Washington, DC 20004
Tel: 202-775-0101
http://www.riaa.com

For information on membership, contact
Society of Professional Audio Recording Services
9 Music Square South, Suite 222
Memphis, TN 37203
Tel: 800-771-7727
Email: spars@spars.com
http://www.spars.com

☐ AUTOMOBILE COLLISION REPAIRERS

OVERVIEW

Automobile collision repairers repair, replace, and repaint damaged body parts of automobiles, buses, and light trucks. They use hand tools and power tools to straighten bent frames and body sections, replace badly damaged parts, smooth out minor dents and creases, remove rust, fill small holes or dents, and repaint surfaces damaged by accident or wear. Some repairers also give repair estimates. There are approximately 183,000 automobile body and related repairers working in the United States.

THE JOB

Automobile collision repairers repair the damage vehicles sustain in traffic accidents and through normal wear. Repairers straighten bent bodies, remove dents, and replace parts that are beyond repair. Just as a variety of skills are needed to build an automobile, so a range of skills is needed to repair body damage to vehicles. Some body repairers specialize in certain areas, such as painting, welding, glass replacement, or air

machine, which uses hydraulic pressure to pull the damaged metal into position. Repairers use specialty measuring equipment to set all components, such as engine parts, wheels, headlights, and body parts, at manufacturer's specifications.

After the frame is straightened, the repairer can begin to work on the car body. Newer composite car bodies often have "panels" that can be individually replaced. Dents in a metal car body can be corrected in several different ways, depending on how deep they are. If any part is too badly damaged to repair, the collision repairers remove it with hand tools, a pneumatic metal-cutting gun, or acetylene torch, and then weld on a replacement. Some dents can be pushed out with hydraulic jacks, pneumatic hammers, prying bars, and other hand tools. To smooth small dents and creases, collision repairers may position small anvils, called dolly blocks, against one side of the dented metal. They then hit the opposite side of the metal with various specially designed hammers. Tiny pits and dimples are removed with pick hammers and punches. Dents that cannot be corrected with this treatment may be filled with solder or a puttylike material that becomes hard like metal after it cures. When the filler has hardened, the collision repairers file, grind, and sand the surface smooth in the correct contour and prepare it for painting. In many shops the final sanding and painting are done by other specialists, usually called *automotive painters*.

Since more than the body is usually damaged in a major automobile accident, repairers have other components to repair. Advanced vehicle systems on new cars such as anti-lock brakes, air bags, and other passive restraint systems require special training to repair. Steering and suspension, electrical components, and glass are often damaged and require repair, removal, or replacement.

Automotive painting is a highly skilled, labor-intensive job that requires a fine eye and attention to detail for the result to match the pre-accident condition. Some paint jobs require that less than the whole vehicle be painted. In this case, the painter must mix pigments to match the original color. This can be difficult if the original paint is faded, but computer technology is making paint matching easier.

A major part of the automobile collision repairer's job is assessing the damage and providing an estimate on the cost to repair it. Sometimes, the damage to a vehicle may cost more to repair than the vehicle is worth. When this happens, the vehicle is said to be "totaled," a term used by collision repairers as well as

bag replacement. All collision repairers should know how to perform common repairs, such as realigning vehicle frames, smoothing dents, and removing and replacing panels.

Vehicle bodies are made from a wide array of materials, including steel, aluminum, metal alloys, fiberglass, and plastic, with each material requiring a different repair technique. Most repairers can work with all of these materials, but as car manufacturers produce vehicles with an increasing proportion of lightweight fiberglass, aluminum, and plastic parts, more repairers specialize in repairing these specific materials.

Collision repairers frequently must remove car seats, accessories, electrical components, hydraulic windows, dashboards, and trim to get to the parts that need repair. If the frame or a body section of the vehicle has been bent or twisted, frame repairers and straighteners can sometimes restore it to its original alignment and shape. This is done by chaining or clamping it to an alignment

insurance companies. Many body repair shops offer towing services and will coordinate the transfer of a vehicle from the accident scene as well as the transfer of a totaled vehicle to a scrap dealer who will salvage the useable parts.

The shop supervisor or repair service estimator prepares the estimate. They inspect the extent of the damage to determine if the vehicle can be repaired or must be replaced. They note the year, model, and make of the car to determine type and availability of parts. Based on past experience with similar types of repair and general industry guidelines, estimates are calculated for parts and labor and then submitted to the customer's insurance company. One "walk around" a car will tell the collision repairer what needs to be investigated. Since a collision often involves "hidden" damage, supervisors write up repair orders with specific instructions so no work is missed or, in some cases, done unnecessarily. Repair orders often indicate only specific parts are to be repaired or replaced. Collision repairers generally work on a project by themselves with minimal supervision. In large, busy shops, repairers may be assisted by helpers or apprentices.

REQUIREMENTS
High School

Technology demands more from the collision repairer than it did 10 years ago. In addition to automotive and shop classes, high school students should take mathematics, English, and computer classes. Adjustments and repairs to many car components require numerous computations, for which good mathematics skills are essential. Reading comprehension skills will help a collision repairer understand complex repair manuals and trade journals that detail new technology. Oral communication skills are also important to help customers understand their options. In addition, computers are common in most collision repair shops. They help repairers keep track of customer histories and parts and often detail repair procedures. Use of computers in repair shops is now the standard, so students will benefit from a basic knowledge of them.

Postsecondary Training

A wide variety of training programs are offered at community colleges, vocational schools, independent organizations, and manufacturers. As automotive technology changes, the materials and methods involved in repair work change. With new high-strength steels, aluminum,

and plastics becoming ever more common in newer vehicles and posing new challenges in vehicle repair, repairers will need special training to detect the many hidden problems that occur beyond the impact spot. Postsecondary training programs provide students with the necessary, up-to-date skills needed for repairing today's vehicles.

Most automobile collision repairers learn their job by working closely with more experienced repairers. New repairers begin by learning how to remove damaged parts, sand body panels, and install repaired parts. They slowly work up to more complex tasks such as removing dents and straightening and aligning damaged body parts. In general, it could take three to four years for an automobile collision repairer to learn all aspects of the job.

Certification or Licensing

Entry-level technicians in the industry can demonstrate their qualifications through certification by the National Automotive Technicians Education Foundation (NATEF), an affiliate of the National Institute for Automotive Service Excellence (ASE). Certification is voluntary, but it assures students that the program they enroll in meets the standards employers expect from their entry-level employees. Many trade and vocational schools throughout the country have affiliation with NATEF. To remain certified, repairers must take the examination again within five years. Another industry-recognized standard of training is provided by the Inter-Industry Conference on Auto Collision Repair (I-CAR). I-CAR provides training for students and experienced technicians alike in the areas of advanced vehicle systems, aluminum repair and welding, complete collision repair, electronics for collision repair, finish matching, and other specialty fields.

Other Requirements

Automobile collision repairers are responsible for providing their own hand tools at an investment of approximately $6,000 to $20,000 or more, depending on the technician's specialty. It is the employer's responsibility to provide the larger power tools and other test equipment. Skill in handling both hand and power tools is essential for any repairer. Since each collision repair job is unique and presents a different challenge, repairers often must be resourceful in their method of repair.

While union membership is not a requirement for collision repairers, many belong to the International Association of Machinists and Aerospace Workers; the

International Union, United Automobile, Aerospace and Agricultural Implement Workers of America; the Sheet Metal Workers International Association; or the International Brotherhood of Teamsters, Chauffeurs, Warehousemen and Helpers of America. Most collision repairers who are union members work for large automobile dealers, trucking companies, and bus lines.

EXPLORING

Many community colleges and park districts offer general auto maintenance, mechanics, and body repair workshops where students can get additional practice working on real cars and learn from experienced instructors. Trade magazines such as *Automotive Body Repair News* (http://www.abrn.com) are an excellent source for learning what's new in the industry. Such publications may be available at larger public libraries or vocational schools. Many journals also post current and archived articles on the Internet.

Working on cars as a hobby provides invaluable first-hand experience in repair work. A part-time job in a repair shop or dealership allows you to get a feel for the general atmosphere and the kind of problems repairers face on the job, and it provides a chance to learn from those already in the business.

Some high school students may gain exposure to automotive repairs through participation in organizations, such as SkillsUSA-Vocational Industrial Clubs of America. VICA coordinates competitions in several vocational areas, including collision repair. The collision repair competition tests students' aptitudes in metal work, MIG welding, painting, alignment of body and frame, painting, estimation of damage to automobiles, and plastic identification and repair. VICA is represented in all 50 states. If your school does not have a VICA chapter, ask your guidance counselor about starting one or participating in a co-op arrangement with another school. See http//www.skillsusa.org for more information.

EMPLOYERS

Automobile collision repairers held about 183,000 jobs in the United States in 2006. Most work for body shops specializing in body repairs and painting, including private shops and shops operated by automobile dealers. Others work for organizations that maintain their own vehicle fleets, such as trucking companies and automobile rental companies. About 15 percent of automobile collision repairers are self-employed, operating small shops in cities large and small.

STARTING OUT

The best way to start out in the field of automobile collision repair is, first, to attend one of the many postsecondary training programs available throughout the country and, second, to obtain certification. Trade and technical schools usually provide job placement assistance for their graduates. Schools often have contacts with local employers who seek highly skilled entry-level employees. Often, employers post job openings at nearby trade schools with accredited programs.

Although postsecondary training programs are considered the best way to enter the field, some repairers learn the trade on the job as apprentices. Their training consists of working for several years under the guidance of experienced repairers. Fewer employers today are willing to hire apprentices because of the time and cost it takes to train them, but since there currently is a shortage of high quality entry-level collision repair technicians, many employers will continue to hire apprentices who can demonstrate good mechanical aptitude and a willingness to learn. Those who do learn their skills on the job will inevitably require some formal training if they wish to advance and stay in step with the changing industry.

Internship programs sponsored by car manufacturers or independent organizations provide students with excellent opportunities to work with prospective employers. Internships can also provide students with valuable contacts who will be able to refer the student to future employers and provide recommendations once they have completed their training. Many students may even be hired by the company at which they interned.

ADVANCEMENT

Like NATEF training programs, currently employed collision repairers may be certified by ASE. Although certification is voluntary, it is a widely recognized standard of achievement for automobile collision repairers and the way many advance in the field. Collision repairers who are certified are more valuable to their employers than those who are not and therefore stand a greater chance of advancement.

Certification is available in four specialty areas: structural analysis and damage repair, nonstructural analysis and damage repair, mechanical and electrical components, and painting and refinishing. Those who have passed all the exams are certified as master body/paint technicians. To maintain their certification, technicians must retake the examination for their specialties every five years. Many employers will hire only accredited technicians, basing salary on their level of accreditation.

With today's complex automobile components and new materials requiring hundreds of hours of study and practice to master, employers encourage their employees to advance in responsibility by learning new systems and repair procedures. A repair shop's reputation will only go as far as its employees are skilled. Those with good communications and planning skills may advance to shop supervisor or service manager at larger repair shops or dealerships. Those who have mastered collision repair may go on to teaching at postsecondary schools or work for certification agencies.

EARNINGS

Salary ranges of collision repairers vary depending on level of experience, type of shop, and geographic location. The median annual salary for automotive body and related repairers was $35,193 in 2006, according to the U.S. Department of Labor. At the lower end of the pay scale, repairers with less experience and repairers who were employed by smaller shops tended to earn less; experienced repairers with management positions earned more. The lowest paid 10 percent earned $21,008 or less, and the top 10 percent $59,716 or more. In many repair shops and dealerships, collision repairers can make more by working on commission, typically earning 40 to 50 percent of the labor costs charged to customers. Employers often guarantee a minimum level of pay in addition to commissions.

Benefits packages vary from business to business. Most repair technicians can expect health insurance and a paid vacation from employers. Other benefits may include dental and eye care, life and disability insurance, and a pension plan. Employers usually cover a technician's work clothes and may pay a percentage of the cost of hand tools they purchase. An increasing number of employers pay all or most of an employee's certification training, dependent on the employee passing the test. A technician's salary can increase through yearly bonuses or profit sharing if the business does well.

WORK ENVIRONMENT

Collision repair work is generally noisy, dusty, and dirty. In some cases, the noise and dirt levels have decreased as new technology such as computers and electrostatic paint guns are introduced. Automobile repair shops are usually well ventilated to reduce dust and dangerous fumes. Because repairers weld and handle hot or jagged pieces of metal and broken glass, they wear safety glasses, masks, and protective gloves. Minor hand and back injuries are the most common problems of technicians. When reaching in hard-to-get-at places or loosening tight bolts, collision repairers often bruise, cut, or burn their hands. With caution and experience, most learn to avoid hand injuries. Working for long periods in cramped or bent positions often results in a stiff back or neck. Collision repairers also lift many heavy objects that can cause injury if not handled carefully; however, this is less of a problem with new cars as automakers design smaller and lighter parts for better fuel economy. Automotive painters wear respirators and other protective gear, and they work in specially ventilated rooms to keep from being exposed to paint fumes and other hazardous chemicals. Painters may need to stand for hours at a time as they work.

By following safety procedures and learning how to avoid typical problems, repairers can minimize the risks involved in this job. Likewise, shops must comply with strict safety procedures to help employees avoid accident or injury. Collision repairers are often under pressure to complete the job quickly. Most repairers work a standard 40-hour week but may be required to work longer hours when the shop is busy or in emergencies.

OUTLOOK

Like many service industries, the collision repair industry is facing a labor shortage of skilled, entry-level workers in many areas of the country. Demand for collision repair services is expected to remain consistent, at the least, as the number of cars in the nation grows, and employment opportunities are expected to increase about as fast as the average through 2016. This demand, paired with technology that will require new skills, translates into a healthy job market for those willing to undergo the training needed. According to *Automotive Body Repair News*, as the need for skilled labor is rising, the number of people pursuing collision repair careers is declining. In many cases, vocational schools and employers are teaming up to recruit new workers. Job opportunities will also arise from a large number of older workers retiring from this field over the next decade.

Changing technology also plays a role in the industry's outlook. New automobile designs have body parts made of steel alloys, aluminum, and plastics—materials that are more time consuming to work with. In many cases, such materials are more prone to damage, increasing the need for body repairs.

The automobile collision repair business is not greatly affected by changes in economic conditions.

Major body damage must be repaired to keep a vehicle in safe operating condition. During an economic downturn, however, people tend to postpone minor repairs until their budgets can accommodate the expense. Nevertheless, body repairers are seldom laid off. Instead, when business is bad, employers hire fewer new workers. During a recession, inexperienced workers face strong competition for entry-level jobs. People with formal training in repair work and automobile mechanics are likely to have the best job prospects in such times.

FOR MORE INFORMATION

For more information on careers, training, and accreditation, contact the following organizations:

Automotive Aftermarket Industry Association
7101 Wisconsin Avenue, NW, Suite 1300
Bethesda, MD 20814-3415
Tel: 301-654-6664
Email: aaia@aftermarket.org
http://www.aftermarket.org

Inter-Industry Conference on Auto Collision Repair
5125 Trillium Boulevard
Hoffman Estates, IL 60192-3600
Tel: 800-422-7872
http://www.i-car.com

National Automotive Technicians Education Foundation
101 Blue Seal Drive, Suite 101
Leesburg, VA 20175-5646
Tel: 703-669-6650
http://www.natef.org

National Institute for Automotive Service Excellence
101 Blue Seal Drive, SE, Suite 101
Leesburg, VA 20175-5646
Tel: 877-273-8324
http://www.asecert.org

☐ AUTOMOBILE SALES WORKERS

OVERVIEW

Automobile sales workers inform customers about new or used automobiles, and they prepare payment, financing, and insurance papers for customers who have purchased a vehicle. It is their job to persuade the customer that the product they are selling is the best choice. They prospect new customers by mail, by telephone, or through personal contacts. To stay informed about their products, sales workers regularly attend training sessions about the vehicles they sell. There are more than 269,000 automobile sales workers employed in the United States.

THE JOB

The automobile sales worker's main task is to sell. Today, many dealerships try to soften the image of salespeople by emphasizing no pressure, even one-price shopping. But automobile dealers expect their employees to sell, and selling in most cases involves some degree of persuasion. The automobile sales worker informs customers of everything there is to know about a particular vehicle. A good sales worker finds out what the customer wants or needs and suggests automobiles that may fit that need—empowering the customer with choice and a feeling that he or she is getting a fair deal.

Since the sticker price on new cars is only a starting point to be bargained down, and since many customers come to dealerships already knowing which car they would like to buy, sales workers spend much of their time negotiating the final selling price.

Most dealerships have special sales forces for new cars, used cars, trucks, recreational vehicles, and leasing operations. In each specialty, sales workers learn all aspects of the product they must sell. They may attend information and training seminars sponsored by manufacturers. New car sales workers, especially, are constantly learning new car features. Sales workers inform customers about a car's performance, fuel economy, safety features, and luxuries or accessories. They are able to talk about innovations over previous models, engine and mechanical specifications, ease of handling, and ergonomic designs. Good sales workers also keep track of competing models' features.

In many ways, used car sales workers have a more daunting mass of information to keep track of. Whereas new car sales workers concentrate on the most current features of an automobile, used car sales workers must keep track of all features from several model years. Good used car dealers can look at a car and note immediately the make, model, and year of a car. Because of popular two- and three-year leasing options, the used car market has increased by nearly 50 percent in the last 10 years.

Successful sales workers are generally good readers of a person's character. They can determine exactly what it is a customer is looking for in a new car. They must be friendly and understanding of customers' needs in order to put them at ease (due to the amount of money involved, car buying is an unpleasant task for most people). They are careful not to oversell the car by providing the customers with information they may not care about or understand, thus confusing them. For example, if a customer only cares about style, sales workers will not impress upon him all of the wonderful intricacies of a new high-tech engine design.

Sales workers greet customers and ask if they have any questions about a particular model. It's very important for sales workers to have immediate and confident answers to all questions about the vehicles they're selling. When a sale is difficult, they occasionally use psychological methods, or subtle "prodding," to influence customers. Some sales workers use aggressive selling methods and pressure the customer to purchase the car. Although recent trends show that more customers are wise to—and put off by—the pressure-sell, competition will keep these types of selling methods prevalent in the industry, but at a toned-down level.

Customers usually make more than one visit to a dealership before purchasing a new or used car. Because one sales worker "works" the customer on the first visit—forming an acquaintanceship and learning the customer's personality—he or she will usually stay with that customer until the sale is made or lost. The sales worker usually schedules times for the customer to come in and talk more about the car in order to stay with the customer through the process and not lose the sale to another sales worker. Sales workers may make follow-up phone calls to make special offers or remind customers of certain features that make a particular model better than the competition, or they may send mailings for the same purpose.

In addition to providing the customer with information about the car, sales workers discuss financing packages, leasing options, and warranty. When the sale is made, they go over the contract with the customer and obtain a signature. Frequently the exact model with all of the features the customer requested is not in the dealership, and the sales worker must place an order with the manufacturer or distributor. When purchasing a new or used vehicle, many customers trade in their old vehicle. Sales workers appraise the trade-in and offer a price.

At some dealerships sales workers also do public relations and marketing work. They establish promotions to get customers into their showrooms, print fliers to distribute in the local community, and make television advertisements. In order to keep their name in the back (or front) of the customer's mind, they may send past

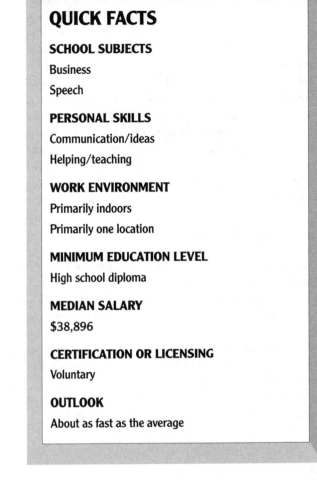

QUICK FACTS

SCHOOL SUBJECTS
Business
Speech

PERSONAL SKILLS
Communication/ideas
Helping/teaching

WORK ENVIRONMENT
Primarily indoors
Primarily one location

MINIMUM EDUCATION LEVEL
High school diploma

MEDIAN SALARY
$38,896

CERTIFICATION OR LICENSING
Voluntary

OUTLOOK
About as fast as the average

customers birthday and holiday cards or similar "courtesies." Most of the larger dealerships also have an auto maintenance and repair service department. Sales workers may help customers establish a periodic maintenance schedule or suggest repair work.

Computers are used at a growing number of dealerships. Customers use computers to answer questions they may have, consult price indexes, check on ready availability of parts, and even compare the car they're interested in with the competition's equivalent. Although computers can't replace human interaction and sell the car to customers who need reassurances, they do help the customer feel more informed and more in control when buying a car.

REQUIREMENTS
High School

Because thorough knowledge of automobiles—from how they work to how they drive and how they are manufactured—is essential for a successful sales worker, automotive maintenance classes in high school are an excellent place to begin. Classes in English, speech, drama, and psychology will help you to achieve the excellent speaking skills you will need to make a good sale and gain customer confidence and respect. Classes in business and mathematics will teach you to manage and prioritize your work load, prepare goals, and work confidently with customer financing packages. Since computers are used in every aspect of the industry, you should take as many computer classes as you can. Speaking a second language will give you an advantage, especially in major cities with large minority populations.

Postsecondary Training

Those who seek management-level positions will have a distinct advantage if they possess a college degree, preferably in business or marketing, but other degrees, whether they be in English, economics, or psychology, are also applicable—just as long as applicants have good management skills and can sell cars. Many schools offer degrees in automotive marketing and automotive aftermarket management that prepare students to take high-level management positions. Even with a two- or four-year degree in hand, many dealerships may not begin new hires directly as managers, but first start them out as sales workers.

Certification or Licensing

By completing the certified automotive merchandiser (CAM) program offered by the National Automobile Dealers Association (NADA), students seeking entry-level positions gain a significant advantage. Certification assures employers that workers have the basic skills they require.

Other Requirements

In today's competitive job market, you will need a high school diploma to land a job that offers growth possibilities, a good salary, and challenges; this includes jobs in the automobile sales industry. Employers prefer to hire entry-level employees who have had some previous experience in automotive services or in retail sales. They look for candidates who have good verbal, business, mathematics, electronics, and computer skills. A number of automotive sales and services courses and degrees are offered today at community colleges, vocational schools, independent organizations, and manufacturers. Sales workers should possess a valid driver's license and have a good driving record.

Sales workers must be enthusiastic, well-organized self-starters who thrive in a competitive environment. They must show excitement and authority about each type of car they sell and convince customers, without being overly pushy, that the car they're interested in is the "right" car, at the fairest price. Sales workers must be able to read a customer's personality and know when to be outgoing and when to pull back and be more reserved. A neat, professional appearance is also very important for sales workers.

EXPLORING

Automobile trade magazines and books, in addition to selling technique and business books, are excellent sources of information for someone considering a career in this field. Local and state automobile and truck dealer associations can also provide you with information on career possibilities in automobile and truck sales. Your local Yellow Pages has a listing under "associations" for dealer organizations in your area.

Students interested in automobile sales work might first stop by their local dealer and ask about training programs and job requirements there. On a busy day at any dealership there will be several sales workers on the floor selling cars. Students can witness the basic selling process by going to dealerships and unobtrusively watching and listening as sales workers talk with customers. Many dealerships hire students part time to wash and clean cars. This is a good way to see the types of challenges and pressures automobile sales workers experience every day. Although it takes a special kind of sales skill set to sell a $25,000 vehicle, any type of retail sales job that requires frequent interaction with customers will prepare students for work as an automobile sales worker.

EMPLOYERS

Franchised automobile dealerships employ the majority of automobile sales workers in the United States. A franchised automobile dealer is a dealer that is formally recognized and authorized by the manufacturer to sell its vehicles. A small number of sales workers are employed by used car dealerships that are strictly independent and not recognized by any manufacturer. Automotive superstores need automobile sales workers as well, although some may argue that these workers aren't truly automobile sales specialists because they tend to have less training and experience in the automotive area.

STARTING OUT

Generally, those just out of high school are not going to land a job as an automobile sales worker; older customers do not feel comfortable making such a large investment through a teenager. Employers prefer to see some previous automotive service experience with certification, such as National Institute of Automotive Service Excellence certification, or postsecondary training in automotive selling, such as NADA's CAM program. Dealerships will hire those with proven sales skill in a different field for sales worker positions and give them on-the-job training.

Employers frequently post job openings at schools that provide postsecondary education in business administration or automotive marketing. Certified automotive technicians or body repairers who think they might eventually like to break into a sales job should look for employment at dealership service centers. They will have frequent contact with sales workers and make connections with dealership managers and owners, as well as become so familiar with one or more models of a manufacturer's cars that they will make well-informed, knowledgeable sales workers.

Some dealerships will hire young workers with little experience in automobile services but who can demonstrate proven skills in sales and a willingness to learn. These workers will learn on the job. They may first be given administrative tasks. Eventually they will accompany experienced sales workers on the showroom floor and learn "hands-on." After about a year, the workers will sell on their own, and managers will evaluate their selling skills in sales meetings and suggest ways they can improve their sales records.

ADVANCEMENT

The longer sales workers stay with a dealership, the larger their client base grows and the more cars are sold. Advancement for many sales workers comes in the form of increased earnings and customer loyalty. Other sales workers may be promoted through a combination of experience and further training or certification.

As positions open, sales workers with proven management skills go on to be assistant and general managers. Managers with excellent sales skills and a good client base may open a new franchise dealership or their own independent dealership.

The Society of Automotive Sales Professionals (SASP), a division of NADA, provides sales workers with advancement possibilities. Once sales workers have completed a certification process and have a minimum of six months' sales experience, they are eligible to participate in SASP seminars that stress improving the car buying process by polishing a sales worker's professional image.

EARNINGS

Earnings for automobile sales workers vary depending on location, size, and method of salary. Previously, most dealerships paid their sales workers either straight commission or salary plus commission. This forced sales workers to become extremely aggressive in their selling strategy—and often too aggressive for many customers. With a new trend toward pressure-free selling, more sales workers are earning a straight salary. Many dealerships still offer incentives such as bonuses and profit sharing to encourage sales. The average hourly wage for automotive sales workers $18.70 in 2006, according to the U.S. Department of Labor. This makes for an annual salary of approximately $38,896 a year. Those who work on a straight commission basis can earn more than $75,000 a year; however, their earnings are minimal during slow periods. Sales workers who are just getting started in the field may earn lower annual salaries for a few years as they work to establish a client base. They may start in the low $20,000s. According to NADA, the average salary for new-car dealership employees was $44,676 in 2004. Benefits vary by dealership but often include health insurance and a paid vacation. An increasing number of employers will pay all or most of an employee's certification training.

WORK ENVIRONMENT

Sales workers for new car dealerships work in pleasant indoor showrooms. Most used car dealerships keep the majority of their cars in outdoor lots where sales workers may spend much of their day. Upon final arrangements for a sale, they work in comfortable office spaces at a desk. Business attire is standard. During slow periods, when competition among dealers is fierce, sales workers often work under pressure. They must not allow "lost" sales to discourage their work. The typical workweek is between 40 and 50 hours, although if business is good, a sales worker will work more. Since most customers shop for cars on the weekends and in the evenings, work hours are irregular.

OUTLOOK

Automobile dealerships are one of the businesses most severely affected by economic recession. Conversely, when the economy is strong, the automobile sales industry tends to benefit. For the sales worker, growth, in any percentage, is good news, as they are the so-called front-line professionals in the industry who are responsible for representing the dealerships and manufacturers and for getting their cars out on the streets. In the late 1990s and early 2000s, automobile sales were especially strong in the United States. However, there have been some setbacks in the industry in recent years. For instance, after a record-breaking year in 2001, sales dropped considerably in 2002. Also, incentives such as rebates and cut-rate financing were in part responsible for the industry's strong showing. These incentives, spurred by a competitive market, cost the industry money and ate into profits at every level.

The automobile sales worker faces many future challenges. A shift in customer buying preferences and experience is forcing sales workers to re-evaluate their selling methods. Information readily available on the Internet helps customers shop for the most competitive financing or leasing package and read reviews on car and truck models that interest them. Transactions are still brokered at the dealer, but once consumers become more familiar with the Internet, many will shop and buy exclusively from home.

Another trend threatening dealers is the automotive superstores, such as CarMax and AutoNation, where customers have a large inventory to select from at a base price and get information and ask questions about a car not from a sales worker, but from a computer. Sales workers are still needed to finalize the sale, but their traditional role at the dealership is lessened.

Nontheless, the number of cars and trucks on U.S. roads is expected to increase, and opportunities in this lucrative, but stressful, career should continue to increase about as fast as the average.

FOR MORE INFORMATION

For information on accreditation and testing, contact

National Automobile Dealers Association
8400 Westpark Drive
McLean, VA 22102
Tel: 800-252-6232
Email: nadainfo@nada.org
http://www.nada.org

For information on certification, contact

National Institute for Automotive Service Excellence
101 Blue Seal Drive, SE, Suite 101
Leesburg, VA 20175-5646
Tel: 877-273-8324
http://www.asecert.org

AUTOMOBILE SERVICE TECHNICIANS

OVERVIEW

Automobile service technicians maintain and repair cars, vans, small trucks, and other vehicles. Using both hand tools and specialized diagnostic test equipment, they pinpoint problems and make the necessary repairs or adjustments. In addition to handling complex and difficult repairs, technicians perform a number of routine maintenance procedures, such as oil changes, tire rotation, and battery replacement. Technicians interact frequently with customers to explain repair procedures and discuss maintenance needs. Approximately 773,000 automotive service technicians work in the United States.

THE JOB

Many automobile service technicians feel that the most exciting part of their work is troubleshooting—locating the source of a problem and successfully fixing it. Diagnosing mechanical, electrical, and computer-related troubles requires a broad knowledge of how cars work, the ability to make accurate observations, and the patience to logically determine what went wrong. Technicians agree that it frequently is more difficult to find the problem than it is to fix it. With experience, knowing where to look for problems becomes second nature.

Generally, there are two types of automobile service technicians: *generalists* and *specialists*. Generalists work under a broad umbrella of repair and service duties. They have proficiency in several kinds of light repairs and maintenance of many different types of automobiles. Their work, for the most part, is routine and basic. Specialists concentrate in one or two areas and learn to master them for many different car makes and models. Today, in light of the sophisticated technology common in new cars, there is an increasing demand for specialists. Automotive systems are not as simple or standard as they used to be: repair technicians must log in many hours of experience to master them. To gain a broad knowledge in auto maintenance and repair, specialists usually begin as generalists.

When a car does not operate properly, the owner brings it to a service technician and describes the problem. At a dealership or larger shop, the customer may talk with a *repair service estimator*, who writes down the customer's description of the problem and relays it to the service technician. The technician may test-drive the car or use diagnostic equipment, such as motor analyzers, spark plug testers, or compression gauges, to determine the problem. If a customer explains that the car's automatic transmission does not shift gears at the right times, the technician must know how the functioning of the transmission depends on the engine vacuum, the throttle pressure, and—more common in newer cars—the onboard computer. Each factor must be thoroughly checked. With each test, clues help the technician pinpoint the cause of the malfunction. After successfully diagnosing the problem, the technician makes the necessary adjustments or repairs. If a part is too badly damaged or worn to be repaired, he or she replaces it after first consulting the car owner, explaining the problem, and estimating the cost.

Normal use of an automobile inevitably causes wear and deterioration of parts. Generalist automobile technicians handle many of the routine maintenance tasks to help keep a car in optimal operating condition. They change oil, lubricate parts, and adjust or replace components of any of the car's systems that might cause a malfunction, including belts, hoses, spark plugs, brakes, filters, and transmission and coolant fluids.

Technicians who specialize in the service of specific parts usually work in large shops with multiple departments, car diagnostic centers, franchised auto service shops, or small independent shops that concentrate on a particular type of repair work.

Tune-up technicians evaluate and correct engine performance and fuel economy. They use diagnostic equipment and other computerized devices to locate malfunctions in fuel, ignition, and emissions-control systems. They adjust ignition timing and valves and may replace spark plugs, points, triggering assemblies in electronic ignitions, and other components to ensure maximum engine efficiency.

Electrical-systems technicians have been in healthy demand in recent years. They service and repair the complex electrical and computer circuitry common in today's automobile. They use both sophisticated diagnostic equipment and simpler devices such as ammeters, ohmmeters, and voltmeters to locate system malfunctions. In addition to possessing excellent electrical skills, electrical-systems technicians need basic mechanical aptitude to get at electrical and computer circuitry located throughout the automobile.

Front-end technicians are concerned with suspension and steering systems. They inspect, repair, and replace front-end parts such as springs, shock absorbers, and

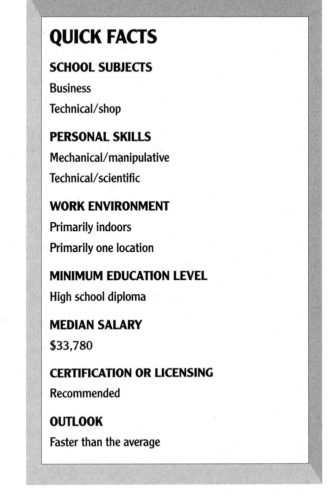

QUICK FACTS

SCHOOL SUBJECTS
Business
Technical/shop

PERSONAL SKILLS
Mechanical/manipulative
Technical/scientific

WORK ENVIRONMENT
Primarily indoors
Primarily one location

MINIMUM EDUCATION LEVEL
High school diploma

MEDIAN SALARY
$33,780

CERTIFICATION OR LICENSING
Recommended

OUTLOOK
Faster than the average

linkage parts such as tie rods and ball joints. They also align and balance wheels.

Brake repairers work on drum and disk braking systems, parking brakes, and their hydraulic systems. They inspect, adjust, remove, repair, and reinstall such items as brake shoes, disk pads, drums, rotors, wheel and master cylinders, and hydraulic fluid lines. Some specialize in both brake and front-end work.

Transmission technicians adjust, repair, and maintain gear trains, couplings, hydraulic pumps, valve bodies, clutch assemblies, and other parts of automatic transmission systems. Transmissions have become complex and highly sophisticated mechanisms in newer model automobiles. Technicians require special training to learn how they function.

Automobile-radiator mechanics clean radiators using caustic solutions. They locate and solder leaks and install new radiator cores. In addition, some radiator mechanics repair car heaters and air conditioners and solder leaks in gas tanks.

Alternative fuel technicians are relatively new additions to the field. This specialty has evolved with the nation's efforts to reduce its dependence on foreign oil by exploring alternative fuels, such as ethanol and electricity.

As more automobiles rely on a variety of electronic components, technicians have become more proficient in the basics of electronics, even if they are not electronics specialists. Electronic controls and instruments are located in nearly all the systems of today's cars. Many previously mechanical functions in automobiles are being replaced by electronics, significantly altering the way repairs are performed. Diagnosing and correcting problems with electronic components often involves the use of specialty tools and computers.

Automobile service technicians use an array of tools in their everyday work, ranging from simple hand tools to computerized diagnostic equipment. Technicians supply their own hand tools at an investment of $6,000 to $25,000 or more, depending on their specialty. It is usually the employer's responsibility to furnish the larger power tools, engine analyzers, and other test equipment.

To maintain and increase their skills and to keep up with new technology, automobile technicians must regularly read service and repair manuals, shop bulletins, and other publications. They must also be willing to take part in training programs given by manufacturers or at vocational schools. Those who have certification must periodically retake exams to keep their credentials.

REQUIREMENTS
High School

In today's competitive job market, aspiring automobile service technicians need a high school diploma to land a job that offers growth possibilities, a good salary, and challenges. There is a big demand in the automotive service industry to fill entry-level positions with well-trained, highly skilled persons. Technology demands more from the technician than it did 10 years ago.

In high school, you should take automotive and shop classes, mathematics, English, and computer classes. Adjustments and repairs to many car components require the technician to make numerous computations, for which good mathematical skills are essential. Good reading skills are also valuable, as a technician must do a lot of reading to stay competitive in today's job market. English classes will prepare you to handle the many volumes of repair manuals and trade journals you will need to remain informed. Computer skills are also vital, as computers are now common in most repair shops. They keep track of customers' histories and parts and

often detail repair procedures. Use of computers in repair shops will only increase in the future.

Look to see if a high school in your area participates in an Automotive Youth Education Service (AYES) program. These programs, certified by the National Institute for Automotive Service Excellence, are partnerships among high school auto repair programs, automotive manufacturers, and franchised automotive dealers. Graduates of AYES programs are widely recognized as some of the best-prepared candidates entering the automotive repair field. For more information, visit http://www.ayes.org.

Postsecondary Training

Employers today prefer to hire only those who have completed some kind of formal training program in automobile mechanics—usually a minimum of two years. A wide variety of such programs are offered at community colleges, vocational schools, independent organizations, and manufacturers. Many community colleges and vocational schools around the country offer accredited postsecondary education. Postsecondary training programs prepare students through a blend of classroom instruction and hands-on practical experience. They range in length from six months to two years or more, depending on the type of program. Shorter programs usually involve intensive study. Longer programs typically alternate classroom courses with periods of work experience. Some two-year programs include courses on applied mathematics, reading and writing skills, and business practices and lead to an associate's degree.

Some programs are conducted in association with automobile manufacturers. Students combine work experience with hands-on classroom study of up-to-date equipment and new cars provided by manufacturers. In other programs, students alternate time in the classroom with internships in dealerships or service departments. These students may take up to four years to finish their training, but they become familiar with the latest technology and also earn a modest salary.

Certification or Licensing

One recognized indicator of quality for entry-level technicians is certification by the National Automotive Technicians Education Foundation (NATEF), an affiliate of the National Institute of Automotive Service Excellence. NATEF's goals are to develop, encourage, and improve automotive technical education for students seeking entry-level positions as automobile service technicians. NATEF certifies many postsecondary programs for training throughout the country. Certification is available in the areas of automatic transmission, brakes, electrical/electronic systems, engine performance, engine repair, heating and air conditioning, manual drive train and axles, and suspension and steering. Certification assures students that the program they enroll in meets the standards employers expect from their entry-level employees. ASE certification is not required, but job applicants who are certified have a competitive advantage over those who are not.

Other Requirements

To be a successful automobile service technician, you must be patient and thorough in your work; a shoddy repair job may put the driver's life at risk. You must have excellent troubleshooting skills and be able to logically deduce the cause of system malfunctions.

EXPLORING

Many community centers offer general auto maintenance and mechanics workshops where you can practice working on real cars and learn from instructors. Trade magazines are excellent sources for learning what's new in the industry and can be found at most public libraries or large bookstores. Many public television stations broadcast automobile maintenance and repair programs that can be of help to beginners to see how various types of cars differ.

Working on cars as a hobby provides valuable firsthand experience in the work of a technician. An after-school or weekend part-time job in a repair shop or dealership can give you a feel for the general atmosphere and kinds of problems technicians face on the job. Oil and tire changes, battery and belt replacement, and even pumping gas may be some of the things you will be asked to do on the job; this work will give you valuable experience before you move on to more complex repairs. Experience with vehicle repair work in the armed forces is another way to pursue your interest in this field.

EMPLOYERS

Because the automotive industry is so vast, automobile service technicians have many choices concerning type of shop and geographic location. Automobile repairs are needed all over the country, in large cities as well as rural areas.

The majority of automobile service technicians work for automotive dealers and independent automotive repair shops and gasoline service stations. The field offers a variety of other employment options as well.

The U.S. Department of Labor estimates that 17 percent of automobile service technicians are self-employed. Other employers include franchises such as PepBoys and Midas that offer routine repairs and maintenance, and automotive service departments of automotive and home supply stores. Some automobile service technicians maintain fleets for taxicab and automobile leasing companies or for government agencies with large automobile fleets.

Technicians with experience and/or ASE certification certainly have more career choices. Some master mechanics may go on to teach at technical and vocational schools or at community colleges. Others put in many years working for someone else and go into business for themselves after they have gained the experience to handle many types of repairs and oversee other technicians.

STARTING OUT

The best way to start out in this field is to attend one of the many postsecondary training programs available throughout the country and obtain accreditation. Trade and technical schools usually provide job placement assistance for their graduates. Schools often have contacts with local employers who need to hire well-trained people. Frequently, employers post job openings at nearby trade schools with accredited programs. Job openings are often listed on the Internet through regional and national automotive associations or career networks.

A decreasing number of technicians learn the trade on the job as apprentices. Their training consists of working for several years under the guidance of experienced mechanics. Fewer employers today are willing to hire apprentices due to the time and money it takes to train them. Those who do learn their skills on the job will inevitably require some formal training if they wish to advance and stay in step with the changing industry.

Intern programs sponsored by car manufacturers or independent organizations provide students with excellent opportunities to actually work with prospective employers. Internships can provide students with valuable contacts who will be able to recommend future employers once they have completed their training. Many students may even be hired by the shop at which they interned.

ADVANCEMENT

Currently employed technicians may be certified by ASE in eight different areas. Those who become certified in all eight areas are known as master mechanics. Although certification is voluntary, it is a widely recognized standard of achievement for automobile technicians and is highly valued by many employers. Certification also provides the means and opportunity to advance. To maintain their certification, technicians must retake the examination for their specialties every five years. Many employers only hire ASE-accredited technicians and base salaries on the level of the technicians' accreditation.

With today's complex automobile components requiring hundreds of hours of study and practice to master, more repair shops prefer to hire specialists. Generalist automobile technicians advance as they gain experience and become specialists. Other technicians advance to diesel repair, where the pay may be higher. Those with good communications and planning skills may advance to shop foreman or service manager at large repair shops or to sales workers at dealerships. Master mechanics with good business skills often go into business for themselves and open their own shops.

EARNINGS

Salary ranges of automobile service technicians vary depending on the level of experience, type of shop the technician works in, and geographic location. Generally, technicians who work in small-town, family-owned gas stations earn less than those who work at dealerships and franchises in metropolitan areas.

According to the U.S. Department of Labor, automobile service technicians had median annual salaries of $33,780 ($16.24 an hour) in 2006. The lowest paid 10 percent made less than $19,073 ($9.17 an hour), and the highest paid 10 percent made more than $56,617 ($27.22 an hour). Since most technicians are paid on an hourly basis and frequently work overtime, their salaries can vary significantly. In many repair shops and dealerships, technicians can earn higher incomes by working on commission. Master technicians who work on commission can earn more than $100,000 annually. Employers often guarantee a minimum level of pay in addition to commissions.

Benefit packages vary from business to business. Most technicians receive health insurance and paid vacation days. Additional benefits may include dental, life, and disability insurance and a pension plan. Employers usually pay for a technician's work clothes and may pay a percentage on hand tools purchased. An increasing number of employers pay for all or most of an employee's certification training, if he or she passes the test. A technician's salary can increase through yearly bonuses or profit sharing if the business does well.

WORK ENVIRONMENT

Depending on the size of the shop and whether it's an independent or franchised repair shop, dealership, or private business, automobile technicians work with anywhere from two to 20 other technicians. Most shops are well lighted and well ventilated. They can frequently be noisy with running cars and power tools. Minor hand and back injuries are the most common problems of technicians. When reaching in hard-to-get-at places or loosening tight bolts, technicians often bruise, cut, or burn their hands. With caution and experience most technicians learn to avoid hand injuries. Working for long periods of time in cramped or bent positions often results in a stiff back or neck. Technicians also lift many heavy objects that can cause injury if not handled carefully; however, this is becoming less of a problem with new cars, as automakers design smaller and lighter parts to improve fuel economy. Some technicians may experience allergic reactions to solvents and oils used in cleaning, maintenance, and repair. Shops must comply with strict safety procedures set by the Occupational Safety and Health Administration and Environmental Protection Agency to help employees avoid accidents and injuries.

The U.S. Department of Labor reports that most technicians work a standard 40-hour week, but 30 percent of all technicians work more than 40 hours a week. Some technicians make emergency repairs to stranded automobiles on the roadside during odd hours.

OUTLOOK

With an estimated 221 million vehicles in operation today, automobile service technicians should feel confident that a good percentage will require servicing and repair. Skilled and highly trained technicians will be in particular demand. Less-skilled workers will face tough competition. The U.S. Department of Labor predicts that this field will grow about faster than the average through 2016, as many automotive repair technicians reach retirement age and will need to be replaced. According to ASE, even if school enrollments were at maximum capacity, the demand for automobile service technicians still would exceed the supply in the immediate future. As a result, many shops are beginning to recruit employees while they are still in vocational or even high school. Opportunities will be best for those who have completed high school and received ASE certification.

Another concern for the industry is the automobile industry's trend toward developing the "maintenance-free" car. Manufacturers are producing high-end cars that require no servicing for their first 100,000 miles. In addition, many new cars are equipped with onboard diagnostics that detect both wear and failure for many of the car's components, eliminating the need for technicians to perform extensive diagnostic tests. Also, parts that are replaced before they completely wear out prevent further damage from occurring to connected parts that are affected by a malfunction or breakdown. Although this will reduce troubleshooting time and the number of overall repairs, the components that need repair will be more costly and require a more experienced (and hence, more expensive) technician.

Most new jobs for technicians will be at independent service dealers, specialty shops, and franchised new car dealers. Because of the increase of specialty shops, fewer gasoline service stations will hire technicians, and many will eliminate repair services completely. Other opportunities will be available at companies or institutions with private fleets (e.g., cab, delivery, and rental companies, and government agencies and police departments).

FOR MORE INFORMATION

For more information on the automotive service industry, contact

Automotive Aftermarket Industry Association
7101 Wisconsin Avenue, Suite 1300
Bethesda, MD 20814-3415
Tel: 301-654-6664
Email: aaia@aftermarket.org
http://www.aftermarket.org

For industry information and job listings, contact

Automotive Service Association
PO Box 929
Bedford, TX 76095-0929
Tel: 800-272-7467
Email: asainfo@asashop.org
http://www.asashop.org

For information and statistics on automotive dealers, contact

National Automobile Dealers Association
8400 Westpark Drive
McLean, VA 22102
Tel: 800-252-6232
Email: nadainfo@nada.org
http://www.nada.org

For information on certified educational programs, careers, and certification, contact

National Automotive Technicians Education Foundation
101 Blue Seal Drive, Suite 101

Leesburg, VA 20175
Tel: 703-669-6650
http://www.natef.org

For information on certification, contact

National Institute for Automotive Service Excellence
101 Blue Seal Drive, SE, Suite 101
Leesburg, VA 20175-5646
Tel: 877-273-8324
http://www.asecert.org

BARBERS

OVERVIEW

Barbers shampoo, cut, trim, and style hair and shave, trim, and shape beards. While barbers are formally trained to perform other services such as coloring and perming hair, most barbers in barbershops do not offer these services. Barbers may also call themselves *barber-stylists*, and a few may even refer to themselves as *tonsorial artists*, an old-fashioned term which is derived from a Latin word meaning "to shear." There are 60,000 barbers working in the United States.

THE JOB

Most barbers in barbershops focus primarily on the basics of men's grooming needs: hair cutting and trimming, shampooing, styling, and beard and mustache trimming and shaping. Many can also perform a brief facial and a scalp and/or neck massage. While some barbers do perform other services, such as tinting or bleaching, most find that few of their customers seek such services, and those that do are more likely to head for a full-service salon. Shaving is far less common in barbershops today than it once was. The safety razor has made shaving at home a relatively quick and easy task, and the art of the straight-edge shave is little more than a relic of tonsorial history.

Most customers who frequent barbershops are men, but some women also patronize barbers. Likewise, most barbers are men, but the field includes some female barbers as well.

The equipment barbers utilize—clippers, razors, shears, combs, brushes, and so forth—must be kept in antiseptic condition. Often barbers must supply their own equipment. Barbers who operate their own shops must handle the details of answering phones and setting

QUICK FACTS

SCHOOL SUBJECTS
Business
Health

PERSONAL SKILLS
Artistic
Mechanical/manipulative

WORK ENVIRONMENT
Primarily indoors
Primarily one location

MINIMUM EDUCATION LEVEL
Some postsecondary training

MEDIAN AVERAGE
$23,150

CERTIFICATION OR LICENSING
Required by all states

OUTLOOK
Faster than the average

appointments, ordering supplies and paying bills, maintaining equipment, and keeping records. If they employ other barbers, they are responsible for the hiring and performance of their staff as well. Barbershops range from one-person operations to larger shops with many chairs and operators.

REQUIREMENTS
High School

Many states require that barbers be high school graduates, although a few states require only an eighth grade education. High school students considering a career as a barber might find it helpful to take courses in health and business. Involvement in theater can provide you with opportunities to practice working on hair and attempting to create different styles as well as give you the opportunity to develop "people skills" you will need later when dealing with the public.

Postsecondary Training

Generally, a barber must complete a certain number of hours of barber school (ranging from 1,000 to 2,000 hours, depending on the state). Most states offer programs that include classroom work, demonstrations, and hands-on work and can be completed in 10 to 24 months. The barber must then pass an examination that includes a written test (and sometimes an oral test) and a practical examination to demonstrate that skills are mastered. A health certificate must also be obtained. In selecting a barber school, a student should be sure the school meets (and preferably exceeds) the state's requirements for licensing. Some schools have waiting lists, so it may be prudent to apply early.

At one time, a one- to two-year apprenticeship was required in many states before a barber was "full-fledged"; this practice is becoming less common as formal training is increasingly emphasized. In a few rural states, an apprenticeship can take the place of formal education, but this is an uncommon and difficult way to acquire sufficient skill and knowledge.

Certification or Licensing

All barbers must be licensed to practice in the state in which they work, although the requirements vary from state to state. Some states have licensing reciprocity agreements that enable barbers to practice in another state without being retested. Some states require that barbers be at least 18 years old in order to be licensed.

Unions were once prevalent among barbers, but they are becoming less common, especially in rural areas. Today there are fewer barbers in the workforce than there were decades ago, and a large percentage—about 46 percent, according to the U.S. Department of Labor—are self-employed. The National Cosmetology Association lists the United Food and Commercial Workers International Union as the principal union that organizes barbers.

Other Requirements

Barbering requires good finger dexterity and stamina, since barbers are required to be on their feet most of the day (although work environments can often be adapted to accommodate workers with disabilities or special needs). Barbers should be neat and well-groomed because they work in close proximity to their customers. Tact and patience are important characteristics, as is being a good listener. The ability to easily carry on light conversation is also important. Roy Bollhoffer, owner of Roy's Barbershop in Highland Park, Illinois, stresses the importance of being a "people-person." Says Bollhoffer about being a barber, "If you don't like people, you're in trouble." Bollhoffer has owned his barbershop for 34 years; he bought it from a barber who started his business just after World War I. Nearly all of Bollhoffer's customers have been with him for many years, and quite a few have patronized his shop for even longer than the 34 years Bollhoffer has been there. Like many barbers, Bollhoffer finds that once customers find a barber they like, they stick with him or her until the customers die or move, or until the barber retires.

To be successful, barbers must understand the importance their customers place on their appearances and seriously strive to provide a look that pleases their customers. An executive in a national association for barbers noted of the profession, "You're in the business of making people happy." Barbers should have a sense of form and style in order to determine what looks would be most flattering for individual customers. A barber must also recognize when a style desired by a customer isn't suited to the customer's features or hair type in order to avoid customer dissatisfaction. These situations require firmness and diplomacy.

EXPLORING

If you are interested in this career, try finding part-time employment in a barbershop or beauty salon to gain exposure to the nature of the work and the working conditions. Another avenue of exploration might be to call a barber school and ask for an opportunity to tour the facilities, observe classes, and question instructors. Of course, nothing compares to talking to someone with firsthand experience; a chat with a local barber is a sure and easy way to obtain helpful and informative feedback.

EMPLOYERS

A barber's domain is almost exclusively the barbershop. While some barbers may find work in a full-service styling salon, most of these businesses are seeking stylists with broader training and experience. Most barbers are self-employed, either owning their own shops or renting a chair at a barbershop. In the days before beauty salons were so prevalent—and before men frequented them—nearly all men had their hair cut by barbers. Today, these men still make up a significant portion of barbershops' clienteles, so opportunities for barbers may be better in areas with a higher concentration of older men. Some barbers are employed as teachers/trainers at barber schools, and some may also serve as inspectors for the State Board of Barber Examiners.

STARTING OUT

In most states, the best way (and often the only way) to enter the field of barbering is to graduate from a barber school that meets the state's requirements for licensing and to pass the state's licensing examination. Nearly all barber schools assist graduates with the process of finding employment opportunities. As barbershops are few in many areas, calling or visiting a barbershop is an excellent way to find employment. In some areas, there may be barbering unions to help in one's job search. While a part-time job in a barbershop or beauty shop can be helpful in determining one's level of interest in the field, satisfying the graduation requirements of an accredited barber school and becoming licensed is usually the only way to enter this occupation.

ADVANCEMENT

The most common form of advancement in the barbering profession is owning one's own shop. This requires business experience and skill as well as proficiency in the barbering profession, and of course start-up requires capital outlay. Those who are successful as owners do reap higher earnings than barbers who rent a booth in a shop or are paid on a commission basis. Some even go on to own a chain of barbershops. In larger barbershops, there may be opportunities for management, but these are relatively rare. The longer a barber is on the job, though, the larger the clientele (and thus the security and income) becomes.

Barbers can increase their opportunities for advancement by becoming licensed as cosmetologists and working in larger beauty shops that provide more complicated, varied, and advanced services. Opportunities for management or specializing in certain services are increasingly plentiful in full-service salons. Many states require a separate license for cosmetology, but often barbering training can be applied toward a cosmetology license. In a few states, the two licenses are combined into one hair styling license.

Related career opportunities may exist if a barber wishes to become an instructor at a barber school or an inspector for the State Board of Barber Examiners.

EARNINGS

Incomes can vary widely depending on a barber's experience, the location of the shop, the number of hours worked, tipping habits of the clientele, and whether or not a barber owns the business. The personality and initiative of a barber also impacts the ability to draw a loyal following. Most barbers receive an hourly wage plus tips. The U.S. Department of Labor reports the median hourly earnings for barbers, plus tips, was $11.13 in 2006 (about $23,150 anually). Wages ranged from less than $7.12 ($13,894 annually) for the lowest paid 10 percent to $20.56 (42,764 annually) for the highest paid 10 percent. Many established barbers and barber/owners earn incomes that well exceed the median.

One of the most frequently cited downsides to being a barber is a lack of benefits, particularly where there are no unions. Many barbers cannot get group insurance, and the cost of individual policies can be high. Also, since most barbers are either self-employed or working for small shops, benefits such as retirement plans, paid vacations, sick days, and so forth are often the exception to the rule.

WORK ENVIRONMENT

Barbers generally enjoy pleasant work surroundings. The barbershop environment is usually friendly, clean, and comfortable. Many barbers can set their own hours, and although many work Saturdays, they typically take Sundays and weeknights off. Of course, this depends largely on the schedules of their clientele; barbers whose clientele consists mostly of retirees rarely find the need to work evenings. Stress levels and job pressures are lower than is the case with most jobs. Established barbers enjoy a unique security in that their clients are usually very loyal and always need haircuts. Most barbers don't share the fears of lay-offs and other job insecurities common to other professions. Compared to their cosmetologist counterparts, barbers are exposed to fewer hair and nail chemicals, which also enhances the work environment. Most barbers have been on the job for many years, and there is clearly a great deal of pride and job enjoyment among barbers. This is a good profession for those who enjoy the company of other people.

OUTLOOK

The U.S. Department of Labor predicts employment of barbers and other personal care workers to grow faster than the average for all occupations through 2016. This will result from general population growth, the increased popularity of personal care services, and the need to replace retiring workers. Since there are currently few qualified candidates, those entering the field may find good opportunities, depending on their location. Says Roy Bollhoffer, "I had another barber here with me for 27 years, but he retired. I'd love to find another barber to bring in, but there is a serious shortage of barbers now. And there will always be people who want to go to a barber. I've made a very nice living here." In all likelihood, the outlook for this profession will be different for various cities, states, and regions of the country.

FOR MORE INFORMATION

For information about the profession as well as a list of licensed training schools, contact

National Accrediting Commission of Cosmetology Arts & Sciences
4401 Ford Avenue, Suite 1300
Alexandria, VA 22302-1432
Tel: 703-600-7600
http://www.naccas.org

For information on careers as a barber, contact
National Association of Barber Boards of America
2703 Pine Street
Arkadelphia, AR 71923
Tel: 501-682-2806
http://www.nationalbarberboards.com

☐ BIOMEDICAL EQUIPMENT TECHNICIANS

OVERVIEW

Biomedical equipment technicians handle the complex medical equipment and instruments found in hospitals, clinics, and research facilities. This equipment is used for medical therapy and diagnosis and includes heart-lung machines, artificial kidney machines, patient monitors, chemical analyzers, and other electrical, electronic, mechanical, or pneumatic devices.

Technicians' main duties are to inspect, maintain, repair, and install this equipment. They disassemble equipment to locate malfunctioning components, repair or replace defective parts, and reassemble the equipment, adjusting and calibrating it to ensure that it operates according to manufacturers' specifications. Other duties of biomedical equipment technicians include modifying equipment according to the directions of medical or supervisory personnel, arranging with equipment manufacturers for necessary equipment repair, and safety-testing equipment to ensure that patients, equipment operators, and other staff members are safe from electrical or mechanical hazards. Biomedical equipment technicians work with hand tools, power tools, measuring devices, and manufacturers' manuals.

Technicians may work for equipment manufacturers as salespeople or as service technicians, or for a health care facility specializing in the repair or maintenance of specific equipment, such as that used in radiology, nuclear medicine, or patient monitoring. In the United States, approximately 38,000 people work as biomedical equipment technicians.

THE JOB

Biomedical equipment technicians are an important link between technology and medicine. They repair, calibrate, maintain, and operate biomedical equipment working under the supervision of researchers, biomedical engineers, physicians, surgeons, and other professional health care providers.

Biomedical equipment technicians may work with thousands of different kinds of equipment. Some of the most frequently encountered are the following: patient monitors; heart-lung machines; kidney machines; blood-gas analyzers; spectrophotometers; X-ray units; radiation monitors; defibrillators; anesthesia apparatus; pacemakers; blood pressure transducers; spirometers; sterilizers; diathermy equipment; patient-care computers; ultrasound machines; and diagnostic scanning machines, such as the CT (computed tomography) scan machine, PET (positron emission tomography) scanner, and MRI (magnetic resonance imaging) machines.

Repairing faulty instruments is one of the chief functions of biomedical equipment technicians. They investigate equipment problems, determine the extent of malfunctions, make repairs on instruments that have had minor breakdowns, and expedite the repair of instruments with major breakdowns, for instance, by writing an analysis of the problem for the factory. In doing this work, technicians rely on manufacturers' diagrams, maintenance manuals, and standard and specialized test instruments, such as oscilloscopes and pressure gauges.

Installing equipment is another important function of biomedical equipment technicians. They inspect and test new equipment to make sure it complies with performance and safety standards as described in the manufacturer's manuals and diagrams, and as noted on the purchase order. Technicians may also check on proper installation of the equipment, or, in some cases, install it themselves. To ensure safe operations, technicians need

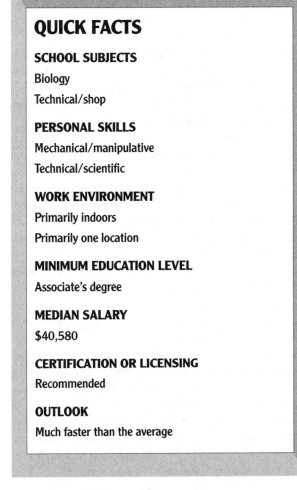

QUICK FACTS

SCHOOL SUBJECTS
Biology
Technical/shop

PERSONAL SKILLS
Mechanical/manipulative
Technical/scientific

WORK ENVIRONMENT
Primarily indoors
Primarily one location

MINIMUM EDUCATION LEVEL
Associate's degree

MEDIAN SALARY
$40,580

CERTIFICATION OR LICENSING
Recommended

OUTLOOK
Much faster than the average

a thorough knowledge of the regulations related to the proper grounding of equipment, and they need to actively carry out all steps and procedures to ensure safety.

Maintenance is the third major area of responsibility for biomedical equipment technicians. In doing this work, technicians try to catch problems before they become more serious. To this end, they take apart and reassemble devices, test circuits, clean and oil moving parts, and replace worn parts. They also keep complete records of all machine repairs, maintenance checks, and expenses.

In all three of these areas, a large part of technicians' work consists of consulting with physicians, administrators, engineers, and other related professionals. For example, they may be called upon to assist hospital administrators as they make decisions about the repair, replacement, or purchase of new equipment. They consult with medical and research staffs to determine whether equipment is functioning safely and properly. They also consult with medical and engineering staffs when called upon to modify or develop equipment. In all of these activities, they use their knowledge of electronics, medical terminology, human anatomy and physiology, chemistry, and physics.

In addition, biomedical equipment technicians are involved in a range of other related duties. Some biomedical equipment technicians maintain inventories of all instruments in the hospital, their condition, location, and operators. They reorder parts and components, assist in providing people with emergency instruments, restore unsafe or defective instruments to working order, and check for safety regulation compliance.

Other biomedical equipment technicians help physicians, surgeons, nurses, and researchers conduct procedures and experiments. In addition, they must be able to explain to staff members how to operate these machines, the conditions under which a certain apparatus may or may not be used, how to solve small operating problems, and how to monitor and maintain equipment.

In many hospitals, technicians are assigned to a particular service, such as pediatrics, surgery, or renal medicine. These technicians become specialists in certain types of equipment. However, unlike electrocardiograph technicians or dialysis technicians, who specialize in one kind of equipment, most biomedical equipment technicians must be thoroughly familiar with a large variety of instruments. They might be called upon to prepare an artificial kidney or to work with a blood-gas analyzer. Biomedical equipment technicians also maintain pulmonary function machines. These machines are used in clinics for ambulatory patients, hospital laboratories, departments of medicine for diagnosis and treatment, and rehabilitation of cardiopulmonary patients.

While most biomedical equipment technicians are trained in electronics technology, there is also a need for technicians trained in plastics to work on the development of artificial organs and for people trained in glass blowing to help make the precision parts for specialized equipment.

Many biomedical equipment technicians work for medical instrument manufacturers. These technicians consult and assist in the construction of new machinery, helping to make decisions concerning materials and construction methods to be used in the manufacture of the equipment.

REQUIREMENTS
High School

There are a number of classes you can take in high school to help you prepare for this work. Science classes, such as chemistry, biology, and physics, will give you the science background you will need for working in a medical environment. Take shop classes that deal with electronics, drafting, or blueprint reading. These classes will give you experience working with your hands, following printed directions, using electricity, and working with machinery. Mathematics classes will help you become comfortable working with numbers and formulas. English classes will help you develop your communication skills, which will be important to have when you deal with a variety of different people in your professional life.

Postsecondary Training

To become qualified for this work, you will need to complete postsecondary education that leads either to an associate's degree from a two-year institution or a bachelor's degree from a four-year college or university. Most biomedical equipment technicians choose to receive an associate's degree. Biomedical equipment technology is a relatively new program in some schools and may also be referred to as *medical electronics technology* or *biomedical engineering technology*. No matter what the name of the program, however, you should expect to receive instruction in such areas as anatomy, physiology, electrical and electronic fundamentals, chemistry, physics, and biomedical equipment construction and design. In addition, you will study safety methods in health care facilities and medical equipment troubleshooting, as it will be your job to be the problem solver. You should also expect to continue taking communication or English classes since communications skills will be essential to your work. In addition to the classroom work, many programs often provide you with practical experience in repairing and servicing equipment in a clinical or laboratory setting under the supervision of an experienced equipment technician. In this way, you learn about electrical components and circuits, the design and construction of common pieces of machinery, and computer technology as it applies to biomedical equipment.

By studying various pieces of equipment, you learn a problem-solving technique that applies not only to the equipment studied, but also to equipment you have not yet seen, and even to equipment that has not yet been invented. Part of this problem-solving technique includes learning how and where to locate sources of information.

A biomedical equipment technician requires continuing education, as biomedical equipment is constantly being improved and refined, and new uses and techniques for the equipment emerge frequently. This aspect of your career development takes place via seminars, self-study, and certification exams.

Some biomedical equipment technicians receive their training in the armed forces. During the course of an enlistment period of four years or less, military personnel can receive training that prepares them for entry-level or sometimes advanced-level positions in the civilian workforce.

Certification or Licensing

The Association for the Advancement of Medical Instrumentation, affiliated with the International Certification Commission for Clinical Engineering and Biomedical Technology, issues a certificate for biomedical equipment technicians that is based on a written examination, work experience, and educational preparation. In some cases, the educational requirements for certification may be waived for technicians with appropriate employment experience. Although certification is not required for employment, it is highly recommended. Technicians with certification have demonstrated that they have attained an overall knowledge of the field and are dedicated to their profession. Many employers prefer to hire technicians who have this certification.

Other Requirements

Biomedical equipment technicians need mechanical ability and should enjoy working with tools. Because this job demands quick decision-making and prompt repairs, technicians should work well under pressure. You should also be extremely precise and accurate in your work, have good communications skills, and enjoy helping others—an essential quality for anyone working in the health care industry.

EXPLORING

You will have difficulty gaining any direct experience in biomedical equipment technology until you are in a training program or working professionally. Your first hands-on opportunities generally come in the clinical and laboratory phases of your education. You can, however, visit school and community libraries to seek out books written about careers in medical technology. You can also join a hobby club devoted to chemistry, biology, radio equipment, or electronics.

Perhaps the best way to learn more about this job is to set up a visit to a local health care facility or to arrange for a biomedical technician to speak to inter-ested students, either on site or at a career exploration seminar hosted by the school. Ask a teacher or guidance counselor for help setting up this sort of session. You may be able to ask the technician about his or her educational background, what a day on the job is like, and what new technologies are on the horizon. Try to visit a school offering a program in biomedical equipment technology and discuss your career plans with an admissions counselor there. The counselor may also be able to provide you with helpful insights about the career and your preparation for it.

Finally, because this work involves the health care field, consider getting a part-time job or volunteering at a local hospital. Naturally, you won't be asked to work with the biomedical equipment, but you will have the opportunity to see professionals on the job and experience being in the medical environment. Even if your duty is only to escort patients to their tests, you may gain a greater understanding of this work.

EMPLOYERS

Many schools place students in part-time hospital positions to help them gain practical experience. Students are often able to return to these hospitals for full-time employment after graduation. Other places of employment include research institutes and biomedical equipment manufacturers. Government hospitals and the military are also employers of biomedical equipment technicians.

STARTING OUT

Most schools offering programs in biomedical equipment technology work closely with local hospitals and industries, and school placement officers are usually informed about openings when they become available. In some cases, recruiters may visit a school periodically to conduct interviews. Also, many schools place students in part-time hospital jobs to help them gain practical experience. Students are often able to return to these hospitals for full-time employment after graduation.

Another effective method of finding employment is to write directly to hospitals, research institutes, or biomedical equipment manufacturers. Other good sources of leads for job openings include state employment offices and newspaper want ads.

ADVANCEMENT

With experience, biomedical equipment technicians can expect to work with less supervision, and in some cases they may find themselves supervising less-experienced technicians. They may advance to positions in which they serve as instructors, assist in research, or have administrative duties. Although many supervisory positions are open to biomedical equipment technicians, some positions are not available without additional education. In large metropolitan hospitals, for instance, the minimum educational requirement for biomedical engineers, who do much of the supervising of biomedical equipment technicians, is a bachelor's degree; many engineers have a master's degree as well.

EARNINGS

Salaries for biomedical equipment technicians vary in different institutions and localities and according to the experience, training, certification, and type of work done by the technician. According to the U.S. Department of Labor, the median annual salary for medical equipment repairers was $40,580 in 2006. The top 10 percent in this profession made $66,160 a year, while the lowest 10 percent made $23,700 per year. In general, biomedical equipment technicians who work for manufacturers have higher earnings than those who work for hospitals. Naturally, those in supervisory or senior positions also command higher salaries. Benefits, such as health insurance and vacation days, vary with the employer.

WORK ENVIRONMENT

Working conditions for biomedical equipment technicians vary according to employer and type of work done. Hospital employees generally work a 40-hour week; their schedules sometimes include weekends and holidays, and some technicians may be on call for emergencies. Technicians working for equipment manufacturers may have to do extensive traveling to install or service equipment.

The physical surroundings in which biomedical equipment technicians work may vary from day to day. Technicians may work in a lab or treatment room with patients or consult with engineers, administrators, and other staff members. Other days, technicians may spend most of their time at a workbench repairing equipment.

OUTLOOK

The U.S. Department of Labor predicts employment for biomedical equipment technicians to grow much faster than the average through 2016. This growth stems from the increasing complexity of and need for biomedical equipment, which creates the need for many knowledgeable technicians. Those with excellent knowledge various

kinds of computer software and electronics will be in high demand.

In hospitals the need for more biomedical equipment technicians exists not only because of the increasing use of biomedical equipment but also because hospital administrators realize that these technicians can help hold down costs. Biomedical equipment technicians do this through their preventive maintenance checks and by taking over some routine activities of engineers and administrators, thus releasing those professionals for activities that only they can perform. Through the coming decades, cost containment will remain a high priority for hospital administrators, and as long as biomedical equipment technicians can contribute to that effort, the demand for them should remain strong.

For the many biomedical equipment technicians who work for companies that build, sell, lease, or service biomedical equipment, job opportunities should also continue to grow.

The federal government employs biomedical equipment technicians in its hospitals, research institutes, and the military. Employment in these areas will depend largely on levels of government spending. In the research area, spending levels may vary; however, in health care delivery, spending should remain high for the near future.

FOR MORE INFORMATION

For information on student memberships, biomedical technology programs, and certification, contact

Association for the Advancement of Medical Instrumentation
1110 North Glebe Road, Suite 220
Arlington, VA 22201-4795
Tel: 800-332-2264
http://www.aami.org

BOILERMAKERS AND BOILERMAKER MECHANICS

OVERVIEW

Boilermakers and *boilermaker mechanics* construct, assemble, and repair boilers, vats, tanks, and other large metal vessels that are designed to hold liquids and gases.

Following blueprints, they lay out, cut, fit, bolt, weld, and rivet together heavy metal plates, boiler tubes, and castings. Boilermaker mechanics maintain and repair boilers and other vessels made by boilermakers. There are approximately 18,000 boilermakers working in the United States.

THE JOB

Some boilermakers and mechanics work at or near the site where the boiler, tank, or vat is installed. Such sites include petroleum refineries, schools, and other institutions with large heating plants, factories where boilers are used to generate power to run machines, factories that make and store products such as chemicals or beer in large tanks, and atomic energy plants. Others work in shops or factories where boilers and other large vessels are manufactured.

Boilermakers who do layout work usually work in a shop or factory. These workers follow drawings, blueprints, and patterns to mark pieces of metal plate and tubing indicating how the metal will be cut and shaped by other workers into the sections of vessels. Once the sections are fabricated, other workers at the shop, called *fitters*, temporarily put together the plates and the framework of the vessels. They check the drawings and other specifications and bolt or tack-weld pieces together to be sure that the parts fit properly.

In doing the final assembly at the site, boilermakers first refer to blueprints and mark off dimensions on the base that has been prepared for the finished vessel. They use measuring devices, straightedges, and transits. They attach rigging equipment, such as hoists, jacks, and rollers, to any prefabricated sections of the vessel that are so large they must be lifted into place with cranes. After crane operators move the sections to the correct positions, the boilermakers fine-tune the alignment of the parts. They use levels and check plumb lines and then secure the sections in place with wedges and turnbuckles. With cutting torches, files, and grinders, they remove irregularities and precisely adjust the fit and finally weld and rivet the sections together. They may also attach tubing, valves, gauges, or other parts to the vessel and then test the container for leaks and defects.

Boilermakers also work in shipbuilding and in repairing the hulls, bulkheads, and decks of iron ships. In a typical repair, boilermakers first remove damaged metal plates by drilling out rivets and cutting off rivet heads with a chipping hammer. Then they take measurements of the damaged plates or make wooden patterns of them so that new plates can be made. They install the new plates, reaming and aligning rivet holes, and then fasten

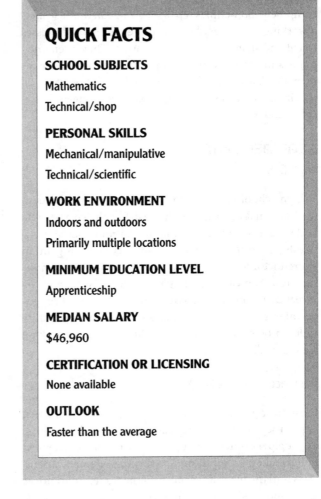

QUICK FACTS

SCHOOL SUBJECTS

Mathematics

Technical/shop

PERSONAL SKILLS

Mechanical/manipulative

Technical/scientific

WORK ENVIRONMENT

Indoors and outdoors

Primarily multiple locations

MINIMUM EDUCATION LEVEL

Apprenticeship

MEDIAN SALARY

$46,960

CERTIFICATION OR LICENSING

None available

OUTLOOK

Faster than the average

on the plates by driving in rivets. Sometimes similar work is done on ships' boilers, condensers, evaporators, loaders, gratings, and stacks.

Field construction boilermakers work outdoors and move from one geographic location to another. They join construction teams in erecting and repairing pressure vessels, air pollution equipment, blast furnaces, water treatment plants, storage tanks, and stacks and liners. They can be involved in the erection of a 750,000-gallon water storage tank, the placement of a nuclear power plant reactor dome, or the construction of components on a hydroelectric power station.

Boilermaker mechanics maintain and repair boilers and other vessels. They routinely clean or direct others to clean boilers, and they inspect fittings, valves, tubes, controls, and other parts. When necessary, they check the vessels to identify specific weaknesses or sources of trouble. They update components, such as burners and boiler tubes, to make them as efficient as possible. They dismantle the units to replace worn or defective parts, using hand and power tools, gas torches, and welding equipment. Sometimes repairs require that they use metalworking machinery such as power shears and presses to cut and shape parts to specification. They strengthen joints and supports, and they put patches on weak areas of metal plates. Like fabrication and installation work, all repairs must be done in compliance with state and local safety codes.

REQUIREMENTS
High School

A high school diploma is required for all applicants to the boilermaking trade. In the past, people have become boilermakers through on-the-job training, but apprenticeships are now strongly recommended. To gain an apprenticeship, an applicant must score well on an aptitude test. You can prepare yourself for this test and the career by taking math classes and shop classes throughout high school. Courses that give you the opportunity to learn blueprint reading, welding, and metalworking are especially helpful.

Postsecondary Training

Formal apprenticeships usually last four years. An apprentice receives practical training while working as a helper under the supervision of an experienced boilermaker. In addition to working, trainees attend classes in the technical aspects of the trade. Apprentices study subjects such as blueprint reading, layout, welding techniques, mechanical drawing, the physics and chemistry of various metals, and applied mathematics. While on the job, apprentices practice the knowledge they have acquired in the classroom. They develop such skills as using rigging and hoisting equipment, welding, riveting, and installing auxiliary devices and tubes onto vessels.

Other Requirements

Mechanical aptitude and manual dexterity are important characteristics for prospective boilermakers. Because the work can be very strenuous, stamina is needed for jobs that require a great deal of bending, stooping, squatting, or reaching. Before they begin work, boilermakers may need to pass a physical examination showing that they are in good enough health to do the work safely. On the job, they must be able to work well despite noisy surroundings, odors, working at heights or in small, enclosed spaces, and other dis-

comforts and dangers. It is also important that they be cautious and careful in their work and that they closely follow safety rules.

EXPLORING

You may be able to observe boilermakers or workers who use similar skills as they work on construction projects or repair and maintenance jobs. For example, welders and equipment operators lifting heavy objects with elaborate rigging can sometimes be seen working at sites where large buildings are being erected. High school shop courses, such as blueprint reading and metalworking, can give you an idea of some of the activities of boilermakers. With the help of shop teachers or guidance counselors, you may be able to arrange to talk with people working in the trade. Information may also be obtained by contacting the local union-management committee in charge of apprenticeships for boilermakers.

EMPLOYERS

Approximately 18,000 boilermakers work in the United States. About 63 percent of boilermakers work in the construction industry. Others work in manufacturing, employed primarily in boiler manufacturing shops, iron and steel plants, petroleum refineries, chemical plants, and shipyards. Still others work for boiler repair firms, for railroads, and in Navy shipyards and federal power facilities.

STARTING OUT

There are a limited number of apprenticeships available in boilermaking; only the best applicants are accepted, and there may be a waiting period before the apprenticeship starts. Sometimes workers begin as helpers in repair shops and enter formal apprenticeships later. These helper jobs are often advertised in newspapers. Vocational and technical schools and sometimes high schools with metal shop courses may also help their graduates locate such positions. Other good approaches are to apply directly to employers and to contact the local office of the state employment service.

ADVANCEMENT

Upon completing their training programs, apprentices qualify as journeymen boilermakers. With experience and the right kind of leadership abilities, boilermakers may be able to advance to supervisory positions. In fabrication shops, layout workers and fitters who start as helpers can learn the skills they need in about two years.

In time, they may move up to become shop supervisors, or they may decide to become boilermakers who work on-site to assemble vessels.

EARNINGS

According to the U.S. Department of Labor, the median salary for boilermakers in 2006 was $46,960. The department also reported that the lowest-paid 10 percent earned less than $30,410 per year, and the highest-paid 10 percent made more than $71,170.

According to the International Brotherhood of Boilermakers, annual earnings vary greatly because of the temporary, cyclical nature of the work. Apprentices start at about 60 percent of journeyman wages. Earnings also vary according to the part of the country where boilermakers work, the industry that employs them, and their level of skill and experience. Pay rates are usually highest for boilermakers doing installation work in the construction industry and lower for those in manufacturing industries, although workers in construction may not be employed as steadily. Workers in the Northeast, the Great Lakes area, and cities in the far West tend to earn the highest wages.

Boilermakers tend to make more than boilermaker mechanics. Among employees in boiler fabrication shops, layout workers generally earn more while fitters earn less. Both layout workers and fitters normally work indoors; therefore, their earnings are not limited by seasonal variations in weather.

Most boilermakers are members of unions, and union contracts set their wages and benefits. The largest union is the International Brotherhood of Boilermakers, Iron Ship Builders, Blacksmiths, Forgers, and Helpers. Other boilermakers are members of the Industrial Union of Marine and Shipbuilding Workers of America; the Oil, Chemical, and Atomic Workers International Union; the United Steelworkers of America; the International Association of Machinists and Aerospace Workers; and the United Automobile, Aerospace, and Agricultural Implement Workers of America. Among the fringe benefits established under union contracts are health insurance, pension plans, and paid vacation time.

WORK ENVIRONMENT

Boilermaking tends to be more hazardous than many other occupations. Boilermakers often work with dangerous tools and equipment; they must manage heavy materials; and they may climb to heights to do installation or repair work. Despite great progress in preventing accidents, the rate of on-the-job injuries for boilermakers remains higher than the average for all manufacturing industries. Employer and union safety programs and standards set by the federal government's Occupational Safety and Health Administration (OSHA) are helping to control dangerous conditions and reduce accidents.

The work often requires physical exertion and may be carried on in extremely hot, poorly ventilated, noisy, and damp places. At times it is necessary to work in cramped quarters inside boilers, vats, or tanks. At other times, workers must handle materials and equipment several stories above ground level. Sometimes installation workers work on jobs that require them to remain away from home for considerable periods of time.

To protect against injury, boilermakers and mechanics use a variety of special clothing and equipment, such as hard hats, safety glasses and shoes, harnesses, and respirators. A 40-hour week is average, but in some jobs, deadlines may require overtime.

OUTLOOK

The U.S. Department of Labor projects that boilermakers will experience faster than average job growth through 2016. One reason for this is the current trend of repairing and retrofitting, rather than replacing, boilers. In addition, the smaller boilers currently being used require less on-site assembly. Finally, the automation of production technologies and the increasing use of imported boilers will cut down on the need for boilermakers.

Another factor contributing to job growth in the energy industry is the passage of the Energy Policy Act of 2005. This law, intended to promote conservation and cleaner technologies in energy production, is expected to result in the building of many new clean-burning coal power plants, which will create jobs for boilermakers. Also, skilled boilermakers will be needed to replace the large number of workers reaching retirement age. Workers who have completed apprenticeships will have the best opportunities.

FOR MORE INFORMATION

For information about boilermaker apprenticeships, contact

Boilermakers National Apprenticeship Program
1017 North 9th Street
Kansas City, KS 66101-2624
Tel: 913-342-2100
Email: info@bnap.com
http://www.bnap.com

For additional career information, contact

International Brotherhood of Boilermakers, Iron Ship
Builders, Blacksmiths, Forgers and Helpers, AFL-CIO
753 State Avenue
Kansas City, KS 66102-2516
Tel: 913-371-2640
http://www.boilermakers.org

BOOKKEEPING AND ACCOUNTING CLERKS

OVERVIEW

Bookkeeping and accounting clerks record financial transactions for government, business, and other organizations. They compute, classify, record, and verify numerical data in order to develop and maintain accurate financial records. There are approximately 2.1 million bookkeeping, accounting, and auditing clerks employed in the United States.

THE JOB

Bookkeeping workers keep systematic records and current accounts of financial transactions for businesses, institutions, industries, charities, and other organizations. The bookkeeping records of a firm or business are a vital part of its operational procedures because these records reflect the assets and the liabilities, as well as the profits and losses, of the operation.

Bookkeepers record these business transactions daily in spreadsheets on computer databases, and accounting clerks often input the information. The practice of posting accounting records directly onto ledger sheets, in journals, or on other types of written accounting forms is decreasing as computerized record keeping becomes more widespread. In small businesses, bookkeepers sort and record all the sales slips, bills, check stubs, inventory lists, and requisition lists. They compile figures for cash receipts, accounts payable and receivable, and profits and losses.

Accounting clerks handle the clerical accounting work; they enter and verify transaction data and compute and record various charges. They may also monitor loans and accounts payable and receivable. More advanced clerks may reconcile billing vouchers, while senior workers review invoices and statements.

Accountants set up bookkeeping systems and use bookkeepers' balance sheets to prepare periodic summary statements of financial transactions. Management relies heavily on these bookkeeping records to interpret the organization's overall performance and uses them to make important business decisions. The records are also necessary to file income tax reports and prepare quarterly reports for stockholders.

Bookkeeping and accounting clerks work in retail and wholesale businesses, manufacturing firms, hospitals, schools, charities, and other types of institutional agencies. Many clerks are classified as *financial institution bookkeeping and accounting clerks, insurance firm bookkeeping and accounting clerks, hotel bookkeeping and accounting clerks,* and *railroad bookkeeping and accounting clerks.*

General bookkeepers and *general-ledger bookkeepers* are usually employed in smaller business operations. They may perform all the analysis, maintain the financial records, and complete any other tasks that are involved in keeping a full set of bookkeeping records. These employees may have other general office duties, such as mailing statements, answering telephone calls, and filing materials. *Audit clerks* verify figures and may be responsible for sending them on to an audit clerk supervisor.

In large companies, an accountant may supervise a department of bookkeepers who perform more specialized work. *Billing and rate clerks* and *fixed capital clerks* may post items in accounts payable or receivable ledgers, make out bills and invoices, or verify the company's rates for certain products and services. *Account information clerks* prepare reports, compile payroll lists and deductions, write company checks, and compute federal tax reports or personnel profit shares. Large companies may employ workers to organize, record, and compute many other types of financial information.

In large business organizations, bookkeepers and accountants may be classified by grades, such as bookkeeper I or II. The job classification determines their responsibilities.

REQUIREMENTS
High School

In order to be a bookkeeper, you will need at least a high school diploma. It will be helpful to have a background in business mathematics, business writing, typing, and computer training. Pay particular attention to developing sound English and communication skills along with mathematical abilities.

Postsecondary Training

Some employers prefer people who have completed a junior college curriculum or those who have attended a post–high school business training program. In many instances, employers offer on-the-job training for various types of entry-level positions. In some areas, work-study programs are available in which schools, in cooperation with businesses, offer part-time, practical on-the-job training combined with academic study. These programs often help students find immediate employment in similar work after graduation. Local business schools may also offer evening courses.

Certification or Licensing

The American Institute of Professional Bookkeepers offers voluntary certification to bookkeepers who have at least two years of full-time experience (or the part-time or freelance equivalent), pass an examination, and sign a code of ethics. Bookkeepers who complete this requirement may use the designation *certified bookkeeper*.

Other Requirements

Bookkeepers need strong mathematical skills and organizational abilities, and they have to be able to concentrate on detailed work. The work is quite sedentary and often tedious, and you should not mind long hours behind a desk. You should be methodical, accurate, and orderly and enjoy working on detailed tasks. Employers look for honest, discreet, and trustworthy individuals when placing their business in someone else's hands.

Once you are employed as a bookkeeping and accounting clerk, some places of business may require you to have union membership. Larger unions include the Office and Professional Employees International Union; the International Union of Electronic, Electrical, Salaried, Machine, and Furniture Workers-Communications Workers of America; and the American Federation of State, County, and Municipal Employees. Also, depending on the business, clerks may be represented by the same union as other manufacturing employees.

EXPLORING

You can gain experience in bookkeeping by participating in work-study programs or by obtaining part-time or summer work in beginning bookkeeping jobs or related office work. Any retail experience dealing with cash management, pricing, or customer service is also valuable.

QUICK FACTS

SCHOOL SUBJECTS

Business

Computer science

Mathematics

PERSONAL SKILLS

Following instructions

Technical/scientific

WORK ENVIRONMENT

Primarily indoors

Primarily one location

MINIMUM EDUCATION LEVEL

High school diploma

MEDIAN SALARY

$30,560

CERTIFICATION OR LICENSING

Voluntary

OUTLOOK

About as fast as the average

You can also volunteer to manage the books for extracurricular student groups. Managing income or cash flow for a club or acting as treasurer for student government are excellent ways to gain experience in maintaining financial records.

Other options are visiting local small businesses to observe their work and talking to representatives of schools that offer business training courses.

EMPLOYERS

Of the approximately 2.1 million bookkeeping, auditing, and accounting clerks, many work for personnel supplying companies; that is, those companies that provide part-time or temporary office workers. Approximately 25 percent of bookkeeping and accounting clerks work part time, according to the U.S. Department of Labor. Many others are employed by government agencies and accounting, tax preparation, and payroll services organizations.

STARTING OUT

You may find jobs or establish contacts with businesses that are interested in interviewing graduates through your guidance or placement offices. A work-study program or internship may result in a full-time job offer. Business schools and junior colleges generally provide assistance to their graduates in locating employment.

You may locate job opportunities by applying directly to firms or responding to ads in newspaper classified sections. State employment agencies and private employment bureaus can also assist in the job search process.

ADVANCEMENT

Bookkeeping workers generally begin their employment by performing routine tasks, such as the simple recording of transactions. Beginners may start as entry-level clerks, cashiers, bookkeeping machine operators, office assistants, or typists. With experience, they may advance to more complex assignments that include computer training in databases and spreadsheets and assume a greater responsibility for the work as a whole.

With experience and education, clerks become department heads or office managers. Further advancement to positions such as office or division manager, department head, accountant, or auditor is possible with a college degree and years of experience. There is a high turnover rate in this field, which increases the promotion opportunities for employees with ability and initiative.

EARNINGS

According to the U.S. Department of Labor, bookkeepers and accounting clerks earned a median income of $30,560 a year in 2006. Earnings are also influenced by such factors as the size of the city where they work and the size and type of business for which they are employed. Clerks just starting out earn approximately $19,760 or less. Those with one or two years of college generally earn higher starting wages. Top-paying jobs average about $46,020 or more a year.

Employees usually receive six to eight paid holidays yearly and one week of paid vacation after six to 12 months of service. Paid vacations may increase to four weeks or more, depending on length of service

and place of employment. Fringe benefits may include health and life insurance, sick leave, and retirement plans.

WORK ENVIRONMENT

The majority of office workers, including bookkeeping workers, usually work a 40-hour week, although some employees may work a 35- to 37-hour week. Bookkeeping and accounting clerks usually work in typical office settings. They are more likely to have a cubicle than an office. While the work pace is steady, it can also be routine and repetitive, especially in large companies where the employee is often assigned only one or two specialized job duties.

Attention to numerical details can be physically demanding, and the work can produce eyestrain and nervousness. While bookkeepers usually work with other people and sometimes under close supervision, they can expect to spend most of their day behind a desk; this may seem confining to people who need more variety and stimulation in their work. In addition, the constant attention to detail and the need for accuracy can place considerable responsibility on the worker and cause much stress.

OUTLOOK

The U.S. Department of Labor predicts a rate of job growth for bookkeepers and accounting clerks that is about as fast as the average for all occupations through 2016. In fact, this job is predicted to have the largest number of new jobs available during the next decade. Recent federal legislation calls for increased accuracy and transparency in financial reporting for organizations of all types, which will create a distinct need for these types of workers. In addition, many companies will continue to outsource routine payroll and accounting functions to bookkeeping agencies. These factors, coupled with a large number of retiring workers needing to be replaced, will lead to favorable job prospects for bookkeeping and accounting clerks. Workers capable of taking on a broad range of responsibilities will enjoy the best opportunities.

FOR MORE INFORMATION

For information on certification and career opportunities, contact
American Institute of Professional Bookkeepers
6001 Montrose Road, Suite 500
Rockville, MD 20852
Email: info@aipb.org

Tel: 800-622-0121
http://www.aipb.org

For information on accredited educational programs, contact
Association to Advance Collegiate Schools of Business
777 South Harbour Island Boulevard, Suite 750
Tampa, FL 33602-5730
Tel: 813-769-6500
http://www.aacsb.edu

For more information on women in accounting, contact
Educational Foundation for Women in Accounting
PO Box 1925
Southeastern, PA 19399-1925
Tel: 610-407-9229
Email: info@efwa.org
http://www.efwa.org

BREWERS

QUICK FACTS

SCHOOL SUBJECTS
Biology
Chemistry

PERSONAL SKILLS
Following instructions
Technical/scientific

WORK ENVIRONMENT
Primarily indoors
Primarily one location

MINIMUM EDUCATION LEVEL
Some postsecondary training

MEDIAN SALARY
$53,810

CERTIFICATION OR LICENSING
Required for certain positions

OUTLOOK
About as fast as the average

OVERVIEW

Brewers oversee the production of many different styles of beer. They develop recipes that consist of various types and blends of the four basic ingredients: barley malt, hops, yeast, and water (and occasionally fruits, wheat, rice, and corn). Brewers add these ingredients into brewing vessels in accordance with the style of beer they are brewing and their own recipe. Brewers also tend to the brewing equipment. They monitor gauges and meters, as well as turn valves, open hatches, and occasionally stir.

THE JOB

Brewers are concerned with all aspects of beer production, from selecting the exact blend and kind of flavoring hops, to the number of minutes the *wort* (liquid formed by soaking mash in hot water and fermenting it) boils. Beer styles and flavors are as multifarious as wine, and the *craftbrewer* (the name given to American brewers who produce quality beers in the European or early-American traditions) can produce any number of beers for any occasion. Like great chefs, craftbrewers take particular pride in their recipes and enjoy presenting their "masterpieces" to others.

There are certain guidelines for each style of beer, but within those guidelines the brewer may experiment to create a truly unique flavor of a particular style. For example, a brewer who is making a pilsner must use bottom-fermenting lager yeasts (as opposed to top-fermenting ale yeasts), a light, dry barley malt (as opposed to a darker, roasted barley malt), and a specific few types of hops (most notably saaz, spalt, tettnanger, and hallertauer). With these basic guidelines observed, the brewer can experiment with such things as blending malts and hops, adding other flavors (such as honey, fruit, herbs, and spices), and varying boiling and lagering times.

The first step in brewing a batch of beer is for the brewer to decide what style he or she wants to brew. There are more than 50 styles of beer, many of which are cousins. Others are completely original and in their own class. All beers fall in one of two categories: ales or lagers. Among the more common styles many American craftbrewers are brewing today are ales (including pale ales, brown ales, and Scotch ales), pilsners, bocks, double bocks, stouts, porters, and wheat beers (commonly know by their German name Weiss- or Weizenbier). With a particular beer style in mind, the brewer will seek the best ingredients to brew it.

The four basic ingredients of beer are malted barley, hops, yeast, and water. Some smaller breweries may use a malt extract. Some beers may call for wheat, rice, or corn in addition to barley. Malted barley not only contributes to the flavor and color of the beer, but more important, it provides food (fermentable sugars) for the yeast to produce alcohol. Brewers have a host of different types of yeast to choose from depending on the particular flavor they seek. There are two main varieties: top-fermenting ale yeasts and bottom-fermenting lager yeasts, and within each of these two varieties there are hundreds of strains, each imparting a different flavor to the beer. Hops come from an herbal flower added to provide a contrasting bitterness and flavor to the sweet malt (called boiling hops), and to add a very important bouquet to the beer (called finishing, or aroma hops). Because beer is about 90 percent water, all serious brewers take the purity of their water very seriously. Water that has been treated with chlorine or that is rich in other minerals can impart unwanted flavors into a beer.

Malted barley must go through a mashing stage in the brewing process. Brewers grind the malted barley in specialized machines so that its husk is removed and the kernel broken. Next they add a precise amount of water and raise the temperature to between 150 and 160 degrees Fahrenheit to dissolve the natural sugars, starches, and enzymes of the barley. Brewers may vary the temperature and time of the mashing process to achieve a desired color or flavor. To complete the mashing process, the brewer strains out the barley grains. The remaining sweetened liquid, called malt extract, is now ready to become the wort.

Initially, wort is concentrated, unhopped beer. The brewer transfers the wort from the mashing vessel to a brewing kettle where boiling hops are added. This is usually just a matter of turning valves. Depending on the style of beer, the brewer will have selected a particular style or blend of hops. Some brewers use the actual hop leaf and others use a pelletized version. The hopped wort is boiled for an hour and a half to two and a half hours according to brewer preferences. After the wort has cooled to 50–60 degrees Fahrenheit for lagers and 60–70 degrees Fahrenheit for ales, the hop leaves or pellet residue are removed in a process called *sparging*, and the wort is now ready for its most vital ingredient, yeast.

To ensure quality and consistency, many brewers culture their own yeast, but some smaller brewpubs or microbreweries use prepackaged yeast. Once the wort is cooled, the brewer transfers it to a starting tank where

the yeast is added and the fermentation process begins. Depending on the style of beer and the desired results, the brewer will choose either an open or closed fermentation. Open fermentation is less common because it leaves the beer susceptible to airborne bacteria. However, some styles of beer require it.

Most beers go through two basic fermentations; some beers require more. The initial contact of the wort and yeast spurs a fervent fermentation that produces alcohol and a foamy head called *kraeusen*. The brewer decides how long he or she wants this fermentation to last, generally between five and 14 days. After the desired time for the primary fermentation, the brewer transfers the beer to a lagering kettle (also called a conditioning kettle) where the beer is allowed to age. The fermentation continues, but at a slower pace. The brewer must strictly regulate the temperature during the lagering time: 60–70 degrees Fahrenheit for ales, and 35–50 degrees Fahrenheit for lagers. After the desired aging or maturation of the beer, anywhere from two weeks to several months, the beer is again transferred to a storage tank where it is ready to be bottled. This step is necessary to leave any yeast or hops sediment behind so it is not present in the bottle or keg.

Brewers add carbonation to their beers either by injecting carbon dioxide into the storage tank just before it is to be bottled or kegged (this is typical of mass-produced beers) or, more common among craftbrewers, by adding a priming sugar, usually dry malt extract or corn sugar diluted in boiled water. If the brewer uses priming sugars, the beer must sit again for one to four weeks before it is ready to be served.

Brewing is both a creative and highly methodical craft requiring precise attention to detail. Brewers must monitor pH (acidity and alkalinity) levels in water and test water purity. They frequently use calculations to predict yields, efficiencies of processes, yeast maturation cycles, alcohol volume, bittering units, and many other factors. They study yeast physiology, metabolism, the biochemistry of fermentation and maturation, and the effects alternative brewing methods as well as bacteria, protozoa, and mold have on beer flavor and color. They constantly study methods of quality control and brewing efficiency.

Some craftbrewers at microbreweries may also help in bottling their beer. Workers at a brewpub (an establishment that is a combination brewery and restaurant) may stand behind the bar to pour drafts as well as work as waitstaff. At small breweries, brewers frequently sterilize their tanks, kettles, hoses, and other brewing equipment. Brewers who have the right resources and live in the right environment may grow, harvest, and store their own hops. Many craftbrewers are responsible for marketing their beer or designing logos. Some manage the brewpub or microbrewery. But a brewer's primary duty is always to brew beer, to experiment and come up with new recipes, and to seek out the right ingredients for the particular style of beer that is being brewed.

REQUIREMENTS
High School

In today's competitive job market, aspiring brewers will need a high school degree to land a job that offers growth possibilities, a good salary, and challenges, including positions in the craftbrewing industry.

High school classes in biology, chemistry, and mathematics will be particularly useful if you are interested in becoming a brewer. Classes in biochemistry and microbiology will prepare you for the more specialized aspects of brewing that serious craftbrewers must master. A background in science and mathematics is needed for brewers to perform basic brewing and engineering calculations and to follow technical discussions on brewing topics. Classes in home economics or family and consumer science can teach you basic kitchen skills, common units of cooking measurement, and the organizational skills you need to prepare and complete complex recipes. If you are interested in running your own microbrewery, be sure to take business, accounting, and computer science classes to help you prepare for managing a business.

Postsecondary Training

Employers today prefer to hire only brewers who have completed some kind of formal training program in brewing sciences, or who have had extensive apprenticeship training at another brewery. The following three institutions are the most prominent U.S. schools offering programs on brewing sciences and the business of brewing. The Siebel Institute of Technology & World Brewing Academy is located in Chicago, Illinois, with a partner campus in Munich, Germany. The Siebel Institute offers courses on specific topics, such as brewing microbiology, and the World Brewing Academy offers a diploma program that lasts 12 weeks and involves work done in Chicago and Munich. The American Brewers Guild is located in Woodland, California. The Craft Brewers Apprenticeship Program of the American Brewers Guild lasts 27 weeks and combines classroom work with hands-on experience. Graduates receive a diploma and job placement assistance. The University Extension, University of California, Davis, Professional Brewing Programs offers certificate options as well as a master brewers program. Although a college degree is not required for admission to the professional brewing programs, you will need to have completed college coursework in the following areas: biological sciences (biology, biochemistry, microbiology), chemistry, physics, mathematics (pre-calculus), and engineering.

It is highly recommended that you complete an organized course of study through one of these programs. Students who learn at a brewing sciences school will have a particular advantage in landing a job as a brewer because employers know graduates have received training in the many highly technical aspects of brewing. Topics covered usually include brewing raw materials, brewhouse theory and practice, fermentation, storage and finishing, packaging and engineering topics, quality control, microbiology laboratory, and sensory evaluation.

Certification or Licensing

Breweries of any size must be licensed both by the state in which they are located and the Bureau of Alcohol, Tobacco, and Firearms, which is part of the U.S. Treasury Department. Owners of breweries are responsible for obtaining and maintaining these licenses.

Other Requirements

Brewers must have an avid appreciation for beer and an excellent sense of taste. They must be able to detect all of a particular beer's subtleties and nuances through taste and aroma. They should also be able to distinguish between styles of beer.

Brewers need good organizational and problem-solving skills as well as creativity. If a batch of beer turns out bad, the brewer must be able, through tests or experience, to pinpoint what went wrong and why. Beer takes time to brew. While the process can be hastened, craftbrewers should have the patience to allow beer to brew in its natural time. Brewers must be able to follow recipes and procedures closely, but they must also know when and how to go beyond a recipe's direction, or when to vary a procedure to achieve a desired result. Since they must be able to legally sample their wares, brewers must be 21 or older.

EXPLORING

Most breweries, whether a microbrewery, a brewpub, or one of the major mass-production breweries, offer tours of their facilities. This is an excellent opportunity to learn what actually goes on in a brewery, to see the brewing equipment and the raw ingredients, and to ask questions. Those 21 and older will be able to sample the various styles of beer at the brewery and ask questions of the masterbrewer.

Homebrewing is a popular trend that has been growing rapidly for the past decade. Those 21 and over can learn firsthand how to brew small batches of beer at home. The equipment and ingredients needed to begin brewing can be found at some larger liquor stores or through mail order.

There are numerous books and magazines available on the subject. *Zymurgy*, the American Homebrewers Association's magazine, focuses on homebrewing issues. *The New Brewer*, the Institute for Brewing Studies' magazine, covers topics of interest to micro- and pubbrewers. Sample articles as well as information on other publications can be found at the Association of Brewers' Web site, http://www.beertown.org. Most brewers began their experience with brewing by brewing first at home. So you're not of legal drinking age yet? Don't worry. You can still learn some of the basic skills of a brewer by making nonalcoholic carbonated drinks, such as sodas. Articles on this topic are frequently found in beer magazines because so much of the same equipment is used to make each.

Some breweries have part-time jobs available to students. They usually entail sanitizing the brewing equipment after a batch has been made or transporting heavy bags of ingredients. This is an excellent opportunity to learn how the brewing machines work, to get to know the various types of ingredients, and to see the types of challenges and pressures brewers face firsthand.

STARTING OUT

The best career path for an aspiring craftbrewer is to begin as a homebrewer, learning the basic methods and science of brewing and possibly developing a personal style. Until recently, many brewers still learned the trade through hands-on experience as an apprentice at a microbrewery or brewpub. Although this is still an option, an increasing number of brewers are completing formal postsecondary training, making the market more competitive. Due to the recent renaissance in American brewing, employers are looking to hire highly qualified brewers who will not require years of on-the-job-training but can immediately begin producing quality beers. An added benefit of getting postsecondary training is the job placement assistance any respected school provides to its graduates.

Currently, however, there are not enough trained craftbrewers to fill the demand, so many breweries still employ apprentices who have some experience in brewing—generally as homebrewers. Apprentices may spend several years learning the craft from a masterbrewer. They usually begin by sanitizing brewing vessels, preparing ingredients for the masterbrewer, and doing some administrative work, all the while taking notes and observing brewing techniques.

Breweries looking for trained craftbrewers often post job openings at brewing schools or advertise in trade magazines or local papers. There are many beer festivals and homebrewing contests where breweries—particularly new breweries—seek out the brewers of winning beers and offer them work.

ADVANCEMENT

Brewers advance as the popularity of their beer increases and continual sales are made. Most microbreweries and brewpubs are led by the so-called *masterbrewer* (often the one who developed the recipe), and depending on the size of the brewery, there may be *general brewers* who help in the brewing process. After demonstrating resourcefulness in technique, or after developing a successful beer recipe on their own, these general brewers may advance to masterbrewer at the brewery where they work, or they may transfer to become masterbrewer at a different brewery. Their work will still be the same, but as masterbrewer, they will be able to relegate work to others and earn a larger salary. After an approximate two-year period of learning the brewing process, an apprentice will advance to become a general brewer or even masterbrewer.

Most brewers are content to remain masterbrewer of a microbrewery or brewpub, but some may advance to management positions if the opportunity arises. *Brewery managers* are responsible for the day-to-day operations of a brewery, including managing finances, marketing, and hiring employees. Many microbreweries are operated by a small staff, and advancement for brewers may simply mean increasing brewery output and doing good business.

EARNINGS

Salaries for those in the brewing business vary considerably based on several factors, including the exact position a person holds, the size of the brewery, its location, the popularity of its beer, and the length of time the brewery has been in business. Brewers running their own microbreweries or brewpubs, like any small business owner, may have very low take-home wages for several years as the business becomes established. According to the Economic Research Institute, masterbrewers with five years of experience average $46,170, with top earnings at $57,250 per year. The institute also reports that those with 10 years of experience average $53,098 annually, and top earnings were $65,000. This is consistent with the U.S. Department of Labor's figures, which state that in 2006, food scientists (which is, essentially, what a brewer is) earned a median salary of $53,810, with the lowest 10 percent earning less than $29,620, and the highest 10 percent earning more than $97,350.

Benefits packages vary from business to business. Brewers running their own businesses must pay for benefits (health insurance, retirement plans, etc.) themselves. Brewers employed by breweries can generally expect health insurance and paid vacation time. Other benefits may include dental and eye care, life and disability insurance, and a pension plan. Many employers will pay for all or part of a brewer's training. A brewer's salary can increase by yearly bonuses or profit sharing if the brewery does well in the course of a year. Most brewers confess that the greatest benefit of their job is free beer.

WORK ENVIRONMENT

Brewers perform a variety of tasks requiring different skills. Most of their time is spent in the brewery preparing the next batch of beer. At many small microbreweries and brewpubs, brewers are responsible for all of the brewery operations. Before preparing a batch of beer, they use hoses and brushes with a sanitizing solution and clean all of the kettles. Since sanitization is a crucial part of brewing, this job must be very thorough and is, therefore, often strenuous. Temperatures in breweries are strictly controlled, in some cases to as low as 40 degrees Fahrenheit.

On brewing days, the brewer weighs and measures ingredients. He or she inspects the brewing equipment to ensure it is both properly sanitized and in working order. Frequently a brewer watches over several different batches of beer all at different stages of production. The most stressful part of a brewer's job is waiting for the beer to be completed and wondering if anything went wrong. Throughout various stages of the brewing process, brewers sample the beer to make certain everything is as it should be. Brewers generally produce the same one to four beer recipes each time they brew. With standardization of the brewing process, most errors can be eliminated. The size of the brewery dictates a craftbrewer's working hours. A small brewery can only produce a limited amount of beer at one time. Brewers may have days when they are not brewing at all. Instead they may perform maintenance on equipment, prepare yeast cultures, or even grow and harvest hops. Many brewers experiment with new styles of beer by brewing small five-gallon batches. Brewers spend a lot of time tasting many different styles and brands of beers to determine what qualities make the beer good and what qualities make it bad, so that they can improve their own beer. Brewers, especially those at small breweries, may work odd hours (until very late at night or very early in the morning) in order to move the brew from one stage in the brewing process to another. Brewers usually work about 40 hours a week. Those who own breweries or brewpubs, however, often work much longer hours than this to complete all the management tasks required of a business.

OUTLOOK

America is currently in the midst of a beer renaissance. An increasing number of people have discovered that beer can be as complex as wine and equally enjoyable. Clearly, taste preferences have changed for a large segment of the beer-drinking population from the bland, almost watery styles of the major beer manufacturers to a more complex, hearty style of the craftbeer producers. Even the major brewers like Miller, Anheuser Busch, and Coors have acknowledged the craftbrewing trend by introducing their own premium-style beers—and to great success.

Although craftbrewing accounts for only a small percentage (about 4 percent) of the U.S. beer market, it is a growing segment of the beer industry. According to the Institute for Brewing Studies, craftbewing has become a $5 billion industry, with roughly 1,390 microbreweries, brewpubs, and regional specialty breweries operating across the United States. Craftbrewers produced approximately 7.5 million barrels of beer in 2007—almost 1 million more than in 2006. As people have become accustomed to the availability of unique tasting beers, they have created a growing market for these products.

Like any small business, just-opened brewpubs and microbreweries will succeed or fail on an individual basis. The craftbrewing industry itself, however, is here to stay. A strong demand for excellent brewers exists, and those with training should have the best opportunities.

FOR MORE INFORMATION

ABG prepares people to work in the craftbrewing field and offers its Craftbrewers Apprenticeship Program both at the school and through distance education. For more information, contact

American Brewers Guild (ABG)
1001 Maple Street
Salisbury, VT 05769-9445
Tel: 800-636-1331

Email: abg@abgbrew.com
http://www.abgbrew.com

Visit the Web site of the Association of Brewers for industry statistics, information on professional brewing and home-brewing, and related publications. Information and links are also available to the American Homebrewers Association and the Institute for Brewing Studies, which are divisions of the Association of Brewers.

Association of Brewers
736 Pearl Street
Boulder, CO 80302-5006
Tel: 303-447-0816
http://www.beertown.org

For information on courses and the diploma in brewing technology, contact

Siebel Institute of Technology & World Brewing Academy
1777 North Clybourn Avenue, Suite 2F
Chicago, IL. 60614-5520
Tel: 312-255-0705
Email: info@siebelinstitute.com
http://www.siebelinstitute.com

For more information about the Professional Brewing Programs offered through the University Extension, University of California, Davis, contact

University Extension
1333 Research Park Drive
Davis, CA 95616-4852
Tel: 800-752-0881
http://universityextension.ucdavis.edu/brewing

☐ BRICKLAYERS AND STONEMASONS

OVERVIEW

Bricklayers are skilled workers who construct and repair walls, partitions, floors, arches, fireplaces, chimneys, and other structures from brick, concrete block, gypsum block, and precast panels made of terra cotta, structural tile, and other masonry materials. *Stonemasons* build stone walls, floors, piers, and other structures, and they set the decorative stone exteriors of structures, such as churches, hotels, and public buildings. Approximately 182,000 bricklayers and stonemasons work in the United States.

THE JOB

When bricklayers and stonemasons begin work on a job, they usually first examine a blueprint or drawing to determine the designer's specifications. Then they measure the work area to fix reference points and guidelines in accordance with the blueprint.

If they are building a wall, bricklayers traditionally start with the corners, or leads, which must be precisely established if the finished structure is to be sound and straight. The corners may be established by more experienced bricklayers, with the task of filling in between the corners left to less experienced workers. Corner posts, or masonry guides, may be used to define the line of the wall, speeding the building process. A first, dry course may be put down without mortar so that the alignment and positioning of the brick can be checked.

In laying brick, bricklayers use a metal trowel to spread a bed or layer of soft mortar on a prepared base. Then they set the brick into the mortar, tapping and working each brick into the correct position. Excess mortar is cut off, and the mortar joints are smoothed with special tools that give a neat, uniform look to the wall. In walls, each layer, or course, is set so that vertical joints do not line up one on top of another but instead form a pleasing, regular pattern. The work must be continually checked for horizontal and vertical straightness with mason's levels, gauge strips, plumb lines, and other equipment. Sometimes it is necessary to cut and fit brick to size using a power saw or hammer and chisel. Around doors and windows, bricklayers generally use extra steel supports in the wall.

Bricklayers must know how to mix mortar, which is made of cement, sand, and water, and how to spread it so that the joints throughout the structure will be evenly spaced, with a neat appearance. They may have helpers who mix the mortar as well as move materials and scaffolding around the work site as needed.

Some bricklayers specialize in working with one type of masonry material only, such as gypsum block, concrete block, hollow tile used in partitions, or terra-cotta products. Other bricklayers, called *refractory masons*, work in the steel and glass manufacturing industries and specialize in installing firebrick and refractory tile linings of furnaces, kilns, boilers, cupolas, and other high-temperature equipment. Still others are employed to construct manholes and catch basins in sewers.

Stonemasons work with two types of stone: natural cut stone, such as marble, granite, limestone, or sandstone; and artificial stone, which is made to order from concrete, marble chips, or other masonry materials. They set the stone in many kinds of structures, including piers, walls, walks, arches, floors, and curbstones. On some projects, the drawings that stonemasons work from specify where to set certain stones that have been previously identified by number. In such cases, helpers may locate the stones and bring them to the masons. Large stones may have to be hoisted into place with derricks.

In building stone walls, masons begin by setting a first course of stones in a bed of mortar, then build upward by alternating layers of mortar and stone courses. At every stage, they may use leveling devices and plumb lines, correcting the alignment of each stone. They often insert wedges and tap the stones into place with rubber mallets. Once a stone is in good position, they remove the wedges, fill the gaps with mortar, and smooth the area using a metal tool called a tuck pointer. Large stones may need to be anchored in place with metal brackets that are welded or bolted to the wall.

Similarly, when masons construct stone floors, they begin by spreading mortar. They place stones, adjusting their positions using mallets and crowbars and periodically checking the levelness of the surface. They may cut some stones into smaller pieces to fit, using hammer and chisel or a power saw with a diamond blade. After all the stones are placed, the masons fill the joints between the stones with mortar and wash off the surface.

Some stonemasons specialize in setting marble. Others work exclusively on setting alberene, which is an acid-resistant soapstone used in industrial settings on floors and for lining vats and tanks. Other specialized stone workers include *composition stone applicators, monument setters, patchers,* and *chimney repairers. Stone repairers* mend broken slabs made of marble and similar stone.

Bricklayers and stonemasons sometimes use power tools, such as saws and drills, but for the most part they use hand tools, including trowels, jointers, hammers, rulers, chisels, squares, gauge lines, mallets, brushes, and mason's levels.

REQUIREMENTS
High School

As with many jobs, employers of bricklayers and stonemasons will often prefer that you have a high school education or at least a GED. Take as many courses as possible in shop, basic mathematics, blueprint reading, and mechanical drawing. Take college prep courses in engineering if your school offers them. It may also help you on the job if you have taken core courses like English and general science and have a driver's license.

Another piece of good advice is to join or help form a student chapter of an organization like the National Association of Home Builders. Membership benefits

QUICK FACTS

SCHOOL SUBJECTS
Mathematics
Technical/shop

PERSONAL SKILLS
Mechanical/manipulative
Technical/scientific

WORK ENVIRONMENT
Primarily outdoors
Primarily multiple locations

MINIMUM EDUCATION LEVEL
High school diploma
Apprenticeship

MEDIAN SALARY
$42,973

CERTIFICATION OR LICENSING
None available

OUTLOOK
About as fast as the average

include issues of various journals in the building industry, low-cost admission to the International Builders' Show, and opportunities to take part in exciting activities like visiting construction sites, sponsoring restoration projects at your school, and helping repair homes for the elderly and underprivileged. Check such Web sites as http://www.hbi.org.

Postsecondary Training

The best way for you to become a bricklayer or stonemason is to complete an apprenticeship. Vocational schools also provide training in these fields. However, many people learn their skills informally on the job simply by observing and helping experienced workers. The disadvantage of this approach is that informal training is likely to be less thorough, and it may take workers much longer to learn the full range of skills necessary for the trade.

Apprenticeship programs are sponsored by contractors or jointly by contractors and unions. Programs that are not sponsored by unions are also available. Applicants for apprenticeships need to be at least 17 years old and in good physical condition. As an apprentice, you would spend about three years learning as you work under the supervision of experienced bricklayers or stonemasons. In addition, you would get at least 144 hours of classroom instruction in related subjects, such as blueprint reading, applied mathematics, and layout work. In the work portion of your apprenticeship, you would begin with simple jobs, like carrying materials and building scaffolds. After becoming familiar with initial tasks, you would eventually take part in a broad range of activities. In the course of an apprenticeship, you can become qualified to work with more than one kind of masonry material.

Other Requirements

In bricklaying and stone masonry, you often have to carry materials and sometimes relatively heavy equipment, such as scaffold parts and rows of brick. Since you'll be mixing mortar and laying brick and stone, you must not mind getting dirty and being on your hands and knees.

You should enjoy doing demanding work and be disciplined and motivated enough to do your job without close and constant supervision. Sometimes, you might be presented with building challenges that require either mental or physical aptitude. The ability to get along with coworkers is also important as many bricklayers and masons work in teams.

EXPLORING

Opportunities are sometimes limited for high school students to directly experience work in the field of bricklaying and stonemasonry. It is fortunate, however, that student groups exist that provide opportunities for experience and exploration. One such group is the National Association of Home Builders Student Chapters Program, which has chapters in high schools and vocational and technical schools. By becoming a member, you get to experience the "real world" of construction, including bricklaying and stone masonry. Some groups visit construction sites; others participate in repairing homes; others help organize repairs on their own school buildings.

Hands-on experience is one of the best ways to explore the building trades. If you are too young to get such experience, at least contact others who have already started their careers. For example, try to contact participants from the International Masonry Institute's Masonry

Camp. One year participants were expected to develop a ferry terminal/visitors' center on Swan's Island, Maine. One camper from Hawaii had this to say: "I learned a great deal more about masonry in the 10 days I was at camp than the six years I was in architecture school. That's something worth shouting from the top of the volcanoes here!" (For more information, visit the IMI's Web site at http://www.imiweb.org.)

EMPLOYERS

Bricklayers and stonemasons are employed in the building industry for such companies as general contractors or specific building contractors, both large and small. Jobs are available across the country but are concentrated in city areas. Those who are skilled in business matters can start their own companies or be contractors; about 24 percent of the approximately 182,000 bricklayers and stonemasons in the United States are self-employed.

STARTING OUT

The two main ways that people start out in these fields are through formal apprenticeship programs and as helpers or laborers who gradually learn their skills on the job. Helper jobs can be found through newspaper want ads and from the local office of the state. If you want to apply for an apprenticeship, you can get more information from local contractors, the state employment service, and the local office of the International Union of Bricklayers and Allied Craftworkers. The Home Builders Institute can also be of help.

Another option may be to enter a bricklaying program at a vocational school. Such a program combines classroom instruction with work experience. If you've taken classes at a vocational school, the placement office there may be able to help you find a job.

ADVANCEMENT

Bricklayers and stonemasons with enough skill and experience may advance to supervisory positions. Some union contracts require a *supervisor* if three or more workers are employed on a job.

Supervisors sometimes become *superintendents* at large construction sites. With additional technical training, bricklayers and stonemasons may become *cost estimators*. *Cost estimators* look at building plans, obtain quotations on masonry material, and prepare and submit bids on the costs of doing the proposed job. Another possible advancement is to become a *city or county inspector* who checks to see if the work done by contractors meets local building code regulations. Some bricklayers and stonemasons go into business for themselves as *contractors*.

EARNINGS

According to the U.S. Department of Labor, the median hourly pay of bricklayers and stonemasons was $20.66 in 2006. A person working full time at this pay rate would have annual earnings of approximately $42,973. Earnings ranged from a low of less than $12.24 per hour (approximately $25,460 annually) to a high of more than $32.43 per hour (about $67,454 yearly) during that same time period.

Of course, earnings for those who work outside can be affected by bad weather, and earnings are lower for workers in areas where the local economy is in a slump. The pay also varies according to geographic region.

The beginning hourly rate for apprentices is about half the rate for experienced workers. In addition to regular pay, various fringe benefits, such as health and life insurance, pensions, and paid vacations, are available to many workers in this field.

WORK ENVIRONMENT

Most bricklayers and stonemasons have a 40-hour workweek. They are usually paid time and a half for overtime and double time for work on Saturdays, Sundays, and holidays.

Most of the work is done outdoors, where conditions may be dusty, hot, cold, or damp. Often workers must stand on scaffolds that are high off the ground. They may need to bend or stoop constantly to pick up materials. They may be on their feet most of the working day, or they may kneel for long periods.

Some of the hazards involved with this work include falling off a scaffold, being hit by falling material, and getting injuries common to lifting and handling heavy material. Whereas poor weather conditions used to affect work schedules and job site conditions, protective sheeting is now used to enclose work areas. The use of this sheeting makes it possible to work through most inclement weather.

Apprentices and experienced workers must furnish their own hand tools and measuring devices. Contractors supply the materials for making mortar, scaffolding, lifts, ladders, and other large equipment used in the construction process.

Well-qualified bricklayers and stonemasons can often find work at wages higher than those of most other construction workers. But because the work is seasonal, bricklayers and stonemasons must plan carefully to make it through any periods of unemployment.

OUTLOOK

Employment for bricklayers and stonemasons is predicted to be very good through 2016, according to the U.S. Department of Labor, with job growth that is about as fast as the average for all occupations. Many workers leave the field each year for less strenuous work, retirement, or other reasons. In addition, the U.S. is experiencing a building boom, and population and business growth will always create the need for new facilities (such as homes, hospitals, long-term care facilities, and offices) and result in a demand for these skilled workers. Restoration of older brick buildings and the popularity of decorative brick in sidewalks, lobbies, and foyers should create a steady demand for these workers in years to come.

During economic downturns, bricklayers and stonemasons, like other workers in construction-related jobs, can expect to have fewer job opportunities and perhaps be laid off.

FOR MORE INFORMATION

This labor union promotes quality construction and builds markets for general contractors. For more information on apprenticeships and training through its National Center for Construction Education and Research, contact

Associated General Contractors of America
2300 Wilson Boulevard, Suite 400
Arlington, VA 22201-5424
Tel: 703-548-3118
Email: info@agc.org
http://www.agc.org

The HBI is the educational arm of the National Association of Home Builders. For more information on education and training programs, contact

Home Builders Institute (HBI)
1201 15th Street NW, Sixth Floor
Washington, DC 20005-2842
Tel: 800-795-7955
http://www.hbi.org

For information on design and technical assistance as well its annual masonry camp for chosen apprentices, contact

International Masonry Institute
The James Brice House
42 East Street
Annapolis, MD 21401-1731
Tel: 410-280-1305
http://www.imiweb.org

For information on available publications, contact
International Union of Bricklayers and Allied Craftworkers
620 F Street, NW
Washington, DC 20004
Tel: 202-783-3788
Email: askbac@bacweb.org
http://www.bacweb.org

For information on specialized education and research programs and apprenticeship opportunities, contact
Mason Contractors Association of America
33 South Roselle Road
Schaumburg, IL 60193
Tel: 847-301-0001
Email: info@masoncontractors.org
http://www.masoncontractors.org

BROADCAST ENGINEERS

OVERVIEW

Broadcast engineers, also referred to as *broadcast technicians*, or *broadcast operators*, operate and maintain the electronic equipment used to record and transmit the audio for radio signals and the audio and visual images for television signals to the public. They may work in a broadcasting station or assist in broadcasting directly from an outside site as a *field technician*. Approximately 38,000 broadcast engineers work in the United States.

THE JOB

Broadcast engineers are responsible for the transmission of radio and television programming, including live and recorded broadcasts. Broadcasts are usually transmitted directly from the station; however, engineers are capable of transmitting signals on location from specially designed, mobile equipment. The specific tasks of the broadcast engineer depend on the size of the television or radio station. In small stations, engineers have a wide variety of responsibilities. Larger stations are able to hire a greater number of engineers and specifically delegate responsibilities to each engineer. In both small and large stations, however, engineers are responsible for the operation, installation, and repair of the equipment.

The *chief engineer* in both radio and television is the head of the entire technical operation and must orchestrate the activities of all the technicians to ensure smooth programming. He or she is also responsible for the budget and must keep abreast of new broadcast communications technology.

Larger stations also have an *assistant chief engineer* who manages the daily activities of the technical crew, controls the maintenance of the electronic equipment, and ensures the performance standards of the station.

Maintenance technicians are directly responsible for the installation, adjustment, and repair of the electronic equipment.

Video technicians usually work in television stations to ensure the quality, brightness, and content of the visual images being recorded and broadcast. They are involved in several different aspects of broadcasting and videotaping television programs. Technicians who are mostly involved with broadcasting programs are often called *video-control technicians*. In live broadcasts using more than one camera, they operate electronic equipment that selects which picture goes to the transmitter for broadcast. They also monitor on-air programs to ensure good picture quality. Technicians mainly involved with taping programs are often called *videotape-recording technicians*. They record performances on videotape using video cameras and tape-recording equipment, and then splice together separate scenes into a finished program; they can create special effects by manipulating recording and re-recording equipment. The introduction of robotic cameras, six-foot-tall cameras that stand on two legs, created a need for a new kind of technician called a video-robo technician. *Video-robo technicians* operate the cameras from a control room computer, using joysticks and a video panel to tilt and focus each camera. With the help of new technology, one person can now effectively perform the work of two or three camera operators. Engineers may work with producers, directors, and reporters to put together videotaped material from various sources. These include networks, mobile camera units, and studio productions. Depending on their employer, engineers may be involved in any number of activities related to editing videotapes into a complete program.

REQUIREMENTS
High School

Take as many classes as you can in mathematics, science, computers, and shop, especially electronics. Speech classes will help you hone your abilities to effectively communicate ideas to others.

Postsecondary Training

An associate's degree in electronics, broadcast technology, or computer networking from a two-year college or technical school is often the minimum requirement to enter this field. However, positions that are more advanced require a bachelor's degree in broadcast communications or a related field. To become a chief engineer, you should aim for a bachelor's degree in electronics or electrical engineering. Because field technicians also act as announcers on occasion, speech courses and experience as an announcer in a school radio station can be helpful. Seeking education beyond a bachelor's degree will further the possibilities for advancement, although it is not required.

Certification or Licensing

The Federal Communications Commission licenses and permits are no longer required of broadcast engineers. However, certification from the Society of Broadcast Engineers (SBE) is desirable, and certified engineers consistently earn higher salaries than uncertified engineers. The SBE offers an education scholarship and accepts student members; members receive a newsletter and have access to the SBE job line.

Other Requirements

Broadcast engineers must have both an aptitude for working with highly technical electronic and computer equipment and minute attention to detail to be successful in the field. You should enjoy both the technical and artistic aspects of working in the radio or television industry. You should also be able to communicate with a wide range of people with various levels of technical expertise.

EXPLORING

Reading association publications is an excellent way to learn more about broadcast engineering. Many of the associations listed at the end of this article offer newsletters and other publications to members—some even post back issues or selected articles on their Web sites. You might also consider reading *Broadcast Engineering* (http://www.broadcastengineering.com), a trade publication for broadcast engineers and technicians.

Experience is necessary to begin a career as a broadcast engineer, and volunteering at a local broadcasting station is an excellent way to gain experience. Many schools have clubs for persons interested in broadcasting. Such clubs sponsor trips to broadcasting facilities, schedule lectures, and provide a place where students can meet others with

QUICK FACTS

SCHOOL SUBJECTS
Computer science
Mathematics

PERSONAL SKILLS
Mechanical/manipulative
Technical/scientific

WORK ENVIRONMENT
Indoors and outdoors
Primarily multiple locations

MINIMUM EDUCATION LEVEL
Some postsecondary training

MEDIAN SALARY
$30,690

CERTIFICATION OR LICENSING
Recommended

OUTLOOK
About as fast as the average

similar interests. Local television station technicians are usually willing to share their experiences with interested young people. They can be a helpful source of informal career guidance. Visits or tours can be arranged by school officials. Tours will allow you to see engineers involved in their work. Most colleges and universities also have radio and television stations where students can gain experience with broadcasting equipment.

Exposure to broadcasting technology also may be obtained through building and operating an amateur, or ham, radio and experimenting with electronic kits. Dexterity and an understanding of home-operated broadcasting equipment will aid in promoting success in education and work experience within the field of broadcasting.

EMPLOYERS

According to the *CIA World Factbook*, there were 13,750 radio stations and 2,218 television stations in the United

States in 2006. These stations might be independently operated or owned and operated by a network. Smaller stations in smaller cities are good starting places, but it is at the larger networks and stations in major cities where the higher salaries are found. Some broadcast engineers work outside of the radio and television industries, producing, for example, corporate employee training and sales programs. Approximately 38,000 broadcast technicians are employed in the United States.

STARTING OUT

In many towns and cities there are public-access cable television stations and public radio stations where high school students interested in broadcasting and broadcast technology can obtain an internship. An entry-level technician should be flexible about job location; most begin their careers at small stations and with experience may advance to larger-market stations.

ADVANCEMENT

Entry-level engineers deal exclusively with the operation and maintenance of their assigned equipment; in contrast, a more advanced broadcast engineer directs the activities of entry-level engineers and makes judgments on the quality, strength, and subject of the material being broadcast.

After several years of experience, a broadcast engineer may advance to *assistant chief engineer*. In this capacity, he or she may direct the daily activities of all of the broadcasting engineers in the station as well as the field engineers broadcasting on location. Advancement to chief engineer usually requires at least a college degree in engineering and many years of experience. A firm grasp of management skills, budget planning, and a thorough knowledge of all aspects of broadcast technology are necessary to become the chief engineer of a radio or television station.

EARNINGS

Larger stations usually pay higher wages than smaller stations, and television stations tend to pay more than radio stations. Also, commercial stations generally pay more than public broadcasting stations. The median annual earnings for broadcast technicians were $30,690 in 2006, according to the U.S. Department of Labor. The department also reported that the lowest paid 10 percent earned less than $15,680 and the highest paid 10 percent earned more than $64,860 during that same period. Experience, job location, and educational background are all factors that influence a person's pay.

WORK ENVIRONMENT

Most engineers work in broadcasting stations that are modern and comfortable. The hours can vary; because most broadcasting stations operate 24 hours a day, seven days a week, there are engineers who must work at night, on weekends, and on holidays. Transmitter technicians usually work behind the scenes with little public contact. They work closely with their equipment and as members of a small crew of experts whose closely coordinated efforts produce smooth-running programs. Constant attention to detail and having to make split-second decisions can cause tension. Since broadcasts also occur outside of the broadcasting station on location sites, field technicians may work anywhere and in all kinds of weather.

OUTLOOK

According to the U.S. Department of Labor, the overall employment of broadcast technicians is expected to grow about as fast as the average for all occupations through 2016. There will be strong competition for jobs in metropolitan areas. In addition, the Department of Labor predicts that a slow growth in the number of new radio and television stations may mean few new job opportunities in the field, but the demand for higher quality broadcasts (especially for digital transmission) will ensure a demand for technicians with solid skills. Technicians trained in the installation of transmitters should have better work prospects as television stations switch from their old analog transmitters to digital transmitters. Job openings will also result from the need to replace existing engineers who often leave the industry for other jobs in electronics.

Some engineers may find work outside of broadcasting. As the new technology becomes more accessible, new industries are discovering the usefulness of visual communications. More and more corporations are creating in-house communications departments to produce their own corporate and industrial videos. Videos effectively explain company policies ranging from public safety (aimed at their customers) to first aid (aimed at their employees). Also, videos of high quality can introduce a company to potential clients in the best light.

In addition to industrial work, *videographers* are in great demand today for the production of commercials, animation, and computer graphics. The field of videography is changing rapidly with the introduction of new and cheaper computer systems and desktop software packages. Maintenance workers will always be in demand, even with the new technology. Someone will always have to be on hand to fix broken equipment and to keep new equipment in good working order.

FOR MORE INFORMATION
Visit the BEA's Web site for useful information about broadcast education and the broadcasting industry.

Broadcast Education Association (BEA)
1771 N Street, NW
Washington, DC 20036-2891
Tel: 888-380-7222
Email: beainfo@beaweb.org
http://www.beaweb.org

For information on union membership, contact
National Association of Broadcast Employees and Technicians
Email: nabet@nabetcwa.org
http://nabetcwa.org

For broadcast education, support, and scholarship information, contact
National Association of Broadcasters
1771 N Street, NW
Washington, DC 20036-2891
Tel: 202-429-5300
Email: nab@nab.org
http://www.nab.org

For information on student membership, scholarships, and farm broadcasting, contact
National Association of Farm Broadcasters
PO Box 500
Platte City, MO 64079-0500
Tel: 816-431-4032
Email: nafboffice@aol.com
http://nafb.com

For information on careers in the cable industry, visit the NCTA's Web site.
National Cable and Telecommunications Association (NCTA)
25 Massachusetts Avenue, NW, Suite 100
Washington, DC 20001
Tel: 202-222-2300
http://www.ncta.com

For scholarship and internship information, contact
Radio-Television News Directors Association and Foundation
1600 K Street, NW, Suite 700
Washington, DC 20006-2838
Tel: 202-659-6510
Email: rtnda@rtnda.org
http://www.rtnda.org

For information on membership, scholarships, and certification, contact
Society of Broadcast Engineers
9102 North Meridian Street, Suite 150
Indianapolis, IN 46260-1896
Tel: 317-846-9000
Email: mclappe@sbe.org
http://www.sbe.org

Visit the society's Web site for information on scholarships, membership for college students, and links to useful resources.
Society of Motion Picture and Television Engineers
3 Barker Avenue
White Plains, NY 10601-1509
Tel: 914-761-1100
http://www.smpte.org

CAMERA OPERATORS

OVERVIEW
Camera operators use motion picture cameras and equipment to photograph subjects or material for movies, television programs, or commercials. They usually use 35- or 16-millimeter cameras or camcorders and a variety of films, lenses, tripods, and filters in their work. Their instructions often come from cinematographers or directors of photography. Approximately 27,000 camera operators work in the United States.

THE JOB
Motion picture camera operators may work on feature films in Hollywood or on location elsewhere. Many work on educational films, documentaries, or television programs. The nature of the camera operator's work depends largely on the size of the production crew. If the film is a documentary or short news segment, the camera operator may be responsible for setting up the camera and lighting equipment as well as for supervising the actors during filming. Equipment that camera operators

QUICK FACTS

SCHOOL SUBJECTS
Art
Mathematics

PERSONAL SKILLS
Communication/ideas
Mechanical/manipulative

WORK ENVIRONMENT
Indoors and outdoors
Primarily multiple locations

MINIMUM EDUCATION LEVEL
High school diploma

MEDIAN SALARY
$40,060

CERTIFICATION OR LICENSING
None available

OUTLOOK
About as fast as the average

ture. They usually add fades, dissolves, superimpositions, and other effects to their films at the request of the *director of photography* (DP), also known as the *director of cinematography* or the *cinematographer*.

Studio camera operators work in a broadcast studio and videotape their subjects—anything from talk-show hosts to soap-opera stars to comedians—from a fixed position.

News camera operators, also called *electronic news gathering (ENG) operators*, work in the field with a reporting team, covering news events live or taping them for later editing and broadcast, although sometimes the camera operator will actually edit footage on the spot for immediate broadcast. Working as this type of camera operator demands quick instincts and editorial judgment, so that relevant (and often unpredictable) events are captured as they happen.

Videographers are camera operators who generally record private ceremonies and special events on videotape. Videographers' subjects can be anything from a wedding to a corporate meeting.

Brian Fass is a cinematographer/camera assistant in New York City. On a project, he works closely with the other professionals to help establish a visual style for the film. "During the project," he says, "I work on setting up the camera in various positions for coverage of scenes and then lighting each chosen angle." Fass has worked as a camera assistant for the Woody Allen films *Everyone Says I Love You* and *Deconstructing Harry*, as well as the Sidney Lumet film *Gloria*.

REQUIREMENTS
High School

Take classes that will prepare you for the technical aspect of the work—courses in photography, journalism, and media arts should give you some hands-on experience with a camera. Mathematics and science can help you understand cameras and filters. You should also take art and art history classes and other courses that will help you develop appreciation of visual styles.

Postsecondary Training

A college degree is not necessary to get a position as a camera operator, but attending film school can help you expand your network of connections if film work is your goal. A bachelor's degree in liberal arts or film studies provides a good background for work in the film industry, but practical experience and industry connections will provide the best opportunities for work. Upon completing an undergraduate program, you may wish to enroll in a master's program at a film school. Schools

typically use include cranes, dollies, mounting heads, and different types of lenses and accessories. Often the camera operator is also responsible for maintenance and repair of all of this equipment.

With a larger crew, the camera operator is responsible only for the actual filming. The camera operator may even have a support team of assistants. The *first assistant camera operator* will typically focus on the cameras, making sure cameras are loaded and operating correctly and conferring with lighting specialists. In larger productions, there are also backup cameras and accessories for use if one should malfunction during filming. *Second assistant camera operators* help the first assistant set up scenes to be filmed and assist in the maintenance of the equipment.

Sometimes camera operators must use shoulder-held cameras. This often occurs during the filming of action scenes for television or motion pictures. *Special effects camera operators* photograph the optical effects segments for motion pictures and television. They create visual illusions that can add mood and tone to the motion pic-

offering well-established programs include the School of Visual Arts in New York, New York University, and the University of Southern California. These schools have film professionals on their faculties and provide a very visible stage for student talent, being located in the two film business hot spots—New York and California. Film school offers overall formal training, providing an education in fundamental skills by working with student productions. Such education is rigorous, but in addition to teaching skills it provides you with peer groups and a network of contacts with students, faculty, and guest speakers that can be of help after graduation.

Many community colleges, technical schools, and photographic institutes offer two-year degree programs in camera technology and operation. Check with your photography instructor or guidance counselor to find out more about programs in your area.

Other Requirements

You must be able to work closely with other members of a crew and to carefully follow the instructions of the cinematographer or director. Since lighting is an integral part of all broadcasts, you should have a thorough understanding of lighting equipment in order to work quickly and efficiently. In addition to the technical aspects of filmmaking, you should also understand the artistic nature of setting up shots. "I'm dyslexic and have always gravitated toward the visual mediums," Brian Fass says. "I feel that this impairment, along with my love of movies, made me turn toward cinematography."

EXPLORING

You should join a photography or camera club, or become involved with the media department of your school. You may have the opportunity then to videotape sports events, concerts, and school plays. You can also learn about photography by working in a camera shop. A part-time job in a camera shop will give you a basic understanding of photographic equipment. Some school districts have television stations where students can learn the basics of camera operation. This kind of hands-on experience is invaluable when it comes time to find work in the field. You can also learn about the film industry by reading such publications as *American Cinematographer* (http://www.ascmag.com) and *Cinefex* (http://www.cinefex.com).

EMPLOYERS

There are approximately 27,000 television, video, and movie camera operators working in the United States. About 17 percent these operators are self-employed. The majority of camera operators who are salaried employees work for the film and television industry at TV stations or film studios. Most jobs are found in large, urban areas.

STARTING OUT

Most entry-level jobs require little formal preparation in photography or camera operation. A college degree is not required by most film or television studios, but you may have to belong to the International Alliance of Theatrical Stage Employees Local 600, the national union for camera operators. An entry-level job as a camera assistant usually begins with assignments such as setting up or loading film into cameras and adjusting or checking lighting. With experience, the assistant may participate in decisions about what to photograph or how to film a particular scene.

Before you receive any paying jobs, you may have to work as a volunteer or intern on a film project. You can look online for postings of openings on film productions, or contact your state's film commission.

ADVANCEMENT

It usually takes two to four years for a motion picture camera operator to learn the techniques necessary for the job. Those who become proficient in their field, after several years of training, may be able to work on film projects as a cinematographer or director of photography. The director of photography supervises other camera operators and works more closely with the directors, producers, and actors in the creation of the film. Some camera operators study cinematography part time while keeping their jobs as camera operators. They may later move to larger studios or command higher salaries. Camera operators who are employed in the television industry might advance by working on more prestigious projects, working for larger stations, or by managing the work of other camera operators.

"I work as an assistant for the money," Brian Fass says, "but hope to jump into work as a DP full-time if the jobs come along. I also own my own Aaton XTR camera package, which makes me more marketable for DP jobs."

EARNINGS

Self-employed camera operators typically work on a project-by-project basis and may have periods of unemployment between jobs. Those working on movies may be paid per day, and their role in the creation of the movie may last anywhere from several weeks to several months. Camera operators who, for example, are salaried employees of a television network have steady, year-round employment. Because of these factors and others, such as area of the country in which the operator works and the size of the employer, salaries vary widely for these professionals. The U.S. Department of Labor reports the median annual earnings of all television, video, and motion picture camera operators as $40,060 in 2006. The department also reports that the lowest paid 10 percent of operators earned less than $18,810 per year, but at the top end of the pay scale, the highest earning 10 percent made more than $84,500 annually.

Salaried employees usually receive benefits such as health insurance, retirement plans, and vacation days. Those who are self-employed must pay for such extras themselves.

WORK ENVIRONMENT

Camera operators work indoors and outdoors. Most work for motion picture studios or in television broadcasting. During filming, a camera operator may spend several weeks or months on location in another city or country. Most often the camera operator lives and works in their home city and works during regular business hours. Hours can be erratic, however, if the film includes scenes that must be shot at night, or if a deadline must be met by after-hours filming.

Much of the work of a camera operator becomes routine after a few years of experience. Camera operators get used to loading and unloading film, carrying cameras and equipment from trucks or workshops into studios or sets, and filming segments over and over again. The glamour of working on motion pictures or television programs may be diminished by the physically demanding work. Also, the actors, directors, and producers are the individuals in the limelight. They often receive credit for the work the camera operators have done.

Many camera operators must be available to work on short notice. Since motion picture camera operators are generally hired to work on one film at a time, there may be long periods during which a camera operator is not working. Few can make a living as self-employed camera operators.

Camera operators working on documentary or news productions may work in dangerous places. Sometimes they must work in uncomfortable positions or make adjustments for imperfect lighting conditions. They usually operate their cameras while standing hours at a time. Deadline pressure is also a constant in the camera operator's work. Working for directors or producers who are on tight budgets or strict schedules may be very stressful.

OUTLOOK

Employment for camera operators is expected to increase about as fast as the average for all occupations through 2016, according to the U.S. Department of Labor. The use of visual images continues to grow in areas such as communication, education, entertainment, marketing, and research and development. More businesses will make use of video training films and public relations projects that use film. Camera operators will also be needed to help create made-for-the-Internet broadcasts. The entertainment industries are also expanding. However, competition for positions is very fierce. Employment will not be as strong in television broadcasting as automation reduces the number of camera operators needed to create television shows, newscasts, and other productions. Camera operators work in what is considered a desirable and exciting field, and they must work hard and be aggressive to get good jobs, especially in Los Angeles and New York.

FOR MORE INFORMATION

For lists of tricks of the trade and favorite films of famous cinematographers, visit the ASC's Web site.

American Society of Cinematographers (ASC)
PO Box 2230
Hollywood, CA 90078-2230
Tel: 800-448-0145
Email: info@theasc.com
http://www.theasc.com

For information on membership benefits, contact this branch of the International Alliance of Theatrical Stage Employees (IATSE):

**International Cinematographers Guild
  (IATSE Local 600)**
National Office/Western Region
7755 Sunset Boulevard
Hollywood, CA 90046-3911
Tel: 323-876-0160
http://www.cameraguild.com

For information on union membership, contact
**National Association of Broadcast Employees
  and Technicians**
Email: nabet@nabetcwa.org
http://nabetcwa.org

Visit the society's Web site for information on scholarships, membership for college students, and links to useful resources.

Society of Motion Picture and Television Engineers
3 Barker Avenue
White Plains, NY 10601-1509
Tel: 914-761-1100
http://www.smpte.org

Visit this Web site, organized by the ASC, for a list of film schools and to learn about the career of cinematographer—the next step on the career ladder for camera operators.

Cinematographer.com
http://www.cinematographer.com

CARDIOVASCULAR TECHNOLOGISTS

OVERVIEW

Cardiovascular technologists assist physicians in diagnosing and treating heart and blood vessel ailments. Depending on their specialties, they operate electrocardiograph machines, perform Holter monitor and stress testing, and assist in cardiac catheterization procedures and ultrasound testing. These tasks help the physicians diagnose heart disease and monitor progress during treatment. Cardiovascular technologists hold approximately 45,000 jobs in the United States.

THE JOB

Technologists who assist physicians in the diagnosis and treatment of heart disease are known as cardiovascular technologists. (Cardio means heart; vascular refers to the blood vessel/circulatory system.) Increasingly, hospitals are centralizing cardiovascular services under one full cardiovascular "service line" overseen by the same administrator. In addition to cardiovascular technologists, the cardiovascular team at a hospital may include *radiology (X-ray) technologists, nuclear medicine technologists, nurses, physician assistants, respiratory technicians,* and *respiratory therapists.* Cardiovascular technologists contribute by performing one or more of a wide range of procedures in cardiovascular medicine, including invasive (enters a body cavity or interrupts normal body functions), noninvasive, peripheral vascular, or echocardiography (ultrasound) procedures. In most facilities, technologists use equipment that is among the most advanced in the medical field; drug therapies also may be used as part of the diagnostic imaging procedures or in addition to them. Technologists' services may be required when the patient's condition is first being explored, before surgery, during surgery (cardiology technologists primarily), or during rehabilitation of the patient. Some of the work is performed on an outpatient basis.

Depending on their specific areas of skill, some cardiovascular technologists are employed in nonhospital

---

QUICK FACTS

SCHOOL SUBJECTS
Biology
Health

PERSONAL SKILLS
Communication/ideas
Technical/scientific

WORK ENVIRONMENT
Primarily indoors
Primarily one location

MINIMUM EDUCATION LEVEL
Some postsecondary training

MEDIAN SALARY
$42,300

CERTIFICATION OR LICENSING
Required in some states

OUTLOOK
Much faster than the average

---

health care facilities. For example, they may work for clinics, mobile medical services, or private doctors' offices. Much of their equipment can go just about anywhere.

Exact job titles of these technologists often vary from one medical facility to another. *Electrocardiograph technologists,* or *EKG technologists,* use an electrocardiograph machine to detect the electronic impulses that come from a patient's heart. The EKG machine records these signals on a paper graph called an electrocardiogram. The electronic impulses recorded by the EKG machine can tell the physician about the action of the heart during and between the individual heartbeats. This in turn reveals important information about the condition of the heart, including irregular heartbeats or the presence of blocked arteries, which the physician can use to diagnose heart disease, monitor progress during treatment, or check the patient's condition after recovery.

To use an EKG machine, the technologist attaches electrodes (small, disk-like devices about the size of a silver dollar) to the patient's chest. Wires attached to the electrodes lead to the EKG machine. Twelve or more leads may be attached. To get a better reading from the electrodes, the technologist may first apply an adhesive gel to the patient's skin to conduct the electrical impulses. The technologist then operates controls on the EKG machine or (more commonly) enters commands for the machine into a computer. The electrodes pick up the electronic signals from the heart and transmit them to the EKG machine. The machine registers and makes a printout of the signals, with a stylus (pen) recording their pattern on a long roll of graph paper.

During the test, the technologist may move the electrodes in order to get readings of electrical activity in different parts of the heart muscle. Since EKG equipment can be sensitive to electrical impulses from other sources, such as other parts of the patient's body or equipment in the room where the EKG test is being done, the technologist must watch for false readings.

After the test, the EKG technologist takes the electrocardiogram off the machine, edits it or makes notes on it, and sends it to the physician (usually a cardiologist, or heart specialist). Physicians may have computer assistance to help them use and interpret the electrocardiogram; special software is available to assist them with their diagnoses.

EKG technologists do not have to repair EKG machines, but they do have to keep an eye on them and know when they are malfunctioning so they can call someone for repairs. They also may keep the machines stocked with paper. Of all the cardiovascular technical positions, EKG technologist positions are the most numerous.

Holter monitoring and stress testing may be performed by *Holter monitor technologists* or *stress test technologists*, respectively, or they may be additional duties of some EKG technologists. In Holter monitoring, electrodes are fastened to the patient's chest, and a small, portable monitor is strapped to the patient's body, often at the waist. The small monitor contains a magnetic tape or cassette that records the action of the heart during activity—as the patient moves, sits, stands, sleeps, etc. The patient is required to wear the Holter monitor for 24 to 48 hours while he or she goes about normal daily activities. When the patient returns to the hospital, the technologist removes the magnetic tape or cassette from the monitor and puts it in a scanner to produce audio and visual representations of heart activity. (Hearing how the heart sounds during activity helps physicians diagnose a possible heart condition.) The technologist reviews and analyzes the information revealed in the tape. Finally, the technologist may print out the parts of the tape that show abnormal heart patterns, or he or she may make a full tape for the physician.

Stress tests record the heart's performance during physical activity. In one type of stress test, the technologist connects the patient to the EKG machine, attaching electrodes to the patient's arms, legs, and chest, and obtains a reading of the patient's resting heart activity and blood pressure. Then, the patient is asked to walk on a treadmill for a designated period of time while the technologist and the physician monitor the heart. The treadmill speed is increased so that the technologist and physician can see what happens when the heart is put under higher levels of exertion.

Cardiology technologists specialize in providing support for cardiac catheterization (tubing) procedures. These procedures are classified as invasive because they require the physician and attending technologists to enter a body cavity or interrupt normal body functions. In one cardiac catheterization procedure—an angiogram—a catheter (tube) is inserted into the heart (usually by way of a blood vessel in the leg) in order to see the condition of the heart blood vessels, whether there is a blockage. In another procedure, known as angioplasty, a catheter with a balloon at the end is inserted into an artery to widen it.

Unlike some of the other cardiovascular technologists, cardiology technologists actually assist in surgical procedures. They may help secure the patient to the table, set up a 35mm video camera or other imaging device under the instructions of the physician (to produce images that assist the physician in guiding the catheter through the cardiovascular system), enter information about the surgical procedure (as it is taking place) into a computer, and provide other support. After the procedure, the technologist may process the angiographic film for use by the physician. Cardiology technologists may also assist during open-heart surgery by preparing and monitoring the patient and placing or monitoring pacemakers.

Vascular technologists and *echocardiographers* are specialists in noninvasive cardiovascular procedures and use ultrasound equipment to obtain and record information about the condition of the heart. Ultrasound equipment is used to send out sound waves to the area of the body being studied; when the sound waves hit the part being studied, they send echoes to the ultrasound machine. The echoes are "read" by the machine, which creates an image on a monitor, permitting the technologist to get an instant "image" of the part of the body and its condition. Vascular technologists are specialists in the use of ultrasound equipment to study blood flow and circulation problems. Echocardiographers are specialists in the use of ultrasound equipment to evaluate the heart and its structures, such as the valves.

Cardiac monitor technicians are similar to and sometimes perform some of the same duties as EKG technologists. Usually working in the intensive care unit or cardio-care unit of the hospital, cardiac monitor technicians keep watch over the patient, monitoring screens to detect any sign that a patient's heart is not beating as it should. Cardiac monitor technicians begin their shift by reviewing the patient's records to familiarize themselves with what the patient's normal heart rhythms should be, what the current pattern is, and what types of problems have been observed. Throughout the shift, cardiac monitor technicians watch for heart rhythm irregularities that need prompt medical attention. Should there be any, they notify a nurse or doctor immediately so that appropriate care can be given.

In addition to these positions, other cardiovascular technologists specialize in a particular aspect of health care. For example, *cardiopulmonary technologists* specialize in procedures for diagnosing problems with the heart and lungs. They may conduct electrocardiograph, phonocardiograph (sound recordings of the heart's valves and of the blood passing through them), echocardiograph, stress testing, and respiratory test procedures.

Cardiopulmonary technologists also may assist on cardiac catheterization procedures, measuring and recording information about the patient's cardiovascular and pulmonary systems during the procedure and alerting the cardiac catheterization team to any problems.

REQUIREMENTS
High School

At a minimum, cardiovascular technologists need a high school diploma or equivalent to enter the field. Although no specific high school classes will directly prepare you to be a technologist, getting a good grounding in basic high school subjects is important to all technologist positions.

During high school, you should take English, health, biology, and typing. You also might consider courses in social sciences to help you understand the social and psychological needs of patients.

Postsecondary Training

In the past, many EKG operators were trained on the job by an EKG supervisor. This still may be true for some EKG technician positions. Increasingly, however, EKG technologists get postsecondary schooling before they are hired. Holter monitoring and stress testing may be part of your EKG schooling, or they may be learned through additional training. Ultrasound and cardiology technologists tend to have the most postsecondary schooling (up to a four-year bachelor's degree) and have

the most extensive academic/experience requirements for credentialing purposes.

You can enter these positions without having had previous health care experience. However, some previous exposure to the business side of health care or even training in related areas is helpful. With academic training or professional experience in nursing, radiology science, or respiratory science, for example, you may be able to move into cardiology technology.

As a rule of thumb, medical employers value postsecondary schooling that gives you actual hands-on experience with patients in addition to classroom training. At many of the schools that train cardiovascular technologists, you work with patients in a variety of health care settings and train on more than one brand of equipment.

Some employers still have a physician or EKG department manager train EKG technicians on the job. Training generally lasts from one to six months. Trainees learn how to operate the EKG machine, how to produce and edit the electrocardiogram, and other related tasks.

Some vocational, technical, and junior colleges have one- or two-year training programs in EKG technology, Holter monitoring, stress testing, or all three; otherwise, EKG technologists may obtain training in Holter and stress procedures after they've already started working, either on the job or through an additional six months or more of schooling. Formal academic programs give technologists more preparation in the subject than is available with most on-the-job training and allow them to earn a certificate (one-year programs) or associate's degree (two-year programs). The American Medical Association (AMA)'s Allied Health Directory has listings of accredited EKG programs.

Ultrasound technologists usually need a high school diploma or equivalent plus one, two, or four years of postsecondary schooling in a trade school, technical school, or community college. Vascular technologists also may be trained on the job. Again, a list of accredited programs can be found in the AMA's Allied Health Directory; also, a directory of training opportunities in sonography is available from the Society of Diagnostic Medical Sonography.

Cardiology technologists tend to have the highest academic requirements of all; for example, a four-year bachelor's degree, a two-year associate's degree, or a certificate of completion from a hospital, trade, or technical cardiovascular program. A two-year program at a junior or community college might include one year of core classes (e.g., mathematics, biology, chemistry, and anatomy) and one year of specialized classes in cardiology procedures.

Cardiac monitor technicians need a high school diploma or equivalent, with additional educational requirements similar to those of EKG technicians.

Certification or Licensing

Some states require licensing of cardiovascular technologists; check with your state's medical board to see if this is the case where you live. Many credentialing bodies for cardiovascular and pulmonary positions exist, including American Registry of Diagnostic Medical Sonographers (ARDMS), Cardiovascular Credentialing International (CCI), and others, and there are more than a dozen possible credentials for cardiovascular technologists. For example, sonographers can take an exam from ARDMS to receive credentialing in sonography. Their credentials may be as registered diagnostic medical sonographer, registered diagnostic cardiac sonographer, or registered vascular technologist. Credentialing requirements for cardiology technologists or ultrasound technologists may include a test plus formal academic and on-the-job requirements. Professional experience or academic training in a related field, such as nursing, radiology science, and respiratory science, may be acceptable as part of these formal academic and professional requirements. As with continuing education, certification is a sign of interest and dedication to the field and is generally favorably regarded by potential employers.

Cardiology is a cutting-edge area of medicine, with constant advancements, and medical equipment relating to the heart is continually updated. Therefore, keeping up with new developments is vital. In addition, technologists who add to their qualifications through taking part in continuing education tend to earn more money and have more employment opportunities. Major professional societies encourage and provide the opportunities for professionals to continue their education.

Other Requirements

Technicians must be able to put patients at ease about the procedure they are to undergo. Therefore, you should be pleasant, patient, alert, and able to understand and sympathize with the feelings of others. When explaining a procedure to patients, cardiovascular technicians should be able to do so in a calm, reassuring, and confident manner.

EXPLORING

Prospective cardiovascular technologists will find it difficult to gain any direct experience on a part-time basis. The first experience with the work generally comes during on-the-job training sessions. You may, however, be able to gain some exposure to patient-care activities in general by signing up for volunteer work at a local hospital. In addition, you can arrange to visit a hospital, clinic, or physician's office where electrocardiographs are taken. In this way, you may be able to watch a technician at work or at least talk to a technician about what the work is like.

EMPLOYERS

There are approximately 45,000 cardiovascular technologists employed in the United States. Most work in hospitals, but employment can be found in physicians' offices, clinics, rehab centers, or anyplace electrocardiographs are taken.

STARTING OUT

Because most cardiovascular technologists receive their initial training on their first job, great care should be taken in finding this first employer. Pay close attention not only to the pay and working conditions, but also to the kind of on-the-job training that is provided for each prospective position. High school vocational counselors may be able to tell you which hospitals have good reputations for EKG training programs. Applying directly to hospitals is a common way of entering the field. Information also can be gained by reading the classified ads in the newspaper and from talking with friends and relatives who work in hospitals.

Finding a first job should be easiest for students who graduate from one- to two-year training programs. First, employers are always eager to hire people who are already trained. Second, these graduates can be less concerned about the training programs offered by their employers. Third, they should find that their teachers and guidance counselors can be excellent sources of information about job possibilities in the area. If the training program includes practical experience, graduates may find that the hospital in which they trained or worked before graduation would be willing to hire them after graduation.

ADVANCEMENT

Opportunities for advancement are best for cardiovascular technologists who learn to do or assist with more complex procedures, such as stress testing, Holter monitoring, echocardiography, and cardiac catheterization. With proper training and experience, these technicians may eventually become cardiovascular technologists, echocardiography technologists, cardiopulmonary technicians, cardiology technologists, or other specialty technicians or technologists.

In addition to these kinds of specialty positions, experienced technicians may also be able to advance to various supervisory and training posts.

EARNINGS

The median salary for cardiovascular technologists was $42,300 in 2006, according to the U.S. Department of Labor. The lowest-paid 10 percent earned less than $23,670, and the highest-paid 10 percent earned more than $67,410 annually. Earnings can vary by size and type of employer. For example, technologists working in doctors' offices had a mean annual income of $41,960, while those in hospitals had a median of $41,950. Those with formal training earn more than those who trained on the job, and those who are able to perform more sophisticated tests, such as Holter monitoring and stress testing, are paid more than those who perform only the basic electrocardiograph tests.

Technologists working in hospitals receive the same fringe benefits as other hospital workers, including medical insurance, paid vacations, and sick leave. In some cases, benefits also include educational assistance, retirement plans, and uniform allowances.

WORK ENVIRONMENT

Cardiovascular technologists usually work in clean, quiet, well-lighted surroundings. They generally work five-day, 40-hour weeks, although technicians working in small hospitals may be on 24-hour call for emergencies, and all technicians in hospitals, large or small, can expect to do occasional evening or weekend work. With the growing emphasis in health care on cost containment, more jobs are likely to develop in outpatient settings, so in the future it is likely that cardiovascular technologists will work more often in clinics, health maintenance organizations, and other nonhospital locations.

Cardiovascular technologists generally work with patients who are ill or who have reason to fear they might be ill. With this in mind, there are opportunities for the technicians to do these people some good, but there is also a chance of causing some unintentional harm as well: A well-conducted test can reduce anxieties or make a physician's job easier; a misplaced electrode or an error in recordkeeping could cause an incorrect diagnosis. Technicians need to be able to cope with these responsibilities and consistently conduct their work in the best interests of their patients.

Part of the technician's job includes putting patients at ease about the procedure they are to undergo. Toward that end, technicians should be pleasant, patient, alert, and able to understand and sympathize with the feelings of others. In explaining the nature of the procedure to patients, cardiovascular technicians should be able to do so in a calm, reassuring, and confident manner.

Inevitably, some patients will try to get information about their medical situation from the technician. In such cases, technicians need to be both tactful and firm in explaining that they are only taking the electrocardiogram; the interpretation is for the physician to make.

Another large part of a technician's job involves getting along well with other members of the hospital staff.

This task is sometimes made more difficult by the fact that in most hospitals there is a formal, often rigid, status structure, and cardiovascular technologists may find themselves in a relatively low position in that structure. In emergency situations or at other moments of frustration, cardiovascular technologists may find themselves dealt with brusquely or angrily. Technicians should not take outbursts or rude treatment personally, but instead should respond with stability and maturity.

OUTLOOK

The overall employment of cardiovascular technologists and technicians should grow much faster than the average through 2016, according to the U.S. Department of Labor. Growth will be primarily due to the increasing numbers of older people who have a higher incidence of heart problems. The labor department, however, projects employment for EKG technicians to decline during this same period as hospitals train other health care personnel to perform basic EKG procedures.

FOR MORE INFORMATION

For information on careers, contact
Alliance of Cardiovascular Professionals
PO Box 2007
Midlothian, VA 23113-9007
Tel: 804-632-0078
http://www.acp-online.org

For information on the medical field, including listings of accredited medical programs, contact
American Medical Association
515 North State Street
Chicago, IL 60610-5453
Tel: 800-621-8335
http://www.ama-assn.org

For information on certification or licensing, contact
American Registry of Diagnostic Medical Sonographers
51 Monroe Street
Plaza East One
Rockville, MD 20850
Tel: 800-541-9754
http://www.ardms.org

For information on credentials, contact
Cardiovascular Credentialing International
1500 Sunday Drive, Suite 102
Raleigh, NC 27607
Tel: 800-326-0268
http://cci-online.org

CARPENTERS

OVERVIEW

Carpenters cut, shape, level, and fasten together pieces of wood and other construction materials, such as wallboard, plywood, and insulation. Many carpenters work on constructing, remodeling, or repairing houses and other kinds of buildings. Other carpenters work at construction sites where roads, bridges, docks, boats, mining tunnels, and wooden vats are built. They may specialize in building the rough framing of a structure, and thus be considered rough carpenters, or they may specialize in the finishing details of a structure, such as the trim around doors and windows, and be finish carpenters. Approximately 1.5 million carpenters work in the United States—the largest segment of the building trades industry.

QUICK FACTS

SCHOOL SUBJECTS
Mathematics
Technical/shop

PERSONAL SKILLS
Following instructions
Mechanical/manipulative

WORK ENVIRONMENT
Indoors and outdoors
Primarily multiple locations

MINIMUM EDUCATION LEVEL
Apprenticeship

MEDIAN SALARY
$36,545

CERTIFICATION OR LICENSING
Voluntary

OUTLOOK
About as fast as the average

THE JOB

The vast majority of carpenters work for contractors involved in building, repairing, and remodeling buildings and other structures. Manufacturing firms, schools, stores, and government bodies employ most other carpenters.

Carpenters do two basic kinds of work: rough carpentry and finish carpentry. *Rough carpenters* construct and install temporary structures and supports and wooden structures used in industrial settings, as well as parts of buildings that are usually covered up when the rooms are finished. Among the structures they build are scaffolds for other workers to stand on, chutes used as channels for wet concrete, forms for concrete foundations, and timber structures that support machinery. In buildings, they may put up the frame and install rafters, joists, subflooring, wall sheathing, prefabricated wall panels and windows, and many other components.

Finish carpenters install hardwood flooring, staircases, shelves, cabinets, trim on windows and doors, and other woodwork and hardware that make the building look complete, inside and outside. Finish carpentry requires especially careful, precise workmanship, since the resulting product must have a good appearance in addition to being sturdy. Many carpenters who are employed by building contractors do both rough and finish work on buildings.

Although they do many different tasks in different settings, carpenters generally follow the same basic steps. First, they review blueprints or plans (or they obtain instructions from a supervisor) to determine the dimensions of the structure to be built and the types of materials to be used. Sometimes local building codes mandate how a structure should be built, so carpenters need to know about such regulations.

Using rulers, framing squares, chalk lines, and other measuring and marking equipment, carpenters lay out how the work will be done. Using hand and power tools, they cut and shape the wood, plywood, fiberglass, plastic, or other materials. Then they nail, screw, glue, or staple the pieces together. Finally, they use levels, plumb bobs, rulers, and squares to check their work, and they make any necessary adjustments. Sometimes carpenters work with prefabricated units for components such as wall panels or stairs. Installing these is, in many ways, a much less complicated task, because much less layout, cutting, and assembly work is needed.

Carpenters who work outside of the building construction field may do a variety of installation and maintenance jobs, such as repairing furniture and installing ceiling tiles or exterior siding on buildings. Other carpenters specialize in building, repairing, or modifying ships, wooden boats, wooden railroad trestles, timber framing in mine shafts, woodwork inside railcars, storage tanks and vats, or stage sets in theaters.

REQUIREMENTS
High School

A high school education is not mandatory for a good job as a carpenter, but most contractors and developers prefer applicants with a diploma or a GED. A good high school background for prospective carpenters would include carpentry and woodworking courses as well as other shop classes; applied mathematics; mechanical drawing; and blueprint reading.

Postsecondary Training

As an aspiring carpenter, you can acquire the skills of your trade in various ways, through formal training programs and through informal on-the-job training. Of the different ways to learn, an apprenticeship is considered the best, as it provides a more thorough and complete foundation for a career as a carpenter than do other kinds of training. However, the limited number of available apprenticeships means that not all carpenters can learn the trade this way.

You can pick up skills informally on the job while you work as a carpenter's helper; many carpenters enter the field this way. You will begin with little or no training and gradually learn as you work under the supervision of experienced carpenters. The skills that you will develop as a helper will depend on the jobs that your employers contract to do. Working for a small contracting company, a beginner may learn about relatively few kinds of carpentry tasks. On the other hand, a large contracting company may offer a wider variety of learning opportunities. Becoming a skilled carpenter by this method can take much longer than an apprenticeship, and the completeness of the training varies. While some individuals are waiting for an apprenticeship to become available they may work as helpers to gain experience in the field.

Some people first learn about carpentry while serving in the military. Others learn skills in vocational educational programs offered in trade schools and through correspondence courses. Vocational programs can be very good, especially as a supplement to other practical training. But without additional hands-on instruction, vocational school graduates may not be adequately prepared to get many jobs in the field because some programs do not provide sufficient opportunity for students to practice and perfect their carpentry skills.

Apprenticeships, which will provide you with the most comprehensive training available, usually last four years. They are administered by employer groups and by local chapters of labor unions that organize carpenters. Applicants must meet the specific requirements of local apprenticeship committees. Typically, you must be at least 17 years old, have a high school diploma, and be able to show that you have some aptitude for carpentry.

Apprenticeships combine on-the-job work experience with classroom instruction in a planned, systematic program. Initially, you will work at such simple tasks as building concrete forms, doing rough framing, and nailing subflooring. Toward the end of your training, you may work on finishing trimwork, fitting hardware, hanging doors, and building stairs. In the course of this experience, you will become familiar with the tools, materials, techniques, and equipment of the trade, and you will learn how to do layout, framing, finishing, and other basic carpentry jobs.

The work experience segment of an apprenticeship is supplemented by about 144 hours of classroom instruction per year. Some of this instruction concerns the correct use and maintenance of tools, safety practices, first aid, building code requirements, and the properties of different construction materials. Other subjects you will study include the principles of layout, blueprint reading, shop mathematics, and sketching. Both on the job and in the classroom, you will learn how to work effectively with members of other skilled building trades.

Certification or Licensing

The United Brotherhood of Carpenters and Joiners of America (UBCJA), the national union for the industry, offers certification courses in a variety of specialty skills. These courses teach the ins and outs of advanced skills—like scaffold construction—that help to ensure worker safety, while at the same time giving workers ways to enhance their abilities and so qualify for better jobs. Some job sites require all workers to undergo training in safety techniques and guidelines specified by the Occupational Safety and Health Administration. Workers who have not passed these courses are considered ineligible for jobs at these sites.

Other Requirements

In general, as a carpenter, you will need to have manual dexterity, good hand-eye coordination, and a good sense of balance. You will need to be in good physical condition, as the work involves a great deal of physical activity. Stamina is much more important than physical strength. On the job, you may have to climb, stoop, kneel, crouch, and reach as well as deal with the challenges of weather.

EXPLORING

Beyond classes such as woodshop or mechanical drawing, there are a number of real-world ways to begin exploring a career in carpentry and the construction trades. Contact trade organizations like the National Association of Home Builders or the Associated General Contractors of America; both sponsor student chapters around the country. Consider volunteering for an organization like Habitat for Humanity; their Youth Programs accept volunteers between the ages of five and 25, and their group building projects provide hands-on experience. If your school has a drama department, look into it—building sets can be a fun way to learn simple carpentry skills. In addition, your local home improvement store is likely to sponsor classes that teach a variety of skills useful around the house; some of these will focus on carpentry.

EMPLOYERS

About one third of the 1.5 million carpenters in the United States work for general-building contractors, and one fifth work for specialty contractors. About 32 percent are self-employed.

Some carpenters work for manufacturing firms, government agencies, retail and wholesale establishments, or schools. Others work in the shipbuilding, aircraft, or railroad industries. Still others work in the arts, for theaters and movie and television production companies as set builders, or for museums or art galleries, building exhibits.

STARTING OUT

Information about available apprenticeships can be obtained by contacting the local office of the state employment service, area contractors that hire carpenters, or the local offices of the United Brotherhood of Carpenters, which cooperates in sponsoring apprenticeship programs. Helper jobs that can be filled by beginners without special training in carpentry may be advertised in newspaper classified ads or with the state employment service. You also might consider contacting potential employers directly.

ADVANCEMENT

Once an applicant has completed and met all the requirements of apprenticeship training, he or she will be considered a *journeyman carpenter*. With sufficient experience, journeymen may be promoted to positions responsible for supervising the work of other carpenters. If a carpenter's background includes exposure to a broad range of construction activities, he or she may eventually advance to a position as a general construction supervisor. A carpenter who is skillful at mathematical computations and has a good knowledge of the construction business may become an *estimator*. An experienced carpenter might one day go into business for himself or herself, doing repair or construction work as an independent contractor.

EARNINGS

According to the U.S. Bureau of Labor Statistics, carpenters had median hourly earnings of $17.57 in 2006. Someone making this wage and working full time for the year would have an income of approximately $36,545. The lowest paid 10 percent of carpenters earned less than $10.87 per hour (or approximately $22,610 per year), and the highest-paid 10 percent made more than $30.45 hourly (approximately $63,336 annually). It is important to note, however, that these annual salaries are for full-time work. Many carpenters, like others in the building trades, have periods of unemployment during the year, and their incomes may not match these.

Starting pay for apprentices can range from $5 to $17 per hour. The wage is increased periodically so that by the fourth year of training apprentice pay is 80 percent of the journeyman carpenter's rate.

Fringe benefits, such as health insurance, pension funds, and paid vacations, are available to most workers in this field and vary with local union contracts. In general, benefits are more likely to be offered on jobs staffed by union workers.

WORK ENVIRONMENT

Carpenters may work either indoors or outdoors. If they do rough carpentry, they will probably do most of their work outdoors. Carpenters may have to work on high scaffolding, or in a basement making cement forms. A construction site can be noisy, dusty, hot, cold, or muddy. Carpenters can expect to be physically active throughout the day, constantly standing, stooping, climbing, and reaching. Some possible hazards of the job include being hit by falling objects, falling off scaffolding or a ladder, straining muscles, and getting cuts and scrapes on fingers and hands. Carpenters who follow recommended safety practices and procedures minimize these hazards.

Work in the construction industry involves changing from one job location to another, and from time to time being laid off because of poor weather, shortages of materials, or simply lack of jobs. Carpenters must be able to arrange their finances so that they can make it through long periods of unemployment.

Though it is not required, many carpenters are members of a union such as the UBCJA. Among many other services, such as the certification courses mentioned previously, the union works with employers, seeking to ensure that members receive equitable pay and work in safe conditions.

OUTLOOK

Although the U.S. Department of Labor predicts employment growth for carpenters to increase about as fast as the average through 2016, job opportunities for carpenters are expected to be very strong. This is because replacement carpenters are needed for the large number of experienced carpenters who leave the field every year for work that is less strenuous. Replacement workers are also needed for the fair amount of workers just starting out in the field who decide to move on to more comfortable occupations. And, of course, replacements are needed for those who retire. Increased home-building, home modifications for the growing elderly population, two-income couples' desire for larger homes, and the growing population of all ages should contribute to the demand for carpenters.

Factors that will hold down employment growth in the field include the use of more prefabricated building parts and improved tools that make construction easier and faster. In addition, a weak economy has a major impact on the building industry, causing companies and individuals to put off expensive building projects until better times. Carpenters with good all-around skills, such as those who have completed apprenticeships, will have the best job opportunities even in difficult times.

FOR MORE INFORMATION

For information on activities and student chapters, contact
Associated General Contractors of America
2300 Wilson Boulevard, Suite 400
Arlington, VA 22201-5424
Tel: 703-548-3118
Email: info@agc.org
http://www.agc.org

For information on apprenticeship and certification, visit
United Brotherhood of Carpenters and Joiners
http://www.carpenters.org

For information on apprenticeships, training programs, and general information about trends in the industry, contact
Home Builders Institute
1201 15th Street, NW, Sixth Floor
Washington, DC 20005-2842
Tel: 202-371-0600
Email: postmaster@hbi.org
http://www.hbi.org

For information about careers in the construction trades and student chapters, contact
National Association of Home Builders
1201 15th Street, NW
Washington, DC 20005-2842
Tel: 800-368-5242
Email: info@nahb.com
http://www.nahb.com

CARTOONISTS AND ANIMATORS

OVERVIEW

Cartoonists and *animators* are artists who draw either still or moving pictures and cartoons to amuse, entertain, educate, and persuade people. While innate creativity and artistic skill are among the job requirements in this field, computers have become increasingly important to the field of animation over the past decade. There are approximately 87,000 multimedia artists and animators and 30,000 fine artists and illustrators working in the United States. Cartoonists and animators are just some of the workers that fall into these categories.

THE JOB

Cartoonists and *animators* draw and animate illustrations for newspapers, books, magazines, publishers, greeting cards, movies, television shows, civic organizations, and private businesses. Cartoons are most often associated with newspaper comics, children's television, and the World Wide Web, but they are also used to highlight and interpret information in publications as well as in advertising.

Whatever their individual specialty, cartoonists and animators translate ideas onto paper or film in order to communicate these ideas to an audience. Sometimes the ideas are original; at other times they are directly related to the news of the day, to the content of a magazine article,

QUICK FACTS

SCHOOL SUBJECTS

Art

Computer science

History

PERSONAL SKILLS

Artistic

Communication/ideas

WORK ENVIRONMENT

Primarily indoors

Primarily one location

MINIMUM EDUCATION LEVEL

High school diploma

MEDIAN SALARY

$41,970

CERTIFICATION OR LICENSING

None available

OUTLOOK

Faster than the average

Comic strip artists tell jokes or short stories with a series of pictures. Each picture is called a frame or a panel, and each frame usually includes words as well as drawings. Comic book artists also tell stories with their drawings, but their stories are longer, and they are not necessarily meant to be funny. In fact, graphic novels such as Art Spiegelman's *Maus*, Frank Miller's *The Dark Knight Returns*, Marjane Satrapi's *Persepolis*, and Chris Ware's *Acme Novelty* comics have blurred the line between comics and serious literature and art.

Animators, or *motion cartoonists*, also draw individual pictures, but they must draw many more for a moving cartoon. Each picture varies only slightly from the ones before and after it in a series. When these drawings are photographed in sequence to make a film that is projected at high speed, the cartoon images appear to be moving. (One can achieve a similar effect by drawing stick figures on the pages of a notepad and then flipping through the pages very quickly.) Animators today also work a great deal with computers.

Other people who work in animation are *prop designers*, who create objects used in animated films, and *layout artists*, who visualize and create the world that cartoon characters inhabit.

Editorial cartoonists comment on society by drawing pictures with messages that are usually funny, but which often have a satirical edge. Their drawings often depict famous politicians. *Portraitists* are cartoonists who specialize in drawing caricatures. Caricatures are pictures that exaggerate someone's prominent features, such as a large nose, to make them recognizable to the public. Most editorial cartoonists are also talented portraitists.

Storyboard artists work in film and television production as well as at advertising agencies. They draw cartoons or sketches that give a client an idea of what a scene or television commercial will look like before it is produced. If the director or advertising client likes the idea, the actions represented by cartoons in the storyboard will be reproduced by actors on film.

or to a new product. After cartoonists come up with ideas, they discuss them with their employers, which include editors, producers, and creative directors at advertising agencies. Next, cartoonists sketch drawings and submit these for approval. Employers may suggest changes, which the cartoonists then make. Cartoonists use a variety of art materials, including pens, pencils, markers, crayons, paints, transparent washes, and shading sheets. They may draw on paper, acetate, or bristol board.

Animators are relying increasingly on computers in various areas of production. Computers are used to color animation art, whereas formerly every frame was painted by hand. Computers also help animators create special effects or even entire films. (One program, Adobe Flash, has given rise to an entire Internet cartoon subculture.)

REQUIREMENTS
High School

If you are interested in becoming a cartoonist or animator, you should study art in high school in addition to following a well-rounded course of study. To comment insightfully on contemporary life through your art, it is useful to study political science, history, and social studies. English and communications classes will also help you to become a better communicator.

Postsecondary Training

Cartoonists and animators do not need to have a college degree, but employers usually look for some art training. Animators must attend art school to learn specific technical skills. Computer training—especially in programs such as Adobe Flash—can be especially valuable.

Other Requirements

Cartoonists and animators must be creative. In addition to having artistic talent, they must generate ideas, although it is not unusual for cartoonists to collaborate with writers for ideas. Whether they create cartoon strips or advertising campaigns, they must be able to come up with concepts and images to which the public will respond. They must have a good sense of humor (or a good dramatic sense) and an observant eye to detect people's distinguishing characteristics and society's interesting attributes or incongruities. They must develop their drawing styles so that they have an individually defined style that appeals to a wide audience.

Cartoonists and animators need to be flexible. Because their art is commercial, they must be willing to accommodate their employers' desires if they are to build a broad clientele and earn a decent living. They must be able to take suggestions and rejections gracefully.

EXPLORING

If you are interested in becoming a cartoonist or an animator, you should submit your drawings to your school paper. You also might want to draw posters to publicize activities, such as sporting events, dances, and meetings.

Scholarship assistance for art students is available from some sources. For example, the Society of Illustrators awards some 125 scholarships annually to student artists from any field. Students do not apply directly; rather, they are selected and given application materials by their instructors. The International Animated Film Society also offers scholarships to high school seniors.

EMPLOYERS

Employers of cartoonists and animators include editors, producers, creative directors at advertising agencies, comics syndicates, newspapers, movie studios, and television networks. In addition, a number of these artists are self-employed, working on a freelance basis. Some do animation on the Web as a part-time business or a hobby.

STARTING OUT

A few places, such as the Walt Disney studios, offer apprenticeships. To enter these programs, applicants must have attended an accredited art school for two or three years.

Formal entry-level positions for cartoonists and animators are rare, but there are several ways for artists to enter the cartooning field. Most cartoonists and animators begin by working piecemeal, selling cartoons to small publications, such as community newspapers, that buy freelance cartoons. Others assemble a portfolio of their best work and apply to publishers or the art departments of advertising agencies. In order to become established, cartoonists and animators should be willing to work for what equals less than minimum wage.

One new way up-and-coming animators have made themselves known to the animating community is by attracting an audience on the World Wide Web. A portfolio of well-executed Web 'toons can help an animator build his or her reputation and get jobs. Some animators, such as the Brothers Chaps (creators of homestarrunner. com), have even been able to turn their Web site into a profitable business.

ADVANCEMENT

Cartoonists' success, like that of other artists, depends on how much the public likes their work. Very successful cartoonists and animators work for prestigious clients at the best wages; some become well known to the public.

EARNINGS

Freelance cartoonists may earn anywhere from $100 to $1,200 or more per drawing, but top dollar generally goes only for big, full-color projects such as magazine cover illustrations. Although the Department of Labor does not give specific information regarding cartoonists' earnings, it does note that the median annual earnings for all types of fine artists were $41,970 in 2006, with the lowest paid 10 percent making less than $18,350 and the highest making more than $79,390. Median annual earnings for multimedia artists and animators were $51,350 in 2006, with 10 percent earning $30,390 or less and 10 percent earning $92,720 and up, although syndicated cartoonists on commission can earn much more. Salaries depend on the work performed. *Cel painters*, as listed in a salary survey conducted by *Animation World*, start at about $750 a week; *animation checkers*, $930 a week; *story sketchers*, $1,500 weekly. Comic strip artists are usually paid according to the number of publications that carry their strip.

Self-employed artists do not receive fringe benefits such as paid vacations, sick leave, health insurance, or pension benefits. Those who are salaried employees of companies, agencies, newspapers, and the like do typically receive these fringe benefits.

WORK ENVIRONMENT

Most cartoonists and animators work in big cities where employers such as television studios, magazine publishers, and advertising agencies are located. They generally work in comfortable environments, at drafting tables or drawing boards with good light. Staff cartoonists work a regular 40-hour workweek but may occasionally be expected to work evenings and weekends to meet deadlines. Freelance cartoonists have erratic schedules, and the number of hours they work may depend on how much money they want to earn or how much work they can find. They often work evenings and weekends but are not required to be at work during regular office hours.

Cartoonists and animators can be frustrated by employers who curtail their creativity, asking them to follow instructions that are contrary to what they would most like to do. Many freelance cartoonists spend a lot of time working alone at home, but cartoonists have more opportunities to interact with other people than do most working artists.

OUTLOOK

Employment for artists and related workers is expected to grow at a faster than average rate through 2016, according to the U.S. Department of Labor. The growing market for Internet content in the form of cartoons and animation will provide healthy job prospects, as will the continued demand for high-quality animation for television, film, and video games. Because so many creative and talented people are drawn to this field, however, competition for jobs will be strong.

More than half of all visual artists are self-employed, but freelance work can be hard to come by, and many freelancers earn little until they acquire experience and establish a good reputation. Competition for work will be keen; those with an undergraduate or advanced degree in art or film will be in demand. Experience in action drawing and computers is a must.

FOR MORE INFORMATION

For membership and scholarship information, contact
International Animated Film Society
2114 Burbank Boulevard
Burbank, CA 91506-1232
Tel: 818-842-8330
Email: info@asifa-hollywood.org
http://www.asifa-hollywood.org

For an art school directory, a scholarship guide, or general information, contact
National Art Education Association
1916 Association Drive

Reston, VA 20191-1590
Tel: 703-860-8000
Email: naea@dgs.dgsys.com
http://www.naea-reston.org

For education and career information, contact
National Cartoonists Society
1133 West Morse Boulevard, Suite 201
Winter Park, FL 32789-2327
http://www.reuben.org

For scholarship information for qualified students in art school, have your instructor contact
Society of Illustrators
Museum of American Illustration
128 East 63rd Street
New York, NY 10021-7303
Tel: 212-838-2560
http://www.societyillustrators.org

CEMENT MASONS

OVERVIEW

Cement masons, who usually work for contractors in the building and construction industries, apply the concrete surfaces in many different kinds of construction projects, ranging from small patios and sidewalks to highways, dams, and airport runways. Cement masons' responsibilities include building forms for holding the concrete, determining the correct mixture of ingredients, and making sure the structure is suitable to the environment. Approximately 229,000 cement masons, concrete finishers, segmental pavers, and terrazzo workers are employed in the United States.

THE JOB

The principal work of cement masons, also known as *concrete masons*, is to put into place and then smooth and finish concrete surfaces in a variety of different construction projects. Sometimes they add colors to the concrete to change its appearance or chemicals to speed up or slow down the amount of time that the concrete takes to harden. They use various tools to create specified surface textures on fresh concrete before it sets. They may also fabricate beams, columns, or panels of concrete.

Cement masons must know their materials well. They must be able to judge how long different concrete mixtures will take to set and how factors such as temperature and wind will affect the curing, or hardening, of the cement. They need to be able to recognize these effects by examining and touching the concrete. They need to know about the strengths of different kinds of concrete and how different surface appearances are produced.

In addition to understanding the materials they work with, cement masons must also be familiar with blueprint reading, applied mathematics, building code regulations, and the procedures involved in estimating the costs and quantities of materials.

On a construction job, the preparation of the site where the concrete will be poured is important. Cement masons begin by setting up the forms that will hold the wet concrete until it hardens into the desired shape. The forms must be properly aligned and allow for the correct dimensions, as specified in the original design. In some structures, reinforcing steel rods or mesh are set into place after the forms are put in position. The cement masons then pour or direct the pouring of the concrete into the forms so that it flows smoothly. The cement masons or their helpers spread and tamp the fresh concrete into place. Then they level the surface by moving a straightedge back and forth across the top of the forms.

Using a large wooden trowel called a bull float, cement masons begin the smoothing operation. This process covers up the larger particles in the wet concrete and brings to the surface the fine cement paste in the mixture. On projects where curved edges are desired, cement masons may use an edger or radius tool, guiding it around the edge between the form and the concrete. They may make grooves or joints at intervals in the surface to help control cracking.

The process continues with more finishing work, done either by hand with a small metal trowel or with a power trowel. This smoothing gets out most remaining irregularities on the surface. To obtain a nonslip texture on driveways, sidewalks, and similar projects, cement masons may pass a brush or broom across or embed pebbles in the surface. Afterward, the concrete must cure to reach its proper strength, a process that can take up to a week.

On structures such as walls and columns with exposed surfaces, cement masons must leave a smooth and uniform finish after the forms are removed. To achieve this, they may rub down high spots with an abrasive material, chip out rough or defective spots with a chisel and hammer, and fill low areas with cement paste. They may finish off the exposed surface with a coating of a cement mixture to create an even, attractive appearance.

Cement masons use a variety of hand and power tools, ranging from simple chisels, hammers, trowels, edgers, and leveling devices to pneumatic chisels, concrete mixers, and troweling machines. Smaller projects, such as sidewalks and patios, may be done by hand, but on large-scale projects, such as highways, power-operated

QUICK FACTS

SCHOOL SUBJECTS
Chemistry
Mathematics
Technical/shop

PERSONAL SKILLS
Mechanical/manipulative
Technical/scientific

WORK ENVIRONMENT
Primarily outdoors
Primarily multiple locations

MINIMUM EDUCATION LEVEL
Apprenticeship

MEDIAN SALARY
$32,656

CERTIFICATION OR LICENSING
None available

OUTLOOK
About as fast as the average

floats and finishing equipment are necessary. Although power equipment can speed up many tasks, most projects have corners or other inaccessible areas that require handwork.

Various cement specialists have jobs that involve covering, leveling, and smoothing cement and concrete surfaces. Among them are *concrete-stone finishers*, who work with ornamental stone and concrete surfaces; *concrete rubbers*, who polish concrete surfaces; and *nozzle cement sprayers*, who use spray equipment to apply cement mixtures to surfaces.

Poured concrete wall technicians make up another occupational group whose activities are related to those of cement masons. These workers use surveying instruments to mark construction sites for excavation and to set up and true (that is, align correctly) concrete forms. They direct the pouring of concrete to form walls of buildings, and, after removing the forms, they may waterproof lower walls and lay drainage tile to promote drainage away from the building. Unlike cement masons, however, poured concrete wall technicians generally get at least two years of technical training in such subjects as surveying and construction methods.

REQUIREMENTS
High School

As with many jobs, if you want to work as a cement mason you will have an advantage if you have graduated from high school or have a GED. Take mathematics courses, and choose shop classes like mechanical drawing and blueprint reading if your school offers these; if it does not offer these specifically, ask your teachers which classes are similar to them. It may also help you on the job if you have taken core courses like English and general science and have a driver's license.

Sometimes, a high school diploma may not be required, but you should have at least taken some kind of vocational-technical classes. If you have no special skills or experience, you might find work as a helper and gradually learn the trade informally over an unspecified number of years by working with experienced masons. In considering applicants for helper jobs, most employers prefer to hire people who are at least 18 and in good physical condition.

Postsecondary Training

It is recommended that you first work as an apprentice to acquire the necessary skills for being a cement mason because apprenticeships provide balanced, in-depth training. Such full-time programs often last two to three years, and they are usually jointly sponsored by local contractors and unions. If you want to apply for an apprenticeship program, you might need to be approved by the local joint labor-management apprenticeship committee. You also might have to take a written test and pass a physical examination.

Training consists of a combination of planned work experience and classroom instruction. On the job as an apprentice, you would learn about the tools and materials of the trade, layout work and finishing techniques, grinding and paving, and job safety. Further classroom instruction involves around 144 hours each year in such related subjects as mathematics, blueprint reading, architectural drawing, procedures for estimating materials and costs, and local building regulations.

Other Requirements

As a cement mason, you will be involved in a great amount of physical, often strenuous, work. You may be required to show your physical fitness by, for example, lifting a 100-pound sack of sand to your shoulder height and carrying it 50 feet.

You should enjoy doing demanding work and be disciplined and motivated enough to do your job without close and constant supervision. The ability to get along with co-workers is important, as most cement masons work in teams. Also, as mentioned, you should have a valid driver's license.

EXPLORING

Since this job involves using your hands to build surfaces and forms, you might like working as a cement mason if you enjoy building things like sculptures or even sandcastles at the beach. But you also have to use your head—you can learn more about your mental aptitude for this kind of work by taking courses like general mathematics, drafting, and various shop classes. In addition, try to find a summer job on a local construction crew to gain valuable firsthand experience. Some people are introduced to the building construction trades, including the work of cement masons, while they are serving in the military, especially with the U.S. Army Corps of Engineers.

Why not help build or repair a walkway where you live? Or ask your local parks department if you can help or at least watch workers making playground areas and skateboard hills. Keep your eyes open for construction work going on in your neighborhood, and ask if you can watch—maybe you'll even be given a hard hat to wear!

EMPLOYERS

Approximately 229,000 cement masons, concrete finishers, segmental pavers, and terrazzo workers are employed in the United States. Most cement masons are employed by concrete contractors or general contractors in the building and construction industries to help build roads, shopping malls, factories, and many other structures. Some cement masons work for large contractors for such big operations as utility companies and public works departments; others work for small contractors to construct buildings such as apartment complexes, shopping malls, and schools. Cement masons who are disciplined and skilled enough in the trade and in business may have the goal of one day starting their own companies, perhaps specializing in walkways, swimming pools, or building foundations.

STARTING OUT

You don't have to attend college to become a cement mason. After graduating from high school or getting a GED, you can either go through a formal apprenticeship training program or get work that offers the opportunity for on-the-job training. For information about becoming an apprentice cement mason, contact local cement contractors, the offices of your state's employment service, or the area headquarters of one of the unions that organize cement masons. Many cement masons are members of either the Operative Plasterers' and Cement Masons' International Association or the International Union of Bricklayers and Allied Craftworkers. Also, don't forget that the Internet is a valuable resource. For example, the Oregon Building Congress has a site (http://www.obcweb.com) that gives information on career descriptions and wages and applying for its apprenticeships.

If you want a job as a trainee, get in touch with contractors in your area who may be hiring helpers. Follow up on job leads from the state employment service and newspaper classified ads.

ADVANCEMENT

Once a beginning cement mason has gained some skills and become efficient in the trade, he or she can specialize in a certain phase of the work. A cement mason may become, for example, a lip-curb finisher, an expansion joint finisher, or a concrete paving-finishing machine operator.

An experienced mason—with good judgment, planning skills, and the ability to deal with people—can try advancing to a supervisory position. Supervisors with a broad understanding of other construction trades may eventually become *job superintendents*, who are in charge of the whole range of activities at the job site. A cement mason may also become an *estimator* for concrete contractors, calculating materials requirements and labor costs. A self-disciplined and highly motivated cement mason can eventually go into business on his or her own by opening a company to do small projects like sidewalks and patios.

EARNINGS

The earnings of cement masons vary widely according to factors such as geographic location, whether they do much overtime work, and how much bad weather or local economic conditions reduce the number of hours worked. Nonunion workers generally have lower wage rates than union workers. The U.S. Department of Labor reports that in 2006 cement masons earned a median wage of $15.70 per hour. A mason doing steady, full-time work at this wage would earn $32,656 annually. The department also reports that at the low end of the pay scale 10 percent of masons earned less than $10.02

per hour (or less than approximately $20,841 annually). At the high end, 10 percent earned more than $27.07 hourly (more than approximately $56,305 yearly). Since the amount of time spent working is limited by weather conditions, many workers' earnings vary from these figures. Apprentices start at wages that are approximately 50 to 60 percent of a fully qualified mason's wage. They receive periodic raises, so in the last phase of training, their wage is between 90 and 95 percent of the experienced worker's pay.

Benefits for cement masons typically include overtime pay, health insurance, and a pension plan.

WORK ENVIRONMENT

Cement masons do strenuous work, and they need to have good stamina. Many work outdoors and with other workers. Although cement masons might not work much in rainy and snowy conditions because cement cannot be poured in such weather, they might frequently work overtime because, once the cement has been poured, the finishing operations must be completed quickly. Temporary heated shelters are sometimes used to extend the time when work can be done.

Masons work in a variety of locations—sometimes on the ground, sometimes on ladders and scaffolds. Cement masons may need to lift or push weights, and they often are kneeling, bending, and stooping. To protect their knees, they routinely wear kneepads; they might also need to wear water-repellent boots and protective clothing.

Common hazards on the job include falling off ladders, being hit by falling objects, having muscle strains, and getting rough hands from contact with wet concrete. By exercising caution and following established job safety practices, masons minimize their exposure to hazardous conditions.

Although most contractors hire workers for 40-hour weeks, many jobs are limited by weather conditions. Masons sometimes have unexpected days off because of rain or snow. Then employers may expect masons to help catch up by working longer than eight hours on days when the weather permits.

OUTLOOK

According to the U.S. Department of Labor, employment for cement masons should grow about as fast as the average through 2016. The number of trained workers is relatively small, and cement masons often leave the profession for less strenuous work. In addition, construction activity is expected to expand during the next decade, and concrete will be an important building material, especially in nonresidential building and construction. Cement masons will be in demand to help build roads, bridges, buildings, subways, shopping malls, and many other structures. Although the productivity of masons will be improved by the introduction of better tools and materials (resulting in the need for fewer workers), cement masons will be needed to replace those who leave the field for retirement or other occupations.

In areas where the local economy is thriving and there are plenty of building projects, there may be occasional shortages of cement masons. At other times, even skilled masons may experience periods of unemployment because of downturns in the economy and declining levels of construction activity.

FOR MORE INFORMATION

For information on apprenticeship and training programs, contact

Associated General Contractors of America
2300 Wilson Boulevard, Suite 400
Arlington, VA 22201-5424
Tel: 703-548-3118
Email: info@agc.org
http://www.agc.org

For information on an annual masonry camp for chosen apprentices, contact

International Masonry Institute
The James Brice House
42 East Street
Annapolis, MD 21401-1731
Tel: 410-280-1305
Email: masonryquestions@imiweb.org
http://www.imiweb.org

For information on available references and publications, contact

International Union of Bricklayers and Allied Craftworkers
620 F Street, NW
Washington, DC 20004
Tel: 202-783-3788
Email: askbac@bacweb.org
http://www.bacweb.org

For information on education and research programs, careers, and apprenticeships, contact

Mason Contractors Association of America
33 South Roselle Road
Schaumburg, IL 60193-1646
Tel: 800-536-2225
http://www.masoncontractors.org

For information on apprenticeship and training programs, contact

Operative Plasterers' and Cement Masons' International Association
14405 Laurel Place, Suite 300
Laurel, MD 20707-6102
Tel: 301-470-4200
Email:opcmiaintl@opcmia.org
http://www.opcmia.org

☐ CHEMICAL TECHNICIANS

OVERVIEW

Chemical technicians assist chemists and chemical engineers in the research, development, testing, and manufacturing of chemicals and chemical-based products. Approximately 61,000 chemical technicians work in the United States.

THE JOB

Most chemical technicians who work in the chemical industry are involved in the development, testing, and manufacturing of plastics, paints, detergents, synthetic fibers, industrial chemicals, and pharmaceuticals. Others work in the petroleum, aerospace, metals, electronics, automotive, and construction industries. Some chemical technicians work in universities and government laboratories.

Technicians may work in any of the fields of chemistry, such as analytical, biochemistry, inorganic, organic, or physical chemistry. Chemical engineering, which is a combination of chemistry and engineering, develops or improves manufacturing processes for making commercial amounts of chemicals, many of which were previously produced only in small quantities in laboratory glassware or a pilot plant.

Within these subfields, chemical technicians work in research and development, design and production, and quality control. In research and development, chemical laboratory technicians often work with Ph.D. chemists and chemical engineers to set up and monitor laboratory equipment and instruments, prepare laboratory setups, and record data.

Technicians often determine the chemical composition, concentration, stability, and level of purity on a wide range of materials. These may include ores, minerals, pollutants, foods, drugs, plastics, dyes, paints, detergents, chemicals, paper, and petroleum products. Although chemists or chemical engineers may design an experiment, technicians help them create process designs, develop written procedures, or devise computer simulations. They also select all necessary glassware, reagents, chemicals, and equipment. Technicians also perform analyses and report test results.

In the design and production area, chemical technicians work closely with chemical engineers to monitor the large-scale production of compounds and to help develop and improve the processes and equipment used. They prepare tables, charts, sketches, diagrams, and flowcharts that record and summarize the collected data.

They work with pipelines, valves, pumps, and metal and glass tanks. Chemical technicians often use their input to answer manufacturing questions, such as how to transfer materials from one point to another, and to build, install, modify, and maintain processing equipment. They also train and supervise production operators. They may operate small-scale equipment for determining process parameters.

Fuel technicians determine viscosities of oils and fuels, measure flash points (the temperature at which fuels catch fire), pour points (the coldest temperature at which the fuel can flow), and the heat output of fuels.

Pilot plant operators make erosion and corrosion tests on new construction materials to determine their suitability. They prepare chemicals for field testing and report on the effectiveness of new design concepts.

Applied research technicians help design new manufacturing or research equipment.

REQUIREMENTS
High School

You should take several years of science and mathematics in high school, and computer training is also important. While a minority of employers still hire high school graduates and place them into their own training programs, the majority prefer to hire graduates of community colleges who have completed two-year chemical technician programs or even bachelor degree recipients. If you plan on attending a four-year college, take at least three years of high school mathematics, including algebra, geometry, and trigonometry; three years of physical sciences, including chemistry; and four years of English.

Postsecondary Training

Graduates of community college programs are productive much sooner than untrained individuals because

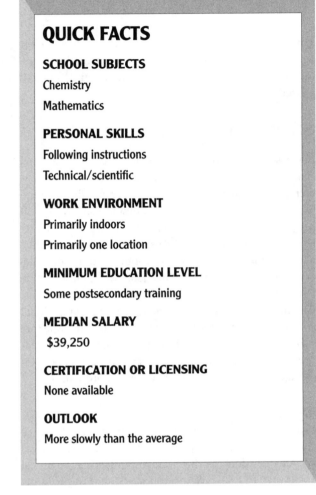

QUICK FACTS

SCHOOL SUBJECTS
Chemistry
Mathematics

PERSONAL SKILLS
Following instructions
Technical/scientific

WORK ENVIRONMENT
Primarily indoors
Primarily one location

MINIMUM EDUCATION LEVEL
Some postsecondary training

MEDIAN SALARY
$39,250

CERTIFICATION OR LICENSING
None available

OUTLOOK
More slowly than the average

they have the technical knowledge, laboratory experience, and skills for the job. Computer course work is necessary, as computers and computer-interfaced equipment are routinely used in the field. Realizing that many students become aware of technical career possibilities too late to satisfy college requirements, many community and technical colleges that offer chemical technician programs may also have noncredit courses that allow students to meet college entrance requirements.

Approximately 40 two-year colleges in the United States have chemical technology programs. Many chemical technicians also hold an associate's degree in process technology—a curriculum that usually covers aspects of chemical processing for all types of substances, from oil to water. Once enrolled in a two-year college program designed for chemical technicians, students should expect to take a number of chemistry courses with strong emphasis on laboratory work and the presentation of data. These courses include basic concepts of modern chemistry, such as atomic structure, descriptive chemistry of both organic and inorganic substances, analytical methods including quantitative and instrumental analysis, and physical properties of substances. Other courses include communications, physics, mathematics, industrial safety, and organic laboratory equipment and procedures.

Other Requirements

Besides the educational requirements, certain personal characteristics are necessary for successful chemical technicians. You must have both the ability and the desire to use mental and manual skills. You should also have a good supply of patience because experiments must frequently be repeated several times. You should be precise and like doing detailed work. Mechanical aptitude and good powers of observation are also needed. You should be able to follow directions closely and enjoy solving problems. Chemical technicians also need excellent organizational and communication skills. Other important qualities are a desire to learn new skills and a willingness to accept responsibility. In addition, you should have good eyesight, color perception, and hand-eye coordination.

EXPLORING

You can explore this field by joining high school science clubs or organizations and taking part in extracurricular activities such as the Junior Engineering Technical Society (JETS). Science contests are a good way to apply principles learned in classes to a special project. You can also subscribe to the American Chemical Society's (ACS's) *ChemMatters*, a quarterly magazine for students taking chemistry in high school. Examples of topics covered in the magazine include the chemistry of lipstick, suntan products, contact lenses, and carbon-14 dating. Also, qualifying students can participate in Project SEED (Summer Education Experience for the Disadvantaged), a program designed to provide high school students from economically disadvantaged homes with the opportunity to experience science research in a laboratory environment.

Once you are in college, you can join the student affiliates of professional associations such as the ACS and the American Institute of Chemical Engineers (AIChE). Membership allows students to experience the professionalism of a career in chemistry. You can also contact ACS or AIChE local chapters to talk with chemists and chemical engineers about what they do. These associations may also help students find summer or co-op work experiences.

EMPLOYERS

Almost all chemical laboratories, no matter their size or function, employ chemical technicians to assist their chemists or chemical engineers with research as well as routine laboratory work. Therefore, chemical technicians can find employment wherever chemistry is involved: in industrial laboratories, in government agencies such as the Department of Health and Human Services and the Department of Agriculture, and at colleges and universities. They can work in almost any field of chemical activity, such as industrial manufacturing of all kinds, pharmaceuticals, food, and production of chemicals. There are approximately 61,000 chemical technicians currently employed in the United States.

STARTING OUT

Graduates of chemical technology programs often find jobs during the last term of their two-year programs. Some companies work with local community colleges and technical schools to maintain a supply of trained chemical technicians. Recruiters regularly visit most colleges where chemical technology programs are offered. Most employers recruit locally or regionally. Because companies hire locally and work closely with technical schools, career services offices are usually successful in finding jobs for their graduates.

Some recruiters also go to four-year colleges and look for chemists with bachelor's degrees. Whether a company hires bachelor's-level chemists or two-year chemical technology graduates depends on both the outlook of the company and the local supply of graduates.

Internships and co-op work are highly regarded by employers, and participation in such programs is a good way to get your foot in the door. Many two- and four-year schools have co-op programs in which full-time students work approximately 20 hours a week for a local company. Such programs may be available to high school seniors as well. Students in these programs develop a good knowledge of the employment possibilities and frequently stay with their co-op employers.

More and more companies are using contract workers to perform technicians' jobs, and this is another way to enter the field. There are local agencies that place technicians with companies for special projects or temporary assignments that last anywhere from a month to a year or more. Many of these contract workers are later hired on a full-time basis.

ADVANCEMENT

Competent chemical technicians can expect to have long-term career paths. Top research and development positions are open to technically trained people, whether they start out with an associate's degree in chemical technology, a bachelor's degree in chemistry, or just a lot of valuable experience with no degree. There are also opportunities for advancement in the areas of technology development and technology management, providing comparable pay for these separate but equal paths. Some companies have the same career path for all technicians, regardless of education level. Other companies have different career ladders for technicians and chemists but will promote qualified technicians to chemists and move them up that path.

Some companies may require additional formal schooling for promotion, and the associate's degree can be a stepping-stone toward a bachelor's degree in chemistry. Many companies encourage their technicians to continue their education, and most reimburse tuition costs. Continuing education in the form of seminars, workshops, and in-company presentations is also important for advancement. Chemical technicians who want to advance must keep up with current developments in the field by reading trade and technical journals and publications.

EARNINGS

Earnings for chemical technicians vary based on their education, experience, employer, and location. The U.S. Department of Labor reports the median hourly wage for chemical technicians as $18.87 in 2006. A technician making this wage and working full-time would earn a yearly salary of approximately $39,250. The top 10 percent earned $28.90 per hour (or $60,112 annually) or more in 2006, while the lowest paid 10 percent earned $11.81 per hour ($24,565 annually). Salaries tend to be highest in private industry and lowest in colleges and universities.

If a technician belongs to a union, his or her wages and benefits depend on the union agreement. However, the percentage of technicians who belong to a union is very small. Benefits depend on the employer, but benefits packages usually include paid vacations and holidays, insurance, and tuition refund plans. Technicians normally work a five-day, 40-hour week. Occasional overtime may be necessary.

WORK ENVIRONMENT

The chemical industry is one of the safest industries in which to work. Laboratories and plants normally have safety committees and safety engineers who closely monitor equipment and practices to minimize hazards. Chemical technicians usually receive safety training both in school and at work to recognize potential hazards and to take appropriate measures.

Most chemical laboratories are clean and well lighted. Technicians often work at tables and benches while operating laboratory equipment and are usually provided office or desk space to record data and prepare reports. The work can sometimes be monotonous and repetitive, as when making samples or doing repetitive testing. Chemical plants are usually clean, and the number of operating personnel for the space involved is often very low.

OUTLOOK

The U.S. Department of Labor expects employment for chemical technicians to grow more slowly than the average for all occupations through 2016, as many chemical companies continue to downsize and use outside contractors for technician work. Despite this prediction, chemical technicians will be in demand as the chemical and pharmaceutical industries work to improve and produce new medicines and personal care products. Chemical technicians will also be needed by businesses that provide environmental services and "earth-friendly" products, analytical development and services, custom or niche products and services, and quality control.

Graduates of chemical technology programs will continue to face competition from bachelor's-level chemists. The chemical and chemical-related industries will continue to become increasingly sophisticated in both their products and their manufacturing techniques. Technicians trained to deal with automation and complex production methods will have the best employment opportunities.

FOR MORE INFORMATION

For general career information, as well as listings of chemical technology programs, internships, and summer job opportunities, contact

American Chemical Society
1155 16th Street, NW
Washington, DC 20036-4801
Tel: 800-227-5558
Email: help@acs.org
http://www.chemistry.org

For information on awards, student chapters, and career opportunities, contact

American Institute of Chemical Engineers
3 Park Avenue
New York, NY 10016-5991
Tel: 800-242-4363
http://www.aiche.org

For information about programs, products, and a chemical engineering career brochure, contact

Junior Engineering Technical Society
1420 King Street, Suite 405
Alexandria, VA 22314-2750
Tel: 703-548-5387
Email: info@jets.org
http://www.jets.org

CHILD CARE WORKERS

OVERVIEW

Child care workers are employed by day care centers, preschools, and other child care facilities and work with infants, toddlers, and preschool-aged children. While parents and guardians are at work, child care providers watch the children and help them develop skills through games and activities. There are approximately 1.4 million child care workers, outside of preschool teachers and teacher assistants, working in the United States.

THE JOB

Anyone who has ever baby-sat or worked with a group of kids in a summer camp knows something about the demands of child care. Professional child care workers take on the responsibility of providing quality care to young children. But the parents don't just expect these workers to simply keep an eye on the kids while they're at work—they also expect child care workers to help the children learn basic skills and to prepare them for their first years of school. Child care workers assist teachers and center directors in coming up with activities that build on children's abilities and curiosity. Child care workers must also pay attention to the individual needs of each child so that they can adapt activities to these specific needs. For example, a worker should plan activities based on the understanding that a three-year-old child has different motor skills and reasoning abilities than a child five years of age. Because child care workers care for babies, toddlers, and kids of pre-kindergarten age, these workers need to provide many different kinds of instruction. Some kids will just be learning how to tie their shoes and button their coats, while others will have begun to develop reading and computer skills. And, of course, the infants require less teaching and more individual atten-

tion from the child care workers—they ensure that the babies are fed, diapered, and held when awake.

Child care workers must call upon a background in child development to create a flexible schedule allowing time for music, art, play time, academics, rest, and other activities. Depending on the size and structure of the center, workers may be assigned to deal with a particular age group, or they may work with many age groups. Liz Rahl, who holds a bachelor's degree in human development, works as an assistant director for the Discovery Academy, a child care center in Omaha, Nebraska. Her mornings begin with caring for the infants—feeding and diapering them. "My job is to provide comfort," she says. "And hopefully some stimulus." She then works with the preschoolers for most of the morning, returning to the infant room to feed them lunch and put them down for their naps, before returning to the preschoolers to assist them with their lunch. When working with the preschoolers, Rahl helps them to develop skills for kindergarten. "They need to know their numbers, one through 15, and to have alphabet recognition. They need to know how to spell their names and to know their addresses and phone numbers. And their social skills have to be on track for kindergarten. They need to know to share and to take turns and to not talk back." Rahl also works with the children on rhyming and other word skills. "And they need to understand pattern schemes, such as triangle, circle, triangle. Or red, red, blue." To help direct the children, the center organizes a different "theme" every few weeks. The theme may center around a holiday or a season, or a specific letter or number that the children should learn. A nursery rhyme or fairy tale may also be part of the theme.

Workers at a child care center have many responsibilities in addition to giving lessons and instruction. Anyone who has worked with children at all knows they need a lot of assistance in a variety of ways. A major portion of a child care worker's day is spent helping children adjust to being away from home and encouraging them to play together. Children who become frightened or homesick need gentle reassurance. Child care workers often help kids with their coats and boots in the winter and also deal with the sniffles, colds, and generally cranky behavior that can occur in young children. These workers supervise snack time, teaching children how to eat properly and clean up after themselves.

Child care workers also work with the parents of each child. It is not unusual for parents to come to a center and observe a child or go on a field trip with the class, and child care workers often take these opportunities to discuss the progress of each child as well as any specific problems or concerns. Rahl makes sure the parents of the children she cares for are aware of the child's progress. "I send home sheets," she says, "listing any problems along with the good things the kids are doing."

REQUIREMENTS

High School

You should take courses in early childhood development when available. Many home economics courses include units in parenting and child care. English courses will help you to develop communication skills important in dealing with children and their parents. In teaching children, you should be able to draw from a wide base of education and interests, so take courses in art, music, science, and physical education.

Postsecondary Training

A high school diploma and some child care experience is usually all that's required to get a job as a child care worker, but requirements vary among employers. Some employers prefer to hire workers who have taken college courses or hold bachelor's degrees; they may also pay better wages to those with some college education. A college program should include course work in a variety of liberal arts subjects, including English, history, and science, as well as nutrition, child development, psychology of the young child, and sociology. Some employers also offer on-the-job training.

Certification or Licensing

Requirements for child care workers vary from state to state. Each state sets its own licensing requirements for child care workers. Some states require that you complete a certain number of continuing education hours every year; these hours may include college courses or research into the subject of child care. CPR training is also often required. National certification isn't required of child care workers, but some organizations do offer it. The Council for Professional Recognition offers the Child Development Associate (CDA) National Credentialing Program. To complete the program and receive the CDA credential, you must do a certain amount of field and course work, and pass a final evaluation. According to the council, there are now more than 200,000 CDAs in the United States and its territories. The National Child Care Association offers the certified childcare professional (CCP) credential. To receive this credential, you must have extensive child care experience, along with special training.

QUICK FACTS

SCHOOL SUBJECTS
Art
Family and consumer science

PERSONAL SKILLS
Communication/ideas
Helping/teaching

WORK ENVIRONMENT
Primarily indoors
Primarily one location

MINIMUM EDUCATION LEVEL
High school diploma

MEDIAN SALARY
$17,630

CERTIFICATION OR LICENSING
Recommended (certification)
Required by certain states (licensing)

OUTLOOK
Faster than the average

Other Requirements

To be a successful child care worker, you should have love and respect for children and a genuine interest in their well-being. You'll also need a great deal of patience and the ability to understand the needs of preschool-aged children in all stages of development. "You need to be able to be on the child's level," Liz Rahl says. "You need to be able to talk directly to them, not down to them." She also emphasizes the importance of a sense of humor. "You need to be laid back, but you can't let them run all over you."

EXPLORING

Talk to neighbors, relatives, and others with small children about baby-sitting some evenings and weekends. Preschools, day care centers, and other child care programs often hire high school students for part-time positions as aides. There are also many volunteer opportunities for working with kids—check with your library or local literacy program about tutoring children and reading to preschoolers. Summer day camps, Bible schools, children's theaters, museums, and other organizations with children's programs also hire high school students as assistants or have need of volunteers.

EMPLOYERS

Both the government and the private sector are working to provide for the enormous need for quality child care. Child care workers should find many job opportunities in private and public preschools, day care centers, government-funded learning programs, religious centers, and Montessori schools. Work is available in small centers or at large centers with many children. Franchisers, like Primrose School Franchising Company and Kids 'R' Kids International, are also providing more employment opportunities. Approximately 1.4 million child care workers are employed in the United; 35 percent of these workers are self-employed.

STARTING OUT

At your first opportunity, you should take part-time work at a child care center to gain firsthand experience. Contact child care centers, nursery schools, Head Start programs, and other preschool facilities to identify job opportunities. The Child Care Bureau estimates that one-third of all child care teachers leave their centers each year: Check the classified section of local newspapers, and you are likely to see many job openings for child care workers. Liz Rahl advises that you get a degree in early child development, so you can advance into a director position if you choose. "And be careful when you choose a child care center," she says. "Make sure you're comfortable with their policies and approaches to child care."

ADVANCEMENT

As child care workers gain experience, they receive salary increases and promotions to such positions as assistant director or preschool teacher. With additional experience and education, they may be able to advance into an administrative position, such as director of a center. Some experienced child care workers with advanced degrees become directors of Head Start programs and other government programs. If a child care worker has a head for business, he or she may choose to open a child care facility. Some child care workers also decide to pursue a degree in education and become certified to teach kindergarten or elementary school.

EARNINGS

Earnings for child care workers depend on their education level, the type of employer, the number of children being cared for, and other such variables. According to the U.S. Department of Labor, the median annual earnings for child care workers in 2006 were $17,630 for full-time work. The lowest paid 10 percent of child care workers made $12,910 or less, while the highest paid 10 percent made more than $27,050. Few child care workers receive full benefits from their employers. Some large day care centers and preschools, however, do offer limited health care coverage and vacation pay.

WORK ENVIRONMENT

Child care workers spend much of their workday on their feet in a classroom or on a playground. Facilities vary from a single room to large buildings. Class sizes also vary; some child care centers serve only a handful of children, while others serve several hundred. Classrooms may be crowded and noisy, but those who love children enjoy all the activity.

Part-time employees generally work between 18 and 30 hours a week, while full-time employees work 35 to 40 hours a week. Part-time work gives the employee flexibility, and for many, this is one of the advantages of the job. "It's a great starter job," Liz Rahl says. The job also allows workers to play with the children and to direct them in games and other activities. "Most adults don't get to have fun at work," she says. She also enjoys watching the children go through all the different stages of development, from infant to preschooler. "It's very rewarding when a preschooler comes in unable to even write a letter," she says, "then soon they're writing their names." Among the children she cares for is her daughter Christa. "The job allows me to be with my child," she says, "so I know what her day's like."

OUTLOOK

Employment for child care workers is projected to increase faster than the average for all occupations through 2016, according to the U.S. Department of Labor. The department predicts that there will be 248,000 new jobs available for child care workers over the next decade, which should lead to healthy employment prospects for those interested in this field. The proportion of children being cared for exclusively by parents or relatives will continue to decline in coming years, which will create a demand for child care workers. In addition, there is high turnover in this field, resulting in the need for many replacement workers. One reason for this turnover rate is the low pay; in order to keep quality employees, center owners may have to charge clients more so that they may better compensate staff members. Jobs will also be available as more child care centers, both nonprofit and for-profit, open to meet the increased demand for child care as more mothers take jobs outside the home. There will be more franchises and national chains offering job opportunities to child care workers, as well as centers that cater exclusively to corporate employees. Child care workers may be working with older children, as more day care centers expand to include elementary school services. Bilingual child care workers will find more job opportunities and better salaries.

FOR MORE INFORMATION

For information about certification, contact

Council for Professional Recognition
2460 16th Street, NW
Washington, DC 20009-3575
Tel: 800-424-4310
http://www.cdacouncil.org

For information about student memberships and training opportunities, contact

National Association of Child Care Professionals
PO Box 90723
Austin, TX 78709-0723
Tel: 800-537-1118
Email: admin@naccp.org
http://www.naccp.org

For information about certification and to learn about the issues affecting child care, visit the NCCA Web site, or contact

National Child Care Association (NCCA)
2025 M Street, NW, Suite 800
Washington, DC 20036-3309
Tel: 800-543-7161
Email: info@nccanet.org
http://www.nccanet.org

❑ COLLECTION WORKERS

OVERVIEW

Collection workers—sometimes known as *bill collectors, collection correspondents,* or *collection agents*—are employed to persuade people to pay their overdue bills.

Some work for collection agencies (which are hired by the business to which the money is owed), while others work for department stores, hospitals, banks, public utilities, and other businesses. Collection workers contact delinquent debtors, inform them of the delinquency, and either secure payment or arrange a new payment schedule. If all else fails, they might be forced to repossess property or turn the account over to an attorney for legal proceedings. There are approximately 434,000 collection workers employed in the United States.

THE JOB

A collection worker's main job is to persuade people to pay bills that are past due. The procedure is generally the same in both collection firms and businesses that employ collection workers. The duties of the various workers may overlap, depending on the size and nature of the company.

When routine billing methods—monthly statements and notice letters—fail to secure payment, the collection worker receives a bad-debt file. This file contains information about the debtor, the nature and amount of the unpaid bill, the last charge incurred, and the date of the last payment. The collection worker then contacts the debtor by phone or mail to request full or partial payment or, if necessary, to arrange a new payment schedule.

Terrence Sheffert is a collection worker for a collection agency based in Chicago. He describes his typical duties as making phone calls and writing letters. "I am usually in the office, on the phone with clients or the people who owe them," he says. "I never actually go out to make collections, but there are some agents who do."

If the bill has not been paid because the customer believes it is incorrect, the merchandise purchased was faulty, or the service billed for was not performed, the collector takes appropriate steps to settle the matter. If, after investigation, the debt collector finds that the debt is still valid, he or she again tries to secure payment.

In cases where the customer has not paid because of a financial emergency or poor money management, the debt collector may arrange a new payment schedule. In instances where the customer goes to great or fraudulent lengths to avoid payment, the collector may recommend that the file be turned over to an attorney. "Every day, we are protecting the clients' interests and getting the money," Sheffert says. "If we can't get it, then we'll call in legal representation to handle it."

When all efforts to obtain payment fail, a collection worker known as a *repossessor* may be assigned to find the merchandise on which the debtor still owes money and return it to the seller. Such goods as furniture or appliances can be picked up in a truck. To reclaim automobiles and other motor vehicles, the repossessor might be forced to enter and start the vehicle with special tools if the buyer does not surrender the key.

In large agencies, some collection workers specialize as *skip tracers*. Skip tracers are assigned to find debtors who "skip" out on their debts—that is, who move without notifying their creditors so that they don't have to pay their bills. Skip tracers act like detectives, searching telephone directories and street listings and making inquiries at post offices in an effort to locate missing debtors. Increasingly such information can be found through online computer databases (some agencies subscribe to a service to collect this information). Skip tracers also try to find out information about a person's whereabouts by contacting former neighbors and employers, local merchants, friends, relatives, and references listed on the original credit application. They follow every lead and prepare a report of the entire investigation.

In some small offices, collection workers perform clerical duties, such as reading and answering correspondence, filing, or posting amounts paid to people's accounts. They might offer financial advice to customers or contact them to inquire about their satisfaction with the handling of the account. In larger companies *credit and loan collection supervisors* might oversee the activities of several other collection workers.

REQUIREMENTS

High School

Most employers prefer to hire high school graduates for collection jobs, but formal education beyond high school is typically not required. High school courses that might prove helpful in this career include those that will help you communicate clearly and properly, such as English and speech. Because collection workers have to talk with people about a very delicate subject, psychology classes might also be beneficial. Finally, computer classes are good choices, since this career, like most others, often requires at least some familiarity with keyboarding and basic computer operation.

Postsecondary Training

Most collection workers learn collection procedures and telephone techniques on the job in a training period spent under the guidance of a supervisor or an experienced collector. The legal restrictions on collection activities, such as when and how calls can be made, are also covered.

Certification or Licensing

Although it is not required by law, some employers require their employees to become certified by the Association of Credit and Collection Professionals, which offers several certifications, including professional collection specialist, creditor collection specialist, healthcare collection specialist, and higher education collection specialist. To learn more, visit http://www.acainternational.org.

Other Requirements

Because this is a people-oriented job, you must have a pleasant manner and voice. You may spend much of your time on the telephone speaking with people about overdue payments, which can be a delicate subject. To succeed as a collector, you must be sympathetic and tactful, yet assertive and persuasive enough to convince debtors to pay their overdue bills. In addition, collectors must be alert, quick-witted, and imaginative to handle the unpredictable and potentially awkward situations that are encountered in this type of work.

Collection work can be emotionally taxing. It involves listening to a bill payer's problems and occasional verbal attacks directed at both the collector and the company. Some people physically threaten repossessors and other collection workers. "The best description of this job would be stressful," Terrence Sheffert says. "Everything about collecting is very stressful." In the face of these stresses, you must be able to avoid becoming upset, personally involved with, or alarmed by angry or threatening debtors. This requires a cool head and an even temperament.

EXPLORING

The best way to explore collection work is to secure parttime or summer employment in a collection agency or credit office. You might also find it helpful to interview a collection worker to obtain firsthand information about the practical aspects of this occupation. Finally, the associations listed at the end of this article may be able to provide further information about the career.

EMPLOYERS

Of the approximately 434,000 collection workers in the United States, approximately 24 percent work for collection agencies. Collection agencies are usually independent companies that are hired by various businesses to collect debt that is owed them. Other bill collectors work for a wide range of organizations and businesses that extend credit to customers. Department stores, hospitals, banks, public utilities, and auto financing companies are examples of businesses that frequently hire bill collectors.

The companies that hire collection workers are located throughout the United States, especially in heavily populated urban areas. Companies that have branch offices in rural communities often locate their collection departments in nearby cities.

STARTING OUT

Terrence Sheffert got started in collection work because it was a family profession. "My whole family is in collecting, so I thought, 'Hey, I'll go for it.'" If you are interested in becoming a collection worker, one easy way to start a job search is to apply directly to collection agencies, credit reporting companies, banks, and major retailers that sell large items. To find collection agencies and credit reporting companies, try doing a simple keyword search on the Internet. Another easy way is to look in your local Yellow Pages—or expand your search by going to the library and looking through Yellow Pages of other cities.

Remember that these sorts of jobs are often more plentiful in more urban areas.

You should also check the classified ads of area newspapers for headings such as "Billing" or "Collection." Finally, job openings may be listed at your local employment office.

ADVANCEMENT

Experienced collection workers who have proven to have above-average ability can advance to management positions, such as supervisors or *collection managers*. These workers generally have responsibility for the operations of a specific shift, location, or department of a collection company. They oversee other collection workers. Other avenues of advancement might include becoming a *credit authorizer*, *credit checker*, or *bank loan officer*. Credit authorizers approve questionable charges against customers' existing accounts by evaluating the customers' computerized credit records and payment histories. Credit checkers in credit bureaus—sometimes also called credit investigators or credit reporters—search for, update, and verify information for credit reports. Loan officers help borrowers fill out loan applications, verify and analyze applications, and decide whether and how much to loan applicants. Some experienced and successful collections workers might open their own agencies. This is Terrence Sheffert's goal. "I hope to advance from collection to management, and then open up my own business," he says.

EARNINGS

Collection workers might receive a salary plus a bonus or commission on the debt amounts they collect. Others work for a flat salary with no commissions. Since the pay system varies among different companies, incomes vary substantially. In 2006, the median hourly wage for bill collectors working full-time was $13.97, according to the U.S. Department of Labor. This hourly wage translates into a yearly income of approximately $29,057. Earnings for collection workers range from less than $19,988 to a high of more than $43,930 annually.

Depending on their employer, some full-time bill collectors receive a benefits package that may include paid holidays and vacations, sick leave, and health and dental insurance.

WORK ENVIRONMENT

Most collectors work in pleasant offices, sit at a desk, and spend a great deal of time on the telephone. Because they spend so much time on the phone, many collectors use phone headsets and program-operated dialing systems. Because most companies use computers to store information about their accounts, the collection worker frequently works on a computer. He or she may sit in front of a computer terminal, reviewing and entering information about the account while talking to the debtor on the phone.

Rarely does a collector have to make a personal visit to a customer. Repossession proceedings are undertaken only in extreme cases.

Terrence Sheffert works a 40-hour week, from 9:00 A.M. to 5:00 P.M., Monday through Friday. Some collection workers stagger their schedules, however. They might start late in the morning and work into the evening, or they might take a weekday off and work on Saturday. Evening and weekend work is common, because debtors are often home during these times.

OUTLOOK

Employment for bill collectors is predicted by the U.S. Department of Labor to grow much faster than the average through 2016. Demand for cash flow is causing businesses to hire more and more debt collectors. Also, America's debt is growing. Due to the relaxed standards for credit cards, which means more people, regardless of their financial circumstances, are able to get credit cards, make purchases on credit, and build up large debts they have difficulty repaying. The Department of Labor also notes that hospitals and physicians' offices are two of the fastest growing employers of bill collectors and collection agencies. This is largely because health insurance plans frequently do not adequately cover payment for medical procedures, and patients are often left with large bills that they have difficulty repaying. Economic recessions also increase the amount of personal debt that goes unpaid. Therefore, unlike many occupations, collection workers usually find that their employment and workloads increase during economic slumps.

FOR MORE INFORMATION

For information on collection work and certification, contact

Association of Credit and Collection Professionals
PO Box 390106
Minneapolis, MN 55439-0106
Tel: 952-926-6547
http://www.acainternational.org

For information on careers and certification, contact the NACM.

National Association of Credit Management (NACM)
8840 Columbia 100 Parkway
Columbia, MD 21045-2158
Tel: 410-740-5560
http://www.nacm.org

COMPUTER-AIDED DESIGN DRAFTERS AND TECHNICIANS

OVERVIEW

Computer-aided design (CAD) drafters and technicians, sometimes called *CAD technicians* or *CAD designers,* use computer-based systems to produce or revise technical illustrations needed in the design and development of machines, products, buildings, manufacturing processes, and other work. They use CAD machinery to manipulate and create design concepts so that they are feasible to produce and use in the real world. There are approximately 253,000 drafters of all kinds working in the United States.

THE JOB

Technicians specializing in CAD technology usually work in the design and drafting activities associated with new product research and development, although many work in other areas such as structural mechanics or piping. CAD technicians must combine drafting and computer skills. They work in any field where detailed drawings, diagrams, and layouts are important aspects of developing new product designs—for example, in architecture, electronics, and in the manufacturing of automobiles, aircraft, computers, and missiles and other defense systems. Most CAD technicians specialize in a particular industry or on one part of a design.

CAD technicians work under the direction and supervision of *CAD engineers and designers,* experts highly trained in applying computer technology to industrial design and manufacturing. These designers and engineers plan how to relate the CAD technology and equipment to the design process. They are also the ones who give assignments to the CAD technicians.

Jackie Sutherland started as a drafter right out of high school, working at a major Midwestern diesel engine manufacturer. Since then, he has moved into a designer's role. In his 25 years on the job, he has seen the transfer from drafting table to CAD workstation.

"I work with everyone from the customer to the engineers, suppliers, pattern makers, and the assembly line from the project concept through the production," says Sutherland of his work as a CAD designer.

Technicians work at specially designed and equipped interactive computer graphics workstations. They call up computer files that hold data about a new product; they then run the programs to convert that information into diagrams and drawings of the product. These are displayed on a video display screen, which then acts as an electronic drawing board. Following the directions of a CAD engineer or designer, the CAD technician enters changes to the product's design into the computer. The technician merges these changes into the data file, and then displays the corrected diagrams and drawings.

The software in CAD systems is very helpful to the user—it offers suggestions and advice and even points out errors. The most important advantage of working with a CAD system is that it saves the technician from the lengthy process of having to produce, by hand, the original and then the revised product drawings and diagrams.

The CAD workstation is equipped to allow technicians to perform calculations, develop simulations, and manipulate and modify the displayed material. Using typed commands at a keyboard, a stylus or light pen for touching the screen display, a mouse, joystick, or other electronic methods of interacting with the display, technicians can move, rotate, or zoom in on any aspect of the drawing on the screen, and project three-dimensional images from two-dimensional sketches. They can make experimental changes to the design and then run tests on the modified design to determine its qualities, such as weight, strength, flexibility, and the cost of materials that would be required. Compared to traditional drafting and design techniques, CAD offers virtually unlimited freedom to explore alternatives, and in far less time.

When the product design is completed and the necessary information is assembled in the computer files, technicians may store the newly developed data, output it on a printer, transfer it to another computer, or send it directly to another step of the automated testing or manufacturing process.

Once the design is approved for production, CAD technicians may use their computers to assist in making detailed drawings of certain parts of the design. They may also prepare designs and drawings of the tools or equipment, such as molds, cutting tools, and jigs, that must be specially made in order to manufacture the product. As the product moves toward production, technicians, drafters, and designers may work closely with those assembling the product to ensure the same quality found with prototype testing.

CAD technicians must keep records of all of their test procedures and results. They may need to present written reports, tables, or charts to document their test results

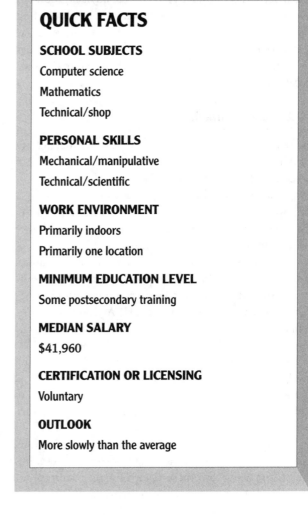

QUICK FACTS

SCHOOL SUBJECTS
Computer science
Mathematics
Technical/shop

PERSONAL SKILLS
Mechanical/manipulative
Technical/scientific

WORK ENVIRONMENT
Primarily indoors
Primarily one location

MINIMUM EDUCATION LEVEL
Some postsecondary training

MEDIAN SALARY
$41,960

CERTIFICATION OR LICENSING
Voluntary

OUTLOOK
More slowly than the average

or other findings. If a particular system, subsystem, or material has not met a testing or production requirement, technicians may be asked to suggest a way to rearrange the system's components or substitute alternate materials.

The company Sutherland works for also uses interoffice and Internet email to communicate with coworkers and the outside world. "I can attach text, a spreadsheet, or a complete three-dimensional CAD model to a message and send it out to several people through a distribution list. It really shortens the cycle of time on a project," he says.

REQUIREMENTS
High School

CAD technicians must be able to read and understand complex engineering diagrams and drawings. The minimum educational requirement for CAD technicians is a high school diploma. If you are a high school student, take courses that provide you with a solid background in algebra, geometry, trigonometry, physics, machine-shop skills, drafting, and electronics, and take whatever computer courses are available. You should also take courses in English, especially those that improve your communication skills.

Postsecondary Training

Increasingly, most prospective CAD technicians are undertaking formal training beyond the high school level, either through a two-year associate's degree program taught at a technical school or community college, or through a four-year college or university program. Employers prefer job applicants who have some form of postsecondary training in drafting.

Such a program should include courses in these areas: basic drafting, machine drawing, architecture, civil drafting (with an emphasis on highways), process piping, electrical, electrical instrumentation, HVAC, and plumbing. There should also be courses in data processing; computer programming, systems, and equipment, especially video display equipment; computer graphics; product design; and computer peripheral equipment and data storage. Some two-year programs may also require you to complete courses in technical writing, communications, social sciences, and the humanities.

In addition, some companies have their own training programs, which can last as long as two years. Requirements for entry into these company-run training programs vary from company to company.

If you are considering a career in CAD technology, it is important to remember that you will be required to take continuing education courses even after you have found a job. This continuing education is necessary because technicians need to know about recent advances in technology that may affect procedures, equipment, terminology, or programming concepts.

"Technology changes so fast in this area," says Jackie Sutherland of his many years in the drafting and designing field.

Certification or Licensing

Certification for CAD technicians is voluntary. Certification in drafting is available from the American Design Drafting Association. The test, called the Drafter Certification Examination, covers basic drafting skills but does not include testing of CAD drafting. Applicants are tested on geometric construction, architectural terms and regulations, and working sketches.

Licensing requirements vary. Licensing may be required for specific projects, such as a construction project, when the client requires it.

Other Requirements

As a CAD technician or drafter, you will need to think logically, have good analytical skills, and be methodical, accurate, and detail-oriented in all your work. You should be able to work as part of a team, as well as independently, since you will spend long periods of time in front of video display screens. Having some artistic skill, particularly in drawing, is also helpful.

"You have to be able to visualize what a part may look like or what a new version of a part may look like," says Sutherland. "You have to have basic common sense but also be able to look into the future."

EXPLORING

There are a number of ways to gain firsthand knowledge about the field of CAD technology. Unfortunately, part-time or summer jobs involved directly with CAD technology are very hard to find; however, drafting-related jobs can sometimes be found, and many future employers will look favorably on applicants with this kind of experience. In addition, jobs related to other engineering fields, such as electronics or mechanics, may be available and can offer you an opportunity to become familiar with the kind of workplace in which technicians may later be employed.

In addition, high school courses in computers, geometry, physics, mechanical drawing, and shop work will give you a feel for the mental and physical activities associated with CAD technology. Other relevant activities include membership in high school science clubs (especially computer and electronics clubs); participating in science fairs; pursuing hobbies that involve computers, electronics, drafting, mechanical equipment, and model building; and reading books and articles about technical topics.

EMPLOYERS

CAD drafters and technicians are employed in a wide variety of industries, including engineering, architecture, manufacturing, construction, communication, utilities, and the government. They are employed by both large and small companies throughout the United States. For some specialties, jobs may be more specific to certain locations. For example, a drafter or designer for the software industry will find the most opportunities in California's Silicon Valley, while an automotive specialist may be more successful finding jobs near Detroit, Michigan.

STARTING OUT

Probably the most reliable method for entering this field is through your school's career services office. This is especially true for students who graduate from a two-year college or technical institute; recruiters from companies employing CAD technicians sometimes visit such schools, and career services office personnel can help students meet with these recruiters.

As a graduate of a postsecondary program, you can conduct your own job search by contacting architects, building firms, manufacturers, high technology companies, and government agencies. You can contact prospective employers by phone, email, or with a letter stating your interest in employment, accompanied by a resume that provides details about your education and job experience. State or private employment agencies may also be helpful, and classified ads in newspapers, professional journals, and at association Web sites may provide additional leads.

ADVANCEMENT

CAD technicians who demonstrate their ability to handle more responsibility can expect to receive promotions after just a few years on the job. They may be assigned to design work that requires their special skills or experience, such as troubleshooting problems with systems they have worked with, or they may be promoted to supervisory or training positions. As trainers, they may teach courses at their workplace or at a local school or community college.

In general, as CAD technicians advance, their assignments become less and less routine, until they may have a hand in designing and building equipment. Technicians who continue their education and earn a bachelor's degree may become data processing managers, engineers, or systems analysts or manufacturing analysts.

Other routes for advancement include becoming a sales representative for a design firm or for a company selling computer-aided design services or equipment. It may also be possible to become an independent contractor for companies using or manufacturing CAD equipment.

EARNINGS

Earnings vary among drafters based on the industry they work in as well as their level of experience and the size of their employer. The U.S. Department of Labor reports the median wage for civil and architectural drafters was $41,960 in 2006. The lowest paid 10 percent of these drafters made less than $27,010 annually; the highest paid

10 percent made more than $63,310 annually. Electrical and electronics drafters had somewhat higher earnings, with an average annual wage of $46,830 in 2006. The lowest paid 10 percent of these drafters earned less than $29,290 per year, and the highest paid 10 percent made more than $74,490 yearly.

Actual salaries vary widely depending on geographic location, exact job requirements, and the training needed to obtain those jobs. With increased training and experience, technicians can earn higher salaries, and some technicians with special skills, extensive experience, or added responsibilities may earn more.

Benefits usually include insurance, paid vacations and holidays, pension plans, and sometimes stock-purchase plans.

WORK ENVIRONMENT

CAD professionals almost always work in clean, quiet, well-lighted, air-conditioned offices. CAD technicians spend most of their days at a workstation. While the work does not require great physical effort, it does require patience and the ability to maintain concentration and attention for extended periods of time. Some technicians may find they suffer from eyestrain from working for long periods in front of a computer monitor.

CAD technicians, because of their training and experience, are valuable employees. They are called upon to exercise independent judgment and to be responsible for valuable equipment. Out of necessity, they also sometimes find themselves carrying out routine, uncomplicated tasks. CAD technicians must be able to respond well to both kinds of demands. Most CAD technicians work as part of a team. They are required to follow orders, and may encounter situations in which their individual contributions are not fully recognized. Successful CAD technicians are those who work well as team members and who can derive satisfaction from the accomplishments of the team as a whole.

OUTLOOK

The U.S. Department of Labor predicts that the employment outlook for drafters will grow more slowly than average through 2016. The best opportunities will be available to those who have skill and experience using CAD systems. Many companies in the near future will feel pressures to increase productivity in design and manufacturing activities, and CAD technology provides some of the best opportunities to improve that productivity.

Another factor that will create a demand for CAD drafters and technicians is the continued focus on safety and quality throughout manufacturing and industrial fields. In order to do business or continue to do business with leading manufacturers, companies and lower-tier suppliers must meet stringent quality guidelines. With this focus on quality as well as safety, companies are scrutinizing their current designs more carefully than ever, requiring more CAD work for new concepts and alterations that will create a better product.

Any economic downturn could adversely affect CAD technicians because many of the industries that they serve—such as auto manufacturing or construction—fluctuate greatly with economic swings. In any event, the best opportunities will be for drafters and technicians proficient in CAD technology who continue to learn, both in school and on the job.

Increasing productivity in the industrial design and manufacturing fields will ensure the long-term economic vitality of our nation; CAD technology is one of the most promising developments in this search for increased productivity. Knowing that they are in the forefront of this important and challenging undertaking provides CAD technicians and drafters with a good deal of pride and satisfaction.

FOR MORE INFORMATION

For information about certification, student drafting contests, and job postings, contact

American Design Drafting Association
105 East Main Street
Newbern, TN 38059-1526
Tel: 731-627-0802
Email: corporate@adda.org
http://www.adda.org

For information about the electrical field or to find the IEEE-USA student branch nearest you, contact

**Institute of Electrical and Electronics Engineers, Inc.
  (IEEE-USA)**
1828 L Street, NW, Suite 1202
Washington, DC 20036-5104
Tel: 202-785-0017
Email: ieeeusa@ieee.org
http://www.ieeeusa.org

For information about scholarships, grants, and student memberships, contact

Society of Manufacturing Engineers
One SME Drive, PO Box 930
Dearborn, MI 48121-0930
Tel: 800-733-4763
http://www.sme.org

☐ COMPUTER AND OFFICE MACHINE SERVICE TECHNICIANS

OVERVIEW

Computer and office machine service technicians install, calibrate, maintain, troubleshoot, and repair equipment such as computers and their peripherals, office equipment, and specialized electronic equipment used in many factories, hospitals, airplanes, and numerous other businesses. There are approximately 175,000 computer and office machine service technicians working in the United States.

THE JOB

Computer and office machine repairers install, fix, and maintain many of the machines used by businesses and households. Some of these workers, called *field technicians,* may travel to work sites as part of a routine service contract or in the event of emergencies. *Bench technicians* work in repair shops located in stores, factories, or service centers. In small companies, repairers may work both in repair shops and at customer locations.

Computer repairers, also known as *computer service technicians* or *data processing equipment repairers,* service mainframe, server, and personal computers; printers; and auxiliary computer equipment. These workers primarily perform hands-on repair, maintenance, and installation of computers and related equipment. In computer subsystem repair, replacement of computer subsystems and components is often more common than repair. Subsystems commonly replaced by computer repairers include video cards, hard drives, and network cards. Defective modules may be given to bench technicians, who use software programs to diagnose the problem and who may repair the modules, if possible.

Office machine and cash register servicers work on photocopiers, cash registers, mail-processing equipment, and fax machines. Common malfunctions in these machines usually can be resolved by cleaning the relevant components. Breakdowns also may result from the failure of commonly used parts. For example, heavy use of a photocopier may wear down the printhead, which applies ink to the final copy. In such cases, the repairer usually replaces the part instead of repairing it.

Computer and office machine repairers use a variety of tools for diagnostic tests and repair. To diagnose malfunctions, they use multimeters to measure voltage, current, resistance, and other electrical properties; signal generators to provide test signals; and oscilloscopes to monitor equipment signals. To diagnose computerized equipment, repairers use software programs. To repair or adjust equipment, workers use hand tools, such as pliers, screwdrivers, soldering irons, and wrenches.

L-3 Communications manufactures computer systems for a diverse group of clients such as Shell Oil, United Airlines, and the Chicago Board of Trade. Besides computer systems, they also offer services such as equipment maintenance contracts and customer training. Joey Arca, a service technician for L-3 Communications, loves the challenge and diversity of his job. He and other members of the staff are responsible for the installation of computer mainframes and systems, as well as training employees on the equipment. A large part of their work is the maintenance, diagnosis, and repair of computer equipment. Since the clients are located throughout the United States, Arca must often travel to different cities in his assigned district. He also presents company products and services to potential clients and bids for maintenance contracts.

"I don't always have to be at the office, which gives me a lot of freedom," says Arca. "Sometimes I call in from my home and get my scheduled appointments for the day." The freedom of not being deskbound does have its downfalls. "One of the most difficult parts of the job is not knowing when a computer will fail. I carry a pager 24/7, and if I get called, I'm bound to a two-hour response time."

Many times work is scheduled before or after regular working hours or on the weekend, because it's important to have the least amount of workday disruption. Arca is successful in his job because he keeps on top of technology that is constantly changing with continuing education classes and training seminars. He is also well versed in both hardware and software, especially system software.

REQUIREMENTS
High School

Traditional high school courses such as mathematics, physical sciences, and other laboratory-based sciences can provide a strong foundation for understanding basic mechanical and electronics principles. English and speech classes can help boost your written and verbal communications skills. Shop classes dealing with electricity, electronics, and blueprint reading are also beneficial.

QUICK FACTS

SCHOOL SUBJECTS
Computer science
Technical/shop

PERSONAL SKILLS
Mechanical/manipulative
Technical/scientific

WORK ENVIRONMENT
Primarily indoors
Primarily multiple locations

MINIMUM EDUCATION LEVEL
Associate's degree

MEDIAN SALARY
$36,483

CERTIFICATION OR LICENSING
Recommended

OUTLOOK
More slowly than the average

Postsecondary Training

You may be able to find work with a high school diploma if you have a lot of practical, hands-on experience in the field. Usually, however, employers require job applicants to have at least an associate's degree in electronics. Joey Arca holds a bachelor of science degree in electrical engineering. He credits specialized classes such as voice and data communications, microprocessor controls, and digital circuits as giving him a good base for his current work environment.

Certification or Licensing

Most employers require certification, though standards vary depending on the company. However many consider certification as a measure of industry knowledge. Certification can also give you a competitive edge when interviewing for a new job or negotiating for a higher salary.

A variety of certification programs are available from the International Society of Certified Electronics Technicians, the Institute for Certification of Computing Professionals, the Computing Technology Industry Association, and Electronics Technicians Association International, among other organizations. After the successful completion of study and examination, you may be certified in fields such as computer, industrial, and electronic equipment. Continuing education credits are required for recertification, usually every two to four years. Arca is certified as a computer technician from the Association of Energy Engineers and the Electronics Technicians Association International.

Other Requirements

A strong technical background and an aptitude for learning about new technologies, good communications skills, and superior manual dexterity will help you succeed in this industry. You'll also need to be motivated to keep up with modern computer and office machine technology. Machines rapidly become obsolete, and so does the service technician's training. When new equipment is installed, service technicians must demonstrate the intellectual agility to learn how to handle problems that might arise.

When asked what kind of people are best suited for this line of work, Arca replies, "task oriented, quantitatively smart, organized, and personable. Also, they need the ability to convey technical terms in writing and orally."

EMPLOYERS

Approximately 175,000 computer and office machine service technicians, including those who work on automated teller machines, are employed in the United States. Potential employers include computer companies and large corporations that need a staff devoted to repairing and maintaining their equipment; electronics, appliance, and office supply stores; electronic and precision equipment repair shops; computer systems design firms; government agencies, and Internet service providers. Many service technicians are employed by companies that contract their services to other businesses. Though work opportunities for service technicians are available nationwide, many jobs are located in large cities where computer companies and larger corporations are based.

STARTING OUT

If your school offers placement services, take advantage of them. Many times, school placements and counseling centers are privy to job openings that are filled before being advertised in the newspaper. Make sure your counselors know of any important preferences, such as location, specialization, and other requirements, so they can best match you to an employer. Do not forget to supply them with an updated resume.

There are also other avenues to take when searching for a job in this industry. Many jobs are advertised in the "Jobs" section of your local newspaper. Look under "Computers" or "Electronics." Also, inquire directly with the personnel department of companies that appeal to you and fill out an application. Trade association Web sites are good sources of job leads; many will post employment opportunities as well as allow you to post your resume.

ADVANCEMENT

Due to the growth of computer products and their influence over the business world, this industry offers a variety of advancement opportunities. Service technicians usually start by working on relatively simple maintenance and repair tasks. Over time, they start working on more complicated projects.

Experienced service technicians may advance to positions of increased responsibility, such as a crew supervisor or a departmental manager. Another advancement route is to become a sales representative for a computer manufacturing company. Technicians develop hands-on knowledge of particular machines and are thus often in the best position to advise potential buyers about important purchasing decisions. Some entrepreneurial-minded servicers might open their own repair business, which can be risky but can also provide many rewards. Unless they fill a certain market niche, technicians usually find it necessary to service a wide range of computers and office machines.

EARNINGS

The U.S. Department of Labor reports that the median hourly earnings for computer, automated teller, and office machine technicians were $17.54 in 2006. A technician earning this amount and working full time would have a yearly income of approximately $36,483. The department also reports that the lowest paid 10 percent of all computer and office machine service technicians (regardless of employer) earned less than $10.65 per hour ($22,152 annually). At the other end of the pay scale, 10 percent earned more than $27.36 per hour (approximately $56,909 annually). Those with certification are typically paid more than those without.

Standard work benefits for full-time technicians include health and life insurance and paid vacation and sick time, as well as a retirement plan. Most technicians are given travel stipends; some receive company cars.

WORK ENVIRONMENT

"I like the freedom of not working in a [typical] office environment and the short workweeks," says Joey Arca. Most service technicians, however, have unpredictable work schedules. Some weeks are quiet and may require fewer work hours. However, during a major computer problem, or worse yet, a breakdown, technicians are required to work around the clock to fix the problem as quickly as possible. Technicians spend a considerable amount of time on call, and must carry a pager in case of work emergencies.

Travel is an integral part of the job for many service technicians, many times amounting to 80 percent of the job time. Arca has even traveled to the Philippines, where he worked on the Tomahawk Missile project at Clark Air Force Base. Since he is originally from the Philippines, he was able to combine work with a visit with friends and family.

OUTLOOK

According to the U.S. Department of Labor, employment for service technicians working with computer and office equipment should grow more slowly than the average for all occupations through 2016. Despite this prediction, demand for qualified and skilled technicians will be steady as corporations, the government, hospitals, and universities worldwide continue their reliance on computers to help manage their daily business. Opportunities are expected to be best for those with knowledge of electronics and working in computer repairs. Those working on office equipment, such as digital copiers, should find a demand for their services to repair and maintain increasingly technically sophisticated office machines.

FOR MORE INFORMATION

For information on internships, student membership, and the magazine Crossroads, *contact*

Association for Computing Machinery
2 Penn Plaza, Suite 701
New York, NY 10121
Tel: 800-342-6626
Email: sigs@acm.org
http://www.acm.org

For information on certification, contact

Electronics Technicians Association International
5 Depot Street
Greencastle, IN 46135-8024

Tel: 800-288-3824
Email: eta@eta-i.org
http://www.eta-i.org

For industry and certification information, contact the following organizations:

ACES International
5241 Princess Anne Road, Suite 110
Virginia Beach, VA 23462-6310
Tel: 800-798-2237
http://www.acesinternational.org

Computing Technology Industry Association
1815 South Meyers Road, Suite 300
Oakbrook Terrace, IL 60181-5228
Tel: 630-678-8300
http://www.comptia.org

Institute for Certification of Computing Professionals
2350 East Devon Avenue, Suite 115
Des Plaines, IL 60018-4610
Tel: 800-843-8227
Email: office@iccp.org
http://www.iccp.org

International Society of Certified Electronics Technicians
3608 Pershing Avenue
Fort Worth, TX 76107-4527
Tel: 800-946-0201
Email: info@iscet.org
http://www.iscet.org

☐ COMPUTER SUPPORT SPECIALISTS

OVERVIEW

Computer support specialists, also known as *technical support specialists*, investigate and resolve problems in computer functioning. They listen to customer complaints, walk customers through possible solutions, and write technical reports based on their work. Computer support specialists have different duties depending on whom they assist and what they fix. Regardless of specialty, all computer support specialists must be very knowledgeable about the products with which they work

QUICK FACTS

SCHOOL SUBJECTS

Computer science

English

Mathematics

PERSONAL SKILLS

Helping/teaching

Technical/scientific

WORK ENVIRONMENT

Primarily indoors

Primarily one location

MINIMUM EDUCATION LEVEL

Some postsecondary training

MEDIAN SALARY

$41,470

CERTIFICATION OR LICENSING

Recommended

OUTLOOK

About as fast as the average

become increasingly reliant on computers, it becomes critical that they function properly all the time. Any computer downtime can be extremely expensive, in terms of work left undone and sales not made, for example. When employees experience problems with their computer system, they call computer support for help. Computer support specialists investigate and resolve problems in computer functioning.

Computer support can generally be broken up into at least three distinct areas, although these distinctions vary greatly with the nature, size, and scope of the company. The three most prevalent areas are user support, technical support, and microcomputer support. Most computer support specialists perform some combination of the tasks explained below.

The jobs of computer support specialists vary according to whom they assist and what they fix. Some specialists help private users exclusively; others are on call to a major corporate buyer. Some work with computer hardware and software, while others help with printer, modem, and fax problems. *User support specialists*, also known as *help desk specialists*, work directly with users who call when they experience problems. The support specialist listens carefully to the user's explanation of the precise nature of the problem and the commands entered that seem to have caused it. Some companies have developed complex software that allows the support specialist to enter a description of the problem and wait for the computer to provide suggestions about what the user should do.

The initial goal is to isolate the source of the problem. If user error is the culprit, the user support specialist explains procedures related to the program in question, whether it is a graphics, database, word processing, or printing program. If the problem seems to lie in the hardware or software, the specialist asks the user to enter certain commands in order to see if the computer makes the appropriate response. If it does not, the support specialist is closer to isolating the cause. The support specialist consults supervisors, programmers, and others in order to outline the cause and possible solutions.

Some *technical support specialists* who work for computer companies are mainly involved with solving problems stemming from the computer system's operating system, hardware, or software. They make exhaustive use of resources, such as colleagues or books, and try to solve the problem through a variety of methods, including program modifications and the replacement of certain hardware or software.

Technical support specialists employed in the information systems departments of large corporations do

and be able to communicate effectively with users from different technical backgrounds. They must be patient and professional with frustrated users and be able to perform well under stress. Computer support is similar to solving mysteries, so support specialists should enjoy the challenge of problem solving and have strong analytical thinking skills. There are approximately 552,000 computer support specialists employed in the United States.

THE JOB

Computers are a vital part of almost every business. Some businesses use computers heavily and in many areas: daily operations, such as employee time clocks; monthly projects, such as payroll and sales accounting; and major reengineering of fundamental business procedures, such as form automation in government agencies, insurance companies, and banks. As more companies

this kind of troubleshooting as well. They also oversee the daily operations of the various computer systems in the company. Sometimes they compare the system's work capacity to the actual daily workload in order to determine if upgrades are needed. In addition, they might help out other computer professionals in the company with modifying commercial software for their company's particular needs.

Microcomputer support specialists are responsible for preparing computers for delivery to a client, including installing the operating system and desired software. After the unit is installed at the customer's location, the support specialists might help train users on appropriate procedures and answer any questions they have. They help diagnose problems that occur, transferring major concerns to other support specialists.

All computer support work must be well documented. Support specialists write detailed technical reports on every problem they work on. They try to tie together different problems on the same software, so programmers can make adjustments that address all of the issues. Record keeping is crucial because designers, programmers, and engineers use technical support reports to revise current products and improve future ones. Some support specialists help write training manuals. They are often required to read trade magazines and company newsletters in order to keep up to date on their products and the field in general.

REQUIREMENTS
High School

A high school diploma is a minimum requirement for computer support specialists. Any technical courses you can take, such as computer science, schematic drawing, or electronics, can help you develop the logical and analytical thinking skills necessary to be successful in this field. Courses in math and science are also valuable for this reason. Since computer support specialists have to deal with both computer programmers on the one hand and computer users who may not know anything about computers on the other, you should take English and speech classes to improve your verbal and written communications skills.

Postsecondary Training

Computer support is a field as old as computer technology itself, so it might seem odd that postsecondary programs in this field are not more common or standardized. The reason behind this is relatively simple: Formal education curricula cannot keep up with the changes, nor can they provide specific training on individual products. Some large corporations might consider educational background, both as a way to weed out applicants and to ensure a certain level of proficiency. Most major computer companies, however, look for energetic individuals who demonstrate a willingness and ability to learn new things quickly and who have general computer knowledge. These employers count on training new support specialists themselves.

Individuals interested in pursuing a job in this field should first determine what area of computer support appeals to them the most and then honestly assess their level of experience and knowledge. Large corporations often prefer to hire people with an associate's degree and some experience. They may also be impressed with commercial certification in a computer field, such as networking. However, if they are hiring from within the company, they will probably weigh experience more heavily than education when making a final decision.

Employed individuals looking for a career change may want to commit themselves to a program of self-study in order to be qualified for computer support positions. Many computer professionals learn a lot of what they know by playing around on computers, reading trade magazines, and talking with colleagues. Self-taught individuals should learn how to effectively demonstrate their knowledge and proficiency on the job or during an interview. Besides self-training, employed individuals should investigate tuition reimbursement programs offered by their company.

High school students with no experience should seriously consider earning an associate's degree in a computer-related technology. The degree shows the prospective employer that the applicant has attained a certain level of proficiency with computers and has the intellectual ability to learn technical processes, a promising sign for success on the job.

There are many computer technology programs that lead to an associate's degree. A specialization in personal computer support and administration is certainly applicable to technical support. Most computer professionals eventually need to go back to school to earn a bachelor's degree in order to keep themselves competitive in the job market and prepare themselves for promotion to other computer fields.

Certification or Licensing

Though certification is not an industry requirement, it is highly recommended. According to HDI, most individuals wishing to qualify to work in a support/help desk environment will need to obtain certification within a month of being on the job. A number of organizations offer several different types of certification. CompTIA: The Computing Technology Industry Association, for example, offers the "A+" certification for entry-level computer service technicians. HDI has training courses and offers a number of certifications for those working in support and help desk positions.

To become certified, you will need to pass a written test and in some cases may need a certain amount of work experience. Although going through the certification process is voluntary, becoming certified will most likely be to your advantage. It will show your commitment to the profession as well as demonstrate your level of expertise. In addition, certification may qualify you for certain jobs and lead to new employment opportunities.

Other Requirements

To be a successful computer support specialist, you should be patient, enjoy challenges of problem solving, and think logically. You should work well under stress and demonstrate effective communication skills. Working in a field that changes rapidly, you should be naturally curious and enthusiastic about learning new technologies as they are developed.

EXPLORING

If you are interested in becoming a computer support specialist, you should try to organize a career day with an employed computer support specialist. Local computer repair shops that offer computer support service might be a good place to contact. Otherwise, you should contact major corporations, computer companies, and even the central office of your school system.

If you are interested in any computer field, you should start working and playing on computers as much as possible; many working computer professionals became computer hobbyists at a very young age. You can surf the Internet, read computer magazines, and join school or community computer clubs.

You might also attend a computer technology course at a local technical/vocational school. This would give you hands-on exposure to typical computer support training. In addition, if you experience problems with your own hardware or software, you should call computer support, paying careful attention to how the support specialist handles the call and asking as many questions as the specialist has time to answer.

EMPLOYERS

Computer support specialists work for computer hardware and software companies, as well as in the information systems departments of large corporations and government agencies. There are approximately 552,000 computer support specialists employed in the United States.

STARTING OUT

Most computer support positions are considered entry-level. They are found mainly in computer companies and large corporations. Individuals interested in obtaining a job in this field should scan the classified ads for openings in local businesses and may want to work with an employment agency for help finding out about opportunities. Since many job openings are publicized by word of mouth, it is also very important to speak with as many working computer professionals as possible. They tend to be aware of job openings before anyone else and may be able to offer a recommendation to the hiring committee.

If students of computer technology are seeking a position in computer support, they should work closely with their school's careeer services office. Many employers inform career services offices at nearby schools of openings before ads are run in the newspaper. In addition, career services office staffs are generally very helpful with resume writing assistance and interviewing techniques.

If an employee wants to make a career change into computer support, he or she should contact the human resources department of the company or speak directly with appropriate management. In companies that are expanding their computing systems, it is often helpful for management to know that current employees would be interested in growing in a computer-related direction. They may even be willing to finance additional education.

ADVANCEMENT

Computer support specialists who demonstrate leadership skills and a strong aptitude for the work may be promoted to supervisory positions within computer support departments. Supervisors are responsible for the more complicated problems that arise, as well as for some administrative duties such as scheduling, interviewing, and job assignments.

Further promotion requires additional education. Some computer support specialists may become commercially certified in computer networking so that they can install, maintain, and repair computer networks. Others may prefer to pursue a bachelor's degree in computer science, either full time or part time. The range of careers available to college graduates varies widely. *Software engineers* analyze industrial, business, and scientific problems and develop software programs to handle them effectively. *Quality assurance engineers* design automated quality assurance tests for new software applications. *Internet quality assurance specialists* work specifically with testing and developing companies' Web sites. *Computer systems programmer-analysts* study the broad computing picture for a company or a group of companies in order to determine the best way to organize the computer systems .

There are limited opportunities for computer support specialists to be promoted into managerial positions. Doing so would require additional education in business but would probably also depend on the individual's advanced computer knowledge.

EARNINGS

Computer support specialist jobs are plentiful in areas where clusters of computer companies are located, such as northern California and Seattle, Washington. Median annual earnings for computer support specialists were $41,470 in 2006, according to the U.S. Department of Labor. The highest paid 10 percent earned more than $68,540, while the lowest paid 10 percent earned less than $25,290. Those who have more education, responsibility, and expertise have the potential to earn much more.

Computer support specialists earned the following median annual salaries by industry in 2006 (according to the U.S. Department of Labor): software publishers, $46,270; management of companies and enterprises, $42,770; computer systems design services, $42,510; colleges and universities, $40,130; and elementary and secondary schools, $37,880.

Most computer support specialists work for companies that offer a full range of benefits, including health insurance, paid vacation, and sick leave. Smaller service or start-up companies may hire support specialists on a contractual basis.

WORK ENVIRONMENT

Computer support specialists work in comfortable business environments. They generally work regular, 40-hour weeks. However, they may be asked to work evenings or weekends or at least be on call during those times in case of emergencies. If they work for service companies, they may be required to travel to clients' sites and log overtime hours.

Computer support work can be stressful, since specialists often deal with frustrated users. Communication problems with people who are less technically qualified may also be a source of frustration. Patience and understanding are essential for handling these problems.

Computer support specialists are expected to work quickly and efficiently and be able to perform under pressure. The ability to do this requires thorough technical expertise and keen analytical ability.

OUTLOOK

The U.S. Department of Labor predicts that employment for computer support specialists will grow about as fast as the average for all occupations through 2016. Each time a new computer product is released on the market or another system is installed, there will be problems, whether from user error or technical difficulty. Therefore, there will always be a need for computer support specialists to solve the problems. Since technology changes so rapidly, it is very important for these professionals to keep up to date on advances. They should read trade magazines, relevant Web sites and blogs, and talk with colleagues in order to know what is happening in the field. Job growth will be weaker than growth during the previous decade as many computer support jobs are being outsourced overseas.

Since some companies stop offering computer support on old products or applications after a designated time, the key is to be flexible with your understanding of technology. This is important for another reason as well: While the industry as a whole will require more computer support specialists in the future, some computer companies may go out of business. It can be a volatile industry for start-ups or young companies dedicated to the development of one product. Computer support specialists interested in working for computer companies should therefore consider living in areas in which many such companies are clustered. In this way, it will be easier to find another job if necessary.

FOR MORE INFORMATION

For information on internships, scholarships, student membership, and the student magazine Crossroads, *contact*
Association for Computing Machinery
2 Penn Plaza, Suite 701
New York, NY 10121-0701
Tel: 800-342-6626
Email: acmhelp@acm.org
http://www.acm.org

For information on certification, contact
CompTIA: Computing Technology Industry Association
1815 South Meyers Road, Suite 300

Oakbrook Terrace, IL 60181-5228
Tel: 630-678-8300
http://www.comptia.org

For more information on this organization's training courses and certification, contact
HDI
102 South Tejon, Suite 1200
Colorado Springs, CO 80903-2231
Tel: 800-248-5667
Email: support@thinkhdi.com
http://www.thinkhdi.com

For information on scholarships, student membership, to read Careers in Computer Science and Computer Engineering, *visit the IEEE's Web site.*
IEEE Computer Society
1828 L Street, NW, Suite 1202
Washington, DC 20036-5104
Tel: 202-371-0101
http://www.computer.org

☐ CONSTRUCTION INSPECTORS

OVERVIEW

Construction inspectors work for federal, state, and local governments. Their job is to examine the construction, alteration, or repair of highways, streets, sewer and water systems, dams, bridges, buildings, and other structures to ensure that they comply with building codes and ordinances, zoning regulations, and contract specifications. Approximately 110,000 construction and building inspectors work in the United States.

THE JOB

This occupation is made up of four broad categories of specialization: building, electrical, mechanical, and public works.

Building inspectors examine the structural quality of buildings. They check the plans before construction, visit the work site a number of times during construction, and make a final inspection when the project is completed. Some building inspectors specialize in areas such as structural steel or reinforced concrete buildings.

Electrical inspectors visit work sites to inspect the installation of electrical systems and equipment. They check wiring, lighting, generators, and sound and security systems. They may also inspect the wiring for elevators, heating and air-conditioning systems, kitchen appliances, and other electrical installations.

Mechanical inspectors inspect plumbing systems and the mechanical components of heating and air-conditioning equipment and kitchen appliances. They also examine gas tanks, piping, and gas-fired appliances. Some mechanical inspectors specialize in elevators, plumbing, or boilers.

Elevator inspectors inspect both the mechanical and the electrical features of lifting and conveying devices, such as elevators, escalators, and moving sidewalks. They also test their speed, load allowances, brakes, and safety devices.

Plumbing inspectors inspect plumbing installations, water supply systems, drainage and sewer systems, water heater installations, fire sprinkler systems, and air and gas piping systems; they also examine building sites for soil type to determine water table level, seepage rate, and similar conditions.

Heating and refrigeration inspectors examine heating, ventilating, air-conditioning, and refrigeration installations in new buildings and approve alteration plans for those elements in existing buildings.

Public works inspectors make sure that government construction of water and sewer systems, highways, streets, bridges, and dams conforms to contract specifications. They visit work sites to inspect excavations, mixing and pouring of concrete, and asphalt paving. They also keep records of the amount of work performed and the materials used so that proper payment can be made. These inspectors may specialize in highways, reinforced concrete, or ditches.

Construction inspectors use measuring devices and other test equipment, take photographs, keep a daily log of their work, and write reports. If any detail of a project does not comply with the various codes, ordinances, or specifications, or if construction is being done without proper permits, the inspectors have the authority to issue a stop-work order.

REQUIREMENTS
High School

People interested in becoming construction inspectors must be high school graduates who have taken courses in drafting, algebra, geometry, and English. Additional shop courses will undoubtedly prove helpful as well.

Postsecondary Training

Employers prefer graduates of an apprenticeship program, community or junior college, or people with at least two years of course work toward an engineering or architectural degree. Required courses include construction technology, blueprint reading, technical math, English, and building inspection.

Most construction inspectors have several years of experience either as a construction contractor or supervisor, or as a craft or trade worker such as a carpenter, electrician, plumber, or pipefitter. This experience demonstrates knowledge of construction materials and practices, which is necessary in inspections. Construction inspectors receive most of their training on the job.

Certification or Licensing

Some states require certification for employment. Inspectors can earn a certificate by passing examinations on construction techniques, materials, and code requirements. The exams are offered by the International Code Council.

Other Requirements

A construction inspector should have experience in construction, have a good driving record, be in good physical shape, have good communication skills, be able to pay attention to details, and have a strong personality. Although there are no standard requirements to enter this occupation, an inspector should be a responsible individual with in-depth knowledge of the construction trades. Inexperience can lead to mistakes that can cost someone a staggering amount of money or even cause a person's death.

The trade is not considered hazardous, but most inspectors wear hard hats as a precaution. Inspectors might need to climb ladders and walk across rooftops, or perhaps trudge up numerous flights of stairs at building projects where elevators are not yet installed. Or they might occasionally find themselves squirming through the dirty, narrow, spider-infested crawl space under a house to check a foundation or crawling across the joists in a cramped, dusty, unfinished attic, inhaling insulation fibers and pesticides.

After the inspection a construction inspector needs to explain his or her findings clearly in reports and should expect to spend many hours answering questions in person, by telephone, and in letters. Because they often deliver bad news, they also need the emotional strength to stand firm on their reports, even when someone calls them a liar or threatens to sue.

On the other hand, an inspector knows that their work is to protect people. For example, they help ensure that a couple's new house will not be apt to burn down from an electrical short, and they might point out less dangerous

QUICK FACTS

SCHOOL SUBJECTS
Mathematics
Technical/shop

PERSONAL SKILLS
Leadership/management
Technical/scientific

WORK ENVIRONMENT
Indoors and outdoors
Primarily multiple locations

MINIMUM EDUCATION LEVEL
High school diploma

MEDIAN SALARY
$46,570

CERTIFICATION OR LICENSING
Required by certain states

OUTLOOK
Faster than the average

problems, such as a malfunctioning septic tank or a leaking roof, that could require expensive repairs.

EXPLORING

Field trips to construction sites and interviews with contractors or building trade officials are good ways to gain practical information about what it is like to work in the industry and how best to prepare for it. Summer jobs at a construction site provide an overview of the work involved in a building project. Students may also seek part-time jobs with a general contracting company, with a specialized contractor (such as a plumbing or electrical contractor), or as a carpenter's helper. Jobs in certain supply houses will help students become familiar with construction materials.

EMPLOYERS

Approximately 110,000 construction and building inspectors are employed in the United States. Approximately 41 percent work for local governments, such as municipal or county building departments. Inspectors employed at the federal level work for such agencies as the Department of Defense or the departments of Housing and Urban Development, Agriculture, and the Interior.

STARTING OUT

People without postsecondary education usually enter the construction industry as a trainee or apprentice. Graduates of technical schools or colleges of construction and engineering can expect to start work as an engineering aide, drafter, estimator, or assistant engineer. Jobs may be found through school career services offices, employment agencies, and unions or by applying directly to contracting company personnel offices. Application may also be made directly to the employment offices of the federal, state, or local governments.

ADVANCEMENT

The federal, state, and large city governments provide formal training programs for their construction inspectors to keep them abreast of new building code developments and to broaden their knowledge of construction materials, practices, and inspection techniques. Inspectors for small agencies can upgrade their skills by attending state-conducted training programs or taking college or correspondence courses. An engineering degree is usually required to become a supervisory inspector.

EARNINGS

The U.S. Department of Labor reports the median annual income for construction and building inspectors was $46,570 in 2006. The lowest paid 10 percent of these workers had annual earnings of less than $29,210; the highest paid 10 percent made more than $72,590. Earnings vary based on the inspector's experience, the type of employer, and the location of the work. Salaries are slightly higher in the North and West than in the South and are considerably higher in large metropolitan areas. Building inspectors earn slightly more than other inspectors.

WORK ENVIRONMENT

Construction inspectors work both indoors and outdoors, dividing their time between their offices and the work sites. Inspection sites are dirty and cluttered with tools, machinery, and debris. Although the work is not considered hazardous, inspectors must climb ladders and stairs and crawl under buildings.

The hours are usually regular, but when there is an accident at a site, the inspector has to remain on the job until reports have been completed. The work is steady year-round, rather than seasonal, as are some other construction occupations. In slow construction periods, inspectors are kept busy examining the renovation of older buildings.

OUTLOOK

As the concern for public safety continues to rise, the demand for inspectors should grow faster than the average through 2016 even if construction activity does not increase. The level of new construction fluctuates with the economy, but maintenance and renovation continue during the downswings, so inspectors are rarely laid off. Applicants who have some college education, are already certified inspectors, or who have experience as carpenters, electricians, or plumbers will have the best opportunities. Construction and building inspectors tend to be older, more experienced workers who have worked in other construction occupations for many years.

FOR MORE INFORMATION

For additional information on a career as a construction inspector, contact the following organizations:

American Construction Inspectors Association
530 South Lake Avenue, Suite 431
Pasadena, CA 91101-3515 Tel: 888-867-2242
Email: office@acia.com.
http://www.acia.com

American Society of Home Inspectors
932 Lee Street, Suite 101
Des Plaines, IL 60016-6546
Tel: 800-743-2744
http://www.ashi.org

International Code Council
5203 Leesburg Pike, Suite 600
Falls Church, VA 22041-3401
Tel: 888-422-7233
http://www.iccsafe.org

COOKS AND CHEFS

OVERVIEW

Cooks and *chefs* are employed in the preparation and cooking of food, usually in large quantities, in hotels, restaurants, cafeterias, and other establishments and institutions. There are almost 3.1 million cooks, chefs, and other food preparation workers employed in the United States.

THE JOB

Cooks and chefs are primarily responsible for the preparation and cooking of foods. Chefs usually supervise the work of cooks; however, the skills required and the job duties performed by each may vary depending upon the size and type of establishment.

Cooks and chefs begin by planning menus. They estimate the amount of food that will be required for a specified period of time, order it from various suppliers, and check it for quantity and quality when it arrives. Following recipes or their own instincts, they measure and mix ingredients for soups, salads, gravies, sauces, casseroles, and desserts. They prepare meats, poultry, fish, vegetables, and other foods for baking, roasting, broiling, and steaming. They use blenders, mixers, grinders, slicers, or tenderizers to prepare the food, and ovens, broilers, grills, roasters, or steam kettles to cook it. During the mixing and cooking, cooks and chefs rely on their judgment and experience to add seasonings; they constantly taste and smell food being cooked and must know when it is cooked properly. To fill orders, they carve meat, arrange food portions on serving plates, and add appropriate gravies, sauces, or garnishes.

Some larger establishments employ specialized cooks, such as banquet cooks, pastry cooks, and broiler cooks. The *garde-manger* designs and prepares buffets, and *pantry cooks* prepare cold dishes for lunch and dinner. Other specialists are *raw shellfish preparers* and *carvers.*

In smaller establishments without specialized cooks, kitchen helpers, or prep cooks, the general cooks may have to do some of the preliminary work themselves, such as washing, peeling, cutting, and shredding vegetables and fruits; cutting, trimming, and boning meat; cleaning and preparing poultry, fish, and shellfish; and baking bread, rolls, cakes, and pastries.

Commercial cookery is usually done in large quantities, and many cooks, including school cafeteria cooks and mess cooks, are trained in "quantity cookery" methods. Numerous establishments today are noted for their specialties in foods, and some cooks work exclusively in the preparation and cooking of exotic dishes, very elaborate meals, or some particular creation of their own for which they have become famous. Restaurants that feature national cuisines may employ international and regional cuisine specialty cooks.

In the larger commercial kitchens, chefs may be responsible for the work of a number of cooks, each preparing and cooking food in specialized areas. They may, for example, employ expert cooks who specialize in frying, baking, roasting, broiling, or sauce cookery. Cooks are often titled by the kinds of specialized cooking they do, such as fry, vegetable, or pastry. Chefs have the major responsibility for supervising the overall preparation and cooking of the food.

Other duties of chefs may include training cooks on the job, planning menus, pricing food for menus, and purchasing food. Chefs may be responsible for determining the weights of portions to be prepared and served. Among their other duties may be the supervision of the work of all members of the kitchen staff. The kitchen staff assists by washing, cleaning, and preparing foods for cooking; cleaning utensils, dishes, and silverware; and assisting in many ways with the overall order and cleanliness of the kitchen. Most chefs spend part of their time striving to create new recipes that will build their reputations as experts. Many, like pastry chefs, focus their attention on particular kinds of food.

Expert chefs who have a number of years of experience may be employed as *executive chefs.* These chefs do little cooking or food preparation—their main responsibilities are management and supervision. Executive chefs interview, hire, and dismiss kitchen personnel, and they

---

QUICK FACTS

SCHOOL SUBJECTS
Family and consumer science
Mathematics

PERSONAL SKILLS
Artistic
Following instructions

WORK ENVIRONMENT
Primarily indoors
Primarily one location

MINIMUM EDUCATION LEVEL
Apprenticeship

MEDIAN SALARY
$34,370

CERTIFICATION OR LICENSING
Required by certain states

OUTLOOK
About as fast as the average

are sometimes responsible for the dining room waiters and other employees. These chefs consult with the restaurant manager regarding the profits and losses of the food service and ways to increase business and cut costs. A part of their time is spent inspecting equipment. Executive chefs are in charge of all food services for special functions such as banquets and parties, and they spend many hours in coordinating the work for these activities. They may supervise the special chefs and assist them in planning elaborate arrangements and creations in food preparation. Executive chefs may be assisted by workers called *sous chefs*.

Smaller restaurants may employ only one or two cooks and workers to assist them. Cooks and assistants work together to prepare all the food for cooking and to keep the kitchen clean. Because smaller restaurants and public eating places usually offer standard menus with little variation, the cook's job becomes standardized. Such establishments may employ specialty cooks, barbecue cooks, pizza bakers, food order expediters, kitchen food assemblers, or counter supply workers. In some restaurants food is cooked as it is ordered; cooks preparing food in this manner are known as *short-order cooks*.

Regardless of the duties performed, cooks and chefs are largely responsible for the reputation and monetary profit or loss of the eating establishment in which they are employed.

REQUIREMENTS

The occupation of chef or cook has specific training requirements. Many cooks start out as kitchen helpers and acquire their skills on the job, but the trend today is to obtain training through high schools, vocational schools, or community colleges.

The amount of training required varies with the position. It takes only a short time to become an assistant or a fry cook, for example, but it requires years of training and experience to acquire the skills necessary to become an executive chef or cook in a fine restaurant.

High School

Although a high school diploma is not required for beginning positions, it is an asset to job applicants. If you are interested in moving beyond low-level positions such as kitchen helper or fry cook, your high school education should include classes in family and consumer science and health. These courses will teach you about nutrition, food preparation, and food storage. Math classes are also recommended; in this line of work you must be comfortable working with fractions, multiplying, and dividing. Since chefs and head cooks often

have management responsibilities, you should also take business courses.

Postsecondary Training

Culinary students spend most of their time learning to prepare food through hands-on practice. At the same time, they learn how to use and care for kitchen equipment. Training programs often include courses in menu planning, determining portion size, controlling food costs, purchasing food supplies in quantity, selecting and storing food, and using leftovers. Students also learn hotel and restaurant sanitation and public health rules for handling food. Courses offered by private vocational schools, professional associations, and university programs often emphasize training in supervisory and management skills.

Professional associations and trade unions sometimes offer apprenticeship programs; one example is the two-year apprenticeship program sponsored by chapters of the American Culinary Federation (ACF) in cooperation with local employers. This program combines classroom work with on-the-job training under the supervision of a qualified chef and is an excellent way to begin your career. For more information, visit the ACF Web site at http://www.acfchefs.org. Some large hotels and restaurants have their own training programs for new employees. The armed forces also offer good training and experience.

Certification or Licensing

To protect the public's health, chefs, cooks, and bakers are required by law in most states to possess a health certificate and to be examined periodically. These examinations, usually given by the state board of health, make certain that the individual is free from communicable diseases and skin infections. The American Culinary Federation offers certification at a variety of levels, such as executive chef and sous chef. In addition to educational and experience requirements, candidates must also pass written tests for each certification. Certification from ACF is recommended as a way to enhance your professional standing and advance your career.

Other Requirements

The successful chef or cook has a keen interest in food preparation and cooking and has a desire to experiment in developing new recipes and new food combinations. Cooks and chefs should be able to work as part of a team and to work under pressure during rush hours, in close quarters, and with a certain amount of noise and confusion. These employees need an even temperament and patience to contend with the public daily and to work closely with many other kinds of employees.

Immaculate personal cleanliness and good health are necessities in this trade. Applicants should possess physical stamina and be without serious physical impairments because of the mobility and activity the work requires. These employees spend many working hours standing, walking, and moving about.

Chefs and cooks must possess a keen sense of taste and smell. Hand and finger agility, hand-eye coordination, and a good memory are helpful. An artistic flair and creative talents in working with food are definitely strengths in this trade.

The principal union for cooks and chefs is UNITE HERE (affiliated with the AFL-CIO).

EXPLORING

You may explore your interest in cooking right at home. Prepare meals for your family, offer to make a special dessert for a friend's birthday, and create your own recipes. Any such hands-on experiences will build your skills and help you determine what type of cooking you enjoy the most.

Volunteer opportunities may be available at local kitchens that serve the homeless or others in need. You can also get a paying part-time or summer job at a fast food or other restaurant. Large and institutional kitchens, for example those in nursing homes, may offer positions such as sandwich or salad maker, soda-fountain attendant, or kitchen helper; while doing one of these jobs, you can observe the work of chefs and cooks.

EMPLOYERS

Cooks and chefs are needed by restaurants of all types and sizes; schools, hospitals, and other institutions; hotels, cruise lines, airlines, and other industries; and catering and bakery businesses. Nearly two-thirds of the 3.1 million chefs, cooks, and food preparation workers employed in the United States work at restaurants, other retail eateries, and drinking establishments. Roughly 15 percent are employed by institutions/cafeterias, such as schools, universities, hospitals, and nursing homes. The rest work at such places as grocery stores, hotels, gas stations, and catering businesses.

STARTING OUT

Apprenticeship programs are one method of entering the trade. These programs usually offer the beginner sound basic training and a regular salary. Upon completion of the apprenticeship, cooks may be hired full time in their place of training or assisted in finding employment with another establishment. Cooks are hired as chefs only after they have acquired a number of years of experience. Cooks who have been formally trained through public or private trade or vocational schools or in culinary institutes may be able to take advantage of school placement services.

In many cases, a cook begins as a kitchen helper or cook's helper and, through experience gained in on-the-job training, is able to move into the job of cook. To do this, people sometimes start out in small restaurants, perhaps as short-order cooks, grill cooks, or sandwich or salad makers, and transfer to larger establishments as they gain experience.

School cafeteria workers who want to become cooks may have an opportunity to receive food-services training. Many school districts, with the cooperation of school food-services divisions of the state departments of education, provide on-the-job training and sometimes summer workshops for interested cafeteria employees. Some community colleges, state departments of education, and school associations offer similar programs. Cafeteria workers who have completed these training programs are often selected to fill positions as cooks.

Job opportunities may be located through employment bureaus, trade associations, unions, contacts with friends, newspaper want ads, or local offices of the state employment service. Another method is to apply directly to restaurants or hotels. Small restaurants, school cafeterias, and other eating places with simple food preparation will provide the greatest number of starting jobs for cooks. Job applicants who have had courses in commercial food preparation will have an advantage in large restaurants and hotels, where hiring standards are often high.

ADVANCEMENT

Advancement depends on the skill, training, experience, originality, and ambition of the individual. It also depends somewhat on the general business climate and employment trends.

Cooks with experience can advance by moving to other places of employment for higher wages or to establishments looking for someone with a specialized skill in preparing a particular kind of food. Cooks who have a number of years of successful job experience may find chef positions open to them; however, in some cases it may take 10 or 15 years to obtain such a position, depending on personal qualifications and other employment factors.

Expert cooks who have obtained supervisory responsibilities as head cooks or chefs may advance to positions as executive chefs or to other types of managerial work. Some go into business for themselves as caterers or restaurant owners; others may become instructors in vocational programs in high schools, colleges, or other academic institutions.

EARNINGS

The salaries earned by chefs and cooks are widely divergent and depend on many factors, such as the size, type, and location of the establishment, and the skill, experience, training, and specialization of the worker. Salaries are usually fairly standard among establishments of the same type. For example, restaurants and diners serving inexpensive meals and a sandwich-type menu generally pay cooks less than establishments with medium-priced or expensive menus. The highest wages are earned at restaurants and hotels known for their elegance.

The U.S. Department of Labor reports the following earnings for cooks and chefs in a variety of positions. In 2006, the median wage-and-salary earning for chefs and head cooks was $34,370 a year, with the lowest paid 10 percent making less than $20,160 and the highest paid 10 percent making more than $60,730 annually. Restaurant cooks had median annual earnings of $20,340 in 2006, with wage-and-salary earnings ranging from les than $14,370 to more than $28,850. Those cooks employed in nursing homes, hospitals, schools, and other institutional settings had median earnings of $20,410.

Chefs and cooks sometimes receive their meals free during working hours and are furnished with any necessary job uniforms. Those working full-time usually receive standard benefits, such as health insurance and vacation and sick days.

WORK ENVIRONMENT

Working conditions vary with the place of employment. Many kitchens are modern, well lighted, well equipped, and air-conditioned, but some older, smaller eating-establishments may be only marginally equipped. The work of cooks can be strenuous, with long hours of standing, lifting heavy pots, and working near hot ovens and ranges. Possible hazards include falls, cuts, and burns, although serious injury is uncommon. Even in the most modern kitchens, cooks, chefs, and bakers usually work amid considerable noise from the operation of equipment and machinery.

Experienced cooks may work with little or no supervision, depending on the size of the food service and the place of employment. Less experienced cooks may work under much more direct supervision from expert cooks or chefs.

Chefs and cooks may work a 40- or 48-hour week, depending on the type of food service offered and certain union agreements. Some food establishments are open 24 hours a day, while others may be open from the very early morning until late in the evening. Establishments open long hours may have two or three work shifts, with some chefs and cooks working day schedules while others work evenings.

All food-service workers may have to work overtime hours, depending on the amount of business and rush-hour trade. These employees work many weekends and holidays, although they may have a day off every week or rotate with other employees to have alternate weekends free. Many cooks are required to work early morning or late evening shifts. For example, doughnuts, breads, and muffins for breakfast service must be baked by 6:00 or 7:00 A.M., which requires bakers to begin work at 2:00 or 3:00 A.M. Some people will find it very difficult to adjust to working such late and irregular hours.

OUTLOOK

Overall the employment of chefs and cooks is expected to increase as fast as the average for all occupations through 2016, according to the U.S. Department of Labor. While some areas (such as institution and cafeteria chefs and cooks) may not see much growth in number of new jobs, turnover rates are high and the need to find replacement cooks and chefs will mean many job opportunities in all areas. The demand for cooks and chefs will also grow as the population increases and lifestyles change. As people earn higher incomes and have more leisure time, they dine out more often and take more vacations. In addition, working parents and their families dine out, or purchase prepared food from grocery or specialty food stores, frequently as a convenience.

FOR MORE INFORMATION

For information on careers, certification, competitions, and scholarships, contact

American Culinary Federation Inc.
180 Center Place Way
St. Augustine, FL 32095-8859
Tel: 800-624-9458
Email: acf@acfchefs.net
http://www.acfchefs.org

For information on careers in baking and cooking, contact

AIB International
1213 Bakers Way
Manhattan, KS 66505-3999
Tel: 800-633-5137
Email: info@aibonline.org
http://www.aibonline.org

For information on culinary education and certification, contact

American Hotel and Lodging Educational Institute
800 North Magnolia Avenue, Suite 1800
Orlando, FL 32803-3271
Tel: 800-752-4567
Email: info@ei-ahla.org
http://www.ei-ahla.org

For information on scholarships, contact

International Association of Culinary Professionals Foundation
455 South Fourth Street, Suite 650
Louisville, KY 40202
Tel: 800-928-4227
http://www.iacp.com

For information on education, scholarships, and careers, contact

National Restaurant Association Educational Foundation
175 West Jackson Boulevard, Suite 1500
Chicago, IL 60604-2814
Tel: 800-765-2122
http://www.nraef.org

For information on culinary schools in Canada, industry news, and a job bank, visit this organization's Web site.

Canadian Culinary Federation
707-1281 West Georgia Street
Vancouver, BC V6E 3J7 Canada
Tel: 506-387-4882
http://www.ccfcc.ca

CORRECTIONS OFFICERS

QUICK FACTS

SCHOOL SUBJECTS
Government
Physical education
Psychology

PERSONAL SKILLS
Communication/ideas
Helping/teaching

WORK ENVIRONMENT
Primarily indoors
Primarily one location

MINIMUM EDUCATION LEVEL
High school diploma

MEDIAN SALARY
$35,760

CERTIFICATION OR LICENSING
Required by certain states

OUTLOOK
Faster than the average

OVERVIEW

Corrections officers guard people who have been arrested and are awaiting trial or who have been tried, convicted, and sentenced to serve time in a penal institution. They search prisoners and their cells for weapons, drugs, and other contraband; inspect windows, doors, locks, and gates for signs of tampering; observe the conduct and behavior of inmates to prevent disturbances or escapes; and make verbal or written reports to superior officers. Corrections officers assign work to inmates and supervise their activities. They guard prisoners who are being transported between jails, courthouses, mental institutions, or other destinations, and supervise prisoners receiving visitors. When necessary, these workers use weapons or force to maintain discipline and order. There are approximately 500,000 corrections officers employed in the United States.

THE JOB

To prevent disturbances or escapes, corrections officers carefully observe the conduct and behavior of inmates at all times. They watch for forbidden activities and infractions of the rules, as well as for poor attitudes or unsatisfactory adjustment to prison life on the part of the inmates. They try to settle disputes before violence can erupt. They may search the prisoners or their living quarters for weapons or drugs and inspect locks, bars on windows and doors, and gates for any evidence of tampering. The inmates are under guard constantly while eating, sleeping, exercising, bathing, and working. They are counted periodically to be sure all are present. Some officers are stationed on towers and at gates to prevent escapes. All rule violations and anything out of the ordinary are reported to a superior officer such as a chief jailer. In case of a major disturbance, corrections officers may use weapons or force to restore order.

Corrections officers give work assignments to prisoners, supervise them as they carry out their duties, and instruct them in unfamiliar tasks. Corrections officers are responsible for the physical needs of the prisoners, such as providing or obtaining meals and medical aid. They assure the health and safety of the inmates by checking the cells for unsanitary conditions and fire hazards.

These workers may escort inmates from their cells to the prison's visiting room, medical office, or chapel. Certain officers, called *patrol conductors*, guard prisoners who are being transported between courthouses, prisons, mental institutions, or other destinations, either by van, car, or public transportation. Officers at a penal institution may also screen visitors at the entrance and accompany them to other areas within the facility. From time to time, they may inspect prisoners' mail, check for contraband, help investigate crimes committed within the prison, or aid in the search for escapees. *Gate tenders* check the identification of all persons entering and leaving the penal institution.

Some police officers specialize in guarding juvenile offenders being held at a police station house or detention room pending a hearing, transfer to a correctional institution, or return to their parents. They often investigate the backgrounds of first offenders to check for a criminal history or to make a recommendation to the magistrate regarding disposition of the case. Lost or runaway children are also placed in the care of these officers until their parents or guardians can be located.

Immigration guards guard aliens held by the immigration service awaiting investigation, deportation, or release.

In most correctional institutions, *psychologists* and *social workers* are employed to counsel inmates with mental and emotional problems. It is an important part of a corrections officer's job, however, to supplement this with informal counseling. Officers may help inmates adjust to prison life, prepare for return to civilian life, and avoid committing crimes in the future. On a more immediate level, they may arrange for an inmate to visit the library, help inmates get in touch with their families, suggest where to look for a job after release from prison, or discuss personal problems. In some institutions, corrections officers may lead more formal group counseling

sessions. As they fulfill more rehabilitative roles, corrections officers are increasingly required to possess a college-level education in psychology, criminology, or related areas of study.

Corrections officers keep a daily record of their activities and make regular reports, either verbal or written, to their supervisors. These reports concern the behavior of the inmates and the quality and quantity of work they do, as well as any disturbances, rule violations, and unusual occurrences that may have taken place.

Head corrections officers supervise and coordinate other corrections officers. They perform roll call and assign duties to the officers; direct the activities of groups of inmates; arrange the release and transfer of prisoners in accordance with the instructions on a court order; maintain security and investigate disturbances among the inmates; maintain prison records and prepare reports; and review and evaluate the performance of their subordinates.

In small communities, corrections officers (who are sometimes called *jailers*) may also act as deputy sheriffs or police officers when they are not occupied with guard duties.

REQUIREMENTS
High School

To work as a corrections officer, candidates generally must meet the minimum age requirement—usually 18 or 21—and have a high school diploma or its equivalent. Individuals without a high school education may be considered for employment if they have qualifying work experience, such as probation and parole experience.

Postsecondary Training

Many states and correctional facilities prefer or require officers to have postsecondary training in psychology, criminology, or related areas of study. Some states require applicants to have one or two years of previous experience in corrections or related police work. Some state governments also require military or related work experience. On the federal level, applicants should have at least two years of college or two years of work or military experience.

Training for corrections officers ranges from the special academy instruction provided by the federal government in some states to the informal, on-the-job training furnished by most states and local governments. The Federal Bureau of Prisons operates a training center in Glynco, Georgia, where new hires generally undergo a three-week program of basic corrections education. Training academies have programs that last from four to eight weeks and instruct trainees on institutional policies, regulations, and procedures; the behavior and custody of inmates; security measures; and report writing. Training in self-defense, the use of firearms and other weapons, and emergency medical techniques is often provided. On-the-job trainees spend two to six months or more under the supervision of an experienced officer. During that period of time, they receive in-house training while gaining actual experience. Periodically, corrections officers may be given additional training as new ideas and procedures in criminal justice are developed.

Certification or Licensing

Numerous certification programs are available to corrections officers; these are optional in most states. Common certifications include self-defense, weapons use, urine analysis, shield and gun, shotgun/handgun, CPR, and cell extraction. Many officers also take advantage of additional training that is offered at their facility, such as suicide prevention, AIDS awareness, use of four-point restraints, and emergency preparedness. At most prisons, there is annual mandatory in-service training that focuses on policies and procedures. The American Correctional Association and the American Jail Association offer certification programs to corrections officers and corrections managers.

Corrections officers who work for the federal government and most state governments are covered by civil service systems or merit boards and may be required to pass a competitive exam for employment. Many states require random or comprehensive drug testing of their officers, either during hiring procedures or while employed at the facility.

Other Requirements

It takes a unique personality to handle the inherent stress of this line of work. In a maximum-security facility, the environment is often noisy, crowded, poorly ventilated, and even dangerous. Corrections officers need the physical and emotional strength to handle the stress involved in working with criminals, some of whom may be violent. A corrections officer has to stay alert and aware of prisoners' actions and attitudes. This constant vigilance can be harder on some people. Work in a minimum-security prison is usually more comfortable, cleaner, and less stressful.

Officers need to use persuasion rather than brute force to get inmates to follow the rules. Certain inmates take a disproportionate amount of time and attention because they are either violent, mentally ill, or victims of abuse by other inmates. Officers have to carry out routine duties while being alert for the unpredictable outbursts. Sound judgment and the ability to think and act quickly are important qualities for corrections officers. With experience and training, corrections officers are usually able to handle volatile situations without resorting to physical force.

The ability to communicate clearly verbally and in writing is extremely important. Corrections officers have to write a number of reports, documenting routine procedures as well as any violations by the inmates. A correction officer's eight-hour shift can easily extend to 10 hours because of the reports that must be written.

An effective corrections officer is not easily intimidated or influenced by the inmates. There is a misconception, however, that corrections officers need to be tough guys. While it's true that a person needs some physical strength to perform the job, corrections officers also need to be able to use their head to anticipate and defuse any potentially dangerous situations between inmates or between guards and inmates.

Most correctional institutions require candidates to be at least 18 years old (sometimes 21 years old), have a high school diploma, and be a U.S. citizen with no criminal record. There are also health and physical strength requirements, and many states have minimum height, vision, and hearing standards. Other common requirements are a driver's license and a job record that shows dependability.

EXPLORING

Because of age requirements and the nature of the work, there are no opportunities for high school students to gain actual experience while still in school. Where the minimum age requirement is 21, prospective corrections officers may prepare for employment by taking college courses in criminal justice or police science. Enrollment in a two- or four-year college degree program in a related field is encouraged. Military service may also offer experience and training in corrections. Social work is another way to gain experience. You may also look into obtaining a civilian job as a clerk or other worker for the police department or other protective service organization. Related part-time, volunteer, or summer work may also be available in psychiatric hospitals and other institutions providing physical and emotional counseling and services. Many online services also have forums for corrections officers and other public safety employees, and these may provide opportunities to read about and communicate with people active in this career.

EMPLOYERS

Three out of five corrections officers work for the government at the local, state, and federal levels in penal institutions and in jobs connected with the penal system. Of the approximately 500,000 corrections officers employed in the United States, roughly 60 percent work in state-run correctional facilities such as prisons, prison camps, and reformatories. Most of the rest are employed at city and county jails or other institutions. Roughly 18,000 work for the federal government and approximately 16,000 are employed by private corrections contractors.

STARTING OUT

To apply for a job as a corrections officer, contact federal or state civil service commissions, state departments of correction, or local correctional facilities and ask for information about entrance requirements, training, and job opportunities. Private contractors and other companies are also a growing source of employment opportunities. Many officers enter this field from social work areas and parole and probation positions.

ADVANCEMENT

Many officers take college courses in law enforcement or criminal justice to increase their chances of promotion. In some states, officers must serve two years in each position before they can be considered for a promotion.

With additional education and training, experienced officers can also be promoted to supervisory or administrative positions such as *head corrections officer, assistant warden,* or *prison director.* Officers who want to continue to work directly with offenders can move into various other positions. For example, *probation and parole officers* monitor and counsel offenders, process their release from prison, and evaluate their progress in becoming productive members of society. *Recreation leaders* organize and instruct offenders in sports, games, and arts and crafts.

EARNINGS

Wages for corrections officers vary considerably depending on their employers and their level of experience. According to the U.S. Department of Labor, the 2006 median annual earnings for corrections officers were $35,760. Median earnings for corrections officers employed by the federal government were $47,750; for those employed by state governments, $36,140; and for those employed by local governments, $32,840. The U.S. Department of Labor reports that overall the lowest paid 10 percent of corrections officers earned less than $23,600 per year in 2006, and the highest paid 10 percent earned more than $58,580.

The U.S. Department of Labor reports higher earnings for supervisors/managers, with a median yearly income of $52,580 in 2006. The lowest paid 10 percent earned less than $33,270, and the highest paid 10 percent earned more than $81,230.

Overtime, night shift, weekend, and holiday pay differentials are generally available at most institutions. Fringe benefits may include health, disability, and life insurance; uniforms or a cash allowance to buy their own uniforms; and sometimes meals and housing. Officers who work for the federal government and for most state governments are covered by civil service systems or merit boards. Some corrections officers also receive retirement and pension plans, and retirement is often possible after 20 to 25 years of service.

WORK ENVIRONMENT

Because prison security must be maintained around the clock, work schedules for corrections officers may include nights, weekends, and holidays. The workweek, however, generally consists of five days, eight hours per day, except during emergencies, when many officers work overtime.

Corrections officers may work indoors or outdoors, depending on their duties. Conditions can vary even within an institution: Some areas are well lighted, ventilated, and temperature-controlled, while others are overcrowded, hot, and noisy. Officers who work outdoors, of course, are subject to all kinds of weather. Correctional institutions occasionally present unpredictable or even hazardous situations. If violence erupts among the inmates, corrections officers may be in danger of injury or death. Although this risk is higher than for most other occupations, corrections work is usually routine.

Corrections officers need physical and emotional strength to cope with the stress inherent in dealing with criminals, many of whom may be dangerous or incapable of change. A correctional officer has to remain alert and aware of the surroundings, prisoners' movements and attitudes, and any potential for danger or violence. Such continual, heightened levels of alertness often create psychological stress for some workers. Most institutions have stress-reduction programs or seminars for their employees, but if not, insurance usually covers some form of therapy for work-related stress.

OUTLOOK

Employment in this field is expected to grow faster than the average for all occupations through 2016, according to the U.S. Department of Labor. The ongoing prosecution of illegal drugs, new tough-on-crime legislation, and increasing mandatory sentencing policies will create a need for more prison beds and more corrections officers.

The extremely crowded conditions in today's correctional institutions have created a need for more corrections officers to guard the inmates more closely and relieve the tensions. A greater number of officers will also be required as a result of the expansion or new construction of facilities. As prison sentences become longer through mandatory minimum sentences set by state law, the number of prisons needed will increase. In addition, many job openings will occur from a characteristically high turnover rate, as well as from the need to fill vacancies caused by the death or retirement of older workers. Traditionally, correction agencies have difficulty attracting qualified employees due to job location and salary considerations.

Because security must be maintained at correctional facilities at all times, corrections officers can depend on steady employment. They are not usually affected by poor economic conditions or changes in government spending. Corrections officers are rarely laid off, even when budgets need to be trimmed. Instead, because of high turnovers, staffs can be cut simply by not replacing those officers who leave.

Most jobs will be found in relatively large institutions located near metropolitan areas, although opportunities for corrections officers exist in jails and other smaller facilities throughout the country. The increasing use of private companies and privately run prisons may limit the growth of jobs in this field as these companies are more likely to keep a close eye on the bottom line. Use of new technologies, such as surveillance equipment, automatic gates, and other devices, may also allow institutions to employ fewer officers.

FOR MORE INFORMATION

For information on training, conferences, and membership, contact

American Correctional Association
206 North Washington Street, Suite 200
Alexandria, VA 22314-2528
Tel: 703-224-0000
http://www.aca.org

American Probation and Parole Association
2760 Research Park Drive
Lexington, KY 40511-8410
Tel: 859-244-8203
Email: appa@csg.org
http://www.appa-net.org

For information on entrance requirements, training, and career opportunities for corrections officers at the federal level, contact

Federal Bureau of Prisons
320 First Street, NW
Washington, DC 20534-0002
Tel: 202-307-3198
http://www.bop.gov

This Web site bills itself as the "Largest Online Resource for News and Information in Corrections."
The Corrections Connection
http://www.corrections.com

COSMETICIANS

OVERVIEW

Cosmeticians specialize in skin care, providing an array of services from applying facial masks, peels, and herbal wraps, to massages, skin analysis, exfoliation, deep cleansing, product recommendations, and makeup application. In addition, cosmeticians provide hair removal services. Most cosmeticians work in beauty salons, day spas, and hotel resorts. Some work with dermatologists and cosmetic surgeons to prepare patients before surgery and during their recovery. There are approximately 22,620 skin care specialists employed in the United States.

THE JOB

Cosmeticians may also be known as *estheticians* (also spelled *aestheticians*) or *skin care specialists.* The word *esthetic* comes from the Greek word meaning harmony, beauty, and perfection. Esthetics is based on an understanding of the skin's anatomy and function. Cosmeticians work to improve the skin's condition and restore its functions. This discipline requires the cosmetician to get to know the client's skin and lifestyle and tailor treatments specifically for the client's needs. Cosmeticians offer a number of appearance-enhancing services that deal with the effects that pollution, lack of exercise, poor nutrition, and stress have on the skin. The cosmetician's job may involve facials, massages, wraps and packs, hydrotherapy treatments, scalp treatments, hair removal services, color analysis, makeup services, and product sales. Before beginning to work with a client, the cosmetician will most likely consult with the individual to determine his or her goals and concerns. It is important that cosmeticians are clear with their clients as to what they should expect from their treatments.

After the initial consultation for a facial, the cosmetician will need to perform a skin analysis in order to

QUICK FACTS

SCHOOL SUBJECTS

Biology

Chemistry

PERSONAL SKILLS

Artistic

Following instructions

WORK ENVIRONMENT

Primarily indoors

Primarily one location

MINIMUM EDUCATION LEVEL

Some postsecondary training

MEDIAN SALARY

$26,170

CERTIFICATION OR LICENSING

Required by certain states

OUTLOOK

About as fast as the average

protect themselves by using gloves and the proper sanitation. These procedures are covered in cosmetician training programs and are regulated by law in most states.

Other services cosmeticians offer include wraps, packs, and hydrotherapy treatments. Often made of herbs, mud, or algae, these treatments remove or redistribute fat cells and retained body water in order to create a temporarily slimmer look. Some wraps and packs actually remove impurities from the body. Hydrotherapy treatments cleanse the body using seawater, fresh water, hot tubs, whirlpool baths, and hydrotherapy tubs.

Cosmeticians also provide cosmetics and makeup consultation and application services. They may assist clients in deciding what colors and makeup to use and how they should apply it to achieve the best results, whether it's for accentuating their features or covering blemishes.

Hair removal services, usually waxing and tweezing, are also offered. Electrolysis is another popular form of hair removal; however, since a special license is required to perform electrolysis, cosmeticians generally wax and tweeze unwanted hair from the face, eyebrows, and other parts of the body.

In addition to working with clients, cosmeticians are expected to keep their work areas clean and implements sanitized. In smaller salons, many make appointments and assist with day-to-day business activities. In larger salons, cosmeticians must be aware of keeping to appointment schedules. They may be juggling two or more clients, at different stages of treatment, at the same time.

Salon managers or owners have managerial responsibilities—accounting and record keeping, hiring, firing, and motivating workers, advertising and public relations, and ordering and stocking supplies and products.

People skills are very important in this career. A critical part of cosmeticians' jobs is to cultivate and maintain a growing clientele for themselves and their salons or spas. Cosmeticians should be sensitive to the client's comfort and have dexterity and a sense of artistry. If the cosmetician's style of skin care is not suited to the client, he or she should be willing to refer the client to another specialist. This builds goodwill toward the cosmetician and the salon or spa.

REQUIREMENTS
High School

If working as a cosmetician interests you, there are a number of classes you can take in high school to prepare for this job. Some vocational high schools offer classes that will prepare you specifically for cosmetology careers.

assess the client's water and oil levels and skin conditions—whether there are blackheads, lines, wrinkles, etc. Once this information is determined, pre-cleansing, deep cleansing, exfoliation (the removal of dead skin), and extractions may follow, depending on the client's skin type. Cosmeticians often blend special cleansers and moisturizers according to their clients' individual skin types.

The application of an appropriate mask for the patron's skin type may follow the cleansing and exfoliation process, along with neck, facial, and shoulder massages. Foot and hand massages may be included as well. In most states, cosmeticians are only licensed to perform hand, foot, and facial massages, and training for these services is usually provided in cosmetology programs. Full body massages require both further training and a special license.

While performing such procedures as extractions, which involve the removal of blackheads, whiteheads, and other skin debris, cosmeticians must be careful to

If you are not attending a vocational high school, you should take science classes, such as biology, chemistry, and human anatomy. These classes will give you an understanding of how the body works as well as how chemicals react with each other. Scientific knowledge will come in handy when you consult with your clients about their allergies and skin conditions. In addition, science classes will give you the background necessary for understanding bacteriology and equipment sanitization—subjects you will most likely study in cosmetician courses following high school. Since you will be working with many different clients in this career, consider taking psychology courses, which will give you an understanding of people and their motivations. Take English and speech classes to develop your communication skills. Finally, take art courses, which will allow you to work with your hands and develop your sense of color.

Postsecondary Training

Once you have completed high school, plan on enrolling in an accredited cosmetology school. A school's accreditation by the National Accrediting Commission of Cosmetology Arts and Sciences means that the school is meeting educational standards set by this national organization. It is important to make sure you will be going to a good school, because having a solid education from a respected program is one of your strongest assets when entering this field. You should also be aware of the licensing requirements for the state in which you hope to work. Make sure that the school you are interested in will allow you to meet these requirements. Depending on the school you choose to attend, you may enter a full cosmetology program to later specialize as a cosmetician, or you may enroll in a cosmetician or esthetician program. In either case your education should include study in skin care, massage techniques, specific areas of the law pertaining to the field, sanitation methods, makeup, and salon management.

Certification or Licensing

A cosmetician needs a license in most states, though the process, laws, and requirements vary from state to state. Licensing usually involves a test of one's skill and knowledge. A few states have reciprocity agreements, which would allow licensed cosmeticians to practice in a different state without additional formal training.

Other Requirements

A friendly, people-oriented personality and good listening skills are essential for this business. Because cosmeticians must work very closely with their clients, interpersonal skills are important. Sensitivity, tactfulness, and patience are particularly vital, especially when dealing with clients who may be unhappy about their appearance or with clients who have unreasonable expectations.

Flexibility is also a necessary trait, considering the long and irregular hours a full-time cosmetician works. Furthermore, the ability to sell has also become a desirable characteristic in cosmeticians, because retail sales are becoming a large part of salon offerings. Finally, a cosmetician should enjoy learning, as he or she may need to take continuing education workshops or seminars in order to keep up with licensing requirements and new developments in the field.

EXPLORING

One of the first activities you may consider in exploring this career is to get a facial or other service provided by a cosmetician. As a client yourself, you will be able to observe the work setting and actually experience the procedure. Often people are best at providing services when they enjoy receiving the service or believe in its benefits.

Next, you may want to research this field by looking at association and trade magazines—the publications cosmeticians read to stay current with their field's trends. Trade publications will give you an idea of what current technical, legal, and fashion issues cosmeticians face.

You may choose to contact cosmetology schools to find out about cosmetician or esthetician programs in your area. Request informational brochures or course listings from the schools and speak to school advisers about the training involved and the nature of the work. A good way to locate cosmetology schools is to conduct an Internet search.

Also, once you have found a cosmetology school you are interested in, ask to set up an informational interview with an instructor or recent graduate. Go to the interview prepared to ask questions. What is the training like? What does this person enjoy about the job? What is the most difficult aspect of the work? By asking such questions you may be able to determine if the field is right for you.

You may also be able to set up an informational interview with a cosmetician who works at a spa or salon near you. Again, go to the interview prepared with questions. By networking in this fashion, you may also develop a mentor relationship. Then you may be able to spend time with your mentor at his or her place of work and observe everyday activities.

Getting a part-time position at a salon or spa on weekends or after school is an excellent way of exploring the field. Because you are working at the spa or salon on a regular basis, you will learn more about what various jobs are like and how the business functions. While on the job, you can observe the interaction between clients and cosmeticians, the interaction among coworkers, the different levels of management, and the general atmosphere. This can help you decide whether this is an area you would like to explore further.

EMPLOYERS

There are roughly 22,620 skin care specialists employed in the United States, and they work in a variety of business settings that provide beauty, fitness and health, or personal care services. They may work for salons, fitness centers, spas, as well as at resorts, large hotels, and even cruise ships. Some work for cosmetology schools as instructors of esthetics. Those with experience and interest in having their own business may decide to run their own salon where they offer a variety of services.

STARTING OUT

After completing a cosmetician or cosmetology program and passing state board exams, you can seek a position as an entry-level cosmetician. Cosmeticians find their jobs through cosmetology schools—salons and spas often recruit directly from schools. Networking in the field is also a viable option for aspiring cosmeticians looking for good work. Reading trade publication classified ads is also a way to locate job openings. Salons and spas most often advertise open positions in newspaper classifieds. There are also some placement agencies that match cosmeticians with salons and spas looking for workers.

ADVANCEMENT

Upon first entering the field, a cosmetician will advance somewhat as he or she gains clientele. A large and steady clientele will translate into higher earnings and greater professional status.

Beyond the entry-level cosmetician, one can move up to *director of cosmeticians* (often called *director of estheticians*). Eventually a cosmetician or esthetician can become a spa or salon manager, then move up to spa or salon director. For many cosmeticians, an ultimate goal is to own a spa or salon. Some cosmeticians open their own salons after being certified and without having to work up the ranks of another spa or salon.

As an alternative to working in a salon or spa, some cosmeticians decide to teach in cosmetology schools or use their knowledge to demonstrate cosmetics and skin care products in department stores. Others become cos-

metics sales representatives or start businesses as beauty consultants. Some cosmeticians work as examiners for state cosmetology boards.

EARNINGS

The U.S. Department of Labor, which groups cosmeticians with barbers, cosmetologists, and workers specializing in personal appearance services, reports that cosmeticians working full time had an annual median income of $26,170 (including tips) in 2006, with salaries ranging from less than $14,440 at the low end to more than $51,040 at the high end. However, salaries for cosmeticians vary widely based on where they work, the method of payment (commission and tips only or commission, salary, and tips), and the clientele. Those working on commission and tips only will find their beginning incomes very low as they work to build a steady clientele. In addition, not every company provides health benefits, which adds extra costs for the entry-level cosmetician who may already be struggling. Some companies pay a salary plus commission, which obviously is better for the entry-level cosmetician who has yet to establish a clientele. Some salaries start at or near minimum wage. When tips are added in, cosmeticians may end up with yearly incomes somewhere between $13,000 and $15,000. Other base salaries may reach the lower to mid-$20,000s.

It is usually not until the cosmetician reaches a manager or director position that he or she will make upwards of $50,000.

WORK ENVIRONMENT

Despite the fact that the field seems elite and glamorous, being a cosmetician is hard work. Through most of the day cosmeticians must work on their feet. Some days are relaxing while others are quite hectic. Cosmeticians and salon owners can easily work more than 40 hours per week. Weekend and lunch-hour time slots are often especially busy. According to Liza Wong, owner of Elite Skin Care, a salon in San Mateo, California, time management is the most difficult aspect of the job. "Cosmeticians must be flexible and willing to work late evenings and on weekends, around their clients' work schedules," says Wong.

On the positive side, it is a very social position. Cosmeticians see a variety of clients each day and perform a variety of services. They learn a lot from their clients—about their lives and their jobs.

OUTLOOK

Liza Wong predicts a big future for cosmeticians. "Americans are just starting to become aware of this field," Wong says. "These services, once only enjoyed by the rich, are becoming more affordable, and as baby boomers are trying to keep their youth and maintain their skin, there will be an increasing demand for skin care." The U.S. Department of Labor predicts that employment for cosmeticians will grow about as fast as the average for all other occupations through 2016. The growing popularity and affordability of day spas that offer full services should provide job opportunities for skin care specialists.

Spending for personal care services is considered by most people to be discretionary. Therefore, during hard economic times, people tend to visit cosmeticians less frequently, which reduces earnings. However, good cosmeticians are rarely laid off solely because of economic downturns.

FOR MORE INFORMATION

For industry news, a listing of accredited schools, and information on financial aid, contact

National Accrediting Commission of Cosmetology Arts and Sciences
4401 Ford Avenue, Suite 1300
Alexandria, VA 22302-1432
Tel: 703-600-7600
http://www.naccas.org

For more industry news, contact
National Cosmetology Association
401 North Michigan Avenue, 22nd Floor
Chicago, IL 60611-4245
Tel: 312-527-6765
http://www.ncacares.org

For a listing of schools by state, check out the following Web site:
Beautyschool.com
http://www.beautyschool.com

For hair styling tips and techniques, job listings, and business advice, visit the following Web site:
Behind the Chair
http://www.behindthechair.com

OVERVIEW

Cosmetologists practice hair-care skills (including washing, cutting, coloring, perming, and applying various conditioning treatments), esthetics (performing skin care

---

QUICK FACTS

SCHOOL SUBJECTS
Art
Business
Speech

PERSONAL SKILLS
Artistic
Mechanical/manipulative

WORK ENVIRONMENT
Primarily indoors
Primarily one location

MINIMUM EDUCATION LEVEL
Some postsecondary training

MEDIAN SALARY
$21,320

CERTIFICATION OR LICENSING
Required by all states

OUTLOOK
Faster than the average

---

treatments), and nail care (grooming of hands and feet). Barbers are not cosmetologists; they undergo separate training and licensing procedures. There are approximately 344,900 hairdressers, hairstylists, and cosmetologists employed in the United States.

THE JOB

Cosmetologists, also known as *hair stylists*, cut, color, perm, straighten, and style their clients' hair, in addition to providing services such as deep conditioning treatments, special-occasion long hair designs, and a variety of hair-addition techniques.

A licensed hair stylist can perform the hair services noted above and also is trained and licensed to do the basics of esthetics and nail technology. To specialize in esthetics or nail technology, additional courses are taken in each of these disciplines—or someone can study just esthetics or just nail technology and get a license in either or both of these areas.

Hair stylists may be employed in shops that have as few as one or two employees, or as many as 20 or more. They may work in privately owned salons or in a salon that is part of a chain. They may work in hotels, department stores, hospitals, nursing homes, resort areas, or on cruise ships. In recent years, a number of hair professionals—especially in big cities—have gone to work in larger facilities, sometimes known as spas or institutes, which offer a variety of health and beauty services. One such business, for example, offers complete hair design/treatment/color services; manicures and pedicures; makeup; bridal services; spa services including different kinds of facials (thermal mask, anti-aging, acne treatment), body treatments (exfoliating sea salt glow, herbal body wrap), scalp treatments, hydrotherapy water treatments, massage therapy, eyebrow/eyelash tweezing and tinting, and hair removal treatments for all parts of the body; a fashion boutique; and even a wellness center staffed with board-certified physicians.

Those who operate their own shops must also take care of the details of business operations. Bills must be paid, orders placed, invoices and supplies checked, equipment serviced, and records and books kept. The selection, hiring, and termination of other workers are also the owner's responsibility. Like other responsible businesspeople, shop and salon owners are likely to be asked to participate in civic and community projects and activities.

Some stylists work for cosmetic/hair product companies. Sean Woodyard, for instance, in addition to being employed as a stylist at a big-city salon, teaches hair coloring for a major national cosmetics/hair care company. When the company introduces a new product or sells an existing product to a new salon, the company hires hair professionals as "freelance educators" to teach the stylists at the salon how to use the product. Woodyard has traveled all over the country during the past six years, while still keeping his full-time job, teaching color techniques at salons, and also participating in demonstrations for the company at trade shows. "I've taught all levels of classes," he says, "from a very basic color demonstration to a very complex color correction class. I've also been responsible for training other educators. I have really enjoyed traveling to other locales and having the opportunity to see other salons and other parts of the beauty and fashion industry."

What Woodyard does at industry shows has varied. He is representing the company, "whether I'm standing behind a booth selling products or working on stage, demonstrating the product, or assisting a guest artist backstage, doing preparatory work. This has given me a real hands-on education, and I've been able to work with some of the top hair stylists in the country."

Woodyard has been working, as he says, "behind the chair" for 14 years. His first job after graduating from cosmetology school was at a small barbershop in his hometown. From there, he moved on to a larger salon and then on to work in a big city. "Work behind the chair led me to want to do color," he said. "This really interested me. I guess wanting to know more about it myself is the reason why I researched it and became so involved with color. As I learned more about hair coloring, I became competent and more confident." The challenge, he said, is to learn the "laws of color"— how to choose a shade to get a specific result on a client's hair. He is now considered a color expert and is the head of the chemical department at his salon. "I've always been involved some way in outside education," Woodyard notes. "I've never been in a job where I have just worked 40 hours behind the chair. I've always been involved in some kind of training. I like to share what I know."

Cosmetologists must know how to market themselves to build their business. Whether they are self-employed or work for a salon or company, they are in business for themselves. It is the cosmetologist's skills and personality that will attract clients to the salon chair. A marketing strategy Woodyard uses is to give several of his business cards to each of his clients. When one of his clients recommends him to a prospective new client, he gives both the old and new client a discount on a hair service.

Karol Thousand is the managing director of corporate school operations for a large cosmetology school that has four campuses in metropolitan areas in two states. She began as a stylist employed by salons and then owned her own shop for seven years. Her business was in an area that was destroyed by a tornado. It was then that she looked at different opportunities to decide the direction of her career. "I looked at the business end of the profession," she said, "and I took some additional business courses and was then introduced to the school aspect of the profession. I have a passion for the beauty business, and as I explored various training programs, I thought to myself, 'Hey, this is something I'd like to do!'"

She managed a cosmetology school in Wisconsin before moving to Chicago for her current position. She said, "This is an empowering and satisfying profession. Not only do you make someone look better, but 99 percent of the time, they will feel better about themselves. In cosmetology, you can have the opportunity several times a day to help change an individual's total look and perspective."

Cosmetologists serving the public must have pleasant, friendly, yet professional attitudes, as well as skill, ability, and an interest in their craft. These qualities are necessary to build a following of steady customers. The nature of their work requires cosmetologists to be aware of the psychological aspects of dealing with all types of personalities. Sometimes this can require diplomacy skills and a high degree of tolerance in dealing with different clients.

"To me," Sean Woodyard admitted, "doing hair is just as much about self-gratification as it is about pleasing the client. It makes me feel good to make somebody else look good and feel good. It's also, of course, a great artistic and creative outlet."

REQUIREMENTS

High School

High school students interested in the cosmetology field can help build a good foundation for postsecondary training by taking subjects in the areas of art, science (especially a basic chemistry course), health, business, and communication arts. Psychology and speech courses could also be helpful.

Postsecondary Training

To become a licensed cosmetologist, you must have completed an undergraduate course of a certain amount of classroom credit hours. The required amount varies from state to state—anywhere from 1,050 to 2,200 hours. The program takes from 10 to 24 months to complete, again depending on the state. Evening courses are also frequently offered, and these take two to four months longer to complete. Applicants must also pass a written test and, in some states, an oral test before they receive a license. Most states will allow a cosmetologist to work as an apprentice until the license is received, which normally just involves a matter of weeks.

A 1,500-hour undergraduate course at a cosmetology school in Illinois is typical of schools around the country. The program consists of theoretical and practical instruction divided into individual units of learning. Students are taught through the media of theory, audiovisual presentation, lectures, demonstrations, practical hands-on experiences, and written and practical testing. All schools have what they call clinic areas or floors, where people can have their hair done (or avail themselves of esthetics or nail services) by students at a discounted price, compared to what they would pay in a regular shop or salon.

One course, Scientific Approach to Hair Sculpture, teaches students how to sculpt straight and curly hair, ethnic and Caucasian, using shears, texturizing tools and techniques, razors, and electric clippers. Teaching tools include mannequins, slip-ons, hair wefts, rectangles, and profiles. People skills segments are part of each course. Among other courses are Scientific Approach to Perm Design, Systematic Approach to Color, and Systematic Approach to Beauty Care. Three different salon prep courses focus on retailing, business survival skills, and practical applications for contemporary design. The program concludes with final testing, as well as extensive reviews and preparations for state board testing through a mock state board written practical examination.

Cosmetology schools teach some aspects of human physiology and anatomy, including the bone structure of the head and some elementary facts about the nervous system, in addition to hair skills. Some schools have now added psychology-related courses to teach good people skills and interpersonal communications.

Karol Thousand noted that, at her school and others throughout the country, "Twenty-five years ago, the courses focused mainly on technical skills. This is still the core focus, but now we teach more interpersonal skills. Our People Skills program helps students understand the individual, the different personality types—to better comprehend how they fit in and how to relate to their clients. We also teach sales and marketing skills—how to sell themselves and their services and products, as well as good business management skills."

Some states offer student internship programs. One such program that was recently initiated in Illinois aims to send better-prepared students/junior stylists into the workforce upon completion of their training from a licensed school. This program allows students to enter into a work-study program for 10 percent of their training in either cosmetology, esthetics, or nail technology. The state requires a student to complete at least 750 hours of training prior to making application for the program.

The program allows a student to experience firsthand the expectations of a salon, to perform salon services to be evaluated by their supervisor, and to experience different types of salon settings. The participating salons have the opportunity to prequalify potential employees before they graduate and work with the school regarding the skill levels of the student interns. This will also enhance job placement programs already in place in the school. The state requires that each participating salon be licensed and registered with the appropriate state department and file proof of registration with the school, along with the name and license number of their cosmetologist who is assigned to supervise students, before signing a contract or agreement.

Certification or Licensing

At the completion of the proper amount of credit hours, students must pass a formal examination before they can be licensed. The exam takes just a few hours. Some states also require a practical (hands-on) test and oral exams.

Most, however, just require written tests. State board examinations are given at regular intervals. After about a month, test scores are available. Those who have passed then send in a licensure application and a specified fee to the appropriate state department. It takes about four to six weeks for a license to be issued.

Temporary permits are issued in most states, allowing students who have passed the test and applied for a license to practice their profession while they wait to receive the actual license. Judy Vargas, manager of the professional services section of the Illinois Department of Financial and Professional Regulation, warns students not to practice without a temporary permit or a license. "This is the biggest violation we see," she said, "and there are penalties of up to $1,000 per violation."

Graduate courses on advanced techniques and new methods and styles are also available at many cosmetology schools. Many states require licensed cosmetologists to take a specified number of credit hours, called continuing education units, or CEUs. Illinois, for instance, requires each licensed cosmetologist to complete 10 to 14 CEUs each year. Licenses must be renewed in all states, generally every year or every two years.

In the majority of states, the minimum age for an individual to obtain a cosmetology license is 16. Because standards and requirements vary from state to state, students are urged to contact the licensing board of the state in which they plan to be employed.

Other Requirements

Hairstyles change from season to season. As a cosmetologist, you will need to keep up with current fashion trends and learn new procedures to create new looks. You should be able to visualize different styles and make suggestions to your clients about what is best for them. And even if you don't specialize in coloring hair, you should have a good sense of color. One of your most important responsibilities will be to make your clients feel comfortable around you and happy with their looks. To do this, you will need to develop both your talking and listening skills.

EXPLORING

Talk to friends or parents of friends who are working in the industry, or just go to a local salon or cosmetology school and ask questions about the profession. Go to the library and get books on careers in the beauty/hair care industry. Search the Internet for related Web sites. Individuals with an interest in the field might seek after-school or summer employment as a general shop helper in a barbershop or a salon. Some schools may permit potential students to visit and observe classes.

EMPLOYERS

Approximately 344,900 hairdressers, hairstylists, and cosmetologists are employed in the United States. The most common employers of hair stylists are, of course, beauty salons. However, hair stylists also find work at department stores, hospitals, nursing homes, spas, resorts, cruise ships, and cosmetics companies. The demand for services in the cosmetology field—hair styling in particular—far exceeds the supply; additionally, the number of salons increases by 2 percent each year. Considering that most cosmetology schools have placement services to assist graduates, finding employment usually is not difficult for most cosmetologists. As with most jobs in the cosmetology field, opportunities will be concentrated in highly populated areas; however, there will be jobs available for hair stylists virtually everywhere. Many hair stylists/cosmetologists aspire ultimately to be self-employed. This can be a rewarding avenue if one has plenty of experience and good business sense (not to mention start-up capital or financial backing); it also requires long hours and a great deal of hard work.

STARTING OUT

To be a licensed cosmetologist/hair stylist, you must graduate from an accredited school and pass a state test. Once that is accomplished, you can apply for jobs that are advertised in the newspapers or over the Internet, or apply at an employment agency specializing in these professions. Most schools have placement services to help their graduates find jobs. Some salons have training programs from which they hire new employees.

Scholarships or grants that can help you pay for your schooling are available. One such program is the Access to Cosmetology Education (ACE) grant. It is sponsored by the American Association of Cosmetology Schools (AACS), the Beauty and Barber Supply Institute Inc., and the Cosmetology Advancement Foundation. Interested students can find out about ACE grants and obtain applications at participating schools, salons, and distributors or through these institutions. The criteria for receiving an ACE grant include approval from an AACS member school, recommendations from two salons, and a high school diploma or GED.

ADVANCEMENT

Individuals in the beauty/hair care industry most frequently begin by working at a shop or salon. Many aspire to be self-employed and own their own shop. There are many factors to consider when contemplating going into your own business. Usually it is essential to obtain experience and financial capital before seeking to own a shop.

The cost of equipping even a one-chair shop can be very high. Owning a large shop or a chain of shops is an aspiration for the very ambitious.

Some pursue advanced educational training in one aspect of beauty culture, such as hair styling or coloring. Others who are more interested in the business aspects can take courses in business management skills and move into shop or salon management, or work for a corporation related to the industry. Manufacturers and distributors frequently have exciting positions available for those with exceptional talent and creativity. Cosmetologists work on the stage as platform artists, or take some additional education courses and teach at a school of cosmetology.

Some schools publish their own texts and other printed materials for students. They want people who have cosmetology knowledge and experience as well as writing skills to write and edit these materials. An artistic director for the publishing venue of one large school has a cosmetology degree in addition to degrees in art. Other cosmetologists might design hairstyles for fashion magazines, industry publications, fashion shows, television presentations, or movies. They might get involved in the regulation of the business, such as working for a state licensing board. There are many and varied career possibilities cosmetologists can explore in the beauty/hair care industry.

EARNINGS

Cosmetologists can make an excellent living in the beauty/hair care industry, but as in most careers, they don't receive very high pay when just starting out. Though their raise in salary may start slowly, the curve quickly escalates. The U.S. Department of Labor reports cosmetologists and hairstylists had a median annual income (including tips) of $21,320 in 2006. The lowest paid 10 percent, which generally included those beginning in the profession, made less than $13,880. The highest paid 10 percent earned more than $39,070. Again, both those salaries include tips. On the extreme upward end of the pay scale, some fashion stylists in New York or Hollywood charge $300 per haircut. Their annual salary can go into six figures. Salaries in larger cities are greater than those in smaller towns; but then the cost of living is higher in the big cities, too.

Most shops and salons give a new employee a guaranteed income instead of commission. If the employee goes over the guaranteed amount, then he or she earns a commission. Usually, this guarantee will extend for the first three months of employment, so that the new stylist can focus on building up business before going on straight commission.

In addition, most salon owners grant incentives for product sales; and, of course, there are always tips. However, true professionals never depend on their tips. If a stylist receives a tip, it is a nice surprise for a job well done, but it is good business practice not to expect these bonuses. All tips must be recorded and reported to the Internal Revenue Service.

The benefits a cosmetologist receives, such as health insurance and retirement plans, depend on the place of employment. A small independent salon cannot afford to supply a hefty benefit package, but a large shop or salon or a member of a chain can be more generous. However, some of the professional associations and organizations offer benefit packages at reasonable rates.

WORK ENVIRONMENT

Those employed in the cosmetology industry usually work a five- or six-day week, which averages approximately 40–50 hours. Weekends and days preceding holidays may be especially busy. Cosmetologists are on their feet a lot and are usually working in a small space. Strict sanitation codes must be observed in all shops and salons, and they are comfortably heated, ventilated, and well lighted.

Hazards of the trade include nicks and cuts from scissors and razors, minor burns when care is not used in handling hot towels or instruments, and occasional skin irritations arising from constant use of grooming aids that contain chemicals. Some of the chemicals used in hair dyes or permanent solutions can be very abrasive; plastic gloves are required for handling and contact. Pregnant women are advised to avoid contact with many of those chemicals present in hair products.

Conditions vary depending on what environment the stylist is working in. Those employed in department store salons will have more of a guaranteed client flow, with more walk-ins from people who are shopping. A freestanding shop or salon might have a more predictable pace, with more scheduled appointments and fewer walk-ins. In a department store salon, for example, stylists have to abide by the rules and regulations of the store. In a private salon, stylists are more like entrepreneurs or freelancers, but they have much more flexibility as to when they come and go and what type of business they want to do.

Stylist Sean Woodyard says, "I've always enjoyed the atmosphere of a salon. There's constant action and something different happening every day. A salon attracts artistic, creative people and the profession allows me to be part of the fashion industry."

Some may find it difficult to work constantly in such close, personal contact with the public at large, especially when they strive to satisfy customers who are difficult to please or disagreeable. The work demands an even temperament, pleasant disposition, and patience.

OUTLOOK

The future looks good for cosmetology. According to the U.S. Department of Labor, employment should grow faster than the average through 2016. Our growing population, the availability of disposable income, and changes in hair fashion that are practically seasonal all contribute to the demand for cosmetologists. In addition, turnover in this career is fairly high as cosmetologists move up into management positions, change careers, or leave the field for other reasons. Competition for jobs at higher paying, prestigious salons, however, is strong.

FOR MORE INFORMATION

For information on cosmetology careers, schools, and the ACE Grant, contact

American Association of Cosmetology Schools
15825 North 71st Street, Suite 100
Scottsdale, AZ 85254-1521
Tel: 800-831-1086
http://www.beautyschools.org

For information on accredited cosmetology programs, contact

National Accrediting Commission of Cosmetology Arts and Sciences
4401 Ford Avenue, Suite 1300
Alexandria, VA 22302-1432
Tel: 703-600-7600
http://www.naccas.org

For information on scholarships, contact

National Cosmetology Association
401 North Michigan Avenue, 22nd Floor
Chicago, IL 60611-4245
Tel: 312-527-6765
http://www.ncacares.org

COST ESTIMATORS

OVERVIEW

Cost estimators use standard estimating techniques to calculate the cost of a construction or manufacturing project. They help contractors, owners, and project planners determine how much a project or product will cost to decide if it is economically viable. There are approximately 221,000 cost estimators employed in the United States.

THE JOB

In the construction industry, the nature of the work is largely determined by the type and size of the project being estimated. For a large building project, for example, the cost estimator reviews architectural drawings and other bidding documents before any construction begins. The estimator then visits the potential construction site to collect information that may affect the way the structure is built, such as the site's access to transportation, water, electricity, and other needed resources. While out in the field, the estimator also analyzes the topography of the land, taking note of its general characteristics, such as drainage areas and the location of trees and other vegetation. After compiling thorough research, the estimator writes a quantity survey, or takeoff. This is an itemized report of the quantity of materials and labor a firm will need for the proposed project.

Large projects often require several estimators, all specialists in a given area. For example, one estimator may assess the electrical costs of a project, while another concentrates on the transportation or insurance costs. In this case, it is the responsibility of a *chief estimator* to combine the reports and submit one development proposal.

In manufacturing, estimators work with engineers to review blueprints and other designs. They develop a list of the materials and labor needed for production. Aiming to control costs but maintain quality, estimators must weigh the option of producing parts in-house or purchasing them from other vendors. After this research, they write a report on the overall costs of manufacturing, taking into consideration influences such as improved employee learning curves, material waste, overhead, and the need to correct problems as manufacturing goes along.

To write their reports, estimators must know current prices for labor and materials and other factors that influence costs. They obtain this data through commercial price books, catalogs, and the Internet, or by calling vendors directly to obtain quotes.

Estimators should also be able to compute and understand accounting and mathematical formulas in order to make their cost reports. Computer programs are frequently used to do the routine calculations, producing more accurate results and leaving the estimator with more time to analyze data.

REQUIREMENTS
High School

To prepare for a job in cost estimating, you should take courses in accounting, business, economics, and mathematics. Because a large part of this job involves comparing calculations, it is essential that you have excellent math skills. English courses with a heavy concentration in writing are also recommended to develop your communication skills. Cost estimators must be able to write clear and accurate reports of their analyses. Finally, drafting and shop courses are also useful since estimators must be able to review and understand blueprints and other design plans.

Postsecondary Training

Though not required for the job, most employers of cost estimators in both construction and manufacturing prefer applicants with formal education. In construction, cost estimators generally have an associate's or bachelor's degree in construction management, construction science, engineering, or architecture. Those employed with manufacturers often have degrees in physical science, business, mathematics, operations research, statistics, engineering, economics, finance, or accounting.

Many colleges and universities offer courses in cost estimating as part of the curriculum for an associate's, bachelor's, or master's degree. These courses cover subjects such as cost estimating, cost control, project planning and management, and computer applications. The Association for the Advancement of Cost Engineering International offers a list of education programs related to cost engineering. Check out the association's Web site, http://www.aacei.org, for more information.

Certification or Licensing

Although it is not required, many cost estimators find it helpful to become certified to improve their standing within the professional community. Obtaining certification proves that the estimator has obtained adequate job training and education. Information on certification procedures is available from organizations such as the American Society of Professional Estimators, the Association for the Advancement of Cost Engineering International, and the Society of Cost Estimating and Analysis.

Other Requirements

To be a cost estimator, you should have sharp mathematical and analytical skills. Cost estimators must work well with others, and be confident and assertive when presenting findings to engineers, business owners, and design professionals. You will need some experience in order to work as a cost estimator in the construction industry; you can do this by completing an internship or cooperative education program.

QUICK FACTS

SCHOOL SUBJECTS
Business
Economics
Mathematics

PERSONAL SKILLS
Leadership/management
Technical/scientific

WORK ENVIRONMENT
Indoors and outdoors
Primarily multiple locations

MINIMUM EDUCATION LEVEL
Some postsecondary training

MEDIAN SALARY
$52,940

CERTIFICATION OR LICENSING
Recommended

OUTLOOK
Faster than the average

EXPLORING

Practical work experience is necessary to become a cost estimator. Consider taking a part-time position with a construction crew or manufacturing firm during your summer vacations. Because of more favorable working conditions, construction companies are the busiest during the summer months and may be looking for additional assistance. Join any business or manufacturing clubs that your school may offer.

Another way to discover more about career opportunities is simply by talking to a professional cost estimator. Ask your school counselor to help arrange an interview with an estimator to ask questions about his or her job demands, work environment, and personal opinion of the job.

EMPLOYERS

Approximately 221,000 cost estimators are employed in the United States: 62 percent by the construction industry and 15 percent by manufacturing companies. Other employers include engineering and architecture firms, business services, government, and a wide range of other industries.

Estimators are employed throughout the country, but the largest concentrations are found in cities or rapidly growing suburban areas. More job opportunities exist in or near large commercial or government centers.

STARTING OUT

Cost estimators often start out working in the industry as laborers, such as construction workers. After gaining experience and taking the necessary training courses, a worker may move into the more specialized role of estimator. Another possible route into cost estimating is through a formal training program, either through a professional organization that sponsors educational programs or through technical schools, community colleges, or universities. School placement counselors can be good sources of employment leads for recent graduates. Applying directly to manufacturers, construction firms, and government agencies is another way to find your first job.

Whether employed in construction or manufacturing, most cost estimators are provided with intensive on-the-job training. Generally, new hires work with experienced estimators to become familiar with the work involved. They develop skills in blueprint reading and learn construction specifications before accompanying estimators to the construction site. In time, new hires learn how to determine quantities and specifications from project designs and report appropriate material and labor costs.

ADVANCEMENT

Promotions for cost estimators are dependent on skill and experience. Advancement usually comes in the form of more responsibility and higher wages. A skilled cost estimator at a large construction company may become a chief estimator. Some experienced cost estimators go into consulting work, offering their services to government, construction, and manufacturing firms.

EARNINGS

Salaries vary according to the size of the construction or manufacturing firm and the experience and education of the worker. According to the U.S. Department of Labor, the median annual salary for cost estimators was $52,940 in 2006. The lowest 10 percent earned less than $31,600 and the highest 10 percent earned more than $88,310. By industry, the mean annual earnings were as follows: nonresidential building construction, $60,870;

residential building construction, $52,460; foundation and exterior contractors, $52,520; and building equipment contractors, $56,170. Starting salaries for graduates of engineering or construction management programs were higher than those with degrees in other fields. A July 2007 salary survey by the National Association of Colleges and Employers reports that candidates with bachelor's degrees in construction science/management were offered average starting salaries of $46,930 a year.

WORK ENVIRONMENT

Much of the cost estimator's work takes place in a typical office setting with access to accounting records and other information. However, estimators must also visit construction sites or manufacturing facilities to inspect production procedures. These sites may be dirty, noisy, and potentially hazardous if the cost estimator is not equipped with proper protective gear such as a hard hat or earplugs. During a site visit, cost estimators consult with engineers, work supervisors, and other professionals involved in the production or manufacturing process.

Estimators usually work a 40-hour week, although longer hours may be required if a project faces a deadline. For construction estimators, overtime hours almost always occur in the summer when most projects are in full force.

OUTLOOK

Employment for cost estimators is expected to increase faster than the average through 2016, according to the U.S. Department of Labor. As in most industries, highly trained college graduates and those with the most experience will have the best job prospects.

Many jobs will arise from the need to replace workers leaving the industry, either to retire or change jobs. In addition, growth within the residential and commercial construction industry is a large cause for much of the employment demand for estimators. The fastest growing areas in construction are in special trade and government projects, including the building and repairing of highways, streets, bridges, subway systems, airports, water and sewage systems, and electric power plants and transmission lines. Additionally, opportunities will be good in residential and school construction, as well as in the construction of nursing and extended care facilities. Cost estimators with degrees in construction management or in construction science, engineering, or architecture will have the best employment prospects. In manufacturing, employment is predicted to remain stable, though growth is not expected to be as strong as in construction. Estimators will be in demand because employers will continue to need their services to control operating costs. Estimators with degrees in engineering, science, mathematics, business administration, or economics will have the best employment prospects in this industry.

FOR MORE INFORMATION

For information on certification and educational programs, contact

American Society of Professional Estimators
2525 Perimeter Place Drive, Suite 103
Nashville, TN 37214-3674
Tel: 888-EST-MATE
Email: info@aspenational.org
http://www.aspenational.org

For information on certification, educational programs, and scholarships, contact

Association for the Advancement of Cost Engineering
International
209 Prairie Avenue, Suite 100
Morgantown, WV 26501-5934
Tel: 800-858-2678
Email: info@aacei.org
http://www.aacei.org

For information on certification, job listings, and a glossary of cost-estimating terms, visit the SCEA Web site:

Society of Cost Estimating and Analysis (SCEA)
527 Maple Avenue East, Suite 301
Vienna, VA 22180
Tel: 703-938-5090
Email: scea@sceaonline.net
http://www.sceaonline.net

☐ COURT REPORTERS

OVERVIEW

Court reporters record every word at hearings, trials, depositions, and other legal proceedings by using a stenotype machine to take shorthand notes. Most court reporters transcribe the notes of the proceedings by using computer-aided transcription systems that print out regular, legible copies of the proceedings. The court reporter must also edit and proofread the final transcript and create the official transcript of the trial or other legal proceeding. Approximately 19,000 court reporters work in the United States.

QUICK FACTS

SCHOOL SUBJECTS
English
Foreign language
Government

PERSONAL SKILLS
Communication/ideas
Following instructions

WORK ENVIRONMENT
Primarily indoors
Primarily multiple locations

MINIMUM EDUCATION LEVEL
Some postsecondary training

MEDIAN SALARY
$45,610

CERTIFICATION OR LICENSING
Required by certain states

OUTLOOK
Much faster than the average

THE JOB

Court reporters are best known as the men or women sitting in the courtroom silently typing to record what is said by everyone involved in the proceedings. While that is true, it is only part of the court reporter's job. The court reporter does a lot more work once he or she leaves the courtroom.

In the courtroom, court reporters use symbols or shorthand forms of complete words to record what is said as quickly as it is spoken on a stenotype machine that looks like a miniature typewriter. The stenotype machine has 24 keys on its keyboard. Each key prints a single symbol. Unlike a typewriter, however, the court reporter using a stenotype machine can press more than one key at a time to print different combinations of symbols. Each symbol or combination represents a different sound, word, or phrase. As testimony is given, the reporter strikes one or more keys to create a phonetic representation of the testimony on a strip of paper, as well as on a computer disk inside the stenotype machine. The court reporter later uses a computer to translate and transcribe the testimony into legible, full-page documents or stores them for reference. Remember, people in court may speak at a rate of between 250 and 300 words a minute, and court reporters must record this testimony word for word and quickly.

Accurate recording of a trial is vital because the court reporter's record becomes the official transcript for the entire proceeding. In our legal system, court transcripts can be used after the trial for many important purposes. If a legal case is appealed, for example, the court reporter's transcript becomes the foundation for any further legal action. The appellate judge refers to the court reporter's transcript to see what happened in the trial and how the evidence was presented.

Because of the importance of accuracy, a court reporter who misses a word or phrase must interrupt the proceedings to have the words repeated. The court reporter may be asked by the judge to read aloud a portion of recorded testimony during the trial to refresh everyone's memory. Court reporters must pay close attention to all the proceedings and be able to hear and understand everything. Sometimes it may be difficult to understand a particular witness or attorney due to poor diction, a strong accent, or a soft speaking voice. Nevertheless, the court reporter cannot be shy about stopping the trial and asking for clarification.

Court reporters must be adept at recording testimony on a wide range of legal issues, from medical malpractice to income tax evasion. In some cases, court reporters may record testimony at a murder trial or a child custody case. Witnessing tense situations and following complicated arguments are unavoidable parts of the job. The court reporter must be able to remain detached from the drama that unfolds in court while faithfully recording all that is said.

After the trial or hearing, the court reporter has more work to do. Using a computer-aided transcription (CAT) program, the stenotype notes are translated to English. The majority of these translated notes are accurate. This rough translation is then edited either by the court reporter or by a *scopist*—an assistant to the court reporter who edits and cleans up the notes. If a stenotype note did not match a word in the court reporter's CAT dictionary during translation, it shows up still in stenotype form. The court reporter must manually change these entries into words and update the dictionary used in translating. If there are any meanings of words or spellings of names that are unfamiliar to the court reporter, research must be done to verify that the correct term or spelling is

used. The court reporter then proofreads the transcript to check for any errors in meaning, such as the word *here* instead of the word *hear*. If necessary or requested by the lawyer or judge, special indexes and concordances are compiled using computer programs. The last step the court reporter must take is printing and binding the transcript to make it an organized and usable document for the lawyers and judge.

In some states, the court reporter is responsible for swearing in the witnesses and documenting items of evidence.

In addition to the traditional method of court reporting discussed above, a number of other methods of reporting have emerged in recent years. In real-time court reporting, the court reporter types the court proceedings on a stenotype machine, which is connected to a computer. The symbols that the court reporter types on the stenotype machine are converted to words that can be read by those involved in the case. This process is known as communications access real-time translation (CART). In addition to its use in court, CART is used in meetings, educational settings, and for closed captioning for the hearing-impaired on television.

In electronic reporting, the court reporter uses audio equipment to record court proceedings. The court reporter is responsible for overseeing the recording process, taking notes to identify speakers and clarify other issues, and ensuring the quality of the recording. Court reporters who specialize in this method are often asked to create a written transcript of the recorded proceeding.

In voice writing, a court reporter wears a hand-held mask (known as a voice silencer) that is equipped with a microphone, and repeats the testimony of all parties involved in the trial. Some reporters translate the voice recording in real time using computer speech recognition technology. Others wait till after the proceedings to create the translation using voice recognition technology or by doing the translation manually.

REQUIREMENTS
High School

To be a court reporter, you need to have a high school diploma or its equivalent. Take as many high-level classes in English as you can and get a firm handle on grammar and spelling. Take typing classes and computer classes to give you a foundation in using computers and a head start in keyboarding skills. Classes in government and business will be helpful as well. Training in Latin can also be a great benefit because it will help you understand the many medical and legal terms that arise during court proceedings. Knowledge of foreign languages can also be helpful because as a court reporter, you will often transcribe the testimony of non-English speakers with the aid of court-appointed translators.

Postsecondary Training

Court reporters are required to complete a specialized training program in shorthand reporting. These programs usually last between two and four years and include instruction on how to enter at least 225 words a minute on a stenotype machine. Other topics include computer operations, transcription methods, English grammar, and the principles of law. For court cases involving medical issues, students must also take courses on human anatomy and physiology. Basic medical and legal terms are also explained.

About 160 postsecondary schools and colleges have two- and four-year programs in court reporting; approximately 70 of these programs are approved by the National Court Reporters Association (NCRA). Many business colleges offer these programs. As a court reporting student in these programs, you must master machine shorthand, or stenotyping, and real-time reporting. The NCRA states that to graduate from one of these programs, you must be able to type at least 225 words per minute and pass tests that gauge your written knowledge and speed.

Certification or Licensing

The NCRA offers several levels of certification for its members. To receive the registered professional reporter certification, you must pass tests that are administered twice a year at more than 100 sites in the United States and overseas. The registered merit reporter certification means you have passed an exam with speeds up to 260 words per minute. The registered diplomate reporter certification is obtained by passing a knowledge exam. This certification shows that the court reporter has gained valuable professional knowledge and experience through years of reporting. The certified real time reporter certification is given to reporters who have obtained the specialized skill of converting the spoken word into written word within seconds. Several other specialized certifications are available for the court reporter.

The American Association of Electronic Reporters and Transcribers also offers the following voluntary certifications: certified electronic court reporter, certified electronic court transcriber, and certified electronic court reporter and transcriber. The National Verbatim Reporters Association offers the following voluntary certifications: certified verbatim reporter, certificate of merit, and real-time verbatim reporter. Contact these organizations for information on requirements for each certification.

Some states require reporters to be notary publics or to be certified through a state certification exam. Currently, more than 40 states grant licenses in either shorthand reporting or court reporting, although not all of these states require a license to work as a court reporter. Licenses are granted after the court reporter passes state examinations and fulfills any prerequisites (usually an approved shorthand reporting program).

Other Requirements

Because part of a court reporter's work is done within the confines of a courtroom, being able to work under pressure is a must. Court reporters need to be able to meet deadlines with accuracy and attention to detail. As stated previously, a court reporter must be highly skilled at the stenotype machine. A minimum of 225 words per minute is expected from a beginning court reporter.

Court reporters must be familiar with a wide range of medical and legal terms and must be assertive enough to ask for clarification if a term or phrase goes by without the reporter understanding it. Court reporters must be as unbiased as possible and accurately record what is said, not what they believe to be true. Patience and perfectionism are vital characteristics, as is the ability to work closely with judges and other court officials.

EXPLORING

Can you see yourself as a court reporter someday? As with any career, you have much to consider. To get an idea of what a court reporter does—at least the work they do in public—attend some trials at your local courts. Instead of focusing on the main players—witnesses, lawyers, judges—keep an eye on the court reporter. If you can, watch several reporters in different courtrooms under different judges to get a perspective on what the average court reporter does. Try to arrange a one-on-one meeting with a court reporter so you can ask the questions you really want answers for. Maybe you can convince one of your teachers to arrange a field trip to a local court.

EMPLOYERS

Approximately 19,000 court reporters are employed in the United States. Many court reporters are employed by city, county, state, or federal courts. Others work for themselves as freelancers or as employees of freelance reporting agencies. These freelance reporters are hired by attorneys to record the pretrial statements, or depositions, of experts and other witnesses. When people want transcripts of other important discussions, freelance reporters may be called on to record what is said at business meetings, large conventions, or similar events.

Most court reporters work in middle- to large-size cities, although they are needed anywhere a court of law is in session. In smaller cities, a court reporter may only work part time.

A new application of court-reporting skills and technology is in the field of television captioning. Using specialized computer-aided transcription systems, reporters can produce captions for live television events, including sporting events and national and local news, for the benefit of hearing-impaired viewers.

STARTING OUT

After completing the required training, court reporters usually work for a freelance reporting company that provides court reporters for business meetings and courtroom proceedings on a temporary basis. Qualified reporters can also contact these freelance reporting companies on their own. Occasionally a court reporter will be hired directly out of school as a courtroom official, but ordinarily only those with several years of experience are hired for full-time judiciary work. A would-be court reporter may start out working as a medical transcriptionist or other specific transcriptionist to get the necessary experience.

Job placement counselors at community colleges can be helpful in finding that first job.

ADVANCEMENT

Skilled court reporters may be promoted to a larger court system or to an otherwise more demanding position, with an accompanying increase in pay and prestige. Those working for a freelance company may be hired permanently by a city, county, state, or federal court. Those with experience working in a government position may choose to become a freelance court reporter and thereby have greater job flexibility and perhaps earn more money. Those with the necessary training, experience, and business skills may decide to open their own freelance reporting company.

According to a study funded by the National Court Reporters Foundation, court reporters advance by assuming more responsibility and greater skill levels; this gives the court reporter credibility in the eyes of the professionals in the legal system. Those advanced

responsibilities include real-time reporting, coding and cross-referencing the official record, assisting others in finding specific information quickly, and helping the judge and legal counsel with procedural matters.

Court reporters can also follow alternative career paths as captioning experts, legal and medical transcriptionists, and cyber-conference moderators.

EARNINGS

Earnings vary according to the skill, speed, and experience of the court reporter, as well as geographic location. Those who are employed by large court systems generally earn more than their counterparts in smaller communities. The median annual income for all court reporters was $45,610 in 2006, according to the U.S. Department of Labor. Ten percent of reporters were paid less than $23,430 annually, and 10 percent had annual earnings of more than $77,770. Incomes can be even higher depending on the reporter's skill level, length of service, and the amount of time the reporter works. Official court reporters not only earn a salary, but also a per-page fee for transcripts. Freelance court reporters are paid by the job and also per page for transcripts.

Court reporters who work in small communities or as freelancers may not be able to work full time. Successful court reporters with jobs in business environments may earn more than those in courtroom settings, but such positions carry less job security.

Those working for the government or full time for private companies usually receive health insurance and other benefits, such as paid vacations and retirement pensions. Freelancers may or may not receive health insurance or other benefits, depending on the policies of their agencies.

WORK ENVIRONMENT

Offices and courtrooms are usually pleasant places to work. Under normal conditions, a court reporter can expect to work a standard 40 hours per week. During lengthy trials or other complicated proceedings, court reporters often work much longer hours. They must be on hand before and after the court is actually in session and must wait while a jury is deliberating. A court reporter often must be willing to work irregular hours, including some evenings. Court reporters must be able to spend long hours transcribing testimony with complete accuracy. There may be some travel involved, especially for freelance reporters and court reporters who are working for a traveling circuit judge. Normally, a court reporter will experience some down time without any transcript orders and then be hit all at once with several.

This uneven workflow can cause the court reporter to have odd hours at times.

Court reporters spend time working with finances as well. Paperwork for record-keeping and tracking invoices, income, and expenses is part of the job.

Long hours of sitting in the same position can be tiring and court reporters may be bothered by eye and neck strain. There is also the risk of repetitive motion injuries, including carpal tunnel syndrome. The constant pressure to keep up and remain accurate can be stressful as well.

OUTLOOK

The U.S. Department of Labor predicts that employment of court reporters should grow faster than the average for all occupations through 2016. Despite the rising number of criminal court cases and civil lawsuits, reduced budgets will limit employment opportunities for court reporters in both state and federal court systems. Job opportunities should be greatest in and around large metropolitan areas, but qualified court reporters should be able to find work in most parts of the country. Court reporters will also find great employment opportunities outside of the legal realm producing captioning for television programs, which is a federal requirement for all television programming, and creating real-time translations for the deaf and hard-of-hearing in legal and academic settings.

As always, job prospects will be best for those with the most training and experience. Because of the reliance on computers in many aspects of this job, computer experience and training are important. Court reporters who are certified—especially with the highest level of certification—will have the most opportunities to choose from.

As court reporters continue to use cutting-edge technology to make court transcripts more usable and accurate, the field itself should continue to grow.

FOR MORE INFORMATION

For information on digital/electronic court reporting and certification, contact

American Association of Electronic Reporters and Transcribers
23812 Rock Circle
Bothell, WA 98021-8573
Tel: 800-233-5306
Email: aaert@blarg.net
http://www.aaert.org

For information on certification and court reporting careers and scholarships, contact

National Court Reporters Association
8224 Old Courthouse Road
Vienna, VA 22182-3808
Tel: 800-272-6272
Email: msic@ncrahq.org
http://www.ncraonline.org

For tips on preparing for certification exams, and for other career information, contact

National Verbatim Reporters Association
207 Third Avenue
Hattiesburg, MS 39401-3868
Tel: 601-582-4345
Email: nvra@aol.com
http://www.nvra.org

This organization represents court reporters who are employed at the federal level.

U.S. Court Reporters Association
4725 North Western Avenue, Suite 240
Chicago, IL 60625
Tel: 800-628-2730
Email: uscra@uscra.org
http://www.uscra.org

☐ CRITICAL CARE NURSES

OVERVIEW

Critical care nurses are specialized nurses who provide highly skilled direct patient care to critically ill patients needing intense medical treatment. Critical care nurses work not only in intensive care units (ICU) and cardiac care units (CCU) of hospitals, but also in the emergency departments, post-anesthesia recovery units, pediatric intensive care units, burn units, and neonatal intensive care units of medical facilities, as well as in other units that treat critically ill patients. According to the "Registered Nurse Population" study done by the Department of Health and Human Services, there are 403,527 nurses in the United States who care for critically ill patients in hospitals.

THE JOB

Critical care nursing is a very challenging job. Because medical facilities employ critical care nurses who work in various units, their job responsibilities vary; however, their main responsibility is providing highly skilled

QUICK FACTS

SCHOOL SUBJECTS
Biology
Chemistry

PERSONAL SKILLS
Helping/teaching
Technical/scientific

WORK ENVIRONMENT
Primarily indoors
Primarily one location

MINIMUM EDUCATION LEVEL
Some postsecondary training

MEDIAN SALARY
$57,280

CERTIFICATION OR LICENSING
Required by all states

OUTLOOK
Much faster than the average

medical and post-surgical care for critically ill patients. Critical care nurses may be assigned one or two patients that they care for as opposed to being involved in the care of several patients.

Brandon Frady, a registered nurse and a certified critical care nurse, works in the pediatrics intensive care unit of an Atlanta children's hospital. He works as a bedside nurse and as a relief charge nurse, meaning that he is not only responsible for caring for his patients, but he is also in charge of the administration of the ward.

Frady is also part of the ground transport team that transports critically ill or injured children within a 150-mile radius to their center. "We are the cutting-edge hospital for pediatric health care," says Frady. "We care for very sick children here and our skills are challenged on a daily basis."

Critical care nursing requires keeping up with the latest medical technology and research as well as medical treatments and procedures. "There is something new to learn every day," Frady says. "We have to learn to operate

very high-tech machines, and we are frequently tested on their use and operation. Plus, we need to know the latest research and treatments available for acutely ill children."

Critical care nursing is a very intense nursing specialty. Patients require constant care and monitoring, says Frady. "Many hospitals are requiring nurses to work 12-hour shifts, which can be very exhausting."

In many cases, critical care nurses are confronted with situations that require them to act immediately on the patients' behalf. The nurse must be a patient advocate, meaning that the nurse must help the patients receive the best possible care and also respect their wishes. They must also provide support and education to the patients and their families.

"Although it can be an emotionally draining job, it can also be very rewarding to know that I helped the child and family get through their medical crisis," Frady relates. "It is especially satisfying when they come back later and thank you for what you have done. The job is very satisfying."

REQUIREMENTS
Postsecondary Training

Critical care nurses must be registered nurses. (See the chapter on Registered Nurses.) Entry-level requirements to become a critical care nurse depend on the institution, its size, whom it serves, and the availability of nurses in that specialty and geographical region. Usually nurses must have some bedside nursing experience before entering the critical care nursing field. However, some hospitals are developing graduate internship and orientation programs that allow new graduates to enter this specialty.

Certification or Licensing

There are critical care nursing certification programs available through the American Association of Critical-Care Nurses (AACN). Some institutions may require certification as a critical care nurse. In addition, registered nurses, regardless of specialty, must be licensed in order to practice in all 50 states and the District of Columbia. Licensing is obtained by passing a national exam.

Other Requirements

Critical care nurses should like working in a fast-paced environment that requires life-long learning. This is a very intense nursing field, and nurses should be able to make critical decisions quickly and intelligently. New medical technology is constantly being developed and implemented. Critical care nurses should be technically inclined and able to learn how to operate new medical equipment without feeling intimidated.

Critical care nurses must be able to deal with major life-and-death crises. Because of the seriousness of their loved one's illness, family members and friends may be difficult to deal with and the nurse must display patience, understanding, and composure during these emotional times. The nurse must be able to communicate with the family and explain medical terminology and procedures to the patient and family so they can understand what is being done and why.

Continuing education is a must in order to stay informed of new treatment options and procedures.

EXPLORING

There are many ways to explore nursing careers. You can visit nursing Web sites, read books on careers in nursing, or talk with your high school guidance counselor or teacher about the career or ask them to set up a talk by a critical care nurse.

If you are already a nursing student, you might consider becoming a student member of the AACN. This will give you access to *Critical Care Nurse, The American Journal of Critical Care*, and other association publications that discuss issues related to critical care nursing.

EMPLOYERS

Contrary to previously held beliefs that critical care nurses work only in intensive care units or cardiac care units of hospitals, today's critical care nurses work in the emergency departments, post-anesthesia recovery units, pediatric intensive care units, burn units, neonatal intensive care units, and in other units that treat critically ill patients.

STARTING OUT

You must first become a registered nurse before you can work as a critical care nurse. Aspiring registered nurses must complete one of the three kinds of educational programs and pass the licensing examination. Registered nurses may apply for employment directly to hospitals, nursing homes, and companies and government agencies that hire nurses. Jobs can also be obtained through school career services offices, by signing up with employment agencies specializing in placement of nursing personnel, or through a state employment office. Other sources of jobs include nurses' associations, professional journals, and newspaper want ads. The AACN also has job listings on its Web site.

ADVANCEMENT

Administrative and supervisory positions in the nursing field go to nurses who have earned at least the bachelor of science degree in nursing. Nurses with many years of experience who are graduates of a diploma program may achieve supervisory positions, but requirements for such promotions have become more difficult in recent years and in many cases require at least the bachelor of science in nursing degree.

EARNINGS

Salary is determined by many factors, including certification and education, place of employment, shift worked, geographical location, and work experience. Findings from a AACN member survey show the largest percentage, 33 percent, averaged between $55,000 and $74,999 annually. The next largest group, 29 percent, earned between $40,000 and $54,999. The top 25 percent made more than $75,000 annually. The U.S. Department of Labor reports the median annual salary for all registered nurses (which includes critical care nurses) was $57,280 in 2006. The lowest paid 10 percent of registered nurses made less than $40,250 per year, and the highest paid 10 percent made more than $83,440. Since critical care nurses must be registered nurses and also have additional training, their salaries should be higher on average than registered nurses who are not in the critical care area.

Flexible schedules and part-time employment opportunities are available for most nurses. Employers usually provide health and life insurance, and some offer educational reimbursements and year-end bonuses to their full-time staff.

WORK ENVIRONMENT

Most critical care nurses work in hospitals in the intensive care unit (ICU), the emergency department, the operating room, or some other specialty unit. Most hospital environments are clean and well lighted. Inner-city hospitals may be in a less than desirable location and safety may be an issue. Generally, critical care nurses who wish to advance in their careers will find themselves working in larger hospitals or medical centers in major cities.

All nursing careers have some health and disease risks; however, adherence to health and safety guidelines greatly minimizes the chance of contracting infectious diseases such as hepatitis and AIDS. Medical knowledge and good safety measures are also needed to limit the nurse's exposure to toxic chemicals, radiation, and other hazards.

OUTLOOK

Nursing specialties will be in great demand in the future. The U.S. Department of Labor estimates the employment of all registered nurses will grow much faster than the average through 2016. According to the AACN, a growing number of hospitals are experiencing a shortage of critical care nurses. Many hospitals needing critical care nurses are offering incentives such as sign-on bonuses. The most critical shortages are in areas that require nurses with experience and highly specialized skills. The highest increase in demand is for those critical care nurses who specialize in a specific area of care, such as cardiovascular ICU, pediatric and neonatal ICU, and open-heart recovery units. Job opportunities vary across the country and may be available in all geographic areas and in large and small hospitals.

FOR MORE INFORMATION

For information on nursing careers and accredited programs, contact

American Association of Colleges of Nursing
One Dupont Circle, NW, Suite 530
Washington, DC 20036-1135
Tel: 202-463-6930
http://www.aacn.nche.edu

For information on certification and fact sheets on critical care nursing, contact

American Association of Critical-Care Nurses (AACN)
101 Columbia
Aliso Viejo, CA 92656-4109
Tel: 800-899-2226
Email: info@aacn.org
http://www.aacn.org

☐ CRUISE SHIP WORKERS

OVERVIEW

Cruise ship workers provide services to passengers on cruise ships. Besides assisting in the operation of the ship, they may serve food and drinks, maintain cabins and public areas, lead shipboard activities, and provide entertainment. There are more than 257,000 workers employed in the U.S. cruise industry.

THE JOB

Many modern cruise ships are similar to floating resorts, offering fine accommodations, gourmet dining, and every possible activity and form of entertainment. It takes a staff of hundreds to ensure the smooth operation of a cruise ship and the comfort of all passengers. All employees, regardless of their rank, are expected to participate in routine lifesaving and safety drills. Crew organization is divided into six different departments (smaller liners may not have as many divisions of organization); the *Captain*, or the *Master of the ship*, oversees the entire crew.

Deck. This department is responsible for the navigation of the ship, and oversees the maintenance of the hull and deck.

Engine. This staff operates and maintains machinery. Together, deck and engine staffs include *officers, carpenters, seamen, maintenance workers, electricians, engineers, repairmen, plumbers,* and *incinerator operators.*

Radio department. *Videographers* are responsible for the maintenance and operation of the ship's broadcast booth, including radio and news telecasts. *Telephonists* help passengers place phone calls shoreside.

Medical department. *Physicians* treat passengers whose maladies range from seasickness to more serious health problems. *Nurses* assist the doctors and provide first aid.

Steward. This department, one of the largest on board, is concerned with the comfort of all passengers. The food staff includes specially trained *chefs* who prepare meals, ranging from gourmet dinners to more casual fare poolside. The *wait staff* serves guests in the formal dining room and provides room service. *Wine stewards* help passengers with wine choices and are responsible for maintaining proper inventories aboard the ship. *Bartenders* mix and serve drinks at many stations throughout the ship. From simple blocks of ice, *sculptors* create works of art that are used to decorate dining room buffets. The housekeeping staff is composed of *executive housekeepers* and *room attendants* who keep cabins and staterooms orderly, supply towels and sheets, and maintain public areas throughout the ship.

Pursers. This large department is responsible for guest relations and services. The *chief purser*, much like a hotel's general manager, is the head of this department and is the main contact for passengers regarding the ship's policies and procedures. *Assistant pursers*, considered junior officers, assist the chief with various duties, such as providing guest services, ship information, monetary exchange, postage, safety deposit boxes, and other duties usually associated with the front desk department of a hotel. The *cruise director* heads the cruise staff and plans daily activities and entertainment. The *youth staff director* plans activities and games specifically designed for children. Ships with a casino on board employ *casino workers*, including *game dealers, cashiers, keno runners*, and *slot machine attendants. Sound and lighting technicians* are needed to provide music and stage lighting for the many entertainment venues found on board. Many *entertainers* are hired to sing, dance, and perform comedy skits and musical revues. *Dance instructors* teach dance classes ranging from ballroom to country. Also, many employees are hired to work in duty-free shops and souvenir stores, beauty parlors, spas, health clubs, and libraries.

Other occupations in the cruise ship industry include *clerical workers, human resources workers, computer specialists,* and *security workers.*

REQUIREMENTS
High School

Cruise lines require at least a high school education, or equivalent, for most entry-level jobs. While in high school, you should concentrate on classes such as geography, sociology, and a foreign language. Fluency in Spanish, French, and Portuguese is highly desirable.

Postsecondary Training

Officer-level positions, or jobs with more responsibility, require college degrees and past work experience. Many employees, especially those on the cruise staff, have an entertainment background. Youth staff members usually have a background in education or recreation.

Certification or Licensing

Most entry-level jobs do not require certification. Some technical positions, such as those in the engine room, may require special training. Physicians and nurses must be licensed to practice medicine. Child-care workers should have experience and proper training in child care. Some cruise line employees may belong to the Seafarers International Union.

Other Requirements

You will need a valid U.S. passport to work in this field. If you hold a passport from another country, you will need to obtain a work visa. Check with your country's embassy for details and requirements.

QUICK FACTS

SCHOOL SUBJECTS
Foreign language
Geography

PERSONAL SKILLS
Leadership/management
Mechanical/manipulative

WORK ENVIRONMENT
Indoors and outdoors
Primarily multiple locations

MINIMUM EDUCATION LEVEL
Varies by job

MEDIAN SALARY
$16,000

CERTIFICATION OR LICENSING
Required for certain positions

OUTLOOK
About as fast as the average

Besides having the proper education, experience, and credentials, employers look for applicants who have excellent communication skills and who are outgoing, hardworking, friendly, and enjoy working with people. It is important to make a positive impression with the passengers, so cruise ship workers should always be properly groomed, neatly dressed, and well behaved at all times.

STARTING OUT

Applicants without college degrees and little shipboard experience are usually assigned to entry-level positions such as wait staff or housekeeping. If you have experience in retail sales, then you may be given a job at the duty-free shop; hospitality experience may land you a position in the purser's office.

Nancy Corbin, Youth Staff Department Manager for Royal Caribbean International, began her career in the cruise ship industry as a youth counselor. Not satisfied with the ship's program for children (or rather, the lack thereof), Corbin and her coworkers revised the schedule of activities and turned the ship's youth counselors into a new department—the youth staff. Today, the youth staff oversees art and science activities, pool parties, talent shows, and theme nights for children ages three to 17.

ADVANCEMENT

Nancy Corbin is still very much involved with the youth staff, though she no longer works on board. Rather, she is stationed shoreside as the youth staff department manager and acts as a liaison for all youth staffs on the cruise line. Where does she see herself in the future? "I'd be interested in a director-type role," Corbin says, "Maybe work as a cruise director."

With cruise experience, a cruise staff member can advance to assistant cruise director, and in turn become cruise director. Assistant pursers can be promoted to chief purser. Even people in entry-level positions can be promoted to jobs with more responsibility and, of course, better pay. Bussers can become assistant waiters and then head waiters. Room stewards can be promoted to housekeeping manager and supervise a team of cleaners or a specific section of the ship.

EXPLORING

Taking a cruise is one of the best ways to observe the varied careers in this industry. Most cruise lines offer competitive prices along with a selection of cruises and destinations.

Also consider inland cruises, which are a less expensive option. In Chicago, for example, there are cruise tours running up and down the city's lakefront and the Chicago River. Some even provide entertainment and dinner shows. Many talented performers hone their skills before "trying out" with the bigger cruise lines.

Some cruise lines will hire college students for some of their entry-level positions. Don't forget to apply early, as these jobs are quickly filled.

If you live near a cruise line office or headquarters, why not call press relations or human resources for a tour of the department?

EMPLOYERS

There are approximately 45 cruise lines with offices in the United States; together, they employ thousands of cruise ship workers. Most employees are contracted to work four or more months at a time. Some major employers include Royal Caribbean International,

The Cunard Line, Holland America, and Disney Cruise Line.

EARNINGS

There are so many variables that it is hard to gauge the salary average for this industry. First, many employees are hired on a contractual basis—anywhere from four to six months for housekeeping, wait staff, and the concessionaires. The size of the cruise line and the region it sails may also affect wages. According to Cruise Services International, the general salary range is between $1,000 and $1,700 per month, plus tips, or $12,000–$20,400 per year. Some employees count on passengers' tips to greatly supplement their income. Restaurant and house staff workers can earn anywhere from $300 to $600 in weekly tips.

Employee benefits include room and board, and all meals while on board. Most cruise lines offer emergency health coverage to their employees, regardless of the length of contract. Full-time employees are also offered health insurance, paid sick and holiday time, stock options, and company discounts.

WORK ENVIRONMENT

Workers in the cruise line industry should not expect to have a lot of free time. Most cruise ship workers work long hours—eight- to 14-hour days, seven days a week are not uncommon. Many employees spend a number of weeks, usually five or more, working at sea, followed by an extended leave ashore.

Being a people person is important in this industry. Cruise ship workers not only are expected to work well with their coworkers, but they have to live with them, too. Accommodations for the crew are especially tight; usually two to four employees are assigned to a room. The crew has dining areas and lounges separate from the passengers, yet total privacy is rare on a cruise ship. Usually, crew members have little access to public areas on their free time. However, when the ship docks at port, crew members on leave are allowed to disembark and go shoreside.

OUTLOOK

The cruise line industry is still one of the fastest growing segments of the travel industry. More than 11 million people cruised in 2005, according to Cruise Lines International Association (CLIA). Nearly 70 new cruise ships were added to the North American Fleet from 2000 to 2005, according to CLIA. Ships are getting bigger and more opulent, and have become travel destinations in themselves. Larger cruise lines pack their ships with every amenity imaginable, including libraries, spas, casinos, and in the case of one of Royal Caribbean International's newest fleet additions—a skating rink and a rock climbing wall. Cruise lines are able to tap into every interest by offering a theme or special interest to their passengers. Several cruise ships are experimenting with smoke-free cruising.

With so many mega-ships in operation, qualified cruise ship workers are still in demand. Entry-level positions such as wait staff and housekeeping will be fairly easy to obtain with the proper paperwork and credentials. A college degree and work experience will be necessary for positions with more responsibility. Fluency in French, Spanish, or Portuguese is a plus. A cruise ship will offer workers the opportunity to travel around the world and meet many people of different nationalities and cultures.

Remember, however, that cruise life is not all fun and travel. Cruise ship workers are expected to work long, hard hours, and be away from their home base for weeks at a time. Many people find the schedule exhausting and opt to find employment ashore.

FOR MORE INFORMATION

CLIA is the official trade organization of the cruise industry. For industry information, contact

Cruise Lines International Association (CLIA)
910 SE 17th Street, Suite 400
Fort Lauderdale, FL 33316
Tel: 754-224-2200
Email: info@cruising.org
http://www.cruising.org

For information on the industry, employment opportunities, and answers to commonly asked questions regarding employment at sea, contact

Cruise Services International
601 Dundas Street West
Box 24070
Whitby, Ontario L1N 8X8, Canada
Tel: 905-430-0361
Email: info@cruisedreamjob.com
http://www.cruisedreamjob.com

For information about the Seafarer's International Union, contact

Seafarers International Union
5201 Auth Way
Camp Springs, MD 20746-4211
Tel: 301-899-0675
http://www.seafarers.org

For industry information and job opportunities, contact the following cruise lines

Cunard Cruise Line
http://www.cunardline.com

Disney Cruise Line
http://www.dcljobs.com

Holland America Line
http://www.hollandamerica.com

Royal Caribbean International
http://www.royalcaribbean.com

☐ CUSTOMER SERVICE REPRESENTATIVES

OVERVIEW

Customer service representatives, sometimes called *customer care representatives*, work with customers of one or many companies, assist with customer problems, or answer questions. Customer service representatives work in many different industries to provide "front-line" customer service in a variety of businesses. Most customer service representatives work in an office setting though some may work in the "field" to better meet customer needs. There are approximately 2.2 million customer service representatives employed in the United States.

THE JOB

Julie Cox is a customer service representative for Affina. Affina is a call center that handles customer service for a variety of companies. Cox works with each of Affina's clients and the call center operators to ensure that each call-in receives top customer service.

Customer service representatives often handle complaints and problems, and Cox finds that to be the case at the call center as well. While the operators who report to her provide customer service to those on the phone, Cox must oversee that customer service while also keeping in mind the customer service for her client, whatever business they may be in.

"I make sure that the clients get regular reports of the customer service calls and check to see if there are any recurring problems," says Cox.

QUICK FACTS

SCHOOL SUBJECTS
Business
English
Speech

PERSONAL SKILLS
Communication/ideas
Helping/teaching

WORK ENVIRONMENT
Primarily indoors
Primarily one location

MINIMUM EDUCATION LEVEL
High school diploma

MEDIAN SALARY
$28,362

CERTIFICATION OR LICENSING
Voluntary

OUTLOOK
Much faster than the average

One of the ways Cox observes if customer service is not being handled effectively is by monitoring the actual time spent on each phone call. If an operator spends a lot of time on a call, there is most likely a problem.

"Our customers are billed per minute," says Cox. "So we want to make sure their customer service is being handled well and efficiently."

Affina's call center in Columbus, Indiana, handles dozens of toll-free lines. While some calls are likely to be focused on complaints or questions, some are easier to handle. Cox and her staff handle calls from people simply wanting to order literature, brochures, or to find their nearest dealer location.

Customer service representatives work in a variety of fields and business, but one thing is common—the customer. All businesses depend on their customers to keep them in business, so customer service, whether handled internally or outsourced to a call center like Affina, is extremely important.

Some customer service representatives, like Cox, do most of their work on the telephone. Others may represent companies in the field, where the customer is actually using the product or service. Still other customer service representatives may specialize in Internet service, assisting customers over the World Wide Web via email or online chats.

Affina's call center is available to their clients 24 hours a day, seven days a week, so Cox and her staff must keep around-the-clock shifts. Not all customer service representatives work a varied schedule; many work a traditional daytime shift. However, customers have problems, complaints, and questions 24 hours a day, so many companies do staff their customer service positions for a longer number of hours, especially to accommodate customers during evenings and weekends.

REQUIREMENTS
High School

A high school diploma is required for most customer service representative positions. High school courses that emphasize communication, such as English and speech, will help you learn to communicate clearly. Any courses that require collaboration with others will also help to teach diplomacy and tact—two important aspects of customer service. Business courses will help you get a good overview of the business world, one that is dependent on customers and customer service. Computer skills are also very important.

Postsecondary Training

While a college degree is not necessary to become a customer service representative, certain areas of postsecondary training are helpful. Courses in business and organizational leadership will help to give you a better feel for the business world. Just as in high school, communications classes are helpful in learning to effectively talk with and meet the needs of other people.

These courses can be taken during a college curriculum or may be offered at a variety of customer service workshops or classes. Julie Cox is working as a customer service representative while she earns her business degree from a local college. Along with her college work, she has taken advantage of seminars and workshops to improve her customer service skills.

Bachelor's degrees in business and communications are increasingly required for managerial positions.

Certification or Licensing

Although it is not a requirement, customer service representative can become certified. The International Customer Service Association offers a manager-level certification program. Upon completion of the program, managers receive the certified customer service professional designation.

Other Requirements

"The best and the worst parts of being a customer service representative are the people," Julie Cox says. Customer service representatives should have the ability to maintain a pleasant attitude at all times, even while serving angry or demanding customers.

A successful customer service representative will most likely have an outgoing personality and enjoy working with people and assisting them with their questions and problems.

Because many customer service representatives work in offices and on the telephone, people with physical disabilities may find this career to be both accessible and enjoyable.

EXPLORING

Julie Cox first discovered her love for customer service while working in retail at a local department store. Explore your ability for customer service by getting a job that deals with the public on a day-to-day basis. Talk with people who work with customers and customer service every day; find out what they like and dislike about their jobs.

There are other ways that you can prepare for a career in this field while you are still in school. Join your school's business club to get a feel for what goes on in the business world today. Doing volunteer work for a local charity or homeless shelter can help you decide if serving others is something that you'd enjoy doing as a career.

Evaluate the customer service at the businesses you visit. What makes that salesperson at The Gap better than the operator you talked with last week? Volunteer to answer phones at an agency in your town or city. Most receptionists in small companies and agencies are called on to provide customer service to callers. Try a nonprofit organization. They will welcome the help, and you will get a firsthand look at customer service.

EMPLOYERS

Customer service representatives are hired at all types of companies in a variety of areas. Because all businesses rely on customers, customer service is generally a high priority for those businesses. Some companies, like call centers, may employ a large number of customer service representatives to serve a multitude of clients, while small businesses may simply have one or two people who are responsible for customer service.

The highest concentation of customer service representatives are employed in four states (Arizona, South Dakota, Texas, and Utah), but opportunities are available throughout the United States. In the United States, approximately 2.2 million workers are employed as customer service representatives.

STARTING OUT

You can become a customer service representative as an entry-level applicant, although some customer service representatives have first served in other areas of a company. This company experience may provide them with more knowledge and experience to answer customer questions. A college degree is not required, but any postsecondary training will increase your ability to find a job in customer service.

Ads for customer service job openings are readily available in newspapers and on Internet job search sites. With some experience and a positive attitude, it is possible to move into the position of customer service representative from another job within the company. Julie Cox started out at Affina as an operator and quickly moved into a customer service capacity.

ADVANCEMENT

Customer service experience is valuable in any business career path. Julie Cox hopes to combine her customer service experience with a business degree and move to the human resources area of her company.

It is also possible to advance to management or marketing jobs after working as a customer service representative. Businesses and their customers are inseparable, so most business professionals are experts at customer relations.

EARNINGS

Earnings vary based on location, level of experience, and size and type of employer. The U.S. Department of Labor reports the median annual income for all customer service representatives as $28,362 in 2006. Salaries ranged from less than $18,117 to more than $45,990. The Association of Support Professionals, which conducts salary surveys of tech support workers at PC software companies, reports that customer service representatives earned a median annual wage of $32,000 in 2006.

Other benefits vary widely according to the size and type of company in which representatives are employed. Benefits may include medical, dental, vision, and life insurance, 401(k) plans, or bonus incentives. Full-time customer service representatives can expect to receive vacation and sick pay, while part-time workers may not be offered these benefits.

WORK ENVIRONMENT

Customer service representatives work primarily indoors, although some may work in the field where the customers are using the product or service. They usually work in a supervised setting and report to a manager. They may spend many hours on the telephone, answering mail, or handling Internet communication. Many of the work hours involve little physical activity.

While most customer service representatives generally work a 40-hour workweek, others work a variety of shifts. Many businesses want customer service hours to coincide with the times that their customers are available to call or contact the business. For many companies, these times are in the evenings and on the weekends, so some customer service representatives work a varied shift and odd hours.

OUTLOOK

The U.S. Department of Labor predicts that employment for customer service representatives will grow much faster than the average through 2016. This is a large field of workers and many replacement workers are needed each year as customer service reps leave this job for other positions, retire, or leave for other reasons. In addition, the Internet and e-commerce should increase the need for customer service representatives who will be needed to help customers navigate Web sites, answer questions over the phone, and respond to emails.

For customer service representatives with specific knowledge of a product or business, the outlook is very good, as quick, efficient customer service is valuable in any business. Additional training and education will also make finding a job as a customer service representative an easier task.

FOR MORE INFORMATION

For information on customer service and other support positions, contact
Association of Support Professionals
122 Barnard Avenue
Watertown, MA 02472-3414
Tel: 617-924-3944
http://www.asponline.com

For information on jobs, training, workshops, and salaries, contact
Customer Care Institute
17 Dean Overlook, NW
Atlanta, GA 30318-1663
Tel: 404-352-9291
Email: info@customercare.com
http://www.customercare.com

For information about the customer service industry, contact
Help Desk Institute
102 South Tejon, Suite 1200
Colorado Springs, CO 80903-2242
Tel: 800-248-5667
Email: support@thinkhdi.com

http://www.thinkhdi.com/For information on international customer service careers, contact
International Customer Service Association
401 North Michigan Avenue
Chicago, IL 60611-4255
Tel: 800-360-4272
Email: icsa@smithbucklin.com
http://www.icsa.com

CUSTOMS OFFICIALS

OVERVIEW

Customs officials are federal workers who are employed by the United States Bureau of Customs and Border Protection (an arm of the Department of Homeland Security) to prevent terrorists and terrorist weapons from entering the United States, enforce laws governing imports and exports, and to combat smuggling and revenue fraud. The Bureau of Customs and Border Protection generates revenue for the government by assessing and collecting duties and excise taxes on imported merchandise. Amid a whirl of international travel and commercial activity, customs officials process travelers, baggage, cargo, and mail, as well as administer certain navigation laws. Stationed in the United States and overseas at airports, seaports, and all crossings, as well as at points along the Canadian and Mexican borders, customs officials examine, count, weigh, gauge, measure, and sample commercial and noncommercial cargoes entering and leaving the United

States. It is their job to determine whether or not goods are admissible and, if so, how much tax, or duty, should be assessed on them. To prevent smuggling, fraud, and cargo theft, customs officials also check the individual baggage declarations of international travelers and oversee the unloading of all types of commercial shipments. Approximately 47,000 customs workers are employed by the Bureau of Customs and Border Protection.

THE JOB

Customs officials perform a wide variety of duties including preventing terrorists and terrorist weapons from entering the United States, controlling imports and exports, and combating smuggling and revenue fraud.

As a result of its merger in 2003 with several other protective and monitoring agencies of the U.S. government, the Bureau of Customs and Border Patrol has created a new position, the *Customs and Border Patrol (CBP) Officer*, which consolidates the skills and responsibilities of three positions in these agencies: the customs inspector, the immigration officer, and the agricultural inspector. These workers are uniformed and armed. A second new position, the *CBP Agriculture Specialist* has been created to complement the work of the CBP Officer. CBP Agriculture Specialists are uniformed, but not armed.

CBP Officers conduct surveillance at points of entry into the United States to prohibit smuggling, detect customs violations, and deter acts of terrorism. They try to catch people illegally transporting smuggled merchandise and contraband such as narcotics, watches, jewelry, chemicals, and weapons, as well as fruits, plants, and meat that may be infested with pests or diseases. On the waterfront, officers monitor piers, ships, and crew members and are constantly on the lookout for items being thrown from the ship to small boats nearby. Customs patrol officers provide security at entrance and exit facilities of piers and airports, make sure all baggage is checked, and maintain security at loading, exit, and entrance areas of customs buildings and during the transfer of legal drug shipments to prevent hijackings or theft. Using informers and other sources, they gather intelligence information about illegal activities. When probable cause exists, they are authorized to take possible violators into custody, using physical force or weapons if necessary. They assist other customs personnel in developing or testing new enforcement techniques and equipment.

CBP Officers also are responsible for carefully and thoroughly examining cargo to make sure that it matches the description on a ship's or aircraft's manifest. They inspect baggage and personal items worn or carried by travelers entering or leaving the United States by ship,

QUICK FACTS

SCHOOL SUBJECTS
English
Government

PERSONAL SKILLS
Communication/ideas
Helping/teaching

WORK ENVIRONMENT
Primarily indoors
Primarily one location

MINIMUM EDUCATION LEVEL
High school diploma

MEDIAN SALARY
$48,148

CERTIFICATION OR LICENSING
None available

OUTLOOK
About as fast as the average

plane, or automobile. CBP Officers are authorized to go aboard a ship or plane to determine the exact nature of the cargo being transported. In the course of a single day they review cargo manifests, inspect cargo containers, and supervise unloading activities to prevent terrorism, smuggling, fraud, or cargo thefts. They may have to weigh and measure imports to see that commerce laws are being followed and to protect American distributors in cases where restricted trademarked merchandise is being brought into the country. In this way, they can protect the interests of American companies.

CBP Officers examine crew and passenger lists, sometimes in cooperation with the police or security personnel from federal government agencies, who may be searching for criminals or terrorists. They are authorized to search suspicious individuals and to arrest these offenders if necessary. They are also allowed to conduct body searches of suspected individuals to check for contraband. They check health clearances and ships' documents in an effort to prevent the spread of disease that may require quarantine.

Individual baggage declarations of international travelers also come under their scrutiny. CBP Officers who have baggage examination duties at points of entry into the United States classify purchases made abroad and, if necessary, assess and collect duties. All international travelers are allowed to bring home certain quantities of foreign purchases, such as perfume, clothing, tobacco, and liquor, without paying taxes. However, they must declare the amount and value of their purchases on a customs form. If they have made purchases above the duty-free limits, they must pay taxes. CBP Officers are prepared to advise tourists about U.S. customs regulations and allow them to change their customs declarations if necessary and pay the duty before baggage inspection. CBP Officers must be alert and observant to detect undeclared items. If any are discovered, it is up to the officer to decide whether an oversight or deliberate fraud has occurred. Sometimes the contraband is held and a hearing is scheduled to decide the case. A person who is caught trying to avoid paying duty is fined. When customs violations occur, officers must file detailed reports and often later appear as witnesses in court.

CBP Agriculture Specialists inspect agricultural and related goods that are imported into the United States. They act as agricultural experts at ports of entry to help protect people from agroterrorism and bioterrorism, as well as monitor agricultural imports for diseases and harmful pests.

CBP Officers and CBP Agriculture Specialists cooperate with special agents for the Federal Bureau of Investigation (FBI), the Drug Enforcement Administration, the Food and Drug Administration, and other government agencies.

Some other specialized careers in the Bureau of Customs and Border Protection are as follows:

Customs pilots, who must have a current Federal Aviation Administration commercial pilot's license, conduct air surveillance of illegal traffic crossing U.S. borders by air, land, or sea. They apprehend, arrest, and search violators and prepare reports used to prosecute the criminals. They are stationed along the Canadian and Mexican borders as well as along coastal areas, flying single- and multiengine planes and helicopters.

Canine enforcement officers train and use dogs to prevent smuggling of all controlled substances as defined by customs laws. These controlled substances include marijuana, narcotics, and dangerous drugs. After undergoing an intensive 15-week basic training course in the National Detector Dog Training Center, where each officer is paired with a dog and assigned to a post, canine enforcement officers work in cooperation with CBP Officers to find and seize contraband and arrest smug-

glers. Canine enforcement officers also use dogs to detect bomb-making materials or other dangerous substances.

Import specialists become technical experts in a particular line of merchandise, such as wine or electronic equipment. They keep up to date on their area of specialization by going to trade shows and importers' places of business. Merchandise for delivery to commercial importers is examined, classified, and appraised by these specialists who must enforce import quotas and trademark laws. They use import quotas and current market values to determine the unit value of the merchandise in order to calculate the amount of money due the government in tariffs. Import specialists routinely question importers, check their lists, and make sure the merchandise matches the description and the list. If they find a violation, they call for a formal inquiry by customs special agents. Import specialists regularly deal with problems of fraud and violations of copyright and trademark laws. If the importer meets federal requirements, the import specialist issues a permit that authorizes the release of merchandise for delivery. If not, the goods might be seized and sold at public auction. These specialists encourage international trade by authorizing the lowest allowable duties on merchandise.

Customs and Border Protection chemists form a subgroup of import specialists who protect the health and safety of Americans. They analyze imported merchandise for textile fibers, lead content, narcotics, and the presence of explosives or other harmful material. In many cases, the duty collected on imported products depends on the chemist's analysis and subsequent report. Customs chemists often serve as expert witnesses in court. Customs laboratories have specialized instruments that can analyze materials for their chemical components. These machines can determine such things as the amount of sucrose in a beverage, the fiber content of a textile product, the lead oxide content of fine crystal, or the presence of toxic chemicals and prohibited additives.

Criminal investigators, or *special agents,* are plainclothes investigators who make sure that the government obtains revenue on imports and that contraband and controlled substances do not enter or leave the country illegally. They investigate smuggling, criminal fraud, and major cargo thefts. Special agents target professional criminals as well as ordinary tourists who give false information on baggage declarations. Often working undercover, they cooperate with CBP Officers and the FBI. Allowed special powers of entry, search, seizure, and arrest, special agents have the broadest powers of search of any law enforcement personnel in the United States. For instance, special agents do not need probable cause or a warrant to justify search or seizure near a border or port of entry. However, in the interior of the United States, probable cause but not a warrant is necessary to conduct a search.

REQUIREMENTS
High School

If you are interested in working for the U.S. Bureau of Customs and Border Protection, you should pursue a well-rounded education in high school. Courses in government, geography and social studies, English, and history will contribute to your understanding of international and domestic legal issues as well as giving you a good general background. If you wish to become a specialist in scientific or investigative aspects of the CBP, courses in the sciences, particularly chemistry, will be necessary and courses in computer science will be helpful. Taking a foreign language, especially Spanish, will also help prepare you for this career.

Postsecondary Training

Applicants to CBP must be U.S. citizens and at least 21 years of age. They must have earned at least a high school diploma, but applicants with college degrees are preferred. Applicants are required to have three years of general work experience involving contact with the public or four years of college.

Like all federal employees, applicants to CBP must pass a physical examination, undergo a security check, and pass a written test. Entrance-level appointments are at grades GS-5 and GS-7, depending on the level of education or work experience.

New CBP Officers participate in a rigorous training program that includes 10 days of pre-Academy orientation; 12 weeks of basic training at the U.S. Customs Explorer Academy; In-Port Training (a combination of on-the-job, computer-based, and classroom training); and Advanced Proficiency Training. CBP Agricultural Specialists receive specialized training from the U.S. Department of Agriculture.

Other Requirements

Applicants must be in good physical condition, possess emotional and mental stability, and demonstrate the ability to correctly apply regulations or instructional material and make clear, concise oral or written reports.

EXPLORING

There are several ways for you to learn about the various positions available at CBP. You can read *Frontline* (http://www.cbp.gov/xp/CustomsToday/cbptoday_about.xml), the official employee newsletter of the United States Bureau of Customs and Border Protection, to learn more about customs work. You can also talk with people employed as customs workers, consult your high school counselors, or contact local labor union organizations and offices for additional information. Information on federal government jobs is available from offices of the state employment service, area offices of the U.S. Office of Personnel Management, and Federal Job Information Centers throughout the country.

Another great way to learn more about this career is to participate in the CBP Explorer Program. CBP Explorers receive practical and hands-on training in law enforcement and criminal justice fields. Applicants must be between the ages of 14 and 21 and have at least a C grade point average in high school or college. Participation in this program is also an excellent starting point for entry into the field. After one year in the program, Explorers can apply to the U.S. Customs Explorer Academy.

EMPLOYERS

The U.S. Customs Service is the sole employer of customs officials. Approximately 47,000 customs officials are employed in the United States.

STARTING OUT

Applicants may enter the various occupations of the Bureau of Customs and Border Protection by applying to take the appropriate civil service examinations. Interested applicants should note the age, citizenship, and experience requirements previously described and realize that they will undergo a background check and a drug test. If hired, applicants will receive exacting, on-the-job training.

ADVANCEMENT

All customs agents have the opportunity to advance through a special system of promotion from within. Although they enter at the GS-5 or GS-7 level, after one year they may compete for promotion to supervisory positions or simply to positions at a higher grade level in the agency. The journeyman level is grade GS-9. Supervisory positions at GS-11 and above are available on a competitive basis. After attaining permanent status (i.e., serving for one year on probation), customs patrol officers may compete to become special agents. Entry-level appointments for customs chemists are made at GS-5. However, applicants with advanced degrees or professional experience in the sciences, or both, should qualify for higher graded positions. Advancement potential exists for the journeyman level at GS-11 and to special-ist, supervisory, and management positions at grades GS-12 and above.

EARNINGS

Entry-level positions at GS-5 began at a base annual pay of $26,264 in 2008, and entry at GS-7 started at $32,534 per year. Most CBP Officers are at the GS-11 position, which had a base annual salary of $48,148 in 2008. Supervisory positions beginning at GS-12 started at $57,709 in 2008. Federal employees in certain cities receive locality pay in addition to their salaries in order to offset the higher cost of living in those areas. Locality pay generally adds from 8.64 percent to 19.04 percent to the base salary. Certain CBP workers are also entitled to receive Law Enforce-ment Availability Pay, which adds another 25 percent to their salaries. All federal workers receive annual cost-of-living salary increases. Federal workers enjoy generous benefits, including health and life insurance, pension plans, and holiday, sick leave, and vacation pay.

WORK ENVIRONMENT

The customs territory of the United States is divided into nine regions that include the 50 states, the District of Columbia, Puerto Rico, and the U.S. Virgin Islands. In these regions there are some 317 ports of entry along land and sea borders. Customs inspectors may be assigned to any of these ports or to overseas work at airports, seaports, waterfronts, border stations, customs houses, or the U.S. Bureau of Customs and Border Protection Headquarters in Washington, D.C. They are able to request assignments in certain localities and usually receive them when possible.

A typical work schedule is eight hours a day, five days a week, but CBP Officers and related employees often work overtime or long into the night. United States entry and exit points must be supervised 24 hours a day, which means that workers rotate night shifts and weekend duty. CBP Officers are sometimes assigned to one-person bor-der points at remote locations, where they may perform immigration and agricultural inspections in addition to regular duties. They often risk physical injury from criminals violating customs regulations.

OUTLOOK

Employment at the Bureau of Customs and Border Pro-tection is steady work that is not affected by changes in the economy. With the increased emphasis on law enforcement, especially the deterrence of terrorism, but also the detection of illegally imported drugs and por-nography and the prevention of exports of sensitive high-technology items, the prospects for steady employment

in the CBP are likely to grow and remain high. The U.S. Department of Labor predicts employment for police and detectives, a category including CBP Officers, to grow about as fast as the average through 2016.

FOR MORE INFORMATION

For career information and to view a short video about CBP Officers, visit the CBP Web site:

U.S. Customs and Border Protection (CBP)
Department of Homeland Security
1300 Pennsylvania Avenue, NW
Washington, DC 20229-0001
Tel: 703-526-4200
http://www.customs.ustreas.gov

DENTAL ASSISTANTS

OVERVIEW

Dental assistants perform a variety of duties in the dental office, including helping the dentist examine and treat patients and completing laboratory and office work. They assist the dentist by preparing patients for dental exams, handing the dentist the proper instruments, tak-ing and processing X rays, preparing materials for mak-ing impressions and restorations, and instructing patients in oral health care. They also perform administrative and clerical tasks so that the office runs smoothly and the dentist's time is available for working with patients. There are approximately 280,000 dental assistants employed in the United States.

THE JOB

Dental assistants help dentists as they examine and treat patients. They usually greet patients, escort them to the examining room, and prepare them by covering their clothing with paper or cloth bibs. They also adjust the headrest of the examination chair and raise the chair to the proper height. Many dental assistants take X rays of patients' teeth and process the film for the dentist to examine. They also obtain patients' dental records from the office files, so the dentist can review them before the examination.

During dental examinations and operations, dental assistants hand the dentist instruments as they are needed and use suction devices to keep the patient's mouth dry. When the examination or procedure is completed, assistants may give the patient after-care instructions for the teeth and mouth. They also provide instructions on infection-control procedures, preventing plaque buildup, and keeping teeth and gums clean and healthy between office visits.

Dental assistants also help with a variety of other clinical tasks. When a dentist needs a cast of a patient's teeth or mouth—used for diagnosing and planning the correction of dental problems—assistants may mix the necessary materials. They may also pour, trim, and polish these study casts. Some assistants prepare materials for making dental restorations, and many polish and clean patients' dentures. Some may perform the necessary laboratory work to make temporary dental replacements.

State laws determine which clinical tasks a dental assistant is able to perform. Dental assistants are not the same as *dental hygienists*, who are licensed to perform a wider variety of clinical tasks such as scaling and polishing teeth. Some states allow dental assistants to apply medications to teeth and gums, isolate individual teeth for treatment using rubber dams, and remove excess cement after cavities have been filled. In some states, dental assistants can actually put fillings in patients' mouths. Dental assistants may also check patients' vital signs, update and check medical histories, and help the dentist with any medical emergencies that arise during dental procedures.

Many dental assistants also perform clerical and administrative tasks. These include receptionist duties, scheduling appointments, managing patient records, keeping dental supply inventories, preparing bills for services rendered, collecting payments, and issuing receipts. Dental assistants often act as business managers who perform all nonclinical responsibilities such as hiring and firing auxiliary help, scheduling employees, and overseeing office accounting.

REQUIREMENTS

High School

Most dental assistant positions are entry level. They usually require little or no experience and no education beyond high school. High school students who wish to work as dental assistants should take courses in general science, biology, health, chemistry, and business management. Typing is also an important skill for dental assistants.

Postsecondary Training

Dental assistants commonly acquire their skills on the job. Many, however, go on to receive training after high school at trade schools, technical institutes, and com-

QUICK FACTS

SCHOOL SUBJECTS
Business
Health

PERSONAL SKILLS
Helping/teaching
Technical/scientific

WORK ENVIRONMENT
Primarily indoors
Primarily one location

MINIMUM EDUCATION LEVEL
High school diploma

MEDIAN SALARY
$30,220

CERTIFICATION OR LICENSING
Recommended

OUTLOOK
Much faster than the average

munity and junior colleges that offer dental assisting programs. The armed forces also train some dental assistants. Students who complete two-year college programs receive associate's degrees, while those who complete one-year trade and technical school programs earn a certificate or diploma. Entrance requirements to these programs require a high school diploma and good grades in high school science, typing, and English. Some postsecondary schools require an interview or written examination, and some require that applicants pass physical and dental examinations. The American Dental Association's Commission on Dental Accreditation accredits about 269 of these programs. Some four- to six-month nonaccredited courses in dental assisting are also available from private vocational schools.

Accredited programs instruct students in dental assisting skills and theory through classes, lectures, and laboratory and preclinical experience. Students take courses in English, speech, and psychology as well as in the biomedical sciences, including anatomy, microbiology, and nutrition. Courses in dental science cover subjects such as oral anatomy and pathology, and dental radiography. Students also gain practical experience in chair-side assisting and office management by working in dental schools and local dental clinics that are affiliated with their program.

Graduates of such programs may be assigned a greater variety of tasks initially and may receive higher starting salaries than those with high school diplomas alone.

Certification or Licensing

Dental assistants may wish to obtain certification from the Dental Assisting National Board. DANB certification is recognized or required in more than 30 states. Certified dental assistant (CDA) accreditation shows that an assistant meets certain standards of professional competence. To take the certification examination, assistants must be high school graduates who have taken a course in cardiopulmonary resuscitation and must have either a diploma from a formal training program accredited by the Commission on Dental Accreditation or two years of full-time work experience with a recommendation from the dentist for whom the work was done.

In more than 30 states dental assistants are allowed to take X rays (under a dentist's direction) only after completing a precise training program and passing a test. Completing the program for CDA certification fulfills this requirement. To keep their CDA credentials, however, assistants must either prove their skills through retesting or acquire further education.

Other Requirements

Dental assistants need a clean, well-groomed appearance and a pleasant personality. Manual dexterity and the ability to follow directions are also important.

EXPLORING

Students in formal training programs receive dental assisting experience as part of their training. High school students can learn more about the field by talking with assistants in local dentists' offices. The American Dental Assistants Association can put students in contact with dental assistants in their areas. Part-time, summer, and temporary clerical work may also be available in dentists' offices.

EMPLOYERS

Approximately 280,000 dental assistants are employed in the United States. Dental assistants are most likely to find employment in dental offices, whether it be a single dentist or a group practice with several dentists, assistants, and hygienists. Other places dental assistants may find jobs include dental schools, hospitals, public health departments, and U.S. Veterans Affairs and Public Health Service hospitals.

STARTING OUT

High school guidance counselors, family dentists, dental schools, dental placement agencies, and dental associations may provide applicants with leads about job openings. Students in formal training programs often learn of jobs through school career services offices.

ADVANCEMENT

Dental assistants may advance in their field by moving to larger offices or clinics, where they can take on more responsibility and earn more money. In small offices they may receive higher pay by upgrading their skills through education. Specialists in the dental field, who typically earn higher salaries than general dentists, often pay higher salaries to their assistants.

Further educational training is required for advancing to positions in dental assisting education. Dental assistants who wish to become dental hygienists must enroll in a dental hygiene program. Because many of these programs do not allow students to apply dental assisting courses toward graduation, dental assistants who think they would like to move into hygienist positions should plan their training carefully.

In some cases, dental assistants move into sales jobs with companies that sell dental industry supplies and materials. Other areas that open to dental assistants include office management, placement services, and insurance companies.

EARNINGS

Dental assistants' salaries are determined by specific responsibilities, the type of office they work in, and the geographic location of their employer. The median annual earnings for dental assistants were $30,220 in 2006, according to the U.S. Department of Labor. The highest paid 10 percent earned more than $43,040 a year, while the lowest paid 10 percent earned less than $20,530 a year.

Salaried dental assistants in a private office typically receive paid vacation, health insurance, and other benefits. Part-time assistants in private offices often receive dental coverage, but do not typically receive other benefits.

WORK ENVIRONMENT

Dental assistants work in offices that are generally clean, modern, quiet, and pleasant. They are also well lighted and well ventilated. In small offices, dental assistants may work solely with dentists, while in larger offices and clinics they may work with dentists, other dental assistants, dental hygienists, and laboratory technicians. Although dental assistants may sit at desks to do office work, they spend a large part of the day beside the dentist's chair where they can reach instruments and materials.

About a third of all dental assistants work 40-hour weeks, sometimes including Saturday hours, and about half work between 31 and 38 hours a week. The remainder work fewer hours, but some part-time workers work in more than one dental office.

Taking X rays poses some risk because regular doses of radiation can be harmful to the body. However, all dental offices must have lead shielding and safety procedures that minimize the risk of exposure to radiation.

OUTLOOK

According to the U.S. Department of Labor, employment for dental assistants is expected to grow much faster than the average through 2016, and is expected to be among the fastest growing occupations. As the population grows, more people will seek dental services for preventive care and cosmetic improvements.

In addition, dentists who earned their dental degrees since the 1970s are more likely than other dentists to hire one or more assistants. Also, as dentists increase their knowledge of innovative techniques such as implantology and periodontal therapy, they generally delegate more routine tasks to assistants so they can make the best use of their time and increase profits.

Job openings will also be created through attrition as assistants leave the field or change jobs.

FOR MORE INFORMATION

For continuing education information and career services, contact

American Dental Assistants Association
35 East Wacker Drive, Suite 1730
Chicago, IL 60601-2211
Tel: 312-541-1550
http://www.dentalassistant.org

For education information, contact
American Dental Association
211 East Chicago Avenue
Chicago, IL 60611-2678

Tel: 312-440-2500
http://www.ada.org

For publications, information on dental schools, and scholarship information, contact
American Dental Education Association
1400 K Street, NW, Suite 1100
Washington, DC 20005-2415
Tel: 202-289-7201
http://www.adea.org

For information on voluntary certification for dental assistants, contact
Dental Assisting National Board
444 North Michigan Avenue, Suite 900
Chicago, IL 60611-3985
Tel: 800-367-3262
Email: danbmail@danb.org
http://www.dentalassisting.com

National Association of Dental Assistants
900 South Washington Street, Suite G13
Falls Church, VA 22046-4009
Tel: 703-237-8616

❑ DENTAL HYGIENISTS

OVERVIEW

Dental hygienists perform clinical tasks, serve as oral health educators in private dental offices, work in public health agencies, and promote good oral health by educating adults and children. Their main responsibility is to perform oral prophylaxis, a process of cleaning teeth by using sharp dental instruments, such as scalers and prophy angles. With these instruments, they remove stains and calcium deposits, polish teeth, and massage gums. There are approximately 167,000 dental hygienists employed in the United States.

THE JOB

In clinical settings, hygienists help prevent gum diseases and cavities by removing deposits from teeth and applying sealants and fluoride to prevent tooth decay. They remove tartar, stains, and plaque from teeth, take X rays and other diagnostic tests, place and remove temporary

QUICK FACTS

SCHOOL SUBJECTS
Biology
Health

PERSONAL SKILLS
Helping/teaching
Technical/scientific

WORK ENVIRONMENT
Primarily indoors
Primarily one location

MINIMUM EDUCATION LEVEL
Associate's degree

MEDIAN SALARY
$62,800

CERTIFICATION OR LICENSING
Required by all states

OUTLOOK
Much faster than the average

fillings, take health histories, remove sutures, polish amalgam restorations, and examine head, neck, and oral regions for disease.

Their tools include hand and rotary instruments to clean teeth, syringes with needles to administer local anesthetic (such as Novocain), teeth models to demonstrate home care procedures, and X-ray machines to take pictures of the oral cavity that the dentist uses to detect signs of decay or oral disease.

A hygienist also provides nutritional counseling and screens patients for oral cancer and high blood pressure. More extensive dental procedures are done by dentists. The hygienist is also trained and licensed to take and develop X rays. Other responsibilities depend on the employer.

Private dentists might require that the dental hygienist mix compounds for filling cavities, sterilize instruments, assist in surgical work, or even carry out clerical tasks such as making appointments and filling in insurance forms. The hygienist might well fill the duties of recep-

tionist or office manager, functioning in many ways to assist the dentist in carrying out the day's schedule.

Although some of these tasks might also be done by a dental assistant, only the dental hygienist is licensed by the state to clean teeth. Licensed hygienists submit charts of each patient's teeth, noting possible decay or disease. The dentist studies these in making further diagnoses.

The *school hygienist* cleans and examines the teeth of students in a number of schools. The hygienist also gives classroom instruction on correct brushing and flossing of teeth, the importance of good dental care, and the effects of good nutrition. They keep dental records of students and notify parents of any need for further treatment.

Dental hygienists may be employed by local, state, or federal public health agencies. These hygienists carry out an educational program for adults and children, in public health clinics, schools, and other public facilities. A few dental hygienists may assist in research projects. For those with further education, teaching in a dental hygiene school may be possible.

Like all dental professionals, hygienists must be aware of federal, state, and local laws that govern hygiene practice. In particular, hygienists must know the types of infection control and protective gear that, by law, must be worn in the dental office to protect workers from infection. Dental hygienists, for example, must wear gloves, protective eyewear, and a mask during examinations. As with most health care workers, hygienists must be immunized against contagious diseases, such as hepatitis.

Dental hygienists are required by their state and encouraged by professional organizations to continue learning about trends in dental care, procedures, and regulations by taking continuing education courses. These may be held at large dental society meetings, colleges and universities, or in more intimate settings, such as a nearby dental office.

REQUIREMENTS

High School

The minimum requirement for admission to a dental hygiene school is graduation from high school. While in high school, you should follow a college preparatory program, which will include courses such as science, mathematics, history, English, and foreign language. It will also be beneficial for you to take health courses.

Postsecondary Training

Two levels of postsecondary training are available in this field. One is a four-year college program offering a bachelor's degree. More common is a two-year program leading to an associate's degree. A bachelor's degree is often preferred by employers, and more schools are likely to require completion of such a degree program in the future. There are about 286 accredited schools in the United States that offer one or both of these courses. Classroom work emphasizes general and dental sciences and liberal arts. Lectures are usually combined with laboratory work and clinical experience.

Certification or Licensing

After graduating from an accredited school, you must pass state licensing examinations, both written and clinical. The American Dental Association Joint Commission on National Dental Examinations administers the written part of the examination. This test is accepted by all states and the District of Columbia. The clinical part of the examination is administered by state or regional testing agencies.

Other Requirements

Aptitude tests sponsored by the American Dental Hygienists' Association are frequently required by dental hygiene schools to help applicants determine whether they will succeed in this field. Skill in handling delicate instruments, a sensitive touch, and depth perception are important attributes that are tested. To be a successful dental hygienist, you should be neat, clean, and personable.

EXPLORING

Work as a dental assistant can be a stepping-stone to a career as a dental hygienist. As a dental assistant, you could closely observe the work of a dental hygienist. You could then assess your personal aptitude for this work, discuss any questions with other hygienists, and enroll in a dental hygiene school where experience as a dental assistant would certainly be helpful.

You may be able to find part-time or summer work in high school as a dental assistant or clerical worker in a dentist's office. You also may be able to arrange to observe a dental hygienist working in a school or a dentist's office or visit an accredited dental hygiene school. The aptitude-testing program required by most dental hygiene schools helps students assess their future abilities as dental hygienists.

EMPLOYERS

Approximately 167,000 dental hygienists are employed in the United States. Dental hygienists can find work in private dentist's offices, school systems, or public health agencies. Hospitals, industrial plants, and the armed forces also employ a small number of dental hygienists.

STARTING OUT

Once you have passed the National Board exams and a licensing exam in a particular state, you must decide on an area of work. Most dental hygiene schools maintain placement services for the assistance of their graduates, and finding a satisfactory position is usually not too difficult.

ADVANCEMENT

Opportunities for advancement, other than increases in salary and benefits that accompany experience in the field, usually require additional study and training. Educational advancement may lead to a position as an administrator, teacher, or director in a dental health program or to a more advanced field of practice. With further education and training, some hygienists may choose to go on to become dentists.

EARNINGS

The dental hygienist's income is influenced by such factors as education, experience, locale, and type of employer. Most dental hygienists who work in private dental offices are salaried employees, although some are paid a commission for work performed or a combination of salary and commission.

According to the U.S. Department of Labor, full-time hygienists earned a median annual salary of $62,800 in 2006. The lowest paid 10 percent of hygienists earned less than $40,450 annually, and the highest 10 percent earned $86,530 or more annually. Salaries in large metropolitan areas are generally somewhat higher than in small cities and towns. In addition, dental hygienists in research, education, or administration may earn higher salaries.

A salaried dental hygienist in a private office typically receives a paid two- or three-week vacation. Part-time or commissioned dental hygienists in private offices usually have no paid vacation.

WORK ENVIRONMENT

Working conditions for dental hygienists are pleasant, with well-lighted, modern, and adequately equipped facilities. Hygienists usually sit while working. State and federal regulations require that hygienists wear masks, protective eyewear, and gloves. Most hygienists do not wear any jewelry. They are required by government infection control procedures to leave their work clothes at work, so many dentists' offices now have laundry facilities to launder work clothes properly. They must also follow proper sterilizing techniques on equipment and instruments to guard against passing infection or disease.

It is common practice among part-time and full-time hygienists to work in more than one office because many dentists schedule a hygienist to come in only two or three days a week. Hygienists frequently piece together part-time positions at several dental offices and substitute for other hygienists who take days off. About 88 percent of hygienists see eight or more patients daily, and 68 percent work in a single practice. Many private offices are open on Saturdays. The work hours of government employees are regulated by the particular agency.

OUTLOOK

The U.S. Department of Labor projects that employment of dental hygienists will grow much faster than the average for all occupations through 2016. In fact, the department predicts that dental hygienists will be among the fastest growing occupations. The demand for dental hygienists is expected to grow as younger generations that grew up receiving better dental care keep their teeth longer.

Population growth, increased public awareness of proper oral home care, and the availability of dental insurance should result in the creation of more dental hygiene jobs. Moreover, as the population ages, there will be a special demand for hygienists to work with older people, especially those who live in nursing homes.

FOR MORE INFORMATION

For education information, contact

American Dental Association
211 East Chicago Avenue
Chicago, IL 60611-2678
Tel: 312-440-2500
http://www.ada.org

For publications, information on dental schools, and scholarship information, contact

American Dental Education Association
1400 K Street, NW, Suite 1100
Washington, DC 20005-2415
Tel: 202-289-7201
http://www.adea.org

For career information and tips for dental hygiene students on finding a job, contact

American Dental Hygienists' Association
444 North Michigan Avenue, Suite 3400
Chicago, IL 60611
Tel: 312-440-8900
Email: mail@adha.net
http://www.adha.org

☐ DESKTOP PUBLISHING SPECIALISTS

OVERVIEW

Desktop publishing specialists prepare reports, brochures, books, cards, and other documents for printing. They create computer files of text, graphics, and page layout. They work with files others have created, or they compose original text and graphics for clients. There are approximately 32,000 desktop publishing specialists employed in the United States.

THE JOB

If you have ever used a computer to design and print a page in your high school paper or yearbook, then you've had some experience in desktop publishing. Not so many years ago, the prepress process (the steps to prepare a document for the printing press) involved metal casts, molten lead, light tables, knives, wax, paste, and a number of different professionals from artists to typesetters. With computer technology, these jobs are becoming more consolidated.

Desktop publishing specialists have artistic talents, proofreading skills, sales and marketing abilities, and a great deal of computer knowledge. They work on computers converting and preparing files for printing presses and other media, such as the Internet and CD-ROM. Much of desktop publishing is called prepress, when specialists typeset, or arrange and transform, text and graphics. They use the latest in design software. Programs such as Photoshop, Illustrator, InDesign, PageMaker (all from software designer Adobe), and QuarkXPress, are the most popular. Some desktop publishing specialists also use CAD (computer-aided design) technology, allowing them to create images and effects with a digitizing pen.

Once they've created a file to be printed, desktop publishing specialists either submit it to a commercial printer or print the pieces themselves. Whereas traditional typesetting costs more than $20 per page, desktop printing can cost less than a penny a page. Individuals hire the services of desktop publishing specialists for creating and printing invitations, advertising and fund-raising brochures, newsletters, flyers, and business cards. Commercial printing involves catalogs, brochures, and reports, while business printing encompasses products used by businesses, such as sales receipts and forms.

Typesetting and page layout work entails selecting font types and sizes, arranging column widths, checking for proper spacing between letters, words, and columns, placing graphics and pictures, and more. Desktop publishing specialists choose from the hundreds of typefaces available, taking the purpose and tone of the text into consideration when selecting from fonts with round shapes or long shapes, thick strokes or thin, serifs or sans serifs. Editing is also an important duty of a desktop publishing specialist. Articles must be updated, or in some cases rewritten, before they are arranged on a page. As more people use their own desktop publishing programs to create print-ready files, desktop publishing specialists will have to be even more skillful at designing original work and promoting their professional expertise to remain competitive.

Darryl Gabriel and his wife Maree own a desktop publishing service in Australia. The Internet has allowed them to publicize the business globally. They currently serve customers in their local area and across Australia, and are hoping to expand more into international Internet marketing. The Gabriels use a computer ("But one is not enough," Darryl says), a laser printer, and a scanner to create business cards, pamphlets, labels, books, and personalized greeting cards. Though they must maintain computer skills, they also have a practical understanding of the equipment. "We keep our prices down by being able to re-ink our cartridges," Darryl says. "This takes a little getting used to at first, but once you get a knack for it, it becomes easier."

Desktop publishing specialists deal with technical issues, such as resolution problems, colors that need to be corrected, and software difficulties. A client may come in with a hand-drawn sketch, a printout of a design, or a file on a diskette, and he or she may want the piece ready to be posted on the Internet or to be published in a high-quality brochure, newspaper, or magazine. Each format presents different issues, and desktop publishing specialists must be familiar with the processes and solutions for each. They may also provide services such as color scanning, laminating, image manipulation, and poster production.

Customer relations are as important as technical skills. Darryl Gabriel encourages desktop publishing specialists to learn how to use equipment and software to their fullest potential. He also advises them to know their customers. "Try and be as helpful as possible to your customers," he says, "so you can provide them with products that they are happy with and that are going to benefit their businesses." He says it is also very important to follow up, calling customers to make sure they are pleased with the work. "If you're able to relate to what the customers want, and if you encourage them to be involved in the initial design

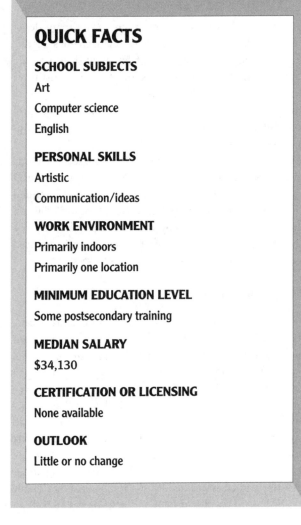

QUICK FACTS

SCHOOL SUBJECTS
Art
Computer science
English

PERSONAL SKILLS
Artistic
Communication/ideas

WORK ENVIRONMENT
Primarily indoors
Primarily one location

MINIMUM EDUCATION LEVEL
Some postsecondary training

MEDIAN SALARY
$34,130

CERTIFICATION OR LICENSING
None available

OUTLOOK
Little or no change

process, then they'll be confident they're going to get quality products."

REQUIREMENTS
High School

Classes that will help you develop desktop publishing skills include computer classes and design and art classes. Computer classes should include both hardware and software, since understanding how computers function will help you with troubleshooting and knowing a computer's limits. Through photography classes you can learn about composition, color, and design elements. Typing, drafting, and print shop classes, if available, will also provide you with the opportunity to gain some indispensable skills. Working on the school newspaper or yearbook will train you on desktop publishing skills as well, including page layout, typesetting, composition, and working under a deadline.

Postsecondary Training

Although a college degree is not a prerequisite, many desktop publishing specialists have at least a bachelor's degree. Areas of study range anywhere from English to graphic design. Some two-year colleges and technical institutes offer programs in desktop publishing or related fields. A growing number of schools offer programs in technical and visual communications, which may include classes in desktop publishing, layout and design, and computer graphics. Four-year colleges also offer courses in technical communications and graphic design. You can enroll in classes related to desktop publishing through extended education programs offered at universities and colleges. These classes, often taught by professionals in the industry, cover basic desktop publishing techniques and advanced lessons on Adobe Photoshop or QuarkXPress.

Other Requirements

Desktop publishing specialists are detail oriented, possess problem-solving skills, and have a sense of design and artistic skills. "People tell me I have a flair for graphic design and mixing the right color with the right graphics," Darryl Gabriel says.

A good eye and patience are critical, as well as endurance to see projects through to the finish. You should have an aptitude for computers, the ability to type quickly and accurately, and a natural curiosity. In addition, a calm temperament comes in handy when working under pressure and constant deadlines. You should be flexible and be able to handle more than one project at a time.

EXPLORING

Experimenting with your home computer, or a computer at school or the library, will give you a good idea as to whether desktop publishing is for you. Play around with various graphic design and page layout programs. If you subscribe to an Internet service, take advantage of any free Web space available to you and design your own home page. Join computer clubs and volunteer to produce newsletters and flyers for school or community clubs. Volunteering is an excellent way to try new software and techniques as well as gain experience troubleshooting and creating final products. Part-time or summer employment with printing shops and companies that have in-house publishing or printing departments are other great ways to gain experience and make valuable contacts.

EMPLOYERS

Approximately 32,000 desktop publishing specialists are employed in the United States. Desktop publishing specialists work for individuals and small business owners. About 34 percent work for newspapers, publishing houses, and directory publishers. Printing shops employ about 24 percent of desktop publishing specialists. Some large companies also contract with desktop publishing services rather than hire full-time designers. Government agencies such as the U.S. Government Printing Office hire desktop publishing specialists to help produce the large number of documents they publish.

Desktop publishing specialists deal directly with their clients, but in some cases they may be subcontracting work from printers, designers, and other desktop publishing specialists. They may also work as consultants, working with printing professionals to help solve particular design problems.

STARTING OUT

To start your own business, you must have a great deal of experience with design and page layout, and a careful understanding of the computer design programs you'll be using. Before striking out on your own, you may want to gain experience as a full-time staff member of a large business. Most desktop publishing specialists enter the field through the production side, or the editorial side of the industry. Those with training as a designer or artist can easily master the finer techniques of production. Printing houses and design agencies are places to check for production artist opportunities. Publishing companies often hire desktop publishing specialists to work in-house or as freelance employees. Working within the industry, you can make connections and build up a clientele.

You can also start out by investing in computer hardware and software, and volunteering your services. By designing logos, letterhead, and restaurant menus, for example, your work will gain quick recognition, and word of your services will spread.

ADVANCEMENT

The growth of Darryl and Maree Gabriel's business requires that they invest in another computer and printer. "We want to expand," Darryl says, "and develop with technology by venturing into Internet marketing and development. We also intend to be a thorn in the side of the larger commercial printing businesses in town."

In addition to taking on more print projects, desktop publishing specialists can expand their business into Web design and page layout for Internet-based magazines.

EARNINGS

There is limited salary information available for desktop publishing specialists, most likely because the job duties of desktop publishing specialists can vary and often overlap with other jobs. The average wage of desktop publishing specialists in the prepress department generally ranges from $15 to $50 an hour. Entry-level desktop publishing specialists with little or no experience generally earn minimum wage. Freelancers can earn from $15 to $100 an hour.

According to the U.S. Department of Labor, median annual earnings of desktop publishing specialists were $34,130 in 2006. The lowest paid 10 percent earned less than $20,550 and the highest paid 10 percent earned more than $55,040. Wage rates vary depending on experience, training, region, and size of the company.

WORK ENVIRONMENT

Desktop publishing specialists spend most of their time working in front of a computer, whether editing text, or laying out pages. They need to be able to work with other prepress professionals, and deal with clients. Hours may vary depending on project deadlines at hand. Some projects may take just a day to complete, while others may take weeks or months. Projects range from designing a logo for letterhead, to preparing a catalog for the printer, to working on a file for a company's Web site.

OUTLOOK

According to the U.S. Department of Labor, employment for desktop publishing specialists is projected to experience little or no change through 2016. This is due in part to technology advances that have made it possible for more people to learn basic desktop publishing skills and incorporate them into their regular jobs. Also, to save the cost of printing and distributing materials, more companies are developing materials for display on the Web rather than creating pages for print publication.

Employment opportunities will continue to be available to replace desktop publishing specialists who move into other positions, retire, or leave the industry for other reasons. Opportunities will be best for specialists with experience in QuarkXPress, Adobe PageMaker, InDesign, Macromedia FreeHand, Adobe Illustrator, Adobe Photoshop, and other programs often used in desktop publishing.

FOR MORE INFORMATION

This organization is a source of financial support for education and research projects designed to promote careers in graphic communications. For more information, contact
Graphic Arts Education and Research Foundation
1899 Preston White Drive
Reston, VA 20191-5468

Tel: 866-381-9839
Email: gaerf@npes.org
http://www.gaerf.org

For career brochures and other information on desktop publishing careers, contact the following organizations:
Graphic Arts Information Network
200 Deer Run Road
Sewickley, PA 15143-2324
Tel: 412-741-6860
Email: gain@piagatf.org
http://www.gain.net

National Association for Printing Leadership
75 West Century Road, Suite 100
Paramus, NJ 07652-1408
Tel: 800-642-6275
http://www.recouncil.org

Society for Technical Communication
901 North Stuart Street, Suite 904
Arlington, VA 22203-1822
Tel: 703-522-4114
Email: stc@stc.org
http://www.stc.org

Visit the following Web site for information on scholarships, competitions, colleges and universities that offer graphic communication programs, and careers:
GRAPHIC COMM Central
Email: gcc@teched.vt.edu
http://teched.vt.edu/gcc

DETECTIVES

OVERVIEW

Detectives are almost always plainclothes investigators who gather difficult-to-obtain information on criminal activity and other subjects. They conduct interviews and surveillance, locate missing persons and criminal suspects, examine records, and write detailed reports. Some make arrests and take part in raids.

THE JOB

The job of a *police detective* begins after a crime has been committed. Uniformed police officers are usually the first to be dispatched to the scene of a crime, however, and it is police officers who are generally required

QUICK FACTS

SCHOOL SUBJECTS
English
Government
History

PERSONAL SKILLS
Leadership/management
Technical/scientific

WORK ENVIRONMENT
Indoors and outdoors
One location with some travel

MINIMUM EDUCATION LEVEL
High school diploma

MEDIAN SALARY
$58,260

CERTIFICATION OR LICENSING
Voluntary (certification)
Required by certain states (licensing)

OUTLOOK
About as fast as the average (police detectives)
Faster than the average (private detectives)

to make out the initial crime report. This report is often the material with which a detective begins an investigation.

Detectives may also receive help early on from other members of the police department. Evidence technicians are sometimes sent immediately to the scene of a crime to comb the area for physical evidence. This step is important because most crime scenes contain physical evidence that could link a suspect to the crime. Fingerprints are the most common physical piece of evidence, but other clues, such as broken locks, broken glass, and footprints, as well as blood, skin, or hair traces, are also useful. If there is a suspect on the scene, torn clothing or any scratches, cuts, and bruises are noted. Physical evidence may then be tested by specially trained crime lab technicians.

It is after this initial stage that the case is assigned to a police detective. Police detectives may be assigned as

many as two or three cases a day, and having 30 cases to handle at one time is not unusual. Because there is only a limited amount of time, an important part of a detective's work is to determine which cases have the greatest chance of being solved. The most serious offenses or those in which there is considerable evidence and obvious leads tend to receive the highest priority. All cases, however, are given at least a routine follow-up investigation.

Police detectives have numerous means of gathering additional information. For example, they contact and interview victims and witnesses, familiarize themselves with the scene of the crime and places where a suspect may spend time, and conduct surveillance operations. Detectives sometimes have informers who provide important leads. Because detectives must often work undercover, they wear ordinary clothes, not police uniforms. Also helpful are existing police files on other crimes, on known criminals, and on people suspected of criminal activity. If sufficient evidence has been collected, the police detective will arrest the suspect, sometimes with the help of uniformed police officers.

Once the suspect is in custody, it is the job of the police detective to conduct an interrogation. Questioning the suspect may reveal new evidence and help determine whether the suspect was involved in other unsolved crimes. Before finishing the case, the detective must prepare a detailed written report. Detectives are sometimes required to present evidence at the trial of the suspect.

Criminal investigation is just one area in which private investigators are involved. Some specialize, for example, in finding missing persons, while others may investigate insurance fraud, gather information on the background of persons involved in divorce or child custody cases, administer lie detection tests, debug offices and telephones, or offer security services. Cameras, video equipment, tape recorders, and lock picks are used in compliance with legal restrictions to obtain necessary information. Some private investigators work for themselves, but many others work for detective agencies or businesses. Clients include private individuals, corporations concerned with theft, insurance companies suspicious of fraud, and lawyers who want information for a case. Whoever the client, the private investigator is usually expected to provide a detailed report of the activities and results of the investigation.

REQUIREMENTS
High School

Because detectives work on a wide variety of cases, if you are interested in this field you are encouraged to take a diverse course load. English, American history, business law, government, psychology, sociology, chemistry, and physics are suggested, as are courses in journalism, computers, and a foreign language. The ability to type is often needed. To become a police detective, you must first have experience as a police officer. Hiring requirements for police officers vary, but most departments require at least a high school diploma.

Postsecondary Training

In some police departments a college degree may be necessary for some or all positions. Many colleges and universities offer courses or programs in police science, criminal justice, or law enforcement. Newly hired police officers are generally sent to a police academy for job training.

After gaining substantial experience in the department—usually about three to five years—and demonstrating the skills required for detective work, a police officer may be promoted to detective. In some police departments, candidates must first take a qualifying exam. For new detectives there is usually a training program, which may last from a few weeks to several months.

Private detective agencies usually do not hire individuals without previous experience. A large number of private investigators are former police officers. Those with no law enforcement experience who want to become private investigators can enroll in special private investigation schools, although these do not guarantee qualification for employment. A college degree is an admissions requirement at some private investigation schools. These schools teach skills essential to detective work, such as how to take and develop fingerprints, pick locks, test for the presence of human blood, investigate robberies, identify weapons, and take photographs. The length of these programs and their admissions requirements vary considerably. Some are correspondence programs, while others offer classroom instruction and an internship at a detective agency. Experience can also be gained by taking classes in law enforcement, police science, or criminal justice at a college or university.

Certification or Licensing

The National Association of Legal Investigators awards the certified legal investigator designation to private detectives and investigators who specialize in cases that deal with negligence or criminal defense investigations.

Private detectives and investigators must be licensed in all states except for Alabama, Alaska, Colorado, Idaho, Mississippi, Missouri, and South Dakota. In general, states that have licensing require applicants to pass a written examination and file a bond. Depending on the state, applicants may also need to have a minimum amount of experience, either as a police officer or as an apprentice under a licensed private investigator. An additional license is sometimes required for carrying a gun.

In almost all large cities the hiring of police officers must follow local civil service regulations. In such cases candidates generally must be at least 21 years old, U.S. citizens, and within the locally prescribed height and weight limits. Other requirements include 20/20 corrected vision and good hearing. Background checks are often done.

The civil service board usually gives both a written and physical examination. The written test is intended to measure a candidate's mental aptitude for police work, while the physical examination focuses on strength, dexterity, and agility.

Other Requirements

Among the most important personal characteristics helpful for detectives are an inquisitive mind, good observation skills, a keen memory, and well-developed oral and written communication skills. The large amount of physical activity involved requires that detectives be in good shape. An excellent moral character is especially important.

EXPLORING

There are few ways of exploring the field of detective work, and actual experience in the field prior to employment is unlikely. Some police departments, however, do hire teenagers for positions as police trainees and interns. If you are interested in becoming a detective, you should talk with your school guidance counselor, your local police department, local private detective agencies, a private investigation school, or a college or university offering police science, criminal justice, or law enforcement courses. In addition, the FBI operates an Honors Internship Program for undergraduate and graduate students that exposes interns to a variety of investigative techniques.

EMPLOYERS

There are more than 861,000 police and detectives in the United States. A large percentage work for police departments or other government agencies. Approximately 52,000 detectives work as private investigators, employed either for themselves, for a private detective firm, or for a business.

STARTING OUT

If you are interested in becoming a detective, you should contact your local police department, the civil service office or examining board, or private detective agencies in your area to determine hiring practices and any special requirements. Newspapers may list available jobs. If you earn a college degree in police science, criminal justice, or law enforcement, you may benefit from your institution's career services or guidance office. Some police academies accept candidates not sponsored by a police department, and for some people this may be the best way to enter police work.

ADVANCEMENT

Advancement within a police department may depend on several factors, such as job performance, length of service, formal education and training courses, and special examinations. Large city police departments, divided into separate divisions with their own administrations, often provide greater advancement possibilities.

Because of the high dropout rate for private investigators, those who manage to stay in the field for more than five years have an excellent chance for advancement. Supervisory and management positions exist, and some private investigators start their own agencies.

EARNINGS

Median annual earnings of police detectives and criminal investigators were $58,260 in 2006, according to the U.S. Department of Labor. The lowest paid 10 percent earned $34,480 or less, while the highest paid 10 percent earned more than $92,590 annually. Median annual earnings were $70,560 in federal government, $51,400 in state government, and $55,550 in local government. Compensation generally increases considerably with experience. Police departments generally offer better than average benefits, including health insurance, paid vacation, sick days, and pension plans.

Median annual earnings of salaried private detectives and investigators were $33,750 in 2006, according to the U.S. Department of Labor. The lowest paid 10 percent earned less than $19,720, and the highest paid 10 percent earned more than $64,380.

Private investigators who are self-employed have the potential for making much higher salaries. Hourly fees of $50 to $150 and even more, excluding expenses, are possible. Detectives who work for an agency may receive benefits, such as health insurance, but self-employed investigators must provide their own.

WORK ENVIRONMENT

The working conditions of a detective are diverse. Almost all of them work out of an office, where they may consult with colleagues, interview witnesses, read documents, or contact people on the telephone.

Their assignments bring detectives to a wide range of environments. Interviews at homes or businesses may be necessary. Traveling is also common. Rarely do jobs expose a detective to possible physical harm or death, but detectives are more likely than most people to place themselves in a dangerous situation.

Schedules for detectives are often irregular, and overtime, as well as night and weekend hours, may be necessary. At some police departments and detective agencies, overtime is compensated with additional pay or time off.

Although the work of a detective is portrayed as exciting in popular culture, the job has its share of monotonous and discouraging moments. For example, detectives may need to sit in a car for many hours waiting for a suspect to leave a building entrance only to find that the suspect is not there. Even so, the great variety of cases usually makes the work interesting.

OUTLOOK

Employment for police detectives is expected to increase about as fast as the average for all other occupations through 2016, according to the U.S. Department of Labor. Many openings will likely result from police detectives retiring or leaving their departments for other reasons.

Employment for private investigators is predicted to grow faster than the average through 2016, although it is important to keep in mind that law enforcement or comparable experience is often required for employment. The use of private investigators by insurance firms, restaurants, hotels, and other businesses is on the rise. Two areas of particular growth are the investigation of the various forms of computer fraud and the conducting of employee background checks.

FOR MORE INFORMATION

Contact the IACP for information about careers in law enforcement.

International Association of Chiefs of Police (IACP)
515 North Washington Street
Alexandria, VA 22314-2357
Tel: 703-836-6767
Email: information@theiacp.org
http://www.theiacp.org

For more information on private investigation, contact
National Association of Investigative Specialists
PO Box 82148
Austin, TX 78708-2148
Tel: 512-719-3595
http://www.pimall.com/nais/nais.j.html

For information on certification, contact

National Association of Legal Investigators
235 North Pine Street
Lansing, MI 48933-1021
Tel: 866-520-6254
Email: info@nalionline.org
http://www.nalionline.org

☐ DIAGNOSTIC MEDICAL SONOGRAPHERS

OVERVIEW

Diagnostic medical sonographers, or *sonographers*, use advanced technology in the form of high-frequency sound waves similar to sonar to produce images of the internal body for analysis by radiologists and other physicians. There are about 46,000 diagnostic medical sonographers employed in the United States.

THE JOB

Sonographers work on the orders of a physician or radiologist. They are responsible for the proper selection and preparation of the ultrasound equipment for each specific exam. They explain the procedure to patients, recording any additional information that may be of later use to the physician. Sonographers instruct patients and assist them into the proper physical position so that the test may begin.

When the patient is properly aligned, the sonographer applies a gel to the skin that improves the diagnostic image. The sonographer selects the transducer, a microphone-shaped device that directs high-frequency sound waves into the area to be imaged, and adjusts equipment controls according to the proper depth of field and specific organ or structure to be examined. The transducer is moved as the sonographer monitors the sound wave display screen in order to ensure that a quality ultrasonic image is being produced. Sonographers must master the location and visualization of human anatomy to be able to clearly differentiate between healthy and pathological areas.

When a clear image is obtained, the sonographer activates equipment that records individual photographic views or sequences as real-time images of the affected area. These images are recorded on computer disk, magnetic tape, strip printout, film, or videotape. The sonographer removes the film after recording and prepares it

for analysis by the physician. In order to be able to discuss the procedure with the physician, if asked, the sonographer may also record any further data or observations that occurred during the exam.

Sonographers can be trained in the following specialties: abdomen, breast, echocardiography, neurosonology, obstetrics/gynecology, ophthalmology, and vascular technology.

Other duties include updating patient records, monitoring and adjusting sonographic equipment to maintain accuracy, and, after considerable experience, preparing work schedules and evaluating potential equipment purchases.

REQUIREMENTS
High School

If you are interested in a career in sonography, you should take high school courses in mathematics, biology, physics,

---

QUICK FACTS

SCHOOL SUBJECTS
Biology
Chemistry

PERSONAL SKILLS
Helping/teaching
Technical/scientific

WORK ENVIRONMENT
Primarily indoors
Primarily one location

MINIMUM EDUCATION LEVEL
Associate's degree

MEDIAN SALARY
$57,160

CERTIFICATION OR LICENSING
Recommended

OUTLOOK
About as fast as the average

anatomy and physiology, and, especially, chemistry. Also, take English and speech classes to improve your communication skills. In this career you will be working with both patients and other medical professionals, and it will be important for you to be able to follow directions as well as explain procedures. Finally, take computer courses to familiarize yourself with using technology.

Postsecondary Training

Instruction in diagnostic medical sonography is offered by hospitals, colleges, universities, technical schools, and the armed forces in the form of hospital certificates, and two-year associate's and four-year bachelor's degree programs. Most sonographers enter the field after completing an associate's degree. The Joint Review Committee on Education in Diagnostic Medical Sonography (a division of the Commission on Accreditation of Allied Health Education Programs) has accredited 147 programs in the United States. Education consists of classroom and laboratory instruction, as well as hands-on experience in the form of internships in a hospital ultrasound department. Areas of study include patient care and medical ethics, general and cross-sectional anatomy, physiology and pathophysiology, applications and limitations of ultrasound, and image evaluation.

Certification or Licensing

After completing their degrees, sonographers may register with the American Registry of Diagnostic Medical Sonographers (ARDMS). Registration allows qualified sonographers to take the National Boards to gain certification, which, although optional, is frequently required by employers. Other licensing requirements may exist at the state level but vary greatly. Three registration categories are available to sonographers: registered diagnostic medical sonographer, registered diagnostic cardiac sonographer, and registered vascular technologist.

Students should also be aware of continuing education requirements that exist to keep sonographers at the forefront of current technology and diagnostic theory. They are required to maintain certification through continuing education classes, which vary from state to state. This continuing education, offered by hospitals and ultrasound equipment companies, is usually offered after regular work hours have ended.

Other Requirements

On a personal level, prospective sonographers need to be technically adept, detail oriented, and precision minded. You need to enjoy helping others and working with a variety of professionals as part of a team. You must be able to follow physician instructions, while maintaining a creative approach to imaging as you complete each procedure. Sonographers need to cultivate a professional demeanor, while still expressing empathy, patience, and understanding in order to reassure patients. This professionalism is also necessary because, in some instances, tragedy such as cancer, untreatable disease, or fetal death is revealed during imaging procedures. As a result, sonographers must be able to skillfully deflect questions better left to the radiologist or the attending physician. Clear communication, both verbal and written, is a plus for those who are part of a health care team.

EXPLORING

Although it is impossible for you to gain direct experience in sonography without proper education and certification, you can gain insight into duties and responsibilities by speaking directly to an experienced sonographer. You can visit a hospital, health maintenance organization, or other locations to view the equipment and facilities used and to watch professionals at work. You may also consider contacting teachers at schools of diagnostic medical sonography or touring their educational facilities. Guidance counselors or science teachers may also be able to arrange a presentation by a sonographer.

EMPLOYERS

Approximately 46,000 sonographers are employed in the United States. More than half of all sonographers are employed by hospitals. However, increasing employment opportunities exist in nursing homes, HMOs, medical and diagnostic laboratories, imaging centers, private physicians' offices, research laboratories, educational institutions, and industry.

STARTING OUT

Those interested in becoming diagnostic medical sonographers must complete a sonographic educational program such as one offered by teaching hospitals, colleges and universities, technical schools, and the armed forces. You should be sure to enroll in an accredited educational program as those who complete such a program stand the best chances for employment.

Voluntary registration with the ARDMS is key to gaining employment. Most employers require registration with ARDMS. Other methods of entering the field include responding to job listings in sonography publications, registering with employment agencies specializing in the health care field, contacting headhunters, or applying to the personnel offices of health care employers. The ARDMS offers a Web site, http://

www.ultrasoundjobs.com, to help sonographers locate jobs in the field.

ADVANCEMENT

Many advancement areas are open to sonographers who have considerable experience, and most importantly, advanced education. Sonographers with a bachelor's degree stand the best chance to gain additional duties or responsibilities. Technical programs, teaching hospitals, colleges, universities, and, sometimes, in-house training programs can provide this further training. Highly trained and experienced sonographers can rise to the position of *chief technologist, administrator,* or *clinical supervisor,* overseeing sonography departments, choosing new equipment, and creating work schedules. Others may become *sonography instructors,* teaching ultrasound technology in hospitals, universities, and other educational settings. Other sonographers may gravitate toward marketing, working as *ultrasound equipment sales representatives* and selling ultrasound technology to medical clients. Sonographers involved in sales may market ultrasound technology for nonmedical uses to the plastics, steel, or other industries. Sonographers may also work as *machinery demonstrators,* traveling at the behest of manufacturers to train others in the use of new or updated equipment.

Sonographers may pursue advanced education in conjunction with or in addition to their sonography training. Sonographers may become certified in computer tomography, magnetic resonance imaging, nuclear medicine technology, radiation therapy, and cardiac catheterization. Others may become diagnostic cardiac sonographers or focus on specialty areas such as obstetrics/gynecology, neurosonography, peripheral vascular doppler, and ophthalmology.

EARNINGS

According to the U.S. Department of Labor, diagnostic medical sonographers earned a median annual income of $57,160 in 2006. The lowest paid 10 percent of this group, which included those just beginning in the field, made approximately $40,960. The highest paid 10 percent, which included those with experience and managerial duties, earned more than $77,520 annually. Median earnings for those who worked in hospitals were $57,670 and for those employed in offices and clinics of medical doctors, $58,050.

Pay scales vary based on experience, educational level, and type and location of employer, with urban employers offering higher compensation than rural areas and small towns. Beyond base salaries, sonographers can expect to enjoy many fringe benefits, including paid vacation, sick and personal days, and health and dental insurance.

WORK ENVIRONMENT

A variety of work settings exist for sonographers, from health maintenance organizations to mobile imaging centers to clinical research labs or industry. In health care settings, diagnostic medical sonographers may work in departments of obstetrics/gynecology, cardiology, neurology, and others.

Sonographers enjoy a workplace that is clean, indoors, well lighted, quiet, and professional. Most sonographers work at one location, although mobile imaging sonographers and sales representatives can expect a considerable amount of travel.

The typical sonographer is constantly busy, seeing as many as 25 patients in the course of an eight-hour day. Overtime may also be required by some employers. The types of examinations vary by institution, but frequent areas include fetal ultrasounds, gynecological (i.e., uterus, ovaries), and abdominal (i.e., gallbladder, liver, and kidney) tests. Prospective sonographers should be aware of the occasionally repetitive nature of the job and the long hours usually spent standing. Daily duties may be both physically and mentally taxing. Although not exposed to harmful radiation, sonographers may nevertheless be exposed to communicable diseases and hazardous materials from invasive procedures. Universal safety standards exist to ensure the safety of the sonographer.

OUTLOOK

According to the U.S. Department of Labor, employment of diagnostic medical sonographers should grow faster than the average for all occupations through 2016. One reason for this growth is that sonography is a safe, nonradioactive imaging process. In addition, sonography has proved successful in detecting life-threatening diseases and in analyzing previously nonimageable internal organs. Sonography will play an increasing role in the fields of obstetrics/gynecology and cardiology. Furthermore, the aging population will create high demand for qualified technologists to operate diagnostic machinery. Approximately three out of four sonographers work in urban areas, and demand for qualified diagnostic medical sonographers exceeds the current supply in some areas of the country, especially rural communities, small towns, and some retirement areas. Those flexible about location and compensation will enjoy the best opportunities in current and future job markets.

A few important factors may slow growth. The health care industry is currently in a state of transition because of public and government debate concerning Medicare, universal health care, and the role of third-party payers in the system. Also, some procedures may prove too costly for insurance companies or government programs to cover. Hospital sonography departments will also be affected by this debate and continue to downsize. Some procedures will be done only on weekends, weeknights, or on an outpatient basis, possibly affecting employment opportunities, hours, and salaries of future sonographers. Conversely, nursing homes, HMOs, mobile imaging centers, and private physicians' groups will offer new employment opportunities to highly skilled sonographers.

Anyone considering a career in sonography should be aware that there is considerable competition for the most lucrative jobs. Those flexible in regard to hours, salary, and location and who possess advanced education stand to prosper in future job markets. Those complementing their sonographic skills with training in other imaging areas, such as magnetic resonance imaging, computer tomography, nuclear medicine technology, or other specialties, will best be able to meet the changing requirements and rising competition of future job markets.

FOR MORE INFORMATION

For information about available jobs and credentials, contact

American Registry of Diagnostic Medical Sonographers
51 Monroe Street, Plaza East One
Rockville, MD 20850-2400
Tel: 800-541-9754
http://www.ardms.org and http://www.ultrasoundcareers.org

For information regarding accredited programs of sonography, contact

Commission on Accreditation of Allied Health Education Programs
1361 Park Street
Clearwater, FL 33756-6039
Tel: 727-210-2350
Email: mail@caahep.org
http://www.caahep.org

For information regarding a career in sonography or to subscribe to the Journal of Diagnostic Medical Sonography, contact

Society of Diagnostic Medical Sonography
2745 Dallas Parkway, Suite 350
Plano, TX 75093-8730
Tel: 800-229-9506
http://www.sdms.org

☐ DIALYSIS TECHNICIANS

OVERVIEW

Dialysis technicians, also called *nephrology technicians* or *renal dialysis technicians*, set up and operate hemodialysis artificial kidney machines for patients with chronic renal failure (CRF). CRF is a condition where the kidneys cease to function normally. Many people, especially diabetics or people who suffer from undetected high blood pressure, develop this condition. These patients require hemodialysis to sustain their lives. In hemodialysis the patient's blood is circulated through the dialysis machine, which filters out impurities, wastes, and excess fluids from the blood. The cleaned blood is then returned to the body. Dialysis technicians also maintain and repair this equipment as well as help educate the patient and family about dialysis.

THE JOB

The National Association of Nephrology Technicians/Technologists (NANT) recognizes three types of dialysis technicians: the *patient care technician*, the *biomedical equipment technician,* and the *dialyzer reprocessing technician*. Dialysis patient-care technicians are responsible for preparing the patient for dialysis, monitoring the procedure, and responding to any emergencies that occur during the treatment. Before dialysis, the technician measures the patient's vital signs (including weight, pulse, blood pressure, and temperature) and obtains blood samples and specimens as required. The technician then inserts tubes into access routes, such as a vein or a catheter, which will exchange blood between the patient and the artificial kidney machine throughout the dialysis session.

While monitoring the process of dialysis, the technician must be attentive, precise, and alert. He or she measures and adjusts blood-flow rates as well as checks and rechecks the patient's vital signs. All of this information is carefully recorded in a log. In addition, the technician must respond to any alarms that occur during the procedure and make appropriate adjustments to the dialysis machine. Should an emergency occur during the session, the technician must be able to administer cardiopulmonary resuscitation (CPR) or other life-saving techniques.

Biomedical equipment technicians are responsible for maintaining and repairing the dialysis machines. Dialyzer reprocessing technicians care for the dialyzers—the apparatus through which the blood is filtered. Each one must be cleaned and bleached after use, then sterilized by filling it with formaldehyde overnight so that it is ready to be used again for the patient's next treatment. To prevent contamination, a dialyzer may only be reused with the same patient, so accurate records must be kept. Some dialysis units reuse plastic tubing as well; this, too, must be carefully sterilized.

While most hemodialysis takes place in a hospital or special dialysis centers, the use of dialysis in the patient's home is becoming more common. In these cases, technicians travel to patients' homes to carry out the dialysis procedures or to instruct family members in assisting with the process.

In many dialysis facilities the duties described above overlap. The dialysis technician's role is determined by a number of factors: the dialysis facility's management plan, the facility's leadership and staff, the technician's skills and background, the unit's equipment and facilities, and the long-term care plans for patients. However, all dialysis technicians work under the supervision of physicians or registered nurses.

REQUIREMENTS
High School

If you are interested in working as a dialysis technician, you should take biology, chemistry, and health classes while in high school. Mathematics classes will also be beneficial, since you will be working with numbers and equations as you determine the appropriate treatment for each patient. English classes will help you develop your communication skills and improve your ability to follow directions and record information. You may also want to take computer classes so that you are comfortable working with technical equipment. Finally, consider taking any class, such as psychology, that will give you insight into dealing with people.

Postsecondary Training

Although there is a movement toward providing more formal academic training in the field of renal dialysis, presently only a few two-year dialysis preparatory programs exist in technical schools and junior colleges. Many people entering the field have some type of experience in a patient-care setting or college training in biology, chemistry, or health-related fields. By far, the majority of technicians learn their skills through on-the-job training at the first hospital or dialysis center where they are employed. Therefore, you should be extremely inquisitive, willing to

QUICK FACTS

SCHOOL SUBJECTS
Biology
Chemistry

PERSONAL SKILLS
Helping/teaching
Technical/scientific

WORK ENVIRONMENT
Primarily indoors
Primarily one location

MINIMUM EDUCATION LEVEL
Some postsecondary training

MEDIAN SALARY
$28,836

CERTIFICATION OR LICENSING
Required by certain states

OUTLOOK
About as fast as the average

learn, and able to work as a team member. Inquire at local hospitals and dialysis centers to find out what type of training they offer and their admission requirements. Training may range from several weeks to a year or more. Typically, the training programs include class study on such topics as anatomy, principles of dialysis, and patient care, as well as supervised clinical practice.

Certification or Licensing

In most states, dialysis technicians are not required to be registered, certified, or licensed. However, several states, such as California and New Mexico, do require practicing dialysis technicians to have certification; in addition, a growing number of states are considering legislation to make certification mandatory. In some states, technicians are required to pass a test before they can work with patients. You will need to check with your state's department of health or licensing board to determine specific requirements for your area.

The Board of Nephrology Examiners Nursing and Technology (BONENT), the National Nephrology Certification Organization, and the Nephrology Nursing Certification Commission offer voluntary certification programs for nurses and technicians. The programs' purposes are to identify safe, competent practitioners, to promote excellence in the quality of care available to kidney patients, and encourage study and advance the science of nursing and technological fields in nephrology. These organizations hope that eventually all dialysis technicians will be certified.

Other Requirements

The ability to talk easily with patients and their families is essential. Kidney patients, especially those who are just beginning dialysis, are confronting a major—and permanent—life change. You must be able to help them deal with the emotional as well as the physical effects of their condition. Good interpersonal skills are crucial, not only in the technician-patient relationship, but in working closely with other technicians and health care professionals as well. Because the slightest mistake can have deadly consequences, a technician must be thorough and detail oriented. Since the technician is responsible for the lives of patients, you must be mature, able to respond to stressful situations calmly, and think quickly in an emergency. Good mathematical skills and a familiarity with the metric system are required. You must be able to calibrate machines and calculate the correct amounts and proportions of solutions to be used as well as quickly determine any necessary changes if there are indications that a patient is not responding to the treatment appropriately.

It can be upsetting to work with people who are ill, and if you have a cheerful disposition and pleasant manner this will help ease the patient's anxiety.

EXPLORING

Volunteering in a hospital, nursing home, dialysis center, or other patient-care facility can give you a taste of what it is like to care for patients. You will soon discover whether you have the necessary disposition to help patients heal both physically and emotionally. Most hospitals have volunteer programs that are open to high school students.

Students interested in the requirements for becoming a dialysis technician may obtain job descriptions from NANT and BONENT. If your interest lies specifically in the area of nursing, you may want to contact the American Nephrology Nurses' Association. Also, several journals discuss the professional concerns of those working in the field as well as other issues such as treatments and quality control.

Until there are a greater number of organized and accredited training programs, those who are interested in the career of the dialysis technician must seek information about educational opportunities from local sources such as high school guidance centers, public libraries, and occupational counselors at technical and community colleges. Specific information is best obtained from dialysis centers, dialysis units of local hospitals, home health care agencies, medical societies, schools of nursing, or individual nephrologists.

EMPLOYERS

Dialysis technicians work throughout the country. They are employed by hospitals, nursing homes, dialysis centers, and health care agencies.

STARTING OUT

The best way to enter this field is through a formal training program in a hospital or other training facility. You may also contact your local hospital and dialysis center to determine the possibility of on-the-job training. Some hospitals pay trainees as they learn.

Other ways to enter this field are through schools of nurse assisting, practical nursing, or nursing programs for emergency medical technicians. The length of time required to progress through the dialysis training program and advance to higher levels of responsibility should be shorter if you first complete a related training program. Most dialysis centers offer a regular program of in-service training for their employees.

ADVANCEMENT

Dialysis technicians who have gained knowledge, skills, and experience advance to positions of greater responsibility within their units and can work more independently. They may also work in supervisory positions. The NANT guidelines encourage a distinction between technicians and technologists, with the latter having additional training and broader responsibilities. Some technologists conduct biochemical analyses or research studies to improve equipment. Not all dialysis units make this distinction.

A technician looking for career advancement in the patient-care sector may elect to enter nurse training; many states require that supervisory personnel in this field are registered nurses. Social, psychological, and counseling services appeal to others who find their greatest satisfaction in interacting with patients and their families.

A dialysis technician interested in biomedical equipment may advance by focusing on machine technology and return to college for a degree in biomedical engineering or other related field.

EARNINGS

Earnings for dialysis technicians are dependent on such factors as their job performance, responsibilities, locality, and length of service. Some employers pay higher wages to certified technicians than to those who are not certified. According to Salary.com, renal dialysis technicians earned an average of $28,836 in 2006. In Salary.com's survey, the lowest 25th percentile earned $26,040 and the highest 75th percentile earned $32,876.

Technicians receive the customary benefits of vacation, sick leave or personal time, and health insurance. Many hospitals or health care centers not only offer in-service training but pay tuition and other education costs as an incentive to further self-development and career advancement.

WORK ENVIRONMENT

Dialysis technicians most often work in a hospital or special dialysis centers. The work environment is usually a clean and comfortable patient-care setting. Some technicians are qualified to administer dialysis in patients' homes, and their jobs may require some local travel. Patients who use dialysis at home need education, assistance, and monitoring. Also, technicians may have to take care of patients when trained family members cannot.

A dialysis technician works a 40-hour week. Patients who work full time or part time often arrange to take their dialysis treatments at times that least interfere with their normal activities, therefore some evening and weekend shifts may be required. Flextime is common in some units, offering four- and even three-day work-weeks. Technicians in hospitals may be on call nights or weekends to serve in emergencies.

The spread of hepatitis and the growing risk of HIV infection have necessitated extra precautions in the field of hemodialysis, as in all fields whose procedures involve possible contact with human blood. All technicians must observe universal precautions, which include the wearing of a protective apron, foot covers, gloves, and a full-face shield.

The work of a technician can also be physically strenuous, especially if the patient is very ill. However, the equipment is mobile and easily moved.

Because the field of renal dialysis is constantly evolving, technicians must keep themselves up to date with technological advances and incorporate new technology as it becomes available. One advantage of being a certified technician is that professional organizations provide journals and offer educational seminars to members.

Although the daily tasks of a dialysis technician can be monotonous, the patients and staff are a diverse group of people. Patients come from all walks of life, all ages, and all levels of society. There is also a great satisfaction in helping critically ill patients stay alive and active. Some patients are carried through a temporary crisis by dialysis treatments and return to normal after a period of time. Other patients may be best treated by kidney transplants. But while they wait for a suitable donated kidney, their lives depend on dialysis treatment.

OUTLOOK

There should continue to be a need for dialysis technicians in the future as the number of people with kidney disease and failure increases. The principal cause of kidney failure, according to the National Kidney Foundation, is diabetes. In 2001, approximately 16 million Americans had diabetes, and the National Kidney Foundation projects this number to increase to 22 million by 2025. Those with kidney failure must have either dialysis or a kidney transplant in order to live. This steadily increasing number of patients in need will mean a continued demand for dialysis technicians.

Technicians make up the largest proportion of the dialysis team, since they can care for only a limited number of patients at a time (the ratio of patient-care technicians to nurses is generally about four to one). There is also a high turnover rate in the field of dialysis technicians, creating many new job openings. Lastly, there is a shortage of trained dialysis technicians in most localities.

A factor that may decrease employment demand is the further development of procedures that may remove the need for dialysis treatments in health care facilities. For instance, if the number of individuals able to participate in home dialysis increases, the staffing requirements and number of dialysis facilities would be affected. Similarly, the growing use of peritoneal dialysis threatens the need for dialysis technicians. In this process the membrane used is the peritoneum (the lining of the abdomen), and the dialysis process takes place within, rather than outside, the patient's body. An increase in the number of kidney transplants could also slow the future demand for dialysis technicians. However, the number of people waiting for transplants is far greater than the number of organs available. Until researchers discover a cure for kidney disease, dialysis technicians will be needed to administer treatment.

FOR MORE INFORMATION

For information on job opportunities, awards, legislative news, and nephrology nursing, contact or visit the following Web site:

American Nephrology Nurses' Association
East Holly Avenue, Box 56
Pitman, NJ 08071-0056

Tel: 856-256-2320
Email: anna@ajj.com
http://www.annanurse.org

For more information about certification, contact
Board of Nephrology Examiners Nursing and Technology
1901 Pennsylvania Avenue, NW, Suite 607
Washington, DC 20006-3405
Tel: 202-462-1252
http://www.bonent.org

Contact the following association for information on scholarships, certification, and the career:
National Association of Nephrology Technicians/
Technologists
PO Box 2307
Dayton, OH 45401-2307
Tel: 877-607-6268
Email: nant@meinet.com
http://www.nant.biz

For information on certification, contact
Nephrology Nursing Certification Commission
East Holly Avenue, Box 56
Pitman, NJ 08071-0056
Tel: 888-884-6622
Email: nncc@ajj.com
http://www.nncc-exam.org/ccht/index.html

The NKF is a voluntary health organization involved with educating the public about kidney and urinary tract diseases as well as organ transplantation. For news relating to these issues, fact sheets, and The Electronic Kidney, *an online newsletter, check out the following Web site:*
National Kidney Foundation (NKF)
30 East 33rd Street
New York, NY 10016-5337
Tel: 800-622-9010
http://www.kidney.org

DIESEL MECHANICS

OVERVIEW

Diesel mechanics repair and maintain diesel engines that power trucks, buses, ships, construction and road building equipment, farm equipment, and some automobiles. They may also maintain and repair non-engine compo-

nents, such as brakes, electrical systems, and heating and air conditioning. Approximately 275,000 diesel mechanics work in the United States.

THE JOB

Most diesel mechanics work on the engines of heavy trucks, such as those used in hauling freight over long distances, or in heavy industries such as construction and mining. Many are employed by companies that maintain their own fleet of vehicles. The diesel mechanic's main task is preventive maintenance to avoid breakdowns, but they also make engine repairs when necessary. Diesel mechanics also frequently perform maintenance on other non-engine components, such as brake systems, electronics, transmissions, and suspensions.

Through periodic maintenance, diesel mechanics keep vehicles or engines in good operating condition. They run through a checklist of standard maintenance tasks, such as changing oil and filters, checking cooling systems, and inspecting brakes and wheel bearings for wear. They make the appropriate repairs or adjustments and replace parts that are worn. Fuel injection units, fuel pumps, pistons, crankshafts, bushings, and bearings must be regularly removed, reconditioned, or replaced.

As more diesel engines rely on a variety of electronic components, mechanics have become more proficient in the basics of electronics. Previously technical functions in diesel equipment (both engine and non-engine parts) are being replaced by electronics, significantly altering the way mechanics perform maintenance and repairs. As new technology evolves, diesel mechanics may need additional training to use tools and computers to diagnose and correct problems with electronic parts. Employers generally provide this training.

Diesel engines are scheduled for periodic rebuilding, usually every 18 months or 100,000 miles. Mechanics rely upon extensive records they keep on each engine to determine the extent of the rebuild. Records detail the maintenance and repair history that helps mechanics determine repair needs and prevent future breakdowns. Diesel mechanics use various specialty instruments to make precision measurements and diagnostics of each engine component. Micrometers and various gauges test for engine wear. Ohmmeters, ammeters, and voltmeters test electrical components. Dynamometers and oscilloscopes test overall engine operations.

Engine rebuilds usually require several mechanics, each specializing in a particular area. They use ordinary hand tools such as ratchets and sockets, screwdrivers, wrenches, and pliers; power tools such as pneumatic wrenches; welding and flame-cutting equipment; and machine tools like lathes and boring machines. Diesel mechanics typically supply their own hand tools at an investment of $6,000 to $25,000, depending upon their specialty. It is the employer's responsibility to furnish the larger power tools, engine analyzers, and other diagnostic equipment.

In addition to trucks and buses, diesel mechanics also service and repair construction equipment such as cranes, bulldozers, earth moving equipment, and road construction equipment. The variations in transmissions, gear systems, electronics, and other engine components of diesel engines may require additional training.

To maintain and increase their skills and to keep up with new technology, diesel mechanics must regularly read service and repair manuals, industry bulletins, and other publications. They must also be willing to take part in training programs given by manufacturers or at vocational schools. Those who have certification must periodically retake exams to keep their credentials. Frequent changes in technology demand that mechanics keep up to date with the latest training.

REQUIREMENTS

High School

A high school diploma is the minimum requirement to land a job that offers growth possibilities, a good salary, and challenges. In addition to automotive and shop classes, high school students should take mathematics, English, and computer classes. Adjustments and repairs to many car components require the mechanic to make numerous computations, for which good mathematical skills will be essential. Diesel mechanics must be voracious readers in order to stay competitive; there are many must-read volumes of repair manuals and trade journals. Computer skills are also important, as computers are common in most repair shops.

Postsecondary Training

Employers prefer to hire those who have completed some kind of formal training program in diesel mechanics, or in some cases automobile mechanics—usually a minimum of two years of education in either case. A wide variety of such programs are offered at community colleges, vocational schools, independent organizations, and manufacturers. Most accredited programs include periods of internship.

Some programs are conducted in association with truck and heavy equipment manufacturers. Students combine work experience with hands-on classroom study of up-to-date equipment provided by manufacturers. In other programs students alternate time in the classroom with internships at manufacturers. Although

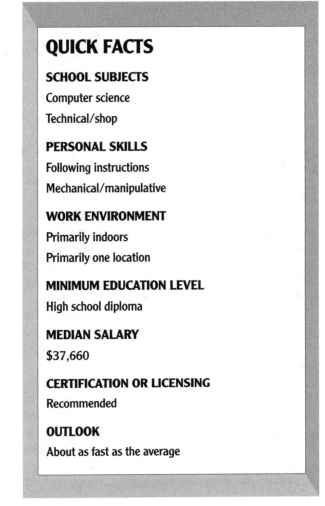

QUICK FACTS

SCHOOL SUBJECTS
Computer science
Technical/shop

PERSONAL SKILLS
Following instructions
Mechanical/manipulative

WORK ENVIRONMENT
Primarily indoors
Primarily one location

MINIMUM EDUCATION LEVEL
High school diploma

MEDIAN SALARY
$37,660

CERTIFICATION OR LICENSING
Recommended

OUTLOOK
About as fast as the average

these students may take up to four years to finish their training, they become familiar with the latest technology and also earn modest salaries as they train.

Certification or Licensing

One indicator of quality for entry-level mechanics recognized by everyone in the industry is certification by the National Institute for Automotive Service Excellence. There are eight areas of certification available in heavy-duty truck repair: gasoline engines; diesel engines; drive train; brakes; suspension and steering; electrical/electronic systems; heating, ventilation, and air conditioning; and preventive maintenance inspection. There are seven areas of certification available in school bus repair: body systems and special equipment, diesel engines, drive train, brakes, suspension and steering, electrical/electronic systems, and air-conditioning systems and controls. Applicants must have at least two years of experience in the field and pass the examinations related to their specialty. To maintain their certification, mechanics must retake the examination for their specialties every five years. The Association of Diesel Specialists also offers voluntary certification to diesel mechanics.

Other Requirements

Diesel mechanics must be patient and thorough in their work. They need to have excellent troubleshooting skills and must be able to logically deduce the cause of system malfunctions. Diesel mechanics also need a Class A driver's license.

EXPLORING

Many community centers offer general auto maintenance workshops where students can get additional practice working on real cars and learn from instructors. Trade magazines such as *Land Line* (http://www.landlinemag.com) and *Overdrive* (http://www.overdriveonline.com) are an excellent source for learning what's new in the trucking industry and can be found at libraries and some larger bookstores. Working part time at a repair shop or dealership can prepare students for the atmosphere and challenges a mechanic faces on the job.

Many diesel mechanics begin their exploration on gasoline engines because spare diesel engines are hard to come by for those who are just trying to learn and experiment. Diesel engines are very similar to gasoline engines except for their ignition systems and size. Besides being larger, diesel engines are distinguished by the absence of common gasoline engine components such as spark plugs, ignition wires, coils, and distributors. Diesel mechanics use the same hand tools as automobile mechanics, however, and in this way learning technical aptitude on automobiles will be important for the student who wishes to eventually learn to work on diesel engines.

EMPLOYERS

Diesel mechanics may find employment in a number of different areas. Many work for dealers that sell semi-trucks and other diesel-powered equipment. About 17 percent of the country's 275,000 diesel mechanics work for local and long distance trucking companies. Others maintain the buses and trucks of public transit companies, schools, or governments or service buses, trucks, and other diesel-powered equipment at automotive repair and maintenance shops, motor vehicle and parts wholesalers, or automotive equipment rental and leasing agencies. Diesel mechanics can find work all over the country, in both large and small cities. Job titles may range from bus maintenance technician to hydraulic system technician, clutch rebuilder, and heavy-duty maintenance mechanic. A small number of diesel mechanics

may find jobs in the railway and industrial sectors and in marine maintenance.

STARTING OUT

The best way to begin a career as a diesel mechanic is to enroll in a postsecondary training program and obtain accreditation. Trade and technical schools nearly always provide job placement assistance for their graduates. Such schools usually have contacts with local employers who need to hire well-trained people. Often, employers post job openings at accredited trade schools in their area.

Although postsecondary training programs are more widely available and popular today, some mechanics still learn the trade on the job as apprentices. Their training consists of working for several years under the guidance of experienced mechanics. Trainees usually begin as helpers, lubrication workers, or service station attendants, and gradually acquire the skills and knowledge necessary for many service or repair tasks. However, fewer employers today are willing to hire apprentices because of the time and cost it takes to train them. Those who do learn their skills on the job inevitably require some formal training if they wish to advance and stay in step with the changing industry.

Intern programs sponsored by truck manufacturers or independent organizations provide students with opportunities to actually work with prospective employers. Internships can provide students with valuable contacts who will be able to recommend future employers once students have completed their classroom training. Many students may even be hired by the company for which they interned.

ADVANCEMENT

Typically, the first step a mechanic must take to advance is to receive certification. Although certification is voluntary, it is a widely recognized standard of achievement for diesel mechanics and the way many advance. The more certification a mechanic has, the more his or her worth to an employer, and the higher he or she advances.

With today's complex diesel engine and truck components requiring hundreds of hours of study and practice to master, more employers prefer to hire certified mechanics. Certification assures the employer that the employee is skilled in the latest repair procedures and is familiar with the most current diesel technology. Those with good communication and planning skills may advance to shop supervisor or service manager at larger repair shops or companies that keep large fleets. Others with good business skills go into business for themselves and open their own shops or work as freelance mechanics. Some master mechanics may teach at technical and vocational schools or at community colleges.

EARNINGS

Diesel mechanics' earnings vary depending upon their region, industry (trucking, construction, railroad), and other factors. Technicians in the West and East tend to earn more than those in other regions, although these distinctions are gradually disappearing.

According to the U.S. Department of Labor, the median hourly pay for all diesel mechanics in 2006 was $18.11, or approximately $37,660 annually, for full-time employment. The department also reported that the lowest paid 10 percent of diesel mechanics earned approximately $11.71 an hour, or $24,370 a year. The highest paid 10 percent earned more than $26.50 an hour, amounting to $55,120 a year. Mechanics who work for companies that must operate around the clock, such as bus lines, may work at night, on weekends, or on holidays and receive extra pay for this work. Some industries are subject to seasonal variations in employment levels, such as construction.

The highest paid diesel mechanics work in motor vehicle manufacturing, and received a mean wage of $26.87 an hour, or $55,890 a year in 2006, according to the U.S. Department of Labor. Those who worked for motor vehicle and parts wholesalers earned a median wage of $18.41 an hour, or $38,290 a year. Those who worked for general freight trucking companies earned a median hourly wage of $17.19, or $35,760 a year, and those who specialized in automotive repair and maintenance earned an average of $17.79 an hour, or $37,000 a year.

Mechanics working for construction companies during peak summer building seasons earn up to $1,000 a week.

Many diesel mechanics are members of labor unions, and their wage rates are established by contracts between the union and the employer. Benefits packages vary from business to business. Mechanics can expect health insurance and paid vacation from most employers. Other benefits may include dental and eye care, life and disability insurance, and a pension plan. Employers usually cover a mechanic's work clothes through a clothing allowance and may pay a percentage of hand-tools purchases. An increasing number of employers pay all or most of an employee's certification training if he or she passes the test. A mechanic's salary can increase by yearly bonuses or profit sharing if the business does well.

WORK ENVIRONMENT

Depending on the size of the shop and whether it is a trucking or construction company, government, or private business, diesel mechanics work with anywhere from two to 20 other mechanics. Most shops are well lighted and well ventilated. They can frequently be noisy due to running trucks and equipment. Hoses are attached to exhaust pipes and led outside to avoid carbon monoxide poisoning.

Minor hand and back injuries are the most common problem for diesel mechanics. When reaching in hard-to-get-at places or loosening tight bolts, mechanics often bruise, cut, or burn their hands. With caution and experience most mechanics learn to avoid hand injuries. Working for long periods of time in cramped or bent positions often results in a stiff back or neck. Diesel mechanics also lift many heavy objects that can cause injury if not handled cautiously; however, most shops have small cranes or hoists to lift the heaviest objects. Some may experience allergic reactions to the variety of solvents and oils frequently used in cleaning, maintenance, and repair. Shops must comply with strict safety procedures to help employees avoid accidents. Most mechanics work between 40- and 50-hour workweeks, but may be required to work longer hours when the shop is busy or during emergencies. Some mechanics make emergency repairs to stranded, roadside trucks or to construction equipment.

OUTLOOK

With diesel technology getting better (smaller, smarter, and less noisy), more light trucks and other vehicles and equipment are switching to diesel engines. Diesel engines are already more fuel efficient than gasoline engines. Also, the increased reliance by businesses on quick deliveries has increased the demand on trucking companies. Many businesses maintain lower inventories of materials, instead preferring to have items shipped more frequently. The increase in diesel-powered vehicles, together with a trend toward increased cargo transportation via trucks, will create jobs for highly skilled diesel mechanics. Less skilled workers will face tough competition. The U.S. Department of Labor predicts employment growth to be about as fast as the average for all occupations through 2016.

Diesel mechanics enjoy good job security. Fluctuations in the economy have little effect on employment in this field. When the economy is bad, people service and repair their trucks and equipment rather than replace them. Conversely, when the economy is good more people are apt to service their trucks and equipment regularly as well as buy new trucks and equipment.

The most jobs for diesel mechanics will open up at trucking companies that hire mechanics to maintain and repair their fleets. Construction companies are also expected to require an increase in diesel mechanics to maintain their heavy machinery, such as cranes, earth-movers, and other diesel powered equipment.

FOR MORE INFORMATION

For information on certification, contact

Association of Diesel Specialists
10 Laboratory Drive, PO Box 13966
Research Triangle Park, NC 27709-3966
Tel: 919-406-8804
Email: info@diesel.org
http://www.diesel.org

For information on the automotive service industry and continuing education programs, contact

Automotive Aftermarket Industry Association
7101 Wisconsin Avenue, Suite 1300
Bethesda, MD 20814-3415
Tel: 301-654-6664
Email: aaia@aftermarket.org
http://www.aftermarket.org

For information on training, accreditation, and testing, contact

I-CAR
5125 Trillium Boulevard
Hoffman Estates, IL 60192-3600
Tel: 800-422-7872
http://www.i-car.com

For career information and information on certified programs, contact

National Automotive Technicians Education Foundation
101 Blue Seal Drive, Suite 101
Leesburg, VA 20175-5646
Tel: 703-669-6650
http://www.natef.org

For information on becoming a certified mechanic, contact

National Institute for Automotive Service Excellence
101 Blue Seal Drive, Suite 101
Leesburg, VA 20175-5646
Tel: 888-273-8378
http://www.asecert.org

☐ DISPENSING OPTICIANS

OVERVIEW

Dispensing opticians measure and fit clients with prescription eyeglasses, contact lenses, other low-vision aids, and sometimes artificial eyes. They help clients select appropriate frames and order all necessary ophthalmic laboratory work. Approximately 66,000 dispensing opticians work in the United States.

THE JOB

Dispensing opticians must be familiar with methods, materials, and operations employed in the optical industry. Their tasks include ensuring that eyeglasses are made according to the optometrist's prescription, determining exactly where the lenses should be placed in relation to the pupils of the eyes, assisting the customer in selecting appropriate frames, preparing work orders for the optical laboratory technician, and sometimes selling optical goods.

Opticians should be good at dealing with people and with handling administrative tasks. They work with the customer to determine which type of frames are best suited to the person's needs. Considerations include the customer's habits, facial characteristics, comfort, and the thickness of the corrective lenses.

The dispensing optician prepares work orders for the ophthalmic laboratory so the technicians can grind the lenses and insert them into the frames. Opticians are responsible for recording lens prescriptions, lens size, and the style and color of the frames.

After the lenses return from the lab, the optician makes sure the glasses are made according to the prescription and that they fit the customer correctly. Opticians use small hand tools and precision instruments to make minor adjustments to the frames. Most dispensing opticians work with prescription eyeglasses, but some work with contact lenses. Opticians must exercise great precision, skill, and patience in fitting contact lenses. They measure the curvature of the cornea, and, following the prescription, prepare complete specifications for the optical technician who manufactures the lens. They must teach the customer how to remove, adjust to, and care for the lenses, a process that can take several weeks.

REQUIREMENTS

High School

A high school diploma is necessary to enter an apprenticeship or other training program in opticianry. If you are interested in this work, you should take courses such as algebra, geometry, biology, and physics while in high school. Mechanical drawing course work is also helpful. Also, be sure to take English classes to hone your written and oral communication skills.

Postsecondary Training

While a number of dispensing opticians learn their skills on the job, many learn their work by completing apprenticeship programs. In addition, the Commission on Opticianry Accreditation has accredited 21 two-year associate's degree programs that lead to work as a dispensing optician. Some employers prefer to hire those with associate's degrees, and this may be an increasing trend. Associate's degree holders are able to advance more rapidly than those who complete an apprenticeship program. Two-year optician programs are offered at community colleges and trade schools and include courses on mechanical optics, geometric optics, ophthalmic dispensing procedures, contact lens practice, business concepts, communications, mathematics, and laboratory work in grinding and polishing procedures.

Some dispensing opticians complete an apprenticeship program offered by optical dispensing companies. These apprenticeships include some of the same subjects as those covered in the two-year associate's degree program and may take two to four years to complete. Some specialized training programs may be offered by contact lens manufacturers and professional societies. These are generally shorter and usually cover a particular area of technical training, such as contact lens fitting.

Certification or Licensing

Currently 21 states require licensing of dispensing opticians. Licensing requires meeting certain educational standards and passing a written examination. Some states require a practical, hands-on examination. To find out more about licensing procedures, contact the licensing board of the state or states in which you plan to work.

Professional credentials may also include voluntary certification. Certification is offered by the American Board of Opticianry/National Contact Lens Examiners.

Some states may permit dispensing opticians to fit contact lenses without certification, provided they have additional training.

Other Requirements

Opticians need to have steady hands and good hand-eye coordination for the tiny, tedious tightening and adjustment jobs that need to be done to glasses. They need to be patient and meticulous when it comes to

QUICK FACTS

SCHOOL SUBJECTS
Biology
Mathematics

PERSONAL SKILLS
Helping/teaching
Technical/scientific

WORK ENVIRONMENT
Primarily indoors
Primarily one location

MINIMUM EDUCATION LEVEL
Apprenticeship

MEDIAN SALARY
$30,300

CERTIFICATION OR LICENSING
Required by certain states

OUTLOOK
About as fast as the average

measuring the cornea for contact lenses or making sure by checking their lens machine that someone's prescription is exactly right. A soothing and confident manner is beneficial for an optician. Opticians touch their customers, when checking the fit of frames, when checking their eyes, when adjusting the finished glasses, or inserting someone's contacts for them initially. A fine sense of touch is an attribute of a good dispensing optician.

Since dispensing opticians very often play a large role in a customer's frame selection, it is important that the optician has a good sense of color and feels comfortable advising the customer. Taking hair and skin color as well as face shape into account is what helps the optician to point out flattering and practical frames for the customer.

There are many qualities important to a dispensing optician, but perhaps the most important of all is good communication skills to be able to obtain the information needed to help customers through the eyewear process.

EXPLORING

Part-time or summer employment in an optical shop is an excellent way of gaining insight into the skills needed to excel in this field. A high school student can also explore opportunities in the field through discussions with professionals already working as dispensing opticians.

EMPLOYERS

There are approximately 66,000 dispensing opticians employed in the United States. About 33 percent work in health and personal care stores, including optical goods stores. Another 33 percent work for ophthalmologists or optometrists who sell glasses directly to patients. Many also work in retail shops or department store showrooms.

STARTING OUT

Since the usual ways of entering the field are either through completion of an apprenticeship program or two-year associate's degree, students can use the services of their school's career services office or they can apply directly to optical stores.

ADVANCEMENT

Skilled dispensing opticians can expect to advance to supervisory or managerial positions in a retail optical store or become sales representatives for manufacturers of eyeglasses or lenses. Some open their own stores. A few opticians, with additional college training, become optometrists.

EARNINGS

The U.S. Department of Labor reported that in 2006 the median annual income for dispensing opticians was $30,300. The lowest paid 10 percent, which typically included those beginning in the field, earned less than $19,290 a year. The highest paid 10 percent earned more than $47,630. Supervisors and those with managerial duties typically earn more than skilled workers, depending on their experience, skills, and responsibilities. Dispensing opticians who own their own stores can earn much more.

WORK ENVIRONMENT

An optician's work requires little physical exertion and is usually performed in a quiet, well-lighted environment. Customer contact is a big portion of the job. Some laboratory work may be required, especially if a dispensing optician works with a larger outfit that makes eyeglasses on the premises. The wearing of safety goggles and other precautions are necessary in a laboratory environment.

Dispensing opticians should expect to work 40 hours a week, although overtime is not unusual. They should be prepared to work evenings and weekends, especially if they work for a large retail establishment.

OUTLOOK

The U.S. Department of Labor predicts the demand for dispensing opticians to grow as fast as the average for all occupations through 2016. One reason for this steady growth is an increase in the number of people who need corrective lenses. Educational programs such as vision screening have made the public more aware of eye problems, therefore increasing the need for dispensing opticians. Insurance programs cover more optical needs, which means that more clients can afford optical care. The wide variety of fashionable frames also has increased demand for eyeglasses.

Employment opportunities should be especially good in larger urban areas because of the greater number of retail optical stores. Those with an associate's degree in opticianry should be most successful in their job search.

FOR MORE INFORMATION

For information on certification, contact

American Board of Opticianry/National Contact Lens Examiners
6506 Loisdale Road, Suite 209
Springfield, VA 22150-1815
Tel: 703-719-5800
Email: mail@abo-ncle.org
http://www.abo-ncle.org

For information on education and training programs, contact the following organizations:

Commission on Opticianry Accreditation
PO Box 4342
Chapel Hill, NC 27515-4342
Tel: 703-468-0566
Email: ellen@coaccreditation.com
http://www.coaccreditation.com

National Academy of Opticianry
8401 Corporate Drive, Suite 605
Landover, MD 20785-2289
Tel: 800-229-4828
Email: info@nao.org
http://www.nao.org

Opticians Association of America
441 Carlisle Drive
Herndon, VA 20170-4884
Tel: 800-443-8997
Email: oaa@oaa.org
http://www.oaa.org

DRYWALL INSTALLERS AND FINISHERS

OVERVIEW

Drywall installers and *drywall finishers* plan and carry out the installation of drywall panels on interior wall and ceiling surfaces of residential, commercial, and industrial buildings. There are approximately 240,000 drywall installers and finishers working in the United States.

THE JOB

Drywall panels are manufactured in standard sizes, such as 4 feet by 12 feet or 4 feet by 8 feet. With such large sizes, the panels are heavy and awkward to handle and often must be cut into pieces. The pieces must be fitted together and applied over the entire surface of walls, ceilings, soffits, shafts, and partitions, including any odd-shaped and small areas, such as those above or below windows.

Installers begin by measuring the wall or ceiling areas and marking the drywall panels with chalk lines and markers. Using a straightedge and utility knife, they score the board along the cutting lines and break off the excess. With a keyhole saw, they cut openings for electrical outlets, vents, air-conditioning units, and plumbing fixtures. Then they fit the pieces into place. They may fasten the pieces directly to the building's inside frame with adhesives before they secure the drywall permanently with screws or nails.

Often the drywall is attached to a metal framework or furring grid that the drywall installers put up for support. When such a framework is used, installers must first study blueprints to plan the work procedures and determine which materials, tools, and assistance they will require. They measure, mark, and cut metal runners and studs and bolt them together to make floor-to-ceiling frames. Furring is anchored in the ceiling to form rectangular spaces for ceiling drywall panels. Then the drywall is fitted into place and screwed to the framework.

Because of the weight of drywall, helpers often assist installers. Large ceiling panels may have to be raised with a special lift. After the drywall is in place, drywall installers may measure, cut, assemble, and install prefabricated metal pieces around windows and doors and in other vulnerable places to protect drywall edges. They may also fit and hang doors and install door hardware such as locks, as well as decorative trim around windows, doorways, and vents.

Drywall finishers, or *tapers*, seal and conceal the joints where drywall panels come together and prepare the walls for painting or papering. Either by hand or with an electric mixer, they prepare a quick-drying sealing material called joint compound, and then spread the paste into and over the joints with a special trowel or spatula. While the paste is still wet, the finishers press perforated paper tape over the joint and smooth it to imbed it in the joint compound and cover the joint line. On large commercial projects, this pasting-and-taping operation is accomplished in one step with an automatic applicator. When the sealer is dry, the finishers spread another two coats of cementing material over the tape and blend it into the wall to completely conceal the joint. Any cracks, holes, or imperfections in the walls or ceiling are also filled with joint compound, and nail and screw heads are covered. After a final sanding of the patched areas, the surfaces are ready to be painted or papered. Drywall finishers may apply textured surfaces to walls and ceilings with trowels, brushes, rollers, or spray guns.

REQUIREMENTS

High School

Most employers prefer applicants who have completed high school, although some hire workers who are not graduates. High school courses in carpentry provide a good background, and mathematics, such as basic math and algebra, are also important.

Postsecondary Training

Many drywall installers and finishers are trained on the job, beginning as helpers who aid experienced workers. Installer helpers carry materials, hold panels, and clean up. They learn how to measure, cut, and install panels. Finisher helpers tape joints and seal nail holes and scratches. In a short time, they learn to install corner guards and to conceal openings around pipes. After they have become skilled workers, both kinds of helpers complete their training by learning how to estimate the costs of installing and finishing drywall.

Other drywall workers learn the trade through apprenticeship programs, which combine classroom study with on-the-job training. A major union in this field, the United Brotherhood of Carpenters and Joiners of America, offers four-year apprenticeships in carpentry that include instruction in drywall installation. A similar four-year program for nonunion workers is conducted by local affiliates of the Associated Builders and Contractors and the National Association of Home Builders. The International Union of Painters and Allied Trades run a two-year apprenticeship for finishers.

Other Requirements

Since drywall installing and finishing is a construction job, employers prefer to hire candidates who are in good physical condition. You will need a certain amount of strength for this job as well as endurance. Also, good coordination is a must.

EXPLORING

It may be possible for students to visit a job site and observe installers and finishers at work. Part-time or summer employment as a helper to drywall workers, carpenters, or painters or even as a laborer on a construction job is a good way to get some practical experience in this field.

EMPLOYERS

Approximately 240,000 drywall installers and finishers are employed in the United States and roughly 56,000 are self-employed. Most drywall installers and finishers work primarily for drywall contractors associated with the construction industry. Typically installers and finishers find work in more heavily populated areas, such as cities, where there is enough work for full-time employment in their specialty.

STARTING OUT

If you want to work in this field, you can start out as an on-the-job trainee or as an apprentice. Those who plan to learn the trade as they work may apply directly to contracting companies for entry-level jobs as helpers. Good places to look for job openings include the offices of the state employment service, the classified ads section in local newspapers, and the local offices of the major unions in the field. Information about apprenticeship possibilities may be obtained from local contractors or local unions.

ADVANCEMENT

Opportunities for advancement are good for those who stay in the trade. Experienced workers who show leadership abilities and good judgment may be promoted to supervisors of work crews. Sometimes they become cost estimators for contractors. Other workers open their own drywall contracting business.

EARNINGS

The annual earnings of drywall workers vary widely. According to the U.S. Department of Labor, the median hourly wage of drywall installers was $17.38 hourly, or $36,140 annually for full-time employment in 2006. The lowest paid 10 percent earned less than $10.90 ($22,68 annually for full-time work), and the highest paid 10 percent earned more than $28.85 ($60,101 for full-time work). Those workers who have managerial duties or their own business may make even more. Apprentices generally receive about half the rate earned by journeymen workers.

Some drywallers are paid according to the hours they work; others are paid based on how much work they complete. For example a contractor might pay installers and finishers five to six cents for every square foot of panel installed. The average worker is capable of installing 35 to 40 panels a day, when each panel measures 4 feet by 12 feet.

Drywall workers usually work a standard workweek of 35 to 40 hours. Construction schedules sometimes require installers and finishers to work longer hours or during evenings or on weekends. Workers who are paid by the hour receive extra pay at these times.

WORK ENVIRONMENT

Drywall installation and finishing can be strenuous work. The large, heavy panels are difficult to handle and frequently require more than one person to maneuver them into position. Workers must spend long hours on their feet, often bending and kneeling. To work high up on walls or on ceilings, workers must stand on stilts, ladders, or scaffolding, risking falls. Another possible hazard is injury from power tools such as saws and nailers. Because sanding creates a lot of dust, finishers wear protective masks and safety glasses.

Drywall installation and finishing is indoor work that can be done in any season of the year. Unlike workers in some construction occupations, drywall workers seldom lose time because of adverse weather conditions.

OUTLOOK

The U.S. Department of Labor predicts that employment for drywall installers and finishers will grow about as fast as the average for all occupations through 2016. Overall increases in the construction industry and high turnover in this field means replacement workers are needed every year. In addition, drywall will continue to be used in many kinds of building construction, providing a demand for workers.

Jobs will be located throughout the country, although they will be more plentiful in metropolitan areas where contractors have enough business to hire full-time drywall workers. In small towns, carpenters often handle drywall installation, and painters may do finishing work. Like other construction trades workers, drywall installers and finishers may go through periods of unemployment or part-time employment when the local economy is in a downturn and construction activity slows.

FOR MORE INFORMATION

For information on the construction industry and educational opportunities, contact

Associated Builders and Contractors
4250 North Fairfax Drive, 9th Floor
Arlington, VA 22203-1607
Tel: 703-812-2000
Email: gotquestions@abc.org
http://www.abc.org

For career and training information for painters, drywall finishers, and others, contact

International Union of Painters and Allied Trades
1750 New York Avenue, NW
Washington, DC 20006-5301

Tel: 202-637-0700
Email: mail@iupat.org
http://www.iupat.org

For an example of an apprenticeship program, check out the following Web site:

Arizona Carpenters Apprenticeship
http://www.azcarpenters.org/apprenticeship.html

For information on union membership and apprenticeship programs, contact

United Brotherhood of Carpenters and Joiners of America
http://www.carpenters.org

ELECTRICIANS

OVERVIEW

Electricians design, assemble, install, test, and repair electrical fixtures and wiring. They work on a wide range of electrical and data communications systems that provide light, heat, refrigeration, air-conditioning, power, and the ability to communicate. There are approximately 705,000 electricians working in the United States.

THE JOB

Many electricians specialize in either construction or maintenance work, although some work in both fields. Electricians in construction are usually employed by electrical contractors. Other *construction electricians* work for building contractors or industrial plants, public utilities, state highway commissions, or other large organizations that employ workers directly to build or remodel their properties. A few are self-employed.

When installing electrical systems, electricians may follow blueprints and specifications or they may be told verbally what is needed. They may prepare sketches showing the intended location of wiring and equipment. Once the plan is clear, they measure, cut, assemble, and install plastic-covered wire or electrical conduit, which is a tube or channel through which heavier grades of electrical wire or cable are run. They strip insulation from wires, splice and solder wires together, and tape or cap the ends. They attach cables and wiring to the incoming electrical service and to various fixtures and machines that use electricity. They install switches,

QUICK FACTS

SCHOOL SUBJECTS
Mathematics
Technical/shop

PERSONAL SKILLS
Mechanical/manipulative
Technical/scientific

WORK ENVIRONMENT
Primarily indoors
Primarily multiple locations

MINIMUM EDUCATION LEVEL
Apprenticeship

MEDIAN SALARY
$43,610

CERTIFICATION OR LICENSING
Required by certain states

OUTLOOK
About as fast as the average

circuit breakers, relays, transformers, grounding leads, signal devices, and other electrical components. After the installation is complete, construction electricians test circuits for continuity and safety, adjusting the setup as needed.

Maintenance electricians do many of the same kinds of tasks, but their activities are usually aimed at preventing trouble before it occurs. They periodically inspect equipment and carry out routine service procedures, often according to a predetermined schedule. They repair or replace worn or defective parts and keep management informed about the reliability of the electrical systems. If any breakdowns occur, maintenance electricians return the equipment to full functioning as soon as possible so that the expense and inconvenience are minimal.

Maintenance electricians, also known as *electrical repairers*, may work in large factories, office buildings, small plants, or wherever existing electrical facilities and machinery need regular servicing to keep them in good

working order. Many maintenance electricians work in manufacturing industries, such as those that produce automobiles, aircraft, ships, steel, chemicals, and industrial machinery. Some are employed by hospitals, municipalities, housing complexes, or shopping centers to do maintenance, repair, and sometimes installation work. Some work for or operate businesses that contract to repair and update wiring in residences and commercial buildings.

A growing number of electricians are involved in activities other than constructing and maintaining electrical systems in buildings. Many are employed to install computer wiring and equipment, telephone wiring, or the coaxial and fiber optics cables used in telecommunications and computer equipment. Electricians also work in power plants, where electric power is generated; in machine shops, where electric motors are repaired and rebuilt; aboard ships, fixing communications and navigation systems; at locations that need large lighting and power installations, such as airports and mines; and in numerous other settings.

All electricians must work in conformity with the National Electrical Code as well as any current state and local building and electrical codes. (Electrical codes are standards that electrical systems must meet to ensure safe, reliable functioning.) In doing their work, electricians try to use materials efficiently, to plan for future access to the area for service and maintenance on the system, and to avoid hazardous and unsightly wiring arrangements, making their work as neat and orderly as possible.

Electricians use a variety of equipment ranging from simple hand tools such as screwdrivers, pliers, wrenches, and hacksaws to power tools such as drills, hydraulic benders for metal conduit, and electric soldering guns. They also use testing devices such as oscilloscopes, ammeters, and test lamps. Construction electricians often supply their own hand tools. Experienced workers may have hundreds of dollars invested in tools.

REQUIREMENTS
High School

If you are thinking of becoming an electrician, whether you intend to enter an apprenticeship or learn informally on the job, you should have a high school background that includes such courses as applied mathematics and science, shop classes that teach the use of various tools, and mechanical drawing. Electronics courses are especially important if you plan to become a maintenance electrician.

Postsecondary Training

Some electricians still learn their trade the same way electrical workers did many years ago—informally on the job while employed as helpers to skilled workers. Especially if that experience is supplemented with vocational or technical school courses, correspondence courses, or training received in the military, electrical helpers may in time become well-qualified crafts workers in some area of the field.

You should be aware, however, that most professionals believe that apprenticeship programs provide the best all-around training in this trade. Apprenticeships combine a series of planned, structured, supervised job experiences with classroom instruction in related subjects. Many programs are designed to give apprentices a variety of experiences by having them work for several electrical contractors doing different kinds of jobs. Typically, apprenticeships last four to five years and provide at least 144 hours of classroom instruction and 2,000 hours of on-the-job training each year. Completion of an apprenticeship is usually a significant advantage in getting the better jobs in the field.

Applicants for apprenticeships generally need to be high school graduates, at least 18 years of age, in good health, and with at least average physical strength. Although local requirements vary, many applicants are required to take tests to determine their aptitude for the work.

Most apprenticeship programs are developed and conducted by state and national contractor associations such as the Independent Electrical Contractors Inc. and the union locals of the International Brotherhood of Electrical Workers. Some programs are conducted as cooperative efforts between these groups and local community colleges and training organizations. In either situation, the apprenticeship program is usually managed by a training committee. An agreement regarding in-class and on-the-job training is usually established between the committee and each apprentice.

Certification or Licensing

Some states and municipalities require that electricians be licensed. To obtain a license, electricians usually must pass a written examination on electrical theory, National Electrical Code requirements, and local building and electrical codes. Electronics specialists receive certification training and testing through the International Society of Certified Electronic Technicians.

Other Requirements

You will need to have good color vision because electricians need to be able to distinguish color-coded wires. Agility and manual dexterity are also desirable characteristics, as are a sense of teamwork, an interest in working outdoors, and a love of working with your hands.

Electricians may or may not belong to a union. While many electricians belong to such organizations as the International Brotherhood of Electrical Workers; the International Union of Electronic, Electrical, Salaried, Machine, and Furniture Workers; Communications Workers of America; the International Association of Machinists and Aerospace Workers; and other unions, an increasing number of electricians are opting to affiliate with independent (nonunion) electrical contractors.

EXPLORING

Hobbies such as repairing radios, building electronics kits, or working with model electric trains will help you understand how electricians work. In addition to sampling related activities like these, you may benefit by arranging to talk with an electrician about his or her job. With the help of a teacher or guidance counselor, it may be possible to contact a local electrical contracting firm and locate someone willing to give an insider's description of the occupation.

EMPLOYERS

Approximately 705,000 electricians are employed in the United States. Electricians are employed in almost every industry imaginable, from construction to telecommunications to health care to transportation and more. Most work for contractors, but many work for institutional employers that require their own maintenance crews, or for government agencies. About 11 percent of electricians are self-employed.

STARTING OUT

People seeking to enter this field may either begin working as helpers or they may enter an apprenticeship program. Leads for helper jobs may be located by contacting electrical contractors directly or by checking with the local offices of the state employment service or in newspaper classified advertising sections. Students in trade and vocational programs may be able to find job openings through the placement office of their school.

If you are interested in an apprenticeship, you may start by contacting the union local of the International Brotherhood of Electrical Workers, the local chapter of Independent Electrical Contractors, or the local apprenticeship training committee. Information on apprenticeship possibilities also can be obtained through the state employment service.

ADVANCEMENT

The advancement possibilities for skilled, experienced electricians depend partly on their field of activity. Those who work in construction may become supervisors, job site superintendents, or estimators for electrical contractors. Some electricians are able to establish their own contracting businesses, although in many areas contractors must obtain a special license. Another possibility for some electricians is to move, for example, from construction to maintenance work, or into jobs in the shipbuilding, automobile, or aircraft industry.

Many electricians find that after they are working in the field, they still need to take courses to keep abreast of new developments. Unions and employers may sponsor classes introducing new methods and materials or explaining changes in electrical code requirements. By taking skill-improvement courses, electricians may also improve their chances for advancement to better-paying positions.

EARNINGS

Most established, full-time electricians working for contractors average earnings of about $21 per hour, or $43,680 per year for full-time work, according to the National Joint Apprenticeship Training Committee—and it is possible to make much more. According to the U.S. Department of Labor, median hourly earnings of electricians were $20.97 in 2006 ($43,610 annually). Wages ranged from less than $12.76 for the lowest paid 10 percent to more than $34.95 an hour for the highest paid 10 percent, or from $26,530 to $72,700 yearly for full-time work. Beginning apprentices earn 40 percent of the base electrician's wage and receive periodic increases each year of their apprenticeship.

Overall, it's important to realize these wages can vary widely, depending on a number of factors, including geographic location, the industry in which an electrician works, prevailing economic conditions, union membership, and others. Wage rates for many electricians are set by contract agreements between unions and employers. In general, electricians working in cities tend to be better paid than those in other areas. Those working as telecommunications or residential specialists tend to make slightly less than those working as linemen or wiremen.

Electricians who are members of the International Brotherhood of Electrical Workers, the industry's labor union, are entitled to benefits including paid vacation days and holidays, health insurance, pensions to help

with retirement savings, supplemental unemployment compensation plans, and so forth.

WORK ENVIRONMENT

Although electricians may work for the same contractor for many years, they work on different projects and at different work sites. In a single year, they may install wiring in a new housing project, rewire a factory, or install computer or telecommunications wiring in an office, for instance. Electricians usually work indoors, although some must do tasks outdoors or in buildings that are still under construction. The standard workweek is approximately 40 hours. In many jobs, overtime may be required. Maintenance electricians often have to work some weekend, holiday, or night hours because they must service equipment that operates all the time.

Electricians often spend long periods on their feet, sometimes on ladders or scaffolds or in awkward or uncomfortable places. The work can be strenuous. Electricians may have to put up with noise and dirt on the job. They may risk injuries such as falls off ladders, electrical shocks, and cuts and bruises. By following established safety practices, most of these hazards can be avoided.

OUTLOOK

Employment of electricians will grow about as fast as the average for all occupations through 2016, according to the U.S. Department of Labor. Growth will result from an overall increase in both residential and commercial construction. In addition, growth will be driven by the ever-expanding use of electrical and electronic devices and equipment. Electricians will be called on to upgrade old wiring and to install and maintain more extensive wiring systems than have been necessary in the past. In particular, the use of sophisticated computer, telecommunications, and data-processing equipment and automated manufacturing systems is expected to lead to job opportunities for electricians.

While the overall outlook for this occupational field is good, the availability of jobs will vary over time and from place to place. Construction activity fluctuates depending on the state of the local and national economy. Thus, during economic slowdowns, opportunities for construction electricians may not be plentiful. People working in this field need to be prepared for periods of unemployment between construction projects. Openings for apprentices also decline during economic downturns. Maintenance electricians are usually less vulnerable to periodic unemployment because they are more likely to work for one employer that needs electrical services on a steady basis. But if they work in an industry where the economy causes big fluctuations in the level of activity—such as automobile manufacturing, for instance—they may be laid off during recessions.

FOR MORE INFORMATION

For more information about the industry, contact

Independent Electrical Contractors
4401 Ford Avenue, Suite 1100
Alexandria, VA 22302-1432
Tel: 703-549-7351
Email: info@ieci.org
http://www.ieci.org

For information about the rules and benefits of joining a labor union, contact

International Brotherhood of Electrical Workers
900 Seventh Street, NW
Washington, DC 20001-3886
Tel: 202-833-7000
http://www.ibew.org

For information on certification, contact

International Society of Certified Electronic Technicians
3608 Pershing Avenue
Fort Worth, TX 76107-4527
Tel: 800-946-0201
Email: info@iscet.org
http://www.iscet.org

For industry information, contact

National Electrical Contractors Association
Three Bethesda Metro Center, Suite 1100
Bethesda, MD 20814-6302
Tel: 301-657-3110
http://www.necanet.org

For background information on apprenticeship and training programs aimed at union workers, contact

National Joint Apprenticeship and Training Committee
301 Prince George's Boulevard, Suite D
Upper Marlboro, MD 20774-7401
http://www.njatc.org

ELECTROLOGISTS

OVERVIEW

Electrologists are trained professionals who remove hair from the skin of patients. The electrologist uses a probe to shoot an electric wave into the papilla, or root, of the hair to kill the root and deter new hair growth. Since the

---

QUICK FACTS

SCHOOL SUBJECTS
Anatomy
Biology
Health

PERSONAL SKILLS
Helping/teaching
Mechanical/manipulative

WORK ENVIRONMENT
Primarily indoors
Primarily one location

MINIMUM EDUCATION LEVEL
Some postsecondary training

MEDIAN SALARY
$19,063

CERTIFICATION OR LICENSING
Voluntary (certification)
Required by certain states (licensing)

OUTLOOK
Faster than the average

---

root may not be destroyed on the first try, it is often necessary to treat the same area many times over a period of months or even years.

THE JOB

Electrologists, who usually conduct business in a professional office, salon, or medical clinic, work with only one patron at a time. This enables them to focus their complete attention and concentration on the delicate treatment they are performing. Since electrolysis can sometimes be uncomfortable, it reassures patrons to know that the practitioner's complete focus is on them and their needs. A high level of professionalism helps patients put their trust in the electrologist and may make them more receptive to the treatment.

Electrologists often begin their work with a personal consultation. It is essential for electrologists to interview potential clients to understand why they want to have the hair removed and what expectations they have about the procedure. The electrologist should explain the process in detail, discussing possible side effects as well as the effectiveness and duration of individual sessions and approximate length of time before the treatments are complete. A good electrologist also may suggest alternate methods of hair removal that may be more cost effective or appropriate for different clients and their needs.

Before beginning a session, the electrologist needs to make sure that the areas to be treated and all instruments used are sterile. A sanitary work environment is crucial for the safety of the electrologist as well as the person undergoing treatment. The electrologist may have an assistant or trainee help with these preparations. The first step in the treatment session is the cleansing of the area of skin that will be treated. Rubbing alcohol or an antiseptic is often used for this purpose. Once the skin is cleansed, hair removal can begin. Electrologists use a round-tipped probe to enter the opening of the skin fold, also known as the hair follicle. The probe also penetrates the papilla, which is the organ beneath the hair root. The electrologist sets the proper amount and duration of the electrical current in advance and presses gently on a floor pedal to distribute that current through the probe. The electrical current helps deaden the tissue, after which the hair can be lifted out gently with a pair of tweezers or forceps.

Electrologists determine the extent of treatments that will be necessary for complete removal of the unwanted hair. They may schedule weekly appointments that last 15, 30, 45, or even 60 minutes. The length of the individual appointments depends on both the amount of hair to be removed and the thickness and depth of the hair. Very coarse hair may take longer to treat, whereas fine hair may be permanently removed in only a few sessions. If a patient is very sensitive to the treatments, the electrologist may set up shorter appointments or schedule more time between sessions. Some electrologists use a gold needle on sensitive clients to minimize adverse reactions, which can include itching, bumps, redness, and pustules. Most of these reactions can be treated with topical ointments and proper skin care.

Electrologists can remove hair from almost any area of the body. The most common areas they treat are the arms, legs, chest, and portions of the face such as upper or lower lip, chin, or cheek. Electrologists should not remove hair from inside the ears or nose or from the eyelids. They should also have the written consent of a physician to remove hair from a mole or birthmark. As with many professions, electrologists should have legitimate malpractice insurance coverage.

As with all cosmetic treatments, the procedure can be fairly expensive. Since electrolysis is performed mainly for aesthetic reasons, it is generally not covered by any health insurance plans. Also, electrolysis is not a "quick fix." Constant maintenance is necessary for some clients, and people often have electrolysis treatments for years in certain areas before the hair root is finally destroyed.

REQUIREMENTS
High School

While you are in high school you should take classes in science, anatomy, physiology, and health if you are interested in pursuing a career as an electrologist. These classes will give you a good understanding of the human body and its functions. Learning about hair and how it grows, in addition to the theories and practices of electrology, can help a potential electrologist decide if this is the proper career path for him or her. In addition, you should consider taking classes in communications, psychology, and bookkeeping, accounting, or business management. These classes will give you skills for working well with people as well as help you if you decide to establish your own practice.

Postsecondary Training

Once you have gotten your high school diploma or equivalency certificate, you can enroll in a trade school or professional school that offers electrolysis training. The quality of these programs may vary, so you should look for programs that offer courses of study in such areas as microbiology, dermatology, neurology, and electricity. You will also learn about proper sterilization and sanitation procedures to avoid infections or injury to yourself or your clients. Classes that cover cell composition, the endocrine system, the vascular pulmonary system, and basic anatomy will also be beneficial to you.

Although the training offered is designed to educate students about the theory of electrolysis and its relation to the skin and tissue, the greater part of the training is of a practical nature. You will spend many training hours learning the purpose and function of the different types of equipment. In addition, hands-on experience with patrons needing different treatments will give you confidence in operating equipment and working with people.

Programs may be offered on a full- or part-time basis. Although tuition varies, some schools offer financial assistance or payment plans to make their programs more affordable. Sometimes lab and materials fees are charged.

Check if the school you are interested in is accredited or associated with any professional organizations. Also, consider what state you want to work in after graduation. Licensing requirements of the various states may affect the length and type of training that the schools offer.

Certification or Licensing

Certification, while voluntary, can indicate your commitment to the profession. A number of certification options are available. For example, the designation of certified professional electrologist (CPE) is offered by the American Electrology Association through the International Board of Electrologists Certification. The Society for Clinical and Medical Hair Removal offers three certification levels through its International Commission for Hair Removal Certification: certified clinical electrologist, certified medical electrologist certification, and certified laser hair removal professional.

Some states require electrologists to be licensed. Those with this requirement offer the licensing examinations through their state health departments. The examination usually covers various topics in the areas of health and cosmetology. Most states require applicants for electrology licensing to have a minimum number of study hours and practical training. They must also pass a written theory examination, a state exam, and a clinical examination. You should become familiar with your state's licensing requirements prior to beginning your training so you can be sure your education provides you with everything necessary to practice.

Other Requirements

Electrologists help people feel good about themselves by improving aspects of their physical appearance. People with excess body hair see the procedure as a way for them to have a "normal" life, in which they do not have to rely on temporary methods to remove hair or hide hairy areas. Electrologists feel a great sense of accomplishment through helping people with the various stages of their treatment and helping them to achieve their hair removal goals. They may sometimes feel the anxiety of a client who is impatient or unrealistic about the results or is nervous about the process. Because electrologists perform personal and sometimes uncomfortable treatments, it is important that they be patient and caring and develop an empathetic working style. A potential electrologist also should not be squeamish, since the procedure involves probes. Since the area to be treated is sometimes delicate, electrologists need to have good visual acuity and coordination to perform the procedures, although special accommodations may be made for practitioners with different abilities.

EXPLORING

To find out more about the field of electrology, try contacting local trade schools for information. Also, some two-year colleges that offer course work in medical technician careers may be able to supply you with literature on programs and training in electrology. If you are particularly interested in the field, make an appointment for an electrolysis consultation and perhaps pursue treatment for yourself.

Cosmetology schools, which are located in many different areas of the country, may also prove helpful for investigating this profession. Most schools and training programs allow interested students to speak with faculty and guidance counselors for further information. Ask if you can sit in on classes or contact a certified electrologist or patient of electrology to find out more about the field and procedures.

EMPLOYERS

Electrologists are employed by salons, professional offices, and medical clinics, or they may be self-employed. In some cases, experienced electrologists may hire newly licensed electrologists as assistants.

STARTING OUT

Many electrologists begin as assistants to a practicing professional. These assistants may handle extra patients when the office is overbooked or have new patients referred to them. In this way, beginning electrologists can build a clientele without having to cover the high costs of equipment, supplies, and office space. Often, trade schools have job placement offices that help new electrologists build a practice. Also, some schools may offer alumni mentor programs, through which the school introduces a new graduate to an established electrologist in order for mutual benefit. The new graduate can introduce new theories and practices to the professional and take care of overflow clients, while the established professional can help the new electrologist build a client base and start his or her own practice.

Some electrologists may choose to open their own business in a medical office complex and receive referrals from their neighboring health care professionals. Clinics or hospitals may also employ electrologists before they get their own office space. Beauty salons and health spas may have an electrologist on staff who can provide initial consultations with clients considering different methods of hair removal.

ADVANCEMENT

As an electrologist becomes more experienced and gains a reputation, he or she often attracts more new patrons and repeat clients. Some electrologists who work as part of a clinic staff may open their own office in a more visible or accessible location.

By obtaining additional training and education, electrologists can often branch out into other fields, including cosmetology and medicine. An electrologist trained in other methods may decide to offer clients additional hair removal procedures, such as waxing, sugaring, or laser hair removal. Electrologists can also become certified to teach the theory and practice of electrology in trade schools. Electrologists may also use their writing skills and practical experience to contribute to trade magazines, journals, and Web sites devoted to the field.

EARNINGS

Because electrologists schedule client treatments that vary in length, their fees are often based on quarter-hour appointments. Rates for a 15-minute treatment may begin at $15 in some cities, while charges in large urban regions may begin at $30. Treatments lasting 30 or 60 minutes in large cities may begin at $50 and $100, respectively. Although rates in smaller towns are often lower, electrologists there still earn a competitive wage for their work.

Salary.com reports that electrologists earned a national median salary of $19,063 in 2006, with the lowest 25 percent earning less than $15,480, and the highest 25 percent earning more than $23,204. The American Electrology Association reports that full-time, established electrologists can earn between $25,000 and $50,000 per year. Electrologists who are employed by a medical clinic or salon may have to contribute a portion of their fees to help cover office space, utilities, and support staff such as receptionists and bookkeepers.

Electrologists employed by a salon or group practice generally get the same benefits as other employees, which may include health, dental, and life insurance, as well as disability coverage, retirement savings plans, and paid vacations. Self-employed electrologists usually must provide these things for themselves.

WORK ENVIRONMENT

Whether the electrologist works in a professional office, a salon, a medical clinic, or a private shop, the nature of the work requires the environment to be clean, comfortable, and professional. Because electrologists perform delicate work, they may operate in spaces that are quiet to allow for greater concentration for the practitioner and to relax the client. Sometimes soothing music is played in the background to help put clients at ease.

A neat and professional appearance is important, so electrologists often wear uniforms or lab coats. As well as being comfortable and practical for the electrologist, a medical uniform may also reassure and comfort the client. Because of the threat of infectious diseases, electrologists may wear eye protection and disposable gloves during the procedure to reduce their risk of exposure. They also wash their hands frequently and maintain a sterile treatment area.

Electrologists generally spend most of their time in an office or treatment room, although not all that time is spent with clients. When not working on clients, electrologists may set up appointments, consult with prospective clients, train an assistant or future electrologist, or check equipment to ensure that it is functioning properly.

OUTLOOK

The U.S. Department of Labor predicts job employment for those in the cosmetology field, which includes electrologists, to increase faster than the average through 2016. Many salons, professional offices, and hospitals and clinics are striving to offer cutting-edge technologies and services to maintain—or gain—a competitive edge, which will create more jobs for electrologists. Further, the demand for electrologists is growing due to the increased awareness of and interest in this service. There are generally greater opportunities for electrologists in larger cities and highly populated areas.

Since electrology has been in practice for over a century, many clients are feeling more comfortable with the procedure. Also, with more disposable income, people who once considered permanent hair removal a luxury are beginning to consider electrolysis an affordable option.

FOR MORE INFORMATION

For information regarding the International Board of Electrologists Certification, careers, and for a directory of accredited schools and specific state requirements relating to electrology, contact

American Electrology Association
Council on Education
3629 Mormon Coulee Road, #D
La Crosse, WI 54601-7369
Tel: 608-788-7274
Email: infoea@electrology.com
http://www.electrology.com

For career, certification, and continuing education information, contact

Society for Clinical and Medical Hair Removal
2810 Crossroads Drive, Suite 3800
Madison, WI 53718-7961
Tel: 608-443-2470
Email: homeoffice@scmhr.org
http://www.scmhr.org

ELECTRO-NEURODIAGNOSTIC TECHNOLOGISTS

OVERVIEW

Electroneurodiagnostic technologists, sometimes called *EEG technologists* or *END technologists*, operate electronic instruments called electroencephalographs. These instruments measure and record the brain's electrical activity. The information gathered is used by physicians (usually neurologists) to diagnose and determine the effects of certain diseases and injuries, including brain tumors, cerebral vascular strokes, Alzheimer's disease, epilepsy, some metabolic disorders, and brain injuries caused by accidents or infectious diseases.

THE JOB

The basic principle behind electroencephalography (EEG) is that electrical impulses emitted by the brain, often called brain waves, vary according to the brain's age, activity, and condition. Research has established that certain brain conditions correspond to certain brain waves. Therefore, testing brain waves can aid the neurologist (a physician specially trained in the study of the brain) in making a diagnosis of a person's illness or injury.

The EEG technologist's first task with a new patient is to take a simplified medical history. This entails asking questions and recording answers about his or her past health status and present illness. These answers provide the technologist with necessary information about the patient's condition. They also provide an opportunity to help the patient relax before the test.

The technologist then applies electrodes to the patient's head. Often, technologists must choose the best combination of instrument controls and placement of electrodes to produce the kind of tracing that has been requested. In some cases, a physician will give special

QUICK FACTS

SCHOOL SUBJECTS
Biology
Mathematics
Physics

PERSONAL SKILLS
Mechanical/manipulative
Technical/scientific

WORK ENVIRONMENT
Primarily indoors
Primarily one location

MINIMUM EDUCATION LEVEL
Some postsecondary training

MEDIAN SALARY
$44,662

CERTIFICATION OR LICENSING
Recommended

OUTLOOK
About as fast as the average

instructions to the technologist regarding the placement of electrodes.

Once in place, the electrodes are connected to the recording equipment. Here, a bank of sensitive electronic amplifiers transmits information to writing instruments. Tracings from each electrode are made on a moving strip of paper or recorded on optical disks in response to the amplified impulses coming from the brain. The resulting graph is a recording of the patient's brain waves.

EEG technologists are not responsible for interpreting the tracings (that is the job of the neurologist); however, they must be able to recognize abnormal brain activity and any readings on the tracing that are coming from somewhere other than the brain, such as readings of eye movement or nearby electrical equipment.

Technologists can make recording changes to better present the abnormal findings for physician interpretation. Stray readings are known as artifacts. Technologists must be able to determine what kinds of artifacts should be expected for an individual patient on the basis of his or her medical history or present illness. They should also be sensitive to these artifacts and be able to identify them if they occur.

Technologists must be able to detect faulty recordings made by human error or by machine malfunctions. When mechanical problems occur, technologists should notify their supervisors so that trained equipment technicians can repair the machine.

Throughout the procedure, electroneurodiagnostic technologists observe the patient's behavior and make detailed notes about any aspect of the behavior that might be of use to the physician in interpreting the tracing. They also keep watch on the patient's brain, heart, and breathing functions for any signs that the patient is in any immediate danger.

During the testing, the patient may be either asleep or awake. In some cases, the physician may want recordings taken in both states. Sometimes drugs or special procedures are prescribed by the physician to simulate a specific kind of condition. Administering the drugs or procedures is often the technologist's responsibility.

EEG technologists need a basic understanding of any medical emergencies that can occur during this procedure. By being prepared, they can react properly if one of these emergencies should arise. For instance, if a patient suffers an epileptic seizure, technologists must know what to do. They must be flexible and able to handle medical crises during procedures.

EEGs are increasingly used on a routine basis in the operating room to monitor patients during major surgery. EEG technologists may also handle other specialized electroencephalograms. For example, in a procedure called ambulatory monitoring, heart and brain activity is tracked over a 24-hour period by a small recording device on the patient's side. In evoked potential testing, a special machine is used to measure the brain's electrical activity in response to specific types of stimuli. In nerve conduction studies, technologists stimulate peripheral nerves with an electrical current and record how long it takes the nerve impulse to reach the muscle. The polysomnogram is a procedure that uses EEG and other physiologic monitors to evaluate sleep and sleep disorders.

Besides conducting various kinds of electroencephalograms, EEG technologists also maintain the machine, perform minor repairs (major repairs require trained equipment technicians), schedule appointments, and order supplies. In some cases, they may have some supervisory responsibilities; however, most supervision is done by registered electroencephalographic technologists.

REQUIREMENTS

High School

You must have a high school diploma for entry into any kind of EEG technologist training program, whether in school or on the job. In general, you will find it helpful to have three years of mathematics (including algebra) and three years of science (including biology, chemistry, and physics). In addition, you should take courses in English, especially those that help improve communication skills, and in social sciences so that you can better understand the social and psychological needs of your patients.

Postsecondary Training

There are two main types of postsecondary training available for EEG technologists: on-the-job training and formal classroom training. Many technologists once received on-the-job training; however, EEG equipment is becoming so sophisticated that many employers prefer to hire EEG technologists with prior formal training.

On-the-job training generally lasts from a few months to one year, depending on the employer's special requirements. Trainees learn how to handle the equipment and carry out procedures by observing and receiving instruction from senior electroencephalographic technologists.

Formal training consists of both practice in the clinical laboratory and instruction in the classroom. The classroom instruction usually focuses on basic subjects such as human anatomy, clinical and internal medicine, psychology, electronics, and instrumentation. The curriculum also includes EEG, evoked potentials, electrode placement and application methods, neurophysiology, neuroanatomy, clinical neurology, neuropsychiatry, and at least an introduction to nerve conduction, polysomnography, and intraoperative neuromonitoring.

The postsecondary programs usually last from one to two years, offering either a certificate or associate's degree upon completion. Hospitals, medical centers, and community or technical colleges offer courses. Currently, there are 18 schools with accredited programs, most of which last two years. The American Society of Electroneurodiagnostic Technologists recommends that students attend schools that are accredited by the Commission on Accreditation of Allied Health Education Programs that offer at least an associate's degree in END technology.

Students who have completed one year of on-the-job training or who have graduated from a formal training program may apply for registration.

Certification or Licensing

The American Board of Registration of Electroencephalographic and Evoked Potential Technologists offers certification as a registered electroencephalographic technologist. Other organizations that offer certification/registration include the American Association of Electrodiagnostic Technologists and the Board of Registered Polysomnographic Technologists. Although registration is not required for employment, it is an acknowledgment of the technologist's training and does make advancement easier. Registration may also provide an increase in salary.

Other Requirements

EEG technologists need good vision and manual dexterity, an aptitude for working with mechanical and electronic equipment, and the ability to get along well with patients, their families, and members of the hospital staff. To be a successful EEG technologist, you must be good with people, quickly recognize what others may be feeling, and personalize treatment to the individual patient's needs. You need to be able to realize that some patients will be very ill, even in the process of dying.

EXPLORING

Prospective EEG technologists will find it difficult to gain any direct experience on a part-time basis in electroencephalography. Your first direct experience with the work will generally come during on-the-job training sessions or in the practical experience portion of your formal training. You may, however, be able to gain some general exposure to patient-care activities by signing up for volunteer work at a local hospital. In addition, you can arrange to visit a hospital, clinic, or doctor's office where electroencephalograms are administered. In this way, you may be able to watch technologists at work or talk to them about what the work is like.

EMPLOYERS

Electroneurodiagnostic technologists typically find work in hospitals, medical centers, clinics, and government agencies that perform EEGs.

STARTING OUT

Technologists often obtain permanent employment in the hospital where they received their on-the-job or work-study training. You can also find employment through classified ads in newspapers and by contacting the personnel offices of hospitals, medical centers, clinics, and government agencies that employ EEG technologists.

ADVANCEMENT

Opportunities for advancement are good for registered EEG technologists. Those without registration will find opportunities for advancement severely limited.

Usually, registered electroneurodiagnostic technologists are assigned to conduct more difficult or specialized electroencephalograms. They also supervise other electroencephalographic technologists, arrange work schedules, and teach techniques to new trainees. They may also establish procedures, manage a laboratory, keep records, schedule appointments, and order supplies.

EEG technologists may advance to *chief electroencephalographic technologists* and thus take on even more responsibilities in laboratory management and in teaching new personnel and students. Chief electroencephalographic technologists generally work under the direction of an electroencephalographer, neurologist, or neurosurgeon.

EARNINGS

According to Salary.com, EEG technologists earned a median salary of $44,662 in 2008. The lowest paid 10 percent earned less than $23,332 and highest paid 10 percent earned more than $65,993. The American Society of Electroneurodiagnostic Technologists reports that earnings depend on education, experience, level of responsibility, type of employment, and geographical region. Salaries for registered EEG technologists tended to be higher than nonregistered technologists with equivalent experience.

The highest salaries for EEG technologists tend to go to those who work as laboratory supervisors, teachers in training programs, and program directors in schools of electroencephalographic technology.

Technologists working in hospitals receive the same fringe benefits as other hospital workers, usually including health insurance, paid vacations, and sick leave. In some cases, the benefits may also include educational assistance, pension plans, and uniform allowances.

WORK ENVIRONMENT

EEG technologists usually work five-day, 40-hour workweeks, with only occasional overtime required. Some hospitals require them to be on call for emergencies during weekends, evenings, and holidays. Technologists doing sleep studies may work most of their hours at night.

EEG technologists often work with people who are ill and may be frightened or emotionally disturbed. As a result, work can be unpredictable and challenging.

Most EEG technologists are employed by hospitals, where the work can vary greatly. In emergency situations, the work is often stressful and hectic as they work closely with other staff members. At other times, conditions are calmer. The EEG technologist often works independently with a patient, spending much time in a darkened room during the tests.

OUTLOOK

Employment opportunities for electroneurodiagnostic technologists are expected to be good, according to the American Society of Electroneurodiagnostic Technologists. According to the association, opportunities will be best in polysomnography and the practice specialties of epilepsy and intraoperative monitoring. Population growth and an increase in the use of electroencephalographs in surgery, diagnosis, monitoring, and research will also create new opportunities in the field. New procedures and technologies that require fewer workers to do the same amount of work and hospitals' use of cross-trained employees to cover many jobs may diminish the need for specially trained technologists.

FOR MORE INFORMATION

For information and an application to start the EEG or Evoked Potential examination process, contact
American Board of Registration of Electroencephalographic and Evoked Potential Technologists
1904 Croydon Drive
Springfield, IL 62703-5223
Tel: 217-553-3758
http://www.abret.org

For a career brochure and information about registration, scholarships, and educational opportunities, contact
American Society of Electroneurodiagnostic Technologists
6501 East Commerce Avenue, Suite 120
Kansas City, MO 64120-2176
Tel: 816-931-1120
Email: info@aset.org
http://www.aset.org

For information on registration, polysomnograms, and sleep disorders, contact
American Association of Sleep Technologists
One Westbrook Corporate Center, Suite 920
Westchester, IL 60154-5767
Tel: 708-492-0796
Email: aast@aastweb.org
http://www.aastweb.org

For information on accredited training programs, contact
Commission on Accreditation of Allied Health Education Programs
1361 Park Street
Clearwater, FL 33756-6039
Tel: 727-210-2350
Email: mail@caahep.org
http://www.caahep.org

ELECTRONICS ENGINEERING TECHNICIANS

OVERVIEW

Electronics engineering technicians work with electronics engineers to design, develop, and manufacture industrial and consumer electronic equipment, including sonar, radar, and navigational equipment, as well as computers, radios, televisions, digital video disc players, stereos, and calculators. They are involved in fabricating, operating, testing, troubleshooting, repairing, and maintaining equipment. Those involved in the development of new electronic equipment help to make changes or modifications in circuitry or other design elements.

Other electronics technicians inspect newly installed equipment or instruct and supervise lower-grade technicians' installation, assembly, or repair activities.

As part of their normal duties, all electronics engineering technicians set up testing equipment, conduct tests, and analyze the results; they also prepare reports, sketches, graphs, and schematic drawings to describe electronics systems and their characteristics. Electronics engineering technicians use a variety of hand and machine tools, including such equipment as bench lathes and drills.

Depending on their specialization, electronics technicians may be *computer laboratory technicians, development instrumentation technicians, electronic communications technicians, nuclear reactor electronics technicians, engineering development technicians,* or *systems testing laboratory technicians.* There are approximately 170,000 electrical and electronics engineering technicians employed in the United States.

THE JOB

Most electronics technicians work in one of three broad areas of electronics: product development, manufacturing and production, or service and maintenance. Technicians involved with service and maintenance are known as *electronics service technicians*.

In the product development area, electronics technicians, or *electronics development technicians*, work directly with engineers or as part of a research team. Engineers draw up blueprints for a new product, and technicians build a prototype according to specifications. Using hand tools and small machine tools, they construct complex parts, components, and subassemblies.

After the prototype is completed, technicians work with engineers to test the product and make necessary modifications. They conduct physical and electrical tests to test the product's performance in various stressful conditions; for example, they test to see how a component will react in extreme heat and cold. Tests are run using complicated instruments and equipment, and detailed, accurate records are kept of the tests performed.

Electronics technicians in the product development field may make suggestions for improvements in the design of a device. They may also have to construct, install, modify, or repair laboratory test equipment.

Electronics drafting is a field of electronics technology closely related to product development. *Electronics drafters*, or *computer-aided design drafters*, convert rough sketches and written or verbal information provided by engineers and scientists into easily understandable schematic, layout, or wiring diagrams to be used in manufacturing the product. These drafters may also prepare a list of components and equipment needed for producing the final product, as well as bills for materials.

Another closely related field is cost estimating. *Cost-estimating technicians* review new product proposals in order to determine the approximate total cost to produce a product. They estimate the costs for all labor, equipment, and materials needed to manufacture the product. The sales department uses these figures to determine at what price a product can be sold and whether production is economically feasible.

In the manufacturing and production phase, the electronics technicians, who are also called *electronics manufacturing and production technicians*, work in a wide variety of capacities, generally with the day-to-day handling of production problems, schedules, and costs. These technicians deal with any problems arising from the production process. They install, maintain, and repair assembly- or test-line machinery. In quality control, they inspect and test products at various stages in the production process. When a problem is discovered, they are involved in determining the nature and extent of it and in suggesting remedies.

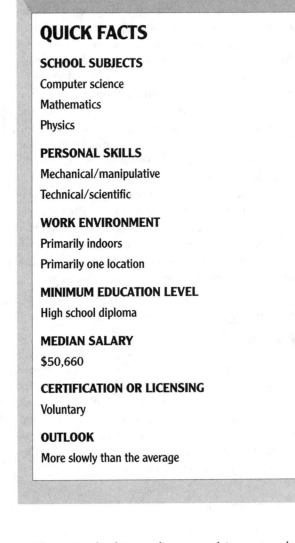

QUICK FACTS

SCHOOL SUBJECTS
Computer science
Mathematics
Physics

PERSONAL SKILLS
Mechanical/manipulative
Technical/scientific

WORK ENVIRONMENT
Primarily indoors
Primarily one location

MINIMUM EDUCATION LEVEL
High school diploma

MEDIAN SALARY
$50,660

CERTIFICATION OR LICENSING
Voluntary

OUTLOOK
More slowly than the average

Those involved in quality control inspect and test the products at various stages of completion. They also maintain and calibrate test equipment used in all phases of manufacturing. They determine the causes for rejection of parts or equipment by assembly-line inspectors and then analyze field and manufacturing reports of product failures.

These technicians may make specific recommendations to their supervisors to eliminate the causes of rejects and may even suggest design, manufacturing, and process changes and establish quality-acceptance levels. They may interpret quality-control standards to the manufacturing supervisors. And they may establish and maintain quality limits on items purchased from other manufacturers, thus ensuring the quality of parts used in the equipment being assembled.

Another area of electronics technology is that of technical writing and editing. *Technical writers* and *technical editors* compile, write, and edit a wide variety of technical information. This includes instructional leaflets, operating manuals, books, and installation and service manuals having to do with the products of the company. To do this, they must confer with design and development engineers, production personnel, salespeople, drafters, and others to obtain the necessary information to prepare the text, drawings, diagrams, parts, lists, and illustrations. They must thoroughly understand how and why the equipment works in order to be able to tell the customer how to use it and the service technician how to install and service it.

At times, technical writers and editors may help prepare technical reports and proposals and write technical articles for engineering societies, management, and other associations. Their job is to produce the means (through printed words and pictures) by which the customer can get the most value out of the purchased equipment.

REQUIREMENTS
High School

A high school diploma is necessary for anyone wishing to pursue a career as an electronics engineering technician. While in high school, you should take algebra, geometry, physics, chemistry, computer science, English, and communications classes. Courses in electronics and introductory electricity are also helpful, as are shop courses and courses in mechanical drawing.

Postsecondary Training

Most employers prefer to hire graduates of two-year postsecondary training programs. These programs provide a solid foundation in the basics of electronics and supply enough general background in science as well as other career-related fields such as business and economics to aid the student in advancing to positions of greater responsibility.

Two-year associate degree programs in electronics technology are available at community colleges and technical institutes. Programs vary quite a bit, but in general, a typical first-year curriculum includes courses in physics for electronics, technical mathematics, communications, AC/DC circuit analysis, electronic amplifiers, transistors, and instruments and measurements.

Typical second-year courses include physics, applied electronics, computer information systems, electronic drafting, electronic instruments and measurements, communications circuits and systems, digital electronics, technical writing, and control circuits and systems.

Students unable to attend a technical institute or community college should not overlook opportunities provided by the military. The military provides extensive training in electronics and other related fields. In addition, some major companies, particularly utilities, hire people straight out of high school and train them through in-house programs. Other companies promote people to technicians' positions from lower-level positions, provided they attend educational workshops and classes sponsored by the company.

Certification or Licensing

Electronics engineering technicians may obtain voluntary certification from the International Society of Certified Electronics Technicians and the Electronics Technicians Association International. This certification is regarded as a demonstration of professional dedication, determination, and expertise.

Other Requirements

You should have an interest in and an aptitude for mathematics and science and should enjoy using tools and scientific equipment. On the personal side, you should be patient, methodical, persistent, and able to get along with different kinds of people. Because technology changes so rapidly, you will need to pursue additional training throughout your career. To work in electronics engineering, you also need to have the ability and desire to learn quickly, an inquisitive mind, and the willingness to read and study materials to keep up to date.

EXPLORING

If you are interested in a career as an electronics engineering technician, you can gain relevant experience by taking shop courses, joining electronics or radio clubs in school, and assembling electronic equipment with commercial kits.

You should take every opportunity to discuss the field with people working in it. Try to visit a variety of different kinds of electronics facilities—service shops, manufacturing plants, and research laboratories—either through individual visits or through field trips organized by teachers or guidance counselors. These visits will provide a realistic idea of the opportunities in the different areas of the electronics industry. You should also take an introductory course in electricity or electronics to test your aptitude, skills, and interest. If you enroll in a community college or technical school, you may be able to secure off-quarter or part-time internships with local employers through your school's job career services office. Internships are valuable ways to gain experience while still in school.

EMPLOYERS

Approximately 170,000 electrical and electronics engineering technicians are employed in the United States. Electronics engineering technicians are employed by companies that design, develop, and manufacture industrial and consumer electronic equipment. Such employers include service shops, manufacturing plants, and research laboratories.

STARTING OUT

You may be able to find your first full-time position through your school's career services office. These offices tend to develop very good working relationships with area employers and can offer you excellent interviewing opportunities.

Another way to obtain employment is through direct contact with a particular company. It is best to write to the personnel department and include a resume summarizing your education and experience. If the company has an appropriate opening, a company representative will schedule an interview with you. There are also many excellent public and commercial employment organizations that can help graduates obtain jobs appropriate to their training and experience. In addition, the classified ads in most metropolitan Sunday newspapers list a number of job openings with companies in the area.

Professional associations compile information on job openings and publish job lists. For example, the International Society of Certified Electronics Technicians offers lists of job openings around the country at its Web site. Information about job openings can also be found in trade magazines on electronics.

ADVANCEMENT

Advancement possibilities in the field of electronics are almost unlimited. Technicians usually begin work under the direct and constant supervision of an experienced technician, scientist, or engineer. As they gain experience or additional education, they are given more responsible assignments, often carrying out particular work programs under only very general supervision. From there, technicians may move into supervisory positions; those with exceptional ability can sometimes qualify for professional positions after receiving additional academic training.

The following short paragraphs describe some of the positions to which electronics technicians can advance.

Electronics technician supervisors work on more complex projects than do electronics technicians. They supervise other technicians and may also have administrative duties, such as making the employee work schedule, assigning laboratory projects to various technicians, overseeing the training progress of new employees, and keeping the workplace clean, organized, and well stocked. In general, they tend to have more direct contact with project managers and project engineers.

Engineering technicians are senior technicians or engineering assistants who work as part of a team of engineers and technicians in research and development of new products. Additional education, resulting in a bachelor of science degree in engineering, is required for this position.

Production test supervisors make detailed analyses of production assembly lines in order to determine where production tests should be placed along the line and the nature and goal of the tests. They may be responsible for designing the equipment setup used in production testing.

Quality control supervisors determine the scope of a product sampling and the kinds of tests to be run on production units. They translate specifications into testing procedures.

Workers who want to advance to engineering positions can become electrical engineers or electronics engineers through additional education. A bachelor of science degree in engineering is required.

All electronics technicians will need to pursue additional training throughout their careers in order to keep up to date with new technologies and techniques. Many employers offer continuing education in the form of in-house workshops or outside seminars. Professional associations also offer seminars and classes on newer technologies and skill building.

EARNINGS

The U.S. Department of Labor reports that in 2006, median annual earnings for electrical and electronics engineering technicians were $50,660. Salaries ranged from less than $30,120 for the lowest paid 10 percent to more than $73,200 for the highest paid 10 percent.

Electronics engineering technicians generally receive premium pay for overtime work on Sundays and holidays and for evening and night-shift work. Most employers offer benefits packages that include paid holidays, paid vacations, sick days, and health insurance. Companies may also offer pension and retirement plans, profit sharing, 401(k) plans, tuition assistance programs, and release time for additional education.

WORK ENVIRONMENT

Because electronic equipment usually must be manufactured in a dust-free, climate-controlled environment, electronics engineering technicians can expect to work in modern, comfortable, well-lighted surroundings. Many electronics plants have been built in industrial parks with ample parking and little traffic congestion. Technicians who work with cable, master antenna television, satellites, and antennas work outside. Frequency of injuries in the electronics industry is far less than in most other industries, and injuries that do occur are usually not serious.

Most employees work a 40-hour workweek, although overtime is not unusual. Some technicians regularly average 50 to 60 hours a week.

OUTLOOK

There is good reason to believe that the electronics industry will remain important through the next decade, but growth and employment opportunities will vary by specialty. Consumer products such as large screen and high-definition televisions, videocassette recorders, digital video disc recorders, compact disc players, personal computers and related hardware, and home appliances with solid-state controls are constantly evolving and in high demand. Other areas driving demand in this field include electronic equipment, medical electronics, and defense-related equipment. Multimedia and interactive products are also expanding rapidly, and many new products are expected in the coming years.

The U.S. Department of Labor estimates that opportunities for electronics engineering technicians will grow more slowly than the average for all occupations through 2016. Foreign design and competition will limit employment growth, and general economic conditions, and levels of government spending may affect certain areas of the field.

Prospective electronics technicians should begin paying attention to certain factors that might affect the areas in which they are thinking of working. For example, workers planning to work for the military or for a military contractor or subcontractor in radar technology need to keep an eye on federal legislation concerning military spending cuts or increases.

The electronics industry is undeniably indispensable to our lives, and although there will be fluctuations in growth for certain subfields, there will be a need for qualified personnel in others. The key to success for an electronics technician is to stay up to date with technology and to be professionally versatile. Building a career on a solid academic foundation and hands-on experience with basic electronics enables an electronics technician to remain competitive in the job market.

FOR MORE INFORMATION

For industry information and to subscribe to Certified Engineering Technician *magazine, contact*
American Society of Certified Engineering Technicians
PO Box 1536
Brandon, MS 39043-1536
Tel: 601-824-8991
http://www.ascet.org

For industry information, contact
Electronic Industries Alliance
2500 Wilson Boulevard
Arlington, VA 22201-3834
Tel: 703-907-7500
http://www.eia.org

For information on certification, contact
Electronics Technicians Association International
Five Depot Street
Greencastle, IN 46135-8024
Tel: 800-288-3824
Email: eta@eta-i.org
http://www.eta-i.org

For information on careers in electrical and electronics engineering, contact
Institute of Electrical and Electronics Engineers Inc.
1828 L Street, NW, Suite 1202
Washington, DC 20036-5104
Tel: 202-785-0017
Email: ieeeusa@ieee.org
http://www.ieee.org

For information on certification, contact
International Society of Certified Electronics Technicians
3608 Pershing Avenue
Fort Worth, TX 76107-4527
Tel: 800-946-0201
Email: info@iscet.org
http://www.iscet.org

Visit the JETS Web site to read the online brochure Engineering Technologists and Technicians.
Junior Engineering Technical Society
1420 King Street, Suite 405
Alexandria, VA 22314-2794
Tel: 703-548-5387
Email: info@jets.org
http://www.jets.org

☐ ELEVATOR INSTALLERS AND REPAIRERS

OVERVIEW

Elevator installers and repairers, also called *elevator constructors* or *elevator mechanics*, are skilled crafts workers who assemble, install, and repair elevators, escalators, dumbwaiters, and similar equipment. They may also be responsible for modernizing this equipment. Approximately 22,000 elevator installers and repairers are employed in the United States.

THE JOB

Elevator installers and repairers may service and update old equipment that has been in operation for many years. Or they may work on new systems, which may be equipped with state-of-the-art microprocessors capable of monitoring a whole elevator system and automatically operating it with maximum possible efficiency. Installing and repairing elevators requires a good understanding of electricity, electronics, and hydraulics.

Installers begin their work by examining plans and blueprints that describe the equipment to be installed. They need to determine the layout of the components, including the framework, guide rails, motors, pumps, cylinders, plunger foundations, and electrical connections. Once the layout is clear, they install the guide rails (for guiding the elevator as it moves up and down) on the walls of the shaft. Then they run electrical wiring in the shaft between floors and install controls and other devices on each floor and at a central control panel. They assemble the parts of the car at the bottom of the shaft. They bolt or weld together the steel frame and attach walls, doors, and parts that keep the car from moving from side to side as it travels up and down the shaft. They also install the entrance doors and doorframes on each floor.

Installers set up and connect the equipment that moves the cars. In cable elevator systems, steel cables are attached to each car and, at their other end, to a large counterweight. Hoisting machinery, often located at the top of the shaft, moves the cables around a pulley, thus moving the elevator car up or down and the counterweight in the opposite direction. In hydraulic systems, the car rests on a hydraulic cylinder that is raised and lowered by a pump, thus moving the elevator car up

QUICK FACTS

SCHOOL SUBJECTS
Mathematics
Technical/shop

PERSONAL SKILLS
Following instructions
Mechanical/manipulative

WORK ENVIRONMENT
Primarily indoors
Primarily multiple locations

MINIMUM EDUCATION LEVEL
Apprenticeship

MEDIAN SALARY
$63,620

CERTIFICATION OR LICENSING
Required (certification)
Required by certain states (licensing)

OUTLOOK
About as fast as the average

and down like an automobile on a lift. New technology also is being developed to run elevators without cables, using magnetic fields instead. Regardless of the type of elevator involved, after the various parts of the elevator system are in place, the elevator installers test the operation of the system and make any necessary adjustments so that the installation meets building and safety code requirements.

In hotels, restaurants, hospitals, and other institutions where food is prepared, elevator installers may work on dumbwaiters, which are small elevators for transporting food and dishes from one part of a building to another. They may also work on escalators, installing wiring, motors, controls, the stairs, the framework for the stairs, and the tracks that keep the stairs in position. Increasingly, installers are working on APMs, or automated people movers, the sort of "moving sidewalks" you might see at an airport.

After elevator and escalator equipment is installed, it needs regular adjustment and maintenance to ensure that the system continues to function in a safe, reliable manner. Elevator repairers routinely inspect the equipment, perform safety tests using meters and gauges, clean parts that are prone to getting dirty, make adjustments, replace worn components, and lubricate bearings and other moving parts.

Repairers also do minor emergency repairs, such as replacing defective parts. Finding the cause of malfunctions often involves troubleshooting. For this reason, repairers need a strong mechanical aptitude. In addition, repairers may work as part of crews that do major repair and modernization work on older equipment.

Elevator installers and repairers use a variety of hand tools, power tools, welding equipment, and electrical testing devices such as digital multimeters, logic probes, and oscilloscopes.

REQUIREMENTS
High School

Employers prefer to hire high school graduates who are at least 18 years of age and in good physical condition. Mechanical aptitude, an interest in machines, and some technical training related to the field are other important qualifications. While you are in high school, therefore, take such classes as machine shop, electronics, and blueprint reading. Mathematics classes will teach you to work with numbers, and applied physics courses will give you a basis for understanding the workings of this equipment. Also, take English classes to enhance your verbal and writing skills. In this work you will be interacting with a variety of people and communication skills will be a necessity.

Postsecondary Training

Union elevator installers and repairers receive their training through the National Elevator Industry (NEI) Educational Program, administered on a local level by committees made up of local employers who belong to the National Elevator Industry Inc., and local branches of the International Union of Elevator Constructors. The programs consist of on-the-job training under the supervision of experienced workers, together with classroom instruction in related subjects. In the work portion of the program, trainees begin with the simplest tasks and gradually progress to more difficult activities. In the classroom, they learn about installation procedures, basic electrical theory, electronics, and job safety.

Union trainees spend their first six months in the industry in a probationary status. Those who com-

plete the period successfully go on to become elevator constructor helpers. After an additional four to five years of required field and classroom education, they become eligible to take a validated mechanic exam. Upon passing this exam, workers become fully qualified journeyman installers and repairers. They may be able to advance more quickly if they already have a good technical background, acquired by taking courses at a postsecondary technical school or junior college.

Certification or Licensing

Certification through the NEI Educational Program's training curriculum is required of new workers in this field. The National Association of Elevator Contractors offers the following voluntary certifications: certified elevator technician and certified accessibility and private residence lift technician. Additionally, most states and municipalities require that elevator installers and repairers pass a licensing examination. This is not true of all areas at this time, but the trend toward mandatory licensure is growing.

Other Requirements

Elevator installers and repairers must be in good physical shape because this job will periodically require them to carry heavy equipment or tools and work in small areas or in awkward positions. Elevator installers and repairers should also enjoy learning. To be successful in this field, they must constantly update their knowledge regarding new technologies, and continuing education through seminars, workshops, or correspondence courses is a must. Elevator installers and repairers need good hand-eye coordination. These workers should not be afraid of heights or of being in confined areas since some of their work may take place in elevator shafts. Also, because elevator installers and repairers frequently work with electrical wiring and wires are typically color-coded based on their function, they need to have accurate color vision.

While union membership is not necessarily a requirement for employment, most elevator installers and repairers are members of the International Union of Elevator Constructors.

EXPLORING

High school courses such as electrical shop, machine shop, and blueprint reading can give you a hands-on sense of tasks that are similar to everyday activities of elevator installers and repairers. A part-time or summer job as a helper at a commercial building site may provide you with the opportunity to observe the conditions that these workers encounter on the job. If you or your guidance counselor can arrange for a tour of an elevator manufacturing firm, this experience will allow you to see how the equipment is built. One of the best ways to learn about the work may be to talk to a professional recommended by local representatives of the International Union of Elevator Constructors.

EMPLOYERS

Approximately 22,000 elevator installers and repairers are employed in the United States and contractors specializing in work with elevators employ the majority. Other elevator installers and repairers work for one of the more than 60 large elevator manufacturers such as Otis or Dover, for government agencies, or for small, local elevator maintenance contractors. Some larger institutions (such as hospitals, which run 24 hours a day) employ their own elevator maintenance and repair crews.

STARTING OUT

If you are seeking information about trainee positions in this field, you can contact the National Elevator Industry Educational Program or the International Union of Elevator Constructors for brochures. The local office of your state's employment service may also be a source of information and job leads.

ADVANCEMENT

When an installer/repairer has completed the approximately five-year training program, met any local licensure requirements, and successfully passed a validated mechanic's exam, he or she is considered fully qualified—a journeyman. After gaining further experience, installers and repairers who work for elevator contracting firms may be promoted to positions such as mechanic-in-charge or supervisor, coordinating the work done by other installers. Other advanced positions include *adjusters*, highly skilled professionals who check equipment after installation and fine-tune it to specifications, and *estimators*, who figure the costs for supplies and labor for work before it is done. Those who work for an elevator manufacturer may move into sales positions, jobs related to product design, or management. Other experienced workers become inspectors employed by the government to inspect elevators and escalators to ensure that they comply with specifications and safety codes.

EARNINGS

Earnings depend on a variety of factors, such as experience and geographical location. Workers who are not fully qualified journeymen earn less than full-time professionals; for example, probationary workers start at about 50 percent of the full wage, and trainees earn about 70 percent of full wage. According to the U.S. Department of Labor, the median hourly wage for fully qualified elevator installers and repairers was $30.59 in 2006. This hourly wage translates into a yearly income of approximately $63,620 for full-time work. The department also reported that the lowest paid 10 percent of installers and repairers made about $17.79 per hour (approximately $36,990 annually), while the highest paid 10 percent earned more than $42.14 per hour (approximately $87,660 annually). In addition to regular wages, union elevator installers and repairers receive other benefits, including health insurance, pension plans, paid holidays and vacations, and some tuition-free courses in subjects related to their work. A change in the union contract called for the institution of a 401(k) retirement program.

WORK ENVIRONMENT

The standard workweek for elevator installers and repairers is 40 hours. Some workers put in overtime hours (for which they are paid extra), and some repairers are on call for 24-hour periods to respond to emergency situations. Most repair work is done indoors, so little time is lost because of bad weather. It frequently is necessary to lift heavy equipment and parts and to work in very hot or cold, cramped, or awkward places.

OUTLOOK

The U.S. Department of Labor predicts employment growth for elevator installers and repairers to be about as fast as the average through 2016. Few new jobs are expected, however, because this occupation is so small. There will also be little need for replacement workers—the turnover in this field is relatively low because the extensive training people go through to gain these jobs results in high wages, which prompts workers to remain in the field. In addition, job outlook is somewhat dependent on the construction industry, particularly for new workers. Because installation of elevators is part of the interior work in new buildings, elevator installers are employed to work on sites about a year after construction begins. So, job availability in this field lags behind boom periods in the construction industry by about a year. Slowdowns in the building industry will eventually catch up to elevator installers, again lagging by about a year as installers complete previously assigned jobs. Due to the growing elderly population in the United States, professionals will also be needed to install and service stair lifts and elevators in homes.

Changes in the union contract that increased the retirement age for elevator installers and repairers brought many older workers back into the workforce in 1998. The NEI Educational Program expects new openings will become available in future years as these older workers retire. In addition, as the technology in the industry becomes more complex, employers will increasingly seek workers who are technically well trained.

FOR MORE INFORMATION

For information on benefits, scholarships, and job opportunities, contact

International Union of Elevator Constructors
7154 Columbia Gateway Drive
Columbia, MD 21046-2132
Tel: 410-953-6150
Email: contact@iuec.org
http://www.iuec.org

For industry news and information on certification and continuing education, contact

National Association of Elevator Contractors
1298 Wellbrook Circle, Suite A
Conyers, GA 30012-8031
Tel: 800-900-6232
http://www.naec.org

For education, scholarship, and career information aimed at women in the construction industry, contact

National Association of Women in Construction
327 South Adams Street
Fort Worth, TX 76104-1002
Tel: 817-877-5551
Email: nawic@nawic.org
http://www.nawic.org

For information on training in the elevator industry, contact

National Elevator Industry Educational Program
11 Larsen Way
Attleboro Falls, MA 02763-1068
Tel: 800-228-8220
http://www.neiep.org

☐ EMERGENCY MEDICAL TECHNICIANS

OVERVIEW

Emergency medical technicians, often called *EMTs*, respond to medical emergencies to provide immediate treatment for ill or injured persons both on the scene and during transport to a medical facility. They function as part of an emergency medical team, and the range of medical services they perform varies according to their level of training and certification. There are approximately 201,000 emergency medical technicians employed in the United States.

THE JOB

EMTs provide on-site emergency care. Their goal is to rapidly identify the nature of the emergency, stabilize the patient's condition, and initiate proper medical procedures at the scene and en route to a hospital. Communities often take great pride in their emergency medical services, knowing that they are as well prepared as possible and that they can minimize the tragic consequences of mishandling emergencies.

The types of treatments an individual is able to give depend mostly on the level of training and certification he or she has completed. *First responders*, the lowest tier of workers in the emergency services, are qualified to provide basic care to the sick and injured since they are often the first to arrive on scene during an emergency. This designation is often held by firefighters, police officers, and other emergency services workers. The most common designation that EMTs hold is *EMT-basic*. A basic EMT can perform CPR, control bleeding, treat shock victims, apply bandages, splint fractures, and perform automatic defibrillation, which requires no interpretation of EKGs. They are also trained to deal with emotionally disturbed patients and heart attack, poisoning, and burn victims. The *EMT-intermediate*, which is the second level of training, is also prepared to start an IV, if needed, or use a manual defibrillator to apply electrical shocks to the heart in the case of a cardiac arrest. A growing number of EMTs are choosing to train for the highest level of certification—the *EMT-paramedic*. With this certification, the individual is permitted to perform more intensive treatment procedures. Often working in close radio contact with a doctor, he or she may give drugs intravenously or orally, interpret EKGs, perform endotracheal intubation, and use more complex life-support equipment.

In the case where a victim or victims are trapped, EMTs first give any medical treatment, and then remove the victim, using special equipment such as the Amkus Power Unit. They may need to work closely with the police or the fire department in the rescue attempt.

EMTs are sent in an ambulance to the scene of an emergency by a dispatcher, who acts as a communications channel for all aspects of emergency medical services. The dispatcher may also be trained as an EMT. It typically is the dispatcher who receives the call for help, sends out the appropriate medical resource, serves as the continuing link between the emergency vehicle and medical facility throughout the situation, and relays any requests for special assistance at the scene.

EMTs, who often work in two-person teams, must be able to get to an emergency scene in any part of their geographic area quickly and safely. For the protection of the public and themselves, they must obey the traffic laws that apply to emergency vehicles. They must be familiar with the roads and any special conditions affecting the choice of route, such as traffic, weather-related problems, and road construction.

Once at the scene, they may find victims who appear to have had heart attacks, are burned, trapped under fallen objects, lacerated, in labor, poisoned, or emotionally disturbed. Because people who have been involved in an emergency are sometimes very upset, EMTs often have to exercise skill in calming both victims and bystanders. They must do their work efficiently and in a reassuring manner.

EMTs are often the first qualified personnel to arrive on the scene, so they must make the initial evaluation of the nature and extent of the medical problem. The accuracy of this early assessment can be crucial. EMTs must be on the lookout for any clues, such as medical identification emblems, indicating that the person has significant allergies, diabetes, epilepsy, or other conditions that may affect decisions about emergency treatment. EMTs must know what questions to ask bystanders or family members if they need more information about a patient.

Once they have evaluated the situation and the patient's condition, EMTs establish the priorities of required care. They administer emergency treatment under standing orders or in accordance with specific instructions received over the radio from a physician. For example, they may have to open breathing passages, perform cardiac resuscitation, treat shock, or restrain emotionally

QUICK FACTS

SCHOOL SUBJECTS
Biology
Health

PERSONAL SKILLS
Helping/teaching
Technical/scientific

WORK ENVIRONMENT
Indoors and outdoors
Primarily multiple locations

MINIMUM EDUCATION LEVEL
Some postsecondary training

MEDIAN SALARY
$27,070

CERTIFICATION OR LICENSING
Required

OUTLOOK
Faster than the average

disturbed patients. The particular procedures and treatments that EMTs may carry out depend partly on the level of certification they have achieved.

People who must be transported to the hospital are put on stretchers or backboards, lifted into the ambulance, and secured for the ride. The choice of hospital is not always up to the EMTs, but when it is they must base the decision on their knowledge of the equipment and staffing needed by the patients. The receiving hospital's emergency department is informed by radio, either directly or through the dispatcher, of details such as the number of persons being transported and the nature of their medical problems. Meanwhile, EMTs continue to monitor the patients and administer care as directed by the medical professional with whom they are maintaining radio contact.

Once at the hospital, EMTs help the staff bring the patients into the emergency department and may assist with the first steps of in-hospital care. They supply whatever information they can, verbally and in writing, for the hospital's records. In the case of a patient's death, they complete the necessary procedures to ensure that the deceased's property is safeguarded.

After the patient has been delivered to the hospital, EMTs check in with their dispatchers and then prepare the vehicle for another emergency call. This includes replacing used linens and blankets; replenishing supplies of drugs, oxygen; and so forth. In addition, EMTs make sure that the ambulance is clean and in good running condition. At least once during the shift, they check the gas, oil, battery, siren, brakes, radio, and other systems.

REQUIREMENTS
High School

While still in high school, interested students should take courses in health and science, driver education, and English. To be admitted to a basic training program, applicants usually must be at least 18 years old and have a high school diploma and valid driver's license. Exact requirements vary slightly between states and training courses. Many EMTs first become interested in the field while in the U.S. Armed Forces, where they may have received training as medics.

Postsecondary Training

The standard basic training program for EMTs was designed by the U.S. Department of Transportation. It is taught in hospitals, community colleges, and police, fire, and health departments across the country. It is approximately 110 hours in length and constitutes the minimum mandatory requirement to become an EMT. In this course, you are taught how to manage common emergencies such as bleeding, cardiac arrest, fractures, and airway obstruction. You also learn how to use equipment such as stretchers, backboards, fracture kits, and oxygen delivery systems.

Successful completion of the basic EMT course opens several opportunities for further training. Among these are a two-day course on removing trapped victims and a five-day course on driving emergency vehicles. Another, somewhat longer course, trains dispatchers. Completion of these recognized training courses may be required for EMTs to be eligible for certain jobs in some areas.

Certification or Licensing

All 50 states have some certification requirement. Certification is only open to those who have completed the standard basic training course. Some states offer new EMTs the choice of the National Registry examination or the state's own certification examination. A majority of states accept national registration in place of their own examination for EMTs who relocate to their states.

After the training program has been successfully completed, the graduate has the opportunity to work toward becoming certified or registered with the National Registry of Emergency Medical Technicians (NREMT). All states have some sort of certification requirement of their own, but many of them accept registration in NREMT in place of their own certification. Applicants should check the specific regulations and requirements for their state.

At present, the NREMT recognizes four levels of competency: first responder, EMT-basic, EMT-intermediate, and EMT-paramedic. Although it is not always essential for EMTs to become registered with one of these ratings, you can expect better job prospects as you attain higher levels of registration.

Candidates for the first responder designation must have completed the standard Department of Transportation training program (or their state's equivalent) and pass both a state-approved practical examination and a written examination.

Candidates for the EMT-basic designation must have completed the standard Department of Transportation training program (or their state's equivalent), have six months' experience, have a current approved CPR credential for the professional rescuer, and pass both a state-approved practical examination and a written examination.

The EMT-intermediate level of competency requires all candidates to have current registration at the basic EMT-basic level. They must also have a certain amount of experience, have a current approved CPR credential for the professional rescuer, and pass both a written test and a practical examination.

To become registered as an EMT-paramedic, or EMT-P, the highest level of registration, candidates must be already registered at the basic or intermediate level. They must have completed a special EMT-P training program and pass both a written and practical examination. Because training is much more comprehensive and specialized than for other EMTs, EMT-Ps are prepared to make more physician-like observations and judgments.

Other Requirements

Anyone who is considering becoming an EMT should have a desire to serve people and be emotionally stable and clearheaded. You must inspire confidence with levelheadedness and good judgment. You must be efficient, neither wasting time nor hurrying through delicate work.

Prospective EMTs need to be in good physical condition. Other requirements include good manual dexterity and motor coordination; the ability to lift and carry up to 125 pounds; good visual acuity, with lenses for correction permitted; accurate color vision, enabling safe driving and immediate detection of diagnostic signs; and competence in giving and receiving verbal and written communication.

EXPLORING

Students in high school usually have little opportunity for direct experience with the emergency medical field. It may be possible to learn a great deal about the health-services field through a part-time, summer, or volunteer job in a hospital or clinic. Such service jobs can provide a chance to observe and talk to staff members concerned with emergency medical services.

High school health courses are a useful introduction to some of the concepts and terminology that EMTs use. You may also be able to take a first-aid class or training in cardiopulmonary resuscitation (CPR). Organizations such as the Red Cross can provide information on local training courses available.

EMPLOYERS

Approximately 201,000 emergency medical technicians are employed in the United States. EMTs are employed by fire departments, private ambulance services, police departments, volunteer emergency medical services squads, hospitals, industrial plants, or other organizations that provide prehospital emergency care.

STARTING OUT

A good source of employment leads for a recent graduate of the basic EMT training program is the school or agency that provided the training. You can also apply directly to local ambulance services, fire departments, and employment agencies.

In some areas, you may face stiff competition if you are seeking full-time paid employment immediately upon graduation. Although you may sometimes qualify for positions with fire and police departments, you are generally more likely to be successful in pursuing positions with private companies.

Volunteer work is an option for EMTs. Volunteers are likely to average eight to 12 hours of work per week. If you are a beginning EMT without prior work experience

in the health field, you may find it advantageous to start your career as a part-time volunteer to gain experience.

Flexibility about the location of a job may help you gain a foothold on the career ladder. In some areas, salaried positions are hard to find because of a strong tradition of volunteer ambulance services. Therefore, if you are willing to relocate where the demand is higher, you should have a better chance of finding employment.

ADVANCEMENT

With experience, EMTs can gain more responsibility while retaining the same job. However, more significant advancement is possible if you move up through the progression of ratings recognized by the NREMT. These ratings acknowledge increasing qualifications, making higher paying jobs and more responsibility easier to obtain.

An avenue of advancement for some EMTs leads to holding an administrative job, such as supervisor, director, operations manager, or trainer. Another avenue of advancement might be further training in a different area of the health care field. Some EMTs eventually move out of the health care field entirely and into medical sales, where their familiarity with equipment and terminology can make them valuable employees.

EARNINGS

Earnings of EMTs depend on the type of employer and individual level of training and experience. Those working in the public sector, for police and fire departments, usually receive a higher wage than those in the private sector, working for ambulance companies and hospitals. Salary levels typically rise with increasing levels of skill, training, and certification.

According to the U.S. Department of Labor, median annual earnings of EMTs and paramedics were $27,070 in 2006. Salaries ranged from less than $17,300 for the lowest 10 paid percent to more than $45,280 for the highest paid 10 percent. For those who worked in local government the mean salary was $32,140, and in hospitals, $30,400.

Benefits vary widely depending on the employer but generally include paid holidays and vacations, health insurance, and pension plans.

WORK ENVIRONMENT

EMTs must work under all kinds of conditions, both indoors and outdoors, and sometimes in very trying circumstances. They must do their work regardless of extreme weather conditions and are often required to do fairly strenuous physical tasks such as lifting, climbing, and kneeling. They consistently deal with situations that many people would find upsetting and traumatic, such as deaths, accidents, and serious injuries.

EMTs usually work irregular hours, including some nights, weekends, and holidays. Those working for fire departments often put in 56 hours a week, while EMTs employed in hospitals, private firms, and police departments typically work a 40-hour week. Volunteer EMTs work much shorter hours.

An additional stress factor faced by EMTs is concern over contracting AIDS or other infectious diseases from bleeding patients. The actual risk of exposure is quite small, and emergency medical programs have implemented procedures to protect EMTs from exposure to the greatest possible degree; however, some risk of exposure does exist, and prospective EMTs should be aware of this.

In spite of the intensity of their demanding job, many EMTs derive enormous satisfaction from knowing that they are able to render such a vital service to the victims of sudden illness or injury.

OUTLOOK

Employment for EMTs is expected to grow faster than the average for all occupations through 2016, according to the U.S. Department of Labor. The proportion of older people, who most use emergency medical services, is growing in many communities, placing more demands on the emergency medical services delivery system and increasing the need for EMTs. There is also high turnover in this occupation (due to limited opportunities for advancement and modest pay), and many openings will occur as current EMTs leave the field.

The employment outlook for paid EMTs depends partly on the community in which they are seeking employment. Many communities perceive the advantages of high-quality emergency medical services and are willing and able to raise tax dollars to support them. In these communities, which are often larger, the employment outlook should remain favorable. Volunteer services are being phased out in these areas, and well-equipped emergency services operated by salaried EMTs are replacing them.

In some communities, however, particularly smaller ones, the employment outlook is not so favorable. Maintaining a high-quality emergency medical services delivery system can be expensive, and financial strains on some local governments could inhibit the growth of these services. Communities may not be able to support the level of emergency medical services that they would oth-erwise like to, and the employment prospects for EMTs may remain limited.

FOR MORE INFORMATION

For industry news and government affairs, contact
American Ambulance Association
8201 Greensboro Drive, Suite 300
McLean, VA 22102-3814
Tel: 800-523-4447
http://www.the-aaa.org

For educational programs and scholarship information, contact
National Association of Emergency Medical Technicians
PO Box 1400
Clinton, MS 39060-1400
Tel: 800-346-2368
Email: info@naemt.org
http://www.naemt.org

For information on testing for EMT certification, contact
National Registry of Emergency Medical Technicians
Rocco V. Morando Building
PO Box 29233
6610 Busch Boulevard
Columbus, OH 43229-1740
Tel: 614-888-4484
http://www.nremt.org

☐ ENERGY CONSERVATION TECHNICIANS

OVERVIEW

Energy conservation technicians identify and measure the amount of energy used to heat, cool, and operate a building or industrial process. They analyze the efficiency of energy use and determine the amount of energy lost through wasteful processes or lack of insulation. After analysis, they suggest energy conservation techniques and install any needed corrective measures.

THE JOB

Energy efficiency and conservation are major concerns in nearly all homes and workplaces. This means that work assignments for energy conservation technicians vary greatly. They may inspect homes, businesses, or industrial buildings to identify conditions that cause energy waste, recommend ways to reduce the waste, and help install corrective measures. When technicians complete an analysis of a problem in energy use and effectiveness, they can state the results in tangible dollar costs, losses, or savings. Their work provides a basis for important decisions on using and conserving energy.

Energy conservation technicians may be employed in power plants, research laboratories, construction firms, industrial facilities, government agencies, or companies that sell and service equipment. The jobs these technicians perform can be divided into four major areas of energy activity: research and development, production, use, and conservation.

In research and development, technicians usually work in laboratories testing mechanical, electrical, chemical, pneumatic, hydraulic, thermal, or optical scientific principles. Typical employers include institutions, private industry, government, and the military. Working under the direction of an engineer, physicist, chemist, or metallurgist, technicians use specialized equipment and materials to perform laboratory experiments. They help record data and analyze it using computers. They may also be responsible for periodic maintenance and repair of equipment.

In energy production, typical employers include solar energy equipment manufacturers, installers, and users; power plants; and process plants that use high-temperature heat, steam, or water. Technicians in this field work with engineers and managers to develop, install, operate, maintain, and repair systems and devices used for the conversion of fuels or other resources into useful energy. Such plants may produce hot water, steam, mechanical motion, or electrical power through systems such as furnaces, electrical power plants, and solar heating systems. These systems may be controlled manually by semiautomated control panels or by computers.

In the field of energy use, technicians might work to improve efficiency in industrial engineering and production line equipment. They also maintain equipment and buildings for hospitals, schools, and multifamily housing.

Technicians working in energy conservation typically work for manufacturing companies, consulting engineers, energy-audit firms, and energy-audit departments of public utility companies. Municipal governments, hotels, architects, private builders, and manufacturers of heating, ventilating, and air-conditioning equipment also hire them. Working in teams under engineers, techni-

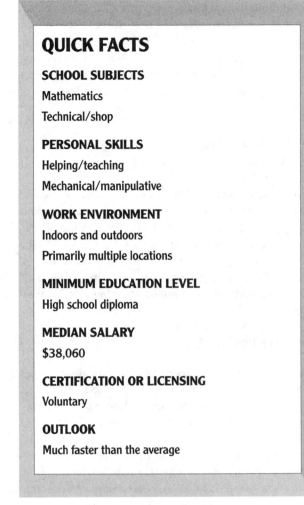

QUICK FACTS

SCHOOL SUBJECTS
Mathematics
Technical/shop

PERSONAL SKILLS
Helping/teaching
Mechanical/manipulative

WORK ENVIRONMENT
Indoors and outdoors
Primarily multiple locations

MINIMUM EDUCATION LEVEL
High school diploma

MEDIAN SALARY
$38,060

CERTIFICATION OR LICENSING
Voluntary

OUTLOOK
Much faster than the average

cians determine building specifications, modify equipment and structures, audit energy use and the efficiency of machines and systems, then recommend modifications or changes to save energy.

If working for a utility company, a technician might work as part of a demand-side management (DSM) program, which helps customers reduce the amount of their electric bill. Under DSM programs, energy conservation technicians visit customers' homes to interview them about household energy use, such as the type of heating system, the number of people home during the day, the furnace temperature setting, and prior heating costs.

Technicians then draw a sketch of the house, measure its perimeter, windows, and doors, and record dimensions on the sketch. They inspect attics, crawl spaces, and basements and note any loose-fitting windows, uninsulated pipes, and deficient insulation. They read hot-water tank labels to find the heat-loss rating and determine the need for a tank insulation blanket. Technicians also examine air furnace filters and heat exchangers to detect dirt or soot buildup that might affect furnace operations. Once technicians identify a problem, they must know how to correct it. After discussing problems with the customer, the technician recommends repairs and provides literature on conservation improvements and sources of loans.

REQUIREMENTS
High School

If you are interested in this field, take classes such as algebra, geometry, physics, chemistry, machine shop, and ecology. These courses and others incorporating laboratory work will provide you with a solid foundation for any postsecondary program that follows. In addition, classes in computer science, drafting (either mechanical or architectural), and public speaking are also very helpful.

Postsecondary Training

Many community colleges and technical institutes provide two-year programs under the specific title of energy conservation and use technology or energy management technology. In addition, schools offer related programs in solar power, electric power, building maintenance, equipment maintenance, and general engineering technology. Though not required for many entry-level jobs, these postsecondary programs can expand career options. With an advanced degree, applicants have a better chance at higher paying jobs, often with private industries.

Advanced training focuses on the principles and applications of physics, energy conservation, energy economics, instrumentation, electronics, electromechanical systems, computers, heating systems, and air-conditioning. A typical curriculum offers a first year of study in physics, chemistry, mathematics, energy technology, energy production systems, electricity and electromechanical devices, and microcomputer operations. The second year of study becomes more specialized, including courses in mechanical and fluid systems, electrical power, blueprint reading, energy conservation, codes and regulations, technical communications, and energy audits.

Considerable time is spent in laboratories, where students gain hands-on experience by assembling, disassembling, adjusting, and operating devices, mechanisms, and integrated systems of machines and controls.

Certification or Licensing

There are no state or federal requirements for certification or licensing of energy conservation technicians. However, certification from the National Institute for Certification in Engineering Technologies and a degree from an accredited technical program are valuable credentials and proof of knowledge and technical skills. The Association of Energy Engineers also offers various certifications to professionals in the field.

Other Requirements

Students entering this field must have a practical understanding of the physical sciences, a good aptitude for math, and the ability to communicate in writing and speech with technical specialists as well as average consumers. Their work requires a clear and precise understanding of operational and maintenance manuals, schematic drawings, blueprints, and computational formulas.

Some positions in electrical power plants require energy conservation technicians to pass certain psychological tests to predict their behavior during crises. Security clearances, arranged by the employer, are required for employment in nuclear power plants and other workplaces designated by the government as high-security facilities.

EXPLORING

To learn more about this profession, ask your career guidance counselor for additional information or for assistance in arranging a field trip to an industrial, commercial, or business workplace to explore energy efficiency.

Utility companies exist in almost every city and employ energy analysts or a team of auditors in their customer service departments. Energy specialists also work for large hospitals, office buildings, hotels, universities, and manufacturing plants. Contact these employers of energy technicians to learn about opportunities for volunteer, part-time, or summer work.

You can also enroll in seminars offered by community colleges or equipment and material suppliers to learn about such topics as building insulation and energy sources. Student projects in energy conservation or part-time work with social service agencies that help low-income citizens meet their energy costs are other options for exploration.

EMPLOYERS

Energy conservation technicians are employed in areas where much energy is used, such as power plants, research laboratories, construction firms, industrial facilities, government agencies, and companies that sell and service equipment. Technicians who focus on research and development work for institutions, private industry, government, and the military. Those who work in energy use are employed by manufacturing facilities, consulting engineering firms, energy audit firms, and energy audit departments of utility companies. Other employers include municipal governments, manufacturers of heating and cooling equipment, private builders, hotels, and architects.

STARTING OUT

Most graduates of technical programs are able to secure jobs in energy conservation before graduation by working with their schools' career services offices. Placement staffs work closely with potential employers, especially those that have hired graduates in recent years. Many large companies schedule regular recruiting visits to schools before graduation.

It is also possible to enter the field of energy conservation on the basis of work experience. People with a background in construction, plumbing, insulation, or heating may enter this field with the help of additional training to supplement their past work experience. Training in military instrumentation and systems control and maintenance is also good preparation for the prospective energy conservation technician. Former navy technicians are particularly sought in the field of energy production.

Opportunities for on-the-job training in energy conservation are available through part-time or summer work in hospitals, major office buildings, hotel chains, and universities. Some regions have youth corps aimed at high school students, such as the Corporation for Youth Energy Corps (CYEC) in New York City's South Bronx. The CYEC offers those who did not complete high school the option of combining work experience and school to earn a general equivalency diploma, get a job, or both.

Some jobs in energy production, such as those in electrical power plants, can be obtained right out of high school. New employees, however, are expected to successfully complete company-sponsored training courses to keep up to date and advance to positions with more responsibility. Graduates with associate's degrees in energy conservation and use, instrumentation, electronics, or electromechanical technology will normally enter employment at a higher level, with more responsibility and higher pay, than those with less education. Jobs in energy research and development almost always require an associate's degree.

ADVANCEMENT

Because the career is relatively new, well-established patterns of advancement have not yet emerged. Nevertheless, technicians in any of the four areas of energy conservation can advance to higher positions, such as senior and supervisory positions. These advanced positions require a combination of formal education, work experience, and special seminars or classes usually sponsored or paid for by the employer.

Technicians can also advance by progressing to new, more challenging assignments. For example, hotels, restaurants, and retail stores hire experienced energy technicians to manage energy consumption. This often involves visits to each location to audit and examine its facilities or procedures to see where energy use can be reduced. The technician then provides training in energy-saving practices. Other experienced energy technicians may be employed as sales and customer service representatives for producers of power, energy, special control systems, or equipment designed to improve energy efficiency.

Technicians with experience and money to invest may start their own businesses, selling energy-saving products, providing audits, or recommending energy-efficient renovations.

EARNINGS

Earnings of energy conservation technicians vary significantly based on the amount of formal training and experience. According to the U.S. Department of Labor, the average annual salary for environmental engineering technicians in engineering and architectural services was $38,060 in 2006. Salaries for all environmental engineering technicians ranged from less than $23,600 to $60,700 or more annually.

Technicians typically receive paid vacations, group insurance benefits, and employee retirement plans. In addition, their employers often offer financial support for all or part of continuing educational programs, which are necessary in order for technicians to keep up to date with technological changes that occur in this developing field.

WORK ENVIRONMENT

Because energy conservation technicians are employed in many different settings, the environment in which they work varies widely. Energy conservation technicians employed in research and development, design, or product planning generally work in laboratories or engineering departments with normal daytime work schedules. Other technicians often travel to customer locations or work in their employer's plant.

Work in energy production and use requires around-the-clock shifts. In these two areas, technicians work either indoors or outdoors at the employer's site. Such assignments require little or no travel, but the work environments may be dirty, noisy, or affected by the weather. Appropriate work clothing must be worn in shop and factory settings, and safety awareness and safe working habits must be practiced at all times.

Energy conservation technicians who work in a plant usually interact with only a small group of people, but those who work for utility companies may have to communicate with the public while providing technical services to their customers. Energy research and development jobs involve laboratory activities requiring social interaction with engineers, scientists, and other technicians. In some cases, technicians may be considered public relations representatives, which may call for special attention to dress and overall appearance.

Job stress varies depending on the job. The pace is relaxed but businesslike in engineering, planning, and design departments and in research and development. However, in more hectic areas, technicians must respond to crisis situations involving unexpected breakdowns of equipment that must be corrected as soon as possible.

OUTLOOK

Since energy use constitutes a major expense for industry, commerce, government, institutions, and private citizens, the demand for energy conservation technicians is likely to remain strong. The U.S. Department of Labor predicts that the employment of environmental engineering technicians is expected to increase much faster than the average for all occupations through 2016. In addition to the financial costs of purchasing natural resources, the added reality of the physical costs of depleting these important resources continues to create a greater demand for trained energy conservation employees. However, employment is influenced by local and national economic conditions.

The utilities industry is in the midst of significant regulatory and institutional changes. Government regulations are moving utility companies toward deregulation, opening new avenues for energy service companies. In the past, energy conservation programs have been dominated by people with engineering and other technical skills. These skills will remain important, but as the industry becomes more customer focused, there will be a growing need for more people with marketing and financial skills.

Utility companies, manufacturers, and government agencies are working together to establish energy effi-ciency standards. The Consortium for Energy Efficiency (http://www.cee1.org) is a collaborative effort involving a group of electric and gas utility companies, government energy agencies, and environmental groups working to develop programs aimed at improving energy efficiency in residential, commercial, and industrial products such as appliances, lighting, geothermal heat pumps, and other systems. Programs such as these will create job opportunities for technicians.

Utility demand-side management (DSM) programs, which have traditionally concentrated on the residential sector, are now focusing more attention on industrial and commercial facilities. With the goal of realizing larger energy savings, lower costs, and more permanent energy-efficient changes, DSM programs are expanding to work with contractors, builders, retailers, distributors, and manufacturers, creating more demand for technicians.

FOR MORE INFORMATION

This trade association represents employees in the petroleum industry. For free videos, fact sheets, and informational booklets available to educators, contact

American Petroleum Institute
1220 L Street, NW
Washington, DC 20005-4070
Tel: 202-682-8000
http://www.api.org

For information on technical seminars, certification programs, conferences, books, and journals, contact

Association of Energy Engineers
4025 Pleasantdale Road, Suite 420
Atlanta, GA 30340-4260
Tel: 770-447-5083
http://www.aeecenter.org

For information on certification programs for engineering technicians and technologists, contact

National Institute for Certification in Engineering Technologies
1420 King Street
Alexandria, VA 22314-2794
Tel: 888-476-4238
Email: tech@nicet.org
http://www.nicet.org

For information on energy efficiency and renewable energy, visit the following Web site:

Energy Efficiency and Renewable Energy
U.S. Department of Energy
http://www.eere.energy.gov

ENVIRONMENTAL TECHNICIANS

OVERVIEW

Environmental technicians, also known as *pollution control technicians*, conduct tests and field investigations to obtain soil samples and other data. Their research is used by engineers, scientists, and others who help clean up, monitor, control, or prevent pollution. An environmental technician usually specializes in air, water, or soil pollution. Although work differs by employer and specialty, technicians generally collect samples for laboratory analysis with specialized instruments and equipment; monitor pollution control devices and systems, such as smokestack air "scrubbers"; and perform various other tests and investigations to evaluate pollution problems. They follow strict procedures in collecting and recording data in order to meet the requirements of environmental laws.

In general, environmental technicians do not operate the equipment and systems designed to prevent pollution or remove pollutants. Instead, they test environmental conditions. In addition, some analyze and report on their findings.

There are approximately 37,000 environmental science and protection technicians, including health technicians, in the United States.

THE JOB

Environmental technicians usually specialize in one aspect of pollution control, such as water pollution, air pollution, or soil pollution. Sampling, monitoring, and testing are the major activities of the job. No matter what the specialty, environmental technicians work largely for or with government agencies that regulate pollution by industry.

Increasingly, technicians input their data into computers. Instruments used to collect water samples or monitor water sources may be highly sophisticated electronic devices. Technicians usually do not analyze the data they collect. However, they may report on what they know to scientists or engineers, either verbally or in writing.

Water pollution technicians monitor both industrial and residential discharge, such as from wastewater treatment plants. They help to determine the presence and extent of pollutants in water. They collect samples from lakes, streams, rivers, groundwater (the water under the earth), industrial or municipal wastewater, or other

QUICK FACTS

SCHOOL SUBJECTS
Biology
Chemistry

PERSONAL SKILLS
Mechanical/manipulative
Technical/scientific

WORK ENVIRONMENT
Indoors and outdoors
One location with some travel

MINIMUM EDUCATION LEVEL
Some postsecondary training

MEDIAN SALARY
$38,090

CERTIFICATION OR LICENSING
Required for certain positions

OUTLOOK
Much faster than the average

sources. Samples are brought to labs, where chemical and other tests are performed. If the samples contain harmful substances, remedial (cleanup) actions will need to be taken. These technicians also may perform various field tests, such as checking the pH, oxygen, and nitrate level of surface waters.

Some water pollution technicians set up monitoring equipment to obtain information on water flow, movement, temperature, or pressure and record readings from these devices. To trace flow patterns, they may inject dyes into the water.

Technicians have to be careful not to contaminate their samples, stray from the specific testing procedure, or otherwise do something to ruin the sample or cause faulty or misleading results.

Depending on the specific job, water pollution technicians may spend a good part of their time outdoors, in good weather and bad, aboard boats, and sometimes near unpleasant smells or potentially hazardous substances.

Field sites may be in remote areas. In some cases, the technician may have to fly to a different part of the country, perhaps staying away from home for a long period of time.

Water pollution technicians play a big role in industrial wastewater discharge monitoring, treatment, and control. Nearly every manufacturing process produces wastewater, but U.S. manufacturers today are required to be more careful about what they discharge with their wastewater.

Some technicians specialize in groundwater, ocean water, or other types of natural waters. *Estuarine resource technicians*, for example, specialize in estuary waters, or coastal areas where fresh water and salt water come together. These bays, salt marshes, inlets, and other tidal water bodies support a wide variety of plant and animal life with ecologically complex relationships. They are vulnerable to destructive pollution from adjoining industries, cities and towns, and other sources. Estuarine resource technicians aid scientists in studying the resulting environmental changes. They may work in laboratories or aboard boats, or may use diving gear to collect samples directly.

Air pollution technicians collect and test air samples (for example, from chimneys of industrial manufacturing plants), record data on atmospheric conditions (such as determining levels of airborne substances from auto or industrial emissions), and supply data to scientists and engineers for further testing and analysis. In labs, air pollution technicians may help test air samples or re-create contaminants. They may use atomic absorption spectrophotometers, flame photometers, gas chromatographs, and other instruments for analyzing samples.

In the field, air pollution technicians may use rooftop sampling devices or operate mobile monitoring units or stationary trailers. The trailers may be equipped with elaborate automatic testing systems, including some of the same devices found in laboratories. Outside air is pumped into various chambers in the trailer where it is analyzed for the presence of pollutants. The results can be recorded by machine on 30-day rolls of graph paper or fed into a computer at regular intervals. Technicians set up and maintain the sampling devices, replenish the chemicals used in tests, replace worn parts, calibrate instruments, and record results. Some air pollution technicians specialize in certain pollutants or pollution sources. For example, *engine emission technicians* focus on exhaust from internal combustion engines.

Soil or *land pollution technicians* collect soil, silt, or mud samples and check them for contamination. Soil can become contaminated when polluted water seeps into the earth, such as when liquid waste leaks from a landfill or other source into surrounding ground. Soil pollution technicians work for federal, state, and local government agencies, for private consulting firms, and elsewhere. (Some soil conservation technicians perform pollution control work.)

A position sometimes grouped with other environmental technicians is that of noise *pollution technician*. Noise pollution technicians use rooftop devices and mobile units to take readings and collect data on noise levels of factories, highways, airports, and other locations in order to determine noise exposure levels for workers or the public. Some test noise levels of construction equipment, chain saws, snow blowers, lawn mowers, or other equipment.

REQUIREMENTS
High School

In high school, key courses include biology, chemistry, and physics. Conservation or ecology courses also will be useful, if offered at your school. Math classes should include at least algebra and geometry, and taking English and speech classes will help to sharpen your communications skills. In addition, work on developing your computer skills while in high school, either on your own or through a class.

Postsecondary Training

Some technician positions call for a high school degree plus employer training. As environmental work becomes more technical and complex, more positions are being filled by technicians with at least an associate's degree. To meet this need, many community colleges across the country have developed appropriate programs for environmental technicians. Areas of study include environmental engineering technologies, pollution control technologies, conservation, and ecology. Courses include meteorology, toxicology, source testing, sampling, and analysis, air quality management, environmental science, and statistics. Other training requirements vary by employer. Some experts advise attending school in the part of the country where you'd like to begin your career so you can start getting to know local employers before you graduate.

Certification or Licensing

Certification or licensing is required for some positions in pollution control, especially those in which sanitation, public health, a public water supply, or a sewage treatment system is involved. For example, the Institute of Professional Environmental Practice offers the qualified environmental professional and the environmental professional intern certifications. See the end of this article for contact information.

Other Requirements

Environmental technicians should be curious, patient, detail-oriented, and capable of following instructions. Basic manual skills are a must for collecting samples and performing similar tasks. Complex environmental regulations drive technicians' jobs; therefore, it's crucial that they are able to read and understand technical materials and to carefully follow any written guidelines for sampling or other procedures. Computer skills and the ability to read and interpret maps, charts, and diagrams are also necessary.

Technicians must make accurate and objective observations, maintain clear and complete records, and be exact in their computations. In addition, good physical conditioning is a requirement for some activities, for example, climbing up smokestacks to take emission samples.

EXPLORING

To learn more about environmental jobs, visit your local library and read some technical and general-interest publications in environmental science. This might give you an idea of the technologies being used and issues being discussed in the field today. You also can visit a municipal health department or pollution control agency in your community. Many agencies are pleased to explain their work to visitors.

School science clubs, local community groups, and naturalist clubs may help broaden your understanding of various aspects of the natural world and give you some experience. Most schools have recycling programs that enlist student help.

With the help of a teacher or career counselor, a tour of a local manufacturing plant using an air- or water-pollution abatement system also might be arranged. Many plants offer tours of their operations to the public. This may provide an excellent opportunity to see technicians at work.

As a high school student, it may be difficult to obtain summer or part-time work as a technician due to the extensive operations and safety training required for some of these jobs. However, it is worthwhile to check with a local environmental agency, nonprofit environmental organizations, or private consulting firms to learn of volunteer or paid support opportunities. Any hands-on experience you can get will be of value to a future employer.

EMPLOYERS

Approximately 37,000 environmental science and protection technicians are employed in the United States. Many jobs for environmental technicians are with the government agencies that monitor the environment, such as the Environmental Protection Agency (EPA), and the Departments of Agriculture, Energy, and Interior.

Water pollution technicians may be employed by manufacturers that produce wastewater, municipal wastewater treatment facilities, private firms hired to monitor or control pollutants in water or wastewater, and government regulatory agencies responsible for protecting water quality.

Air pollution technicians work for government agencies such as regional EPA offices. They also work for private manufacturers producing airborne pollutants, research facilities, pollution control equipment manufacturers, and other employers.

Soil pollution technicians may work for federal or state departments of agriculture and EPA offices. They also work for private agricultural groups that monitor soil quality for pesticide levels.

Noise pollution technicians are employed by private companies and by government agencies such as the Occupational Safety and Health Administration (OSHA).

STARTING OUT

Graduates of two-year environmental programs are often employed during their final term by recruiters who visit their schools. Specific opportunities will vary depending on the part of the country, the segment of the environmental industry, the specialization of the technician (air, water, or land), the economy, and other factors. Many beginning technicians find the greatest number of positions available in state or local government agencies.

Most schools provide job-hunting advice and assistance. Direct application to state or local environmental agencies, employment agencies, or potential employers can also be a productive approach. If you hope to find employment outside your current geographic area, you may get good results by checking with professional organizations or by reading advertisements in technical journals, many of which have searchable job listings on the Internet.

ADVANCEMENT

The typical hierarchy for environmental work is technician (two years of postsecondary education or less), technologist (two years or more of postsecondary training), technician manager (perhaps a technician or technologist with many years of experience), and scientist or engineer (four-year bachelor of science degree or more, up to Ph.D. level).

In some private manufacturing or consulting firms, technician positions are used for training newly recruited professional staff. In such cases, workers with four-year degrees in engineering or physical science are likely to be promoted before those with two-year degrees. Employees of government agencies usually are organized under civil service systems that specify experience, education, and other criteria for advancement. Private industry promotions are structured differently and will depend on a variety of factors.

EARNINGS

Pay for environmental technicians varies widely depending on the nature of the work they do, training and experience required for the work, type of employer, geographic region, and other factors. Public-sector positions tend to pay less than private-sector positions.

According to the U.S. Department of Labor, the average annual salary for environmental science and protection technicians was $38,090 in 2006. Salaries ranged from less than $23,600 to more than $60,700. Technicians who work for local government earned mean annual salaries of $43,050 in 2006; those who were employed by state government earned $43,810. Technicians who become managers or supervisors can earn up to $50,000 per year or more. Technicians who work in private industry or who further their education to secure teaching positions can also expect to earn higher than average salaries.

No matter which area they specialize in, environmental technicians generally enjoy fringe benefits such as paid vacation, holidays and sick time, and employer-paid training. Technicians who work full time (and some who work part time) often have health insurance benefits. Technicians who are employed by the federal government may get additional benefits, such as pension and retirement benefits.

WORK ENVIRONMENT

Conditions range from clean and pleasant indoor offices and laboratories to hot, cold, wet, bad-smelling, noisy, or even hazardous settings outdoors. Anyone planning a career in environmental technology should realize the possibility of exposure to unpleasant or unsafe conditions at least occasionally in his or her career. Employers often can minimize these negatives through special equipment and procedures. Most laboratories and manufacturing companies have safety procedures for potentially dangerous situations.

Some jobs involve vigorous physical activity, such as handling a small boat or climbing a tall ladder. For the most part, technicians need only to be prepared for moderate activity. Travel may be required; technicians go to urban, industrial, or rural settings for sampling.

Because their job can involve a considerable amount of repetitive work, patience and the ability to handle routine are important. Yet, particularly when environmental technicians are working in the field, they also have to be ready to use their resourcefulness and ingenuity to find the best ways of responding to new situations.

OUTLOOK

Demand for environmental technicians is expected to increase much faster than the average for all occupations through 2016. Those trained to handle increasingly complex technical demands will have the upper hand. Environmental technicians will be needed to regulate waste products; to collect air, water, and soil samples for measuring levels of pollutants; to monitor compliance with environmental regulations; and to clean up contaminated sites.

Demand will be higher in some areas of the country than others depending on specialty; for example, air pollution technicians will be especially in demand in large cities, such as Los Angeles and New York, which face pressure to comply with national air quality standards. Amount of industrialization, stringency of state and local pollution control enforcement, health of local economy, and other factors also will affect demand by region and specialty. Perhaps the greatest factors affecting environmental work are continued mandates for pollution control by the federal government. As long as the federal government is supporting pollution control, the environmental technician will be needed.

FOR MORE INFORMATION

For job listings and certification information, contact
Air & Waste Management Association
420 Fort Duquesne Boulevard
One Gateway Center, 3rd Floor
Pittsburgh, PA 15222-1435
Tel: 412-232-3444

Email: info@awma.org
http://www.awma.org

For information on the engineering field and technician certification, contact

American Society of Certified Engineering Technicians
PO Box 1536
Brandon, MS 39043-1536
Tel: 601-824-8991
http://www.ascet.org

The following organization is an environmental careers resource for high school and college students.

Environmental Careers Organization
30 Winter Street, 6th Floor
Boston, MA 02108-4720
Tel: 617-426-4375
http://www.eco.org

For information on environmental careers and student employment opportunities, contact

Environmental Protection Agency
Ariel Rios Building
1200 Pennsylvania Avenue, NW
Washington, DC 20460-0001
Tel: 202-260-2090
Email: public-access@epa.gov
http://www.epa.gov

For information on certification, contact

Institute of Professional Environmental Practice
600 Forbes Avenue
339 Fisher Hall
Pittsburgh, PA 15282
Tel: 412-396-1703
Email: ipep@duq.edu
http://www.ipep.org

For job listings and scholarship opportunities, contact

National Ground Water Association
601 Dempsey Road
Westerville, OH 43081-8978
Tel: 800-551-7379
Email: ngwa@ngwa.org
http://www.ngwa.org

For information on conferences and workshops, contact

Water Environment Federation
601 Wythe Street
Alexandria, VA 22314-1994
Tel: 800-666-0206
http://www.wef.org

FINANCIAL INSTITUTION TELLERS, CLERKS, AND RELATED WORKERS

OVERVIEW

Financial institution tellers, clerks, and related workers perform many tasks in banks and other savings institutions. Tellers work at teller windows where they receive and pay out money, record customer transactions, cash checks, sell traveler's checks, and perform other banking duties. The most familiar teller is the commercial teller, who works with customers, handling check cashing, deposits, and withdrawals. Specialized tellers are also employed, especially at large financial institutions. Clerks' and related workers' jobs usually vary with the size of the institution. In small banks, a clerk or related worker may perform a combination of tasks, while in larger banks an employee may be assigned to one specialized duty. All banking activities are concerned with the safekeeping, exchange, record keeping, credit, and other uses of money. There are approximately 608,000 tellers employed in the United States.

THE JOB

Several different types of tellers may work at a financial institution, depending on its size. The teller the average bank customer has the most contact with, however, is the commercial teller, also known as a *paying and receiving teller*. These tellers service the public directly by accepting customers' deposits and providing them with receipts, paying out withdrawals and recording the transactions, cashing checks, exchanging money for customers to provide them with certain kinds of change or currency, and accepting savings account deposits. At the beginning of the workday, each teller is given a cash drawer containing a certain amount of cash from the vault. During the day, this is the money they use for transactions with customers. Their work with the money and their record keeping must be accurate. At the end of their shifts, the tellers' cash drawers are recounted, and the amount must match up with the transactions done that day. A teller who has problems balancing his or her drawer will not be employed for very long.

QUICK FACTS

SCHOOL SUBJECTS
Business
Computer science
Mathematics

PERSONAL SKILLS
Following instructions
Mechanical/manipulative

WORK ENVIRONMENT
Primarily indoors
Primarily one location

MINIMUM EDUCATION LEVEL
Some postsecondary training

MEDIAN SALARY
$30,000

CERTIFICATION OR LICENSING
None available

OUTLOOK
About as fast as the average

Head tellers and *teller supervisors* train tellers, arrange work schedules, and monitor the tellers' records of the day's transactions. If there are any problems in balancing the cash drawers, the head teller or supervisor must try to figure out where the error occurred and reconcile the differences.

At large financial institutions, tellers may perform specialized duties and are identified by the transactions they handle. *Note tellers*, for example, are responsible for receiving and issuing receipts or payments on promissory notes and recording these transactions correctly. *Discount tellers* are responsible for issuing and collecting customers' notes. *Foreign banknote tellers* work in the exchange department, where they buy and sell foreign currency. When customers need to trade their foreign currency for U.S. currency, these tellers determine the current value of the foreign currency in dollars, count out the bills requested by the customer, and make change.

These tellers may also sell foreign currency and traveler's checks for people traveling out of the country. *Collection and exchange tellers* accept payments in forms other than cash—contracts, mortgages, and bonds, for example.

While tellers' work involves much interaction with the public, most of the work done by clerks and other related workers is completed behind the scenes. Clerks and related workers are responsible for keeping depositors' money safe, the bank's investments healthy, and government regulations satisfied. All such workers assist in processing the vast amounts of paperwork that a bank generates. This paperwork may consist of deposit slips, checks, financial statements to customers, correspondence, record transactions, and reports for internal and external use. Depending on their job responsibilities, clerks may prepare, collect, send, index, or file these documents. In addition, they may talk with customers and other banks, take telephone calls, and perform other general office duties.

The tasks clerks and related workers perform also depend on the size of the financial institution. Duties may be more generalized in smaller facilities and very specialized at larger institutions. The nature of the bank's business and the array of services it offers may also determine a clerk's duties. Services may differ somewhat in a commercial bank from those in a savings bank, trust company, credit union, or savings and loans. In the past, banks generally lent money to businesses while savings and loan and credit unions lent to individuals, but these differences are slowly disappearing over time.

Collection clerks process checks, coupons, and drafts that customers present to the financial institution for special handling. *Commodity-loan clerks* keep track of commodities (usually farm products) used as collateral by the foreign departments of large banks.

Banks employ *bookkeepers* to keep track of countless types of financial and administrative information. *Bookkeeping clerks* file checks, alphabetize paperwork to assist senior bookkeepers, and sort and list various other kinds of material.

Proof machine operators handle a machine that, in one single operation, can sort checks and other papers, add their amounts, and record totals. *Transit clerks* sort and list checks and drafts on other banks and prepare them for mailing back to those banks. *Statement clerks* send customers their account statements listing the withdrawals and deposits they have made. *Bookkeeping machine operators* maintain records of the various deposits, checks, and other items that are credited to or charged against customer accounts. Often they cancel checks and file them, provide customers with information about account balances, and prepare customers' statements for mailing.

Messengers deliver checks, drafts, letters, and other business papers to other financial institutions, business firms, and local and federal government agencies. Messengers who work only within the bank are often known as *pages*. *Trust-mail clerks* keep track of mail in trust departments.

Other clerks—*collateral-and-safekeeping clerks*, *reserves clerks*, and *interest clerks*—collect and record information about collateral, reserves, and interest rates and payments. *Letter-of-credit clerks* keep track of letters of credit for export and import purposes. *Wire-transfer clerks* operate machines that direct the transfer of funds from one account to another.

Many banks now use computers to perform the routine tasks that workers formerly did by hand. To operate these new machines, banks employ *computer operators*, *tabulating machine operators*, *microfilming machine operators*, and *electronic reader-sorter operators*. *Encoder operators* run machines that print information on checks and other papers in magnetic ink so that machines can read them. *Control clerks* keep track of all the data and paperwork transacted through the electronic data processing divisions.

In addition to working in banks, people employed by financial institutions may work at savings and loan associations, personal finance companies, credit unions, government agencies, and large businesses operating credit offices. Although tellers, clerks, and other workers' duties may differ among institutions, the needs for accuracy and honesty are the same. Financial institutions are usually pleasant, quiet places to work and have very up-to-date equipment and business machines. People who work in banking should be of good character and enjoy precision and detailed work.

REQUIREMENTS
High School

Most banks today prefer to hire individuals who have completed high school. If you take courses in bookkeeping, mathematics, business arithmetic, and business machines while in high school, you may have an advantage when applying for a job. In addition, anyone working in a bank should be able to use computers, so be sure to take computer science courses. Take English, speech, and foreign language classes to improve your communication skills, which you will need when interacting with customers and other workers. Some banks are interested in hiring college graduates (or those who have completed

at least two years of college training) who can eventually move into managerial positions. Exchange clerks may be expected to know foreign languages.

Postsecondary Training

Once hired, tellers, clerks, and related workers typically receive on-the-job training. At large institutions, tellers usually receive about one week of classroom training and then undergo on-the-job training for several weeks before they are allowed to work independently. Smaller financial institutions may only provide the on-the-job training in which new tellers are supervised in their work by experienced employees. Clerks may also need to undergo classroom instruction; for example, a bookkeeping clerk may need to take a class covering a certain computer program.

To enhance your possibility of getting a job as well as increase your skills, you may want to take business-related courses or courses for those in the financial industry at a local community college. Courses that may be helpful to take include records management, office systems and procedures, and computer database programming. Those with the most skills and training will find they usually have the best possibilities for advancing.

Numerous educational opportunities will be available to you once you have begun working—and gaining experience—in the financial world. For example, the educational division of the American Bankers Association—the American Institute of Banking—has a vast array of adult education classes in business fields and offers training courses in numerous parts of the country that enable people to earn standard or graduate certificates in bank training. Individuals may also enroll in correspondence study courses.

Other Requirements

Because the work involves many details, a prime requirement for all bank employees is accuracy. Even the slightest error can cause untold extra hours of work and inconvenience or even monetary loss. A pleasing and congenial personality and the ability to get along well with fellow workers and the public are also necessary in this employment.

The physical requirements of the work are not very demanding, although many of these workers spend much of the day standing, which can be tiring. While working in this field, you will be expected to be neat, clean, and appropriately dressed for business.

Banks occasionally require lie detector tests of applicants, as well as fingerprint and background investigations if the job requires handling currency and finances. Those employees handling money or having access to confidential financial information may have to qualify for a personal bond. Some banks now require pre-employment drug testing, and random testing for drugs while under employment is becoming more typical.

Although integrity and honesty are important traits for an employee in any type of work, they are absolutely necessary if you hope to be employed in banks and other financial institutions where large sums of money are handled every day. Workers must also exhibit sound judgment and intelligence in their job performance.

EXPLORING

You can explore the jobs in this field by visiting local financial institutions and talking with the directors of personnel or with people who work in these jobs. You should also consider serving as treasurer for your student government or a club that you are interested in. This will give you experience working with numbers and handling finances, as well as the opportunity to demonstrate responsibility. Learn about finances and the different kinds of financial instruments available by reading publications such as the business section of your local paper and *Money* magazine (also online at http://money. cnn.com).

Sometimes banks offer part-time employment to young people who feel they have a definite interest in pursuing a career in banking or those with business and clerical skills. Other types of part-time employment— where you learn basic business skills, how to interact with the public, and how to work well with other employees—may also be valuable training for those planning to enter these occupations.

EMPLOYERS

Approximately 608,000 workers are employed as tellers in the United States; about 33 percent of them work part time. Financial institution tellers, clerks, and related workers are employed by commercial banks and other depository institutions and by mortgage banks and other nondepository institutions.

STARTING OUT

Private and state employment agencies frequently list available positions for financial institution tellers, clerks, and related workers. Newspaper help-wanted advertisements carry listings for such employees. Some large financial institutions visit schools and colleges to recruit qualified applicants to fill positions on their staff.

If you are interested in a job as a financial institution teller or clerk, try contacting the director of personnel at a bank or other institution to see if any positions are available. If any jobs are open, you may be asked to come in and fill out an application. It is very important, however, to arrange the appointment first by telephone or mail because drop-in visits are disruptive and seldom welcome.

If you know someone who is willing to give you a personal introduction to the director of personnel or to the officers of a bank, you may find that this will help you secure employment. Personal and business references can be important to bank employers when they hire new personnel.

Many financial institution clerks begin their employment as trainees in certain types of work, such as business machine operation or general or specialized clerical duties. Employees may start out as file clerks, transit clerks, or bookkeeping clerks and in some cases as pages or messengers. In general, beginning jobs are determined by the size of the institution and the nature of its operations. In banking work, employees are sometimes trained in related job tasks so that they might be promoted later.

ADVANCEMENT

Many banks and financial institutions follow a "promote-from-within" policy. Promotions are usually given on the basis of past job performance and consider the employee's seniority, ability, and general personal qualities. Clerks who have done well and established good reputations may be promoted to teller positions. Tellers, in turn, may be promoted to head teller or supervisory positions such as department head. Some head tellers may be transferred from their main branch bank to a smaller branch bank where they have greater responsibilities.

Employees who show initiative in their jobs and pursue additional education may advance into low-level officer positions, such as assistant trust officer. The Bank Administration Institute and the American Institute of Banking (a division of the American Bankers Association) offer courses in various banking topics that can help employees learn new skills and prepare for promotions.

Advancement into the higher-level positions typically requires the employee to have a college or advanced degree.

EARNINGS

The earnings of financial institution workers vary by their specific duties, size and type of institution, and area of the country. According to the U.S. Department of Labor, full-time tellers earned a median annual income of about

$22,140 in 2006. Salaries ranged from less than $16,770 for the lowest paid 10 percent to more than $30,020 for the highest paid 10 percent.

The Department of Labor also reports that bookkeeping, accounting, and auditing clerks earned a median full-time salary of $30,560 a year in 2006. The lowest paid 10 percent earned less than $19,760, and the highest paid 10 percent earned more than $46,020 a year.

Financial institution tellers, clerks, and related workers may receive up to 12 paid holidays a year, depending on their locale. A two-week paid vacation is common after one year of service and can increase to three weeks after 10 or 15 years of service. Fringe benefits usually include group life and health insurance, hospitalization, and jointly financed retirement plans.

WORK ENVIRONMENT

Most financial institution workers work a 40-hour week. Tellers may need to work irregular hours or overtime, since many banks stay open until 8:00 p.m. on Fridays and are open Saturday mornings to accommodate their customers. Bank clerks and accounting department employees may have to work overtime at least once a week and often at the close of each month's banking operations to process important paperwork. Check-processing workers who are employed in large financial institutions may work late evening or night shifts. Those employees engaged in computer operations may also work evening or night shifts because this equipment is usually run around the clock. Pay for overtime work is usually straight compensation.

Banks and other depository institutions are usually air-conditioned, pleasantly decorated, and comfortably furnished. Financial institutions have excellent alarm systems and many built-in features that offer protection to workers and facilities. Although the work is not physically strenuous, tellers do have to spend much of their time on their feet. The work clerks and others perform is usually of a very repetitive nature, and the duties are very similar from day to day. Most of the work is paperwork, computer entry, data processing, and other mechanical processes. Clerks do not frequently have contact with customers or clients. Tellers, on the other hand, have extended contact with the public and must always remain polite, even under trying circumstances. Tellers, clerks, and others must be able to work closely with each other, sometimes on joint tasks, as well as under supervision.

OUTLOOK

Job outlooks, naturally, vary by position. The U.S. Department of Labor predicts that employment of financial institution tellers will grow about as fast as the average for all occupations through 2016. Until recently, there was a projected decline caused by overexpansion by banks and competition from companies offering bank-like services, along with the increasing use of automatic teller machines, banking by telephone and computer, and other technologies has resulted in either increased teller efficiency or removed the need for tellers altogether. However, the increased numbers of bank branches, together with longer hours and more services offered to draw in more customers, will require more tellers. Prospects are best for those who have excellent customer skills and are knowledgeable about financial services.

Employment for clerks and related workers is predicted to grow more slowly than the average for all occupations through 2016. Again, mergers, closings, and the use of computers and automated technologies contribute to containing the number of new positions available. Due to their repetitive natures, these jobs have a high turnover rate. Most job openings come from the need to find replacement workers for those who have left. In addition, financial institutions need to employ a large number of people to function properly.

It seems likely that the increasing use of computers and electronic data processing methods will only continue to curtail the numbers of workers needed for these positions. Nevertheless, because of the large size of these occupations, there should be many opportunities for replacement workers.

FOR MORE INFORMATION

The ABA has general information about the banking industry and information on education available through the American Institute of Banking.

American Bankers Association (ABA)
1120 Connecticut Avenue, NW
Washington, DC 20036-3902
Tel: 800-226-5377
http://www.aba.com

The Bank Administration Institute (BAI) offers a number of online courses such as "Introduction to Checks" and "Cash Handling Techniques." For more education information, visit its Web site.

Bank Administration Institute (BAI)
One North Franklin, Suite 1000
Chicago, IL 60606-3421
Tel: 888-284-4078
Email: info@bai.org
http://www.bai.org

 FIREFIGHTERS

OVERVIEW

Firefighters are responsible for protecting people's lives and property from the hazards of fire and other emergencies. They provide this protection by fighting fires to prevent property damage and by rescuing people trapped or injured by fires or other accidents. Through inspections and safety education, firefighters also work to prevent fires and unsafe conditions that could result in dangerous, life-threatening situations. They assist in many types of emergencies and disasters in everyday life. Although in many rural areas firefighters serve on a volunteer basis, this article is mainly concerned with describing full-time career firefighters. There are approximately 293,000 paid firefighters working in the United States.

THE JOB

The duties of career firefighters vary with the size of the fire department and the population of the city in which they are employed. However, each firefighter's individual responsibilities are well defined and clear-cut. In every fire department there are divisions of labor among firefighters. For example, when their department goes into action, firefighters know whether they are to rescue people caught in fires, raise ladders, connect hoses to water hydrants, or attempt to break down doors, windows, or walls with fire axes so that other firefighters can enter the area with water hoses.

Firefighters may fight a fire in a massive building giving off intense heat, or they may be called to extinguish nothing more than a small brush fire or a blazing garbage can. Firefighters on duty at fire stations must be prepared to go on an alarm call at any moment. Time wasted may result in more damage or even loss of life. Firefighters wear protective suits to prevent their hands and bodies from injury, including protective gloves, helmets, boots, coats, and self-contained breathing apparatuses. Because of the mass confusion that occurs at the scene of a fire and the dangerous nature of the work, the firefighters are organized into details and units. They work under the supervision of commanding officers, such as fire captains, battalion chiefs, or the fire chief. These officers may reassign the firefighters' duties at any time, depending on the needs of a particular situation.

Once firefighters have extinguished a fire, they often remain at the site for a certain length of time to make sure that the fire is completely out. *Fire investigators* or *fire marshals* may examine the scene to determine the causes of the fire, especially if it resulted in injury or death or may have been set intentionally. They seek clues to the type of fuel or the place where the fire may have started. They may also determine that the fire was the result of arson—that is, it was set deliberately—and they will examine the scene for evidence that will lead them to suspects. These officials may arrest suspected arsonists and testify in court against them.

Firefighters often answer calls requesting emergency medical care, such as help in giving artificial respiration to drowning victims or emergency aid for heart attack victims on public streets. They may also administer emergency medical care. Many fire departments operate emergency medical services. Most firefighters are cross-trained to participate in both fire and emergency activities.

Some firefighters are assigned as *fire inspectors.* Their work is to prevent fires. They inspect buildings for trash, chemicals, and other materials that could easily ignite; for poor, worn-out, or exposed wiring; for inadequate alarm systems, blocked hallways, or impassable exits; and for other conditions that pose fire hazards. These conditions are usually reported to the owners of the property for correction; if not corrected, the owners could be fined and held criminally liable if any fires occur. Fire inspectors also check to see that public buildings are operated in accordance with fire codes and city ordinances and that the building management complies with safety regulations and fire precautions. Often firefighters are called on to give speeches on fire prevention before school and civic groups.

While firefighters are on station duty and between alarm calls, they perform various duties on a regular basis. They must keep all firefighting equipment in first-class condition for immediate use. This includes polishing and lubricating mechanical equipment, keeping water hoses dry and stretched into shape, and keeping their own personal protective gear in good repair. They hold practice drills for improving response times and firefighting techniques to become as efficient and proficient as possible.

Many firefighters study while on duty to improve their skills and knowledge of firefighting and emergency medical techniques. They also prepare themselves for examinations, which are given regularly and which determine to some extent their opportunities for promotion. They are often required to participate in training programs to hone their skills and learn new techniques.

Since many firefighters must live at the fire station for periods of 24 hours at a time, housekeeping duties and cleaning chores are performed by the on-duty firefighters on a rotation basis. In some small towns, firefighters are only employed on a part-time basis. They are on alarm call from their homes, except perhaps for practice drills. Usually in such situations, only a fire chief and assistant live at the station and are employed full time.

Firefighters work in other settings as well. Many industrial plants employ fire marshals who are in charge of fire-prevention and firefighting efforts and personnel. At airports, potential or actual airplane crashes bring out crash, fire, and rescue workers who prevent or put out fires and save passengers and crewmembers.

The job of firefighters has become more complicated in recent years due to the use of increasingly sophisticated equipment. In addition, many firefighters have assumed additional responsibilities. For example, firefighters work with emergency medical services providing emergency medical treatment, assisting in the rescue and recovery from natural disasters such as earthquakes and tornadoes, as well as manmade disasters, such as the control and cleanup of oil spills and other hazardous chemical incidents, or rescuing victims of bombings. The work of firefighters is very dangerous. The nature of the work demands training, practice, courage, and teamwork. However, firefighting is more than a physical activity that requires strength and alertness. It is also a science that demands continual study and learning.

REQUIREMENTS

High School

Most job opportunities open to firefighters today require applicants to have a high school education. Because much of the work firefighters do is focused around emergency medical services and extinguishing fires, classes in related sciences such as anatomy, physics, and biology are helpful. Courses in English and speech to improve written and spoken communication skills are important as well.

Postsecondary Training

Once high school is completed, there are a variety of options available in both two- and four-year degree programs that specifically focus on fire science and emergency medical certificates. Both are extremely helpful when competing for a position.

In most cases, applicants are required to pass written intelligence tests. Some municipalities may require a civil service examination. Formal education is an asset to potential firefighters because part of their training involves a continuous education program, and a person's

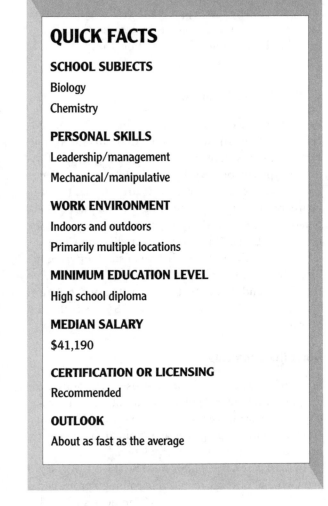

QUICK FACTS

SCHOOL SUBJECTS
Biology
Chemistry

PERSONAL SKILLS
Leadership/management
Mechanical/manipulative

WORK ENVIRONMENT
Indoors and outdoors
Primarily multiple locations

MINIMUM EDUCATION LEVEL
High school diploma

MEDIAN SALARY
$41,190

CERTIFICATION OR LICENSING
Recommended

OUTLOOK
About as fast as the average

educational progress may affect future opportunities for advancement.

Many junior and community colleges offer two-year firetechnology programs. Courses involve the study of physics and hydraulics as they apply to pump and nozzle pressures. Fundamentals of chemistry are taught to provide an understanding of chemical methods of extinguishing fires. Skill in communications—both written and spoken—is also emphasized.

Beginning firefighters may receive six to 12 or more weeks of intensive training, either as on-the-job training or through formal fire department training schools. Training is given both in the classroom and in the field, where new firefighters are taught the fundamentals of firefighting, fire prevention, ventilation, emergency medical procedures, the use and care of equipment, and general job duties and skills, including search and rescue techniques. Trainees may also be given instruction in local building codes and fire ordinances. After this period, new firefighters generally serve a six-month to one-year probationary apprenticeship. Apprentice firefighters usually start out on the job as ladder handlers or hose handlers and are given additional responsibilities with training and experience.

Certification or Licensing

Regulations vary by state, but firefighters do not generally need certification before they are hired, and certification is voluntary but recommended. Certification is typically offered through a state's fire academy, fire-service certification board, fire-service training board, or other agency regulating fire and public safety personnel. Certification programs are accredited by the International Fire Service Accreditation Congress (IFSAC), which provides a listing of states offering the Firefighter I and Firefighter II designations. To become certified, candidates must pass written and practical tests. (Contact information for the IFSAC is at the end of this article.)

Other Requirements

Strict physical examinations are usually required for the job of firefighter. Applicants must also pass rigorous physical performance tests, which may include running, climbing, and jumping. These examinations are clearly defined by local civil service regulations.

In most cases, firefighters must be at least 18 years of age. Generally, the age range for becoming a professional firefighter is between 18 and 35. Candidates must also meet height and weight requirements. Applicants are required to have good vision (20/20 vision is required in some departments), no physical impairments that could keep them from doing their jobs, and great physical stamina. Many cities have residency requirements for their fire department personnel. Most firefighters join the International Association of Fire Fighters (AFL-CIO) when they are hired.

Usually the individuals who score the highest on their tests have the best chances of getting jobs as firefighters. Those who gained firefighting experience in the military or who have served as volunteer community firefighters may receive preferential consideration on their job applications. Applicants with emergency medical service and training are often in demand as firefighters.

A mechanical aptitude is an asset to a person in this career. Also important are a congenial temperament and the ability to adapt to uncertain situations that call for teamwork. Firefighters must be willing to follow the orders of their superiors. Firefighters need sound judg-

ment, mental alertness, and the ability to reason and think logically in situations demanding courage and bravery. The ability to remain calm and compassionate is a valued asset, as firefighters must cope with the emotions of those they are helping, emotions that range from those of distraught homeowners to burn victims.

EXPLORING

You can explore this occupation by talking with local firefighters. You may also be able to get permission to sit in on some of the formal training classes for firefighters offered by city fire departments. In some cases, depending on the size and regulations of the town or city department, you may be able to gain experience by working as a volunteer firefighter.

Some fire departments offer explorer and cadet programs for high-school age students to become involved in if they are interested in the job of firefighter. Many fire departments also offer programs that allow civilians to ride along on calls. This is a good way to spend several hours in a fire station and actually respond to calls to get a feel for whether this is the career that is right for you. Community colleges offer classes that high school students may take to begin preparing for a career as a firefighter. In addition, any volunteer work, especially in service-related fields such as hospitals and hospices that provide care to people in need, can help students prepare for the jobs that firefighters do every day.

Courses in lifesaving and first aid will offer you experience in these aspects of the firefighter's job. You can explore these areas through community training courses and the training offered by the Boy Scouts of America or the American Red Cross. Individuals serving in the military may request training and assignment to firefighting units to gain experience.

EMPLOYERS

More than nine out of every 10 career firefighters are employed by local government. Some very large cities have several thousand firefighters, while small towns might only have a few. The remainder work in fire departments on federal and state installations, such as military bases, airports, and the U.S. Forestry Department. Private fire brigades employ a very small number of firefighters. Most volunteers work for departments that protect fewer than 25,000 people. More than half of all volunteer firefighters are located in small, rural departments that protect fewer than 9,999 people, according to the National Volunteer Fire Council. Many industries have their own fire protection staffs and private fire brigades.

STARTING OUT

You can enter this occupation by applying to take the local civil service examinations. This usually requires passing the physical health, physical performance, and written general intelligence examinations.

If you successfully pass all of the required tests and receive a job appointment, you may serve a probationary period during which you receive intensive training. After the completion of this training, you may be assigned to a fire department or engine company for specific duties.

In some small towns and communities, applicants may enter this occupation through on-the-job training as volunteer firefighters or by applying directly to the local government for the position.

ADVANCEMENT

Firefighters are generally promoted from within the department, first to the position of firefighter, first grade. After they demonstrate successful job performance and gain experience, firefighters may be promoted to positions as lieutenants, captains, deputies, battalion chiefs, assistant chiefs, deputy chiefs, and finally fire chief. Firefighters may sometimes work three to five years or more to receive a promotion to lieutenant. Promotions usually depend upon the firefighter's position rating, which is determined by seniority, job performance, and scores made on the periodic written examinations.

EARNINGS

The median hourly pay for firefighters was $19.80 in 2006 (or $41,190 annually based on a 40-hour workweek), according to the U.S. Department of Labor. Of all firefighters, 10 percent earned less than $9.93 (or $20,660 annually), while the top paid 10 percent earned more than $31.80 (or $66,140 annually). The Department of Labor also reports that firefighters employed by local government earned a median hourly salary of $20.52 (or $42,680 annually) in 2006; those employed by the federal government earned a median hourly salary of $19.65 (or $40,860 annually) in 2006. Many firefighters receive longevity pay for each year they remain in service, which may add as much as $1,000 per year to their salaries. Firefighters also earn overtime pay and are usually given shift, weekend, and holiday pay differentials. In addition, firefighters generally receive a uniform allowance and are eligible to retire after 25 years of service or if disabled in the line of duty. Benefits, including health, life, and disability insurance, vary widely according to the community.

Fire lieutenants, captains, and fire chiefs earned salaries that ranged from $56,511 to $95,271 in 2006, according to the U.S. Department of Labor, although fire chiefs in larger cities may earn much more. Inspectors and investigators earned an average of $48,050 per year in 2006.

WORK ENVIRONMENT

The work of firefighters can often be exciting; the job, however, is one of grave responsibilities. Someone's life or death often hangs in the balance. The working conditions are frequently dangerous and involve risking one's life in many situations. Floors, walls, or even entire buildings can cave-in on firefighters as they work to save lives and property in raging fires. Exposure to smoke, fumes, chemicals, and gases can end a firefighter's life or cause permanent injury.

New equipment that can make the firefighter's job much safer is constantly being developed and tested. For example, special masks that allow firefighters to see in the dense and smoky environments they enter have been introduced. These masks display heat sources close in temperature to the human body, allowing firefighters to locate victims in rooms otherwise impenetrable. With developments like these, firefighters will be able to save many more victims and drastically reduce the danger to them.

In many fire departments, firefighters may be on duty and live at fire stations for long periods of time. They may work 24-hour shifts followed by either 48 or 72 hours off. Firefighters can also work in split shifts, which require that they work nine-hour days and 15-hour night tours or 10-hour days and 14-hour night tours. After each set of day tours, firefighters receive 72 hours off, and after each set of night tours, they receive 48 hours off. Workweeks can range from 40 to almost 56 hours; across the United States and Canada, firefighters worked an average week of 50 hours.

This occupation requires a great deal of physical strength and stamina, so firefighters must work to keep themselves physically fit and in condition. They must be mentally alert at all times. Firefighters may be called into action at any time of the day or night and be required to work in all types of weather conditions, sometimes for long hours. Firefighters must do their work in a highly organized team effort to be effective, since a great deal of excitement and public confusion is usually present at the site of a fire.

Firefighters know that their work is essential for the public welfare, and they receive a great deal of personal satisfaction, as well as admiration and respect from society.

OUTLOOK

Firefighting is forecasted to remain a very competitive field, and the number of people interested in becoming firefighters will outweigh the number of available positions in most areas. Employment of firefighters is expected to grow about as fast as the average for all occupations through 2016, according to the U.S. Department of Labor.

Most new jobs will be created as small communities grow and augment their volunteer staffs with career firefighters. There are also growing numbers of "call" firefighters, who are paid only when responding to fires. Little growth is expected in large, urban fire departments. Some local governments are expected to contract for firefighting services with private companies. In some fire departments, the hours of each work shift have been shortened, and two people may be employed to cover a shift normally worked by one person. Most job growth will occur as volunteer firefighting departments are converted to paid positions. Layoffs of firefighters are uncommon, given the essential nature of fire protection to communities.

FOR MORE INFORMATION

For news in the firefighting field, visit the IAFC's Web site.
International Association of Fire Chiefs (IAFC)
4025 Fair Ridge Drive, Suite 300
Fairfax, VA 22033-2868
Tel: 703-273-0911
http://www.iafc.org

The IAFF's Web site has a virtual academy with information on scholarships for postsecondary education.
International Association of Fire Fighters (IAFF)
1750 New York Avenue, NW, Suite 300
Washington, DC 20006-5395
Tel: 202-737-8484
http://www.iaff.org

For more information on certification, contact
International Fire Service Accreditation Congress
Oklahoma State University
1700 West Tyler
Stillwater, OK 74078-8075
Tel: 405-744-8303
http://www.ifsac.org

For information on fire safety issues, careers in fire protection, and public education, contact
National Fire Protection Association
One Batterymarch Park
Quincy, MA 02169-7471
Tel: 617-770-3000
Email: public_affairs@nfpa.org
http://www.nfpa.org

☐ FIRE SAFETY TECHNICIANS

OVERVIEW

Fire safety technicians work to prevent fires. Typical services they perform include conducting safety inspections and planning fire protection systems. In the course of their job, fire safety technicians recognize fire hazards, apply technical knowledge, and perform services to control and prevent fires. There are approximately 361,000 fire department workers. Approximately 66,000 of these are technically prepared inspectors, supervisors, or technical workers.

THE JOB

Fire safety technicians are employed by local fire departments, fire insurance companies, industrial organizations, government agencies, and businesses dealing with fire protection equipment and consulting services.

Fire science specialists employed by insurance companies make recommendations for fire protection and safety measures in specific buildings. As part of their duties they help set insurance rates, examine water supply and sprinkler facilities, and make suggestions to correct hazardous conditions. They may be part of an arson investigation squad or work with adjusters to determine the amount of personal injury or property loss caused by fire.

In industry, fire safety technicians are often part of an industrial safety team. They inspect areas for possible fire hazards and formulate company procedures in case of fire. They make periodic inspections of firefighting equipment such as extinguishers, hoses and hydrants, fire doors, automatic alarms, and sprinkler systems. An important part of their duties is to hold fire prevention seminars to keep department heads and key workers aware and alert to potential fire hazards in their particular areas. Technicians also teach these employees what to do in case of fire or other emergencies.

Because of the large number of people occupying their facilities, many restaurants, large hotels, and entertainment or recreational centers employ fire safety technicians. There is a great hazard of fire from food cooking in kitchens, lint in laundries, and sparks that fall on draperies and bedding. The possible loss of life from fire makes it necessary to have the best possible fire-protection program.

Many government agencies employ fire safety technicians. They are largely responsible for inspecting government buildings, property and storage, or handling systems for reducing fire hazards. They arrange for installation of adequate alarm systems and fire protection devices. They may be required to organize a firefighting unit in a government agency or assist with designing sprinkler systems in buildings.

Companies that manufacture fire-protection devices and alarm systems employ many technicians. Their training enables them to explain technical functions to customers and to give advice on installation and use. They also help to place smoke detectors and other fire prevention or extinguishing devices in the correct locations to give the greatest protection from fire, and they service fire protection devices after they are installed. Fire extinguishers, for example, must be regularly inspected to be certain that they function properly. *Fire extinguisher servicers* are technicians trained to perform inspections, tests, and maintenance of fire extinguishers and may also instruct people on their use. Private companies specializing in fire safety equipment often employ them.

Public education is also an important area of activity for fire control and safety technicians. By working with the public through schools, businesses, and service clubs and organizations, they can expand the level of understanding about the dangers of fire and teach people about methods of fire protection and fire prevention.

Newly hired technicians generally receive on-the-job orientation before they are given full responsibility in an entry-level position. Examples of entry-level positions are described in the following paragraphs.

Fire insurance inspectors inspect buildings and offices and make recommendations for fire protection and general safety conditions.

Fire insurance underwriters help set rates to conform to company policies and building codes.

Fire insurance adjusters determine losses due to fire and compute rates for adjustment and settling claims.

Fire protection engineering technicians draft plans for the installation of fire protection systems for buildings and structures. Using their knowledge of drafting and fire protection codes, they analyze architectural blueprints and specifications to determine which type and size of fire protection system is required to meet fire protection codes and then estimate its cost. During building construction, they work with the superintendent to ensure proper installation of the system. They may specialize in a specific kind of fire protection system, such as foam, water, dry chemicals, or gas. After a fire

QUICK FACTS

SCHOOL SUBJECTS
Chemistry
Mathematics

PERSONAL SKILLS
Following instructions
Technical/scientific

WORK ENVIRONMENT
Indoors and outdoors
One location with some travel

MINIMUM EDUCATION LEVEL
Associate's degree

MEDIAN SALARY
$38,500

CERTIFICATION OR LICENSING
Recommended

OUTLOOK
About as fast as the average

they may inspect fire-damaged buildings to check for malfunctioning systems.

Fire inspectors check firefighting equipment and report any potential fire hazards. They recommend changes in equipment, practice, materials, or methods to reduce fire hazards.

Plant protection inspectors inspect industrial plants for fire hazards, report findings, and recommend action. Fire alarm superintendents inspect alarm systems in government buildings and institutions.

Fire service field instructors hold training sessions throughout a state to keep firefighters up-to-date on firefighting methods and techniques. They may also inspect small fire departments and report on personnel and equipment.

REQUIREMENTS

While a high school diploma is often sufficient to obtain employment as a firefighter, aspiring fire safety technicians should plan to attend a two-year, postsecondary program in fire technology or a four-year program in fire protection engineering.

High School

While in high school, you should study the physical sciences. You should take either physics or chemistry courses that include laboratory work. Fire science demands some knowledge of hydraulics, physics, and chemistry. For example, laying out sprinkler systems requires skills that are introduced in high school mechanical drawing courses. Algebra and geometry are also recommended, as well as English and writing courses.

Postsecondary Training

Fire protection and safety technology programs are now available at more than 200 technical institutes, community colleges, and universities. These programs provide in-depth education in the fire science specialization for people seeking to work for industries, institutions, or government as fire safety technicians. These programs are also available to members of fire departments or related fire specialists.

Courses in these programs include physics and hydraulics as they apply to pump and nozzle pressures. Fundamentals of chemistry are taught to help students understand chemical methods of extinguishing fires and the chemistry of materials and combustion. Communications skills are also emphasized.

Typical courses in the first year of a two-year program include firefighting tactics and strategy, fire protection equipment and alarm systems, fundamentals of fire suppression, introductory fire technology, chemistry (especially combustion and chemistry of materials), mathematics, and communications skills.

Second-year courses may include building construction for fire protection, hazardous materials, fire administration, industrial fire protection, applied physics, introduction to fire prevention, and applied economics.

Like most professional workers in high-technology careers, fire safety technicians must continue to study during their careers to keep up with new developments in the field. Improved fire detection and prevention instruments, equipment, and methods for making materials fireproof are being developed all the time.

Certification or Licensing

The Board of Certified Safety Professionals (BCSP) offers the designations associate safety professional (ASP) and certified safety professional (CSP). Although the BCSP does not offer a specific certification unique to fire safety technicians, anyone wishing to advance in the field of fire safety should get the ASP and CSP designations. These credentials demonstrate that the technician has completed a high level of education, has passed written examinations, and has acquired a certain amount of professional experience.

The National Institute for Certification in Engineering Technologies offers certification to fire protection workers in the following specialty areas: Automatic Sprinkler System Layout, Fire Alarm Systems, Inspection and Testing of Water-Based Systems, and Special Hazards Suppression Systems. Contact the institute for information on requirements for each certification.

Other Requirements

Those who wish to work in fire science technology in fire departments may train as technicians and apply for specialist jobs in large fire departments. Others may choose to enter the fire department as untrained firefighters. For the latter group, very rigid physical examinations are usually required. Firefighters must keep themselves physically fit and conditioned since they may be required to do hard work in all types of weather and sometimes for long hours.

Firefighters must be able to follow orders and to accept the discipline that is necessary for effective teamwork. While on active call, firefighters usually work under the close supervision of commanding officers such as battalion chiefs or assistant fire chiefs. Their work requires highly organized team efforts to be effective, since there is usually a great deal of excitement and confusion at fires.

Because of the physical demands of the profession, physical performance tests are required and may include running, climbing, and jumping. These examinations are clearly defined by local civil service regulations but may vary from one community to another.

In most cases, prospective firefighters must be at least 18 years of age. They must also meet height and weight requirements. Applicants must have good vision (20/20 vision is required in some departments), no hindering physical impairments, and strong stamina. Some fire departments require that applicants be nonsmokers.

Fire science technicians, who do not work as firefighters but as industrial or government inspectors and consultants, do not need unusual physical strength. These technicians must be able to read and write with ease and communicate well.

For fire safety technicians in industry or government, no licenses are usually required. Favorable academic records and an appropriate two-year degree or certificate are given special consideration by most employers. Becoming a member of the Society of Fire Protection Engineers is a valuable mark of achievement of which employers take note.

For those who want to enter fire departments as firefighters and work toward technician-level tasks, civil service examinations are required in most cases.

Firefighters are a highly organized occupational group; many firefighters belong to the International Association of Fire Fighters.

EXPLORING

If your are still in high school, your guidance department and science teachers should be able to provide you with some introductory information about the various careers in fire protection, safety, and prevention. You can visit your local fire department, look at the equipment, and talk with the firefighters and their commanding officers. In some departments, you may be able to gain experience by working as a volunteer firefighter.

In addition, many fire departments have Fire Explorer Posts that give high school students an opportunity to learn more about jobs in fire service. Local or community colleges also have courses in fire science and prevention that high school students can take.

Courses in lifesaving and first aid also offer helpful experience. Summer jobs as aides with the government park and forest service are available as well. In these jobs, you may learn about fire prevention, control, and detection in forest and grassland conservation work.

It is usually possible to arrange a visit with an insurance company to learn about the huge economic losses caused by fire. Large insurance offices often have agents or officers who can describe fire technician jobs or services in inspection, fire insurance, rate setting or claim settlement, and fire prevention services. You can also obtain part-time or summer jobs with fire equipment manufacturing, supply, and service companies.

EMPLOYERS

Challenging job opportunities are available for fire safety technicians. Most are employed by public or private fire departments and the rest work for large corporations overseeing the design and operation of fire prevention systems. Insurance companies hire fire safety technicians to survey the facilities they insure and to perform research, testing, and analysis. Fire safety technicians and fire protection engineers work in various levels of government and in branches of the armed services, where they help develop and enforce building and fire prevention codes. Fire safety technicians also are employed by fire equipment and systems manufacturing companies, hospitals and health-care facilities, industrial and chemical companies, testing and certifying laboratories, transportation companies, and universities and colleges.

STARTING OUT

Graduates of programs in technical colleges, community colleges, technical institutes, or universities usually secure jobs before they graduate. They are hired by company recruiters sent to school career services offices, which arrange interviews for graduating students. The placement officers or fire science instructors usually keep contacts open to help place their current graduates.

Some schools have cooperative work-study programs where students study part time and work part time for pay. Employers who participate in cooperative programs provide experience in different tasks so the student learns about various aspects of the job. Often, students in such programs are hired permanently by the cooperating employer.

Some students may find jobs in fire departments that are large enough to need special technicians outside the ranks of regular firefighters. Others may choose to become firefighters and advance to technical positions.

Some fire departments place new employees on probation, a period during which they are intensively trained. After training is completed, they may be assigned to specific duties.

Students with a high school diploma or its equivalent can enter a fire department apprenticeship program. These programs run from three to four years, combining intensive on-the-job training with active firefighting service, and include related study in the science and theory of firefighting. These apprenticeship programs may or may not be union sponsored.

Even after completing an apprenticeship program, fire safety technicians seeking to advance to the level of supervisor or inspector must continue to study. Part-time courses are available in community colleges or technical institutes.

In some small communities, applicants may enter through on-the-job training as volunteer firefighters or by direct application for such an appointment.

ADVANCEMENT

Examples of advanced positions are described in the following paragraphs.

Fire prevention analysts analyze overall fire prevention systems in an organization and confer with fire inspectors to obtain detailed information and recommend policies and programs for fire prevention.

Fire protection engineers combine their engineering and management skills to perform a broad range of jobs. Some work as fire protection designers, creating systems that automatically detect and suppress fires. Some design fire alarm, smoke control, emergency lighting, communication, and exit systems. These engineers also perform fire safety evaluations of buildings and industrial complexes. Some research the behavior and control of fire. Others analyze risk management and assessment for industrial applications. Fire protection engineers also investigate fires or explosions, preparing technical reports or providing expert courtroom testimony on the facts of the incident.

"The difference between fire safety technicians and fire protection engineers is that the engineers usually look at the big picture," according to Morgan Hurley, technical director at the Society of Fire Protection Engineers. "Technicians specialize in one specific system, such as sprinklers or smoke alarms. Engineers expand on that knowledge."

Deputy fire marshals inspect possible fire hazards and analyze the amount of loss resulting from a fire. If necessary, they have the authority to condemn buildings. They report cases of arson and work with district attorneys to prosecute arsonists. This is an appointed position, although those holding the position usually have considerable fire experience.

Fire captains work under the supervision of a *fire chief* on a military base or in a municipal area. They are responsible for fire protection in a specific location. Fire chiefs are responsible for all firefighting units in a municipal area. Several fire captains may report to and support the activities of this administrator.

Other possible advancements include an officer position in the fire prevention bureau or branching out into the building department.

Owners of fire equipment or consulting businesses employ fire prevention and control technicians and specialists, who contract for, deliver, and install equipment and provide training and other services in fire prevention.

EARNINGS

Beginning salaries for fire safety technicians tend to be higher than those of other technicians. This is partly due to the shortage of qualified personnel in the field. Starting salaries are approximately $20,500 to $22,000. Expe-

rienced technicians earn salaries that average between $33,000 to $44,000 per year. Those who advance to positions of great responsibility may earn $60,000 per year or more.

The Society of Fire Protection Engineers reports that the average starting salary for fire protection engineers was $47,000 in 2005. Professionals with considerable experience had mean earnings of $85,000. Top engineers can earn more than $100,000 annually. According to the International City-County Management Association, fire prevention/code inspectors earned salaries that ranged from $45,951 to $58,349 in 2006.

Benefits usually include compensatory time off or overtime pay for hours worked beyond the regular work schedule. Other benefits include liberal pension plans, disability benefits, and early retirement options. Also included are paid vacations, paid sick leave, and in some cases, paid holidays or compensatory time off for holidays worked.

WORK ENVIRONMENT

Fire safety technicians may experience danger when assisting or observing firefighting or when inspecting and analyzing structures damaged or destroyed by fire. Floors, walls, or entire buildings can collapse on firefighters as they work to save lives and property. Exposure to smoke, fumes, chemicals, and gases can injure or kill. Most of the duties, however, are performed in offices where the surroundings are clean, safe, and comfortable.

When performing routine inspections, these workers must follow safety regulations and wear protective clothing when appropriate. They must be familiar with the environments they inspect and analyze.

Fire safety technicians must have a natural curiosity about everything that relates to fire. They must be patient and willing to study the physics and chemistry of fire, as well as fire prevention and control. They must also be able to think systematically and objectively as they analyze fire hazards, damages, and prevention.

Technicians must be observant and understand how human factors of carelessness, thoughtlessness, fatigue, or haste may cause fires. One of the great challenges of this career is to learn how to teach people to avoid the mistakes that cause fires and to establish safety procedures and controls that prevent fires.

Fire is one of the most feared and destructive hazards. Fire science technicians can find continuing satisfaction and challenge in saving lives and property by preventing fires.

OUTLOOK

Technical careers in fire prevention and control are predicted to grow about as fast as the average for all other occupations. In the future, these technicians will probably be needed in more places than ever before. The greatest increase in employment will be in industry. More industries are finding that the cost of replacing buildings and property destroyed by fire is greater than the yearly cost of fire protection and the expertise and equipment of these specialists.

New fire prevention and control techniques must be developed as technology continues to change. Skilled and ambitious fire safety technicians will be needed to address and monitor this changing technology.

FOR MORE INFORMATION

The following organization offers general information on careers in fire safety:

American Society of Safety Engineers
1800 East Oakton Street
Des Plaines, IL 60018-2187
Tel: 847-699-2929
Email: customerservice@asse.org
http://www.asse.org

For information on the ASP and CSP certifications, contact
Board of Certified Safety Professionals
208 Burwash Avenue
Savoy, IL 61874-9510
Tel: 217-359-9263
http://www.bcsp.com

For information on fire prevention careers, contact
National Fire Protection Association
One Batterymarch Park
Quincy, MA 02169-7471
Tel: 617-770-3000
Email: public_affairs@nfpa.org
http://www.nfpa.org

For information on training programs, contact
National Fire Sprinkler Association
40 Jon Barrett Road
Patterson, NY 12563-2164
Tel: 845-878-4200, ext. 133
Email: info@nfsa.org
http://www.nfsa.org

For information on certification, contact
National Institute for Certification in Engineering Technologies

1420 King Street
Alexandria, VA 22314-2794
Tel: 888-476-4238
http://www.nicet.org

For information on student chapters, a list of universities that offer programs in fire protection engineering, and a copy of Careers in Fire Protection Engineering, *contact*
Society of Fire Protection Engineers
7315 Wisconsin Avenue, Suite 620E
Bethesda, MD 20814-3234
Tel: 301-718-2910
http://www.sfpe.org

FITNESS DIRECTORS

OVERVIEW

Fitness directors organize and schedule exercise classes and programs for health clubs, resorts, cruise lines, corporations, and other institutions. They work with other fitness professionals, such as personal trainers, nutritionists, and health care personnel, to deliver the best services for the individuals who use the fitness facility. Fitness directors must balance the needs of their staff with the needs of the paying customers. To do this, directors listen to suggestions from staff and clients regarding program changes or additions, instructor criticisms, and any other comments to make sure the fitness facility runs smoothly and paying customers are happy.

THE JOB

Fitness directors are a crucial part of sports and health facilities. They coordinate the schedules of exercise instructors and personal trainers. They also make sure that their institution offers a wide variety of options to keep customers happy. For example, a fitness director who works at a nursing home must plan and direct classes that appeal to an older population. This director ensures that instructors have experience working with the elderly and then arranges for a class that is low-impact or held in a swimming pool. Exercise classes can be held even while clients remain seated.

On a cruise ship, fitness directors must cater to a wide variety of clients. There may be children on board

QUICK FACTS

SCHOOL SUBJECTS
Health
Physical education

PERSONAL SKILLS
Communication/ideas
Helping/teaching

WORK ENVIRONMENT
Primarily indoors
Primarily multiple locations

MINIMUM EDUCATION LEVEL
Some postsecondary training

MEDIAN SALARY
$32,800

CERTIFICATION OR LICENSING
Voluntary

OUTLOOK
Much faster than the average

who would enjoy exercising through games while their parents might enjoy a step aerobics class to help counter all the food eaten that day at the buffet. This balancing act can be a large part of the fitness director's job.

In addition to planning class schedules, directors oversee the overall operation of the fitness facility, making sure equipment and rooms are clean, exercise machines are operating correctly, and the temperature of rooms is comfortable.

Directors must also be observant and make improvements to the programming schedule. For example, perhaps a water aerobics class has not been well attended and is taking up unnecessary lanes in the pool. The facility's fitness director, after talking to lap swimmers that exercise at that time, might decide to eliminate or move the water aerobics class to another time slot, or simply reserve fewer lanes for the class. These are the types of adjustments that directors make on a monthly, if not weekly, basis to keep customers happy.

Because many clients may feel uncomfortable making suggestions or complaints about a class directly to an instructor, fitness directors also serve as a sounding board. Perhaps during an aerobics class, participants are having a hard time hearing the instructor over the music. In this case, a class member can bring the complaint to the attention of the fitness director, who in turn might provide the instructor with a cordless microphone to use during class. Fitness directors keep the peace in health and sports facilities and, as a result, help to keep the facilities in business.

REQUIREMENTS
High School

If you are interested in working in a health and fitness facility, take science and physical education classes and get involved in sports activities. It is also important to take home economics classes, which include lessons in diet and nutrition. Business courses can help you prepare for the management aspect of the job.

Postsecondary Training

Fitness directors should have a background in exercise science to be able to serve their clients and understand the needs of their fitness facility. Associate's and bachelor's degree programs in health education, exercise and sports science, fitness program management, and athletic training are offered in colleges all over the country. Typical classes include nutrition education and consulting, anatomy and physiology, business management, biochemistry, and kinesiology. Because the job of fitness director is a higher management position, most employers will require a bachelor's degree in a sports fitness field and many years of experience in the fitness industry.

Certification or Licensing

Certification in fitness or exercise science is highly recommended (if not required) to work in a management-level position at a fitness facility. Because there are many kinds of certification available, you should choose a certifying board that offers scientifically based exams and requires continuing education credits. The American Council on Exercise (ACE) and the American Fitness Professionals & Associates (AFPA) are just two of the many organizations with certification programs. Some employers also require that their fitness staff members be certified in cardiopulmonary resuscitation (CPR).

Other Requirements

Fitness directors not only need to know about the industry in which they work, but they also have to be comfortable with managing staff. This requires organization, flexibility, and strong communication skills. A friendly disposition and good people skills are also essential.

EXPLORING

To explore this career, be sure to get fit yourself! If your school offers exercise classes or some other after-school fitness program, sign up and note what you like and dislike about instructor methods or the environment. If there is an affordable gym or health club in your community, take a tour and even a sample class or two. Some clubs offer guest passes for a small fee so prospective members can try out a facility before committing to a membership.

While at the facility, talk to an instructor, manager, or trainer about his or her job and work environment and how to best break into the industry. This way, you can learn about what goes into developing, running, and maintaining a fitness program.

You may even be able to obtain a part-time job at your school or community recreation and fitness center. This would give you the chance to see if you enjoy working in fitness.

EMPLOYERS

Fitness directors work in health clubs, gyms, corporate fitness centers, daycare centers, nursing homes, hospitals, rehabilitation centers, resorts, and even for cruise lines. Health and sports centers are located in urban, suburban, and rural areas all over the country.

STARTING OUT

Most fitness directors start out in another career within the sports, health care, or fitness industries. They may start out as personal trainers, aerobics instructors, or physical therapists, and move into managerial positions that involve more responsibility and earning potential. Those looking to break into a fitness career should be sure they have the appropriate knowledge and certifications before applying for positions. Health and fitness centers within gyms, resorts, corporate buildings, and cruise ships may advertise open positions in the newspaper or online at their Web sites. Professional associations, such as the Medical Fitness Association and the Aerobics and Fitness Association of America, have job boards that post openings in centers all over the country.

ADVANCEMENT

Because the job of fitness director is a higher-level management position, advancement is limited to moving to the same position within a larger fitness institution or becoming an owner of a fitness facility.

EARNINGS

Because many fitness directors start out in other positions, earnings can vary. Many individuals who eventually become directors major in exercise science. According to the American Society of Exercise Physiologists, the salaries for those who have earned degrees in exercise science are as follows: bachelor's, $18,000–$25,000; master's, $22,000–$32,000; and doctorate, $30,000–$60,000.

Once in a management position, fitness directors can earn much more, but their salaries still vary considerably depending on their experience and the size and location of their facility. Managers of personal service workers (the category under which the U.S. Department of Labor classifies fitness directors) earned median annual salaries of $32,800 in 2006. The lowest paid 10 percent earned less than $19,940, and the highest paid 10 percent earned $56,960 or more per year.

WORK ENVIRONMENT

With the pressure of balancing the needs of both clients and staff members, the job of fitness director can be demanding. However, the majority of directors work in comfortable workplaces. Most facilities maintain a cool temperature, are clean and well lit, and have well-cared-for equipment. Directors who work part time usually have to pay for their own benefits.

OUTLOOK

Opportunities within the fitness industry should grow much faster than the average through 2016. In general, people are much more knowledgeable about exercise and nutrition. Businesses and medical professionals are promoting exercise as beneficial for both good health and increased work productivity. As baby boomers grow older, they will increasingly rely on gyms, health clubs, and other fitness facilities to stay in shape. Knowledge of special weight training, stretching exercises, and diets for seniors will also drive older individuals to fitness institutions in the years to come.

FOR MORE INFORMATION

For a listing of jobs and certification information, contact
Aerobics and Fitness Association of America
15250 Ventura Boulevard, Suite 200

Sherman Oaks, CA 91403-3297
Tel: 877-968-7263
http://www.afaa.com

For general health and fitness topics, and to learn about certification, contact
American Council on Exercise
4851 Paramount Drive
San Diego, CA 92123-1449
Tel: 888-825-3636
Email: support@acefitness.org
http://www.acefitness.org

For information on certification, contact
American Fitness Professionals & Associates
PO Box 214
Ship Bottom, NJ 08008-0234
Tel: 609-978-7583
Email: afpa@afpafitness.com
http://www.afpafitness.com

For information on exercise physiology and certification, contact
American Society of Exercise Physiologists
College of St. Scholastica
1200 Kenwood Avenue
Duluth, MN 55811-4199
Tel: 218-723-6472
http://www.asep.org

For a listing of jobs in the fitness industry, contact
Medical Fitness Association
PO Box 73103
Richmond, VA 23235-8026
Tel: 804-897-5701
Email: info@medicalfitness.org
http://www.medicalfitness.org

FLIGHT ATTENDANTS

OVERVIEW

Flight attendants are responsible for the safety and comfort of airline passengers from the initial boarding to disembarkment. They are trained to respond to emergencies and passenger illnesses. Flight attendants are required on almost all national and international commercial flights. There are approximately 97,000 flight attendants employed in the United States.

THE JOB

Flight attendants perform a variety of preflight and inflight duties. At least one hour before takeoff, they attend a briefing session with the rest of the flight crew; carefully check flight supplies, emergency life jackets, oxygen masks, and other passenger safety equipment; and see that the passenger cabins are neat, orderly, and furnished with pillows and blankets. They also check the plane galley to see that food and beverages are on board and that the galley is secure for takeoff.

Attendants welcome the passengers on the flight and check their tickets as they board the plane. They show the passengers where to store briefcases and other small pieces of luggage, direct them to their cabin section for seating, and help them put their coats and carry-on luggage in overhead compartments. They often give special attention to elderly or disabled passengers and those traveling with small children.

Before takeoff, a flight attendant speaks to the passengers as a group, usually over a loudspeaker. He or she welcomes the passengers and gives the names of the crew and flight attendants, as well as weather, altitude, and safety information. As required by federal law, flight attendants demonstrate the use of lifesaving equipment and safety procedures and check to make sure all passenger seatbelts are fastened before takeoff.

Upon takeoff and landing and during any rough weather, flight attendants routinely check to make sure passengers are wearing their safety belts properly and have their seats in an upright position. They may distribute reading materials to passengers and answer any questions regarding flight schedules, weather, or the geographic terrain over which the plane is passing. Sometimes they call attention to points of interest that can be seen from the plane. They observe passengers during the flight to ensure their personal comfort and assist anyone who becomes airsick or nervous.

During some flights, attendants serve prepared breakfasts, lunches, dinners, or between-meal refreshments. They are responsible for certain clerical duties, such as filling out passenger reports and issuing reboarding passes. They keep the passenger cabins neat and comfortable during flights. Attendants serving on international flights may provide customs and airport information and sometimes translate flight information or passenger instructions into a foreign language. Most flight attendants work for commercial airlines. A small number, however, work on private airplanes owned and operated by corporations or private companies.

REQUIREMENTS

High School

Flight attendants need to have at least a high school education. A broad education is important to allow flight attendants to cope with the variety of situations they will encounter on the job. Beginning foreign language studies in high school will open up the possibility of working on international flights later.

Postsecondary Training

Airlines increasingly prefer applicants with a college-level education. Business training and experience working with the public are also preferred. Attendants employed by international airlines are usually required to be able to converse in a foreign language.

Most large airline companies maintain their own training schools for flight attendants. Training programs may last from four to seven weeks. Some smaller airlines send their applicants to the schools run by the bigger airlines. A few colleges and schools offer flight attendant training, but these graduates may still be required to complete an airline's training program.

Airline training programs usually include classes in company operations and schedules, flight regulations and duties, first aid, grooming, emergency operations and evacuation procedures, flight terminology, and other types of job-related instruction. Flight attendants also receive 12 to 14 hours of additional emergency and passenger procedures training each year. Trainees for international flights are given instruction on customs and visa regulations and are taught procedures for terrorist attacks. Near the end of the training period, trainees are taken on practice flights, in which they perform their duties under supervision.

An on-the-job probationary period, usually six months, follows training school. During this time, experienced attendants pay close attention to the performance, aptitudes, and attitudes of the new attendants. After this period, new attendants serve as reserve personnel and fill in for attendants who are ill or on vacation. While on call, these reserve attendants must be available to work on short notice.

Certification or Licensing

Certification by the Federal Aviation Administration (FAA) is required of all flight attendants. For certifica-

QUICK FACTS

SCHOOL SUBJECTS
Psychology
Speech

PERSONAL SKILLS
Communication/ideas
Helping/teaching

WORK ENVIRONMENT
Primarily indoors
Primarily multiple locations

MINIMUM EDUCATION LEVEL
Some postsecondary training

MEDIAN SALARY
$53,780

CERTIFICATION OR LICENSING
Required

OUTLOOK
About as fast as the average

tion it is necessary to successfully complete training that includes aircraft evacuation procedures, handling medical emergencies, fire fighting, and security procedures as established by the FAA and the Transportation Security Administration (TSA). For certification, flight attendants also must perform the assigned duties of a cabin crewmember and complete an approved proficiency check.

Other Requirements

Airlines in the United States require flight attendants to be U.S. citizens, have permanent resident status, or have valid work visas. In general, applicants must be at least 18 to 21 years old, although some airlines have higher minimum age requirements. They should be at least five feet, two inches tall in order to reach overhead compartments, and their weight should be in proportion to their height.

Airlines are particularly interested in employing people who are intelligent, poised, resourceful, and able to work in a tactful manner with the public. Flight attendants must have excellent health, good vision, and the ability to speak clearly. Young people who are interested in this occupation need to have a congenial temperament, a pleasant personality, and the desire to serve the public. They must be able to think clearly and logically, especially in emergency situations, and they must be able to follow instructions working as team members of flight crews.

EXPLORING

Opportunities for experience in this occupation are almost nonexistent until you have completed flight attendant training school. You may explore this occupation by talking with flight attendants or people in airline personnel offices. Airline companies and private training schools publish many brochures describing the work of flight attendants and send them out upon request.

Any part-time or full-time job in customer service, such as food service, hospitality, or retail sales, would offer a good introduction to the kind of work flight attendants do. You might also try volunteering for jobs that require people skills, such as diplomacy, listening, helping, and explaining.

EMPLOYERS

Approximately 97,000 professionally trained flight attendants are employed in the United States. Commercial airlines employ the vast majority of all flight attendants, most of whom are stationed in the major cities that serve as their airline's home base. A very small number of flight attendants work on company-owned or private planes.

STARTING OUT

Individuals who are interested in becoming flight attendants should apply directly to the personnel divisions of airline companies. The names and locations of these companies may be obtained by writing to the Air Transport Association. Addresses of airline personnel division offices can also be obtained from almost any airline office or ticket agency. Some major airlines have personnel recruiting teams that travel throughout the United States interviewing prospective flight attendants. Airline company offices can provide interested people with information regarding these recruitment visits, which are sometimes announced in newspaper advertisements in advance.

ADVANCEMENT

A number of advancement opportunities are open to flight attendants. They may advance to supervisory positions such as *first flight attendant* (sometimes known as the *flight purser* or the *supervising flight attendant*), or become an *instructor* or *airline recruitment representative*. They may also have the opportunity to move into the position of *chief attendant*, representing all flight attendants in a particular division or area. Although the rate of turnover in this field was once high, more people are making careers as flight attendants, and competition for available supervisory jobs is very high.

Many flight attendants who no longer qualify for flight duty because of health or other factors move into other jobs with the airlines. These jobs may include reservation agent, ticket agent, or personnel recruiter. They may also work in the public relations, sales, air transportation, dispatch, or communications divisions. Trained flight attendants may also find similar employment in other transportation or hospitality industries such as luxury cruise ship lines.

EARNINGS

Beginning flight attendants earned a median salary of $15,849 in 2006, according to the Association of Flight Attendants, although earnings vary by airline. Median annual earnings of all flight attendants were $53,780 in 2006, according to the U.S. Department of Labor. The middle 50 percent earned between $33,320 and $77,410. Salaries ranged from less than $24,250 for the lowest paid 10 percent to more than $99,300 for the highest paid 10 percent. Wage and work schedule requirements are established by union contract. Most flight attendants are members of the Transport Workers Union of America or the Association of Flight Attendants.

Flight attendants are limited to a specific number of flying hours. In general, they work approximately 80 hours of scheduled flying time and an additional 35 hours of ground duties each month. They receive extra compensation for overtime and night flights. Flight attendants on international flights customarily earn higher salaries than those on domestic flights. Most airlines give periodic salary increases until a maximum pay ceiling is reached. Flight assignments are often based on seniority, with the most senior flight attendants having their choice of flight times and destinations.

Airlines usually pay flight attendants in training either living expenses or a training salary. Companies usually pay flight attendants' expenses such as food, ground transportation, and overnight accommodations while they are on duty or away from home base. Some airlines may require first-year flight attendants to furnish their own uniforms, but most companies supply them.

Fringe benefits include paid sick leave and vacation time, free or reduced air travel rates for attendants and their families, and, in some cases, group hospitalization and life insurance plans and retirement benefits.

WORK ENVIRONMENT

Flight attendants are usually assigned to a home base in a major city or large metropolitan area. These locations include cites such as New York, Chicago, Boston, Atlanta, Miami, Los Angeles, San Francisco, and St. Louis. Some airlines assign attendants on a rotation system to home bases, or they may give preference to the requests of those with rank and seniority on bids for certain home bases. Those with the longest records of service may be given the most desirable flights and schedules.

Flight attendants need to be flexible in their work schedules, mainly because commercial airlines maintain operations 24 hours a day throughout the entire year. They may be scheduled to work nights, weekends, and on holidays, and they may find that some of their allotted time off occurs away from home between flights. They are often away from home for several days at a time. They work long days, but over a year's time, a flight attendant averages about 156 days off, compared with 96 days off for the average office worker.

The work performed by flight attendants may be physically demanding in some respects. For most of the flight, they are usually on their feet servicing passengers' needs, checking safety precautions, and, in many cases, serving meals and beverages. Working with the public all day can be draining. Flight attendants are the most visible employees of the airline, and they must be courteous to everyone, even passengers who are annoying or demanding. There is a certain degree of risk involved in any type of flight work. Flight attendants may suffer minor injuries as they perform their duties in a moving aircraft. They may suffer from irregular sleeping and eating patterns, dealing with stressful passengers, working in a pressurized environment, and breathing recycled air. Flight attendants also face risk of injury or death from hijackings. Since the terrorist attacks of September 11, 2001, comprehensive security measures and upgrades have been implemented by airlines and the Department of Transportation to ensure the safety of travelers and industry workers.

The combination of free time and the opportunity to travel are benefits that many flight attendants enjoy. For those who enjoy helping and working with people, being a flight attendant may be a rewarding career.

OUTLOOK

The U.S. Department of Labor predicts that employment opportunities for flight attendants will grow about as fast as the average through 2016. The terrorist attacks of September 11, 2001, had a great impact on the airline industry and several thousand flight attendants were laid off. The airline industry predicts a slow economic recovery as passengers only gradually return to the skies in pre-terrorist attack numbers. Economic and political conditions are likely to affect all airline employees over the next few years.

Even in the best of times, finding employment as a flight attendant is highly competitive, and since some job restrictions at airlines have been abolished, the once high rate of turnover for flight attendants has declined. Even though the number of job openings is expected to grow, airlines receive thousands of applications each year. Most of the job openings through 2016 will arise from replacement of flight attendants who retire or transfer to other jobs. Students interested in this career will have a competitive advantage if they have a college degree and prior work experience in customer relations or public contact. Courses in business, psychology, sociology, geography, speech, communications, first aid and emergency medical techniques such as CPR, and knowledge of foreign languages and cultures will make the prospective flight attendant more attractive to the airlines.

FOR MORE INFORMATION

For industry and statistical information, as well as to read the Airline Handbook *online, visit ATA's Web site.*

Air Transport Association (ATA)
1301 Pennsylvania Avenue, NW, Suite 1100
Washington, DC 20004-1707
Tel: 202-626-4000
Email: ata@airlines.org
http://www.airlines.org

For information on union membership, contact
Association of Flight Attendants
501 Third Street, NW
Washington, DC 20001-2760
Tel: 202-434-1300
Email: afatalk@afanet.org
http://www.afanet.org/afa

For information on aviation safety, statistics, and regulations, contact
Federal Aviation Administration
800 Independence Avenue, SW

Washington, DC 20591-0001
Tel: 866-835-5322
http://www.faa.gov

This Web site offers information on careers and job issues and links to discussion forums and other aviation-related sites.

Flight Attendants.org
http://www.flightattendants.org

FLORISTS

OVERVIEW

Florists, or *floral designers*, arrange live or cut flowers, potted plants, foliage, or other decorative items, according to basic design principles, to make eye-pleasing creations. Designers make such arrangements for birthdays, weddings, funerals, or other occasions. They are employed by local flower shops or larger national chains, grocery stores, or establish at-home businesses. There are more than 87,000 floral design workers employed in the United States.

THE JOB

From simple birthday bouquets to lavish wedding arrangements, floral designers define a sentiment, a mood, or make an impression, using flowers as their medium of expression. Along with live flowers, designers may use silk flowers or foliage, fresh fruit, and twigs, or incorporate decorative items such as candles, balloons, ribbons, and stuffed animals to their arrangements. Good equipment—foam, wire, wooden or plastic picks, shears, florist's knife, tape, and a variety of containers—is essential. Techniques such as wiring flower stems or shading the tips of blooms with paint or glitter are often used to give floral arrangements a finished look. Familiarity with different species of flowers and plants, as well as creativity and knowledge of the elements of design are what distinguish a good floral designer.

Floral designers are fortunate to have a number of employment paths from which to choose. Some designers are employed at flower shops, while some opt to work independently. Aurora Gagni, owner of Floral Elegance, is one such entrepreneur. A registered nurse by training but creative by nature, Gagni always enjoyed making crafts. "I would see a picture of a flower arrangement in a magazine and try to duplicate it," she says, "but I

would always add and experiment and make it my own creation." Gagni made floral arrangements, wreaths, and displays for family, friends, and coworkers, who in turn would spread word of her abilities. "At one point, I found myself giving bow-making lessons at work!" In time, Gagni had a steady and growing number of customers who relied on her skills.

What persuaded Gagni to give up nursing and go into business for herself? "My kids!" she answers. Indeed, this job perk is an attractive one, especially for someone juggling a career with family. Gagni conducts her business almost entirely from her home, and is available for the "many little things"—driving to and from sports events, delivering forgotten lunch boxes, and, of course, homework.

Gagni tackles a variety of floral requests, but weddings are her specialty. While a typical wedding day lasts a few hours, the planning stage can take months. "Usually, the bride and groom look at my book," Gagni says, "and decide if they like my work." If so, the contract is "closed"—the contract agreement is signed, a budget is set, and a down payment is made—several months before the wedding day. Soon after, designs are made, keeping the budget in mind. Many brides wish for orchids with a carnation budget. "I try to accommodate what type of flower, or color, or look the customer wants," Gagni explains, sometimes making alternate suggestions, especially if price is an issue, or if the flower is difficult to obtain. Gagni orders necessary supplies weeks in advance and scouts for upcoming sales. She notifies her floral wholesalers in advance of any flowers that are seasonal or difficult to obtain. Also, she visits the church and reception hall to check on details such as size, location, and any restrictions. The quickest route to both destinations is also mapped out to ensure prompt delivery of the flowers.

Gagni periodically checks in with the bride about any last-minute changes. Oftentimes, more corsages or more banquet table centerpieces are needed to accommodate extra guests. Bows are tied and secured with wire about two weeks before the wedding. Three days before the wedding, flowers are picked and kept fresh in buckets of water treated with floral preservatives. The actual arranging, done in Gagni's basement, is begun the night before the wedding—bricks of floral foam, treated with water and preservatives, keep the flowers in place. Bouquets and corsages are delivered to the bride's home on the morning of the wedding; and ribbons, flower arrangements, and corsages for the groom's party, are brought to the location of the ceremony. Gagni then goes to the hall to set up for the reception. Final touch-ups are given to table centerpieces, the head table is decorated, and the last details are tackled.

Gagni hires additional help for large contracts, especially to assist with the final arrangements. Her children also help when needed, and her husband is her unofficial delivery driver.

Most retail floral businesses keep a relatively small staff. Sales workers help customers place their orders; they also take care of phone orders. Drivers are hired to make deliveries. Sometimes assistant designers are employed.

REQUIREMENTS

High School

Take art and design classes while in high school. After all, "creativity" is an important buzzword in this industry. Biology classes would be helpful in learning about plants and flowers. Do you have aspirations of owning a flower establishment? Sign up for business-related courses and computer classes—they will help make you a better entrepreneur.

Postsecondary Training

In the past, floral designers learned their craft on the job, usually working as an assistant or apprentice to an experienced designer. Most designers today, however, pursue advanced education resulting in a certificate or degree. While this education is not mandatory in the industry, it does give candidates an advantage when they apply for design positions. There are numerous universities that offer degrees in floriculture and horticulture, as well as community colleges and independent schools that offer certification in floral design.

Programs vary from school to school, lasting anywhere from days to years depending on the type of degree or certificate. The American Floral Art School, a state-approved and licensed vocational school located in Chicago, offers courses in modern floral design, with class schedules from one to three weeks. The curriculum includes the fundamentals of artistic floral design, general instruction in picking or wiring, tinting, and arranging flowers, different types of arrangements and their containers, fashion flowers and wedding flowers, and flower shop management. When you are choosing a school to attend, consider the course offerings as well as your career goals. For example, the Boston-based Rittners School of Floral Design offers classes that emphasize floral business skills, a must if you plan on starting your own shop. Some distance education is also available. The Society of American Florists,

QUICK FACTS

SCHOOL SUBJECTS
Agriculture
Art
Business

PERSONAL SKILLS
Artistic
Following instructions
Leadership/management

WORK ENVIRONMENT
Primarily indoors
Primarily one location

MINIMUM EDUCATION LEVEL
High school diploma

MEDIAN SALARY
$21,700

CERTIFICATION OR LICENSING
Recommended

OUTLOOK
Decline

headquartered in Virginia, has an online learning center through which various courses are offered.

Other Requirements

Most people do not wake up one morning and decide to become a floral designer. If you do not have creative and artistic inclinations, you are already a step behind the rest. A good floral designer enjoys and understands plants and flowers, and can visualize a creation from the very first daffodil. Are you able to work well under pressure and deadlines, and effectively deal with vendors or wholesalers? These are daily requirements of the job. Also, be prepared to greet and accommodate all types of customers, from impatient grooms to nervous brides to grieving families. A compassionate and patient personality will help you go far in this field.

EXPLORING

Considering a future in floral design? Now is the best time to determine if this career is the right one for you. As a high school student without experience, it is doubtful you will be hired as a floral designer; but working as a cashier, flower delivery person, or an assistant is a great way to break into the industry.

What about taking some classes to test your talent? Michaels, a national arts and crafts retailer, offers floral design workshops. Look for similar workshops in your area. Park district programs also have design classes, especially during the holiday seasons. Such programs are relatively inexpensive—most times the fee is just enough to cover materials used in class.

Learn the industry firsthand—why not spend a day at work with a floral designer? Explain your interest to your local florist and ask if he or she would be willing to let you observe.

EMPLOYERS

Approximately 87,000 floral designers are employed in the United States. Small, independently owned flower shops are the most common employers of florists. Large, national chains, such as Teleflora and FTD, supply additional jobs. Flower departments, now a staple in larger grocery stores, also employ floral designers. Approximately 33 percent of floral designers are self-employed.

STARTING OUT

Some floral designers get their start by working as assistant designers. Others, especially if they are certified, may be hired as floral designers. Experienced designers may concentrate in a certain area, such as weddings, and become wedding specialists.

Aurora Gagni needed to apply for a tax identification number before she officially "opened" her business. This number is necessary to establish accounts with wholesalers and greenhouses, as well as for tax purposes. It would be wise to consult with business or legal experts regarding income tax issues, promotion and advertising, and other matters dealing with operating your own business.

Professionals in floral design maintain a portfolio of their best designs. A portfolio is useful when applying for membership in floral associations, classes, and when wooing potential clients.

ADVANCEMENT

Advancement in this field depends on the interest of the individual. Some floral designers are content to work at small local shops, especially if they have created a name for themselves in the area they serve. Others decide to try employment with larger national chains such as Teleflora, or 1-800-FLOWERS. Superstore grocery chains now boast full-service floral departments, creating many job opportunities for designers.

Do you possess an entrepreneurial nature? Maybe owning a floral business—either based in your home or established in the middle of your town's business district—is in your future. Still other options include entering the field of landscape design; interior landscaping for offices, shopping centers, and hotels; or a large floral design specialty. Imagine working on a float for Pasadena's Tournament of Roses Parade.

Many of Aurora Gagni's contracts are for weddings, so it makes sense that her business branches out accordingly. Party favors, cake toppers, and the veil and cord—elements unique in many ethnic wedding ceremonies—are some items Gagni customizes for her clients.

EARNINGS

Experience counts for a lot when it comes to a designer's salary. Geographic location also plays a part in salary differences. Floral designers on the East and West Coasts traditionally enjoy higher than average salaries, compared to floral designers in other parts of the United States. Stores located in large urban areas tend to have higher annual sales than those in rural areas, resulting in higher pay for their employees.

According to the U.S. Department of Labor, florists had median annual earnings of $21,700 in 2006. Well-established floral designers with a steady customer base can earn more than $33,650 annually. Less experienced florists may earn less than $15,040 annually. The Department of Labor also reports that florists employed in grocery stores earned a mean annual salary of $24,870 in 2006.

Depending on the store, designers may be offered sick leave and vacation time, health and life insurance, as well as other benefits.

WORK ENVIRONMENT

Flowers can be purchased almost anywhere, from small, strip-mall flower shops to large national chains to the neighborhood grocery store. This availability means that floral designers can work almost anywhere—from remote, rural areas to busy cities.

Retail floral designers can expect to have comfortable work surroundings. Most floral shops are cool, clean, and well decorated to help attract customers.

Glass refrigerators filled with fresh flowers, live plants and flower arrangements, and arts and crafts are typical items in any flower shop. Workstations for making floral pieces are usually found in the back of the store, along with supplies, containers, and necessary equipment.

Expect to spend the majority of the time on your feet—either standing while working on an arrangement, consulting with customers regarding types of flowers, or on a flower-buying expedition. Most retail-based designers work a normal eight-hour workday with a day off during the week. Weekends are especially busy (often because of weddings) and holidays notoriously so. Christmas, Mother's Day, and Valentine's Day are peak times for floral orders. Long work hours are the norm during these times to accommodate the heavy demand for flowers.

Most designers, if contracted to work a wedding, will travel to the church or the banquet hall to make sure the church arrangements or the table arrangements are properly set up.

OUTLOOK

Employment in floral design is expected to decline moderately through 2016, according to the U.S. Department of Labor, however employment opportunities should remain good due in part to the high turnover rate for this occupation. In addition, at least one flower shop is situated in even the smallest of towns. The emergence of full-service floral departments in grocery stores, as well as opportunities in Internet floral shops, have contributed to job availability. Floral experts who are able to create exciting and original designs will be in high demand. Certified designers may have an edge for the best jobs.

A growing population with large disposable incomes is good news for this industry. Sending flowers to mark an occasion is an old tradition that still has impact today. However, advancement in this career is limited unless you choose to enter management or open a business. Also, starting hourly pay for floral designers is considerably lower than in other design fields.

FOR MORE INFORMATION

For information on classes and schedules, contact
American Floral Art School
634 South Wabash Avenue, Suite 210
Chicago, IL 60605-1808
Tel: 312-922-9328
http://www.americanfloralartschool.com

For information on student chapters and scholarships available through the AIFD Foundation, contact
American Institute of Floral Designers (AIFD)
720 Light Street
Baltimore, MD 21230-3850
Tel: 410-752-3318
Email: AIFD@assnhqtrs.com
http://www.aifd.org

Contact the Rittners School of Floral Design for career and education information. You can also visit its Web site for information on classes and information on how to care for and arrange floral materials.
Rittners School of Floral Design
345 Marlborough Street
Boston, MA 02115-1713
Tel: 617-267-3824
Email: stevrt@tiac.net
http://www.floralschool.com

For education information, including online courses offered through the SAF, contact
Society of American Florists (SAF)
1601 Duke Street
Alexandria, VA 22314-3406
Tel: 800-336-4743
http://www.safnow.org

For fun and interesting information about flowers, visit the SAF's Aboutflowers.com Web site.
Aboutflowers.com
http://www.aboutflowers.com

FORESTRY TECHNICIANS

OVERVIEW

Forestry technicians work as members of a forest management team under the direction of a professional forester. They collect data and information needed to make decisions about resources and resource depletion. They also help plan, supervise, and conduct the operations necessary to maintain and protect forest growth, including harvesting, replanting, and marketing of forest products. Forestry technicians understand the inventory methods and management skills required to produce wood fiber and forest products. They help manage forests and wildlife areas

QUICK FACTS

SCHOOL SUBJECTS

Earth science

Mathematics

PERSONAL SKILLS

Following instructions

Technical/scientific

WORK ENVIRONMENT

Primarily outdoors

Primarily multiple locations

MINIMUM EDUCATION LEVEL

Some postsecondary training

MEDIAN SALARY

$30,880

CERTIFICATION OR LICENSING

Required for certain positions

OUTLOOK

Little or no change

and control fires, insects, and disease. Forestry technicians may also survey land, measure the output of forest products, and operate logging and log-handling equipment. Approximately 34,000 forest and conservation technicians are employed in the United States.

THE JOB

Forestry technicians perform duties that require scientific training and skill, frequently doing work that was once performed by professional foresters. Most are employed in forest land management and administration; they may be involved in timber production, recreation, wildlife forage, water regulation, preservation for scientific studies and special uses, or a combination of these areas.

Nate Benson, a forestry technician employed by the National Park Service, is the leader of a prescribed fire module. The module, one of only nine in the nation, uses fire as a forest management resource. "We ignite and manage fires for ecological, cultural, and hazard fuel benefits," Benson says. "Many different ecosystems are dependent upon fire. You need to burn out the smaller trees to let the larger ones persist." Burning wildlands in a planned and controlled manner can also decrease the chances of an unplanned and uncontrolled forest fire. "If the understory gets too heavy, it becomes more of a fire hazard," Benson says. "You'll want to burn it off to reduce the fuel load."

While not all forestry technicians perform the same types of duties, their day-to-day work includes general activities for managing and harvesting a forest. The first major step in the cycle is planting trees to replace those that have been cut down, harvested, or lost to disease or fire. Technicians tend and care for maturing trees by thinning them to obtain the best growth, spraying them with pesticides when necessary, and protecting them from fire or other damage. Periodic measuring or scaling of trees to determine the amount of lumber they will produce is necessary in planning for harvesting and marketing.

Harvesting and marketing the trees is the last step. In preparing for harvesting, access roads for logging machinery and trucks are planned, surveyed, and built, sometimes with the use of aerial photography. Technicians must understand the land surveys and be able to interpret aerial photographs. After harvesting is complete, the land is reconditioned and the cycle begins again.

The work of a forestry technician is more complicated than it was just a few decades ago. Equipment and methods used to detect, prevent, and fight tree diseases and parasites have developed rapidly, as has the machinery used for harvesting, with powerful log handlers and loaders now being commonly used.

A forestry technician's work includes many different kinds of activities. In addition to the various duties required for each step of the tree-growing cycle, each forest area is managed with a particular objective, which affects the specific duties of the technician. Because the management plan for each area differs, the nature of technicians' jobs varies considerably.

Benson spends about half of his time in the Great Smoky Mountains National Park, where he is based. The remainder of the time, he and his six-person crew travel to other forested areas, wherever they are needed. He says some of his days are spent in the office, setting up logistical needs, creating "burn plans" for various regions, and tending to basic administrative tasks. Other days he spends in the field.

"On a day in the field, we travel to a particular park service unit and play a variety of different roles in the burning," he says. "We may assist with ignition by using a drip torch, or we may be involved in holding the fire behind the fire line to contain it. We may also be monitoring the fire, taking weather and fire behavior observations." Benson says that depending upon the size and complexity of the unit to be burned, projects may take anywhere from a day to a week to complete.

Forestry technicians employed by the federal government, like Benson, may specialize in a specific area of forestry. More often, however, they work as assistants to professional foresters in research connected with watershed management, timber management, wildlife management, forest genetics, fire control, disease and insect control, recreational development, and other matters. Many communities also now employ forestry technicians in the management of their municipal watersheds and in their parks and recreation development programs.

Some forestry technicians are employed by private industry, where they "cruise" timber (measure the volume of standing trees to determine their lumber content), survey logging roads, prepare maps and charts, and mark trees for cutting or thinning.

Following are descriptions of specialized positions that are held by forestry technicians. These positions may be found within federal or state agencies or the private forestry industry. Each requires a different mix of skills and abilities.

Information and education technicians write news releases and act as public relations specialists in nature centers.

Survey assistants locate and mark boundary lines. They also assist in the clearing of forests and construction of logging roads, prepare maps of surveys, and work on land appraisal and acquisition problems for private, state, and federal employers.

Biological aides work in insect and disease prevention and control. They record and analyze data, run experiments under supervision, and prepare maps to show damage done to forests by parasites.

Technical research assistants gather and analyze field data to assist scientists in basic and applied research problems that relate to timber, watershed, and wildlife management.

Sawmill buyers purchase high-grade logs for milling and furniture manufacture.

Pulp buyers purchase pulp logs for use in paper mills and other pulp and paper companies.

Lumber inspectors and/or graders grade and calculate the volume of hardwood and softwood lumber at mills or in retail and wholesale yards.

Tree-nursery management assistants help operate and manage tree nurseries. They keep records, hire tempo-rary personnel, and supervise tree production during planting season. These technicians may also run seed tests and analyze data, operate and maintain equipment, and help supervise forest planting-stock production.

Wildlife technicians conduct fieldwork for various game commissions and federal agencies engaged in fish and game preservation and management. They capture, tag, and track animals with radio collars to establish territories and animal survival records. Wildlife technicians also help take wildlife censuses and maintain daily crew records.

REQUIREMENTS

Nate Benson's educational path did not lead him immediately into forestry. After receiving a bachelor's degree in Latin American studies, he began working for the National Park Service on a seasonal basis. Because he enjoyed the work so much, he went back to school for a master's degree in forestry and became a forestry technician.

High School

The best way to enter this field is to graduate from a formal program in forest technology. Almost all forest technology programs require a high school diploma, and most require applicants to have taken two courses in advanced mathematics and one course in physics. Courses in chemistry, biology, earth sciences, and any other courses in natural resources are excellent choices. Because you will need good writing and public speaking skills, English and speech classes are also recommended.

Postsecondary Training

Whether at a technical institute or a junior or community college, prospective technicians usually take a two-year program to receive an associate's degree. The Society of American Foresters (SAF) gives recognition to schools that offer associate's degrees in forestry technology (or its equivalent). For a listing of recognized schools, visit the SAF's Web site, http://www.safnet.org.

Since forestry technicians must learn both scientific theory and applied science practices, the technical program is a demanding one. It requires organized classroom study and considerable time in the laboratory or field. Students must learn about the kinds of trees and plants that grow in a forest, and how they relate to or affect other plants. Technicians also learn about measuring and calculating the amount of lumber in a tree. This is called mensuration, or forest measurements.

Students in forestry technician programs take mathematics, communications, botany, engineering, and technical forestry courses. The specific types of forestry courses taken vary, depending upon the climate in a given locale and the nature of local forestry practice.

A typical first year's study in a two-year forestry program might include the following courses: elementary forest surveying, communication skills, technical mathematics, dendrology (tree identification), botany of forests, forest orientation, technical reporting, elementary forest measurements, applied silviculture (how plants relate to each other), forest soils, computer applications, and elementary business management.

A typical second year's courses might include the following: personnel management, forest business methods, timber harvesting, advanced forest surveying and map drafting, outdoor recreation and environmental control, wildlife ecology, elements of social science, forest products utilization, forest protection, forest insect and disease control, forest fire control, advanced forest measurements, and aerial photographic interpretation.

Since student technicians also need practical experience working in a forest to learn many of the aspects of their jobs, almost all forestry technician programs require actual work experience in forested areas. Some schools arrange summer jobs for students between the first and second years of study. Many forestry technician programs also own or use a small sawmill where students can learn the basic elements of sawmill operation.

A special feature of some programs is a second-year seminar that includes visits to tree nurseries, sawmills, paper mills, veneer mills, wallboard manufacturing plants, and furniture factories. These visits help students understand how forest products are processed, used, measured, and classified by levels of quality. They also give students a better understanding of different types of companies that employ forestry technicians.

Certification or Licensing

In some states, forestry technicians need to be licensed to perform certain duties. For example, those working with pesticides or chemicals must be trained and licensed in their use. Technicians who make surveys of land for legal public property records are also required to hold a license.

Other Requirements

Forestry technicians must have a genuine enthusiasm for outdoor work. "You need to enjoy working outside, to have the ability to work in often extreme weather condi-

tions, and to love learning more about the resource you're working with," Nate Benson says. "It's a great opportunity to work outdoors and do something you enjoy."

Because the job is often tough and physically demanding, technicians should have good health and stamina. In dealing with dangerous or emergency situations, such as forest fires, it is necessary that technicians be able to think clearly and act calmly and efficiently.

It is of great importance that technicians be able to work without supervision. Often working in rural and remote areas, they may be isolated from a supervisor and other workers for days or weeks at a time. To be successful in this career, you must be self-sufficient, resourceful, and able to tolerate solitude.

Despite the remoteness of most forestry work, effective communication skills are extremely important. Technicians must deal with other workers, members of the public who use the forest for recreation, and conservationists who protect fish, game, and plant life. Technicians may also supervise and coordinate the activities of laborers and field workers. Communication skills also are needed to prepare oral and written reports.

Forestry technicians must be able to apply both theoretical knowledge and specialized occupational skills. They need to be familiar with certain principles of engineering, biology, mathematics, and statistics and know how to operate a computer.

EXPLORING

There are a number of ways you can learn more about a career in forest technology. High school guidance counselors may be able to provide you with materials and information on the career. Community and technical colleges may also have career information centers or other services that can provide information. For information about what the actual day-to-day work is like, you might visit a park or public land area and talk with forestry technicians about the specifics of their jobs.

For even more hands-on information, you might consider getting a summer or part-time job in forestry-related work, such as timber harvesting, clearing, or planting operations. State forestry departments, federal agencies, private companies, or environmental groups are all potential sources of summer or part-time work. The National Wildlife Federation's *Conservation Directory* lists names and addresses of state and federal land management agencies and other groups concerned with the environment.

EMPLOYERS

Approximately 34,000 forest and conservation technicians are employed in the United States. About 76 percent of all technicians work for federal and state governments. In the federal government, most jobs are in the U.S. Department of Agriculture's Forest Service or the Department of Interior's Bureau of Land Management. Opportunities in the federal government also exist with the Natural Resources Conservation Service, the National Park Service, and the U.S. Army Corps of Engineers.

State governments also employ forestry technicians to provide services to private forestland owners and to manage state forest lands. In many states, the Cooperative Extension Service and the Department of Natural Resources have forestry positions. County and municipal governments may also have forestry positions.

There are also a number of employment opportunities in the private sector. Technicians work with companies that manage forestlands for lumber, pulpwood, and other products. Companies that use forest products and suppliers of forestry equipment and materials also hire forestry technicians. Other employers include private estates, tree service companies, and forestry consulting firms.

STARTING OUT

For Nate Benson, a full-time job in forest technology was not easy to come by. "I worked seasonally for 10 years and went back to school to get my master's degree before I got a full-time position," he says. "Initially, it's hard to get career positions in federal land management agencies. You can work seasonally for a long time and not necessarily get a break."

Graduates of technical forestry programs have the best prospects for entering this profession. Although a two-year degree is not a requirement, you will find it much more difficult to find a job without one.

Technicians who have graduated from a college program usually learn about employment leads from their school's career services office, instructors, or guidance staff members. Students who have worked in forestry part time or during summers may be hired on a permanent basis after graduation. Working seasonally, as Benson did, may also be a good way to break into the field.

If you choose to pursue a career in the private sector, you should apply directly to companies that employ forestry technicians.

ADVANCEMENT

Forestry technicians can advance in a number of different ways. Technicians who are federal employees advance to higher grades and better salaries after attaining a certain number of years of experience. However, according to Nate Benson, competition for advancement can be fierce. "In the Park Service, part of the problem you run

into is that it's a wide-based pyramid, and there aren't that many positions to move into," he says. "It's pretty competitive."

Some advancement opportunities require additional schooling. For example, a forestry technician who wants to become a forester needs to complete a four-year degree program. Other forestry technicians advance by moving into research work. Following are potential positions to which a technician can advance.

Timber cruisers supervise crews in the measurement of trees for volume computations. They keep records, run statistical analyses of volumes, and mark timber for sale. They recommend logging methods and use aerial photographs to locate future timber harvesting areas.

Forest-fire control technicians maintain fire control supplies in a central area and report fires by radio-telephone. They recruit, train, and supervise forest-fire wardens and crews, sometimes dispatching and serving as crew leaders in fire suppression. They also conduct investigations into the causes of fires. They also educate communities in fire prevention.

Refuge managers supervise work crews in game and fish management. They help plant food plots for wildlife and other plants for habitat improvement. They patrol restricted areas, conduct census studies, and make maps.

Sawmill managers supervise sawmills, oversee crew and production schedules, and keep payroll records.

Kiln operators supervise and control the kiln schedules for correct drying of lumber. They run drying tests and submit reports on loads of drying lumber.

Forest recreation technicians supervise the operation and maintenance of outdoor recreation facilities. They are responsible not only for tactful enforcement of rules but also for fire watches.

Assistant logging superintendents control harvesting and loading operations for timber sales. They help maintain safety, keep payroll and supply records, and write technical reports for superintendents.

Forestry consultants fill an increasingly important role in forestry by providing forestry services to people whose property or business does not require a permanent, full-time forester.

Experienced forestry technicians may also build rewarding careers in research. *Research technicians* perform many varied functions, such as obtaining data for computer analysis, helping develop new chemical fire retardants, and designing machines to prepare forest soils for planting. Research technicians work for private industries, large cities, or state and federal government agencies.

EARNINGS

Salary levels vary greatly depending on employer and area of forestry. According to the U.S. Department of Labor, median wages for forest and conservation technicians were $30,880 in 2006. The top paid 10 percent of forest and conservation technicians earned more than $49,380, and the bottom paid 10 percent earned less than $22,450 a year. Forestry technicians who work for the federal government averaged $40,534 in 2007.

Those employed by government agencies typically earn less than technicians employed by private industries. Positions with the federal government tend to pay slightly higher wages than those in state governments.

Benefits usually include paid holidays, vacation and sick days, and insurance and retirement plans, although these vary by employer. Some employers offer part or full tuition reimbursement for job-related schooling.

WORK ENVIRONMENT

Working hours for forestry technicians are fairly normal. Most technicians work eight-hour days, five days a week. In case of fires or other unusual situations, however, longer hours may be necessary.

Some of the work is physically demanding. In addition, technicians working in the field may occasionally have to deal with hazardous conditions such as forest fires.

For many technicians, most of the working day is spent outdoors, even in unpleasant weather, in settings that are sparsely settled, primitive, and remote. Many forest areas do not have paved roads, and large areas have only a few roads or trails that are passable.

Technicians who work in laboratories or offices generally have well-lit, modern, and comfortable surroundings.

The twin purposes of forestry—protecting natural resources while promoting their use—present challenges to forestry technicians. Many technicians find satisfaction both in assisting in the conservation and improvement of the forest and in providing an essential public service.

OUTLOOK

Employment growth is predicted to experience little or no change in forestry-related employment through 2016, according to the *Occupational Outlook Handbook*. Most job openings will result from technicians leaving the field or being promoted to other areas. However, competition will be strong; technicians with good preparation in forestry technology and machinery management will have an advantage over less prepared applicants in the job market.

The increased awareness for protecting the environment will continue the demand for conservation and forestry workers, especially in state and local governments. Forestry technicians who have knowledge of urban forestry and geographic information systems will have especially strong employment opportunities, according to the U.S. Department of Labor. Budgetary constraints, however, will affect hiring, particularly at the federal and state levels of government.

One promising area of future employment for forestry technicians is in the area of forest recreation. Ever-increasing numbers of people are enjoying the forests. These resources must be managed for the protection of the users, as well as of the resources themselves, and such management requires the expertise of foresters and forestry technicians.

In addition, new uses for wood and wood products are continually being found. Meeting this growing demand requires an increasing supply of timber and pulp. Forestry technicians who specialize in land management and the various aspects of logging and sawmill work will play a valuable role in assuring this supply. Research technicians who help find improved methods of planting, growing, and timber and pulp production will be needed in greater numbers.

FOR MORE INFORMATION

For information on forests in the United States and to read selections from American Forests *magazine, visit American Forests' Web site.*

American Forests
PO Box 2000
Washington, DC 20013-2000
Tel: 202-773-1944
Email: info@amfor.org
http://www.americanforests.org

The NWF's Web site provides information on conservation, jobs, and the online Conservation Directory, *a directory of environmental groups around the country and the world. The* Conservation Directory *is also available in print form.*

National Wildlife Federation (NWF)
11100 Wildlife Center Drive
Reston, VA 20190-5362
Tel: 800-822-9919
http://www.nwf.org

For a list of recognized associate degree programs and other information on careers in forestry, contact

Society of American Foresters
5400 Grosvenor Lane

Bethesda, MD 20814-2198
Tel: 866-897-8720
Email: safweb@safnet.org
http://www.safnet.org

For information about government careers in forestry, contact
USDA Forest Service
1400 Independence Avenue, SW
Washington, DC 20250-0003
Tel: 202-205-8333
http://www.fs.fed.us

☐ FRANCHISE OWNERS

OVERVIEW

A franchise owner contracts with a company to sell that company's products or services. After paying an initial fee and agreeing to pay the company a certain percentage of revenue, the franchise owner can use the company's name, logo, and guidance. McDonald's, Subway, and KFC are some of the top franchised companies that have locations all across the country. Franchises, however, are not limited to the fast food industry. Today, franchises are available in a wide variety of business areas including computer service, lawn care, real estate, and even hair salons. According to the International Franchise Association (IFA), franchises generate 18 million jobs in the United States and yield more than $1.5 trillion in economic output a year.

THE JOB

Today, industry experts report that franchises are responsible for nearly 50 percent of all retail sales in the United States, and this figure is expected to grow through the 21st century. Franchisers (those companies that sell franchise businesses) and franchisees (those who buy the businesses) are sharing in the more than $1.5 trillion a year that franchise businesses take in. While everyone probably has a favorite business or two—maybe the neighborhood Krispy Kreme with its fresh crullers or the 7-11 market down the street with its gallon-sized sodas—not everyone may realize that these are franchised establishments. For those interested in starting their own businesses, becoming franchisees may offer just the right mix of risk and security. Any new business

---

QUICK FACTS

SCHOOL SUBJECTS
Business
Mathematics

PERSONAL SKILLS
Following instructions
Leadership/management

WORK ENVIRONMENT
Primarily indoors
Primarily one location

MINIMUM EDUCATION LEVEL
Some postsecondary training

MEDIAN SALARY
Varies widely

CERTIFICATION OR LICENSING
Required by certain franchisers (certification)
Required by certain states (licensing)

OUTLOOK
About as fast as the average

---

venture comes with a certain amount of risk, but franchises offer the new owners the security of a name and product that customers are used to and are willing to seek out. Someone with money to invest, the willingness to work hard and sometimes long hours, and the desire to operate a retail business may be able to become the successful franchisee, sharing in the franchiser's success.

There's a franchise for practically every type of product and service imaginable. In addition to the familiar McDonald's and Burger King, other franchise operations exist: businesses that offer temporary employment services, maid services, weight control centers, and custom picture framing, to name a few. The IFA, in fact, reports that there are approximately 75 different industries that make use of the franchise system. No matter what business a person is interested in, there are probably franchise opportunities available.

Depending on the size and nature of the franchise, owners' responsibilities will differ. Those who are able to make a large initial investment may also be able to hire managers and staff members to assist them. Those running a smaller business will need to handle most, if not all, of the job responsibilities themselves. Though there should be assistance from the franchiser in terms of training, marketing guidance, and established business systems, the business is essentially the franchisee's own. The franchisee has paid an initial franchise fee, makes royalty payments to the franchiser, purchased equipment, and rented business space. Any franchisee must handle administrative details, such as record keeping, creating budgets, and preparing reports for the franchiser. A franchisee is also responsible for hiring (and firing) employees, scheduling work hours, preparing payroll, and keeping track of inventory. Using the franchiser's marketing methods, the franchisee advertises the business. The practices and systems of franchisers differ, so those interested in this work need to carefully research the franchise before buying into it.

Some owners work directly with the clientele. Of course, someone who owns multiple units of the McDonald's franchise probably won't be taking orders at the counter; but someone who owns a single unit of a smaller operation, like a pool maintenance service, may be actively involved in the work at hand, in dealing with the customers, and in finding new customers.

Donna Weber of Redmond, Washington, owns a Jazzercise franchise. Jazzercise is the world's largest dance fitness franchise corporation, with more than 7,200 instructors leading 32,000 classes weekly. "I own and teach seven Jazzercise classes a week in two suburbs around the Seattle area," Weber says. After investing with an initial low franchise fee, Weber went through considerable training and testing; the training involves instruction on exercise physiology, dance/exercise technique, and safety issues, as well as instruction on the business aspect of owning a franchise. After training, Weber received certification and started her business. She pays a monthly fee to Jazzercise and in return receives choreography notes to new songs and videos demonstrating the exercises.

In addition to conducting classes, Weber spends some part of every workday preparing paperwork for the corporate headquarters. "I keep track of my students' attendance and write personal postcards to those I haven't seen in a while, those who are having birthdays, those who need some personal recognition for a job well done, etc.," says Weber, who must also regularly learn new routines. "I teach three different formats," she says, "regular aerobics, step, and a circuit-training class each week, so there is a lot of prep to do a good, safe class."

The franchisee's experience will be affected by the name recognition of the business. If it's a fairly new business, the franchisee may have to take on much of the responsibility of promoting it. If it is a well-established business, customers and clients already know what to expect from the operation.

REQUIREMENTS
High School

Business, math, economics, and accounting courses will be the most valuable to you in preparing for franchise ownership. Before buying into a franchise, you'll have to do a lot of research into the company, analyzing local demographics to determine whether a business is a sound investment. English classes will help you develop the research skills you'll need. In addition, you will need to hone your communication skills, which will be essential in establishing relationships with franchisers and customers. Take computer classes since it is virtually impossible to work in today's business world without knowing how to use a computer or the Web. If you already know of a particular area that interests you—such as food service, fashion, or fitness—take classes that will help you learn more about it. Such classes may include home economics, art, dance, or physical education.

Postsecondary Training

Because there are such a variety of franchise opportunities available, there is no single educational path for everyone to take on the road to owning a franchise. Keep in mind, however, that when franchisers review your application for the right to purchase a unit, they'll take into consideration your previous experience in the area. Obviously, a real estate company is unlikely to take a risk on you if you've never had any experience as a broker. In addition, there are some franchise opportunities that require degrees; for example, to own an environmental consulting agency, a business that helps companies meet government environmental standards, you'll have to be an engineer or geologist. But there are also many companies willing to sell to someone wanting to break into a new business. Franchisers will often include special training as part of the initial franchise fee.

Experts in the field stress the importance of gaining work experience before starting out with your own business. Hone your sales, management, and people skills and take the time to learn about the industry that interests you. Even if you don't plan on getting a college degree, consider taking some college-level courses in subjects such as business and finance. One recent survey of franchisees found that more than 80 percent had attended college or had a college degree. This reflects the fact that many franchisees have worked for many years in other professions in order to have the money and security needed for starting new businesses. Some organizations and schools, for example, the Schulze School of Entrepreneurship at the University of St. Thomas (http://www.stthomas.edu/cob/schoolofentrepreneurship/default.html), offer courses for prospective franchisees.

Certification or Licensing

Some franchisers have their own certification process and require their franchisees to go through training. You may also want to receive the certified franchise executive credential offered by the Institute of Certified Franchise Executives, an organization affiliated with the IFA. This certification involves completing a certain number of courses in topics such as economics and franchise law, participating in events such as seminars or conventions, and work experience. Although certification is voluntary, it will show your level of education and commitment to the field as well as give you the opportunity to network with other franchise professionals.

You may also need to obtain a small business license to own a franchise unit in your state. Regulations vary depending on the state and the type of business, so it is important that you check with your state's licensing board for specifics before you invest in a franchise.

Other Requirements

As with any small business, you need self-motivation and discipline in order to make your franchise unit successful. Though you'll have some help from your franchiser, the responsibilities of ownership are your own. You'll also need a good credit rating to be eligible for a bank loan, or you'll need enough money of your own for the initial investment. You should be fairly cautious—many people are taken every year in fraudulent franchise schemes. But at the same time, you should feel comfortable taking some risks.

EXPLORING

One relatively easy way to learn about franchising is to do some research on the Web. The International Franchise Association, for example, hosts a very informative Web site (http://www.franchise.org). The association also offers the magazine *Franchising World*. Also, check out your public library or bookstores for the many business magazines that report on small business opportunities. Many of these magazines, such as *Entrepreneur* (http://www.entrepreneur.com), publish special editions dealing specifically with franchises.

Join your high school's business club, a group that may give you the opportunity to meet business leaders in your community. Find a local franchise owner and ask to meet with him or her for an informational interview. Discuss the pros and cons of franchise ownership, find out about the owner's educational and professional background, and ask them for general advice. Also, most franchise companies will send you brochures about their franchise opportunities. Request some information and read about what's involved in owning a franchise unit.

Think about what industry interests you, such as services, fast food, health and fitness, or computers. Come up with your own ideas for a franchise business and do some research to find out if this business already exists. If it does, there may be a part-time or summer job opportunity there for you. If it doesn't, keep the idea in mind for your future but go ahead and get some work experience now. Many franchises hire high school students, and even if you end up working at a Subway when what you're really interested in is lawn care, you'll still be gaining valuable experience dealing with customers, handling sales, and working with others.

EMPLOYERS

There are a number of franchise directories available that list hundreds of franchise opportunities in diverse areas. While some franchisers sell units all across the country, others only do business in a few states. Some of the most successful franchises can guarantee franchisees great revenue, but these franchise units can require hundreds of thousands of dollars in initial investment.

Many franchisees own more than one franchise unit with a company; some even tie two different franchises together in a practice called "cross-branding." For example, a franchisee may own a pizza franchise, as well as an ice cream franchise housed in the same restaurant. Another combination owners find popular is having a convenience store that also houses a fast food outlet.

STARTING OUT

Before you invest a cent, or sign any papers, you should do extensive research into the franchise, particularly if it's a fairly new company. There are many disreputable franchise operations, so you need to be certain of what you're investing in. Lawyers and franchise consultants offer their services to assist people in choosing franchises; some consultants also conduct seminars. The Federal Trade Commission (FTC) publishes *The FTC Consumer Guide to Buying a Franchise* and other relevant publications. The IFA also provides free franchise-buying advice.

You'll need money for the initial franchise fee and for the expenses of the first few years of business. You may pursue a loan from a bank, from business associates, or you may use your own savings. In some cases your start-up costs will be very low; in others you'll need money for a computer, rental of work space, equipment, signs, and staff. According to the IFA, total start-up costs can range from $20,000 or less to more than $1 million, depending on the franchise selected and whether it is necessary to own or lease real estate to operate the business. Moreover, the initial franchise fee for most franchisers is between $20,000 and $28,000.

Some franchises can cost much less. Donna Weber's Jazzercise franchise required an initial $600 franchise fee. Though her business has been successful, she must share her gross income. "Twenty percent of that goes back to Jazzercise each month as a fee, I pay about 23 percent of the gross for monthly rent, and 8.6 percent to the state of Washington for sales tax collected on the price of my tickets. There are lots of women grossing $75,000 a year doing this, and there are some who choose to do this for fun and make nothing in return. It's all in how you make it work for you."

ADVANCEMENT

A new franchise unit usually takes a few years to turn profitable. Once the business has proven a success, franchisees may choose to invest in other franchise units with the same company. Franchise owners may also be able to afford to hire management and other staff to take on some of the many responsibilities of the business.

EARNINGS

The earnings for franchisees vary greatly, depending on such factors as the type of franchise they own, the amount of money a franchisee was able to initially invest without taking a loan, the franchise's location, and the number of franchise units the franchisee owns. An International Franchise Association survey of 1,000 franchise owners found that the average yearly salary of this group was $91,630. Approximately 24 percent made more than $100,000 annually.

Since franchisees run their own businesses, they generally do not have paid sick days or holidays. In addition, they are typically responsible for providing their own insurance and retirement plans.

WORK ENVIRONMENT

Owning a franchise unit can be demanding, requiring work of 60 to 70 hours a week, but owners have the satisfaction of knowing that their business's success is a result of their own hard work. Some people look for franchise opportunities that are less demanding and may only require a part-time commitment.

Franchise owners who handle all the business details personally may consider this work to be very stressful. In addition, dealing with the hiring, management, and sometimes firing of staff can also be difficult. In some situations, much of a franchisee's work will be limited to an office setting; in other situations, such as with a home inspection service or a maid service, the franchisee drives to remote sites to work with clients. Some franchises are mobile in nature, and these will involve a lot of traveling within a designated region.

OUTLOOK

While some experts say that the success rate of franchises is very high and a great deal of money can be made with a franchise unit, others say franchising isn't as successful as starting an independent business. According to the U.S. Department of Commerce, less than 5 percent of franchised outlets have failed each year since 1971. However, when reporting figures, franchisers don't always consider a unit as failing if it is under different ownership, but still in operation. The employment outlook will depend on factors such as the economy—a downturn in the economy is always most difficult for new businesses—as well as the type of franchise. Overall, though, growth should be steady and about as fast as the average.

FOR MORE INFORMATION

For information about buying a franchise and a list of AAFD-accredited franchisers, contact

American Association of Franchisees & Dealers (AAFD)
PO Box 81887
San Diego, CA 92138-1887
Tel: 800-733-9858
Email: Benefits@aafd.org
http://www.aafd.org

Visit the FTC's Web site for information on franchising, including the publication A Consumer Guide to Buying a Franchise.

Federal Trade Commission (FTC)
600 Pennsylvania Avenue, NW

Washington, DC 20580-0002
Tel: 202-326-2222
http://www.ftc.gov

For more information on franchising as well as a free newsletter, contact

FranchiseHelp
101 Executive Boulevard, 2nd Floor
Elmsford, NY 10523-1316
Tel: 800-401-1446
Email: company@franchisehelp.com
http://www.franchisehelp.com

For general information about franchising, specific franchise opportunities, and publications, contact the IFA

International Franchise Association (IFA)
1501 K Street, NW, Suite 350
Washington, DC 20005-1412
Tel: 202-628-8000
http://www.franchise.org

☐ FUNERAL HOME WORKERS

QUICK FACTS

SCHOOL SUBJECTS
Biology
Business
Psychology

PERSONAL SKILLS
Helping/teaching
Leadership/management

WORK ENVIRONMENT
Primarily indoors
One location with some travel

MINIMUM EDUCATION LEVEL
Some postsecondary training

MEDIAN SALARY
$49,620 (funeral directors); $37,480 (embalmers)

CERTIFICATION OR LICENSING
Required

OUTLOOK
About as fast as the average

OVERVIEW

The funeral director, also called a *mortician* or *undertaker*, handles all the arrangements for burial and funeral services of the deceased, in accordance with family's wishes. This includes the removal of the body to the funeral home, securing information and filing for the death certificate, and organizing the service and burial plans. The director also supervises the personnel who prepare bodies for burial. An *embalmer* uses chemical solutions to disinfect, preserve, and restore the body and employs cosmetic aids to simulate a lifelike appearance. A *mortuary science technician* works under the direction of a funeral director to perform embalming and related funeral service tasks. Most are trainees working to become licensed embalmers and funeral directors. *Funeral attendants* perform various tasks during a funeral such as arranging flowers and lighting around the casket, escorting mourners during services, and issuing and storing funeral equipment before and after services.

Funeral home workers are employed throughout the world in small communities as well as large metropolitan areas. Because cultures and religions affect burial customs, funeral home workers must be sensitive and knowledgeable to these differences.

There are approximately 29,000 funeral directors, 9,000 embalmers, and 33,000 funeral attendants employed in the United States.

THE JOB

Funeral directors are responsible for all the details related to the funeral ceremony and burial. The law determines some of their tasks, such as compliance with sanitation and health-related standards. Other responsibilities are administrative and logistical, such as securing information and filing the death certificate. Finally, custom and practice dictate some tasks.

Directors handle all the paperwork that needs to be filed, such as the death certificate, obituary notices, and may even assist the family in applying for the transfer of insurance policies, pensions, or other funds.

They assist the family of the deceased in the choice of casket, type of funeral service, and preparation of the remains, which may be burial, cremation, or entombment. Part of the director's job is to be a caregiver and, at times, a counselor. They must deal respectfully and sympathetically with families of the deceased, guiding them through decisions they may not be prepared to make and taking great care that their wishes are carried out.

First, the funeral director arranges for the body to be transported to the funeral home. The director then makes complete arrangements for the funeral ceremony, determining first the place and time of the service. If there is to be a religious ceremony, it is the director's responsibility to contact the appropriate clergy. Directors oversee the selection and playing of music, notify pallbearers, and arrange the placement of the casket and floral displays in the viewing parlor or chapel. If a service is held in the funeral home, the director arranges seating for guests. After the service, the director organizes the procession of cars to the cemetery, or wherever arrangements have been made for the disposal of remains. Funeral directors may have to make arrangements for transporting a body to another state for burial.

Most directors are also trained, licensed, and practicing embalmers. Embalming is a required sanitary process done to the body within 24 hours of death to preserve the remains for burial services. If a body is not being autopsied, it is brought to a funeral home where it is washed with a germicidal soap. The body is placed in a lifelike position, and an incision is made in a major artery and vein where a tube pumps a preservative and disinfectant solution through the entire circulatory system. Circulation of the chemical solution eventually replaces all blood with the embalming fluid. In addition, embalmers remove all other gases and liquids from the body, replacing it with disinfectant chemicals for preservation.

The preparation of an autopsied body can be much more complex, depending on the condition of the deceased. The embalmer may repair disfigured parts of the body and improve the facial appearance, using wax, cotton, plaster of paris, and cosmetics. When the embalming process is complete, the body is dressed and put in a casket.

Mortuary science technicians assist directors and embalmers in the funeral home. They are usually involved in a training process that will ultimately lead to a job as a licensed funeral director, embalmer, or both. Technicians may assist in various phases of the embalming process. Since embalming fluids are available in different chemical compositions and color tints, learning the various formulas is one important part of the technician's job. The technician may also be responsible for helping in the application of cosmetics to the body to create a natural, lifelike appearance. It is important that they use the proper products and techniques for applying them, since the result must satisfy and comfort those who view the body. (In some funeral homes, a licensed cosmetologist called a *mortuary cosmetologist* may perform these cosmetic services.) After the cosmetic application is complete, the technician may assist with the dressing and placement of the body for the funeral service. Finally, the technician may be responsible for cleaning the embalming area and equipment in accordance with required standards of sanitation.

Mortuary science technicians may also perform duties related to the actual funeral service. They may prepare the casket for the service and transport it to the cemetery. They also assist in receiving and ushering mourners to their seats at the service, organizing and managing the funeral procession, or any other tasks that are necessary for the occasion.

Funeral attendants perform a variety of tasks during a funeral, including placing the casket in a chapel or parlor before the service, arranging flower offerings and lighting around the casket, escorting mourners, closing the casket after the services, and issuing and storing equipment used before, during, and after the service.

REQUIREMENTS
High School

If you are interested in entering the field of mortuary science, consider taking classes in algebra, chemistry, biology, physics, and any other laboratory courses available. In addition, a psychology class might be helpful since funeral home workers must deal with distraught families and friends of deceased persons.

Postsecondary Training

Almost all states require funeral service practitioners to have completed postsecondary training in mortuary science varying from nine months to four years. Several colleges and universities now offer two- and four-year programs in funeral service. The American Board of Funeral Service Education accredits about 55 mortuary science programs. A typical curriculum at a school of mortuary science would include courses in anatomy, embalming practices, funeral customs, psychology, accounting, and public health laws. Laboratory study is essential in many of the courses and can account for up to a quarter of the program.

After completion of at least a two-year program, the graduate can apply to work as a mortuary science technician. Graduates who want to obtain a license in either embalming or funeral directing must work as an apprentice in an established funeral home for one to three years, depending on the state's requirements. Some schools of mortuary science have arrangements with local area funeral homes to provide students with either a work-study program or a period of school-supervised funeral service work (residency or apprenticeship).

Rather than extensive post-secondary training, funeral attendants receive short-term, on-the-job training at the funeral home where they are employed.

Certification or Licensing

All states require embalmers and funeral directors to be licensed. Some states grant a combination single license covering the activity of both the embalmer and funeral director. In order to maintain licensure, a growing number of states require continuing education classes.

After successfully completing their formal education, including apprenticeship, prospective funeral service practitioners must pass a state board examination that usually consists of written and oral tests and demonstration of skills. Those who wish to practice in another state may have to pass that state's examination as well, although some states have reciprocity arrangements to waive this requirement.

Other Requirements

A strong sense of understanding, empathy, and a genuine desire to help people at a time of great stress are essential qualities for anyone wanting to work at a funeral home. Workers must be tactful and discrete in all contacts with the bereaved family and friends. Funeral service workers must always be compassionate and sympathetic, but also remain strong and confident to accomplish the necessary tasks of the job. Funeral home workers must also be good listeners. For example, when details such as cosmetics and clothing are discussed, they must be especially attentive to the client's wishes.

The work sometimes requires physical strength for lifting the deceased or their caskets. Good coordination is also needed to perform the precise procedures used in embalming, restoration, and cosmetology.

EXPLORING

Ask your high school guidance counselor for information on mortuary science or check out your public and school library for useful books, magazines, and pamphlets. Local funeral homes are the most direct source of information. Arrange a visit with a funeral director and embalming staff to learn about the nature of the work and the importance and intricacies of funeral service. After becoming acquainted with local funeral homes, ask around to see if you can work part time, handling either clerical or custodial duties. Finally, check out the organizations listed at the end of this article for more career information.

EMPLOYERS

Funeral directors are usually employed by a funeral home or are in the business themselves. There are about 29,000 funeral directors in the United States, approximately 20 percent of whom are self-employed. The majority of embalmers and mortuary science technicians are also employed by funeral homes, though a small amount work for hospitals and medical schools. Funeral attendants are generally employed by funeral homes as well. Employers for these professions are located worldwide.

STARTING OUT

After attending an accredited school of mortuary science for two to four years, beginning workers start out as a mortuary science technicians, working under the supervision of a licensed director or embalmer.

Most mortuary science schools provide placement assistance for graduates. Additionally, since many schools require internship programs, students are often able to obtain permanent jobs where they have trained.

ADVANCEMENT

For many years, most funeral homes were family businesses. Younger members of the family or their husbands or wives were expected to move up into managerial positions when the older members retired. This is changing, however, as the majority are entering the field today having no prior background or family connection. Therefore, the potential for advancement into managerial positions is considerably greater than in the past.

The natural progression in the field is from mortuary science technician to fully licensed embalmer, funeral director, or both. With licensing comes more opportunity for advancement. While many people who enter this field aspire to eventually own their own funeral homes, there are other possibilities as well. One advanced specialty, for example, is that of *trade embalmers*, who embalm under contract for funeral homes. Their work typically includes restorative treatment. Also, an increasing number specialize in selling funeral and burial arrangements in advance. Providing the option to make plans ahead of time can give clients peace of mind. Finally, with sufficient financial backing, funeral service practitioners may establish their own businesses or purchase a portion or all of an existing one.

The percentage of mortuary science graduates who pursue advancement outside the funeral home is small. However, opportunities do exist. Funeral supply manufacturers employ licensed funeral service personnel because of their familiarity with the products and their ability to handle technical problems. Workers may be employed in customer relations or product sales.

EARNINGS

Salaries of funeral home workers vary depending on experience, services performed, level of formal education, and location. According to the U.S. Department of Labor, the median annual salary for funeral directors was $49,620 in 2006. The lowest paid 10 percent earned less than $28,410 and the highest paid 10 percent earned more than $91,800 a year. The department also reports that embalmers earned a median annual salary of $37,480 in 2006. Salaries ranged from a low of $23,290 for the lowest paid 10 percent to a high of $59,900 or more per year for the highest paid 10 percent. Funeral attendants earned annual salaries ranging from less than $13,780 to more than $32,390 with median earnings of $20,350 in 2006.

According to the American Board of Funeral Service Education, starting salaries for new funeral service licensees often closely approximate those of starting teachers in the same community.

In some metropolitan areas, many funeral home employees are unionized; in these cases, salaries are determined by union contracts and are generally higher than regions in which employees have not organized a union.

Benefits may vary depending on the position and the employer.

WORK ENVIRONMENT

In firms employing two or more licensees, funeral workers generally have a set schedule of eight-hour days, five or six days a week. However, because services may be needed at any hour of the day or night, shifts are usually arranged so that someone is always available at night and on weekends.

In smaller firms, employees generally work long hours at odd times and often remain on call and within a short distance of the funeral home. Some may work in shifts, such as all days one week and all nights the next. Occasionally, overtime may be necessary.

Employees who transport bodies and accompany the funeral procession to the cemetery are frequently required to lift heavy weights and to be outdoors in inclement weather. Sometimes directors and embalmers must handle the remains of those who have died of contagious diseases, though the risk of infection, given the strict sanitary conditions required in all funeral homes, is minimal.

In this field, much of workers' time is spent trying to help families work through their grief. Because they are exposed daily to such intense emotion, as well as death and sometimes unpleasant or upsetting sights, there is the chance that the work may be depressing or emotionally draining. Employees need to be aware of that possibility and be able to approach situations philosophically and with a clear head.

Many who enter this field find that their occupation can be very rewarding because the work they do may help the family and friends of the deceased adjust at a time when they are greatly stressed by grief. They help provide an essential social service and one that, when well done, brings comfort and satisfaction.

OUTLOOK

Employment for funeral directors should grow about as fast as the average for all occupations through 2016. The need to replace those retiring (more directors are 55 or older than in other occupations) or leaving the profession will spur a demand for newly trained directors. Employment for embalmers and funeral attendants is predicted to grow faster than the average for all occupations through 2016.

Despite this demand, there are a limited number of employers in any geographical area, and it might be wise for prospective students to check with employers in their area to see what the chances for employment will be. If possible, students should try to arrange postgraduate employment while they are still in school.

Job security in the funeral service industry is relatively unaffected by economic downturns. Despite the flux and movement in the population, funeral homes are a stable institution. The average firm has been in its community for more than 40 years, and funeral homes with a history of over 100 years are not uncommon.

FOR MORE INFORMATION

For information on careers in the funeral service industry, colleges that offer programs in mortuary science, and scholarships, contact

American Board of Funeral Service Education

3432 Ashland Avenue, Suite U

St. Joseph, MO 64506-1333

Tel: 816-233-3747

Email: exdir@absfe.org

http://www.abfse.org

Visit the NFDA's Web site to read the career brochure Thinking about a Career in Funeral Service?

National Funeral Directors Association (NFDA)

13625 Bishop's Drive

Brookfield, WI 53005-6607

Tel: 800-228-6332

Email: nfda@nfda.org

http://www.nfda.org

GAMING OCCUPATIONS

QUICK FACTS

SCHOOL SUBJECTS

English

Mathematics

PERSONAL SKILLS

Communication/ideas

Following instructions

WORK ENVIRONMENT

Primarily indoors

Primarily one location

MINIMUM EDUCATION LEVEL

High school diploma

MEDIAN SALARY

$26,000

CERTIFICATION OR LICENSING

Required by all states

OUTLOOK

Much faster than the average

OVERVIEW

The gaming industry supports gambling as a form of recreation in such venues as traditional casinos, riverboats, Native American reservation casinos, racing tracks, and state lotteries. Gaming employees, running the gamut from entry-level service workers to game dealers to casino and track managers, are needed to keep such facilities operating smoothly. The American Gaming Association claims that the gaming industry employs approximately 354,000 workers, and that an additional 450,000 workers are employed in related businesses. The U.S. Department of Labor estimates that gaming services workers hold approximately 174,000 jobs.

THE JOB

The gaming industry relies on a variety of workers for specific customer services and operational tasks. One example of a service position is that of cashier. Cashiers may be categorized as either coin cashiers or change persons. Basically, these employees work in a cage or at a station on the gaming floor and make change and sell coins to patrons for slot machines. They may pay off slot machine jackpots and keep records of all transactions. At the end of each shift, they count and balance their money drawers. Cashiers also provide information to guests, call for cocktail servers to visit the slot area, and provide other customer services. The duties performed by cashiers in this capacity are similar to those of a host.

Cage cashiers sell gaming chips to patrons for roulette, card, and dice games. These workers operate the main cashier cage in the casino and act much like a banker. They may provide the slot cashiers with additional change. They take in cash, accept checks when appropriate, charge guests' credit cards for currency advances, and check credit references. Likewise, these workers must balance their cash drawers and keep records of their cash transactions.

Slot key persons, or *slot attendants,* coordinate and supervise the operation of slot machines. They must verify and handle payoffs for winnings, reset the slot machines, and refill the machines with money. Slot key persons must be able to make minor repairs or adjustments to the machines, as needed.

Dealers conduct the gaming tables for poker, blackjack, baccarat, craps, or roulette. These workers exchange real currency for casino currency, in the form of either chips or coins. They explain the rules of the game and wagering guidelines, ask patrons to place their bets, conduct the game, and make appropriate payoffs and collect losing bets. In poker the dealer shuffles and deals the cards to the players, and the casino takes its winnings as a percentage of the pot. *Blackjack dealers* deal themselves a hand of cards and try to win money for the "house," or the casino.

Games such as baccarat, craps, and roulette are conducted by more than one employee. Baccarat requires three dealers, two of whom collect money for bets and the third who calls the game rules. *Craps dealers* also collect money for bets at the game table and exchange money for chips. A manager called a *box person* supervises the exchange of money for chips, and another assistant, called the *stick handler,* collects the dice after they have been thrown, passing them to the next shooter. Because craps is a fast game, there is a greater potential for cheating, so three people work this particular table. *Roulette dealers* sell chips, take bets, spin the roulette wheel, toss the ball in, and announce the winners. In busy games, chips are collected, passed, racked, and sorted by color by the *chip mucker.*

Other game attendants include *keno runners,* who pick up keno tickets, money, and bet orders from patrons who are in the lounge or playing at another gaming table and deliver these to the *keno writer.* The keno writer calls the game, punches the game draw cards, and changes the paper color with each new game. The keno writer also takes players' tickets, makes copies, and checks or calculates payoffs at the request of players. *Runners* take the copies back to the players, check for winning tickets, take winning tickets to the payoff window, and return winnings to the players.

Bingo is another popular form of gambling that is found in many cities across the country. People who work in bingo parlors are *bingo paymasters,* who sell the playing cards and pay money to the winners, and *bingo callers,* who operate the device that chooses the numbers, call out the numbers, check winners' cards, and announce the payouts. Many parlors have *bingo package preparers* who put together packets of bingo cards and special games.

Shift supervisors, floor bosses, and *pit bosses* oversee the performance of the game attendants. Sometimes these workers monitor one or more game tables, while at other times this work is performed by staff dealers. Shift supervisors may be responsible for all the casino games being played during a shift.

The role of *casino hosts* is a visible one. They cover the gaming floor, greet guests, and make sure everyone is enjoying themselves. Some aspects of their job are similar to that of a hotel concierge. Customers may request that dinner or room reservations be made or tickets obtained for special casino functions. Some casinos have *executive casino hosts* designated to care for premium customers, especially high rollers.

"And they're off!" A good *race announcer* adds to the excitement of any race. Besides giving horse, owner, and trainer information prior to the start of the race, an announcer will declare each horse's final odds and racing colors. During the race, the announcer will give a detailed, neck-by-neck account of the race.

REQUIREMENTS
High School

For many positions in the gaming industry educational requirements are minimal, although a high school education is preferable and personal requirements such as good diction, reliability, a good memory, and personal motivation are necessary. Good mathematical skills for making change and calculating odds are also important. Most casinos have basic math tests all applicants must pass to be considered for employment. High school math, English, and speech classes will help you develop the skills necessary for this work.

Postsecondary Training

If you are interested in a job with a higher level of responsibility, consider obtaining an associate's or bachelor's degree, emphasizing courses in business management or hospitality. Some colleges and universities—such as Morrisville State College, Northeast Wisconsin Technical College, San Diego State University, and Tulane University—offer certificates or degrees in casino management, tribal gaming, and other areas.

Certification or Licensing

According to the government publication *Occupational Outlook Quarterly,* all gaming workers must be licensed by a regulatory agency such as the state gaming commission or control board. In addition, many schools in resort areas offer training classes that lead to certification for workers in specific games and skills. Other schools may offer certification to students who have learned all the games. This award is called a certificate of professional casino croupier and can prepare an employee for nearly any game table position. In most states, applicants must have a license, or gaming badge, in order to participate in a training session.

Each casino establishes its own requirements for the training employees must have, but many casinos now offer in-house training programs to promising employees at no charge. Kim Torri, a games trainer for Empress Casinos, says eligible candidates must be employees of the casino for no shorter than three months, pass a math test, have a license from the Illinois Gaming Board (or the gaming board in their state), and have an excellent work record and recommendations. Openings at this particular training program are determined by the casino's demand for new dealers. Dealers are taught game rules, shuffling and dealing techniques, and the house regulations and procedures. In the game of blackjack, they learn to control and protect the table. Certain bases, the first and last seats at the table especially, are vulnerable to cheating.

Completion of the training program will not automatically land you a job. Dealers must showcase their skills and training at a casino game audition. Competition for good jobs is usually intense. Though some casinos only require good casino work experience as a prerequisite of their employees, your best bet will be to get certification.

Union representation for gaming workers is very strong in Las Vegas and less strong in Atlantic City. Work permits are required in both locations. The minimum age for receiving work permits is 21. Some casinos require FBI fingerprint clearance for gaming workers, and many require their employees to be bonded. Prospective employees must also have no criminal background.

Other Requirements

People in this industry must be able to work in hectic, stressful environments and enjoy meeting and working with a wide variety of people. Workers should have good communication skills, be pleasant and courteous, and enjoy their work. Quick thinking and calculating skills are necessary in almost all positions in a casino. Workers must also be responsible, alert, and completely trustworthy, since they work around large amounts of money.

Workers should understand the importance of giving good service to guests and be able to handle frustrated, unruly, or angry patrons with tact. They may face the prospect of dealing with people who do not know when to stop gambling. Rogelio Dizon, a dealer at an Illinois casino, offers the following advice: "Don't be shy, and be prepared to deal with all kinds of people and their levels of gambling experience." Dizon's training has taught him to spot potential problems and notify management without creating a disturbance in the casino.

EXPLORING

Because casino gambling and employment is generally restricted to people who are at least 18 or 21 years old, it is very difficult for high school students to get first-hand experience in this field. Most casino jobs for a high school student will be limited to those in gift shops and eateries. However, part-time and summer jobs in restaurants, hotels, amusement parks, and other areas of the hospitality and entertainment industries will give you a feel for working with the public. Cashier jobs are also good ways to gain experience in handling money. Participating in school fairs, carnivals, state fairs, and other places where skill-type games are played may also offer insight into the gaming industry.

Potential sources for information for this occupation include individual casinos, the departments of tourism in the states that allow gambling, and hotel and motel associations. Don't forget to consult the horse racing industry and the American Gaming Association. Casinos can offer information about the types of jobs available for skilled or unskilled workers. You can also consult your local library for information on the gambling industry.

STARTING OUT

Applicants should contact the personnel officers of casinos, hotels, and resorts for information on openings and entry-level requirements. Previous experience may be difficult to obtain if the applicant lives in an area that prohibits gambling. Previous work experience in the hospitality industry, however, is a big advantage for beginners. Applicants may want to contact casinos prior to the heavy vacation season or be willing to accept part-time employment and work their way up. Many casino schools have job placement services for their graduates. Check for this perk before enrolling.

ADVANCEMENT

Advancement often comes to employees who demonstrate professionalism, have self-confidence, and establish good work records. Part-time employees may be offered full-time positions as slot cashiers or keno runners, who may advance to become cage cashiers or keno writers. Dealers generally begin at minimum wager tables and advance to tables featuring higher stakes as they gain experience and sharpen their skills.

Most supervisory positions require additional education and training as well as experience in the casino. Positions such as executive casino host, casino manager, or director of table games, require leadership, managerial skills, and keen perception. Experienced supervisors with advanced education can move into management positions in other fields such as hospitality or tourism. Another option is to become a casino games trainer.

EARNINGS

Wages for this occupation vary depending on the job. The latest survey conducted by the American Gaming Association found the national average salary for gaming employees to be about $26,000, including benefits and tips. Table dealers for such games as blackjack, craps, and poker are paid on an hourly basis, but their wages are greatly supplemented by customers' tips. According to 2006 U.S. Department of Labor data, gaming dealers earned a median salary of $14,730; gaming and sport book writers and runners, $18,800; gaming change persons and booth cashiers, $20,675; slot key workers, $22,720; gaming cage workers, $23,150; gaming supervisors, $41,160; and gaming managers, $62,820.

Unlike most professions, the weekend and evening hours are the prime shift for a gaming worker, because these shifts are the busiest playing times and generally bring in the most tips. "Tips are pooled together," says Rogelio Dizon, "and divided evenly among all employees from that shift."

Benefits may include gift shop discounts, health insurance, paid vacations, additional compensation for working holidays, and pension plans. Some casinos provide uniforms, usually a tuxedo or a vest, at a discount, or free of charge.

WORK ENVIRONMENT

Some gaming workers may sit while working, but most remain on their feet throughout their shift. Dealers stationed at handicapped tables are able to sit since such tables are positioned lower than others to accommodate wheelchairs. Because many casinos operate 24 hours a day, workers may be assigned to work late at night. Weekend work is common, but these shifts are usually preferred, because there are usually more players, and therefore, more tips.

While casinos are usually pleasant, comfortable, and attractive places, the activity inside them may result in considerable noise and potential distraction. This can cause stress in many people, as can the emotions of players who are on a losing streak. Employees must concentrate for long periods of time, work quickly, and often have little opportunity to talk with the gamblers. Many games rely on hand signals or short phrases for communication, so the worker must remain alert at all times. Many casinos have designated smoke-free areas, though most high stakes tables are located in smoking sections. This is a disadvantage for people sensitive to cigarette smoke. Evening hours are the busiest and may remain busy until early hours of the morning. Numerous breaks are necessary to relieve the stress. Rogelio Dizon and his fellow dealers are given 20-minute breaks every hour.

OUTLOOK

The public's interest in gambling, new gaming venues, and the growth of casinos throughout the country will keep this industry growing much faster than the average for all occupations through 2016, according to the U.S. Department of Labor. The newer casinos, particularly in Las Vegas, are larger than ever before, and many casinos are open until late in the evening or 24 hours a day. Where employment in the gaming industry was formerly limited to Nevada, and later, Atlantic City, opportunities are now available in almost every region of the country. Many Native American tribes around the country, exercising their rights as sovereign nations, have established large casinos that attract many customers to their territories. There are 423 Indian gaming operations with 249 tribal/state compacts in 28 states, according to the National Indian Gaming Association. Some of the most successful Native American casinos include the Foxwoods Resort Casino in Connecticut and the Mystic Lake Casino in Minnesota.

The growing number and size of casinos will increase demand for qualified employees to work service and managerial positions. In addition, many casinos take on additional employees during their busy seasons, and many opportunities are available for part-time as well as full-time employees.

Opportunities for cage cashiers will grow about as fast as the average as more casinos incorporate technology that reduces the amount of cash managed by employees. There is a high level of turnover in this particular occupation, which will create some openings as cage cashiers pursue other gaming or leave the field for other opportunities.

FOR MORE INFORMATION

For background information regarding the gaming industry, and salary and industry figures, contact
American Gaming Association
1299 Pennsylvania Avenue, NW, Suite 1175
Washington, DC 20004-2400
Tel: 202-552-2675
Email: info@americangaming.org
http://www.americangaming.org

For information on the Native American gambling industry, contact
National Indian Gaming Association
224 2nd Street, SE

Washington, DC 20003-1943

Tel: 202-546-7711

Email: info@indiangaming.org

http://www.indiangaming.org

For information regarding vocational training as a dealer, contact

Reno Tahoe Dealers School and Bartenders School

3702 South Virginia Street, Suite H2

Reno, NV 89502-6034

Tel: 775-329-5665

http://www.renodealingschool.com

For casino salary information in Nevada, contact

Nevada Department of Employment, Training and Rehabilitation

Information Development and Processing

Research and Analysis Bureau

500 East Third Street

Carson City, NV 89713-0001

Tel: 775-684-0450

http://detr.state.nv.us

❑ GENERAL MAINTENANCE MECHANICS

QUICK FACTS

SCHOOL SUBJECTS

Mathematics

Technical/shop

PERSONAL SKILLS

Mechanical/manipulative

Technical/scientific

WORK ENVIRONMENT

Indoors and outdoors

Primarily one location

MINIMUM EDUCATION LEVEL

High school diploma

MEDIAN SALARY

$31,910

CERTIFICATION OR LICENSING

Voluntary

OUTLOOK

About as fast as the average

OVERVIEW

General maintenance mechanics, sometimes called *maintenance technicians* or *building engineers,* repair and maintain machines, mechanical equipment, and buildings, and work on plumbing, electrical, and controls. They also do minor construction or carpentry work and routine preventive maintenance to keep the physical structures of businesses, schools, factories, and apartment buildings in good condition. They also maintain and repair specialized equipment and machinery found in cafeterias, laundries, hospitals, offices, and factories. There are approximately 1.4 million general maintenance mechanics employed in the United States, working in almost every industry.

THE JOB

General maintenance mechanics perform almost any task that may be required to maintain a building or the equipment in it. They may be called on to replace faulty electrical outlets, fix air-conditioning motors, install water lines, build partitions, patch plaster or drywall, open clogged drains, dismantle, clean, and oil machinery, paint windows, doors, and woodwork, repair institutional-size dishwashers or laundry machines, and see to many other problems. Because of the diverse nature of the responsibilities of maintenance mechanics, they have to know how to use a variety of materials and be skilled in the use of most hand tools and ordinary power tools. They also must be able to recognize when they cannot handle a problem and must recommend that a specialized technician be called.

General maintenance mechanics work in many kinds of settings. Mechanics who work primarily on keeping industrial machines in good condition may be called *factory maintenance workers* or *mill maintenance workers,* while those mechanics that concentrate on the maintenance of a building's physical structure may be called *building maintenance workers and technicians.*

Once a problem or defect has been identified and diagnosed, maintenance mechanics must plan the repairs. They may consult blueprints, repair manuals, and parts catalogs to determine what to do. They obtain supplies and new parts from a storeroom or order them from a distributor. They install new parts in place of worn or broken ones, using hand tools, power tools, and sometimes, electronic test devices and other specialized equipment. In some situations, maintenance mechanics may fix an old part or even fabricate a new part. To do this, they may need to set up and operate machine tools, such as lathes or milling machines, and operate gas- or arc-welding equipment to join metal parts together.

One of the most important kinds of duties general maintenance mechanics perform is routine preventive maintenance to correct defects before machinery breaks down or a building begins to deteriorate. This type of maintenance keeps small problems from turning into large, expensive ones. Mechanics often inspect machinery on a regular schedule, perhaps following a checklist that includes such items as inspecting belts, checking fluid levels, replacing filters, oiling moving parts, and so forth. They keep records of the repair work done and the inspection dates. Repair and inspection records can be important evidence of compliance with insurance requirements and government safety regulations.

New buildings often have computer-controlled systems, so mechanics that work in them must have basic computer skills. For example, newer buildings might have light sensors that are electronically controlled and automatically turn lights on and off. The maintenance mechanic has to understand how to make adjustments and repairs.

In small establishments, one mechanic may be the only person working in maintenance, and thus may be responsible for almost any kind of repair. In large establishments, however, tasks may be divided among several mechanics. For example, one mechanic may be assigned to install and set up new equipment, while another may handle preventive maintenance.

REQUIREMENTS
High School

Many employers prefer to hire helpers or mechanics who are high school graduates, but a diploma is not always required. High school courses that will prepare you for this occupation include mechanical drawing, metal shop, electrical shop, woodworking, blueprint reading, general science, computer science, and applied mathematics.

Postsecondary Training

Some mechanics learn their skills by working as helpers to people employed in building trades, such as electricians or carpenters. Other mechanics attend trade or vocational schools that teach many of the necessary skills. Becoming fully qualified for a mechanic's job usually requires one to four years of on-the-job training or classroom instruction, or some combination of both.

Certification or Licensing

There are some certification and training programs open to maintenance mechanics. The BOMI Institute International, for example, offers the designation of systems maintenance technician (SMT) to applicants who have completed courses in boilers, heating systems, and applied mathematics; refrigeration systems and accessories; air handling, water treatment, and plumbing systems; electrical systems and illumination; and building control systems. Technicians who have achieved SMT status can go on and become certified as systems maintenance administrators (SMAs) by taking further classes in building design and maintenance, energy management, and supervision. The Association for Facilities Engineering offers the certified plant engineer and certified plant maintenance manager designations to applicants who pass an examination and satisfy job experience requirements. While not necessarily required for employment, employees with certification may become more valuable assets to their employers and may have better chances at advancement.

Other Requirements

General maintenance mechanics need to have good manual dexterity and mechanical aptitude. People who enjoy taking things apart and putting them back together are good candidates for this position. Since some of the work, such as reaching, squatting, and lifting, requires physical strength and stamina, reasonably good health is necessary. Mechanics also need the ability to analyze and solve problems and to work effectively on their own without constant supervision.

EXPLORING

Shop classes can give you a good indication of your mechanical aptitude and of whether or not you would enjoy maintenance work. The best way to experience the work these mechanics do, however, is to get a summer or part-time job as a maintenance helper in a factory, apartment complex, or similar setting. If such a job is not available, you might try talking with a maintenance mechanic to get a fuller, more complete picture of his or her responsibilities.

EMPLOYERS

General maintenance mechanics are employed in factories, hospitals, schools, colleges, hotels, offices, stores, malls, gas and electric companies, government agencies, and apartment buildings throughout the United States. Statistics from the U.S. Department of Labor indicate that there are approximately 1.4 million people in the field. Approximately 20 percent are employed in manufacturing industries. Others are employed in service industries, such as elementary and secondary schools, colleges and universities, hospitals and nursing homes, and hotels, office and apartment buildings, government agencies, and utility companies.

STARTING OUT

General maintenance mechanics usually start as helpers to experienced mechanics and learn their skills on the job. Beginning helpers are given the simplest jobs, such as changing light bulbs or making minor drywall repairs. As general maintenance mechanics acquire skills, they are assigned more complicated work, such as troubleshooting malfunctioning machinery.

Job seekers in this field usually apply directly to potential employers. Information on job openings for mechanic's helpers can often be found through newspaper classified ads, school career services offices, and the local offices of the state employment service. Graduates of trade or vocational schools may be able to get referrals and information from their school's career services office. Union offices may also be a good place to learn about job opportunities.

ADVANCEMENT

Some general maintenance mechanics who are employed in large organizations may advance to supervisory positions. Another possibility is to move into one of the traditional building trades and become a craftworker, such as a plumber or electrician. In smaller organizations, opportunities for promotion are limited, although increases in pay may result from an employee's good performance and increased value to the employer.

EARNINGS

Earnings for general maintenance mechanics vary widely depending on skill, geographical location, and industry. The U.S. Department of Labor reports that general main-

tenance mechanics and repairers earned median annual salaries of $31,910 in 2006. Earnings ranged from less than $19,140 to more than $50,840.

Almost all maintenance mechanics receive a benefits package that includes health insurance, paid vacation, sick leave, and a retirement plan. Mechanics earn overtime pay for work in excess of 40 hours per week.

WORK ENVIRONMENT

General maintenance mechanics work in almost every industry and in a wide variety of facilities. In most cases, they work a 40-hour week. Some work evening or night shifts or on weekends; they may also be on call for emergency repairs. In the course of a single day, mechanics may do a variety of tasks in different parts of a building or in several buildings, and they may encounter different conditions in each spot. Sometimes they have to work in hot or cold conditions, on ladders, in awkward or cramped positions, among noisy machines, or in other uncomfortable places. Sometimes they must lift heavy weights. On the job, they must stay aware of potential hazards such as electrical shocks, burns, falls, and cuts and bruises. By following safety regulations and using tools properly, they can keep such risks to a minimum.

The mechanic who works in a small establishment may be the only maintenance worker and is often responsible for doing his or her job with little direct supervision. Those who work in larger establishments usually report to a maintenance supervisor who assigns tasks and directs their activities.

OUTLOOK

Employment of general maintenance mechanics is expected to grow about as fast as the average for all occupations through 2016, according to the U.S. Department of Labor. Although the rate of construction of new apartment and office buildings, factories, hotels, schools, and stores is expected to be slower than in the past, most of these facilities still require the services of maintenance mechanics. This is a large occupation with a high turnover rate. In addition to newly created jobs, many openings will arise as experienced mechanics transfer to other occupations or leave the labor force.

General maintenance mechanics who work for manufacturing companies may be subject to layoffs during bad economic times, when their employers are under pressure to cut costs. Most mechanics, however, are not usually as vulnerable to layoffs related to economic conditions.

FOR MORE INFORMATION

For information on certification, contact

Association for Facilities Engineering
12100 Sunset Hills Road, Suite 130
Reston, VA 20190-3221
Tel: 513-489 2473
Email: info@afe.org
http://www.afe.org

This organization provides education programs for commercial property professionals, including building engineers and technicians.

BOMA International
1101 15th Street, NW, Suite 800
Washington, DC 20005-5021
Tel: 202-408-2662
Email: info@boma.org
http://www.boma.org

For information on professional certifications, contact

BOMI Institute International
One Park Place, Suite 475
Annapolis, MD 21401-3479
Tel: 800-235-2664
Email: service@bomi-edu.org
http://www.bomi-edu.org

For information on general maintenance careers in building maintenance and construction, contact

Mechanical Contractors Association of America
1385 Piccard Drive
Rockville, MD 20850-4329
Tel: 301-869-5800
http://www.mcaa.org/careers

☐ GLAZIERS

OVERVIEW

Glaziers select, cut, fit, and install all types of glass and glass substitutes such as plastics. They install windows, mirrors, shower doors, glass tabletops, display cases, skylights, special items such as preassembled stained glass and leaded glass window panels, and many other glass items. There are approximately 55,000 glaziers employed in the United States.

THE JOB

Glaziers install different kinds of glass in different places. They put insulating glass where it is desirable to keep heat or sound on one side and laminated glass in doors and windows where safety is a concern. They install large structural glass panels on building exteriors to create walls that admit natural light. They install mirrors, storefronts, automobile windows, and sunroom additions to homes. Glaziers may also occasionally work with plastics, granite, marble, steel, and aluminum.

In most of these applications, the glass is precut to size in a shop or factory and comes to the work site mounted in a frame. Because glass is heavy and easily breakable, glaziers may need to use a hoist or a crane to move larger pieces into position. The glass is held with suction cups and gently guided into place.

When it is in place, glaziers often put the glass on a bed of putty or another kind of cement inside a metal or wooden frame and secure the glass with metal clips, metal or wooden molding, bolts, or other devices. They may put a rubber gasket around the outside edges to clamp the glass in place and make a moisture-proof seal. In windows, glaziers may pack a putty-like glazing compound into the joints at the edges of the glass in the molding that surrounds the open space. They trim off the excess compound with a glazing knife for a neat appearance.

Sometimes glaziers must manually cut glass to size at a work site. They put uncut glass on a rack or cutting table and measure and mark the cutting line. They use a cutting tool such as a small, sharp wheel of hard metal, which cuts the glass when rolled firmly over the surface. After making a cut, they break off the excess by hand or with a notched tool.

In some situations, glaziers cut and fasten together pieces of metal. When installing storefront windows, for example, they cut the drain moldings and face moldings that fit around the opening. They screw the drain molding into position and place plate glass into position against the metal. Then they bolt the face molding around the edges and attach metal corner pieces. When installing glass doors, they fit hinges and bolt on handles, locks, and other hardware.

Some workers in glazing occupations specialize in other kinds of glass installations. Among these workers are *aircraft safety glass installers*, who cut and install laminated safety glass in airplane windows and windshields; *auto glass installers*, who replace pitted or broken windows and windshields in motor vehicles; *refrigerator glaziers*, who install the plate glass windows in refrigerator display cases and walk-in coolers; and *glass installers*, who work in planing mills where they fit glass into newly manufactured millwork products, such as doors, window sashes, china cabinets, and office partitions.

REQUIREMENTS
High School

The best way for glaziers to learn their trade is by completing an apprenticeship program. Requirements for admission to apprenticeship programs are set by the local administrators of each program. Typically, applicants need to be high school graduates, at least 17 years old, in good physical condition, with proven mechanical aptitude. Some previous high school or vocational school courses in applied mathematics, shop, blueprint reading, and similar subjects are desirable as preparation for work in glazing occupations.

Postsecondary Training

Apprenticeships last three to four years and combine on-the-job training with classroom instruction in related subjects. Apprenticeship programs are operated by the National Glass Association in cooperation with local committees representing unions and employers or local contractor groups.

Apprentices spend roughly 6,000 hours working under the supervision of experienced glaziers in planned programs that teach all aspects of the trade. Apprentices learn how to use tools and equipment; how to handle, measure, cut, and install glass, molding, and metal framing; and how to install glass doors. Their formal classroom instruction, about 144 hours each year of the apprenticeship, covers subjects such as glass manufacturing, selecting glass for specific purposes, estimating procedures, mathematics, blueprint reading, construction techniques, safety practices, and first aid.

Many glaziers learn their skills informally on the job. They are hired in helper positions and gradually pick up skills as they assist experienced workers. When they start, they are assigned simple tasks, like carrying glass; later they may get the opportunity to cut glass and do other more complex tasks. Glaziers who learn informally on the job often do not receive as thorough training as apprentices do, and their training usually takes longer.

Certification and Licensing

The National Glass Association offers a voluntary certification program to glaziers. Applicants who satisfy specific work experience requirements and pass a written examination receive the designation, certified glass installer. Certification must be renewed every three years. The association also offers certification to auto glass replacement technicians and auto glass repair technicians.

QUICK FACTS

SCHOOL SUBJECTS
Mathematics
Technical/shop

PERSONAL SKILLS
Following instructions
Mechanical/manipulative

WORK ENVIRONMENT
Primarily indoors
Primarily multiple locations

MINIMUM EDUCATION LEVEL
Apprenticeship

MEDIAN SALARY
$34,610

CERTIFICATION OR LICENSING
Voluntary

OUTLOOK
About as fast as the average

Other Requirements

To be a successful glazier, you should have good eyesight, be in good physical condition, and not be afraid of heights. You should have excellent manual dexterity and be familiar with the tools and processes associated with this career. Strong communication skills will help you to work well with other glaziers and your supervisors.

EXPLORING

Hobbies that require manual dexterity, using a variety of hand tools, and attention to detail offer good experience. Working with stained glass, making decorative objects such as windowpanes, lampshades, and ornaments, is an excellent hobby for the prospective glazier.

For a more direct look at this career, you may be able to get a part-time or summer job as a helper at a construction site or in a glass shop. If this cannot be arranged, it may be possible to talk with someone employed in a glass shop or as a glazier in construction work to get an insider's view of the field.

EMPLOYERS

Most glaziers work in construction, renovation, and repair of buildings and are employed by construction companies, glass suppliers, or glazing contractors. A good number of glaziers work for manufacturers who need glass installed in some of their products. Many glaziers who work in construction are members of the International Union of Painters and Allied Trades, a labor union.

STARTING OUT

People who would like to enter this field either as apprentices or on-the-job trainees can obtain more information about local opportunities by contacting area glazing contractors, the local offices of the state employment service, or local offices of the International Union of Painters and Allied Trades. Information about apprenticeships may also be available through the state apprenticeship agency. Job leads for helper positions may also be listed in newspaper classified ads.

ADVANCEMENT

Experienced glaziers usually have only a few possible avenues for advancement. In some situations, they can move into supervisory positions, directing the work done by other glazing workers at construction sites or in shops or factories. Or they can become *estimators*, figuring the costs for labor and materials before jobs are done. Advancement for glaziers often consists of pay increases without changes in job activity.

EARNINGS

Earnings of glaziers vary substantially in different parts of the country. A recent study suggested that annual earnings can average from about $20,000 to about $40,000, depending on geographical location. Glaziers covered by union contracts generally earn more than nonunion workers. The U.S. Department of Labor reports that in 2006, median hourly earnings of glaziers were $16.64—or $34,610 annually. Hourly wages ranged from less than $10.19 ($21,190 annually) to $30.52 ($63,490 annually) or more. Glaziers in Chicago, Newark (N.J.), Santa Barbara and Oakland (Calif.), and St. Louis (Mo.) received the highest wages. However, bad weather, periods of unemployment, and other factors can mean that the number of hours glaziers work, and thus their real earnings, are considerably lower than the high hourly figures suggest.

Glaziers who work under union contracts usually make more money than workers who are not union members. Wages for apprentices usually start at approximately 40 to 50 percent of the skilled glazier's rate and increase every six months throughout the training period.

WORK ENVIRONMENT

Glaziers who are employed by construction companies, glass suppliers, or glazing contractors may have to drive trucks that carry glass and tools to and from job sites. Working on buildings may require them to be outdoors, sometimes in unpleasant weather. Bad weather can also cause the shutdown of job activities, limiting the hours glaziers work and thus also limiting their pay. Glaziers typically work 40-hour weeks and receive compensation for overtime.

Glaziers in construction often have to work at great heights, on scaffolding, or in buildings that are not yet completed. On the job, they must frequently bend, kneel, lift objects, and move about. The hazards they need to guard against include cuts from broken glass, falls from heights, and muscle strains caused by using improper techniques to lift heavy pieces of glass.

OUTLOOK

Due to growth in residential and nonresidential construction, employment in this field is expected to increase about as fast as the average for all occupations through 2016. Glass will most likely continue to be popular for its good looks and its practical advantages, and further improvements in glass and glass products may make glass still more desirable as a construction material. A growing focus on energy management and the growing trend toward the installation of safety glass in many government and commercial buildings, will also increase demand for qualified glaziers.

Nonetheless, glaziers who work in construction should realize that there will be variations from time to time and place to place in the opportunities available to them. They should expect to go through periods of unemployment, and they must plan for these times. During economic downturns, construction activity is significantly reduced, and jobs for construction craftworkers, including glaziers, become scarce. Also, construction jobs are almost always of limited length, and workers may be unemployed between projects. On the other hand, when the level of construction activity is high in a region, there may be more jobs available than there are skilled workers to fill them. In general, jobs will be most abundant in and around cities, where most glass shops and glazing contractors are located.

FOR MORE INFORMATION

For information about the career of glazier and apprentice-ships, contact

Construction Employers Association
950 Keynote Circle, Suite 10
Cleveland, OH 44131-1802
Tel: 216-398-9860
http://www.ceacisp.org

For information about union membership, contact

International Union of Painters and Allied Trades
1750 New York Avenue, NW
Washington, DC 20006-5301
Tel: 202-637-0700
http://www.iupat.org

For information on certification, contact

National Glass Association
8200 Greensboro Drive, Suite 302
McLean, VA 22102-3881
Tel: 866-342-5642
http://www.glass.org

For information on the glass industry, visit

Glasslinks.com
http://www.glasslinks.com

GRAPHIC DESIGNERS

OVERVIEW

Graphic designers are practical artists whose creations are intended to express ideas, convey information, or draw attention to a product. They design a wide variety of materials including advertisements, displays, packaging, signs, computer graphics and games, book and magazine covers and interiors, animated characters, and company logos to fit the needs and preferences of their various clients. There are approximately 261,000 graphic designers employed in the United States.

THE JOB

Graphic designers are not primarily fine artists, although they may be highly skilled at drawing or painting. Most designs commissioned to graphic designers involve both

---

QUICK FACTS

SCHOOL SUBJECTS
Art
Computer science

PERSONAL SKILLS
Artistic
Communication/ideas

WORK ENVIRONMENT
Primarily indoors
Primarily one location

MINIMUM EDUCATION LEVEL
Some postsecondary training

MEDIAN SALARY
$39,900

CERTIFICATION OR LICENSING
None available

OUTLOOK
About as fast as the average

---

artwork and copy (words). Thus, the designer must not only be familiar with the wide range of art media (photography, drawing, painting, collage, etc.) and styles, but he or she must also be familiar with a wide range of typefaces and know how to manipulate them for the right effect. Because design tends to change in a similar way to fashion, designers must keep up to date with the latest trends. At the same time, they must be well grounded in more traditional, classic designs.

Graphic designers can work as *in-house designers* for a particular company, as staff designers for a graphic design firm, or as *freelance designers* working for themselves. Some designers specialize in designing advertising materials or packaging. Others focus on corporate identity materials such as company stationery and logos. Some work mainly for publishers, designing book and magazine covers and page layouts. Some work in the area of computer graphics, creating still or animated graphics for computer software, videos, or motion pictures.

A highly specialized type of graphic designer, the *environmental graphic designer*, designs large outdoor signs. Depending on the project's requirements, some graphic designers work exclusively on the computer, while others may use both the computer and drawings or paintings created by hand.

Whatever the specialty and whatever their medium, all graphic designers take a similar approach to a project, whether it is for an entirely new design or for a variation on an existing one. Graphic designers begin by determining the needs and preferences of clients and potential users, buyers, or viewers.

For example, if a graphic designer is working on a company logo, he or she will likely meet with company representatives to discuss such points as how and where the company is going to use the logo and what size, color, and shape preferences company executives might have. Project budgets must be respected: A design that may be perfect in every way but that is too costly to reproduce is basically useless. Graphic designers may need to compare their ideas with similar ones from other companies and analyze the image they project. They must have a good knowledge of how various colors, shapes, and layouts affect the viewer psychologically.

After a plan has been conceived and the details worked out, the graphic designer does some preliminary designs (generally two or three) to present to the client for approval. The client may reject the preliminary designs entirely and request a new one, or he or she may ask the designer to make alterations. The designer then goes back to the drawing board to attempt a new design or make the requested changes. This process continues until the client approves the design.

Once a design has been approved, the graphic designer prepares the piece for professional reproduction, or printing. The printer may require what is called a mechanical, in which the artwork and copy are arranged on a white board just as it is to be photographed, or the designer may be asked to submit an electronic copy of the design. Either way, designers must have a good understanding of the printing process, including color separation, paper properties, and halftone (photograph) reproduction.

REQUIREMENTS
High School

While in high school, take any art and design courses that are available. Computer classes are also helpful, particularly those that teach page layout programs or art and photography manipulation programs. Working on the school newspaper or yearbook can provide valuable design experience. You could also volunteer to design flyers or posters for school events.

Postsecondary Training

More graphic designers are recognizing the value of formal training; at least two out of three people entering the field today have a college degree or some college education. About 250 colleges and art schools offer art and graphic design programs that are accredited by the National Association of Schools of Art and Design. At many schools, graphic design students must take a year of basic art and design courses before being accepted into the bachelor's degree program. In addition, applicants to the bachelor's degree programs in graphic arts may be asked to submit samples of their work to prove artistic ability. Many schools and employers depend on samples, or portfolios, to evaluate the applicants' skills in graphic design.

Many programs increasingly emphasize the importance of using computers for design work. Computer proficiency will be very important in the years to come. Interested individuals should select an academic program that incorporates computer training into the curriculum, or train themselves on their own.

A bachelor of fine arts program at a four-year college or university may include courses such as principles of design, art and art history, painting, sculpture, mechanical and architectural drawing, architecture, computer design, basic engineering, fashion designing and sketching, garment construction, and textiles. Such degrees are desirable but not always necessary for obtaining a position as a graphic designer.

Other Requirements

As with all artists, graphic designers need a degree of artistic talent, creativity, and imagination. They must be sensitive to beauty, have an eye for detail, and have a strong sense of color, balance, and proportion. Much of these qualities come naturally to potential graphic designers, but skills can be developed and improved through training, both on the job and in professional schools, colleges, and universities.

More and more graphic designers need solid computer skills and working knowledge of several of the common drawing, image editing, and page layout programs. Graphic design can be done on both Macintosh systems and on PCs; in fact, many designers have both types of computers in their studios.

With or without specialized education, graphic designers seeking employment should have a good portfolio containing samples of their best work. The graphic designer's portfolio is extremely important and can make a difference when an employer must choose between two otherwise equally qualified candidates.

A period of on-the-job training is expected for all beginning designers. The length of time it takes to become fully qualified as a graphic designer may run from one to three years, depending on prior education and experience, as well as innate talent.

EXPLORING

If you are interested in a career in graphic design, there are a number of ways to find out whether you have the talent, ambition, and perseverance to succeed in the field. Take as many art and design courses as possible while still in high school and become proficient at working on computers. To get an insider's view of various design occupations, you could enlist the help of art teachers or school guidance counselors to make arrangements to tour design firms and interview designers.

While in school, seek out practical experience by participating in school and community projects that call for design talents. These might include such activities as building sets for plays, setting up exhibits, planning seasonal and holiday displays, and preparing programs and other printed materials. If you are interested in publication design, work on the school newspaper or yearbook is invaluable.

Part-time and summer jobs are excellent ways to become familiar with the day-to-day requirements of a design job and gain some basic related experience. Possible places of employment include design studios, design departments in advertising agencies and manufacturing companies, department and furniture stores, flower shops, workshops that produce ornamental items, and museums. Museums also use a number of volunteer workers. Inexperienced people are often employed as sales, clerical, or general assistants; those with a little more education and experience may qualify for jobs in which they have a chance to develop actual design skills and build portfolios of completed design projects.

EMPLOYERS

Graphic designers hold approximately 261,000 jobs. They work in many different industries, including the wholesale and retail trade (such as department stores, furniture and home furnishings stores, apparel stores, and florist shops); manufacturing industries (such as machinery, motor vehicles, aircraft, metal products, instruments, apparel, textiles, printing, and publishing); service industries (such as business services, engineering, and architecture); construction firms; and government agencies. Public relations and publicity firms, advertising agencies, and mail-order houses all have graphic design departments. The publishing industry is a primary employer of graphic designers, including book publishers, magazines, newspapers, and newsletters.

About 25 percent of all graphic designers are self-employed, a higher proportion than is found in most other occupations. These freelance designers sell their services to multiple clients.

STARTING OUT

The best way to enter the field of graphic design is to have a strong portfolio. Potential employers rely on portfolios to evaluate talent and how that talent might be used to fit the company's needs. Beginning graphic designers can assemble a portfolio from work completed at school, in art classes, and in part-time or freelance jobs. The portfolio should continually be updated to reflect the designer's growing skills so it will always be ready for possible job changes.

Those just starting out can apply directly to companies that employ designers. Many colleges and professional schools have placement services to help graduates find positions, and sometimes it is possible to get a referral from a previous part-time employer or volunteer coordinator.

ADVANCEMENT

As part of their on-the-job training, beginning graphic designers generally are given simpler tasks and work under direct supervision. As they gain experience, they move up to more complex work with increasingly less supervision. Experienced graphic designers, especially those with leadership capabilities, may be promoted to chief designer, design department head, or other supervisory positions.

Graphic designers with strong computer skills can move into other computer-related positions with additional education. Some may become interested in graphics programming in order to further improve computer design capabilities. Others may want to become involved with multimedia and interactive graphics. Video games, touch-screen displays in stores, and even laser light shows are all products of multimedia graphic designers.

When designers develop personal styles that are in high demand in the marketplace, they sometimes go into business for themselves. Freelance design work can be erratic, however, so usually only the most experienced designers with an established client base can count on consistent full-time work.

EARNINGS

The range of salaries for graphic designers is quite broad. Salaries depend primarily on the nature and scope of the employer. The U.S. Department of Labor reports that in 2006, graphic designers earned a median salary of $39,900; the highest paid 10 percent earned $69,730 or more, while the lowest paid 10 percent earned $24,120 or less.

The American Institute of Graphic Arts/Aquent Salary Survey 2006 reports that designers earned a median salary of $38,500 in 2006, while senior designers earned a median of $50,000 annually. Salaried designers who advance to the position of creative/design director earned a median of $76,000 a year. The owner of a consulting firm can make $110,000 or more annually.

Self-employed designers can earn a lot one year and substantially more or less the next. Their earnings depend on individual talent and business ability, but, in general, are higher than those of salaried designers. Although like any self-employed individual, freelance designers must pay their own insurance costs and taxes and are not compensated for vacation or sick days.

Graphic designers who work for large corporations receive full benefits, including health insurance, paid vacation, and sick leave.

WORK ENVIRONMENT

Most graphic designers work regular hours in clean, comfortable, pleasant offices or studios. Conditions vary depending on the design specialty. Some graphic designers work in small establishments with few employees; others work in large organizations with large design departments. Some deal mostly with their coworkers; others may have a lot of public contact. Freelance designers are paid by the assignment. To maintain a steady income, they must constantly strive to please their clients and to find new ones. At times, graphic designers may have to work long, irregular hours in order to complete an especially ambitious project.

OUTLOOK

Employment for qualified graphic designers is expected to grow about as fast as the average for all occupations through 2016; employment should be especially strong for those involved with Web site design and animation. As computer graphic and Web-based technology continues to advance, there will be a need for well-trained computer graphic designers. Companies that have always used graphic designers will expect their designers to perform work on computers. Companies for which graphic design was once too time consuming or costly are now sprucing up company newsletters and magazines, among other things, requiring the skills of design professionals.

Because the design field appeals to many talented individuals, competition is expected to be strong in all areas. Beginners and designers with only average talent or without formal education and technical skills may encounter some difficulty in finding a job.

FOR MORE INFORMATION

For more information about careers in graphic design, contact

American Institute of Graphic Arts
164 Fifth Avenue
New York, NY 10010-5901
Tel: 212-807-1990
http://www.aiga.org

Visit the NASAD's Web site for information on schools.

National Association of Schools of Art and Design (NASAD)
11250 Roger Bacon Drive, Suite 21
Reston, VA 20190-5248
Tel: 703-437-0700
Email: info@arts-accredit.org
http://nasad.arts-accredit.org

If you are interested in working in environmental design, contact

Society for Environmental Graphic Design
1000 Vermont Avenue, Suite 400
Washington, DC 20005-4921
Tel: 202-638-5555
Email: segd@segd.org
http://www.segd.org

To read an online newsletter featuring competitions, examples of top designers' work, and industry news, visit the SPD's Web site.

Society of Publication Designers (SPD)
17 East 47th Street, 6th Floor
New York, NY 10017-1920
Tel: 212-223-3332
Email: mail@spd.org
http://www.spd.org

HEATING AND COOLING TECHNICIANS

OVERVIEW

Heating and cooling technicians work on systems that control the temperature, humidity, and air quality of enclosed environments. They help design, manufacture, install, and maintain climate-control equipment. They provide people with heating and air-conditioning in such structures as shops, hospitals, malls, theaters, factories, restaurants, offices, apartment buildings, and private homes. They may work to provide temperature-sensitive products such as computers, foods, medicines, and precision instruments with climate-controlled environments. They may also provide comfortable environments or refrigeration in such modes of transportation as ships, trucks, planes, and trains. There are approximately 292,000 heating and cooling technicians employed in the United States.

THE JOB

Many industries today depend on carefully controlled temperature and humidity conditions while manufacturing, transporting, or storing their products. Many common foods are readily available only because of extensive refrigeration. Less obviously, numerous chemicals, drugs, explosives, oil, and other products our society uses must be produced using refrigeration processes. For example, some room-sized computer systems need to be kept at a certain temperature and humidity; spacecraft must be able to withstand great heat while exposed to the rays of the sun and great cold when the moon or earth blocks the sun, and at the same time maintain a steady internal environment; the air in tractor trailer cabs must be regulated so that truck drivers can spend long hours behind the wheel in maximum comfort and safety. Each of these applications represents a different segment of a large and very diverse industry.

Heating and cooling technicians may work in installation and maintenance (which includes service and repairs), sales, or manufacturing. The majority of technicians who work in installation and maintenance work for heating and cooling contractors; manufacturers of air-conditioning, refrigeration, and heating equipment; dealers and distributors; or utility companies.

QUICK FACTS

SCHOOL SUBJECTS
Mathematics
Technical/shop

PERSONAL SKILLS
Following instructions
Mechanical/manipulative

WORK ENVIRONMENT
Indoors and outdoors
Primarily multiple locations

MINIMUM EDUCATION LEVEL
High school diploma
Apprenticeship

MEDIAN SALARY
$37,660

CERTIFICATION OR LICENSING
Required for certain positions

OUTLOOK
About as fast as the average

Technicians who assemble and install air-conditioning, refrigeration, and heating systems and equipment work from blueprints. Experienced technicians read blueprints that show them how to assemble components and how the components should be installed into the structure. Because structure sizes and climate-control specifications vary, technicians have to pay close attention to blueprint details. While working from the blueprints, technicians use algebra and geometry to calculate the sizes and contours of ductwork as they assemble it.

Heating and cooling technicians work with a variety of hardware, tools, and components. For example, in joining pipes and ductwork for an air-conditioning system, technicians may use soldering, welding, or brazing equipment, as well as sleeves, couplings, and elbow joints. Technicians handle and assemble such components as motors, thermometers, burners, compressors, pumps, and fans. They must join these parts together when building climate-control units and then connect this equipment to the ductwork, refrigerant lines, and power source.

As a final step in assembly and installation, technicians run tests on equipment to ensure that it functions properly. If the equipment is malfunctioning, technicians must investigate in order to diagnose the problem and determine a solution. At this time, they adjust thermostats, reseal piping, and replace parts as needed. They retest the equipment to determine whether the problem has been remedied, and they continue to modify and test it until everything checks out as functioning properly.

Some technicians may specialize on only one type of cooling, heating, or refrigeration equipment. For example, *window air-conditioning unit installers and servicers* work on window units only. *Air-conditioning and refrigeration technicians* install and service central air-conditioning systems and a variety of refrigeration equipment. Air-conditioning installations may range from small wall units, either water- or air-cooled, to large central plant systems. Commercial refrigeration equipment may include display cases, walk-in coolers, and frozen-food units such as those in supermarkets, restaurants, and food processing plants.

Other technicians are *furnace installers*, also called *heating-equipment installers*. Following blueprints and other specifications, they install oil, gas, electric, solid fuel (such as coal), and multifuel heating systems. They move the new furnace into place and attach fuel supply lines, air ducts, pumps, and other components. Then they connect the electrical wiring and thermostatic controls and, finally, check the unit for proper operation.

Technicians who work in maintenance perform routine service to keep systems operating efficiently and respond to service calls for repairs. They perform tests and diagnose problems on equipment that has been installed in the past. They calibrate controls, add fluids, change parts, clean components, and test the system for proper operation. For example, in performing a routine service call on a furnace, technicians will adjust blowers and burners, replace filters, clean ducts, and check thermometers and other controls.

Technicians who maintain oil- and gas-burning equipment are called *oil-burner mechanics* and *gas-burner mechanics*, or *gas-appliance servicers*. They usually perform more extensive maintenance work during the warm weather, when the heating system can be shut down. During the summer, technicians replace oil and air filters; vacuum vents, ducts, and other parts that accumulate soot and ash; and adjust the burner so that it achieves maximum operating efficiency. Gas-burner

mechanics may also repair other gas appliances such as cooking stoves, clothes dryers, water heaters, outdoor lights, and grills.

Other heating and cooling technicians who specialize in a limited range of equipment include evaporative cooler installers, hot-air furnace installer-and-repairers, and air and hydronic balancing technicians, radiant heating installers, and geothermal heating and cooling technicians.

In their work on refrigerant lines and air ducts, heating and cooling technicians use a variety of hand and power tools, including hammers, wrenches, metal snips, electric drills, measurement gauges, pipe cutters and benders, and acetylene torches. To check electrical circuits, burners, and other components, technicians work with volt-ohmmeters, manometers, and other testing devices.

REQUIREMENTS
High School

In high school, students considering the heating and cooling field should take algebra, geometry, English composition, physics, computer applications and programming, and classes in industrial arts or shop. Helpful shop classes include mechanical drawing and blueprint reading, power and hand tools operations, and metalwork. Shop courses in electricity and electronics provide a strong introduction into understanding circuitry and wiring and teach students to read electrical diagrams. Classes in computer-aided design are also helpful, as are business courses.

Postsecondary Training

Although postsecondary training is not mandatory to become a heating, air-conditioning, and refrigeration technician, employers prefer to hire technicians who have training from a technical school, junior college, or apprenticeship program. Vocational-technical schools, private trade schools, and junior colleges offer both one- and two-year programs. Graduates of two-year programs usually receive an associate's degree in science or in applied science. Certificates, rather than degrees, are awarded to those who complete one-year programs. Although no formal education is required, most employers prefer to hire graduates of two-year applications-oriented training programs. This kind of training includes a strong background in mathematical and engineering theory. However, the emphasis is on the practical uses of such theories, not on explorations of their origins and development, such as one finds in engineering programs.

The following organizations accredit heating and cooling technology programs: HVAC Excellence, the National Center for Construction Education and Research, and the Partnership for Air-Conditioning, Heating, and Refrigeration Accreditation.

Formal apprenticeship programs typically last three to five years and combine classroom education with on-the-job training. Programs are offered by local chapters of the following organizations: Air Conditioning Contractors of America, Mechanical Contractors Association of America, Plumbing-Heating-Cooling Contractors Association, Sheet Metal Workers International Association, United Association of Journeymen and Apprentices of the Plumbing and Pipefitting Industry of the United States and Canada, Associated Builders and Contractors, and National Association of Home Builders.

Certification or Licensing

Voluntary certification for various specialties is available through professional associations. The heating and cooling industry recently adopted a standard certification program for experienced technicians. The program is available to both installation and service technicians and is offered by North American Technician Excellence. Technicians must take and pass a core exam (covering safety, tools, soft skills, principles of heat transfer, and electrical systems) and one specialty exam of their choice (covering installation and service). The specialties available are air-conditioning, air distribution, gas heating, heat pumps, hydronics, and oil heating. Technicians who become certified as a service technician are automatically certified as an installation technician without additional testing. Certification must be renewed every five years.

The Refrigerating Engineers & Technicians Association offers the certified assistant refrigeration operator and certified industrial refrigeration operator designations to heating and cooling technicians who specialize in industrial plant refrigeration. Contact the association for more information. The Air-Conditioning and Refrigeration Institute offers certification to technicians who work for the Environmental Protection Agency (EPA). HVAC Excellence offers certification to professionals at a variety of skill levels.

Technicians who handle refrigerants must receive approved refrigerant recovery certification, which is a requirement of the EPA and requires passing a special examination. The following certifications levels are available: Type I (servicing small appliances), Type II (high-pressure refrigerants), and Type III (low-pressure refrigerants). Exams are administered by unions, trade schools, and contractor associations approved by the EPA.

In some areas of the field, for example, those who work with design and research engineers, certification is increasingly the norm and viewed as a basic indicator of competence. Even where there are no firm requirements, it generally is better to be qualified for whatever license or certification is available.

Other Requirements

Persons interested in the heating and cooling field need to have an aptitude for working with tools, manual dexterity and manipulation, and the desire to perform challenging work that requires a high level of competence and quality. Students who are interested in how things work, who enjoy taking things apart and putting them back together, and who enjoy troubleshooting for mechanical and electrical problems may enjoy a career in air-conditioning, refrigeration, and heating.

EXPLORING

A student trying to decide on a career in heating and cooling technology may have to base the choice on a variety of indirect evidence. Part-time or summer work is usually not available to high school students because of their lack of the necessary skills and knowledge. It may be possible, however, to arrange field trips to service shops, companies that develop and produce heating and cooling equipment, or other firms concerned with the environmental control field. Such visits can provide a firsthand overview of the day-to-day work. A visit with a local contractor or to a school that conducts a heating and cooling technology training program can also be very helpful.

EMPLOYERS

Approximately 292,000 heating and cooling technicians are employed in the United States. While most heating and cooling technicians work directly with the building, installation, and maintenance of equipment via heating and cooling firms, some technicians work in equipment sales. These technicians are usually employed by manufacturers or dealers and distributors and are hired to explain the equipment and its operation to prospective customers. These technicians must have a thorough knowledge of their products. They may explain newly developed equipment, ideas, and principles, or assist dealers and distributors in the layout and installation of unfamiliar components. Some technicians employed as sales representatives contact prospective buyers and help them plan air-conditioning, refrigeration, and heating systems. They help the client select appropriate equipment and estimate costs.

Other technicians work for manufacturers in engineering or research laboratories, performing many of the same assembling and testing duties as technicians who work for contractors. However, they perform these operations at the manufacturing site rather than traveling to work sites as most contractors' technicians do. Technicians aid engineers in research, equipment design, and equipment testing. Technicians in a research laboratory may plan the requirements for the various stages of fabricating, installing, and servicing climate-control and refrigeration systems; recommend appropriate equipment to meet specified needs; and calculate heating and cooling capacities of proposed equipment units. They also may conduct operational tests on experimental models and efficiency tests on new units coming off the production lines. They might also investigate the cause of breakdowns reported by customers, and determine the reasons and solutions.

Engineering-oriented technicians employed by manufacturers may perform tests of new equipment, or assist engineers in fundamental research and development, technical report writing, and application engineering. Other engineering technicians serve as *liaison representatives*, coordinating the design and production engineering for the development and manufacture of new products.

Technicians may also be employed by utility companies to help ensure that their customers' equipment is using energy efficiently and effectively. *Utility technicians*, often called *energy conservation technicians*, may conduct energy evaluations of customers' systems, compile energy surveys, and provide customer information.

Technicians may also work for consulting firms, such as engineering firms or building contractors who hire technicians to estimate costs, determine air-conditioning and heating load requirements, and prepare specifications for climate-control projects.

Some large institutions such as hospitals, universities, factories, office complexes, and sports arenas employ heating and cooling technicians directly, maintaining their own climate-control staffs.

Some technicians also open up their own businesses, either as heating and cooling contractors or consultants specializing in sales, parts supply, service, and installation.

STARTING OUT

Many students in two-year programs work at a job related to their area of training during the summer between the first and second years. Their employers may hire them on a part-time basis during the second year and make offers of full-time employment after graduation. Even if such a job offer cannot be made, the employer may be aware of other companies that are hiring and help the student with suggestions and recommendations, provided the student's work record is good.

Some schools make work experience part of the curriculum, particularly during the latter part of their program. This is a valuable way for students to gain practical experience in conjunction with classroom work.

It is not unusual for graduates of two-year programs to receive several offers of employment, either from contacts they have made themselves or from companies that routinely recruit new graduates. Representatives of larger companies often schedule interview periods at schools with two-year air-conditioning, refrigeration, and heating technician programs. Other, usually smaller, prospective employers may contact specific faculty advisors who in turn make students aware of opportunities that arise.

In addition to using their schools' career services office, resourceful students can independently explore other leads by applying directly to local heating and cooling contractors; sales, installation, and service shops; or manufacturers of air-conditioning, refrigeration, and heating equipment. State employment offices may also post openings or provide job leads. Finally, student membership in the local chapter of a trade association, such as one of those listed at the end of this article, will often result in good employment contacts.

ADVANCEMENT

There is such a wide range of positions within this field that workers who gain the necessary skills and experience have the flexibility to choose between many different options and types of positions. As employees gain on-the-job work experience, they may decide to specialize in a particular aspect or type of work. They may be able to be promoted into positions requiring more responsibilities and skills through experience and demonstrated proficiency, but in some cases additional training is required.

Many workers continue to take courses throughout their careers to upgrade their skills and to learn new techniques and methods used within the industry. Training can take the form of a class offered by a manufacturer regarding specific equipment or it may be a more extensive program resulting in certification for a specific area or procedure. Skill improvement programs that offer advanced training in specialized areas are available through vocational-technical institutes and trade associations. Technicians with an interest in the engineering aspect of the industry may go back to school to get a bachelor of science degree in heating and cooling engineering or mechanical engineering.

Technicians increase their value to employers and themselves with continued training. For example, a technician employed by a manufacturer may progress to the position of *sales manager*, who acts as liaison with distributors and dealers, promoting and selling the manufacturer's products, or to a *field service representative*, who solves unusual service problems of dealers and distributors in the area. Technicians working for dealers and distributors or contractors may advance to a *service manager* or supervisory position, overseeing other technicians who install and service equipment. Another possible specialization is mechanical design, which involves designing piping, ductwork, controls, and the distribution systems for consulting engineers, mechanical contractors, manufacturers, and distributors. Technicians who do installation and maintenance may decide to move into sales or work for the research and development department of a manufacturing company.

Some technicians also open up their own businesses, becoming heating and cooling contractors, consultants, self-employed service technicians, or specializing in sales and parts distribution.

EARNINGS

The earnings of heating and cooling technicians vary widely according to the level of training and experience, the nature of their work, type of employer, region of the country, and other factors. Heating and cooling technicians had median hourly earnings of $18.11 (or $37,660 annually) in 2006, according to the U.S. Department of Labor. The lowest paid 10 percent earned less than $11.38 (or $23,680 annually), while the top paid 10 percent earned more than $28.57 (or $59,430 annually).

Heating and cooling apprentices usually earn about 50 percent of the wage rate paid to experienced workers. This percentage rises as apprentices gain experience and skill training in the field.

Many employers offer medical insurance and paid vacation days, holidays, and sick days, although the actual benefits vary from employer to employer. Some companies also offer tuition assistance for additional training.

WORK ENVIRONMENT

Working conditions for heating and cooling technicians vary considerably, depending on the area of the industry in which they work. For the most part, the hours are regular, although certain jobs in production may involve shift work, and service technicians may have to be on call some evenings and weekends to handle emergency repairs.

Technicians who work in installation and service may work in a variety of environments ranging from industrial plants to construction sites and can include both indoor and outdoor work. Technicians may encounter extremes in temperature when servicing outdoor and rooftop equipment and cramped quarters when servicing indoor commercial and industrial equipment. They often have to lift heavy objects as well as stoop, crawl, and crouch when making repairs and installations. Working conditions can include dirt, grease, noise, and safety hazards. Hazards include falls from rooftops or scaffolds, electric shocks, burns, and handling refrigerants and compressed gases. With proper precautions and safety measures, however, the risk from these hazards can be minimized.

Technicians who work in laboratories usually work in the research and development departments of a manufacturing firm or an industrial plant. Technicians employed by distributors, dealers, and consulting engineers usually work in an office or similar surroundings and are subject to the same benefits and conditions as other office workers. Some technicians, such as sales representatives or service managers, go out periodically to visit customers or installation and service sites.

OUTLOOK

Employment in the heating and cooling field is expected to increase about as fast as the average for all occupations through 2016, according to the U.S. Department of Labor. Some openings will occur when experienced workers retire or transfer to other work. Other openings will be generated because of a demand for new climate-control systems for residences and industrial and commercial users. In addition, many existing systems are being upgraded to provide more efficient use of energy and to provide benefits not originally built into the system. There is a growing emphasis on improving indoor air and making equipment more environmentally friendly. Systems that use chloroflurocarbons (CFCs) need to be retrofitted or replaced with new equipment, since regulations banning CFC production became effective in 2000.

Comfort is only one of the major reasons for environmental control. Conditioned atmosphere is a necessity in any precision industry where temperature and humidity can affect fine tolerances. As products and processes become more complex and more highly automated, the need for closely controlled conditions becomes increasingly important. For example, electronics manufacturers must keep the air bone-dry for many parts of their production processes to prevent damage to parts and to maintain nonconductivity. Pharmaceutical and food manufacturers rely on pure, dirt-free air. High-speed multicolor printing requires temperature control of rollers and moisture control for the paper racing through the presses. There is every reason to expect that these and other sophisticated industries will rely more in the coming years on precision control of room conditions. The actual amount of industry growth for these applications will hinge on the overall health of the nation's economy and the rate of manufacturing.

Technicians who are involved in maintenance and repair are not as affected by the economy as workers in some other jobs. Whereas in bad economic times a consumer may postpone building a new house or installing a new air-conditioning system, hospitals, restaurants, technical industries, and public buildings will still require skilled technicians to maintain their climate-control systems. Technicians who are versed in more than one aspect of the job have greater job flexibility and can count on fairly steady work despite any fluctuations in the economy.

FOR MORE INFORMATION

For information on certification and publications, contact
Air-Conditioning and Refrigeration Institute
4100 North Fairfax Drive, Suite 200
Arlington, VA 22203-1623
Tel: 703-524-8800
Email: ari@ari.org
http://www.ari.org

For information on careers and educational programs, contact
Air Conditioning Contractors of America
2800 Shirlington Road, Suite 300
Arlington, VA 22206-3607
Tel: 703-575-4477
http://www.acca.org

For information on careers, contact
American Society of Heating, Refrigerating and Air-Conditioning Engineers
1791 Tullie Circle, NE
Atlanta, GA 30329-2305
Tel: 404-636-8400
Email: ashrae@ashrae.org
http://www.ashrae.org

For information on accredited programs and certification, contact
HVAC Excellence
PO Box 491
Mt. Prospect, IL 60056-0491
Tel: 800-394-5268
http://www.hvacexcellence.org

For information on certification programs, contact
North American Technician Excellence
4100 North Fairfax Drive, Suite 210
Arlington, VA 22203-1623
Tel: 877-420-6283
http://www.natex.org

For information on accredited training programs, contact
Partnership for Air-Conditioning, Heating, Refrigeration Accreditation
4100 North Fairfax Drive, Suite 210
Arlington, VA 22203-1623
Tel: 703-524-8800
http://www.pahrahvacr.org

For information on union membership, contact
Plumbing-Heating-Cooling Contractors Association
PO Box 6808
180 South Washington Street
Falls Church, VA 22046-2900
Tel: 800-533-7694
Email: naphcc@naphcc.org
http://www.phccweb.org

For information on industrial plant refrigeration certification, contact
Refrigerating Engineers & Technicians Association
PO Box 1819
Salinas, CA 93902-1819
Tel: 831-455-8783
Email: info@reta.com
http://www.reta.com

For information on heating and cooling and the sheet metal industry, contact
Sheet Metal and Air Conditioning Contractors' National Association
4201 Lafayette Center Drive
Chantilly, VA 20151-1209
Tel: 703-803-2980
Email: info@smacna.org
http://www.smacna.org

Check out the following Web site, created by a coalition of organizations representing the heating, air-conditioning, and refrigeration industry

Cool Careers
PO Box 4361
Washington, DC 20044-9361
Email: info@coolcareers.org
http://www.coolcareers.org

HISTOLOGIC TECHNICIANS

OVERVIEW

Histologic technicians perform basic laboratory procedures to prepare tissue specimens for microscopic examination. They process specimens to prevent deterioration and cut them using special laboratory equipment. They stain specimens with special dyes and mount the tissues on slides. Histologic technicians work closely with pathologists and other medical personnel to detect disease and illness.

THE JOB

Histologic technicians use delicate instruments, which are often computerized, to prepare tissues for microscopic scrutiny and diagnosis. They must also perform quality control tests and keep accurate records of their work.

After a tissue sample is taken, the first step in preparing it for study is known as fixation. This is usually done by a pathologist or scientist. The specimen is examined, described, trimmed to the right size, and placed in special fluids to preserve it.

When the fixed specimen arrives at the histology lab, the histologic technician removes the water and replaces it with melted wax, which moves into the tissue and provides support for the delicate cellular structure as it cools and hardens. Then the technician places small pieces of wax-soaked tissue in larger blocks of wax, a step called embedding, which prevents the tissue from collapsing during the next step of the process.

The technician then sections the specimen by mounting it on a microtome, a scientific instrument with a very sharp blade. The microtome cuts thin slices of tissue, often only one cell thick. The technician cuts many sections of tissue, usually one after another so they form a ribbon, which is placed in warm water until

QUICK FACTS

SCHOOL SUBJECTS
Biology
Chemistry
Health

PERSONAL SKILLS
Following instructions
Technical/scientific

WORK ENVIRONMENT
Primarily indoors
Primarily one location

MINIMUM EDUCATION LEVEL
Associate's degree

MEDIAN SALARY
$32,840

CERTIFICATION OR LICENSING
Voluntary (certification)
Required by certain states (licensing)

OUTLOOK
Faster than the average

it flattens out. Then the prepared sections are laid on microscope slides.

Next the technician stains each tissue specimen by adding chemicals and then places a coverslip over the sample to protect it. Different stains highlight different tissue structures or abnormalities in the cells, which aids in the diagnosis and study of diseases.

A second, quicker technique is used to prepare samples and make diagnoses while the patient is still in the operating room. In these cases, tissue specimens are frozen instead of being embedded in wax. It is important for a technician to work swiftly, accurately, and cooperate with the rest of the team during this procedure because surgeries cannot be completed until test results are delivered.

Histologic technicians work with a lot of machines in the lab, such as robotic stainers, tissue processors, and cover slippers, but they must have the knowledge to perform all the functions manually should the equipment malfunction. They must also work closely with a team of researchers, as well as other laboratory and medical personnel.

REQUIREMENTS

High School

Biology, chemistry, mathematics, and computer science courses are necessary to develop the preliminary technical skills needed for histotechnology programs. Classes in communication, such as speech and English, are also helpful to reinforce your written and verbal skills.

Postsecondary Training

You can become a histologic technician with a high school diploma and on-the-job training, but a college degree or other formal training is becoming more generally recommended.

You can enter the field with an associate's degree from an accredited college or university and participation in supervised, hands-on experience in clinical settings. You may also prepare for the profession through a one- or two-year certificate program at an accredited institution, such as a hospital. These programs combine classroom studies along with clinical and laboratory experience.

Certification or Licensing

Certification is not required for entry-level histologic technicians, but it can aid in your hiring and the advancement of your career. The Board of Registry of the American Society for Clinical Pathology is the main certifying organization for professions in laboratory medicine. Applicants can qualify for the Board of Registry exam in two ways. They can complete an accredited program in histotechnology within five years of applying to take the exam or earn an associate's degree from an accredited college or university and combine it with one year of experience. Some states also require that all laboratory personnel be licensed; check your individual state department of health for requirements.

Other Requirements

To be a successful histologic technician, you should be patient, attentive to detail, and be able to concentrate well under pressure when necessary. Good color vision and manual dexterity are important for the meticulous work involved. Some laboratory work can also be repetitive, requiring technicians to perform the same part of a procedure all day long. Finally, you must be honest and willing to admit mistakes made, because people's lives may depend on how well you do your job.

EXPLORING

To learn more about this career, take a tour of a local hospital or laboratory to see histologic technicians at work. Read as much as you can about histology and clinical laboratory science. Ask your biology teacher or counselor to arrange an information interview with a histologic technician.

EMPLOYERS

A histologic technician has the opportunity to work in many fields of medicine and science. Most are employed by hospitals or by industrial laboratories that specialize in chemical, petrochemical, pharmaceutical, cosmetic, or household products. Other employers include medical clinics, universities, government organizations, and biomedical companies. Regional laboratories for large health systems hire employees to work flexible shifts since their laboratories operate seven days a week, 24 hours a day. This arrangement could allow a student to attend college classes while working.

STARTING OUT

You can apply directly to laboratory facilities in your area, contact your local employment office, or check your local newspaper's help wanted ads. If you complete a training program, placement assistance is often available to graduates.

ADVANCEMENT

Some histologic technicians become laboratory supervisors. Others specialize in certain areas of histotechnology such as orthopedic implants or diseases of the lungs. Technicians who have more education and experience are more likely to be promoted. In the future, an associate's degree is likely to become the standard requirement for entering the field and being promoted. Returning to school and earning a bachelor's degree will also provide opportunities for advancement into other medical or business fields.

EARNINGS

According to the U.S. Department of Labor, in 2006 the median annual salary for medical and clinical laboratory technicians, a category that includes histologic technicians, was $32,840. The lowest paid 10 percent earned

$21,830 or less, while the highest paid 10 percent earned $50,250 or more annually.

In general, geographic location, experience, level of education, type of employer, and work performed determine the salary range for histologic technicians. Education, certification, experience, and specialization can increase earnings for histologic technicians.

Benefits such as vacation time, sick leave, health insurance, and other fringe benefits vary by employer, but are usually consistent with other full-time health care workers.

WORK ENVIRONMENT

Histologic technicians work in laboratories that are well ventilated. Most of the tissue processors that they use are enclosed, minimizing inhalation of odors and chemical fumes. Histologic technicians occasionally work with hazardous chemicals but wear protective clothing and carefully monitor exposure levels. They also face the risk of contact with disease through tissue samples. However, the steps involved in preparing specimens generally kill any living organisms.

Some histologic technicians may spend a great deal of time standing or sitting in one position and performing one type of operation, though most are able to rotate jobs. They must also deal with government regulations and spend time complying with required reports and organizing paperwork. Technicians who work for large laboratories or hospitals may be required to work rotating shifts, including weekends and holidays.

OUTLOOK

Employment for clinical laboratory workers is expected to grow faster than the average for all occupations through 2016, according to the *Occupational Outlook Handbook*. Advances in technology will have both positive and negative effects on employment in this career. The development of new tests and procedures is expected to increase opportunities, but at the same time many tests are being simplified so that health care professionals and patients can perform them themselves.

FOR MORE INFORMATION

For general information about careers in medicine, contact
American Medical Association
515 North State Street
Chicago, IL 60610-5453
Tel: 800-621-8335
http://www.ama-assn.org

For information on histologic technician careers and certification, contact
American Society for Clinical Pathology
33 West Monroe, Suite 1600
Chicago, IL 60603-5308
Tel: 800-267-2727
http://www.ascp.org

For information on accredited schools, contact
National Accrediting Agency for Clinical Laboratory Sciences
8410 West Bryn Mawr Avenue, Suite 670
Chicago, IL 60631-3402
Tel: 773-714-8880
Email: info@naacls.org
http://www.naacls.org

For career information and a list of schools of histotechnology, contact
National Society for Histotechnology
10320 Little Patuxent Parkway, Suite 804
Columbia, MD 21044-3349
Tel: 443-535-4060
Email: histo@nsh.org
http://www.nsh.org

For links to a variety of histologic-related resources, visit
The Histotech's Home Page
http://www.histology.to/main.html

HOME HEALTH CARE AIDES

OVERVIEW

Home health care aides, also known as *homemaker-home health aides* or *home attendants*, serve elderly and infirm persons by visiting them in their homes and caring for them. Working under the supervision of nurses or social workers, they perform various household chores that clients are unable to perform for themselves as well as attend to patients' personal needs. Although they work primarily with the elderly, home health care aides also attend to clients with disabilities or those needing help with small children. There are approximately 787,000 home health aides employed in the United States.

QUICK FACTS

SCHOOL SUBJECTS

Family and consumer science

Health

PERSONAL SKILLS

Following instructions

Helping/teaching

WORK ENVIRONMENT

Primarily indoors

Primarily multiple locations

MINIMUM EDUCATION LEVEL

High school diploma

MEDIAN SALARY

$19,240

CERTIFICATION OR LICENSING

Required for certain positions

OUTLOOK

Much faster than the average

THE JOB

Home health care aides enable elderly persons to stay in their own homes. For some clients, just a few visits a week are enough to help them look after themselves. Although physically demanding, the work is often emotionally rewarding. Home health care aides may not have access to equipment and facilities such as those found in hospitals, but they also don't have the hospital's frantic pace. Home health care aides are expected to take the time to get to know their clients and their individual needs. They perform their duties within the client's home environment, which often is a much better atmosphere than the impersonal rooms of a hospital.

In addition to the elderly, home health care aides assist people of any age who are recovering at home following hospitalization. They also help children whose parents are ill, disabled, or neglectful. Aides may be trained to supply care to people suffering from specific illnesses such as AIDS, Alzheimer's disease, or cancer, or patients with developmental disabilities who lack sufficient daily living skills.

Clients unable to feed themselves may depend on home health care aides to shop for food, prepare their meals, feed them, and clean up after meals. Likewise, home health care aides may assist clients in dressing and grooming, including washing, bathing, cleaning teeth and nails, and fixing the clients' hair.

Massages, alcohol rubs, whirlpool baths, and other therapies and treatments may be a part of a client's required care. Home health care aides may work closely with a physician or home nurse in giving medications and dietary supplements and helping with exercises and other therapies. They may check pulses, temperatures, and respiration rates. Occasionally, they may change nonsterile dressings, use special equipment such as a hydraulic lift, or assist with braces or artificial limbs.

Home health care aides working in home care agencies are supervised by a registered nurse, physical therapist, or social worker who assigns them specific duties. Aides report changes in patients' conditions to the supervisor or case manager.

Household chores are often another aspect of the home health care aide's responsibilities. Light housekeeping, such as changing and washing bed linens, doing the laundry and ironing, and dusting, may be necessary. When a home health care aide looks after the children of a disabled or neglectful parent, work may include making lunches for the children, helping them with their homework, or providing companionship and adult supervision in the evening.

Personal attention and comfort are important aspects of an aide's care. Home health care aides can provide this support by reading to children, playing checkers or a computer game, or visiting with an elderly client. Often just listening to a client's personal problems will help the client through the day. Because elderly people do not always have the means to venture out alone, a home health care aide may accompany an ambulatory patient to the park for an afternoon stroll or to the physician's office for an appointment.

REQUIREMENTS

High School

Many programs require only a high school diploma for entry-level positions. Previous or additional course work in home economics, cooking, sewing, and meal planning are very helpful, as are courses that focus on family living and home nursing.

Postsecondary Training

Health care agencies usually focus their training on first aid, hygiene, and the principles of health care. Cooking and nutrition, including meal preparation for patients with specific dietary needs, are often included in the program. Home health care aides may take courses in psychology and child development as well as family living. Because of the need for hands-on work, aides usually learn how to bathe, dress, and feed patients as well as how to help them walk upstairs or get up from bed. The more specific the skill required for certain patients, the more an agency is likely to have more comprehensive instruction.

Most agencies will offer free training to prospective employees. Such training may include instruction on how to deal with depressed or reluctant patients, how to prepare easy and nutritious meals, and tips on housekeeping. Specific course work on health and sanitation may also be required.

Certification or Licensing

Home Care University, a subsidiary of the National Association for Home Care and Hospice, offers the home care aide certification to applications who complete educational and skill requirements and pass a written examination. Contact the association for more information.

The federal government has enacted guidelines for home health aides whose employers receive reimbursement from Medicare. Federal law requires home health aides to pass a competency test covering 12 areas: communication skills; documentation of patient status and care provided; reading and recording vital signs; basic infection control procedures; basic body functions; maintenance of a healthy environment; emergency procedures; physical, emotional, and developmental characteristics of patients; personal hygiene and grooming; safe transfer techniques; normal range of motion and positioning; and basic nutrition.

Federal law suggests at least 75 hours of classroom and practical training supervised by a registered nurse. Training and testing programs may be offered by the employing agency, but they must meet the standards of the Centers for Medicare and Medicaid Services. Training programs vary depending upon state regulations.

Other Requirements

Caring for people in their own homes can be physically demanding work. Lifting a client for baths and exercise, helping a client up and down stairs, performing housework, and aiding with physical therapy all require that an aide be in good physical condition. Aides do not have the equipment and facilities of a hospital to help them with their work, and this requires adaptability and ingenuity. Oftentimes they must make do with the resources available in a typical home.

An even temperament and a willingness to serve others are important characteristics for home health care aides. People in this occupation should be friendly, patient, sensitive to others' needs, and tactful. At times an aide will have to be stern in dealing with uncooperative patients or calm and understanding with those who are angry, confused, despondent, or in pain. Genuine warmth and respect for others are important attributes. Cheerfulness and a sense of humor can go a long way in establishing a good relationship with a client, and a good relationship can make working with the client much easier.

Home health care aides must be willing to follow instructions and abide by the health plan created for each patient. Aides provide an important outreach service, supporting the care administered by the patient's physician, therapist, or social worker. They are not trained medical personnel, however, and must know the limits of their authority.

EXPLORING

Home health care aides are employed in many different areas. Interested students can learn more about the work by contacting local agencies and programs that provide home care services and requesting information on the organization's employment guidelines or training programs. Visiting the county or city health department and contacting the personnel director may provide useful information as well. Often, local organizations sponsor open houses to inform the community about the services they provide. This could serve as an excellent opportunity to meet the staff involved in hiring and program development and to learn about job opportunities. In addition, it may be possible to arrange to accompany a home health care aide on a home visit.

EMPLOYERS

Approximately 787,000 home health aides are employed in the United States. The primary employers of home health care aides are local social service agencies that provide home care services. Such agencies often have training programs for prospective employees. Home health care aides might also find employment with hospitals that operate their own community outreach programs. Most hospitals, however, hire home health care aides through agencies.

STARTING OUT

Some social service agencies enlist the aid of volunteers. By contacting agencies and inquiring about such openings, aspiring home care aides can get an introduction to the type of work this profession requires. Also, many agencies or nursing care facilities offer free training to prospective employees.

Checking the local Yellow Pages for agencies that provide health care to the aged and disabled or family service organizations can provide a list of employment prospects. Nursing homes, public and private health care facilities, and local chapters of the Red Cross and United Way are likely to hire entry-level employees. The National Association for Home Care and Hospice can also supply information on reputable agencies and departments that employ home care aides.

ADVANCEMENT

As home health care aides develop their skills and deepen their experience, they may advance to management or supervisory positions. Those who find greater enjoyment working with clients may branch into more specialized care and pursue additional training. Additional experience and education often bring higher pay and increased responsibility.

Aides who wish to work in a clinic or hospital setting may return to school to complete a nursing degree. Other related occupations include social worker, physical or occupational therapist, and dietitian. Along with a desire for advancement, however, must come the willingness to meet additional education and experience requirements.

EARNINGS

Earnings for home health care aides are comparable to the salaries of nursing and psychiatric aides and nurse assistants. Depending on the agency, considerable flexibility exists in working hours and patient load. For many aides who begin as part-time employees, the starting salary is usually the minimum hourly wage. For full-time aides with significant training or experience, earnings may be around $6 to $8 per hour. According to the U.S. Department of Labor, median hourly earnings of home health aides were $9.34 in 2006, or $19,240 annually. Wages ranged from less than $7.06 ($14,680 annually) to more than $13.00 an hour ($27,030 annually).

Aides are usually paid only for the time worked in the home. They normally are not paid for travel time between jobs.

Vacation policies and benefits packages vary with the type and size of the employing agency. Many full-time home health care aides receive one week of paid vacation following their first year of employment, and they often receive two weeks of paid vacation each year thereafter. Full-time aides may also be eligible for health insurance and retirement benefits. Some agencies also offer holiday or overtime compensation.

WORK ENVIRONMENT

Health aides in a hospital or nursing home setting work at a much different pace and in a much different environment than the home health care aide. With home care, aides can take the time to sit with their clients and get to know them. Aides spend a certain amount of time with each client and can perform their responsibilities without the frequent distractions and demands of a hospital. Home surroundings differ from situation to situation. Some homes are neat and pleasant, while others are untidy and depressing. Some patients are angry, abusive, depressed, or otherwise difficult; others are pleasant and cooperative.

Because home health care aides usually have more than one patient, the hours an aide works can fluctuate based on the number of clients and types of services needed. Many clients may be ill or have disabilities. Some may be elderly and have no one else to assist them with light housekeeping or daily errands. These differences can dictate the type of responsibilities a home care aide has for each patient.

Working with the infirm or disabled can be a rewarding experience as aides enhance the quality of their clients' lives with their help and company. However, the personal strains—on the clients as well as the aides—can make the work challenging and occasionally frustrating. There can be difficult emotional demands that aides may find exhausting. Considerable physical activity is involved in this line of work, such as helping patients to walk, dress, or take care of themselves. Traveling from one home to another and running various errands for patients can also be tiring and time-consuming, or it can be a pleasant break.

OUTLOOK

As government and private agencies develop more programs to assist the dependent, the need for home health care aides will continue to grow. Because of the physical and emotional demands of the job, there is high turnover and, therefore, frequent job openings for home health care aides.

Also, the number of people 70 years of age and older is expected to increase substantially, and many of them will require at least some home care. Rising health care costs are causing many insurance companies to consider alternatives to hospital treatment, so many insurance providers now cover home care services. In addition, hospitals and nursing homes are trying to balance the demand for their services and their limitations in staff and physical facilities. The availability of home health care aides can allow such institutions as hospitals and nursing homes to offer quality care to more people. The U.S. Department of Labor projects that employment of home health aides will grow much faster than the average through 2016.

FOR MORE INFORMATION

For certification information and statistics on the home health care industry, visit the association's Web site.

National Association for Home Care and Hospice
228 Seventh Street, SE
Washington, DC 20003-4306
Tel: 202-547-7424
http://www.nahc.org

For information on caring for the elderly, visit
ElderWeb
http://www.elderweb.com

HOTEL CONCIERGES

OVERVIEW

Concierges assist hotel guests and help make their stays pleasant and comfortable. Guests may use their services to book tours, airline reservations, or car rentals. Concierges are experts in what their particular city has to offer. Many times they may be asked to recommend restaurants, shows, or museums as well as give directions to other points of interest. Concierges may also be asked to plan cocktail receptions, dinner meetings, or small parties for hotel guests. There are approximately 20,000 concierges employed in the United States.

THE JOB

Concierges are the most visible and active ambassadors of hotel hospitality. Their basic duty is to provide hotel guests with services to help make their stay as comfortable, enjoyable, and memorable as possible. Many of the requests concierges receive are for directions to city attractions, recommendations for tours or restaurants, or help dealing with airlines or car rental agencies. Concierges obtain out-of-town newspapers, arrange for the pickup of dry cleaning, or reserve show tickets. Concierges also

work with other departments in the hotel to prepare for large groups, VIP guests, or any guest that may have special needs. Sometimes, welcome letters or baskets of fruit are sent to such guests by the concierge desk. However, concierge duties do not end there. Many hotels provide different levels of concierge service, depending on the type of guest. Penthouse guests can enjoy a private reception with a separate concierge department to meet their needs as well as serve them afternoon tea and hot hors d'oeuvres and drinks during the cocktail hour. Some concierge desks also host similar cocktail hours in the lobby.

Sometimes, a request can be more involved. Concierges have been known to plan large dinners or receptions on short notice, design entire travel itineraries complete with lodging and tours, rent airplanes or helicopters, secure the front row seats to a sold-out concert or sporting event, or even fill a room with flowers to set the mood for a marriage proposal. Concierges are trained to use their resources and

QUICK FACTS

SCHOOL SUBJECTS
Business
Mathematics
Speech

PERSONAL SKILLS
Helping/teaching
Leadership/management

WORK ENVIRONMENT
Primarily indoors
Primarily one location

MINIMUM EDUCATION LEVEL
High school diploma

MEDIAN SALARY
$24,600

CERTIFICATION OR LICENSING
Recommended

OUTLOOK
Faster than the average

contacts to serve the guest in whatever manner possible. They will, however, refuse to help the guest in any acts unlawful or unkind—no illegal drugs, prostitution, or practical jokes that may be deemed hurtful.

Concierges also spend a considerable amount of time researching restaurants, tours, museums, and other city attractions. Since a recommendation can bring additional business, many tour operators will pay special attention to visiting concierges.

REQUIREMENTS

High School

A well-rounded high school education is a good starting point for the career of concierge. Speech and writing classes will help you learn how to effectively communicate with hotel guests and coworkers. Fluency in another language, especially French, Japanese, or Spanish, can also be extremely helpful in this field.

Postsecondary Training

A college degree is not required to be a concierge. In fact, many successful and established concierges have a variety of educational and employment backgrounds—from managers to artists to teachers. However, in today's competitive job market it pays to have an edge. A well-rounded education, such as a liberal arts degree or a degree from a concierge program, could only help.

Certification or Licensing

Though not a requirement, certification is viewed by many as a measurement of professional achievement. The Educational Institute of the American Hotel and Lodging Association offers certification classes for concierges.

High school juniors and seniors who are interested in working in the hospitality industry can take advantage of the Educational Institute of the American Hotel and Lodging Association's Lodging Management Program. The program combines classroom learning with work experience in the hospitality industry. Graduating seniors who pass examinations and work in the lodging industry for at least 30 days receive the certified rooms division specialist designation. Visit http://www.lodging-management.org for more information.

Other Requirements

Decorum is a key word in this industry. A good concierge is always well groomed and dressed neatly. No matter how difficult the situation, concierges should always be polite and pleasant. They never gossip about the guests. If a guest has a strange request, the concierge should always be very discreet so as not to embarrass the guest or the hotel.

What separates an adequate concierge from a great one? "What you look for in a concierge," offers Diana Nelson, Chief Concierge at San Francisco's Grand Hyatt Hotel, "is an attitude. It's the feeling someone has in making a difference in a person's stay."

EXPLORING

Try to find part-time or seasonal work in order to gain working experience. Your part-time job need not be in a hotel (although that's the best place to make contacts); consider working in the customer service department of a department store. What about working as a junior assistant for a wedding consultant or party caterer? If you are always recruited to show out-of-town relatives the city sights, then at least get paid for your efforts by working for a tour company.

EMPLOYERS

Look for jobs in large cities like New York, Los Angeles, and Chicago; tourist-heavy areas, such as California and Florida; and the convention and entertainment mecca of Las Vegas. Employment opportunities are plentiful abroad, although European standards and training may be different from those found in the United States.

Concierges also work in other aspects of business. Besides hotels, concierges work in some large apartment buildings and condominiums. The concierge services provided at one Chicago high-rise apartment building include taking clothes to the cleaners, watering plants, and caring for pets when occupants are out of town. Large upscale department stores, such as Nordstrom, offer concierge services for their shoppers, from complimentary coat and package checking to restaurant and store information and tours.

STARTING OUT

At most hotels, new hires are not allowed to sit at the lobby desk until they are properly trained. The first few days are spent going over the basic philosophy of being a concierge and the hotel's expectations of employees. Many concierge trainees come from other departments of the hotel, such as the front desk. Diana Nelson likes to start trainees in the Regency Club, a special service provided by the Grand Hyatt to their VIP guests. Here, special guests can relax and be served gourmet food and drinks. The pace in the Regency Club is slower, but expectations are high when it comes to service because of the clientele; this makes a great training ground before concierges are allowed to work the lobby, where according to Nelson, "you almost have to be able to do three or four things at the same time—with a lot of ease."

There is no typical path to this career. Some concierges have only a high school education. Being a graduate of a hotel or concierge program will, however, give you an edge in getting hired. Many schools with such programs offer job placement services. Also, check hotel industry publications as they often post employment opportunities. Les Clefs d'Or USA takes great pride in the worldwide networking program it provides its members.

ADVANCEMENT

There are many opportunities for concierges who want to advance to other hotel departments. Because a concierge's duties are very people-oriented, similar positions, such as front desk manager, should be considered. A concierge who has a degree in hotel management or business, and work experience, as well as superior management skills, could vie for the position of general manager.

The extremely ambitious can also start their own concierge businesses. *Personal concierges* are personal assistants to those too busy to organize their homes or run errands. For a fixed price, known as a *retainer*, personal concierges are responsible for a set of weekly duties; special requests, such as planning dinner parties or buying Christmas gifts, are charged extra.

EARNINGS

The U.S. Department of Labor reports that concierges earned salaries that ranged from less than $15,910 to $38,210 or more in 2006. The median annual salaary was $24,600 in 2006. An experienced concierge, with Les Clefs d'Or USA status, working at a large urban hotel, can expect to earn around $50,000 a year, according to the International Concierge Institute. Concierges employed by hotels typically receive benefits such as paid vacations, sick and holiday time, health insurance, and some type of employee hotel discount, depending on the establishment.

Concierge service is a free service provided to the guests by the hotel. A concierge, especially a good one, is often given tips or gifts by grateful hotel patrons. Concierges, ethically, cannot and will not press for tips. The hotel guest decides whether to tip, and if so, how much.

WORK ENVIRONMENT

Most concierges have workstations, usually a desk or a counter, prominently situated in the main lobby. Concierges spend much of the day on their feet, greeting guests, making phone calls, running errands, or doing whatever it takes to make things happen. A considerable amount of time is spent in the field, trying out new restaurants, visiting museums, and researching new tours. Concierges need to be up on what's new and happening in their city. Flexibility is imperative in this job since there is no such thing as "a typical day." A good concierge must be ready to deal with a single guest or a group of 20, always in a cheerful and courteous manner. Situations can get hectic, especially when it's the middle of the tourist season or the hotel is full of conventioneers.

OUTLOOK

Job opportunities look bright for those interested in a concierge career, with employment opportunities expected to increase faster than the average of all occupations through 2016, according to the U.S. Department of Labor. Busier lifestyles leave little time for mundane chores or last-minute details. Once shy of or intimidated by the concierge desk, savvy travelers now realize this is a free service available for their convenience. Some hotels have experimented with computerized kiosks advertising tours and restaurants. These displays are less personal, however, and since listings are in essence a paid advertisement, they do not provide a true recommendation.

Hotel general managers realize that a concierge department can provide the ultimate in guest services; and it is that type of service that makes a hotel a true luxury hotel. Even many smaller hotels, especially those that cater to business travelers, are now providing concierge service. The best hotels will look for concierges with experience, membership in an organization like Les Clefs d'Or USA, and connections with people in local restaurants, transportation companies, special events organizations, and tourism councils.

FOR MORE INFORMATION

For information on hotel careers, contact

American Hotel and Lodging Association
1201 New York Avenue, NW, Suite 600
Washington, DC 20005-3931
Tel: 202-289-3100
Email: info@ahla.com
http://www.ahla.com

For information on internships, scholarships, or certification requirements, contact

**Educational Institute of the American Hotel
    and Lodging Association**
800 North Magnolia Avenue, Suite 300
Orlando, FL 32803-3271
Tel: 800-752-4567
Email: eiinfo@ahla.com
http://www.ei-ahla.org

For more information on concierge careers and opportunities, contact

Les Clefs d'Or USA
68 Laurie Avenue
Boston, MA 02132
Phone: 617-469-5397
Email: Info@lcdusa.org45
http://lcdusa.org

For information on local chapters, certification, and publications, contact

National Concierge Association
Email: info@nationalconciergeassociation.com
http://www.nationalconciergeassociation.com

☐ HUMAN SERVICES WORKERS

OVERVIEW

Under the supervision of social workers, psychologists, sociologists, and other professionals, *human services workers* offer support to families, the elderly, the poor, and others in need. They teach life and communication skills to people in mental health facilities or substance abuse programs. Employed by agencies, shelters, halfway houses, and hospitals, they work individually with clients or in group counseling. They also direct clients to social services and benefits. There are approximately 339,000 human services workers employed in the United States.

THE JOB

A group of teenagers in a large high school are concerned about the violence that threatens them every day. They have seen their friends and classmates hurt in the school's hallways, on the basketball court, and in the parking lot. In a place built for their education, they fear for their safety, and each of them has something to say about it. They have something to say to the administration, to the parents, and, most of all, to the kids who carry guns and knives to school. Human services workers come to their aid. Human services workers step in to support the efforts of social workers, psychologists, and other professional agencies or programs. Human services workers may work in a school, a community center, a housing project, or a hospital. They may work as aides, assistants, technicians, or counselors. In the case of the high school students who want to improve conditions in their school, human services workers serve

as group leaders under the supervision of a *school social worker*, meeting with some of the students to discuss their fears and concerns. They also meet with administrators, faculty, and parents. Eventually, they conduct a school-wide series of group discussions—listening, taking notes, offering advice, and most important, empowering people to better their communities and their lives.

The term "human services" covers a wide range of careers, from counseling prison inmates to counseling the families of murder victims, from helping someone with a disability find a job to caring for the child of a teenage mother during the school day. From one-on-one interaction to group interaction, from paperwork to footwork, the human services worker is focused on improving the lives of others.

As society changes, so do the concerns of human services workers. New societal problems (such as the rapid spread of AIDS among teenagers and the threat of gang violence) require special attention, as do changes in the population (such as the increasing number of elderly people living on their own and the increasing number of minimum-wage workers unable to fully provide for their families). New laws and political movements also affect human services workers because many social service programs rely heavily on federal and state aid. Although government policy makers are better educated than the policy makers of years past, social service programs are more threatened than ever before. Despite all these changes in society and the changes in the theories of social work, some things stay the same—human services workers care about the well-being of individuals and communities. They are sensitive to the needs of diverse groups of people, and they are actively involved in meeting the needs of the public.

Human services workers have had many of the same responsibilities throughout the years. They offer their clients counseling, representation, emotional support, and the services they need. Although some human services workers assist professionals with the development and evaluation of social programs, policy analysis, and other administrative duties, most work directly with clients.

This direct work can involve aid to specific populations, such as ethnic groups, women, and the poor. Many human services workers assist poor people in numerous ways. They interview clients to identify needed services. They care for clients' children during job or medical appointments and offer clients emotional support. They determine whether clients are eligible for food stamps, Medicaid, or other welfare programs. In some food stamp programs, aides advise low-income family members how to plan, budget, shop for, and prepare balanced meals, often accompanying or driving clients to the store and offering suggestions on the most nutritious and economical food to purchase.

Some aides serve tenants in public housing projects. They are employed by housing agencies or other groups to help tenants relocate. They inform tenants of the use of facilities and the location of community services, such as recreation centers and clinics. They also explain the management's rules about sanitation and maintenance. They may at times help resolve disagreements between tenants and landlords.

Members of specific populations call on the aid of human services workers for support, information, and representation. The human services worker can provide these clients with counseling and emotional support and direct them to support groups and services. Social workers work with human services workers to reach out to the people; together, they visit individuals, families, and neighborhood groups to publicize the supportive services available.

Other clients of human services workers are those experiencing life-cycle changes. Children, adolescents, and the elderly may require assistance in making transitions. Human services workers help parents find proper day care for their children. They educate young mothers about how to care for an infant. They counsel children struggling with family problems or peer pressure. They offer emotional support to gay, lesbian, and bisexual teenagers and involve them in support groups. Some programs help the elderly stay active and help them prepare meals and clean their homes. They also assist the elderly in getting to and from hospitals and community centers and stay in touch with these clients through home visits and telephone calls.

Some human services workers focus on specific problems, such as drug and alcohol abuse. Human services workers assist in developing, organizing, and conducting programs dealing with the causes of and remedies for substance abuse. Workers may help individuals trying to overcome drug or alcohol addiction to master practical skills, such as cooking and doing laundry, and teach them ways to communicate more effectively with others. Domestic violence is also a problem receiving more attention, as more and more people leave abusive situations. Shelters for victims require counselors, assistants, tutors, and day care personnel for their children. Human services workers may also teach living and communication skills in homeless shelters and mental health facilities.

Record keeping is an important part of the duties of human services workers, because records may affect a client's eligibility for future benefits, the proper assessment of a program's success, and the prospect of future funding. Workers prepare and maintain records and case

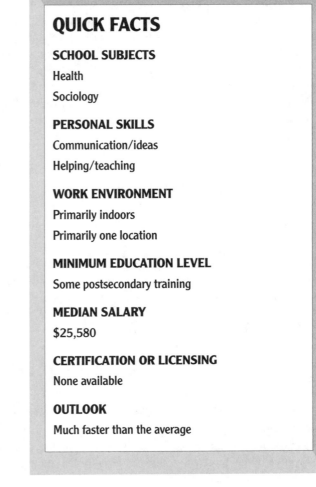

QUICK FACTS

SCHOOL SUBJECTS
Health
Sociology

PERSONAL SKILLS
Communication/ideas
Helping/teaching

WORK ENVIRONMENT
Primarily indoors
Primarily one location

MINIMUM EDUCATION LEVEL
Some postsecondary training

MEDIAN SALARY
$25,580

CERTIFICATION OR LICENSING
None available

OUTLOOK
Much faster than the average

files of every person with whom they work. They record clients' responses to the various programs and treatment. They must also track costs in group homes in order to stay within budget.

REQUIREMENTS
High School

Some employers hire people with only a high school education, but these employees might find it hard to move beyond clerical positions. Interested high school students should plan to attend a college or university and should take classes in English, mathematics, political science, psychology, and sociology.

Postsecondary Training

Certificate and associate's degree programs in human services or mental health are offered at community and junior colleges, vocational-technical institutes, and other postsecondary institutions. It is also possible to pursue a bachelor's degree in human services. Almost 500 human services education programs exist; academic programs such as these prepare students for occupations in the human services. Because the educators at these colleges and universities stay in regular contact with the social work employers in their area, the programs are continually revised to meet the changing needs of the field. Students are exposed early and often to the kinds of situations they may encounter on the job.

Undergraduate and graduate programs typically include courses in psychology, sociology, crisis intervention, family dynamics, therapeutic interviewing, rehabilitation, and gerontology.

Other Requirements

Many people perform human services work because they want to make a difference in their community. They may also like connecting on a personal level with other people, offering them emotional support, helping them sort out problems, and teaching them how to care for themselves and their families. A genuine interest in the lives and concerns of others and sensitivity to their situations are important to a human services worker. An artistic background can also be valuable in human services. Some programs in mental health facilities, domestic violence shelters, and other group homes use art therapy. Painting, music, dance, and creative writing are sometimes incorporated into counseling sessions, providing a client with alternative modes of expression.

In addition to the rewarding aspects of the job, a human services worker must be prepared to take on difficult responsibilities. The work can be very stressful. The problems of some populations—such as prison inmates, battered women and children, substance abusers, and the poor—can seem insurmountable. Their stories and day-to-day lives can seem tragic. Even if human services workers are not counseling clients, they are working directly with clients on some level. Just helping a person fill out an application or prepare a household budget requires a good disposition and the ability to be supportive. Clients may not welcome help and may not even care about their own well-being. In these cases, a human services worker must remain firm but supportive and encouraging. Patience is very important, whatever the area of human service.

The workload for a human services worker can also be overwhelming. An agency with limited funding cannot always afford to hire the number of employees it needs. A human services worker employed by an understaffed agency will probably be overworked. This can sometimes result in employee burnout.

EXPLORING

To get an idea of the requirements of human service, you can volunteer your time to a local human services agency or institution. Church organizations also involve young people in volunteer work, as do the Red Cross, the Boy Scouts, and the Girl Scouts. Volunteer work could include reading to blind or elderly people and visiting nursing homes and halfway homes. You might get involved organizing group recreation programs at the YMCA or YWCA or performing light clerical duties in an office. You could also encourage any high school organizations to which you belong to become actively involved in charity work.

Some members of high school organizations also perform social services within their own schools, educating classmates on the dangers of gangs, unsafe sex, and substance abuse. By being actively involved in your community, you can gain experience in human services as well as build up a history of volunteer service that will impress future employers.

EMPLOYERS

Approximately 339,000 human services workers are employed in the United States. They are employed in a variety of settings, including agency offices, community centers, group homes, halfway houses, mental health facilities, hospitals, shelters, and the private homes of clients. About 30 percent of human services workers are employed by state and local governments in public welfare agencies and facilities for people with physical and mental disabilities.

STARTING OUT

Students may find jobs through their high school counselors or local and state human services agencies. Sometimes summer jobs and volunteer work can develop into full-time employment upon graduation. Employers try to be selective in their hiring because many human services jobs involve direct contact with people who are impaired and therefore vulnerable to exploitation. Experience with helping others is a definite advantage.

ADVANCEMENT

Job performance has some bearing on pay raises and advancement for human services workers. However, career advancement almost always depends on formal education, such as a bachelor's or master's degree in social work, counseling, rehabilitation, or some other related field. Many employers encourage their workers to further their education and some may even reimburse part of the costs of school. In addition, many employers provide in-service training such as seminars and workshops.

EARNINGS

Salaries of human services workers depend in part on their employer and amount of experience. According to the U.S. Department of Labor, median annual earnings of social and human service assistants were $25,580 in 2006. Salaries ranged from less than $16,180 to more than $40,780.

WORK ENVIRONMENT

Most human services workers work a standard 40-hour week, spending time both in the office and in the field interviewing clients and performing other support services. Some weekend and evening work may be required, but compensatory time off is usually granted. Workers in residential settings generally work in shifts. Because group homes need 24-hour staffing, workers usually work some evenings and weekends.

Work conditions are affected by the size and location of the town in which the work is found. The societal problems of large, urban areas are different from those of small, rural areas. In a city, human services workers deal with issues of crime, racism, gang warfare, and violence in the schools. These problems can exist in smaller communities as well, but human services workers in rural areas focus more on work with the elderly and the poor. Rural communities typically have an older population, with people living deeper in the country and farther from public and private services. This can require more transportation time. The social services in rural areas, because of lower salaries and poorer facilities, typically have trouble attracting workers.

Offices and facilities may be clean and cheerful, or they may be dismal, cramped, and inadequately equipped. While out in the field with clients, workers may also find themselves in dangerous, squalid areas. In a large city, workers can rely on public transportation, whereas workers in a rural community must often drive long distances.

OUTLOOK

Employment for human services workers will grow much faster than the average through 2016, according to the U.S. Department of Labor. The best opportunities will be in job-training programs, residential care facilities, and private social service agencies, which include such services as adult daycare and meal delivery programs. Correctional facilities are also expected to employ many more human services workers. Because counseling inmates and offenders can be undesirable work, there are a number of high-paying jobs available in that area.

New ideas in treating people with disabilities or mental illness also influence employment growth in group homes and residential care facilities. Public concern for the homeless—many of whom are former mental patients who were released under service reductions in the 1980s—as well as for troubled teenagers, and those with substance abuse problems, is likely to bring about new community-based programs and group residences.

Job prospects in public agencies are not as bright as they once were because of fiscal policies that tighten eligibility requirements for federal welfare and other payments. State and local governments are expected to remain major employers, however, as the burden of providing social services such as welfare, child support, and nutrition programs is shifted from the federal government to the state and local level. In larger cities, such as New York or Washington, D.C., jobs in the public sector will be more plentiful than in smaller cities because of the higher demand. There is also a higher burnout rate in the larger cities, resulting in more job opportunities as people vacate their positions for other careers.

FOR MORE INFORMATION

For more information on careers in counseling, contact
American Counseling Association
5999 Stevenson Avenue
Alexandria, VA 22304-3304
Tel: 800-347-6647
http://www.counseling.org

To access the online publication Choices: Careers in Social Work, *visit the NASW's Web site:*
National Association of Social Workers (NASW)
750 First Street, NE, Suite 700
Washington, DC 20002-4241
http://www.naswdc.org

For information on student memberships, scholarships, and master's degree programs in human services, visit the NOHS Web site.
National Organization for Human Services (NOHS)
90 Madison Street, Suite 206
Denver, CO 80206-5411
Tel: 303-320-5430
http://www.nationalhumanservices.org

For information on employment with government human service agencies, contact
U.S. Department of Health and Human Services
200 Independence Avenue, SW
Washington, DC 20201-0004
Tel: 877-696-6775
http://www.hhs.gov

The following is a job search Web site for social services and social work positions:
SocialService.Com
http://www.socialservice.com

INDUSTRIAL ENGINEERING TECHNICIANS

OVERVIEW

Industrial engineering technicians assist industrial engineers in their duties: they collect and analyze data and make recommendations for the efficient use of personnel, materials, and machines to produce goods or to provide services. They may study the time, movements, and methods a worker uses to accomplish daily tasks in production, maintenance, or clerical areas.

Industrial engineering technicians prepare charts to illustrate workflow, floor layouts, materials handling, and machine utilization. They make statistical studies, analyze production costs, prepare layouts of machinery and equipment, help plan workflow and work assignments, and recommend revisions to revamp production methods or improve standards. As part of their job, industrial engineering technicians often use equipment such as computers, timers, and video cameras. There are approximately 75,000 industrial engineering technicians employed in the United States.

THE JOB

The type of work done by an industrial engineering technician depends on the location, size, and products of the company for which he or she works. Usually a technician's duties fall into one or more of the following areas: work measurement, production control, wage and job evaluation, quality control, or plant layout.

Industrial engineering technicians involved in methods engineering analyze new and existing products to determine the best way to make them at the lowest cost. In these analyses, *methods engineering technicians* recommend which processing equipment to use; determine how fast materials can be processed; develop flowcharts; and consider all materials handling, movement, and storage aspects of the production.

The *materials handling technician* studies the current methods of handling material, then compares and evaluates alternatives. The technician will suggest changes that reduce physical effort, make handling safer, and lower costs and damage to products.

Work measurement technicians study the production rate of a given product and determine how much time is needed for all the activities involved. They do this by timing the motions necessary for a complete operation, analyzing tapes of workers, and consulting historical statistics collected in the factory. *Time study technicians* analyze and determine elements of work, their order, and the time required to produce a part.

The engineering technicians in production control often work in scheduling departments, where they coordinate many complex details to ensure product delivery on a specified date. To do this, *production control technicians* must know the products and assemblies to be made, the routes to be used through the plant, and the time required for the process. These technicians also issue orders to manufacture products, check machine loads, and maintain constant surveillance of the master schedules. Production control technicians also work in dispatching offices, where they issue orders to the production areas, watch department machine loads, report progress of products, and expedite the delivery of needed parts to avoid delays.

Inventory control technicians maintain inventories of raw materials, semifinished products, completed products, packaging materials, and supplies. They ensure an adequate supply of raw materials, watch for obsolete parts, and prevent damage or loss to products.

In quality control, technicians work with inspection departments to maintain quality standards set by production engineers. They check all incoming materials and forecast the quality of obtainable materials. *Quality control technicians* use a variety of techniques to perform duties that include part-drawing surveillance, checking of parts with inspection tools, identifying trouble, and providing corrective procedures.

Cost control technicians compare actual product costs with budgeted allowances. These technicians investigate cost discrepancies, offer corrective measures, and analyze results.

Budget technicians gather figures and facts to project and graph break-even points. They help prepare budgets for management and present the effects of production schedules on profitability.

Technicians working in the area of wage and job evaluation gather and organize information pertaining to the skill, manual effort, education, and other factors involved in the jobs of all hourly employees. This information helps to set salary ranges and establish job descriptions.

Plant layout technicians work with materials handling personnel, supervisors, and management to help make alterations in manufacturing facilities. These technicians study old floor plans; consider all present and future aspects of operations; and revise, consult, and then propose layouts to production and management personnel.

REQUIREMENTS

High School

In high school, take classes in algebra, geometry, calculus, chemistry, physics, trigonometry, and English. Mechanical drawing, metal shop, and communications will also be helpful. Computers have become the most used tool in industrial engineering, so computer science classes are critical if you are considering a career in this field. Also recommended are courses in shop sketching, blueprint reading, mechanical drawing, and model making, if available.

Postsecondary Training

Most employers prefer to hire someone with at least a two-year degree in engineering technology although it is possible to qualify for some jobs with no formal training. Training is available at technical institutes, junior and community colleges, extension divisions of universities, public and private vocational-technical schools, and through some technical training programs in the armed services.

Most two-year associate's programs accredited by the Accreditation Board for Engineering and Technology (ABET) include first-year courses in mathematics, orthographic and isometric sketching, blueprint reading, manufacturing processes, communications, technical reporting, introduction to numerical control, and introduction to computer-aided design (CAD).

Typical second-year courses include methods, operation, and safety engineering; industrial materials; statistics; quality control; computer control of industrial processes; plant layout and materials handling; process planning and manufacturing costs; production problems; psychology and human relations; and industrial organization and institutions. Since the type and quality of programs and schools vary considerably, prospective students are advised to consider ABET-accredited programs first.

Certification or Licensing

To give recognition and encouragement to industrial engineering technicians, the National Institute for Certification in Engineering Technologies has established a certification program that some technicians may wish to consider. Although certification is not generally required by employers, those with certification often have a competitive advantage when it comes to hiring and promotions. Certification is available at various levels, each combining a written examination in a specialty field with a specified amount of job-related experience.

QUICK FACTS

SCHOOL SUBJECTS
Computer science
Mathematics

PERSONAL SKILLS
Communication/ideas
Technical/scientific

WORK ENVIRONMENT
Primarily indoors
Primarily one location

MINIMUM EDUCATION LEVEL
Associate's degree

MEDIAN SALARY
$46,810

CERTIFICATION OR LICENSING
Voluntary

OUTLOOK
About as fast as the average

Other Requirements

You should be adept at compiling and organizing data and be able to express yourself clearly and persuasively both orally and in writing. You should be detail oriented and enjoy solving problems.

EXPLORING

Opportunities to gain experience in high school are somewhat limited. However, you can obtain part-time work or summer jobs in industrial settings, even if not specifically in the industrial engineering area. Although this work may consist of menial tasks, it offers firsthand experience and demonstrates interest to future employers. Part-time jobs often lead to permanent employment, and some companies offer tuition reimbursement for educational costs.

You might also consider joining a science or engineering club, such as the Junior Engineering Technical Society

(JETS). JETS offers academic competitions and conducts design contests in which students learn and apply science and engineering principles. It also publishes the *Pre-Engineering Times*, a newsletter that will be of interest if you are interested in engineering. It contains information on engineering specialties, competitions, schools, scholarships, and other resources. Visit http://www.jets.org/newsletter/index.cfmto read the publication. Insights into the industrial engineering field can also be obtained in less direct ways. Professional associations regularly publish newsletters (such as *Certified Engineering Technician*, which is published by the American Society of Certified Engineering Technicians) and other information relevant to the technician. Industrial firms frequently advertise or publish articles in professional journals or in business and general interest magazines that discuss innovations in plant layout, cost control, and productivity improvements. By reading these articles, you can acquaint yourself with and stay informed on developments in the field.

EMPLOYERS

Approximately 75,000 industrial engineering technicians are employed in the United States. These technicians most often work in durable goods manufacturing, such as electronic and electrical machinery and equipment, industrial machinery and equipment, instruments, and transportation equipment. Others work in the automotive and aerospace industries. Some technicians are employed by engineering and business services companies that do contract engineering work. The U.S. Departments of Defense, Transportation, Agriculture, and Interior are also major employers, along with state and municipal governments.

STARTING OUT

Many industrial engineering technicians find their first jobs through interviews with company recruiters who visit campuses. In many cases, students are invited to visit the prospective employer's plant for further consultation and to become better acquainted with the area, product, and facilities. For many students, the career services office of their college or technical school is the best source of possible jobs. Local manufacturers or companies are in constant contact with these facilities, so they have the most up-to-date job listings.

ADVANCEMENT

As industrial engineering technicians gain additional experience, and especially if they pursue further education, they become candidates for advancement. Con-

tinuing education is fast becoming the most important tool for advancement. Many employers encourage their employees to pursue continuing education and will reimburse education costs.

The typical advancement path for industrial engineering technicians is to become a supervisor, an industrial engineer, or possibly a chief industrial engineer.

Here are some examples of positions to which technicians might aspire:

Production control managers supervise all production control employees, train new technicians, and coordinate manufacturing departments.

Production supervisors oversee manufacturing personnel and compare departmental records of production, scrap, and expenditures with departmental allowances.

Plant layout engineers supervise all plant-layout department personnel, estimate costs, and confer directly with other department heads to obtain information needed by the layout department.

Managers of quality control supervise all inspection and quality control employees, select techniques, teach employees new techniques, and meet with tool room and production people when manufacturing tolerances or scrap become a problem.

Chief industrial engineers supervise all industrial engineering employees, consult with department heads, direct departmental projects, set budgets, and prepare reports.

EARNINGS

Salaries for industrial engineering technicians vary according to the product being manufactured, geographic location, and the education and skills of the technician. The U.S. Department of Labor reports that industrial engineering technicians earned salaries that ranged from less than $30,190 to more than $79,180 in 2006, with a median salary of $46,810. Industrial engineering technicians who worked in the aerospace product and parts manufacturing industry earned a mean salary of $61,730 in 2006. Technicians employed in data processing, hosting, and related services earned an average salary of 73,720 in 2006. In addition to salary, most employers offer paid vacation time, holidays, insurance and retirement plans, and tuition assistance for work-related courses.

WORK ENVIRONMENT

Industrial engineering technicians generally work indoors. Depending on their jobs, they may work in the shop or office areas or in both. The type of plant facilities depends on the product. For example, an electronics plant producing small electronic products requiring very exacting tolerances has very clean working conditions.

Industrial engineering technicians often travel to other locations or areas. They may accompany engineers to technical conventions or on visits to other companies to gain insight into new or different methods of operation and production.

Continuing education plays a large role in the life of industrial engineering technicians. They may attend classes or seminars, keeping up to date with emerging technology and methods of managing production efficiently.

Hours of work may vary and depend on factory shifts. Industrial engineering technicians are often asked to get jobs done quickly and to meet very tight deadlines.

OUTLOOK

As products become more technically demanding to produce, competitive pressures will force companies to improve and update manufacturing facilities and product designs. Thus, employment for well-trained industrial engineering technicians will grow about as fast as the average for all occupations through 2016, according to the U.S. Department of Labor. Opportunities will be best for individuals who have up-to-date skills. As technology becomes more sophisticated, employers will continue to seek technicians who require the least amount of additional job training.

The employment outlook varies by area of specialization and industry. For example, changing and increasing numbers of environmental and safety regulations may lead companies to revise some of their procedures and practices, and new technicians may be needed to assist in these changeovers. Technicians whose jobs are defense-related may experience improved opportunities because of recent increases to the defense budget.

Prospective technicians should keep in mind that advances in technology and management techniques make industrial engineering a constantly changing field. Technicians will be able to take advantage of new opportunities only if they are willing to continue their training and education throughout their careers.

FOR MORE INFORMATION

For information on accredited educational programs, contact

Accreditation Board for Engineering and Technology
111 Market Place, Suite 1050
Baltimore, MD 21202-7116
Tel: 410-347-7700
http://www.abet.org

For information about membership in a professional society specifically created for certified engineering technicians, contact

American Society of Certified Engineering Technicians
PO Box 1356
Brandon, MS 39043-1356
Tel: 601-824-8991
Email: general-manager@ascet.org
http://www.ascet.org

For information on careers and training as an industrial engineer, contact

Institute of Industrial Engineers
3577 Parkway Lane, Suite 200
Norcross, GA 30092-2833
Tel: 800-494-0460
http://www.iienet.org

Visit the society's Web site to read the online brochures Engineering Technologists and Technicians *and* Industrial Engineering.

Junior Engineering Technical Society
1420 King Street, Suite 405
Alexandria, VA 22314-2750
Tel: 703-548-5387
Email: info@jets.org
http://www.jets.org

For information on certification, contact

National Institute for Certification in Engineering Technologies
1420 King Street
Alexandria, VA 22314-2794
Tel: 888-476-4238
http://www.nicet.org

INDUSTRIAL MACHINERY MECHANICS

OVERVIEW

Industrial machinery mechanics, often called *machinery maintenance mechanics* or *industrial machinery repairers*, inspect, maintain, repair, and adjust industrial production and processing machinery and equipment to ensure its proper operation in various industries. There are

QUICK FACTS

SCHOOL SUBJECTS

Mathematics

Technical/shop

PERSONAL SKILLS

Mechanical/manipulative

Technical/scientific

WORK ENVIRONMENT

Primarily indoors

Primarily one location

MINIMUM EDUCATION LEVEL

Apprenticeship

MEDIAN SALARY

$41,050

CERTIFICATION OR LICENSING

None available

OUTLOOK

About as fast as the average

approximately 345,000 industrial machinery mechanics employed in the United States.

THE JOB

The types of machinery on which industrial machinery mechanics work are as varied as the types of industries operating in the United States today. Mechanics are employed in metal stamping plants, printing plants, chemical and plastics plants, and almost any type of large-scale industrial operation that can be imagined. The machinery in these plants must be maintained regularly. Breakdowns and delays with one machine can hinder a plant's entire operation, which is costly for the company.

Preventive maintenance is a major part of mechanics' jobs. They inspect the equipment, oil and grease moving components, and clean and repair parts. They also keep detailed maintenance records on the equipment they service. They often follow blueprints and engineering specifications to maintain and fix equipment.

When breakdowns occur, mechanics may partially or completely disassemble a machine to make the necessary repairs. They replace worn bearings, adjust clutches, and replace and repair defective parts. They may have to order replacement parts from the machinery's manufacturer. If no parts are available, they may have to make the necessary replacements, using milling machines, lathes, or other tooling equipment. After the machine is reassembled, they may have to make adjustments to its operational settings. They often work with the machine's regular operator to test it. When repairing electronically controlled machinery, mechanics may work closely with electronic repairers or electricians who maintain the machine's electronic parts.

Often these mechanics can identify potential breakdowns and fix problems before any real damage or delays occur. They may notice that a machine is vibrating, rattling, or squeaking, or they may see that the items produced by the machine are flawed. Many types of new machinery are built with programmed internal evaluation systems that check the accuracy and condition of equipment. This assists mechanics in their jobs, but it also makes them responsible for maintaining the checkup systems.

Machinery installations are becoming another facet of a mechanic's job. As plants retool and invest in new equipment, they rely on mechanics to properly situate and install the machinery. In many plants, millwrights traditionally did this job, but as employers increasingly seek workers with multiple skills, industrial machinery mechanics are taking on new responsibilities.

Industrial machinery mechanics use a wide range of tools when doing preventive maintenance or making repairs. For example, they may use simple tools such as a screwdriver and wrench to repair an engine or a hoist to lift a printing press off the ground. Sometimes they solder or weld equipment. They use power and hand tools and precision measuring instruments. In some shops, mechanics troubleshoot the entire plant's operations. Others may become experts in electronics, hydraulics, pneumatics, or other specialties.

REQUIREMENTS
High School

While most employers prefer to hire those who have completed high school, opportunities do exist for those without a diploma as long as they have had some kind of related training. While you are in high school, take courses in mechanical drawing, general mathematics, algebra, and geometry. Other classes that will help prepare you for this career are physics, computer science, and electronics. Any class that gives you experience in blueprint reading adds to your qualifications.

Postsecondary Training

In the past, most industrial machinery mechanics learned the skills of the trade informally by spending several years as helpers in a particular factory. Currently, as machinery has become more complex, more formal training is necessary. Today, many mechanics learn the trade through apprenticeship programs sponsored by a local trade union. Apprenticeship programs usually last four years and include both on-the-job and related classroom training. In addition to the use and care of machine and hand tools, apprentices learn the operation, lubrication, and adjustment of the machinery and equipment they will maintain. In class they learn shop mathematics, blueprint reading, safety, hydraulics, welding, and other subjects related to the trade.

Students may also obtain training through vocational or technical schools. Useful programs are those that offer machine shop courses and provide training in electronics and numerical control machine tools.

Other Requirements

Students interested in this field should possess mechanical aptitude and manual dexterity. Good physical condition and agility are necessary because as a mechanic you will sometimes have to lift heavy objects, crawl under large machines, or climb to reach equipment located high above the factory floor.

Mechanics are responsible for valuable equipment and are often called upon to exercise considerable independent judgment. Because of technological advances, you should be willing to learn the requirements of new machines and production techniques. When a plant purchases new equipment, the equipment's manufacturer often trains plant employees in proper operation and maintenance. Technological change requires mechanics to be adaptable and to have inquiring minds.

EXPLORING

If you are interested in this field, you should take as many shop courses as you can. Exploring and repairing machinery, such as automobiles and home appliances, will also sharpen your skills. In addition, try landing part-time work or a summer job in an industrial plant that gives you the opportunity to observe industrial repair work being done.

EMPLOYERS

Approximately 345,000 industrial machinery mechanics are employed in the United States. These mechanics work in a wide variety of plants and are employed in every part of the country, although employment is concentrated in industrialized areas. According to the U.S. Department of Labor, two-thirds of all industrial machinery mechanics work in manufacturing industries such as chemicals, motor vehicles, food processing, textile mill products, primary metals, and fabricated metal products. Others work for public utilities, government agencies, and mining companies.

STARTING OUT

Jobs can be obtained by directly applying to companies that use industrial equipment or machinery. The majority of mechanics work for manufacturing plants. These plants are found in a wide variety of industries, including the automotive, plastics, textile, electronics, packaging, food, beverage, and aerospace industries. Chances for job openings may be better at a large plant. New workers are generally assigned to work as helpers or trainees.

Prospective mechanics also may learn of job openings or apprenticeship programs through local unions. Industrial mechanics may be represented by one of several unions, depending on their industry and place of employment. These unions include the International Union, United Automobile, Aerospace, and Agricultural Implement Workers of America; the United Steelworkers of America; the United Auto Workers; the International Union of Electronic, Electrical, Salaried, Machine, and Furniture Workers; the United Brotherhood of Carpenters and Joiners of America; and the International Association of Machinists and Aerospace Workers. According to the U.S. Department of Labor, approximately 25 percent of all industrial machinery mechanics are members of a union. Private and state employment offices are other good sources of job openings.

ADVANCEMENT

Those who begin as helpers or trainees usually become journeymen in four years. Although opportunities for advancement beyond this rank are somewhat limited, industrial machinery mechanics who learn more complicated machinery and equipment can advance into higher-paying positions. The most highly skilled mechanics may be promoted to master mechanics. Those who demonstrate good leadership and interpersonal skills can become supervisors. Skilled mechanics also have the option of becoming machinists, numerical control tool programmers, precision metalworkers, packaging machinery technicians, and robotics technicians. Some of these positions do require additional training, but the skills of a mechanic readily transfer to these areas.

EARNINGS

In 2006, median hourly earnings for industrial machinery mechanics were $19.74 (or $41,050 annually), according to the U.S. Department of Labor. The lowest paid 10 percent earned less than $12.84 an hour (or $26,710 annually). The highest paid 10 percent earned $29.85 or more per hour (or $62,080 annually). Apprentices generally earn lower wages and earn incremental raises as they advance in their training. Earnings vary based on experience, skills, type of industry, and geographic location. Those working in union plants generally earn more than those in nonunion plants. Most industrial machinery mechanics are provided with benefit packages, which can include paid holidays and vacations; medical, dental, and life insurance; and retirement plans.

WORK ENVIRONMENT

Industrial machinery mechanics work in all types of manufacturing plants, which may be hot, noisy, and dirty or relatively quiet and clean. Mechanics frequently work with greasy, dirty equipment and need to be able to adapt to a variety of physical conditions. Because machinery is not always accessible, mechanics may have to work in stooped or cramped positions or on high ladders.

Although working around machinery poses some danger, this risk is minimized with proper safety precautions. Modern machinery includes many safety features and devices, and most plants follow good safety practices. Mechanics often wear protective clothing and equipment, such as hard hats and safety belts, glasses, and shoes.

Mechanics work with little supervision and need to be able to work well with others. They need to be flexible and respond to changing priorities, which can result in interruptions that pull a mechanic off one job to repair a more urgent problem. Although the standard workweek is 40 hours, overtime is common. Because factories and other sites cannot afford breakdowns, industrial machinery mechanics may be called to the plant at night or on weekends for emergency repairs.

OUTLOOK

The U.S. Department of Labor predicts that employment for industrial machinery mechanics will grow about as fast as the average for all occupations through 2016. Some industries will have a greater need for mechanics than others. Much of the new automated production equipment that companies are purchasing has its own self-diagnostic capabilities and is more reliable than older equipment. Although this machinery still needs to be maintained, most job openings will stem from the replacement of transferring or retiring workers.

Certain industries are extremely susceptible to changing economic factors and reduce production activities in slow periods. During these periods, companies may lay off workers or reduce hours. Mechanics are less likely to be laid off than other workers as machines need to be maintained regardless of production levels. Slower production periods and temporary shutdowns are often used to overhaul equipment. Nonetheless, employment opportunities are generally better at companies experiencing growth or stable levels of production.

Because machinery is becoming more complex and automated, mechanics need to be more highly skilled than in the past. Mechanics who stay up to date with new technologies, particularly those related to electronics and computers, should find favorable employment opportunities over the next decade.

FOR MORE INFORMATION

For information about apprentice programs, contact the UAW.

International Union, United Automobile, Aerospace, and Agricultural Implement Workers of America (UAW)
8000 East Jefferson Avenue
Detroit, MI 48214-3963
Tel: 313-926-5000
http://www.uaw.org

For information about the machining industry and career opportunities, contact

National Tooling and Machining Association
9300 Livingston Road
Fort Washington, MD 20744-4998
Tel: 800-248-6862
Email: info@ntma.org
http://www.ntma.org

For industry information, contact

Precision Machined Products Association
6700 West Snowville Road
Brecksville, OH 44141-3212
Tel: 440-526-0300
http://www.pmpa.org

INSTRUMENTATION TECHNICIANS

OVERVIEW

Instrumentation technicians are skilled craftsworkers who do precision work and are involved in the field of measurement and control. Technicians inspect, test, repair, and adjust instruments that detect, measure, and record changes in industrial environments. They work with theoretical or analytical problems, helping engineers improve instrument and system performance.

THE JOB

Instrumentation technicians work with complex instruments that detect, measure, and record changes in industrial environments. As part of their duties, these technicians perform tests, develop new instruments, and install, repair, inspect, and maintain the instruments. Examples of such instruments include altimeters, pressure gauges, speedometers, and radiation detection devices.

Some instrumentation technicians operate the laboratory equipment that produces or records the effects of certain conditions on the test instruments, such as vibration, stress, temperature, humidity, pressure, altitude, and acceleration. Other technicians sketch, build, and modify electronic and mechanical fixtures, instruments, and related apparatuses.

As part of their duties, technicians might verify the dimensions and functions of devices assembled by other technicians and craftsworkers, plan test programs, and direct technical personnel in carrying out these tests. Instrumentation technicians also perform mathematical calculations on instrument readings and test results so they can be used in graphs and written reports.

Instrumentation technicians work with three major categories of instruments: 1) pneumatic and electropneumatic equipment, which includes temperature and flow transmitters and receivers and devices that start or are started by such things as pressure springs, diaphragms, and bellows; 2) hydraulic instrumentation, which includes hydraulic valves, hydraulic valve operators, and electrohydraulic equipment; and 3) electrical and electronic equipment, which includes electrical sensing elements and transducers, electronic recorders, electronic telemetering systems, and electronic computers.

In some industries, a technician might work on equipment from each category, while in other industries a technician might be responsible for only one specific

QUICK FACTS

SCHOOL SUBJECTS
Mathematics
Physics
Technical/shop

PERSONAL SKILLS
Mechanical/manipulative
Technical/scientific

WORK ENVIRONMENT
Primarily indoors
Primarily one location

MINIMUM EDUCATION LEVEL
Associate's degree

MEDIAN SALARY
$46,250

CERTIFICATION OR LICENSING
Voluntary

OUTLOOK
About as fast as the average

type of task. The different levels of responsibility depend also on the instrumentation technician's level of training and experience.

Instrumentation technicians may hold a variety of different positions. *Mechanical instrumentation technicians*, for example, handle routine mechanical functions. They check out equipment before operation, calibrate it during operation, rebuild it using standard replacement parts, mount interconnecting equipment from blueprints, and perform routine repairs using common hand tools. They must be able to read both instrumentation and electronic schematic diagrams. *Instrumentation repair technicians* determine the causes of malfunctions and make repairs. Such repairs usually involve individual pieces of equipment, as distinguished from entire systems. This job requires experience, primarily laboratory-oriented, beyond that of mechanical instrumentation technicians.

Troubleshooting instrumentation technicians make adjustments to instruments and control systems, calibrate equipment, set up tests, diagnose malfunctions, and revise existing systems. Their work is performed either on-site or at a workbench. Advanced training in mathematics, physics, and graphics is required for this level of work. Technicians who are involved in the design of instruments are called *instrumentation design technicians*. They work under the supervision of a design engineer. Using information prepared by engineers, they build models and prototypes and prepare sketches, working drawings, and diagrams. These technicians also test out new system designs, order parts, and make mock-ups of new systems.

Technicians in certain industries have more specialized duties and responsibilities. *Biomedical equipment technicians* work with instruments used during medical procedures. They receive special training in the biomedical area in which their instruments are used. For more information on this career, see the article Biomedical Equipment Technicians.

Calibration technicians, also known as *standards laboratory technicians*, work in the electronics industry and in aerospace and aircraft manufacturing. As part of their inspection of systems and instruments, they measure parts for conformity to specifications, and they help develop calibration standards, devise formulas to solve problems in measurement and calibration, and write procedures and practical guides for other calibration technicians.

Electromechanical technicians work with automated mechanical equipment controlled by electronic sensing devices. They assist mechanical engineers in the design and development of such equipment, analyze test results, and write reports. The technician follows blueprints, operates metalworking machines, builds instrument housings, installs electrical equipment, and calibrates instruments and machinery. Technicians who specialize in the assembly of prototype instruments are known as *development technicians*. *Fabrication technicians* specialize in the assembly of production instruments.

Nuclear instrumentation technicians work with instruments at a nuclear power plant. These instruments control the various systems within the nuclear reactor, detect radiation, and sound alarms in case of equipment failure. *Instrument sales technicians* work for equipment manufacturing companies. They analyze customer needs, outline specifications for equipment cost and function, and sometimes do emergency troubleshooting.

REQUIREMENTS

High School

Math and science courses, such as algebra, geometry, physics, and chemistry, are essential prerequisites to becoming an instrumentation technician. In addition, machine and electrical shop courses will help you become familiar with electrical, mechanical, and electronic technology. Classes in mechanical drawing and computer-aided drafting are also beneficial. Instrumentation technicians also need good writing and communication skills, so be sure to take English, composition, and speech classes.

Postsecondary Training

The basic requirement for an entry-level job is completion of a two-year technical program or equivalent experience in a related field. Such equivalent experience may come from work in an electronics or manufacturing firm or any job that provides experience working with mechanical or electrical equipment.

Technical programs beyond high school can be found in community colleges as well as technical schools. Programs are offered in many different disciplines in addition to instrumentation technology. Programs may be in electronics or in electrical, mechanical, biomedical, or nuclear technology.

Most programs allow technicians to develop hands-on and laboratory skills as well as learn theory. Classes are likely to include instruction on electronic circuitry, computer science, mathematics, and physics. Courses in basic electronics, electrical theory, and graphics are also important. Technical writing is helpful, as most technicians will prepare technical reports. Industrial economics, applied psychology, and plant management courses are helpful to those who plan to move into customer service or design.

Certification or Licensing

Instrumentation technicians who graduate from a recognized technical program may become certified by the National Institute for Certification in Engineering Technologies, although this is usually not a required part of a job. Certification is available at various levels, each combining a written exam in one of more than 25 specialty fields with a specified amount of job-related experience. Instrumentation technicians who specialize in biomedical equipment repair can receive voluntary certification from the Board of Examiners for Biomedical Equipment

Technicians. ISA—The Instrumentation, Systems, and Automation Society also offers certification for technicians who are involved in automation, control, maintenance, and manufacturing.

Other Requirements

To be an instrumentation technician, you need mathematical and scientific aptitude and the patience to methodically pursue complex questions. A tolerance for following prescribed procedures is essential, especially when undertaking assignments requiring a very precise, unchanging system of problem solving. Successful instrumentation technicians are able to provide solutions quickly and accurately even in stressful situations.

EXPLORING

As a way to test your abilities and learn more about calibration work try building small electronic equipment. Kits for building radios and other small appliances are available in some electronics shops. This will give you a basic understanding of electronic components and applications.

Some communities and schools also have clubs for people interested in electronics. They may offer classes that teach basic skills in construction, repair, and adjustment of electrical and electronic products. Model building, particularly in hard plastic and steel, will give you a good understanding of how to adapt and fit parts together. It may also help develop your hand skills if you want to work with precision instruments.

Visits to industrial laboratories, instrument shops, research laboratories, power installations, and manufacturing companies that rely on automated processes can expose you to the activities of instrumentation technicians. During such visits, you might be able to speak with technicians about their work or with managers about possible openings in their company. Also, you might look into getting a summer or part-time job as a helper on an industrial maintenance crew.

EMPLOYERS

Employers of instrumentation technicians include oil refineries, chemical and industrial laboratories, electronics firms, aircraft and aeronautical manufacturers, and biomedical firms. Companies involved in space exploration, oceanographic research, and national defense systems also employ instrumentation technicians. In addition, they work in various capacities in such industries as automotives, food, metals, ceramics, pulp and paper, power, textiles, pharmaceuticals, mining, metals, and pollution control.

STARTING OUT

Many companies recruit students prior to their graduation. Chemical and medical research companies especially need maintenance and operations technicians and usually recruit at schools where training in these areas is strong. Similarly, many industries in search of design technicians recruit at technical institutes and community colleges where the program is likely to meet their needs.

Students may also get assistance in their job searches through their schools' career services office, or they may learn about openings through ads in the newspapers. Prospective employees can also apply directly to a company in which they are interested.

ADVANCEMENT

Entry-level technicians develop their skills by learning tasks on their employers' equipment. Those with good academic records may, upon completion of an employer's basic program, move to an advanced level in sales or another area where a general understanding of the field is more important than specific laboratory skills. Technicians who have developed proficiency in instrumentation may choose to move to a supervisory or specialized position that requires knowledge of a particular aspect of instrumentation.

EARNINGS

Earnings for instrumentation technicians vary by industry, geographic region, educational background, experience, and level of responsibility. According to the U.S. Department of Labor, median annual earnings of precision instrument and equipment repairers were $46,250 in 2006. Median annual earnings of electromechanical technicians were $44,720 in 2006. Salaries ranged from less than $29,830 to more than $68,700. Electrical and electronic engineering technicians had median annual earnings of $50,660 in 2006, and mechanical engineering technicians earned $45,850. Medical equipment repairers earned average salaries of $40,580. Employee benefits vary, but can include paid vacations and holidays, sick leave, insurance benefits, 401(k) plans, profit sharing, pension plans, and tuition assistance programs.

WORK ENVIRONMENT

Working conditions vary widely for instrumentation technicians. An oil refinery plant job is as different from space mission instrumentation work as a nuclear reactor instrumentation job is different from work in the operating room of a hospital. All these jobs use similar principles, however, and instrumentation technicians can master new areas by applying what they have learned previously. For technicians who would like to travel, the petroleum industry, in particular, provides employment opportunities in foreign countries.

Instrumentation technicians' tasks may range from the routine to the highly complex and challenging. A calm, professional approach to work is essential. Calibration and adjustment require the dexterity and control of a watch-maker. Consequently, a person who is easily excited or impatient is not well suited to this kind of employment.

OUTLOOK

Employment opportunities for most instrumentation technicians will grow about as fast as the average through 2016. Opportunities will be best for graduates of post-secondary technical training programs. As technology becomes more sophisticated, employers will continue to look for technicians who are skilled in new technology and require a minimum of additional job training.

Most developments in automated manufacturing techniques, including robotics and computer-controlled machinery, rely heavily on instrumentation devices. The emerging fields of air and water pollution control are other areas of growth. Scientists and technicians measure the amount of toxic substances in the air or test water with the use of instrumentation.

Oceanography, including the search for undersea deposits of oil and minerals, is another expanding field for instrumentation technology, as is medical diagnosis, including long-distance diagnosis by physicians through the use of sensors, computers, and telephone lines.

One important field of growth is the teaching profession. As demand rises for skilled technicians, qualified instructors with combined knowledge of theory and application will be needed. Opportunities already exist, not only in educational institutions but also in those industries that have internal training programs.

FOR MORE INFORMATION

For information on educational programs and medical instrument certification, contact
Association for the Advancement of Medical Instrumentation
1110 North Glebe Road, Suite 220
Arlington, VA 22201-4795
Tel: 703-525-4890
Email: certifications@aami.org
http://www.aami.org

For information on careers and accredited programs, contact
Institute of Electrical and Electronics Engineers
1828 L Street, NW, Suite 1202

Washington, DC 20036-5104
Tel: 202-785-0017
Email: ieeeusa@ieee.org
http://www.ieee.org

For information on careers and student membership, contact
ISA—The Instrumentation, Systems, and Automation Society
67 Alexander Drive
Research Triangle Park, NC 27709
Tel: 919-549-8411
Email: info@isa.org
http://www.isa.org

For information on careers and student clubs, contact
Junior Engineering Technical Society (JETS)
1420 King Street, Suite 405
Alexandria, VA 22314-2750
Tel: 703-548-5387
Email: info@jets.org
http://www.jets.org

For information on certification, contact
National Institute for Certification in Engineering Technologies
1420 King Street
Alexandria, VA 22314-2794
Tel: 888-476-4238
http://www.nicet.org

INSURANCE POLICY PROCESSING WORKERS

OVERVIEW

Insurance policy processing workers perform a variety of clerical and administrative tasks that ensure that insurance applications and claims are handled in an efficient and timely manner. They review new applications, make adjustments to existing policies, work on policies that are to be reinstated, check the accuracy of company records, verify client information, and compile information used in claim settlement. Insurance policy processing personnel also handle business correspondence relating to any of the above duties. They use computers, word processors, calculators, and other office equipment in the course of their work. There are approximately 254,000 insurance policy processing workers employed in the United States.

THE JOB

Insurance policy processing workers are involved in all aspects of handling insurance applications and settling claims (or requests from policy holders regarding payment). The individual policies are sold by an *insurance agent* or *broker*, who sends the policies to processing workers and waits to see whether the company accepts the policy under the terms as written. The agent or the customer may contact policy processing workers many times during the life of a policy for various services. *Claims examiners* review settled insurance claims to verify that payments have been made according to company procedures and are in line with the information provided in the claim form. These professionals may also need to contact policy processing clerks in the course of reviewing settlements. While a policy processing worker may be assigned a variety of tasks, insurance companies increasingly rely on specialists to perform specific functions.

Claims clerks review insurance claim forms for accuracy and completeness. Frequently, this involves calling or writing the insured party or other people involved to secure missing information. After placing this data in a claims file, the clerk reviews the insurance policy to determine the coverage. Routine claims are transmitted for payment; if further investigation is needed, the clerk informs the claims supervisor.

Claims supervisors not only direct the work of claims clerks but also are responsible for informing policy owners and beneficiaries of the procedures for filing claims. They submit claim liability statements for review by the actuarial department and inform department supervisors of the status of claims.

Reviewers review completed insurance applications to ensure that all questions have been answered by the applicants. They contact insurance agents to inform them of any problems with the applications, and if none are found, reviewers suggest that policies be approved and delivered to policyholders. Reviewers may collect premiums from new policyholders and provide management with updates on new business.

Policy-change clerks compile information on changes in insurance policies, such as a change in beneficiaries, and determine if the proposed changes conform to company policy and state law. Using rate books and knowledge of specific types of policies, these clerks calculate new premiums and make appropriate adjustments to accounts. Policy-change clerks may help write a new

QUICK FACTS

SCHOOL SUBJECTS
Business
Computer science
Mathematics

PERSONAL SKILLS
Following instructions
Leadership/management

WORK ENVIRONMENT
Primarily indoors
Primarily one location

MINIMUM EDUCATION LEVEL
High school diploma

MEDIAN SALARY
$31,120

CERTIFICATION OR LICENSING
None available

OUTLOOK
Little or no change

policy with the client's specified changes or prepare a rider to an existing policy.

Cancellation clerks cancel insurance policies as directed by insurance agents. They compute any refund due and mail any appropriate refund and the cancellation notice to the policyholder. Clerks also notify the bookkeeping department of the cancellation and send a notice to the insurance agent.

Revival clerks approve reinstatement of customers' insurance policies if the reason for the lapse in service, such as an overdue premium, is corrected within a specified time limit. They compare answers given by the policyholder on the reinstatement application with those previously approved by the company and examine company records to see if there are any circumstances that make reinstatement impossible. Revival clerks calculate the irregular premium and the reinstatement penalty due when the reinstatement is approved, type notices of company action (approval or denial of reinstatement), and send this notification to the policyholder.

Insurance checkers verify the accuracy and completeness of insurance company records by comparing the computations on premiums paid and dividends due on individual forms. They then check that information against similar information on other applications. They also verify personal information on applications, such as the name, age, address, and value of property of the policyholder, and they proofread all material concerning insurance coverage before it is sent to policyholders.

Insurance agents must apply to insurance companies in order to represent the companies and sell their policies. *Agent-contract clerks* evaluate the ability and character of prospective insurance agents and approve or reject their contracts to sell insurance for a company. They review the prospective agent's application for relevant work experience and other qualifications and check the applicant's personal references to see if they meet company standards. Agent-contract clerks correspond with both the prospective agent and company officials to explain their decision to accept or reject individual applications.

Medical-voucher clerks analyze vouchers sent by doctors who have completed medical examinations of insurance applicants and approve payment of these vouchers based on standard rates. These clerks note the doctor's fee on a form and forward the form and the voucher to the insurance company's bookkeeper or other appropriate personnel for further approval and payment.

REQUIREMENTS
High School

A high school diploma is usually sufficient for beginning insurance policy processing workers. To prepare yourself for this job, you should take courses in English, mathematics, and computer science while in high school. In addition, take as many business-related courses as possible, such as typing, word processing, and bookkeeping.

Postsecondary Training

Community colleges and vocational schools often offer business education courses that provide training for insurance policy processing workers. You may want to consider taking these courses to improve your possibilities for advancement to supervisory positions.

Other Requirements

In order to succeed in this field, you should have some aptitude with business machines, the ability to concen-

trate for long periods of time on repetitious tasks, and mathematical skills. Legible handwriting is a necessity. Because you will often work with policyholders and other workers, you must be able to communicate effectively and work well with others. In addition, you need to be familiar with state and federal insurance laws and regulations. You should find systematic and orderly work appealing and enjoy working on detailed tasks.

Other personal qualifications include dependability, trustworthiness, and a neat personal appearance. Insurance policy processing personnel who work for the federal government may need to pass a civil service examination.

EXPLORING

You can get experience in this field by assuming clerical or bookkeeping responsibilities for a school club or other organization. In addition, some school work-study programs may have opportunities with insurance companies for part-time on-the-job training. It may also be possible to get a part-time or summer job with an insurance company.

You can get training in office procedures and the operation of business machinery and computers through evening courses offered by business schools. Another way to gain insight into the responsibilities of insurance policy processing workers is to talk to someone already working in the field.

EMPLOYERS

Approximately 254,000 insurance claims and policy processing clerks are employed in the United States. Insurance companies are the principal employers of insurance policy processing workers. These workers may perform similar duties for real estate firms and the government.

STARTING OUT

If you are interested in securing an entry-level position, you should contact insurance agencies directly. Jobs may also be located through help-wanted advertisements or by visiting industry-related Web sites.

Some insurance companies may give you an aptitude test to determine your ability to work quickly and accurately. Work assignments may be made on the basis of the results of this test.

ADVANCEMENT

Many inexperienced workers begin as file clerks and advance to positions in policy processing. Insurance policy processing workers usually begin their employment handling more routine tasks, such as reviewing insurance applications to ensure that all the questions have been answered. With experience, they may advance to more complicated tasks and assume a greater responsibility for complete assignments. Those who show desire and ability may be promoted to clerical supervisory positions, with a corresponding increase in pay and work responsibilities. To become a claims adjuster or an underwriter, it is usually necessary to have a college degree or have taken specialized courses in insurance. Many such courses are available from local business or vocational colleges and various industry trade groups.

The high turnover rate among insurance policy processing workers increases opportunities for promotions. The number and kind of opportunities, however, may depend on the place of employment and the ability, training, and experience of the employee.

EARNINGS

Insurance policy processing workers' salaries are varied, depending on such factors as the worker's experience and the size and location of the employer. Generally, those working for large companies in big cities earn the highest salaries. According to the U.S. Department of Labor, the median yearly income for insurance policy processing clerks was $31,120 in 2006. Salaries ranged from less than $21,390 to $46,490 or more.

As full-time employees of insurance companies, policy processing workers usually receive the standard fringe benefits of vacation and sick pay, health insurance, and retirement plans.

WORK ENVIRONMENT

As is the case with most office workers, insurance policy processing employees work an average of 37 to 40 hours a week. Although the work environment is usually well ventilated and lighted, the job itself can be fairly routine and repetitive, with most of the work taking place at a desk. Policy processing workers often interact with other insurance professionals and policyholders, and they may work under close supervision.

Because many insurance companies offer 24-hour claims service to their policyholders, some claims clerks may work evenings and weekends. Many insurance workers are employed part time or on a temporary basis.

OUTLOOK

The U.S. Department of Labor predicts that employment opportunities for insurance processing workers will experience little or no change through 2016. This is due to the increased use of data processing machines and other types of automated equipment that increase worker productivity and result in the need for fewer workers.

Many jobs will result from workers retiring or otherwise leaving the field. Employment opportunities should be best in and around large metropolitan areas, where the majority of large insurance companies are located. There should be an increase in the number of opportunities for temporary or part-time work, especially during busy business periods.

FOR MORE INFORMATION

For general information about the insurance industry, contact

Insurance Information Institute
110 William Street
New York, NY 10038-3901
Tel: 212-346-5500
http://www.iii.org

For information on educational programs, contact

Insurance Institute of America/American Institute for CPCU
720 Providence Road, Suite 100
Malvern, PA 19355-3433
Tel: 800-644-2101
Email: customersupport@cpcuiia.org
http://www.aicpcu.org

For information on the Canadian insurance industry, contact

Insurance Institute of Canada
18 King Street East, 6th Floor
Toronto, ON M5C 1C4 Canada
Tel: 416-362-8586
Email: IIOmail@insuranceinstitute.ca
http://www.insuranceinstitute.ca

☐ LABORATORY TESTING TECHNICIANS

OVERVIEW

Laboratory testing technicians conduct tests on countless substances and products. Their laboratory duties include measuring and evaluating materials and running quality

QUICK FACTS

SCHOOL SUBJECTS
Computer science
Government
Mathematics

PERSONAL SKILLS
Following instructions
Leadership/management

WORK ENVIRONMENT
Indoors and outdoors
Primarily multiple locations

MINIMUM EDUCATION LEVEL
Some postsecondary training

MEDIAN SALARY
$32,840

CERTIFICATION OR LICENSING
None

OUTLOOK
Faster than the average

control tests. They work in a variety of unrelated fields, such as medicine, metallurgy, manufacturing, geology, and meteorology. Therefore, students interested in a career as a laboratory testing technician should look for job titles such as metallurgical, medical, or pharmaceutical technicians.

THE JOB

Laboratory testing technicians usually assist scientists in conducting tests on many substances and products. They are trained to use the required tools and instruments. Those who serve as *quality control technicians* test products to see that they are safe to use and meet performance specifications. Most of these technicians either work for testing laboratories or in research and development centers. They may test toys for safety by looking for small, separable parts, sharp edges, and fragility. Or they may test electric toasters for correct wiring,

tendency to smoke or spark, and for proper grounding. In short, laboratory testing technicians in quality control are responsible for certifying that a product or material will perform according to specifications.

Not only do technicians test new products for safety and durability but they also perform failure analyses to determine the cause of the problem and how it can be prevented. Technicians also evaluate incoming materials, such as metals, ceramics, and chemicals, before they are used to verify that their suppliers have shipped the specified products. *Materials technicians* prepare specimens, set up equipment, run heating and cooling tests, and record test results. These tests are designed to determine how a certain alloy functions in a variety of test conditions. These technicians work with the test materials and assess the equipment used to perform the tests. For example, a technician may run tests to determine the proper temperature settings for a furnace. Some technicians may oversee the work of others to see if they are doing their assignments correctly.

Those who work in the medical field are called *medical technicians* or *clinical technicians*. They work in hospitals, universities, doctors' offices, and research laboratories. They set up equipment and perform tests on body fluids, tissues, and cells; perform blood counts; and identify parasites and bacteria. Medical technicians also work in veterinary and pharmaceutical laboratories.

Some *geological technicians* test shale, sand, and other earthen materials to find the petroleum and/or mineral content. Tests are run on core samples during oil well drilling to determine what's present in the well bore. Technicians who specialize in testing ores and minerals for metal content are called *assayers*.

Regardless of the specific nature of the tests technicians have conducted, they must always keep detailed records of every step. Laboratory technicians often do a great deal of writing and must make charts, graphs, and other displays to illustrate results. They may be called on to interpret test results, to draw overall conclusions, and to make recommendations. Occasionally, laboratory testing technicians are asked to appear as witnesses in court to explain why a product failed and who may be at fault.

REQUIREMENTS
High School

If working as a laboratory testing technician sounds interesting to you, you can prepare for this work by taking at least two years of mathematics and a year each of chemistry and physics in high school. You should also consider taking shop classes to become accustomed to working with tools and to develop manual dexterity. Classes in English and writing will provide you with good experience in doing research and writing reports. Take computer classes so that you become familiar with using this tool. If you know of a specific area that you want to specialize in, such as geology or medicine, you will benefit by taking relevant courses, such as earth science or biology.

Postsecondary Training

A high school diploma is the minimum requirement for finding work as a laboratory testing technician. However, a two-year associate's degree in engineering or medical technology or metallurgy—depending on the field you want to specialize in—is highly recommended. Many community colleges or technical schools offer two-year degree programs in a specific technology. Completing the associate's degree will greatly enhance your resume, help you in finding full-time positions, and allow you to advance rapidly in your field. Some technicians, such as medical technicians, may also receive appropriate training through the armed forces or through hospital certification programs.

Certification or Licensing

Depending on what type of laboratory technician you want to be, you may need certification or licensing. For example, certification for those who work as medical technicians is voluntary, but it is highly recommended and some employers may even require it. Organizations offering certification include the American Medical Technologists, the American Association of Bioanalysts, the Board of Registry of the American Society for Clinical Pathology, and the National Credentialing Agency for Laboratory Personnel. In addition, a number of states require that laboratory workers be licensed. Check with your state's occupational licensing board to find out specific requirements for your area. In addition, make sure any program or community college you are considering attending will provide the courses and experience you need for licensing.

Other Requirements

Laboratory technicians should be detail oriented and enjoy figuring out how things work. They should like problem solving and troubleshooting. For example, if you enjoy disassembling and reassembling your bicycle or tinkering with your car stereo, you will probably enjoy being a laboratory testing technician. Laboratory technicians must have the patience to repeat a test many times,

perhaps even on the same material. They must be able to follow directions carefully but also should be independent and motivated to work on their own until their assigned tasks are completed.

EXPLORING

Due to the precision and training required in the field, it is unlikely that as a high school student you will be able to find a part-time or summer job as a laboratory testing technician. However, you can explore the career by contacting local technical colleges and arranging to speak with a professor in the school's technician program. Ask about the required classes, the opportunities available in your area, and any other questions you have. Through this connection you may also be able to contact a graduate of the program and arrange for an informational interview with him or her. Although you probably won't be able to get work as a laboratory testing technician at this point, some research companies and plants do offer summer jobs to high school students to work in their offices or mail rooms. While you won't necessarily get hands-on technical experience in these jobs, you will get to experience the work environment.

EMPLOYERS

Laboratory technicians work in almost every type of manufacturing industry that employs chemists or chemical engineers. They are needed wherever testing is carried on, whether it is for developing new products or improving current manufacturing procedures or for quality control purposes. They are employed by such companies as Baxter, Heinz, Shell, and Eastman Kodak. Laboratory technicians also can find positions in research institutions and in government laboratories such as those run by the federal Departments of Health, Agriculture, and Commerce. They may assist biochemists, metallurgists, meteorologists, geologists, or other scientific personnel in large and small laboratories located all over the country.

STARTING OUT

Technical schools often help place graduating technicians. Many laboratories contact these schools directly looking for student employees or interns. Students can also contact local manufacturing companies and laboratories to find out about job openings in their area. Technicians often begin as trainees who are supervised by more experienced workers. As they gain experience, technicians take on more responsibilities and are allowed to work more independently.

ADVANCEMENT

Skilled laboratory technicians may be promoted to manager or supervisor of a division in their company. For example, a quality control technician who has become an expert in testing computer monitors may be put in charge of others who perform this task. This supervisor may assign project duties and organize how and when results will be recorded and analyzed, and may also help other technicians solve problems they encounter when running tests. Experienced technicians may form their own testing laboratories or return to school to become engineers, physicists, or geologists.

EARNINGS

Earnings for laboratory testing technicians vary based on the type of work they do, their education and experience, and even the size of the laboratory and its location. For example, the U.S. Department of Labor reported that in 2006, the median annual earnings of medical and clinical laboratory technicians were $32,840. Salaries ranged from less than $21,830 to $50,250 or more annually. Geological technicians had median earnings of $46,155 in 2006.

Salaries increase as technicians gain experience and as they take on supervisory responsibility. Most companies that employ laboratory testing technicians offer medical benefits, sick leave, and vacation time. However, these benefits will depend on the individual employer.

WORK ENVIRONMENT

Laboratory testing technicians typically work a 40-hour week. During especially busy times or in special circumstances, they may be required to work overtime. Most technicians work in clean, well-lighted laboratories where attention is paid to neatness and organization. Some laboratory testing technicians have their own offices, while others work in large single-room laboratories.

Some technicians may be required to go outside their laboratories to collect samples of materials for testing at locations, which can be hot, cold, wet, muddy, and uncomfortable.

OUTLOOK

Overall, employment for laboratory workers is expected to grow about as fast as the average through 2016. Environmental concerns and dwindling natural resources are causing many manufacturers to look for better ways to develop ores, minerals, and other substances from the earth. Laboratory technicians will be needed to test new production procedures as well as prototypes of new products.

Some specialties may face growth that is slightly slower than the average; for example, those who work with stone, clay, glass, fabricated metal products, and transportation equipment may experience this slow growth.

Faster-than-average employment growth is expected for medical and clinical technicians. Employment possibilities at testing laboratories will be affected by advances in technology. New testing procedures that are developed will lead to an increase in the testing that is done. However, increased automation will mean each technician can complete more work.

Technicians in any specialty who have strong educational backgrounds, keep up with developing technologies, and demonstrate knowledge of testing equipment will have the best employment opportunities.

FOR MORE INFORMATION

This organization has information on certification for medical laboratory technicians.

American Association of Bioanalysts
906 Olive Street, Suite 1200
St. Louis, MO 63101-1434
Tel: 314-241-1445
Email: aab@aab.org
http://www.aab.org

The ACS provides career information and has information on new developments in the field.

American Chemical Society (ACS)
1155 16th Street, NW
Washington, DC 20036-4801
Tel: 800-227-5558
Email: service@acs.org
http://www.chemistry.org

Contact this organization for certification information.

American Medical Technologists
10700 West Higgins Road, Suite 150
Rosemont, IL 60018-3707
Tel: 847-823-5169
http://www.amt1.com

For information on certification specialties, contact

American Society for Clinical Pathology
33 West Monroe, Suite 1600
Chicago, IL 60603-5308
Tel: 312-541-4999
Email: info@ascp.org
http://www.ascp.org

For information on certification, contact

National Credentialing Agency for Laboratory Personnel
PO Box 15945-289
Lenexa, KS 66285
Tel: 913-438-5110, ext. 4647
Email: nca-info@goamp.com
http://www.nca-info.org

This society offers student membership and provides industry news.

The Minerals, Metals, and Materials Society
184 Thorn Hill Road
Warrendale, PA 15086-7514
Tel: 800-759-4867
http://www.tms.org

LANDSCAPERS AND GROUNDS MANAGERS

OVERVIEW

Landscapers and *grounds managers* plan, design, and maintain gardens, parks, lawns, and other landscaped areas and supervise the care of the trees, plants, and shrubs that are part of these areas. Specific job responsibilities depend on the type of area involved. Landscapers and grounds managers direct projects at private homes, parks, schools, arboretums, office parks, shopping malls, government offices, and botanical gardens. They are responsible for purchasing material and supplies and for training, directing, and supervising employees. Grounds managers maintain the land after the landscaping designs have been implemented. They may work alone or supervise a grounds staff. They may have their own business or be employed by a landscaping firm. There are approximately 1.5 million grounds maintenance workers in the United States; about 202,000 of these workers are in management positions.

THE JOB

There are many different types of landscapers and grounds managers, and their specific job titles depend on the duties involved. One specialist in this field is the *landscape contractor*, who performs landscaping work on a contract basis for homeowners, highway

QUICK FACTS

SCHOOL SUBJECTS
Biology
Chemistry

PERSONAL SKILLS
Helping/teaching
Mechanical/manipulative

WORK ENVIRONMENT
Primarily indoors
Primarily one location

MINIMUM EDUCATION LEVEL
Master's degree

MEDIAN SALARY
$50,000

CERTIFICATION OR LICENSING
Required by all states

OUTLOOK
Faster than the average

departments, operators of industrial parks, and others. Landscape contractors confer with prospective clients and study the landscape design, drawings, and bills of material to determine the amount of landscape work required. They plan the installation of lighting or sprinkler systems, erection of fences, and the types of trees, shrubs, and ornamental plants required. They inspect the grounds and calculate labor, equipment, and materials costs. They also prepare and submit bids, draw up contracts, and direct and coordinate the activities of landscape laborers who mow lawns, plant shrubbery, dig holes, move topsoil, and perform other related tasks.

Industrial-commercial grounds managers maintain areas in and around industrial or commercial properties by cutting lawns, pruning trees, raking leaves, and shoveling snow. They also plant grass and flowers and are responsible for the upkeep of flowerbeds and public passageways. These types of groundskeepers may repair and maintain fences and gates and also operate sprinkler systems and other equipment.

Parks-and-grounds managers maintain city, state, or national parks and playgrounds. They plant and prune trees; haul away garbage; repair driveways, walks, swings, and other equipment; and clean comfort stations.

Landscape supervisors supervise and direct the activities of landscape workers who are engaged in pruning trees and shrubs, caring for lawns, and performing related tasks. They coordinate work schedules, prepare job cost estimates, and deal with customer questions and concerns.

Landscapers maintain the grounds of private or business establishments. They care for hedges, gardens, and other landscaped areas. They mow and trim lawns, plant trees and shrubs, apply fertilizers and other chemicals, and repair walks and driveways.

Many *arboriculture technicians* work as landscapers or grounds managers. Below is a listing of some careers in this area.

Tree surgeons prune and treat ornamental and shade trees to improve their health and appearance. This may involve climbing with ropes, working in buckets high off the ground, spraying fertilizers and pesticides, or injecting chemicals into the tree trunk or root zone in the ground. *Tree-trimming supervisors* coordinate and direct the activities of workers engaged in cutting away tree limbs or removing trees that interfere with electric power lines. They inspect power lines and direct the placement of removal equipment. Tree-trimming supervisors answer consumer questions when trees are located on private property.

Pest management scouts survey landscapes and nurseries regularly to locate potential pest problems including insects, diseases, and weeds before they become hard to control in an effective, safe manner. Scouts may specialize in the treatment of a particular type of infestation, such as gypsy moths or boll weevils.

Lawn-service workers plant and maintain lawns. They remove leaves and dead grass and apply insecticides, fertilizers, and weed killers as necessary. Lawn-service workers also use aerators and other tools to pierce the soil to make holes for the fertilizer and de-thatchers to remove built-up thatch.

Horticulturists conduct experiments and investigations into the problems of breeding, production, storage, processing, and transit of fruits, nuts, berries, flowers, and trees. They also develop new plant varieties and determine methods of planting, spraying, cultivating, and harvesting.

A *city forester* advises communities on the selection, planting schedules, and proper care of trees. They also plant, feed, spray, and prune trees and may supervise other workers in these activities. Depending on the situation, landscapers and groundskeepers may perform these functions alone or with city foresters.

Turfgrass consultants analyze turfgrass problems and recommend solutions. They also determine growing techniques, mowing schedules, and the best type of turfgrass to use for specified areas. Depending on the geographic area of the country, lawn-service companies regularly use such consultants.

On golf courses, landscapers and grounds managers are employed as *greenskeepers*. There are two types of greenskeepers: *Greenskeepers I* supervise and coordinate the activities of workers engaged in keeping the grounds and turf of a golf course in good playing condition. They consult with the greens superintendent to plan and review work projects; they determine work assignments, such as fertilizing, irrigating, seeding, mowing, raking, and spraying; and they mix and prepare spraying and dusting solutions. They may also repair and maintain mechanical equipment.

Greenskeepers II follow the instructions of Greenskeepers I as they maintain the grounds of golf courses. They cut the turf on green and tee areas; dig and rake grounds to prepare and cultivate new greens; connect hose and sprinkler systems; plant trees and shrubs; and operate tractors as they apply fertilizer, insecticide, and other substances to the fairways or other designated areas.

Greens superintendents supervise and coordinate the activities of greenskeepers and other workers engaged in constructing and maintaining golf course areas. They review test results of soil and turf samples, and they direct the application of fertilizer, lime, insecticide, or fungicide. Their other duties include monitoring the course grounds to determine the need for irrigation or better care, keeping and reviewing maintenance records, and interviewing and hiring workers.

REQUIREMENTS
High School

In general, a high school diploma is necessary for most positions, and at least some college training is needed for those with supervisory or specialized responsibilities. High school students interested in this career should take classes in English, mathematics, chemistry, biology, and as many courses as possible in horticulture and botany.

Postsecondary Training

Those interested in college training should enroll in a two- or four-year program in horticulture, landscape management, or agronomy. Classes might include landscape maintenance and design, turfgrass management, botany, and plant pathology. Course work should be selected with an area of specialization in mind. Those wishing to have managerial responsibilities should take courses in personnel management, communications, and business-related courses such as accounting and economics.

Many trade and vocational schools offer landscaping, horticulture, and related programs. Several extension programs are also available that allow students to take courses at home.

Certification or Licensing

Licensing and certification differ by state and vary according to specific job responsibilities. For example, in most states landscapers and grounds managers need a certificate to spray insecticides or other chemicals. Landscape contractors must be certified in some states.

Several professional associations offer certification programs for workers in the field. The Professional Landcare Network offers the following certification designations: certified landscape professional: exterior and interior; certified landscape technician: interior; and certified landscape technician: exterior; certified turfgrass professional; and certified ornamental landscape professional. The Professional Grounds Management Society offers the certified grounds manager and the certified grounds technician certifications. The American Society for Horticultural Sciences offers the certified horticulturist and professional horticulturist designations.

Landscapers and grounds managers who specialize in the care of golf courses and sports fields can receive certification from the Golf Course Superintendents Association of America or the Sports Turf Managers Association.

Contractors and other self-employed people may also need a license to operate their businesses.

Other Requirements

Aspiring landscapers and grounds managers should have "green thumbs," and an interest in preserving and maintaining natural areas. They should also be reasonably physically fit, have an aptitude for working with machines, and display good manual dexterity.

All managerial personnel must carefully supervise their workers to ensure that they adhere to environmental regulations as specified by the Environmental Protection Agency and other local and national government agencies.

EXPLORING

Part-time work at a golf course, lawn-service company, greenhouse, botanical garden, or other similar enterprise is an excellent way of learning about this field. Many companies gladly hire part-time help, especially during the busy summer months. In addition, there are numerous opportunities mowing lawns, growing flowers, and tending gardens. You can also join garden clubs, visit local flower shops, and attend botanical shows.

The American Public Gardens Association (APGA) has a very strong internship program and offers a directory of internships in more than 100 public gardens throughout the United States. APGA is a valuable resource to those individuals interested in gaining practical experience. Visit their Web site at http://www.publicgardens.org. Finally, a summer job mowing lawns and caring for a neighbor's garden is an easy, simple introduction to the field.

EMPLOYERS

Landscapers and grounds managers are employed by golf courses, lawn-service companies, greenhouses, nurseries, botanical gardens, and public parks. Many people in this field start their own businesses.

STARTING OUT

Summer or part-time jobs often lead to full-time employment with the same employer. Those who enroll in a college or other training programs can receive help in finding work from the school's career services office. In addition, directly applying to botanical gardens, nurseries, or golf courses is common practice. Jobs may also be listed in newspaper want ads as well as via online job posting sites, such as Service Magic, which is targeted directly to the landscaping business (http://www.servicemagic.com), and via more general sites, such as Monster (http://www.monster.com) and Yahoo! hotjobs (http://www.hotjobs.com). Most landscaping and related companies provide on-the-job training for entry-level personnel.

ADVANCEMENT

In general, landscapers and grounds managers can expect to advance as they gain experience and additional educational training. For example, a greenskeeper with a high school diploma usually must have at least some college training to become a greens superintendent. It is also possible to go into a related field, such as selling equipment used in maintaining lawns and other natural areas.

Those in managerial positions may wish to advance to a larger establishment or go into consulting work. In some instances, skilled landscapers and grounds managers may start their own consulting or contracting business.

EARNINGS

Salaries depend on the experience and education level of the worker, the type of work being done, and geographic location. The *Occupational Outlook Handbook* reports the following median annual salaries for workers in this industry in 2006: first-line supervisors/managers of landscaping, lawn service, and groundskeeping workers, $37,294; tree trimmers and pruners, $28,246; pesticide handlers, sprayers, and applicators, vegetation, $26,707; and landscaping and groundskeeping workers, $21,258. Landscape contractors and others who run their own businesses earn between $25,000 and $50,000 per year, with those with a greater ability to locate customers earning even more. According to the Golf Course Superintendents Association of America, the average base salary for golf course superintendents was $73,766 in 2007.

Fringe benefits vary from employer to employer but generally include medical insurance and some paid vacation.

WORK ENVIRONMENT

Landscapers and grounds managers spend much of their time outside. Those with administrative or managerial responsibilities spend at least a portion of their workday in an office. Most of the outdoor work is done during daylight hours, but work takes place all year round in all types of weather conditions. Most people in the field work 37 to 40 hours a week, but overtime is especially likely during the summer months when landscapers and grounds managers take advantage of the longer days and warmer weather. Workweeks may be shorter during the winter. Weekend work is highly likely. Managerial personnel should be willing to work overtime updating financial records and making sure the business accounts are in order.

Much of the work can be physically demanding and most of it is performed outdoors in one extreme or another. Workers shovel dirt, trim bushes and trees, constantly bend down to plant flowers and shrubbery, and may have to climb ladders or the tree itself to prune branches or diagnose a problem. There is some risk of injury using

planting and pruning machinery and some risk of illness from handling and breathing pesticides, but proper precautions should limit any job-related hazards.

OUTLOOK

Employment for this field is expected to grow faster than the average for all occupations through 2016, according to the *Occupational Outlook Handbook*. Landscapers and their services will be in strong demand due to increased construction of buildings, shopping malls, homes, and other structures. Upkeep and renovation of existing landscapes will create jobs as well. There is also a high degree of turnover in this field as many workers transfer to better-paying occupations, retire, or leave the field for other reasons.

Another factor for job growth is the increase in amount of disposable incomes. In order to have more leisure time, people are beginning to contract out for lawn care and maintenance. The popularity of home gardening will create jobs with local nurseries and garden centers. Jobs should be available with government agencies as well as in the private sector.

Nonseasonal work will be more prevalent in states such as California, Arizona, and Florida, where mild climates warrant landscaping and lawn maintenance year-round.

FOR MORE INFORMATION

For information on certification and training programs and to read the online publication Careers in Horticulture, *visit the ASHS Web site.*
American Society for Horticultural Sciences (ASHS)
113 South West Street, Suite 200
Alexandria, VA 22314-2851
Tel: 703-836-4606
http://www.ashs.org

For comprehensive information on golf course management careers, internships, job listings, turfgrass management programs, and certification, contact
Golf Course Superintendents Association of America
1421 Research Park Drive
Lawrence, KS 66049-3859
Tel: 800-472-7878
Email: infobox@gcsaa.org
http://www.gcsaa.org

For information on career opportunities and education, contact
Professional Grounds Management Society
720 Light Street

Baltimore, MD 21230-3816
Tel: 800-609-7467
http://www.pgms.org

For information on careers and certification, contact
Professional Landcare Network
950 Herndon Parkway, Suite 450
Herndon, VA 20170-5531
Tel: 800- 395-2522
http://www.landcarenetwork.org

For certification information, contact
Sports Turf Managers Association
805 New Hampshire, Suite E
Lawrence, KS 66044-2774
Tel: 800-323-3875
http://www.stma.org

For more information on arboriculture, contact
Tree Care Industry Association
3 Perimeter Road, Unit I
Manchester, NH 03103-3341
Tel: 800-733-2622
http://www.treecareindustry.org

For profiles of professional working in a variety of careers, visit
Awesome Careers in Horticulture & Crop Science
http://enplant.osu.edu/careers/index.html

LEGAL SECRETARIES

OVERVIEW

Legal secretaries, sometimes called *litigation secretaries* or *trial secretaries,* assist lawyers by performing the administrative and clerical duties in a law office or firm. Legal secretaries spend most of their time writing legal correspondence, preparing legal documents, performing research, and answering incoming calls and emails. Legal secretaries read and review many law journals to check for any new court decisions that may be important for cases pending at that time. Legal secretaries also maintain files and records, take notes during meetings or hearings, and assume all other general secretarial duties. Approximately 275,000 legal secretaries work in law offices and firms in the United States today.

QUICK FACTS

SCHOOL SUBJECTS
English
Government
Journalism

PERSONAL SKILLS
Communication/ideas
Following instructions

WORK ENVIRONMENT
Primarily indoors
Primarily one location

MINIMUM EDUCATION LEVEL
Some postsecondary training

MEDIAN SALARY
$38,190

CERTIFICATION OR LICENSING
Recommended

OUTLOOK
About as fast as the average

THE JOB

Legal secretaries must be able to handle all the duties of a general secretary plus all the specific responsibilities that come with working for a lawyer. Although every law office or firm may vary in the exact duties required for the position, in general, most legal secretaries spend their time managing information that comes in and goes out of the law office. According to professional legal secretary Alexis Montgomery, a typical day starts with setting priorities. "Each day begins with reviewing the work to be done, which requires reading snail mail, email, and faxes to see how they might affect the day's priorities." Next, she says, the work is addressed according to priority. Work can include any number of things ranging from attending legal meetings to filling out trial and courtroom requests.

Legal secretaries may type letters and legal documents, such as subpoenas, appeals, and motions; handle incoming and outgoing mail; maintain a detailed filing system; and deliver legal documents to the court. Besides these duties, legal secretaries spend much of their time making appointments with clients, and dealing with client questions. "An important part of being an effective legal secretary is fielding telephone calls and all client contact efficiently and courteously," says Montgomery. "Often the client's primary contact is with the legal secretary and client satisfaction depends heavily on how helpful and courteous that contact is perceived." The legal secretary is a sort of personal assistant to one or more lawyers as well, and must maintain the calendars and schedules for the office. "Always knowing where your attorney can be found or whether another attorney can assist the client is an important part of the process," says Montgomery.

Legal secretaries are also called upon to conduct research for the cases that are current within the office. They may research and write legal briefs on a topic or case that is relevant to the lawyer's current cases. According to Rebecca Garland, a legal advocate who was trained as a legal secretary but is now using those skills to assist victims of domestic violence in obtaining personal protection orders, research often takes up an entire workday. "You may spend one whole day working on a legal brief for one client, and then spend the next day working on small things for several different cases." Legal secretaries spend many hours researching cases in law libraries, public libraries, and on the Internet. Part of this research includes scouring legal journals and magazines looking for relevant laws and courtroom decisions that may affect the clientele.

Legal secretaries are also record keepers. They help lawyers find information such as employment, medical, and criminal records. They also keep records from all previous clients and court cases for future use. Legal secretaries must also track and use various forms, such as trial request, client application, and accident report forms. "The bottom line is that legal secretaries process the paperwork generated by their attorneys," says Alexis Montgomery.

REQUIREMENTS
High School

Because a legal secretary must be able to communicate the attorney's ideas in written and oral form, it's important to get a firm grounding in English (especially writing), spelling, typing, and public speaking. Computers are used in most law offices, so be sure to gain computer experience while in high school. Government and political science courses will get you started on the road to

legal knowledge as well. Classes that give you experience with research are also important. Rebecca Garland says, "Learning how to do research in the school or community library will go a long way in learning how to do research in a law library."

Postsecondary Training

Many legal secretaries get their training through established one- or two-year legal secretary programs. These programs are available at most business, vocational, and junior colleges. You could also obtain a four-year degree to get a more well-rounded education. Courses taken should focus on specific skills and knowledge needed by a legal secretary, such as personal computers, keyboarding, English, legal writing, editing, researching, and communication. The National Association of Legal Secretaries also offers basic and advanced legal secretary training courses. (See their contact information at the end of this article.)

As businesses continue to expand worldwide, employers are increasingly looking for candidates with bachelor's degrees and professional certifications.

Certification or Licensing

Two general legal secretary certifications are offered by the National Association of Legal Secretaries. After some preliminary office training, you can take an examination to receive the accredited legal secretary (ALS) designation. This certification is for legal secretaries with education, but little to no experience. Legal secretaries with three years of experience can become certified as a professional legal secretary (PLS). The PLS certification designates a legal secretary with exceptional skills and experience.

Other specific legal secretary certifications are given by Legal Secretaries International Inc. You can become board certified in civil litigation, probate, real estate, business law, criminal law, or intellectual property. Applicants must have a minimum of five years of law experience and pass an examination.

Other Requirements

To be employed as a legal secretary, you must learn a great deal of legal terminology and court structures and practices. Whether through study or experience, you must be able to grasp the inner workings of the law. You must also be able to quickly learn computer programs, especially word processing and database programs, and be able to use them skillfully. The ability to prioritize and balance different tasks is also necessary for the job. Legal secretaries must be organized and focused to handle their varying responsibilities.

EXPLORING

Does a career as a legal secretary sound interesting? If so, suggest a career day at your school (if one isn't already scheduled) where professionals from a variety of careers give presentations. Be sure to let your career counselor know that you would like to have a legal secretary come as a guest speaker. Or you can ask your political science or government teacher to take your class on a field trip to a law library. Many law offices hire "runners" to deliver and file documents. Check with local law offices and offer your services for the summer or after school. You may also find it helpful to contact a local law firm and ask a legal secretary there if you can conduct an information interview.

EMPLOYERS

Approximately 275,000 legal secretaries are employed in the United States. The majority of legal secretaries work for law offices or law firms. Some government agencies on the state and national level also employ legal secretaries. More law firms and offices are located in Washington, D.C., and in larger metropolitan areas, so these regions offer more opportunities. However, most law offices and firms are now online. The Internet enables workers to send information easily from the law office to the courtroom, so offices are not forced to be located close to the courts. Legal secretaries are in demand anywhere lawyers practice.

STARTING OUT

Many legal secretaries get their first job through the career services offices of their college or vocational school. Still other legal secretaries start by working part time, gaining experience toward a first full-time position. Alexis Montgomery started out that way: "My first employment was as a staff secretary on a newspaper. Thereafter I worked as a 'floater' in a medium-sized law firm. [A *floater* is a secretary who is not assigned to any particular lawyer, but fills in for absent secretaries and handles overflow.] This job was my first exposure to the field and provided on-the-job training as a legal secretary." Montgomery also adds that working as a floater exposes you to a wide variety of legal practices—useful when deciding which area you want to specialize in. Don't forget to contact the local law offices in your area and let them know you are available; often direct contact now can lead to a job later.

ADVANCEMENT

Experienced legal secretaries are often promoted to oversee less experienced legal secretaries. Some firms have senior legal secretaries who are given more responsibility and less supervision duties. "In many cases more experienced legal secretaries do the drafting of letters and documents and pass them on to the attorney for revision or signature," says Montgomery. "As one becomes more experienced and proficient, the work of a legal secretary tends to blend into what is regarded as paralegal work." Legal secretaries may continue their education and become paralegals themselves. Many of the skills legal secretaries obtain can be transferred to almost any other office setting.

EARNINGS

According to the U.S. Department of Labor, the average salary for legal secretaries was approximately $38,190 in 2006. Salaries ranged from less than $23,890 to more than $58,770. An attorney's rank in the firm will also affect the salary of his or her legal secretary; secretaries who work for a partner will earn higher salaries than those who work for an associate. Certified legal secretaries generally receive higher pay.

Most law firms provide employees with sick days, vacation days, and holidays. Health insurance, 401(k) plans, and profit sharing may be offered as well. Some law firms offer in-house training or pay for off-site classes to increase their secretarial skills.

WORK ENVIRONMENT

Legal secretaries spend the majority of their day behind their desk at a computer. They spend lengthy periods of time typing or writing, which may cause hand and wrist strain. Long hours staring at a computer monitor may also cause eyestrain. Legal secretaries work with lawyers, other legal secretaries, clients, court personnel, library personnel, and other support workers. Senior legal secretaries supervise some legal secretaries; others are left largely unsupervised. Most legal secretaries are full-time employees who work a 40-hour week. Some are part-time workers who move into full-time status as they gain more experience. Because the legal secretary's work revolves around the lawyer, many secretaries work long hours of overtime. Alexis Montgomery comments, "It is the nature of litigation; often overtime and weekend work is necessary to meet the deadlines that pop up, no matter how carefully one tries to anticipate them."

OUTLOOK

Because the legal services industry as a whole is growing, legal secretaries will be in demand. An increased need for lawyers in such areas as intellectual property cases will leave lawyers in need of assistance with their caseloads. Qualified legal secretaries will have plentiful job opportunities, especially in the larger metropolitan areas.

Technological advances in recent years have revolutionized traditional secretarial tasks such as typing or keeping correspondence. The use of email, scanners, and the Internet will make secretaries more productive in coming years. The downside to these advancements is a possible decrease in demand: Fewer workers are needed to do the same workload. For the legal profession, however, advances in technology have only expanded the responsibilities for secretaries. According to the *Occupational Outlook Handbook*, employment for legal secretaries will grow about as fast as the average for all occupations through 2016.

FOR MORE INFORMATION
For information about certification, careers, and job listings, contact

Legal Secretaries International Inc.
2302 Fannin Street, Suite 500
Houston, TX 77002-9136
http://www.legalsecretaries.org

For information on certification, job openings, and more, contact

National Association of Legal Secretaries
159 East 41st Street
Tulsa, OK 74105-3830
Tel: 918-582-5188
Email: info@nals.org
http://www.nals.org

☐ LIBRARY TECHNICIANS

OVERVIEW
Library technicians, sometimes called *library technical assistants,* work in all areas of library services, supporting professional librarians or working independently to help people access information. They order and catalog books, help library patrons locate materials, and make the library's services and facilities readily available. Technicians verify bibliographic information on orders and perform basic cataloging of materials received. They answer routine questions about library services and refer questions requiring professional help to librarians. Technicians also help with circulation desk operations and oversee the work of stack workers, library aides, and other clerical workers. They circulate audiovisual equipment and materials and inspect items upon return. Approximately 121,000 library technicians are employed in the United States.

THE JOB
Work in libraries falls into three general categories: technical services, user services, and administrative services. Library technicians may have responsibilities in any of these areas.

In technical services, library technicians are involved with acquiring resources and then organizing them so the material can be easily accessed. They process order requests, verify bibliographic information, and prepare order forms for new materials, such as books, magazines, journals, videos, digital video discs (DVDs), and CD-ROMs. They perform routine cataloging of new materials and record information about the new materials in computer files or on cards to be stored in catalog drawers. The *acquisitions technicians, classifiers,* and *catalogers* who perform these functions make information available for the library users. Technicians who work for interlibrary loan departments may arrange for one library to borrow materials from another library or for a library to temporarily display a special collection. They might make basic repairs to damaged books or refer the materials to a preservation department for more comprehensive conservation. A *circulation counter attendant* helps readers check out materials and collects late fines for overdue books. *Media technicians* operate audiovisual equipment for library media programs and maintain the equipment in working order. They often prepare graphic artwork and television programs.

Under the guidance of librarians in user services, technicians work directly with library patrons and help them to access the information needed for their research. They direct library patrons to the computer or card catalog in response to inquiries and assist with identifying the library's holdings. They describe the general arrangement of the library for new patrons and answer basic questions about the library's collections. They may also help patrons use microfiche and microfilm equipment. They may help them locate materials in an interlibrary system's computerized listing of holdings. *Reference library technicians* specialize in locating and researching information. *Children's library technicians* and *young-adult library technicians* specialize in getting children and young adults interested in books, reading, and learning by sponsoring summer reading programs, reading hours, puppet shows, literacy contests, and other fun activities.

Technicians who work in administrative services help with the management of the library. They might help prepare budgets, coordinate the efforts of different departments within the library, write policy and procedures, and work to develop the library's collection. If they have more responsibility, they might supervise and coordinate staff members, recruit and supervise volunteers, organize fund-raising efforts, sit on community boards, and develop programs to promote and encourage reading and learning in the community.

The particular responsibilities of a library technician vary according to the type of library. *Academic library technicians* work in university or college libraries, assisting professors and students in their research needs. Their work revolves around handling reference materials and specialized journals. *School library technicians* work with *school library media specialists,* assisting teachers and students in utilizing the print and nonprint resources of a school library media center.

Library technicians also work in special libraries maintained by government agencies, corporations, law firms, advertising agencies, museums, professional associations, medical centers, religious organizations, and research laboratories. Library technicians in special libraries deal with information tailored to the specific needs and interests of the particular organization. They may also organize bibliographies, prepare abstracts and indexes of current periodicals, or research and analyze information on particular issues.

Library technicians develop and index computerized databases to organize information collected in the library. They also help library patrons use computers to access the information stored in their own databases or in remote databases. With the increasing use of automated information systems, many libraries hire *automated system technicians* to help plan and operate computer systems and *information technicians* to help design and develop information storage retrieval systems and procedures for collecting, organizing, interpreting, and classifying information.

In the past, library technicians functioned solely as the librarian's support staff, but this situation has evolved over the years. Library technicians continue to refer questions or problems requiring professional experience and judgment to librarians. However, with the increasing use of computer systems in libraries, library technicians now perform many of the technical and user service responsibilities once performed by librarians, thereby freeing librarians to focus more on acquisitions and administra-

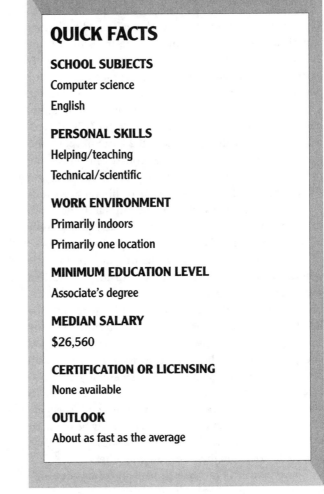

QUICK FACTS

SCHOOL SUBJECTS
Computer science
English

PERSONAL SKILLS
Helping/teaching
Technical/scientific

WORK ENVIRONMENT
Primarily indoors
Primarily one location

MINIMUM EDUCATION LEVEL
Associate's degree

MEDIAN SALARY
$26,560

CERTIFICATION OR LICENSING
None available

OUTLOOK
About as fast as the average

tive responsibilities. In some cases a library technician may handle the same responsibilities as a librarian, even in place of a librarian.

REQUIREMENTS
High School

If you are considering a career as a library technician, you should take a college preparatory course load. Classes in English, history, literature, foreign languages, computers, and mathematics are crucial to giving you a strong background in the skills you will need as a library technician. Strong verbal and writing skills are especially important, so take all the classes you can to help you develop facility in speaking and writing. Any special knowledge of a particular subject matter can also be beneficial. For instance, if you have a strong interest in geography, you may want to consider pursuing a technical assistant position in a map room of a library.

Postsecondary Training

The technical nature of the work performed by library technicians, especially when working in technical services, is prompting more and more libraries to hire only high school graduates who have gone on to complete a two-year program in library technology. Many enroll in a two-year certificate program that, upon graduation, bestows the title *library technical assistant* (LTA). Typical programs include courses in the basic purpose and functions of libraries; technical courses in processing materials, cataloging acquisitions, library services, and use of the Internet; and one year of liberal arts studies. Persons entering such programs should understand that the library-related courses they take will not apply toward a professional degree in library science.

For some positions, a bachelor's degree may be required in a specific area, such as art history for work in a museum library, or sociology for a position at a YMCA library. Specialized study in a foreign language may be helpful, since most libraries have materials in many languages, and all of those materials must be cataloged and processed for library patrons to use. Also, not all library users speak English; a library employee who is able to communicate with all users in person, as well as via email, on the telephone, and in writing is especially effective. While in college, you will probably be required to take courses in the liberal arts: sociology, psychology, speech, history, and literature, among others.

Some smaller libraries, especially in rural communities, may hire persons with only a high school education for library technician positions. Some libraries may hire individuals who have prior work experience, and some may provide their own training for inexperienced individuals. On the other hand, some libraries may only hire library technicians who have earned associate's or bachelor's degrees.

Other Requirements

Whatever your educational or training background, you should demonstrate aptitude for careful, detailed, analytical work. You should enjoy problem solving and working with people as well as with books and other library materials. Good interpersonal skills are invaluable, since library technicians often have much public contact. As a library technician, you should possess patience and flexibility and should not mind being interrupted frequently to answer questions from library patrons.

You should also exhibit good judgment; you'll need to know when you can effectively assist a user and when the problem must be referred to a professional librarian.

Since there are many tasks that must get done in order to make materials available to users, you must have excellent time-management skills. Technicians who supervise the work of others must be able to manage effectively, explain procedures, set deadlines, and follow through with subordinates. You should also feel comfortable reporting to supervisors and working alongside other technicians in a team atmosphere.

EXPLORING

Personal experience as a library patron is the first opportunity for you to see if a library career would be of interest. You can get a good idea of the general atmosphere of a library by browsing for books, searching in electronic encyclopedias for a school research project, or using a library's Internet connection to access all kinds of information. Using libraries yourself will also give you an idea of the types of services that a library provides for its patrons.

If you are interested in a career as a library technician, talk with librarians and library technicians at your school or community library. A visit to a large or specialized library would also be helpful in providing a view of the different kinds of libraries that exist.

There may also be opportunities to work as a library volunteer at a public library or in the school library media center. Some grammar schools or high schools have library clubs as a part of their extracurricular activities. If your school doesn't have a library club, contact your school librarian and get some friends together to start your own group. Part-time or summer work as a shelving clerk or typist may also be available in some libraries.

EMPLOYERS

There are approximately 121,000 library technicians employed in the United States. Most library technicians work in grammar school, high school, college, university, and public libraries. The rest work for government libraries, in special libraries for privately held institutions, and in corporate libraries. Many types of organizations employ library technicians. For example, library technicians are key personnel at archives, zoos, museums, hospitals, fraternal organizations, historical societies, medical centers, law firms, professional societies, advertising agencies, and virtual libraries. In general, wherever there is a library, library technicians are needed.

STARTING OUT

Since specific training requirements vary from library to library, if you are interested in a career as a library technician, you should be familiar with the requirements of the libraries in which you hope to work. In some small libraries, for instance, a high school diploma may be sufficient, and a technician might not need a college degree. However, since most libraries require their library technicians to be graduates of at least a two-year associate's degree program, you should have earned or be close to earning this degree before applying.

In most cases, graduates of training programs for library technicians may seek employment through the career services offices of their community colleges. Job applicants may also approach libraries directly, usually by contacting the personnel officer of the library or the human resources administrator of the organization. Civil service examination notices, for those interested in government service, are usually posted in community colleges as well as in government buildings and on government Web sites.

Many state library agencies maintain job hotlines listing openings for prospective library technicians. State departments of education also may keep lists of openings available for library technicians. If you are interested in working in a school library media center, you should remember that most openings occur at the end of the school year and are filled for the following year.

ADVANCEMENT

The trend toward requiring more formal training for library technicians suggests that advancement opportunities will be limited for those lacking such training. In smaller libraries and less-populated areas, the shortage of trained personnel may lessen this limitation. Nonetheless, those with adequate or above-average training will perform the more interesting tasks.

Generally, library technicians advance by taking on greater levels of responsibility. A new technician, for instance, may check materials in and out at the library's circulation desk and then move on to inputting, storing, and verifying information. Experienced technicians in supervisory roles might be responsible for budgets and personnel or the operation of an entire department. Library technicians will find that experience, along with continuing education courses, will enhance their chances for advancement.

Library technicians might also advance by pursuing a master's degree in library and information science and becoming a librarian. With experience, additional courses, or an advanced degree, technicians can also advance to higher paying positions outside of the library setting.

EARNINGS

Salaries for library technicians vary depending on such factors as the type of library, geographic location, and specific job responsibilities. According to the U.S. Department of Labor, the median annual salary for all library technicians in 2006 was $26,560. The lowest paid 10 percent made less than $15,820, while the highest paid 10 percent earned more than $42,850. The U.S. Department of Labor also reported that library technicians employed by the federal government had mean annual salaries of $43,238 in 2006.

Benefits vary according to employer, but most full-time library technicians receive the same benefits as other employees, which may include the following: health insurance, dental insurance, paid vacations, paid holidays, compensated sick time, and retirement savings plans. Library technicians in grammar schools and high schools generally work fewer hours during summers and holidays when students are not in class, although these "down" times are often used to finish up backlogged projects. Technicians who work in corporate libraries may receive special perks as part of their benefits plan, such as stock in the company or discounts on products the company produces or markets. Many colleges and universities offer their employees discounted or free classes to help them earn a higher degree. Most employers offer training sessions to their technicians to keep them informed of new developments in library services and technology,

WORK ENVIRONMENT

Libraries usually have clean, well-lit, pleasant work atmospheres. Hours are regular in company libraries and in school library media centers, but academic, public, and some specialized libraries are open longer hours and may require evening and weekend work, usually on a rotating basis.

Some tasks performed by library technicians, like calculating circulation statistics, can be repetitive. Technicians working in technical services may develop headaches and eyestrain from working long hours in front of a computer screen. Heavy public contact in user services may test a technician's tact and patience. However, a library's atmosphere is generally relaxed and interesting. The size and type of library will often determine the duties of library technicians. A technician working in a small branch library might handle a wide range of responsibilities. Sometimes a technician working in a school, rural, or special library might be the senior staff member, with full responsibility for all technical, user, and administrative services and staff supervision. A technician working in a large university or public library might focus on only one task all of the time.

Libraries are presently responding to decreased government funding by cutting budgets and reducing staff, often leaving an overwhelming workload for the remaining staff members. Because library technicians earn less money than librarians do, libraries often replace librarians with technicians. This situation can lead to resentment in the working relationship among colleagues. In addition, there is also an ongoing struggle to define the different responsibilities of the librarian and technician. Despite the difference in the educational requirements for the two jobs—librarians require a master's degree and technicians an associate's degree—some of the responsibilities do overlap. Library technicians may find it frustrating that, in some cases, they are performing the same tasks as librarians and yet do not command as high a salary.

OUTLOOK

The U.S. Department of Labor predicts that employment for library technicians will grow about as fast as the average through 2016. Job openings will result from technicians leaving the field for other employment or retirement, as well as from libraries looking to stretch their budgets by hiring library technicians to handle computer-oriented tasks previously overseen by librarians. Since a library technician earns less than a librarian, a library may find it more economical to hire the technician. The continued growth of special libraries in medical, business, and law organizations will lead to growing opportunities for technicians who develop specialized skills. A technician who has excellent computer skills and is able to learn quickly will be highly employable, as will a technician who shows the drive to gain advanced degrees and accept more responsibility.

FOR MORE INFORMATION

For information on library careers, a list of accredited schools, scholarships and grants, and college student membership, contact

American Library Association
50 East Huron Street
Chicago, IL 60611-2729
Tel: 800-545-2433
Email: library@ala.org
http://www.ala.org

For information on education and awards programs, contact

Association for Educational Communications and Technology
1800 North Stonelake Drive, Suite 2
Bloomington, IN 47404-1517
Tel: 877-677-2328
http://www.aect.org

For information on continuing education programs and publications, contact

Library & Information Technology Association
c/o American Library Association
50 East Huron Street
Chicago, IL 60611-2795
Tel: 800-545-2433, ext. 4270
Email: lita@ala.org
http://www.lita.org

For information on the wide variety of careers in special libraries, contact

Special Libraries Association
331 South Patrick Street
Alexandria, VA 22314-3501
Tel: 703-647-4900
Email: sla@sla.org
http://www.sla.org

For information on library technician careers in Canada, contact

Alberta Association of Library Technicians
PO Box 700
Edmonton, AB T5J 2L4 Canada
Tel: 866-350-2258
http://www.aalt.org

To request information on education programs in Canada and scholarships, contact

Canadian Library Association
328 Frank Street
Ottawa, ON K2P 0X8 Canada
Tel: 613-232-9625
Email: info@cla.ca
http://www.cla.ca

☐ LICENSED PRACTICAL NURSES

OVERVIEW

Licensed practical nurses (LPNs), a specialty of the nursing profession, are sometimes called *licensed vocational nurses*. LPNs are trained to assist in the care and treatment of patients. They may assist registered nurses and physicians or work under various other circumstances. They perform many of the general duties of nursing and may be responsible for some clerical duties. LPNs work in hospitals, public health agencies, nursing homes, or in home health. Approximately 749,000 licensed practical nurses are employed in the United States.

THE JOB

Licensed practical nurses work under the supervision of a registered nurse, or a physician. They are responsible for many general duties of nursing such as administering prescribed drugs and medical treatments to patients, taking patients' temperatures and blood pressures, assisting in the preparation of medical examination and surgery, and performing routine laboratory tests. LPNs help with therapeutic and rehabilitation sessions; they may also participate in the planning, practice, and evaluation of a patient's nursing care.

A primary duty of an LPN is to ensure that patients are clean and comfortable, and that their needs, both physical and emotional, are met. They sometimes assist patients with daily hygiene such as bathing, brushing teeth, and dressing. Many times they provide emotional comfort by simply talking with the patient.

LPNs working in nursing homes have duties similar to those of LPNs employed by hospitals. They provide bedside care, administer medications, develop care plans, and supervise nurse assistants. Those working in doctors' offices and clinics are sometimes required to perform clerical duties such as keeping records, maintaining files and paperwork, as well as answering phones and tending the appointment book. Home health LPNs, in addition to their nursing duties, may sometimes prepare and serve meals to their patients.

REQUIREMENTS
High School

Some LPN programs do not require a high school diploma, but it is highly recommended, particularly if you want to be eligible for advancement opportunities. To prepare for a career as an LPN, you should study biology, chemistry, physics, and science while in high school. English and mathematics courses are also helpful.

Postsecondary Training

Those interested in a career as an LPN usually enroll in a practical nursing program after graduating from high school. There are about 1,500 state-approved programs in the United States that provide practical nursing training. Many LPNs graduate from a technical or vocational school, or from a community or junior college. The

---

QUICK FACTS

SCHOOL SUBJECTS
Biology
Chemistry

PERSONAL SKILLS
Helping/teaching
Technical/scientific

WORK ENVIRONMENT
Primarily indoors
Primarily multiple locations

MINIMUM EDUCATION LEVEL
Some postsecondary training

MEDIAN SALARY
$36,550

CERTIFICATION OR LICENSING
Voluntary (certification)
Required by all states (licensing)

OUTLOOK
About as fast as the average

---

remainder are enrolled in colleges, hospital programs, or high schools. Most programs last 12 months, with time spent for both classroom study and supervised clinical care. Courses include basic nursing concepts, anatomy, physiology, medical-surgical nursing, pediatrics, obstetrics, nutrition, and first aid. Clinical practice is most often in a hospital setting.

Certification or Licensing

The National Federation of Licensed Practical Nurses offers voluntary certification for LPNs who specialize in IV therapy or gerontology. The National Association for Practical Nurse Education and Service offers voluntary certification for LPNs who specialize in long-term care or pharmacology. Contact these organizations for more information.

All 50 states and the District of Columbia require graduates of a state-approved practical nursing program to take a licensing examination that has been developed by the National Council of State Boards of Nursing.

Other Requirements

Stamina, both physical and mental, is a must for this occupation. LPNs may be assigned to care for heavy or immobile patients or patients confused with dementia. Patience and a caring, nurturing attitude are valuable qualities to possess in order to be a successful LPN. As part of a health care team, LPNs must be able to follow orders and work under close supervision.

EXPLORING

High school students can explore an interest in this career by reading books or by checking out Web sites devoted to the nursing field. You should also take advantage of any information available in your school career center. An excellent way to learn more about this career firsthand is to speak with the school nurse or local public health nurse. Visits to the local hospital can give you a feel for the work environment. Volunteer work at a hospital, community health center, or even the local Red Cross chapter can provide valuable experience. Some high schools offer membership in Future Nurses organizations.

EMPLOYERS

Approximately 749,000 licensed practical nurses are employed in the United States. The U.S. Department of Labor reports that 26 percent of LPNs work in hospitals, 26 percent work in nursing facilities, and 12 percent work in physicians' offices and clinics. Others are employed by home health care agencies, public health agencies, schools, residential care facilities, temp agencies, and government agencies.

STARTING OUT

After they fulfill licensing requirements, LPNs should check with human resource departments of hospitals, nursing homes, and clinics for openings. State employment agencies and employment agencies that specialize in health professions are other ways to find work, as are school career services centers. Newspaper classified ads, nursing associations, and professional journals are great sources of job opportunities.

ADVANCEMENT

A large percent of LPNs use their license and experience as a stepping-stone for other occupations in the health field, many of which offer more responsibility and higher salaries. For example, with additional training, some LPNs become medical technicians, surgical attendants, optometric assistants, or psychiatric technicians. Many LPNs return to school to become registered nurses. Hospitals often offer LPNs the opportunity for more training, seminars, workshops, and clinical sessions to sharpen their nursing skills.

EARNINGS

According to the U.S. Department of Labor, LPNs earned an average of $36,550 annually in 2006. Ten percent earned less than $26,380, and 10 percent earned more than $50,480. Many LPNs are able to supplement their salaries with overtime pay and shift differentials. One-fifth of all LPNs work part time.

WORK ENVIRONMENT

Most LPNs work 40-hour weeks, less if part time. As with other health professionals, they may be asked to work during nights, weekends, or holidays to provide 24-hour care for their patients. Nurses are usually given pay differentials for these shifts.

LPNs employed in hospitals and nursing homes, as well as in clinics, enjoy clean, well-lighted, and generally comfortable work environments. The nature of their work calls for LPNs to be on their feet for most of the shift—providing patient care, dispensing medication, or assisting other health personnel.

OUTLOOK

Employment for LPNs is expected to grow about as fast as the average for all occupations through 2016, according to the U.S. Department of Labor. A growing elderly population requiring long-term health care is the primary factor for the demand of qualified LPNs. Traditionally, hospitals have provided the most job opportunities for LPNs. However, this source will only provide a moderate number of openings in the future. Inpatient population is not expected to increase significantly. Also, in many hospitals, certified nursing attendants are increasingly taking over many of the duties of LPNs.

Employment for LPNs in most non-hospital settings is expected to grow faster than the average. The increasing number of people age 65 and over and technological innovations that allow for more treatments at home will create much-faster-than-average employment opportunities for LPNs who work in home health care services.

Employment growth that is about as fast as the average is predicted for LPNs in nursing homes. Due to advanced medical technology, people are living longer, though many will require medical assistance. Private medical practices will also be excellent job sources because many medical procedures are now being performed on an outpatient basis in doctors' offices.

FOR MORE INFORMATION

For information on education programs and careers, contact the following organization:

American Association of Colleges of Nursing
One Dupont Circle, NW, Suite 530
Washington, DC 20036-1135
Tel: 202-463-6930
http://www.aacn.nche.edu

For information on licensing, contact

National Council of State Boards of Nursing
111 East Wacker Drive, Suite 2900
Chicago, IL 60601-4277
Tel: 312-525-3600
Email: info@ncsbn.org
http://www.ncsbn.org

For career and certification information, contact the following organizations

National Association for Practical Nurse Education and Service
1940 Duke Street, Suite 200
Alexandria, VA 22314-3452
Tel: 703-933-1003
Email: napnes@napnes.org
http://www.napnes.org

National Federation of Licensed Practical Nurses
605 Poole Drive
Garner, NC 27529-5203
Tel: 919-779-0046
http://www.nflpn.org

Discover Nursing, sponsored by Johnson & Johnson Health Care Systems, provides information on nursing careers, nursing schools, and scholarships.

Discover Nursing
http://www.discovernursing.com

LIFEGUARDS AND SWIMMING INSTRUCTORS

OVERVIEW

Lifeguards and swimming instructors watch over and teach swimmers at public and private pools, beaches, health clubs, summer camps, private resorts, and public

parks. Lifeguards enforce local laws and the particular regulations of their facility, and provide assistance to swimmers in need. One of their greatest responsibilities is preventing injuries and fatal accidents in or around water. Instructors hold group or individual swimming lessons. Most of their students are children, though instructors teach swimmers of all ages. Both lifeguards and instructors are trained professionals in the techniques of water rescue, cardiopulmonary resuscitation (CPR), and first aid.

THE JOB

Lifeguards patrol beaches, lakes, swimming pools, and other water areas to ensure safety of the patrons and management of the facility. They monitor water activities to make sure all swimmers are safe. If swimmers go too far from shore or leave the designated swimming zone, the lifeguard is responsible for signaling the swimmer back to safer waters. In some cases, the lifeguard must physically bring the swimmer back. They also watch for any roughhousing in the water, as this may cause

QUICK FACTS

SCHOOL SUBJECTS
Health
Physical education

PERSONAL SKILLS
Helping/teaching
Leadership/management

WORK ENVIRONMENT
Indoors and outdoors
Primarily one location

MINIMUM EDUCATION LEVEL
High school diploma

MEDIAN SALARY
$10/hour

CERTIFICATION OR LICENSING
Required by all states

OUTLOOK
About as fast as the average

potential danger and injury. Lifeguards who are posted at lakes and ocean beaches must be on the watch for strong currents, changing weather conditions, and dangerous animals, such as jellyfish or sharks.

Lifeguards also enforce local laws or facility regulations. They must notify patrons if they are breaking beach rules such as drinking alcoholic beverages, using glass containers, swimming with pets, or driving motorized vehicles. Swimming pools usually ban similar items; some pools also enforce certain time periods based on age.

Lifeguards keep watch from tower stations or elevated chairs. The height is advantageous because it allows the lifeguard clear visibility of the facility, and it also keeps the station in the public's view. Whistles, megaphones, and binoculars are helpful tools for maintaining order. Lifeguards also use equipment such as floatation devices, ropes, poles, and small boats during rescue attempts. They must be well versed in CPR and other first-aid techniques—such knowledge may mean the difference between life and death with drowning victims. Lifeguards not only need to be strong swimmers, but they must be levelheaded, calm, and ready to react in emergency situations.

Many lifeguards also work as swimming instructors. Instructors are hired by public pools, private swim clubs, and schools to teach proper swimming techniques. Instructors show students (generally children or young adults) how to swim using different strokes and breathing techniques. They also may teach students how to rescue or resuscitate swimmers during emergencies.

REQUIREMENTS
High School

Most facilities require their lifeguards and instructors to have a high school diploma, or a GED equivalent. High school classes in physical education (especially swimming) and health will be helpful for this career.

Postsecondary Training

If you aspire to hold a pool or beach management position, such as pool manager or instructor supervisor or use your swimming training in a related career, then it would be wise to work toward a college degree. Consider degrees in health, recreation, or business.

Certification or Licensing

All lifeguards and instructors must be certified to work. Depending on their skill level, lifeguards must pass a training program, from basic lifeguard training to head

lifeguard to aquatic professional. The basic lifeguard course lasts approximately six days and tests swimming skills. You will need to be able to swim 500 yards (no time frame) and tread water for one minute—as well as demonstrate your physical endurance, professionalism, and skills in using lifesaving equipment and techniques, CPR, and first aid. Head lifeguard courses teach advanced techniques in injury prevention, selection and training of guards, team building, and emergency response planning. To successfully complete the program, guards must attend and participate in the course, pass a written test, and demonstrate their guarding skills in the pool.

Instructors also must obtain certification to prove their teaching and swimming skills. The American Red Cross offers the designation water safety instructor to individuals 16 years of age or older. To earn this designation, candidates must attend and participate in the course, pass a written test, and prove their skills in techniques such as shallow and deep-water diving, rescue and lifesaving techniques, and demonstrate ability in all swimming strokes.

Other Requirements

Most training and certification programs require applicants to be at least 15 years of age. You should be in excellent physical condition, trustworthy, and able to exercise good judgment in serious situations. These jobs come with a tremendous amount of responsibility. Lifeguards are relied upon to keep water patrons safe and maintain order at their facility. Instructors are trusted with groups of small children who are not yet skilled at swimming.

EXPLORING

Do you want to test the waters now? If you are interested in lifeguarding, the United States Lifesaving Association offers junior lifeguard programs to students ages nine to 17. Participants learn water and beach safety and first-aid techniques, as well as build self-confidence in the water.

Another way to explore these careers is by talking to lifeguards and instructors at your local pool or beach. Ask them how they got their jobs and learned their swimming and guarding techniques. They may recommend certain programs for you to explore further. Finally, you can learn more about the work of lifeguards by reading *American Lifeguard Magazine* (http://www.usla.org/LGtoLG/mag.asp).

EMPLOYERS

Lakes and beaches are not the only work venues for lifeguards and swimming instructors. Hotels, schools, park districts, and health clubs all have swimming facilities, as well as public pools and institutions, such as the YMCA. Most places hire lifeguards and instructors on a temporary or seasonal basis. Opportunities for full-time employment are greater in areas that have warm weather year-round.

STARTING OUT

There is no standard way to enter this field. Many lifeguards and instructors find employment at facilities they normally frequent, or by word of mouth. The newspaper want ads are a good source—check under "Swimming Instructor," or "Lifeguard." Also, consider compiling a list of swimming facilities in your area and send job inquiries to those that interest you.

ADVANCEMENT

Many guards and instructors, employed on a temporary or seasonal basis, return to their jobs every summer until they finish school. There are quite a number of lifeguards and instructors who use their passion for the water and skills acquired while on the job as a basis for a full-time career. Dave Zielinski is a perfect example—he worked many summers as a lifeguard for his local YMCA. Today, he is employed as a customer service support manager for the Chicago chapter of the American Red Cross. Says Zielinski, "Lifeguarding gives an exciting avenue for those who enjoy the water."

There are other options as well. With hard work, ample experience, and further education, lifeguards and instructors can move into managerial positions such as *head lifeguard*, who assists managers and oversees all other guards; *aquatics manager*, who is responsible for the maintenance and operation of a pool; or *instructor supervisor*, who is involved in the hiring, training, and managing of all staff instructors. Highly skilled swimmers may choose to work as *aquatic specialists*, who run lifeguarding and instructor training programs or may even train professional swimmers.

EARNINGS

Earnings vary depending on several factors—facility or venue, hours worked, and certification status of the individual. According to Payscale.com, median hourly rates for lifeguards varied according to years of experience in the field: $7.63 per hour, less than one year of lifeguarding experience; $9.15 per hour, five to nine years or experience; $11.82 per hour, 10 to 19 years' experience. Lifeguard supervisors are paid $10 to $17 an hour.

Instructors may be paid per hour or per class. In general, they earn more for giving private lessons than teaching group sessions. According to a job posting on the summer employment Web site for the city of Raleigh, North Carolina, a swim instructor can earn $10 per hour.

Full-time employees are often offered a benefits package consisting of paid vacation time, sick leave, health insurance, and a retirement plan.

WORK ENVIRONMENT

Employment in the sun, surf, and the outdoors may be the ideal work atmosphere for some. However, these jobs are anything but cushy. Lifeguards have a tremendous amount of responsibility when on duty. They must always be ready to prevent accidents and react quickly during emergencies, while resisting the distractions of the job environment. Similarly, instructors have to stay alert while teaching, especially when instructing young children. Instructors also have the added stress of teaching young students who may not enjoy their time in the pool, and as a result, may not cooperate or be on their best behavior.

Though instructors teach classes of varying lengths, most lifeguards work eight-hour shifts. Depending on the size of the facility, guards work in pairs or teams. "Expect long hours in the sun," says Dave Zielinski—especially if you are stationed outdoors.

OUTLOOK

The outlook for lifeguards and instructors is mixed. Public interest in health and physical fitness is increasing steadily. Also, water amusement parks, a collection of swimming pools, wave pools, and water slides, are gaining in popularity. Combined with lakes, beaches, private and public swimming pools, not to mention pools located within high schools and universities, the opportunity for employment is plentiful. However, most lifeguard and instructor positions are part-time, or seasonal, mainly during the summer months. There are some swimming facilities open year-round, though these jobs are rare. Many students take lifeguard or instructor positions to supplement their income until they finish school. Those who desire to have a full-time career as a lifeguard or instructor should seek the best training available, and consider a college education, as well as advanced training in swimming and lifesaving procedures and techniques.

FOR MORE INFORMATION

For information regarding certification, education, or class schedules, contact
American Red Cross
2025 E Street, NW

Washington, DC 20006-5009
Tel: 703-206-6000
http://www.redcross.org

For information on careers and the junior lifeguard program, contact
United States Lifesaving Association
Tel: 866-FOR-USLA
http://www.usla.org

For industry information, tryouts, or job descriptions, contact
US Ocean Safety Inc.
http://www.usos.com

LINE INSTALLERS AND CABLE SPLICERS

OVERVIEW

Line installers and cable splicers construct, maintain, and repair the vast network of wires and cables that transmit electric power, telephone, and cable television lines to commercial and residential customers. Line construction and cable splicing is a vital part of the communications system. Workers are involved in linking electricity between generation plants and homes and other buildings, merging phone communications between telephone central offices and customers, and bringing cable television stations to residences and other locations. There are approximately 275,000 line installers and cable splicers working in the United States.

THE JOB

In the installation of new telephone and electric power lines, workers use power-driven machinery to first dig holes and erect the poles or towers that are used to support the cables. (In some areas, lines must be buried underground, and in these cases installers use power-driven equipment to dig and to place the cables in underground conduits.) These line installers, also called *outside plant technicians* and *construction line workers,* climb the poles using metal rungs (or they use truck-mounted work platforms) and install the necessary equipment and cables.

Installers who work with telephone lines usually leave the ends of the wires free for cable splicers to connect afterward; installers who work with electric power lines usually do the splicing of the wires themselves. For work on electric power lines, insulators must first be set into the poles before cables are attached. To join sections of power line and to conduct transformers and electrical accessories, line installers splice, solder, and insulate the conductors and related wiring. In some cases, line installers must attach other equipment—such as transformers, circuit breakers, and devices that deter lightning—to the line poles.

In addition to working with lines for electric power and telephones, installers set up lines for cable television transmission. Such lines carry broadcast signals from microwave towers to customer bases. Cable television lines are hung on the same poles with power and phone lines, or they are buried underground. In some cases, installers must attach other wires to the customer's premises in order to connect the outside lines to indoor television sets.

After line installers have completed the installation of underground conduits or poles, wires, and cables, cable splicers complete the line connections; they also rearrange wires when lines are changed. To join the individual wires within the cable, splicers must cut the lead sheath and insulation from the cables. They then test or phase out each conductor to identify corresponding conductors in adjoining cable sections according to electrical diagrams and specifications. At each splice, they either wrap insulation around the wires and seal the joint with a lead sleeve or cover the splice with some other type of closure. Sometimes they fill the sheathing with pressurized air so that leaks can be located and repaired.

In the past, copper was the material of choice for cables, but fiber optics are now replacing the outdated material. Fiber optic cables are hair-thin strands of glass that transmit signals more efficiently than do copper wires. For work with fiber optic cable, splicing is performed in workshop vans located near the splice area. Splicers of copper cables do their work on aerial platforms, down in manholes, in basements, or in underground vaults where the cables are located.

Preventive maintenance and repair work occupy major portions of the line installer's and cable splicer's time. When wires or cables break or poles are knocked down, workers are sent immediately to make emergency repairs. Such repair work is usually necessary after the occurrence of such disasters as storms and earthquakes. The *line crew supervisor* is notified when there is a break in a line and is directed to the trouble spot by workers who keep a check on the condition of all lines in given areas. During the course of routine periodic inspection, the line installer also makes minor repairs and line changes. Workers often use electric and gas pressure tests to detect possible trouble.

To allow for the demands of high-speed, high-definition transmissions, many telecommunications companies are installing fiber optic cables. The use of hybrid fiber/coax systems requires far less maintenance than traditional copper-based networks. Line installers and cable splicers will spend significantly less time repairing broken wires and cables once hybrid fiber/coax systems become more prevalent. As the cost of fiber cables decrease and become more in line with the costs of copper cables, more cable companies will make the switch.

Included in this occupation are many specialists, such as the following: section line maintainers, tower line repairers, line construction checkers, tower erectors, and cable testers. Other types of related workers include troubleshooters, test desk trouble locators, steel-post installers, radio interference investigators, and electric powerline examiners.

REQUIREMENTS
High School

You'll need math courses to prepare for the technical nature of this career. While in high school, you should also take any shop classes that will teach you the principles of electricity and how to work with it. In addition, you will benefit from taking any classes that deal with electricity at a vocational or technical college in your area. Other high school shop classes, such as machinery, will give you the opportunity to work with tools and improve your hand-eye coordination. Science classes that involve lab work will also be beneficial. Take computer classes so that you will be able to use this tool in your professional life. Because you may be frequently interacting with customers, take English, speech, and other courses that will help you develop communication skills.

Postsecondary Training

Many companies prefer to hire applicants with a high school diploma or the equivalent. Although specific educational courses are not required, you'll need certain qualifications. It is helpful to have some knowledge of the basic principles of electricity and the procedures involved in line installation; such information can be obtained through attending technical programs or having been a member of the armed forces. Many employers, particularly for cable television installation, prefer to hire

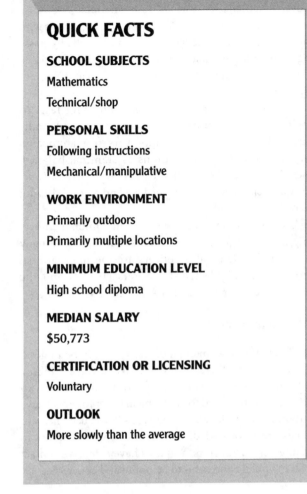

QUICK FACTS

SCHOOL SUBJECTS
Mathematics
Technical/shop

PERSONAL SKILLS
Following instructions
Mechanical/manipulative

WORK ENVIRONMENT
Primarily outdoors
Primarily multiple locations

MINIMUM EDUCATION LEVEL
High school diploma

MEDIAN SALARY
$50,773

CERTIFICATION OR LICENSING
Voluntary

OUTLOOK
More slowly than the average

applicants who have received some technical training or completed a trade school or technical program that offers certification classes in technology such as fiber optics. Training can also be obtained through special classes offered through trade associations. The Society of Cable Telecommunications Engineers (SCTE) offers seminars that provide hands-on, technical training.

In many companies, entry-level employees must complete a formal apprenticeship program combining classroom instruction with supervised on-the-job training. These programs often last several years and are administered by both the employer and the union representing the employees. The programs may involve computer-assisted instruction as well as hands-on experience with simulated environments.

Certification or Licensing

Though not a requirement for employment, certification demonstrates to employers that a line installer has achieved a certain level of technical training and has been proven qualified to perform certain functions. The SCTE offers several certification designations to applicants who show technical knowledge and practical skills by passing both multiple-choice and essay-based examinations. (Contact information for the SCTE is listed at the end of this article.)

Employers may also give preemployment tests to applicants to determine verbal, mechanical, and mathematical aptitudes; some employers test applicants for such physical qualifications as stamina, balance, coordination, and strength. Workers who drive a company vehicle need a driver's license and a good driving record.

Unions represent many workers, and union membership may be required. Two unions that represent many line installers and cable splicers are the International Brotherhood of Electrical Workers (IBEW) and the Communications Workers of America (CWA).

Other Requirements

You'll need to have manual dexterity and to be in good physical shape. Much of your work will involve climbing poles and ladders, so you'll need to feel comfortable with heights. You also need to be strong in order to carry heavy equipment up poles and ladders. Also, because lines and cables are color coded, you should have the ability to distinguish such colors. You may have extensive contact with the public and need to be polite and courteous.

EXPLORING

In high school or vocational school, you can test your ability and interest in the occupations of line installer and cable splicer through courses in mathematics, electrical applications, and machine shop. Hobbies that involve knowledge of and experience with electricity also provide valuable practical experience. To observe line installers and cable splicers at work, it may be possible to have a school counselor arrange a field trip by calling the public relations office of the local telephone or cable television company.

Direct training and experience in telephone work may be gained in the armed forces. Frequently, those who have received such training are given preference for job openings and may be hired in positions above the entry level.

EMPLOYERS

There are approximately 275,000 line installers and cable splicers working in the United States. Most work for tele-

phone or cable television companies. They also find work with electric power companies. Some installers also work for the freelance construction companies that contract with telecommunications companies.

STARTING OUT

Those who meet the basic requirements and are interested in becoming either a line installer or a cable splicer may inquire about job openings by directly contacting the personnel offices of local telephone companies, utility companies, and cable television providers.

Those enrolled in a trade school or technical institute may be able to find out about job openings through their school's career services department. Occasionally, employers will contact teachers and program administrators, so it is helpful to check with them also. Some positions are advertised through classified advertisements in the newspaper. Because many line installers are members of unions such as the CWA and the IBEW, job seekers can contact their local offices for job leads and assistance or visit these unions' Web sites.

ADVANCEMENT

Entry-level line installers are generally hired as helpers, trainees, or ground workers; cable splicers tend to work their way up from the position of line installer.

After successfully completing an on-the-job training program, the employee will be assigned either as a line crewmember under the guidance of a line supervisor or as a cable splicer's helper under the guidance of experienced splicers. Cable splicers' helpers advance to positions of qualified cable splicers after three to four years of working experience.

Both the line installer and the cable splicer must continue to receive training throughout their careers, not only to qualify for advancement but also to keep up with the technological changes that occur in the industry. It usually takes line installers about six years to reach top pay for their job; top pay for cable splicers is earned after about five to seven years of work experience.

In companies represented by unions, opportunities for advancement may be based on seniority. Workers who demonstrate technical expertise in addition to certain personal characteristics, such as good judgment, planning skills, and the ability to deal with people, may progress to foremen or line crew supervisors. With additional training, the line installer or the cable splicer may advance to telephone installer, telephone repairer, communications equipment technician, or another higher ranked position.

EARNINGS

For line installers and cable splicers, earnings vary according to different regions of the country, and as with most occupations, work experience and length of service determine advances in scale. Telecommunications line installers and repairers had a median hourly wage of $24.41 in 2006, which made a yearly income of approximately $50,773. The lowest paid 10 percent of all of these workers made less than $13.96 per hour ($29,037 per year), while the highest paid 10 percent made $34.20 or more per hour ($71,136 per year). Electrical line installers and repairers had a median hourly wage of $24.41 in 2006, according to the U.S. Department of Labor. This hourly wage translated into a yearly income of approximately $50,773. When emergencies arise and overtime is necessary during unscheduled hours, workers are guaranteed a minimum rate of pay that is higher than their regular rate.

Beginning workers and those with only a few years of experience make significantly less than more experienced workers. As mentioned earlier, the turnover rate in these occupations is low; therefore, many workers are in the higher wage categories. Also, cable splicers who work with fiber optics tend to earn more than those who work with copper cables.

Telecommunications companies often provide workers with many benefits. Although benefits vary from company to company, in general, most workers receive paid holidays, vacations, and sick leaves. In addition, most companies offer medical, dental, and life insurance plans. Some companies offer pension plans.

WORK ENVIRONMENT

Most line installers and cable splicers work standard 40-hour weeks, though evening and weekend work is not unusual. For example, line installers and cable splicers who work for construction companies may need to schedule their work around contractors' activities and then be required to rush to complete a job on schedule. Shift work, such as four 10-hour days or working Tuesday through Saturday, is common for many workers. Most workers earn extra pay for any work over 40 hours a week.

Some workers are on call 24 hours a day and need to be available for emergencies. Both occupations require that workers perform their jobs outdoors, often in severe weather conditions when emergency repairs are needed. Construction line installers usually work in crews of two to five persons, with a supervisor directing the work of several of these crews. Work may involve extensive travel, including overnight trips during emergencies to distant locations.

There is a great deal of climbing involved in these occupations, and some underground work must be done in stooped and cramped conditions. Cable splicers sometimes perform their work on board a marine craft if they are employed with an underwater cable crew.

The work can be physically demanding and poses significant risk of injury from shocks or falls. The hazards of this work have been greatly reduced, though, by concerted efforts to establish safety standards. Such efforts have been put forward by the telecommunications companies, utility companies, and appropriate labor unions.

OUTLOOK

The U.S. Department of Labor anticipates that employment for line installers and cable splicers will grow more slowly than the average for all occupations through 2016, though the trend will vary among industries. For example, little or no employment growth is expected for those working specifically for electric companies, while those working as telephone or cable television installers are predicted to have better job opportunities. There tends to be a low rate of employee turnover, but new employees will be needed to replace those who retire or leave the field.

FOR MORE INFORMATION

For information about union representation, contact the following organizations:

Communications Workers of America
501 Third Street, NW
Washington, DC 20001-2797
Tel: 202-434-1100
http://www.cwa-union.org

International Brotherhood of Electrical Workers
900 Seventh Street, NW
Washington, DC 20001-3886
Tel: 202-833-7000
http://www.ibew.org

For information on careers and the cable industry, contact
National Cable and Telecommunications Association
25 Massachusetts Avenue, NW, Suite 100
Washington, DC 20001-1434
Tel: 202-222-2300
http://www.ncta.com

For information on training seminars and certification, contact
Society of Cable Telecommunications Engineers
140 Philips Road
Exton, PA 19341-1318

Tel: 800-542-5040
Email: scte@scte.org
http://www.scte.org

For information about conferences, special programs, and membership, contact
Women in Cable Telecommunications
14555 Avion Parkway, Suite 250
Chantilly, VA 20151-1117
Tel: 703-234-9810
http://www.wict.org

LOCKSMITHS

OVERVIEW

Locksmiths, or *lock experts*, are responsible for all aspects of installing and servicing locking devices, such as door and window locks for buildings, door and ignition locks for automobiles, locks on such objects as combination safes and desks, and electronic access control devices. Locksmiths are often considered to be artisans or craftspeople who combine ingenuity with mechanical aptitude. There are approximately 26,000 locksmiths employed in the United States.

THE JOB

The aspects of the locksmith profession differ, depending on whether one works for one's own business, in a shop for a master locksmith, or as an in-house lock expert for a large establishment, such as an apartment complex or a high-rise office building. However, the essential nature of the work for all locksmiths can be described in general terms. Basically, they sell, service, and install locks, spending part of their working time in locksmith shops and part of it at the sites they are servicing. Locksmiths install locks in homes, offices, factories, and many other types of establishments. In addition to maintaining the working mechanics of lock devices, locksmiths usually perform functions that include metalworking, carpentry, and electronics.

The basic equipment used by the locksmith includes a workbench, various tools, a key machine and supplies. Tools may include broken key extractors, drills, files, key blanks, springs, C-clamps, circular hole cutters, hammers, and screwdrivers.

While at the shop, locksmiths work on such portable items as padlocks and luggage locks, as well as on an endless number of keys. When they need to do work at a customer's site, they usually drive to the site in a work van that carries an assortment of the locksmith's most common equipment and supplies. When on site, they perform whatever function is needed for each specific job, be it opening locks whose keys have been lost, preparing master-key systems for such places as hotels and apartment complexes, removing old locks and installing modern devices, or rewiring electronic access control devices. Because locks are commonly found on doors and other building structures, lock experts often put their carpentry skills to use when doors have to be fitted for locks. And because locking devices are increasingly made with electronic parts, locksmiths must use their knowledge and skill to work with electronic door openers, electromagnetic locks, and electrical keyless locks.

Lock experts may spend part of their working day providing service to those who have locked themselves out of their houses, places of work, or vehicles. When keys are locked inside, locksmiths must pick the lock. If keys are lost, new ones often must be made. Locksmiths often repair locks by taking them apart to examine, clean, file, and adjust the cylinders and tumblers. Combination locks present a special task for locksmiths; they must be able to open a safe, for example, if its combination lock does not work smoothly. Manipulating combination locks requires expert, precise skills that are honed by much practice. The technique requires that the locksmith listen for vibrations and for the interior mechanism to indicate a change in direction while the dial is carefully rotated; this is repeated until the mechanism has been accurately turned. If it is not possible to open the lock through these methods, the device may be drilled.

Locksmiths work in any community large enough to need their services, but most jobs are available in large metropolitan areas. Some locksmiths work in shops for other professionals, and others work for large hardware or department stores. Also, many open their own businesses. Independent locksmiths must perform all the tasks needed to run any type of business, such as keeping books and tax records, preparing statements, ordering merchandise, and advertising. A locksmith's clients may include individual home or automobile owners as well as large organizations such as hospitals, housing developments, military bases, and federal agencies. Industrial complexes and huge factories may employ locksmiths to install and maintain complete security systems, and other establishments, such as school systems and hotels, employ locksmiths to regularly install or change locks. Many locksmiths are getting more involved in the security aspect of the profession and may be required to analyze security needs and propose, monitor, and maintain security systems for businesses and residences.

REQUIREMENTS
High School

No special educational requirements are needed to become a locksmith. Most employers prefer applicants who have graduated from high school. Helpful school classes include metal shop, mathematics, mechanical drawing, computers, and electronics, if available.

Postsecondary Training

There are locksmiths who have learned their skills from professionals in the business, but many workers learn the trade by either attending a community college or trade school or completing an accredited correspondence course. A number of trade schools in the United States follow a curriculum based on all practical aspects of the locksmith trade. They teach the correct application of the current range of security devices, including the theory and practice of electronic access control, as well as the servicing and repairing of mortise, cylindrical, and bit-key locks. Students learn to recognize keys by their manufacturer and practice cutting keys by hand as well as by machine. Some courses allow students to set up a sample master-key system for clients such as a business or apartment complex. In addition to these fundamentals, pupils also learn to use carpentry tools and jigs to install common locking devices. Finally, they learn about automobile lock systems (how to enter locked automobiles in emergencies and how to remove, service, and repair ignition locks) and combination locks (how to service interchangeable core cylinders and manipulate combinations). The objective of such training is to teach the prospective locksmith all basic responsibilities. After completing a training course, the graduate should be able to meet customer demand and standards of the trade with minimum supervision.

Many persons interested in a locksmith career learn the trade by taking correspondence courses, which include instructions, assignments, tools, and model locks and keys. Lessons may be supplemented with supervised on-the-job training with a consenting master locksmith.

Certification or Licensing

Many cities and states require that locksmiths be licensed and bonded. In some areas, locksmiths may have to be fingerprinted and pay a fee to be licensed.

QUICK FACTS

SCHOOL SUBJECTS
Mathematics
Technical/shop

PERSONAL SKILLS
Mechanical/manipulative
Technical/scientific

WORK ENVIRONMENT
Indoors and outdoors
Primarily multiple locations

MINIMUM EDUCATION LEVEL
Some postsecondary training

MEDIAN SALARY
$33,560

CERTIFICATION OR LICENSING
Voluntary (certification)
Required by certain states (licensing)

OUTLOOK
Much faster than average

Area and state locksmith associations may require that their members be certified. The Associated Locksmiths of America (ALA) offers the following certification designations: registered locksmith, certified registered locksmith, certified professional locksmith, and the highest level, certified master locksmith. The ALA also offers the following certification designations to locksmiths who specialize in installing and servicing locks and other security devices on safes and vaults: certified professional safetech and certified master safetech. Contact the ALA for more information.

Other Requirements

Locksmiths must be able to plan and schedule jobs and to use the right tools, techniques, and materials for each. Good vision and hearing are necessary for working with combination locks, and eye-hand coordination is essential when working with tiny locks and their intricate interiors. A good locksmith should have both a delicate touch and an understanding of the nature of mechanical devices.

Each lost key, broken lock, and security problem will present a unique challenge that the locksmith must be prepared to remedy on the spot. Locksmiths, therefore, must be able to think well on their feet. Locksmiths also have a responsibility to be reliable, accurate, and, most important, honest, since their work involves the security of persons and valuables. Customers must be able to count on their skill, dependability, and integrity. In addition, locksmiths must be aware of laws that apply to elements of their jobs, such as restrictions on duplicating master keys, making safe deposit box keys, and opening automobiles whose keys are not available. It is suggested that the locksmith-to-be consult with a lawyer to discuss the legal responsibilities of the trade.

EXPLORING

High school machine shop classes will provide you with a degree of experience in using a variety of hand tools, some of which may be used in the trade. If you are interested in learning specifically about types of locks and how to work with them, read *The Complete Book of Locks and Locksmithing* (New York: McGraw-Hill Professional, 2005) or other books about the trade that may be available at local libraries or bookstores.

It is a good idea to contact organizations that are involved with the locksmithing trade. You might request information from the Associated Locksmiths of America, whose objective is to educate and provide current information to those involved in the physical security industry. Another method of finding out more about the career is to talk with someone already employed as a locksmith.

EMPLOYERS

Approximately 26,000 locksmiths are employed in the United States. The largest demand for locksmiths is in larger metropolitan areas. Locksmith shops or large hardware or department stores hire many locksmiths. Numerous large factories, resorts, hotels and industrial facilities hire locksmiths to install and change their locks and to maintain their security systems. Many locksmiths open their own businesses and provide services to home or automobile owners, as well as to hospitals, hotels, motels, businesses, government facilities, and housing developments.

The increased use of security systems in businesses and residences offers many additional employment options for locksmiths. These jobs may require additional training and skills, however.

STARTING OUT

Since locksmithing is a vocation that requires skill and experience, it is unlikely that the untrained job seeker will be able to begin immediately in the capacity of locksmith. Beginners might consider contacting local shops to inquire about apprenticeships. In some cases, skilled locksmiths may be willing to teach their trade to a promising worker in exchange for low-cost labor. Another method is to check with state employment offices for business and industry listings of job openings for locksmiths. Some locksmith trade organizations may post job openings or apprenticeships.

Students enrolled in a trade school can obtain career counseling and job placement assistance. Trade school graduates should be qualified to begin work in established locksmith shops doing basic work both in the shop and on the road; others become in-house locksmiths for businesses and other establishments.

ADVANCEMENT

Most locksmiths regard their work as a lifetime profession. They stay abreast of new developments in the field so that they can increase both their skills and earnings. As they gain experience, industrial locksmiths may advance from apprentices to journeymen to master locksmiths, and then to any of several kinds of supervisory or managerial positions.

After having worked in the field for a number of years, many lock experts decide to establish their own shops and businesses. In so doing, they tend to build working relationships with a list of clients and, in effect, can grow their business at their own flexible rate. Self-employed locksmiths are responsible for all the tasks that are required to run a business, such as planning, organizing, bookkeeping, and marketing.

Another advancement opportunity lies in becoming a specialist in any of a number of niches. Some locksmiths work exclusively with combination locks, for example, or become experts with automobile devices. One of the most promising recent specialty growth areas is that of electronic security. Such safety devices and systems are becoming standard equipment for large establishments such as banks, hotels, and many industries, as well as residences and autos, and their popularity is creating a need for skilled locksmiths to install and service them.

EARNINGS

Locksmithing can be a lucrative occupation, depending upon the geographic region of the country and the type of work done. Geographically, wages for locksmiths tend to follow the pattern of general earnings of all occupations; that is, workers on the East Coast tend to earn the most and those in the South and Southwest the least.

Entry-level locksmiths with no experience generally start out with wages between minimum wage and $8 an hour, although in some areas wages may be higher. Experienced locksmiths earned an average of $33,560 annually in 2006, according to the U.S. Department of Labor. Locksmiths with considerable experience and a large clientele can earn more than $51,170 annually. Locksmiths who specialize in high-security electronic systems may earn much more than that. Full-time employees can usually expect general fringe benefits.

Self-employed locksmiths may be small business operators who earn less than some salaried employees, or they may head larger operations and earn more than the average through contracts with numerous clients.

WORK ENVIRONMENT

Locksmiths who are self-employed often work up to 60 hours per week; apprentices and locksmiths working in industries and institutions, however, usually work standard 40-hour workweeks. Some locksmith businesses may offer after-hour services. These employers may require locksmiths to answer service calls at any time of the day or night, including weekends.

Locksmiths stand during much of their working time, but they also often need to crouch, bend, stoop, and kneel. Sometimes they are required to lift heavy gates, doors, and other objects when dealing with safes, strong rooms, or lock fittings.

Locksmith workshops are usually well lit, well heated, and well ventilated. Some shops, particularly mobile ones, however, may be crowded and small, requiring that workers move carefully around fixtures and stock. Some locksmiths work outdoors, installing or repairing protective or warning devices. Some workers who work at other sites may have to do considerable driving. Locksmiths may work alone or may be required at times to work with others at stores, banks, factories, schools, and other facilities. Physical injuries are not common, but minor ones can occur from soldering irons, welding equipment, electric shocks, flying bits from grinders, and sharp lock or key edges.

OUTLOOK

The U.S. Department of Labor predicts that employment for locksmiths will grow much faster than average through 2016. Population growth and an expanding public awareness of the need for preventive measures against home, business, and auto burglary continue to create needs for security devices and their mainte-

nance. Also, many individuals and firms are replacing older lock and alarm systems with the latest developments in computerized equipment. Consequently, opportunities will be best for those workers who are able to install and service electronic security systems.

The locksmith trade itself has remained stable, with few economic fluctuations, and locksmiths with an extensive knowledge of their trade are rarely unemployed.

FOR MORE INFORMATION

For information on schools and colleges that offer locksmith classes, contact

Accrediting Commission of Career Schools and Colleges of Technology
2101 Wilson Boulevard, Suite 302
Arlington, VA 22201-3062
Tel: 703-247-4212
Email: info@accsct.org
http://www.accsct.org

For information on locksmithing careers, certification, education, and scholarships, contact

Associated Locksmiths of America
3500 Easy Street
Dallas, TX 75247
Tel: 800-532-2562
Email: education@aloa.org
http://www.aloa.org

For a list of accredited home-study programs in locksmithing, contact

Distance Education and Training Council
1601 18th Street, NW
Washington, DC 20009-2529
Tel: 202-234-5100
Email: detc@detc.org
http://www.detc.org

MAKEUP ARTISTS

OVERVIEW

Makeup artists prepare actors for performances on stage and before cameras. They read scripts and consult with directors, producers, and technicians to design makeup effects for each individual character. They apply makeup and prosthetics and build and style wigs. They also create special makeup effects.

QUICK FACTS

SCHOOL SUBJECTS

Art

Theater/dance

PERSONAL SKILLS

Artistic

Communication/ideas

WORK ENVIRONMENT

Indoors and outdoors

Primarily multiple locations

MINIMUM EDUCATION LEVEL

Some postsecondary training

MEDIAN SALARY

$31,820

CERTIFICATION OR LICENSING

None available

OUTLOOK

Faster than the average

THE JOB

Some of makeup artist Vincent Guastini's creations have involved turning Alanis Morissette into God and Matt Damon and Ben Affleck into angels. These effects for the film *Dogma* hearken back to the earliest examples of theatrical makeup, back to the Middle Ages when makeup effects were used to represent God, angels, and devils. But Guastini is not relying on the simple symbolic face painting of the past; this production demanded that he design complicated animatronic wings, detailed rubber masks, and radio-controlled mechanical creatures. With a crew of some of the top makeup artists in the business, Guastini created effects using rubber, plastic, fiberglass, latex paints, radio-control units from model airplanes, and steel cables. "As well as," Guastini says, "the old standby of a makeup kit filled with grease paints, makeup, rubber glues, brushes, and powders."

From a seven-foot-tall alien for the film *Metamorphosis: The Alien Factor* to the animatronic killer doll Chucky in *Child's Play III*, Guastini has created some very bizarre and disturbing effects. "Movies like *Star Wars* and horror movies left an impact on me as a kid," Guastini says, citing his inspirations. He is also called upon to create less extreme transformations with makeup; his production company worked on *The Last of the Mohicans*, which involved applying wounds and prosthetics to hundreds of actors and extras.

Not every project involves prosthetics and special effects. Makeup artists also apply "clean" makeup, which is a technique of applying foundations and powders to keep actors and models looking natural under the harsh lighting of stage and film productions. Makeup artists accent, or downplay, an actor's natural features. They conceal an actor's scars, skin blemishes, tattoos, and wrinkles, as well as apply these same things when needed for the character. Having read the script and met with the director and technicians, makeup artists take into consideration many factors: the age of the characters, the setting of the production, the time period, lighting effects, and other details that determine how an actor should appear. Historical productions require a great deal of research to learn about the hair and clothing styles of the time. Makeup artists also style hair; apply wigs, bald caps, beards, and sideburns; and temporarily color hair. In many states, however, makeup artists are limited in the hair services they can perform; some productions bring in locally licensed cosmetologists for hair cutting, dye jobs, and perms.

After much preparation, the makeup artist becomes an important backstage presence during a production. Throughout the making of a film, makeup artists arrive early for work every day. On the set of *Dogma*, preparing an actor's makeup took four to six hours. "We were always the first to arrive and the last to leave the set," Guastini says of his crew of artists. Makeup artists are required to maintain the actors' proper makeup throughout filming and to help the actors remove the makeup at the end of the day. With the aid of fluorescent lighting, makeup artists apply the makeup, and they keep their eyes on the monitors during filming to make sure the makeup looks right. Guastini's production crew is also responsible for the mechanical creatures they create. "We must do constant repairs and upkeep on any mechanical creatures, making sure they're in working order," Guastini says.

Most makeup artists for film are in business for themselves, contracting work from studios, production companies, and special effects houses on a freelance basis. They may supplement their film work with projects for TV, video, commercials, industrial films, and photo shoots for professional photographers. Makeup artists for theater may also work freelance or be employed full time by a theater or theater troupe. Makeup artists for theater find work with regional theaters, touring shows, and recreational parks.

REQUIREMENTS

High School

Does becoming a makeup artist sound interesting to you? If so, there are a number of classes you can take in high school to help prepare you for this profession. Take all the art classes you can, including art history if this is offered at your school. Photography courses will help you understand the use of light and shadow. Courses in illustration, painting, and drawing will help you to develop the skills you'll need for illustrating proposed makeup effects. Learning about sculpting is important, as creating special makeup effects with rubber, prosthetics, and glue is often much like sculpting from clay. Other helpful classes for you to take are anatomy and chemistry. Anatomy will give you an understanding of the human body, and chemistry will give you insight into the products you will be using. If your school offers drama classes, be sure to take these. In drama class you will gain an understanding of all the different elements—such as scripts, actors, and location—needed for a production. Computer classes will give you exposure to this technology, which you may use in the future to design projects. Try experimenting with makeup and special effects on your own. Take photographs of your efforts in order to build a portfolio of your work. Finally, because this work is typically done on a freelance basis and you will need to manage your business accounts, it will be helpful for you to take math, business, and accounting classes.

Postsecondary Training

There are a number of postsecondary educational routes you can take to become a makeup artist. If you have experience and a portfolio to show off your work, you may be able to enter the business right out of high school. This route is not always advisable, however, because your chances for establishing a successful freelance career without further training are slim. You must be very ambitious, enthusiastic, and capable of seeking out successful mentors willing to teach you the ropes. This can mean a lot of time working for free or for very little pay.

Another route you can take is to get specific training for makeup artistry through vocational schools. One advantage of this route is that after graduating from the program, you will be able to use the school's place-

ment office, instructors, and other graduates as possible networking sources for jobs. Probably the most highly respected schools for makeup artists in film are the Joe Blasco schools, which have several locations across the country. Topics you might study at a Joe Blasco school include beauty makeup, old age makeup, bald cap, hairwork, and monster makeup. Some people in the business have cosmetology degrees, also offered by vocational schools. A cosmetology course of study, however, is not typically geared toward preparing you for makeup artistry work in the entertainment industry.

A third route you can take is to get a broad-based college or university education that results in either a bachelor's or master's degree. Popular majors for makeup artists include theater, art history, film history, photography, and fashion merchandising. In addition to makeup courses, it is important to take classes in painting, illustration, computer design, and animation. A master of fine arts degree in theater or filmmaking will allow you to gain hands-on experience in production as well as working with a faculty of practicing artists.

Other Requirements

Patience and the ability to get along well with people are important for a makeup artist—throughout a film production, the actors will spend many hours in the makeup chair. Though many actors will be easy to work with, you may have to put up with much irritability, as well as overwhelming egos. Producers and directors can also be difficult to work with. And, as you gain more experience, you may have more knowledge about filmmaking than some of the producers of the projects. This may put you in frustrating situations, and you may see time wasted in costly mistakes.

Attention to detail is important; you must be quick to spot any makeup problems before they are filmed. Such responsibilities can be stressful—a whole production team will be relying on you to properly apply makeup that will look good on film. If your work isn't up to par, the whole production will suffer. Work as a makeup artist requires as much creativity and ingenuity as any other filmmaking task. The directors and actors rely on the makeup artists to come up with interesting makeup effects and solutions to filming problems. "It's important to be original in your work," Vincent Guastini advises. Guastini is also an example of the importance of ambition and dedication—within five years of graduating from high school, he began work on his first motion picture. A year after that first assignment, he had developed a list of clients and put together a team of special effects artists. Because of the tough, competitive nature of the entertainment industry, makeup artists must be persistent and enthusiastic in their pursuit of work.

As a makeup artist, you may want to consider joining a union. The International Alliance of Theatrical Stage Employees, Moving Picture Technicians, Artists and Allied Crafts of the United States, Its Territories, and Canada represents workers in theater, film, and television production. Hair stylists, makeup artists, engineers, art directors, and set designers are some of the professionals who belong to the more than 500 local unions affiliated with the alliance. Union membership is not required of most makeup artists for film and theater, but it can help individuals negotiate better wages, benefits, and working conditions. Theaters in larger cities may require union membership of makeup artists, while smaller, regional theaters across the country are less likely to require membership.

EXPLORING

High school drama departments or local community theaters can provide you with great opportunities to explore the makeup artist's work. Volunteer to assist with makeup during a stage production and you will learn about the materials and tools of a makeup kit, as well as see your work under stage lights. A high school video production team or film department may also offer you opportunities for makeup experience.

Most states have their own film commissions that are responsible for promoting film locales and inviting film productions to the local area. These film commissions generally need volunteers and may have internships for students. By working for a film commission, you will learn about productions coming to your state and may have the chance to work on the production. Film industry publications such as *Variety* (http://www.variety.com) can alert you to internship opportunities.

The summer is a great time for students interested in stage production to gain firsthand experience. There are probably local productions in your area, but summer theaters often promote positions nationally. The Theatre Communications Group publishes a directory of nonprofit professional theaters across the country. Its bimonthly publication, *ARTSEARCH*, provides information on summer theater positions and internships. (More information can be found at the end of this chapter.)

Finally, explore this career by reading other publications for the field. For example, check out *Make-Up Artist Magazine* (http://www.makeupmag.com), a bimonthly publication with profiles of makeup artists for film as well as how-to columns and product information.

EMPLOYERS

Although makeup artists work in a wide variety of circumstances, from theater to television to movies, they usually are self-employed, contracting individual jobs. Theater troupes, touring shows, and amusement parks may hire makeup artists on to their staffs, but in the film industry, makeup artists work on a freelance basis. Large cities and metropolitan areas will provide the majority of jobs for makeup artists, particularly those cities associated with thriving theaters, movie or television studios, fashion photography, and modeling/talent agencies. Although there may be some jobs in smaller towns, they will most likely be along the lines of industrial films, corporate videos, and photographic shoots—not very promising for those who wish to make a living in this line of work. Those who aspire to work exclusively as makeup artists gravitate toward the big cities.

STARTING OUT

You should keep a photographic record of all the work you do for theater and film productions, including photos of any drawings or sculptures you have done for art classes. It's important to have a portfolio to send along with your resume to effects shops, makeup departments, and producers. "Be prepared to work for free or for little money at the start," Vincent Guastini advises, "just to hook up with the right person who will hire you the next time out." To build up a portfolio of photographs, experiment in art classes and at home with makeup and special effects, and photograph the results. Check with local TV studios about work in their makeup departments. Locally produced newscasts, children's programming, documentaries, and commercials offer opportunities for makeup artists. Commercials are often quick productions (between one and three days) with small casts, and they pay well. Department stores hire makeup artists to demonstrate and sell cosmetic products onsite in the stores, which may be a starting position for those who want to earn a salary while getting on-the-job training and practice.

Because of the freelance nature of the business, you will be going from project to project. This requires you to constantly seek out work. Read industry trade magazines like *Variety,* and don't be shy about submitting your portfolio to producers and studios. Self-promotion will be an important part of your success as a makeup artist.

ADVANCEMENT

Many makeup artists start as assistants or volunteers on a production, making contacts and connections while on the job. They eventually take on projects for which they are in charge of makeup departments and designing makeup effects. They may also establish their own production companies and make their own films or stage their own plays. "I would love to direct someday," Vincent Guastini says about his future, "or produce a film, but the project the first time out should be a really solid, visually exciting film that incorporates my current talents."

Successful, experienced makeup artists can pick and choose their projects and work as much as they like. In the early years, makeup artists must frequently take on a variety of different projects just for the money; however, as they become established in the field and develop a solid reputation, they can concentrate on projects specific to their interests.

EARNINGS

Makeup artists usually contract with a production, negotiating a daily rate. This rate can vary greatly from project to project, depending on the budget of the production, the prestige of the project, and other factors. Even well-established makeup artists occasionally forgo payment to work on the low-budget independent productions of filmmakers they respect.

Independent contractors don't draw steady, yearly salaries. This means they may work long hours for several weeks, then, upon completion of a production, go without work for several weeks. Unless makeup artists are part of the union, they may be without benefits, having to provide all their own health insurance. An experienced makeup artist can make between $500 to $700 a day on a film with a sizable budget; some of the top makeup artists in the business command around $1,000 a day. Theatrical makeup artists can make comparable daily wages on Broadway, or in a theater in a large city; some small theaters, however, may only pay around $50 a day.

Because of such variables as the unsteady nature of the work, the makeup artist's experience, and even where he or she works, the yearly incomes for these individuals vary widely. Some makeup artists may show yearly earnings little higher than those resulting from the minimum wage. Others may have annual income in the hundreds of thousands of dollars. The U.S. Department of Labor reports that makeup artists, theatrical and performance, had median annual salaries of $31,820 in 2006. Salaries ranged from less than $14,500 to more than $70,750.

WORK ENVIRONMENT

Long hours, deadlines, and tight budgets can result in high stress on a movie set. Because makeup artists move from production to production, they work with different groups of people all the time, and in different locales and settings. Although this allows makeup artists the opportunity to travel, it may also cause them feel displaced. While working on a production, they may have to forgo a social life, working long hours to design effects and prepare the actors for filming. The workdays may be twice as long as in the average workplace, and those work hours may be a stressful combination of working hurriedly and then waiting.

For those passionate about the work, however, any uncomfortable or frustrating conditions are easily overlooked. "I like creating something from nothing and seeing it alive and moving," Vincent Guastini says, in regard to the creatures he has constructed for special effects. He also appreciates the travel and variety. "I like the people I meet," he says, "and the job is always different, no matter the project or effect."

When working for the theater, the conditions are generally more controlled. With the exception of outdoor productions, theatrical makeup artists work in the dressing and makeup rooms of theaters and concert halls. The work can be very stressful, however, as the actors hurry to prepare for live productions.

OUTLOOK

The U.S. Department of Labor predicts employment of makeup artists and other personal appearance workers will grow faster than the average through 2016. Makeup artists will find their opportunities increasing in the film and television industries. Digital TV has made it possible for hundreds of cable channels to be piped into our homes. The original programming needed to fill the schedules of these new channels results in jobs for makeup artists. Makeup effects artists will find challenging and well-paying work as the film industry pushes the envelope on special effects. These makeup artists may be using computers more and more, as digital design has become an important tool in creating film effects.

Funding for theaters, some of which comes from the National Endowment for the Arts, is always limited and may be reduced during economic downturns or when productions are unpopular. During these times many theaters may be unable to hire the cast and crew needed for new productions. There has been a revived interest in Broadway, however, due to highly successful musicals like *Rent* and *The Lion King*. This interest could result in better business for traveling productions, as well as regional theaters across the country.

There will be a continuing need for makeup artists in still photography to prepare models for catalog and magazine shoots.

FOR MORE INFORMATION

For information on the Alliance, a union representing more than 110,000 members in entertainment and related fields in the United States and Canada, contact

International Alliance of Theatrical Stage Employees, Moving Picture Technicians, Artists and Allied Crafts of the United States, Its Territories, and Canada
1430 Broadway, 20th Floor
New York, NY 10018-3348
Tel: 212-730-1770
http://www.iatse-intl.org

For information about how to order a copy of or subscription to Make-Up Artist Magazine, *contact*

Make-Up Artist Magazine
4018 NE 112th Avenue, Suite D-8
Vancouver, WA 98682-5703
Tel: 800-805-6648
http://www.makeupmag.com

For information about theater jobs and a sample copy of ARTSEARCH, *contact*

Theatre Communications Group
520 Eighth Avenue, 24th Floor
New York, NY 10018-4156
Tel: 212-609-5900
Email: tcg@tcg.org
http://www.tcg.org

For information about the Joe Blasco schools and careers in makeup artistry, visit

Joe Blasco Makeup Training and Cosmetics
http://www.joeblasco.com

❑ MARBLE SETTERS, TILE SETTERS, AND TERRAZZO WORKERS

OVERVIEW

Marble setters, tile setters, and terrazzo workers are employed in the masonry and stonework trades covering interior and exterior walls, floors, and other surfaces with marble, tile, and terrazzo. Setters in each of these distinct trades work primarily with the material indicated by their title.

These workers are employed in the general construction industries building such things as libraries, schools, hospitals, and apartment complexes. Terrazzo workers tend to be most concentrated in the warm southern states of Texas, California, and Florida. There are more than 79,000 marble setters, tile setters, and terrazzo workers employed in the United States.

THE JOB

Part builders and part artists, marble setters, tile setters, and terrazzo workers work on newly constructed or remodeled buildings. Tile and terrazzo are used mainly on interior building surfaces, while marble (in large pieces) is used primarily as exterior facing.

In marble work, the material to be used is generally delivered to the site ready to be applied, so little cutting and polishing is required. Machine hoists and marble helpers aid in lifting and carrying large marble blocks. Helpers do most of the mixing of cement and mortar, which leaves the setters free to concentrate on their work. It takes only one look at a wall that has been improperly laid (where the joint lines do not run true) to realize the importance of accuracy for these workers. Where color is used, an improper blending of hues can ruin the appearance of the whole job.

When setting marble, the workers first lay out the job. Then they apply a special plaster mixture to the backing material and set the marble pieces in place. These pieces may have to be braced until they are firmly set. Special grout is packed into the joints between the marble pieces, and the joints are slightly indented. This indenting is known as "pointing up."

Tile setters attach tile (thin slabs of clay or stone) to floors, walls, and ceilings with mortar or specially prepared tile cement. They set a sheet of metal mesh to the surface to be tiled and then apply the cement to it, raking it with a tool similar to a yard rake. When this "scratch coat" has dried, they put a second coat of cement to the mesh and to the tiles and set the tiles in place. Some smaller sized tile comes in sheets made by fastening a number of tiles to a special paper backing so that they do not have to be set individually. Glassy, non-porous tile is used primarily for floors, and duller, more porous tile is used for walls. After the tile is set in place, the setters tap it with a block of wood or a tool handle to even out the surface. They finish by applying grout (fine cement) to the set tile, scraping it with a tool to remove the excess grout and wiping it with a wet sponge.

Terrazzo workers lay a base (first course) of fine, dry concrete and level it with a straightedge. They then place metal strips wherever a joint will be placed or where design or color delineations are to be made. This metal stripping is embedded in the first course of concrete. Then the terrazzo workers pour the top course of concrete—a mortar containing marble or granite chips—and roll and level it. Different-colored stone chips are used to color whatever pattern has been planned for the finished floor. In a few days, after the concrete has hardened, the floor is ground smooth and polished with large polishing machines.

Unlike many construction jobs, these occupations are relatively free from routine. Each job is slightly different, and workers rely on their training and ingenuity to a great extent. Marble setters, tile setters, and terrazzo workers generally do not have immediate supervisors on the job. They often manage their own time, schedule their work, and have the responsibility of doing whatever is necessary to provide the best possible job. Because these workers have an opportunity to plan the job, see that the material is delivered on time, and follow the work through the cleanup phase, they often feel a greater sense of satisfaction from the completed job than construction workers who are responsible for only one part of the total job.

REQUIREMENTS
High School

If you want to apply for jobs in these three trades, you should be at least 17 or 18 years old to qualify for labor-management apprenticeship programs. You should also have graduated from high school or have received a GED. Take at least some courses that involve using hand tools, reading blueprints, and taking precise measurements. Other courses that will be helpful include general math and core English. Taking art courses will increase your knowledge and perception of colors (which is helpful in the marble and tile trades), and many vocational courses will help you improve your manual dexterity. In addition, since being in good physical condition is often necessary in these jobs, participate in sports and general physical education classes.

Postsecondary Training

The best way to train for work in these masonry and tile trades is to participate in an apprenticeship program. In each of these trades, such programs are sponsored

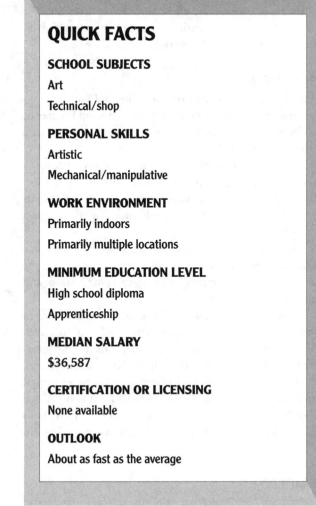

QUICK FACTS

SCHOOL SUBJECTS
Art
Technical/shop

PERSONAL SKILLS
Artistic
Mechanical/manipulative

WORK ENVIRONMENT
Primarily indoors
Primarily multiple locations

MINIMUM EDUCATION LEVEL
High school diploma
Apprenticeship

MEDIAN SALARY
$36,587

CERTIFICATION OR LICENSING
None available

OUTLOOK
About as fast as the average

by local unions and contractors, and they usually consist of about three or four years of on-the-job training and related classroom instruction. In on-the-job training, you learn from professional setters how to handle the tools and other materials of the job. You'll become familiar with such jobs as edging, jointing, and using a straightedge. In class, you will learn blueprint reading, layout work, basic mathematics, safety, cost estimating, and shop practice.

Other Requirements

As with other jobs in the building industries, it is often necessary to have a driver's license so you can operate vehicles on the job and get to job sites that are not accessible by public transportation. You may be required to pass a physical exam and written test at the end of your apprenticeship. You should enjoy doing demanding work and be disciplined and motivated enough to do your job without close and constant supervision. The ability to get along with coworkers is important, as many employees in these trades work in teams.

EXPLORING

Find an interesting construction site and watch workers and apprentices on their jobs. Ask a shop teacher or counselor to arrange an information interview with a worker in the field.

Look into the International Masonry Institute's National Training Center in Bowie, Maryland. Once you become an apprentice, you could try to qualify for its 12-week program, which includes housing, food, and a nominal wage.

During one of your summer vacations, try to get some work at construction sites or for general contractors; the work may include mixing mortar, carrying, lifting, and keeping the work area clean.

Finally, if you have access to the Internet, one of the easiest ways to explore these trades is to check out the Web sites of such organizations as the International Masonry Institute (http://www.imiweb.org), which offers a National Terrazzo Training Program; and the International Union of Bricklayers and Allied Craftworkers (http://www.bacweb.org). These sites will lead to information on training and apprenticeship programs.

EMPLOYERS

More than 79,000 marble, tile, and terrazzo workers in the United States are employed mainly in the construction industry. Most of those who work with terrazzo have jobs with specialty contractors installing artistic, decorative floors and walls; some are self-employed and may specialize in small jobs. Tile setters are more often self-employed, working on smaller, residential projects like bathrooms, kitchens, and other niches.

STARTING OUT

If you are interested in this work, you should explore apprenticeship programs. In addition, the local office of the state employment service may be a source of information about apprenticeship training and other programs. Local offices of workers' unions can help, as well as local contractors, who often advertise job openings in the help wanted ads.

Although formal three- or four-year apprenticeships are often available in these trades, many workers learn the work informally by working a certain number of years as a helper, watching and participating in the work firsthand with experienced craftspeople.

After being accepted for a job, new employees are referred for clearance to the union and, after a period of time working, are given positions as helpers. When an opening occurs for a skilled worker, the best-qualified person with the most seniority is recommended for the position.

ADVANCEMENT

Skilled tile, terrazzo, and marble setters may become supervisors with the responsibility of managing work crews for large contractors. They can also become self-employed and do contracting on their own. Self-employed contractors must know not only the skills of the trade but also the principles of business. These skills include sales, bidding, bookkeeping, and supervising workers.

EARNINGS

According to the U.S. Department of Labor, median hourly earnings of tile and marble setters were $17.59 (or $36,587 annually) in 2006. Wages ranged from less than $10.26 (or $21,341 annually) to more than $29.95 an hour (or $62,296 annually). Earnings of tile and marble setters vary by union membership and geographic location. The highest wages are paid in urban areas. Earnings for tile setters are usually highest in the North and on the West Coast and lowest in the South.

Apprentices start at about 50 percent of the skilled worker's salary and increase periodically up to 95 percent during the final stage of the training. Many opportunities are available for overtime work, which usually pays time-and-a-half, or one-and-a-half times the regular wage. Most workers are union members and are thus eligible for the following benefits: retirement plans, hospital and life insurance, and paid holidays and vacations.

WORK ENVIRONMENT

At building sites, tile setters work mostly inside, while marble and terrazzo workers work both indoors and outdoors. Construction sites are often noisy, with different kinds of building equipment being operated. The work is often demanding and requires some strength and physical fitness; workers will find themselves bending, kneeling, lifting, carrying, and reaching. Once they have been given instructions on the details of a particular job, they are expected to work without constant supervision and sometimes with the cooperation of other workers. Most workers can expect 40-hour workweeks at times when the construction project is proceeding as planned;

however, when such factors as inappropriate weather restrict operations, workers may be expected to work fewer hours until conditions change and then overtime when the work can continue.

OUTLOOK

Employment for terrazzo workers will increase over the next several years because of the popularity of terrazzo in warm, southwestern states like California and Texas, as well as in Florida. Employment opportunities for tile and marble setters is expected to grow about as fast as the average through 2016, according to the U.S. Department of Labor. Growth will result from more construction of shopping malls, hospitals, schools, restaurants, and other structures in which tile is used extensively, but growth will be offset somewhat by the increasing use of tile substitutes, such as plastic or fiberglass tub and shower enclosures.

Marble setters, tile setters, and terrazzo workers will find better employment opportunities in more populated urban and suburban areas where more buildings are being constructed and remodeled. Workers may find that work is steadier in climates that allow year-round construction.

FOR MORE INFORMATION

For information on apprenticeship training, contact

International Masonry Institute
The James Brice House
42 East Street
Annapolis, MD 21401-1731
Tel: 410-280-1305
Email: masonryquestions@imiweb.org
http://www.imiweb.org

For information on training and employment, contact

International Union of Bricklayers and Allied Craftworkers
620 F Street, NW
Washington, DC 20004-1618
Tel: 202-783-3788
Email: askbac@bacweb.org
http://www.bacweb.org

For information on national standards and continuing educational seminars, contact

National Terrazzo and Mosaic Association
201 North Maple, Suite 208
Purcellville, VA 20132-6102
Tel: 800-323-9736
Email: info@ntma.com
http://www.ntma.com

For information on union membership, contact

United Brotherhood of Carpenters and Joiners of America
http://www.carpenters.org

☐ MARINE SERVICES TECHNICIANS

OVERVIEW

Marine services technicians inspect, maintain, and repair marine vessels, from small boats to large yachts. They work on vessels' hulls, engines, transmissions, navigational equipment, and electrical, propulsion, and refrigeration systems. Depending on their specialty, they may also be known as *motorboat mechanics*, *marine electronics technicians*, or *fiberglass technicians*. Marine services technicians may work at boat dealerships, boat repair shops, boat engine manufacturers, or marinas. Naturally, jobs are concentrated near large bodies of water and coastal areas.

THE JOB

Marine services technicians work on the more than 16 million boats and other watercraft owned by people in the United States. They test and repair boat engines, transmissions, and propellers; rigging, masts, and sails; and navigational equipment and steering gear. They repair or replace defective parts and sometimes make new parts to meet special needs. They may also inspect and replace internal cabinets, refrigeration systems, electrical systems and equipment, sanitation facilities, hardware, and trim.

Workers with specialized skills often have more specific titles. For example, *motorboat mechanics* work on boat engines—those that are inboard, outboard, and inboard/outboard. Routine maintenance tasks include lubricating, cleaning, repairing, and adjusting parts.

Motorboat mechanics often use special testing equipment, such as engine analyzers, compression gauges, ammeters, and voltmeters, as well as other computerized diagnostic equipment. Technicians must know how to disassemble and reassemble components and refer to service manuals for directions and specifications. Motorboat workers often install and repair electronics, sanitation, and air-conditioning systems. They need a

QUICK FACTS

SCHOOL SUBJECTS
Mathematics
Technical/shop

PERSONAL SKILLS
Following instructions
Mechanical/manipulative

WORK ENVIRONMENT
Indoors and outdoors
One location with some travel

MINIMUM EDUCATION LEVEL
Some postsecondary training

MEDIAN SALARY
$33,197

CERTIFICATION OR LICENSING
Required for certain positions

OUTLOOK
About as fast as the average

Technicians who are *field repairers* go to the vessel to do their work, perhaps at the marina dock. *Bench repairers*, on the other hand, work on equipment brought into shops.

Some technicians work only on vessel hulls. These are usually made of either wood or fiberglass. *Fiberglass repairers* work on fiberglass hulls, of which most pleasure crafts today are built. They reinforce damaged areas of the hull, grind damaged pieces with a sander, or cut them away with a jigsaw and replace them using resin-impregnated fiberglass cloth. They finish the repaired sections by sanding, painting with a gel-coat substance, and then buffing.

REQUIREMENTS
High School

Most employers prefer to hire applicants who have a high school diploma. If you are interested in this work, take mathematics classes and shop classes in metals, woodwork, and electronics while you are in high school. These classes will give you experience completing detailed and precise work. Shop classes will also give you experience using a variety of tools and reading blueprints. Take computer classes; you will probably be using this tool throughout your career for such things as diagnostic and design work. Science classes, such as physics, will also be beneficial to you. And English classes will help you hone your reading and research skills, which will be needed when you consult technical manuals for repair and maintenance information throughout your career.

Postsecondary Training

Many marine services technicians learn their trade on the job. They find entry-level positions as general boatyard workers, doing such jobs as cleaning boat bottoms, and work their way into the position of service technician. Or they may be hired as trainees. They learn how to perform typical service tasks under the supervision of experienced mechanics and gradually complete more difficult work. The training period may last for about three years.

Other technicians decide to get more formal training and attend vocational or technical colleges for classes in engine repair, electronics, and fiberglass work. Some schools, such as Northwest Technical College in Minnesota and Washington County Community College in Maine, have programs specifically for marine technicians (see For More Information at the end of this chapter). These schools often offer an associate's degree in

set of general and specialized tools, often provided by their employers; many mechanics gradually acquire their own tools, often spending thousands of dollars on this investment.

Marine electronics technicians work with vessels' electronic safety and navigational equipment, such as radar, depthsounders, loran (long-range navigation), autopilots, and compass systems. They install, repair, and calibrate equipment for proper functioning. Routine maintenance tasks include checking, cleaning, repairing, and replacing parts. Electronics technicians check for common causes of problems, such as loose connections and defective parts. They often rely on schematics and manufacturers' specification manuals to troubleshoot problems. These workers also must have a set of tools, including hand tools such as pliers, screwdrivers, and soldering irons. Other equipment, often supplied by their employers, includes voltmeters, ohmmeters, signal generators, ammeters, and oscilloscopes.

areas such as applied science. Classes students take may include mathematics, physics, electricity, schematic reading, and circuit theory. Boat manufacturers and other types of institutions, such as the American Boatbuilders and Repairers Association, Mystic Seaport Museum (http://www.mysticseaport.org/), and the WoodenBoat School (http://www.thewoodenboatschool.com/), offer skills training through less formal courses and seminars that often last several days or a few weeks. The military services can also provide training in electronics.

Certification or Licensing

Those who test and repair marine radio transmitting equipment must have a general radio-telephone operator license from the Federal Communications Commission.

Certification for technicians in the marine electronics industry is voluntary, and is administered by the National Marine Electronics Association. There are three grades of certification for workers in this industry: the certified marine electronic technician (CMET) designation for technicians with one year of experience, the advanced CMET designation for those with three years of experience, and the senior CMET designation for those with 10 years of experience. Basic certification is by written examination and the employer's verification as to the technician's proficiency in the repair of basic radar, voice SSB, VHF, depth sounders, and autopilots. The higher degrees of certification are earned by meeting all previous grade requirements plus satisfactorily completing a factory training course or having the employer attest to the technician's proficiency in repairing advanced equipment.

Other Requirements

Most technicians work outdoors some of the time, and they are often required to test-drive the vessels they work on. This is considered an added benefit by many workers. Some workers in this field maintain that one of the most important qualities for a technician is a pleasant personality. Boat owners are often very proud of and attached to their vessels, so workers need to have both respect and authority when communicating with customers.

Technicians also need to be able to adapt to the cyclical nature of this business. They are often under a lot of pressure in the summer months, when most boat owners are enjoying the water and calling on technicians for service. On the other hand, they often have gaps in their work during the winter; some workers receive unemployment compensation at this time.

Motorboat technicians' work can sometimes be physically demanding, requiring them to lift heavy outboard motors or other components. Electronics technicians, on the other hand, must be able to work with delicate parts, such as wires and circuit boards. They should have good eyesight, color vision, and good hearing (to listen for malfunctions revealed by sound).

Some marine services technicians may be required to provide their own hand tools. These tools are usually acquired over a period of time, but the collection may cost the mechanic hundreds if not thousands of dollars.

EXPLORING

This field lends itself to a lot of fun ways to explore job opportunities. Of course, having a boat of your own and working on it is one of the best means of preparation. If friends, neighbors, or relatives have boats, take trips with them and see how curious you are about what makes the vessel work. Offer to help do repairs to the boat, or at least watch while repairs are made and routine maintenance jobs are done. Clean up the deck, sand an old section of the hull, or polish the brass. If a boat just isn't available to you, try to find some type of engine to work on. Even working on an automobile engine will give you a taste of what this type of work is like.

Some high schools have co-op training programs through which students can look for positions with boat-related businesses, such as boat dealerships or even marinas. Check with your guidance counselor about this possibility. You also can read trade magazines such as *Boating Industry* (http://www.boating-industry.com) and the online forum *Professional Boatbuilder* (http://www.proboat.com). These periodicals offer information monthly or bimonthly on the pleasure boat industry, as well as on boat design, construction, and repair.

EMPLOYERS

Marine services technicians are employed by boat retailers, boat repair shops, boat engine manufacturers, boat rental firms, resorts, and marinas. The largest marinas are in coastal areas, such as Florida, New York, California, Texas, Massachusetts, and Louisiana; smaller ones are located near lakes and water recreation facilities such as campgrounds. Manufacturers of large fishing vessels also employ technicians for on-site mechanical support at fishing sites and competitive events. These workers often follow professionals on the fishing circuit, traveling from tournament to tournament maintaining the vessels.

STARTING OUT

A large percentage of technicians get their start by working as general boatyard laborers—cleaning boats, cutting grass, painting, and so on. After showing interest and ability, they can begin to work with experienced technicians and learn skills on the job. Some professional organizations, such as Marine Trades Association of New Jersey (http://www.mtanj.org/) and Michigan Boating Industries Association (http://www.mbia.org/), offer scholarships for those interested in marine technician training.

For those technicians who have attended vocational or technical colleges, career services offices of these schools may have information about job openings.

ADVANCEMENT

Many workers consider management and supervisory positions as job goals. After working for a number of years on actual repairs and maintenance, many technicians like to manage repair shops, supervise other workers, and deal with customers more directly. These positions require less physical labor but more communication and management skills. Many workers like to combine both aspects by becoming self-employed; they may have their own shops, attract their own jobs, and still get to do the technical work they enjoy.

Advancement often depends on an individual's interests. Some become marina managers, manufacturers' salespersons, or field representatives. Others take a different direction and work as boat brokers, selling boats. Marine surveyors verify the condition and value of boats; they are independent contractors hired by insurance companies and lending institutions such as banks.

EARNINGS

According to the U.S. Department of Labor, the median yearly earnings of motorboat mechanics were $33,197 in 2005. The middle 50 percent earned between $26,333 and $41,621. Salaries ranged from less than $20,675 to more than $50,752 a year.

Technicians in small shops tend to receive few fringe benefits, but larger employers often offer paid vacations, sick leave, and health insurance. Some employers provide uniforms and tools and pay for work-related training. Many technicians who enjoy the hands-on work with boats claim that the best benefit is to take repaired boats out for test-drives.

WORK ENVIRONMENT

Technicians who work indoors are often in well-lit and ventilated shops. The work is cleaner than that on cars because there tends to be less grease and dirt on marine engines; instead, workers have to deal with water scum, heavy-duty paint, and fiberglass. In general, marine work is similar to other types of mechanical jobs, where workers encounter such things as noise when engines are being run and potential danger with power tools and chemicals. Also similar to other mechanics' work, sometimes technicians work alone on a job and at other times they work on a boat with other technicians. Unless a technician is self-employed, his or her work will likely be overseen by a supervisor of some kind. For any repair job, the technician may have to deal directly with customers.

Some mechanics, such as those who work at marinas, work primarily outdoors—and in all kinds of weather. In boats with no air conditioning, the conditions in the summer can be hot and uncomfortable. Technicians often have to work in tight, uncomfortable places to perform repairs. Sailboats have especially tight access to inboard engines.

There is usually a big demand for service just before Memorial Day and the Fourth of July. In the summer, workweeks can average 60 hours. But in winter, the week can involve less than 40 hours of work, with layoffs common at this time of year. Work tends to be steadier throughout the year in the warmer climates of the United States.

OUTLOOK

According to the U.S. Department of Labor, employment opportunities for small engine mechanics, including marine services technicians, are expected to grow about as fast as the average for all occupations through 2016. As boat design and construction become more complicated, the outlook will be best for well-trained technicians. Most marine craft purchases are made by the over-40 age group, which is expected to increase over the next decade. The growth of this population segment should help expand the market for motorboats and increase the demand for qualified mechanics.

The availability of jobs will be related to the health of the pleasure boat industry. One interesting demographic trend that will influence job opportunities is the shift of the population to the South and West, where warm-weather seasons are longer and thus attract more boating activity.

An increase in foreign demand for U.S. pleasure vessels will mean more opportunities for workers in this field. U.S. manufacturers are expected to continue to develop foreign markets and establish more distribution channels. However, legislation in the United States may require boat operator licenses and stricter emission standards, which might lead to a decrease in the number of boats sold and maintained here.

FOR MORE INFORMATION

For industry information, contact

American Boatbuilders and Repairers Association
50 Water Street
Warren, RI 02885-3034
Tel: 401-247-0318
http://www.abbra.org

To find out whether there is a marine association in your area, contact

Marine Retailers Association of America
PO Box 1127
Oak Park, IL 60304-0127
Tel: 708-763-9210
Email: mraa@mraa.com
http://www.mraa.com

For information on certification, the industry, and membership, contact

National Marine Electronics Association
7 Riggs Avenue
Severna Park, MD 21146-3819
Tel: 410-975-9425
Email: info@nmea.org
http://www.nmea.org

For educational information, contact the following:

Northwest Technical College
905 Grant Avenue, SE
Bemidji, MN 56601-4907
Tel: 800-942-8324
http://www.ntcmn.edu

Washington County Community College
Eastport Campus
16 Deep Cove Road
Eastport, ME 04631-3218
Tel: 800-806-0433
Email: admissions@wctc.org
http://www.wccc.me.edu

MASSAGE THERAPISTS

OVERVIEW

Massage therapy is a broad term referring to a number of health-related practices, including Swedish massage,

---

> **QUICK FACTS**
>
> **SCHOOL SUBJECTS**
> Health
> Physical education
>
> **PERSONAL SKILLS**
> Helping/teaching
> Mechanical/manipulative
>
> **WORK ENVIRONMENT**
> Primarily indoors
> Primarily one location
>
> **MINIMUM EDUCATION LEVEL**
> Some postsecondary training
>
> **MEDIAN SALARY**
> $33,405
>
> **CERTIFICATION OR LICENSING**
> Recommended (certification)
> Required by certain states (licensing)
>
> **OUTLOOK**
> Faster than the average

sports massage, Rolfing, Shiatsu and acupressure, trigger point therapy, and reflexology. Although the techniques vary, most *massage therapists* (or *massotherapists*) press and rub the skin and muscles. Relaxed muscles, improved blood circulation and joint mobility, reduced stress and anxiety, and decreased recovery time for sprains and injured muscles are just a few of the potential benefits of massage therapy. Massage therapists are sometimes called *bodyworkers*. The titles *masseur* and *masseuse*, once common, are now rare among those who use massage for therapy and rehabilitation. There are approximately 118,000 massage therapists employed in the United States.

THE JOB

Massage therapists work to produce physical, mental, and emotional benefits through the manipulation of the body's soft tissue. Auxiliary methods, such as the movement of joints and the application of dry and steam heat, are also used. Among the potential physical benefits are the release of muscle tension and stiffness, reduced blood pressure, better blood circulation, a shorter healing time for sprains and pulled muscles, increased flexibility and greater range of motion in the joints, and reduced swelling from edema (excess fluid buildup in body tissue). Massage may also improve posture, strengthen the immune system, and reduce the formation of scar tissue.

Mental and emotional benefits include a relaxed state of mind, reduced stress and anxiety, clearer thinking, and a general sense of well-being. Physical, mental, and emotional health are all interconnected: Being physically fit and healthy can improve emotional health, just as a positive mental attitude can bolster the immune system to help the body fight off infection. A release of muscle tension also leads to reduced stress and anxiety, and physical manipulation of sore muscles can help speed the healing process.

There are many different approaches a massage therapist may take. Among the most popular are Swedish massage, sports massage, Rolfing, Shiatsu and acupressure, and trigger point therapy.

In Swedish massage, the traditional techniques are effleurage, petrissage, friction, and tapotement. Effleurage (stroking) uses light and hard rhythmic strokes to relax muscles and improve blood circulation. It is often performed at the beginning and end of a massage session. Petrissage (kneading) is the rhythmic squeezing, pressing, and lifting of a muscle. For friction, the fingers, thumb, or palm or heel of the hand are pressed into the skin with a small circular movement. The massage therapist's fingers are sometimes pressed deeply into a joint. Tapotement (tapping), in which the hands strike the skin in rapid succession, is used to improve blood circulation.

During the session the client, covered with sheets, lies undressed on a padded table. Oil or lotion is used to smooth the skin. Some massage therapists use aromatherapy, adding fragrant essences to the oil to relax the client and stimulate circulation. Swedish massage may employ a number of auxiliary techniques, including the use of rollers, belts, and vibrators; steam and dry heat; ultraviolet and infrared light; and saunas, whirlpools, steam baths, and packs of hot water or ice.

Sports massage is essentially Swedish massage used in the context of athletics. A light massage generally is given before an event or game to loosen and warm the muscles. This reduces the chance of injury and may improve performance. After the event, the athlete is massaged more deeply to alleviate pain, reduce stiffness, and promote healing.

Rolfing, developed by American Ida Rolf, involves deep, sometimes painful massage. Intense pressure is applied to various parts of the body. Rolfing practitioners believe that emotional disturbances, physical pain, and other problems can occur when the body is out of alignment—for example, as a result of poor posture. This method takes 10 sessions to complete.

Like the ancient Oriental science of acupuncture, Shiatsu and acupressure are based on the concept of meridians, or invisible channels of flowing energy in the body. The massage therapist presses down on particular points along these channels to release blocked energy and untie knots of muscle tension. For this approach, the patient wears loosely fitted clothes, lies on the floor or on a futon, and is not given oil or lotion for the skin.

Trigger point therapy, a neuromuscular technique, focuses in on a painful area, or trigger point, in a muscle. A trigger point might be associated with a problem in another part of the body. Using the fingers or an instrument, such as a rounded piece of wood, concentrated pressure is placed on the irritated area in order to "deactivate" the trigger point.

All of these methods of massage can be altered and intermingled depending on the client's needs. Massage therapists can be proficient in one or many of the methods, and usually tailor a session to the individual.

REQUIREMENTS
High School

Since massage therapists need to know more than just technical skills, many practitioners use the basic knowledge learned in high school as a foundation to build a solid career in the field. During your high school years, you should take fundamental science courses, such as chemistry, anatomy, and biology. These classes will give you a basic understanding of the human body and prepare you for the health and anatomy classes you will take while completing your postsecondary education. English, psychology, and other classes relating to communications and human development will also be useful as the successful massage therapist is able to express his or her ideas with clients as well as understand the clients' reactions to the therapy. If you think you might wish to run your own massage therapy business someday, computer and business courses are essential. Finally, do not neglect your own physical well-being. Take physical education and health courses to strengthen your body and your understanding of your own conditioning.

Postsecondary Training

The best way to become a successful massage therapist is to attend an accredited massage therapy school after you have finished high school. There are approximately 300 state-accredited schools located throughout the United States. More than 80 of these schools are accredited or approved by the Commission on Massage Therapy Accreditation (COMTA), a major accrediting agency for massage therapy programs and an affiliate of the American Massage Therapy Association (AMTA). COMTA-accredited and -approved schools must provide at least 500 hours of classroom instruction. Studies should include such courses as anatomy, physiology, theory and practice of massage therapy, and ethics. In addition, students should receive supervised hands-on experience. Most programs offer students the opportunity to participate at clinics, such as those providing massage services at hospices, hospitals, and shelters, or at school clinics that are open to the general public.

Massage therapy training programs typically take about a year to complete. Students can specialize in particular disciplines, such as infant massage or rehabilitative massage. Basic first aid and cardiopulmonary resuscitation (CPR) must also be learned. When choosing a school, you should pay close attention to the philosophy and curricula of the program, since a wide range of program options exists. Also, keep in mind that licensure requirements for massage therapists vary by state. For example, some state medical boards require students to have completed more than 500 hours of instruction before they can be recognized as massage therapists. Part of your process for choosing a school, therefore, should include making sure that the school's curriculum will allow you to meet your state's requirements.

Certification or Licensing

Currently, 38 states and the District of Columbia regulate the practice of massage therapy, requiring licensure, certification, or registration. Because requirements for licensing, certification, registration, and even local ordinances vary, however, you will need to check with your state's department of regulatory agencies to get specifics for your area. Typically, requirements include completing an accredited program and passing a written test and a demonstration of massage therapy techniques.

The National Certification Board for Therapeutic Massage and Bodywork offers two national certification examinations for massage therapists: the National Certification Examination for Therapeutic Massage and Bodywork and the National Certification Exami-

nation for Therapeutic Massage. To learn more about each exam, visit http://www.ncbtmb.com. Certification is highly recommended, since it demonstrates a therapist's high level of education and achievement. Certification may also make a therapist a more desirable candidate for job openings.

Other Requirements

Physical requirements of massage therapists generally include the ability to use their hands and other tools to rub or press on the client's body. Manual dexterity is usually required to administer the treatments, as is the ability to stand for at least an hour at a time. Special modifications or accommodations can often be made for people with different abilities.

If you are interested in becoming a massage therapist, you should be, above all, nurturing and caring. Constance Bickford, a certified massage therapist in Chicago, thinks that it is necessary to be both flexible and creative: easily adaptable to the needs of the client, as well as able to use different techniques to help the client feel better. Listening well and responding to the client is vital, as is focusing all attention on the task at hand. Massage therapists need to tune in to their client rather than zone out, thinking about the grocery list or what to cook for supper. An effective massage is a mindful one, where massage therapist and client work together toward improved health.

To be a successful massage therapist, you should also be trustworthy and sensitive. Someone receiving a massage may feel awkward lying naked in an office, with only a sheet for cover, and listening to music while a stranger kneads his or her muscles. A good massage therapist will make the client feel comfortable in what could potentially be perceived as a vulnerable situation.

Therapists considering opening up their own business should be prepared for busy and slow times. In order to both serve their clients well and stay in business, they should be adequately staffed during rush seasons, and must be financially able to withstand dry spells.

EXPLORING

The best way to become familiar with massage therapy is to get a massage. Look for a certified therapist in your area and make an appointment for a session. If you can afford it, consider going to several different therapists who offer different types of massage. Also, ask if you can set up an informational interview with one of the therapists. Explain that you are interested in pursuing this career, and come to the interview prepared to ask questions. What is this massage therapist's educational background? Why was he or she drawn to the job? What is the best part of this work? By talking to a massage therapist, you may also have the chance to develop a mentoring relationship with him or her.

A less costly approach is to find a book on massage instruction at a local public library or bookstore. Massage techniques can then be practiced at home. Books on self-massage are available. Many books discuss in detail the theoretical basis for the techniques. Videos that demonstrate massage techniques are available as well.

Consider volunteering at a hospice, nursing home, or shelter. This work will give you experience in caring for others and help you develop good listening skills. It is important for massage therapists to listen well and respond appropriately to their clients' needs. The massage therapist must make clients feel comfortable, and volunteer work can help foster the skills necessary to achieve this.

EMPLOYERS

Approximately 118,000 massage therapists are employed in the United States. After graduating from an accredited school of massage therapy, there are a number of possibilities for employment. Doctors' offices, hospitals, clinics, health clubs, resorts, country clubs, cruise ships, community service organizations, and nursing homes, for example, all employ massage therapists. Some chiropractors have a massage therapist on staff to whom they can refer patients. A number of massage therapists run their own businesses. Most opportunities for work will be in larger, urban areas with population growth, although massage therapy is slowly spreading to more rural areas as well.

STARTING OUT

There are a number of resources you can use to locate a job. The AMTA offers job placement information to certified massage therapists who belong to the organization. Massage therapy schools have career services offices. Newspapers often list jobs. Some graduates are able to enter the field as self-employed massage therapists, scheduling their own appointments and managing their own offices.

Networking is a valuable tool in maintaining a successful massage therapy enterprise. Many massage therapists get clients through referrals, and often rely on word of mouth to build a solid customer base. Beginning massage therapists might wish to consult businesses about arranging onsite massage sessions for their employees.

Health fairs are also good places to distribute information about massage therapy practices and learn about other services in the industry. Often, organizers of large sporting events will employ massage therapists to give massages to athletes at the finish line. These events may include marathons and runs or bike rides held to raise money for charitable organizations.

ADVANCEMENT

For self-employed massage therapists, advancement is measured by reputation, the ability to attract clients, and the fees charged for services. Health clubs, country clubs, and other institutions have supervisory positions for massage therapists. In a community service organization, massage therapists may be promoted to the position of health service director. Licensed massage therapists often become instructors or advisors at schools for massage therapy. They may also make themselves available to advise individuals or companies on the short- and long-term benefits of massage therapy, and how massage therapy can be introduced into professional work environments.

EARNINGS

The earnings of massage therapists vary greatly with the level of experience and location of practice. Therapists in New York and California, for example, typically charge higher rates than those in other parts of the country. Some entry-level massage therapists earn as little as minimum wage (ending up with a yearly income of around $12,168), but with experience, a massage therapist can charge from $45 to $70+ for a one-hour session.

The U.S. Department of Labor reports that massage therapists earned a median salary of $33,405 a year in 2006. The lowest 10 percent earned $15,558 or less, while the highest 10 percent earned $70,366 or more.

Approximately two-thirds of all massage therapists are self employed, and self-employed therapists are not paid for the time spent on bookkeeping, maintaining their offices, waiting for customers to arrive, and looking for new clients. In addition, they must pay a self-employment tax and provide their own benefits. With membership in some national organizations, self-employed massage therapists may be eligible for group life, health, liability, and renter's insurance through the organization's insurance agency.

Massage therapists employed by a health club usually get free or discounted memberships to the club. Those who work for resorts or on cruise ships can get free or discounted travel and accommodations, in addition to full access to facilities when not on duty. Massage therapists employed by a sports team often get to attend the team's sporting events.

WORK ENVIRONMENT

Massage therapists work in clean, comfortable settings. Because a relaxed environment is essential, the massage room may be dim, and soft music, scents, and oils are often used. Since massage therapists may see a number of people per day, it is important to maintain a hygienic working area. This involves changing sheets on the massage table after each client, as well as cleaning and sterilizing any implements used, and washing hands frequently.

Massage therapists employed by businesses may use a portable massage chair—that is, a padded chair that leaves the client in a forward-leaning position ideal for massage of the back and neck. Some massage therapists work out of their homes or travel to the homes of their clients.

The workweek of a massage therapist is typically 35 to 40 hours, which may include evenings and weekends. On average, 20 hours or fewer per week are spent with clients, and the other hours are spent making appointments and taking care of other business-related details.

Since the physical work is sometimes demanding, massage therapists need to take measures to prevent repetitive stress disorders, such as carpal tunnel syndrome. Also, for their own personal safety, massage therapists who work out of their homes or have odd office hours need to be particularly careful about scheduling appointments with unknown clients.

OUTLOOK

The industry predicts a strong employment outlook for massage therapists through the next several years. The growing acceptance of massage therapy as an important health care discipline has led to the creation of additional jobs for massage therapists in many sectors.

One certified massage therapist points to sports massage as one of the fastest growing specialties in the field. The increasing popularity of professional sports has given massage therapists new opportunities to work as key members of a team's staff. Their growing presence in sports has made massage therapy more visible to the public, spreading the awareness of the physical benefits of massage.

Massages aren't just for athletes. According to the 2007 American Massage Therapy Association Consumer Survey, 24 percent of Americans surveyed had a massage within the 12 months preceding the survey. The survey also found that people are getting massages not just for medical reasons, but to relax and reduce stress.

There is a growing opportunity for massage therapists in the corporate world. Many employers eager to hold on to good employees offer perks, such as workplace massages. As a result, many massage therapists are working as mobile business consultants.

FOR MORE INFORMATION

For information on careers and education programs, contact

American Massage Therapy Association
500 Davis Street
Evanston, IL 60201-4668
Tel: 877-905-2700
Email: info@amtamassage.org
http://www.amtamassage.org

For information on careers in the field, state board requirements, and training programs, contact

Associated Bodywork and Massage Professionals
1271 Sugarbush Drive
Evergreen, CO 80439-9766
Tel: 800-458-2267
Email: expectmore@abmp.com
http://www.abmp.com or
http://www.massagetherapy.com

For information on accreditation and programs, contact

Commission on Massage Therapy Accreditation
1007 Church Street, Suite 302
Evanston, IL 60201-5912
Tel: 847-869-5039
Email: info@comta.org
http://www.comta.org

For information about state certification and education requirements, contact

National Certification Board for Therapeutic Massage and Bodywork
1901 South Meyers Road, Suite 240
Oakbrook Terrace, IL 60181-5243
Tel: 800-296-0664
http://www.ncbtmb.com

MECHANICAL ENGINEERING TECHNICIANS

OVERVIEW

Mechanical engineering technicians work under the direction of mechanical engineers to design, build, maintain, and modify many kinds of machines,

QUICK FACTS

SCHOOL SUBJECTS

English

Mathematics

Physics

PERSONAL SKILLS

Mechanical/manipulative

Technical/scientific

WORK ENVIRONMENT

Primarily indoors

Primarily one location

MINIMUM EDUCATION LEVEL

Associate's degree

MEDIAN SALARY

$45,820

CERTIFICATION OR LICENSING

Voluntary

OUTLOOK

About as fast as the average

mechanical devices, and tools. They work in a wide range of industries and in a variety of specific jobs within every industry.

Mechanical engineering technicians review mechanical drawings and project instructions, analyze design plans to determine costs and practical value, sketch rough layouts of proposed machines or parts, assemble new or modified devices or components, test completed assemblies or components, analyze test results, and write reports. There are approximately 48,000 mechanical engineering technicians employed in the United States.

THE JOB

Mechanical engineering technicians are employed in a broad range of industries. Technicians may specialize in any one of many areas including biomedical equipment, measurement and control, products

manufacturing, solar energy, turbo machinery, energy resource technology, and engineering materials and technology.

Within each application, a technician may be involved with various aspects of the work. One phase is research and development. In this area, the mechanical technician may assist an engineer or scientist in the design and development of anything from a ballpoint pen to a sophisticated measuring device. These technicians prepare rough sketches and layouts of the project being developed.

In the design of an automobile engine, for example, engineering technicians make drawings that detail the fans, pistons, connecting rods, and flywheels to be used in the engine. They estimate cost and operational qualities of each part, taking into account friction, stress, strain, and vibration. By performing these tasks, they free the engineer to accomplish other research activities.

A second common type of work for mechanical engineering technicians is testing. For products such as engines, motors, or other moving devices, technicians may set up prototypes of the equipment to be tested and run performance tests. Some tests require one procedure to be done repeatedly, while others require that equipment be run over long periods of time to observe any changes in operation. Technicians collect and compile all necessary data from the testing procedures and prepare reports for the engineer or scientist.

In order to manufacture a product, preparations must be made for its production. In this effort, mechanical engineering technicians assist in the product design by making final design layouts and detailed drawings of parts to be manufactured and of any special manufacturing equipment needed. Some test and inspect machines and equipment or work with engineers to eliminate production problems.

Other mechanical engineering technicians examine plans and drawings to determine what materials are needed and prepare lists of these materials, specifying quality, size, and strength. They also may estimate labor costs, equipment life, and plant space needed. After the product is manufactured, some mechanical engineering technicians may help solve storage and shipping problems, while others assist in customer relations when product installation is required.

Some engineering technicians work with *tool designers,* who prepare sketches of designs for cutting tools, jigs, special fixtures, and other devices used in mass production. Frequently, they redesign existing tools to improve their efficiency.

REQUIREMENTS

High School

Preparation for this career begins in high school. Although entrance requirements to associate's degree programs vary somewhat from school to school, mathematics and physical science form the backbone of a good preparatory curriculum. Classes should include algebra, geometry, science, computer science, mechanical drawing, shop, and communications.

Postsecondary Training

Associate's degree or two-year mechanical technician programs are designed to prepare students for entry-level positions. Most programs accredited by the Accreditation Board for Engineering and Technology offer one year of basic training with a chance to specialize in the second year. The first year of the program generally consists of courses in college algebra and trigonometry, science, and communication skills. Other classes introduce students to the manufacturing processes, drafting, and language of the industry.

The second year's courses focus on mechanical technology. These include fluid mechanics, thermodynamics, tool and machine design, instruments and controls, production technology, electricity, and electronics. Many schools allow their students to choose a major in the second year of the program, which provides training for a specific area of work in the manufacturing industry.

Certification or Licensing

Many mechanical engineering technicians choose to become certified by the National Institute for Certification in Engineering Technologies. To become certified, a technician must combine a specific amount of job-related experience with a written examination. Certifications are offered at several levels of expertise. Such certification is generally voluntary, although obtaining certification shows a high level of commitment and dedication that employers find highly desirable.

Mechanical engineering technicians are encouraged to become affiliated with professional groups, such as the American Society of Certified Engineering Technicians, that offer continuing education sessions for members. Some mechanical engineering technicians may be required to belong to unions.

Other Requirements

To work as a mechanical engineering technician, you need mathematical and mechanical aptitude. You will need to understand abstract concepts and apply scientific principles to problems in the shop or laboratory, in both the design and the manufacturing process. You should be interested in people and machines and have the ability to carry out detailed work. You should be able to analyze sketches and drawings and possess patience, perseverance, and resourcefulness. Additionally, you must have good communication skills and be able to present both spoken and written reports.

EXPLORING

You may be able to obtain part-time or summer work in a machine shop or factory. This type of work usually consists of sweeping floors and clearing out machine tools, but it will also give you an opportunity to view the field firsthand and also demonstrate your interest to future employers. Field trips to industrial laboratories, drafting studios, or manufacturing facilities can offer overall views of this type of work. Hobbies like automobile repair, model making, and electronic kit assembly can also be helpful. Finally, if you are in high school and interested in the engineering field, consider joining JETS, the Junior Engineering Technical Society.

EMPLOYERS

Many of the 48,000 mechanical engineering technicians employed in the United States work in durable goods manufacturing, primarily making electrical and electronic machinery and equipment, industrial machinery and equipment, instruments and related products, and transportation equipment. A sizable percentage work in service industries, mostly in engineering and business services companies that do contract work for government, manufacturing, and other organizations.

The federal government employs mechanical engineering technicians in the Departments of Defense, Transportation, Agriculture, and Interior as well as the Tennessee Valley Authority and the National Aeronautics and Space Administration. State and municipal governments also employ mechanical engineering technicians.

STARTING OUT

Schools offering associate's degrees in mechanical engineering technology and two-year technician programs usually help graduates find employment. At most colleges, in fact, company recruiters interview prospective graduates during their final semester of school. As a result, many students receive job offers before graduation. Other graduates may prefer to apply directly to employers, use newspaper classified ads, or apply through public or private employment services.

ADVANCEMENT

As mechanical engineering technicians remain with a company, they become more valuable to the employer. Opportunities for advancement are available to those who are willing to accept greater responsibilities either by specializing in a specific field, taking on more technically complex assignments, or by assuming supervisory duties. Some technicians advance by moving into technical sales or customer relations. Mechanical technicians who further their education may choose to become tool designers or mechanical engineers.

EARNINGS

Salaries for mechanical engineering technicians vary depending on the nature and location of the job, employer, amount of training the technician has received, and number of years of experience.

According to the U.S. Department of Labor, the average annual salary for mechanical engineering technicians was $45,820 in 2006. In general, mechanical engineering technicians who develop and test machinery and equipment under the direction of an engineering staff earn between $30,000 and $50,000 a year. Mechanical engineering technicians at the start of their careers earned around $25,000 a year or less, while senior technicians with specialized skills and experience earned much more, between $50,000 and $70,000 or more a year.

These salaries are based upon the standard 40-hour workweek. Overtime or premium time pay may be earned for work beyond regular daytime hours or workweek. Other benefits, depending on the company and union agreements, include paid vacation days, insurance, retirement plans, profit sharing, and tuition-reimbursement plans.

WORK ENVIRONMENT

Mechanical engineering technicians work in a variety of conditions, depending on their field of specialization. Technicians who specialize in design may find that they spend most of their time at the drafting board or computer. Those who specialize in manufacturing may spend some time at a desk, but also spend considerable time in manufacturing areas or shops.

Conditions also vary by industry. Some industries require technicians to work in foundries, die-casting rooms, machine shops, assembly areas, or punch-press areas. Most of these areas, however, are well lighted, heated, and ventilated. Moreover, most industries employing mechanical engineering technicians have strong safety programs.

Mechanical engineering technicians are often called upon to exercise decision-making skills, to be responsible for valuable equipment, and to act as effective leaders. At other times they carry out routine, uncomplicated tasks. Similarly, in some cases, they may coordinate the activities of others, while at other times, they are the ones supervised. They must be able to respond well to both types of demands. In return for this flexibility and versatility, mechanical engineering technicians are usually highly respected by their employers and coworkers.

OUTLOOK

Job opportunities for mechanical engineering technicians are expected to grow about as fast as the average through 2016, according to the U.S. Department of Labor. Manufacturing companies will be looking for more ways to apply the advances in mechanical technology to their operations. Opportunities will be best for technicians who are skilled in new manufacturing concepts, materials, and designs. Many job openings also will be created by people retiring or leaving the field.

However, the employment outlook for engineering technicians is influenced by the economy. Hiring will fluctuate with the ups and downs of the nation's overall economic situation.

FOR MORE INFORMATION

For information on colleges and universities offering accredited programs in engineering technology, contact
Accreditation Board for Engineering and Technology
111 Market Place, Suite 1050
Baltimore, MD 21202-7116
Tel: 410-347-7700
http://www.abet.org

For information about membership in this professional society for engineering technicians, contact
American Society of Certified Engineering Technicians
PO Box 1356
Brandon, MS 39043-1356
Tel: 601-824-8991
Email: general-manager@ascet.org
http://www.ascet.org

For information about the field of mechanical engineering, contact

American Society of Mechanical Engineers
Three Park Avenue
New York, NY 10016-5990
Tel: 800-843-2763
Email: infocentral@asme.org
http://www.asme.org

For information on technician careers and high school programs that provide opportunities to learn about engineering technology, contact

Junior Engineering Technical Society
1420 King Street, Suite 405
Alexandria, VA 22314-2750
Tel: 703-548-5387
Email: info@jets.org
http://www.jets.org

For information on certification, contact

National Institute for Certification in Engineering Technologies
1420 King Street
Alexandria, VA 22314-2794
Tel: 888-476-4238
http://www.nicet.org

MEDICAL ASSISTANTS

QUICK FACTS

SCHOOL SUBJECTS
Biology
Mathematics

PERSONAL SKILLS
Helping/teaching
Technical/scientific

WORK ENVIRONMENT
Primarily indoors
Primarily one location

MINIMUM EDUCATION LEVEL
Some postsecondary training

MEDIAN SALARY
$26,290

CERTIFICATION OR LICENSING
Voluntary

OUTLOOK
Much faster than the average

OVERVIEW

Medical assistants help physicians in offices, hospitals, and clinics. They keep medical records, help examine and treat patients, and perform routine office duties to allow physicians to spend their time working directly with patients. Medical assistants are vitally important to the smooth and efficient operation of medical offices. There are approximately 417,000 medical assistants employed in the United States.

THE JOB

Depending on the size of the office, medical assistants may perform clerical or clinical duties, or both. The larger the office, the greater the chance that the assistant will specialize in one type of work.

In their clinical duties, medical assistants help physicians by preparing patients for examination or treatment. They may check and record patients' blood pressure, pulse, temperature, height, and weight. Medical assistants often ask patients questions about their medical histories and record the answers in the patient's file. In the examining room, the medical assistant may be responsible for arranging medical instruments and handing them to the physician as requested during the examination. Medical assistants may prepare patients for X rays and laboratory examinations, as well as administer electrocardiograms. They may apply dressings, draw blood, and give injections. Medical assistants also may give patients instructions about taking medications, watching their diet, or restricting their activities before laboratory tests or surgery. In addition, medical assistants may collect specimens such as throat cultures for laboratory tests and may be responsible for sterilizing examining room instruments and equipment.

Medical assistants are responsible for preparing examining rooms for patients and keeping examining and waiting rooms clean and orderly. After each examination, they straighten the examining room and dispose of used linens and medical supplies. Sometimes medical assistants keep track of office and medical supply inventories and order necessary supplies. They may deal with pharmaceutical and medical supply company representatives when ordering supplies.

At other times, medical assistants may perform a wide range of administrative tasks. *Medical secretaries* and *medical receptionists* also perform administrative activities in medical offices, but these workers are distinguished from medical assistants by the fact that they rarely perform clinical functions. The administrative and clerical tasks that medical assistants may complete include typing case histories and operation reports; keeping office files, X rays, and other medical records up to date; keeping the office's financial records; preparing and sending bills and receiving payments; and transcribing dictation from the physician. Assistants may also answer the telephone, greet patients, fill out insurance forms, schedule appointments, take care of correspondence, and arrange for patients to be admitted to the hospital. Most medical assistants use word processors and computers for most record-keeping tasks.

Some medical assistants work in ophthalmologists' offices, where their clinical duties involve helping with eye examinations and treatments. They use special equipment to test and measure patients' eyes and check for disease. They administer eye drops and dressings and teach patients how to insert and care for contact lenses. They may maintain surgical instruments and help physicians during eye surgery. Other medical assistants work as *optometric assistants*, who may be required to prepare patients for examination and assist them in eyewear selection; *chiropractor assistants*, whose duties may include treatment and examination of patients' muscular and skeletal problems; and *podiatric assistants*, who assist podiatrists during examinations and surgery, take and develop X rays, and make castings of patients' feet.

REQUIREMENTS
High School

Medical assistants usually need a high school diploma, but in many cases receive specific training on the job. High school courses in the sciences, especially biology, are helpful, as are courses in algebra, English, bookkeeping, typing, computers, and office practices.

Postsecondary Training

Formal training for medical assistants is available at many trade schools, community and junior colleges, and universities. College programs generally award an associate's degree and take two years to complete. Other programs can last as long as a year and award a diploma or certificate. Prior to enrolling in any school program, you should check its curriculum and verify its accreditation.

Schools for medical assistants may be accredited by either the Commission on Accreditation of Allied Health Education Programs, which has approved approximately 2,000 medical programs; the Accrediting Bureau of Health Education Schools, which has accredited approximately 170 medical assisting programs; or the National Commission for Certifying Agencies, which has accredited more than 190 programs representing 78 organizations. Course work includes biology, anatomy, physiology, and medical terminology, as well as typing, transcribing, shorthand, record keeping, and computer skills. Perhaps most importantly, these programs provide supervised, hands-on clinical experience in laboratory techniques, first-aid procedures, proper use of medical equipment, and clinical procedures. You also learn administrative duties and procedures in medical offices and receive training in interpersonal communications and medical ethics.

Certification or Licensing

Voluntarily certification is available from certain professional organizations. The registered medical assistant credential is awarded by American Medical Technologists, and the American Association of Medical Assistants awards a credential for certified medical assistant. Ophthalmic assistants can receive the following designations from the Joint Commission on Allied Health Personnel in Ophthalmology: certified ophthalmic assistant, certified ophthalmic technician, and certified ophthalmic medical technologist. Medical assistants generally do not need to be licensed. Some states require medical assistants to pass a test or take a course before they can perform certain tasks like taking X rays.

Other Requirements

To be a successful medical assistant, you must be able to interact with patients and other medical personnel and be able to follow detailed directions. In addition, you must be dependable and compassionate and have the desire to help people. Medical assistants must also respect patients' privacy by keeping medical information confidential. Overall, medical assistants who help patients feel at ease in the doctor's office and other medical settings and have good communication skills and a desire to serve should do well in this job.

EXPLORING

Students in postsecondary school medical assistant programs will have the chance to explore the field through the supervised clinical experience required by the various programs. Others may wish to gain additional experience by volunteering at hospitals, nursing homes, or clinics to get a feel for the work involved in a medical environment. You may want to talk with the medical assistants in your own or other local physicians' offices to find out more about the work they do.

EMPLOYERS

About 417,000 medical assistants are employed in physicians' offices, clinics, hospitals, health maintenance organizations, and other medical facilities. Approximately 62 percent work in private doctors' offices and 12 percent work in hospitals. Another 11 percent work in optometrists', podiatrists', and chiropractors' offices and other health care facilities.

STARTING OUT

Students enrolled in college or other postsecondary school medical assistant programs may learn of available positions through their school career services offices. High school guidance counselors may have information about positions for students about to graduate. Newspaper want ads and state employment offices are other good places to look for leads. You may also wish to call local physicians' offices to find out about unadvertised openings.

ADVANCEMENT

Experienced medical assistants may be able to move into managerial or administrative positions without further education, but moving into a more advanced clinical position, such as nursing, requires more education. As more and more clinics and group practices open, more office managers will be needed, and these are positions that well-qualified, experienced medical assistants may be able to fill. As with most occupations, today's job market gives medical assistants with computer skills more opportunities for advancement.

EARNINGS

The earnings of medical assistants vary widely, depending on experience, skill level, and location. According to the U.S. Department of Labor, median annual earnings of medical assistants were $26,290 in 2006. The lowest 10 percent earned less than $18,860, and the highest 10 percent earned more than $36,840 a year. Mean annual earnings of medical assistants who worked in offices of physicians were $26,620 and in hospitals they were $27,340.

Medical assistants usually receive six or seven paid holidays a year, as well as annual paid vacation days. They often receive health and life insurance, a retirement plan, sick leave, and uniform allowances.

WORK ENVIRONMENT

Most medical assistants work in pleasant, modern surroundings. The average medical assistant works 40 hours a week, including some Saturday and evening hours. Sterilizing equipment and handling medical instruments require care and attentiveness. As most professionals in the health sciences will attest, working with people who are ill may be upsetting at times, but it can also have many personal rewards.

OUTLOOK

Employment for medical assistants will grow much faster than the average for all occupations through 2016, according to the U.S. Department of Labor. Most openings will occur to replace workers who leave their jobs, but many will be the result of a predicted surge in the number of physicians' offices, clinics, and other outpatient care facilities. The growing number of elderly Americans who need medical treatment is also a factor for this increased demand for health services. In addition, new and more complex paperwork for medical insurance, malpractice insurance, government programs, and other purposes will create a growing need for assistants in medical offices.

Many physicians prefer experienced and formally trained medical assistants, so these workers will have the best employment outlook. Word-processing skills, computer skills, and formal certification are all definite assets.

FOR MORE INFORMATION

For information on accreditation and testing, contact
Accrediting Bureau of Health Education Schools
7777 Leesburg Pike, Suite 314-North
Falls Church, VA 22043-2411

Tel: 703-917-9503
Email: info@abhes.org
http://www.abhes.org

For career and certification information, contact the following organizations:

American Association of Medical Assistants
20 North Wacker Drive, Suite 1575
Chicago, IL 60606-2963
Tel: 312-899-1500
http://www.aama-ntl.org

American Medical Technologists
10700 West Higgins Road
Park Ridge, IL 60018-3707
Tel: 847-823-5169
http://www.amt1.com

For information on podiatric medical assisting careers and certification, contact

American Society of Podiatric Medical Assistants
2124 South Austin Boulevard
Cicero, IL 60804-2012
Tel: 888-882-7762
http://www.aspma.org

For information on accredited programs, contact

Commission on Accreditation of Allied Health Education Programs
1361 Park Street
Clearwater, FL 33756-6039
Tel: 727-210-2350
Email: mail@caahep.org
http://www.caahep.org

For information on accredited programs and certification, contact the following organizations:

Joint Commission on Allied Health Personnel in Ophthalmology
2025 Woodlane Drive
St. Paul, MN 55125-2998
Tel: 800-284-3937
Email: jcahpo@jcahpo.org
http://www.jcahpo.org/newsite/index.htm

National Commission for Certifying Agencies
2025 M Street, NW, Suite 800
Washington, DC 20036-3309
Tel: 202-367-1165
Email: info@noca.org
http://www.noca.org

MEDICAL LABORATORY TECHNICIANS

OVERVIEW

Medical laboratory technicians, also known as *clinical laboratory technicians*, perform routine tests in medical laboratories. These tests help physicians and other professional medical personnel diagnose and treat disease. Technicians prepare samples of body tissue; perform laboratory tests, such as urinalysis and blood counts; and make chemical and biological analyses of cells, tissue, blood, or other body specimens. They usually work under the supervision of a medical technologist or a laboratory director. Medical laboratory technicians may work in many fields, or specialize in one specific medical area, such as cytology (the study of cells), hematology (the study of blood, especially on the cellular level), serology (the study and identification of antibodies found in the blood), or histology (the study of body tissue). There are approximately 319,000 medical laboratory technicians and technologists employed in the United States.

THE JOB

Medical laboratory technicians may be generalists in the field of laboratory technology; that is, they may be trained to carry out many different kinds of medical laboratory work. Alternatively, they may specialize in one type of medical laboratory work, such as cytology, hematology, blood bank technology, serology, or histology. The following paragraphs describe the work of generalists and those in the specialty fields of cytology, histology, and blood bank technology.

Medical laboratory technicians who work as generalists perform a wide variety of tests and laboratory procedures in chemistry, hematology, urinalysis, blood banking, serology, and microbiology. By performing these tests and procedures, they help to develop vital data on the blood, tissues, and fluids of the human body. This data is then used by physicians, surgeons, pathologists, and other medical personnel to diagnose and treat patients.

The tests and procedures that these technicians perform are more complex than the routine duties assigned to laboratory assistants, but do not require specialized knowledge like those performed by more highly trained medical technologists. In general, medical laboratory technicians work with only limited supervision. This means that while the tests they perform may have well-established procedures, the technicians themselves must exercise independent judgment. For instance, they must be able to discriminate between very similar colors or shapes, correct their own errors using established strategies, and monitor ongoing quality control measures.

To carry out these responsibilities, medical laboratory technicians need a sound knowledge of specific techniques and instruments and must be able to recognize factors that potentially influence both the procedures they use and the results they obtain.

In their work, medical laboratory technicians frequently handle test tubes and other glassware and use precision equipment, such as microscopes and automated blood analyzers. (Blood analyzers determine the levels of certain blood components like cholesterol, sugar, and hemoglobin.) Technicians are often responsible for making sure machines are functioning and supplies are adequately stocked.

Medical laboratory technicians who specialize in cytology are usually referred to as *cytotechnicians*. Cytotechnicians prepare and stain body cell samplings using special dyes that accentuate the delicate patterns of the cytoplasm, and structures such as the nucleus. Mounted on slides, the various features of the specimen then stand out brightly under a microscope. Using microscopes that magnify cells perhaps 1,000 times, cytotechnicians screen out normal samplings and set aside those with minute irregularities (in cell size, shape, and color) for further study by a pathologist.

Medical laboratory technicians specializing in histology are usually referred to as *histologic technicians* or *tissue technicians*. Histology is the study of the structure and chemical composition of the tissues, and histologic technicians are mainly concerned with detecting tissue abnormalities and assisting in determining appropriate treatments for the disease conditions associated with the abnormalities.

Medical laboratory technicians who specialize in blood bank technology perform a wide variety of routine tests related to running blood banks, offering transfusion services, and investigating blood diseases and reactions to transfusions. Examples of tasks frequently performed by medical laboratory technicians specializing in this field include donor screening, determining blood types, performing tests of patients' blood counts, and assisting physicians in the care of patients with blood-related problems.

QUICK FACTS

SCHOOL SUBJECTS

Biology

Chemistry

PERSONAL SKILLS

Following instructions

Technical/scientific

WORK ENVIRONMENT

Primarily indoors

Primarily one location

MINIMUM EDUCATION LEVEL

Some postsecondary training

MEDIAN SALARY

$49,700

CERTIFICATION OR LICENSING

Required by certain states

OUTLOOK

Faster than average

REQUIREMENTS
High School

To be hired as a medical laboratory technician, you must have a high school diploma and one or two years of postsecondary training. No specific kind of high school training is required; however, you must be able to meet the admissions requirements of institutions offering post-high school training. In general, courses in biology, chemistry, mathematics, English, and computer science will be most helpful in a career as a medical laboratory technician.

Postsecondary Training

After high school, prospective technicians enroll in one- or two-year training programs accredited by the American Medical Association's Committee on Allied Health Education and Accreditation, the Accrediting Bureau of Health Education Schools, or the National Accrediting Agency for Clinical Laboratory Sciences. One-year programs include both classroom work and practical laboratory training, and focus on areas such as medical ethics and conduct, medical terminology, basic laboratory solutions and media, manipulation of cytological and histological specimens, blood collecting techniques, and introductions to basic hematology, serology, blood banking, and urinalysis.

To earn an associate's degree, you must complete a two-year post-high school program. Like certificate programs, associate's degree programs include classroom instruction and practical training. Courses are taught both on campus and in local hospitals. On-campus courses focus on general knowledge and basic skills in laboratory testing associated with hematology, serology, chemistry, microbiology, and other pertinent biological and medical areas. The clinical training program focuses on basic principles and skills required in medical diagnostic laboratory testing.

Certification or Licensing

Students who have earned an associate's degree are eligible for certification from several different agencies, including the Board of Registry of the American Society for Clinical Pathology, the American Medical Technologists, the National Credentialing Agency for Laboratory Personnel, and the American Association of Bioanalysts.

Prospective medical laboratory technicians who think they might want to specialize in cytology or blood bank technology should definitely consider the two-year program, which will best prepare them for the additional education they may need later.

In addition to completing the educational programs described above, prospective technicians need to pass an examination after graduation to receive certification. In some states, this certificate is all that is required for employment. In other states, state licensure is also required. School officials are the best source of information regarding state requirements.

Other Requirements

Besides fulfilling the academic requirements, medical laboratory technicians must have good manual dexterity, normal color vision, the ability to follow instructions, and a tolerance for working under pressure.

EXPLORING

It is difficult for people interested in a career in medical laboratory technology to gain any direct experience through part-time employment. There are some other ways, however, to learn more about this career on a firsthand basis. Perhaps the best way is to arrange a visit to a hospital, blood bank, or commercial medical laboratory to see technicians at work at their jobs. Another way to learn about this kind of work in general, and about the training required in particular, is to visit an accredited school of medical laboratory technology to discuss career plans with the admissions counselor at the school. You can also write to the sources listed at the end of this article for more reading material on medical laboratory technology. Finally, you should remember that high school science courses with laboratory sections will give you exposure to some of the kinds of work you might do later in your career.

EMPLOYERS

Medical laboratory technicians are employed where physicians work, such as in hospitals, clinics, offices of physicians, blood blanks, and commercial medical laboratories. Approximately 319,000 medical laboratory technicians and technologists are employed in the United States, with more than half working in hospitals.

STARTING OUT

Graduates of medical laboratory technology schools usually receive assistance from faculty and school placement services to find their first jobs. Hospitals, laboratories, and other facilities employing medical laboratory technicians may notify local schools of job openings. Often the hospital or laboratory at which you receive your practical training will offer full-time employment after graduation. Positions may also be secured using the various registries of certified medical laboratory workers. Newspaper job advertisements and commercial placement agencies are other sources of help in locating employment.

ADVANCEMENT

Medical laboratory technicians often advance by returning to school to earn a bachelor's degree. This can lead to positions as medical technologists, histological technologists, cytotechnologists, or specialists in blood bank technology.

Other technicians advance by gaining more responsibility while retaining the title of technician. For instance, with experience, these workers can advance to supervisory positions or other positions assigning work to be done by other medical laboratory workers. Medical laboratory technicians may also advance by training to do very specialized or complex laboratory or research work.

EARNINGS

Salaries of medical laboratory technicians vary according to employer and geographical area. According to the U.S. Bureau of Labor Statistics, median annual earnings of medical and clinical laboratory technicians were $49,700 in 2006. Salaries ranged from less than $34,660 to more than $69,260. Fifty percent of workers in this field earned between $41,680 and $58,560 annually. Medical laboratory technicians who go on to earn their bachelor's degrees and certification as medical technologists can expect an increase in annual earnings.

Most medical laboratory technicians receive paid vacations and holidays, sick leave, health insurance, and retirement benefits.

WORK ENVIRONMENT

Medical laboratory technicians work in clean, well-lit, and usually air-conditioned settings. There may, however, be unpleasant odors and some infectious materials involved in the work. In general, there are few hazards associated with these odors and materials as long as proper methods of sterilization and handling of specimens, materials, and equipment are used.

Medical laboratory technicians often spend much of their days standing or sitting on stools. A 40-hour, five-day week is normal, although those working in hospitals can expect some evening and weekend work.

Medical laboratory technicians derive satisfaction from knowing their work is very important to patients and their physicians. Although the work involves new patient samples, it also involves some very repetitive tasks that some people may find trying. Additionally, the work must often be done under time pressure, even though it is often very painstaking.

Another factor that aspiring medical laboratory technicians should keep in mind is that advancement opportunities are limited, although they do exist. To maximize their chances for advancement, medical laboratory technicians must consider getting additional training.

OUTLOOK

The U.S. Department of Labor predicts job growth for medical laboratory technicians to be faster than the average through 2016. Competition for jobs, however, may be strong. One reason for this increased competition is the overall national effort to control health care costs. Hospitals, where most medical laboratory technicians are employed, will seek to control costs in part through cutting down on the amount of laboratory testing they do and, consequently, the personnel they require.

Despite such cutbacks, though, the overall amount of medical laboratory testing will probably increase, as much of medical practice today relies on high-quality laboratory testing. However, because of the increased use of automation, this increase in laboratory testing probably will not lead to an equivalent growth in employment.

One other technological factor that will influence employment in this field is the development of laboratory-testing equipment that is easier to use. This means that some testing that formerly had to be done in hospitals can now be done in physicians' offices and other non-hospital settings. This development will slow growth in hospital laboratory employment; however, it should increase the number of technicians hired by medical groups and clinics, medical and diagnostic laboratories, and other ambulatory health care services such as blood and organ banks. In addition, equipment that is easier to use may also lead to technicians being able to do more kinds of testing, including some tests that used to be done only by medical technologists.

Despite these growth projections, aspiring technicians should keep in mind that medical laboratory testing is an absolutely essential element in today's medicine. For well-trained technicians who are flexible in accepting responsibilities and willing to continue their education throughout their careers, employment opportunities should remain good.

FOR MORE INFORMATION

For information on accreditation and testing, contact
Accrediting Bureau of Health Education Schools
7777 Leesburg Pike, Suite 314-North
Falls Church, VA 22043-2411
Tel: 703-917-9503
Email: info@abhes.org
http://www.abhes.org

For information on certification, contact
American Association of Bioanalysts
906 Olive Street, Suite 1200
St. Louis, MO 63101-1434
Tel: 314-241-1445
Email: aab@aab.org
http://www.aab.org

For career and certification information, contact
American Medical Technologists
10700 West Higgins Road, Suite 150
Park Ridge, IL 60018-3707
Tel: 847-823-5169
http://www.amt1.com

For information on clinical laboratory careers and certification, contact

American Society for Clinical Laboratory Science
6701 Democracy Boulevard, Suite 300
Bethesda, MD 20817-7500
Tel: 301-657-2768
http://www.ascls.org

For information on certification, contact

American Society for Clinical Pathology
33 West Monroe, Suite 1600
Chicago IL 60603-5617
Tel: 800-267-2727
Email: info@ascp.org
http://www.ascp.org

For information on accredited programs, contact the following organizations:

Commission on Accreditation of Allied Health Education Programs
1361 Park Street
Clearwater, FL 33756-6039
Tel: 727-210-2350
Email: mail@caahep.org
http://www.caahep.org

National Accrediting Agency for Clinical Laboratory Sciences
8410 West Bryn Mawr Avenue, Suite 670
Chicago, IL 60631
Tel: 773-714-8880
Email: info@naacls.org
http://www.naacls.org

For information on certification, contact

National Credentialing Agency for Laboratory Personnel
PO Box 15945-289
Lenexa, KS 66285-5945
Tel: 913-895-4613
Email: nca-info@goamp.com
http://www.nca-info.org

MEDICAL RECORD TECHNICIANS

OVERVIEW

In any hospital, clinic, or other health care facility, permanent records are created and maintained for all the patients treated by the staff. Each patient's medical record describes in detail his or her condition over time. Entries include illness and injuries, operations, treatments, outpatient visits, and the progress of hospital stays. *Medical record technicians* compile, code, and maintain these records. They also tabulate and analyze data from groups of records in order to assemble reports. They review records for completeness and accuracy; assign codes to the diseases, operations, diagnoses, and treatments according to detailed standardized classification systems; and post the codes on the medical record. They transcribe medical reports; maintain indices of patients, diseases, operations, and other categories of information; compile patient census data; and file records. In addition, they may direct the day-to-day operations of the medical records department. They maintain the flow of records and reports to and from other departments, and sometimes assist medical staff in special studies or research that draws on information in the records. There are approximately 170,000 medical record technicians employed in the United States.

THE JOB

A patient's medical record consists of all relevant information and observations of any health care workers who have dealt with the patient. It may contain, for example, several diagnoses, X-ray and laboratory reports, electrocardiogram tracings, test results, and drugs prescribed. This summary of the patient's medical history is very important to the physician in making speedy and correct decisions about care. Later, information from the record is often needed in authenticating legal forms and insurance claims. The medical record documents the adequacy and appropriateness of the care received by the patient and is the basis of any investigation when the care is questioned in any way.

Patterns and trends can be traced when data from many records are considered together. Many different groups use these types of statistical reports. Hospital administrators, scientists, public health agencies, accrediting and licensing bodies, people who evaluate the effectiveness of current programs or plan future ones, and medical reimbursement organizations are examples of some groups that rely on health care statistics. Medical records can provide the data to show whether a new treatment or medication really works, the relative effectiveness of alternative treatments or medications, or patterns that yield clues about the causes or methods of preventing certain kinds of disease.

Medical record technicians are involved in the routine preparation, handling, and safeguarding of individual records as well as the statistical information extracted from groups of records. Their specific tasks and the scope of their responsibilities depend a great deal on the size and type of the employing institution. In large organizations, there may be a number of technicians and other employees working with medical records. The technicians may serve as assistants to the medical record administrator as needed or may regularly specialize in some particular phase of the work done by the department. In small facilities, however, technicians often carry out the whole range of activities and may function fairly independently, perhaps bearing the full responsibility for all day-to-day operations of the department. A technician in a small facility may even be a department director. Sometimes technicians handle medical records and also spend part of their time helping out in the business or admitting office.

Whether they work in hospitals or other settings, medical record technicians must organize, transfer, analyze, preserve, and locate vast quantities of detailed information when needed. The sources of this information include physicians, nurses, laboratory workers, and other members of the health care team.

In a hospital, a patient's cumulative record goes to the medical record department at the end of the hospital stay. A technician checks over the information in the file to be sure that all the essential reports and data are included and appear accurate. Certain specific items must be supplied in any record, such as signatures, dates, the patient's physical and social history, the results of physical examinations, provisional and final diagnoses, periodic progress notes on the patient's condition during the hospital stay, medications prescribed and administered, therapeutic treatments, surgical procedures, and an assessment of the outcome or the condition at the time of discharge. If any item is missing, the technician sends the record to the person who is responsible for supplying the information. After all necessary information has been received and the record has passed the review, it is considered the official document describing the patient's case.

The record is then passed to a *medical record coder*. Coders are responsible for assigning a numeric code to every diagnosis and procedure listed in a patient's file. Most hospitals in the United States use a nationally accepted system for coding. The lists of diseases, procedures, and conditions are published in classification manuals that medical records personnel refer to frequently. By reducing information in different forms to a single consistent coding system, the data contained in the record is rendered much easier to handle, tabulate,

QUICK FACTS

SCHOOL SUBJECTS
Computer science
Health
English

PERSONAL SKILLS
Following instructions
Technical/scientific

WORK ENVIRONMENT
Primarily indoors
Primarily one location

MINIMUM EDUCATION LEVEL
Associate's degree

MEDIAN SALARY
$28,030

CERTIFICATION OR LICENSING
Recommended

OUTLOOK
Faster than average

and analyze. It can be indexed under any suitable heading, such as by patient, disease, type of surgery, physician attending the case, and so forth. Cross-indexing is likely to be an important part of the medical record technician's job. Because the same coding systems are used nearly everywhere in the United States, the data may be used not only by people working inside the hospital, but may also be submitted to one of the various programs that pool information obtained from many institutions.

After the information on the medical record has been coded, technicians may use a packaged computer program to assign the patient to one of several hundred diagnosis-related groupings, or DRGs. The DRG for the patient's stay determines the amount of money the hospital will receive if the patient is covered by Medicare or one of the other insurance programs that base their reimbursement on DRGs.

Because information in medical records is used to determine how much hospitals are paid for caring for patients, the accuracy of the work done by medical records personnel is vital. A coding error could cause the hospital or patient to lose money.

Another vital part of the job concerns filing. Regardless of how accurately and completely information is gathered and stored, it is worthless unless it can be retrieved promptly. If paper records are kept, technicians are usually responsible for preparing records for storage, filing them, and getting them out of storage when needed. In some organizations, technicians supervise other personnel who carry out these tasks.

In many health care facilities, computers, rather than paper, are used for nearly all the medical record keeping. In such cases, medical and nursing staff make notes on an electronic chart. They enter patient-care information into computer files, and medical record technicians access the information using their own terminals. Computers have greatly simplified many traditional routine tasks of the medical records department, such as generating daily hospital census figures, tabulating data for research purposes, and updating special registries of certain types of health problems, such as cancer and stroke.

In the past, some medical records that were originally on paper were later photographed and stored on microfilm, particularly after they were a year or two old. Medical record technicians may be responsible for retrieving and maintaining those films. It is not unusual for a health care institution to have a combination of paper and microfilm files as well as computerized record storage, reflecting the evolution of technology for storing information.

Confidentiality and privacy laws have a major bearing on the medical records field. The laws vary in different states for different types of data, but in all cases, maintaining the confidentiality of individual records is of major concern to medical records workers. All individual records must be in secure storage but also be available for retrieval and specified kinds of properly authorized use. Technicians may be responsible for retrieving and releasing this information. They may prepare records to be released in response to a patient's written authorization, a subpoena, or a court order. This requires special knowledge of legal statutes and often requires consultation with attorneys, judges, insurance agents, and other parties with legitimate rights to access information about a person's health and medical treatment.

Medical record technicians may participate in the quality assurance, risk management, and utilization review activities of a health care facility. In these cases, they may serve as data abstractors and data analysts, reviewing records against established standards to ensure quality of care. They may also prepare statistical reports for the medical or administrative staff that reviews appropriateness of care.

With more specialized training, medical record technicians may participate in medical research activities by maintaining special records, called registries, related to such areas as cancer, heart disease, transplants, or adverse outcomes of pregnancies. In some cases, they are required to abstract and code information from records of patients with certain medical conditions. These technicians also may prepare statistical reports and trend analyses for the use of medical researchers.

REQUIREMENTS
High School

If you are contemplating a career in medical records, you should take as many high school English classes as possible, because technicians need both written and verbal communication skills to prepare reports and communicate with other health care personnel. Basic math or business math is very desirable because statistical skills are important in some job functions. Biology courses will help to familiarize you with the terminology that medical record technicians use. Other science courses, computer training, typing, and office procedures are also helpful.

Postsecondary Training

Most employers prefer to hire medical record technicians who have completed a two-year associate's degree program accredited by the American Medical Association's Commission on Accreditation of Allied Health Programs and the American Health Information Management Association (AHIMA). There are 245 of these accredited programs available throughout the United States, mostly offered in junior and community colleges. They usually include classroom instruction in such subjects as anatomy, physiology, medical terminology, medical record science, word processing, medical aspects of recordkeeping, statistics, computers in health care, personnel supervision, business management, English, and office skills.

In addition to classroom instruction, the student is given supervised clinical experience in the medical records departments of local health care facilities. This provides students with practical experience in performing many of the functions learned in the classroom and the opportunity to interact with health care professionals.

Certification or Licensing

Medical record technicians who have completed an accredited training program are eligible to take a national qualifying examination to earn the credential of registered health information technician (RHIT). Most health care institutions prefer to hire individuals with an RHIT credential as it signifies that they have met the standards established by the AHIMA as the mark of a qualified health professional. AHIMA also offers certification to medical coders and health information administrators.

Other Requirements

Medical records are extremely detailed and precise. Sloppy work could have serious consequences in terms of payment to the hospital or physician, validity of the patient records for later use, and validity of research based on data from medical records. Therefore, a prospective technician must have the capacity to do consistently reliable and accurate routine work. Records must be completed and maintained with care and attention to detail. You may be the only person who checks the entire record, and you must understand the responsibility that accompanies this task.

The technician needs to be able to work rapidly as well as accurately. In many medical record departments, the workload is very heavy, and you must be well organized and efficient in order to stay on top of the job. You must be able to complete your work accurately, in spite of interruptions, such as phone calls and requests for assistance. You also need to be discreet, as you will deal with records that are private and sometimes sensitive.

Computer skills are also essential, and some experience in transcribing dictated reports may be useful.

EXPLORING

To learn more about this and other medical careers, you may be able to find summer, part-time, or volunteer work in a hospital or other health care facility. Sometimes such jobs are available in the medical records area of an organization. You may also be able to arrange to talk with someone working as a medical record technician or administrator. Faculty and counselors at schools that offer medical record technician training programs may also be good sources of information. You can also learn more about this profession by reading journals and other literature available at a public library.

EMPLOYERS

Although two out of five of the 170,000 medical record technicians employed in the United States work in hospitals, many work in other health care settings, including health maintenance organizations (HMOs), industrial clinics, skilled nursing facilities, rehabilitation centers, large group medical practices, ambulatory care centers, and state and local government health agencies. Technicians also work for computer firms, consulting firms, and government agencies. Records are maintained in all of these facilities, although record-keeping procedures vary.

Not all medical record technicians are employed in a single health care facility; some serve as consultants to several small facilities. Other technicians do not work in health care settings at all. They may be employed by health and property liability insurance companies to collect and review information on medical claims. A few are self-employed, providing medical transcription services.

STARTING OUT

Most successful medical record technicians are graduates of two-year accredited programs. Graduates of these programs should check with their schools' placement offices for job leads. Those who have taken the accrediting exam and have become certified can use AHIMA's resume referral service.

You may also apply directly to the personnel departments of hospitals, nursing homes, outpatient clinics, and surgery centers. Many job openings are also listed in the classified advertising sections of local newspapers and with private and public employment agencies.

ADVANCEMENT

Medical record technicians may be able to achieve some advancement and salary increase without additional training simply by taking on greater responsibility in their job function. With experience, technicians may move to supervisory or department head positions, depending on the type and structure of the employing organization. Another means of advancing is through specialization in a certain area of the job. Some technicians specialize in coding, particularly Medicare coding or tumor registry. With a broad range of experience, a medical record technician may be able to become an independent consultant. Generally, technicians with an associate's degree and the RHIT designation are most likely to advance.

More assured job advancement and salary increase come with the completion of a bachelor's degree in medical record administration. The bachelor's degree, along with AHIMA accreditation, makes the technician eligible for a supervisory position, such as department director. Because of a general shortage of medical record administrators, hospitals often assist technicians who are working toward a bachelor's degree by providing flexible scheduling and financial aid or tuition reimbursement.

EARNINGS

The salaries of medical record technicians are greatly influenced by the location, size, and type of employing institution, as well as the technician's training and experience. According to the U.S. Department of Labor, the median annual earnings of medical records and health information technicians were $28,030 in 2006. Salaries ranged from less than $19,060 to more than $45,260.

According to AHIMA, beginning technicians with a bachelor's degree can expect to earn between $30,000 and $50,000 a year. With five years of experience, technicians can earn up to $75,000 annually.

In general, medical record technicians working in large urban hospitals make the most money, and those in rural areas make the least. Like most hospital employees, medical record technicians usually receive paid vacations and holidays, life and health insurance, and retirement benefits.

WORK ENVIRONMENT

Medical records departments are usually pleasantly clean, well-lit, and air-conditioned areas. Sometimes, however, paper or microfilm records are kept in cramped, out-of-the-way quarters. Although the work requires thorough and careful attention to detail, there may be a constant bustle of activity in the technician's work area, which can be disruptive. The job is likely to involve frequent routine contact with nurses, physicians, hospital administrators, other health care professionals, attorneys, and insurance agents. On occasion, individuals with whom the technicians may interact are demanding or difficult. In such cases, technicians may find that the job carries a high level of frustration.

A 40-hour workweek is the norm, but because hospitals operate on a 24-hour basis, the job may regularly include night or weekend hours. Part-time work is sometimes available.

The work is extremely detailed and may be tedious. Some technicians spend the majority of their day sitting at a desk, working on a computer. Others may spend hours filing paper records or retrieving them from storage.

In many hospital settings, the medical record technician experiences pressure caused by a heavy workload. As the demands for health care cost containment and productivity increase, medical record technicians may be required to produce a significantly greater volume of high-quality work in shorter periods of time.

Nonetheless, the knowledge that their work is significant for patients and medical research can be very personally satisfying for medical record technicians.

OUTLOOK

Employment prospects through 2016 are expected to be very good. The U.S. Department of Labor predicts that employment in this field will grow faster than average. The demand for well-trained medical record technicians will grow rapidly and will continue to exceed the supply. This expectation is related to the health care needs of a population that is both growing and aging, and the trend toward more technologically sophisticated medicine and greater use of diagnostic procedures. It is also related to the increased requirements of regulatory bodies that scrutinize both costs and quality of care of health care providers. Because of the fear of medical malpractice lawsuits, doctors and other health care providers are documenting their diagnoses and treatments in greater detail. Also, because of the high cost of health care, insurance companies, government agencies, and courts are examining medical records with a more critical eye. These factors combine to ensure a healthy job outlook for medical record technicians.

Opportunities will be best in offices of physicians, particularly in large group practices, nursing care facilities, home health care services, and outpatient care centers.

Technicians with associate's degrees and RHIT status will have the best prospects, and the importance of such qualifications is likely to increase.

FOR MORE INFORMATION

For information on earnings, careers in health information management, and accredited programs, contact

American Health Information Management Association
233 North Michigan Avenue, Suite 2150
Chicago, IL 60601-5800
Tel: 312-233-1100
Email: info@ahima.org
http://www.ahima.org

For a list of schools offering accredited programs in health information management, contact

Commission on Accreditation of Allied Health Education Programs
1361 Park Street
Clearwater, FL 33756-6039
Tel: 727-210-2350
http://www.caahep.org

MEDICAL SECRETARIES

OVERVIEW

Medical secretaries perform administrative and clerical work in medical offices, hospitals, or private physicians' offices. They answer phone calls, order supplies, handle correspondence, bill patients, complete insurance forms, and transcribe dictation. Medical secretaries also handle bookkeeping, greet patients, schedule appointments, arrange hospital admissions, and schedule surgeries. There are approximately 408,000 medical secretaries employed throughout the United States.

THE JOB

Medical secretaries play important roles in the health care profession. They transcribe dictation, prepare correspondence, and assist physicians or medical scientists with reports, speeches, articles, and conference proceedings. Medical secretaries also record simple medical histories, arrange for patients to be hospitalized, and order supplies. Most need to be familiar with insurance rules, billing practices, and hospital or laboratory procedures.

Doctors rely on medical secretaries to keep administrative operations under control. Secretaries are the information clearinghouses for the office. They schedule appointments, handle phone calls, organize and maintain paper and electronic files, and produce correspondence for the office. Medical secretaries must have basic technical skills to operate office equipment such as facsimile machines, photocopiers, and switchboard systems. Increasingly, they use computers to run spreadsheet, word-processing, database-management, or desktop publishing programs.

REQUIREMENTS

High School

Most employers require medical secretaries to have a high school diploma and be able to type between 60 and 90 words per minute. In order to handle more specialized duties, you must be familiar with medical terms and procedures and be able to use medical software programs. In addition, you need to have basic math skills and strong written and verbal communication skills to write up correspondence and handle patient inquiries. English, speech, and health classes will help you prepare for this career.

QUICK FACTS

SCHOOL SUBJECTS
English
Health
Speech

PERSONAL SKILLS
Communication/ideas
Following instructions

WORK ENVIRONMENT
Primarily indoors
Primarily one location

MINIMUM EDUCATION LEVEL
High school diploma

MEDIAN SALARY
$28,090

CERTIFICATION OR LICENSING
Voluntary

OUTLOOK
About as fast as the average

Postsecondary Training

One- and two-year programs are offered by many vocational, community, and business schools covering the skills needed for secretarial work. For more specialized training, some schools offer medical secretarial programs, covering the basics such as typing, filing, and accounting, as well as more specialized courses on medical stenography, first aid, medical terminology, and medical office procedures.

Certification or Licensing

Certification is not required for a job as a medical secretary, but obtaining it may bring increased opportunities, earnings, and responsibility. The International Association of Administrative Professionals offers the certified professional secretary (CPS) and certified administrative professional (CAP) designations. To achieve CPS or CAP certification, you must meet certain experience requirements and pass a rigorous exam covering a number of general secretarial topics.

Other Requirements

To succeed as a medical secretary, you must be trustworthy and use discretion when dealing with confidential medical records. You must also have a pleasant and confident personality for handling the public and a desire to help others in a dependable and conscientious manner.

EXPLORING

The best way to learn about this career is to speak with an experienced medical secretary about his or her work. Ask your school guidance counselor to set up an information interview with a medical secretary, or arrange a tour of a medical facility so you can see secretaries in action.

EMPLOYERS

Approximately 408,000 medical secretaries are employed in the United States. Medical secretaries work in private physicians' offices, hospitals, outpatient clinics, emergency care facilities, research laboratories, and large health organizations, such as the Mayo Medical Clinic. The Mayo Clinic branches, located in Florida, Minnesota, and Arizona, employ more than 1,000 medical secretaries who work for nearly 2,500 physicians and scientists. A majority of medical secretaries work with one or two physicians practicing in a clinical outpatient care setting. The remainder provide support to physicians and scientists in clinical and research laboratories, hospitals, or Mayo Clinic's medical school.

STARTING OUT

To find work in this field, you should apply directly to hospitals, clinics, and physicians' offices. Potential positions might be listed with school or college placement centers or in newspaper want ads. Networking with medical secretaries is another inside track to job leads, because employers tend to trust employee recommendations.

ADVANCEMENT

Promotions for secretaries who work in doctors' offices are usually limited to increases in salary and responsibilities. Medical secretaries employed by clinics or hospitals can advance to executive positions, such as senior secretary, clerical supervisor, or office manager; or into more administrative jobs, such as medical records clerk, administrative assistant, or unit manager.

EARNINGS

The U.S. Department of Labor reports that medical secretaries earned a median annual salary of $28,090 in 2006. Salaries ranged from less than $19,750 to more than $40,870. The median salary in 2006 for medical secretaries employed in general medical and surgical hospitals was $28,810.

Most employers offer vacation, sick leave, and medical benefits. Many also include life, dental, and vision care insurance, retirement benefits, and profit sharing.

WORK ENVIRONMENT

Medical secretaries usually work 40 hours a week, Monday through Friday, during regular business hours. However, some work extended hours one or two days a week, depending on the physician's office hours. They do their work in well-lit, pleasant surroundings, but could encounter stressful emergency situations.

OUTLOOK

While the demand for secretaries in the general sector is expected to grow more slowly than the average for all occupations, the U.S. Department of Labor projects a higher demand for medical secretaries, expecting the occupation to grow as fast as the average through 2016.

Health services are demanding more from their support personnel and are increasing salary levels accordingly. Technological advances are making secretaries more productive and able to handle the duties once done by managers or other staff. The distribution of work has shifted; secretaries receive fewer requests for typing and filing jobs. Instead, they do more technical work requiring computer skills beyond keyboarding. The job outlook appears brightest for those who are up to date on the latest programs and technological advances.

FOR MORE INFORMATION

For information on training to become a medical secretary, contact

Arlington Career Institute
901 Avenue K
Grand Prairie, TX 75050-2636
Tel: 800-394-5445
http://www.arlingtoncareerinstitute.edu

For information on professional certification, contact
International Association of Administrative Professionals
PO Box 20404
10502 NW Ambassador Drive

Kansas City, MO 64195-0404
Tel: 816-891-6600
Email: service@iaap-hq.org
http://www.iaap-hq.org

The Mayo Clinic is a major employer of medical secretaries. Visit its Web site for more information.
Mayo Clinic
http://www.mayo.edu

MEDICAL TRANSCRIPTIONISTS

OVERVIEW

Doctors and other health care professionals often make tape recordings documenting what happened during their patients' appointments or surgical procedures. *Medical transcriptionists* listen to these tapes and transcribe, or type, reports of what the doctor said. The reports are then included in patients' charts. Medical transcriptionists work in a variety of health care settings, including hospitals, clinics, and doctors' offices, as well as for transcription companies or out of their own homes. There are approximately 98,000 medical transcriptionists working in the United States. Medical transcriptionists are also called *medical transcribers*, *medical stenographers*, or *medical language specialists*.

THE JOB

Medical transcriptionists transcribe (type into printed format) a dictated (oral) report recorded by a doctor or another health care professional. They work for primary care physicians as well as health care professionals in various medical specialties, including cardiology, immunology, oncology, podiatry, radiology, and urology. The medical transcriptionist usually types up the report while listening to the recording through a transcriber machine's headset, using a foot pedal to stop or rewind the recording as necessary. Some doctors dictate over the telephone, and others use the Internet.

The report consists of information gathered during a patient's office appointment or hospital visit and covers the patient's medical history and treatment. Doctors dictate information about patient consultations, physical examinations, results from laboratory work or X rays, medical tests, psychiatric evaluations, patient diagnosis

QUICK FACTS

SCHOOL SUBJECTS
Biology
English
Health

PERSONAL SKILLS
Communication/ideas
Technical/scientific

WORK ENVIRONMENT
Primarily indoors
Primarily one location

MINIMUM EDUCATION LEVEL
Some postsecondary training

MEDIAN SALARY
$29,952

CERTIFICATION OR LICENSING
Recommended

OUTLOOK
Faster than the average

and prognosis, surgical procedures, a patient's hospital stay and discharge, autopsies, and so on. Often doctors will use abbreviations while dictating. The medical transcriptionist must type out the full names of those abbreviations.

Because the report becomes a permanent part of a patient's medical record and is referred to by the same doctor or other members of the patient's health care team during future office visits or when determining future medical treatment, it must be accurate. This includes dates and the spelling of medications, procedures, diseases, medical instruments and supplies, and laboratory values.

After typing up a report, medical transcriptionists review it and make corrections to grammar, punctuation, and spelling. They read it to be sure it is clear, consistent, and complete and does not contain any errors. Medical transcriptionists are expected to edit for clarity and make grammar corrections; therefore, the final report does not need to be identical to the original dictation in those respects.

Being a medical transcriptionist is not all about typing and proofreading. Medical transcriptionists are very familiar with medical terminology. When recording their reports, doctors use medical terms that are relevant to a patient's condition and treatment. Such terms might be names of diseases or medications. Medical transcriptionists understand what these medical terms mean and how they are spelled. They understand enough about various diseases and their symptoms, treatments, and prognoses as to be able to figure out what a doctor is saying if the recording is a little garbled. They have a good understanding of medicine and know about human anatomy and physiology. If what the doctor says on the tape is unclear, a medical transcriptionist often has to determine the appropriate word or words based on the context. However, medical transcriptionists never guess when it comes to medications, conditions, medical history, and treatments. A patient could receive improper and even damaging treatment if a diagnosis is made based on a report containing errors. Medical transcriptionists contact the doctor if they are uncertain or they leave a blank in the report, depending on the employer's or client's expectations and guidelines. After the medical transcriptionist reviews the report, it is given to the doctor, who also reviews it and then signs it if it is acceptable—or returns it to the transcriptionist for correction, if necessary. Once it has been signed, the report is placed in the patient's permanent medical file.

Many medical transcriptionists use voice recognition software to electronically create documents from oral dictation, eliminating much of their typing work. Medical transcriptionists still have to review the transcription for accuracy and format.

While some transcriptionists only do transcribing, other transcriptionists, often those who work in doctors' offices or clinics, may have additional responsibilities. They may deal with patients, answer the phone, handle the mail, and perform other clerical tasks. And transcriptionists may be asked to file or deliver the reports to other doctors, lawyers, or other people who request them.

A growing number of medical transcriptionists work out of their homes, either telecommuting as employees or subcontractors or as self-employed workers. As technology becomes more sophisticated, this trend is likely to continue. Medical transcriptionists who work out of their homes have some degree of mobility and can live where they choose, taking their jobs with them.

These workers must keep up to date with their medical resources and equipment. Because terminology continues to change, medical transcriptionists regularly buy revised editions of some of the standard medical resources.

REQUIREMENTS
High School

English and grammar classes are important in preparing you to become a medical transcriptionist. Focus on becoming a better speller. If you understand the meanings of word prefixes and suffixes (many of which come from Greek and Latin), it will be easier for you to learn medical terminology, since many terms are formed by adding a prefix and/or a suffix to a word or root. If your high school offers Greek or Latin classes, take one; otherwise, try to take Greek or Latin when you continue your studies after high school.

Biology and health classes will give you a solid introduction to the human body and how it functions, preparing you to take more advanced classes in anatomy and physiology after you graduate. Be sure to learn how to type by taking a class or teaching yourself. Practice typing regularly to build up your speed and accuracy. Word-processing and computer classes are also useful.

Postsecondary Training

Some junior, community, and business colleges and vocational schools have medical transcription programs. You can also learn the business of medical transcription by taking a correspondence course. To be accepted into a medical transcription program, you might need to have a minimum typing speed. The Association for Healthcare Documentation Integrity (AHDI) recommends that medical transcriptionists complete a two-year program offering an associate's degree, but this is not necessary for you to find a job.

You should take courses in English grammar as well as medical terminology, anatomy, physiology, and pharmacology. Some of the more specific classes you might take include Medicolegal Concepts and Ethics, Human Disease and Pathophysiology, Health Care Records Management, and Medical Grammar and Editing. Certain programs offer on-the-job training, which will help when you are looking for full-time employment.

The AHDI has a mentoring program for students who are studying medical transcription. Students can make important contacts in the field and learn much from experienced professionals.

Certification or Licensing

The AHDI awards two voluntary certifications: certified medical transcriptionist (CMT), and registered medical transcriptionist (RMT). The CMT designation requires at least two years of experience in acute care. Medical transcriptionists with less than two years of acute care experience, but who successfully pass the AHDI Level 1 registered medical transcriptionist exam, may become RMTs. Certification is good for three years, at which point recertification is necessary to keep the CMT or RMT designation. (There are also certain other requirements, which are detailed at the AHDI Web site, http://www.ahdionline.org.)

While medical transcriptionists do not need to be certified to find a job, it is highly recommended as a sign of achievement and professionalism. CMTs will probably more readily find employment and earn higher salaries.

Other Requirements

A love of language and grammar is an important quality, and accuracy and attention to detail are absolute musts for a medical transcriptionist. It is essential that you correctly type up information as spoken by the doctor on the tape recording. You must be able to sift through background sounds on the tape and accurately record what the doctor says. Doctors dictate at the same time they are with a patient or later from their office or maybe even as they go about their daily routine, perhaps while eating, driving in traffic, or walking along a busy street. In each of these cases, the recording will likely include background noises or conversations that at times drown out or make unclear what the doctor is saying.

Many doctors grew up outside of the United States and do not speak English as their first language, so they may not have a thorough understanding of English or they may speak with an accent. You must have a good ear to be able to decipher what these doctors are saying.

In addition to having accurate typing skills, you will also need to type quickly if you want to earn higher wages and get more clients. A solid understanding of word-processing software will help you to be more productive. An example of this is the use of macros, or keystroke combinations that are used for repetitive actions, such as typing the same long, hard-to-spell word or phrase time and again. If you suffer from repetitive strain injuries, then this would not be a suitable profession.

Flexibility is also important because you must be able to adapt to the different skills and needs of various health care professionals.

Medical transcriptionists should be able to concentrate and be prepared to sit in one place for long periods at a time, either typing or reading. For this reason, it is important that you take regular breaks. An ability to work independently will help you whether you are self-employed or have an office position, since you do most of your work sitting at a computer.

Medical transcriptionists are required to keep patient records confidential, just as doctors are, so integrity and discretion are important.

EXPLORING

There is plenty of accessible reading material aimed at medical transcriptionists. This is a good way to learn more about the field and decide if it sounds interesting to you. Several of the Web sites listed at the end of this article feature self-tests and articles about medical transcription. Marylou Bunting, a home-based certified medical transcriptionist, recommends that you get a medical dictionary and PDR (*Physicians' Desk Reference*) to familiarize yourself with terminology. See if your local library has the *Journal of the American Association for Medical Transcription* and browse through some issues. The Internet is a great resource for would-be medical transcriptionists. Find a bulletin board or mailing list and talk to professionals in the field, perhaps conducting an informational interview.

Bunting also suggests that you "put yourself in a medical setting as soon and as often as you can." Ask if your doctor can use your help in any way or apply for a volunteer position at a local hospital. Ask to be assigned to the hospital's medical records department, which won't give you the opportunity to transcribe, but will give you some experience dealing with medical records.

EMPLOYERS

According to the *Occupational Outlook Handbook,* there are about 98,000 medical transcriptionists working in the United States. About 41 percent work in hospitals and 29 percent work in doctors' offices and clinics. Others work for laboratories, home health care services, medical centers, colleges and universities, medical libraries, insurance companies, transcription companies, temp agencies, and even veterinary facilities. Medical transcriptionists can also find government jobs, with public health or veterans hospitals.

STARTING OUT

It can be difficult to get started in this field, especially if you do not have any work experience. Some medical transcriptionists start out working as administrative assistants or receptionists in doctors' offices. They become acquainted with medical terminology and office procedures, and they make important contacts in the medical profession.

Marylou Bunting recommends that you try to get an informal apprenticeship position since on-the-job experience seems to be a prerequisite for most jobs. Or perhaps you can find an internship position with a transcription company. Once you have some experience, you can look for another position through classified ads, job search agencies, or Internet resources. You can also find job leads through word-of-mouth and professional contacts.

ADVANCEMENT

There are few actual advancement opportunities for medical transcriptionists. Those who become faster and more accurate will have an easier time securing better paying positions or lining up new clients. Skilled and experienced medical transcriptionists can become supervisors of transcription departments or managers of transcription companies, or they might even form their own transcription companies. Some also become teachers, consultants, or authors or editors of books on the subject of medical transcription.

EARNINGS

Medical transcriptionists are paid in a variety of ways, depending on the employer or client. Payment might be made based on the number of hours worked or the number of lines transcribed. Monetary incentives might be offered to hourly transcriptionists achieving a high rate of production.

The U.S. Department of Labor reports that in 2006, the lowest 10 percent of all medical transcriptionists earned an annual salary of $21,258, and the highest paid 10 percent earned $41,912, annually. The median annual salary was $29,952. Medical transcriptionists who worked in hospitals earned $30,410 annually and those who worked in offices and clinics of medical doctors earned $29,120. Medical transcriptionists who are certified earn higher average salaries than transcriptionists who have not earned certification.

Medical transcriptionists working in a hospital or company setting can expect to receive the usual benefits, including paid vacation, sick days, and health insurance. Tuition reimbursement and 401(k) plans may also be offered. Home-based medical transcriptionists who are employed by a company may be entitled to the same benefits that in-house staff members get—it is important to check with each individual company to be sure. Self-employed medical transcriptionists have to make arrangements for their own health and retirement plans and other benefits.

WORK ENVIRONMENT

Most medical transcriptionists work in an office setting, either at their employer's place of business or in their own homes. They generally sit at desks in front of computers and have transcribers or dictation machines and medical reference books at hand. Home-based workers and sometimes even office workers must invest a substantial amount of money in reference books and equipment on an ongoing basis, to keep up with changes in medical terminology and technology.

Transcriptionists who are not self-employed usually put in a 40-hour week. Some medical transcriptionists working in hospitals are assigned to the second or third shift. Independent contractors, on the other hand, clock their hours when they have work to do. Sometimes this will be part-time or on the weekends or at night. If they are busy enough, some work more hours than in the normal workweek.

Because medical transcriptionists spend such a long time typing at a computer, the risk of repetitive stress injuries is present. Other physical problems may also occur, including eyestrain from staring at a computer screen and back or neck pain from sitting in one position for long periods at a time.

OUTLOOK

As Internet security issues are resolved, its use for receiving dictation and returning transcriptions will likely become more popular. The Internet offers a quick way to communicate and transfer documents, which is useful for medical transcriptionists who work far away from their employers or clients. As voice recognition technology improves and better recognizes complex medical terminology, it, too, will be used more and medical transcriptionists will do less typing.

Even with these technological advances, there will continue to be a need for medical transcriptionists. They will still have to review electronically created documents. And given that people are living longer, they will require more medical tests and procedures, which will all need to be documented and transcribed. The U.S. Department of Labor reports that employment of medical transcriptionists is expected to grow faster than the average through 2016.

FOR MORE INFORMATION

AHDI works to set standards in education and practice in the medical transcription field.

Association for Healthcare Documentation Integrity (ADHI)
4230 Kiernan Avenue, Suite 130
Modesto, CA 95356-9322
Tel: 800-982-2182
Email: ahdi@ahdionline.org
http://www.ahdionline.org

This publication contains an assortment of articles of interest to health information management professionals, including medical transcriptionists.

Advance for Health Information Professionals
http://www.advanceforhim.com

This Web site features articles and resources for medical transcriptionists and those wanting to learn more about the field.

Keeping Abreast of Medical Transcription
http://www.wwma.com/kamt

For an overview of the job, several language resources and tests, and sample reports, visit

Medword—Medical Transcription
http://www.medword.com

This networking resource for professionals includes discussion forums and interviews.

MT Daily
http://www.mtdaily.com

See this Web site for an extensive glossary, a huge list of "stumper terms" for medical transcriptionists, links to other medical-related dictionaries and resources, sample operative reports, book suggestions, chat forums, and classified ads.

MT Desk
http://www.mtdesk.com

☐ MERCHANDISE DISPLAYERS

OVERVIEW

Merchandise displayers, sometimes known as *visual merchandisers*, design and install displays of clothing, accessories, furniture, and other products to attract customers. They set up these displays in windows and showcases and on the sales floors of retail stores. Display workers who specialize in dressing mannequins are known as *model dressers*. Those who specialize in installing displays in store windows are known as w*indow dressers* or *window trimmers*. These workers use their artistic flair and imagination to create excitement and customer interest in the store. They also work with other types of merchandising to develop exciting images, product campaigns, and shopping concepts. There are approximately 87,000 merchandise displayers and window trimmers employed in the United States.

THE JOB

Using their imagination and creative ability, as well as their knowledge of color harmony, composition, and other fundamentals of art and interior design, merchandise

---

QUICK FACTS

SCHOOL SUBJECTS
Art
Technical/shop
Theater/dance

PERSONAL SKILLS
Artistic
Mechanical/manipulative

WORK ENVIRONMENT
Primarily indoors
Primarily one location

MINIMUM EDUCATION LEVEL
High school diploma

MEDIAN SALARY
$23,820

CERTIFICATION OR LICENSING
None available

OUTLOOK
About as fast as the average

displayers in retail establishments create an idea for a setting designed to show off merchandise and attract customers' attention. Often the display is planned around a theme or concept. After the display manager approves the design or idea, the display workers create the display. They install background settings, such as carpeting, wallpaper, and lighting, gather props and other accessories, arrange mannequins and merchandise, and place price tags and descriptive signs where they are needed.

Carpenters, painters, or store maintenance workers may assist displayers in some of these tasks. Displayers may use merchandise from various departments of the store or props from previous displays. Sometimes they borrow from other stores special items that their business doesn't carry , such as toys or sports equipment. The displays are dismantled and new ones installed every few weeks. In very large stores that employ many display workers, displayers may specialize in carpentry, painting, making signs, or setting up interior or window displays. A *display director* usually supervises and coordinates the display workers' activities and confers with other managers to select merchandise to be featured.

Ambitious and talented display workers have many possible career avenues. The importance of visual merchandising is being recognized more and more as retail establishments compete for consumer dollars. Some display workers can advance to display director or even to a position in store planning.

In addition to traditional stores, the skills of visual marketing workers are now in demand in many other types of establishments. Restaurants often try to present a distinct image to enhance the dining experience. Outlet stores, discount malls, and entertainment centers also use visual marketing to establish their identities with the public. Chain stores often need to make changes in or redesign all their stores and turn to display professionals for their expertise. Consumer product manufacturers also are heavily involved in visual marketing. They hire display and design workers to come up with exciting concepts, such as in-store shops, that present a unified image of the manufacturer's products and are sold as complete units to retail stores.

There are also opportunities for employment with store fixture manufacturers. Many companies build and sell specialized props, banners, signs, displays, and mannequins and hire display workers as sales representatives to promote their products. The display workers' understanding of retail needs and their insight into the visual merchandising industry make them valuable consultants.

Commercial decorators prepare and install displays and decorations for trade and industrial shows, exhibitions, festivals, and other special events. Working from blueprints, drawings, and floor plans, they use woodworking power tools to construct installations (usually referred to as booths) at exhibition halls and convention centers. They install carpeting, drapes, and other decorations, such as flags, banners, and lights. They arrange furniture and accessories to attract the people attending the exhibition. Special event producers, coordinators, and party planners may also seek out the skills of display professionals.

This occupation appeals to imaginative, artistic individuals who find it rewarding to use their creative abilities to visualize a design concept and transform it into reality. Original, creative displays grow out of an awareness of current design trends and popular themes. Although display workers use inanimate objects such as props and materials, an understanding of human motivations helps them create displays with strong customer appeal.

REQUIREMENTS
High School

To work as a display worker, you must have at least a high school diploma. Important high school subjects include art, woodworking, mechanical drawing, and merchandising.

Postsecondary Training

Some employers require college courses in art, interior decorating, fashion design, advertising, or related subjects. Community and junior colleges that offer advertising and marketing courses may include display work in the curriculum. Fashion merchandising schools and fine arts institutes also offer courses useful to display workers.

Much of the training for display workers is gained on the job. They generally start as helpers for routine tasks, such as carrying props and dismantling sets. Gradually, they are permitted to build simple props and work up to constructing more difficult displays. As they become more experienced, display workers who show artistic talent may be assigned to plan simple designs. The total training time varies depending on the beginner's ability and the variety and complexity of the displays.

Other Requirements

Besides education and experience, you will also need creative ability, manual dexterity, and mechanical aptitude to do this work. You should possess the strength and physical ability needed to be able to carry equipment and climb ladders. You also need agility to work in close quarters without upsetting the props.

EXPLORING

To explore the work of merchandise displayers, try to get a part-time or summer job with a department or retail store or at a convention center. This will give you an overview of the display operations in these establishments. Photographers and theater groups need helpers to work with props and sets, although some may require previous experience or knowledge related to their work. Your school's drama and photo clubs may offer opportunities to learn basic design concepts. You also should read about this line of work; *Display & Design Ideas* magazine (http://www.ddimagazine.com) publishes articles on the field and related subjects.

EMPLOYERS

Approximately 87,000 merchandise displayers and window trimmers are employed in the United States. Most work in department and clothing stores, but many are employed in other types of retail stores, such as variety, drug, and shoe stores. Some have their own design businesses, and some are employed by design firms that handle interior and professional window dressing for small stores. Employment of display workers is distributed throughout the country, with most of the jobs concentrated in large towns and cities.

STARTING OUT

School placement offices may have job listings for display workers or related positions. Individuals wishing to become display workers can apply directly to retail stores, decorating firms, or exhibition centers. Openings may also be listed in the classified ads of newspapers.

A number of experienced merchandise displayers choose to work as freelance designers. Competition in this area, however, is intense, and it takes time to establish a reputation, build a list of clients, and earn an adequate income. Freelancing part time while holding down another job provides a more secure income for many display workers. Freelancing also provides beginners with opportunities to develop a portfolio of photographs of their best designs, which they can then use to sell their services to other stores.

ADVANCEMENT

Display workers with supervisory ability can become regional managers. Further advancement may lead to a position as a display director or head of store planning.

Another way to advance is by starting a freelance design business. This can be done with very little financial investment, although freelance design workers must spend many long hours generating new business and establishing a reputation in the field.

Experienced display workers also may be able to transfer their skills to jobs in other art-related fields, such as interior design or photography. This move, however, requires additional training.

EARNINGS

According to the U.S. Department of Labor, the median annual earnings of merchandise displayers were $23,820 in 2006. The lowest 10 percent earned less than $15,630 and the highest 10 percent earned more than $341,370. Displayers working in clothing stores such as department stores earned a median salary of $32,280 in 2006.

Freelance displayers may earn as much as $37,000 a year, but their income depends entirely on their talent, reputation, number of clients, and amount of time they work.

WORK ENVIRONMENT

Display workers usually work 35 to 40 hours a week, except during busy seasons, such as Christmas. Selling promotions and increased sales drives during targeted seasons can require the display staff to work extra hours in the evening and on weekends.

The work of constructing and installing displays requires prolonged standing, bending, stooping, and working in awkward positions. There is some risk of falling off ladders or being injured from handling sharp materials or tools, but serious injuries are uncommon.

OUTLOOK

Employment for display workers is expected to grow about as fast as the average for all occupations through 2016, according to the U.S. Department of Labor. Growth in this profession is expected due to an expanding retail sector and the increasing popularity of visual merchandising. Most openings will occur as older, experienced workers retire or leave the occupation.

Fluctuations in our nation's economy affect the volume of retail sales because people are less likely to spend money during recessionary times. For display workers, this can result in layoffs or hiring freezes.

FOR MORE INFORMATION

For information on student membership, scholarship opportunities, schools with student chapters, and additional career materials, contact

American Society of Interior Designers
608 Massachusetts Avenue, NE
Washington, DC 20002-6006
Tel: 202-546-3480
http://www.asid.org

For membership information, contact
Institute of Store Planners
25 North Broadway
Tarrytown, NY 10591-3221
Tel: 914-332-0040
Email: info@ispo.org
http://www.ispo.org

To read about industry events and news, check out the following magazine's Web site:
Display & Design Ideas
http://www.ddimagazine.com

MILLWRIGHTS

OVERVIEW

Millwrights install, assemble, and maintain heavy industrial machinery and other equipment. If necessary, they construct foundations for certain large assemblies. They may also dismantle, operate, or repair these machines. Approximately 55,000 millwrights are employed in the United States.

THE JOB

Millwrights are highly skilled workers whose primary function is to install heavy machinery. When machinery arrives at the job site, it must be unloaded, inspected, and moved into position. For light machinery, millwrights use rigging and hoisting devices such as pulleys and cables to lift and position equipment. For heavier jobs, they are assisted by hydraulic lift-truck or crane operators. To decide what type of device is needed to position machinery, millwrights must know the load-bearing properties of ropes, cables, hoists, and cranes.

New machinery sometimes requires a new foundation. Millwrights either prepare the foundation themselves or supervise its construction. To do this, they must be able to work with concrete, wood, and steel, and read blueprints and schematic diagrams to make any electrical connections.

When installing machinery, millwrights fit bearings, align gears and wheels, attach motors, and connect belts according to the manufacturer's instructions. They may use hand and power tools, cutting torches, welding machines, and soldering guns. In order to modify parts to fit specifications, they use metalworking equipment such as lathes and grinders.

Millwrights must be very precise in their work and have good mathematical skills to measure angles, material thicknesses, and small distances with tools such as squares, calipers, and micrometers. When a high level of precision is required, such as on a production line, lasers may be used for alignment.

Once machinery is installed, millwrights may do repair or preventive maintenance work such as oiling and greasing parts and replacing worn components.

Millwrights may be hired to change the placement of existing machines in a plant or mill to set up a new production line or improve efficiency. Their contribution is key to the planning of complicated production processes. In large shops and plants, they may update machinery placement to improve the production process. They may even move and reassemble machinery each time a new production run starts. In smaller factories, however, machinery is rearranged only to increase production and improve efficiency. Millwrights consult with supervisors, planners, and engineers to determine the proper placement of equipment based on floor loads, workflow, safety measures, and other important concerns.

The increasing use of automation in many industries means that millwrights are responsible for installing and maintaining more sophisticated machines. When working with this more complicated machinery, millwrights are assisted by computer or electronic experts, electricians, and manufacturers' representatives.

REQUIREMENTS
High School

Employers prefer applicants with a high school diploma or equivalency. You should take courses in science, mathematics, and shop to give you a technical and mechanical foundation. Any class with an emphasis on mechanical reasoning, such as mechanical drawing, blueprint reading, hydraulics, and machine shop, is of particular value.

Postsecondary Training

Millwrights receive their training either through a formal apprenticeship program or through community colleges combined with informal on-the-job training. Apprenticeships last for four to five years and combine hands-on training with classroom instruction. During the program, apprentices gain experience dismantling, moving, erecting, and repairing machinery. They may also work with concrete and receive instruction in carpentry, welding, and sheet metal work. Classes focus on mathematics, blueprint reading, hydraulics, electricity, and computers.

Other Requirements

To handle the physical demands involved in the work, applicants should be in good health and physically fit. A high level of coordination and mechanical aptitude is necessary to read complicated diagrams and work with the machinery. Communication and interpersonal skills are also needed for giving instructions and working in teams.

EXPLORING

One of the best ways to find out more about this career is to talk with a working millwright. Develop a list of questions to ask, such as details about the responsibilities, hours, pay, and how he or she first got into the work. You could also visit an industrial setting that employs millwrights to watch these workers in action. Local unions that represent millwrights can also provide you with information on the career.

EMPLOYERS

There are approximately 55,000 millwrights employed in the United States. Millwrights work in every state but are concentrated in highly industrial areas. Most are employed in industries that manufacture durable goods, such as automobiles, steel, and metal products, or in construction. Others work in plants that manufacture paper, chemicals, knit goods, and other items, or with utility companies. Manufacturers and retailers of industrial machinery often employ millwrights, usually under contract, to install machines for their customers.

STARTING OUT

The usual entry method is through an apprenticeship. Most apprentices start out with unskilled or semiskilled work in a plant or factory. As they gain experience and job openings become available, they move into positions requiring more skilled labor. Openings are generally filled according to experience and seniority.

ADVANCEMENT

Most advancement for millwrights comes in the form of higher wages. With the proper training, skill, and seniority, however, workers can move to supervisory positions or work as trainers for apprentices. Others may choose to become self-employed contractors.

QUICK FACTS

SCHOOL SUBJECTS
Mathematics
Technical/shop

PERSONAL SKILLS
Mechanical/manipulative
Technical/scientific

WORK ENVIRONMENT
Indoors and outdoors
One location with some travel

MINIMUM EDUCATION LEVEL
Apprenticeship

MEDIAN SALARY
$45,635

CERTIFICATION OR LICENSING
None available

OUTLOOK
More slowly than the average

EARNINGS

Millwrights are typically paid by the hour. According to the *Occupational Outlook Handbook*, hourly earnings averaged $21.94 (or $45,635 annually) in 2006. The lowest 10 percent earned less than $13.84 an hour (or $28,787 annually) and the highest 10 percent earned more than $34.39 an hour (or $71,531 annually).

Most workers in this field receive a benefits package that includes life and health insurance, paid vacation and sick leave, and a retirement pension.

Salary rates can vary depending on experience, geographic location, industry, and union membership. Approximately 50 percent of millwrights are represented by labor unions, one of the highest rates of membership for one profession. The International Union, United Automobile, Aerospace, and Agricultural Implement Workers of America; the International Association of Machinists and Aerospace Workers; and the United Brotherhood of Carpenters and Joiners of America are three unions to which millwrights belong.

WORK ENVIRONMENT

Approximately one-third of all millwrights work more than 40 hours a week. They often work overtime and in varying shifts to accommodate production schedules. Millwrights may be called to work at unusual times or for longer hours during emergencies. An equipment breakdown can affect an entire plant's operation and be very costly, so machines need to be immediately tended to when problems arise. Rearranging whole production lines often requires long hours.

Depending on the industry, working conditions vary from indoors to outdoors, and from working at one location to having to travel. In manufacturing jobs, millwrights work indoors in a shop setting. In construction jobs, they may work outside, in all weather conditions. Millwrights that do contract work may travel from plant to plant. Others are employed by a single manufacturer and remain on site much of the time.

What is consistent throughout the profession is the amount of labor involved. Millwrights often endure hard physical labor in surroundings made unpleasant by heat, noise, grime, and cramped spaces. In addition, the work can be hazardous at times, although protective gear and other safety regulations serve to protect workers from injury.

OUTLOOK

Employment for millwrights is expected to grow more slowly than the average for all occupations through 2016, according to the U.S. Department of Labor. New automation, the introduction of new, labor-saving technologies, limited growth in industrial construction, and the use of lower paid workers for installation and maintenance of machinery are contributing to this slow growth.

However, millwrights will still be needed to keep existing machinery in working order, dismantle outdated machinery, and install new equipment. Many openings will arise each year as experienced workers transfer to other jobs or retire.

FOR MORE INFORMATION

For information about training and education programs, as well as legislative issues affecting the construction industry, contact

Associated General Contractors of America
2300 Wilson Boulevard, Suite 400
Arlington, VA 22201-3308
Tel: 703-548-3118
Email: info@agc.org
http://agc.org

For information on union membership, contact the following organizations:

International Association of Machinists and Aerospace Workers
9000 Machinists Place
Upper Marlboro, MD 20772-2687
Tel: 301-967-4500
http://www.iamaw.org/

International Union, United Automobile, Aerospace, and Agricultural Implement Workers of America
Solidarity House
8000 East Jefferson Avenue
Detroit, MI 48214-2699
Tel: 313-926-5000
http://www.uaw.org

For information on available publications, conventions and seminars, contact

National Tooling & Machining Association
9300 Livingston Road
Fort Washington, MD 20744-4998
Tel: 800-248-6862
Email: info@ntma.org
http://www.ntma.org

To learn about apprenticeships and training programs and the benefits of union membership, visit the following Web site:

United Brotherhood of Carpenters and Joiners of America
101 Constitution Avenue, NW
Washington, DC 20001-2192
Tel: 202-546-6206
http://www.carpenters.org

MUSICAL INSTRUMENT REPAIRERS AND TUNERS

OVERVIEW

Musical instrument repairers and tuners work on a variety of instruments, often operating inside music shops or repair shops to keep the pieces in tune and in proper condition. Those who specialize in working on pianos or pipe organs may travel to the instrument's location to work. Instrument repairers and tuners usually specialize in certain families of musical instruments, such as stringed or brass instruments. Depending on the instrument, they may be skilled in working with wood, metal, electronics, or other materials. There are approximately 6,000 music instrument repairers and tuners employed in the United States.

HISTORY

The world's first musical instrument was the human body. Paleolithic dancers clapped, stamped, chanted, and slapped their bodies to mark rhythm. Gourd rattles, bone whistles, scrapers, hollow branch, and conch shell trumpets, wooden rhythm pounders and knockers, and bull-roarers followed. By the early Neolithic times, people had developed drums that produced two or more pitches and pottery and cane flutes that gave several notes. The musical bow, a primitive stringed instrument and forerunner of the jaw harp, preceded the bow-shaped harp (about 3000 B.C.) and the long-necked lute (about 2000 B.C.).

The history of the pipe organ stretches back to the third century B.C., when the Egyptians developed an organ that used waterpower to produce a stream of air. A few centuries later, organs appeared in Byzantium that used bellows (a device that draws air in and then expels it with great force) to send air through the organ pipes. From that time until about 1500 A.D., all the features of the modern pipe organ were developed.

The first version of the violin, played by scraping a taut bow across several stretched strings, appeared in Europe around 1510. The end of the 16th century saw the development of the violin as it is known today. Over the next 100 years, violin making reached its greatest achievements in the area around Cremona, Italy, where families of master craftsmen, such as the Stradivaris, the Guarneris, and the Amatis, set a standard for quality that never has been surpassed. Today, their violins are coveted by players around the world for their tonal quality.

The modern piano is the end product of a gradual evolution from plucked string instruments, such as the harp, to instruments employing hammers of one kind or another to produce notes by striking the strings. By the late 1700s, the immediate ancestor of the modern piano had been developed. Improvements and modifications (most involving new materials or manufacturing processes) took place throughout the 19th century, resulting in today's piano.

In addition to the stringed instruments, contemporary orchestral instruments also include the woodwind, brass, and percussion families. Woodwinds include the flute,

QUICK FACTS

SCHOOL SUBJECTS
Music
Technical/shop

PERSONAL SKILLS
Artistic
Mechanical/manipulative

WORK ENVIRONMENT
Primarily indoors
One location with some travel

MINIMUM EDUCATION LEVEL
Some postsecondary training

MEDIAN SALARY
$29,200

CERTIFICATION OR LICENSING
Voluntary

OUTLOOK
More slowly than the average

clarinet, oboe, bassoon, and saxophone. Brass instruments include the French horn, trumpet, cornet, trombone, and tuba. All require some professional care and maintenance at some time. The modern electronic organ is a descendent of the pipe organ. In 1934, Laurens Hammond, an American inventor, patented the first practical electronic organ, an instrument that imitates the sound of the pipe organ but requires much less space and is more economical and practical to own and operate. The development of electronic and computer technology produced the first synthesizers and synthesized instruments, which are used widely today.

THE JOB

All but the most heavily damaged instruments usually can be repaired by competent, experienced craftsworkers. In addition, instruments require regular maintenance and inspection to ensure that they play properly and to prevent small problems from becoming major ones.

Stringed-instrument repairers perform extremely detailed and difficult work. The repair of violins, violas, and cellos might be considered the finest woodworking done in the world today. Because their sound quality is so beautiful, some older, rarer violins are worth millions of dollars, and musicians will sometimes fly halfway around the world to have rare instruments repaired by *master restorers*. In many ways, the work of these master craftspeople may be compared to the restoration of fine art masterpieces.

When a violin or other valuable stringed instrument needs repair, its owner takes the instrument to a repair shop, which may employ many repairers. If the violin has cracks in its body, it must be taken apart. The pieces of a violin are held together by a special glue that allows the instrument to be dismantled easily for repair purposes. The glue, which is made from hides and bones and has been used for more than 400 years, is sturdy but does not bond permanently with the wood.

To repair a crack in the back of a violin, the repairer first pops the back off the instrument. After cleaning the crack with warm water, the repairer glues the crack and attaches cleats or studs above the crack on the inside to prevent further splitting. The repairer reassembles the violin and closes the outside of the crack with fill varnish. Lastly, the repairer treats the crack scrupulously with retouching varnish so that it becomes invisible.

The repairer does not complete every step immediately after the previous one. Depending on the age and value of the instrument, a repair job can take three weeks or longer. Glues and varnishes need to set, and highly detailed work demands much concentration. The repairer also needs to do research to isolate the original type of varnish on the instrument and match it precisely with modern materials. The repairer usually has more than one repair job going at any one time.

A major restoration, such as the replacement of old patchwork or the fitting of inside patches to support the instrument, requires even more time. A large project can take two years or longer. A master restorer can put 2,000 or more hours into the repair of a valuable violin that has nothing more than a few cracks in its finish. Since many fine instruments are worth $2 million or more, they need intense work to preserve the superior quality of their sound. The repairer cannot rush the work, must concentrate on every detail, and complete the repair properly or risk other problems later on.

While all instruments are not made by Stradivari, they still need to be kept in good condition to be played well. Owners bring in their violins, violas, and cellos to the repair shop every season for cleaning, inspecting

joints, and gluing gaps. The work involves tools similar to woodworker's tools, such as carving knives, planes, and gouges. The violin repairer will often need to play the instrument to check its condition and tune it. Bow rehairers maintain the quality of the taut, vibrating horsehair string that is stretched from end to end of the resilient wooden bow.

Wind-instrument repairers require a similar level of skill to that required of stringed-instrument repairers. However, as the quality of sound is more standard among manufacturers, old instruments do not necessarily play any better than new ones, and these instruments do not command the same value as a fine violin.

The repairer first needs to determine the extent of repairs that the instrument warrants. The process may range from a few minor repairs to bring the instrument up to playing condition to a complete overhaul. After fixing the instrument, the repairer also will clean both the inside and outside and may replate the metal finish on a scuffed or rusty instrument.

For woodwinds such as clarinets and oboes, common repairs include fixing or replacing the moving parts of the instrument, including replacing broken keys with new keys, cutting new padding or corks to replace worn pieces, and replacing springs. If the body of the woodwind is cracked in any sections, the repairer will take the instrument apart and attempt to pin or glue the crack shut. In some situations, the repairer will replace the entire section or joint of the instrument.

Repairing brass instruments such as trumpets and French horns requires skill in metal working and plating. The pieces of these instruments are held together by solder, which the repairer must heat and remove to take the instrument apart for repair work. To fix dents, the repairer will unsolder the piece and work the dent out with hammers and more delicate tools and seal splits in the metal with solder as well. A final buffing and polishing usually removes any evidence of the repair.

If one of the valves of the brass instrument is leaking, the repairer may replate it and build up layers of metal to fill the gaps. At times, the repairer will replace a badly damaged valve with a new valve from the instrument manufacturer, but often the owner will discard the entire instrument because the cost of making a new valve from raw materials is prohibitive. Replacement parts are usually available from the manufacturer, but parts for older instruments are sometimes difficult or impossible to find. For this reason, many repairers save and stockpile discarded instruments for their parts.

Piano technicians and *piano tuners* repair and tune pianos so that when a key is struck it will produce its correctly pitched note of the musical scale. A piano may go out of tune for a variety of reasons, including strings that have stretched or tightened from age, temperature change, relocation, or through use. Tuners use a special wrench to adjust the pins that control the tension on the strings. Piano tuners usually are specially trained for such work, but piano technicians may also perform tuning in connection with a more thorough inspection or overhaul of an instrument.

A piano's performance is also affected by problems in any of the thousands of moving parts of the action or by problems in the sounding board or the frame holding the strings. These are problems that the technician is trained to analyze and correct. They may involve replacing or repairing parts or making adjustments that enable the existing parts to function more smoothly.

The life of a piano—that is, the period of time before it can no longer be properly tuned or adjusted to correct operational problems—is usually estimated at 20 years. Because the harp and strong outer wooden frame are seldom damaged, technicians often rebuild pianos by replacing the sounding board and strings, refurbishing and replacing parts where necessary, and refinishing the outer case.

In all their work, from tuning to rebuilding, piano technicians discover a piano's problems by talking to the owner and playing the instrument themselves. They may dismantle a piano partially on-site to determine the amount of wear to its parts and look for broken parts. They use common hand tools such as hammers, screwdrivers, and pliers. To repair and rebuild pianos, they use a variety of specialized tools for stringing and setting pins.

For *pipe organ technicians*, the largest part of the job is repairing and maintaining existing organs. This primarily involves tuning the pipes, which can be time consuming, even in a moderate-sized organ.

To tune a flue pipe, the technician moves a slide that increases or decreases the length of the speaking (note-producing) part of the pipe, varying its pitch. The technician tunes a reed pipe by varying the length of the brass reed inside the pipe.

To tune an organ, the technician tunes either the A or C pipes by matching their notes with those of a tuning fork or electronic note-producing device. He or she then tunes the other pipes in harmony with the A or C notes. This may require a day or more for a moderate-sized organ and much longer for a giant concert organ.

Pipe organ technicians also diagnose, locate, and correct problems in the operating parts of the organ and perform preventive maintenance on a regular basis. To do this, they work with electric wind-generating equipment and with slides, valves, keys, air channels, and other equipment that enables the organist to produce the desired music.

Occasionally, a new organ is installed in a new or existing structure. Manufacturers design and install the largest organs. Each is unique, and the designer carefully supervises its construction and installation. Often, designers individually create moderate-sized organs specifically for the structure, usually churches, in which they will be played. Technicians follow the designer's blueprints closely during installation. The work involves assembling and connecting premanufactured components, using a variety of hand and power tools. Technicians may work in teams, especially when installing the largest pipes of the organ.

Although the electronic organ imitates the sound of the pipe organ, the workings of the two instruments have little in common. The electronic organ consists of electrical and electronic components and circuits that channel electrical current through various oscillators and amplifiers to produce sound when a player presses each key. It is rare for an oscillator or other component to need adjustment in the way an organ pipe needs to be adjusted to tune it. A technician tunes an electronic organ by testing it for electronic malfunction and replacing or repairing the component, circuit board, or wire.

The work of the *electronic organ technician* is closer to that of the television repair technician than it is to that of the pipe organ technician. The technician often begins looking for the source of a problem by checking for loose wires and solder connections. After making routine checks, technicians consult wiring diagrams that enable them to trace and test the circuits of the entire instrument to find malfunctions. For instance, an unusual or irregular voltage in a circuit may indicate a problem. Once the problem has been located, the technician often solves it by replacing a malfunctioning part, such as a circuit board.

These technicians work with common electrician's tools: pliers, wire cutters, screwdriver, soldering iron, and testing equipment. Technicians can make most repairs and adjustments in the customer's home. Because each manufacturer's instruments are arranged differently, technicians follow manufacturers' wiring diagrams and service manuals to locate trouble spots and make repairs. In larger and more complex instruments, such as those in churches and theaters, this may require a day or more of searching and testing.

Other types of repairers work on a variety of less common instruments. Percussion tuners and repairers work on drums, bells, congas, timbales, cymbals, and castanets. They may stretch new skins over the instrument, replace broken or missing parts, or seal cracks in the wood.

Accordion tuners and repairers work on free-reed portable accordions, piano accordions, concertinas, harmoniums, and harmonicas. They repair leaks in the bellows of an instrument, replace broken or damaged reeds, and perform various maintenance tasks. Other specialists in instrument repair include fretted-instrument repairers, harp regulators, trombone-slide assemblers, metal-reed tuners, tone regulators, and chip tuners.

Some musical repairers work as *musical instrument designers and builders.* They work in musical instrument factories or as freelancers designing and building instruments in their own workshops. Almost any type of instrument can be designed and built, but musical instrument builders most often craft guitars, banjos, violins, and flutes.

In addition to repairing, designing, or building instruments, those who run their own shops perform duties similar to others in the retail business. They order stock from instrument manufacturers, wait on customers, handle their accounting and billing work, and perform other duties.

REQUIREMENTS
High School

No matter what family of instruments interests you, you should start preparing for this field by gaining a basic knowledge of music. Take high school classes in music history, music theory, and choir, chorus, or other singing classes. By learning to read music, developing an ear for scales, and understanding tones and pitches, you will be developing an excellent background for this work. Also, explore your interest in instruments (besides your own voice) by taking band or orchestra classes or private music lessons. By learning how to play an instrument, you will also learn how a properly tuned and maintained instrument should sound. If you find yourself interested in instruments with metal parts, consider taking art or shop classes that provide the opportunity to do metal working. These classes will allow you to practice soldering and work with appropriate tools. If you are interested in piano or stringed instruments, consider taking art or shop classes that offer woodworking. In these classes, you will learn finishing techniques and use tools that you may relate to the building and maintaining of the bodies of these instruments.

Because instrument repair of any type is precision work, you will benefit from taking mathematics classes such as algebra and geometry. Since many instrument repairers and tuners are self-employed, take business or accounting classes to prepare for this possibility. Finally, take English classes to develop your research, reading, and communication skills. You will often need to consult technical instruction manuals for repair and maintenance work. You will also need strong communication skills that will help you broaden your client base as well as help you explain to your clients what work needs to be done.

Postsecondary Training

There are two main routes to becoming a music instrument repairer and tuner: extensive apprenticeship or formal education through technical or vocational schools. Apprenticeships, however, can be difficult to find. You will simply need to contact instrument repair shops and request a position as a trainee. Once you have found a position, the training period may last from two to five years. You will get hands-on experience in working with the instruments as well as by having other duties around the shop, such as selling any products offered.

Depending on the family of instruments you want to work with, there are a number of technical or vocational schools that offer either courses or full-time programs in repair and maintenance work. Professional organizations may have information on such schools. The National Association of Professional Band Instrument Repair Technicians, for example, provides a listing of schools offering programs in band instrument repair. The Piano Technicians Guild has information on both full-time programs and correspondence courses. Wind-instrument repairers can learn their craft at one of the handful of vocational schools in the country that offers classes in instrument repair. Entrance requirements vary among schools, but all require at least a high school diploma or GED. Typical classes that are part of any type of instrument repair and tuning education include acoustics, tool care and operation, and small business practices. Depending on what instrument you choose to specialize in, you may also study topics such as buffing, dent removal, plating, soldering, or woodworking. You may also be required to invest in personal hand tools and supplies, and you may need to make tools that are not available from suppliers.

If you are interested in working with electronic organs, you will need at least one year of electronics technical training to learn organ repair skills. Electronics training is available from community colleges and technical and vocational schools. The U.S. Armed Forces also offer excellent training in electronics, which you can apply to instrument work. Electronic organ technicians also may attend training courses offered by electronic organ manufacturers.

It is important to keep in mind that even those who take courses or attend school for their postsecondary training will need to spend years honing their skills.

A number of instrument repairers and tuners have completed some college work or have a bachelor's degree. Although no colleges award bachelor's degrees in instrument repair, people who major in some type of music performance may find this background adds to their understanding of the work.

Certification or Licensing

The Piano Technicians Guild helps its members improve their skills and keep up with developments in piano technology. Local chapters offer refresher courses and seminars in new developments, and courses offered by manufacturers are publicized in guild publications. The guild also administers a series of tests that can lead to certification as a registered piano technician.

Other Requirements

Personal qualifications for people in this occupational group include keen hearing and eyesight, mechanical aptitude, and manual dexterity. You should be resourceful and able to learn on the job, because every instrument that needs repair is unique and requires individual care. You must also have the desire to learn throughout your professional life by studying trade magazines and manufacturers' service manuals related to new developments in their field. You can also improve your skills in training programs and at regional and national seminars. Instrument manufacturers often offer training in the repair of their particular products.

Other qualifications for this career relate to your instrument specialty. For example, if you want to work as a piano technician, you should be able to communicate clearly when talking about a piano's problems and when advising a customer. A pleasant manner and good appearance are important to instill confidence. While the physical strength required for moving a piano is not often needed, you may be required to bend or stand in awkward positions while working on the piano. If you are interested in working as a pipe organ technician, you will need the ability to follow blueprints and printed instructions to plan and execute repair or installation work.

And any repairer and tuner who works in a store selling musical instruments should be comfortable working with the public.

EXPLORING

One of the best ways to explore this field is to take some type of musical instrument lessons. This experience will help you develop an ear for tonal quality and acquaint you with the care of your instrument. It will also put you in contact with those who work professionally with music. You may develop a contact with someone at the store where you have purchased or rented your instrument, and, naturally, you will get to know your music teacher. Ask these people what they know about the repair and tuning business. Your high school or local college music departments can also be excellent places for meeting those who work with instruments. Ask teachers in these departments whom they know working in instrument repair. You may be able to set up an informational interview with a repairer and tuner you find through these contacts. Ask the repairer about his or her education, how he or she got interested in the work, what he or she would recommend for someone considering the field, and any other questions you may have.

Part-time and summer jobs that are related closely to this occupation may be difficult to obtain because full-time trainees usually handle the routine tasks of a helper. Nevertheless, it is worth applying for such work at music stores and repair shops in case they do not use full-time trainees. General clerical jobs in stores that sell musical instruments may help familiarize you with the language of the field and may offer you the opportunity to observe skilled repairers at work.

EMPLOYERS

Approximately 6,000 people work as musical instrument repairers and tuners of all types in the United States. About one in six are self-employed and may operate out of their own homes. The majority of the rest work in repair shops and music stores and for manufacturers. Large cities with extensive professional music activity, both in the United States and in Europe, are the best places for employment. Musical centers such as Chicago, New York, London, and Vienna are the hubs of the repair business for stringed instruments, and any repairer who wishes a sufficient amount of work may have to relocate to one of these cities.

Some piano technicians work in factories where pianos are made. They may assemble and adjust pianos or inspect the finished instruments. Some technicians work in shops that rebuild pianos. Many piano repairers and tuners work in customers' homes.

Most of the few hundred pipe organ technicians in the United States are self-employed. These pipe organ technicians are primarily engaged in repairing and tuning existing organs. A small number are employed by organ manufacturers and are engaged in testing and installing new instruments. The great expense involved in manufacturing and installing a completely new pipe organ decreases demand and makes this type of work scarce.

STARTING OUT

Vocational schools and community colleges that offer instrument repair training can usually connect recent graduates with repair shops that have job openings. Those who enter the field through apprenticeships work at the local shop where they are receiving their training. Professional organizations may also have information on job openings.

ADVANCEMENT

Repairers and tuners may advance their skills by participating in special training programs. A few who work for large dealers or repair shops may move into supervisory positions. Some instrument repair technicians become instructors in music instrument repair programs at community colleges and technical institutes.

Another path to advancement is to open one's own musical repair shop and service. Before doing this, however, the worker should have adequate training to survive the strong competition that exists in the tuning and repair business. In many cases, repairers may need to continue working for another employer until they develop a clientele large enough to support a full-time business.

A few restorers of stringed instruments earn worldwide reputations for their exceptional skill. Their earnings and the caliber of their customers both rise significantly when they become well known. It takes a great deal of hard work and talent to achieve such professional standing, however, and this recognition only comes after years in the field. At any one time, there may be perhaps 10 restorers in the world who perform exceptional work, while another 100 or so are known for doing very good work. The work of these few craftspeople is always in great demand.

EARNINGS

Wages vary depending on geographic area and the worker's specialty, skill, and speed at making repairs. Full-time instrument repairers and tuners had a median income of $29,200 in 2006, according to the U.S. Bureau of Labor Statistics. The highest paid 10 percent earned $69,280 or more per year, and the lowest paid earned less than $16,230 annually. Some helpers work for the training they get and receive no pay. Repairers and tuners who are self-employed earn more than those who work for music stores or instrument manufacturers, but their income is generally less stable. Repairers who gain an international reputation for the quality of their work earn the highest income in this field.

Repairers and tuners working as employees of manufacturers or stores often receive some benefits, including health insurance, vacation days, and holiday and sick pay. Self-employed repairers and tuners must provide these for themselves.

WORK ENVIRONMENT

Repairers and tuners work in shops, homes, and instrument factories, surrounded by the tools and materials of their trade. The atmosphere is somewhat quiet but the pace is often busy. Since repairers and tuners are usually paid by the piece, they have to concentrate and work diligently on their repairs. Piano technicians and tuners generally perform their work in homes, schools, churches, and other places where pianos are located.

Instrument tuners and repairers may work more than 40 hours a week, especially during the fall and winter, when people spend more time indoors playing musical instruments. Self-employed tuners and repairers often work evenings and weekends, when it is more convenient to meet with customers.

As noted, many repairs demand extreme care and often long periods of time to complete. For large instruments, such as pianos and pipe organs, repairers and tuners may have to work in cramped locations for some length of time, bending, stretching, and using tools that require physical strength to handle. Tuning pianos and organs often requires many hours and can be tedious work.

The field at times may be very competitive, especially among the more prestigious repair shops for stringed instruments. Most people at the major repair shops know each other and vie for the same business. There is often a great deal of pressure from owners to fix their instruments as soon as possible, but a conscientious repairer cannot be rushed into doing a mediocre job. In spite of these drawbacks, repair work is almost always interesting, challenging, and rewarding. Repairers never do the same job twice, and each instrument comes with its own set of challenges. The work requires repairers to call on their ingenuity, skill, and personal pride every day.

OUTLOOK

Job opportunities for musical instrument repairers and tuners are expected to grow more slowly than the average through 2016, according to the U.S. Department of Labor. This is a small, specialized field, and replacement needs will be the source of most jobs. Because training positions and school programs are relatively difficult to find, those with thorough training and education will have the best employment outlook.

It is a luxury for most owners to have their instruments tuned and repaired, and they tend to postpone these services when money is scarce. Tuners and repairers therefore may lose income during economic downturns. In addition, few trainees are hired at repair shops or music stores when business is slow.

FOR MORE INFORMATION

For information on organ and choral music fields, contact

American Guild of Organists
475 Riverside Drive, Suite 1260
New York, NY 10115-0055
Tel: 212-870-2310
Email: info@agohq.org
http://www.agohq.org

The GAL is an international organization of stringed-instrument makers and repairers. Visit the FAQ section of its Web site for information on building and repairing instruments and choosing a training program.

Guild of American Luthiers (GAL)
8222 South Park Avenue
Tacoma, WA 98408-5226
Tel: 253-472-7853
http://www.luth.org

For information about band instrument repair and a list of schools offering courses in the field, contact

National Association of Professional Band Instrument Repair Technicians
PO Box 51
Normal, IL 61761-0051
Tel: 309-452-4257
http://www.napbirt.org

For information on certification, contact

Piano Technicians Guild
4444 Forest Avenue
Kansas City, KS 66106-3750
Tel: 913-432-9975
Email: ptg@ptg.org
http://www.ptg.org

MUSICIANS

OVERVIEW

Musicians perform, compose, conduct, arrange, and teach music. Performing musicians may work alone or as part of a group, or ensemble. They may play before live audiences in clubs or auditoriums, or they may perform on television or radio, in motion pictures, or in a recording studio. Musicians usually play either classical, popular (including rock and country), jazz, or folk music, but many musicians play several musical styles. Musicians, singers, and related workers hold approximately 264,000 jobs in the United States.

THE JOB

Instrumental musicians play one or more musical instruments, usually in a group and in some cases as featured soloists. Musical instruments are usually classified in several distinct categories according to the method by which they produce sound: strings (e.g., violins, cellos, basses), which make sounds by vibrations from bowing or plucking; woodwinds (e.g., oboes, clarinets, saxophones), which make sounds by air vibrations through reeds; brass (e.g., trumpets, French horns, trombones), which make sounds by air vibrations through metal; and percussion (e.g., drums, pianos, triangles), which produce sounds by striking. Instruments can also be classified as electric or acoustic, especially in popular music. Synthesizers are another common instrument, and computer and other electronic technology are increasingly used for creating music.

Like other instrumental musicians, *singers* use their own voice as an instrument to convey music. They aim to express emotion through lyric phrasing and characterization.

Musicians may play in symphony orchestras, dance bands, jazz bands, rock bands, country bands, or other groups, or they might go it alone. Some musicians may play in recording studios either with their group or as a session player for a particular recording. Recordings are in the form of records, tapes, compact discs, videotape cassettes, and digital video discs. *Classical musicians* perform in concerts, opera performances, and chamber music concerts, and they may also play in theater orchestras, although theater music is not normally classical. The most talented ones may work as soloists with orchestras or alone in recitals. Some classical musicians accompany singers and choirs, and they may also perform in churches, temples, and other religious settings.

QUICK FACTS

SCHOOL SUBJECTS
English
Music

PERSONAL SKILLS
Artistic
Communication/ideas

WORK ENVIRONMENT
Indoors and outdoors
Primarily multiple locations

MINIMUM EDUCATION LEVEL
High school diploma

MEDIAN SALARY
$41,038

CERTIFICATION OR LICENSING
Required for certain positions

OUTLOOK
About as fast as the average

Musicians who play popular music make heavy use of such rhythm instruments as piano, bass, drums, and guitar. *Jazz musicians* also feature woodwind and brass instruments, especially the saxophone and trumpet, and they extensively utilize the bass. Synthesizers are also commonly used jazz instruments; some music is performed entirely on synthesizers, which can be programmed to imitate a variety of instruments and sounds. Musicians in jazz, blues, country, and rock groups play clubs, festivals, and concert halls and may perform music for recordings, television, and motion picture soundtracks. Occasionally, they appear in a movie themselves. Other musicians compose, record, and perform entirely with electronic instruments, such as synthesizers and other devices. In the late 1970s, rap artists began using turntables as musical instruments, and later, samplers, which record a snippet of other songs and sounds, as part of their music.

Instrumental musicians and singers use their skills to convey the form and meaning of written music. They work to achieve precision, fluency, and emotion within a piece of music, whether through an instrument or through their own voice. Musicians practice constantly to perfect their techniques.

Many musicians supplement their incomes through teaching; others teach as their full-time occupation, perhaps playing jobs occasionally. *Voice and instrumental music teachers* work in colleges, high schools, elementary schools, conservatories, and in their own studios; often they give concerts and recitals featuring their students. Many professional musicians give private lessons. Students learn to read music, develop their voices, breathe correctly, and hold their instruments properly.

Choral directors lead groups of singers in schools and other organizations. Church choirs, community oratorio societies, and professional symphony choruses are among the groups that employ choral directors outside of school settings. Choral directors audition singers, select music, and direct singers in achieving the tone, variety, intensity, and phrasing that they feel is required. *Orchestra conductors* do the same with instrumental musicians. Many work in schools and smaller communities, but the best conduct large orchestras in major cities. Some are resident instructors, while others travel constantly, making guest appearances with major national and foreign orchestras. They are responsible for the overall sound and quality of their orchestras.

Individuals also write and prepare music for themselves or other musicians to play and sing. *Composers* write the original music for symphonies, songs, or operas using musical notation to express their ideas through melody, rhythm, and harmony. *Arrangers* and *orchestrators* take a composer's work and transcribe it for the various orchestra sections or individual instrumentalists and singers to perform; they prepare music for film scores, musical theater, television, or recordings. *Copyists* assist composers and arrangers by copying down the various parts of a composition, each of which is played by a different section of the orchestra. *Librettists* write words to opera and musical theater scores, and lyricists write words to songs and other short musical pieces. A number of songwriters compose both music and lyrics, and many are musicians who perform their own songs.

REQUIREMENTS

High School

If you are interested in becoming a musician, you will probably have begun to develop your musical skills long before you entered high school. While you are in high school, however, there are a number of classes you can take that will help you broaden your knowledge. Naturally, take band, orchestra, or choir classes depending on your interest. In addition, you should also take mathematics classes, since any musician needs to understand counting, rhythms, and beats. Many professional musicians write at least some of their own music, and a strong math background is very helpful for this. If your high school offers courses in music history or appreciation, be sure to take these. Finally, take classes that will improve your communication skills and your understanding of people and emotions, such as English and psychology. If you are interested in working in the classical music field, you will most likely need a college degree to succeed in this area. Therefore, be sure to round out your high school education by taking other college preparatory classes. Finally, no matter what type of musician you want to be, you will need to devote much of your after-school time to your private study and practice of music.

Postsecondary Training

Depending on your interest, especially if it is popular music, further formal education is not required. College or conservatory degrees are only required for those who plan to teach in institutions. Nevertheless, you will only benefit from continued education.

Scores of colleges and universities have excellent music schools, and there are numerous conservatories that offer degrees in music. Many schools have noted musicians on their staff, and music students often have the advantage of studying under a professor who has a distinguished career in music. By studying with someone like this, you will not only learn more about music and performance, but you will also begin to make valuable connections in the field. You should know that having talent and a high grade point average do not always ensure entry into the top music schools. Competition for positions is extremely tough. You will probably have to audition, and only the most talented are accepted.

College undergraduates in music school generally take courses in music theory, harmony, counterpoint, rhythm, melody, ear training, applied music, and music history. Courses in composing, arranging, and conducting are available in most comprehensive music schools. Students will also have to take courses such as English and psychology along with a regular academic program.

Certification or Licensing

Musicians who want to teach in state elementary and high schools must be state certified. To obtain a state cer-

tificate, musicians must satisfactorily complete a degree-granting course in music education at an institution of higher learning. About 600 institutions in the United States offer programs in music education that qualify students for state certificates. Music education programs include many of the same courses mentioned earlier for musicians in general. They also include education courses and supervised practice teaching. To teach in colleges and universities or in conservatories generally requires a graduate degree in music. Widely recognized musicians, however, sometimes receive positions in higher education without having obtained a degree.

The American Guild of Organists offers a number of voluntary, professional certifications to its members. Visit the guild's Web site (http://www.agohq.org) for more information.

Other Requirements

Hard work and dedication are key factors in a musical career, but music is an art form, and like those who practice any of the fine arts, musicians will succeed according to the amount of musical talent they have. Those who have talent and are willing to make sacrifices to develop it are the ones most likely to succeed. How much talent and ability one has is always open to speculation and opinion, and it may take years of studying and practice before musicians can assess their own degree of limitation.

There are other requirements necessary to becoming a professional musician that are just as important as training, education, and study. Foremost among these is a love of music strong enough to endure the arduous training and working life of a musician. To become an accomplished musician and to be recognized in the field requires an uncommon degree of dedication, self-discipline, and drive. Musicians who would move ahead must practice constantly with a determination to improve their technique and quality of performance. Musicians also need to develop an emotional toughness that will help them deal with rejection, indifference to their work, and ridicule from critics, which will be especially prevalent early in their careers. There is also praise and adulation along the way, which is easier to take, but also requires a certain psychological handling.

For musicians interested in careers in popular music, little to no formal training is necessary. Many popular musicians teach themselves to play their instruments, which often results in the creation of new and exciting playing styles. Quite often, popular musicians do not even know how to read music. Some would say that many rock musicians do not even know how to play their instruments. This was especially true in the early days of the punk era (c. late 1970s–early 1980s). Most musicians, however, have a natural talent for rhythm and melody.

Many musicians often go through years of paying their dues—that is, receiving little money, respect, or attention for their efforts. Therefore, they must have a strong sense of commitment to their careers and to their creative ideas.

Professional musicians generally hold membership in the American Federation of Musicians (AFL-CIO), and concert soloists also hold membership in the American Guild of Musical Artists (AFL-CIO). Singers can belong to a branch of Associated Actors and Artists of America (AFL-CIO). Music teachers in schools often hold membership in MENC: The National Association for Music Education (formerly Music Educators National Conference).

EXPLORING

The first step to exploring your interest in a musical career is to become involved with music. Elementary schools, high schools, and institutions of higher education all present a number of options for musical training and performance, including choirs, ensembles, bands, and orchestras. You may also have chances to perform in school musicals and talent shows. Those involved with services at churches, synagogues, or other religious institutions have excellent opportunities for exploring their interest in music. If you can afford to, take private music lessons.

Besides learning more about music, you will most likely have the chance to play in recitals arranged by your teacher. You may also want to attend special summer camps or programs that focus on the field. Interlochen Center for the Arts (http://www.interlochen.org), for example, offers summer camps for students from the elementary to the high school level. College, university, and conservatory students gain valuable performance experience by appearing in recitals and playing in bands, orchestras, and school shows. The more enterprising students in high school and in college form their own bands and begin earning money by playing while still in school.

It is important for you to take advantage of every opportunity to audition so that you become comfortable with this process. There are numerous community amateur and semiprofessional theater groups throughout the United States that produce musical plays and operettas, in which beginning musicians can gain playing experience.

EMPLOYERS

Most musicians work in large urban areas and are particularly drawn to the major recording centers, such as Chicago, New York City, Los Angeles, Nashville, and Miami Beach. Many find work in churches, temples, schools, clubs, restaurants, and cruise lines, at weddings, in opera and ballet productions, and on film, television, and radio. Religious organizations are the largest single source of work for musicians.

Full-time positions as a musician in a choir, symphony orchestra, or band are few and are held only by the most talented. Musicians who are versatile and willing to work hard will find a variety of opportunities available, but all musicians should understand that work is not likely to be steady or provide much security. Many musicians support themselves in another line of work while pursuing their musical careers on a part-time basis. Busy musicians often hire agents to find employers and negotiate contracts or conditions of employment.

STARTING OUT

Young musicians need to get involved in as many playing situations as they can in their school and community musical groups. They should audition as often as possible, because experience at auditioning is very important. Whenever possible, they should take part in seminars and internships offered by orchestras, colleges, and associations. The National Orchestral Association (http://www.nationalorchestral.org) offers training programs for musicians who want a career in the orchestral field.

Musicians who want to perform with established groups, such as choirs and symphony orchestras, enter the field by auditioning. Recommendations from teachers and other musicians often help would-be musicians obtain the opportunity to audition. Concert and opera soloists are also required to audition. Musicians must prepare themselves thoroughly for these auditions, which are demanding and stressful. A bad audition can be very discouraging for the young musician.

Popular musicians often begin playing at low-paying social functions and at small clubs or restaurants. If people like their performances, they usually move on to bookings at larger rooms in better clubs. Continued success leads to a national reputation and possible recording contracts. Jazz musicians tend to operate in the same way, taking every opportunity to audition with established jazz musicians.

Music teachers enter the field by applying directly to schools. College and university placement offices often have listings of positions. Professional associations frequently list teaching openings in their newsletters and journals, as do newspapers. Music-oriented journals—such as the American Federation of Musicians' journal *International Musician* (http://www.afm.org/resources/international-musician)—are excellent sources to check for job listings.

ADVANCEMENT

Popular musicians, once they have become established with a band, advance by moving up to more famous bands or by taking leadership of their own group. Bands may advance from playing small clubs to larger halls and even stadiums and festivals. They may receive a recording contract; if their songs or recordings prove successful, they can command higher fees for their contracts. Symphony orchestra musicians advance by moving to the head of their section of the orchestra. They can also move up to a position such as assistant or associate conductor. Once instrumental musicians acquire a reputation as accomplished artists, they receive engagements that are of higher status and remuneration, and they may come into demand as soloists. As their reputations develop, both classical and popular musicians may receive attractive offers to make recordings and personal appearances.

Popular and opera singers move up to better and more lucrative jobs through recognition of their talent by the public or by music producers and directors and agents. Their advancement is directly related to the demand for their talent and their own ability to promote themselves.

Music teachers in elementary and secondary schools may, with further training, aspire to careers as supervisors of music of a school system, a school district, or an entire state. With further graduate training, teachers can qualify for positions in colleges, universities, and music conservatories, where they can advance to become department heads. Well-known musicians can become artists-in-residence in the music departments of institutions of higher learning.

EARNINGS

It is difficult to estimate the earnings of the average musician, because what a musician earns is dependent upon his or her skill, reputation, geographic location, type of music, and number of engagements per year.

According to the American Federation of Musicians, musicians in the major U.S. symphony orchestras earned salaries of between $16,800 and $108,160 during the 2004–05 performance season. The season for these major orchestras, generally located in the largest U.S. cities, ranges from 24 to 52 weeks. Featured musicians and soloists can earn much more, especially those with an international reputation. According to the U.S. Department of Labor, median annual earnings of musicians, singers, and related workers were $19.73 per hour or $41,038 in 2006. The lowest paid 10 percent earned $7.08 per hour or about $14,726 annually, while the highest paid 10 percent earned $57.37 per hour or $119,330 annually.

Popular musicians are usually paid per concert or gig. A band just starting out playing a small bar or club may be required to play three sets a night, and each musician may receive next to nothing for the entire evening. Often, bands receive a percentage of the cover charge at the door. Some musicians play for drinks alone. On average, however, pay per musician ranges from $30 to $300 or more per night. Bands that have gained recognition and a following may earn far more, because a club owner can usually be assured that many people will come to see the band play. The most successful popular musicians, of course, can earn millions of dollars each year. By the end of the 1990s, some artists, in fact, had signed recording contracts worth $20 million or more.

Musicians are well paid for studio recording work, when they can get it. For recording film and television background music, musicians are paid a minimum of about $185 for a three-hour session; for record company recordings they receive a minimum of about $235 for three hours. Instrumentalists performing live earn anywhere from $30 to $300 per engagement, depending on their degree of popularity, talent, and the size of the room they play.

The salaries received by music teachers in public elementary and secondary schools are the same as for other teachers. According to the U.S. Department of Labor, public elementary and high school teachers had median yearly earnings of $43,580 and $48,690, respectively, in 2006. Music teachers in colleges and universities have widely ranging salaries. Most teachers supplement their incomes through private instruction and by performing in their off hours.

Most musicians do not, as a rule, work steadily for one employer, and they often undergo long periods of unemployment between engagements. Because of these factors, few musicians can qualify for unemployment compensation. Unlike other workers, most musicians also do not enjoy such benefits as sick leave or paid vacations. Some musicians, on the other hand, who work under contractual agreements, do receive benefits, which usually have been negotiated by artists unions, such as the American Federation of Musicians.

WORK ENVIRONMENT

Work conditions for musicians vary greatly. Performing musicians generally work in the evenings and on weekends. They also spend much time practicing and rehearsing for performances. Their workplace can be almost anywhere, from a swanky club to a high school gymnasium to a dark, dingy bar. Many concerts are given outdoors and in a variety of weather conditions. Performers may be given a star's dressing room, share a mirror in a church basement, or have to change in a bar's storeroom. They may work under the hot camera lights of film or television sets or tour with a troupe in subzero temperatures. They may work amid the noise and confusion of a large rehearsal of a Broadway show or in the relative peace and quiet of a small recording studio. Seldom are two days in a performer's life alike.

Many musicians and singers travel a great deal. More prominent musicians may travel with staffs that make their arrangements and take care of wardrobes and equipment. Their accommodations are usually quite comfortable, if not luxurious, and they generally play in major urban centers. Lesser known musicians may have to take care of all their own arrangements and put up with modest accommodations in relatively remote places. Some musicians perform on the streets, at subway or bus stations, and other places likely to have a great deal of passersby. Symphony orchestra musicians probably travel less than most, but musicians in major orchestras usually travel first class.

The chief characteristic of musical employment is its lack of continuity. Few musicians work full time and most experience periods of unemployment between engagements. Most work other jobs to supplement their music or performing incomes. Those who are in great demand generally have agents and managers to help direct their careers.

Music teachers affiliated with institutions work the same hours as other classroom teachers. Many of these teachers, however, spend time after school and on weekends directing and instructing school vocal and instrumental groups. Teachers may also have varied working conditions. They may teach in a large urban school, conducting five different choruses each day, or they may work in several rural elementary schools and spend much time driving from school to school.

College or university instructors may divide their time between group and individual instruction. They may teach several musical subjects and may be involved with planning and producing school musical events. They may also supervise student music teachers when they do their practice teaching.

Private music teachers work part or full time out of their own homes or in separate studios. The ambiance of their workplace would be in accordance with the size and nature of their clientele.

OUTLOOK

It is difficult to make a living solely as a musician, and this will continue because competition for jobs will be as intense as it has been in the past. Most musicians must hold down other jobs while pursuing their music careers. Thousands of musicians are all trying to make it in the music industry. Musicians are advised to be as versatile as possible, playing various kinds of music and more than one instrument. More importantly, they must be committed to pursuing their craft.

The U.S. Department of Labor predicts that employment of musicians will grow about as fast as the average through 2016. Slower-than-average growth is predicted for self-employed musicians. The demand for musicians will be greatest in theaters and restaurants as the public continues to spend more money on recreational activities. The outlook is favorable in churches and other religious organizations. The increasing numbers of cable television networks and new television programs will likely cause an increase in employment for musicians. Digital recording technology has also made it easier and less expensive for musicians to produce and distribute their own recordings. Few musicians, however, will earn substantial incomes from these efforts. Popular musicians may receive many short-term engagements in nightclubs, restaurants, and theaters, but these engagements offer little job stability. The supply of musicians for virtually all types of music will continue to exceed the demand for the foreseeable future.

FOR MORE INFORMATION

For information on membership in a local union nearest you, developments in the music field, a searchable database of U.S. and foreign music schools, and articles on careers in music, visit the following Web site:

American Federation of Musicians
1501 Broadway, Suite 600
New York, NY 10036-5505
Tel: 212-869-1330
http://www.afm.org

The AGMA is a union for professional musicians. Its Web site has information on upcoming auditions, news announcements for the field, and membership information.

American Guild of Musical Artists (AGMA)
1430 Broadway, 14th Floor
New York, NY 10018-3308

Tel: 212-265-3687
Email: AGMA@MusicalArtists.org
http://musicalartists.org

For information on voluntary certifications, contact
American Guild of Organists
475 Riverside Drive, Suite 1260
New York, NY 10115-1260
Tel: 212-870-2310
Email: info@agohq.org
http://www.agohq.org

For information on the music summer camps program, contact
Interlochen Center for the Arts
PO Box 199
Interlochen, MI 49643-0199
Tel: 231-276-7200
Email: admissions@interlochen.org
http://www.interlochen.org

This organization supports public outreach programs, promotes music education, and offers information on the career of music teacher.
MENC: The National Association for Music Education
1806 Robert Fulton Drive
Reston, VA 20191-5462
Tel: 800-336-3768
http://www.menc.org

For information on membership, competitions for music students, and resources for music teachers, contact
Music Teachers National Association
441 Vine Street, Suite 505
Cincinnati, OH 45202-2811
Tel: 888-512-5278
http://www.mtna.org

NASM is an association of music schools, colleges, and universities. Visit the Web site for a listing of NASM-accredited institutions.
National Association of Schools of Music (NASM)
11250 Roger Bacon Drive, Suite 21
Reston, VA 20190-5248
Tel: 703-437-0700
Email: info@arts-accredit.org
http://nasm.arts-accredit.org

This organization offers networking opportunities, career information, and a mentoring program for women in music.

Women In Music—National Network
1450 Oddstad Drive
Redwood City, CA 94063-2607
Tel: 866-305-7963
Email: info@womeninmusic.com
http://www.womeninmusic.com

NANNIES

OVERVIEW

Nannies, also known as *au pairs*, are caregivers who care for children in the parents' homes. The children usually range in age from infant to 10 or 12 years old. The nanny's responsibilities may include supervising the nursery, organizing play activities, taking the children to appointments or classes, and keeping the children's quarters clean and intact. They may be responsible for supervising the child part of the day or the entire day.

In a large and growing percentage of American families, both parents hold full-time jobs and require full-time child care, which has resulted in increased employment opportunities for nannies. In many other families, parents are opting for part-time work or running businesses out of their homes. Although this allows the parents to be with their children more than if they worked a traditional job, the unpredictability of children's needs makes a nanny's help welcome. A growing segment of parents prefer that their children be cared for at home as opposed to taking them to day care or a babysitter. Thus, the nanny has become a viable and often satisfactory solution.

THE JOB

Nannies perform their child care duties in the homes of the families that employ them. Unlike other kinds of household help, nannies are specifically concerned with the needs of the children in their charge. Nannies prepare the children's meals, making sure they are nutritious, appealing, and appetizing. They may do grocery shopping specifically for the children. Nannies may attend to the children during their mealtimes and oversee their training in table manners and proper etiquette. They also clean up after the children's meals. If there is an infant in the family, a nanny will wash and sterilize bottles and feed the infant. It is not part of a nanny's regular duties to cook for the adult members of the household or do domestic chores outside of those required for the children.

QUICK FACTS

SCHOOL SUBJECTS
Family and consumer science
Psychology

PERSONAL SKILLS
Communication/ideas
Helping/teaching

WORK ENVIRONMENT
Primarily indoors
Primarily one location

MINIMUM EDUCATION LEVEL
High school diploma

MEDIAN SALARY
$17,630

CERTIFICATION OR LICENSING
Voluntary

OUTLOOK
Faster than the average

Nannies are responsible for keeping order in the children's quarters. They may clean the bedrooms, nursery, and playrooms, making sure beds are made with clean linens and sufficient blankets. Nannies may also wash and iron the children's clothing and do any necessary mending. They make sure that the clothing is neatly put away. With older children, the nanny may begin instructions in orderliness and neatness, teaching children how to organize their possessions.

Nannies bathe and dress the children and instill proper grooming skills. Children often seek the assistance of their nanny in getting ready for family parties or holidays. As the children get older, nannies help them learn how to dress themselves and take care of their appearance.

Not only are nannies responsible for the care and training of their charges, but they also act as companions and guardians. They plan games and learning activities for the children and supervise their play, encouraging fair-

ness and good sportsmanship. They may be responsible for planning activities to commemorate holidays, special events, or birthdays. These activities may center on field trips, arts and crafts, or parties. Nannies may travel with families on trips and vacations, or they may take the children on short excursions without their families. Nannies must be detail oriented when it comes to the children entrusted to their care. They keep records of illnesses, allergies, and injuries. They also note learning skills and related progress as well as personal achievements, such as abilities in games or arts and crafts. Later, they relate these events and achievements to the parents.

Nannies act as the parents' assistants by focusing closely on the children and fostering the behavior expected of them. They are responsible for carrying out the parents' directions for care and activities. By setting good examples and helping the children follow guidelines established by their parents, nannies encourage the development of happy and confident personalities.

REQUIREMENTS

High School

From an educational standpoint, nannies usually are required to have at least a high school diploma or equivalent (GED). Helpful high school classes include health, psychology, and home economics. English and communications classes are also useful, as they provide skills that will help in everyday dealings with the children and their parents. Nannies usually must also have a valid driver's license, since they may be asked to chauffeur the children to doctors' appointments or other outings.

Postsecondary Training

There are several schools that offer specialized nanny training usually lasting between 12 and 16 weeks. These programs are typically accredited by individual state agencies. Employers generally prefer applicants who have completed an accredited program. Graduates of accredited programs also can command higher salaries.

Two- and four-year programs are available at many colleges and include courses on early childhood education, child growth and development, and child care. College course work in nanny training may also focus on communication, family health, first aid, child psychology, and food and nutrition. Classes may include play and recreational games, arts and crafts, children's literature, and safety and health. Because nannies may be responsible for children of various ages, the course work focuses on each stage of childhood development and the particular needs of individual children. Special emphasis is given to the care of infants. Professional nanny schools may also give instruction on family management, personal appearance, and appropriate conduct.

Certification or Licensing

Nannies who have graduated from a nanny school that is accredited by the American Council of Nanny Schools can use the title "certified professional nanny." Some employers look for nannies who have earned a child development associate or certified childcare professional credential. Certification shows potential employers your commitment to the work as well as your level of training.

Other Requirements

Nannies must possess an even and generous temperament when working with children. They must be kind, affectionate, and genuinely interested in the child's well-being and development. Good physical condition, energy, and stamina are also necessary for success in this career. Nannies must be able to work well on their own initiative and have sound judgment to handle any small crises or emergencies that arise. They must know how to instill discipline and carry out the parents' expectations.

They should be loyal and committed to the children and respect the families for whom they work. In some cases, this is difficult, since nannies are often privy to negative elements of family life, including the emotional problems of parents and their neglect of their children. Nannies need to recognize that they are not part of the family and should not allow themselves to become too familiar with its members. When they disagree with the family on matters of raising the children, they should do so with tact and the realization that they are only employees. Finally, it is imperative that they be discreet about confidential family matters. A nanny who gossips about family affairs is likely to be rapidly dismissed.

EXPLORING

Babysitting is an excellent way to gain child care experience. Often, a babysitter cares for children without any supervision, thereby learning child management and personal responsibility. Volunteer or part-time work at day care centers, nurseries, or elementary schools can also be beneficial.

Talk to a nanny to get further information. There are several placement agencies for prospective nannies, and one of them might be able to set up a meeting or phone interview with someone who works in the field.

Gather information about nannies either from the library or from sources listed at the end of this article.

EMPLOYERS

Mid- to upper-income parents who seek in-home child care for their children usually employ nannies. These opportunities are generally available across the country in large cities and affluent suburbs. Most nannies are placed in homes by placement agencies, by employment agencies, or through government-authorized programs.

STARTING OUT

Most schools that train nannies offer placement services. In addition, it is possible to register with an employment agency that places child care workers. Currently, there are more than 200 agencies that specialize in placing nannies. Some agencies conduct recruitment drives or fairs to find applicants. Newspaper classified ads may also list job openings for nannies.

Prospective nannies should screen potential employers carefully. Applicants should ask for references from previous nannies, particularly if a family has had many prior nannies, and talk with one or more of them, if possible. There are many horror stories in nanny circles about past employers, and the prospective worker should not assume that every employer is exactly as he or she appears to be at first. Nannies also need to make sure that the specific duties and terms of the job are explicitly specified in a contract. Most agencies will supply sample contracts.

ADVANCEMENT

More than half of the nannies working in this country are under the age of 30. Many nannies work in child care temporarily as a way to support themselves through school. Many nannies leave their employers to start families of their own. Some nannies, as their charges grow older and start school, may work for a new family every few years, which may result in better paying positions.

Other advancement opportunities for nannies depend on the personal initiative of the nanny. Some nannies enroll in college to get the necessary training to become teachers or child psychologists. Other nannies may establish their own child care agencies or schools for nannies.

EARNINGS

According to the U.S. Department of Labor, child care workers providing residential care (a group that includes nannies) had median annual earnings of $17,630 in 2006. The Department of Labor also reports that of all child care workers in 2006, 10 percent earned less than $12,910 per year, and 10 percent earned more than $27,050 per year.

In reality, however, nannies often work more than 40 hours per week, and their pay may not be based on an hourly rate, but rather will be a flat amount that may range from $250 to $400 or more per week. These weekly earnings translate into yearly incomes ranging from $13,000 to $20,800 or more. Income also depends on such factors as the number of children, length of time with a family, and level of previous experience. Some employers provide room and board but in return offer lower pay. Presently, the highest demands for nannies are in large cities on the West and East coasts. High demand can result in higher wages.

Some nannies may be asked to travel with the family. If it is a business-oriented trip, a nanny may be compensated with wages as well as additional days off upon return. If the travel is for vacation, a nanny may get paid a bonus for working additional days. Some employers choose not to take their nannies along when they travel, and these nannies may not earn any wages while the family is gone. Such situations can be a financial disadvantage for the nanny who has been promised full-time work and full-time pay. It is recommended that nannies anticipate possible scenarios or situations that may affect their working schedules and wages and discuss these issues with employers in advance.

Nannies often have work contracts with their families that designate wages, requirements, fringe benefits, and salary increases. Health insurance, worker's compensation, and Social Security tax are sometimes included in the benefits package. Annual pay raises vary, with increases of 7 or 8 percent being on the high end of the scale.

WORK ENVIRONMENT

No other job involves as intimate a relationship with other people and their children as the nanny's job. Because nannies often live with their employers, it is important that they choose their employer with as much care as the employer chooses them. All necessary working conditions need to be negotiated at the time of hire. Nannies should be fair, flexible, and able to adapt to changes easily. Because nannies work in their employers' homes, their working conditions vary greatly. Some nannies are live-ins, sharing the home of their employer because of convenience or because of the number or age of children in the family. Newborn babies need additional care that may require the nanny to live on the premises.

It is also common for nannies to live with their families during the week and return to their own homes on the weekends. When nannies live in the family's home, they usually have their own quarters or a small apartment that is separate from the rest of the family's bedrooms and offers some privacy. Sometimes the nanny's room is next to the children's room so it is possible for the nanny to respond immediately if help is needed.

Nannies who are not live-ins may expect to stay at the home for long periods of time, much longer than a traditional 9-to-5 job. Since it is often the nanny's responsibility to put the children to bed in the evening, a nanny may not return home until late evening. Often, nannies are asked to stay late or work weekends if the parents have other engagements.

The work of a nanny can often be stressful or unpleasant. Many employers expect their nannies to do things unrelated to their job, such as clean the house, run errands, walk dogs, or babysit for neighborhood children. Some employers may be condescending, rude, and critical. Some mothers, while they need and want the services of a nanny, grow resentful and jealous of the bonds the nanny forms with the children.

Nannies have very few legal rights with regard to their jobs and have little recourse to deal with unfair employers. Job security is very poor, as parents have less need for nannies as their children get older and start school. In addition, nannies are often fired with no notice and sometimes no explanation due to the whims of their employers. Leaving behind a job and the children they have taken care of and grown close to can be emotionally difficult for workers in this field.

The work is often strenuous, requiring a great deal of lifting, standing, and walking or running. The work is also mentally taxing, as young children demand constant attention and energy. However, it can be very rewarding for nannies as they grow close to the children, helping with their upbringing and care. In the best cases, the nanny becomes an integral part of the family he or she works for and is treated with professionalism, respect, and appreciation.

OUTLOOK

The U.S. Department of Labor predicts employment for all child care workers to be faster than the average through 2016. The continuing trend of both parents working outside the home ensures that nannies will remain in demand. Even if many of these parents switch to part-time jobs, there will still be a need for qualified child care providers. Presently, the demand for nannies outweighs the supply, and graduating nannies may find themselves faced with several job offers. In addition, the long hours and low pay make for a high turnover rate in this field, and replacement workers are in steady demand. It may be years before the gap between the number of positions open and the availability of nannies diminishes.

FOR MORE INFORMATION

For information on educational standards, certification, and professional support, contact the following organizations:

Council for Professional Recognition
2460 16th Street, NW
Washington, DC 20009-3547
Tel: 800-424-4310
http://www.cdacouncil.org

English Nanny & Governess School
37 South Franklin Street
Chagrin Falls, OH 44022-3212
Tel: 800-733-1984
http://www.nanny-governess.com

GoAuPair is an exchange program that places foreign students between the ages of 18 and 26 in American homes as au pairs for one year. For more information, contact

GoAuPair
151 East 6100 South, Suite 200
Murray, UT 84107-7489
Tel: 888-287-2471
Email: inforequest@goaupair.com
http://www.goaupair.com

For information on a career as a nanny and earnings, contact

International Nanny Association
3801 Kirby Drive, Suite 540
Houston, TX 77098-4127
Tel: 888-878-1477
http://www.nanny.org

This organization is a national support group run by nannies for nannies. For information on its national network, newsletters, and yearly conferences, contact

Association of Professional Nannies
10 Ashbury Court
Bluffton, SC 29910-8855
Tel: 641-715-3800 (Access Code: 69185)
http://www.nannyassociation.com

NUCLEAR MEDICINE TECHNOLOGISTS

OVERVIEW

Nuclear medicine technologists prepare and administer chemicals known as radiopharmaceuticals (radioactive drugs) used in the diagnosis and treatment of certain diseases. These drugs are administered to a patient and absorbed by specific locations in the patient's body, thus allowing technologists to use diagnostic equipment to image and analyze their concentration in certain tissues or organs. Technicians also perform laboratory tests on patients' blood and urine to determine certain body

QUICK FACTS

SCHOOL SUBJECTS
Biology
Computer science
Mathematics

PERSONAL SKILLS
Helping/teaching
Technical/scientific

WORK ENVIRONMENT
Primarily indoors
Primarily one location

MINIMUM EDUCATION LEVEL
Associate's degree

MEDIAN SALARY
$62,300

CERTIFICATION OR LICENSING
Required by certain states

OUTLOOK
Faster than the average

chemical levels. There are approximately 20,000 nuclear medicine technologists employed in the United States.

THE JOB

Nuclear medicine technologists work directly with patients, preparing and administering radioactive drugs. All work is supervised by a physician. Because of the nature of radioactive material, the drug preparation requires adherence to strict safety precautions. The Nuclear Regulatory Commission oversees all safety procedures.

After administering the drug to the patient, the technologist operates a gamma scintillation camera that takes pictures of the radioactive drug as it passes through or accumulates in parts of the patient's body. These images are then displayed on a computer screen, where the technologist and physician can examine them. The images can be used to diagnose diseases or disorders in such organs as the heart, brain, lungs, liver, kidneys, and bones. Nuclear medicine is also used for therapeutic purposes, such as to destroy abnormal thyroid tissue or ease the pain of a terminally ill patient.

Nuclear medicine technologists also have administrative duties. They must document the procedures performed, check all diagnostic equipment and record its use and maintenance, and keep track of the radioactive drugs administered. These technologists may also perform laboratory testing of a patient's body specimens, such as blood or urine. In addition, they provide the attending physician with up-to-date medical records for his or her review.

REQUIREMENTS
High School

To prepare for this work, you should take plenty of high school classes in math and science, including algebra, geometry, biology, chemistry, and physics. If your school offers anatomy classes, take those as well. Health courses may also be beneficial. Because using technology will be a large part of this work, be sure to take computer science classes. Also, because you will have considerable interaction with patients as well as other health care professionals, take English courses to improve your communication skills.

Postsecondary Training

There are several ways to become a nuclear medicine technologist. You can complete at minimum a two-year certificate program, a two-year associate's degree

program, or a four-year bachelor's degree program in nuclear medicine technology. Professional training is available at some colleges as part of a bachelor's or associate's program, and it ranges from two to four years in length. Some hospitals and technical schools also offer certificate training programs. Whatever program you decide to attend, make sure it is accredited by the Joint Review Committee on Educational Programs in Nuclear Medicine Technology (JRCNMT). Information on accredited programs is available at the JRC-NMT Web site, http://www.jrcnmt.org. There are 100 accredited training programs in the United States and Puerto Rico.

Some educational programs are designed for individuals who already have a background in a related health care field, such as radiologic technology, sonography, or nursing. These programs are usually one year in length. A good knowledge of anatomy and physiology is helpful. Course work in nuclear medicine technologist programs includes radiation biology and protection, radioactivity and instrumentation, radiopharmaceuticals and their use on patients, and therapeutic nuclear medicine.

Certification or Licensing

Nuclear medicine technologists must know the minimum federal standards for use and administration of nuclear drugs and equipment. More than half of all states now require technologists to be licensed. Certification or registration are also available through the Nuclear Medicine Technology Certification Board (NMTCB) and the American Registry of Radiologic Technologists (ARRT). Many nuclear medicine technologist positions, especially those in hospitals, are open only to certified or registered technologists. Information on becoming registered or certified is available from the ARRT and the NMTCB. (See the end of this article for contact information.)

Other Requirements

Those interested in a nuclear medicine technology career should have a strong sense of teamwork, compassion for others, and self-motivation.

EXPLORING

Individuals cannot get hands-on experience without the necessary qualifications. However, it is possible to become familiar with the job responsibilities by talking with practicing nuclear medicine technologists or teachers involved in the field. In addition, volunteer experience at local hospitals or nursing homes provides a good introduction to what it is like to work in a health care setting.

EMPLOYERS

There are approximately 20,000 nuclear medicine technologists in the United States, with most employed by hospitals. Nuclear medicine technologists are employed at health clinics, nuclear medical equipment development facilities, research facilities, and private laboratories.

STARTING OUT

Graduates of specialized training programs and two- and four-year programs usually receive placement assistance from their educational institutions, which have a vested interest in placing as many graduates as possible. Help wanted ads in local papers and professional journals are also good sources of job leads, as is participation in professional organizations, which gives members opportunities to network.

ADVANCEMENT

Growth in the field of nuclear medicine should lead to advancement opportunities. Advancement usually takes the form of promotion to a supervisory position, with a corresponding increase in pay and responsibilities. Due to increased competition for positions in large metropolitan hospitals, technologists who work at these institutions may need to transfer to another hospital or city to secure a promotion. Hospitals in rural areas have much less competition for positions and therefore are more likely to give promotions.

Promotions, which are more easily attained by earning a bachelor's degree, are normally to positions of supervisor, chief technologist, or nuclear medicine department administrator. Some technologists may advance by leaving clinical practice to teach or work with equipment development and sales.

EARNINGS

Naturally, individual earnings vary based on factors such as a person's level of education and experience. Also, those who work overtime and on-call can add to their yearly income. The U.S. Department of Labor reports that the median annual salary for all nuclear medicine technologists was $62,300 in 2006. The lowest paid 10 percent of technologists earned less than $46,490 annually, and the highest paid 10 percent made more than $82,310 per year. Technologists who worked in general medical and surgical hospitals had median earnings of $61,230. Typical benefits for hospital workers include health insurance, paid vacations and sick leave, and pension plans.

WORK ENVIRONMENT

Nuclear medicine technologists usually set their own schedules and can expect to work 35 to 40 hours a week, although larger hospitals often require overtime. Night and weekend work can also be expected. Because the job usually takes place inside a hospital or other health care facility, the environment is always clean and well lighted. The placing or positioning of patients on the diagnostic equipment is sometimes required, so a basic physical fitness level is necessary. There is a small chance of low-level contamination from the radioactive material or from the handling of body fluids. Strict safety precautions, including the use of shielded syringes and gloves and the wearing of badges that measure radiation, greatly reduce the risk of contamination.

OUTLOOK

According to the U.S. Department of Labor, employment of nuclear medicine technologists should grow faster than the average through 2016. According to a 2006 article in *ScienceDaily*, in 2005, 19.7 nuclear medicine procedures were performed on 17.2 million people in more than 7,200 medical sites in the United States—a 15 percent increase from 2001. Advances in medical diagnostic procedures could lead to increased use of nuclear medicine technology in the diagnosis and treatment of more diseases, including cancer treatment and cardiology. In addition, as the country's population ages there will be a growing number of middle-aged and older persons, who are the main users of diagnostic tests. A growing population using these tests will create a demand for more professionals to administer the procedures. Most new job opportunities are expected to be in areas with large hospitals.

FOR MORE INFORMATION

For information about career opportunities as a nuclear medicine technologist, contact

American Society of Radiologic Technologists
15000 Central Avenue, SE
Albuquerque, NM 87123-3917
Tel: 800-444-2778
http://www.asrt.org

For information on certification and state licensing, contact the following organizations:

American Registry of Radiologic Technologists
1255 Northland Drive
St. Paul, MN 55120-1155
Tel: 651-687-0048
http://www.arrt.org

Joint Review Committee on Educational Programs in Nuclear Medicine Technology
2000 West Danforth Road, Suite 130, #203
Edmond, OK 73003-4687
Tel: 405-285-0546
Email: jrcnmt@coxinet.net
http://www.jrcnmt.org

Nuclear Medicine Technology Certification Board
3558 Habersham at Northlake, Building I
Tucker, GA 30084-4009
Tel: 404-315-1739
Email: board@nmtcb.org
http://www.nmtcb.org

For information on nuclear medicine, professional development, and education, contact
Society of Nuclear Medicine
1850 Samuel Morse Drive
Reston, VA 20190-5316
Tel: 703-708-9000
http://www.snm.org

NUMERICAL CONTROL TOOL PROGRAMMERS

OVERVIEW

Numerical control tool programmers, also called *computer numerical control tool programmers*, develop programs that enable machine tools to produce parts automatically. These precisely made parts are used in automobiles, airplanes, industrial machinery, and other durable goods. There are approximately 158,000 numerical control programmers and operators in the United States.

THE JOB

Numerical control tool programmers write the programs that direct machine tools to perform functions automatically. Programmers must understand how the various machine tools operate and know the working properties of the metals and plastics that are used in the process.

Writing a program for a numerically controlled tool involves several steps. Before tool programmers can begin writing a program, they must analyze the blueprints of whatever function is to be performed or item to be made. Programmers then determine the steps and tools needed. After all necessary computations have been made, the programmers write the program.

Programmers almost always use computers to write the programs, using computer-aided design (CAD) systems. The growing use of this technology has increased productivity, translating designs directly into machine instructions without the need for coded programming. CAD systems allow programmers to more easily modify existing programs for other jobs with similar specifications.

To ensure that a program has been properly designed, tool programmers often perform a test or trial run. Trial runs help ensure that a machine is functioning properly and that the resulting product is according to plan. However, because problems found during a trial run could damage expensive machinery and tools, tests are increasingly done using computer simulations.

REQUIREMENTS
High School

High school courses in computer science, algebra, geometry, and English provide the basics needed to become a CNC programmer. More specific courses in blueprint reading, drafting, and computer-aided design are also useful. In addition, shop classes in metalworking can provide an understanding of machinery operations.

Postsecondary Training

Employers prefer to hire skilled machinists or tool operators to work as CNC programmers. Workers are usually trained through formal apprenticeships or postsecondary programs, or informally on the job. Apprenticeship programs usually last four years and include training in machine operations, program writing, computer-aided design and manufacturing, and analysis of drawings and design data. Classes include blueprint reading and drawing, machine tools, industrial mathematics, computers, and operation and maintenance of CNC machines.

Formal apprentice programs are becoming rare as more programmers receive training through community or technical colleges. Associate's degrees are available in areas such as manufacturing technology and automated manufacturing systems. Typical classes include machine shop, numerical control fundamentals, technical mechanics, advanced NC programming, introduction to robotic technology, and computer-assisted manufacturing.

For specialized types of programming, such as in aerospace or shipbuilding, employers often require a four-year degree in engineering in addition to technical skills and work experience.

Other Requirements

Numerical control tool programmers must have an understanding of machine tool operations, possess analytical skills, and show a strong aptitude for mathematics and computers. They also need good written and verbal communication skills to instruct machine operators and other engineers how to use and adjust programs. In addition, as new developments in technology bring new computer languages, methods, and equipment, numerical control tool programmers must be willing to learn new skills. Employers generally arrange and pay for courses to keep their programmers up to date on the latest trends and technology.

EXPLORING

If you are interested in a career as a tool programmer, you can test your interest and aptitude by taking shop and other vocational classes. You can also visit firms that employ numerical control tool programmers and talk directly with them to gain practical information about their jobs. Summer or part-time work at manufacturing firms and machine shops is a great way to find out more about the job and gain hands-on experience.

EMPLOYERS

Most numerical control tool programmers work in cities where factories and machine shops are concentrated, such as the Northeast, Midwest, and West Coast regions. They work for many types and sizes of businesses. Among the largest employers are the aerospace and automobile industries and other manufacturers of durable goods. Approximately 158,000 numerical control programmers and operators are employed in the United States.

STARTING OUT

Tool programming generally is not considered an entry-level job; most employers prefer to hire skilled machinists or those with technical training. Students who want to enter the job directly from formal training at a college or technical school can find job assistance through their school's placement services. Prospective programmers

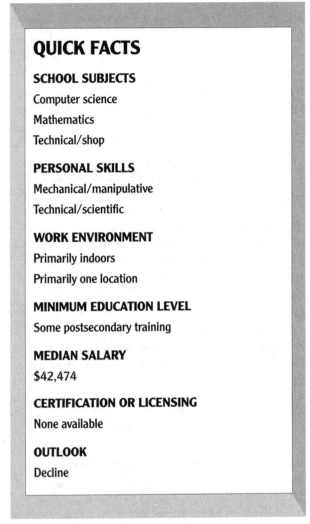

QUICK FACTS

SCHOOL SUBJECTS
Computer science
Mathematics
Technical/shop

PERSONAL SKILLS
Mechanical/manipulative
Technical/scientific

WORK ENVIRONMENT
Primarily indoors
Primarily one location

MINIMUM EDUCATION LEVEL
Some postsecondary training

MEDIAN SALARY
$42,474

CERTIFICATION OR LICENSING
None available

OUTLOOK
Decline

may also learn of openings through state and private employment offices, newspaper ads, and the Internet.

ADVANCEMENT

Advancement opportunities are somewhat limited for tool programmers. Employees may advance to higher paying jobs by transferring to larger or more established manufacturing firms or shops. Experienced tool programmers who demonstrate good interpersonal skills and managerial ability can be promoted to supervisory positions.

EARNINGS

The median hourly salary for numeric control tool programmers was $20.42 (or $42,474 annually) in 2006, according to the U.S. Department of Labor. The lowest 10 percent earned less than $13.11 (or $27,269 annually), and the highest 10 percent earned more than $31.85 (or $66,248 annually).

Benefits vary but may include paid vacations and holidays; personal leaves; medical, dental, vision, and life insurance; retirement plans; profit sharing; and tuition assistance programs.

WORK ENVIRONMENT

Numerical control tool programmers generally work a 40-hour week, although overtime is common during peak periods. To justify the costly investments in machinery, some employers extend hours of operation, requiring CNC programmers to work evening and weekend shifts.

Programmers work in comfortable office surroundings, set apart from the noisier, more hazardous shop floor. Their work is more analytical and, as a result, less physically demanding than the work of machinists and other tool operators.

OUTLOOK

According to the *Occupational Outlook Handbook*, the employment of numerical control tool programmers is expected to decline through 2016. Initially, employment of CNC programmers was made possible by the introduction of new automation, but recent technological advancements are reducing the demand for such workers. Newer, user-friendly technology now allows some programming and minor adjustments to be made on the shop floor by machinists and machine operators rather than by skilled CNC programmers. Fewer programmers are needed to translate designs into CNC machine tool instructions, as new software is able to do this automatically. Employment is also influenced by economic cycles. As the demand for machined goods falls, programmers involved in this production may be laid off or forced to work fewer hours.

However, employers continue to have difficulty finding workers with the necessary skills and experience to fill open programmer positions. Additionally, many openings will arise as numerical control tool programmers leave jobs to retire or switch occupations.

FOR MORE INFORMATION

For information on apprenticeships, contact

International Union, United Automobile, Aerospace, and Agricultural Implement Workers of America
Solidarity House
8000 East Jefferson Avenue
Detroit, MI 48214-2699
Tel: 313-926-5000
http://www.uaw.org

For information on careers and educational programs, contact the following organizations:

National Tooling & Machining Association
9300 Livingston Road
Fort Washington, MD 20744-4914
Tel: 800-248-6862
http://www.ntma.org

Precision Machined Products Association
6700 West Snowville Road
Brecksville, OH 44141-3292
Tel: 440-526-0300
http://www.pmpa.org

NURSE ASSISTANTS

OVERVIEW

Nurse assistants (also called *nurse aides*, *orderlies*, or *hospital attendants*) work under the supervision of nurses and handle much of the personal care needs of the patients. This allows the nursing staff to perform their primary duties more effectively and efficiently. Nurse assistants help move patients, assist in patients' exercise and nutrition needs, and oversee patients' personal hygiene. Nurse assistants may also be required to take patients to other areas of the hospital for treatment, therapy, or diagnostic testing. They are required to keep charts of their work with their patients for review by other medical personnel and to comply with required reporting. There are about 1.4 million nurse assistants in the United States, and more than 50 percent of them are employed in nursing homes.

THE JOB

Nurse assistants generally help nurses care for patients in hospital or nursing home settings. Their duties include tending to the daily care of the patients, including bathing them, helping them with their meals, and checking their body temperature and blood pressure. In addition, they often help persons who need assistance with their personal hygiene and answer their call lights when they need immediate assistance.

The work can be strenuous, requiring the lifting and moving of patients. Nurse assistants must work with partners or in groups when performing the more strenuous tasks to ensure their safety as well as the patient's. Some requirements of the job can be as routine as changing sheets and helping a patient or resident with phone calls, while other requirements can be as difficult and unattractive as assisting a resident with elimination and cleaning up a resident or patient who has vomited.

Nurse assistants may be called upon to perform the more menial and unappealing tasks of health and personal care, but they also have the opportunity to develop meaningful relationships with patients. In a nursing home, nursing assistants work closely with residents, often gaining their trust and friendship.

REQUIREMENTS
High School

Although a high school diploma is not always required to work as a nurse assistant, there are a number of high school classes that can help you do this work. Communication skills are valuable for a nurse assistant to have, so take English classes. Science courses, such as biology and anatomy, and family and consumer science, health, and nutrition classes are also helpful. Some high schools offer courses directly related to nurse assistant training. These classes may include body mechanics, infection control, and resident/patient rights.

Postsecondary Training

Nurse assistants are not required to have a college degree, but they may have to complete a short training course at a community college or vocational school. These training courses, usually taught by a registered nurse, teach basic nursing skills and prepare students for the state certification exam. Nurse assistants typically begin the training courses after getting their first job as an assistant, and the course work is often incorporated into their on-the-job training.

Many people work as nurse assistants as they pursue other medical professions such as a premedical or nursing program.

Certification or Licensing

Some states require nurse assistants to be certified no matter where they work. The Omnibus Budget Reconciliation Act of 1987 requires nurse assistants working in nursing homes to undergo special training. Nursing homes can hire inexperienced workers as nurse assistants, but they must have at least 75 hours of training and pass a competency evaluation program within four months of being

QUICK FACTS

SCHOOL SUBJECTS
Biology
Health

PERSONAL SKILLS
Following instructions
Helping/teaching

WORK ENVIRONMENT
Primarily indoors
Primarily multiple locations

MINIMUM EDUCATION LEVEL
High school diploma

MEDIAN SALARY
$22,194

CERTIFICATION OR LICENSING
Required for certain positions

OUTLOOK
Faster than the average

hired. Those who fulfill these requirements are then certified and placed on the state registry of nurse aides.

Other Requirements

You must care about the patients in your care, and you must show a genuine understanding and compassion for the ill, the disabled, and the elderly. Because of the rigorous physical demands placed on you, you should be in good health and have good work habits. Along with good physical health, you should have good mental health and a cheerful disposition. The job can be emotionally demanding, requiring patience and stability. You should be able to work as a part of a team and also be able to take orders and follow through on your responsibilities.

EXPLORING

Because a high school diploma is frequently not required of nursing aides, many high school students are hired by nursing homes and hospitals for part-time work. Job opportunities may also exist in a hospital or nursing home kitchen, introducing you to diet and nutrition. These jobs will give you an opportunity to become familiar with the hospital and nursing home environments. Also, volunteer work can familiarize you with the work nurses and nurse assistants perform, as well as introduce you to basic medical terminology.

EMPLOYERS

Approximately 52 percent of the 1.4 million nurse assistants in the United States are employed in nursing homes, and another 29 percent worked in hospitals. Others are employed in halfway houses, retirement centers, homes for persons with disabilities, and private homes.

STARTING OUT

Because of the high demand for nurse assistants, you can apply directly to the health facilities in your area, contact your local employment office, or check your local newspaper's help wanted ads as well as the Internet.

ADVANCEMENT

For the most part, there is not much opportunity for advancement with this job. To advance in a health care facility requires additional training. After becoming familiar with the medical and nursing home environments and gaining some knowledge of medical terminology, some nurse assistants enroll in nursing programs or pursue other medically related careers.

Many facilities are recognizing the need to retain good health care workers and are putting some training and advancement programs in place for their employees.

EARNINGS

Salaries for most health care professionals vary by region, population, and size and kind of institution. The pay for nurse assistants in a hospital is usually more than in a nursing home.

According to the U.S. Department of Labor, nurse assistants earned median hourly wages of $10.67 in 2006. For full-time work at 40 hours per week, this hourly wage translates into a yearly income of approximately $22,194. The lowest paid 10 percent earned less than $7.78 per hour (approximately $16,182 per year), and the highest paid 10 percent earned more than $14.99 per hour (approximately $31,179 annually).

Benefits are usually based on the hours worked, length of employment, and the policies of the facility. Some offer paid vacation and holidays, medical or hospital insurance, and retirement plans. Some also provide free meals to their workers.

WORK ENVIRONMENT

The work environment in a health care or long-term care facility can be hectic at times and very stressful. Some patients may be uncooperative and may actually be combative. Often there are numerous demands that must be met at the same time. Nurse assistants are required to be on their feet most of the time, and they often have to help lift or move patients. Most facilities are clean and well lighted, but nurse assistants do have the possibility of exposure to contagious diseases, although using proper safety procedures minimizes their risk.

Nurse assistants generally work a 40-hour workweek, with some overtime. The hours and weekly schedule may be irregular, depending on the needs of the institution. Nurse assistants are needed around the clock, so work schedules may include night shift or swing-shift work.

OUTLOOK

There will continue to be many job opportunities for nurse assistants; the U.S. Department of Labor predicts that this occupation will grow faster than the average through 2016. Because of the physical and emotional demands of the job, and because of the lack of advancement opportunities, there is a high employee turnover rate. Additional opportunities may be available as different types of care facilities are developed and as facilities try to curb operating costs.

More nurse assistants will also be required as government and private agencies develop more programs to assist people with disabilities, dependent people, and the increasing aging population.

FOR MORE INFORMATION

For additional information on nurse assistant careers and training, contact the following organizations:

National Association of Health Care Assistants
1201 L Street, NW
Washington, DC 20005
Tel: 800-784-6049
http://www.nahcacares.org

National Network of Career Nursing Assistants
3577 Easton Road
Norton, OH 44203-5661
Tel: 330-825-9342
Email: cnajeni@aol.com
http://www.cna-network.org

OCCUPATIONAL THERAPY ASSISTANTS AND AIDES

OVERVIEW

Occupational therapy assistants (also called OTAs) help people with mental, physical, developmental, or emotional limitations using a variety of activities to improve basic motor functions and reasoning abilities. They work under the direct supervision of an occupational therapist, and their duties include helping to plan, implement, and evaluate rehabilitation programs designed to regain patients' self-sufficiency and to restore their physical and mental functions. There are 25,000 occupational therapy assistants employed in the United States. *Occupational therapy aides* help OTAs and occupational therapists by doing such things as clerical work, preparing therapy equipment for a client's use, and keeping track of supplies. Approximately 8,200 occupational therapy aides are employed in the United States.

THE JOB

Occupational therapy is used to help provide rehabilitation services to persons with mental, physical, emotional, or developmental disabilities. The goal of occupational therapy is to improve a patient's quality of life by compensating for limitations caused by age, illness, or injury. It differs from physical therapy because it focuses not only on physical rehabilitation, but also on psychological well-being. Occupational therapy emphasizes improvement of the activities of daily living—including such functions as personal hygiene, dressing, eating, and cooking.

Occupational therapy assistants, under the supervision of the therapist, implement patient care plans and activities. They help patients improve mobility and productivity using a variety of activities and exercises. They may use adaptive techniques and equipment to help patients perform tasks many take for granted. A reacher, a long-handled device that pinches and grabs small items, may be used to pick up keys from the floor or a book from the shelf. Therapy assistants may have patients mix ingredients for a cake or flip a grilled cheese sandwich using a special spatula. Activities such as danc-

QUICK FACTS

SCHOOL SUBJECTS
Health
Psychology

PERSONAL SKILLS
Helping/teaching
Mechanical/manipulative

WORK ENVIRONMENT
Primarily indoors
Primarily one location

MINIMUM EDUCATION LEVEL
Associate's degree (assistants)
High school diploma (aides)

MEDIAN SALARY
$42,060 (assistants)
$25,020 (aides)

CERTIFICATION OR LICENSING
Required (assistants)
None available (aides)

OUTLOOK
Much faster than the average

ing, playing cards, or throwing a ball are fun, yet they help improve mobility and give the patients a sense of self-esteem. Therapists evaluate an activity, minimize the number of steps, and streamline movement so the patient will be less fatigued.

Assistants may also help therapists evaluate a patient's progress, change care plans as needed, make therapy appointments, and complete paperwork.

Occupational therapy aides are responsible for materials and equipment used during therapy. They assemble and clean equipment and make certain the therapists and assistants have what they need for a patient's therapy session. A therapy aide's duties are more clerical in nature. They answer telephones, schedule appointments, order supplies and equipment, and complete insurance forms and other paperwork.

REQUIREMENTS

High School

According to the U.S. Department of Labor, most occupational therapy aides receive on-the-job training, while occupational therapy assistants require further education after high school. For either position, however, a high school diploma is a must. Prepare for these careers by taking classes in biology, health, and social sciences. Anyone interested in doing this work must also be able to communicate clearly, follow directions, and work as part of a team. English or communication classes can help you improve on these skills.

In addition, admissions officers at postsecondary programs are favorably impressed if you have experience in the health care field. If you cannot find a paid job, consider volunteering at a local hospital or nursing home during your high school years.

Postsecondary Training

While occupational therapy aides receive on-the-job training, occupational therapy assistants must have either an associate's degree or certificate from an accredited OTA program. Programs are accredited by the Accreditation Council for Occupational Therapy Education (ACOTE), which is part of the American Occupational Therapy Association (AOTA). In 2007, there were 126 programs fully accredited by the ACOTE; in addition, a number of programs were on "inactive status," meaning that they were not currently accepting new students but may reactivate (begin accepting students again) in the future. A full listing of programs, as well as their contact information, is available on the AOTA Web site at http://www.aota.org.

Generally, programs take two years to complete. Studies include courses such as human anatomy, psychology of adjustment, biology, human kinesiology, therapeutic media, and techniques. Most schools also require their students to take a number of general classes as well to round out their education. These may be courses such as English, business math, and management. In addition to class work, you will be required to complete a period of supervised fieldwork, which will give you hands-on experience with occupational therapy.

Certification or Licensing

Occupational therapy aides do not require certification or licensing. Occupational therapy assistants must pass the certifying test of the National Board for Certification in Occupational Therapy. After passing this test, assistants receive the designation certified occupational therapy assistant. Licensure requirements for assistants vary by state, so you will need to check with the licensing board of the state in which you want to work for specific information.

Other Requirements

Occupational therapy assistants and aides must be able to take directions. OTAs should have a pleasant disposition, strong people skills, and a desire to help those in need. Assistants must also be patient and responsible. Aides, too, should be responsible. They also need to be detail oriented in order to keep track of paperwork and equipment. It is important for assistants and aides to work well as a team.

EXPLORING

A visit to your local hospital's occupational therapy department is the best way to learn about this field. Speak with occupational therapists, assistants, and aides to gain an understanding of the work they do. Also, the AOTA and other related organizations might be able to provide career information. School guidance and job centers, and the library, are good information sources.

EMPLOYERS

There are approximately 25,000 occupational therapy assistants and 8,200 occupational therapy aides employed in the United States. Approximately 29 percent of all assistants and aides work in a hospital setting, 23 percent are employed by offices of physicians and occupational therapists, and 21 percent work in nursing facilities. Others work in community care facilities for the elderly, home health care services, outpatient rehabilitation centers, and state government agencies.

STARTING OUT

The career services department of your local community college or technical school can provide a listing of jobs available in the occupational therapy field. Job openings are usually posted in hospital human resource departments. Professional groups are also a good source of information, providing information on professional development, networking and educational opportunities, as well as employment listings.

ADVANCEMENT

After some experience, occupational therapy assistants can be promoted to *lead assistant*. Lead assistants are responsible for making work schedules of other assistants and for the training of occupational therapy students. Since occupational therapy assistants work under the supervision of an occupational therapist, there is little room for advancement. Aides may return to school and train to become occupational therapy assistants. Some assistants and aides return to school to become occupational therapists. Some shift to other health care careers.

EARNINGS

According to the U.S. Department of Labor, the median yearly income of occupational therapy assistants was $42,060 in 2006. Salaries ranged from less than $26,050 to $58,270 or more annually. Naturally, experience, location, and type of employer all factor into the salaries paid.

The importance of education, though, cannot be overlooked, as assistants tend to earn more than aides. Median annual earnings of occupational therapist aides were $25,020 in 2006, according to the U.S. Department of Labor. Salaries ranged from less than $17,060 to $44,130 or more annually.

Benefits for full-time workers depend on the employer. They generally include health and life insurance, paid sick and vacation time, holiday pay, and a retirement plan.

WORK ENVIRONMENT

Most occupational therapy assistants and aides work during the day, although depending on the place of employment, some evening or weekend work may be required. Most therapy is done in a hospital or clinic setting that is clean, well lighted, and generally comfortable.

Occupational therapy assistants often use everyday items, settings, and activities to help rehabilitate their patients. Such props include kitchen settings, card games, dancing, or exercises. Therapy assistants should be in good physical shape, since heavy lifting—of patients as well as equipment—is a daily part of the job. Therapy assistants should also have stamina, since they are on their feet for much of the day.

OUTLOOK

According to the *Occupational Outlook Handbook*, employment for occupational therapy assistants and aides will grow much faster than the average through 2016. Only a small number of new jobs will actually be available, however, due to the size of these occupations. Occupational growth will stem from an increased number of people with disabilities and elderly people. Although more people are living well into their 70s, 80s, and, in some cases, 90s, they often need the kinds of services occupational therapy provides. Medical technology has greatly improved, saving many lives that

in the past would be lost through accidents, stroke, or other illnesses. Such people need rehabilitation therapy as they recuperate. Hospitals and employers are hiring more therapy assistants to help with the workload and to reduce costs.

FOR MORE INFORMATION

For additional information on careers, education, and news related to the field, contact

American Occupational Therapy Association (AOTA)
4720 Montgomery Lane
PO Box 31220
Bethesda, MD 20824-1220
Tel: 301-652-2682
http://www.aota.org

For information on certification, contact
National Board for Certification in Occupational Therapy
12 South Summit Avenue, Suite 100
Gaithersburg, MD 20877-4150
Tel: 301-990-7979
Email: info@nbcot.org
http://www.nbcot.org

☐ OFFICE ADMINISTRATORS

OVERVIEW

Office administrators direct and coordinate the work activities of office workers within an office. They supervise office clerks and other workers in their tasks and plan department activities with other supervisory personnel. Administrators often define job duties and develop training programs for new workers. They evaluate the progress of their clerks and work with upper-management officials to ensure that the office staff meets productivity and quality goals. Office administrators often meet with office personnel to discuss job-related issues or problems, and they are responsible for maintaining a positive office environment. There are approximately 1.5 million office administrators employed in the United States.

THE JOB

As modern technology and an increased volume of business communications become a normal part of daily business, offices are becoming more complicated places in

QUICK FACTS

SCHOOL SUBJECTS

Business

Mathematics

Speech

PERSONAL SKILLS

Communication/ideas

Leadership/management

WORK ENVIRONMENT

Primarily indoors

Primarily one location

MINIMUM EDUCATION LEVEL

Associate's degree

MEDIAN SALARY

$43,510

CERTIFICATION OR LICENSING

Voluntary

OUTLOOK

Little change or more slowly than the average

the strengths and weaknesses of each worker, as well as the ability to determine what needs to be done and when it must be completed. For example, if a supervisor knows that one worker is especially good at filing business correspondence, that person will probably be assigned important filing tasks. Office administrators often know how to do many of the tasks done by their subordinates and assist or relieve them whenever necessary.

Office administrators not only train clerical workers and assign them job duties but also recommend increases in salaries, promote workers when approved, and occasionally fire them. Therefore, they must carefully observe clerical workers performing their jobs (whether answering the telephones, opening and sorting mail, or inputting computer data) and make positive suggestions for any necessary improvements. Managers who can communicate effectively, both verbally and in writing, will be better able to carry out this kind of work. Motivating employees to do their best work is another important component of an office administrator's responsibilities.

Office administrators must be very good at human relations. Differences of opinion and personality clashes among employees are inevitable in almost any office, and the administrator must be able to deal with grievances and restore good feelings among the staff. Office administrators meet regularly with their staff, alone and in groups, to discuss and solve any problems that might affect people's job performance.

Planning is a vital and time-consuming portion of the job responsibilities of office administrators. Not only do they plan the work of subordinates, they also assist in planning current and future office space needs, work schedules, and the types of office equipment and supplies that need to be purchased.

Office administrators must always keep their superiors informed as to the overall situation in the clerical area. If there is a delay on an important project, for example, upper management must know the cause and the steps being taken to expedite the matter.

REQUIREMENTS

High School

A high school diploma is essential for this position, and a college degree is highly recommended. You should take courses in English, speech and communications, mathematics, sociology, history, and as many business-related courses, such as typing and bookkeeping, as possible. Knowledge of a wide variety of computer software programs is also very important.

which to work. By directing and coordinating the activities of clerks and other office workers, office administrators are an integral part of an effective organization.

The day-to-day work of office administrators, also known as office managers, involves organizing and overseeing many different activities. Although specific duties vary with the type and size of the particular office, all supervisors and managers have several basic job responsibilities. The primary responsibility of the office administrator is to run the office; that is, whatever the nature of the office's business, the office administrator must see to it that all workers have what they need to do their work.

Office administrators are usually responsible for interviewing prospective employees and making recommendations on hiring. They train new workers, explain office policies, and explain performance criteria. Office administrators are also responsible for delegating work responsibilities. This requires a keen understanding of

Postsecondary Training

In college, pursue a degree in business administration or at least take several courses in business management and operations. In some cases, an associate's degree is considered sufficient for a supervisory position, but a bachelor's degree will make you more attractive to employers and help in advancement.

Many community colleges and vocational schools offer business education courses that help train office administrators. The American Management Association has a Self-Study Certificate Program in several areas, including customer service management, human resources management, general management, strategic leadership, and others. (See contact information at the end of this article.)

Colleges and universities nationwide offer bachelor's degrees in business administration; a few may offer programs targeted to specific industries, such as medical administration or hotel management.

Certification and Licensing

The International Association of Administrative Professionals offers voluntary certification to administrative professionals. Applicants who meet experience requirements and who pass an examination may use the designation, certified administrative professional (CAP). The Institute of Certified Professional Managers offers the certified manager (CM) designation to applicants who pass examinations that cover the foundations of management, planning and organizing, and leading and controlling.

Other Requirements

Offices can be hectic places. Deadlines on major projects can create tension, especially if some workers are sick or overburdened. Office administrators must constantly juggle the demands of their superiors with the capabilities of their subordinates. Thus, they need an even temperament and the ability to work well with others. Additional important attributes include organizational ability, attention to detail, dependability, and trustworthiness. Since many offices promote administrators from clerical work positions within their organization, relevant work experience is also helpful.

EXPLORING

You can get general business experience by taking on clerical or bookkeeping responsibilities with a school club or other organization. Volunteering in your school office is an ideal introduction to office work. This will allow you to become more familiar with computer programs often used in offices and practice business skills such as opening and sorting mail, answering telephones, and filing documents.

Community colleges and other institutions may offer basic or advanced computer training courses for students of all ages. After high school, you may want to explore work-study programs where you can work part time and gain on-the-job training with local businesses while earning your degree.

EMPLOYERS

Approximately 1.5 million office administrators are employed in the United States. Administrators are needed in all types of offices that have staffs large enough to warrant a manager. The federal government is a major employer of office administrators. Other job opportunities are found in private companies with large clerical staffs, such as banks, telecommunications companies, wholesalers, retail establishments, business service firms, health care facilities, schools, and insurance companies.

STARTING OUT

To break into this career, you should contact the personnel offices of individual firms directly. This is especially appropriate if you have previous clerical experience. College placement offices or other job placement offices may also know of openings. You can also locate jobs through help wanted advertisements. Another option is to sign up with a temporary employment service. Working as a "temp" provides the advantage of getting a firsthand look at a variety of office settings and making many contacts.

Often, a firm will recruit office administrators from its own clerical staff. A clerk with potential supervisory abilities may be given periodic supervisory responsibilities. Later, when an opening occurs for an administrator, that person may be promoted to a full-time position.

ADVANCEMENT

Skilled administrators may be promoted to group manager positions. Promotions, however, often depend on the individual's level of education and other appropriate training, such as training in the company's computer system. Firms usually encourage their employees to pursue further education and may even pay for some tuition costs. Supervisory and management skills can be obtained through company training or community colleges and local vocational schools.

Some companies will prepare office clerks for advancement to administrative positions by having them work in several company departments. This broad experience allows the administrator to better coordinate numerous activities and make more knowledgeable decisions.

EARNINGS

According to Salary.com, in April 2008, the median annual salary for office managers ranged between $45,493 and $64,413, depending upon experience.

According to the U.S. Department of Labor, office administrators earned median annual salaries of $43,510 in 2006. Fifty percent earned between $32,910 and $54,630 a year. The lowest paid 10 percent earned less than $26,530, and the top 10 percent earned over $71,340.

The size and geographic location of the company and the person's individual skills can be key determinants of earnings. Higher wages will be paid to those who work for larger private companies located in and around major metropolitan areas. Full-time workers also receive paid vacations and health and life insurance. Some companies offer year-end bonuses and stock options.

WORK ENVIRONMENT

As is the case with most office workers, office administrators work an average of 35 to 40 hours a week, although overtime is not unusual. Depending on the company, night, weekend, holiday, or shift work may be expected. Most offices are pleasant places to work. The environment is usually well ventilated and well lighted, and the work is not physically strenuous. The administrator's job can be stressful, however, as it entails supervising a variety of employees with different personalities, temperaments, and work habits.

OUTLOOK

According to the U.S. Department of Labor, employment of office administrators is projected to experience little change or grow more slowly than the average for all occupations through 2016. The increased use of data processing and other automated equipment as well as corporate downsizing may reduce the number of administrators in the next decade. However, this profession will still offer good employment prospects because of its sheer size. A large number of job openings will occur as administrators transfer to other industries or leave the workforce for other reasons. Since some clerical occupations will be affected by increased automation, some office administrators may have smaller staffs and be asked to perform more professional tasks.

The federal government should continue to be a good source for job opportunities. Private companies, particularly those with large clerical staffs, such as hospitals, banks, and telecommunications companies, should also have numerous openings. Employment opportunities will be especially good for those trained to operate computers and other types of modern office machinery.

FOR MORE INFORMATION

For information on seminars, conferences, and news on the industry, contact

American Management Association
1601 Broadway
New York, NY 10019-7420
Tel: 212-586-8100
Email: customerservice@amanet.org
http://www.amanet.org

For information on certification, contact

Institute of Certified Professional Managers
James Madison University
MSC 5504
Harrisonburg, VA 22807-0002
Tel: 800-568-4120
http://www.icpm.biz/

For career and certification information, contact

International Association of Administrative Professionals
10502 NW Ambassador Drive
PO Box 20404
Kansas City, MO 64195-0404
Tel: 816-891-6600
Email: service@iaap-hq.org
http://www.iaap-hq.org

For information about programs for students in kindergarten through high school, and information on local chapters, contact

Junior Achievement
One Education Way
Colorado Springs, CO 80906-4477
Tel: 719-540-8000
Email: newmedia@ja.org
http://www.ja.org

For career information, contact

National Management Association
2210 Arbor Boulevard
Dayton, OH 45439-1580
Tel: 937-294-0421
Email: nma@nma1.org
http://www.nma1.org

OFFICE CLERKS

OVERVIEW

Office clerks perform a variety of clerical tasks that help an office run smoothly, including file maintenance, mail sorting, and record keeping. In large companies, office clerks might have specialized tasks such as inputting data into a computer, but in most cases, clerks are flexible and have many duties including typing, answering telephones, taking messages, making photocopies, and preparing mailings. Office clerks usually work under close supervision, often with experienced clerks directing their activities. There are approximately 3.2 million office clerks employed in the United States.

THE JOB

Office clerks usually perform a variety of tasks as part of their overall job responsibility. They may type or file bills, statements, and business correspondence. They may stuff envelopes, answer telephones, and sort mail. Office clerks also enter data into computer databases, run errands, and operate office equipment such as photocopiers, fax machines, and switchboards. In the course of an average day, an office clerk usually performs a combination of these and other clerical tasks, spending an hour or so on one task and then moving on to another as directed by an office manager or other supervisor.

An office clerk may work with other office personnel, such as a bookkeeper or accountant, to maintain a company's financial records. The clerk may type and mail invoices and sort payments as they come in, keep payroll records, or take inventories. With more experience, the clerk may be asked to update customer files to reflect receipt of payments and verify records for accuracy.

Office clerks often deliver messages from one office worker to another, an especially important responsibility in larger companies. Clerks may relay questions and answers from one department head to another. Similarly, clerks may relay messages from people outside the company or employees who are outside of the office to those working in house. Office clerks may also work with other personnel on individual projects, such as preparing a yearly budget or making sure a mass mailing gets out on time.

Administrative clerks assist in the efficient operation of an office by compiling business records; providing information to sales personnel and customers; and preparing and sending out bills, policies, invoices, and other business correspondence. Administrative clerks

---

QUICK FACTS

SCHOOL SUBJECTS
Business
English
Mathematics

PERSONAL SKILLS
Communication/ideas
Following instructions

WORK ENVIRONMENT
Primarily indoors
Primarily one location

MINIMUM EDUCATION LEVEL
High school diploma

MEDIAN SALARY
$23,710

CERTIFICATION OR LICENSING
None available

OUTLOOK
About as fast as the average

---

may also keep financial records and prepare the payroll. File clerks review and classify letters, documents, articles, and other information and then file this material so it can be quickly retrieved at a later time. They contribute to the smooth distribution of information at a company.

Some clerks have titles that describe where they work and the jobs they do. For example, congressional-district aides work for the elected officials of their U.S. congressional district. Police clerks handle routine office procedures in police stations, and concrete products dispatchers work with construction firms on building projects.

REQUIREMENTS
High School

To prepare for a career as an office clerk, you should take courses in English, mathematics, and as many business-related subjects as possible, such as keyboarding and bookkeeping. Community colleges and vocational schools often offer business education courses that provide training for general office workers.

Postsecondary Training

A high school diploma is usually sufficient for beginning office clerks, although business courses covering office machine operation and bookkeeping are also helpful. To succeed in this field, you should have computer skills, the ability to concentrate for long periods of time on repetitive tasks, good English and communication skills, and mathematical abilities. Legible handwriting is also a necessity.

Other Requirements

To find work as an office clerk, you should have an even temperament, strong communication skills, and the ability to work well with others. You should find systematic and detailed work appealing. Other personal qualifications include dependability, trustworthiness, and a neat personal appearance.

EXPLORING

You can gain experience by taking on clerical or bookkeeping responsibilities with a school club or other organization. In addition, some school work-study programs may provide opportunities for part-time, on-the-job training with local businesses. You may also be able to get a part-time or summer job in a business office by contacting businesses directly or enlisting the aid of a guidance counselor. Training in the operation of business machinery (computers, word processors, and so on) may be available through evening courses offered by business schools and community colleges.

EMPLOYERS

Approximately 3.2 million office clerks are employed throughout the United States. Major employers include local government, health care, and social assistance organizations; administrative and support services companies; finance and insurance companies; or professional, scientific, and technical services industries. Smaller companies also hire office workers and sometimes offer a greater opportunity to gain experience in a variety of clerical tasks.

STARTING OUT

To secure an entry-level position, you should contact businesses or government agencies directly. Newspaper ads, temporary-work agencies, and the Internet are also good sources for finding jobs in this area. Most companies provide on-the-job training, during which company policies and procedures are explained.

ADVANCEMENT

Office clerks usually begin their employment performing more routine tasks such as delivering messages and sorting and filing mail. With experience, they may advance to more complicated assignments and assume a greater responsibility for the entire project to be completed. Those who demonstrate the desire and ability may move to other clerical positions, such as secretary or receptionist. Clerks with good leadership skills may become group managers or supervisors. To be promoted to a professional occupation such as accountant, a college degree or other specialized training is usually necessary.

The high turnover rate that exists among office clerks increases promotional opportunities. The number and kind of opportunities, however, usually depend on the place of employment and the ability, education, and experience of the employee.

EARNINGS

Salaries for office clerks vary depending on the size and geographic location of the company and the skills of the worker. According to the U.S. Department of Labor, the median salary for full-time office clerks was $23,710 in 2006. The lowest paid 10 percent earned less than $14,850, while the highest paid group earned more than $37,600.

Full-time workers generally also receive paid vacations, health insurance, sick leave, and other benefits.

WORK ENVIRONMENT

As is the case with most office workers, office clerks work an average 37- to 40-hour week. They usually work in comfortable surroundings and are provided with modern equipment. Although clerks have a variety of tasks and responsibilities, the job itself can be fairly routine and repetitive. Clerks often interact with accountants and other office personnel and may work under close supervision.

OUTLOOK

Although employment of office clerks is expected to grow only about as fast as the average through 2016, there will still be many jobs available due to the vastness of this field and a high turnover rate. With the increased use of data processing equipment and other types of automated office machinery, more and more employers are hiring people proficient in a variety of office tasks. Industries that generally have the strongest demand for qualified administrative staff include health care, mortgage and title, and nonprofits. Other industries that will provide good opportunities include construction, technology, and transportation.

Because they are so versatile, office workers can find employment in virtually any kind of industry, so their overall employment does not depend on the fortunes of any single sector of the economy. In addition to private companies, the federal government should continue to be a good source of jobs. Employment opportunities should be especially good for those trained in various computer skills as well as other office machinery. Temporary and part-time work opportunities should also increase, especially during busy business periods.

FOR MORE INFORMATION

For information on seminars, conferences, and news on the industry, contact

National Association of Executive Secretaries and Administrative Assistants
900 South Washington Street, Suite G-13
Falls Church, VA 22046-4009
Tel: 703-237-8616
http://www.naesaa.com

For free office career and salary information, and job listings, visit

OfficeTeam
http://www.officeteam.com

OPERATING ENGINEERS

OVERVIEW

Operating engineers operate various types of power-driven construction machines such as shovels, cranes, tractors, bulldozers, pile drivers, concrete mixers, and pumps. There are approximately 494,000 operating engineers employed in the United States.

THE JOB

Operating engineers work for a variety of construction companies as well as manufacturers and state agencies.

QUICK FACTS

SCHOOL SUBJECTS
Mathematics
Technical/shop

PERSONAL SKILLS
Following instructions
Mechanical/manipulative

WORK ENVIRONMENT
Primarily outdoors
Primarily multiple locations

MINIMUM EDUCATION LEVEL
Some postsecondary training

MEDIAN SALARY
$36,899

CERTIFICATION OR LICENSING
None available

OUTLOOK
About as fast as the average

Whatever the employer, operating engineers run power shovels, cranes, derricks, hoists, pile drivers, concrete mixers, paving machines, trench excavators, bulldozers, tractors, and pumps. They use these machines to move construction materials, earth, logs, coal, grain, and other material. Generally, operating engineers move the materials over short distances: around a construction site, factory, or warehouse or on and off trucks and ships. They also do minor repairs on the equipment, as well as keep them fueled and lubricated. They often are identified by the machines they operate.

Bulldozer operators operate the familiar bulldozer, a tractor-like vehicle with a large blade across the front for moving rocks, trees, earth, and other obstacles from construction sites. They also operate trench excavators, road graders, and similar equipment.

Crane and tower operators lift and move materials, machinery, or other heavy objects with mechanical booms and tower and cable equipment. Although some cranes are used on construction sites, most are used in manufacturing and other industries.

Excavation and loading machine operators handle machinery equipped with scoops, shovels, or buckets to excavate earth at construction sites and to load and move loose materials, mainly in the construction and mining industries.

Hoist and winch operators lift and pull heavy loads using power-operated equipment. Most work in loading operations in construction, manufacturing, logging, transportation, public utilities, and mining.

Operating engineers use various pedals, levers, and switches to run their machinery. For example, crane operators may rotate a crane on its chassis, lift and lower its boom, or lift and lower the load. They also use various attachments to the boom such as buckets, pile drivers, or heavy wrecking balls. When a tall building is being constructed, the crane and its operator may be positioned several hundred feet off the ground.

Operating engineers must have very precise knowledge about the capabilities and limitations of the machines they operate. To avoid tipping over their cranes or damaging their loads, crane operators must be able to judge distance and height and estimate their load size. They must be able to raise and lower the loads with great accuracy. Sometimes operators cannot see the point where the load is to be picked up or delivered. At these times, they follow the directions of other workers using hand or flag signals or radio transmissions.

The range of skills of the operating engineer is broader than in most building trades as the machines themselves differ in the ways they operate and the jobs they do. Some operators know how to work several types of machines, while others specialize with one machine.

REQUIREMENTS
High School

A high school education or its equivalent is valuable for the operating engineer and is a requirement for apprenticeship training. Mathematics, physics, and shop classes can provide useful preparation for operating construction equipment.

Postsecondary Training

There are two ways to become an operating engineer: through a union apprentice program or on-the-job training. The apprenticeship, which lasts three years, has at least two advantages: the instruction is more complete, which results in greater employment opportunities, and both labor and management know that the apprentice

is training to be a machine operator. Applicants to an apprenticeship program generally must be between the ages of 18 and 30.

Besides learning on the job, the apprentice also receives some classroom instruction in grade-plans reading, elements of electricity, physics, welding, and lubrication services. Despite the advantages of apprenticeships, most apprenticeship programs are difficult to enter because the number of apprentices is limited to the number of skilled workers already in the field.

Other Requirements

Operating engineers must have excellent mechanical aptitude and skillful coordination of eye, hand, and foot movements. In addition, because reckless use of the machinery may be dangerous to other workers, it is necessary to have a good sense of responsibility and seriousness on the job.

Operating engineers should be healthy and strong. They need the temperament to withstand dirt and noise and to endure all kinds of weather conditions. Many operating engineers belong to the International Union of Operating Engineers.

EXPLORING

You may be able to gain practical experience with operating machines by observing them in action by working as a laborer or machine operator's helper in a construction job during the summer. Such jobs may be available on local, state, and federal highway and building construction programs.

EMPLOYERS

Construction equipment operators hold approximately 494,000 jobs in the United States. They work for contractors who build highways, dams, airports, skyscrapers, buildings, and other large-scale projects. They also work for utility companies, manufacturers, factories, mines, steel mills, and other firms that do their own construction work. Many work for state and local public works and highway departments.

STARTING OUT

Once apprentices complete their training, their names are put on a list; as positions open up, they are filled in order from the list of available workers. People who do not complete an apprenticeship program may apply directly to manufacturers, utilities, or contractors who employ operating engineers for entry-level jobs as machine operator's helpers.

ADVANCEMENT

Some operating engineers (generally those with above-average ability and interest, as well as good working habits) advance to job supervisor and occasionally construction supervisor. Some are able to qualify for higher pay by training themselves to operate more complicated machines.

EARNINGS

The median annual salary for all operating engineers and other construction equipment operators was approximately $36,899 in 2006, according to the U.S. Department of Labor. Salaries ranged from less than $24,003 to more than $64,106 a year.

Often, workers are paid by the hour. Rates vary according to the area of the country and the employer. In highway and street construction, the median hourly salary was $19.88 in 2006. Those working in heavy construction (except highway work) earned $17.63 an hour. In local government, operating engineers made approximately $15.95 an hour.

WORK ENVIRONMENT

Operating engineers consider dirt and noise a part of their jobs. Some of the machines on which they work constantly shake and jolt them. This constant movement, along with the strenuous, outdoor nature of the work, makes this a physically tiring job. Since the work is done almost entirely outdoors in almost any kind of weather, operating engineers must be willing to work under conditions that are often unpleasant.

OUTLOOK

Employment of all operating engineers is projected to grow about as fast as the average through 2016. Although job growth will be somewhat limited by increased efficiency brought about by automation, there will be many opportunities for operating engineers. Operating engineers will be needed to assist with the repair of highways, bridges, dams, harbors, airports, subways, water and sewage systems, power plants, and transmission lines. Construction of schools, office and other commercial buildings, and residential property will also stimulate demand for these workers. However, the construction industry is very sensitive to changes in the overall economy, so the number of openings may fluctuate from year to year.

FOR MORE INFORMATION

For information on training, contact
> Associated General Contractors of America
> 2300 Wilson Boulevard., Suite 400

> Arlington, VA 22201-5426
> Tel: 703-548-3118
> Email: info@agc.org
> http://www.agc.org

For information on careers, apprenticeships, and union membership, contact
> **International Union of Operating Engineers**
> 1125 17th Street, NW
> Washington, DC 20036-4707
> Tel: 202-429-9100
> http://www.iuoe.org

For information on training, contact
> **National Center for Construction Education and Research**
> 3600 NW 43rd Street, Building G
> Gainesville, FL 32606-8137
> http://www.nccer.org

PAINTERS AND PAPERHANGERS

OVERVIEW

For both practical purposes and aesthetic appeal, building surfaces are often painted and decorated with various types of coverings. Although painting and paperhanging are two separate skills, many building trades craftsworkers do both types of work. *Painters* apply paints, varnishes, enamels, and other types of finishes to decorate and protect interior and exterior surfaces of buildings and other structures. *Paperhangers* cover interior walls and ceilings with decorative paper, fabric, vinyls, and other types of materials. There are approximately 473,000 painters and paperhangers working in the United States.

THE JOB

Workers in the painting and paperhanging trades often perform both functions: Painters may take on jobs that involve hanging wallpaper, and paperhangers may work in situations where they are responsible for painting walls and ceilings. However, although there is some overlap in the work, each trade has its own characteristic skills.

Painters must be able to apply paint thoroughly, uniformly, and rapidly to any type of surface. To do this, they must be skilled in handling brushes and other painting tools and have a working knowledge of the various

QUICK FACTS

SCHOOL SUBJECTS
Mathematics
Technical/shop

PERSONAL SKILLS
Artistic
Following instructions

WORK ENVIRONMENT
Indoors and outdoors
Primarily multiple locations

MINIMUM EDUCATION LEVEL
Apprenticeship

MEDIAN SALARY
$31,200 (Painters)
$33,717 (Paperhangers)

CERTIFICATION OR LICENSING
None available

OUTLOOK
About as fast as the average

characteristics of paints and finishes—their durability, suitability, and ease of handling and application.

Preparation of the area to be painted is an important duty of painters, especially when repainting old surfaces. They first smooth the surface, removing old, loose paint with a scraper, paint remover (usually a liquid solution), wire brush, or paint-removing gun (similar in appearance to a hairdryer) or a combination of these items. If necessary, they remove grease and fill nail holes, cracks, and joints with putty, plaster, or other types of filler. Often, a prime coat or sealer is applied to further smooth the surface and make the finished coat level and well blended in color.

Once the surface is prepared, painters select premixed paints or prepare paint by mixing required portions of pigment, oil, and thinning and drying substances. (For purposes of preparing paint, workers must have a thorough knowledge of the composition of the various mate-

rials they use and of which materials mix well together.) They then paint the surface using a brush, spray gun, or roller. Choosing the most appropriate tool for applying paint is one of the most important decisions a painter must make because using incorrect tools often slows down the work and produces unacceptable results. Spray guns are used generally for large surfaces or objects that do not lend themselves to brush work, such as lattices, cinder and concrete blocks, and radiators.

Many painters specialize in working on exterior surfaces only, painting house sidings and outside walls of large buildings. When doing work on tall buildings, scaffolding (raised supportive platforms) must be erected to allow the painter to climb to his or her position at various heights above the ground; workers might also use swing-like and chair-like platforms hung from heavy cables.

The first task of the paperhanger is similar to that of the painter: to prepare the surface to be covered. Rough spots must be smoothed, holes and cracks must be filled, and old paint, varnish, and grease must be removed from the surface. In some cases, old wallpaper must be removed by brushing it with solvent, soaking it down with water, or steaming it with portable steamer equipment. In new work, the paperhangers apply sizing, which is a prepared glazing material used as filler to make the plaster less porous and to ensure that the paper sticks well to the surface.

After erecting any necessary scaffolding, the paperhangers measure the area to be covered and cut the paper to size. They then mix paste and apply it to the back of the paper, which is then placed on the wall or ceiling and smoothed into place with brushes or rollers. In placing the paper on the wall, paperhangers must make sure that they match any design patterns at the adjacent edges of paper strips, cut overlapping ends, and smooth the seams between each strip.

REQUIREMENTS
High School

Although a high school education is not essential, it is preferred that workers have at least the equivalent, such as a GED diploma. Shop classes can help prepare you for the manual work involved in painting and paperhanging, while art classes will help you develop an eye for color and design. Chemistry classes will be useful in dealing with the paints, solvents, and other chemicals used in this work.

Postsecondary Training

To qualify as a skilled painter or paperhanger, a person must complete either an apprenticeship or an on-the-job training program. The apprenticeship program, which often combines painting and paperhanging, consists of three years of carefully planned activity, including work experience and related classroom instruction (approximately 144 hours of courses each year). During this period, the apprentice becomes familiar with all aspects of the craft: use of tools and equipment, preparation of surfaces as well as of paints and pastes, application methods, coordination of colors, reading of blueprints, characteristics of wood and other surfaces, cost-estimating methods, and safety techniques. Courses often involve the study of mathematics as well as practice sessions on the techniques of the trade.

On-the-job training programs involve learning the trade informally while working for two to three years under the guidance of experienced painters or paperhangers. The trainees usually begin as helpers until they acquire the necessary skills and knowledge for more difficult jobs. Workers without formal apprenticeship training are more easily accepted in these crafts than in most of the other building trades.

Other Requirements

Basic skills requirements are the same for both painters and paperhangers. Most employers prefer to hire applicants in good physical condition, with manual dexterity and a good sense of color. For protection of their own health, applicants should not be allergic to paint fumes or other materials used in the trade.

EXPLORING

You can explore the work of painters and paperhangers by reading trade journals and watching instructional videos or television programs. Those who already have some experience in the trade should keep up with the news by reading such publications as the monthly *Painters and Allied Trades Journal*, available to members of the International Union of Painters and Allied Trades (http://www.iupat.org/about/publications.html). Look for educational books and videos at your local library. The projects tackled on television home improvement shows almost always feature the work of painters or paperhangers to some extent.

Certainly, painting and paperhanging in your own home or apartment provide valuable firsthand experience, often impossible to obtain in other fields. Also valuable is the experience gained with a part-time or summer job as a helper to skilled workers who are already in the trade. Those who have done satisfactory part-time work sometimes go on to work full time for the same employer after a certain period of time.

EMPLOYERS

There are approximately 473,000 painters and paperhangers employed in the United States; most of them are painters and trade union members. Approximately 42 percent of these workers are self-employed. Jobs are found mainly with contractors who work on projects such as new construction, remodeling, and restoration; others are found as maintenance workers for such establishments as schools, apartment complexes, and high-rise buildings.

STARTING OUT

If you wish to become an apprentice, you should contact employers, your state's employment service bureau or apprenticeship agency, or the union headquarters of the International Union of Painters and Allied Trades. You must, however, have the approval of the joint labor-management apprenticeship committee before you can enter the occupation by this method. If the apprentice program is filled, you may wish to enter the trade as an on-the-job trainee. In this case, you usually should contact employers directly to begin work as a helper.

ADVANCEMENT

Successful completion of one of the two types of training programs is necessary before individuals can become qualified, skilled painters or paperhangers. If workers have management ability and good planning skills, and if they work for a large contracting firm, they may advance to the following positions: *supervisor*, who supervises and coordinates activities of other workers; *painting and decorating contract estimator*, who computes material requirements and labor costs; or *superintendent*, who oversees a large contract painting job.

Some painters and paperhangers, once they have acquired enough capital and business experience, go into business for themselves as painting and decorating contractors. These self-employed workers must be able to take care of all standard business affairs, such as bookkeeping, insurance and legal matters, advertising, and billing.

EARNINGS

Painters and paperhangers tend to earn more per hour than many other construction workers, but their total annual incomes may be less because of work time lost due to poor weather and periods of layoffs between contract assignments. In 2006, median hourly earnings of painters, construction and maintenance were $15 (or $31,200 annually), according to the U.S. Department of Labor.

Hourly wages ranged from less than $9.97 (or $20,738 annually) to more than $25.62 (or $53,290 annually). In general, paperhangers make more than painters. The Department of Labor reports that paperhangers earned a median hourly salary of $16.21 (or $33,717 annually) in 2006. Wages ranged from less $10.34 ($21,507 annually) to $26.77 ($55,682 annually). Hourly wage rates for painting and paperhanging apprentices usually start at 40 to 50 percent of the rate for experienced workers and increase periodically. Wages often vary depending on the geographic location of the job.

WORK ENVIRONMENT

Most painters and paperhangers have a standard 40-hour workweek, and they usually earn extra pay for working overtime. Their work requires them to stand for long periods of time, to climb, and to bend. Painters work both indoors and outdoors, because their job may entail painting interior surfaces as well as exterior siding and other areas; paperhangers work exclusively indoors. Because these occupations involve working on ladders and often with electrical equipment such as power sanders and paint sprayers, workers must adhere to safety standards.

OUTLOOK

Employment of painters and paperhangers is expected to grow about as fast as the average for all occupations through 2016, according to the U.S. Department of Labor. Most job openings will occur as other workers retire, transfer, or otherwise leave the occupation. Turnover is very high in this trade. Openings for paperhangers will be fewer than those for painters, however, because this is a smaller specialized trade.

Increased construction will generate a need for more painters to work on new buildings and industrial structures. However, this will also lead to increased competition among self-employed painters and painting contractors for the better jobs. Newer types of paint have made it easier for inexperienced persons to do their own painting, but this does not affect the employment outlook much because most painters and paperhangers work on industrial and commercial projects and are not dependent on residential work.

FOR MORE INFORMATION

For information on union membership, contact
International Union of Painters and Allied Trades
1750 New York Avenue, NW
Washington, DC 20006-5301

Tel: 202-637-0700
Email: mail@iupat.org
http://www.iupat.org

For additional information about becoming a painter or paperhanger, contact the following organizations:
National Association of Home Builders
1201 15th Street, NW
Washington, DC 20005-2842
Tel: 800-368-5242
http://www.nahb.com

Painting and Decorating Contractors of America
1801 Park 270 Drive, Suite 220
St. Louis, MO 63146-4020
Tel: 800-332-7322
http://www.pdca.org

PARALEGALS

OVERVIEW

Paralegals, also known as *legal assistants*, assist in trial preparations, investigate facts, prepare documents such as affidavits and pleadings, and, in general, do work customarily performed by lawyers. Approximately 238,000 paralegals and legal assistants work in law firms, businesses, and government agencies all over the United States; the majority work with lawyers and legislators.

THE JOB

A paralegal's main duty is to do everything a lawyer needs to do but does not have time to do. Although the lawyer assumes responsibility for the paralegal's work, the paralegal may take on all the duties of the lawyer except for setting fees, appearing in court, accepting cases, and giving legal advice.

Paralegals spend much of their time in law libraries, researching laws and previous cases and compiling facts to help lawyers prepare for trial. Paralegals often interview witnesses as part of their research as well. After analyzing the laws and facts that have been compiled for a particular client, the paralegal often writes a report that the lawyer may use to determine how to proceed with the case. If a case is brought to trial, the paralegal helps prepare legal arguments and draft pleadings to be filed in court. They also organize and store files and correspondence related to cases.

Not all paralegal work centers on trials. Many paralegals work for corporations, agencies, schools, and financial institutions. *Corporate paralegals* create and maintain contracts, mortgages, affidavits, and other documents. They assist with corporate matters, such as shareholder agreements, contracts, and employee benefit plans. Another important part of a corporate paralegal's job is to stay on top of new laws and regulations to make sure the company is operating within those parameters.

Some paralegals work for the government. They may prepare complaints or talk to employers to find out why health or safety standards are not being met. They often analyze legal documents, collect evidence for hearings, and prepare explanatory material on various laws for use by the public. For example, a *court administrator paralegal* is in charge of keeping the courthouse functioning; tasks include monitoring personnel, handling the case load for the court, and general administration.

Other paralegals are involved in community or public-service work. They may help specific groups, such as poor or elderly members of the community. They may file forms, research laws, and prepare documents. They may represent clients at hearings, although they may not appear in court on behalf of a client.

Many paralegals work for large law firms, agencies, and corporations and specialize in a particular area of law. Some work for smaller firms and have a general knowledge of many areas of law. Paralegals have varied duties, and must be familiar with certain computer software and database programs, as well as the Internet, in order to accomplish their work.

REQUIREMENTS
High School

While in high school, take a broad range of subjects, including English, social studies or government, computer science, and languages, especially Spanish and Latin. Because legal terminology is used constantly, word origins and vocabulary should be a focus.

Postsecondary Training

Requirements for paralegals vary by employer. Some paralegals start out as legal secretaries or clerical workers and gradually are given more training and responsibility. The majority, however, choose formal training and education programs.

Formal training programs usually range from one to three years and are offered in a variety of educational

QUICK FACTS

SCHOOL SUBJECTS
Computer science
English
Government

PERSONAL SKILLS
Communication/ideas
Following instructions

WORK ENVIRONMENT
Primarily indoors
Primarily multiple locations

MINIMUM EDUCATION LEVEL
Some postsecondary training

MEDIAN SALARY
$43,040

CERTIFICATION OR LICENSING
Voluntary

OUTLOOK
Much faster than the average

settings: four-year colleges and universities, law schools, community and junior colleges, business schools, proprietary schools, and paralegal associations. Admission requirements vary, but good grades in high school and college are always an asset. There are approximately 1,000 paralegal programs, about 260 of which have been approved by the American Bar Association. The National Federation of Paralegal Associations reports that 85 percent of all paralegals receive formal paralegal education.

Some paralegal programs require a bachelor's degree for admission; others do not require any college education. In either case, those who have a college degree usually have an edge over those who do not.

Certification or Licensing

Paralegals are not required to be licensed or certified. Instead, when lawyers employ paralegals, they often follow guidelines designed to protect the public from the practice of law by unqualified persons.

Paralegals may, however, opt to be certified. To do so, they may take and pass an extensive two-day test conducted by the National Association of Legal Assistants (NALA) Certifying Board. Paralegals who pass the test may use the title certified legal assistant (CLA) after their names. In 1994, the National Federation of Paralegal Associations established the Paralegal Advanced Competency Exam (PACE), as a means for paralegals who fill education and experience requirements to acquire professional recognition. Paralegals who pass this exam and maintain the continuing education requirement may use the designation "registered paralegal" (RP).

Other Requirements

Communication skills, both verbal and written, are vital to working as a paralegal. You must be able to turn research into reports that a lawyer or corporate executive can use. You must also be able to think logically and learn new laws and regulations quickly. Research skills, computer skills, and people skills are other necessities.

EXPLORING

If you are interested in a career as a paralegal, but you are not positive yet, do not worry. There are several ways you can explore the career of a paralegal. Colleges, universities, and technical schools have a wealth of information available for the asking. Elizabeth Houser, a practicing paralegal, recommends contacting schools that have paralegal programs directly. "Ask questions. They are helpful and will give you a lot of information about being a paralegal," she says.

Look for summer or part-time employment as a secretary or in the mailroom of a law firm to get an idea of the nature of the work. If paid positions are not available, offer yourself as a volunteer to the law offices in town. Ask your guidance counselor to help you set up a volunteer/internship agreement with a lawyer.

Talk to your history or government teacher about organizing a trip to a lawyer's office and a courthouse. Ask your teacher to set aside time for you to talk to paralegals working there and to their supervising attorneys.

If you have access to a computer, search the Web for information on student organizations that are affiliated with the legal profession. You can also contact the organizations listed at the end of this article for general information.

EMPLOYERS

Paralegals and legal assistants hold approximately 238,000 jobs. The majority work for lawyers in law offices or in law firms. Other paralegals work for the government, namely for the Federal Trade Commission, Justice Department, Treasury Department, Internal Revenue Service, Department of the Interior, and many other agencies and offices. Paralegals also work in the business community. Anywhere legal matters are part of the day-to-day work, paralegals are usually handling them. Paralegals fit in well in business because many smaller corporations must deal with legal regulations but don't necessarily need an attorney or a team of lawyers.

Paralegals in business can be found all over the country. Larger cities employ more paralegals who focus on the legal side of the profession, and government paralegals will find the most opportunities in state capitals and Washington, D.C.

STARTING OUT

Although some law firms promote legal secretaries to paralegal status, most employers prefer to hire individuals who have completed paralegal programs. To have the best opportunity at getting a quality job in the paralegal field, you should attend a paralegal school. In addition to providing a solid background in paralegal studies, most schools help graduates find jobs. Even though the job market for paralegals is expected to grow rapidly through to at least 2016, those with the best credentials will get the best jobs.

For Elizabeth Houser, the internship program was the springboard to her first paralegal position. "The paralegal program of study I took required an internship. I was hired directly from that internship experience."

The National Federation of Paralegal Associations recommends using job banks that are sponsored by paralegal associations across the country. For paralegal associations that may be able to help, see the addresses listed at the end of this article. Many jobs for paralegals are posted on the Internet as well.

ADVANCEMENT

There are no formal advancement paths for paralegals. There are, however, some possibilities for advancement, as large firms are beginning to establish career programs for paralegals.

For example, a person may be promoted from a paralegal to a head legal assistant who supervises others. In addition, a paralegal may specialize in one area of law, such as environmental, real estate, or medical malpractice. Many paralegals also advance by moving from small to large firms.

Expert paralegals who specialize in one area of law may go into business for themselves. Rather than work for one firm, these freelance paralegals often contract their services to many lawyers. Some paralegals with bachelor's degrees enroll in law school to train to become lawyers.

Paralegals can also move horizontally by taking their specialized knowledge of the law into another field, such as insurance, occupational health, or law enforcement.

EARNINGS

Salaries vary greatly for paralegals. The size and location of the firm and the education and experience of the employee are some factors that determine the annual earnings of paralegals.

The U.S. Department of Labor reports that paralegals and legal assistants had median annual earnings of $43,040 in 2006. The highest 10 percent earned more than $67,540, while the lowest 10 percent earned less than $27,450. According to the 2008 National Utilization and Compensation Survey Report conducted by the National Association of Legal Assistants, the average total compensation (including bonuses) earned by legal assistants in 2007 was above $50,000, and some higher level paralegals earned more than $80,000.

WORK ENVIRONMENT

Paralegals often work in pleasant and comfortable offices. Much of their work is performed in a law library. Some paralegals work out of their homes in special employment situations. When investigation is called for, paralegals may travel to gather information. Most paralegals work a 40-hour week, although long hours are sometimes required to meet court-imposed deadlines. Longer hours—sometimes as much as 90 hours per week—are usually the normal routine for paralegals starting out in law offices and firms.

Many of the paralegal's duties involve routine tasks, so they must have a great deal of patience. However, paralegals may be given increasingly difficult assignments over time. Paralegals are often unsupervised, especially as they gain experience and a reputation for quality work. Elizabeth Houser does much of her work unsupervised. "You get to put a lot of yourself into what you do and that provides a high level of job satisfaction," she says.

OUTLOOK

Employment for paralegals is expected to grow much faster than the average through 2016, according to the

U.S. Department of Labor. One reason for the expected rapid growth in the profession is the financial benefits of employing paralegals. The paralegal, whose duties fall between those of the legal secretary and those of the attorney, helps make the delivery of legal services more cost effective to clients. The growing need for legal services among the general population and the increasing popularity of prepaid legal plans is creating a tremendous demand for paralegals in private law firms. In the private sector, paralegals can work in banks, insurance companies, real estate and title insurance firms, and corporate legal departments. In the public sector, there is a growing need for paralegals in the courts and community legal service programs, government agencies, and consumer organizations.

The growth of this occupation, to some extent, is dependent on the economy. Businesses are less likely to pursue litigation cases when profit margins are down, thus curbing the need for new hires.

FOR MORE INFORMATION

For information regarding accredited educational facilities, contact

American Association for Paralegal Education
19 Mantua Road
Mt. Royal, NJ 08061-1006
Tel: 856-423-2829
Email: info@aafpe.org
http://www.aafpe.org

For general information about careers in the law field, contact

American Bar Association
321 North Clark Street, 14th Floor
Chicago, IL 60610-7598
Tel: 800-285-2221
http://www.abanet.org

For career information, contact

Association of Legal Administrators
75 Tri-State International, Suite 222
Lincolnshire, IL 60069-4435
Tel: 847-267-1252
http://www.alanet.org

For information about educational and licensing programs, certification, and paralegal careers, contact

National Association of Legal Assistants
1516 South Boston Avenue, Suite 200
Tulsa, OK 74119-4013
Tel: 918-587-6828

Email: nalanet@nala.org
http://www.nala.org

For information about almost every aspect of becoming a paralegal, contact
National Federation of Paralegal Associations
PO Box 2016
Edmonds, WA 98020-9516
Tel: 425-967-0045
Email: info@paralegals.org
http://www.paralegals.org

For information about employment networks and school listings, contact
National Paralegal Association
PO Box 406
Solebury, PA 18963-0406
Tel: 215-297-8333
Email: admin@nationalparalegal.org
http://www.nationalparalegal.org

❑ PERSONAL TRAINERS

OVERVIEW

Personal trainers, often known as *fitness trainers*, assist health-conscious people with exercise, weight training, weight loss, diet and nutrition, and medical rehabilitation. During one training session, or over a period of several sessions, trainers teach their clients how to achieve their health and fitness goals. They train in the homes of their clients, their own studio spaces, or in health clubs. More than 235,000 personal trainers work in the United States, either independently or on the staff of a fitness center.

THE JOB

Remember the first time you ever went to the gym? The weight machines may have resembled medieval forms of torture. So, to avoid the weight training, you stuck to the treadmill. Or maybe you called upon the services of a personal trainer. Personal trainers help their clients achieve health and fitness goals. They instruct on the proper use of exercise equipment and weight machines and may suggest diet and nutrition tips.

If you've reached your own workout goals, then you may be ready to help others reach theirs. "You have to

believe in working out and eating healthy," advises Emelina Edwards, a personal trainer in New Orleans. For 12 years she's been in the business of personal training, a career she chose after whipping herself into great shape at the age of 46. Now, at 58, she has a lot of firsthand experience in training, nutrition, aerobic exercise, and stress management. Edwards says, "You have to practice what you preach."

And practice Edwards does—not only does she devote time every day to her own weight training, jogging, and meditation, but she works with three to five clients in the workout facility in her home. She has a total of about 20 clients, some of whom she assists in one-on-one sessions, and others in small groups. Her clients have included men and women from the ages of 20 to 80 who are looking to improve their general physical condition or to work on specific ailments.

When meeting with a client for the first time, Edwards gets a quick history of his or her physical problems and medical conditions. "If problems are serious," Edwards says, "I check with their doctor. If mild, I explain to them what I believe will help." When she discovered that four out of five people seeking her help suffered from back problems, she did a great deal of research on back pain and how to alleviate it through exercise. "I teach people how to do for themselves," she says. "Sometimes I see a person once, or for three or four sessions, or forever."

In addition to working directly with clients, Edwards is active promoting her line of "Total Body Rejuvenation" products. These products, consisting of audiotapes and books, are based on her years of experience and the many articles she has written for fitness publications. When she's not training clients, writing articles, and selling products, she's reading fitness publications to keep up on the business, as well as speaking at public events. "When I realized I loved training," she says, "I thought of all the things I could relate to it. So along with the training, I began to write about it, and to give talks on health and fitness."

Successful personal trainers do not necessarily have to keep as busy as Edwards. They may choose to specialize in certain areas of personal training. They may work as an *athletic trainer*, helping athletes prepare for sports activities. They may specialize in helping with the rehabilitation treatment of people with injuries and other physical problems. Yoga, dance, martial arts, indoor cycling, boxing, and water fitness have all become aspects of special training programs. People call upon personal trainers to help them quit smoking, to assist with healthy pregnancies, and to maintain mental and emotional stability. Whatever the problem, whether mental or physical, people are turning to exercise and nutrition to help them deal with it.

Many personal trainers have their own studios or home gyms where they train their clients; others go into the homes of their clients. Because of the demands of the workplace, many personal trainers also work in offices and corporate fitness centers. Though most health clubs hire their own trainers to assist with club members, some hire freelance trainers as independent contractors. These independent contractors are not considered staff members and do not receive employee benefits.

REQUIREMENTS
High School

If you are interested in health and fitness, you are probably already taking physical education classes and involved in sports activities. It is also important to take health courses and courses like home economics, which include lessons in diet and nutrition. Business courses can help you prepare for the management aspect of running your own personal training service. Science courses such as biology, chemistry, and physiology are important for your understanding of muscle groups, food and drug reactions, and other concerns of exercise science. If you are not interested in playing on sports teams, you may be able to volunteer as an assistant. These positions will allow you to learn about athletic training as well as rehabilitation treatments.

Postsecondary Training

A college education is not required to work as a personal trainer, but you can benefit from one of the many fitness-related programs offered at colleges across the country. Some relevant college programs include health education, exercise and sports science, fitness program management, and athletic training. These programs include courses in therapeutic exercise, nutrition, aerobics, and fitness and aging. The IDEA Health and Fitness Association recommends a bachelor's degree from a program that includes at least a semester each in anatomy, kinesiology, and exercise physiology. IDEA offers scholarships to students seeking careers as fitness professionals.

If you are not interested in a full four-year program, many schools offer shorter versions of their bachelor's programs. Upon completing a shorter program, you'll receive either an associate's degree or certification from the school. Once you have established yourself in the business, continuing education courses are important for you to keep up with the advances in the industry. IDEA is

QUICK FACTS

SCHOOL SUBJECTS
Health
Physical education

PERSONAL SKILLS
Communication/ideas
Helping/teaching

WORK ENVIRONMENT
Primarily indoors
Primarily multiple locations

MINIMUM EDUCATION LEVEL
Some postsecondary training

MEDIAN SALARY
$25,910

CERTIFICATION OR LICENSING
Recommended

OUTLOOK
Much faster than the average

one of many organizations that offer independent study courses, conferences, and seminars.

Certification or Licensing

There are so many schools and organizations that offer certification to personal trainers that it has become a concern in the industry. Without more rigid standards, the profession could suffer at the hands of less experienced, less skilled trainers. Some organizations only require membership fees and short tests for certification. Emelina Edwards isn't certified and doesn't believe that certification is necessary. "Experience is what counts," she says.

However, the U.S. Department of Labor reports that personal trainers must be certified in the fitness field to find employment, and health clubs look for certified trainers when hiring independent contractors. If you are seeking certification, you should choose a certifying board that offers scientifically based exams and requires continuing education credits. The American Council on Exercise, the National Federation of Professional Trainers, and the American Fitness Professionals and Associates are just a few of the many groups with certification programs.

Other Requirements

Physical fitness and knowledge of health and nutrition are the most important assets of personal trainers. "The more intelligently you can speak to someone," Edwards says, "the more receptive they'll be." Your clients will also be more receptive to patience and friendliness. "I'm very enthusiastic and positive," she says regarding the way she works with her clients. You should be able to explain things clearly, recognize progress, and encourage it. You should be comfortable working one-on-one with people of all ages and in all physical conditions. An interest in reading fitness books and publications is important to your continuing education.

EXPLORING

Your high school may have a weight-training program, or some other extracurricular fitness program, as part of its athletic department; in addition to signing up for the program, you can assist the faculty who manage it. That way, you can learn about what goes into developing and maintaining such a program. If your school doesn't have a fitness program, seek one out at a community center, or join a health club.

You should also try the services of a personal trainer. By conditioning yourself and eating a healthy diet, you'll get a good sense of the duties of a personal trainer. Any number of books and magazines address issues of health and nutrition and offer weight-training advice. The IDEA publishes several helpful health- and career-related publications including *IDEA Fitness Journal* and *IDEA Trainer Success*.

Finally, seek out part-time work at a gym or health club to meet trainers and learn about weight machines and certification programs.

EMPLOYERS

The U.S. Department of Labor reports that in 2006, more than 235,000 fitness workers held jobs in the United States. Personal trainers are employed by people of all ages. Individuals hire the services of trainers, as do companies for the benefit of their employees. Though most health clubs hire personal trainers full time, some clubs hire trainers on an independent contractor basis. Sports and exercise programs at community colleges hire trainers part time to conduct classes.

Personal trainers can find clients in most major cities in all regions of the country. In addition to health clubs and corporate fitness centers, trainers find work at YMCAs, aerobics studios, and hospital fitness centers.

STARTING OUT

Most people who begin personal training do so after successful experiences with their own training. Once they've developed a good exercise regimen and healthy diet plan for themselves, they may feel ready to help others. Emelina Edwards had hit a low point in her life, and had turned to weight training to help her get through the difficult times. "I didn't have a college degree," she says, "and I needed something to do. All I had was weight training." She then called up all the women she knew, promoting her services as a personal trainer. Through the benefit of word-of-mouth, Edwards built up a clientele.

Some trainers begin by working part time or full time for health clubs and, after making connections, they go into business for themselves. As with most small businesses, personal trainers must promote themselves through classified ads, flyers posted in community centers, and other forms of advertisement. Many personal trainers have published guides on how to establish businesses. IDEA offers a book called *The Successful Trainer's Guide to Marketing: How to Get Clients and Make Money*, which offers advice on how to attract clients.

ADVANCEMENT

After personal trainers have taken on as many individual clients as they need to maintain a business, they may choose to lead small group training sessions or conduct large aerobics classes. Some trainers join forces with other trainers to start their own fitness centers. Trainers who are employed by fitness centers may be promoted to the position of *personal training director*. These workers supervise and schedule other personal trainers and manage department budgets.

Emelina Edwards has advanced her business by venturing out into other areas of fitness instruction, such as publishing books and speaking to groups. "I want to develop more in the public speaking arena," she says. Right now, she only speaks to local groups—she'd like to go national. "I'd also like to break into the Latin market," she says. "The interest is there, and the response has been great."

EARNINGS

Hourly fees for personal trainers can range anywhere from less than $20 to $100 or more, depending upon years of experience and reputation in the field. Personal trainers who offer specialized instruction (such as in yoga, martial arts, or indoor cycling), or who work with their own clients in their own homes, can charge higher hourly rates. The U.S. Department of Labor reports that in 2006, the median annual salary for fitness trainers, which includes personal trainers, was $25,910. The lowest paid 10 percent earned $14,880 or less and the highest paid 10 percent earned $56,750 or more. A 2008 Salary. com survey found the middle 50 percent of personal trainers earning between $36,668 and $62,407.

WORK ENVIRONMENT

Personal training is obviously a physically demanding job, but anybody who is in good shape and who eats a healthy diet should be able to easily handle the demands. Personal trainers who work out of their homes will enjoy familiar and comfortable surroundings. Trainers who work in a gym as independent contractors will also experience a comfortable workplace. Most good gyms maintain a cool temperature, keep the facilities clean and well lit, and care for the weight machines. Whether in a gym or at home, personal trainers work directly with their clients, usually in one-on-one training sessions. In this teaching situation, the workplace is usually quiet and conducive to learning.

As with most self-employment, sustaining a business can be both rewarding and difficult. Many trainers appreciate being able to keep their own hours, and to work as little, or as much, as they care to. By setting their own schedules, they can arrange time for their personal workout routines. But, without an employer, there's less security, no benefits, and no steady paycheck. Personal trainers have to regularly promote their services and be ready to take on new clients.

OUTLOOK

Fitness training will continue to enjoy strong growth in the near future. The U.S. Department of Labor predicts employment opportunities for personal trainers and other fitness workers to grow much faster than the average through 2016. As the baby boomers grow older, they will increasingly rely on the services of personal trainers. Boomers have long been interested in health and fitness, and they will carry this into their old age. A knowledge of special weight training, stretching exercises, and diets for seniors will be necessary for personal trainers in the years to come. Trainers will actively promote their services to senior centers and retirement communities.

With the number of health publications and fitness centers, people are much more knowledgeable about exercise and nutrition. This could increase business for personal trainers, as people better understand the necessity of proper training and seek out professional assistance. Trainers may also be going into more of their clients' homes as people set up their own workout stations complete with weights and treadmills. In the health and medical field, new developments are constantly affecting how people eat and exercise. Personal trainers must keep up with these advances, as well as with any new trends in fitness and dieting.

FOR MORE INFORMATION

For general health and fitness topics, and to learn about certification, contact
American Council on Exercise
4851 Paramount Drive
San Diego, CA 92123-1449
Tel: 888-825-3636
http://www.acefitness.org

For information on certification, contact
American Fitness Professionals and Associates
PO Box 214
Ship Bottom, NJ 08008-0234
Tel: 609-978-7583
Email: afpa@afpafitness.com
http://www.afpafitness.com

IDEA conducts surveys, provides continuing education, and publishes a number of books and magazines relevant to personal trainers. For information about the fitness industry in general, and personal training specifically, contact
IDEA Health and Fitness Association
10455 Pacific Center Court
San Diego, CA 92121-4339
Tel: 800-999-4332 ext. 7
Email: contact@ideeafit.com
http://www.ideafit.com

For information on certification, contact
National Federation of Professional Trainers
PO Box 4579
Lafayette, IN 47903-4579
Tel: 800-729-6378
http://www.nfpt.com

PHARMACY TECHNICIANS

OVERVIEW

Pharmacy technicians provide technical assistance for pharmacists and work under their direct supervision.

QUICK FACTS

SCHOOL SUBJECTS

Biology

Chemistry

PERSONAL SKILLS

Following instructions

Technical/scientific

WORK ENVIRONMENT

Primarily indoors

Primarily one location

MINIMUM EDUCATION LEVEL

Some postsecondary training

MEDIAN SALARY

$25,626

CERTIFICATION OR LICENSING

Voluntary

OUTLOOK

Much faster than the average

They usually work in chain or independent drug stores, hospitals, community ambulatory care centers, home health care agencies, nursing homes, and the pharmaceutical industry. They perform a wide range of technical support functions and tasks related to the pharmacy profession. They maintain patient records; count, package, and label medication doses; prepare and distribute sterile products; and fill and dispense routine orders for stock supplies such as over-the-counter products. There are approximately 285,000 pharmacy technicians employed in the United States.

THE JOB

The roles of the pharmacist and pharmacy technician expanded greatly in the 1990s. The pharmacist's primary responsibility is to ensure that medications are used safely and effectively through clinical patient counseling and monitoring. In order to provide the highest quality of pharmaceutical care, pharmacists now focus on providing clinical services. As a result, pharmacy technicians' duties have evolved into a more specialized role known as pharmacy technology. Pharmacy technicians perform more of the manipulative functions associated with dispensing prescriptions. Their primary duties are drug-product preparation and distribution, but they are also concerned with the control of drug products. Technicians assemble, prepare, and deliver requested medication. Technicians are responsible for record keeping, and they record drug-related information on specified forms, frequently doing this part of the work on computers. Depending on a technician's experience, he or she may order pharmaceuticals and take inventory of controlled substances, such as Valium and Ritalin.

Technicians who work in hospitals have the most varied responsibilities of all pharmacy technicians. In a hospital, technicians fill total parenteral nutrition preparations and standard and chemotherapy IVs (intravenous solutions) for patients under doctors' orders. Other duties that a hospital pharmacy technician may be required to do include filling "stat," or immediate, orders and delivering them; preparing special emergency carts stocked with medications; and monitoring defibrillators and resuscitation equipment. In an emergency, pharmacy technicians respond with doctors and nurses, rushing the cart and other equipment to the emergency site. They also keep legal records of the events that occur during an emergency. Technicians work in the hospital's outpatient pharmacy, which is similar to a commercial drugstore, and assist the pharmacist in dispensing medication.

Tamara Britton works as a technician in a hospital. Because the hospital pharmacy is open 24 hours a day, Tamara has worked all three shifts. Her work involves using a computer to create labels for large IV bags and "piggybacks" (small-volume IV bags). She stacks the IVs on carts, then delivers them to the appropriate nurse stations. She also delivers medications through a process known as "tubing and shagging." Two "tubes," or lines, (similar to those at a bank's drive-through) run through the entire hospital to every nurse unit. "Shagging" is the process of placing the nurse unit's medications in baggies; the meds are then shot through the tubes to the proper units. Tamara also prepares drug carts with the aid of a RxOBOT; this robotic arm is in a glassed-off room, and fills the drawers of the carts with the correct medication for individual patients. Britton places coded labels on the drawers of the carts. She explains, "I put the drawers with labels facing Robota (we named her), and a conveyor belt takes them in the room for Robota to fill with all of the patients' existing meds for the day. The tray, after filling, drops down to a lower conveyor belt that brings the drawer back to me, which I replace in the cart."

As their roles increase, trained technicians have become more specialized. Some specialized types of pharmacy technicians include *narcotics control pharmacy technicians, operating room pharmacy technicians, emergency room pharmacy technicians, nuclear pharmacy technicians,* and *home health care pharmacy technicians.* Specially trained pharmacy technicians are also employed as *data entry technicians, lead technicians, supervisors,* and *technician managers.*

REQUIREMENTS
High School

You should take courses in mathematics and science (especially chemistry and biology), because you will be dealing with patient records and drug dosages. Health classes can help you get a basic understanding of the health care industry and various medical treatments. Take English and speech classes to help you develop your writing and communication skills. You will be using a computer a lot to maintain records and prepare labels, so take courses in computer fundamentals.

Postsecondary Training

In the past, pharmacy technicians received most of their training on the job in hospital and community pharmacy training programs. Since technician functions and duties have changed greatly in recent years, most pharmacy technicians today receive their education through formal training programs offered through community colleges, vocational/technical schools, hospital community pharmacies, and government programs throughout the United States. Program length usually ranges from six months to two years, and leads to a certificate, diploma, or associate's degree in pharmacy technology. A high school diploma usually is required for entry into a training program. The American Society of Health-System Pharmacists (ASHP) is the national accrediting organization for pharmacy technician training programs. ASHP can provide you with information on approved programs across the country (see address at end of this article).

In a pharmacy technician training program, you will receive classroom instruction and participate in supervised clinical apprenticeships in health institutions and community pharmacies. Courses include introduction to pharmacy and health care systems, pharmacy laws and ethics, medical terminology, chemistry, and microbiology. Most pharmacy technicians continue their education even

after their formal training ends by reading professional journals and attending training or informational seminars, lectures, review sessions, and audiovisual presentations.

Certification or Licensing

Certification is voluntary in most states, but required by some states and employers. Two organizations administer national certification exams: the Pharmacy Technician Certification Board (PTCB) and the Institute for the Certification of Pharmacy Technicians. Those who pass the test can use the certified pharmacy technician designation. After receiving certification, you will be required to complete 20 hours of continuing education every two years as part of the qualifications for recertification. Even though it is not required in every state, certification is recommended to enhance your credentials, demonstrate to employers your commitment to the profession, and possibly qualify you for higher pay.

Other Requirements

You must be precision-minded, honest, and mature as you are depended on for accuracy and high levels of quality control, especially in hospitals. "I pay attention to details," Tamara Britton says, "and try to catch all my own mistakes before a pharmacist checks my work." You need good communications skills in order to successfully interact with pharmacists, supervisors, and other technicians. You must be able to follow written and oral instructions precisely because a wide variety of people, including physicians, nurses, pharmacists, and patients, rely on your actions. You also need some computer aptitude in order to effectively record pharmaceutical data.

EXPLORING
Ask your school's guidance or career counselor to help you arrange for a pharmacy technician to talk to a group of students interested in this career. Your counselor may also be able to help you arrange for an informational interview with a pharmacy technician. You can then meet one-on-one with the technician and ask him or her about the work. Volunteer work at a local hospital or nursing home will provide you with an excellent opportunity to be in an environment similar to the one in which many professional technicians work. As a volunteer, you can hone your communication skills and learn about medical settings by interacting with both patients and medical staff. You may even have the opportunity to meet and talk with pharmacy technicians. Finally, look for a part-time or summer job at a local retail pharmacy. Although your

duties may be limited to stocking the shelves, working the cash register, or making deliveries, you will still gain valuable experience by working in this environment and interacting with trained pharmacists and technicians. By doing this, you may even be able to find a mentor who is willing to give you advice about education and the pharmacy technician career.

EMPLOYERS

Approximately 285,000 pharmacy technicians are employed in the United States. Most opportunities for pharmacy technicians are in retail, with chain pharmacy companies and supermarkets, as well as with independent pharmacies. Technicians also work in hospitals and long-term care facilities as well as in clinics at military bases, prisons, and colleges. Technicians are also finding work with home health care agencies, mail-order and Internet pharmacies, and with the federal government.

STARTING OUT

In some cases you may be able to pursue education and certification while employed as a pharmacy technician. Some chain drugstores pay the certification fees for their techs and also reward certified techs with higher hourly pay. This practice will probably increase—industry experts predict a need for pharmacists and technicians as more chain drug stores open across the country, and more pharmacies offer 24-hour service.

Pharmacy technicians often are hired by the hospital or agency where they interned. If you don't find employment this way, you can use employment agencies or newspaper ads to help locate job openings. Pharmacy technician Tamara Britton found her hospital job in the classifieds. "There was an ad that said 'use your data entry skills and become a pharmacy technician.' They tested me on data entry and then interviewed me and gave me the job. They trained me on all I needed to know to do the job."

ADVANCEMENT

Depending on where they are employed, technicians may direct or instruct newer pharmacy technicians, make schedules, or move to purchasing or computer work. Some hospitals have a variety of tech designations, based on experience and responsibility, with a corresponding increase in pay. Some pharmacy techs return to school to pursue a degree in pharmacy.

EARNINGS

According to the U.S. Department of Labor, pharmacy technicians had median annual earnings of $25,626 in 2006. The lowest paid 10 percent of technicians earned less than $17,805, while the highest paid 10 percent made $36,712 or more. Pharmacy technicians earned the following median salaries in 2006 by type of employer: general medical and surgical hospitals, $28,829; grocery stores, $26,582; pharmacies and drug stores, $23,920.

Benefits that technicians receive depend on their employers but generally include medical and dental insurance, retirement savings plans, and paid sick, personal, and vacation days.

WORK ENVIRONMENT

Pharmacy technicians work in clean, well-lit, pleasant, and professional surroundings. They may wear scrubs or other uniforms in hospitals, especially in the IV room. In a retail drugstore, a technician may be allowed to wear casual clothing along with a smock. Most pharmacy settings are extremely busy, especially hospital and retail. "I feel like I'm part of a system," Tamara Britton says, "to help the sick get better and maybe keep people from dying." Like any other occupation that demands skill, speed, and accuracy, the pharmacy technician job can be stressful. Because most hospitals, nursing homes, health care centers, and retail pharmacies are open between 16 and 24 hours a day, multiple shifts, weekend, and holiday hours are usually required.

OUTLOOK

The U.S. Department of Labor projects much faster than average employment growth for pharmacy technicians through 2016. As the role of the pharmacist shifts to consultation, more technicians will be needed to assemble and dispense medications. Furthermore, new employment avenues and responsibilities will mirror that of the expanding and evolving role of the pharmacist. A strong demand is emerging for technicians with specialized training to work in specific areas, such as emergency room and nuclear pharmacy. An increasing number of pharmacy technicians will be needed as the number of older Americans (who, on average, require more prescription medication than younger generations) continues to rise.

Those who want to work as pharmacy technicians should be aware that in the future, they may need more education to gain certification because of the growing number of complex medications and new drug therapies on the market. Mechanical advances in the pharmaceutical field, such as robot-picking devices and automatic counting equipment, may eradicate some of the duties pharmacy technicians previously performed, yet there will remain a need for skilled technicians to clean and maintain such devices. Traditionally, pharmacists have been required to check the work of technicians; however, in some states, hospitals are allowing techs to check the work of other techs.

FOR MORE INFORMATION

Contact AAPT for more information on membership and continuing education.

American Association of Pharmacy Technicians (AAPT)
PO Box 1447
Greensboro, NC 27402-1447
Tel: 877-368-4771
Email: aapt@pharmacytechnician.com
http://www.pharmacytechnician.com

For more information on accredited pharmacy technician training programs, contact

American Society of Health-System Pharmacists (ASHP)
7272 Wisconsin Avenue
Bethesda, MD 20814-4836
Tel: 301-657-3000
http://www.ashp.org

For industry information and employment opportunities in retail, contact

National Association of Chain Drug Stores
413 North Lee Street
Alexandria, VA 22314-2301
Tel: 703-549-3001
http://www.nacds.org

To learn more about certification and training, contact

Pharmacy Technician Certification Board
1100 15th Street, NW, Suite 730
Washington, DC 20005-1707
Tel: 800-363-8012
http://www.ptcb.org

Pharmacy Week *is a newsletter for professionals and pharmacy students. Check out the Web site for articles, industry news, job listings, and continuing education information.*

Pharmacy Week
http://www.pharmacyweek.com

PHOTOGRAPHERS

OVERVIEW

Photographers take and sometimes develop and print pictures of people, places, objects, and events, using a variety of cameras and photographic equipment. They

---

QUICK FACTS

SCHOOL SUBJECTS
Art
Chemistry

PERSONAL SKILLS
Artistic
Communication/ideas

WORK ENVIRONMENT
Indoors and outdoors
Primarily multiple locations

MINIMUM EDUCATION LEVEL
Some postsecondary training

MEDIAN SALARY
$26,170

CERTIFICATION OR LICENSING
None available

OUTLOOK
About as fast as the average

---

work in the publishing, advertising, public relations, science, and business industries, as well as provide personal photographic services. They may also work as fine artists. There are approximately 122,000 photographers employed in the United States.

THE JOB

Photography is both an artistic and technical occupation. There are many variables in the process that a knowledgeable photographer can manipulate to produce a clear image or a more abstract work of fine art. First, photographers know how to use cameras and can adjust focus, shutter speeds, aperture, lenses, and filters. They know about the types and speeds of films. Photographers also know about light and shadow, deciding when to use available natural light and when to set up artificial lighting to achieve desired effects.

Some photographers send their film to laboratories, but some develop their own negatives and make their own prints. These processes require knowledge about chemicals such as developers and fixers and how to use enlarging equipment. Photographers must also be familiar with the large variety of papers available for printing photographs, all of which deliver a different effect. Most photographers continually experiment with photographic processes to improve their technical proficiency or to create special effects.

Digital photography is a rapidly growing technology. With digital photography, film is replaced by microchips that record pictures in digital format. Pictures can then be downloaded onto a computer's hard drive. Photographers use special software to manipulate the images on screen. Digital photography is used primarily for electronic publishing and advertising, but it is increasingly being used for photos in newspapers and other traditional print publications.

Photographers usually specialize in one of several areas: portraiture, commercial and advertising photography, photojournalism, fine art, educational photography, or scientific photography. There are subspecialties within each of these categories. A *scientific photographer*, for example, may specialize in aerial or underwater photography. A *commercial photographer* may specialize in food or fashion photography.

Some photographers write for trade and technical journals, teach photography in schools and colleges, act as representatives of photographic equipment manufacturers, sell photographic equipment and supplies, produce documentary films, or do freelance work.

REQUIREMENTS

High School

While in high school, take as many art classes and photography classes that are available. Chemistry is useful for understanding developing and printing processes. You can learn about photo manipulation software and digital photography in computer classes, and business classes will help if you are considering a freelance career.

Postsecondary Training

Formal educational requirements depend upon the nature of the photographer's specialty. For instance, photographic work in scientific and engineering research generally requires an engineering background with a degree from a recognized college or institute.

A college education is not required to become a photographer, although college training probably offers the most

promising assurance of success in fields such as industrial, news, or scientific photography. There are degree programs at the associate's, bachelor's, and master's levels. Many schools offer courses in cinematography, although very few have programs leading to a degree in this specialty. Many men and women, however, become photographers with no formal education beyond high school.

To become a photographer, you should have a broad technical understanding of photography plus as much practical experience with cameras as possible. Take many different kinds of photographs with a variety of cameras and subjects. Learn how to develop photographs and, if possible, build your own darkroom or rent one. Experience in picture composition, cropping prints (cutting images to a desired size), enlarging, and retouching are all valuable. Familiarizing yourself with computer software programs such as Adobe Photoshop will also be helpful.

Other Requirements

You should possess manual dexterity, good eyesight and color vision, and artistic ability to succeed in this line of work. You need an eye for form and line, an appreciation of light and shadow, and the ability to use imaginative and creative approaches to photographs or film, especially in commercial work. In addition, you should be patient and accurate and enjoy working with detail.

Self-employed (or freelance) photographers need good business skills. They must be able to manage their own studios, including hiring and managing assistants and other employees, keeping records, and maintaining photographic and business files. Marketing and sales skills are also important to a successful freelance photography business.

EXPLORING

Photography is a field that anyone with a camera can explore. To learn more about this career, you can join high school camera clubs, yearbook or newspaper staffs, photography contests, and community hobby groups. You can also seek a part-time or summer job in a camera shop or work as a developer in a laboratory or processing center.

EMPLOYERS

About 122,000 photographers work in the United States, more than half of whom are self-employed. Most jobs for photographers are provided by photographic or commercial art studios; other employers include newspapers and magazines, radio and TV broadcasting, government agencies, and manufacturing firms. Colleges, universities, and other educational institutions and associations employ photographers to prepare promotional and educational materials.

STARTING OUT

Some photographers enter the field as apprentices, trainees, or assistants. Trainees may work in a darkroom, camera shop, or developing laboratory. They may move lights and arrange backgrounds for a commercial or portrait photographer or motion picture photographer. Assistants spend many months learning this kind of work before they move into a job behind a camera.

Many large cities offer schools of photography, which may be a good way to start in the field. Beginning press photographers may work for one of the many newspapers and magazines published in their area. Other photographers choose to go into business for themselves as soon as they have finished their formal education. Setting up a studio may not require a large capital outlay, but beginners may find that success does not come easily.

ADVANCEMENT

Because photography is such a diversified field, there is no usual way in which to get ahead. Those who begin by working for someone else may advance to owning their own businesses. Commercial photographers may gain prestige as more of their pictures are placed in well-known trade journals or popular magazines. Press photographers may advance in salary and the kinds of important news stories assigned to them. A few photographers may become celebrities in their own right by making contributions to the art world or the sciences.

EARNINGS

The U.S. Department of Labor reports that in 2006, salaried photographers earned median annual salaries of $26,170. Salaries ranged from less than $18,680 to more than $56,640. Self-employed photographers often earn more than salaried photographers, but their earnings depend on general business conditions. In addition, self-employed photographers do not receive the benefits that a company provides its employees.

Scientific photographers, who combine training in science with photographic expertise, usually start at higher salaries than other photographers. Salary.com reports that in 2008, the middle 50 percent of scientific photographers earned annual base salaries that ranged between $32,864 and $50,661. They also usually receive consistently larger advances in salary than do others, so that their income, both as beginners and as experienced photographers, places them well above the average in their field. Photographers in salaried jobs usually receive benefits such as paid holidays, vacations, and sick leave and medical insurance.

WORK ENVIRONMENT

Work conditions vary based on the job and employer. Many photographers work a 35- to 40-hour workweek, but freelancers and news photographers often put in long, irregular hours. Commercial and portrait photographers work in comfortable surroundings. Photojournalists seldom are assured physical comfort in their work and may in fact face danger when covering stories on natural disasters or military conflicts. Some photographers work in research laboratory settings; others work on aircraft; and still others work underwater. For some photographers, conditions change from day to day. One day they may be photographing a hot and dusty rodeo; the next they may be taking pictures of a dogsled race in Alaska.

In general, photographers work under pressure to meet deadlines and satisfy customers. Freelance photographers have the added pressure of uncertain incomes and have to continually seek out new clients.

For specialists in fields such as fashion photography, breaking into the field may take years. Working as another photographer's assistant is physically demanding when carrying equipment is required.

For freelance photographers, the cost of equipment can be quite expensive, with no assurance that the money spent will be repaid through income from future assignments. Freelancers in travel-related photography, such as travel and tourism photographers and photojournalists, have the added cost of transportation and accommodations. For all photographers, flexibility is a major asset.

OUTLOOK

Employment of photographers will increase about as fast as the average for all occupations through 2016, according to the *Occupational Outlook Handbook*. The demand for new images should remain strong in education, communication, entertainment, marketing, and research. As the Internet continues to grow, and more newspapers and magazines turn to electronic publishing, demand for digital images will continue to rise. Additionally, as the population grows and many families have more disposable income to spend, the demand should increase for photographers who specialize in portraiture, especially of children.

Photography is a highly competitive field. There are far more photographers than positions available. Only those who are extremely talented and highly skilled can support themselves as self-employed photographers.

Many photographers take pictures as a sideline while working another job.

FOR MORE INFORMATION

The ASMP promotes the rights of photographers, educates its members in business practices, and promotes high standards of ethics.

American Society of Media Photographers (ASMP)
150 North Second Street
Philadelphia, PA 19106-1912
Tel: 215-451-2767
http://www.asmp.org

The NPPA maintains a job bank, provides educational information, and makes insurance available to its members. It also publishes News Photographer *magazine.*

National Press Photographers Association (NPPA)
3200 Croasdaile Drive, Suite 306
Durham, NC 27705-2588
Tel: 919-383-7246
Email: info@nppa.com
http://www.nppa.org

This organization provides training, publishes its own magazine, and offers various services for its members.

Professional Photographers of America
229 Peachtree Street, NE, Suite 2200
Atlanta, GA 30303-1608
Tel: 800-786-6277
Email: csc@ppa.com
http://www.ppa.com

For information on student membership, contact

Student Photographic Society
229 Peachtree Street, NE, Suite 2200
Atlanta, GA 30303-1608
Tel: 866-886-5325
Email: info@studentphoto.com
http://www.studentphoto.com

PHYSICAL THERAPY ASSISTANTS

OVERVIEW

Physical therapy assistants help to restore physical function in people with injury, birth defects, or disease. They assist physical therapists with a variety of techniques, such as exercise, massage, heat, and water therapy.

Physical therapy assistants work directly under the supervision of physical therapists. They teach and help patients improve functional activities required in their daily lives, such as walking, climbing, and moving from one place to another. The assistants observe patients during treatments, record the patients' responses and progress, and report these to the physical therapist, either orally or in writing. They fit patients for and teach them to use braces, artificial limbs, crutches, canes, walkers, wheelchairs, and other devices. They may make physical measurements to assess the effects of treatments or to evaluate patients' range of motion, length and girth of body parts, and vital signs. Physical therapy assistants act as members of a team and regularly confer with other members of the physical therapy staff. There are approximately 60,000 physical therapy assistants employed in the United States.

THE JOB

Physical therapy personnel work to prevent, diagnose, and rehabilitate, to restore physical function, prevent permanent disability as much as possible, and help people achieve their maximum attainable performance. For many patients, this objective involves daily living skills, such as eating, grooming, dressing, bathing, and other basic movements that unimpaired people do automatically without thinking.

Physical therapy may alleviate conditions such as muscular pain, spasm, and weakness, joint pain and stiffness, and neuromuscular incoordination. These conditions may be caused by any number of disorders, including fractures, burns, amputations, arthritis, nerve or muscular injuries, trauma, birth defects, stroke, multiple sclerosis, and cerebral palsy. Patients of all ages receive physical therapy services; they may be severely disabled or they may need only minimal therapeutic intervention.

Physical therapy assistants always work under the direction of a qualified physical therapist. Other members of the health team may be a physician or surgeon, nurse, occupational therapist, psychologist, or vocational counselor. Each of these practitioners helps establish and achieve realistic goals consistent with the patient's individual needs. Physical therapy assistants help perform tests to evaluate disabilities and determine the most suitable treatment for the patient. Then, as the treatment progresses, they routinely report the patient's condition to the physical therapist. If they observe a patient having serious problems during treatment, the assistants notify the therapist as soon as possible. Physical therapy assistants generally perform complicated therapeutic procedures decided by the physical therapist. Assistants may also initiate routine procedures independently.

These procedures may include physical exercises, which are the most varied and widely used physical treatments. Exercises may be simple or complicated, easy or strenuous, active or passive. Active motions are performed by the patient alone and strengthen or train muscles. Passive exercises involve the assistant moving the body part through the motion, which improves mobility of the joint but does not strengthen muscle. For example, for a patient with a fractured arm, both active and passive exercise may be appropriate. The passive exercises may be designed to maintain or increase the range of motion in the shoulder, elbow, wrist, and finger joints, while active resistive exercises strengthen muscles weakened by disuse. An elderly patient who has suffered a stroke may need guided exercises aimed at keeping the joints mobile, regaining the function of a limb, walking, or climbing stairs. A child with cerebral palsy who would otherwise never walk may be helped to learn coordination exercises that enable crawling, sitting balance, standing balance, and, finally, walking.

Patients sometimes perform exercises in bed or immersed in warm water. Besides its usefulness in alleviating stiffness or paralysis, exercise also helps to improve circulation, relax tense muscles, correct posture, and aid the breathing of patients with lung problems.

Other treatments that physical therapy assistants may administer include massages; traction for patients with neck or back pain; ultrasound and various kinds of heat treatment for diseases such as arthritis that inflame joints or nerves; cold applications to reduce swelling, pain, or hemorrhaging; and ultraviolet light.

Physical therapy assistants train patients to manage devices and equipment that they either need temporarily or permanently. For example, they instruct patients on how to walk with canes or crutches using proper gait and on how to maneuver well in a wheelchair. They also teach patients how to apply, remove, care for, and cope with splints, braces, and artificial body parts.

Physical therapy personnel must often work on improving the emotional state of patients, preparing them psychologically for treatments. The overwhelming sense of hopelessness and lack of confidence that afflict many disabled patients can reduce the patients' success in achieving improved functioning. The health team must be attuned to both the physical and nonphysical aspects of patients to assure that treatments are most beneficial. Sometimes physical therapy personnel work

QUICK FACTS

SCHOOL SUBJECTS
Biology
Health

PERSONAL SKILLS
Helping/teaching
Mechanical/manipulative

WORK ENVIRONMENT
Primarily indoors
Primarily one location

MINIMUM EDUCATION LEVEL
Associate's degree

MEDIAN SALARY
$41,360

CERTIFICATION OR LICENSING
Required by certain states

OUTLOOK
Much faster than the average

with patients' families to educate them on how to provide simple physical treatments and psychological support at home.

In addition, physical therapy assistants may perform office duties: They schedule patients, keep records, handle inventory, and order supplies. *Physical therapy aides* may also handle these duties.

REQUIREMENTS
High School

Does this work sound interesting to you? If so, you can prepare for it while still in high school by taking biology, health, and mathematics classes. Psychology, sociology, and even social studies classes will be helpful, because they will give you an understanding of people. And, since you will be working so closely with clients as well as other professionals, you will need excellent communication skills. So, take English courses and other classes that will improve these skills, such as speech. It's also a good idea to take computer classes since almost all employers require their employees to have computer skills.

Postsecondary Training

To do this work, you will need a degree from an accredited physical therapy assistant program. Accreditation is given by the Commission on Accreditation in Physical Therapy Education (CAPTE), which is part of the American Physical Therapy Association (APTA). These programs, leading to an associate's degree, are usually offered at community and junior colleges. Typically lasting two years, the programs combine academic instruction with a period of supervised clinical practice in a physical therapy setting. According to APTA, there are 233 accredited schools offering assistant programs as well as several programs in development. Information about these programs can be found on APTA's Web site, http://www.apta.org. The first year of study is typically taken up with general course work, while the second year is focused on professional classes. Classes you can expect to take include mathematics, biology, applied physical sciences, psychology, human growth and development, and physical therapist assistant procedures such as massage, therapeutic exercise, and heat and cold therapy.

In recent years, admission to accredited programs has been fairly competitive, with three to five applicants for each available opening.

Some physical therapy assistants begin their careers while in the armed forces, which operate training programs. While these programs are not sufficient for state licensure and do not award degrees, they can serve as an excellent introduction to the field for students who later enter more complete training programs.

Certification or Licensing

Many states require regulation of physical therapy assistants in the form of registration, certification, or licensure. Typically, graduation from an CAPTE-accredited program and passing a written exam are needed for licensing. Because requirements vary by state, you will need to check with your state's licensure board for specific information.

Other Requirements

Physical therapy assistants must have stamina, patience, and determination, but at the same time they must be able to establish personal relationships quickly and successfully. They should genuinely like and understand people, both under normal conditions and under the stress of illness. An outgoing personality is highly desirable as is the ability to instill confidence and enthusiasm in patients. Much of the work of physical retraining and restoring is very repetitive, and assistants may not perceive any progress for long periods of time. Patients may seem unable or unwilling to cooperate at times. In such cases, assistants need boundless patience, to appreciate small gains and build on them. When restoration to good health is not attainable, physical therapist assistants must help patients adjust to a different way of life and find ways to cope with their situation. Creativity is an asset to devising methods that help disabled people achieve greater self-sufficiency. Assistants should be flexible and open to suggestions offered by their coworkers and willing and able to follow directions closely.

Because the job can be physically demanding, physical therapy assistants must be reasonably strong and enjoy physical activity. Manual dexterity and good coordination are needed to adjust equipment and assist patients. Assistants should be able to lift, climb, stoop, and kneel.

EXPLORING

While still in high school, you can experience this work by getting summer or part-time employment or by volunteering in the physical therapy department of a hospital or clinic. Also, many schools, both public and private, have volunteer assistance programs for work with disabled students. You can also gain direct experience by working with disabled children in a summer camp.

These opportunities will provide you with direct job experience that will help you determine if you have the personal qualities necessary for this career. If you are unable to get direct experience, you should talk to a physical therapist or physical therapy assistant during career-day programs at your high school. It may also be possible for you to arrange to visit a physical therapy department, watch the staff at work, and ask questions.

EMPLOYERS

Physical therapy assistants are employed in hospitals, rehabilitation centers, schools for the disabled, nursing homes, community and government health agencies, physicians' or physical therapists' offices, and facilities for the mentally disabled. There are approximately 60,000 physical therapy assistants employed in the United States.

STARTING OUT

One good way to find a job is to access the resources available at the career services office of your educational institution. Alternatively, you can apply to the physical therapy departments of local hospitals, rehabilitation centers, extended-care facilities, and other potential employers. Openings are listed in the classified ads of newspapers, professional journals, and with private and public employment agencies. In locales where training programs have produced many physical therapy assistants, competition for jobs may be keen. In such cases, you may want to widen your search to areas where there is less competition, especially suburban and rural areas.

ADVANCEMENT

With experience, physical therapy assistants are often given greater responsibility and better pay. In large health care facilities, supervisory possibilities may open up. In small institutions that employ only one physical therapist, the physical therapist assistant may eventually take care of all the technical tasks that go on in the department, within the limitations of his or her training and education.

Physical therapy assistants with degrees from accredited programs are generally in the best position to gain advancement in any setting. They sometimes decide to earn a postbaccalaureate degree in physical therapy and become fully qualified physical therapists.

EARNINGS

Salaries for physical therapy assistants vary considerably depending on geographical location, employer, and level of experience. Physical therapy assistants earned median annual salaries of $41,360 in 2006, according to the U.S. Department of Labor. The lowest 10 percent earned less than $26,190; the highest 10 percent earned more than $57,220. According to Salary.com, the national average median salary for physical therapy assistants in 2008 was $41,487, with 50 percent earning between $37,272 and $45,703, annually.

Fringe benefits vary, although they usually include paid holidays and vacations, health insurance, and pension plans.

WORK ENVIRONMENT

Physical therapy is generally administered in pleasant, clean, well-lighted, and well-ventilated surroundings. The space devoted to physical therapy services is often large, in order to accommodate activities such as gait training and exercises and procedures requiring equipment. Some procedures are given at patients' bedsides.

In the physical therapy department, patients come and go all day, many in wheelchairs, on walkers, canes, crutches, or stretchers. The staff tries to maintain a purposeful, harmonious, congenial atmosphere as they and the patients work toward the common goal of restoring physical efficacy.

The work can be exhausting. Physical therapy assistants may be on their feet for hours at a time, and they may have to move heavy equipment, lift patients, and help them to stand and walk. Most assistants work daytime hours, five days a week, although some positions require evening or weekend work. Some assistants work on a part-time basis.

The combined physical and emotional demands of the job can exert a considerable strain. Prospective assistants would be wise to seek out some job experience related to physical therapy so that they have a practical understanding of their psychological and physical capacities. By exploring their suitability for the work, they can make a better commitment to the training program.

Job satisfaction can be great for physical therapy assistants as they can see how their efforts help to make people's lives much more rewarding.

OUTLOOK

Employment prospects are very good for physical therapy assistants; the U.S. Department of Labor predicts that employment will grow much faster than the average through 2016. Many new positions for physical therapy assistants are expected to open up as hospital programs that aid the disabled expand and as long-term facilities seek to offer residents more adequate services.

A major contributing factor is the increasing number of Americans aged 65 and over. This group tends to suffer a disproportionate amount of the accidents and chronic illnesses that necessitate physical therapy services. Many from the baby boom generation are reaching the age common for heart attacks, thus creating a need for more cardiac and physical rehabilitation. Legislation that requires appropriate public education for all disabled children also may increase the demand for physical therapy services. As more adults engage in strenuous physical exercise, more musculoskeletal injuries will result, thus increasing demand for physical therapy services.

FOR MORE INFORMATION

For additional education and career information, contact
American Physical Therapy Association
1111 North Fairfax Street
Alexandria, VA 22314-1488
Tel: 800-999-2782
http://www.apta.org

For information on accredited programs, contact
Commission on Accreditation in Physical Therapy
Education (CAPTE)
Email: accreditation@apta.org
http://www.apta.org/CAPTE

PLASTERERS

OVERVIEW

Plasterers apply coats of plaster to interior walls, ceilings, and partitions of buildings to produce fire-resistant and relatively soundproof surfaces. They also work on exterior building surfaces and do ornamental forming and casting work. Their work is similar to that of drywall workers, who use drywall rather than plaster to build interior walls and ceilings. Plasterers who specialize in exterior plastering are known as *stucco masons*. There are approximately 61,000 plasterers and stucco masons employed in the United States.

THE JOB

Plasterers work on building interiors and exteriors. They apply plaster directly to masonry, wire, wood, metal, or lath. (Lath is a supportive reinforcement made of wood or metal that is attached to studs to form walls and ceilings.) These surfaces are designed to hold the plaster in position until it dries. After checking the specifications and plans made by the builder, architect, or foreman, plasterers put a border of plaster of the desired thickness on the top and bottom of the wall. After this border has hardened sufficiently, they fill in the remaining portion of the wall with two coats of plaster. The surface of the wall area is then leveled and smoothed with a straightedged tool and darby (a long flat tool used for smoothing). They then apply the third or finishing coat of plaster, which is the last operation before painting or paperhanging. This coat may be finished to an almost velvet smoothness or into one of a variety of decorative textures used in place of papering.

When plastering cinder block and concrete, plasterers first apply what is known as a brown coat of gypsum plaster as a base. The second coat, called the white coat, is lime-based plaster. When plastering metal lath foundations, they first apply a scratch coat with a trowel, spread it over the lath, and scratch the surface with a rake-like tool to make ridges before it dries so that the next coat—the

brown coat—will bond tightly. Next, the plasterer sprays or trowels the plaster for the brown coat and smoothes it. The finishing coat is either sprayed on or applied with a hawk (a basic spackling tool) and trowel. Plasterers also use brushes and water for the finishing coat. The final coat is a mix of lime, water, and plaster of Paris that sets quickly and is smooth and durable.

The plasterer sometimes works with plasterboard or sheetrock, which are types of wallboard that come ready for installation. When working with such wallboard, the plasterer cuts and fits the wallboard to the studding and joists of ceilings and interior walls. When installing ceilings, workers perform as a team.

Stucco masons are plasterers who specialize in exterior plastering. They apply a weather-resistant decorative covering of Portland cement plaster to lath in the same manner as interior plastering or with the use of a spray gun. In exterior work, however, the finish coat usually consists of a mixture of white cement and sand or a patented finish material that may be applied in a variety of colors and textures.

Decorative and ornamental plastering is the specialty of highly skilled *molding plasterers*. This work includes molding or forming and installing ornamental plaster panels and trim. Some molding plasterers also cast intricate cornices and recesses used for indirect lighting. Such work is rarely used today because of the great degree of skill involved and the high cost.

In recent years, most plasterers began using machines to spray plaster on walls, ceilings, and structural sections of buildings. Machines that mix plaster have been in general use for many years.

REQUIREMENTS
High School

Although a high school or trade school education is not mandatory, it is highly recommended. In high school or vocational school, you should take mechanical drawing, drafting, woodwork, and other shop courses. Classes in mathematics will sharpen your skills in the applied mathematics of layout work.

Postsecondary Training

To qualify as a journeyman plasterer, you must complete either an apprenticeship or on-the-job training program. The apprenticeship program consists of two to three years of carefully planned activity combined with approximately 6,000 to 8,000 hours of work experience and an annual 144 hours of related classroom instruction. An apprenticeship is usually the best start, since it includes on-the-job training as well as formal instruction.

On-the-job training consists of working for two or more years under the supervision of experienced plasterers. The trainee usually begins as a helper or laborer and learns the trade informally by observing or being taught by other plasterers.

Other Requirements

Most employers prefer to hire applicants who are at least 18 years old, in good physical condition, and have a high degree of manual dexterity.

EXPLORING

To observe the plasterer at work, field trips to construction sites may be arranged by a school counselor or you can arrange an interview on your own. An excellent first-hand experience in this trade would be to obtain a part-time or summer job as a plasterer's helper or laborer.

EMPLOYERS

Most plasterers work for independent plastering contractors and are members of unions, either the Operative Plasterers' and Cement Masons' International Association of the United States and Canada or the International Union of Bricklayers and Allied Craftworkers. Approximately 61,000 plasterers and stucco masons are employed in the United States. Although they are employed throughout the country, many workers in this field, especially stucco masons, work in Florida, California, and the Southwest on exterior stucco with decorative finishes.

STARTING OUT

Those who wish to become apprentices usually contact local plastering contractors, the state employment service bureau, or the appropriate union headquarters. In most places, the local branch of the Operative Plasterers' and Cement Masons' International Association of the United States and Canada is the best place to inquire about apprenticeships. The Bureau of Apprenticeship and Training, U.S. Department of Labor, and the state employment office are also good places to contact for information.

If the apprenticeship program is filled, applicants may wish to enter the field as on-the-job trainees. In this case, they usually contact a plastering contractor directly and begin work as helpers or laborers. They learn about the work by mixing the plaster, helping plasterers with scaffolding, and carrying equipment.

QUICK FACTS

SCHOOL SUBJECTS
Art
Technical/shop

PERSONAL SKILLS
Artistic
Mechanical/manipulative

WORK ENVIRONMENT
Primarily indoors
Primarily multiple locations

MINIMUM EDUCATION LEVEL
Apprenticeship

MEDIAN SALARY
$34,694

CERTIFICATION OR LICENSING
None available

OUTLOOK
About as fast as the average

ADVANCEMENT

Most plasterers learn the full range of plastering skills. They develop expertise in finish plastering as well as rough coat plastering. They also learn the spray gun technique and become proficient spray gun plasterers. With additional training, they may specialize in exterior work as stucco masons or in ornamental plastering as molding plasterers.

If they have certain personal characteristics such as the ability to deal with people and good judgment and planning skills, plasterers may progress to become supervisors or job estimators. Many plasterers become self-employed, and some eventually become contractors.

EARNINGS

The median earnings for plasterers were $34,694 in 2006, according to the U.S. Department of Labor. Earnings ranged from less than $22,547 to more than $56,805. Plasterers may receive traditional fringe benefits, such as health insurance and paid vacation days.

WORK ENVIRONMENT

Most plasterers have a regular 40-hour workweek with occasional overtime when necessary to meet a contract deadline. Overtime work is usually compensated at the rate of one and a half times the regular hourly wage. The workday may start earlier than most (7:00 A.M.), but it also usually ends earlier (3:00 P.M.). Some plasterers face layoffs between jobs, while others may work with drywall or ceiling tile as required by their contractors when there is no plastering work to be done.

Most of the work is performed indoors, plastering walls and ceilings and forming and casting ornamental designs. Plasterers also work outdoors, doing stuccowork and Exterior Insulated Finish Systems (exterior systems that include Styrofoam insulation board and two thin coats of polymer and acrylic modified materials). They often work with other construction workers, including carpenters, plumbers, and pipefitters. Plasterers must do a considerable amount of standing, stooping, and lifting. They often get plaster on their work clothes and dust in their eyes and noses.

Plasterers take pride in seeing the results of their work—something they have helped to build a structure that will last a long time. Their satisfaction with progress on the job, day by day, may be a great deal more than in jobs where the worker never sees the completed product or where the results are less obvious.

As highly skilled workers, plasterers have higher earnings, better chances for promotion, and more opportunity to go into business for themselves than other workers. They can usually find jobs in almost any part of the United States.

OUTLOOK

Employment opportunities for plasterers are expected to increase about as fast as the average through 2016, according to the U.S. Department of Labor. A growing number of people are starting to appreciate the attractive finishes that plaster provides. Plasterers' employment prospects usually rise and fall with the economy, and are especially connected with the health of the construction industry.

Recent improvements in both plastering materials and methods of application are expected to increase the scope of the craft and create more job opportunities. To name a few such developments: more lightweight plasters are being used because of excellent soundproofing and acoustical qualities; machine plastering and insulating finishes are becoming more widespread; and the use of plaster veneer or high-density plaster in creating a finished surface is being used increasingly in new buildings. Plaster veneer, or thin-coat plastering, is a thin coat of plaster that can be finished in one coat. It is made of

lime and plaster of Paris and can be mixed with water at the job site. It is often applied to a special gypsum base on interior surfaces. Exterior systems have also changed to include more Exterior Insulated Finish Systems.

FOR MORE INFORMATION

For information on scholarships and education in the wall and ceiling industry, contact

Association of the Wall and Ceiling Industry
513 West Broad Street, Suite 210
Falls Church, VA 22046-3257
Tel: 703-538-1600
http://www.awci.org

For information on the lath and plaster industry, contact
International Institute for Lath and Plaster
Lath & Plaster Information Bureau
PO Box 3922
Palm Desert, CA 92260-3922
Tel: 760-837-9094
http://www.iilp.org

For information about construction trades, training, and union membership, contact
International Union of Bricklayers and Allied Craftworkers
620 F Street, NW
Washington, DC 20004-1618
Tel: 202-783-3788
Email: askbac@bacweb.org
http://www.bacweb.org

For information on membership and apprenticeships, contact
Operative Plasterers' and Cement Masons' International Association of the United States and Canada
11720 Beltsville Drive, Suite 700
Beltsville, MD 20705-3104
Tel: 301-623-1000
Email: opcmiaintl@opcmia.org
http://www.opcmia.org

PLUMBERS AND PIPEFITTERS

OVERVIEW

Plumbers and *pipefitters* assemble, install, alter, and repair pipes and pipe systems that carry water, steam, air, or other liquids and gases for sanitation and industrial purposes as well as other uses. Plumbers also install plumbing fixtures, appliances, and heating and refrigerating units. There are approximately 569,000 plumbers and pipefitters working in the United States.

THE JOB

Because little difference exists between the work of the plumber and the pipefitter in most cases, the two are often considered to be one trade. However, some craftsworkers specialize in one field or the other, especially in large cities.

The work of pipefitters differs from that of plumbers mainly in its location and the variety and size of pipes used. Plumbers work primarily in residential and commercial buildings, whereas pipefitters are generally employed by large industrial concerns—such as oil refineries, refrigeration plants, and defense establishments—where more complex systems of piping are used. Plumbers assemble, install, and repair heating, water, and drainage systems, especially those that must be connected to public utilities systems. Some of their jobs include replacing burst pipes and installing and repairing sinks, bathtubs, water heaters, hot water tanks, garbage disposal units, dishwashers, and water softeners. Plumbers also may work on septic tanks, cesspools, and sewers. During the final construction stages of both commercial and residential buildings, plumbers install heating and air-conditioning units and connect radiators, water heaters, and plumbing fixtures.

Most plumbers follow set procedures in their work. After inspecting the installation site to determine pipe location, they cut and thread pipes, bend them to required angles by hand or machines, and then join them by means of welded, brazed, caulked, soldered, or threaded joints. To test for leaks in the system, they fill the pipes with water or air. Plumbers use a variety of tools, including hand tools such as wrenches, reamers, drills, braces and bits, hammers, chisels, and saws; power machines that cut, bend, and thread pipes; gasoline torches; and welding, soldering, and brazing equipment.

Specialists include diesel engine pipefitters, steamfitters, ship and boat building coppersmiths, industrial-gas fitters, gas-main fitters, prefab plumbers, and pipe cutters.

REQUIREMENTS
High School

A high school diploma is especially important for getting into a good apprenticeship program. High school preparation should include courses in mathematics, chemistry, and physics, as well as some shop courses.

Postsecondary Training

To qualify as a plumber, a person must complete either a formal apprenticeship or an informal on-the-job training program. To be considered for the apprenticeship program, individuals must pass an examination administered by the state employment agency and have their qualifications approved by the local joint labor-management apprenticeship committee.

The apprenticeship program for plumbers consists of four or five years of carefully planned activity combining direct training with at least 144 hours of formal classroom instruction each year. The program is designed to give apprentices diversified training by having them work for several different plumbing or pipefitting contractors.

On-the-job training, on the other hand, usually consists of working for five or more years under the guidance

QUICK FACTS

SCHOOL SUBJECTS
Chemistry
Physics

PERSONAL SKILLS
Following instructions
Mechanical/manipulative

WORK ENVIRONMENT
Primarily indoors
Primarily multiple locations

MINIMUM EDUCATION LEVEL
Apprenticeship

MEDIAN SALARY
$42,765

CERTIFICATION OR LICENSING
Required by certain states

OUTLOOK
About as fast as the average

of an experienced craftworker. Trainees begin as helpers until they acquire the necessary skills and knowledge for more difficult jobs. Frequently, they supplement this practical training by taking trade (or correspondence) school courses.

Certification or Licensing

A license is required for plumbers in many places. To obtain this license, plumbers must pass a special examination to demonstrate their knowledge of local building codes as well as their all-around knowledge of the trade. To become a plumbing contractor in most places, a master plumber's license must be obtained.

Other Requirements

To be successful in this field, you should like to solve a variety of problems and should not object to being called on during evenings, weekends, or holidays to perform emergency repairs. As in most service occupations, plumbers should be able to get along well with all kinds of people. You should be a person who works well alone, but who can also direct the work of helpers and enjoy the company of those in the other construction trades.

EXPLORING

Although opportunities for direct experience in this occupation are rare for those in high school, there are ways to explore the field. Speaking to an experienced plumber or pipefitter will give you a clearer picture of day-to-day work in this field. Pursuing hobbies with a mechanical aspect will help you determine how much you like such hands-on work.

EMPLOYERS

Plumbers and pipefitters hold about 569,000 jobs. Approximately 55 percent work for mechanical and plumbing contractors engaged in new construction, repair, modernization, or maintenance work. About 12 percent of all plumbers and pipefitters are self-employed.

STARTING OUT

Applicants who wish to become apprentices usually contact local plumbing, heating, and air-conditioning contractors who employ plumbers, the state employment service bureau, or the local branch of the United Association of Journeymen and Apprentices of the Plumbing and Pipe Fitting Industry of the United States and Canada. Individual contractors or contractor associations often sponsor local apprenticeship programs. Apprentices very commonly go on to permanent employment with the firms with which they apprenticed.

ADVANCEMENT

If plumbers have certain qualities, such as the ability to deal with people and good judgment and planning skills, they may progress to such positions as supervisor or job estimator for plumbing or pipefitting contractors. If they work for a large industrial company, they may advance to the position of job superintendent. Many plumbers go into business for themselves. Eventually they may expand their activities and become contractors, employing other workers.

EARNINGS

Plumbers and pipefitters had median earnings of $42,765 in 2006, according to the U.S. Department of Labor. Wages ranged from less than $25,584 to $72,363 or more. Pay rates for apprentices usually start at 50 percent of the experienced worker's rate, and increase by 5 percent every six months until a rate of 95 percent is reached. Benefits for union workers usually include health insurance, sick time, and vacation pay, as well as pension plans.

WORK ENVIRONMENT

Most plumbers have a regular 40-hour workweek with extra pay for overtime. Unlike most of the other building trades, this field is little affected by seasonal factors. The work of the plumber is active and strenuous. Standing for prolonged periods and working in cramped or uncomfortable positions are often necessary. Possible risks include falls from ladders, cuts from sharp tools, and burns from hot pipes or steam. Working with clogged pipes and toilets can also be smelly.

OUTLOOK

Employment opportunities for plumbers are expected to grow about as fast as the average for all jobs through 2016, according to the U.S. Department of Labor. Construction projects are usually only short-term in nature and more plumbers will find steady work in renovation, repair, and maintenance. Since pipework is becoming more important in large industries, more workers will be needed for installation and maintenance work, especially where refrigeration and air-conditioning equipment are used. Employment opportunities fluctuate with local economic conditions, although the plumbing industry is less affected by economic trends than other construction trades.

FOR MORE INFORMATION

For more information about becoming a plumber or pipefitter, contact the following organizations:

Plumbing-Heating-Cooling Contractors Association
180 South Washington Street
PO Box 6808
Falls Church, VA 22046-2900
Tel: 800-533-7694
http://www.phccweb.org

United Association of Journeymen and Apprentices of the Plumbing and Pipe Fitting Industry of the United States and Canada
901 Massachusetts Avenue, NW
Washington, DC 20001-4397
Tel: 202-628-5823
http://www.ua.org

For information on state apprenticeship programs, visit
Employment & Training Administration
U.S. Department of Labor
http://www.doleta.gov

POLICE OFFICERS

QUICK FACTS

SCHOOL SUBJECTS
Physical education
Psychology

PERSONAL SKILLS
Communication/ideas
Leadership/management

WORK ENVIRONMENT
Indoors and outdoors
Primarily multiple locations

MINIMUM EDUCATION LEVEL
High school diploma

MEDIAN SALARY
$47,460

CERTIFICATION OR LICENSING
None available

OUTLOOK
About as fast as the average

OVERVIEW

Police officers perform many duties relating to public safety. Their responsibilities include not only preserving the peace, preventing criminal acts, enforcing the law, investigating crimes, and arresting those who violate the law, but also directing traffic, controlling crowds at public events, and working in community relations. Police officers are employed at the federal, state, county, and city level.

State police officers patrol highways and enforce the laws and regulations that govern the use of those highways, in addition to performing general police work. Police officers are under oath to uphold the law 24 hours a day. There are approximately 861,000 police and detectives employed in the United States.

THE JOB

Depending on the orders they receive from their commanding officers, police may direct traffic during the rush-hour periods and at special events when traffic is unusually heavy. They may patrol public places such as parks, streets, and public gatherings to maintain law and order. Police are sometimes called upon to prevent or break up riots and to act as escorts at funerals, parades, and other public events. They may administer first aid in emergency situations, assist in rescue operations of various kinds, investigate crimes, issue tickets to violators of traffic or parking laws or other regulations, or arrest drunk drivers. Officers in small towns may have to perform all these duties and administrative work as well.

As officers patrol their assigned beats, either on foot, bicycle, horseback, motorcycle, or in cars, they must be alert for any situations that arise and be ready to take appropriate action. Many times they must be alert to identify stolen cars, identify and locate lost children, and identify and apprehend escaped criminals and others wanted by various law enforcement agencies. While on patrol, they keep in constant contact with headquarters and their fellow officers by calling in regularly on two-way radios. Although their profession may at times be dangerous, police officers are trained not to endanger their own lives or the lives of ordinary citizens. If they need assistance, they radio for additional officers.

In large city police departments, officers usually have more specific duties and specialized assignments. The police departments generally are comprised of special work divisions such as communications, criminal investigation, firearms identification, fingerprint identification and forensic science, accident prevention, and administrative services. In very large cities, police departments may have special work units such as the harbor patrol, canine corps, mounted police, vice squad, fraud or bank squad, traffic control, records control, and rescue units. A few of the job titles for these specialties are *identification and records commanders and officers, narcotics and vice detectives or investigators, homicide squad commanding officers, detective chiefs, traffic lieutenants, sergeants, parking enforcement officers, public safety officers, accident-prevention squad officers, safety instruction police officers,* and *community relations lieutenants.*

In very large city police departments, officers may fill positions as police chiefs, precinct sergeants and captains, desk officers, booking officers, police inspectors, identification officers, complaint evaluation supervisors and officers, and crime prevention police officers. Some officers work as plainclothes detectives in criminal investigation divisions. Internal affairs investigators are employed to police the police. Other specialized police officers include police commanding officers, who act as supervisors in missing persons and fugitive investigations; and officers who investigate and pursue nonpayment and fraud fugitives. Many police departments employ police clerks, who perform administrative and community-oriented tasks.

A major responsibility for state police officers (sometimes known as *state troopers* or *highway patrol officers*) is to patrol the highways and enforce the laws and regulations of those traveling on them. Riding in patrol cars equipped with two-way radios, they monitor traffic for troublesome or dangerous situations. They write traffic tickets and issue warnings to drivers who are violating traffic laws or otherwise not observing safe driving practices. They radio for assistance for drivers who are stopped because of breakdowns, flat tires, illnesses, or other reasons. They direct traffic around congested areas caused by fires, road repairs, accidents, and other emergencies. They may check the weight of commercial vehicles to verify that they are within allowable limits, conduct driver examinations, or give safety information to the public.

In the case of a highway accident, officers take charge of the activities at the site by directing traffic, giving first aid to any injured parties, and calling for emergency equipment such as ambulances, fire trucks, or tow trucks. They write up a report to be used by investigating officers who attempt to determine the cause of the accident.

In addition to these responsibilities, state police officers in most states do some general police work. They are often the primary law enforcement agency in communities or counties that have no police force or a large sheriff's department. In those areas, they may investigate such crimes as burglary and assault. They also may assist municipal or county police in capturing lawbreakers or controlling civil disturbances.

Most police officers are trained in the use of firearms and carry guns. Police in special divisions, such as chemical analysis and handwriting and fingerprint identification, have special training to perform their work. Police officers often testify in court regarding cases with which they have been involved. Police personnel are required to complete accurate and thorough records of their cases.

REQUIREMENTS
High School

The majority of police departments today require that applicants have a high school education. Although a high school diploma is not always required, related work experience is generally required.

If you are interested in pursuing this career, you will find the subjects of psychology, sociology, English, law, mathematics, U.S. government and history, chemistry, and physics most helpful. Because physical stamina is very important in this work, sports and physical education are also valuable. Knowledge of a foreign language is especially helpful, and bilingual officers are often in great demand. If specialized and advanced positions in law enforcement interest you, pursue studies leading to college programs in criminology, criminal law, criminal psychology, or related areas.

Postsecondary Training

The best chance for advancement is by getting some postsecondary education, and many police departments now require a two- or four-year degree, especially for more specialized areas of police work. Many junior colleges and universities offer two- and four-year degree programs in law enforcement, police science, and administration of justice. Many police departments require a two-year degree to make lieutenant and a bachelor's degree to make captain. The armed forces also offer training and opportunities in law enforcement that can be applied to civilian police work.

Newly recruited police officers must pass a 12- to 14-week training program at their agency's police academy. After training, they are usually placed on a probationary period lasting from three to six months. In small towns and communities, a new officer may get his or her training on the job by working with an experienced officer. Inexperienced officers are never sent out on patrol alone but are always accompanied by veteran officers.

Large city police departments give classroom instruction in laws, accident investigation, city ordinances, and traffic control. These departments also give instruction in the handling of firearms, methods of apprehension and arrest, self-defense tactics, and first-aid techniques. Both state and municipal police officers are trained in safe driving procedures and maneuvering an automobile at high speeds.

Other Requirements

Police job appointments in most large cities and in many smaller cities and towns are governed by local civil service regulations. You will be required to pass written tests designed to measure your intelligence and general aptitude for police work. You will also be required to pass physical examinations, which usually include tests of physical agility, dexterity, and strength. Your personal history, background, and character will undergo careful scrutiny because honesty and law-abiding characteristics are essential traits for law enforcement officers. Another important requirement is that you have no arrest record.

To be a police officer, you must be at least 20 years of age (or older for some departments), and some municipalities stipulate an age limit of not more than 35 years. You must have, in some cases, 20/20 uncorrected vision, good hearing, and weight proportionate to your height. You will also be required to meet locally prescribed weight and height rules for your gender. Most regulations require that you be a U.S. citizen, and many police departments have residency requirements.

If you hope to be a police officer, you should enjoy working with people and be able to cooperate with others. Because of the stressful nature of much police work, you must be able to think clearly and logically during emergency situations, have a strong degree of emotional control, and be capable of detaching yourself from incidents.

Physical fitness training is a mandatory, continuing activity in most police departments, as are routine physical examinations. Police officers can have no physical disabilities that would prevent them from carrying out their duties.

EXPLORING

A good way to explore police work is to talk with various law enforcement officers. Most departments have community outreach programs and many have recruitment programs as well. You may also wish to visit colleges offering programs in police work or write for information on their training programs.

In some cases, high school graduates can explore this occupation by seeking employment as police cadets in large city police departments. These cadets are paid employees who work part time in clerical and other duties. They attend training courses in police science on a part-time basis. When you reach the age of at least 20, you will be eligible to apply for regular police work. Some police departments also hire college students as interns.

EMPLOYERS

Police officers hold approximately 861,000 jobs in the United States. According to the U.S. Department of Labor, approximately 79 percent of police officers are employed by local governments. State police agencies employ approximately 11 percent of officers, and about 7 percent of officers work for federal agencies. Some also work for educational services, rail transportation, and contract investigation and security services.

STARTING OUT

If you are interested in police work, you should apply directly to local civil service offices or examining boards to qualify as a candidate for police officer. In some locations, written examinations may be given to groups at specified times. For positions in smaller communities that do not follow civil service methods, you should apply directly to the police department or city government offices in that community. If you are interested in becoming a state police officer, you can apply directly to the state civil service commission or the state police headquarters, which are usually located in the state capital.

ADVANCEMENT

Advancement in these occupations is determined by several factors. An officer's eligibility for promotion may depend on a specified length of service, job performance, formal education and training courses, and results of written examinations. Those who become eligible for promotion are listed on the promotional list along with other qualified candidates. Promotions generally become available from six months to three years after starting, depending on the department. As positions of different or higher rank become open, candidates are promoted to fill them according to their position on the list. Lines of promotion usually begin with officer third grade and progress to grade two and grade one. Other possible promotional opportunities include the ranks of detective, sergeant, lieutenant, or captain. Many promotions require additional training and testing. Advancement to the very top-ranking positions, such as division, bureau, or department director or chief, may be made by direct political appointment. Officers who have come up through the ranks hold most of these top positions.

Large city police departments offer the greatest number of advancement opportunities. Most of the larger departments maintain separate divisions, which require administration workers, line officers, and more employees in general at each rank level. Officers may move into areas that they find challenging, such as criminal investigation or forensics.

Most city police departments offer various types of in-service study and training programs. These programs allow police departments to keep up-to-date on the latest police science techniques and are often required for those who want to be considered for promotion. Police academies, colleges, and other educational institutions provide training courses. Some of the subjects offered are civil defense, foreign languages, and forgery detection. Some municipal police departments share the cost with their officers or pay all educational expenses if the officers are willing to work toward a college degree in either police work or police administration. Independent study is also often required.

Intensive 12-week administrative training courses are offered by the National Academy of the Federal Bureau of Investigation in Washington, D.C. A limited number of officers are selected to participate in this training program.

Advancement opportunities on police forces in small communities are considerably more limited by the rank and number of police personnel needed. Other opportunities for advancement may be found in related police, protective, and security service work with private companies, state and county agencies, and other institutions.

EARNINGS

According to the U.S. Department of Labor, police officers earned an annual average salary of $47,460 in 2006; the lowest 10 percent earned less than $27,310 a year, while the highest 10 percent earned $72,450 or more annually. Police detectives earned median salaries of $58,260 a year in 2006, with a low of less than $34,480 and a high of more than $92,590. Salaries for police officers range widely based on geographic location. Police departments in the West and North generally pay more than those in the South.

Most police officers receive periodic and annual salary increases up to a limit set for their rank and length of service. Police departments generally pay special compensation to cover the cost of uniforms. They usually provide any equipment required such as firearms and handcuffs. Overtime pay may be given for certain work shifts or emergency duty. In these instances, officers are usually paid straight or time-and-a-half pay, while extra time off is sometimes given as compensation.

Because most police officers are civil service employees, they receive generous benefits, including health insurance and paid vacation and sick leave, and enjoy increased job security. In addition, most police departments offer retirement plans and retirement after 20 or 25 years of service, usually at half pay.

WORK ENVIRONMENT

Police officers work under many different types of circumstances. Much of their work may be performed outdoors, as they ride in patrol cars or walk the beats assigned to them. In emergency situations, no consideration can be made for weather conditions, time of day or night, or day of the week. Police officers may be on call 24 hours a day; even when they are not on duty, they are usually required by law to respond to emergencies or criminal activity. Although they are assigned regular work hours, individuals in police work must be willing to live by an unpredictable and often erratic work schedule. The work demands constant mental and physical alertness as well as great physical strength and stamina.

Police work generally consists of an eight-hour day and a five-day week, but police officers may work night and weekend shifts and on holidays. Emergencies may add many extra hours to an officer's day or week. The occupation is considered dangerous. Some officers are killed or wounded while performing their duties. Their work can involve unpleasant duties and expose them to sordid, depressing, or dangerous situations. They may be called on to deal with all types of people under many types of circumstances. While the routine of some assigned duties may become boring, the dangers of police work are often stressful for the officers and their families. Police work in general holds the potential for the unknown and unexpected, and most people who pursue this work have a strong passion for and commitment to police work.

OUTLOOK

Employment of police officers and detectives is expected to increase about as fast as the average for all occupations through 2016, according to the U.S. Department of Labor. Strong competition for jobs will exist at the federal level and in most state police departments. Opportunities will be best in local police departments, especially those which are located in high-crime areas or that offer relatively lower pay than other departments.

The opportunities that become available, however, may be affected by technological, scientific, and other changes occurring today in police work. Automation in traffic control is limiting the number of officers needed in this area, while the increasing reliance on computers throughout society is creating demands for new kinds of police work. New approaches in social science and psychological research are also changing the methodology used in working with public offenders. These trends indicate a future demand for more educated, specialized personnel.

This occupation has a very low turnover rate. However, new positions will open as current officers retire, leave the force, or move into higher positions. Retirement ages are relatively low in police work compared to other occupations. Many officers retire while in their 40s and then pursue a second career. In response to increasing crime rates and threats of terrorism, some police departments across the country are expanding the number of patrol officers; however, budget problems faced by many municipalities may limit growth.

In the past decade, private security firms have begun to take over some police activities such as patrolling public places. Some private companies have even been contracted to provide police forces for some cities. Many companies and universities also operate their own police forces.

FOR MORE INFORMATION

Created by the American Federation of Police and Concerned Citizens and the National Association of Chiefs of Police, the American Police Hall of Fame and Museum offers summer camps, scholarships, and other information for young people interested in police work.

American Police Hall of Fame and Museum
6350 Horizon Drive
Titusville, FL 32780-8002
Tel: 321-264-0911
Email: policeinfo@aphf.org
http://www.aphf.org

The National Association of Police Organizations is a coalition of police unions and associations that work to advance the interests of law enforcement officers through legislation, political action, and education.

National Association of Police Organizations
317 South Patrick Street
Alexandria, VA 22314-3501
Tel: 703-549-0775
Email: info@napo.org
http://www.napo.org

PRESCHOOL TEACHERS

OVERVIEW

Preschool teachers promote the general education of children under the age of five. They help students develop physically, socially, and emotionally; work with them on language and communications skills; and help cultivate their cognitive abilities. They also work with families to support parents in raising their young children and reinforcing skills at home. They plan and lead activities developed in accordance with the specific ages and needs of the children. It is the goal of all preschool teachers to help students develop the skills, interests, and individual creativity that they will use for the rest of their lives. Many schools and districts consider *kindergarten teachers*, who teach students five years of age, to be preschool teachers. For the purposes of this article, kindergarten teachers will be included in this category. There are approximately 437,000 preschool teachers and 170,000 kindergarten teachers in the United States.

THE JOB

Preschool teachers plan and lead activities that build on children's abilities and curiosity and aid them in developing skills and characteristics that help them grow. Because children develop at varying skill levels as well as have different temperaments, preschool teachers need to develop a flexible schedule with time allowed for music, art, playtime, academics, rest, and other activities.

Preschool teachers plan activities that encourage children to develop skills appropriate to their developmental needs. For example, they plan activities based on the understanding that a three-year-old child has different motor skills and reasoning abilities than a child of five years of age. They work with the youngest students on learning the days of the week and the recognition of colors, seasons, and animal names and

QUICK FACTS

SCHOOL SUBJECTS

Art

English

Family and consumer science

PERSONAL SKILLS

Communication/ideas

Helping/teaching

WORK ENVIRONMENT

Primarily indoors

Primarily one location

MINIMUM EDUCATION LEVEL

Some postsecondary training

MEDIAN SALARY

$22,680

CERTIFICATION OR LICENSING

Required for certain positions

OUTLOOK

About as fast as the average

another, sing songs, have show and tell, talk about the weather and do calendar events. We then move on to language arts, which may include talking to children about rules, good listening, helping, sharing, etc., using puppets, work papers, games, and songs."

Preschool teachers adopt many parental responsibilities for the children. They greet the children in the morning and supervise them throughout the day. Often these responsibilities can be quite demanding and complicated. In harsh weather, for example, preschool teachers contend not only with boots, hats, coats, and mittens, but also with the inevitable sniffles, colds, and generally cranky behavior that can occur in young children. For most children, preschool is their first time away from home and family for an extended period of time. A major portion of a preschool teacher's day is spent helping children adjust to being away from home and encouraging them to play together. This is especially true at the beginning of the school year. They may need to gently reassure children who become frightened or homesick.

In both full-day and half-day programs, preschool teachers supervise snack time, helping children learn how to eat properly and clean up after themselves. Proper hygiene, such as hand washing before meals, is also stressed. Other activities include storytelling, music, and simple arts and crafts projects. Full-day programs involve a lunch period and at least one naptime. Programs usually have exciting activities interspersed with calmer ones. Even though the children get naptime, preschool teachers must be energetic throughout the day, ready to face, with good cheer, the many challenges and demands of young children.

Preschool teachers also work with the parents of each child. It is not unusual for parents to come to preschool and observe a child or go on a field trip with the class. Preschool teachers often take these opportunities to discuss the progress of each child as well as any specific problems or concerns. Scheduled meetings are available for parents who cannot visit the school during the day. Solutions to fairly serious problems are worked out in tandem with the parents, often with the aid of the director of the preschool, or in the case of an elementary school kindergarten, with the principal or headmaster.

Kindergarten teachers usually have their own classrooms, made up exclusively of five-year-olds. Although these teachers do not have to plan activities for a wide range of ages, they need to consider individual developmental interests, abilities, and backgrounds represented by the students. Kindergarten teachers usually spend more time helping students with academic skills than

characteristics. They help older students with number and letter recognition and even simple writing skills. Preschool teachers help children with such simple, yet important, tasks as tying shoelaces and washing hands before snack time. Attention to the individual needs of each child is vital; preschool teachers need to be aware of these needs and capabilities, and when possible, adapt activities to the specific needs of the individual child. Self-confidence and the development of communication skills are encouraged in preschools. For example, teachers may give children simple art projects, such as finger painting, and have children show and explain their finished projects to the rest of the class. Show and tell, or "sharing time" as it is often called, gives students opportunities to speak and listen to others.

"A lot of what I teach is based on social skills," says June Gannon, a preschool teacher in Amherst, New Hampshire. "During our circle time, we say hello to one

do other preschool teachers. While a teacher of a two-, three-, and four-year-old classroom may focus more on socializing and building confidence in students through play and activities, kindergarten teachers often develop activities that help five-year-olds acquire the skills they will need in grade school, such as introductory activities on numbers, reading, and writing.

REQUIREMENTS
High School

If you are interested in the field of preschool teaching, take child development, home economics, and other classes that involve you with child care, such as family and consumer science classes. You will also need a fundamental understanding of the general subjects you will be introducing to preschool students, so take English, science, and math. Also, take classes in art, music, and theater to develop creative skills.

Postsecondary Training

Specific education requirements for preschool and kindergarten teachers vary from state to state and also depend on the specific guidelines of the school or district. Many schools and child care centers require preschool teachers to have a bachelor's degree in early childhood education or a related field, but others accept adults with a high school diploma and some child care experience. Some preschool facilities offer on-the-job training to their teachers, hiring them as assistants or aides until they are sufficiently trained to work in a classroom alone. A college degree program should include course work in a variety of liberal arts subjects, including English, history, and science as well as nutrition, child development, psychology of the young child, and sociology.

Several groups offer on-the-job training programs for prospective preschool teachers. For example, the American Montessori Society offers a career program for aspiring preschool teachers. This program requires a three-month classroom-training period followed by one year of supervised on-the-job training.

Certification or Licensing

Licensing requirements for preschool teachers usually vary by state. Many states accept the child development associate credential (awarded by the Council for Professional Recognition) or an associate or bachelor's degree as sufficient requirement for work in a preschool facility. Individual state boards of education can provide specific

licensure information. Kindergarten teachers working in public elementary schools almost always need teaching certification similar to that required by other elementary school teachers in the school. Other types of licensure or certification may be required, depending upon the school or district. These may include first-aid or cardiopulmonary resuscitation (CPR) training. In addition, kindergarten (through high school) teachers who want to show competency beyond the licensing requirements can receive national certification from the National Board for Professional Teaching Standards.

Other Requirements

Because young children look up to adults and learn through example, it is especially important that as a preschool teacher, you be a good role model. "Remember how important your job is," June Gannon says. "Everything you say and do will affect these children." Gannon also emphasizes being respectful of the children and keeping a sense of humor. "I have patience and lots of heart for children," Gannon says. "You definitely need both."

EXPLORING
Preschools, daycare centers, and other childcare programs often hire high school students for part-time positions as aides. You may also find many volunteer opportunities to work with children. Check with your library or local literacy program about tutoring children and reading to preschoolers. Summer day camps or religious schools with preschool classes also hire high school students as counselors or counselors-in-training. Discussing the field with preschool teachers and observing in their classes are other good ways to discover specific job information and explore your aptitude for this career.

EMPLOYERS
There are approximately 437,000 preschool teachers employed in the United States, as well as 170,000 kindergarten teachers. Six of every 10 mothers of children under the age of six are in the labor force, and the number is rising. Both government and the private sector are working to fill the enormous need for quality childcare. Preschool teachers will find many job opportunities in private and public preschools, including daycare centers, government-funded learning programs, churches, and Montessori schools. They may find work in a small center, or with a large preschool with many students and classrooms. Preschool franchises, like Primrose Schools (http://www.primroseschools.com) and Kids 'R' Kids

International (http://www.kidsrkids.com), are also providing more opportunities for preschool teachers.

STARTING OUT

Before becoming a preschool teacher, June Gannon gained a lot of experience in child care. "I have worked as a special education aide and have taken numerous classes in childhood education," she says. "I am a sign language interpreter and have taught deaf children in a public school inclusion program."

If you hope to become a preschool teacher, you can contact child care centers, nursery schools, Head Start programs, and other preschool facilities to identify job opportunities. Often, jobs for preschool teachers are listed in the classified section of newspapers. In addition, many school districts and state boards of education maintain job listings of available teaching positions. If no permanent positions are available at preschools, you may be able to find opportunities to work as a substitute teacher. Most preschools and kindergartens maintain a substitute list and refer to it frequently.

ADVANCEMENT

Many teachers advance by becoming more skillful in what they do. Skilled preschool teachers, especially those with additional training, usually receive salary increases as they become more experienced. A few preschool teachers with administrative ability and an interest in administrative work advance to the position of director. Administrators need to have at least a master's degree in child development or a related field and have to meet any state or federal licensing regulations. Some become directors of Head Start programs or other government programs. A relatively small number of experienced preschool teachers open their own facilities. This entails not only the ability to be an effective administrator but also the knowledge of how to operate a business. Kindergarten teachers sometimes have the opportunity to earn more money by teaching at a higher grade level in the elementary school. This salary increase is especially true when a teacher moves from a half-day kindergarten program to a full-day grade school classroom.

EARNINGS

Although there have been some attempts to correct the discrepancies in salaries between preschool teachers and other teachers, salaries in this profession tend to be lower than for teaching positions in public elementary and high schools. Because some preschool programs are held only in the morning or afternoon, many preschool teachers work only part time. As part-time workers, they often do not receive medical insurance or other benefits and may get paid minimum wage to start.

According to the U.S. Department of Labor, preschool teachers earned a median salary of $22,680 per year in 2006. Annual salaries for these workers ranged from less than $14,870 to $39,960 or more. The department reports that kindergarten teachers (which the department classifies separately from preschool teachers) earned median annual salaries of $43,580 in 2006. The lowest 10 percent earned less than $28,590, while the highest 10 percent earned $71,410 or more.

WORK ENVIRONMENT

Preschool teachers spend much of their workday on their feet in a classroom or on a playground. Facilities vary from a single room to large buildings. Class sizes also vary; some preschools serve only a handful of children, while others serve several hundred. Classrooms may be crowded and noisy, but anyone who loves children will enjoy all the activity. "The best part about working with children," Gannon says, "is the laughter, the fun, the enjoyment of watching the children grow physically, emotionally, and intellectually."

Many children do not go to preschool all day, so work may be part time. Part-time employees generally work between 18 and 30 hours a week, while full-time employees work 35 to 40 hours a week. Part-time work gives the employee flexibility, and for many, this is one of the advantages of the job. Some preschool teachers teach both morning and afternoon classes, going through the same schedule and lesson plans with two sets of students.

OUTLOOK

Employment opportunities for preschool teachers are expected to increase about as fast as the average for all occupations through 2016, according to the U.S. Department of Labor. Specific job opportunities vary from state to state and depend on demographic characteristics and level of government funding. Jobs should be available at private child care centers, nursery schools, Head Start facilities, public and private kindergartens, and laboratory schools connected with universities and colleges. In the past, the majority of preschool teachers were female, and although this continues to be the case, more males are becoming involved in early childhood education.

One-third of all childcare workers leave their centers each year, often because of the low pay and lack of benefits. This will mean plenty of job openings for preschool teachers and possibly improved benefit plans, as centers attempt to maintain qualified preschool teachers.

Employment for all teachers, including preschool teachers, will vary by region and state. The U.S. Department of Labor predicts that Southern and Western states, particularly Utah, California, Idaho, Hawaii, Alaska, and New Mexico, will have strong increases in enrollments, while schools located in the Northeast and Midwest may experience declines in enrollment.

FOR MORE INFORMATION

For information on training programs, contact

American Montessori Society
281 Park Avenue South
New York, NY 10010-6102
Tel: 212-358-1250
Email: info@amshq.org
http://www.amshq.org

For information about certification, contact the following organizations:

Council for Professional Recognition
2460 16th Street, NW
Washington, DC 20009-3575
Tel: 800-424-4310
http://www.cdacouncil.org

National Board for Professional Teaching Standards
1525 Wilson Blvd., Suite 500
Arlington, VA 22209-2451
Tel: 800-228-3224
http://www.nbpts.org

For general information on preschool teaching careers, contact

National Association for the Education of Young Children
1313 L Street, NW, Suite 500
Washington, DC 20005-4110
Tel: 800-424-2460
Email: naeyc@naeyc.org
http://www.naeyc.org

For information about student memberships and training opportunities, contact

National Association of Child Care Professionals
PO Box 90723
Austin, TX 78709-0723
Tel: 800-537-1118
Email: admin@naccp.org
http://www.naccp.org

PUBLIC TRANSPORTATION OPERATORS

OVERVIEW

Public transportation operators include drivers of school buses, intercity buses, local commuter buses, and local transit railway systems, such as subways and streetcars. Many drivers run a predetermined route within a city or metropolitan area, transporting passengers from one designated place to another. Intercity drivers travel between cities and states, transporting passengers and luggage on more lengthy trips. Some public transportation operators are required to handle additional special duties, such as transporting disabled passengers. There are approximately 653,000 public transportation operators employed in the United States.

REQUIREMENTS

High School

While still in high school, take English and speech classes to improve your communication skills. Math skills may also be needed to calculate fares and make change. Finally, sign up for a driver's education class to learn the rules of the road.

Postsecondary Training

Qualifications and standards for bus drivers are established by state and federal regulations. Federal regulations require drivers who operate vehicles designed to transport 16 or more passengers to obtain a commercial license (CDL). In order to receive a CDL, applicants must pass a written exam and a driving test in the type of vehicle they will be operating. Drivers must also take a written examination on the Motor Carrier Safety Regulations of the U.S. Department of Transportation.

While many states' minimum age requirement for drivers is 18, federal regulations require that interstate bus drivers be at least 21 years old and in good general health. They must pass a physical exam every two years, checking for good hearing, vision, and reflexes. They must also be able to speak, read, and write English well enough to fill out reports, read signs, and talk to passengers. In addition to these minimum requirements, many employers prefer drivers over 24 years old with at least a

QUICK FACTS

SCHOOL SUBJECTS

Mathematics

Speech

PERSONAL SKILLS

Following instructions

Mechanical/manipulative

WORK ENVIRONMENT

Primarily indoors

Primarily multiple locations

MINIMUM EDUCATION LEVEL

High school diploma

MEDIAN SALARY

$32,094

CERTIFICATION OR LICENSING

Required by all states

OUTLOOK

About as fast as the average

high school diploma and previous truck or bus driving experience. Bus companies and local transit systems train their drivers with two to eight weeks of classroom and on-the-road instruction. In the classroom, trainees learn federal and company work policies, state and local driving regulations, and other general safe driving practices. They also learn how to handle the public, read schedules, determine fares, and keep records.

School bus drivers are required to obtain a commercial driver's license with a school bus endorsement from the state in which they live. To receive this endorsement, they must pass a written test and demonstrate necessary skills in a bus of the same type that they would be driving on their route. These tests are specific to school buses and are in addition to the testing required to receive a commercial license and the passenger endorsement. For subway operator jobs, local transit companies prefer applicants 21 years of age or older with at least a high school diploma. As with bus

drivers, good vision, hearing, and reflexes are necessary, as well as a clean driving record.

New operators are generally trained both in the classroom and on the job in programs that range from a few weeks to six months. Operators must then pass qualifying exams covering operations, troubleshooting, and emergency procedures.

Other Requirements

Bus and rail car drivers must have good reflexes and quick reaction time, and must drive safely under all circumstances. Because operators are required to deal regularly with passengers, it is also important that they be courteous and level-headed. An even temperament comes in handy when driving in heavy or fast-moving traffic or during bad weather conditions. Drivers should be able to stay alert and attentive to the task at hand. They must be dependable and responsible, because the lives of their passengers are in their hands.

EXPLORING

Any job that requires driving can provide you with important experience for a job as a public transportation operator. Possibilities include a part-time or summer job as a delivery driver.

You may also benefit from talking personally with a bus driver or subway operator. Those already employed with bus or rail companies can give you a good, detailed description of the pros and cons of the position.

EMPLOYERS

There are approximately 653,000 bus drivers currently employed in the United States. More than 70 percent are employed by a school system or a company that provides contract school bus service. The second largest group of bus drivers work for private and local transit systems, and the remainder work as intercity and charter drivers. There are approximately 11,000 subway and streetcar operators, located almost exclusively in major urban areas.

STARTING OUT

If you are interested in the field, you should directly contact public transportation companies as well as government and private employment agencies. Labor unions, such as the Amalgamated Transit Union, might know about available jobs. Positions for drivers can also be found in the classified section of the newspaper.

After completing the training program, new drivers often initially are given only special or temporary assignments—for example, substituting for a sick employee, driving an extra bus or rail car during commuter rush hours, or driving a charter bus to a sporting event. These new drivers may work for several years in these part-time, substitute positions before gaining enough seniority for a regular route.

ADVANCEMENT

Advancement is usually measured by greater pay and better assignments or routes. For example, senior drivers or rail car operators may have routes with lighter traffic, weekends off, or higher pay rates. Although opportunities for promotion are limited, one option for advancement is to move into supervisory or training positions. Experienced drivers can become dispatchers (workers who assign drivers their bus or train route, determine whether buses or trains are running on time, and send out help when there is a breakdown or accident). Other managerial positions also exist. Experienced subway or streetcar operators, for example, may become station managers.

EARNINGS

Earnings for public local transportation operators vary by location and experience. According to the U.S. Department of Labor, the 2006 median salary for local and intercity bus drivers was $32,094. The lowest 10 percent earned less than $19,260 and the highest 10 percent earned more than $50,086. School bus drivers on average made less, with a median salary of $24,814. The lowest 10 percent earned less than $13,640 and the highest 10 percent earned $36,628 or more. Subway and streetcar operators earned salaries that ranged from $31,160 to $57,150 or more, with a median of $48,980.

Almost all public transportation operators belong to a union, such as the Amalgamated Transit Union or the Transport Workers Union of America. Wages and benefits packages are usually determined through bargaining agreements between these unions and the management of the transit system. Benefits often include paid health and life insurance, sick leave, free transportation on their line or system, and as much as four weeks of vacation per year.

WORK ENVIRONMENT

Public transportation operators work anywhere from 20 to 40 hours per week. The U.S. Department of Transportation restricts all drivers from working more than 10 hours per day or more than 60 hours in seven days or 70 hours in eight days. New drivers often work part time, though they may be guaranteed a minimum number of hours.

Schedules for intercity bus drivers may require working nights, weekends, and holidays. Drivers may also have to spend nights away from home, staying in hotels at company expense. Senior drivers who have regular routes typically have regular working hours and set schedules, while others must be prepared to work on short notice.

Local transit drivers and subway operators usually have a five-day workweek, with Saturdays and Sundays considered regular workdays. Some of these employees work evenings and night shifts. To accommodate commuters, many work split shifts, such as four hours in the morning and four hours in the afternoon and evening, with time off in between.

The lack of direct supervision is one of the advantages of being a public transportation operator. Intercity bus drivers may also enjoy traveling as a benefit. Disadvantages include weekend, holiday, or night shifts, and, in some cases, being called to work on short notice. Operators with little seniority may be laid off when business declines.

Although driving a bus or rail car is usually not physically exhausting, operators are exposed to tension from maneuvering their vehicle on heavily congested streets or through crowded stations. They also may feel stressed from dealing with passengers—including those who are unruly or difficult.

OUTLOOK

Employment for public transportation operators is expected to grow about as fast as the average for all occupations through 2016, according to the *Occupational Outlook Handbook*. As the population increases, local and intercity travel will also increase. Future government efforts to reduce traffic and pollution through greater funding of public transportation could also greatly improve job opportunities. In addition, thousands of job openings are expected to occur each year because of the need to replace workers who retire or leave the occupation.

Because many of these positions offer relatively high wages and attractive benefits, however, job seekers may face heavy competition. Those who have good driving records and are willing to work in rapidly growing metropolitan areas will have the best opportunities.

FOR MORE INFORMATION

For transit news and links to local chapters, contact
Amalgamated Transit Union
5025 Wisconsin Avenue, NW
Washington, DC 20016-4139
Tel: 202-537-1645
http://www.atu.org

For salary statistics and other career information, contact
American Public Transportation Association
1666 K Street, NW
Washington, DC 20006-2803
Tel: 202-496-4800
http://www.apta.com

For information on school transportation careers, contact
National School Transportation Association
113 South West Street, 4th Floor
Alexandria, VA 22314-2858
Tel: 800-222-6782
Email: info@yellowbuses.org
http://www.yellowbuses.org

For information on careers in public transportation, contact
Transport Workers Union of America
1700 Broadway, 2nd Floor
New York, NY 10019-5905
http://www.twu.com

RADIOLOGIC TECHNOLOGISTS

OVERVIEW

Radiologic technologists operate equipment that creates images of a patient's body tissues, organs, and bones for the purpose of medical diagnoses and therapies. These images allow physicians to know the exact nature of a patient's injury or disease, such as the location of a broken bone or the confirmation of an ulcer.

Before an X-ray examination, radiologic technologists may administer drugs or chemical mixtures to the patient to better highlight internal organs. They place the patient in the correct position between the X-ray source and film and protect body areas that are not to be exposed to radiation. After determining the proper duration and intensity of the exposure, they operate the controls to beam X rays through the patient and expose the photographic film.

They may operate computer-aided imaging equipment that does not involve X rays and may help to treat diseased or affected areas of the body by exposing the patient to specified concentrations of radiation for prescribed times. Radiologic technologists and technicians hold about 196,000 jobs in the United States.

THE JOB

All radiological work is done at the request of and under the supervision of a physician. Just as a prescription is required for certain drugs to be dispensed or administered, so must a physician's request be issued before a patient can receive any kind of imaging procedure.

There are four primary disciplines in which radiologic technologists may work: radiography (taking X-ray pictures or radiographs), nuclear medicine, radiation therapy, and sonography. In each of these medical imaging methods, the technologist works under the direction of a physician who specializes in interpreting the pictures produced by X rays, other imaging techniques, or radiation therapy. Technologists can work in more than one of these areas. Some technologists specialize in working with a particular part of the body or a specific condition.

X-ray pictures, or radiographs, are the most familiar use of radiologic technology. They are used to diagnose and determine treatment for a wide variety of afflictions, including ulcers, tumors, and bone fractures. Chest X-ray pictures can determine whether a person has a lung disease. Radiologic technologists who operate X-ray equipment first help the patient prepare for the radiologic examination. After explaining the procedure, they may administer a substance that makes the part of the body being imaged more clearly visible on the film. They make sure that the patient is not wearing jewelry or other metal that would obstruct the X rays. They position the person sitting, standing, or lying down so that the correct view of the body can be radiographed, and then they cover adjacent areas with lead shielding to prevent unnecessary exposure to radiation.

The technologist positions the X-ray equipment at the proper angle and distance from the part to be radiographed and determines exposure time based on the location of the particular organ or bone and thickness of the body in that area. The controls of the X-ray machine are set to produce pictures of the correct density, contrast, and detail. Placing the photographic film closest to the body part being x-rayed, the technologist takes the requested images, repositioning the patient as needed. Typically, there are standards regarding the number of views to be taken of a given body part. The film is then developed for the radiologist or other physician to interpret.

In a fluoroscopic examination (a more complex imaging procedure that examines the gastrointestinal area), a beam of X rays passes through the body and onto a fluorescent screen, enabling the physician to see the internal organs in motion. For these, the technologist first prepares a solution of barium sulfate to be administered to the patient, either rectally or orally, depending on the exam. The barium sulfate increases the contrast between the digestive tract and surrounding organs, making the image clearer. The technologist follows the physician's guidance in positioning the patient, monitors the machine's controls, and takes any follow-up radiographs as needed.

Radiologic technologists may learn other imaging procedures such as computed tomography (CT) scanning, which uses X rays to get detailed cross-sectional images of the body's internal structures, and MRI, which uses radio waves, powerful magnets, and computers to obtain images of body parts. These diagnostic procedures are becoming more common and usually require radiologic technologists to undergo additional on-the-job training.

Other specialties within the radiography discipline include mammography and cardiovascular interventional technology. In addition, some technologists may focus on radiography of joints and bones, or they may be involved in such areas as angiocardiography (visualization of the heart and large blood vessels) or neuroradiology (the use of radiation to diagnose diseases of the nervous system).

Radiologic technologists perform a wide range of duties, from greeting patients and putting them at ease by explaining the procedures to developing the finished film. Their administrative tasks include maintaining patients' records, recording equipment usage and maintenance, organizing work schedules, and managing a radiologist's private practice or hospital's radiology department. Some radiologic technologists teach in programs to educate other technologists.

REQUIREMENTS
High School

If this career interests you, take plenty of math and science classes in high school. Biology, chemistry, and physics classes will be particularly useful to you. Take computer classes to become comfortable working with this technology. English classes will help you improve your communication skills. You will need these skills both when interacting with the patients and when working as part of a health care team. Finally, consider taking photography classes. Photography classes will give you experience with choosing film, framing an image, and developing photographs.

Postsecondary Training

After high school, you will need to complete an education program in radiography. Programs range in length from one to four years. Depending on length, the programs award a certificate, associate's degree, or bachelor's degree. Two-year associate's degree programs are the most popular option.

Educational programs are available in hospitals, medical centers, colleges and universities, and vocational and technical institutes. It is also possible to get radiologic technology training in the armed forces.

To enter an accredited program, you must be a high school graduate; some programs require one or two years of higher education. Courses in radiologic technology education programs include anatomy, physiology, patient care, physics, radiation protection, medical ethics, principles of imaging, medical terminology, radiobiology, and pathology. For some supervisory or administrative jobs in this field, a bachelor's or master's degree may be required.

Certification or Licensing

Radiologic technologists can become certified through the American Registry of Radiologic Technologists (ARRT) after graduating from an accredited program in radiography, radiation therapy, or nuclear medicine. After becoming certified, many technologists choose to register with the ARRT. Registration is an annual procedure required to maintain the certification. Registered technologists meet the following three criteria: They agree to comply with the ARRT rules and regulations, comply with the ARRT standards of ethics, and meet continuing education requirements. Only technologists who are currently registered can designate themselves as ARRT Registered Technologists and use the initials RT after their names. Although registration and certification are voluntary, many jobs are open only to technologists who have acquired these credentials.

In addition to being registered in the various imaging disciplines, radiologic technologists can receive advanced qualifications in each of the four radiography specializations: mammography, CT, MRI, and cardiovascular interventional technology. As the work of radiologic technologists grows increasingly complex and employment opportunities become more competitive, the desirability of registration and certification will also grow.

An increasing number of states have set up licensing requirements for radiologic technologists. As of 2007, 40 states and Puerto Rico require radiologic technologists to be licensed. You will need to check with the state in which you hope to work about specific requirements there.

Other Requirements

Radiologic technologists should be responsible individuals with a mature and caring nature. They should be personable and enjoy interacting with all types of people, including those who are very ill. A compassionate attitude is essential to deal with patients who may be frightened or in pain.

EXPLORING

There is no way to gain direct experience in this profession without the appropriate qualifications. However, it is possible to learn about the duties of radiologic technologists by talking with them and observing the facilities and equipment they use. It is also possible to have interviews with teachers of radiologic technology. Ask your guidance counselor or a science teacher to help you contact local hospitals or schools with radiography programs to locate technologists who are willing to talk to an interested student.

As with any career in health care, volunteering at a local hospital, clinic, or nursing home provides an excellent opportunity for you to explore your interest in the field. Most hospitals are eager for volunteers, and working in such a setting will give you a chance to see health care professionals in action as well as to have some patient contact.

EMPLOYERS

There are approximately 196,000 radiologic technologists working in the United States. According to the U.S. Department of Labor, more than half of these technologists work in hospitals. Radiologic technologists also find employment in doctors' offices and clinics, at X-ray labs, and in outpatient care centers.

STARTING OUT

With more states regulating the practice of radiologic technology, certification by the appropriate accreditation body for a given specialty is quickly becoming a necessity for employment. If you get your training from a school that lacks accreditation or if you learn on the job, you may have difficulty in qualifying for many positions, especially those with a wide range of assignments. If you are enrolled in a hospital educational program, you may be able to get a job with the hospital upon completion of the program. If you are in a degree program, get help in finding a job through your school's placement office.

ADVANCEMENT

More than half of all radiologic technologists are employed in hospitals where there are opportunities for advancement to administrative and supervisory positions such as chief technologist or technical administrator. Other technologists develop special clinical skills in advanced imaging procedures, such as CT scanning or MRI. Some radiologic technologists qualify as instructors, while others work as sales representatives or instructors with equipment manufacturers. Radiologic technologists who hold bachelor's degrees have more opportunities for advancement. The technologist who wishes to become a teacher or administrator will find that a master's degree and considerable experience are necessary.

EARNINGS

Salaries for radiologic technologists compare favorably with those of similar health care professionals. According to the U.S. Department of Labor, median annual earnings of radiologic technologists and technicians were $48,170 in 2006. The lowest paid 10 percent, which typically includes those just starting out in the field, earned less than $32,750. The highest paid 10 percent, which typically includes those with considerable experience, earned more than $68,920.

Median annual earnings of radiologic technologists and technicians who worked in medical and diagnostic laboratories were $51,280 in 2006. Those who worked in hospitals earned a median of $48,830, and those who worked in offices and clinics of medical doctors earned $45,500.

Most technologists take part in their employers' vacation and sick leave provisions. In addition, most employers offer benefits such as health insurance and pensions.

WORK ENVIRONMENT

Full-time technologists generally work eight hours a day, 40 hours a week. In addition, they may be on call for some night emergency duty or weekend hours, which pays in equal time off or additional compensation.

In diagnostic radiologic work, technologists perform most of their tasks while on their feet. They move around a lot and often are called upon to lift patients who need help in moving.

Great care is exercised to protect technologists from radiation exposure. Each technologist wears a badge that measures radiation exposure, and records are kept of total exposure accumulated over time. Other routine precautions include the use of safety devices (such as lead aprons, lead gloves, and other shielding) and the use of disposable gowns, gloves, and masks. Careful attention to safety procedures has greatly reduced or eliminated radiation hazards for the technologist.

Radiologic technology is dedicated to conserving life and health. Technologists derive satisfaction from their work, which helps promote health and alleviate human suffering. Those who specialize in radiation therapy need to be able to handle the close relationships they inevitably develop while working with very sick or dying people over a period of time.

OUTLOOK

Overall, employment for radiologic technologists is expected to grow faster than the average through 2016, according to the U.S. Department of Labor. A major reason for this growth is the increasing elderly population in the United States, which will create a need for radiologic technologists' services. The demand for qualified technologists in some areas of the country far exceeds the supply. This shortage is particularly acute in rural areas and small towns. Those who are willing to relocate to these areas may have increased job prospects. Radiologic technologists who are trained to do more than one type of imaging procedure will also find that they have increased job opportunities. Finally, those specializing in sonography are predicted to have more opportunities than those working only with radiographs. One reason for this is ultrasound's increasing popularity due to its lack of possible side effects.

In the years to come, increasing numbers of radiologic technologists will be employed in settings outside of hospitals, such as physicians' offices, clinics, health maintenance organizations, laboratories, government agencies, and diagnostic imaging centers. This pattern will be part of the overall trend toward lowering health care costs by delivering more care outside of hospitals. Technological advancements have enabled more procedures to be performed outside the hospital setting. Nevertheless, hospitals will remain the major employers of radiologic technologists for the near future. Because of the increasing importance of radiologic technology in the diagnosis and treatment of disease, it is unlikely that hospitals will do fewer radiologic procedures than in the past. Instead, they try to do more on an outpatient basis and on weekends and evenings. This should increase the demand for part-time technologists and thus open more opportunities for flexible work schedules.

FOR MORE INFORMATION

For information on certification and educational programs, contact
American Registry of Radiologic Technologists
1255 Northland Drive
St. Paul, MN 55120-1155
Tel: 651-687-0048
http://www.arrt.org

For information about the field, a catalog of educational products, and to access their job bank, contact
American Society of Radiologic Technologists
15000 Central Avenue, SE
Albuquerque, NM 87123-3917
Tel: 800-444-2778
customerinfo@asrt.org
http://www.asrt.org

For career and education information, contact
Canadian Association of Medical Radiation Technologists
1000-85 Albert Street
Ottawa, ON
K1P 5G4 Canada
Tel: 613-234-0012
http://www.camrt.ca

For a list of accredited education programs, contact
Joint Review Committee on Education in Radiologic Technology
20 N. Wacker Drive, Suite 2850
Chicago, IL 60606-3182
Tel: (312) 704-5300
http://www.jrcert.org

For an educational resource guide, contact
Society of Diagnostic Medical Sonography
2745 Dallas Parkway, Suite 350
Plano, TX 75093-8730
Tel: 800-229-9506
http://www.sdms.org

REAL ESTATE AGENTS AND BROKERS

OVERVIEW

Real estate brokers are businesspeople who sell, rent, or manage the property of others. *Real estate agents* are salespeople who are either self-employed or hired by brokers. Sometimes, the term agent is applied to both real estate brokers and agents. There are approximately 564,000 real estate agents and real estate brokers employed in the United States. Real estate agents hold more than 75 percent of these jobs

THE JOB

The primary responsibility of real estate brokers and agents is to help clients buy, sell, rent, or lease a piece of real estate. Real estate is defined as a piece of land or property and all improvements attached to it. The property may be residential, commercial, or agricultural. When people wish to put property up for sale or rent, they contract with real estate brokers to arrange the sale and to represent them in the transaction. This contract with a broker is called a listing.

One of the main duties of brokers is to actively solicit listings for the agency. They develop leads for potential listings by distributing promotional items, by advertising in local publications, and by showing other available properties in open houses. They also spend a great deal of time on the phone exploring leads gathered from various sources, including personal contacts.

Once a listing is obtained, real estate agents analyze the property to present it in the best possible light to prospective buyers. They have to recognize and promote the property's strong selling points. A residential real estate agent might emphasize such attributes as a home's layout or proximity to schools, for example. Agents develop descriptions to be used with photographs of the property in ads and promotions. To make a piece of real estate more attractive to prospective buyers, agents may also advise homeowners on ways to improve the look of their property to be sold.

Agents are also responsible for determining the fair market value for each property up for sale. They compare their client's real estate with similar properties in the area that have recently been sold to decide upon a fair asking price. The broker and any agents of the brokerage work to obtain the highest bid for a property because their earnings are dependent on the sale price. Owners usually sign a contract agreeing that if their property is sold, they will pay the agent a percentage of the selling price.

When the property is ready to be shown for sale, agents contact buyers and arrange a convenient time for them to see the property. If the property is vacant, the broker usually retains the key. To adjust to the schedules of potential buyers, agents frequently show properties in the late afternoon or evening and on weekends. Because a representative of the broker's firm is usually on the premises in each house, weekend showings are a good way to put part-time or beginning agents to work.

An agent may have to meet several times with a prospective buyer to discuss and view available properties. When the buyer decides on a property, the agent must bring the buyer and seller together at terms agreeable to both. In many cases, different brokers will represent the seller and buyer. Agents may have to present several counteroffers to reach a compromise suitable to both parties.

Once the contract is signed by both the buyer and the seller, the agent must see to it that all terms of the contract are carried out before the closing date. For example, if the seller has agreed to repairs or a home inspection, the agent must make sure it is carried out or the sale cannot be completed.

Brokers often provide buyers with information on loans to finance their purchase. They also arrange for title searches and title insurance. A broker's knowledge, resourcefulness, and creativity in arranging financing that is favorable to the buyer can mean the difference between success and failure in closing a sale. In some cases, agents assume the responsibilities of closing the sale, but the closing process is increasingly handled by lawyers or loan officers.

Commercial or agricultural real estate agents operate in much the same fashion. Their clients usually have specific and prioritized needs. For example, a trucking firm might require their property to be located near major highways. These real estate specialists often conduct extensive searches to meet clients' specifications. They usually make fewer but larger sales, resulting in higher commissions.

In addition to selling real estate, some brokers rent and manage properties for a fee. Some brokers combine other types of work, such as selling insurance or practicing law, with their real estate businesses.

REQUIREMENTS
High School

There are no standard educational requirements for the real estate field. However, high school courses in English, business, and math would help to prepare you for communicating with clients and handling sales.

Postsecondary Training

An increasing percentage of real estate agents and brokers have some college education. As property transactions have become more complex, many employers favor applicants with more education. Courses in statistics, economics, sociology, marketing, finance, business administration, and law are helpful. Many colleges also offer specific courses or even degrees in real estate.

Certification or Licensing

Every state (and the District of Columbia) requires that real estate agents and brokers be licensed. For the general license, most states require agents to be at least 18 years old, have between 30 and 90 hours of classroom training, and pass a written examination on real estate fundamentals and relevant state laws. Prospective brokers must pass a more extensive examination and complete between 60 and 90 hours of classroom training. Additionally, many

QUICK FACTS

SCHOOL SUBJECTS
Business
English
Mathematics

PERSONAL SKILLS
Communication/ideas
Helping/teaching

WORK ENVIRONMENT
Primarily indoors
Primarily multiple locations

MINIMUM EDUCATION LEVEL
High school diploma

MEDIAN SALARY
$39,760 (agents)
$60,790 (brokers)

CERTIFICATION OR LICENSING
Required

OUTLOOK
About as fast as average

states require brokers to have prior experience selling property or a formal degree in real estate.

State licenses usually must be renewed annually without examination, but many states require agents to fulfill continuing education requirements in real estate for renewal. Agents who move to another state must qualify under the licensing laws of that state. To supplement minimum state requirements, many agents take courses in real estate principles, laws, financing, appraisal, and property development and management.

Other Requirements

Successful brokers and agents must be willing to study the changing trends of the industry to keep their skills updated. Residential real estate agents must keep up with the latest trends in mortgage financing, construction, and community development. They must have a thorough knowledge of the housing market in their assigned communities so they can identify which neighborhoods will best fit their clients' needs and budgets, and they must be familiar with local zoning and tax laws. Agents and brokers must also be good negotiators to act as go-betweens between buyers and sellers.

In most cases, educational experience is less important than the right personality. Brokers want agents who possess a pleasant personality, exude honesty, and maintain a neat appearance. Agents must work with many different types of people and inspire their trust and confidence. They need to express themselves well and show enthusiasm to motivate customers. They should also be well organized and detail-oriented, and have a good memory for names, faces, and business details.

EXPLORING

Contact local real estate brokers and agents for useful information on the field and to talk one-on-one with an employee about their job. You can also obtain information on licensing requirements from local real estate boards or from the real estate departments of each state. Securing part-time and summer employment in a real estate office will provide you with practical experience.

EMPLOYERS

There are approximately 564,000 real estate agents and brokers currently employed in the United States. Many work part time, supplementing their income with additional jobs in law, finance, or other fields.

Agents work in small offices, larger organizations, or for themselves. (Six out of ten real estate agents and brokers are self-employed.) Opportunities exist at all levels, from large real estate firms specializing in commercial real estate to smaller, local offices that sell residential properties. Much of agents' work is independent; over time, they can develop their own client bases and set their own schedules.

STARTING OUT

The typical entry position in this field is as an agent working for a broker with an established office. Another opportunity may be through inside sales, such as with a construction firm building new housing developments. Prospective agents usually apply directly to local real estate firms or are referred through public and private employment services. Brokers looking to hire agents may run newspaper advertisements or list openings on employment Web sites. Starting out, prospective agents often contact firms in their own communities, where

their knowledge of area neighborhoods can work to their advantage.

The beginning agent must choose between the advantages of joining a small or a large organization. In a small office, the newcomer will train informally under an experienced agent. Their duties will be broad and varied but possibly menial. However, this is a good chance to learn all the basics of the business, including gaining familiarity with the computers used to locate properties or sources of financing. In larger firms, the new agent often proceeds through a more standardized training process and specializes in one aspect of the real estate field, such as commercial real estate, mortgage financing, or property management.

ADVANCEMENT

While many successful agents develop professionally by expanding the quality and quantity of their services, others seek advancement by entering management or by specializing in residential or commercial real estate. An agent may enter management by becoming the head of a division of a large real estate firm. Other agents purchase an established real estate business, join one as a partner, or set up their own offices. Self-employed agents must meet state requirements and obtain a broker's license.

Agents who wish to specialize have a number of available options. They may develop a property management business. In return for approximately 5 percent of the gross receipts, *property managers* operate apartment houses or multiple-tenant business properties for their owners. Property managers are in charge of renting (including advertising, tenant relations, and collecting rents), building maintenance (heating, lighting, cleaning, and decorating), and accounting (financial recording and filing tax returns).

Agents can also become *appraisers*, estimating the current market value of land and buildings, or *real estate counselors*, advising clients on the suitability of available property. Experienced brokers can also join the real estate departments of major corporations or large government agencies.

EARNINGS

Compensation in the real estate field is based largely upon commission. Agents usually split commissions with the brokers who employ them, in return for providing the office space, advertising support, sales supervision, and the use of the broker's good name. When two or more agents are involved in a transaction (for example, one agent listing the property for sale and another selling it), the commission is usually divided between the two on the basis of an established formula. Agents can earn more if they both list and sell the property.

According to the U.S. Department of Labor, median annual earnings of salaried real estate agents, including commission, were $39,760 in 2006. Salaries ranged from less than $20,170 to more than $111,500.

Median annual earnings of salaried real estate brokers, including commission, were $60,790 in 2006, and the middle 50 percent of salaries for brokers ranged from less than $37,800 to more than $102,180 a year.

Agents and brokers may supplement their incomes by appraising property, placing mortgages with private lenders, or selling insurance. Since earnings are irregular and economic conditions unpredictable, agents and brokers should maintain sufficient cash reserves for slack periods.

WORK ENVIRONMENT

One glance at the property advertisements in any newspaper will offer a picture of the high degree of competition found within the field of real estate. In addition to full-time workers, the existence of many part-time agents increases competition.

Beginning agents must accept the frustration inherent in the early months in the business. Earnings are often irregular before a new agent has built a client base and developed the skills needed to land sales.

After agents become established, many work more than 40 hours a week, including evenings and weekends to best cater to their clients' needs. Despite this, agents work on their own schedules and are free to take a day off when they choose. Some do much of their work out of their own homes. However, successful agents will spend little time in an office; they are busy showing properties to potential buyers or meeting with sellers to set up a listing.

Real estate positions are found in every part of the country but are concentrated in large urban areas and in smaller, rapidly growing communities. Regardless of the size of the community in which they work, good agents should know its economic life, the personal preferences of its citizens, and the demand for real estate.

OUTLOOK

According to the *Occupational Outlook Handbook*, employment of agents and brokers is expected to grow about as fast as the average for all occupations through 2016. Turnover within the field is high; new job opportunities surface as agents retire or transfer to other types of work.

The country's expanding population also creates additional demand for real estate services. A trend toward mobility, usually among Americans in their prime working years, indicates a continued need for real estate professionals. In addition, a higher percentage of affluence among this working group indicates that more Americans will be able to own their own homes.

An increase in agents' use of technology, such as computers, faxes, and databases, has greatly improved productivity. Computer-generated images now allow agents and customers to view multiple property listings without leaving the office. However, the use of this technology may eliminate marginal jobs, such as part-time workers, who may not be able invest in this technology and compete with full-time agents. Job growth is potentially limited by the fact that many potential customers are conducting their own searches for property using the Internet.

The field of real estate is easily affected by changes in the economy. Periods of prosperity bring a lot of business. Conversely, a downturn leads to a lower number of real estate transactions, resulting in fewer sales and commissions for agents and brokers.

FOR MORE INFORMATION

For information on licensing, contact

Association of Real Estate License Law Officials
8361 Sangre de Cristo Road
Littleton, CO 80127
Tel: 303-979-6190
Email: mailbox@arello.org
http://www.arello.org

For information on state and local associations, professional designations, real estate courses, and publications, contact

National Association of Realtors
430 North Michigan Avenue
Chicago, IL 60611-4011
Tel: 800-874-6500
http://www.realtor.org

For information on commercial real estate, contact

Society of Industrial and Office Realtors
1201 New York Avenue, NW, Suite 350
Washington, DC 20005-6126
Tel: 202-449-8200
Email: admin@sior.com
http://www.sior.com

RECEPTIONISTS

OVERVIEW

Receptionists—so named because they receive visitors in places of business—have the important job of giving a business's clients and visitors a positive first impression. Also called *information clerks*, these front-line workers are the first communication sources who greet clients and visitors to an office, answer their questions, and direct them to the people they wish to see. Receptionists also answer telephones, take and distribute messages for other employees, and make sure no one enters the office unescorted or unauthorized. Many receptionists perform additional clerical duties. *Switchboard operators* perform similar tasks but primarily handle equipment that receives an organization's telephone calls. There are more than 1.2 million receptionists employed throughout the United States.

THE JOB

The receptionist is a specialist in human contact: The most important part of a receptionist's job is dealing with people in a courteous and effective manner. Receptionists greet customers, clients, patients, and salespeople, take their names, and determine the nature of their business and the person they wish to see. The receptionist then pages the requested person, directs the visitor to that person's office or location, or makes an appointment for a later visit. Receptionists usually keep records of all visits by writing down the visitor's name, purpose of visit, person visited, and date and time.

Most receptionists answer the telephone at their place of employment; many operate switchboards or paging systems. These workers usually take and distribute messages for other employees and may receive and distribute mail. Receptionists may perform a variety of other clerical duties, including keying in and filing correspondence and other paperwork, proofreading, preparing travel vouchers, and preparing outgoing mail. In some businesses, receptionists are responsible for monitoring the attendance of other employees. In businesses where employees are frequently out of the office on assignments, receptionists may keep track of their whereabouts to ensure that they receive important phone calls and messages. Many receptionists use computers and word processors in performing their clerical duties.

Receptionists are partially responsible for maintaining office security, especially in large firms. They may require all visitors to sign in and out and carry visitors' passes during their stay. Since visitors may not enter most offices unescorted, receptionists usually accept and sign for packages and other deliveries.

Receptionists are frequently responsible for answering inquiries from the public about a business's nature and operations. To answer these questions efficiently and in a manner that conveys a favorable impression, a receptionist must be as knowledgeable as possible about the business's products, services, policies, and practices and familiar with the names and responsibilities of all other employees. They must be careful, however, not to divulge classified information such as business procedures or employee activities that a competing company might be able to use. This part of a receptionist's job is so important that some businesses call their receptionists information clerks.

A large number of receptionists work in physicians' and dentists' offices, hospitals, clinics, and other health care establishments. Workers in medical offices receive patients, take their names, and escort them to examination rooms. They make future appointments for patients and may prepare statements and collect bill payments. In hospitals, receptionists obtain patient information, assign patients to rooms, and keep records on the dates they are admitted and discharged.

In other types of industries, the duties of these workers vary. Receptionists in hair salons arrange appointments for clients and may escort them to stylists' stations. Workers in bus or train companies answer inquiries about departures, arrivals, and routes. In-file operators collect and distribute credit information to clients for credit purposes. Registrars, park aides, and tourist-information assistants may be employed as receptionists at public or private facilities. Their duties may include keeping a record of the visitors entering and leaving the facility, as well as providing information on services that the facility provides. Information clerks, automobile club information clerks, and referral-and-information aides provide answers to questions by telephone or in person from current or potential clients and keep a record of all inquiries.

Switchboard operators may perform specialized work, such as operating switchboards at police district offices to take calls for assistance from citizens. Or, they may handle airport communication systems, including public address paging systems and courtesy telephones, or serve as answering-service operators, who record and deliver messages for clients who cannot be reached by telephone.

REQUIREMENTS
High School

You can prepare for a receptionist or switchboard operator position by taking courses in business procedures, office machine operation, business math, English, and public speaking. You should also take computer science courses, as computers are used in nearly all offices.

Postsecondary Training

Most employees require receptionists to have a high school diploma. Some businesses prefer to hire workers who have completed post-high school courses at a junior college or business school. If you are interested in post-high school education, you may find courses in basic bookkeeping and principles of accounting helpful. This type of training may lead to a higher paying receptionist job and a better chance for advancement. Many employers require typing, switchboard, computer, and other clerical skills, but they may provide some on-the-job training, as the work is typically entry level.

Other Requirements

To be a good receptionist, you must be well groomed, have a pleasant voice, and be able to express yourself clearly. Because you may sometimes deal with demanding people, a smooth, patient disposition and good judgment are important. All receptionists need to be courteous and tactful. A good memory for faces and names also proves very valuable. Most important are good listening and communications skills and an understanding of human nature.

EXPLORING

A good way to obtain experience in working as a receptionist is through a high school work-study program. Students participating in such programs spend part of their school day in classes and the rest working for local businesses. This arrangement will help you gain valuable practical experience before you look for your first job. High school guidance counselors can provide information about work-study opportunities.

EMPLOYERS

According to the U.S. Department of Labor, approximately 1.2 million people are employed as receptionists. Almost 90 percent of these work in service-providing industries. Among service-providing industries, health care and social assistance offices employed almost one-third of receptionists. Factories, wholesale and retail stores, and real estate industries also employ a large percentage of these workers. Almost one-third of receptionists work part time.

QUICK FACTS

SCHOOL SUBJECTS
Business
Computer science
English

PERSONAL SKILLS
Communication/ideas
Following instructions

WORK ENVIRONMENT
Primarily indoors
Primarily one location

MINIMUM EDUCATION LEVEL
High school diploma

MEDIAN SALARY
$22,900

CERTIFICATION OR LICENSING
None available

OUTLOOK
Faster than the average

STARTING OUT

While you are in high school, you may be able to learn of openings with local businesses through your school guidance counselors or newspaper want ads. Local state employment offices frequently have information about receptionist work. You should also contact area businesses for whom you would like to work; many available positions are not advertised in the paper because they are filled so quickly. Temporary-work agencies are a valuable resource for finding jobs, too, some of which may lead to permanent employment. Friends and relatives may also know of job openings.

ADVANCEMENT

Advancement opportunities are limited for receptionists, especially in small offices. The more clerical skills and education workers have, the greater their chances for promotion to such better-paying jobs as secretary, administrative assistant, or bookkeeper. College or business school training can help receptionists advance to higher-level positions. Many companies provide training for their receptionists and other employees, helping workers gain skills for job advancement.

EARNINGS

Earnings for receptionists vary widely with the education and experience of the worker and type, size, and geographic location of the business. The median annual salary for receptionists was $22,900 in 2006, according to the U.S. Department of Labor. According to an Office Team salary survey, receptionists had starting salaries ranging from $21,000 to $26,750 in 2007. The lowest paid 10 percent earned less than $15,683, while the highest paid 10 percent earned more than $33,758.

Receptionists are usually eligible for paid holidays and vacations, sick leave, medical and life insurance coverage, and a retirement plan of some kind.

WORK ENVIRONMENT

Because receptionists usually work near or at the main entrance to the business, their work area is one of the first places a caller sees. Therefore, these areas are usually pleasant and clean and are carefully furnished and decorated to create a favorable, businesslike impression. Work areas are almost always air-conditioned, well lit, and relatively quiet, although a receptionist's phone rings frequently. Receptionists work behind a desk or counter and spend most of their workday sitting, although some standing and walking is required when filing or escorting visitors to their destinations. The job may be stressful at times, especially when a worker must be polite to rude callers.

Most receptionists work 35–40 hours a week. Some may work weekend and evening hours, especially those in medical offices. Switchboard operators may have to work any shift of the day if their employers require 24-hour phone service, such as hotels and hospitals. These workers usually work holidays and weekend hours.

OUTLOOK

Employment for receptionists is expected to grow faster than the average occupation through 2016, according to the *Occupational Outlook Handbook.* Many openings will occur due to the occupation's high turnover rate. Opportunities will be best for those with wide clerical skills and work experience. Growth in jobs for receptionists is expected to be greater than for other clerical

positions because automation will have little effect on the receptionist's largely interpersonal duties and because of an anticipated growth in the number of businesses providing services. In addition, more and more businesses are learning how valuable a receptionist can be in furthering their public relations efforts and helping them convey a positive image. Opportunities should be especially good in rapid services industries, such as physician's offices, law firms, temporary help agencies, and consulting firms.

FOR MORE INFORMATION

For information on careers, contact

International Association of Administrative
   Professionals
10502 NW Ambassador Drive
PO Box 20404
Kansas City, MO 64195-0404
Tel: 816-891-6600
Email: service@iaap-hq.org
http://www.iaap-hq.org

☐ RECREATION WORKERS

OVERVIEW

Recreation workers help groups and individuals enjoy and use their leisure time constructively. They organize and administer physical, social, and cultural programs. They also operate recreational facilities and study recreation needs. There are approximately 320,000 recreation workers employed in the United States.

THE JOB

Recreation workers plan, organize, and direct recreation activities for people of all ages, social and economic levels, and degrees of physical and emotional health. The exact nature of their work varies and depends on their individual level of responsibility.

Recreation workers employed by local governments and voluntary agencies include *recreation supervisors* who coordinate recreation center directors, who in turn supervise *recreation leaders* and *aides.* With the help of volunteer workers, they plan and carry out programs at community centers, neighborhood playgrounds, recreational and rehabilitation centers, prisons, hospitals, and homes for children and the elderly, often working in cooperation with social workers and sponsors of the various centers.

Recreation supervisors plan programs to meet the needs of the people they serve. Well-rounded programs may include arts and crafts, dramatics, music, dancing, swimming, games, camping, nature study, and other pastimes. Special events may include festivals, contests, pet and hobby shows, and various outings. Recreation supervisors also create programs for people with special needs, such as the elderly or people in hospitals. Supervisors have overall responsibility for coordinating the work of the recreation workers who carry out the programs and supervise several recreation centers or an entire region.

Recreation center directors run the programs at their respective recreation buildings, indoor centers, playgrounds, or day camps. In addition to directing the staff of the facility, they oversee the safety of the buildings and equipment, handle financial matters, and prepare reports.

Recreation or activity leaders, with the help of *recreation aides*, work directly with assigned groups and are responsible for the daily operations of a recreation program. They organize and lead activities such as drama, dancing, sports and games, camping trips, and other recreations. They give instruction in crafts, games, and sports, and they work with other staff on special projects and events. Leaders help train and direct volunteers and perform other tasks as required by the director.

In industry, *recreation leaders* plan social and athletic programs for employees and their families. Bowling leagues, softball teams, picnics, and dances are examples of company-sponsored activities. In addition, an increasing number of companies are providing exercise and fitness programs for their employees.

Camp counselors lead and instruct children and adults in nature-oriented forms of recreation at camps or resorts. Activities usually include swimming, hiking, horseback riding, and other outdoor sports and games, as well as instruction in nature and folklore. Camp counselors teach skills such as wood crafting, leather working, and basket weaving. Some camps offer specialized instruction in subjects such as music, drama, gymnastics, and computers. In carrying out the programs, camp counselors are concerned with the safety, health, and comfort of the campers. Counselors are supervised by a camp director.

Another type of recreation worker is the *social director*, who plans and organizes recreational activities for guests in hotels and resorts or for passengers aboard a ship. Social directors usually greet new arrivals and introduce them to other guests, explain the recreational facilities, and encourage guests to participate in planned activities. These activities may include card parties, games, contests, dances, musicals, or field trips and may require setting up equipment, arranging for transportation, or planning decorations, refreshments, or entertainment. In general, social directors try to create a friendly atmosphere, paying particular attention to lonely guests and trying to ensure that everyone has a good time.

REQUIREMENTS

For some recreation positions, a high school diploma or an associate's degree in parks and recreation, social work, or other human service discipline is sufficient preparation. However, most full-time career positions require a bachelor's degree, and a graduate degree is often a necessity for high-level administrative posts.

QUICK FACTS

SCHOOL SUBJECTS
Physical education
Theater/dance

PERSONAL SKILLS
Following instructions
Helping/teaching

WORK ENVIRONMENT
Indoors and outdoors
Primarily one location

MINIMUM EDUCATION LEVEL
High school diploma

MEDIAN SALARY
$20,470

CERTIFICATION OR LICENSING
Required for certain positions

OUTLOOK
About as fast as the average

High School

High school students interested in recreation work should get a broad liberal arts and cultural education and acquire at least a working knowledge of arts and crafts, music, dance, drama, athletics, and nature study.

Postsecondary Training

Acceptable college majors include parks and recreation management, leisure studies, fitness management, and related disciplines. A degree in any liberal arts field may be sufficient if the person's education includes courses relevant to recreation work.

In industrial recreation, employers usually prefer applicants with a bachelor's degree in recreation and a strong background in business administration. Some jobs require specialized training in a particular field, such as art, music, drama, or athletics. Others need special certifications, such as a lifesaving certificate to teach swimming.

There are about 100 parks and recreation curriculums at the bachelor's degree level accredited by the National Recreation and Park Association (NRPA). Students may also pursue a master's degree or doctorate (Ph.D.) in the field.

Certification or Licensing

Many recreation professionals apply for certification as evidence of their professional competence. The NRPA, the American Camp Association, and the Employee Services Management Association award certificates to individuals who meet their standards. More than 40 states have adopted NRPA standards for park/recreation professionals.

The federal government employs many recreation leaders in national parks, the armed forces, the Department of Veterans Affairs, and correctional institutions. It may be necessary to pass a civil service examination to qualify for these positions.

Other Requirements

Personal qualifications for recreation work include a desire to work with people, an outgoing personality, an even temperament, and the ability to lead and influence others. Recreation workers should have good health and stamina and should be able to stay calm and think clearly and quickly in emergencies.

EXPLORING

Young people interested in this field should obtain related work experience as part-time or summer workers or vol-unteers in recreation departments, neighborhood centers, camps, and other organizations.

EMPLOYERS

There are about 320,000 recreation workers, not counting summer workers or volunteers, employed in the United States. About 32 percent work for local governments, primarily in parks and recreation departments, and about 10 percent are employed by civic, social, fraternal, or religious membership organizations such as the Boy Scouts, YWCA, or Red Cross. Others work in social service organizations, such as centers for seniors and adult day care, and residential-care facilities, such as halfway houses, nursing homes, institutions for delinquent youths, and group homes or commercial recreation establishments and private industry.

STARTING OUT

College placement offices are useful in helping graduates find employment. Most college graduates begin as either recreation leaders or specialists and, after several years of experience, they may become recreation directors. A few enter trainee programs leading directly to recreation administration within a year or so. Those with graduate training may start as recreation directors.

ADVANCEMENT

Recreation leaders without graduate training will find advancement limited, but it is possible to obtain better paying positions through a combination of education and experience. With experience it is possible to become a recreation director. With further experience, directors may become supervisors and eventually head of all recreation departments or divisions in a city. Some recreation professionals become consultants.

EARNINGS

Full-time recreation workers earned a median salary of $20,470 a year, as of 2006. Wages ranged from $14,150 a year to more than $35,780 a year. Some top-level managers can make considerably more.

Recreational therapists had median earnings of $34,990 in 2006, according to the U.S. Department of Labor.

WORK ENVIRONMENT

Physical conditions vary greatly from outdoor parks to nursing homes for the elderly. A recreation worker can choose the conditions under which he or she would like to work. Recreation workers with an interest in the outdoors may become camp counselors. Those who have an interest in travel may seek a job as a social director on a cruise ship. There are opportunities for people who want to help the elderly or mentally handicapped, as well as for people with an interest in drama or music.

Generally, recreation workers must work while others engage in leisure activities. Most recreation workers work 40-hour weeks. But they should expect, especially those just entering the field, some night and weekend work. A compensating factor is the pleasure of helping people enjoy themselves.

Many of the positions are part-time or seasonal, and many full-time recreation workers spend more time performing management duties than in leading hands-on activities.

OUTLOOK

The U.S. Department of Labor predicts that employment opportunities for recreation workers will increase about as fast as the average through 2016. The expected expansion in the recreation field will result from increased leisure time and income for the population as a whole, along with a continuing interest in fitness and health and a growing elderly population in nursing homes, senior centers, and retirement communities. There also is a demand for recreation workers to conduct activity programs for special needs groups.

Two areas promising the most favorable opportunities for recreation workers are the commercial recreation and social service industries. Commercial recreation establishments include amusement parks, sports and entertainment centers, wilderness and survival enterprises, tourist attractions, vacation excursions, hotels and other resorts, camps, health spas, athletic clubs, and apartment complexes. New employment opportunities will arise in social service agencies such as senior centers, halfway houses, children's homes, and day-care programs for the mentally or developmentally disabled.

Recreation programs that depend on government funding are most likely to be affected in times of economic downturns when budgets are reduced. During such times, competition will increase significantly for jobs in the private sector. Due to such predicted budget reductions, employment for recreation workers in local government is predicted to grow more slowly than the average for all other occupations.

In any case, competition is expected to be keen because the field is open to college graduates regardless of major; as a result, there are more applicants than there are job openings. Opportunities will be best for individuals who

have formal training in recreation and for those with previous experience.

FOR MORE INFORMATION

For information regarding industry trends, accredited institutions, and conventions, contact

American Association for Physical Activity and Recreation
1900 Association Drive
Reston, VA 20191-1598
Tel: 703-476-3400
http://www.aahperd.org/aapar

For information on certification qualifications, contact

American Camp Association
5000 State Road 67 North
Martinsville, IN 46151-7902
Tel: 765-342-8456
http://www.acacamps.org

For information on membership, internships, and certification, contact

Employee Services Management Association
568 Spring Road, Suite D
Elmhurst, IL 60126-3868
Tel: 630-559-0020
http://www.esmassn.org

For information on the recreation industry, career opportunities, and certification qualifications, contact

National Recreation and Park Association
22377 Belmont Ridge Road
Ashburn, VA 20148-4501
Tel: 703-858-0784
http://www.nrpa.org

REGISTERED NURSES

OVERVIEW

Registered nurses (RNs) help individuals, families, and groups to improve and maintain health and to prevent disease. They care for the sick and injured in hospitals and other health care facilities, physicians' offices, private homes, public health agencies, schools, camps, and industry. Some registered nurses are employed in private practice. RNs hold about 2.5 million jobs in the United States.

QUICK FACTS

SCHOOL SUBJECTS

Biology

Chemistry

Health

PERSONAL SKILLS

Helping/teaching

Technical/scientific

WORK ENVIRONMENT

Primarily indoors

Primarily multiple locations

MINIMUM EDUCATION LEVEL

Some postsecondary training

MEDIAN SALARY

$57,280 to $83,440+

OUTLOOK

Much faster than the average

THE JOB

Registered nurses work under the direct supervision of nursing departments and in collaboration with physicians. Two-thirds of all nurses work in hospitals, where they may be assigned to general, operating room, or maternity room duty. They may also care for sick children or be assigned to other hospital units, such as emergency rooms, intensive care units, or outpatient clinics. There are many different kinds of RNs.

General duty nurses work together with other members of the health care team to assess the patient's condition and to develop and implement a plan of health care. These nurses may perform such tasks as taking patients' vital signs, administering medication and injections, recording the symptoms and progress of patients, changing dressings, assisting patients with personal care, conferring with members of the medical staff, helping prepare a patient for surgery, and completing any number of duties that require skill and understanding of patients' needs.

Surgical nurses oversee the preparation of the operating room and the sterilization of instruments. They assist surgeons during operations and coordinate the flow of patient cases in operating rooms.

Maternity nurses, or *neonatal nurses*, help in the delivery room, take care of newborns in the nursery, and teach mothers how to feed and care for their babies.

The activities of staff nurses are directed and coordinated by *head nurses* and *charge nurses*. Heading up the entire nursing program in the hospital is the *nursing service director*, who administers the nursing program to maintain standards of patient care. The nursing service director advises the medical staff, department heads, and the hospital administrator in matters relating to nursing services and helps prepare the department budget.

Private duty nurses may work in hospitals or in a patient's home. They are employed by the patient they are caring for or by the patient's family. Their service is designed for the individual care of one person and is carried out in cooperation with the patient's physician.

Office nurses usually work in the office of a dentist, physician, or health maintenance organization (HMO). An office nurse may be one of several nurses on the staff or the only staff nurse. If a nurse is the only staff member, this person may have to combine some clerical duties with those of nursing, such as serving as receptionist, making appointments for the doctor, helping maintain patient records, sending out monthly statements, and attending to routine correspondence. If the physician's staff is a large one that includes secretaries and clerks, the office nurse will concentrate on screening patients, assisting with examinations, supervising the examining rooms, sterilizing equipment, providing patient education, and performing other nursing duties.

Occupational health nurses, or *industrial nurses*, are an important part of many large firms. They maintain a clinic at a plant or factory and are usually occupied in rendering preventive, remedial, and educational nursing services. They work under the direction of an industrial physician, nursing director, or nursing supervisor. They may advise on accident prevention, visit employees on the job to check the conditions under which they work, and advise management about the safety of such conditions. At the plant, they render treatment in emergencies.

School nurses may work in one school or in several, visiting each for a part of the day or week. They may supervise the student clinic, treat minor cuts or injuries, or give advice on good health practices. They may examine students to detect conditions of the eyes or teeth that require attention. They also assist the school physician.

Community health nurses, also called *public health nurses*, require specialized training for their duties. Their job usually requires them to spend part of the time traveling from one assignment to another. Their duties may differ greatly from one case to another. For instance, in one day they may have to instruct a class of expectant mothers, visit new parents to help them plan proper care for the baby, visit an aged patient requiring special care, and conduct a class in nutrition. They usually possess many varied nursing skills and often are called upon to resolve unexpected or unusual situations.

Administrators in the community health field include *nursing directors*, *educational directors*, and *nursing supervisors*. Some nurses go into nursing education and work with nursing students to instruct them on theories and skills they will need to enter the profession. Nursing instructors may give classroom instruction and demonstrations or supervise nursing students on hospital units. Some instructors eventually become nursing school directors, university faculty, or deans of a university degree program. Nurses also have the opportunity to direct staff development and continuing education programs for nursing personnel in hospitals.

Advanced practice nurses are nurses with training beyond that required to have the RN designation. There are four primary categories of nurses included in this category: *nurse-midwives*, *clinical nurse specialists*, *nurse anesthetists*, and *nurse practitioners*.

Some nurses are consultants to hospitals, nursing schools, industrial organizations, and public health agencies. They advise clients on such administrative matters as staff organization, nursing techniques, curricula, and education programs. Other administrative specialists include *educational directors* for the state board of nursing, who are concerned with maintaining well-defined educational standards, and *executive directors* of professional nurses' associations, who administer programs developed by the board of directors and the members of the association.

Some nurses choose to enter the armed forces. All types of nurses, except private duty nurses, are represented in the military services. They provide skilled nursing care to active-duty and retired members of the armed forces and their families. In addition to basic nursing skills, *military nurses* are trained to provide care in various environments, including field hospitals, on-air evacuation flights, and onboard ships. Military nurses actively influence the development of health care through nursing research. Advances influenced by military nurses include the development of the artificial kidney (dialysis unit) and the concept of the intensive care unit.

REQUIREMENTS

High School

If you are interested in becoming a registered nurse, you should take high school mathematics and science courses, including biology, chemistry, and physics. Health courses will also be helpful. English and speech courses should not be neglected because you must be able to communicate well with patients.

Postsecondary Training

There are three basic kinds of training programs that you may choose from to become a registered nurse: associate's degree (ADN), bachelor's degree (BSN), and diploma. The choice of which of the three training programs to pursue depends on your career goals. A bachelor's degree in nursing is required for most supervisory or administrative positions, for jobs in public health agencies, and for admission to graduate nursing programs. A master's degree is usually necessary to prepare for a nursing specialty or to teach. For some specialties, such as nursing research, a Ph.D. is essential.

There are approximately 709 bachelor's degree programs in nursing in the United States. It requires four (in some cases, five) years to complete. The graduate of this program receives a BSN degree. The ADN is awarded after completion of a two-year study program that is usually offered in a junior or community college. There are approximately 850 ADN programs in the United States. You receive hospital training at cooperating hospitals in the general vicinity of the community college. The diploma program, which usually lasts three years, is conducted by hospitals and independent schools, although the number of these programs is declining, with roughly 70 programs in existence. At the conclusion of each of these programs, you become a graduate nurse, but not, however, a registered nurse. To obtain the RN designation you must pass a licensing examination required in all states.

Nurses can pursue postgraduate training that allows them to specialize in certain areas, such as emergency room, operating room, premature nursery, or psychiatric nursing. This training is sometimes offered through hospital on-the-job training programs.

Certification or Licensing

All states and the District of Columbia require a license to practice nursing. To obtain a license, graduates of approved nursing schools must pass a national examination. Nurses may be licensed in more than one state, either by examination or by the endorsement of a license issued by another state. The Nurse Licensure Compact Agreement allows a nurse who is licensed and permanently resides in one of the member states to practice in the other member states without obtaining additional licensure. In 2007, 21 states were members of the compact. In some states, continuing education is a condition for license renewal. Different titles require different education and training levels.

Other Requirements

You should enjoy working with people, especially those who may experience fear or anger because of an illness. Patience, compassion, and calmness are qualities needed by anyone working in this career. In addition, you must be able to give directions as well as follow instructions and work as part of a health care team. Anyone interested in becoming a registered nurse should also have a strong desire to continue learning, because new tests, procedures, and technologies are constantly being developed within medicine.

EXPLORING

You can explore your interest in nursing in a number of ways. Read books on careers in nursing and talk with high school guidance counselors, school nurses, and local public health nurses. Visit hospitals to observe the work and talk with hospital personnel to learn more about the daily activities of nursing staff.

Some hospitals now have extensive volunteer service programs in which high school students may work after school, on weekends, or during vacations in order both to render a valuable service and to explore their interests in nursing. There are other volunteer work experiences available with the Red Cross or community health services. Camp counseling jobs sometimes offer related experiences. The Internet is full of resources about nursing. Check out Nursing Net (http://www.nursingnet.org), and the American Nurses Association's Nursing World (http://www.nursingworld.org).

EMPLOYERS

Approximately 2.5 million registered nurses are employed in the United States. Inpatient and outpatient hospital departments account for about three out of five jobs for registered nurses. Nurses are employed by hospitals, managed-care facilities, long-term care facilities, clinics, industry, private homes, schools, camps, and government agencies. One out of five nurses works part time.

STARTING OUT

The only way to become a registered nurse is through completion of one of the three kinds of educational programs, plus passing the licensing examination, known as the NCLEX-RN. Registered nurses may apply for employment directly to hospitals, nursing homes, home care agencies, temporary nursing agencies, companies, and government agencies that hire nurses. Jobs can also be obtained through school placement offices, by signing up with employment agencies specializing in placement of nursing personnel, or through the state employment office. Other sources of jobs include nurses' associations, professional journals, and newspaper want ads.

ADVANCEMENT

Increasingly, administrative and supervisory positions in the nursing field go to nurses who have earned at least the bachelor of science degree in nursing. Nurses with many years of experience who are graduates of a diploma program may achieve supervisory positions, but requirements for such promotions have become more difficult in recent years and in many cases require at least the BSN degree.

Nurses with bachelor's degrees are usually those who are hired as public health nurses. Nurses with master's degrees are often employed as clinical nurse specialists, faculty, nurse educators and instructors, supervisors, or administrators.

RNs can pursue further education to become advanced practice nurses, who have greater responsibilities and command higher salaries.

EARNINGS

According to the U.S. Department of Labor, registered nurses had median annual earnings of $57,280 in 2006. Salaries ranged from less than $40,250 to more than $83,440. Earnings of RNs vary according to employer. According to the *Occupational Outlook Handbook*, those who worked at hospitals earned $58,550; those working in home health care services earned $54,190; and RNs who worked at nursing and personal care facilities earned $52,490.

Salary is determined by several factors: setting, education, and work experience. Most full-time nurses are given flexible work schedules as well as health and life insurance; some are offered education reimbursement and year-end bonuses. A staff nurse's salary is often limited only by the amount of work he or she is willing to take on. Many nurses take advantage of overtime work and shift differentials. About 10 percent of all nurses hold more than one job.

WORK ENVIRONMENT

Most nurses work in facilities that are clean and well lighted and where the temperature is controlled, although some work in rundown inner-city hospitals in less-than-ideal conditions. Usually, nurses work eight-hour shifts. Those in hospitals generally work any of three shifts: 7:00 A.M. to 3:00 P.M.; 3:00 P.M. to 11:00 P.M.; or 11:00 P.M. to 7:00 A.M. Many hospitals, however, are now moving to twelve-hour shifts.

Nurses spend much of the day on their feet, either walking or standing. Handling patients who are ill or infirm can also be very exhausting. Nurses who come in contact with patients with infectious diseases must be especially careful about cleanliness and sterility. Although many nursing duties are routine, many responsibilities are unpredictable. Sick persons are often very demanding, or they may be depressed or irritable. Despite this, nurses must maintain their composure and should be cheerful to help the patient achieve emotional balance. They must also maintain composure when interacting with the patient's family and loved ones, who may be concerned about the patient's well-being and the care they are receiving. Ethical issues in medicine and health care are also concerns.

Community health nurses may be required to visit homes that are in poor condition or very dirty. They may also come in contact with social problems, such as family violence. The nurse is an important health care provider and in many communities the sole provider.

Both the office nurse and the industrial nurse work regular business hours and are seldom required to work overtime. In some jobs, such as where nurses are on duty in private homes, they may frequently travel from home to home and work with various cases.

OUTLOOK

The nursing field is the largest of all health care occupations, and employment prospects for nurses are excellent. The U.S. Department of Labor projects that registered nurses will have one of the largest numbers of new jobs for all professions through 2016.

There has been a serious shortage of nurses in recent years. The shortage will be exacerbated by the increasing numbers of baby-boomer aged nurses who are expected to retire, creating more open positions than there are graduates of nursing programs. Job dissatisfaction and burnout are other reasons for the large turnover in this field.

The much faster than average job growth in this field is also a result of improving medical technology that will allow for treatments of many more diseases and health conditions. Nurses will be in strong demand to work with the rapidly growing population of senior citizens in the United States.

Approximately 59 percent of all nursing jobs are found in hospitals. However, because of administrative cost cutting, increased nurse's workload, and rapid growth of outpatient services, hospital nursing jobs will experience slower than average growth within the nursing profession. Employment in home care and nursing homes is expected to grow rapidly. Though more people are living well into their 80s and 90s, many need the kind of long-term care available at a nursing home. Also, because of financial reasons, patients are being released from hospitals sooner and admitted into nursing homes. Many nursing homes have facilities and staff capable of caring for long-term rehabilitation patients, as well as those afflicted with Alzheimer's. Many nurses will also be needed to help staff the growing number of outpatient facilities, such as HMOs, chemotherapy centers, dialysis centers, group medical practices, and ambulatory surgery centers.

Nursing specialties will be in great demand. There are, in addition, many part-time employment possibilities, with about one in four RNs working part time.

FOR MORE INFORMATION

Visit the AACN Web site to access a list of member schools and to read the online pamphlet Your Nursing Career: A Look at the Facts.

American Association of Colleges of Nursing (AACN)
One Dupont Circle, NW
Suite 530
Washington, DC 20036-1110
Tel: 202-463-6930
http://www.aacn.nche.edu

For information about opportunities as an RN, contact
American Nurses Association
8515 Georgia Avenue, Suite 400
Silver Spring, MD 20910-3403
Tel: 800-274-4262
http://www.nursingworld.org

For information about state-approved programs and information on nursing, contact the following organizations:
National League for Nursing
61 Broadway, 33rd Floor
New York, NY 10006-2701
Tel: 212-363-5555
http://www.nln.org

National Organization for Associate Degree Nursing
7794 Grow Drive
Pensacola, FL 32514-7072
Tel: 850-484-6948
Email: noadn@puetzamc.com
http://www.noadn.org

Discover Nursing, sponsored by Johnson & Johnson Health Care Systems, provides information on nursing careers, nursing schools, and scholarships.
Discover Nursing
http://www.discovernursing.com

RESERVATION AND TICKET AGENTS

OVERVIEW

Reservation and ticket agents are employed by airlines, bus companies, railroads, large hotel chains, and cruise lines to help customers in several ways. Reservation agents make and confirm travel arrangements for passengers by using computers and manuals to determine timetables, taxes, and other information. They usually work in reservation call centers, answering telephone or email inquiries and offering travel arrangement suggestions and information such as routes, schedules, fares, and types of accommodations. They also change or confirm transportation and lodging reservations.

Ticket agents sell tickets in terminals or in separate offices. Like reservation agents, they also use computers and manuals containing scheduling, boarding, and rate information to plan routes and calculate ticket costs. They determine whether seating is available, answer customer inquiries, check baggage, and direct passengers to proper places for boarding. They may also announce arrivals and departures and assist passengers in boarding. There are approximately 165,000 reservation and ticket agents employed in the United States.

THE JOB

Airline reservation agents are sales agents who work in large central offices run by airline companies. Their primary job is to book and confirm reservations for passengers on scheduled flights. At the request of the customer or a ticket agent, they plan the itinerary and other travel arrangements. While many agents still use timetables, airline manuals, reference guides, and tariff books, most of this work is performed using specialized computer programs.

Computers are used to make, confirm, change, and cancel reservations. After asking for the passenger's destination, desired travel time, and airport of departure, reservation agents type the information into a computer and quickly obtain information on all flight schedules and seating availability. If the plane is full, the agent may suggest an alternative flight or check to see if space is available on another airline that flies to the same destination. Agents may even book seats on competing airlines, especially if their own airline can provide service on the return trip.

Reservation agents also answer telephone and email inquiries about such things as schedules, fares, arrival and departure times, and cities serviced by their airline. They may maintain an inventory of passenger space available so they can notify other personnel and ticket stations of changes and try to book all flights to capacity. Some reservation agents work in more specialized areas, handling calls from travel agents or booking flights for members of frequent flyer programs. Agents working with international airlines must also be informed of visa regulations and other travel developments. This information is usually supplied by the senior reservation agent, who supervises and coordinates the activities of the other agents.

In the railroad industry, *train reservation clerks* perform similar tasks. They book seats or compartments for passengers, keep station agents and clerks advised on available space, and communicate with reservation clerks in other towns.

General transportation ticket agents for any mode of travel (air, bus, rail, or ship) sell tickets to customers at terminals or at separate ticket offices. Like reservation agents, they book space for customers. In addition, they use computers to prepare and print tickets, calculate fares, and collect payment. At the terminals they check and tag luggage, direct passengers to the proper areas for boarding, keep records of passengers on each departure, and help with customer problems, such as lost baggage or missed connections. *Airline ticket agents* may have additional duties, such as paging arriving and departing passengers and finding accommodations or new travel arrangements for passengers in the event of flight cancellations.

In airports, *gate agents* assign seats, issue boarding passes, make public address announcements of departures and arrivals, and help elderly or disabled passengers board the planes. In addition, they may also provide information to disembarking passengers about ground transportation, connecting flights, and local hotels.

Regardless of where they work, reservation and transportation ticket agents must be knowledgeable about their companies' policies and procedures, as well as the standard procedures of their industry. They must be aware of the availability of special promotions and services and be able to answer any questions customers may have.

REQUIREMENTS
High School

Reservation and ticket agents are generally required to have at least a high school diploma. Applicants should be able to type and have good communication and problem-solving skills. Because computers are being used more and more in this field, you should have a basic knowledge of computers and computer software. Previous experience working with the public is also helpful for the job. Knowledge of geography and foreign languages are other valuable skills, especially for international service agents.

Postsecondary Training

Some college is preferred, although it is not considered essential for the job. Some colleges now offer courses specifically designed for ticket reservations.

Reservation agents are given several weeks of classroom instruction. Here you will be taught how to read schedules, calculate fares, and plan itineraries. They learn how to use computer programs to get information and reserve space efficiently. They also study company policies, safety and security procedures, and government regulations that apply to the industry.

Transportation ticket agents receive less training, consisting of about one week of classroom instruction. They learn how to read tickets and schedules, assign seats, and tag baggage. This is followed by one week of on-the-job training, working alongside an experienced agent. After mastering the simpler tasks, the new ticket agents are trained to reserve space, make out tickets, and handle the boarding gate.

Other Requirements

Because you will be in constant contact with the public, professional appearance, a clear and pleasant speaking voice, and a friendly personality are important qualities. You need to be tactful in keeping telephone time to a

QUICK FACTS

SCHOOL SUBJECTS
Business
Computer science
English

PERSONAL SKILLS
Communication/ideas
Helping/teaching

WORK ENVIRONMENT
Primarily indoors
Primarily one location

MINIMUM EDUCATION LEVEL
Some postsecondary training

MEDIAN SALARY
$28,540

CERTIFICATION OR LICENSING
None available

OUTLOOK
Little or no change in growth

minimum without alienating your customers. In addition, you should enjoy working with people, have a good memory, and be able to maintain your composure when working with harried or unhappy travelers. Agents form a large part of the public image of their company.

Although not a requirement, many agents belong to labor unions such as the Transport Workers Union of America and the International Brotherhood of Teamsters.

EXPLORING

You may wish to apply for part-time or summer work with transportation companies in their central offices or at terminals. A school counselor can help you arrange an information interview with an experienced reservation and transportation ticket agent. Talking to an agent directly about his or her duties can help you to become more familiar with transportation operations.

EMPLOYERS

Reservation and ticket agents hold approximately 165,000 jobs in the United States. Commercial airlines are the main employers. However, other transportation companies, such as rail, ship, and bus lines, also require their services.

STARTING OUT

To find part-time or summer work, apply directly to the personnel or employment offices of transportation companies. Ask your school counselor or college placement director for information about job openings, requirements, and possible training programs. Additionally, contact transportation unions for lists of job openings.

ADVANCEMENT

With experience and a good work record, some reservation and ticket agents can be promoted to supervisory positions. They can also become city and district sales managers for ticket offices. Beyond this, opportunities for advancement are limited. However, achieving seniority within a company can give an agent the first choice of shifts and available overtime.

EARNINGS

According to the U.S. Department of Labor, reservation and transportation ticket agents earned median salaries of approximately $28,540 in 2006. The lowest paid 10 percent of these workers made less than $17,670 per year, while the highest paid 10 percent earned more than $45,400 annually.

Most agents can earn overtime pay; many employers also pay extra for night work. Benefits vary according to the place of work, experience, and union membership; however, most receive vacation and sick pay, health insurance, and retirement plans. Agents, especially those employed by the airlines, often receive free or reduced-fare transportation for themselves and their families.

WORK ENVIRONMENT

Reservation and ticket agents generally work 40 hours per week. Those working in reservations typically work in cubicles with their own computer terminals and telephone headsets. They are often on the telephone and behind their computers all day long. Conversations with customers and computer activity may be monitored and recorded by their supervisors for evaluation and quality reasons. Agents might also be required to achieve sales or reservations quotas. During holidays or when special promotions and discounts are being offered, agents are especially busy. At these times or during periods of severe weather, passengers may become frustrated. Handling customer frustrations can be stressful, but agents must maintain composure and a pleasant manner when speaking and emailing with customers.

Ticket agents working in airports and train and bus stations face a busy and noisy environment. They may stand most of the day and lift heavy objects such as luggage and packages. During holidays and busy times, their work can become extremely hectic as they process long lines of waiting customers. Storms and other factors may delay or even cancel flights, trains, and bus services. Like reservation agents, ticket agents may be confronted with upset passengers, but must be able to maintain composure at all times.

OUTLOOK

According to the U.S. Department of Labor, employment for reservation and ticket agents is expected to show little or no change in growth for all occupations through 2016. Technology is changing the way consumers purchase tickets. Ticketless travel and electronic ticketing—automated reservations ticketing—is reducing the need for agents. In addition, many airports now have computerized kiosks that allow passengers to reserve and purchase tickets themselves. Passengers can also access information about fares and flight times on the Internet, where they can also make reservations and purchase tickets. However, for security reasons, all of these services cannot be fully automated, so the need for reservation and transportation ticket agents will never be completely eliminated.

Most openings will occur as experienced agents transfer to other occupations or retire. Competition for jobs is fierce due to declining demand, low turnover, and because of the glamour and attractive travel benefits associated with the industry.

Overall, the transportation industry will remain heavily dependent on the state of the economy. During periods of recession or public fear about the safety of air travel, passenger travel generally declines and transportation companies are less likely to hire new workers, or may even resort to layoffs. Although terrorist threats have greatly affected the transportation industry, the World Tourism Organization (UNWTO) predicts that the industry will rebound in the long term. The economic need for business travel—as well as the public's desire for personal travel—will not be permanently altered by external events, states the UNWTO.

FOR MORE INFORMATION

For information on the airline industry, contact
Federal Aviation Administration
800 Independence Avenue, SW, Room 810
Washington, DC 20591-0004
Tel: 866-835-5322
http://www.faa.gov

For information on careers in the airline industry, visit
Avjobs.com
http://www.avjobs.com

For statistics on international travel and tourism, visit the following Web site:
World Tourism Organization
Capitán Haya 42
28020 Madrid, Spain
Email: omt@unwto.org
http://www.unwto.org

☐ RESPIRATORY THERAPISTS AND TECHNICIANS

OVERVIEW

Respiratory therapists, also known as respiratory care practitioners, evaluate, treat, and care for patients with deficiencies or abnormalities of the cardiopulmonary (heart/lung) system by either providing temporary relief from chronic ailments or administering emergency care where life is threatened. They are involved with the supervision of other respiratory care workers in their area of treatment. *Respiratory technicians* have many of the same responsibilities as therapists; however, technicians do not supervise other respiratory care workers.

Working under a physician's direction, these workers set up and operate respirators, mechanical ventilators, and other devices. They monitor the functioning of the equipment and the patients' response to the therapy and maintain the patients' charts. They also assist patients with breathing exercises, and inspect, test, and order repairs for respiratory therapy equipment. They may demonstrate procedures to trainees and other health care personnel. Approximately 122,000 respiratory therapy workers are employed in the United States.

QUICK FACTS

SCHOOL SUBJECTS
Health
Mathematics

PERSONAL SKILLS
Helping/teaching
Technical/scientific

WORK ENVIRONMENT
Primarily indoors
Primarily one location

MINIMUM EDUCATION LEVEL
Associate's degree

MEDIAN SALARY
$39,120 (technicians)
$47,420 (therapists)

LICENSING
Recommended

OUTLOOK
Faster than the average

THE JOB

Respiratory therapists and technicians treat patients with various cardiorespiratory problems. They may provide care that affords temporary relief from chronic illnesses such as asthma or emphysema, or they may administer life-support treatment to victims of heart failure, stroke, drowning, or shock. These specialists often mean the difference between life and death in cases involving acute respiratory conditions, as may result from head injuries or drug poisoning. Adults who stop breathing for longer than three to five minutes rarely survive without serious brain damage, and an absence of respiratory activity for more than nine minutes almost always results in death. Respiratory therapists carry out their duties under a physician's direction and supervision. Technicians typically work under the supervision of a respiratory therapist and physician, following specific instructions. Therapists and technicians set up and operate special devices to treat patients who need temporary or emergency relief from breathing difficulties. The equipment may include respirators, positive-pressure breathing machines, or environmental control systems. Aerosol inhalants are administered to confine medication to the lungs. Respiratory therapists often treat patients who have undergone surgery because anesthesia depresses normal respiration, thus the patients need some support to restore their full breathing capability and to prevent respiratory illnesses.

In evaluating patients, therapists test the capacity of the lungs and analyze the oxygen and carbon dioxide concentration and potential of hydrogen (pH), a measure of the acidity or alkalinity level of the blood. To measure lung capacity, therapists have patients breathe into an instrument that measures the volume and flow of air during inhalation and exhalation. By comparing the reading with the norm for the patient's age, height, weight, and gender, respiratory therapists can determine whether lung deficiencies exist. To analyze oxygen, carbon dioxide, and pH levels, therapists draw an arterial blood sample, place it in a blood gas analyzer, and relay the results to a physician.

Respiratory therapists watch equipment gauges and maintain prescribed volumes of oxygen or other inhalants. Besides monitoring the equipment to be sure it is operating properly, they observe the patient's physiological response to the therapy and consult with physicians in case of any adverse reactions. They also record pertinent identification and therapy information on each patient's chart and keep records of the cost of materials and the charges to the patients.

Therapists instruct patients and their families on how to use respiratory equipment at home, and they may demonstrate respiratory therapy procedures to trainees and other health care personnel. Their responsibilities include inspecting and testing equipment. If it is faulty, they either make minor repairs themselves or order major repairs.

Respiratory therapy workers include therapists, technicians, and assistants. Differences between respiratory therapists' duties and those of other respiratory care workers' include supervising technicians and assistants, teaching new staff, and bearing primary responsibility for the care given in their areas. At times the respiratory therapist may need to work independently and make clinical judgments on the type of care to be given to a patient. Although technicians can perform many of the same activities as a therapist (for example, monitoring equipment, checking patient responses, and giving medicine), they do not make independent decisions about what type of care to give. Respiratory assistants clean, sterilize, store, and generally take care of the equipment but have very little contact with patients.

REQUIREMENTS
High School

To prepare for a career in this field while you are still in high school, take health and science classes, including biology, chemistry, and physics. Mathematics and statistics classes will also be useful to you since much of this work involves using numbers and making calculations. Take computer science courses to become familiar with using technical and complex equipment and to become familiar with programs you can use to document your work. Since some of your responsibilities may include working directly with patients to teach them therapies, take English classes to improve your communication skills. Studying a foreign language may also be useful.

Postsecondary Training

Formal training is necessary for entry to this field. Training is offered at the postsecondary level by hospitals, medical schools, colleges and universities, trade schools, vocational-technical institutes, and the armed forces. The Committee on Accreditation for Respiratory Care (CoARC) has accredited more than 350 programs nationwide. A listing of these programs is available on CoARC's Web site, http://www.coarc.com. To be eligible for a respiratory therapy program, you must have graduated from high school.

Accredited respiratory therapy programs combine class work with clinical work. Programs vary in length, depending on the degree awarded. A certificate program generally takes one year to complete, an associate's degree usually takes two years, and a bachelor's degree program typically takes four years. In addition, it is important to note that some advanced-level programs will prepare you for becoming a registered respiratory therapist (RRT), while entry-level programs will prepare you for becoming a certified respiratory therapist (CRT). RRT-prepared graduates will be eligible for jobs as respiratory therapists once they have been certified. CRT-prepared graduates, on the other hand, are only eligible for jobs as respiratory technicians after certification. The areas of study for both therapists and technicians cover human anatomy and physiology, chemistry, physics, microbiology, and mathematics. Technical studies include courses such as patient evaluation, respiratory care pharmacology, pulmonary diseases, and care procedures. There are no standard hiring requirements for assistants. Department heads in charge of hiring set the standards and may require only a high school diploma.

Certification and Licensing

The National Board for Respiratory Care (NBRC) offers voluntary certification to graduates of CoARC-accredited programs. The certifications, as previously mentioned, are registered respiratory therapist (RRT) and certified respiratory therapist (CRT). You must have at least an associate's degree to be eligible to take the CRT exam. Anyone desiring certification must take the CRT exam first. After successfully completing this exam, those who are eligible can take the RRT exam. CRTs who meet further education and experience requirements can qualify for the RRT credential.

Certification is highly recommended because most employers require this credential. Those who are designated CRT or are eligible to take the exam are qualified for technician jobs that are entry-level or generalist positions. Employers usually require those with supervisory positions or those in intensive care specialties to have the RRT (or RRT eligibility).

A license is required to practice as a respiratory therapist, except in Alaska and Hawaii. Also, most employers require respiratory therapists to maintain a cardiopulmonary resuscitation (CPR) certification. The NBRC Web site provides helpful contact information for state licensure agencies at http://www.nbrc.org/StateLicAgencies.htm.

Other Requirements

Respiratory therapists must enjoy working with people. You must be sensitive to your patients' physical and psychological needs because you will be dealing with people who may be in pain or who may be frightened. The work of this occupational group is of great significance. Respiratory therapists are often responsible for the lives and well being of people already in critical condition. You must pay strict attention to detail, be able to follow instructions and work as part of a team, and remain cool in emergencies. Mechanical ability and manual dexterity are necessary to operate much of the respiratory equipment. Respiratory therapists must also be computer literate.

EXPLORING

Those considering advanced study may obtain a list of accredited educational programs in respiratory therapy by writing to the American Association for Respiratory Care at the address listed at the end of this article or visiting their Web site. Formal training in this field is available in hospitals, vocational-technical institutes, private trade schools, and other noncollegiate settings as well. Local hospitals can provide information on training opportunities. School vocational counselors may be sources of additional information about educational matters and may be able to set up interviews with or lectures by a respiratory therapy practitioner from a local hospital.

Hospitals are excellent places to obtain part-time and summer employment. They have a continuing need for helpers in many departments. Even though the work may not be directly related to respiratory therapy, you will gain knowledge of the operation of a hospital and may be in a position to get acquainted with respiratory therapists and observe them as they carry out their duties. If part-time or temporary work is not available, you may wish to volunteer your services.

EMPLOYERS

More than four out of five respiratory therapy jobs were in hospital departments of respiratory care, anesthesiology, or pulmonary medicine. The rest are employed by oxygen equipment rental companies, ambulance services, nursing homes, home health agencies, and physicians' offices. Many respiratory therapists (13 percent, as opposed to 5 percent in other occupations) hold a second job.

STARTING OUT

Graduates of CoARC-accredited respiratory therapy training programs may use their school's placement offices to help them find jobs. Otherwise, they may apply directly to the individual local health care facilities.

High school graduates may apply directly to local hospitals for jobs as respiratory therapy assistants. If your goal is to become a therapist or technician, however, you will need to enroll in a formal respiratory therapy educational program.

ADVANCEMENT

Many respiratory therapists start out as assistants or technicians. With appropriate training courses and experience, they advance to the therapist level. Respiratory therapists with sufficient experience may be promoted to assistant chief or chief therapist. With graduate education, they may be qualified to teach respiratory therapy at the college level or move into administrative positions such as director. Respiratory therapists in home health care and equipment rental firms may become branch managers. Others use the knowledge gained as a respiratory therapist to work in another industry, such as developing, marketing, or selling pharmaceuticals and medical devices.

EARNINGS

Respiratory therapists earned a median salary of $47,420 in 2006, according to the *Occupational Outlook Handbook*. The lowest 10 percent earned less than $35,200, and the highest 10 percent earned more than $64,190. Median annual earnings of respiratory therapy technicians were $39,120 in 2006. Salaries ranged from less than $25,940 to more than $56,220.

Hospital workers receive benefits that include health insurance, paid vacations and sick leave, and pension plans. Some institutions provide additional benefits, such as uniforms and parking, and offer free courses or tuition reimbursement for job-related courses.

WORK ENVIRONMENT

Respiratory therapists generally work in extremely clean, quiet surroundings. They usually work 40 hours a week, which may include nights and weekends because hospitals are in operation 24 hours a day, seven days a week. The work requires long hours of standing and may be very stressful during emergencies.

A possible hazard is that the inhalants these employees work with are highly flammable. The danger of fire is minimized, however, if the workers test equipment regularly and are strict about taking safety precautions. As do workers in many other health occupations, respiratory therapists run a risk of catching infectious diseases. Careful adherence to proper procedures minimizes the risk.

OUTLOOK

Employment growth for respiratory therapists is expected to grow at a faster than average rate through 2016, despite the fact that efforts to control rising health care costs has reduced the number of job opportunities in hospitals.

The increasing demand for therapists is the result of several factors. The fields of neonatal care and gerontology are growing, and there are continuing advances in treatments for victims of heart attacks and accidents and for premature babies.

Employment opportunities for respiratory therapists and technicians should be very favorable in the rapidly growing field of home health care, although this area accounts for only a small number of respiratory therapy jobs. In addition to jobs in home health agencies and hospital-based home health programs, there should be numerous openings for respiratory therapists in equipment rental companies and in firms that provide respiratory care on a contract basis.

FOR MORE INFORMATION

For information on scholarships, continuing education, job listings, and careers in respiratory therapy, contact
American Association for Respiratory Care
9425 North MacArthur Boulevard, Suite 100
Irving, TX 75063-4706
Tel: 972-243-2272
Email: info@aarc.org
http://www.aarc.org

For more information on allied health care careers as well as a listing of accredited programs, contact
Commission on Accreditation of Allied Health Education Programs
1361 Park Street
Clearwater, FL 33756-6039
Tel: 727-210-2350
Email: mail@caahep.org
http://www.caahep.org

For a list of CoARC-accredited training programs, contact
Committee on Accreditation for Respiratory Care (CoARC)
1248 Harwood Road
Bedford, TX 76021-4244
Tel: 817-283-2835
Email: info@coarc.com
http://www.coarc.com

For information on licensing and certification, contact
National Board for Respiratory Care
18000 W. 105th Street
Olathe, KS 66061-7543
Tel: 913-895-4900
http://www.nbrc.org

RESTAURANT AND FOOD SERVICE MANAGERS

OVERVIEW

Restaurant and food service managers are responsible for the overall operation of businesses that serve food. Food service work includes the purchasing of a variety of food, selection of the menu, preparation of the food, and, most importantly, maintenance of health and sanitation levels.

It is the responsibility of managers to oversee staffing for each task in addition to performing the business and accounting functions of restaurant operations. There are approximately 350,000 food service managers employed in the United States.

THE JOB

Restaurant and food service managers work in restaurants ranging from elegant hotel dining rooms to fast food restaurants. They also may work in food service facilities ranging from school cafeterias to hospital food services. Whatever the setting, these managers coordinate and direct the work of the employees who prepare and serve food and perform other related functions. *Restaurant managers* set work schedules for wait staff and host staff. *Food service managers* are responsible for buying the food and equipment necessary for the operation of the restaurant or facility, and they may help with menu planning. They inspect the premises periodically to ensure compliance with health and sanitation regulations. Restaurant and food service managers perform many clerical and financial duties, such as keeping records, directing payroll operations, handling large sums of money, and taking inventories. Their work usually involves much contact with customers and vendors, such as taking suggestions, handling complaints, and creating a friendly atmosphere. Restaurant managers generally supervise any advertising or sales promotions for their operations.

In some very large restaurants and institutional food service facilities, one or more *assistant managers* and an *executive chef* or *food manager* assist the manager. These specially trained assistants oversee service in the dining room and other areas of the operation and supervise the kitchen staff and preparation of all foods served.

Restaurant and food service managers are responsible for the success of their establishments. They continually analyze every aspect of its operation and make whatever changes are needed to guarantee its profitability.

These duties are common, in varying degrees, to both owner-managers of relatively small restaurants and to nonowner-managers who may be salaried employees in large restaurants or institutional food service facilities. The owner-manager of a restaurant is more likely to be involved in service functions, sometimes operating the cash register, waiting on tables, and performing a wide variety of tasks.

REQUIREMENTS

Educational requirements for restaurant and food service managers vary greatly. In many cases, no specific requirements exist and managerial positions are filled by

QUICK FACTS

SCHOOL SUBJECTS
Business
Health

PERSONAL SKILLS
Communication/ideas
Leadership/management

WORK ENVIRONMENT
Primarily indoors
Primarily one location

MINIMUM EDUCATION LEVEL
High school diploma

MEDIAN SALARY
$43,020

CERTIFICATION OR LICENSING
None available

OUTLOOK
More slowly than the average

promoting experienced food and beverage preparation and service workers. However, as more colleges offer programs in restaurant and institutional food service management—programs that combine academic work with on-the-job experience—more restaurant and food service chains are seeking individuals with this training.

Postsecondary Training

Almost 1,000 colleges and universities offer four-year programs in restaurant and hospitality management or institutional food service management leading to a bachelor's degree; a growing number of university programs offer graduate degrees in hospitality management or similar fields. Some individuals qualify for management training by earning an associate's degree or other formal award below the bachelor's degree level from one of the more than 800 community and junior colleges, technical institutes, or other institutions that offer programs in these fields. Students hired as *management trainees* by restaurant chains and food service management companies undergo vigorous training programs.

Certification or Licensing

The National Restaurant Association Educational Foundation offers a voluntary foodservice management professional certification to restaurant and food service managers. The National Restaurant Association Educational Foundation awards the food service manager (FMP) designation to managers who achieve a qualifying score on a written examination, complete a series of courses that cover a range of food service management topics, and meet standards of work experience in the field.

Other Requirements

Experience in all areas of restaurant and food service work is an important requirement for successful managers. Managers must be familiar with the various operations of the establishment: food preparation, service operations, sanitary regulations, and financial functions.

One of the most important requirements for restaurant and food service managers is to have good business knowledge. They must possess a high degree of technical knowledge in handling business details, such as buying large items of machinery and equipment and large quantities of food. Desirable personality characteristics include poise, self-confidence, and an ability to get along with people. Managers may be on their feet for long periods, and the hours of work may be both long and irregular.

EXPLORING

Practical restaurant and food service experience is usually easy to get. In colleges with curriculum offerings in these areas, summer jobs in all phases of the work are available and, in some cases, required. Some restaurant and food service chains provide on-the-job training in management.

EMPLOYERS

Restaurants and food service make up one of the largest and most active sectors of the nation's economy. Employers include restaurants of various sizes, hotel dining rooms, ships, trains, institutional food service facilities, and many other establishments where food is served. No matter the size or style of the establishment, managers are needed to oversee the operation and to ensure that records are kept, goals are met, and things run smoothly.

STARTING OUT

Many restaurants and food service facilities provide self-sponsored, on-the-job training for prospective managers. There are still cases in which people work hard and move up the ladder within the organization's workforce, finally arriving at the managerial position. More and more, people with advanced education and specialized training move directly into manager-trainee positions and then on to managerial positions.

ADVANCEMENT

In large restaurants and food service organizations, promotion opportunities frequently arise for employees with knowledge of the overall operation. Experience in all aspects of the work is an important consideration for the food service employee who desires advancement. The employee with knowledge of kitchen operations may advance from pantry supervisor to food manager, assistant manager, and finally restaurant or food service manager. Similar advancement is possible for dining room workers with knowledge of kitchen operations.

Advancement to top executive positions is possible for managers employed by large restaurant and institutional food service chains. A good educational background and some specialized training are increasingly valuable assets to employees who hope to advance.

EARNINGS

The earnings of salaried restaurant and food service managers vary a great deal, depending on the type and size of the establishment. According to the U.S. Department of Labor's *Occupational Outlook Handbook*, median annual earnings of food service managers were $43,020 in 2006. The lowest paid 10 percent earned less than $27,400, and the highest paid 10 percent earned more than $70,810. Those in charge of the largest restaurants and institutional food service facilities often earn more than $70,000. Managers of fast food restaurants average about $25,000 per year. In addition to a base salary, most managers receive bonuses based on profits, which can range from $2,000 to $7,500 a year.

WORK ENVIRONMENT

Work environments are usually pleasant. There is usually a great deal of activity involved in preparing and serving food to large numbers of people, and managers usually work 40 to 48 hours per week. In some cafeterias, especially those located within an industry or business establishment, hours are regular, and little evening work is required. Many restaurants serve late dinners, however, necessitating the manager to remain on duty during a late-evening work period.

Many restaurants furnish meals to employees during their work hours. Annual bonuses, group-plan pensions, hospitalization, medical, and other benefits may be offered to restaurant managers.

OUTLOOK

Employment for well-qualified restaurant and food service managers will grow more slowly than the average through 2016, with a projected growth of 5 percent. This will not limit opportunities, however. New restaurants are always opening to meet increasing demand. Those willing to relocate to other areas may also find more opportunities. Jobs are located throughout the country, with large cities and resort areas providing more opportunities for full-service dining positions. It has been estimated that at least 44 percent of all of the food consumed in the United States is eaten in restaurants and hotels.

Many job openings will arise from the need to replace managers retiring from the workforce. Also, population growth will result in an increased demand for eating establishments and, in turn, a need for managers to oversee them. As the elderly population increases, managers will be needed to staff dining rooms located in hospitals and nursing homes.

Economic downswings have a great effect on eating and drinking establishments. During a recession, people have less money to spend on luxuries such as dining out, thus hurting the restaurant business. However, greater numbers of working parents and their families are finding it convenient to eat out or purchase carryout food from a restaurant.

FOR MORE INFORMATION

For information on restaurant management careers, education, and certification, contact the following organizations:

International Council on Hotel, Restaurant and Institutional Education
2810 North Parham Road, Suite 230
Richmond VA 23294-4434
Tel: 804-346-4800
Email: info@chrie.org
http://www.chrie.org

National Restaurant Association Educational Foundation
175 West Jackson Boulevard, Suite 1500
Chicago, IL 60604-2814
Tel: 800-765-2122
Email: info@restaurant.org
http://www.nraef.org

Canadian Restaurant and Foodservices Association
316 Bloor Street West
Toronto, ON M5S 1W5 Canada
Tel: 800-387-5649
Email: info@crfa.ca
http://www.crfa.ca

RETAIL MANAGERS

OVERVIEW

Retail managers are responsible for the profitable operation of retail trade establishments. They oversee the selling of food, clothing, furniture, sporting goods, novelties, and many other items. Their duties include hiring, training, and supervising other employees, maintaining the physical facilities, managing inventory, monitoring expenditures and receipts, and maintaining good public relations. Retail managers hold about 2.2 million jobs in the United States.

THE JOB

Retail managers are responsible for every phase of a store's operation. They often are one of the first employees to arrive in the morning and the last to leave at night. Their duties include hiring, training, and supervising other employees, maintaining the physical facilities, managing inventory, monitoring expenditures and receipts, and maintaining good public relations.

Perhaps the most important responsibility of retail managers is hiring and training qualified employees. Managers then assign duties to employees, monitor their progress, promote employees, and increase salaries when appropriate. When an employee's performance is not satisfactory, a manager must find a way to improve the performance or, if necessary, fire him or her.

Managers should be good at working with all different kinds of people. Differences of opinion and personality clashes among employees are inevitable, however, and the manager must be able to restore good feelings among the staff. Managers often have to deal with upset customers, and must attempt to restore goodwill toward the store when customers are dissatisfied.

Retail managers keep accurate and up-to-date records of store inventory. When new merchandise arrives, the manager ensures items are recorded, priced, and displayed or shelved. They must know when stock is getting low and order new items in a timely manner.

QUICK FACTS

SCHOOL SUBJECTS
Business
Mathematics

PERSONAL SKILLS
Helping/teaching
Leadership/management

WORK ENVIRONMENT
Primarily indoors
Primarily one location

MINIMUM EDUCATION LEVEL
High school diploma

MEDIAN SALARY
$33,960

LICENSING
None available

OUTLOOK
More slowly than the average

Some managers are responsible for merchandise promotions and advertising. The manager may confer with an advertising agency representative to determine appropriate advertising methods for the store. The manager also may decide what products to put on sale for advertising purposes.

The duties of store managers vary according to the type of merchandise sold, the size of the store, and the number of employees. In small, owner-operated stores, managers often are involved in accounting, data processing, marketing, research, sales, and shipping. In large retail corporations, however, managers may be involved in only one or two of these activities.

REQUIREMENTS
High School

You will need at least a high school education in order to become a retail manager. Helpful courses include busi-

ness, mathematics, marketing, and economics. English and speech classes are also important. These courses will teach you to communicate effectively with all types of people, including employees and customers. Computer courses will also be of use.

Postsecondary Training

Most retail stores prefer applicants with a college degree, and many hire only college graduates. Liberal arts, social sciences, and business are the most common degrees held by retail managers.

To prepare for a career as a retail store manager, take courses in accounting, business, marketing, English, advertising, and computer science. If you are unable to attend college as a full-time student, consider getting a job in a store to gain experience and attend college part time. All managers, regardless of their education, must have good marketing, analytical, communication, and people skills.

Many large retail stores and national chains have established formal training programs, including classroom instruction, for their new employees. The training period may last a week or as long as one year. Training programs for retail franchises are generally extensive, covering all functions of the company's operation, including budgeting, marketing, management, finance, purchasing, product preparation, human resource management, and compensation. Training for a department store manager, for example, may include working as a salesperson in several departments in order to learn about the store's operations.

Other Requirements

To be a successful retail manager, you should have good communication skills, enjoy working with and supervising people, and be willing to put in very long hours. Diplomacy often is necessary when creating schedules for workers and in disciplinary matters. There is a great deal of responsibility in retail management and such positions often are stressful. A calm disposition and ability to handle stress will serve you well.

EXPLORING

If you are interested in becoming a retail manager, you may be able to find part-time, weekend, or summer jobs in a clothing store, supermarket, or other retail trade establishment. You can gain valuable work experience through such jobs and will have the opportunity to observe the retail industry to determine whether you are interested in pursuing a career in it. It also is useful to read periodicals that publish articles on the retail field, such as *Stores Online* (http://www.stores.org), published by the National Retail Federation.

EMPLOYERS

There are about 2.2 million retail managers in the United States, and about one-third are self-employed (many are store owners). Nearly every type of retail business requires management, though small businesses may be run by their owners. Wherever retail sales are made there is an opportunity for a management position, though most people have to begin in a much lower job. The food industry employs more workers than nearly any other, and retail food businesses always need managers, though smaller businesses may not pay very well. In general, the larger the business and the bigger the city, the more a retail manager can earn. Most other retail managers work in grocery and department stores, motor vehicle dealerships, and clothing and accessory stores.

STARTING OUT

Many new college graduates are able to find managerial positions through their schools' placement service. Some of the large retail chains recruit on college campuses.

Not all store managers, however, are college graduates. Many store managers are promoted to their positions from jobs of less responsibility within their organization. Some may be in the retail industry for more than a dozen years before being promoted. Those with more education often receive promotions faster.

Regardless of educational background, people who are interested in the retail industry should consider working in a retail store at least part time or during the summer. Although there may not be an opening when the application is made, there often is a high turnover of employees in retail management, and vacancies occur frequently.

ADVANCEMENT

Advancement opportunities in retailing vary according to the size of the store, where the store is located, and the type of merchandise sold. Advancement also depends on the individual's work experience and educational background.

A store manager who works for a large retail chain, for example, may be given responsibility for a number of stores in a given area or region or transferred to a larger store in another city. Willingness to relocate to a new city may increase an employee's promotional opportunities.

Some managers decide to open their own stores after they have acquired enough experience in the retail indus-

try. After working as a retail manager for a large chain of clothing stores, for example, a person may decide to open a small boutique.

Sometimes becoming a retail manager involves a series of promotions. A person who works in a supermarket, for example, may advance from clerk, checker, or bagger to a regular assignment in one of several departments in the store. After a period of time, he or she may become an assistant manager and eventually, a manager.

EARNINGS

Salaries depend on the size of the store, the responsibilities of the job, and the number of customers served. According to the U.S. Department of Labor, median annual earnings of supervisors of retail sales workers, including commission, were $33,960 in 2006. Salaries ranged from less than $21,420 to more than $59,710 per year. Median annual earnings of grocery store managers in 2006 were $33,390, and managers of clothing stores earned $33,140. Those who managed home building supply stores ranked among the highest paid at $35,820. Managers who oversee an entire region for a retail chain can earn more than $100,000.

In addition to a salary, some stores offer their managers special bonuses, or commissions, which are typically connected to the store's performance. Many stores also offer employee discounts on store merchandise.

WORK ENVIRONMENT

Most retail stores are pleasant places to work, and managers often are given comfortable offices. Many, however, work long hours. Managers often work six days a week and as many as 60 hours a week, especially during busy times of the year such as the Christmas season. Because holiday seasons are peak shopping periods, it is extremely rare that managers can take holidays off or schedule vacations around a holiday, even if the store is not open on that day.

Although managers usually can get away from the store during slow times, they must often be present if the store is open at night. It is important that the manager be available to handle the store's daily receipts, which usually are put in a safe or taken to a bank's night depository at the close of the business day.

OUTLOOK

Employment of retail managers is expected to grow more slowly than the average for all occupations through 2016. Although retailers have reduced their management staff to cut costs and make operations more efficient, there still are good opportunities in retailing. Internet stores and e-commerce ventures will present many new opportunities for retail managers, for example. However, competition for all jobs will probably continue to increase, and computerized systems for inventory control may reduce the need for some managers. Applicants with the best educational backgrounds and work experience will have the best chances of finding jobs. There will always be a need for retail managers, however, as long as retail stores exist. Retail manager positions are rarely affected by corporate restructuring at retail headquarters; this has a greater impact on home office staff.

FOR MORE INFORMATION

For materials on educational programs in the retail industry and to read the industry publication, STORES *magazine, contact*

National Retail Federation
325 7th Street, NW, Suite 1100
Washington, DC 20004-2818
Tel: 800-673-4692
http://www.nrf.com

For information on jobs in retail, contact
Retail Industry Leader's Association
1700 North Moore Street, Suite 2250
Arlington, VA 22209-2793
Tel: 703-841-2300
http://www.imra.org

RETAIL SALES WORKERS

OVERVIEW

Retail sales workers assist customers with purchases by identifying their needs, showing or demonstrating merchandise, receiving payment, recording sales, and wrapping their purchases or arranging for their delivery. They are sometimes called *sales clerks*, *retail clerks*, or *salespeople*. There are approximately 4.5 million retail salespersons employed in the United States.

THE JOB

Salespeople work in more than a hundred different types of retail establishments in a variety of roles. Some, for example, work in small specialty shops where, in addition to

waiting on customers, they might check inventory, order stock from sales representatives (or by telephone, email, or mail), place newspaper display advertisements, prepare window displays, and rearrange merchandise for sale.

Other salespeople may work in specific departments, such as the furniture department, of a large department store. The employees in a department work in shifts to provide service to customers six or seven days a week. To improve their sales effectiveness and knowledge of merchandise, they attend regular staff meetings. Advertising, window decorating, sales promotion, buying, and market research specialists support the work of retail salespeople.

Whatever they are selling, the primary responsibility of retail sales workers is to interest customers in the merchandise. This might be done by describing the product's features, demonstrating its use, or showing various models and colors. Some retail sales workers must have specialized knowledge, particularly those who sell such expensive, complicated products as stereos, appliances, and personal computers.

In addition to selling, most retail sales workers make out sales checks; receive cash, checks, and charge payments; bag or package purchases; and give change and receipts. Depending on the hours they work, retail sales workers might have to open or close the cash register. This might include counting the money in the cash register; separating charge slips, coupons, and exchange vouchers; and making deposits at the cash office. The sales records they keep are normally used in inventory control. Sales workers are usually held responsible for the contents of their registers, and repeated shortages are cause for dismissal in many organizations.

Sales workers must be aware of any promotions the store is sponsoring and know the store's policies and procedures, especially on returns and exchanges. Also, they often must recognize possible security risks and know how to handle such situations.

Consumers often form their impressions of a store by its sales force. To stay ahead in the fiercely competitive retail industry, employers are increasingly stressing the importance of providing courteous and efficient service. When a customer wants an item that is not on the sales floor, for example, the sales worker might be expected to check the stockroom and, if necessary, place a special order or call another store to locate the item.

REQUIREMENTS
High School

Employers generally prefer to hire high school graduates for most sales positions. Such subjects as English, speech, and mathematics provide a good background for these jobs. Many high schools and two-year colleges have special programs that include courses in merchandising, principles of retailing, and retail selling.

Postsecondary Training

In retail sales, as in other fields, the level of opportunity tends to coincide with the level of a person's education. In many stores, college graduates enter immediately into on-the-job training programs to prepare them for management assignments. Successful and experienced workers who do not have a degree might also qualify for these programs. Useful college courses include economics, business administration, and marketing. Many colleges offer majors in retailing. Executives in many companies express a strong preference for liberal arts graduates, especially those with some business courses or a master's degree in business administration.

Other Requirements

The retail sales worker must be in good health. Many selling positions require standing most of the day. The sales worker must have stamina to face the grueling pace of busy times, such as weekends and the Christmas season, while at the same time remaining pleasant and effective. Personal appearance is important. Salespeople should be neat and well groomed and have an outgoing personality.

A pleasant speaking voice, natural friendliness, tact, and patience are all helpful personal characteristics. The sales worker must be able to converse easily with strangers of all ages. In addition to interpersonal skills, sales workers must be equally good with figures. They should be able to add and subtract accurately and quickly and operate cash registers and other types of business machines.

Most states have established minimum standards that govern retail employment. Some states set a minimum age of 14, require at least a high school diploma, or prohibit more than eight hours of work a day or 48 hours in any six days. These requirements are often relaxed during the Christmas season.

EXPLORING

Because of its seasonal nature, retailing offers numerous opportunities for temporary or part-time sales experience. Most stores add extra personnel for the Christmas season. Vacation areas may hire sales employees, usually high school or college students, on a seasonal basis.

QUICK FACTS

SCHOOL SUBJECTS

English

Mathematics

Speech

PERSONAL SKILLS

Communication/ideas

Helping/teaching

WORK ENVIRONMENT

Primarily indoors

Primarily one location

MINIMUM EDUCATION LEVEL

High school diploma

MEDIAN SALARY

$19,760

CERTIFICATION OR LICENSING

None available

OUTLOOK

About as fast as the average

Fewer sales positions are available in metropolitan areas during the summer, as this is frequently the slowest time of the year.

Many high schools and junior colleges have developed "distributive education" programs that combine courses in retailing with part-time work in the field. The distributive education student may receive academic credit for this work experience in addition to regular wages. Store owners cooperating in these programs often hire students as full-time personnel upon completion of the program.

EMPLOYERS

There are many different types of retail establishments, ranging from small specialty shops that appeal to collectors to large retailers that sell everything from eyeglasses to DVD players. The largest employers of retail salespersons are department stores, clothing and accessories stores, building material and garden equipment stores, and motor vehicle dealers. Retail sales workers can have just one or two coworkers or well over 100, depending on the size of the establishment.

STARTING OUT

If they have openings, retail stores usually hire beginning salespeople who come in and fill out an application. Major department stores maintain extensive personnel departments, while in smaller stores the manager might do the hiring. Occasionally, sales applicants are given an aptitude test.

Young people might be hired immediately for sales positions. Often, however, they begin by working in the stockroom as clerks, helping to set up merchandise displays, or assisting in the receiving or shipping departments. After a while they might be moved up to a sales assignment.

Training varies with the type and size of the store. In large stores, the beginner might benefit from formal training courses that cover sales techniques, store policies, the mechanics of recording sales, and an overview of the entire store. Programs of this type are usually followed by on-the-job sales supervision. The beginner in a small store might receive personal instruction from the manager or a senior sales worker, followed by supervised sales experience.

College graduates and people with successful sales experience often enter executive training programs (sometimes referred to as flying squads because they move rapidly through different parts of the store). As they rotate through various departments, the trainees are exposed to merchandising methods, stock and inventory control, advertising, buying, credit, and personnel. By spending time in each of these areas, trainees receive a broad retailing background designed to help them as they advance into the ranks of management.

ADVANCEMENT

Large stores have the most opportunities for promotion. Retailing, however, is a mobile field, and successful and experienced people can readily change employment. This is one of the few fields where, if the salesperson has the necessary initiative and ability, advancement to executive positions is possible regardless of education.

When first on the job, sales workers develop their career potential by specializing in a particular line of merchandise. They become authorities on a certain product line, such as sporting equipment, women's suits, or building materials. Many good sales workers prefer

the role of the *senior sales worker* and remain at this level. Others might be asked to become supervisor of a section. Eventually they might develop into a *department manager, floor manager, division or branch manager,* or *general manager.*

People with sales experience often enter related areas, such as buying. Other retail store workers advance into support areas, such as personnel, accounting, public relations, and credit.

Young people with ability find that retailing offers the opportunity for unusually rapid advancement. One study revealed that half of all retail executives are under 35 years of age. It is not uncommon for a person under 35 to be in charge of a retail store or department with an annual sales volume of over $1,000,000. Conversely, a retail executive who makes bad merchandising judgments might quickly be out of a job.

EARNINGS

Most beginning sales workers start at the federal minimum wage, which is $5.85 an hour. The federal minimum wage will rise to $6.55 in the summer of 2008 and to $7.25 in the summer of 2009. Wages vary greatly, depending primarily on the type of store and the degree of skill required. Businesses might offer higher wages to attract and retain workers. Some sales workers make as much as $18 an hour or more.

Department stores or retail chains might pay more than smaller stores. Higher wages are paid for positions requiring a greater degree of skill. Many sales workers also receive a commission (often 4 to 8 percent) on their sales or are paid solely on commission. According to the *Occupational Outlook Handbook,* median hourly earnings of retail salespersons, including commission, were $9.50 in 2006. A yearly salary for full-time work therefore averages $19,760. Wages ranged from less than $6.79 ($14,123 a year) to more than $18.48 an hour ($38,438 a year). Sales workers in new and used car dealerships earned median wages of $18.70 an hour; in lumber and other building materials, $11.37; in department stores, $8.70; and in clothing stores, $8.53.

Salespeople in many retail stores are allowed a discount on their own purchases, ranging from 10 to 50 percent. This privilege is sometimes extended to the worker's family. Many clothing stores require employees to purchase clothes to wear while on the job, usually at a deep discount. Meals in the employee cafeterias maintained by large stores might be served at a price that is below cost. Many stores provide sick leave, medical and life insurance, and retirement benefits for full-time workers. Most stores give paid vacations.

WORK ENVIRONMENT

Retail sales workers generally work in clean, comfortable, well-lighted areas. Those with seniority have reasonably good job security. When business is slow, stores might curtail hiring and not fill vacancies that occur. Most stores, however, are able to weather mild recessions in business without having to release experienced sales workers. During periods of economic recession, competition among salespeople for job openings can become intense.

With nearly two million retail stores across the country, sales positions are found in every region. An experienced salesperson can find employment in almost any state. The vast majority of positions, however, are located in large cities or suburban areas.

The five-day, 40-hour workweek is the exception rather than the rule in retailing. Most salespeople can expect to work some evening and weekend hours, and longer than normal hours might be scheduled during Christmas and other peak periods. In addition, most retailers restrict the use of vacation time between Thanksgiving and early January. Most sales workers receive overtime pay during Christmas and other rush seasons. Part-time salespeople generally work at peak hours of business, supplementing the full-time staff. Because competition in the retailing business is keen, many retailers work under pressure. The sales worker might not be directly involved but will feel the pressures of the industry in subtle ways. The sales worker must be able to adjust to alternating periods of high activity and dull monotony. No two days—or even customers—are alike. Because some customers are hostile and rude, salespeople must learn to exercise tact and patience at all times.

OUTLOOK

About 4.5 million people are employed as sales workers in retail stores of all types and sizes. The employment of sales personnel should grow about as fast as the average for all occupations through 2016, according to the U.S. Department of Labor. Turnover among sales workers is much higher than average. Many of the expected employment opportunities will stem from the need to replace workers. Other positions will result from existing stores' staffing for longer business hours or reducing the length of the average employee workweek.

As drug, variety, grocery, and other stores have rapidly converted to self-service operations, they will need fewer sales workers. At the same time, many products, such as stereo components, electrical appliances, computers, and sporting goods, do not lend themselves to self-service operations. These products require extremely skilled sales workers to assist customers and explain the benefits of various makes and models. On balance, as easy-to-sell goods will be increasingly marketed in self-service stores, the demand in the future will be strongest for sales workers who are knowledgeable about particular types of products.

During economic recessions, sales volume and the resulting demand for sales workers generally decline. Purchases of costly items, such as cars, appliances, and furniture, tend to be postponed during difficult economic times. In areas of high unemployment, sales of all types of goods might decline. Since turnover of sales workers is usually very high, however, employers often can cut payrolls simply by not replacing all those who leave.

There should continue to be good opportunities for temporary and part-time workers, especially during the holidays. Stores are particularly interested in people who, by returning year after year, develop good sales backgrounds.

FOR MORE INFORMATION

For materials on educational programs in the retail industry, contact

National Retail Federation
325 7th Street, NW, Suite 1100
Washington, DC 20004-2818
Tel: 800-673-4692
http://www.nrf.com

ROBOTICS TECHNICIANS

OVERVIEW

Robotics technicians assist robotics engineers in a wide variety of tasks relating to the design, development, production, testing, operation, repair, and maintenance of robots and robotic devices.

THE JOB

The majority of robotics technicians work within the field of computer-integrated manufacturing or programmable automation. Using computer science technology, robotics engineers design and develop robots and other automated equipment, including computer software used to program robots. Robotics technicians assist in all phases of robotics engineering. They install, repair, and maintain finished robots. Others help design and develop new kinds of robotics equipment. Technicians who install,

QUICK FACTS

SCHOOL SUBJECTS

Computer science

Mathematics

PERSONAL SKILLS

Mechanical/manipulative

Technical/scientific

WORK ENVIRONMENT

Primarily indoors

Primarily one location

MINIMUM EDUCATION LEVEL

High school diploma

MEDIAN SALARY

$45,850

CERTIFICATION OR LICENSING

None available

OUTLOOK

About as fast as the average

repair, and maintain robots and robotic equipment need knowledge of electronics, electrical circuitry, mechanics, pneumatics, hydraulics, and computer programming. They use hand and power tools, testing instruments, manuals, schematic diagrams, and blueprints.

Before installing new equipment, technicians review the work order and instructional information; verify that the intended site in the factory is correctly supplied with the necessary electrical wires, switches, circuit breakers, and other parts; position and secure the robot in place, sometimes using a crane or other large tools and equipment; and attach various cables and hoses, such as those that connect a hydraulic power unit with the robot. After making sure that the equipment is operational, technicians program the robot for specified tasks, using their knowledge of its programming language. They may write the detailed instructions that program robots or reprogram a robot when changes are needed.

Once robots are in place and functioning, they may develop problems. Technicians then test components and locate faulty parts. When the problem is found, they may replace or recalibrate parts. Sometimes they suggest changes in circuitry or programming, or may install different end-of-arm tools on robots to allow machines to perform new functions. They may train robotics operators in how to operate robots and related equipment and help establish in-house basic maintenance and repair programs at new installations.

Companies that only have a few robots don't always hire their own robotics technicians. Instead they use *robot field technicians* who work for a robotic manufacturer. These technicians travel to manufacturing sites and other locations where robots are used to repair and service robots and robotic equipment.

Technicians involved with the design and development of new robotic devices are sometimes referred to as *robotics design technicians*. As part of a design team, they work closely with robotics engineers. The robotics design job starts as the engineers analyze the tasks and settings to be assigned and decide what kind of robotics system will best serve the necessary functions. Technicians involved with robot assembly, sometimes referred to as *robot assemblers*, commonly specialize in one aspect of robot assembly. Materials handling technicians receive requests for components or materials, then locate and deliver them to the technicians doing the actual assembly or those performing tests on these materials or components. Mechanical assembly technicians put together components and subsystems and install them in the robot. Electrical assembly technicians do the same work as mechanical assembly technicians but specialize in electrical components such as circuit boards and automatic switching devices. Finally, some technicians test the finished assemblies to make sure the robot conforms to the original specifications.

Other kinds of robotics technicians include *robot operators*, who operate robots in specialized settings, and *robotics trainers*, who train other employees in the installation, use, and maintenance of robots.

Robotics technicians may also be referred to as *electromechanical technicians*, *manufacturing technicians*, *robot mechanics*, *robotics repairmen*, *robot service technicians*, and *installation robotics technicians*.

REQUIREMENTS
High School

In high school, you should take as many science, math, and computer classes as possible. Recommended courses are biology, chemistry, physics, algebra, trigonometry, geometry, calculus, graphics, computer science, English, speech, composition, social studies, and drafting. In addition, take shop and vocational classes that teach blueprint and electrical schematic reading, the use of hand tools, drafting, and the basics of electricity and electronics.

Postsecondary Training

Because changes occur so rapidly within this field, it is often recommended that technicians get a broad-based education that encompasses robotics but does not focus solely on robotics. Programs that provide the widest career base are those in automated manufacturing, which includes robotics, electronics, and computer science.

Although the minimum educational requirement for a robotics technician is a high school diploma, many employers prefer to hire technicians who have received formal training beyond high school. Two-year programs are available in community colleges and technical institutes that grant an associate's degree in robotics. The armed forces also offer technical programs that result in associate's degrees in electronics, biomedical equipment, and computer science. The military uses robotics and other advanced equipment and offers excellent training opportunities to members of the armed forces. This training is highly regarded by many employers and can be an advantage in obtaining a civilian job in robotics.

Other Requirements

Because the field of robotics is rapidly changing, one of the most important requirements for a person interested in a career in robotics is the willingness to pursue additional training on an ongoing basis during his or her career. After completing their formal education, engineers and technicians may need to take additional classes in a college or university or take advantage of training offered through their employers and professional associations.

Robotics technicians need manual dexterity, good hand-eye coordination, and mechanical and electrical aptitude.

EXPLORING

Because robotics is a relatively new field, it is important to learn as much as possible about current trends and recent technologies. Reading books and articles in trade magazines provides an excellent way to learn about what is happening in robotics technologies and expected future trends. A trade magazines with informative articles is *Robotics & Automation*.

You can become a robot hobbyist and build your own robots or buy toy robots and experiment with them. Complete robot kits are available through a number of companies and range from simple, inexpensive robots to highly complex robots with advanced features and accessories. A number of books that give instructions and helpful hints on building robots can be found at most public libraries and bookstores. In addition, relatively inexpensive and simple toy robots are available from electronics shops, department stores, and mail order companies.

You can also participate in competitions. An annual competition, the International Aerial Robotics Competition, is sponsored by the Association for Unmanned Vehicle Systems International. This competition, which requires teams of students to build complex robots, is open to college students. FIRST Robotics Competition (FRC) challenges teams of young people and their mentors to solve a common problem in a six-week timeframe using a standard "kit of parts" and a common set of rules. Teams build robots from the parts and enter them in competitions. Visit http://www.usfirst.org for more information.

Robotic Autonomy is a new summer robotics camp offered by Carnegie Mellon University in collaboration with NASA/Ames Research Center. The course introduces high school juniors and seniors to the electronics, mechanics, and computer science of robotics during the summer. See http://www-2.cs.cmu.edu/~robocamp for details or visit http://robotics.arc.nasa.gov for robotics information and activities.

Another great way to learn about robotics is to attend trade shows. Many robotics and automated machinery manufacturers exhibit their products at shows and conventions. Numerous such trade shows are held every year in different parts of the country. Information about these trade shows is available through association trade magazines and periodicals such as *Managing Automation* (http://www.managingautomation.com).

Other activities that foster knowledge and skills relevant to a career in robotics include membership in high school science clubs, participation in science fairs, and pursuing hobbies that involve electronics, mechanical equipment, and model building.

EMPLOYERS

Robotics technicians are employed in virtually every manufacturing industry. With the trend toward automation continuing—often via the use of robots—people trained in robotics can expect to find employment with almost all types of manufacturing companies in the future.

STARTING OUT

In the past, most people entered robotics technician positions from positions as automotive workers, machinists, millwrights, computer repair technicians, and computer operators. Companies retrained them to troubleshoot and repair robots rather than hire new workers. Although this still occurs today, there are many more opportunities for formal education and training specifically in robotics engineering, and robotics manufacturers are more likely to hire graduates of robotics programs, both at the technician and engineer levels.

Graduates of two- and four-year programs may learn about available openings through their schools' job placement services. It also may be possible to learn about job openings through want ads in newspapers, job Web sites, and trade magazines.

In many cases, it will be necessary to research companies that manufacture or use robots and apply directly to them.

Job opportunities may be good at small start-up companies or a start-up robotics unit of a large company. Many times these employers are willing to hire inexperienced workers as apprentices or assistants. Then, when their sales and production grow, these workers have the best chances for advancement.

Other places to search for employment include your college's job placement services, advertisements in professional magazines, Web sites, and newspapers, or job fairs.

ADVANCEMENT

After several years on the job, robotics technicians who have demonstrated their ability to handle more responsibility may be assigned some supervisory work or, more likely, will train new technicians. Experienced technicians and engineers may teach courses at their workplace or find teaching opportunities at a local school or community college.

Other routes for advancement include becoming a sales representative for a robotics manufacturing or design firm or working as an independent contractor for companies that use or manufacture robots.

With additional training and education, such as a bachelor's degree, technicians can become eligible for positions as robotics engineers.

EARNINGS

The U.S. Department of Labor reports that median annual earnings of electrical and electronics engineering technicians were $50,660 in 2006, and the average annual salary for mechanical engineering technicians was $45,850. Technicians with considerable experience and a college degree can earn $73,200 or more.

Employers offer a variety of benefits that can include the following: paid holidays, vacations, personal days, and sick leave; medical, dental, disability, and life insurance; 401(k) plans, pension and retirement plans; profit sharing; and educational assistance programs.

WORK ENVIRONMENT

Robotics technicians may work either for a company that manufactures robots or a company that uses robots. Most companies that manufacture robots are relatively clean, quiet, and comfortable environments. Technicians may work in an office or on the production floor. A large number of robotics manufacturers are found in California, Michigan, Illinois, Indiana, Pennsylvania, Ohio, Connecticut, Texas, British Columbia, and Ontario, although companies exist in many other states and parts of Canada.

Technicians who work in a company that uses robots may work in noisy, hot, and dirty surroundings. Conditions vary based on the type of industry within which one works. Automobile manufacturers use a significant number of robots, as do manufacturers of electronics components and consumer goods and the metalworking industry. Workers in a foundry work around heavy equipment and in hot and dirty environments. Workers in the electronics industry generally work in very clean and quiet environments. Some robotics personnel are required to work in clean room environments, which keep electronic components free of dirt and other contaminants. Workers in these environments wear facemasks, hair coverings, and special protective clothing.

Some technicians may confront potentially hazardous conditions in the workplace. Robots, after all, are often designed and used precisely because the task they perform involves some risk to humans: handling laser beams, arc-welding equipment, radioactive substances, or hazardous chemicals. When they design, test, build, install, and repair robots, it is inevitable that some engineers and technicians will be exposed to these same risks. Plant safety procedures protect the attentive and cautious worker, but carelessness in such settings can be especially dangerous.

In general, most technicians work 40-hour workweeks, although overtime may be required for special projects or to repair equipment that is shutting down a production line. Some technicians, particularly those involved in maintenance and repairs, may work shifts that include evening, late night, or weekend work.

Field service technicians travel to manufacturing sites to repair robots. Their work may involve extensive travel and overnight stays. They may work at several sites in one day or stay at one location for an extended period for more difficult repairs.

OUTLOOK

Employment opportunities for robotics technicians are closely tied to economic conditions in the United States and in the global marketplace. The Robotics Industry Association (RIA) reports that the robotics market gained 24 percent in the fourth quarter of 2007, reversing the decline from 2006. Sales of robots to industries like automotive, food, consumer goods, and pharmaceuticals increased. The area of promising growth are materials handling robots that handle payloads greater than 10 pounds and for arc-welding robots, both of which declined less than the industry average. RIA estimates that some 178,000 robots are now working in U.S. factories, making the United States the world's second largest robotics user, next to Japan. There are an estimated one million robots worldwide.

The U.S. Department of Labor predicts the fields of mechanical, electronics, and computer hardware engineering will grow as fast as the average occupation through 2016. Job opportunities for engineering technicians will also grow as fast as the average. Competition for technician jobs with be stiff, and opportunities will be best for those that have advanced degrees.

The use of industrial robots is expected to grow as robots become more programmable and flexible and as manufacturing processes become more automated. Growth is also expected in nontraditional applications, such as education, health care, security, and nonindustrial purposes. Future employment in robotics will depend on future demand for new applications, as well as available capital to spend on research and development.

FOR MORE INFORMATION

For information on competitions and student membership, contact
Association for Unmanned Vehicle Systems International
2700 South Quincy Street, Suite 400
Arlington, VA 22206-2242
Tel: 703-845-9671
http://www.auvsi.org

For career information, company profiles, training seminars, and educational resources, contact
Robotic Industries Association
900 Victors Way

PO Box 3724
Ann Arbor, MI 48106-2735
Tel: 734-994-6088
http://www.roboticsonline.com

For information on careers and educational programs, contact
Robotics and Automation Society
Institute of Electrical and Electronics Engineers
1828 L Street, NW, Suite 1202
Washington, DC 20036-5104
Tel: 202-785-0017
http://www.ncsu.edu/IEEE-RAS

For information on educational programs, competitions, and student membership in SME, contact
Society of Manufacturing Engineers (SME)
One SME Drive
Dearborn, MI 48121-2408
Tel: 800-733-4763
http://www.sme.org

 ROOFERS

OVERVIEW

Roofers install and repair roofs of buildings using a variety of materials and methods, including built-up roofing, single-ply roofing systems, asphalt shingles, tile, and slate. They may also waterproof and damp-proof walls, swimming pools, and other building surfaces. Roughly 156,000 roofers are employed in the United States.

THE JOB

Although roofers usually are trained to apply most kinds of roofing, they often specialize in either sheet membrane roofing or prepared roofing materials such as asphalt shingles, slate, or tile.

One kind of sheet membrane roofing is called built-up roofing. Built-up roofing, used on flat roofs, consists of roofing felt (fabric saturated in bitumen, a tar-like material) laid into hot bitumen. To prepare for putting on a built-up roof, roofers may apply a layer of insulation to the bare roof deck. Then they spread molten bitumen over the roof surface, lay down overlapping layers of roofing felt, and spread more hot bitumen over the felt, sealing the seams and making the roof watertight. They repeat this process several times to build up as many

QUICK FACTS

SCHOOL SUBJECTS

Mathematics

Technical/shop

PERSONAL SKILLS

Following instructions

Mechanical/manipulative

WORK ENVIRONMENT

Primarily outdoors

Primarily multiple locations

MINIMUM EDUCATION LEVEL

Apprenticeship

MEDIAN SALARY

$32,261

CERTIFICATION OR LICENSING

Required by all states

OUTLOOK

About as fast as the average

To apply asphalt shingles, a very common roofing material on houses, roofers begin by cutting strips of roofing felt and tacking them down over the entire roof. They nail on horizontal rows of shingles, beginning at the low edge of the roof and working up. Sometimes they must cut shingles to fit around corners, vent pipes, and chimneys. Where two sections of roof meet, they nail or cement flashing, which consists of strips of metal or shingle that make the joints watertight.

Tile and slate shingles, which are more expensive types of residential roofing, are installed slightly differently. First, roofing felt is applied over the wood base. Next, the roofers punch holes in the slate or tile pieces so that nails can be inserted, or they embed the tiles in mortar. Each row of shingles overlaps the preceding row.

Metal roofing is applied by specially trained roofers or by sheet metal workers. One type of metal roof uses metal sections shaped like flat pans, soldered together for weatherproofing and attached by metal clips to the wood below. Another kind of metal roofing, called "standing seam roofing," has raised seams where the sections of sheet metal interlock. A small but growing number of buildings now have "green" roofs that incorporate plants. A "green" roof begins with a single- or multi-ply waterproof layer. After it is proven to be leak free, roofers put a root barrier over it, and then layers of soil, in which trees and grass are planted. Roofers are usually responsible for making sure the roof is watertight and can withstand the weight and water needs of the plants. There are also efforts in the industry to make roofing more energy-efficient and many contractors are now using "green" products in the construction of roofs.

Some roofers waterproof and damp-proof walls, swimming pools, tanks, and structures other than roofs. To prepare surfaces for waterproofing, workers smooth rough surfaces and roughen glazed surfaces. Then they brush or spray waterproofing material on the surface. Damp-proofing is done by spraying a coating of tar or asphalt onto interior or exterior surfaces to prevent the penetration of moisture.

Roofers use various hand tools in their work, including hammers, roofing knives, mops, pincers, caulking guns, rollers, welders, chalk lines, and cutters.

REQUIREMENTS

High School

Most employers prefer to hire applicants at least 18 years of age who are in good physical condition and have a good sense of balance. Although a high school education

layers as desired. They then give the top a smooth finish or embed gravel in the top for a rough surface.

Single-ply roofing, a relatively new roofing method, uses a waterproof sheet membrane and employs any of several different types of chemical products. Some roofing consists of polymer-modified bituminous compounds that are rolled out in sheets on the building's insulation. The compound may be remelted on the roof by torch or hot anvil to fuse it to or embed it in hot bitumen in a manner similar to built-up roofing. Other single-ply roofing is made of rubber or plastic materials that can be sealed with contact adhesive cements, solvent welding, hot air welding, or other methods. Still another type of single-ply roofing consists of spray-in-place polyurethane foam with a polymeric coating. Roofers who apply these roofing systems must be trained in the application methods for each system. Many manufacturers of these systems require that roofers take special courses and receive certification before they are authorized to use the products.

or its equivalent is not required, it is generally preferred. Students can also take courses that familiarize them with some of the skills that are a regular part of roofing work. Beneficial courses include shop, basic mathematics, and mechanical drawing.

Postsecondary Training

Roofers learn the skills they need through on-the-job training or by completing an apprenticeship. Most roofers learn informally on the job while they work under the supervision of experienced roofers. Beginners start as helpers, doing simple tasks like carrying equipment and putting up scaffolding. They gradually gain the skills and knowledge they need for more difficult tasks. Roofers may need four or more years of on-the-job training to become familiar with all the materials and techniques they need to know.

Apprenticeship programs generally provide more thorough, balanced training. Apprenticeships are three years in length and combine a planned program of work experience with formal classroom instruction in related subjects. The work portion of the apprenticeship includes a minimum of 2,000 paid hours each year under the guidance of experienced roofers. Classroom instruction, amounting to at least 144 hours per year, covers such topics as safety practices, how to use and care for tools, and arithmetic.

Certification or Licensing

In addition to apprenticeship experience or on-the-job training, all roofers should receive safety training that is in compliance with standards set by the Occupational Safety and Health Administration (OSHA). Workers can get safety training through their employer or through OSHA's Outreach Training Program.

In addition, the educational arm of the National Roofing Contractors Association and the Roofing Industry Educational Institute have combined to provide various educational resources, including seminars, customized training programs, and certificate programs. For more information on these programs, visit the Web site http://www.nrca.net.

Other Requirements

A roofer with a fear of heights will not get far in his or her career. Roofers need a good sense of balance and good hand-eye coordination. Since this work can be dangerous, roofers need to pay attention to detail and be able to follow directions precisely. They should enjoy working outdoors and working with their hands. Roofers may work with architects and other construction workers as well as interact with customers, so they must be able to work as part of a team. To advance in this field, to the position of *estimator* for example, a roofer should also have strong communication and mathematical skills.

EXPLORING

High school or vocational school students may be able to get firsthand experience of this occupation through a part-time or summer job as a roofer's helper. It may be possible to visit a construction site to observe roofers at work, but a close look is unlikely, as roofers do most of their work at heights.

EMPLOYERS

There are approximately 156,000 people employed as roofers in the United States. Most work for established roofing contractors. Approximately 20 percent of roofers are self-employed.

STARTING OUT

People who are planning to start out as helpers and learn on the job can directly contact roofing contractors to inquire about possible openings. Job leads may also be located through the local office of the state employment service or newspaper classified ads. Graduates of vocational schools may get useful information from their schools' placement offices.

People who want to become apprentices can learn about apprenticeships in their area by contacting local roofing contractors, the state employment service, or the local office of the United Union of Roofers, Waterproofers and Allied Workers.

ADVANCEMENT

Experienced roofers who work for roofing contractors may be promoted to supervisory positions in which they are responsible for coordinating the activities of other roofers. Roofers also may become estimators, calculating the costs of roofing jobs before the work is done. Roofers, who have the right combination of personal characteristics, including good judgment, the ability to deal with people, and planning skills, may be able to go into business for themselves as independent roofing contractors.

EARNINGS

The earnings of roofers vary widely depending on how many hours they work, geographical location, skills and experience, and other factors. Sometimes bad weather prevents them from working, and some weeks they work fewer than 20 hours. They make up for lost time in other weeks, and if they work longer hours than the standard workweek (usually 40 hours), they receive extra pay for the overtime. While roofers in northern states may not work in the winter, most roofers work year-round.

In 2006, median hourly earnings of roofers were $15.51, according to the *Occupational Outlook Handbook*, or a $32,261 yearly salary for full-time work. Wages ranged from less than $9.81 (or a full-time salary of $20,405) to more than $26.79 (or a full time salary of $55,723). Median annual earnings for foundation, structure, and building exterior contractors were $15.54 (or a full-time salary of $32,323).

Hourly rates for apprentices usually start at about 40 percent of the skilled worker's rate and increase periodically until the pay reaches 90 percent of the full rate during the final six months.

WORK ENVIRONMENT

Roofers work outdoors most of the time they are on the job. They work in the heat and cold, but not in wet weather. Roofs can get extremely hot during the summer. The work is physically strenuous, involving lifting heavy weights, prolonged standing, climbing, bending, and squatting. Roofers must work while standing on surfaces that may be steep and quite high; they must use caution to avoid injuries from falls while working on ladders, scaffolding, or roofs.

OUTLOOK

Employment for roofers is expected to increase at about the same rate as the average for all occupations through 2016. Roofers will continue to be in demand for the construction of new buildings, and roofs tend to need more maintenance and repair work than other parts of buildings. About 75 percent of roofing work is on existing structures. Roofers will always be needed for roof repairs and replacement, even during economic downturns when construction activity generally decreases. Also, damp-proofing and waterproofing are expected to provide an increasing proportion of the work done by roofers.

Turnover in this job is high because roofing work is strenuous, hot, and dirty. Many workers consider roofing a temporary job and move into other construction trades. Since roofing is done during the warmer part of the year, job opportunities will probably be best during spring and summer.

FOR MORE INFORMATION

For information on membership benefits and about becoming a professional roofer, contact the following organizations:

National Roofing Contractors Association
10255 West Higgins Road, Suite 600
Rosemont, IL 60018-5607
Tel: 847-299-9070
Email: nrca@nrca.net
http://www.nrca.net

United Union of Roofers, Waterproofers and Allied Workers
1660 L Street, NW, Suite 800
Washington, DC 20036-5646
Tel: 202-463-7663
Email: roofers@unionroofers.com
http://www.unionroofers.com

For information on the Roofing Safety Program and other educational programs, contact

Roofing Industry Educational Institute
10255 West Higgins Road, Suite 600
Rosemont, IL 60018-5607
Tel: 847-299-9070
http://www.nrca.net/riei

☐ SALES REPRESENTATIVES

OVERVIEW

Sales representatives, also called *sales reps*, sell the products and services of manufacturers and wholesalers. They look for potential customers or clients such as retail stores, other manufacturers or wholesalers, government agencies, hospitals, and other institutions; explain or demonstrate their products to these clients; and attempt to make a sale. The job may include follow-up calls and visits to ensure the customer is satisfied.

Sales representatives work under a variety of titles. Those employed by manufacturers are typically called *manufacturers' sales workers* or *manufacturers' representatives*. Those who work for wholesalers are sometimes called *wholesale trade sales workers* or *wholesale sales representatives*. A *manufacturers' agent* is a self-employed salesperson who agrees to represent the products of various companies. A *door-to-door sales worker* usually represents just one company and sells products directly to consumers, typically in their homes. Approximately 2 million people work as manufacturers' and wholesale sales representatives in the United States.

THE JOB

Manufacturers' representatives and wholesale sales representatives sell goods to retail stores, other manufacturers and wholesalers, government agencies, and various institutions. They usually do so within a specific geographical area. Some representatives concentrate on just a few products. An electrical appliance salesperson, for example, may sell 10 to 30 items ranging from food freezers and air conditioners to waffle irons and portable heaters. Representatives of drug wholesalers, however, may sell as many as 50,000 items.

The duties of sales representatives usually include locating and contacting potential new clients, keeping a regular correspondence with existing customers, determining their clients' needs, and informing them of pertinent products and prices. They also travel to meet with clients, show them samples or catalogs, take orders, arrange for delivery, and possibly provide installation. A sales representative also must handle customer complaints, keep up to date on new products, and prepare reports. Many salespeople attend trade conferences, where they learn about products and make sales contacts.

Finding new customers is one of sales representatives' most important tasks. Sales representatives often follow leads suggested by other clients, from advertisements in trade journals, and from participants in trade shows and conferences. They may make "cold calls" to potential clients. Sales representatives frequently meet with and entertain prospective clients during evenings and weekends.

Representatives who sell highly technical machinery or complex office equipment often are referred to as *sales engineers* or *industrial sales workers*. Because their products tend to be more specialized and their clients' needs more complex, the sales process for these workers tends to be longer and more involved. Before recommending a product, they may, for example, carefully analyze a customer's production processes, distribution methods, or office procedures. They usually prepare extensive sales presentations that include information on how their products will improve the quality and efficiency of the customer's operations.

Some sales engineers, often with the help of their company's research and development department, adapt products to a customer's specialized needs. They may

QUICK FACTS

SCHOOL SUBJECTS

Business

Mathematics

Speech

PERSONAL SKILLS

Communication/ideas

Helping/teaching

WORK ENVIRONMENT

Indoors and outdoors

Primarily multiple locations

MINIMUM EDUCATION LEVEL

High school diploma

MEDIAN SALARY

$49,610

CERTIFICATION OR LICENSING

None available

OUTLOOK

About as fast as the average

provide the customer with instructions on how to use the new equipment or work with installation experts who provide this service. Some companies maintain a sales assistance staff to train customers and provide specific information. This permits sales representatives to devote a greater percentage of their time to direct sales contact.

Other sales workers, called *detail people*, do not engage in direct selling activities but strive instead to create a better general market for their companies' products. A detail person for a drug company, for example, may call on physicians and hospitals to inform them of new products and distribute samples.

The particular products sold by the sales representative directly affect the nature of the work. Salespeople who represent sporting goods manufacturers may spend most of their time driving from town to town calling on retail stores that carry sporting equipment. They may visit with coaches and athletic directors of high schools and colleges. A representative in this line may be a former athlete or coach who knows intimately the concerns of his or her customers.

Food manufacturers and wholesalers employ large numbers of sales representatives. Because these salespeople usually know the grocery stores and major chains that carry their products, their main focus is to ensure the maximum sales volume. Representatives negotiate with retail merchants to obtain the most advantageous store and shelf position for displaying their products. They encourage the store or chain to advertise their products, sometimes by offering to pay part of the advertising costs or by reducing the selling price to the merchant so that a special sale price can be offered to customers. Representatives check to make sure that shelf items are neatly arranged and that the store has sufficient stock of their products.

Sales transactions can involve huge amounts of merchandise, sometimes worth millions of dollars. For example, in a single transaction, a washing-machine manufacturer, construction company, or automobile manufacturer may purchase all the steel products it needs for an extended period of time. Salespeople in this field may do much of their business by telephone because the product they sell is standardized and, to the usual customer, requires no particular description or demonstration.

Direct, or door-to-door, selling has been an effective way of marketing various products, such as appliances and housewares, cookware, china, tableware and linens, foods, drugs, cosmetics and toiletries, costume jewelry, clothing, and greeting cards. Like other sales representatives, *door-to-door sales workers* find prospective buyers, explain and demonstrate their products, and take orders. Door-to-door selling has waned in popularity, and Internet-based selling has taken over much of the door-to-door market.

Several different arrangements are common between companies and their door-to-door sales workers. Under the direct company plan, for example, a sales representative is authorized to take orders for a product, and the company pays the representative a commission for each completed order. Such workers may be employees of the company and may receive a salary in addition to a commission, or they may be independent contractors. They usually are very well trained. Sales workers who sell magazine subscriptions may be hired, trained, and supervised by a *subscription crew leader*, who assigns representatives to specific areas, reviews the orders they take, and compiles sales records.

Under the exhibit plan a salesperson sets up an exhibit booth at a place where large numbers of people are expected to pass, such as a state fair, trade show, or product exposition. Customers approach the booth and schedule appointments with the salespersons for later demonstrations at home.

The dealer plan allows a salesperson to function as the proprietor of a small business. The salesperson, or dealer, purchases the product wholesale from the company and then resells it to consumers at the retail price, mainly through door-to-door sales.

Under various group plans, a customer is contacted by a salesperson and given the opportunity to sponsor a sales event. In the party plan, for example, the sales representative arranges to demonstrate products at the home of a customer, who then invites a group of friends for the party. The customer who hosts the party receives free or discounted merchandise in return for the use of the home and for assembling other potential customers for the salesperson.

Finally, the COD plan allows representatives to sell products on a cash-on-delivery (COD) basis. In this method, the salesperson makes a sale, perhaps collecting an advance deposit, and sends the order to the company. The company, in turn, ships the merchandise directly to the customer, who in this case makes payment to the delivery person, or to the salesperson. The product is then delivered to the customer and the balance collected.

Whatever the sales plan, door-to-door sales workers have some advantages over their counterparts in retail stores. Direct sellers, for example, do not have to wait for the customer to come to them; they go out and find the buyers for their products. The direct seller often carries only one product or a limited line of products and thus is much more familiar with the features and benefits of the merchandise. In general, direct sellers get the chance to demonstrate their products where they will most likely be used—in the home.

There are drawbacks to this type of selling. Many customers grow impatient or hostile when salespeople come to their house unannounced and uninvited. It may take several visits to persuade someone to buy the product. In a brief visit, the direct seller must win the confidence of the customer, develop the customer's interest in a product or service, and close the sale.

REQUIREMENTS
High School

A high school diploma is required for most sales positions, although an increasing number of salespeople are graduates of two- or four-year colleges. In high school, take classes such as business, mathematics, psychology, speech, and economics that will teach you to deal with customers and financial transactions.

Postsecondary Training

Some areas of sales work require specialized college work. Those in engineering sales, for example, usually have a college degree in a relevant engineering field. Other fields that demand specific college degrees include chemical sales (chemistry or chemical engineering), office systems (accounting or business administration), and pharmaceuticals and drugs (biology, chemistry, or pharmacy). Those in less technical sales positions usually benefit from course work in English, speech, psychology, marketing, public relations, economics, advertising, finance, accounting, and business law.

Other Requirements

To be a successful sales representative, you should enjoy working with people. You should also be persuasive, self-confident and enthusiastic, and self-disciplined. You must be able to handle rejection since only a small number of your sales contacts will result in a sale.

EXPLORING

If you are interested in becoming a sales representative, try to get part-time or summer work in a retail store. Working as a telemarketer also is useful. Some high schools and junior colleges offer programs that combine classroom study with work experience in sales.

Various opportunities exist to gain experience in direct selling. You can take part in sales drives for school or community groups, for instance.

Occasionally manufacturers hire college students for summer assignments. These temporary positions provide an opportunity for the employer and employee to appraise each other. A high percentage of students hired for these specialized summer programs become career employees after graduation. Some wholesale warehouses also offer temporary or summer positions.

EMPLOYERS

In the United States, 2 million people work as manufacturers' and wholesale sales representatives. More thanhalf of these salespeople work in wholesale, many as sellers of machinery. Many others work in mining and manufacturing. Food, drugs, electrical goods, hardware, and clothing are among the most common products sold by sales representatives.

STARTING OUT

Firms looking for sales representatives sometimes list openings with high school and college placement offices, as well as with public and private employment agencies. In many areas, professional sales associations refer people to suitable openings. Contacting companies directly also is recommended. A list of manufacturers and wholesalers can be found in telephone books and industry directories, which are available at public libraries.

Although some high school graduates are hired for manufacturers' or wholesale sales jobs, many join a company in a nonselling position, such as office, stock, or shipping clerk. This experience allows an employee to learn about the company and its products. From there, he or she eventually may be promoted to a sales position.

Most new representatives complete a training period before receiving a sales assignment. In some cases new salespeople rotate through several departments of an organization to gain a broad exposure to the company's products. Large companies often use formal training programs lasting two years or more, while small organizations frequently rely on supervised sales experience.

Direct selling usually is an easy field to enter. Direct sale companies advertise for available positions in newspapers, online, in sales workers' specialty magazines, and on television and radio. Many people enter direct selling through contacts they have had with other door-to-door sales workers. Most firms have district or area representatives who interview applicants and arrange the necessary training. Part-time positions in direct selling are common.

ADVANCEMENT

New representatives usually spend their early years improving their sales ability, developing their product knowledge, and finding new clients. As sales workers gain experience they may be shifted to increasingly large territories or more difficult types of customers. In some organizations, experienced sales workers narrow their focus. For example, an office equipment sales representative may work solely on government contracts.

Advancement to management positions, such as *regional or district manager*, also is possible. Some representatives, however, choose to remain in basic sales. Because of commissions, they often earn more money than their managers do, and many enjoy being in the field and working directly with their customers.

A small number of representatives decide to become *manufacturers' agents*, or self-employed salespeople who handle products for various organizations. Agents perform many of the same functions as sales representatives but usually on a more modest scale.

Door-to-door sales workers also have advancement possibilities. Some are promoted to supervisory roles and recruit, train, and manage new members of the sales force. Others become *area, branch, or district managers*. Many managers of direct selling firms began as door-to-door sales workers.

EARNINGS

Many beginning sales representatives are paid a salary while receiving their training. After assuming direct responsibility for a sales territory, they may receive only a commission (a fixed percentage of each dollar sold). Also common is a modified commission plan (a lower rate of commission on sales plus a low base salary). Some companies provide bonuses to successful representatives.

Because manufacturers' and wholesale sales representatives typically work on commission, salaries vary widely. Some made as little as $26,030 a year in 2006, according to the U.S. Department of Labor. The most successful representatives earn more than $121,850. However, the median annual salaries for sales representatives were $49,610 for those working with technical and scientific products, and $54,900 for those working in other aspects of wholesale and manufacturing, including commissions. Most sales representatives make between $35,000 and $71,000 a year.

Earnings can be affected by changes in the economy or industry cycles, and great fluctuations in salary from year to year or month to month are common. Employees who travel usually are reimbursed for transportation, hotels, meals, and client entertainment expenses. Door-to-door sales workers usually earn a straight commission on their sales, ranging from 10 to 40 percent of an item's suggested retail price.

Sales engineers earned salaries that ranged from $47,010 to $127,680 or more in 2006, according to the Department of Labor.

Sales representatives typically receive vacation days, medical and life insurance, and retirement benefits. However, manufacturers' agents and some door-to-door sales workers do not receive benefits.

WORK ENVIRONMENT

Salespeople generally work long and irregular hours. Those with large territories may spend all day calling and meeting customers in one city and much of the night traveling to the place where they will make the next day's calls and visits. Sales workers with a small territory may do little overnight travel but, like most sales workers, may spend many evenings preparing reports, writing up orders, and entertaining customers. Several times a year, sales workers may travel to company meetings and participate in trade conventions and conferences. Irregular working hours, travel, and the competitive demands of the job can be disruptive to ordinary family life.

Sales work is physically demanding. Representatives often spend most of the day on their feet. Many carry heavy sample cases or catalogs. Occasionally, sales workers assist a customer in arranging a display of the company's products or moving stock items. Many door-to-door sellers work in their own community or nearby areas, although some cover more extensive and distant territories. They often are outdoors in all kinds of weather. Direct sellers must treat customers, even those who are rude or impatient, with tact and courtesy.

OUTLOOK

Employment for manufacturers' and wholesale sales representatives is expected to grow at an average rate through 2016, according to the U.S. Department of Labor. Because of continued economic growth and an increasing number of new products on the market, more sales representatives will be needed to explain, demonstrate, and sell these products to customers. The Department of Labor notes that job opportunities will be better for wholesale sales representatives as compared to manufacturing sales representatives, as manufacturing firms will rely less on in-house sales personnel. They will instead employ the services of independent sales workers, who are paid exclusively on a commission basis. Although this decreases overhead costs for manufacturers, the instability of self-employment is a deterrent in the field of independent sales. Thus, competition for in-house sales positions with wholesalers will be stiff, and jobs will go to applicants with the most experience and technical knowledge. Computers and other information technology are also making sales representatives more effective and productive, allowing sales representatives to handle more clients, and thus hindering job growth somewhat.

Future opportunities will vary greatly depending upon the specific product and industry. For example, as giant food chains replace independent grocers, fewer salespeople will be needed to sell groceries to individual stores. By contrast, greater opportunities will probably exist in the air-conditioning field, and advances in consumer electronics and computer technology also may provide many new opportunities.

FOR MORE INFORMATION

For a list of marketing programs and detailed career information, contact

Direct Marketing Association
1120 Avenue of the Americas
New York, NY 10036-6700
Tel: 212-768-7277
http://www.the-dma.org

For referrals to industry trade associations, contact

Manufacturers' Agents National Association
One Spectrum Pointe, Suite 150
Lake Forest, CA 92630-2282
Tel: 877-626-2776
Email: MANA@MANAonline.org
http://www.manaonline.org

SECRETARIES

OVERVIEW

Secretaries, also called *administrative assistants*, perform a wide range of jobs that vary greatly from business to business. However, most secretaries key in documents, manage records and information, answer telephones, handle correspondence and emails, schedule appointments, make travel arrangements, and sort mail. The amount of time secretaries spend on these duties depends on the size and type of the office as well as on their own job training. There are approximately 4.2 million secretaries employed in the United States.

THE JOB

Secretaries perform a variety of administrative and clerical duties. The goal of all their activities is to assist their employers in the execution of their work and to help their companies conduct business in an efficient and professional manner.

Secretaries' work includes processing and transmitting information to the office staff and to other organizations. They operate office machines and arrange for their repair or servicing. These machines include computers, typewriters, dictating machines, photocopiers, switchboards, and fax machines. Secretaries also order office supplies and perform regular duties such as answering phones, sorting mail, managing files, taking dictation, and composing and keying in letters.

QUICK FACTS

SCHOOL SUBJECTS
Business
Computer science
English

PERSONAL SKILLS
Communication/ideas
Following instructions

WORK ENVIRONMENT
Primarily indoors
Primarily one location

MINIMUM EDUCATION LEVEL
High school diploma

MEDIAN SALARY
$37,240

CERTIFICATION OR LICENSING
Voluntary

OUTLOOK
As fast as the average

Some offices have word-processing centers that handle all of the firm's typing. In such a situation, *administrative secretaries* take care of all secretarial duties except for typing and dictation. This arrangement leaves them free to respond to correspondence, prepare reports, do research and present the results to their employers, and otherwise assist the professional staff. Often these secretaries work in groups of three or four so that they can help each other if one secretary has a workload that is heavier than normal.

In many offices, secretaries make appointments for company executives and keep track of the office schedule. They make travel arrangements for the professional staff or for clients, and occasionally are asked to travel with staff members on business trips. Other secretaries might manage the office while their supervisors are away on vacation or business trips.

Secretaries take minutes at meetings, write up reports, and compose and type letters. They often will find their responsibilities growing as they learn the business. Some are responsible for finding speakers for conferences, planning receptions, and arranging public relations programs. Some write copy for brochures or articles before making the arrangements to have them printed or microfilmed, or they might use desktop publishing software to create the documents themselves. They greet clients and guide them to the proper offices, and they often supervise and train other staff members and newer secretaries, especially in the use of computer software programs.

Some secretaries perform very specialized work. *Legal secretaries* prepare legal papers including wills, mortgages, contracts, deeds, motions, complaints, and summonses. They work under the direct supervision of an attorney or paralegal. They assist with legal research by reviewing legal journals and organizing briefs for their employers. They must learn an entire specialized vocabulary that is used in legal papers and documents.

Medical secretaries take medical histories of patients; make appointments; prepare and send bills to patients; track and collect bills; process insurance billing; maintain medical files; and pursue correspondence with patients, hospitals, and associations. They assist physicians or medical scientists with articles, reports, speeches, and conference proceedings. Some medical secretaries are responsible for ordering medical supplies. They, too, need to learn an entire specialized vocabulary of medical terms and be familiar with laboratory or hospital procedures.

Technical secretaries work for engineers and scientists preparing reports and papers that often include graphics and mathematical equations that are difficult to format on paper. The secretaries maintain a technical library and help with scientific papers by gathering and editing materials.

Social secretaries, often called *personal secretaries*, arrange all of their employer's social activities. They handle private as well as business social affairs and may plan parties, send out invitations, or write speeches for their employers. Social secretaries are often hired by celebrities or high-level executives who have busy social calendars to maintain.

Many associations, clubs, and nonprofit organizations have membership secretaries who compile and send out newsletters or promotional materials while maintaining membership lists, dues records, and directories. Depending on the type of club, the secretary may be the one who gives out information to prospective members and who keeps current members and related organizations informed of upcoming events.

Education secretaries work in elementary or secondary schools or on college campuses. They take care of all clerical duties at the school. Their responsibilities may include preparing bulletins and reports for teachers, parents, or students, keeping track of budgets for school supplies or student activities, and maintaining the school's calendar of events. Depending on the position, they may work for school administrators, principals, or groups of teachers or professors. Other education secretaries work in administration offices, state education departments, or service departments.

REQUIREMENTS
High School

You will need at least a high school diploma to enter this field. To prepare for a career as a secretary, take high school courses in business, English, and speech. Keyboarding and computer science courses will also be helpful.

Postsecondary Training

To succeed as a secretary, you will need good office skills that include rapid and accurate keyboarding skills and good spelling and grammar. You should enjoy handling details. Some positions require typing a minimum number of words per minute, as well as shorthand ability. Knowledge of word processing, spreadsheet, and database management is important, and most employers require it. Some of these skills can be learned in business education courses taught at vocational and business schools. Special training programs are available for students who want to become medical or legal secretaries or administrative technology assistants.

Certification or Licensing

Qualifying for the designations certified professional secretary (CPS) or certified administrative professional (CAP) is increasingly recognized in business and industry as a consideration for promotion as a senior level secretary. The International Association of Administrative Professionals gives the examinations required for these certifications. Secretaries with limited experience can become an accredited legal secretary (ALS) by obtaining certification from the Certifying Board of the National Association of Legal Secretaries. Those with at least three years of experience in the legal field can be certified as a professional legal secretary (PLS) from this same organization. Legal Secretaries International offers the certified legal secretary specialist designation in areas such as business law, probate, criminal law, and civil litigation to those who have at least five years of law-related experience and who pass an examination.

Other Requirements

Personal qualities are important in this field of work. As a secretary, you will often be the first employee that clients meet, and therefore you must be friendly, poised, and professionally dressed. Because you must work closely with others, you should be personable and tactful. Discretion, good judgment, organizational ability, and initiative are also important. These traits will not only get you hired but will also help you advance in your career.

Some employers encourage their secretaries to take advanced courses and to be trained to use any new piece of equipment in the office. Requirements vary widely from company to company.

EXPLORING

High school guidance counselors can give interest and aptitude tests to help you assess your suitability for a career as a secretary. Local business schools often welcome visitors, and sometimes offer courses that can be taken in conjunction with a high school business course. Work-study programs will also provide you with an opportunity to work in a business setting to get a sense of the work performed by secretaries.

Part-time or summer jobs as *receptionists*, *file clerks*, and *office clerks* are often available in various offices. These jobs are the best indicators of future satisfaction in the secretarial field. You may find a part-time job if you are computer-literate. Cooperative education programs arranged through schools and "temping" through an agency also are valuable ways to acquire experience. In general, any job that teaches basic office skills is helpful.

EMPLOYERS

There are 4.2 million secretaries employed throughout the United States, making this profession one of the largest in the country. Of this total, 275,000 specialize as legal secretaries and 408,000 work as medical secretaries. Secretaries are employed in almost every type of industry. From health care, banking, financial services, and real estate to construction, manufacturing, transportation, communications, and retail and wholesale trade. A large number of secretaries are employed by federal, state, and local governments.

STARTING OUT

Most people looking for work as secretaries find jobs through the newspaper want ads, online job sites, or by applying directly to local businesses. Both private employment offices and state employment services place secretaries, and business schools help their graduates find suitable jobs. Temporary-help agencies also are an excellent way to find jobs, some of which may turn into permanent ones.

ADVANCEMENT

Secretaries often begin by assisting executive secretaries and work their way up by learning the way their business operates. Initial promotions from a secretarial position are usually to jobs such as *secretarial supervisor*, *office manager*, or *administrative assistant*. Depending on other personal qualifications, college courses in business, accounting, or marketing can help the ambitious secretary enter middle and upper management. Training in computer skills can also lead to advancement. Secretaries who become proficient in word processing, for instance, can get jobs as instructors or as sales representatives for software manufacturers.

Many legal secretaries, with additional training and schooling, become *paralegals*. Secretaries in the medical field can advance into the fields of radiological and surgical records or medical transcription.

EARNINGS

Salaries for secretaries vary widely by region; type of business; and the skill, experience, and level of responsibility of the secretary. Secretaries (except legal, medical, and executive) earned an average of $27,450 annually in 2006. Medical secretaries earned salaries averaging $28,0900, and ranging from less than $19,750 to $40,870 or more per year in 2006, according to the U. S. Department of Labor. Legal secretaries made an average of $39,6700 in 2006. Salaries for legal secretaries ranged from $23,870 to more than $58,770 annually. An attorney's rank in the firm will also affect the earnings of a legal secretary; secretaries who work for a partner will earn higher salaries than those who work for an associate. The median salary for executive secretaries and executive administrative assistants was $37,240 in 2006, with salaries ranging from less than $25,190 to more than $56,740.

Secretaries, especially those working in the legal profession, earn considerably more if certified. Most secretaries receive paid holidays and two weeks vacation after a year of work, as well as sick leave. Many offices provide benefits including health and life insurance, pension plans, overtime pay, and tuition reimbursement.

WORK ENVIRONMENT

Most secretaries work in pleasant offices with modern equipment. Office conditions vary widely, however. While some secretaries have their own offices and work for one or two executives, others share crowded workspace with other workers.

Most office workers work 35–40 hours a week. Very few secretaries work on the weekends on a regular basis, although some may be asked to work overtime if a particular project demands it.

The work is not physically strenuous or hazardous, although deadline pressure is a factor and sitting for long periods of time can be uncomfortable. Many hours spent in front of a computer can lead to eyestrain or repetitive-motion problems for secretaries. Most secretaries are not required to travel. Part-time and flexible schedules are easily adaptable to secretarial work.

OUTLOOK

The U.S. Department of Labor predicts that overall employment for secretaries will grow as fast as the average through 2016. Secretaries and administrative assistants will have among the largest numbers of new jobs. Industries such as administrative and support services, health care and social assistance, private education services, and professional, scientific, and technical services will create the most new job opportunities. As common with large occupations, the need to replace retiring workers and those leaving the field will generate many openings.

Computers, fax machines, electronic mail, copy machines, voice message systems, and scanners are some technological advancements that have greatly improved the work productivity of secretaries. Company downsizing and restructuring, in some cases, have redistributed traditional secretarial duties to other employees. There has been a growing trend in assigning one secretary to assist two or more managers, adding to this field's decline. Though more professionals are using personal computers for their correspondence, some administrative duties will still need to be handled by secretaries. The personal aspects of the job and responsibilities such as making travel arrangements, scheduling conferences, and transmitting staff instructions have not changed.

Many employers currently complain of a shortage of capable secretaries. Those with skills (especially computer skills) and experience will have the best chances for employment. Specialized secretaries should attain certification in their field to stay competitive.

FOR MORE INFORMATION

For information on the certified professional secretary designation, contact
International Association of Administrative Professionals
10502 NW Ambassador Drive
PO Box 20404
Kansas City, MO 64195-0404
Tel: 816-891-6600
Email: service@iaap-hq.org
http://www.iaap-hq.org

For information about certification, contact
Legal Secretaries International Inc.
2302 Fannin Street, Suite 500
Houston, TX 77002-9136
http://www.legalsecretaries.org

For information on the certified professional legal secretary and the accredited legal secretary designations, contact
NALS
8159 East 41st Street
Tulsa, OK 74145-3312
Tel: 918-582-5188
Email: info@nals.org
http://www.nals.org

For information regarding union representation, contact
Office & Professional Employees International Union
265 West 14th Street, Sixth Floor
New York, NY 10011-7103
Tel: 800-346-7348
http://www.opeiu.org

For employment information, contact
OfficeTeam
2884 Sand Hill Road
Menlo Park, CA 94025-7072
Tel: 800-804-8367
http://www.officeteam.com

☐ SECURITY CONSULTANTS AND GUARDS

OVERVIEW

Security consultants and *security guards* are responsible for protecting public and private property against theft, fire, vandalism, illegal entry, and acts of violence. They may work for commercial or government organizations or private individuals. More than one million security workers are employed in the United States.

THE JOB

A security consultant is engaged in protective service work. Anywhere that valuable property or information is present or people are at risk, a security consultant may be called in to devise and implement security plans that offer protection. Security consultants may work for a variety of clients, including large stores, art museums, factories, laboratories, data processing centers, and political candidates. They are involved in preventing theft, vandalism, fraud, kidnapping, and other crimes. Specific job responsibilities depend on the type and size of the client's company and the scope of the security system required.

Security consultants always work closely with company officials or other appropriate individuals in the development of a comprehensive security program that will fit the needs of individual clients. After discussing goals and objectives with the relevant company executives, consultants study and analyze the physical conditions and internal operations of a client's operation. They learn much by simply observing day-to-day operations.

The size of the security budget also influences the type of equipment ordered and methods used. For example, a large factory that produces military hardware may fence off its property and place electric eyes around the perimeter of the fence. They may also install perimeter alarms and use passkeys to limit access to restricted areas. A smaller company may use only entry-control mechanisms in specified areas. The consultant may recommend sophisticated technology, such as closed-circuit surveillance or ultrasonic motion detectors, alone or in addition to security personnel. Usually, a combination of electronic and human resources is used.

Security consultants not only devise plans to protect equipment but also recommend procedures on safeguarding and possibly destroying classified material. Increasingly, consultants are being called on to develop strategies to safeguard data processing equipment. They may have to develop measures to safeguard transmission lines against unwanted or unauthorized interceptions.

Once a security plan has been developed, the consultant oversees the installation of the equipment, ensures that it is working properly, and checks frequently with the client to ensure that the client is satisfied. In the case of a crime against the facility, a consultant investigates the nature of the crime (often in conjunction with police

QUICK FACTS
SCHOOL SUBJECTS
Business
Psychology
PERSONAL SKILLS
Communication/ideas
Mechanical/manipulative
WORK ENVIRONMENT
Indoors and outdoors
One location with some travel
MINIMUM EDUCATION LEVEL
Associate's degree (security consultants)
High school diploma (security guards)
MEDIAN SALARY
$21,530
CERTIFICATION OR LICENSING
Recommended
OUTLOOK
Faster than the average

or other investigators) and then modifies the security system to safeguard against similar crimes in the future.

Many consultants work for security firms that have several types of clients, such as manufacturing and telecommunications plants and facilities. Consultants may handle a variety of clients or work exclusively in a particular area. For example, one security consultant may be assigned to handle the protection of nuclear power plants and another to handle data processing companies.

Security consultants may be called on to safeguard famous individuals or persons in certain positions from kidnapping or other type of harm. They provide security services to officers of large companies, media personalities, and others who want their safety and privacy protected. These consultants, like bodyguards, plan and review client travel itineraries and usually accompany the client on trips, checking accommodations and appointment locations along the way. They often check the backgrounds of people who will interact with the client, especially those who see the client infrequently.

Security consultants are sometimes called in for special events, such as sporting events and political rallies, when there is no specific fear of danger but rather a need for overall coordination of a large security operation. The consultants oversee security preparation—such as the stationing of appropriate personnel at all points of entry and exit—and then direct specific responses to any security problems.

Security officers develop and implement security plans for companies that manufacture or process material for the federal government. They ensure that their clients' security policies comply with federal regulations in such categories as the storing and handling of classified documents and restricting access to authorized personnel only.

Security guards have various titles, depending on the type of work they do and the setting in which they work. They may be referred to as patrollers (who are assigned to cover a certain area), bouncers (who eject unruly people from places of entertainment), golf-course rangers (who patrol golf courses), or gate tenders (who work at security checkpoints).

Many security guards are employed during normal working hours in public and commercial buildings and other areas with a good deal of pedestrian traffic and public contact. Others patrol buildings and grounds outside normal working hours, such as at night and on weekends. Guards usually wear uniforms and may carry a nightstick. Guards who work in situations where they may be called upon to apprehend criminal intruders are usually armed. They may also carry a flashlight, a whistle, a two-way radio, and a watch clock, which is used to record the time at which they reach various checkpoints.

Guards in public buildings may be assigned to a certain post or they may patrol an area. In museums, art galleries, and other public buildings, guards answer visitors' questions and give them directions; they also enforce rules against smoking, touching art objects, and so forth. In commercial buildings, guards may sign people in and out after hours and inspect packages being carried out of the building. Bank guards observe customers carefully for any sign of suspicious behavior that may signal a possible robbery attempt. In department stores, security guards often work with undercover detectives to watch for theft by customers or store employees. Guards at large public gatherings such as sporting events and conventions keep traffic moving, direct people to their seats, and eject unruly spectators. Guards employed at airports limit access to boarding areas to passengers only. They make sure people entering passenger areas have valid tickets and observe passengers and their baggage as they pass through X-ray machines and metal detection equipment.

After-hours guards are usually employed at industrial plants, defense installations, construction sites, and transport facilities such as docks and railroad yards. They make regular rounds on foot or, if the premises are very large, in motorized vehicles. They check to be sure that no unauthorized persons are on the premises, that doors and windows are secure, and that no property is missing. They may be equipped with walkie-talkies to report in at intervals to a central guard station. Sometimes guards perform custodial duties, such as turning on lights and setting thermostats.

In a large organization, a *security officer* is often in charge of the guard force; in a small organization, a single worker may be responsible for all security measures. As more businesses purchase advanced electronic security systems to protect their properties, more guards are being assigned to stations where they monitor perimeter security, environmental functions, communications, and other systems. In many cases, these guards maintain radio contact with other guards patrolling on foot or in motor vehicles. Some guards use computers to store information on matters relevant to security such as visitors or suspicious occurrences during their time on duty.

Security guards work for government agencies or for private companies hired by government agencies. Their task is usually to guard secret or restricted installations domestically or in foreign countries. They spend much of their time patrolling areas, which they may do on foot, on horseback, or in automobiles or aircraft. They may monitor activities in an area through the use of surveillance cameras and video screens. Their assignments usually include detecting and preventing unauthorized activities, searching for explosive devices, standing watch during secret and hazardous experiments, and performing other routine police duties within government installations.

Security guards are usually armed and may be required to use their weapons or other kinds of physical force to prevent some kinds of activities. They are usually not, however, required to remove explosive devices from an installation. When they find such devices, they notify a bomb disposal unit, which is responsible for removing and then defusing or detonating the device.

REQUIREMENTS
High School

A high school diploma is preferred for security guards and required for security consultants, who should also go on to obtain a college degree. Security guards must be high school graduates. In addition, they should expect to receive from three to six months of specialized training in security procedures and technology. If you would like to be a security guard, you should take mathematics courses while in high school to ensure that you can perform basic arithmetic operations with different units of measure; compute ratios, rates, and percentages; and interpret charts and graphs.

You should take English courses to develop your reading and writing skills. You should be able to read manuals, memos, textbooks, and other instructional materials and write reports with correct spelling, grammar, and punctuation. You should also be able to speak to small groups with poise and confidence.

Postsecondary Training

Most companies prefer to hire security consultants who have at least a college degree. An undergraduate or associate's degree in criminal justice, business administration, or related field is best. Course work should be broad and include business management, communications, computer courses, sociology, and statistics. As the security consulting field becomes more competitive, many consultants choose to get a master's in business administration (MBA) or other graduate degree.

Although there are no specific educational or professional requirements, many security guards have had previous experience with police work or other forms of crime prevention. It is helpful if a person develops an expertise in a specific area. For example, if you want to work devising plans securing data processing equipment, it is helpful to have previous experience working with computers.

Certification or Licensing

Many security consultants are certified by the American Society for Industrial Security to be certified protection professionals. To be eligible for certification, a consultant must pass a written test and have 10 years' work and educational experience in the security profession. Information on certification is available from , a professional organization to which many security consultants belong.

Virtually every state has licensing or registration requirements for security guards who work for contract security agencies. Registration generally requires that a person newly hired as a guard be reported to the licensing authorities, usually the state police department or special state licensing commission. To be granted a license, indi-

viduals generally must be 18 years of age, have no convictions for perjury or acts of violence, pass a background investigation, and complete classroom training on a variety of subjects, including property rights, emergency procedures, and capture of suspected criminals.

Other Requirements

For security guards, general good health (especially vision and hearing), alertness, emotional stability, and the ability to follow directions are important characteristics. Military service and experience in local or state police departments are assets. Prospective guards should have clean police records. Some employers require applicants to take a polygraph examination or a written test that indicates honesty, attitudes, and other personal qualities. Most employers require applicants and experienced workers to submit to drug screening tests as a condition of employment.

For some hazardous or physically demanding jobs, guards must be under a certain age and meet height and weight standards. For top-level security positions in facilities such as nuclear power plants or vulnerable information centers, guards may be required to complete a special training course. They may also need to fulfill certain relevant academic requirements.

Guards employed by the federal government must be U.S. armed forces veterans, have some previous experience as guards, and pass a written examination. Many positions require experience with firearms. In many situations, guards must be bonded.

Security technicians need good eyesight and should be in good physical shape, able to lift at least 50 pounds, climb ladders, stairs, poles, and ropes, and maintain their balance on narrow, slippery, or moving surfaces. They should be able to stoop, crawl, crouch, and kneel with ease.

EXPLORING

Part-time or summer employment as a *clerk* with a security firm is an excellent way to gain insight into the skills and temperament needed to become a security consultant. Discussions with professional security consultants are another way of exploring career opportunities in this field. You may find it helpful to join a safety patrol at school.

If you are interested in a particular area of security consulting, such as data processing, for example, you can join a club or association to learn more about the field. This is a good way to make professional contacts.

Opportunities for part-time or summer work as security guards are not generally available to high school students. You may, however, work as a *lifeguard*, on a *safety patrol*, and as a *school hallway monitor*, which can provide helpful experience.

EMPLOYERS

Security services is one of the largest employment fields in the United States. More than one million persons are employed in the security industry in the United States. Industrial security firms and guard agencies, also called contract security firms, employ more than half of all guards, while the remainder are in-house guards employed by various establishments.

STARTING OUT

People interested in careers in security services generally apply directly to security companies. Some jobs may be available through state or private employment services. People interested in security technician positions should apply directly to government agencies.

Beginning security personnel receive varied amounts of training. Training requirements are generally increasing as modern, highly sophisticated security systems become more common. Many employers give newly hired security guards instruction before they start the job and also provide several weeks of on-the-job training. Guards receive training in protection, public relations, report writing, crisis deterrence, first aid, and drug control.

Those employed at establishments that place a heavy emphasis on security usually receive extensive formal training. For example, guards at nuclear power plants may undergo several months of training before being placed on duty under close supervision. Guards may be taught to use firearms, administer first aid, operate alarm systems and electronic security equipment, handle emergencies, and spot and deal with security problems.

Many of the less strenuous guard positions are filled by older people who are retired police officers or armed forces veterans. Because of the odd hours required for many positions, this occupation appeals to many people seeking part-time work or second jobs.

Most entry-level positions for security consultants are filled by those with a bachelor's or associate's degree in criminal justice, business administration, or a related field. Those with a high school diploma and some experience in the field may find work with a security consulting firm, although they usually begin as security guards and become consultants only after further training.

Because many consulting firms have their own techniques and procedures, most require entry-level personnel to complete an on-the-job training program, during the course of which they learn company policies.

ADVANCEMENT

In most cases, security guards receive periodic salary increases, and guards employed by larger security companies or as part of a military-style guard force may increase their responsibilities or move up in rank. A guard with outstanding ability, especially with some college education, may move up to the position of chief guard, gaining responsibility for the supervision and training of an entire guard force in an industrial plant or a department store, or become director of security services for a business or commercial building. A few guards with management skills open their own contract security guard agencies; other guards become licensed private detectives. Experienced guards may become bodyguards for political figures, executives, and celebrities, or choose to enter a police department or other law enforcement agency. Additional training may lead to a career as a corrections officer.

Increased training and experience with a variety of security and surveillance systems may lead security guards into higher-paying security consultant careers. Security consultants with experience may advance to management positions or they may start their own private consulting firms. Instruction and training of security personnel is another advancement opportunity for security guards, consultants, and technicians.

EARNINGS

Earnings for security consultants vary greatly depending on the consultant's training and experience. Entry-level consultants with bachelor's degrees commonly start at $26,000 to $32,000 per year. Consultants with graduate degrees begin at $34,000 to $41,000 per year, and experienced consultants may earn $50,000 to $100,000 per year or more. Many consultants work on a per-project basis, with rates of up to $75 per hour.

Average starting salaries for security guards and technicians vary according to their level of training and experience, and the location where they work. Median annual earnings for security guards were $21,530 in 2006, according to the U.S. Department of Labor. Experienced security guards earned more than $35,840 per year in 2006, while the least experienced security guards earned less than $15,030 annually. Entry-level guards working for contract agencies may receive little more than the minimum wage. In-house guards generally earn higher wages and have greater job security and better advancement potential.

WORK ENVIRONMENT

Consultants usually divide their time between their offices and a client's business. Much time is spent analyzing various security apparatuses and developing security proposals. The consultant talks with a variety of employees at a client's company, including the top officials, and discusses alternatives with other people at the consulting firm. A consultant makes a security proposal presentation to the client and then works with the client on any modifications. Consultants must be sensitive to budget issues and develop security systems that their clients can afford.

Consultants may specialize in one type of security work (nuclear power plants, for example) or work for a variety of large and small clients, such as museums, data processing companies, and banks. Although there may be a lot of travel and some work may require outdoor activity, there will most likely be no strenuous work. A consultant may oversee the implementation of a large security system but is not involved in the actual installation process. A consultant may have to confront suspicious people but is not expected to do the work of a police officer.

Security guards and technicians may work indoors or outdoors. In high-crime areas and industries vulnerable to theft and vandalism, there may be considerable physical danger. Guards who work in museums, department stores, and other buildings and facilities remain on their feet for long periods of time, either standing still or walking while on patrol. Guards assigned to reception areas or security control rooms may remain at their desks for the entire shift. Much of their work is routine and may be tedious at times, yet guards must remain constantly alert during their shift. Guards who work with the public, especially at sporting events and concerts, may have to confront unruly and sometimes hostile people. Bouncers often confront intoxicated people and are frequently called upon to intervene in physical altercations.

Many companies employ guards around the clock in three shifts, including weekends and holidays, and assign workers to these shifts on a rotating basis. The same is true for security technicians guarding government facilities and installations. Those with less seniority will likely have the most erratic schedules. Many guards work alone for an entire shift, usually lasting eight hours. Lunches and other meals are often taken on the job, so that constant vigilance is maintained.

OUTLOOK

Employment for guards and other security personnel is expected to increase faster than the average career through 2016, as crime rates rise with the overall population growth. Public concern about crime, vandalism, and terrorism continues to increase. Many job openings will be created as a result of the high turnover of workers in this field.

A factor adding to this demand is the trend for private security firms to perform duties previously handled by police officers, such as courtroom security. Private security companies employ security technicians to guard many government sites, such as nuclear testing facilities. Private companies also operate many training facilities for government security technicians and guards, as well as providing police services for some communities.

FOR MORE INFORMATION

For information on educational programs and certification procedures, contact
American Society for Industrial Security
1625 Prince Street
Alexandria, VA 22314-2818
Tel: 703-519-6200
Email: asis@asisonline.org
http://www.asisonline.org

For information on union membership, contact
Security, Police, and Fire Professionals of America
25510 Kelly Road
Roseville, MI 48066-4932
Tel: 800-228-7492
http://www.spfpa.org

SHEET METAL WORKERS

OVERVIEW

Sheet metal workers fabricate, assemble, install, repair, and maintain ducts used for ventilating, air-conditioning, and heating systems. They also work with other articles of sheet metal, including roofing, siding, gutters, downspouts, partitions, chutes, and stainless steel kitchen and beverage equipment for restaurants. Not included in this group are employees in factories where sheet metal items are mass-produced on assembly lines. There are approximately 189,000 sheet metal workers employed in the United States.

THE JOB

Most sheet metal workers handle a variety of tasks in fabricating, installing, and maintaining sheet metal

QUICK FACTS

SCHOOL SUBJECTS
Chemistry
Mathematics

PERSONAL SKILLS
Following instructions
Technical/scientific

WORK ENVIRONMENT
Primarily indoors
One location with some travel

MINIMUM EDUCATION LEVEL
Apprenticeship

MEDIAN SALARY
$37,357

CERTIFICATION OR LICENSING
Required by all states

OUTLOOK
About as fast as the average

products. Some workers concentrate on just one of these areas. Skilled workers must know about the whole range of activities involved in working with sheet metal.

Many sheet metal workers are employed by building contracting firms that construct or renovate residential, commercial, and industrial buildings. Fabricating and installing air-conditioning, heating, and refrigeration equipment is often a big part of their job. Some workers specialize in adjusting and servicing equipment that has already been installed so that it can operate at peak efficiency. Roofing contractors, the federal government, and businesses that do their own alteration and construction work also employ sheet metal workers. Other sheet metal workers are employed in the shipbuilding, railroad, and aircraft industries or in shops that manufacture specialty products such as custom kitchen equipment or electrical generating and distributing machinery.

Fabricating is often done in a shop away from the site where the product is to be installed. When fabricating products, workers usually begin by studying blueprints

or drawings. After determining the amounts and kinds of materials required for the job, they make measurements and lay out the pattern on the appropriate pieces of metal. They may use measuring tapes and rulers and figure dimensions with the aid of calculators. Then, following the pattern they have marked on the metal, they cut out the sections with hand or power shears or other machine tools. They may shape the pieces with a hand or machine brake, which is a type of equipment used for bending and forming sheet metal, and punch or drill holes in the parts. As a last step before assembly, workers inspect the parts to verify that all of them are accurately shaped. Then they fasten the parts together by welding, soldering, bolting, riveting, cementing, or using special devices such as metal clips. After assembly, it may be necessary to smooth rough areas on the fabricated item with a file or grinding wheel.

Computers play an increasingly important role in several of these tasks. Computers help workers plan the layout efficiently, so that all the necessary sections can be cut from the metal stock while leaving the smallest possible amount of waste sheet metal. Computers also help guide saws, shears, and lasers that cut metal, as well as other machines that form the pieces into the desired shapes.

If the item has been fabricated in a shop, it is taken to the installation site. There, the sheet metal workers join together different sections of the final product. For example, they may connect sections of duct end to end. Some items, such as sections of duct, can be bought factory-made in standard sizes, and workers modify them at the installation site to meet the requirements of the situation. Once finished, ductwork may be suspended with metal hangers from ceilings or attached to walls. Sometimes sheet metal workers weld, bolt, screw, or nail items into place. To complete the installation, they may need to make additional sheet metal parts or alter the items they have fabricated.

Some tasks in working with sheet metal, such as making metal roofing, are routinely done at the job site. Workers measure and cut sections of roof paneling, which interlock with grooving at the edges. They nail or weld the paneling to the roof deck to hold it in place and put metal molding over joints and around the edges, windows, and doors to finish off the roof.

REQUIREMENTS
High School

Requirements vary slightly, but applicants for sheet metal training programs must be high school graduates. High school courses that provide a good background include shop classes, mechanical drawing, trigonometry, and geometry.

Postsecondary Training

The best way to learn the skills necessary for working in this field is to complete an apprenticeship. Apprenticeships generally consist of a planned series of on-the-job work experiences plus classroom instruction in related subjects. The on-the-job training portion of apprenticeships, which last at least four years, includes about 8,000 hours of work. The classroom instruction totals approximately 600 hours, spread over the years of the apprenticeship. The training covers all aspects of sheet metal fabrication and installation.

Apprentices get practical experience in layout work, cutting, shaping, and installing sheet metal. They also learn to work with materials that may be used instead of metal, such as fiberglass and plastics. Under the supervision of skilled workers, they begin with simple tasks and gradually work up to the most complex. In the classroom, they learn blueprint reading, drafting, mathematics, computer operations, job safety, welding, and the principles of heating, air-conditioning, and ventilating systems.

Apprenticeships may be run by joint committees representing locals of the Sheet Metal Workers' International Association, an important union in the field, and local chapters of the Sheet Metal and Air Conditioning Contractors' National Association. Other apprenticeships are run by local chapters of a contractor group, the Associated Builders and Contractors.

A few sheet metal workers learn informally on the job while they are employed as helpers to experienced workers. They gradually develop skills when opportunities arise for learning. Like apprentices, helpers start out with simple jobs and in time take on more complicated work. However, the training that helpers get may not be as balanced as that for apprentices, and it may take longer for them to learn all that they need to know. Helpers often take vocational school courses to supplement their work experience.

Even after they have become experienced and well qualified in their field, sheet metal workers may need to take further training to keep their skills up to date. Such training is often sponsored by union groups or paid for by their employers.

Other Requirements

Sheet metal workers need to be in good physical condition, with good manual dexterity, eye-hand coordination, and the ability to visualize and understand shapes and forms.

EXPLORING

High school students can gauge their aptitude for and interest in some of the common activities of sheet metal workers by taking courses such as metal shop, blueprint reading, and mechanical drawing. A summer or part-time job as a helper with a contracting firm that does sheet metal work could provide an excellent opportunity to observe workers on the job. If such a job cannot be arranged, it may be possible to visit a construction site and perhaps to talk with a sheet metal worker who can give an insider's view of this job.

EMPLOYERS

Most workers in this field are employed by sheet metal contractors; some workers with a great deal of experience go into business for themselves. Many sheet metal workers are members of the Sheet Metal Workers' International Association.

STARTING OUT

People who would like to enter an apprentice program in this field can seek information about apprenticeships from local employers of sheet metal workers, such as sheet metal contractors or heating, air-conditioning, and refrigeration contractors; from the local office of the Sheet Metal Workers' International Association; or from the local Sheet Metal Apprentice Training office, the joint union-management apprenticeship committee. Information on apprenticeship programs also can be obtained from the local office of the state employment service or the state apprenticeship agency.

People who would rather enter this field as on-the-job trainees can contact contractors directly about possibilities for jobs as helpers. Leads for specific jobs may be located through the state employment service, online, or newspaper classified ads. Graduates of vocational or technical training programs may get assistance from the placement office at their schools.

ADVANCEMENT

Skilled and experienced sheet metal workers who work for contractors may be promoted to positions as *supervisors* and eventually *job superintendents*. Those who develop their skills through further training may move into related fields, such as welding. Some sheet metal workers become specialists in particular activities, such as design and layout work or estimating costs of installations. Some workers eventually go into business for themselves as *independent sheet metal contractors*.

EARNINGS

Sheet metal workers earned a median hourly wage of $17.96 in 2006, according to the *Occupational Outlook Handbook*. This amounts to a yearly salary of $37,357. Overall, hourly earnings ranged from less than $10.36 ($21,549 a year) to more than $32.30 ($67,184 a year). Earnings vary in different parts of the country and tend to be highest in industrialized urban areas. Earnings also vary by industry, with federal government jobs paying sheet metal workers the highest hourly rates. Apprentices begin at about 40 to 50 percent of the rate paid to experienced workers and receive periodic pay increases throughout their training. Some workers who are union members are eligible for supplemental pay from their union during periods of unemployment or when they are working less than full time.

WORK ENVIRONMENT

Most sheet metal workers have a regular 40-hour workweek and receive extra pay for overtime. Most of their work is performed indoors, so they are less likely to lose wages due to bad weather than many other craftworkers involved in construction projects. Some work is done outdoors, occasionally in uncomfortably hot or cold conditions.

Workers sometimes have to work high above the ground (like when they install gutters and roofs) and sometimes in awkward, cramped positions (when they install ventilation systems in buildings). Workers may have to be on their feet for long periods, and they may have to lift heavy objects. Possible hazards of the trade include cuts and burns from machinery and equipment, as well as falls from ladders and scaffolding. Workers must use effective safety practices to avoid injuries and sometimes wear protective gear such as safety glasses. Sheet metal fabrication shops are usually well ventilated and properly heated and lighted, but at times they are quite noisy.

OUTLOOK

The U.S. Department of Labor predicts that employment for sheet metal workers will grow about as fast as the average career through 2016. Employment growth will be related to several factors. Many new residential, commercial, and industrial buildings will be constructed, requiring the skills of sheet metal workers, and many older buildings will need to have new energy-efficient heating, cooling, and ventilating systems installed to replace outdated systems. Existing equipment will need routine maintenance and repair. Decorative sheet metal products are becoming more popular for some uses, a trend that is expected to provide an increasing amount of employment for sheet metal workers. Still, most of the demand for new workers in this field will be to replace experienced people who are transferring to other jobs or leaving the workforce altogether.

Job prospects will vary somewhat with economic conditions. In general, the economy is closely tied to the level of new building construction activity. During economic downturns, workers may face periods of unemployment, while at other times there may be more jobs than skilled workers available to take them. But overall, sheet metal workers are less affected by economic ups and downs than some other craftworkers in the construction field. This is because activities related to maintenance, repair, and replacement of old equipment compose a significant part of their job, and even during an economic slump, building owners are often inclined to go ahead with such work. Opportunities should be particularly good for individuals who have apprenticeship training or who are certified welders.

FOR MORE INFORMATION

For industry and career information, contact the following organizations:

International Training Institute for the Sheet Metal and Air-Conditioning Industry
601 North Fairfax Street, Suite 240
Alexandria, VA 22314-2054
Tel: 703-739-7200
http://www.sheetmetal-iti.org

Sheet Metal and Air Conditioning Contractors' National Association
4201 Lafayette Center Drive
Chantilly, VA 20151-1209
Tel: 703-803-2980
Email: info@smacna.org
http://www.smacna.org

☐ SURGICAL TECHNOLOGISTS

OVERVIEW

Surgical technologists, also called *surgical technicians* or *operating room technicians*, are members of the surgical team who work in the operating room with surgeons, nurses, anesthesiologists, and other personnel before, during, and after surgery. They ensure a safe and sterile environment. To prepare a patient for surgery, they may wash, shave, and disinfect the area where the incision will be made. They arrange the equipment, instruments, and supplies in the operating room according to the preference of the surgeons and nurses. During the operation, they adjust lights and other equipment as needed. They count sponges, needles, and instruments used during the operation, hand instruments and supplies to the surgeon, and hold retractors and cut sutures as directed. They maintain specified supplies of fluids (for example, saline, plasma, blood, and glucose), and may assist in administering these fluids. Following the operation, they may clean and restock the operating room and wash and sterilize the used equipment using germicides, autoclaves, and sterilizers, although in most larger hospitals these tasks are done by other central service personnel. There are approximately 86,000 surgical technologists employed in the United States.

THE JOB

Surgical technologists are health professionals who work in the surgical suite with surgeons, anesthesiologists, registered nurses, and other surgical personnel delivering surgical patient care.

In general, the work responsibilities of surgical technologists may be divided into three phases: preoperative (before surgery), intraoperative (during surgery), and postoperative (after surgery). Surgical technologists may work as the *scrub person*, *circulator*, or *surgical first assistant*.

In the preoperative phase, surgical technologists prepare the operating room by selecting and opening sterile supplies such as drapes, sutures, sponges, electrosurgical devices, suction tubing, and surgical instruments. They assemble, adjust, and check nonsterile equipment to ensure that it is in proper working order. Surgical technologists also operate sterilizers, lights, suction machines, electrosurgical units, and diagnostic equipment.

When patients arrive in the surgical suite, surgical technologists may assist in preparing them for surgery by providing physical and emotional support, checking charts, and observing vital signs. They properly position the patient on the operating table, assist in connecting and applying surgical equipment and monitoring devices, and prepare the incision site by cleansing the skin with an antiseptic solution.

During surgery, surgical technologists have primary responsibility for maintaining the sterile field. They

---

QUICK FACTS

SCHOOL SUBJECTS
Biology
Health

PERSONAL SKILLS
Helping/teaching
Technical/scientific

WORK ENVIRONMENT
Primarily indoors
Primarily one location

MINIMUM EDUCATION LEVEL
Some postsecondary training

MEDIAN SALARY
$36,080

CERTIFICATION OR LICENSING
Recommended

OUTLOOK
Much faster than the average

---

constantly watch that all members of the team adhere to aseptic techniques so the patient does not develop a postoperative infection. As the scrub person, they most often function as the sterile member of the surgical team who passes instruments, sutures, and sponges during surgery. After "scrubbing," which involves the thorough cleansing of the hands and forearms, they put on a sterile gown and gloves and prepare the sterile instruments and supplies that will be needed. After other members of the sterile team have scrubbed, they assist them with gowning and gloving and applying sterile drapes around the operative site.

Surgical technologists must anticipate the needs of surgeons during the procedure, passing instruments and providing sterile items in an efficient manner. Checking, mixing, and dispensing appropriate fluids and drugs in the sterile field are other common tasks. They share with the circulator the responsibility for accounting for sponges, needles, and instruments before, during, and after surgery. They may hold retractors or instruments, sponge or suction the operative site, or cut suture material as directed by the surgeon. They connect drains and tubing and receive and prepare specimens for subsequent pathologic analysis.

Surgical technologists most often function as the scrub person, but may function in the nonsterile role of *circulator*. The circulator does not wear a sterile gown and gloves, but is available to assist the surgical team. As a circulator, the surgical technologist obtains additional supplies or equipment, assists the anesthesiologist, keeps a written account of the surgical procedure, and assists the scrub person.

Surgical first assistants, who are technologists with additional education or training, provide aid in retracting tissue, controlling bleeding, and other technical functions that help surgeons during the procedure.

After surgery, surgical technologists are responsible for preparing and applying dressings, including plaster or synthetic casting materials, and for preparing the operating room for the next patient. They may provide staffing in postoperative recovery rooms where patients' responses are carefully monitored in the critical phases following general anesthesia.

Some of these responsibilities vary, depending on the size of the hospital and department in which the surgical technologist works; they also vary based on geographic location and health care needs of the local community.

REQUIREMENTS
High School

During your high school years, you should take courses that develop your basic skills in mathematics, science, and English. You also should take all available courses in health and biology.

Postsecondary Training

Surgical technology education is available through postsecondary programs offered by community and junior colleges, vocational and technical schools, the military, universities, and structured hospital programs in surgical technology. A high school diploma is required for entry into any of these programs.

More than 400 of these programs are accredited by the Commission on Accreditation of Allied Health Education Programs (CAAHEP). The accredited programs vary from nine to twelve months for a diploma or certificate, to two years for an associate's degree. You can expect to take courses in medical terminology, communications, anatomy, physiology, microbiology, pharmacology, medical ethics, and legal responsibilities. You gain a thorough knowledge of patient preparation and care, surgical procedures, surgical instruments and equipment, and principles of asepsis (how to prevent infection). In addition to classroom learning, you receive intensive supervised clinical experience in local hospitals, which is an important component of your education.

Certification or Licensing

Increasing numbers of hospitals are requiring certification as a condition of employment. Surgical technologists may earn a professional credential by passing a nationally administered certifying examination. To take the examination, you must be currently or previously certified or be a graduate of a CAAHEP-accredited program. The National Board of Surgical Technology and Surgical Assisting (NBSTSA) is the certifying agency for the profession. Those who pass the exam and fulfill education and experience requirements are granted the designation of certified surgical technologist (CST). To renew the four-year certificate, the CST must earn continuing education credits or retake the certifying examination. The NBSTSA also offers an advanced credential for surgical first assistants; this exam awards the designation of CST certified first assistant (CST/CFA). Another certification for surgical technologists can be obtained from the National Center for Competency Testing. To take the certification exam, candidates must either complete an accredited training program, attend a two-year hospital on-the-job training program, or have seven years of experience in the field. Upon passing the exam, surgical technologists obtain the designation of Tech in Surgery-Certified, TS-C (NCCT). This certification must be renewed every five years either through reexamination or continuing education.

Other Requirements

Surgical technologists must possess an educational background in the medical sciences, a strong sense of responsibility, a concern for order, and an ability to integrate a number of tasks at the same time. You need good manual dexterity to handle awkward surgical instruments with speed and agility. In addition, you need physical stamina to stand through long surgical procedures.

EXPLORING

It is difficult to gain any direct experience on a part-time basis in surgical technology. The first opportunities for direct experience generally come in the clinical and laboratory phases of your educational programs. However, interested students can explore some aspects of this career in several ways. You or your teachers can arrange a visit to a hospital, clinic, or other surgical setting in order to learn about the work. You also can visit a school with a CAAHEP-accredited program. During such a visit, you can discuss career plans with the admissions counselor. In addition, volunteering at a local hospital or nursing home can give you insight into the health care environment and help you evaluate your aptitude to work in such a setting.

EMPLOYERS

Most surgical technologists are employed in hospital operating rooms, clinics, and surgical centers. They also work in delivery rooms, cast rooms, emergency departments, ambulatory care areas, and central supply departments. Surgical technologists may also be employed directly by surgeons as private scrubs or as surgical first assistants in a surgical team. Surgical teams are used in specialized surgeries, such as liver transplants.

STARTING OUT

Graduates of programs are often offered jobs in the same hospital in which they received their clinical training. Programs usually cooperate closely with hospitals in the area, which are usually eager to employ technologists educated in local programs. Available positions are also advertised in newspaper want ads.

ADVANCEMENT

With increased experience, surgical technologists can serve in management roles in surgical services departments and may work as *central service managers*, *surgery schedulers*, and *materials managers*. The role of *surgical first assistant* on the surgical team requires additional training and experience and is considered an advanced role.

Surgical technologists must function well in a number of diverse areas. Their competency with multiple skills is demonstrated by their employment in organ and tissue procurement/preservation, cardiac catheterization laboratories, medical sales and research, and medical-legal auditing for insurance companies. A number are *instructors* and *directors* of surgical technology programs.

EARNINGS

Salaries vary greatly in different institutions and localities. According to the U.S. Department of Labor, the average salary for surgical technologists was $36,080 in 2006, and ranged from $25,490 to $51,1400 a year (excluding overtime). Some technologists with experience earn much more. Most surgical technologists are required to be periodically on call—available to work on short notice in cases of emergency—and can earn overtime from such work. Graduates of educational programs usually receive salaries higher than technologists without formal education. In general, technologists working on the East Coast and West Coast earn more than surgical technologists in other parts of the country. Surgical first assistants and private scrubs employed directly by surgeons tend to earn more than surgical technologists employed by hospitals.

WORK ENVIRONMENT

Surgical technologists naturally spend most of their time in the operating room. Operating rooms are cool, well lighted, orderly, and extremely clean. Technologists are often required to be on their feet for long intervals, during which their attention must be closely focused on the operation.

Members of the surgical team, including surgical technologists, wear sterile gowns, gloves, caps, masks, and eye protection. This surgical attire is meant not only to protect the patient from infection but also to protect the surgical team from any infection or bloodborne diseases that the patient may have. Surgery is usually performed during the day; however, hospitals, clinics, and other facilities require 24-hour-a-day coverage. Most surgical technologists work regular 40-hour weeks, although many are required to be periodically on call.

Surgical technologists must be able to work under great pressure in stressful situations. The need for surgery is often a matter of life and death, and one can never assume that procedures will go as planned. If operations do not go well, nerves may fray and tempers flare. Technologists must understand that this is the result of stressful conditions and should not take this anger personally.

In addition, surgical technologists should have a strong desire to help others. Surgery is performed on people, not machines. Patients literally entrust their lives to the surgical team, and they rely on them to treat them in a dignified and professional manner. Individuals with these characteristics find surgical technology a rewarding career in which they can make an important contribution to the health and well-being of their community.

OUTLOOK

According to the U.S. Department of Labor, the field of surgical technology is projected to experience rapid job growth through 2016. Population growth, longevity, and improvement in medical and surgical procedures have all contributed to a growing demand for surgical services and hence for surgical technologists. As long as the rate at which people undergo surgery continues to increase, there will continue to be a need for this profession. Also, as surgical methods become increasingly complex, more surgical technologists will likely be needed. Technological advances, such as fiber optics and laser technology, will also permit a larger number of new surgical procedures to be performed and also will allow surgical technologists to assist with a greater number of procedures.

An increasing number of surgical procedures are being performed in the offices of physicians and ambulatory surgical centers, requiring the skills of surgical technologists. As a result, employment for technologists in these nonhospital settings should grow much faster than the average.

FOR MORE INFORMATION

For information on education programs and certification, contact the following organizations:

Association of Surgical Technologists
6 West Dry Creek Circle, Suite 200
Littleton, CO 80120-8031
Tel: 303-694-9130
http://www.ast.org

National Board of Surgical Technology and Surgical Assisting
6 West Dry Creek Circle, Suite 100
Littleton, CO 80120-8031
Tel: 800-707-0057
http://www.nbstsa.org

☐ SURVEYING AND MAPPING TECHNICIANS

OVERVIEW

Surveying and mapping technicians help determine, describe, and record geographic areas or features. They are usually the leading assistant to the professional surveyor, civil engineer, and mapmaker. They operate modern surveying and mapping instruments and may participate in other operations. Technicians must have a basic knowledge of the current practices and legal implications of surveys to establish and record property size, shape, topography, and boundaries. They often super-

vise other assistants during routine surveying conducted within the bounds established by a professional surveyor. There are approximately 76,000 surveying and mapping technicians working in the United States.

THE JOB

As essential assistants to civil engineers, surveyors, and mapmakers, surveying and mapping technicians are usually the first to be involved in any job that requires precise plotting. This includes highways, airports, housing developments, mines, dams, bridges, and buildings of all kinds.

The surveying and mapping technician is a key worker in field parties and major surveying projects and is often assigned the position of chief instrument worker under the surveyor's supervision. Technicians use a variety of surveying instruments, including the theodolite, transit, level, and other electronic equipment, to measure distances or locate a position. Technicians may be rod workers, using level rods or range poles to make elevation and distance measurements. They may also be chain workers, measuring shorter distances using a surveying chain or a metal tape. During the survey, it is important to accurately record all readings and keep orderly field notes to check for accuracy.

Surveying and mapping technicians may specialize if they join a firm that focuses on one or more particular types of surveying. In a firm that specializes in land surveying, technicians are highly skilled in technical measuring and tasks related to establishing township, property, and other tract-of-land boundary lines. They help the professional surveyor with maps, notes, and title deeds. They help survey the land, check the accuracy of existing records, and prepare legal documents such as deeds and leases.

Similarly, technicians who work for highway, pipeline, railway, or power line surveying firms help to establish grades, lines, and other points of reference for construction projects. This survey information provides the exact locations for engineering design and construction work.

Technicians who work for geodetic surveyors help take measurements of large masses of land, sea, or space. These measurements must take into account the curvature of Earth and its geophysical characteristics. Their findings set major points of reference for smaller land surveys, determining national boundaries, and preparing maps.

Technicians may also specialize in hydrographic surveying, measuring harbors, rivers, and other bodies of water. These surveys are needed to design navigation systems, prepare nautical maps and charts, establish property boundaries, and plan for breakwaters, levees, dams, locks, piers, and bridges.

Mining surveying technicians are usually on the geological staffs of either mining companies or exploration companies. In recent years, costly new surveying instruments have changed the way they do their jobs. Using highly technical machinery, technicians can map underground geology, take samples, locate diamond drill holes, log drill cores, and map geological data derived from boreholes. They also map data on mine plans and diagrams and help the geologist determine ore reserves. In the search for new mines, technicians operate delicate instruments to obtain data on variations in Earth's magnetic field, its conductivity, and gravity. They use their data to map the boundaries of areas for potential further exploration.

Surveying and mapping technicians may find topographical surveys to be interesting and challenging work. These surveys determine the contours of the land and indicate such features as mountains, lakes, rivers, forests, roads, farms, buildings, and other distinguishable landmarks. In topographical surveying, technicians help take aerial or land photographs with photogrammetric equipment installed in an airplane or ground station that can take pictures of large areas. This method is widely used to measure farmland planted with certain crops and to verify crop average allotments under government production planning quotas.

A large number of survey technicians are employed in construction work. Technicians are needed from start to finish on any job. They check the construction of a structure for size, height, depth, level, and form specifications. They also use measurements to locate the critical construction points as specified by design plans, such as corners of buildings, foundation points, center points for columns, walls, and other features, floor or ceiling levels, and other features that require precise measurements and location.

Technological advances such as the Global Positioning System (GPS) and Geographic Information Systems (GIS) have revolutionized surveying and mapping work. Using these systems, surveying teams can track points on the Earth with radio signals transmitted from satellites and store this information in computer databases. As more of these systems are developed, many mapping specialists are being called *geographic information specialists.*

REQUIREMENTS
High School

If you are interested in becoming a surveying and mapping technician, take mathematics courses, such as alge-

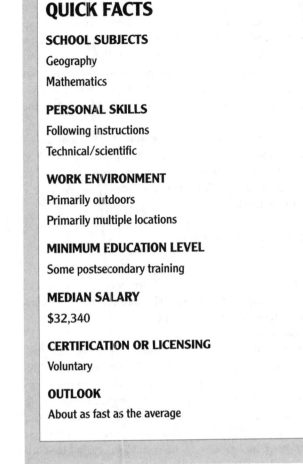

QUICK FACTS

SCHOOL SUBJECTS
Geography
Mathematics

PERSONAL SKILLS
Following instructions
Technical/scientific

WORK ENVIRONMENT
Primarily outdoors
Primarily multiple locations

MINIMUM EDUCATION LEVEL
Some postsecondary training

MEDIAN SALARY
$32,340

CERTIFICATION OR LICENSING
Voluntary

OUTLOOK
About as fast as the average

bra, geometry, and trigonometry, as well as mechanical drawing in high school. Physics, chemistry, and biology are other valuable classes that will help you gain laboratory experience. Reading, writing, and comprehension skills as well as knowledge of computers are also vital in surveying and mapping, so English and computer science courses are also highly recommended.

Postsecondary Training

Though not required to enter the field, graduates of accredited postsecondary training programs for surveying, photogrammetry, and mapping are in the best position to become surveying and mapping technicians. Postsecondary training is available from institutional programs and correspondence schools. These demanding technical programs generally last two years with a possible field study in the summer. First-year courses include English, composition, drafting, applied mathematics, surveying and measurements, construction materials and methods, applied physics, statistics, and computer applications. Second-year courses cover subjects such as technical physics, advanced surveying, photogrammetry and mapping, soils and foundations, technical reporting, legal issues, and transportation and environmental engineering. Contact the American Congress on Surveying and Mapping (ACSM) for a list of accredited programs (see the end of this article for contact information).

With additional experience and study, technicians can specialize in geodesy, topography, hydrography, or photogrammetry. Many graduates of two-year programs later pursue a bachelor's degree in surveying, engineering, or geomatics.

Certification or Licensing

Unlike professional land surveyors, there are no certification or licensing requirements for becoming a surveying and mapping technician. However, technicians who seek government employment must pass a civil service examination.

Many employers prefer certified technicians for promotions into higher positions with more responsibility. ACSM offers the voluntary survey technician certification at four levels. With each level, the technician must have more experience and pass progressively challenging examinations. If the technician hopes one day to work as a surveyor, he or she must be specially certified to work in his or her state. The National Society of Professional Surveyors (NSPS), a member organization of the ACSM, sponsors a comprehensive national certification program for survey technicians leading to the designation of certified survey technician.

Other Requirements

To be a successful surveying and mapping technician, you must be patient, orderly, systematic, accurate, and objective in your work. You must be willing to work cooperatively and have the ability to think and plan ahead. Because of the increasing technical nature of their work, you must have computer skills to be able to use highly complex equipment such as GPS and GIS technology.

EXPLORING

One of the best opportunities for experience is to work part time or during your summer vacation for a construction firm or a company involved in survey work. Even if the job does not involve direct contact with survey crews, you may be able to observe their work and converse with them to discover more about their daily activities. Another possibility is to work for a government agency overseeing land use. The Bureau of Land Management, for example, has employment opportunities for students who qualify, as well as many volunteer positions. The Forest Service also offers temporary positions for students.

EMPLOYERS

There are approximately 76,000 surveying and mapping technicians working in the United States. Almost two-thirds of technicians find work with engineering or architectural service firms. The federal government also employs a number of technicians to work for the U.S. Geological Survey, the Bureau of Land Management, the National Oceanic and Atmospheric Administration, the national Imagery and Mapping Agency, and the Forest Service. State and local governments also hire surveying and mapping technicians to work for highway departments and urban planning agencies. Construction firms and oil, gas, and mining companies also hire technicians.

STARTING OUT

If you plan on entering surveying straight from high school, you may first work as an apprentice. Through on-the-job training and some classroom work, apprentices build up their skills and knowledge of the trade to eventually become surveying and mapping technicians.

If you plan to attend a technical institute or four-year college, check out your school's placement service for help in arranging examinations or interviews. Employers of surveying technicians often send recruiters to schools before graduation and arrange to employ promising graduates. Some community or technical colleges have work-study programs that provide cooperative part-time or summer work for pay. Employers involved with these programs often hire students full time after graduation.

Finally, many cities have employment agencies that specialize in placing technical workers in positions in surveying, mapping, construction, mining, and related fields. Check your local newspaper, telephone book, or surf the Web to see if your town offers these services.

ADVANCEMENT

Possibilities for advancement are linked to levels of formal education and experience. As technicians gain experience and technical knowledge, they can advance to positions of greater responsibility and eventually work as chief surveyor. To advance into this position, technicians will most likely need a two- or four-year degree in surveying and many years of experience. Also, all 50 states require surveyors to be licensed, requiring varying amounts of experience, schooling, and examinations.

Regardless of the level of advancement, all surveying and mapping technicians must continue studying to keep up with the technological developments in their field and enhance their computer skills. Technological advances in computers, lasers, and microcomputers will continue to change job requirements. Studying to keep up with changes combined with progressive experience gained on the job will increase the technician's opportunity for advancement.

EARNINGS

According to the U.S. Department of Labor, the 2006 median hourly salary for all surveying and mapping technicians, regardless of the industry, was $32,340. The lowest-paid 10 percent earned less than $20,020, and the highest-paid 10 percent earned over $53,310. Technicians working for the public sector in federal, state, and local governments generally earn more than those working in the private sector for engineering and architectural services. In 2006, surveying and mapping technicians working for the federal government made a median salary of $37,550 per year.

WORK ENVIRONMENT

Surveying and mapping technicians usually work about 40 hours a week except when overtime is necessary. The peak work period for many kinds of surveying work is during the summer months when weather conditions are most favorable. However, surveying crews are exposed to all types of weather conditions.

Some survey projects involve certain hazards depending upon the region and the climate as well as local plant and animal life. Field survey crews may encounter snakes and poison ivy. They are subject to heat exhaustion, sunburn, and frostbite. Some projects, particularly those being conducted near construction projects or busy highways, impose dangers of injury from cars and flying debris. Unless survey technicians are employed for office assignments, their work location changes from survey to survey. Some assignments may require technicians to be away from home for varying periods of time.

While on the job, technicians who supervise other workers must take special care to observe good safety practices. Construction and mining workplaces usu-ally require hard hats, special clothing, and protective shoes.

OUTLOOK

Surveying and mapping technicians are expected to enjoy worse job prospects than other workers in the surveying field, because of increased use of new technologies used in surveying and mapping such as GPS and GIS. According to the *Occupational Outlook Handbook,* however, employment is expected to grow about as fast as the average for all occupations through 2016.

One of the factors that is expected to increase the demand for surveying services, and therefore surveying technicians, is growth in urban and suburban areas. New streets, homes, shopping centers, schools, and gas and water lines will require property and boundary line surveys. Other factors are the continuing state and federal highway improvement programs and the increasing number of urban redevelopment programs. The expansion of industrial and business firms and the relocation of some firms in large undeveloped areas are also expected to create a need for surveying services.

The need to replace workers who have either retired or transferred to other occupations will also provide opportunities. In general, technicians with more education and skill training will have more job options.

FOR MORE INFORMATION

For more information on accredited surveying programs, contact

Accreditation Board for Engineering and Technology Inc.
111 Market Place, Suite 1050
Baltimore, MD 21202-4012
Tel: 410-347-7700
Email: accreditation@abet.org
http://www.abet.org

For information on careers, scholarships, certification, and educational programs, contact

American Congress on Surveying and Mapping
6 Montgomery Village Avenue, Suite 403
Gaithersburg, MD 20879-3546
Tel: 240-632-9716
Email: info@acsm.net
http://www.acsm.net

For information about the Bureau of Land Management and its responsibilities, visit its Web site.

Bureau of Land Management
Office of Public Affairs

1849 C Street, Room 406-LS
Washington, DC 20240-0001
Tel: 202-452-5125
http://www.blm.gov

For more information on Geographic Information Systems (GIS), visit the following Web site:
GIS.com
    http://www.gis.com

 SURVEYORS

OVERVIEW

Surveyors mark exact measurements and locations of elevations, points, lines, and contours on or near Earth's surface. They measure distances between points to determine property boundaries and to provide data for map-making, construction projects, and other engineering purposes. There are approximately 148,000 surveyors, cartographers, photogrammetrists, and surveying technicians employed in the United States. Of those, about 60,000 are *surveyors* and about 12,000 are *cartographers* and *photogrammetrists*.

THE JOB

On proposed construction projects, such as highways, airstrips, and housing developments, it is the surveyor's responsibility to make necessary measurements through an accurate and detailed survey of the area. The surveyor usually works with a field party consisting of several people. Instrument assistants, called *surveying and mapping technicians*, handle a variety of surveying instruments including the theodolite, transit, level, surveyor's chain, rod, and other electronic equipment. In the course of the survey, it is important that all readings be recorded accurately and field notes maintained so that the survey can be checked for accuracy.

Surveyors may specialize in one or more particular types of surveying.

Land surveyors establish township, property, and other tract-of-land boundary lines. Using maps, notes, or actual land title deeds, they survey the land, checking for the accuracy of existing records. This information is used to prepare legal documents such as deeds and leases. *Land surveying managers* coordinate the work of surveyors, their parties, and legal, engineering, architec-

tural, and other staff involved in a project. In addition, these managers develop policy, prepare budgets, certify work upon completion, and handle numerous other administrative duties.

Highway surveyors establish grades, lines, and other points of reference for highway construction projects. This survey information is essential to the work of the numerous engineers and the construction crews who build the new highway.

Geodetic surveyors measure large masses of land, sea, and space that must take into account the curvature of Earth and its geophysical characteristics. Their work is helpful in establishing points of reference for smaller land surveys, determining national boundaries, and preparing maps. Geodetic computers calculate latitude, longitude, angles, areas, and other information needed for mapmaking. They work from field notes made by an engineering survey party and also use reference tables and a calculating machine or computer.

Marine surveyors measure harbors, rivers, and other bodies of water. They determine the depth of the water through measuring sound waves in relation to nearby land masses. Their work is essential for planning and constructing navigation projects, such as breakwaters, dams, piers, marinas, and bridges, and for preparing nautical charts and maps.

Mine surveyors make surface and underground surveys, preparing maps of mines and mining operations. Such maps are helpful in examining underground passages within the levels of a mine and assessing the volume and location of raw material available.

Geophysical prospecting surveyors locate and mark sites considered likely to contain petroleum deposits. *Oil-well directional surveyors* use sonic, electronic, and nuclear measuring instruments to gauge the presence and amount of oil- and gas-bearing reservoirs. *Pipeline surveyors* determine rights-of-way for oil construction projects, providing information essential to the preparation for and laying of the lines.

Photogrammetric engineers determine the contour of an area to show elevations and depressions and indicate such features as mountains, lakes, rivers, forests, roads, farms, buildings, and other landmarks. Aerial, land, and water photographs are taken with special equipment able to capture images of very large areas. From these pictures, accurate measurements of the terrain and surface features can be made. These surveys are helpful in construction projects and in the preparation of topographical maps. Photogrammetry is particularly helpful in charting areas that are inaccessible or difficult to travel.

REQUIREMENTS

High School

Does this work interest you? If so, you should prepare for it by taking plenty of math and science courses in high school. Take algebra, geometry, and trigonometry to become comfortable making different calculations. Earth science, chemistry, and physics classes should also be helpful. Geography will help you learn about different locations, their characteristics, and cartography. Benefits from taking mechanical drawing and other drafting classes include an increased ability to visualize abstractions, exposure to detailed work, and an understanding of perspectives. Taking computer science classes will prepare you for working with technical surveying equipment.

Postsecondary Training

Depending on state requirements, you will need some postsecondary education. The quickest route is by earning a bachelor's degree in surveying or engineering combined with on-the-job training. Other entry options include obtaining more job experience combined with a one- to three-year program in surveying and surveying technology offered by community colleges, technical institutes, and vocational schools.

Certification or Licensing

All 50 states require that surveyors making property and boundary surveys be licensed or registered. The requirements for licensure vary, but most require a degree in surveying or a related field, a certain number of years of experience, and passing of examinations in land surveying. Generally, the higher the degree obtained, the less experience required. Those with bachelor's degrees may need only two to four years of on-the-job experience, while those with a lesser degree may need up to 12 years of prior experience to obtain a license. Information on specific requirements can be obtained by contacting the licensure department of the state in which you plan to work. If you are seeking employment in the federal government, you must take a civil service examination and meet the educational, experience, and other specified requirements for the position.

Other Requirements

The ability to work with numbers and perform mathematical computations accurately and quickly is very important. Other helpful qualities are the ability to visu-

alize and understand objects in two and three dimensions (spatial relationships) and the ability to discriminate between and compare shapes, sizes, lines, shadings, and other forms (form perception).

Surveyors walk a great deal and carry equipment over all types of terrain so endurance and coordination are important physical assets. In addition, surveyors direct and supervise the work of their team, so you should be good at working with other people and demonstrate leadership abilities.

EXPLORING

While you are in high school, begin to familiarize yourself with terms, projects, and tools used in this profession by reading books and magazines on the topic. One magazine that is available online is *Professional Surveyor Magazine* at http://www.profsurv.com. One of the best opportunities for experience is a summer job with a construction outfit or company that requires survey work.

QUICK FACTS

SCHOOL SUBJECTS
Geography
Mathematics

PERSONAL SKILLS
Communication/ideas
Technical/scientific

WORK ENVIRONMENT
Primarily outdoors
Primarily multiple locations

MINIMUM EDUCATION LEVEL
Some postsecondary training

MEDIAN SALARY
$48,290

CERTIFICATION OR LICENSING
Required

OUTLOOK
Much faster than the average

Even if the job does not involve direct contact with survey crews, it will offer an opportunity to observe surveyors and talk with them about their work.

Some colleges have work-study programs that offer on-the-job experience. These opportunities, like summer or part-time jobs, provide helpful contacts in the field that may lead to future full-time employment. If your college does not offer a work-study program and you can't find a paying summer job, consider volunteering at an appropriate government agency. The U.S. Geological Survey and the Bureau of Land Management usually have volunteer opportunities in select areas.

EMPLOYERS

According to the U.S. Department of Labor, almost two-thirds of surveying workers in the United States are employed in engineering, architectural, and surveying firms. Federal, state, and local government agencies are the next largest employers of surveying workers, and the majority of the remaining surveyors work for construction firms, oil and gas extraction companies, and public utilities. Only a small number of surveyors are self-employed.

STARTING OUT

Apprentices with a high school education can enter the field as equipment operators or surveying assistants. Those who have postsecondary education can enter the field more easily, beginning as surveying and mapping technicians.

College graduates can learn about job openings through their schools' placement services or through potential employers that may visit their campus. Many cities have employment agencies that specialize in seeking out workers for positions in surveying and related fields. Check your local newspaper or telephone book to see if such recruiting firms exist in your area.

ADVANCEMENT

With experience, workers advance through the leadership ranks within a surveying team. Workers begin as assistants and then can move into positions such as senior technician, party chief, and, finally, licensed surveyor. Because surveying work is closely related to other fields, surveyors can move into electrical, mechanical, or chemical engineering or specialize in drafting.

EARNINGS

In 2006, surveyors earned a median annual salary of $48,290. According to the U.S. Department of Labor, the middle 50 percent earned between $35,720 and $42,230 a year. The lowest-paid 10 percent were paid less than $26,690, and the highest-paid 10 percent earned over $79,910 a year. In general, the federal government paid the highest wages to its surveyors, $72,180 a year in 2006.

Most positions with the federal, state, and local governments and with private firms provide life and medical insurance, pension, vacation, and holiday benefits.

WORK ENVIRONMENT

Surveyors work 40-hour weeks except when overtime is necessary to meet a project deadline. The peak work period is during the summer months when weather conditions are most favorable. However, it is not uncommon for the surveyor to be exposed to adverse weather conditions.

Some survey projects may involve hazardous conditions, depending on the region and climate as well as the plant and animal life. Survey crews may encounter snakes, poison ivy, and other hazardous plant and animal life, and may suffer heat exhaustion, sunburn, and frostbite while in the field. Survey projects, particularly those near construction projects or busy highways, may impose dangers of injury from heavy traffic, flying objects, and other accidental hazards. Unless the surveyor is employed only for office assignments, the work location most likely will change from survey to survey. Some assignments may require the surveyor to be away from home for periods of time.

OUTLOOK

The U.S. Department of Labor predicts the employment of surveyors to grow much faster than the average occupation through 2016. The outlook is best for surveyors who have college degrees and advanced field experience. Increasing demand for fast, accurate, and complete geographic information will be the main source of growth for these occupations. The widespread use of technology, such as the Global Positioning System and Geographic Information Systems, will provide jobs to surveyors with strong technical and computer skills.

Growth in urban and suburban areas (with the need for new streets, homes, shopping centers, schools, gas and water lines) will provide employment opportunities. State and federal highway improvement programs and local urban redevelopment programs also will provide jobs for surveyors. The expansion of industrial and business firms and the relocation of some firms to large undeveloped tracts will also create job openings. However, construction projects are closely tied to the state of the economy, so employment may fluctuate from year to year.

FOR MORE INFORMATION

For information on state affiliates and colleges and universities offering land surveying programs, contact

American Congress on Surveying and Mapping
6 Montgomery Village Avenue, Suite 403
Gaithersburg, MD 20879-3546
Tel: 240-632-9716
Email: info@acsm.net
http://www.acsm.net

For information on awards and recommended books to read, contact or check out the following Web sites:

American Association for Geodetic Surveying
6 Montgomery Village Avenue, Suite 403
Gaithersburg, MD 20879-3546
Tel: 240-632-9716
http://www.aagsmo.org/

National Society of Professional Surveyors
6 Montgomery Village Avenue, Suite 403
Gaithersburg, MD 20879
Tel: 240-632-9716
http://www.nspsmo.org

For information on photogrammetry and careers in the field, contact

American Society for Photogrammetry and Remote Sensing
5410 Grosvenor Lane, Suite 210
Bethesda, MD 20814-2160
Tel: 301-493-0290
http://www.asprs.org

For information on volunteer opportunities with the federal government, contact

Bureau of Land Management
Office of Public Affairs
1849 C Street, Room 406-LS
Washington, DC 20240-0001
Tel: 202-452-5125
http://www.blm.gov

U.S. Geological Survey
12201 Sunrise Valley Drive
Reston, VA 20192-0002
Tel: 703-648-4000
http://www.usgs.gov

☐ TAX PREPARERS

OVERVIEW

Tax preparers prepare income tax returns for individuals and small businesses for a fee, for either quarterly or yearly filings. They help to establish and maintain business records to expedite tax preparations and may advise clients on how to save money on their tax payments. There are approximately 100,000 tax preparers employed in the United States.

THE JOB

Tax preparers help individuals and small businesses keep the proper records to determine their legally required tax and file the proper forms. They must be well acquainted with federal, state, and local tax laws and use their knowledge and skills to help taxpayers take the maximum number of legally allowable deductions.

The first step in preparing tax forms is to collect all the data and documents that are needed to calculate the client's tax liability. The client has to submit documents such as tax returns from previous years, wage and income statements, records of other sources of income, statements of interest and dividends earned, records of expenses, property tax records, and so on. The tax preparer then interviews the client to obtain further information that may have a bearing on the amount of tax owed. If the client is an individual taxpayer, the tax preparer will ask about any important investments, extra expenses that may be deductible, contributions to charity, and insurance payments; events such as marriage, childbirth, and new employment are also important considerations. If the client is a business, the tax preparer may ask about capital gains and losses, taxes already paid, payroll expenses, miscellaneous business expenses, and tax credits.

Once the tax preparer has a complete picture of the client's income and expenses, the proper tax forms and schedules needed to file the tax return can be determined. While some taxpayers have very complex finances that take a long time to document and calculate, others have typical, straightforward returns that take less time. Often the tax preparer can calculate the amount a taxpayer owes, fill out the proper forms, and prepare the complete return in a single interview. When the tax return is more complicated, the tax preparer may have to collect all the data during the interview and perform the calculations later. If a client's taxes are

QUICK FACTS

SCHOOL SUBJECTS
Business
Mathematics

PERSONAL SKILLS
Following instructions
Helping/teaching

WORK ENVIRONMENT
Primarily indoors
Primarily one location

MINIMUM EDUCATION LEVEL
Some postsecondary training

MEDIAN SALARY
$27,360

CERTIFICATION OR LICENSING
Required by certain states

OUTLOOK
Decline

unusual or very complex, the tax preparer may have to consult tax law handbooks and bulletins.

Computers are the main tools used to figure and prepare tax returns. The tax preparer inputs the data onto a spreadsheet, and the computer calculates and prints out the tax form. Computer software can be very versatile and may even print up data summary sheets that can serve as checklists and references for the next tax filing.

Tax preparers often have another tax expert or preparer check their work, especially if they work for a tax service firm. The second tax preparer will check to make sure the allowances and deductions taken were proper and that no others were overlooked. They also make certain that the tax laws are interpreted properly and that calculations are correct. It is very important that a tax preparer's work is accurate and error-free, and clients are given a guarantee covering additional taxes or fines if the preparer's work is found to be incorrect. Tax preparers are required by law to sign every return they complete

for a client and provide their Social Security number or federal identification number. They must also provide the client with a copy of the tax return and keep a copy in their own files.

REQUIREMENTS

High School

Although there are no specific postsecondary educational requirements for tax preparers, you should certainly get your high school diploma. While you are in high school there are a number of classes you can take that will help prepare you for this type of work. You should take mathematics classes. Accounting, bookkeeping, and business classes will also give you a feel for working with numbers and show you the importance of accurate work. In addition, take computer classes. You will need to be comfortable using computers, since much tax work is done using this tool. Finally, take English classes. English classes will help you work on your research, writing, and speaking skills—important communication skills to have when you work with clients.

Postsecondary Training

Once you have completed high school, you may be able to find a job as a tax preparer at a large tax-preparing firm. These firms, such as H & R Block, typically require their tax preparers to complete a training program in tax preparation. If you would like to pursue a college education, many universities offer individual courses and complete majors in the area of taxation. Another route is to earn a bachelor's degree or master's degree in business administration with a minor or concentration in taxation. A few universities offer master's degrees in taxation.

In addition to formal education, tax preparers must continue their professional education. Both federal and state tax laws are revised every year, and the tax preparer is obligated to understand these new laws thoroughly by January 1 of each year. Major tax reform legislation can increase this amount of study even further. One federal reform tax bill can take up thousands of pages, and this can mean up to 60 hours of extra study in a single month to fully understand all the intricacies and implications of the new laws. To help tax preparers keep up with new developments, the National Association of Tax Professionals offers more than 200 workshops every year. Tax service firms also offer classes explaining tax preparation to both professionals and individual taxpayers.

Certification or Licensing

Licensing requirements for tax preparers vary by state, and you should be sure to find out what requirements there are in the state where you wish to practice. Since 2002, for example, tax preparers in California have been required to register with the California Tax Education Council, a nonprofit corporation established by the California State Legislature to oversee tax preparation. Tax preparers who apply for registration in that state must be at least 18 years old. In addition, they need to have 60 hours of formal, approved instruction in basic income tax law, theory, and practice, or two years of professional experience in preparing personal income tax returns.

The Internal Revenue Service (IRS) offers an examination for tax preparers. Those who complete the test successfully are called enrolled agents and are entitled to legally represent any taxpayer in any type of audit before the IRS or state tax boards. (Those with five years' experience working for the IRS as an auditor or in a higher position can become enrolled agents without taking the exam.) The four-part test is offered annually and takes two days to complete. There are no education or experience requirements for taking the examination, but the questions are roughly equivalent to those asked in a college course. Study materials and applications may be obtained from local IRS offices. The IRS does not oversee seasonal tax preparers, but local IRS offices may monitor some commercial tax offices.

The Institute of Tax Consultants offers an annual open book exam to obtain the title of certified tax preparer (CTP). Certification also requires 30 hours of continuing education each year.

Other Requirements

Tax preparers should have an aptitude for math and an eye for detail. They should have strong organizational skills and the patience to sift through documents and financial statements. The ability to communicate effectively with clients is also key to be able to explain complex tax procedures and to make customers feel confident and comfortable. Tax preparers also need to work well under the stress and pressure of deadlines. They must also be honest, discreet, and trustworthy in dealing with the financial and business affairs of their clients.

EXPLORING

If a career in tax preparation sounds interesting, you should first gain some experience by completing income tax returns for yourself and for your family and friends. These returns should be double-checked by the actual taxpayers who will be liable for any fees and extra taxes if the return is prepared incorrectly. You can also look for internships or part-time jobs in tax service offices and tax preparation firms. Many of these firms operate nationwide, and extra office help might be needed as tax deadlines approach and work becomes hectic. The IRS also trains people to answer tax questions for its 800-number telephone advisory service; they are employed annually during early spring.

Try also to familiarize yourself with the tax preparation software available on the Internet and utilize Web sites to keep abreast of changing laws, regulations, and developments in the industry. The National Association of Tax Professionals offers sample articles from its publications, *TAXPRO Quarterly* and *TAXPRO Monthly*, online. (See end of article for contact information.)

EMPLOYERS

Tax preparers may work for tax service firms that conduct most of their business during tax season. Other tax preparers may be self-employed and work full or part time.

STARTING OUT

Because tax work is very seasonal, most tax firms begin hiring tax preparers in December for the upcoming tax season. Some tax service firms will hire tax preparers from among the graduates of their own training courses. Private and state employment agencies may also have information and job listings, as will classified newspaper ads. You should also consult your school guidance offices to establish contacts in the field.

There are a large number of Internet sites for this industry, many of which offer job postings. Many large tax preparation firms, such as H & R Block, also have their own Web pages.

ADVANCEMENT

Some tax preparers may wish to continue their academic education and work toward becoming *certified public accountants*. Others may want to specialize in certain areas of taxation, such as real estate, corporate, or nonprofit work. Tax preparers who specialize in certain fields are able to charge higher fees for their services.

Establishing a private consulting business is also an option. Potential proprietors should consult with other self-employed practitioners to gain advice on how to start a private practice. Several Internet sites also give valuable advice on establishing a tax business.

EARNINGS

According to the U.S. Department of Labor, the median annual income for tax preparers was approximately $27,360 in 2006. Salaries range from less than $17,859 to more than $56,301 annually. Incomes can vary widely from these figures, however, due to a number of factors. One reason is that tax preparers generally charge a fee per tax return, which may range from $30 to $1,500 or more, depending on the complexity of the return and the preparation time required. Therefore, the number of clients a preparer has, as well as the difficulty of the returns, can affect the preparer's income. Another factor affecting income is the amount of education a tax preparer has. Seasonal or part-time employees, typically those with less education, usually earn minimum wage plus commission. Enrolled agents, certified public accountants, and other professional preparers, typically those with college degrees or more, usually charge more. Finally, it is important to realize that fees vary widely in different parts of the country. Tax preparers in large cities and in the western United States generally charge more, as do those who offer year-round financial advice and services.

WORK ENVIRONMENT

Tax preparers generally work in office settings that may be located in neighborhood business districts, shopping malls, or other high-traffic areas. Employees of tax service firms may work at storefront desks or in cubicles during the three months preceding the April 15 tax-filing deadline. In addition, many tax preparers work at home to earn extra money while they hold a full-time job.

The hours and schedules that tax preparers work vary greatly, depending on the time of year and the manner in which workers are employed. Because of the changes in tax laws that occur every year, tax preparers often advise their clients throughout the year about possible ways to reduce their tax obligations. The first quarter of the year is the busiest time, and even part-time tax preparers may find themselves working very long hours. Workweeks can range from as little as 12 hours to 40 or 50 or more, as tax preparers work late into the evening and on weekends. Tax service firms are usually open seven days a week and 12 hours a day during the first three months of the year. The work is demanding, requiring heavy concentration and long hours sitting at a desk and working on a computer.

OUTLOOK

The U.S. Department of Labor predicts that employment for tax preparers will decline through 2016. Although tax laws are constantly evolving and people look to tax preparers to save time, money, and frustration, new tax programs and online resources are easing the process of preparing taxes, lessening the need for outside help. Information is available at the touch of a button on tax laws and regulations. Tax tips are readily available, as are online seminars and workshops. Computers are increasingly expediting the process of tabulating and storing data. Recent surveys of employers in large metropolitan areas have found an adequate supply of tax preparers; prospects for employment may be better in smaller cities or rural areas.

The IRS currently offers taxpayers and businesses the option to "e-file," or electronically file their tax returns on the Internet. While some people may choose to do their own electronic filing, the majority of taxpayers will still rely on tax preparers—licensed by the IRS as Electronic Return Originators—to handle their returns.

FOR MORE INFORMATION

For information on the certified tax preparer designation, contact

Institute of Tax Consultants
7500 212th SW, Suite 205
Edmonds, WA 98026-7641
Tel: 425-774-3521
http://taxprofessionals.homestead.com/welcome.
   html

For industry information, contact

National Association of Tax Consultants
PO Box 90276
Portland, OR 97290-0276
Tel: 800-745-6282
http://www.natctax.org

For information on educational programs, publications, and online membership, contact

National Association of Tax Professionals
720 Association Drive
PO Box 8002
Appleton, WI 54912-8002
Tel: 800-558-3402
Email: natp@natptax.com
http://www.natptax.com

For training programs, contact

H & R Block
http://www.hrblock.com

For information on becoming certified as an enrolled agent, check out the IRS Web site:

Internal Revenue Service
Department of the Treasury
http://www.irs.ustreas.gov

☐ TAXIDERMISTS

QUICK FACTS

SCHOOL SUBJECTS
Art
Biology
Technical/shop

PERSONAL SKILLS
Artistic
Mechanical/manipulative

WORK ENVIRONMENT
Primarily indoors
Primarily one location

MINIMUM EDUCATION LEVEL
Some postsecondary training

MEDIAN SALARY
$30,000

CERTIFICATION OR LICENSING
Required

OUTLOOK
About as fast as the average

OVERVIEW

Taxidermists preserve and prepare animal skins and parts to create lifelike animal replicas. Taxidermists prepare the underpadding and mounting to which the skin will be attached, model the structure to resemble the animal's body, and then attach appropriate coverings, such as skin, fur, or feathers. They may add details, such as eyes or teeth, to make a more realistic representation. The animals they mount or stuff may be for private or public display. Museums frequently display creations from taxidermists to exhibit rare, exotic, or extinct animals. Hunters also use taxidermists' services to mount fishing and hunting trophies for display.

THE JOB

Taxidermists use a variety of methods to create realistic, lifelike models of birds and animals. Although specific processes and techniques vary, most taxidermists follow a series of basic steps.

First, they must remove the skin from the carcass of the animal with special knives, scissors, and pliers. The skin must be removed very carefully to preserve the natural state of the fur or feathers. Once the skin is removed, it is preserved with a chemical solution.

Some taxidermists still make the body foundation, or skeleton, of the animal. These foundations are made with a variety of materials, including clay, plaster, burlap, papier-mâché, wire mesh, and glue. Other taxidermists, however, use ready-made forms, which are available in various sizes; taxidermists simply take measurements of the specimen to be mounted and order the proper size from the supplier. Metal rods are often used to achieve the desired mount for the animal.

The taxidermist uses special adhesives or modeling clay to attach the skin to the foundation or form. Then artificial eyes, teeth, and tongues are attached. Sometimes taxidermists use special techniques, such as airbrushing color or sculpting the eyelids, nose, and lips. They may need to attach antlers, horns, or claws.

Finally they groom and dress the fur or feathers with styling gel, if necessary, to enhance the final appearance of the specimen.

Taxidermists work with a variety of animal types, including one-cell organisms, large game animals, birds, fish, and reptiles. They even make models of extinct animal species, based on detailed drawings or paintings. The specific work often depends on the area of the country where the taxidermist is employed, since the types of animals hunted vary by region.

REQUIREMENTS
High School

High school classes in art, woodworking, and metal shop may help develop the skills necessary for this career. Also, a class or classes in biology might be helpful for learning the bodily workings of certain animals.

Postsecondary Training

In the United States, several schools offer programs or correspondence courses in taxidermy. Courses often last from four to six weeks, and subjects such as laws and legalities, bird mounting, fish mounting, deer, small mammals, diorama-making, airbrush painting, and form-making are covered. Taxidermists who hope to work in museums should expect to take further training and acquire additional skills in related subjects, which they can learn in museum classes.

Self-employed taxidermists need accounting, advertising, and marketing courses to help in the management of a business, including maintaining an inventory of chemicals and supplies, advertising and promotion, and pricing their work.

Certification or Licensing

Taxidermists are required to be licensed in most states, with specific licensing requirements varying from state to state. Many taxidermists choose to become members of national or local professional associations. The largest of these, the National Taxidermists Association, offers the designation of certified taxidermist to members who have met specific requirements. Members may be certified in one or all four categories of specialization: mammals, fish, birds, and reptiles. Certification indicates that they have reached a certain level of expertise and may allow them to charge a higher price for their work.

Other Requirements

Successful taxidermy requires many skills. You must have good manual dexterity, an eye for detail, knowledge of animal anatomy, and training in the taxidermy processes.

EXPLORING

Because taxidermy is a specialized occupation, there are few opportunities for part-time or summer work for students, although some larger companies hire apprentices to help with the workload. However, you may learn more by ordering videotapes and practicing with mounting kits to experience the mounting process. Other good learning opportunities include speaking to a museum taxidermist or writing to schools or associations that offer courses in taxidermy. Check with the National Taxidermists Association for upcoming conventions and seminars that are open to the public. Time spent at such an event would provide not only a solid learning experience, but also a chance to meet and mingle with the pros.

EMPLOYERS

Taxidermists can be found throughout the United States and abroad. Experienced and established taxidermists, especially those with a large client base, will often hire apprentices, or less experienced taxidermists, to assist with larger projects or undertake smaller jobs. Contact the National Taxidermists Association for a listing of such employers. The majority of taxidermists, about 70 to 80 percent, are self-employed.

STARTING OUT

Taxidermy is a profession that requires experience. Most workers start out as hobbyists in their own homes, and eventually start doing taxidermy work part time professionally. Later, after they have built up a client base, they may enter the profession full time. Jobs in existing taxidermy shops or businesses are difficult to find because most taxidermists are self-employed and prefer to do the work themselves. However, in some cases, it may be possible to become a journeyman or apprentice and work for an already established taxidermist on either an hourly basis or for a percentage of the selling price of the work they are doing.

Jobs in museums are often difficult to obtain; applicants should have a background in both taxidermy and general museum studies. Taxidermy schools primarily train their students to become self-employed but may sometimes offer job placement as well.

ADVANCEMENT

Advancement opportunities are good for those with the proper skills, education, and experience. Taxidermists who can work on a wide range of projects will have the best chances of advancing. Since larger game animals bring more money, one method of advancing would be to learn the skills necessary to work on these animals. Taxidermists who develop a large customer base may open their own shop. Workers employed in museums may advance to positions with more responsibilities and higher pay.

EARNINGS

A taxidermist's level of experience, certification, speed, and quality of work are all factors that significantly affect income. Most taxidermists will charge by the inch or the weight of the animal. Fees can range from $100 to $2,500, depending on the size of the animal and the style of the mount. Difficult mounts or unusual background accessories may add significantly to the final price. For example, an open mouth on an animal, as opposed to a droopy mouth or a closed mouth, can add about $100 to the price of a mounting. In addition, the region of the country and the type of game typically hunted and mounted are important variables. Most new taxidermists might expect to earn about $15,000 annually. Those with five to 10 years of experience and proven skills can earn $30,000 or more. Some exceptional taxidermists can earn upwards of $50,000 annually. Museum workers might also expect to average $25,000 to $30,000 yearly.

Because most taxidermists are self-employed or work for a very small operation, few have any sort of benefits package. Those who work in museums, however, may be offered health insurance and paid vacations and sick leave.

WORK ENVIRONMENT

Most taxidermists work 40 hours a week, although overtime is not uncommon during certain times of the year. Taxidermists with their own shops may have to work long hours, especially when first starting out. They often work with strong chemicals, glues, hand and power tools, and possibly diseased animals. If working on smaller animals and birds, they can sit or stand. However, creating larger mammal displays requires more physical work, such as climbing or squatting.

Taxidermists find it satisfying to see a project from beginning to completion. There is also the element of pride in good craftsmanship; it can be gratifying for workers to use their talents to recreate extremely realistic and lifelike animal forms.

OUTLOOK

The job outlook for taxidermists should be good over the next decade. Although jobs in museums may be scarce, the demand for hunting and fishing trophies continues to provide work for taxidermists. It is not unusual for qualified taxidermists to have a year's worth of work backlogged. In addition, many museums and other educational institutions actively seek models of animal and bird species that are nearing extinction. Talented taxidermists who can take on a variety of projects should be able to find steady employment. Those with an eye for unique poses and mounts, or unusual expressions, will be in high demand.

FOR MORE INFORMATION

For information on the industry, certification, taxidermy schools, trade magazines, association membership, and career opportunities, contact the following organizations:
National Taxidermists Association
108 Branch Drive

Slidell, LA 70461-1912
Tel: 866-662-9054
Email: ntahq@aol.com
http://www.nationaltaxidermists.com

United Taxidermist Association
http://www.nationaltaxidermist.com

For information on training in taxidermy, including a list of schools, workshops, books, magazines, videos, and links to state taxidermy associations, see
Taxidermy.net
http://www.taxidermy.net

TEACHER AIDES

OVERVIEW

Teacher aides, also called *teacher assistants* or *paraprofessionals*, perform a wide variety of duties to help teachers run a classroom. Teacher aides prepare instructional materials, help students with classroom work, and supervise students in the library, on the playground, and at lunch. They perform administrative duties such as photocopying, keeping attendance records, and grading papers. There are approximately 1.3 million teacher aides employed in the United States.

THE JOB

Teacher aides work in public, private, and parochial preschools and elementary and secondary schools. Their duties vary depending on the classroom teacher, school, and school district. Some teacher aides specialize in one subject, and some work in a specific type of school setting. These settings include bilingual classrooms, gifted and talented programs, classes for learning disabled students and those with unique physical needs, and multi-age classrooms. These aides conduct the same type of classroom work as other teacher aides, but they may provide more individual assistance to students.

No matter what kind of classroom they assist in, teacher aides will likely copy, compile, and hand out class materials, set up and operate audiovisual equipment, arrange field trips, and type or word-process materials. They organize classroom files, including grade reports, attendance, and health records. They may also obtain library materials and order classroom supplies.

QUICK FACTS

SCHOOL SUBJECTS

Art

English

History

PERSONAL SKILLS

Helping/teaching

Leadership/management

WORK ENVIRONMENT

Primarily indoors

Primarily one location

MINIMUM EDUCATION LEVEL

High school diploma

MEDIAN SALARY

$20,740

CERTIFICATION OR LICENSING

None available

OUTLOOK

About as fast as the average

answered correctly. The clerk then records this score and averages students' test scores to determine their grades for the course.

Under the teacher's supervision, teacher aides may work directly with students in the classroom. They listen to a group of young students read aloud or involve the class in a special project such as a science fair, art project, or drama production. With older students, teacher aides provide review or study sessions prior to exams or give extra help with research projects or homework. Some teacher aides work with individual students in a tutorial setting, helping in areas of special need or concern. They may work with the teacher to prepare lesson plans, bibliographies, charts, or maps. They may help to decorate the classroom, design bulletin boards and displays, and arrange workstations. Teacher aides may also participate in parent-teacher conferences to discuss students' progress.

Many teacher assistants work extensively with special education students. As schools become more inclusive and integrate special education students into general education classrooms, teacher assistants increasingly assist students with disabilities. They attend to the physical needs of students with disabilities, including feeding, teaching good grooming habits, or assisting students riding the school bus.

REQUIREMENTS
High School

Courses in English, history, social studies, mathematics, art, drama, physical education, and the sciences will provide you with a broad base of knowledge. This knowledge will enable you to help students learn in these same subjects. Knowledge of a second language can be an asset, especially when working in schools with bilingual student, parent, or staff populations. Courses in child care, home economics, and psychology are also valuable for this career. You should try to gain some experience working with computers; students at many elementary schools and even preschools now do a large amount of computer work, and computer skills are important in performing clerical duties.

Postsecondary Training

Postsecondary requirements for teacher aides depend on the school or school district and the kinds of responsibilities the aides have. In districts where aides perform mostly clerical duties, applicants may need only to have a high school diploma or a general equivalency diploma (GED).

Teacher aides may be in charge of keeping order in classrooms, school cafeterias, libraries, hallways, and playgrounds. Often, they wait with preschool and elementary students coming to or leaving school and make sure all students are accounted for. When a class leaves its room for such subjects as art, music, physical education, or computer lab, teacher aides may go with the students to help the teachers of these other subjects.

Another responsibility of teacher aides is correcting and grading homework and tests, usually for objective assignments and tests that require specific answers. They use answer sheets to mark students' papers and examinations and keep records of students' scores. In some large schools, an aide may be called a *grading clerk* and be responsible only for scoring objective tests and computing and recording test scores. Often using an electronic grading machine or computer, the grading clerk totals errors found and computes the percentage of questions

Those who work in the classroom may be required to take some college courses and attend in-service training and special teacher conferences and seminars. Some schools and districts may help you pay some of the costs involved in attending these programs. Often community and junior colleges have certificate and associate's programs that prepare teacher aides for classroom work, offering courses in child development, health and safety, and child guidance. Teacher aides who work in Title I schools—those with a large proportion of students from low-income households—must have college training or proven academic skills. They face new federal requirements as of 2006: aides must hold a two-year or higher degree, have a minimum of two years of college, or pass a rigorous state or local assessment.

Newly hired aides participate in orientation sessions and formal training at the school. In these sessions, aides learn about the school's organization, operation, and philosophy. They learn how to keep school records, operate audiovisual equipment, check books out of the library, and administer first aid.

Many schools prefer to hire teacher aides who have some experience working with children; some schools prefer to hire workers who live within the school district. Schools may also require that you pass written exams and health physicals. You must be able to work effectively with both children and adults and should have good verbal and written communication skills. Teacher aides who speak a second language, especially Spanish, are in great demand for communicating with growing numbers of students and parents whose primary language is not English.

Other Requirements

You must enjoy working with children and be able to handle their demands, problems, and questions with patience and fairness. You must be willing and able to follow instructions, but also should be able to take the initiative in projects. Flexibility, creativity, and a cheerful outlook are definite assets for anyone working with children. You should find out the specific job requirements from the school, school district, or state department of education in the area where you would like to work. Requirements vary from school to school and state to state. It is important to remember that an aide who is qualified to work in one state, or even one school, may not be qualified to work in another.

EXPLORING

You can gain experience working with children by volunteering to help with religious education classes at your place of worship. You may volunteer to help with scouting troops or work as a counselor at a summer camp. You may have the opportunity to volunteer to help coach a children's athletic team or work with children in after-school programs at community centers. Babysitting is a common way to gain experience in working with children and to learn about the different stages of child development.

EMPLOYERS

Approximately 1.3 million workers are employed as teacher assistants in the United States. About 40 percent of teacher assistants work part time. With the national shortage of teachers, aides can find work in just about any preschool, elementary, or secondary school in the country. Teacher aides also assist in special education programs and in group-home settings. Aides work in both public and private schools.

STARTING OUT

You can apply directly to schools and school districts for teacher aide positions. Many school districts and state departments of education maintain job listings, bulletin boards, and hotlines that list available job openings. Teacher aide jobs are often advertised in the classified section of the newspaper. Once you are hired as a teacher aide, you will spend the first months in special training and will receive a beginning wage. After six months or so, you'll have regular responsibilities and possibly a wage increase.

ADVANCEMENT

Teacher aides usually advance only in terms of increases in salary or responsibility, which come with experience. Aides in some districts may receive time off to take college courses. Some teacher aides choose to pursue bachelor's degrees and fulfill the licensing requirements of the state or school to become teachers

Some aides, who find that they enjoy the administrative side of the job, may move into *school or district office staff* positions. Others choose to get more training and then work as *resource teachers, tutors, guidance counselors,* or *reading, mathematics, or speech specialists.* Some teacher aides go into *school library work* or become *media specialists.* While it is true that most of these jobs require additional training, the job of teacher aide is a good place to begin.

EARNINGS

Teacher aides are usually paid on an hourly basis and usually only during the nine or 10 months of the school calendar. Salaries vary depending on the school or district, region of the country, and the duties the aides perform. Median annual earnings of teacher assistants in 2006 were $20,740, according to the U.S. Department of Labor. Salaries ranged from less than $13,910 to more than $31,610.

Benefits such as health insurance and vacation or sick leave may also depend on the school or district as well as the number of hours a teacher aide works. Many schools employ teacher aides only part-time and do not offer such benefits. Other teacher aides may receive the same health and pension benefits as the teachers in their school and be covered under collective bargaining agreements.

WORK ENVIRONMENT

Teacher aides work in a well-lit, comfortable, wheelchair-accessible environment, although some older school buildings may be in disrepair with unpredictable heating or cooling systems. Most of their work will be indoors, but teacher aides will spend some time outside before and after school, and during recess and lunch hours, to watch over the students. They are often on their feet, monitoring the halls and lunch areas and running errands for teachers. Although this work is not physically strenuous, working closely with children can be stressful and tiring.

Teacher aides find it rewarding to help students learn and develop. The pay, however, is not as rewarding

OUTLOOK

Growth in this field is expected to be about as fast as the average through 2016 because of an expected gradual increase in the school enrollments, but especially the student population that requires assistance of teacher aides, including special education students and students for whom English is not their first language. As the number of students in schools increases, new schools and classrooms will be added, and more teachers and teacher aides will be hired. A shortage of teachers will cause administrators to hire more aides to help with larger classrooms. Because of increased responsibilities for aides, state departments of education will likely establish standards of training.

The No Child Left Behind Act may also increase demand for teacher aides, due to a greater focus on educational quality and accountability. Teachers will need aides to help students prepare for standardized testing and assist those students who perform poorly on standardized tests.

The field of special education (working with students with specific learning, emotional, or physical concerns or disabilities) is expected to grow rapidly, and more aides will be needed in these areas. The 1997 Individuals with Disabilities Education Act requires a more specialized training for aides working with students with disabilities. Teacher aides who want to work with young children in day care or extended day programs will have a relatively easy time finding work because more children are attending these programs while their parents are at work.

FOR MORE INFORMATION

To learn about current issues affecting paraprofessionals in education, visit the AFT Web site or contact
American Federation of Teachers (AFT)
555 New Jersey Avenue, NW
Washington, DC 20001-2029
Tel: 202-879-4400
http://www.aft.org

To order publications or read current research and other information, contact
Association for Childhood Education International
17904 Georgia Avenue, Suite 215
Olney, MD 20832
Tel: 800-423-3563
Email: headquarters@acei.org
http://www.acei.org

For information about training programs and other resources, contact
National Resource Center for Paraprofessionals
Utah State University
6526 Old Main Hill
Logan, UT 84322-6526
Tel: 435-797-7272
Email: info@nrcpara.org
http://www.nrcpara.org

TRAVEL AGENTS

OVERVIEW

Travel agents assist individuals or groups who will be traveling by planning their itineraries, making transportation, hotel, and tour reservations, obtaining or preparing tickets, and performing related services. There are more than 101,000 travel agents employed in the United States.

THE JOB

The travel agent may work as a *salesperson, travel consultant, tour organizer, travel guide, bookkeeper,* or *small busi-*

ness executive. If the agent operates a one-person office, he or she usually performs all of these functions. Other travel agents work in offices with dozens of employees, which allows them to specialize in certain areas. In such offices, one staff member may become an authority on sea cruises, another may work on trips to the Far East, and a third may develop an extensive knowledge of either low-budget or luxury trips. In some cases, travel agents are employed by national or international firms and can draw upon very extensive resources.

As salespeople, travel agents must be able to motivate people to take advantage of their services. Travel agents study their customers' interests, learn where they have traveled, appraise their financial resources and available time, and present a selection of travel options. Customers are then able to choose how and where they want to travel with a minimum of effort.

Travel agents consult a variety of published and computer-based sources for information on air transportation departure and arrival times, airfares, and hotel ratings and accommodations. They often base their recommendations on their own travel experiences or those of colleagues or clients. Travel agents may visit hotels, resorts, and restaurants to rate their comfort, cleanliness, and quality of food and service.

As travel consultants, agents give their clients suggestions regarding travel plans and itineraries, information on transportation alternatives, and advice on the available accommodations and rates of hotels and motels. They also explain and help with passport and visa regulations, foreign currency and exchange, climate and wardrobe, health requirements, customs regulations, baggage and accident insurance, traveler's checks or letters of credit, car rentals, tourist attractions, and welcome or tour services. In the event of changes in itinerary in the middle of a trip, travel agents intercede on the traveler's behalf to make alternate booking arrangements.

Many travel agents only sell tours that are developed by other organizations. The most skilled agents, however, often organize tours on a wholesale basis. This involves developing an itinerary, contracting a knowledgeable person to lead the tour, making tentative reservations for transportation, hotels, and side trips, publicizing the tour through descriptive brochures, advertisements, and other travel agents, scheduling reservations, and handling last-minute problems. Sometimes tours are arranged at the specific request of a group or to meet a client's particular needs.

In addition to other duties, travel agents may serve as *tour guides*, leading trips ranging from one week to six months to locations around the world. Agents often

QUICK FACTS

SCHOOL SUBJECTS
Business
Computer science
Geography

PERSONAL SKILLS
Communication/ideas
Helping/teaching

WORK ENVIRONMENT
Indoors and outdoors
One location with some travel

MINIMUM EDUCATION LEVEL
High school diploma

MEDIAN SALARY
$29,210

CERTIFICATION OR LICENSING
Required by certain states

OUTLOOK
Little or no growth

find tour leadership a useful way to gain personal travel experience. It also gives them the chance to become thoroughly acquainted with the people in the tour group, who may then use the agent to arrange future trips or recommend the agent to friends and relatives. Tour leaders are usually reimbursed for all their expenses or receive complimentary transportation and lodging. Most travel agents, however, arrange for someone to cover for them at work during their absence, which may make tour leadership prohibitive for self-employed agents.

Agents serve as bookkeepers to handle the complex pattern of transportation and hotel reservations that each trip entails. They work directly with airline, steamship, railroad, bus, and car rental companies. They make direct contact with hotels and sightseeing organizations or work indirectly through a receptive operator in the city involved. These arrangements require a great deal of accuracy because mistakes could result in a client being left stranded in a foreign or remote area. After reservations are made, agents write up or obtain tickets, write out itineraries, and send out bills for the reservations involved. They also send out confirmations to airlines, hotels, and other companies.

Travel agents must promote their services. They present slides or movies to social and special interest groups, arrange advertising displays, create Web sites, and suggest company-sponsored trips to business managers.

REQUIREMENTS
High School

A high school diploma is the minimum requirement for becoming a travel agent. If you are interested in pursuing a career as an agent, be certain to take some computer courses, as well as typing or keyboarding courses, in your class schedule. Since much of your work as a travel agent will involve computerized reservation systems, it is important to have effective keyboarding skills and to be comfortable working with computers.

Because being able to communicate clearly with clients is central to this job, any high school course that enhances communication skills, such as English or speech, is a good choice. Proficiency in a foreign language, while not a requirement, might be helpful in many cases, such as when you are working with international travelers. Finally, geography, social studies, and business mathematics are classes that may also help prepare you for various aspects of the travel agent's work.

You can also begin learning about being a travel agent while still in high school by getting a summer or part-time job in travel and tourism. If finding a part-time or summer job in a travel agency proves impossible, you might consider looking for a job as a reservation agent for an airline, rental car agency, or hotel.

Postsecondary Training

Travel courses are available from certain colleges, private vocational schools, and adult education programs in public high schools. Some colleges and universities grant bachelor's and master's degrees in travel and tourism. Although college training is not required for work as a travel agent, it can be very helpful and is expected to become increasingly important. It is predicted that in the future most agents will be college graduates. Travel schools provide basic reservation training and other training related to travel agents' functions, which is help-

ful but not required. Much of the training for this field happens on the job.

A liberal arts or business administration background is recommended for a career in this field. Useful liberal arts courses include foreign languages, geography, English, communications, history, anthropology, political science, art and music appreciation, and literature. Pertinent business courses include transportation, business law, hotel management, marketing, office management, and accounting. As in many other fields, computer skills are increasingly important.

Certification or Licensing

To be able to sell passage on various types of transportation, you must be approved by the conferences of carriers involved. These are the Airlines Reporting Corporation, the International Air Transport Association, and the Cruise Lines International Association. To sell tickets for these individual conferences, you must be clearly established in the travel business and have a good personal and business background. Not all travel agents are authorized to sell passage by all of the above conferences. Naturally, if you wish to sell the widest range of services, you should seek affiliation with all three.

Currently, travel agents are not required to be federally licensed. The following states require some form of registration or licensing: California, Florida, Hawaii, Illinois, Iowa, Ohio, Oregon, Rhode Island, and Washington.

Travel agents may choose to become certified by the Travel Institute, formerly known as the Institute of Certified Travel Agents. The Travel Institute offers certification programs leading to the designations of certified travel associate (CTA) and certified travel counselor (CTC). In order to become a CTA, you must have 18 months of experience as a travel agent and pass a written test. In order to become a CTC, you must have five years of experience, have attained CTA status, take a 12-course program, and pass a final exam. While not a requirement, certification by the Travel Institute will help you progress in your career.

The Travel Institute also offers travel agents a number of other programs such as sales skills development courses and destination specialist courses, which provide a detailed knowledge of various geographic regions of the world.

Other Requirements

The primary requisite for success in the travel field is a sincere interest in travel. Your knowledge of and travel experiences with major tourist centers, various hotels, and local customs and points of interest make you a more effective and convincing source of assistance. Yet the work of travel agents is not one long vacation. They operate in a highly competitive industry.

As a travel agent, you must be able to make quick and accurate use of transportation schedules and tariffs. You must be able to handle addition and subtraction quickly. Almost all agents make use of computers to get the very latest information on rates and schedules and to make reservations.

You will work with a wide range of personalities as a travel agent, so skills in psychology and diplomacy will be important for you to have. You must also be able to generate enthusiasm among your customers and be resourceful in solving any problems that might arise. Knowledge of foreign languages is useful because many customers come from other countries, and you will be in frequent contact with foreign hotels and travel agencies.

EXPLORING

Any type of part-time experience with a travel agency will be helpful if you're interested in pursuing this career. A small agency may welcome help during peak travel seasons or when an agent is away from the office. If your high school or college arranges career conferences, you may be able to invite a speaker from the travel industry. Visits to local travel agents will also provide you with helpful information.

If you are already pursuing a travel or hospitality career in college, you might also consider joining the Future Travel Professionals Club, organized by the American Society of Travel Agents (ASTA). Membership allows you to network with professional members of the ASTA, attend chapter meetings, be eligible for scholarships, and receive two newsletters. For more information contact the ASTA (see sources at the end of this article).

EMPLOYERS

There are about 101,000 travel agents employed in the United States. Agents may work for commercial travel agents, work in the corporate travel department of a large company, or be self-employed. Travel agencies employ more than 8 out of 10 salaried agents. About one-tenth of agents are self-employed.

In addition to the regular travel business, a number of travel jobs are available with oil companies, automobile clubs, and transportation companies. Some jobs in travel are on the staffs of state and local governments seeking to encourage tourism.

STARTING OUT

As you start searching for a career in the travel field, you may begin by working for a company involved with transportation and tourism. Fortunately, a number of positions exist that are particularly appropriate if you are young and have limited work experience. Airlines, for example, hire flight attendants, reservation agents, and ticket clerks. Railroads and cruise line companies also have clerical positions; the rise in their popularity in recent years has resulted in more job opportunities. Those with travel experience may secure positions as tour guides. Organizations and companies with extensive travel operations may hire employees whose main responsibility is making travel arrangements.

Since travel agencies tend to have relatively small staffs, most openings are filled as a result of direct application and personal contact. While evaluating the merits of various travel agencies, you may wish to note whether the agency's owner belongs to ASTA. This trade group may also help in several other ways. It also sponsors the nationwide travel agent proficiency (TAP) test along with the Travel Institute, which is a certification designation specifically designed for entry-level travel agents. This test provides entry-level workers with a competitive edge. It also sponsors adult night school courses in travel agency operation in some metropolitan areas and many online certification courses in travel specialties. Visit ASTA's Web site for further information.

ADVANCEMENT

Advancement opportunities within the travel field are limited to growth in terms of business volume or extent of specialization. Successful agents, for example, may hire additional employees or set up branch offices. A travel agency worker who has held his or her position for a while may be promoted to become a travel assistant. Travel assistants are responsible for answering general questions about transportation, providing current costs of hotel accommodations, and providing other information.

Travel agents may also advance to work as a corporate travel manager. Corporate travel managers work for companies, not travel agencies. They book all business travel for a company's employees.

Travel bureau employees may decide to go into business for themselves. Agents may show their professional status by belonging to ASTA, which requires its members to have three years of satisfactory travel agent experience and approval by at least two carrier conferences.

EARNINGS

Travel agency income comes from commissions paid by hotels, car rental companies, cruise lines, and tour operators. Due to the rising popularity of Internet travel sites, which enable customers to book their own flights, airlines no longer pay commissions to travel agents. This has been a big blow to those in this career, and it is a trend that will probably continue.

Travel agents typically earn a straight salary. Salaries of travel agents ranged from $18,100 to $46,270, with a median annual wage of $29,210. In addition to experience level, the location of the firm is also a factor in how much travel agents earn. Agents working in larger metropolitan areas tend to earn more than their counterparts in smaller cities.

Small travel agencies provide a smaller-than-average number of fringe benefits such as retirement, medical, and life insurance plans. Self-employed agents tend to earn more than those who work for others, although the business risk is greater. Also, a self-employed agent may not see much money for the first year or two, since it often takes time to establish a client base that is large enough to make a profit. Those who own their own businesses may experience large fluctuations in income because the travel business is extremely sensitive to swings in the economy.

One of the benefits of working as a travel agent is the chance to travel at a discounted price. Major airlines offer special agent fares, which are often only 25 percent of regular cost. Hotels, car rental companies, cruise lines, and tour operators also offer reduced rates for travel agents. Agents also get the opportunity to take free or low-cost group tours sponsored by transportation carriers, tour operators, and cruise lines. These trips, called "fam" trips, are designed to familiarize agents with locations and accommodations so that agents can better market them to their clients.

WORK ENVIRONMENT

The job of the travel agent is neither as simple nor as glamorous as some might expect. Travel is a highly competitive field. Since almost every travel agent can offer the client the same service, agents must depend on repeat customers for much of their business. Their reliability, courtesy, and effectiveness in past transactions will determine whether they will get repeat business.

Travel agents also work in an atmosphere of keen competition for referrals. They must resist direct or indirect pressure from travel-related companies that have provided favors in the past (free trips, for example) and book all trips based only on the best interests of clients.

Most agents work a 40-hour week, although this frequently includes working a half-day on Saturday or an occasional evening. During busy seasons (typically from January through June), overtime may be necessary. Agents may receive additional salary for this work or be given compensatory time off.

As they gain experience, agents become more effective. One study revealed that 98 percent of all agents had more than three years' experience in some form of the travel field. Almost half had 20 years experience or more in this area.

OUTLOOK

The U.S. Department of Labor predicts that employment of travel agents will show little or no growth through 2016. Most airlines and other travel suppliers now offer consumers the option of making their own travel arrangements through online reservation services, which are readily accessible through the Internet. Thus, travelers are becoming less dependent upon agents to make travel arrangements for them. The American Society of Travel Agents reports that approximately 21 million consumers were booking their travel arrangements exclusively online as of June 2002. Additionally, airlines have eliminated the flat commission they pay travel agencies. This has reduced the income of many agencies, thereby making them less profitable and less able to hire new travel agents. Since these innovations are recent, their full effect on travel agents has not yet been determined.

However, consumers should continue to spend more on travel and tourism over the next decade, which will help employment prospects for travel agents. There will also be many opportunities to plan tour services for foreign visitors vacationing in the United States, and to arrange frequent trips for businesses with overseas offices. Despite the challenges travel agents face, there are still many people who prefer their services over online booking, as they appreciate the efficiency, value, professional knowledge, and face-to-face contact that travel agents provide.

FOR MORE INFORMATION

Visit the ASTA Web site to read the online pamphlet Becoming a Travel Agent *for a nominal fee.*

American Society of Travel Agents (ASTA)
1101 King Street, Suite 200
Alexandria, VA 22314-2944
Tel: 703-739-2782
Email: askasta@astahq.com
http://www.asta.org

For information regarding the travel industry and certification, contact

The Travel Institute
148 Linden Street, Suite 305
Wellesley, MA 02482-7900
Tel: 800-542-4282
Email: info@thetravelinstitute.com
http://www.icta.com

For information on travel careers in the U.S. government, contact

Society of Government Travel Professionals
4938 Hampden Lane
Bethesda, MD 20814-2914-
Tel: 202-363-7487
Email: info@sgtp.org
http://www.sgtp.org

For general information on the travel industry, contact

Travel Industry Association of America
1100 New York Avenue, NW, Suite 450
Washington, DC 20005-3934
Tel: 202-408-8422
http://www.tia.org

TRUCK DRIVERS

QUICK FACTS

SCHOOL SUBJECTS
Business
Technical/shop

PERSONAL SKILLS
Following instructions
Mechanical/manipulative

WORK ENVIRONMENT
Primarily outdoors
Primarily multiple locations

MINIMUM EDUCATION LEVEL
Apprenticeship

MEDIAN SALARY
$35,048

CERTIFICATION OR LICENSING
Required

OUTLOOK
About as fast as the average

OVERVIEW

Truck drivers generally are distinguished by the distance they travel. *Over-the-road drivers*, also known as *long-distance drivers or tractor-trailer drivers*, haul freight over long distances in large trucks and tractor-trailer rigs that are usually diesel-powered. Depending on the specific operation, over-the-road drivers also load and unload the shipments and make minor repairs to vehicles. *Short-haul drivers* or *pickup and delivery drivers* operate trucks that transport materials, merchandise, and equipment within a limited area, usually a single city or metropolitan area. There are approximately 3.4 million truck drivers employed in the United States.

THE JOB

Truckers drive trucks of all sizes, from small straight trucks and vans to tanker trucks and tractors with multiple trailers. The average tractor-trailer rig is no more than 102 inches wide, excluding the mirrors, 13 feet and six inches tall, and just under 70 feet in length. The engines in these vehicles range from 250 to 600 horsepower.

Over-the-road drivers operate tractor-trailers and other large trucks that are often diesel-powered. These drivers generally haul goods and materials over long distances and frequently drive at night. Whereas many other truck drivers spend a considerable portion of their time loading and unloading materials, over-the-road drivers spend most of their working time driving.

At the terminal or warehouse where they receive their load, drivers get ready for long-distance runs by checking over the vehicle to make sure all the equipment and systems are functioning and that the truck is loaded properly and has the necessary fuel, oil, and safety equipment.

Some over-the-road drivers travel the same routes repeatedly and on a regular schedule. Other companies require drivers to do unscheduled runs and work when dispatchers call with an available job. Some long-distance runs are short enough that drivers can get to the destination, remove the load from the trailer, replace it with another load, and return home all in one day. Many runs, however, take up to a week or longer, with various stops. Some companies assign two drivers to long runs, so that one can sleep while the other drives. This method ensures that the trip will take the shortest amount of time possible.

In addition to driving their trucks long distances, over-the-road drivers have other duties. They must inspect their vehicles before and after trips, prepare reports on accidents, and keep daily logs. They may load and unload some shipments or hire workers to help with these tasks at the destination. Drivers of long-distance moving vans, for example, do more loading and unloading work than most other long-haul drivers. Drivers of vehicle-transport trailer trucks move new automobiles or trucks from manufacturers to dealers and also have additional duties. At plants where the vehicles are made, transport drivers drive new vehicles onto the ramps of transport trailers. They secure the vehicles in place with chains and clamps to prevent them from swaying and rolling. After driving to the destination, the drivers remove the vehicles from the trailers.

Over-the-road drivers must develop a number of skills that differ from the skills needed for operating smaller trucks. Because trailer trucks vary in length and number of wheels, skilled operators of one type of trailer may need to undergo a short training period if they switch to a new type of trailer. Over-the-road drivers must be able to maneuver and judge the position of their trucks and must be able to back their huge trailers into precise positions.

Local truck drivers generally operate the smaller trucks and transport a variety of products. They may travel regular routes or routes that change as needed. Local drivers include delivery workers who supply fresh produce to grocery stores and drivers who deliver gasoline in tank trucks to gas stations. Other local truck drivers, such as those who keep stores stocked with baked goods, may sell their employers' products as well as deliver them to customers along a route. These drivers are known as *route drivers* or *route-sales drivers.*

Often local truck drivers receive their assignments and delivery forms from dispatchers at the company terminal each day. Some drivers load goods or materials on their trucks, but in many situations dockworkers have already loaded the trucks in such a way that the unloading can be accomplished along the route with maximum convenience and efficiency.

Local drivers must be skilled at maneuvering their vehicles through the worst driving conditions, including bad weather and traffic-congested areas. The ability to pull into tight parking spaces, negotiate narrow passageways, and back up to loading docks is essential.

Some drivers have *helpers* who travel with them and assist in unloading at delivery sites, especially if the loads are heavy or bulky or when there are many deliveries scheduled. Drivers of some heavy trucks, such as dump trucks and oil tank trucks, operate mechanical levers, pedals, and other devices that assist with loading and unloading cargo. Drivers of moving vans generally have a crew of helpers to aid in loading and unloading customers' household goods and office equipment.

Once a local driver reaches his or her destination, he or she sometimes obtains a signature acknowledging that the delivery has been made and may collect a payment from the customer. Some drivers serve as intermediaries between the company and its customers by responding to customer complaints and requests.

Each day, local drivers have to make sure that their deliveries have been made correctly. At the end of the day, they turn in their records and the money they collected. Local drivers may also be responsible for doing routine maintenance on their trucks to keep them in good working condition. Otherwise, any mechanical problems are reported to the maintenance department for repair.

REQUIREMENTS
High School

High school students interested in working as truck drivers should take courses in driver training and automobile mechanics. In addition, some bookkeeping, mathematics, and business courses will teach methods that help in keeping accurate records of customer transactions.

Postsecondary Training

Drivers must know and meet the standards set by both state and federal governments for the particular work they do and the type of vehicle they drive. In some companies, new employees can informally learn the skills appropriate for the kind of driving they do from experienced drivers. They may ride with and watch other employees of the company, or they may take a few hours of their own time to learn from an experienced driver. For jobs driving some kinds of trucks, companies require new employees to attend classes that range from a few days to several weeks.

One of the best ways to prepare for a job driving large trucks is to take a tractor-trailer driver training course. Programs vary in the amount of actual driving experience they provide. Programs that are certified by the Professional Truck Driver Institute meet established guidelines for training and generally provide good preparation for drivers. Another way to determine whether programs are adequate is to check with local companies that hire drivers and ask for their recommendations. Completing a certified training program helps potential truck drivers learn specific skills, but it does not guarantee a job. Vehicles and the freight inside trucks can represent a large investment to companies that employ truck drivers. Therefore, they seek to hire responsible and reliable drivers in order to protect their investment. For this reason, many employers set various requirements of their own that exceed state and federal standards.

Certification or Licensing

Truck drivers must meet federal requirements and any requirements established by the state where they are based. All drivers must obtain a state commercial driver's license (CDL). Truck drivers involved in interstate commerce must meet requirements of the U.S. Department of Transportation. They must be at least 21 years old and pass a physical examination that requires good vision and hearing, normal blood pressure, and normal use of arms and legs (unless the applicant qualifies for a waiver). Drivers must then pass physicals every two years and meet other requirements, including a minimum of 20/40 vision in each eye and no diagnosis of insulin-dependent diabetes or epilepsy.

Other Requirements

Many drivers work with little supervision, so they need to have a mature, responsible attitude toward their job. In jobs where drivers deal directly with company customers, it is especially important for the drivers to be pleasant, courteous, and able to communicate well with people. Helping a customer with a complaint can mean the difference between losing and keeping a client.

EXPLORING

High school students interested in becoming truck drivers may be able to gain experience by working as drivers' helpers during summer vacations or in part-time delivery jobs. Many people get useful experience in driving vehicles while they are serving in the armed forces. It may also be helpful to talk with employers of local or over-the-road truck drivers or with the drivers themselves.

The Internet provides a forum for prospective truck drivers to explore their career options. Two online magazines—*Overdrive* (http://www.etrucker.com) and *Land Line Magazine* (http://www.landlinemag.com)—provide a look at issues in the trucking industry and a list of answers to frequently asked questions for people interested in trucking careers.

EMPLOYERS

Over-the-road and local drivers may be employed by either private carriers or for-hire carriers. Food store chains and manufacturing plants that transport their own goods are examples of private carriers. There are two kinds of for-hire carriers: trucking companies serving the general public (common carriers) and trucking firms transporting goods under contract to certain companies (contract carriers).

Drivers who work independently are known as *owner-operators*. They own their own vehicles and often do their own maintenance and repair work. They must find customers who need goods transported, perhaps through personal references or by advertising their services. For example, many drivers find contract jobs through "Internet truck stops," where drivers can advertise their services and companies can post locations of loads they need transported. Some independent drivers establish long-term contracts with just one or two clients, such as trucking companies.

STARTING OUT

Prospective over-the-road drivers can gain commercial driving experience as local truck drivers and then attend a tractor trailer–driver training program. Driving an intercity bus or dump truck is also suitable experience for aspiring over-the-road truck drivers. Many newly hired long-distance drivers start by filling in for regular drivers or helping out when extra trips are necessary. They are assigned regular work when a job opens up.

Many truck drivers hold other jobs before they become truck drivers. Some local drivers start as *drivers' helpers*, loading and unloading trucks and gradually taking over some driving duties. When a better driving position opens up, helpers who have shown they are reliable and responsible may be promoted. Members of the armed forces who have gained appropriate experience may get driving jobs when they are discharged.

Job seekers may apply directly to firms that use drivers. Listings of specific job openings are often posted at local offices of the state employment service and in the classified ads in newspapers. Many jobs, however, are not posted. Looking in the yellow pages under trucking and moving and storage can provide names of specific companies to solicit. Also, large manufacturers and retailing companies sometimes have their own fleets. Many telephone calls, emails, and letters may be required, but they can lead to a potential employer. Personal visits, when appropriate, sometimes get the best results.

ADVANCEMENT

Some over-the-road drivers who stay with their employers advance by becoming *safety supervisors*, *driver supervisors*, or *dispatchers*. Many over-the-road drivers look forward to going into business for themselves by acquiring their own tractor-trailer rigs. This step requires a significant initial investment and a continuing good income to cover expenses. Like many other small business owners, independent drivers sometimes have a hard time financially. Those who are their own mechanics and have formal business training are in the best position to do well.

Local truck drivers can advance by learning to drive specialized kinds of trucks or by acquiring better schedules or other job conditions. Some may move into positions as dispatchers and, with sufficient experience, they eventually become supervisors or terminal managers. Other local drivers decide to become over-the-road drivers to receive higher wages.

EARNINGS

Wages of truck drivers vary according to their employer, size of the truck they drive, product being hauled, geographical region, and other factors. Drivers who are employed by for-hire carriers have higher earnings than those who work independently or for private carriers.

Pay rates for over-the-road truck drivers are often figured using a cents-per-mile rate. Most companies pay between 20 and 30 cents per mile, but large companies are advertising higher rates to attract good drivers. Drivers employed by J. B. Hunt, the nation's largest publicly held trucking company, can earn up to 41 cents a mile and earn an average of $1,000 a week.

Tractor-trailer drivers usually have the highest earnings; average hourly pay generally increases with the size of the truck. Drivers in the South have lower earnings than those in the Northeast and West. The U.S. Department of Labor reports that median hourly earnings of heavy truck and tractor-trailer drivers were $16.85 in 2006 ($35,048 a year). Wages ranged from less than $10.80 to more than $25.39 an hour (from $22,464 to $52,811 a year for full-time work). Median hourly earnings of light or delivery services truck drivers were $12.17, and wages ranged from less than $7.47 to more than $21.23 an hour ($15,538 to $44,158 a year). Median hourly earnings of driver/sales workers, including commission, were $9.99, and wages ranged from less than $6.19 to more than $20.30 an hour ($12,875 to $42,224 a year).

In addition to their wages, the majority of truck drivers receive benefits, many of which are determined by agreements between their unions and company management. The benefits may include health insurance coverage, pension plans, paid vacation days, and work uniforms.

WORK ENVIRONMENT

Although there is work for truck drivers in even the smallest towns, most jobs are located in and around larger metropolitan areas. About 25 percent of all drivers work for for-hire carriers, and another 25 percent work for private carriers. Less than 10 percent are self-employed.

Even with modern improvements in cab design, driving trucks is often a tiring job. Although some local drivers work 40-hour weeks, many work eight hours a day, six days a week, or more. Some drivers, such as those who bring food to grocery stores, often work at night or very early in the morning. Drivers who must load and unload their trucks may do a lot of lifting, stooping, and bending.

It is common for over-the-road truck drivers to work at least 50 hours a week. However, federal regulations require that drivers cannot be on duty for more than 60 hours in any seven-day period. Furthermore, after drivers have driven for 10 hours, they must be off duty for at least eight hours before they can drive again. Drivers often work the maximum allowed time to complete long runs in as little time as possible. In fact, most drivers drive 10 to 12 hours per day and make sure they have proper rest periods. A driver usually covers between 550 and 650 miles daily. The sustained driving, particularly at night, can be fatiguing, boring, and sometimes very stressful, as when traffic or weather conditions are bad.

Local drivers may operate on schedules that easily allow a social and family life, but long-distance drivers often find that difficult. They may spend a considerable amount of time away from their homes and families, including weekends and holidays. After they try it, many people find they do not want this way of life. On the other hand, some people love the lifestyle of the over-the-road driver. Many families are able to find ways to work around the schedule of a truck-driving spouse. In some cases, the two people assigned to a long-distance run are a husband and wife team.

OUTLOOK

The employment of truck drivers is expected to increase about as fast as the average rate for all other occupations through 2016. Employment of light and heavy truck drivers will be faster than the average, because of continually increasing amounts of consumer goods that need to be transported quickly and safely. Employment of driver/sales workers will be slower than the average as companies move more sales positions into central offices.

The need for trucking services is directly linked to the growth of the nation's economy. During economic downturns, when the pace of business slows, some drivers may receive fewer assignments and thus have lower earnings, or they may be laid off. Drivers employed in some vital industries, such as food distribution, are less affected by an economic recession. On the other hand, people who own and operate their own trucks usually suffer the most.

A large number of driver jobs become available each year. Most openings develop when experienced drivers transfer to other fields or leave the workforce entirely. There is a considerable amount of turnover in the field. Beginners are able to get many of these jobs. Competition is expected to remain strong for the more desirable jobs, such as those with large companies or the easiest routes.

FOR MORE INFORMATION

For further information and literature about a career as a truck driver, contact the following organizations:

American Trucking Associations
950 North Glebe Road, Suite 210
Arlington, VA 22203-1824
Tel: 703-838-1700
http://www.truckline.com

Professional Truck Driver Institute
555 E. Braddock Road Road
Alexandria, VA 22314-4654
Tel: 703-647-7015http://www.ptdi.org

☐ VETERINARY TECHNICIANS

OVERVIEW

Veterinary technicians provide support and assistance to veterinarians. They work in a variety of environments, including zoos, animal hospitals, clinics, private practices, kennels, and laboratories. Their work may involve large or small animals or both. Although most veterinary technicians work with domestic animals, some profes-

QUICK FACTS

SCHOOL SUBJECTS
Biology
Chemistry

PERSONAL SKILLS
Helping/teaching
Technical/scientific

WORK ENVIRONMENT
Primarily indoors
Primarily one location

MINIMUM EDUCATION LEVEL
Associate's degree

MEDIAN SALARY
$26,790

CERTIFICATION OR LICENSING
Required by certain states

OUTLOOK
Much faster than the average

sional settings may require treating exotic or endangered species. There are approximately 71,000 veterinary technicians employed in the United States.

THE JOB

Many pet owners depend on veterinarians to maintain the health and well-being of their pets. Veterinary clinics and private practices are the primary settings for animal care. In assisting veterinarians, veterinary technicians play an integral role in the care of animals within this particular environment.

A veterinary technician is the person who performs much of the laboratory testing procedures commonly associated with veterinary care. In fact, approximately 50 percent of a veterinary technician's duties involve laboratory testing. Laboratory assignments usually include taking and developing X rays, performing parasitology tests, and examining various samples taken from the animal's body, such as blood and stool. A veterinary technician may also assist the veterinarian with necropsies in an effort to determine the cause of an animal's death.

In a clinic or private practice, a veterinary technician assists the veterinarian with surgical procedures. This generally entails preparing the animal for surgery by shaving the incision area and applying a topical antibacterial agent. Surgical anesthesia is administered and controlled by the veterinary technician. Throughout the surgical process, the technician tracks the surgical instruments and monitors the animal's vital signs. If an animal is very ill and has no chance for survival, or an overcrowded animal shelter is unable to find a home for a donated or stray animal, the veterinary technician may be required to assist in euthanizing it.

During routine examinations and checkups, veterinary technicians will help restrain the animals. They may perform ear cleaning and nail clipping procedures as part of regular animal care. Outside the examination and surgery rooms, veterinary technicians perform additional duties. In most settings, they record, replenish, and maintain pharmaceutical equipment and other supplies.

Veterinary technicians also may work in a zoo. Here, job duties, such as laboratory testing, are quite similar, but practices are more specialized. Unlike in private practice, the *zoo veterinary technician* is not required to explain treatment to pet owners; however, he or she may have to discuss an animal's treatment or progress with zoo veterinarians, zoo curators, and other zoo professionals. A zoo veterinary technician's work also may differ from private practice in that it may be necessary for the technician to observe the animal in its habitat, which could require working outdoors. Additionally, zoo veterinary technicians usually work with exotic or endangered species. This is a very competitive and highly desired area of practice in the veterinary technician field. There are only a few zoos in each state; thus, a limited number of job opportunities exist within these zoos. To break into this area of practice, veterinary technicians must be among the best in the field.

Veterinary technicians also work in research. Most research opportunities for veterinary technicians are in academic environments with veterinary medicine or medical science programs. Again, laboratory testing may account for many of the duties; however, the veterinary technicians participate in very important animal research projects from start to finish.

Technicians are also needed in rural areas. Farmers require veterinary services for the care of farm animals such as pigs, cows, horses, dogs, cats, sheep, mules, and chickens. It is often essential for the veterinarian and technician to drive to the farmer's residence because animals are usually treated on-site.

Another area in which veterinary technicians work is that of animal training, such as at an obedience school or with show business animals being trained for the circus or movies. Veterinary technicians may also be employed in information systems technology, where information on animals is compiled and provided to the public via the Internet.

No matter what the setting, a veterinary technician must be an effective communicator and proficient in basic computer applications. In clinical or private practice, it is usually the veterinary technician who conveys and explains treatment and subsequent animal care to the animal's owner. In research and laboratory work, the veterinary technician must record and discuss results among colleagues. In most practical veterinary settings, the veterinary technician must record various information on a computer.

REQUIREMENTS
High School

Veterinary technicians must have a high school diploma. High school students who excel at math and science have a strong foundation on which to build. Those who have had pets or who simply love animals and would like to work with them also fit the profile of a veterinary technician.

Postsecondary Training

The main requirement is the completion of a two- to four-year college-based accredited program. Upon graduation, the student receives an associate's or bachelor's degree. Currently, there are more than 130 accredited programs in the United States. A few states do their own accrediting, using the American Veterinary Medical Association (AVMA) and associated programs as benchmarks.

Most accredited programs offer thorough course work and preparatory learning opportunities to the aspiring veterinary technician. Typical courses include mathematics, chemistry, humanities, biological science, communications, microbiology, liberal arts, ethics/jurisprudence, and basic computers.

Once the students complete this framework, they move on to more specialized courses. Students take advanced classes in animal nutrition, animal care and management, species/breed identification, veterinary anatomy/physiology, medical terminology, radiography and other clinical procedure courses, animal husbandry, parasitology, laboratory animal care, and large/small animal nursing.

Veterinary technicians must be prepared to assist in surgical procedures. In consideration of this, accredited programs offer surgical nursing courses. In these courses, a student learns to identify and use surgical instruments, administer anesthesia, and monitor animals during and after surgery.

In addition to classroom study, accredited programs offer practical courses. Hands-on education and training are commonly achieved through a clinical practicum, or internship, where the student has the opportunity to work in a clinical veterinary setting. During this period, a student is continuously evaluated by the participating veterinarian and encouraged to apply the knowledge and skills learned.

Certification or Licensing

Although the AVMA determines the majority of the national codes for veterinary technicians, state codes and laws vary. Most states offer registration or certification, and the majority of these states require graduation from an AVMA-accredited program as a prerequisite for taking the examination, known as the National Veterinary Technician (NVT) exam. Most colleges and universities assist graduates with registration and certification arrangements. To keep abreast of new technology and applications in the field, practicing veterinary technicians may be required to complete a determined number of annual continuing education courses.

Other Requirements

As a veterinarian technician, you should be able to meet, talk, and work well with a variety of people. An ability to communicate with the animal owner is as important as diagnostic skills.

In clinical or private practice, it is usually the veterinary technician who conveys and explains treatment and subsequent animal care to the animal's owner. Technicians may have to help euthanize (that is, humanely kill) an animal that is very sick or severely injured and cannot get well. As a result, they must be emotionally stable and help pet owners deal with their grief and loss.

EXPLORING

High school students can acquire exposure to the veterinary field by working with animals in related settings. For example, a high school student may be able to work as a part-time animal attendant or receptionist in a private veterinary practice. Paid or volunteer positions may be available at kennels, animal shelters, and training

schools. However, direct work with animals in a zoo is unlikely for high school students.

EMPLOYERS

Veterinary technicians are employed by veterinary clinics, animal hospitals, zoos, schools, universities, and animal training programs. In rural areas, farmers hire veterinary technicians as well as veterinarians. Jobs for veterinary technicians in zoos are relatively few, since there are only a certain number of zoos across the country. Those veterinary technicians with an interest in research should seek positions at schools with academic programs for medical science or veterinary medicine. The majority of veterinary technicians find employment in animal hospitals or private veterinary practices, which exist all over the country. However, there are more job opportunities for veterinary technicians in more densely populated areas.

STARTING OUT

Veterinary technicians who complete an accredited program and become certified or registered by the state in which they plan to practice are often able to receive assistance in finding a job through their college's placement offices. Students who have completed internships may receive job offers from the place where they interned.

Veterinary technician graduates may also learn of clinic openings through classified ads in newspapers. Opportunities in zoos and research facilities are usually listed in specific industry periodals such as *Veterinary Technician Magazine.*

ADVANCEMENT

Where a career as a veterinary technician leads is entirely up to the individual. Opportunities are unlimited. With continued education, veterinary technicians can move into allied fields such as veterinary medicine, nursing, medical technology, radiology, and pharmacology. By completing two more years of college and receiving a bachelor's degree, a *veterinary technician* can become a *veterinary technologist.* Advanced degrees can open the doors to a variety of specialized fields. There are currently efforts to standardize requirements for veterinary technicians. A national standard would broaden the scope of educational programs and may create more opportunities in instruction for veterinary professionals with advanced degrees.

EARNINGS

Earnings are generally low for veterinary technicians in private practices and clinics, but pay scales are steadily climbing due to the increasing demand. Better-paying jobs are in zoos and in research. Those fields of practice are very competitive (especially zoos) and only a small percentage of highly qualified veterinary technicians are employed in them.

Most veterinary technicians are employed in private or clinical practice and research. The U.S. Department of Labor reports that the median annual salary for veterinary technicians and technologists was $26,790 in 2006. The lowest-paid 10 percent made less than $18,283 annually, and the highest-paid 10 percent made more than $38,854 annually. Earnings vary depending on practice setting, geographic location, level of education, and years of experience. Benefits vary and depend on each employer's policies.

WORK ENVIRONMENT

Veterinary technicians generally work 40-hour weeks, which may include a few long weekdays and alternated or rotated Saturdays. Hours may fluctuate, as veterinary technicians may need to have their schedules adjusted to accommodate emergency work.

A veterinary technician must be prepared for emergencies. In field or farm work, they often have to overcome weather conditions in treating the animal. Injured animals can be very dangerous, and veterinary technicians have to exercise extreme caution when caring for them. A veterinary technician also handles animals that are diseased or infested with parasites. Some of these conditions, such as ringworm, are contagious, so the veterinary technician must understand how these conditions are transferred to humans and take precautions to prevent the spread of diseases.

People who become veterinary technicians care about animals. For this reason, maintaining an animal's well-being or helping to cure an ill animal is very rewarding work. In private practice, technicians get to know the animals they care for. This provides the opportunity to actually see the animals' progress. In other areas, such as zoo work, veterinary technicians work with very interesting, sometimes endangered, species. This work can be challenging and rewarding in the sense that they are helping to save a species and continuing efforts to educate people about these animals. Veterinary technicians who work in research gain satisfaction from knowing their work contributes to promoting both animal and human health.

OUTLOOK

Employment for veterinary technicians will grow much faster than the average for all other occupations through 2016, according to the U.S. Department of Labor. Veterinary medicine is a field that is not adversely affected by the economy, so it does offer stability. The public's love for pets coupled with higher disposable incomes will encourage continued demand for workers in this occupation.

FOR MORE INFORMATION

For more information on careers, schools, and resources, contact the following organizations:

American Veterinary Medical Association
1931 North Meacham Road, Suite 100
Schaumburg, IL 60173-4360
Tel: 847-925-8070
Email: avmainfo@avma.org
http://www.avma.org

Association of Zoo Veterinary Technicians
http://www.azvt.org

National Association of Veterinary Technicians in America
50 S. Pickett Street, Suite 110
Alexandria, VA 22304-7207
Tel: 703-740-8737
http://www.navta.net

For information on veterinary careers in Canada, contact
Canadian Veterinary Medical Association
339 Booth Street
Ottawa, ON K1R 7K1 Canada
Tel: 613-236-1162
Email: admin@cvma-acmv.org
http://www.canadianveterinarians.net

☐ WASTEWATER TREATMENT PLANT OPERATORS AND TECHNICIANS

OVERVIEW

Wastewater treatment plant operators control, monitor, and maintain the equipment and treatment processes in wastewater (sewage) treatment plants. They remove or neutralize the chemicals, solid materials, and organisms in wastewater so that the water is not polluted when it is returned to the environment. There are approximately 111,000 water and liquid waste treatment plant operators currently working in the United States.

Wastewater treatment plant technicians work under the supervision of wastewater treatment plant operators. Technicians take samples and monitor treatment to ensure treated water is safe for its intended use. Depending on the level of treatment, water is used for human consumption or for nonconsumptive purposes, such as field irrigation or discharge into natural water sources. Some technicians also work in labs, where they collect and analyze water samples and maintain lab equipment.

THE JOB

Wastewater from homes, public buildings, and industrial plants is transported through sewer pipes to treatment plants. The wastes include both organic and inorganic substances, some of which may be highly toxic, such as lead and mercury. Wastewater treatment plant operators and technicians regulate the flow of incoming wastewater by adjusting pumps, valves, and other equipment, either manually or through remote controls. They keep track of the various meters and gauges that monitor the purification processes and indicate how the equipment is operating. Using the information from these instruments, they control the pumps, engines, and generators that move the untreated water through the processes of filtration, settling, aeration, and sludge digestion. They also operate chemical-feeding devices, collect water samples, and perform laboratory tests, so that the proper level of chemicals, such as chlorine, is maintained in the wastewater. Technicians may record instrument readings and other information in logs of plant operations. These logs are supervised and monitored by operators. Computers are commonly used to monitor and regulate wastewater treatment equipment and processes. Specialized software allows operators to store and analyze data, which is particularly useful when something in the system malfunctions.

The duties of operators and technicians vary somewhat with the size and type of plant where they work. In small plants one person per shift may be able to do all the necessary routine tasks. But in larger plants, there may be a number of operators, each specializing in just a few activities and working as part of a team that includes engineers, chemists, technicians, mechanics, helpers, and other employees. Some facilities are equipped to handle both wastewater treatment and treatment of the clean water supplied to municipal water systems, and plant operators may be involved with both functions.

QUICK FACTS

SCHOOL SUBJECTS
Chemistry
Mathematics

PERSONAL SKILLS
Mechanical/manipulative
Technical/scientific

WORK ENVIRONMENT
Indoors and outdoors
Primarily one location

MINIMUM EDUCATION LEVEL
Some postsecondary training

MEDIAN SALARY
$36,070

CERTIFICATION OR LICENSING
Required by certain states

OUTLOOK
Faster thanthe average

Other routine tasks that plant operators and technicians perform include maintenance and minor repairs on equipment such as valves and pumps. They may use common hand tools such as wrenches and pliers and special tools adapted specifically for the equipment. In large facilities, they also direct attendants and helpers who take care of some routine tasks and maintenance work. The accumulated residues of wastes from the water must be removed from the plant, and operators may dispose of these materials. Some of this final product, or sludge, can be reclaimed for uses such as soil conditioners or fuel for the production of electricity.

Technicians may also survey streams and study basin areas to determine water availability. To assist the engineers they work with, technicians prepare graphs, tables, sketches, and diagrams to illustrate survey data. They file plans and documents, answer public inquiries, help train new personnel, and perform various other support duties.

Plant operators and technicians sometimes have to work under emergency conditions, such as when heavy rains flood the sewer pipes, straining the treatment plant's capacity, or when there is a chlorine gas leak or oxygen deficiency in the treatment tanks. When a serious problem arises, they must work quickly and effectively to solve it as soon as possible.

REQUIREMENTS

High School

A high school diploma or its equivalent is required for a job as a wastewater treatment plant operator or technician, and additional specialized technical training is generally preferred for both positions. A desirable background for this work includes high school courses in chemistry, biology, mathematics, and computers; welding or electrical training may be helpful as well. Other characteristics that employers look for include mechanical aptitude and the ability to perform mathematical computations easily. You should be able to work basic algebra and statistics problems. Future technicians may be required to prepare reports containing statistics and other scientific documentation. Communications, statistics, and algebra are useful for this career path. Such courses enable the technician to prepare graphs, tables, sketches, and diagrams to illustrate surveys for the operators and engineers they support.

Postsecondary Training

As treatment plants become more technologically complex, workers who have previous training in the field are increasingly at an advantage. Specialized education in wastewater technology is available in two-year programs that lead to an associate's degree and one-year programs that lead to a certificate. Such programs, which are offered at some community and junior colleges and vocational-technical institutes, provide a good general knowledge of water pollution control and will prepare you to become an operator or technician. Beginners must still learn the details of operations at the plant where they work, but their specialized training increases their chances for better positions and later promotions.

Many operators and technicians acquire the skills they need during a period of on-the-job training. Newly hired workers often begin as attendants or operators-in-training. Working under the supervision of experienced operators, they pick up knowledge and skills by observing other workers and by doing routine tasks such as recording meter readings, collecting samples, and general cleaning and plant maintenance. In larger plants, trainees may study supplementary written material pro-

vided at the plant, or they may attend classes in which they learn plant operations.

Wastewater treatment plant operators and technicians often have various opportunities to continue learning about their field. Most state water pollution control agencies offer training courses for people employed in the field. Subjects covered by these training courses include principles of treatment processes and process control, odors and their control, safety, chlorination, sedimentation, biological oxidation, sludge treatment and disposal, and flow measurements. Correspondence courses on related subject areas also are available. Some employers help pay tuition for workers who take related college-level courses in science or engineering.

Certification or Licensing

Workers who control operations at wastewater treatment plants must be certified by most states. To obtain certification, operators must pass an examination given by the state. There is no nationwide standard, so different states administer different tests. Many states issue several classes of certification, depending on the size of the plant the worker is qualified to control. Certification may be beneficial even if it is not a requirement and no matter how much experience a worker already has. In Illinois, for example, operators who have the minimum state certification level are automatically eligible for higher pay than those without any certification, although certification is not a requirement of employment.

Other Requirements

Operators and technicians must be familiar with the provisions of the Federal Water Pollution Control Act (Clean Water Act) and various state and local regulations that apply to their work. Whenever they become responsible for more complex processes and equipment, they must become acquainted with a wider scope of guidelines and regulations. In larger cities and towns especially, job applicants may have to take a civil service exam or other tests that assess their aptitudes and abilities.

EXPLORING

It may be possible to arrange to visit a wastewater treatment plant to observe its operations. It can also be helpful to investigate courses and requirements of any programs in wastewater technology or environmental resources programs offered by a local technical school or college. Part-time or summer employment as a helper in a wastewater treatment plant could be a very helpful experience, but such a job may be hard to find. However, a job in any kind of machine shop can provide you with an opportunity to become familiar with handling machinery and common tools.

Ask wastewater plant operators or technicians in your city if you can interview them about their jobs. Learning about water conservation and water quality in general can be useful. Government agencies or citizen groups dedicated to improving water quality or conserving water can educate you about water quality and supply in your area.

EMPLOYERS

Three-quarters of the approximately 111,000 wastewater treatment plant operators in the United States are employed by local governments; others work for the federal government, utility companies, or private sanitary services that operate under contracts with local governments. Jobs are located throughout the country, with the greatest numbers found in areas with high populations.

Wastewater treatment plant operators and technicians can find jobs with state or federal water pollution control agencies, where they monitor plants and provide technical assistance. Examples of such agencies are the Army Corps of Engineers and the Environmental Protection Agency. These jobs normally require vocational-technical school or community college training. Other experienced wastewater workers find employment with industrial wastewater treatment plants, companies that sell wastewater treatment equipment and chemicals, large utilities, consulting firms, or vocational-technical schools.

STARTING OUT

Graduates of most postsecondary technical programs and some high schools can get help in locating job openings from the placement office of the school they attended. Another source of information is the local office of the state employment service. Job seekers may also directly contact state and local water pollution control agencies and the personnel offices of wastewater treatment facilities in desired locations.

In some plants, a person must first work as a wastewater treatment plant technician before becoming an operator or working in a supervisory position. Wastewater treatment plant technicians have many of the same duties as a plant operator but less responsibility. They inspect, study, and sample existing water treatment systems and evaluate new structures for efficacy and safety. Support work and instrumentation reading make up the bulk of the technician's day.

The Internet has become a useful resource for finding job leads. Professional associations, such as the Water Environment Federation (http://www.wef.org), offer job listings in the wastewater field as part of their Web site. Such sites are a good place for someone getting started in the field, as they also list internship or trainee positions available. Also, an Internet search using the words "wastewater treatment plant operator or technician" will generate a list of Web sites that may contain job postings and internship opportunities.

ADVANCEMENT

As operators gain skills and experience, they are assigned tasks that involve more responsibility for more complex activities. Some technicians advance to become operators. Some operators advance to become *plant supervisors* or *plant superintendents*. The qualifications that superintendents need are related to the size and complexity of the plant. In smaller plants, experienced operators with some postsecondary training may be promoted to superintendent positions. In larger plants, educational requirements are increasing along with the sophistication and complexity of their systems, and superintendents usually have bachelor's degrees in engineering or science.

Some operators and technicians advance by transferring to a related job. Such jobs may require additional schooling or training to specialize in water pollution control, commercial wastewater equipment sales, or teaching wastewater treatment in a vocational or technical school.

EARNINGS

Salaries of wastewater treatment plant operators and technicians vary depending on factors such as the size of the plant, the workers' job responsibilities, and their level of certification. According to the U.S. Department of Labor, water and liquid waste treatment plant operators earned median annual salaries of $36,070 in 2006. The lowest-paid 10 percent earned $21,860 or less, while the highest-paid 10 percent earned $55,120 or more a year. In local government, plant operators earned a median salary of $36,200 in 2006.

In addition to their pay, most operators and technicians receive benefits such as life and health insurance, a pension plan, and reimbursement for education and training related to their job.

WORK ENVIRONMENT

In small towns, plant operators may only work part time or may handle other duties as well as wastewater treatment. The size and type of plant also determine the range of duties. In larger plants with many employees, operators and technicians usually perform more specialized functions. In some cases, they may be responsible for monitoring only a single process. In smaller plants, workers likely will have a broader range of responsibilities. Wastewater treatment plants operate 24 hours a day, every day of the year. Operators and technicians usually work one of three eight-hour shifts, often on a rotating basis so that employees share the evening and night work. Overtime is often required during emergencies.

The work takes operators and technicians both indoors and outdoors. They must contend with noisy machinery and may have to tolerate unpleasant odors, despite the use of chlorine and other chemicals to control odors. The job involves moving about, stooping, reaching, and climbing. Operators and technicians often get their clothes dirty. Slippery sidewalks, dangerous gases, and malfunctioning equipment are potential hazards on the job, but by following safety guidelines, workers can minimize their risk of injury.

OUTLOOK

Employment in this field is expected to grow faster than the average for all occupations through 2016. The number of job applicants in this field is generally low due to the unclean and physically demanding nature of the work. However, this relative lack of competition means that you can enter the field with ease, given you have adequate experience. The growth in demand for wastewater treatment will be related to the overall growth of the nation's population and economy. New treatment plants will probably be built, and existing ones will be upgraded, requiring additional trained personnel to manage their operations. Other openings will arise when experienced workers retire or transfer to new occupations. Operators and technicians with formal training will have the best chances for new positions and promotions.

Workers in wastewater treatment plants are rarely laid off, even during a recession, because wastewater treatment is essential to public health and welfare. In the future more wastewater professionals will probably be employed by private companies that contract to manage treatment plants for local governments.

FOR MORE INFORMATION

For current information on the field of wastewater management, contact:

American Water Works Association
6666 West Quincy Avenue
Denver, CO 80235-3098
Tel: 303-794-7711
http://www.awwa.org

For information on education and training, contact the following organizations:

Environmental Careers Opportunities, Inc.
700 Graves Street
Charlottesville, VA 22902-5722
Tel: 800-315-9777
http://www.ecojobs.com

National Environmental, Safety and Health Training Association
PO Box 10321
Phoenix, AZ 85064-0321
Tel: 602-956-6099
http://www.neshta.org

For career information, contact or visit the following Web site:

Water Environment Federation
601 Wythe Street
Alexandria, VA 22314-1994
Tel: 800-666-0206
http://www.wef.org

WEBMASTERS

OVERVIEW

Webmasters design, implement, and maintain Internet Web sites for corporations, educational institutions, not-for-profit organizations, government agencies, or other institutions. Webmasters should have working knowledge of network configurations, interface, graphic design, software development, business, writing, marketing, and project management. Because the function of a webmaster encompasses so many different responsibilities, the position is often held by a team of individuals in a large organization.

THE JOB

Because the idea of designing and maintaining a Web site is relatively new, there is no complete, definitive job description for webmasters. Many of their job responsibilities depend on the goals and needs of the particular organization for which they work. There are, however, some basic duties that are common to almost all webmasters.

Webmasters, specifically site managers, first secure space on the Web for the site they are developing. This is done by contracting with an Internet service provider. The provider serves as a sort of storage facility for the organization's online information, usually charging a set monthly fee for a specified amount of megabyte space. The webmaster may also be responsible for establishing a uniform resource locator, or URL, for the Web site he or she is developing. The URL serves as the site's online "address" and must be registered with InterNIC, the Web URL registration service.

The webmaster is responsible for developing the actual Web site for his or her organization. In some cases, this may involve actually writing the text content of the pages. More commonly, however, the webmaster is given the text to be used and is merely responsible for programming it in such a way that it can be displayed on a Web page. In larger companies webmasters specialize in content, adaptation, and presentation of data.

In order for text to be displayed on a Web page, it must be formatted using hypertext markup language (HTML). HTML is a system of coding text so that the computer that is "reading" it knows how to display it. For example, text could be coded to be a certain size or color or to be italicized or boldface. Paragraphs, line breaks, alignment, and margins are other examples of text attributes that must be coded in HTML.

Although it is less and less common, some webmasters code text manually, by actually typing the various commands into the body of the text. This method is time consuming, however, and mistakes are easily made. More often, webmasters use a software program that automatically codes text. Some word-processing programs, such as WordPerfect, even offer HTML options.

Along with coding the text, the webmaster must lay out the elements of the Web site in such a way that it is visually pleasing, well organized, and easy to navigate. He or she may use various colors, background patterns, images, tables, or charts. These graphic elements can come from image files already on the Web, software clip-art files, or images scanned into the computer with an electronic scanner. In some cases, when an organization is using the Web site to promote its product or service, the webmaster may work with a marketing specialist or department to develop a page.

Some Web sites have several directories or "layers." That is, an organization may have several Web pages, organized in a sort of "tree," with its home page connected, via hypertext links, to other pages, which may in turn be linked to other pages. The webmaster is responsible for organizing the pages in such a way that a visitor can easily browse through them and find what he or she is looking for. Such webmasters are called programmers

QUICK FACTS

SCHOOL SUBJECTS
Computer science
Mathematics

PERSONAL SKILLS
Communication/ideas
Technical/scientific

WORK ENVIRONMENT
Primarily indoors
Primarily one location

MINIMUM EDUCATION LEVEL
Some postsecondary training

MEDIAN SALARY
$46,480

CERTIFICATION OR LICENSING
Voluntary

OUTLOOK
Much faster than the average

and developers; they are also responsible for creating Web tools and special Web functionality.

For webmasters who work for organizations that have several different Web sites, one responsibility may be making sure that the "style" or appearance of all the pages is the same. This is often referred to as "house style." In large organizations, such as universities, where many different departments may be developing and maintaining their own pages, it is especially important that the webmaster monitor these pages to ensure consistency and conformity to the organization's requirements. In almost every case, the webmaster has the final authority for the content and appearance of his or her organization's Web site. He or she must carefully edit, proofread, and check the appearance of every page.

Besides designing and setting up Web sites, most webmasters are charged with maintaining and updating existing sites. Most sites contain information that changes regularly. Some change daily or even hourly. Depending on his or her employer and the type of Web site, the webmaster may spend a good deal of time updating and remodeling the page. He or she is also responsible for ensuring that the hyperlinks contained within the Web site lead to the sites they should. Since it is common for links to change or become obsolete, the webmaster usually performs a link check every few weeks.

Other job duties vary, depending on the employer and the position. Some try to make sites work faster and test, update, or fix parts of the site that need improvement. Most webmasters are responsible for receiving and answering email messages from visitors to the organization's Web site. Some webmasters keep logs and create reports on when and how often their pages are visited and by whom. Depending on the company, Web sites count anywhere from 300 to 1.4 billion visits, or "hits," a month. Some create and maintain order forms or online "shopping carts" that allow visitors to the Web site to purchase products or services. Some may train other employees on how to create or update Web pages. Finally, webmasters may be responsible for developing and adhering to a budget for their departments.

REQUIREMENTS

High School

High school students who are interested in becoming webmasters should take as many computer science classes as they can. Mathematics classes are also helpful. Finally, because writing skills are important in this career, English classes are good choices.

Postsecondary Training

A number of community colleges, colleges, and universities offer classes and certificate programs for webmasters, but there is no standard educational path or requirement for becoming a webmaster. While many have bachelor's degrees in computer science, information systems, or computer programming, liberal arts degrees, such as English, are not uncommon. There are also webmasters who have degrees in engineering, mathematics, and marketing.

Certification or Licensing

There is strong debate within the industry regarding certification. Some, mostly corporate chief executive officers, favor certification. They view certification as a way to gauge an employee's skill and expertise. Others argue, however, that it is nearly impossible to test knowledge of technology that is constantly changing and improving. Despite the split of opinion, webmaster certification

programs are available at many colleges, universities, and technical schools throughout the United States. Programs vary in length, anywhere from three weeks to nine months or more. Topics covered include client/server technology, Web development, programs, and software and hardware. The International Webmasters Association and World Organization of Webmasters also offer voluntary certification programs.

Should webmasters be certified? Though it's currently not a prerequisite for employment, certification can only enhance a candidate's chance at landing a webmaster position.

What most webmasters have in common is a strong knowledge of computer technology. Most people who enter this field are already well versed in computer operating systems, programming languages, computer graphics, and Internet standards. When considering candidates for the position of webmaster, employers usually require at least two years of experience with World Wide Web technologies. In some cases, employers require that candidates already have experience in designing and maintaining Web sites. It is, in fact, most common for someone to move into the position of webmaster from another computer-related job in the same organization.

Other Requirements

Webmasters should be creative. It is important for a Web page to be designed well in order to attract attention. Good writing skills and an aptitude for marketing are also excellent qualities for anyone considering a career in Web site design.

EXPLORING

One of the easiest ways to learn about what a webmaster does is to spend time surfing the Web. By examining a variety of Web sites to see how they look and operate, you can begin to get a feel for what goes into a home page.

An even better way to explore this career is to design your own personal Web page. Many Internet servers offer their users the option of designing and maintaining a personal Web page for a very low fee. A personal page can contain virtually anything that you want to include, from snapshots of friends to audio files of favorite music to hypertext links to other favorite sites.

EMPLOYERS

The majority of webmasters working today are full-time employees, according to *Interactive Week*. They are employed by Web design companies, businesses, schools or universities, not-for-profit organizations, government agencies—in short, any organization that requires a presence on the Web. Webmasters may also work as freelancers or operate their own Web design businesses.

STARTING OUT

Most people become webmasters by moving into the position from another computer-related position within the same company. Since most large organizations already use computers for various functions, they may employ a person or several people to serve as computer "specialists." If these organizations decide to develop their own Web sites, they frequently assign the task to one of these employees who is already experienced with the computer system. Often, the person who ultimately becomes an organization's webmaster at first just takes on the job in addition to his or her other, already established duties.

Another way that individuals find jobs in this field is through online postings of job openings. Many companies post webmaster position openings online because the candidates they hope to attract are very likely to use the Internet for a job search. Therefore, the prospective webmaster should use the Web to check job-related newsgroups. He or she might also use a Web search engine to locate openings.

ADVANCEMENT

Experienced webmasters employed by a large organization may be able to advance to the position of *chief Web officer*. Chief Web officers supervise a team of webmasters and are responsible for every aspect of a company's presence on the Web. Others might advance by starting their own business, designing Web sites on a contractual basis for several clients rather than working exclusively for one organization.

Opportunities for webmasters of the future are endless due to the continuing development of online technology. As understanding and use of the World Wide Web increase, there may be new or expanded job duties in the future for individuals with expertise in this field.

EARNINGS

According to the U.S. Department of Labor, the median salary for webmasters was between $46,480 and $78,060 a year, but pay ranged from less than $36,2600 to $100,000 or more. In some cases, the demand for webmasters is so great that some companies are offering stock options, sign-on bonuses, and other perks, in addition to high salaries. However, many webmasters move into the position from another position within their company or have taken on the task in addition to other duties. These employees are often paid approximately the same salary they were already making.

Depending on the organization for which they work, webmasters may receive a benefits package in addition to salary. A typical benefits package would include paid vacations and holidays, medical insurance, and perhaps a pension plan.

WORK ENVIRONMENT

Although much of the webmaster's day may be spent alone, it is nonetheless important that he or she be able to communicate and work well with others. Depending on the organization for which he or she works, the webmaster may have periodic meetings with graphic designers, marketing specialists, writers, or other professionals who have input into Web site development. In many larger organizations, there is a team of webmasters rather than just one. Although each team member works alone on his or her own specific duties, the members may meet frequently to discuss and coordinate their activities.

Because technology changes so rapidly, this job is constantly evolving. Webmasters must spend time reading and learning about new developments in online communication. They may be continually working with new computer software or hardware. Their actual job responsibilities may even change, as the capabilities of both the organization and the Web itself expand. It is important that these employees be flexible and willing to learn and grow with the technology that drives their work.

Because they don't deal with the general public, most webmasters are allowed to wear fairly casual attire and to work in a relaxed atmosphere. In most cases, the job calls for standard working hours, although there may be times when overtime is required.

OUTLOOK

According to the U.S. Department of Labor, the field of computer and data processing services is projected to be among the fastest growing industries for the next decade. As a result, the employment rate of webmasters and other computer specialists is expected to grow much faster than the average rate for all occupations through 2016.

There can be no doubt that computer, and specifically online, technology will continue its rapid growth for the next several years. Likewise, then, the number of computer-related jobs, including that of webmaster, should also increase. As more and more businesses, not-for-profit organizations, educational institutions, and government agencies choose to "go online," the total number of Web sites will grow, as will the need for experts to design them.

Companies view Web sites not as temporary experiments, but rather as important and necessary business and marketing tools. Growth will be largest for Internet content developers (webmasters responsible for the information displayed on a Web site) and chief Web officers.

One thing to keep in mind, however, is that when technology advances extremely rapidly, it tends to make old methods of doing things obsolete. If current trends continue, the responsibilities of the webmaster will be carried out by a group or department instead of a single employee, in order to keep up with the demands of the position. It is possible that in the next few years, changes in technology will make the Web sites as we know it today a thing of the past. Another possibility is that, like desktop publishing, user-friendly software programs will make Web site design so easy and efficient that it no longer requires an "expert" to do it well. Webmasters who are concerned with job security should be willing to continue learning and using the very latest developments in technology, so that they are prepared to move into the future of online communication, whatever it may be.

FOR MORE INFORMATION

For information on training and certification programs, contact the following organizations:

International Webmasters Association
119 East Union Street, Suite F
Pasadena, CA 91103-3950
Tel: 626-449-3709
http://www.iwanet.org

World Organization of Webmasters
PO Box 1743
Folsom, CA 95630-1888
Tel: 916-989-2933
Email: info@joinwow.org
http://www.joinwow.org

WIRELESS SERVICE TECHNICIANS

OVERVIEW

Wireless service technicians are responsible for maintaining a specified group of cell sites, including the radio towers, cell site equipment, and often the building and grounds for the sites. Technicians routinely visit and monitor the functioning of the on-site equipment, performing preventive testing and maintenance. They are also responsible for troubleshooting and remedying problems that might arise with any of their sites. Most wireless service technicians spend their work time at various locations, visiting each of their cell sites as necessary.

THE JOB

Wireless service technicians are sometimes also called *cell site technicians, field technicians,* or *cell site engineers.* These workers maintain cell sites—which consist of a radio tower and computerized equipment. Each cell site covers a geographic territory that varies in size. When someone places a wireless call within a particular cell site's geographic territory, radio waves are transmitted to that cell site's antenna. The antenna picks up the radio waves and transmits them through cables to computerized equipment that is typically located in a building adjacent to the antenna. This equipment then "reads" the radio waves, turns them into a computerized code, and sends the information on to a "switching center." At the switching center, the call is transferred to its destination—which might be another wireless phone or a traditional wireline phone.

The equipment at each cell site—the antenna and computerized equipment—are important pieces of the wireless telecommunications network. If a cell site stops functioning for some reason, wireless users within that site's coverage area may not be able to use their mobile phones. Since many people rely on these devices to receive or transmit important or emergency information, a lapse in coverage can be very serious. Wireless service technicians are responsible for maintaining and troubleshooting the equipment and operations of the cell sites. The majority of cellular communication is currently voice transmissions. However, wireless service is increasingly being used to transmit data, for purposes such as Internet access. The data transmission equipment may be a separate, peripheral part of the cell site equipment, and the technician is responsible for maintaining it as well.

Wireless service technicians typically perform both routine, preventive maintenance and troubleshooting of equipment that has malfunctioned. Routine maintenance might include scheduled visits to each cell site to check power levels and computer functions. Technicians often carry laptop computers, which contain sophisticated testing software. By connecting their laptop computers to the cell site equipment, technicians can test to make sure the equipment is functioning as it should. Wireless carriers may also have backup equipment, such as generators and batteries, at their cell sites to ensure that even if the primary system fails, wireless coverage is still maintained. Technicians may periodically check this backup equipment to make sure it is functional and ready to be used in case of emergency. In addition to maintaining the actual cell site computer equipment, wireless service technicians may be responsible for routine and preventive maintenance of the radio tower itself and the building and grounds of the site. In many cases, technicians do not perform the actual physical maintenance on the tower and grounds themselves. Rather, they contract with other service providers to do so and are then responsible for ensuring that the work meets appropriate standards and is done when needed.

The frequency of the scheduled visits to individual cell sites depends on the technician's employer and the number of sites the technician is responsible for. For example, a technician who is responsible for 10 to 15 sites might be required to visit each site monthly to perform routine, preventive maintenance. In some cases, these sites may be very close together—perhaps within blocks of each other. In other cases, in less populated areas, the sites may be more than 20 miles apart.

When cell site equipment malfunctions, wireless service technicians are responsible for identifying the problem and making sure that it is repaired. Technicians run diagnostic tests on the equipment to determine where the malfunction is. If the problem is one that can be easily solved—for example, by replacing a piece of equipment—the technician handles it. If it is something more serious, such as a problem with the antenna or with the local wireline telecommunications system, the technician calls the appropriate service people to remedy the situation.

In addition to routine maintenance and troubleshooting responsibilities, wireless service technicians may have a range of other duties. They may test the wireless system by driving around the coverage area while using a mobile phone. They may work with technicians in the switching center to incorporate new cell sites into the network and make sure that the wireless calls are smoothly transmitted from one cell to another.

REQUIREMENTS
High School

If you are interested in pursuing a career as a wireless service technician, you should take high school classes

QUICK FACTS

SCHOOL SUBJECTS
Computer science
Physics

PERSONAL SKILLS
Mechanical/manipulative
Technical/scientific

WORK ENVIRONMENT
Primarily outdoors
Primarily multiple locations

MINIMUM EDUCATION LEVEL
Associate's degree

MEDIAN SALARY
$52,430

CERTIFICATION OR LICENSING
None available

OUTLOOK
About as fast as the average

that will prepare you for further schooling in electronics. Physics classes will provide the background necessary to understand the theory of electronics. Because wireless service technician jobs are so heavily computer-oriented, computer classes are also excellent choices. Other important classes are those that will provide you with the basic abilities needed both in college and in the workplace—such as English, speech, and mathematics courses.

Postsecondary Training

A two-year associate's degree in a technical field is the minimum educational level needed to become a wireless service technician. Many technicians obtain degrees in electronics or electronic technology. For these degrees, course work would likely include both classes and laboratory work in circuit theory, digital electronics, microprocessors, computer troubleshooting, telecommunications, and data communications technology. Other students might opt for degrees in telecommunications management or computer science. Students working toward a telecommunications degree might take classes on such subjects as local area networks, advanced networking technologies, network management, and programming. Computer science courses might include such topics as programming, operating systems, computer languages, and network architecture. Although most wireless service technicians have two-year degrees, some may have four-year degrees in computer science, telecommunications, electronic engineering, or other similar subjects.

No matter what sort of educational background new technicians have, they have to learn about the specific equipment used by their employers. Most wireless carriers send their technicians through formal education programs, which are typically offered by equipment manufacturers. In these programs, new technicians learn the operating specifics of the equipment they will be maintaining. A new technician is usually given a smaller number of cell sites to manage when he or she first begins and may be paired with a more experienced technician who can answer questions and conduct on-the-job training.

Other Requirements

The ability to work independently is one of the most important characteristics of a good wireless service technician. Most technicians work on their own, traveling from site to site and performing their duties with little or no supervision. The willingness to learn and to adapt to change is another key personality trait of successful wireless service technicians. Finally, because so much of the job involves traveling between cell sites, a technician must have a valid driver's license and good driving record.

EXPLORING

If you think you might be interested in becoming a wireless service technician, you might first want to explore the ins and outs of electronics, which is a key part of the technician's job. There are numerous books on electronics and electronic theory, geared to various levels of expertise. Check with your high school or local public library to see what you can find on this topic. In addition, many hobby shops or specialty science stores have electronics kits and experiments that allow young people to get some hands-on experience with how electronic circuits work.

To find out more about wireless communications specifically, you might again check for books or magazine articles on the subject in local libraries. You might also

contact a wireless provider in your area and ask to talk with a cell technician about his or her job.

EMPLOYERS

There are dozens of wireless service providers, both large and small, all over the United States. Anywhere that there is wireless service—that is, anywhere that you can use a cellular phone—there is a cell site, owned and maintained by a wireless provider. Some of the largest wireless providers are AT&T Wireless, Verizon Wireless, Sprint , T-Mobile, U.S. Cellular, and Qwest. All of these companies have Web sites, and most maintain a listing of available jobs on their site.

In addition to these major players, there are smaller wireless carriers sprinkled throughout the United States in virtually every medium-sized and large community. You should be able to find a list of them by asking your local librarian for help or by doing a key word search on "wireless service providers" on the Internet.

STARTING OUT

One of the best ways to start looking for a job as a wireless service technician is to visit the Web sites of several wireless providers. Many wireless companies maintain jobs sections on their sites, which list available positions. Another possibility is to browse through wireless industry publications, such as *Wireless Week* (http://www.wirelessweek. com), *Telephony Online* (http://www.telephonyonline. com), and *Wireless Review*, which is part of the *Telephony Online* site (http://www.wirelessreview.com).

Another way to find your first wireless technician's job is to look for and attend technical job fairs, expos, or exchanges. Because technically and technologically skilled employees are so much in demand, communities frequently have events to allow employers to network with and meet potential employees. Watch local newspapers for similar events in your community. Finally, an excellent source of job leads will be your college's placement office. Many wireless companies visit schools that offer the appropriate degree programs to recruit qualified students for employees. Some companies even offer a co-op program, in which they hire students on a part-time basis while they are still in school.

ADVANCEMENT

In some companies, a natural path of advancement for a wireless service technician is becoming a switch technician or switch engineer. The switch technician works at the "switching center," which controls the routing of the wireless phone calls.

Another avenue of advancement might be to move into system performance. System performance workers strive to maximize the performance of the wireless system. They run tests and make adjustments to ensure that the system is providing the best possible coverage in all areas and that signals from the different cell sites do not interfere with each other.

EARNINGS

Because there is such a demand for qualified and dependable employees in the wireless field, the qualified wireless technician can expect to receive a good salary. According to the U.S. Department of Labor, telecommunications equipment installers and repairers earned a median salary of $52,430 a year.

The job generally comes with other benefits as well. Many wireless companies provide their service technicians with company vehicles. Cellular phones and laptop computers, which technicians need to perform their work, are also common perks. Finally, most major wireless service providers offer a benefits package to their employees, which often includes health insurance, paid vacation, holiday, and sick days, and a pension or 401(k) plan.

WORK ENVIRONMENT

Cell site technicians who are in charge of several cell sites spend their workweek visiting the different sites. Depending on how far apart the sites are, this may mean driving a substantial distance. While the actual computer equipment is located inside a building at each cell site location, any work or routine checking of the radio tower requires outside work, in varying kinds of weather.

This is important because the management of cell sites is a 24-hour-a-day, seven-day-a-week business. If an alarm system goes off at three in the morning, a cell site technician must respond. The ability to access the system remotely from his or her laptop computer may save the technician an actual trip to the site. Because the sites must be maintained continuously, wireless service technicians are likely to sometimes work unusual hours. Most wireless service technicians are not very closely supervised. They generally set their own schedules (with management concurrence) and work alone and independently. They may, however, have to work closely at times with other company employees to integrate new sites into the system, make modifications to the system, or troubleshoot problems.

OUTLOOK

According to the U. S. Department of Labor, employment in the telecommunications industry is expected to grow at a rate that is slightly slower than the average. This is mainly due to vast improvements in telecommunications equipment and the automation of system monitoring and repair. However, rising demand for wireless services and the creation of new wireless networks should ensure job opportunities for workers in this segment of the industry.

There are several reasons for the growing popularity of wireless service. It has become more and more important to have telephone, Internet, and text messaging access at all times. A second reason for the increase in usage is that coverage areas are increasingly broad and comprehensive. As more and more cell sites are added, more and more parts of the United States have cellular service. Areas that previously had no wireless service are being covered—and consequently, more people have access to and use for cellular phones and pagers.

A third factor in the growth is the continuous improvement in cellular phones and services due to technological advances. One of the most recent innovations is digital communication technology called "personal communications services" (PCS). PCS is expected to increase wireless phone use by offering better quality and range. New technologies are also increasingly allowing people to transmit data as well as voice over wireless connections. Examples of wireless data communication include such applications as text messaging and Internet access.

In recent years there has also been an increase in the number of wireless companies. This growth was spurred by the Federal Communications Commission's partial deregulation of the industry in 1993, which allowed for as many as nine carriers in a geographic market. This competition has added a large number of technicians' jobs and is expected to continue to do so.

FOR MORE INFORMATION

For job postings, links to wireless industry recruiters, industry news, and training information, contact
Cellular Telecommunications and Internet Association
1400 16th Street, NW, Suite 600
Washington, DC 20036-2217
Tel: 202-785-0081
http://www.ctia.org

For information on the wireless industry in Canada, contact
Canadian Wireless Telecommunications Association
130 Albert Street, Suite 1110
Ottawa, ON K1P 5G4
Canada
Tel: 613-233-4888
Email: info@cwta.ca
http://www.cwta.ca

☐ YOGA AND PILATES INSTRUCTORS

OVERVIEW

Yoga and pilates instructors lead specialized exercise, stretching, and meditation classes for people of all ages. They demonstrate techniques in front of the class and then watch members perform the movements, making suggestions and form adjustments as needed. Classes range from introductory to intermediate to advanced, and they may be aimed at specific groups, such as children or the elderly. *Yoga instructors* lead their class through a series of asanas, or poses, aimed at building strength, flexibility, and balance. *Pilates instructors* teach a series of movements that are more fluid than the poses used in yoga. Pilates also builds strength and flexibility but focuses on training the individual's core, or center.

THE JOB

Yoga and pilates instructors teach alternatives to the more traditional exercises of aerobics, weight training, or interval training classes. With yoga, the instructors' methods vary greatly based on the type of yoga they teach. Some instructors begin class seated or even lying down, encouraging class members to relax their muscles and focus on their breathing. After a few minutes of breathing exercises, the instructor leads the class into the various asanas, or yoga poses. These poses have Sanskrit names, though the instructor may use the English terminology for the benefit of the class, instructing students to get into the downward dog position or child's pose. Again, depending on the yoga method, poses may be fluid, with quicker movement from position to position, or instructors may tell class members to hold poses for as long as three or four minutes, encouraging strength and control.

Most yoga classes are done barefoot on the floor, using a thin, rubber mat to keep class members from slipping while in poses. Other equipment, such as foam blocks, ropes, or cloth straps, may also be used in the poses, usually to help with form or assist in the tougher positions.

During the class, yoga instructors verbally describe and demonstrate moves in front of the class. They also walk around and survey the movements of class members, making slight adjustments to members' form to prevent injury, encourage good practice, and improve their skills.

Pilates is similar to yoga in that class participants are led through different motions. However, unlike yoga poses that are often held for minutes at a time, pilates encompasses more fluid movement of the arms and legs using what is called core strength. This strength comes from the body's torso, from the top of the rib cage to the lower abdomen.

The job of pilates instructor is similar to that of a yoga teacher. Pilates teachers also demonstrate and describe motions and check class members' form and technique. Some classes include equipment such as an apparatus called The Reformer, which is a horizontal framework of straps and strings that is used for more than 100 exercises. Class members can tone, build, lengthen, and strengthen muscles by adjusting the equipment's springs to create different levels of resistance.

Both yoga and pilates instructors have to prepare for their classes ahead of time to choose the exercises and equipment to be used or whether to focus on one method or area of the body. Good instructors are available after class for questions and advice. Instructors should also be open to class suggestions and comments to make the class the best it can be.

REQUIREMENTS

High School

You will need at least a high school diploma to work as a yoga or pilates instructor. In high school, take anatomy, biology, psychology, and physical education. In addition, get involved in weight lifting, dance, sports, and other activities that will help you to stay fit and learn more about exercise.

Postsecondary Training

Although a college degree isn't always necessary to work in the fitness field, you will be more attractive to employers if your qualifications contain a balance of ability and education. Useful college courses include anatomy, physiology, psychology, kinesiology, biomechanics, chemistry, physics, first aid and safety, health, and nutrition.

Certification or Licensing

Most qualified yoga and pilates instructors become certified through a professional association, such as the Yoga Alliance or the Pilates Center. For example, the Pilates Center offers a comprehensive program consisting of training on proper form, the purpose of each exercise, how to assess and adjust class members' posture and form, and how to properly pace the class to create an effective and comprehensive class. A certificate is awarded to those who complete a minimum of 60 hours of formal lecture and 750 hours of apprentice work and pass several written and practical tests.

It is important to note that there are no nationally recognized standards for either yoga or pilates instruction. "Certified" training can be as short as a weekend course or as long as a multiyear program that is the equivalent of a college degree. According to the American Yoga Association, because yoga was historically passed down from teacher to student on an individual basis (creating many varieties and methods), it is unlikely that a standard training program for instruction will be created. Be sure to investigate your yoga or pilates training program to ensure that it is a quality program, and one suited to your own approach.

Other Requirements

Yoga and pilates instructors are expected to be flexible and physically fit, but they do not have to be in super-human shape. Though the American Yoga Association has established a list of strict qualities that instructors should adhere to (maintain a vegetarian diet, act ethically), the basic qualities of every good instructor are the same: to be knowledgeable and passionate about your craft and be a patient and thorough instructor.

EXPLORING

The best way to explore these careers is to experience a yoga or pilates class firsthand. In fact, you should attend several classes to learn the basics of the practice and build your skills. Ask to talk to the instructor after class about his or her job and how to get started. The instructor may recommend a certification program or give you names of other professionals to talk to about the practice.

You may also want to see if a local gym or community center has part-time positions available. Even if you are just working at the front desk, you will be able to see if you enjoy working in a health facility.

EMPLOYERS

Yoga and pilates instructors work in fitness centers, gymnasiums, spas, dance studios, and community centers. Most employers are for-profit businesses, but some are community-based, such as the YMCA or a family center. Other job possibilities can be found in corporate fitness centers, colleges, nursing homes, hospitals, and resorts. In smaller towns, positions can be found in health care facilities, schools, and community centers.

STARTING OUT

If you have been attending yoga or pilates classes regularly, ask your instructor for ideas on training programs and if he or she knows of any job leads.

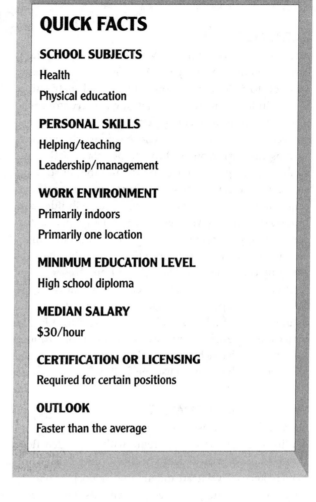

QUICK FACTS

SCHOOL SUBJECTS
Health
Physical education

PERSONAL SKILLS
Helping/teaching
Leadership/management

WORK ENVIRONMENT
Primarily indoors
Primarily one location

MINIMUM EDUCATION LEVEL
High school diploma

MEDIAN SALARY
$30/hour

CERTIFICATION OR LICENSING
Required for certain positions

OUTLOOK
Faster than the average

Often, facilities that provide training or internships will hire or provide job assistance to individuals who have completed programs. Students can also find jobs through classified ads and by applying to health and fitness clubs, YMCAs, YWCAs, community centers, local schools, park districts, religious groups, and other fitness organizations. Many companies now provide fitness facilities to their employees. As a result, students should consider nearby companies for prospective instructor positions.

ADVANCEMENT

Yoga and pilates instructors who have taught for several years and have the proper training can move into an instructor trainer position or, if they have the necessary capital, they may choose to establish their own private studio. To own a yoga or pilates studio, the instructor should be confident in his or her ability to attract new clients or be willing to ask old clients to move from their old class location to the new studio. With a bachelor's degree in either sports physiology or exercise physiology, instructors can advance to the position of health club director or to teach corporate wellness programs.

EARNINGS

According to the Pilates Method Alliance, pilates instructors usually charge $10 to $30 for group classes and $50 to $100 for an hour of personal instruction. CareerBuilder.com reports that yoga instructors who teach in community college extension programs earn an average of $35 per hour. Those who teach in private studios can earn from $30 to $40 per class, with some facilities paying more based on the number of students attending the class. Those who teach in corporate settings can earn $75 an hour or more. CareerBuilder.com reports that, in Los Angeles, successful yoga instructors can earn approximately $50,000 per year. Some highest-profile teachers earn more than $150,000 a year by charging their clients up to $250 an hour!

A compensation survey by health and fitness organization IDEA reports that many employers offer health insurance and paid sick and vacation time to full-time employees. They also may provide discounts on products sold in the club (such as shoes, clothing, and equipment) and free memberships to use the facility.

WORK ENVIRONMENT

Yoga and pilates classes are generally held indoors, in a studio or quiet room, preferably with a wooden floor. Classes can get crowded and hectic at times. Instructors need to keep a level head and maintain a positive personality in order to motivate class participants. They need to lead challenging, yet enjoyable, classes so that members return for more instruction.

OUTLOOK

Health professionals have long recommended daily aerobic exercise and resistance training to maintain weight, build strength, and improve overall health. But more recently, health professionals have added another recommendation: work on flexibility, posture, and stress reduction. These new concerns have given yoga and pilates a boost in popularity.

The U.S. Department of Labor predicts that the job outlook for fitness instructors should remain very strong over the next several years. As the average age of the population increases, yoga and pilates instructors will find more opportunities to work with the elderly in retirement homes and assisted-living communities. Large companies and corporations, after realizing the stress reduction benefits of these "softer" forms of exercise, also hire yoga and pilates instructors to hold classes for their employees.

FOR MORE INFORMATION

For more information about the practice, teaching, and origin of yoga, contact

American Yoga Association
PO Box 19986
Sarasota, FL 34276-2986
Tel: 941-927-4977
http://www.americanyogaassociation.org

For fitness facts and articles, visit IDEA's Web site.

IDEA: The Health and Fitness Association
10455 Pacific Center Court
San Diego, CA 92121-4339
Tel: 800-999-4332, ext. 7
Email: contact@ideafit.com
http://www.ideafit.com

For training and certification information, contact

The Pilates Center
4800 Baseline Road, Suite D206
Boulder, CO 80303-2699
Tel: 303-494-3400
Email: info@thepilatescenter.com
http://www.thepilatescenter.com

For information about learning to practice and teach pilates, contact

Pilates Method Alliance
PO Box 370906
Miami, FL 33137-0906
Tel: 866-573-4945
Email: info@pilatesmethodalliance.org
http://www.pilatesmethodalliance.org

INDEX